China's Southwest

Damian Harper,

Tienlon Ho, Thomas Huhti, Korina Miller, Eilís Quinn

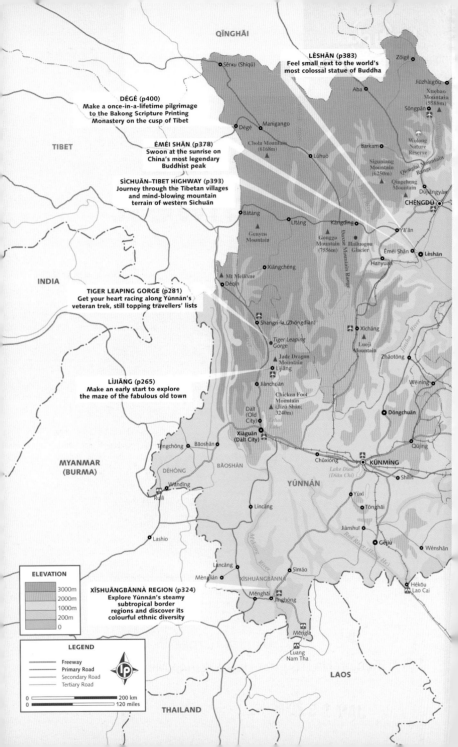

QĪNGHǍI

LÈSHĀN (p383)
Feel small next to the world's most colossal statue of Buddha

DÉGÉ (p400)
Make a once-in-a-lifetime pilgrimage to the Bakong Scripture Printing Monastery on the cusp of Tibet

TIBET

ÉMÉI SHĀN (p378)
Swoon at the sunrise on China's most legendary Buddhist peak

SÌCHUĀN–TIBET HIGHWAY (p393)
Journey through the Tibetan villages and mind-blowing mountain terrain of western Sìchuān

INDIA

TIGER LEAPING GORGE (p281)
Get your heart racing along Yúnnán's veteran trek, still topping travellers' lists

LÌJIĀNG (p265)
Make an early start to explore the maze of the fabulous old town

MYANMAR (BURMA)

XĪSHUĀNGBǍNNÀ REGION (p324)
Explore Yúnnán's steamy subtropical border regions and discover its colourful ethnic diversity

ELEVATION
3000m
2000m
1000m
200m
0

LEGEND
Freeway
Primary Road
Secondary Road
Tertiary Road

0   200 km
0   120 miles

THAILAND

Sêrxu (Shíqú)
Zöigê
Jiùzhàigōu
Aba
Xuebao Mountain (5588m)
Sōngpān
Dégé   Manigango
Chola Mountain (6168m)
Lúhuò
Barkam
Wolong Nature Reserve
Siguniang Mountain (6250m)
Qionglai Mountain Range
Qingcheng Mountain
Dūjiāngyàn
CHÉNGDŪ
Bātáng   Lǐtáng
Kāngdìng
Ya'ān
Genyen Mountain
Gongga Mountain (7556m)
Hailuogou Glacier
Éméi Shān   Lèshān
Hanyuán
Xiāngchéng
Mt Meilixue
Déqīn
Shangri-la (Zhōngdiàn)
Xīchāng
Luoji Mountain
Tiger Leaping Gorge
Zhāotōng
Jade Dragon Mountain
Lìjiāng
Weining
Jiànchuān
Chicken Foot Mountain (Jīzú Shān; 3240m)
Dōngchuān
Dàlǐ (Old City)
Ěrhai Lake
Qūjìng
Xiàguān (Dàlǐ City)
Tengchōng   Bǎoshān
Chūxióng
KŪNMÍNG
Lake Dian (Diàn Chí)
Shílín
BǍOSHĀN
DÉHÓNG
Wǎnding
Rúilì
YÚNNÁN
Yùxī
Tónghǎi
Líncāng
Jiànshuǐ
Gèjiù
Wénshān
Lashio
Líncāng
Simáo
Mènglián
XĪSHUĀNGBǍNNÀ
Hékǒu
Lao Cai
Ménghǎi   Jǐnghóng
Měnglà
Luang Nam Tha

LAOS

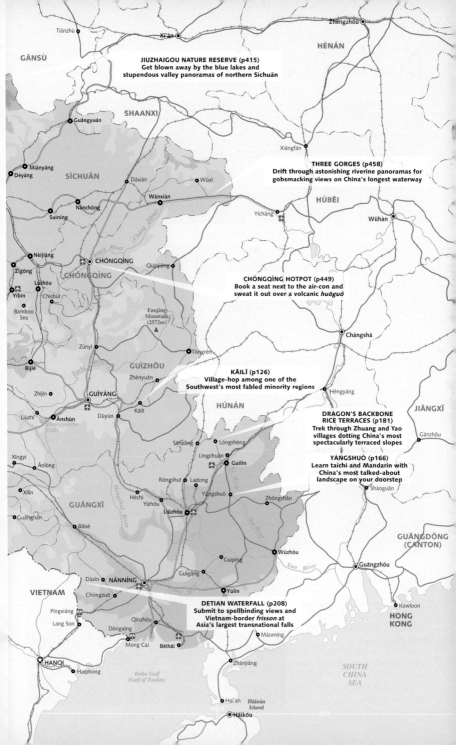

JIUZHAIGOU NATURE RESERVE (p415)
Get blown away by the blue lakes and
stupendous valley panoramas of northern Sìchuān

THREE GORGES (p458)
Drift through astonishing riverine panoramas for
gobsmacking views on China's longest waterway

CHÓNGQÌNG HOTPOT (p449)
Book a seat next to the air-con and
sweat it out over a volcanic *huǒguǒ*

KǍILǏ (p126)
Village-hop among one of the
Southwest's most fabled minority regions

**DRAGON'S BACKBONE
RICE TERRACES (p181)**
Trek through Zhuang and Yao
villages dotting China's most
spectacularly terraced slopes

YÁNGSHUÒ (p166)
Learn taichi and Mandarin with
China's most talked-about
landscape on your doorstep

DETIAN WATERFALL (p208)
Submit to spellbinding views and
Vietnam-border *frisson* at
Asia's largest transnational falls

On the Road

DAMIAN HARPER
Coordinating Author
January at the Dragon's Backbone Rice Terraces outside Lóngshèng frequently sees the fantastic landscape swathed in copious mists. The winter views may be a bit touch and go, but the cloud cover has a silver lining: there's hardly anyone else about.

EILÍS QUINN
Dozens of bags and a half dozen mangy, sheep-sized dogs crowded the aisles of the Litáng–Bātáng bus. Tibetan villagers hoisted a decapitated yak on the roof, carried the head inside and dropped it in the only clear space – between my feet. To their amusement, I spent the rest of the trip battling all six dogs for their dinner. When we finally arrived in Bātáng at 10pm that night it was one of the happiest days of my entire trip.

THOMAS HUHTI
Stop number one, legs aren't ready for the up-and-down of mountain walking with even a day pack, so this is the typical pose: exhausted-but-don't-sit-on-the-pig-poop. Bǎoshān is such an extraordinary place. I could have sat there all day, but then a pony train came along and made me move.

TIENLON HO
Flying about 30 stories above the surface of the Wu River in Wǔlóng is wildly exhilarating, especially when you're zipping along cables that are squeaking like a baby elephant. Immediately after this photo was taken, I gracelessly crash-landed into a pile of mattresses.

KORINA MILLER
I'm in the remote and very frozen town of Tóngrén, Guìzhōu and have just rounded a bend in a lane to run headlong into a parade in full swing, complete with a 20-person dragon. I'm instantly plied with sweets, hello-hello-hellos and big grins – it's not hard to get into that festive spirit in Southwest China.

See full author bios page 513

Sacred Sights

JOHN BORTHWICK

Find solitude in a Buddhist temple on Éméi Shān (Emei Mountain; p378), Sìchuān

KORINA MILLER

Meet the timeless gaze of the Grand Buddha (Dàfó; p383) in Lèshān, Sìchuān

KEREN SU

Join pilgrims circumambulating the Bakong Scripture Printing Monastery (p400) in Dégé, Sìchuān

Scenic Marvels & Natural Wonders

KORINA MILLER

Visit the spectacular Huangguoshu Falls (p115) in Guìzhōu, the largest waterfalls in Asia

BRADLEY MAYHEW

Enjoy a tranquil moment on Lugu Lake (Lúgū Hú; p285), Yúnnán

Watch sunrise on the Li River (p166), Yángshuò, Guǎngxī

KEREN SU

See giant pandas up close in the Giant Panda Research Centre (p375), Wolong Nature Reserve, Sìchuān

Gaze down at the Dragon's Backbone Rice Terraces (p181), Lóngshèng, Guǎngxī

Marvel at the terraced natural limestone pools in Huanglong National Park, Sìchuān (p414)

Great Escapes

Visit the Nujiang Valley (p297), a sublime 320km-long river gorge in Yúnnán

Be awe-struck by Chola Mountain (p393) on the northern route of the Sichuān–Tibet Highway

Trek the Tiger Leaping Gorge (p281), Yúnnán, one of the deepest gorges in the world

Contents

Regional Map Contents

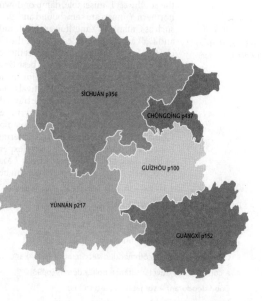

SÌCHUĀN p356

CHÓNGQÌNG p437

GUÌZHŌU p100

YÚNNÁN p217

GUĂNGXĪ p152

Getting Started

From low-cost DIY independent adventuring to luxury tours, China's Southwest is accessible to literally any budget. Getting around much of the region is straightforward as flights, trains and buses link the major destinations although travellers to remoter regions such as the mountainous wilds of west Sìchuān will need to prepare for some heavy-duty bus rides and a flexible itinerary. The Itineraries chapter (p16) can provide you with ideas for planning your route through the Southwest.

WHEN TO GO

The optimum seasons to visit the Southwest are spring (March to May) and autumn (September to October), when average temperatures are either warming up or tapering off, although the region can realistically be visited any time of the year (p467). It all depends on which area you wish to visit. Altitude is largely the deciding factor in frequently dramatic temperature variations within and between provinces. Summer is largely very hot, but the climate of Yúnnán alone ranges from the muggy subtropics of Xīshuāngbǎnnà to the chill north climbing into Tibet, with considerable disparity in between. Chóngqìng famously simmers like one of its notorious hotpots in July, while altitudinous Western Sìchuān is much, much cooler in the depths of summer.

Winter visits are not ideal although not impossible. Some parts of the Southwest, such as southern Guǎngxī province and Xīshuāngbǎnnà, may enjoy temperate winter months but much – although not all – of the rest of the Southwest is miserable, damp or downright frozen. Western Sìchuān and northern Yúnnán are snowbound and glacial in winter, and tourist drawcards such as Guìlín and Yángshuò are bleak and disappointing, although Kūnmíng and Dàlǐ are generally pleasant. See the Climate sections in each destination chapter for details on prevailing weather conditions by province.

Minority festivals can be the best time to see villages and destinations; consult the destination chapters for the lowdown on these and also see the boxed text p14 for the top 10 festivals in the region.

Major public holidays can make travel difficult, and sights can be crammed with holidaying Chinese. Manoeuvring around China with 1.3 billion others at the Chinese New Year (p470) can be daunting, but you also get to see China at its most colourful and entertaining. Hotel room prices (see the boxed text, opposite) become very expensive during the May Day holiday (a week-long holiday for many from 1 May) and National Day on 1 October (also week-long), and train tickets can be difficult to procure.

See Climate Charts (p467) for more information.

DON'T LEAVE HOME WITHOUT...

- Checking the visa situation (p476)
- Checking travel advisory bureaus
- Checking on your recommended vaccinations (p494) and travel medications
- A copy of your travel insurance policy details (p493)
- Good deodorant – sometimes hard to find
- Reading matter for those unremitting bus trips
- A sense of adventure

HOTEL ROOMS

Rack rates are quoted for hotels in this book, although generally the only time you will pay the full rate is during the major holiday periods, namely the first week of May, the first week of October and the Chinese New Year. At other times you can expect to receive discounts ranging between 10% and 50%. This does not apply to youth hostels or budget guesthouses, which tend to have set rates and are often much less busy during the holiday period, when the Chinese enjoy splashing out.

COSTS & MONEY

China is an increasingly expensive travel destination. The good news is that, unless you default to staying at tourist hotels, eating at tourist restaurants and shopping in tourist zones, the Southwest remains highly affordable and accessible to cheap exploration. Whereas China's more affluent and booming regions such as Běijīng, Shànghǎi and Hong Kong can be prohibitively pricey, the Southwest remains full of surprising travel bargains. As the Southwest is less wealthy than more developed parts of China, this also means that even if you want to spend your money, there are limits to how much you can realistically spend.

Accommodation will be your principal day-to-day expense. In this department, travellers in every budget bracket should find what they want, although the luxury end of the hotel market is not well represented outside of the really big urban destinations such as Chóngqìng. This book covers all budgets. Beds can be found from as little as Y8 a night at Chinese guesthouses, or from around Y20 for a dorm bed at a youth hostel, but can soar to as much as US$300 a night at a five-star hotel in Běijīng.

It depends where you go and where you stay, but the ultra cost-conscious can theoretically survive on as little as Y50 a day, although this precludes long-distance journeys, taxi trips, shopping or buying entrance tickets, and requires finding the cheapest beds in town and dining at low-cost restaurants or street stalls. On average, however, most budget travellers can bank on living on between Y60 and Y250 a day.

Those on midrange budgets can live quite comfortably for between Y250 and Y500 per day, while travellers aiming to maximise their comforts can easily spend upwards of Y500, depending on where they travel to. Spikes in all of the above accompany air travel, long-distance train travel and expensive entrance tickets to top sights where daily budgets can be blown in one go.

Food is reasonably priced throughout China's Southwest, and the frugal can eat for as little as Y25 a day, but expect a very simple diet. Transport costs can be kept to a minimum by travelling by bus or hard-seat on the train. Train travel is reasonable, and is generally about half the price of air travel. Flying in China is expensive, but discounting is the norm and those with less time will find it indispensable for covering vast distances or getting somewhere in a hurry.

Everything in China has its price and if anyone has worked out a way to charge someone else for something, it will be done. The principle of making a sight free in order to lure travellers in huge quantities to spend money on the local service industry does not exist in China, where short-term gain is typically the only economic principle at work.

Consequently, entrance tickets to sights in China's Southwest are virtually unavoidable and can be a major expense. A typical day of sightseeing in a large city can mean having to buy half-a-dozen entry tickets, and drawcard sights, such as Éméi Shān (Y120; p378) and Emerald Pagoda Lake (Y190; p292) are costly. Other sights have a general admission fee for access to the

HOW MUCH?

Cigarettes: from Y3.5

International Herald Tribune from a five-star hotel: Y23

City bus ticket: Y1

Hour in an internet café: Y1.5-Y3

City map: Y5

TOP 10

CHINA'S SOUTHWEST

Tibet
Nepal Bhutan
East China Sea

TREKS

1 Tackle Tiger Leaping Gorge (p281), the granddaddy of all Yúnnán treks – and still full of beans

2 Village-hop among the drum towers and wind and rain bridges of Sānjiāng (p184)

3 Walk the demanding Kawa Karpo Trek (p296) – but don't forget your Tibet permit

4 Ramble through the awe-inspiring scenery of the Nujiang Valley (p297)

5 Take in some serious trekking from Shítóuchéng (p278) to Lugu Lake (p285)

6 Trek the karst valley panoramas around stunning Déhāng (p214) in western Húnán

7 Clamber to the sacred summit of Éméi Shān (p378), possibly China's most famous holy Buddhist peak

8 Trek among the gorgeous Tibetan villages around Dānbā (p396)

9 Explore gob-smacking scenery at Yading Nature Reserve (p407), on foot or horseback

10 Visit breathtaking Jiuzhaigou Nature Reserve (p415), one of China's scenic marvels

SINGULAR SPOTS

Think you've seen it all before? The Southwest is bursting with unexpected surprises and side-trips.

1 Get the proper perspective on the bizarre Yin-Yang diagram of Tàijítú (p257)

2 Opt for a beancurd blast in Shípíng (p315)

3 Sidestep the prehistoric ferns of Chìshuǐ (p149)

4 Discover the magnificent Qiang watchtowers (p396) of Suōpō (p397)

5 Wonder at the startling ethnology of Xīngměng's (p309) Mongolian ancestry

6 Breeze over to Weizhou Island (p204) – China's largest volcanic island and haven for a remote pair of Catholic churches

7 Wander the flagstones of the ancient fortified town of Láitān (p456) in Chóngqìng

8 Submit to the authentic village charms of historic Nuòdèng (p248)

9 Bask in the yellow spring glow of Luópíng's (p302) monochromatic rapeseed fields

10 Delve into one of Yúnnán's old salt capitals at ancient Hēijǐng (p241)

FESTIVALS

The following festivals are recommended events taking place every year across the Southwest.

1 Spring Festival, 1st day of the first lunar month (usually late January or February) – Chinese New Year mayhem in the Southwest (p470)

2 Water-Splashing Festival, Xīshuāngbǎnnà (p326), 13 to 15 April

3 Lítáng Horse Festival, usually over 10 days from 1 August, Lítáng (p402)

4 Third Moon Fair, 15th day of the third lunar month (usually April), Dàlǐ (p259)

5 Dragon Boat Festival (p471), 5th day of the fifth lunar month (usually late May or June): Guìlín (p160), Nánníng (p192), Chóngqìng (p447), Shídòng (p132), Chóng'ān (p133), Zhènyuǎn (p141), Lèshān (p383)

6 Lusheng Festival, first lunar month (usually February), Guizhōu (p101)

7 Walking Around the Mountain Festival, 8th day of the fourth lunar month, Kāngdìng (p388)

8 Three Temples Festival, 23rd to 25th days of the fourth lunar month (usually May), Dàlǐ (p259)

9 Mid-Autumn Festival, 15th day of the eighth lunar month (usually September or October), throughout the Southwest (p471)

10 Festival of Songs, a three-day festival usually in July, August or September, Shíbǎoshān (p276)

area or complex, but then individual sights within charge their own admission fees or you are required to buy a more expensive through ticket (通票; *tōngpiào*) that should allow access across the board. It can all get costly and sometimes frustrating as ticket prices routinely outstrip inflation.

Whatever your budget, learn to haggle. Since you're using a new currency, take your time to accurately convert prices and see what locals are paying for the same goods.

TRAVEL LITERATURE

Also see the Yúnnán chapter (p216) for a list of recommended Yúnnán-specific titles.

River Town: Two Years on the Yangtze (2001), by Peter Hessler, is full of poignant and telling episodes during the author's posting as an English teacher in the town of Fúlíng on the Yangzi River. Hessler perfectly captures the experience of being a foreigner in today's China in his observations of the local people.

A vivid and gritty account of his penniless three-year meandering around China in the 1980s, *Red Dust*, by Ma Jian, traces the author's flight from the authorities in Běijīng to the remotest corners of the land.

An occasionally hilarious account of travel around this huge country, *Fried Eggs with Chopsticks* (2005), by Polly Evans, is perhaps the perfect partner to pack for those long bus journeys.

Soul Mountain (2001), by Gāo Xíngjiàn (高行健), winner of the Nobel Prize for Literature in 2000, tells the story of a voyage through the wilds of Sìchuān and Yúnnán in search of Líng Shān (Soul Mountain).

Yak Butter and Black Tea: A Journey Into Tibet (1998), by Wade Brackenbury, is an account of the author's two-year adventure with a French photographer trying to hike into the Drung Valley in northwestern Yúnnán.

'Red Dust, by Ma Jian, traces the author's flight from the authorities in Běijīng to the remotest corners of the land.'

INTERNET RESOURCES

Chinese Culture Club (www.chinesecultureclub.org) Resourceful and popular Běijīng-based cultural organisation with a catalogue of trips to the Southwest. Office in Shànghǎi.

Ecotourism in Northwest Yúnnán (www.northwestyunnan.com) Ecotourism tours around the Lìjiāng region.

Nature Conservancy (www.nature.org/wherewework/asiapacific/china) Environmental protection organisation with several projects in China's Southwest including protection of the Yúnnán Golden Monkey.

WWFChina (www.wwfchina.org/english/) Website covering the World Wildlife Fund for Nature's activities and programs in China.

YunnanExplorer.com (www.yunnanexplorer.com) Handy information on Yúnnán province, including a selection of absorbing features on local history.

1 Tackle Tiger Leaping Gorge (p281), the granddaddy of all Yúnnán treks – and still full of beans

2 Village-hop among the drum towers and wind and rain bridges of Sānjiāng (p184)

3 Walk the demanding Kawa Karpo Trek (p296) – but don't forget your Tibet permit

4 Ramble through the awe-inspiring scenery of the Nujiang Valley (p297)

5 Take in some serious trekking from **Shí**tóuchéng (p278) to Lugu Lake (p285)

6 Trek the karst valley panoramas around stunning Déhāng (p214) in western Húnán

Itineraries

CLASSIC ROUTES

THE LONG SOUTHWEST LOOP

Five to Six Weeks/
Chéngdū to Kūnmíng

Spend several days in **Chéngdū** (p358) exploring the sights and surrounding diversions (including **Éméi Shān**, p378, and **Lèshān**, p383) before heading to the stunning **Jiuzhaigou Nature Reserve** (p415), **Huanglong National Park** (p414) and **Sōngpān** (p411) in the north of Sìchuān for a week's exploration. From Jiuzhaigou Nature Reserve, fly to **Chóngqìng** (p436) for a few days, visiting **Dàzú** (p453), exploring the trekking and climbing possibilities of **Wǔlóng County** (p455) and the magnificent village of **Láitān** (p456). From Chóngqìng, consider drifting through the **Three Gorges** (p458) before journeying to **Guìyáng** (p101) in Guìzhōu, possibly via **Chìshuǐ** (p147). Visit the dramatic **Huangguoshu Falls** (p115) and **Maling Gorge** (p124) before pressing on to **Kūnmíng** (p220). Returning to Guìyáng, continue east to **Kǎilǐ** (p126) and the fascinating minority villages of eastern Guìzhōu; take a week or so to explore the region before continuing southeast to **Sānjiāng** (p184) and **Lóngshèng** (p180). Spend four days visiting **Guìlín** (p154) and **Yángshuò** (p166) before travelling from Guìlín to Kūnmíng in Yúnnán to tour the province's highlights, including **Dàlǐ** (p257), **Lìjiāng** (p265) and **Xīshuāngbǎnnà** (p324).

This comprehensive journey takes you through all of the drawcard destinations in the Southwest, from Sìchuān province to Yúnnán. You will experience the thrilling diversity of scenic Jiuzhaigou Nature Reserve, the minority villages of Guìzhōu, the mind-boggling landscape of Yángshuò and the beauty of Yúnnán.

THE SHORTER SOUTHWEST LOOP

**Three to Four Weeks/
Guìlín to Chéngdū**

Using **Guìlín** (p154) as a scenic base, pop down to **Yángshuò** (p166) by bus or boat for several days' exploration of its outstanding karst landscapes. Trek the sights of **Lóngshèng** (p180) and **Sānjiāng** (p184), from where side trips into Guìzhōu and the minority regions of Húnán offer tantalising tasters of the provinces. Take the train or plane from Guìlín to **Kūnmíng** (p220) in Yún-nán for several days and visit the surrounding sights. Hop on a bus, train or plane to **Xiàguān** (p242) and bus it to **Dàlǐ** (p257) for several days exploring the sights in this fantastic region. Linked to Xiàguān by bus, the Naxi town of **Lìjiāng** (p265) is the classic gateway to breathtaking treks along **Tiger Leaping Gorge** (p281). Consider a journey to **Lugu Lake** (p285) on the border with Sìchuān, or travel to **Shangri-la** (p287) in northern Yúnnán for several days. Adventurous travellers may opt for the rigorous and adventurous overland route to Chéngdū in Sìchuān by bus via **Xiāngchéng**, **Lǐtáng** and **Kāngdìng** (p19). Overland journeys to Lhasa in Tibet from Shangri-la (p291) are also an option, but you will need to arrange a tour and a Tibet permit. From Shangri-la you can fly back to Kūnmíng and either continue south to explore **Xīshuāngbǎnnà** (p324) in the deep south of Yúnnán or fly from Kūnmíng to **Chéngdū** (p358). From Chéngdū journey to the Big Buddha at **Lèshān** (p383) and conclude your adventure by climbing the sacred Buddhist mountain of **Éméi Shān** (p378) before returning to Chéngdū for transport links to the rest of the Southwest and China.

This extensive route embraces many of the Southwest's highlights, while allowing for a wide-ranging tour of magnificent Yúnnán province and providing options for adventurous detours. The journey could be done in three weeks, but a month would allow more time to explore the region.

ROADS LESS TRAVELLED

WESTERN SÌCHUÃN & THE TIBETAN BORDERLANDS

Two to Three Weeks/
Chéngdū to Dégé or Sêrxu (Shíqú)

Due to altitude, this trip through the west and northwest of Sìchuān should not be attempted during the big freeze from November to March and April, only during the warmer months of late spring or summer (and even then be fully prepared for sudden temperature drops). From **Chéngdū** (p358) take a bus to **Kāngdìng** (p387) in western Sìchuān and consider expeditions to its surrounding sights, such as the monastery of **Gònggā Gompa** (p390), but note that trekking around and climbing Gongga Mountain (Gònggā Shān) is strictly for experienced hikers and climbers; travelling in groups is also highly advised. Return to Kāngdìng and journey north to **Dānbā** (p395) to spend as long as you require discovering the landscape, strewn with Tibetan villages, including **Zhōng Lù Zàngzhài Diāoqún Gǔyízhǐ** (p396), **Shuǐqiàzi Cūn** (p397) and the **Qiang Watchtowers** of **Suōpō** (p397). From Dānbā, you could hop on a bus via the back route to the Tibetan villages around **Mǎ'ěrkāng** (p409) to open up the wonders of northern Sìchuān (p409), or get a long-distance bus to **Gānzī** (p393) along the Sìchuān–Tibet Hwy (northern route) and explore the monasteries in the area. From Gānzī, you can reach the cusp of Tibet at **Dégé** (p400) via **Manigango** (p399), or journey up to **Sêrxu** (Shíqú; p401) in the northwest on the road to Qīnghǎi beyond.

Traversing the wilds of western Sìchuān, this spectacular route transports you through astonishing mountain scenery to the edges of Tibet and north towards Qīnghǎi. A two-week tour is possible, but try to allow more time to savour the landscape and its sheer potential for adventure.

WESTERN SÌCHUĀN TO YÚNNÁN

**Two to Three or Four Weeks/
Kāngdìng to Déqīn**

This magnificent route also begins in **Kāngdìng** (p390) in western Sìchuān, but leads onto the southern arm of the Sìchuān–Tibet Hwy. Spend several days sightseeing around Kāngdìng before the eight-hour bus trip to the Tibetan town of **Lǐtáng** (p402). Spend several days here trekking in the hills and see the Lǐtáng section (p402) and the Health chapter (p499) for details about altitude sickness. From Lǐtáng, either take a long, long bus journey to **Bātáng** (p405) on the edges of western Sìchuān and Tibet, or head south towards **Shangri-la** (p287) in Yúnnán via **Xiāngchéng** (p406). For some excellent trekking in the magnificent **Yading Nature Reserve** (p407), go via **Dàochéng** (p407). Continue south from Xiāngchéng to Shangri-la to spend several days exploring the sights. You can delve south to **Jiànchuān** (p274) from **Lìjiāng** (p265) to jump on the bus to the time-locked caravan-route village of **Shāxī** (p277) and explore little-visited **Nuòdèng** (p248), or journey to **Bǎoshān** (p278) from Lìjiāng to explore the village of **Shítóuchéng** (p278), and even weigh up the exhilarating three- or seven-day trek to **Lugu Lake** (p285). Alternatively, head north by bus to **Déqīn** (p294) and the truly wild north of Yúnnán or consider the overland journey to Lhasa in Tibet from Shangri-la (p291), but you will need to arrange a tour and a permit for this. Flights also link Shangri-la and Lhasa.

This rugged journey from western Sìchuān to the north of Yúnnán, with a diversion to the fringes of Tibet, is one of China's most exhilarating adventures. It can be done in two weeks, but three weeks to a month would allow a more thorough expedition.

TAILORED TRIPS

THE TRADITIONAL VILLAGE & TOWN TOUR

From **Guìlín** (p154) visit **Jiāngtóuzhōu** (p164) in beautiful karst surroundings and take a bus to **Dàxū** (p165) on the Li River. Overnight amid the historic architecture of **Huángyáo** (p179), then explore Zhuang and Yao villages around **Lóngshèng** (p180), Dong villages near **Sānjiāng** (p184), the lovely panorama around **Déhāng** (p214) and the ancient river town of **Fènghuáng** (p212). From Fènghuáng backtrack to Huáihuà and take the train west to **Kǎilǐ** (p126) in Guìzhōu province, via **Zhènyuǎn's** (p140) historic old town. From here

explore the region's minority villages – Xījiāng (p130), Lángdé (p130), Shíqiáo (p131), the villages around Táijiāng (p132) and the ancient village of Lónglǐ (p133). Take the train to **Guìyáng** (p101) to visit the Ming town of **Qīngyán** (p108) before continuing north to **Chóngqìng** (p436) where you can admire **Ciqikou Ancient Town** (p443) and journey to the historic walled village of **Láitān** (p456). From Chóngqìng head northwest to Chéngdū (p358) in Sìchuān and daytrip to the Hakka village of **Luódài** (p371), or riverside town of **Huánglóng Xī** (p372). Travel to **Làngzhōng** (p376), northeast of Chéngdū, to explore its old town. From Chéngdū, tackle the Sìchuān–Tibet Hwy (p387) west of **Kāngdìng** (p387) – scenically littered with Tibetan villages and stupendous scenery.

SCENIC SENSATION ROUTE

From **Guìlín** (p154) journey to **Lóngshèng** (p180) and **Yángshuò** (p166), and stay several days amid the stupendous karst setting. From Nánníng travel to **Detian Waterfall** (p208), close to the Vietnam border. Backtrack to Nánníng and fly or take the train to **Guìyáng** (p101) before busing over to the breathtaking **Huangguoshu Falls** (p115) and continuing on to Xīngyì and **Maling Gorge** (p124). If it's spring, make a beeline for **Luópíng** (p302) in Yúnnán, a short journey from Xīngyì's never-ending bright yellow fields. Continue to Kūnmíng and down the southeast to the spectacular **Yuanyang Rice Terraces** (p323). Return to Kūnmíng and journey to **Xiàguān** (p242) and on to **Liùkù** (p297) for treks along the **Nujiang Valley** (p297) or continue to Lìjiāng (p265) for a trek

through **Tiger Leaping Gorge** (p281), with views of **Yùlóng Xuěshān** (p274). Near Lìjiāng is **Lugu Lake** (p285) and the stunning sights around **Shangri-la** (p287). **Déqīn** (p294), **Kawa Karpo Mountain** (p296) and **Mingyong Glacier** (p295) lie further north still towards Tibet. Bus travel to **Yading Nature Reserve** (p407) via **Dàochéng** (p407) in Sìchuān is possible from Shangri-la, as are buses to **Chéngdū** (p358) via Kāngdìng and **Hailuogou Glacier Park** (p392) and the options along the Sìchuān–Tibet Hwy. Alternatively, from Kūnmíng fly to Chéngdū to take a trip to **Jiuzhaigou Nature Reserve** (p415), then sail through the magnificent **Three Gorges** (p458) from Chóngqìng to Yíchāng; here flights, buses and planes connect with the rest of China.

Destination Southwest China

A siesta from China's instinct to put in the overtime, a holiday from the national overdrive and an unspoiled getaway from China's ever more water-less north, China's Southwest is a lush and invigorating region of the Middle Kingdom. This is remote China at its most diverse and exotic.

China's Southwest is an essential counterbalance to the nation's impatient and shrill powerhouses. If you want your China the Gucci way – go to Shànghǎi, Hong Kong or Běijīng; and stay put. If however, you're angling for astonishing scenic beauty, wild mountainous treks, riveting displays of ethnic culture and the irresistible allure of the immense outdoors, China's Southwest is a fascinating and rewarding destination.

Everything you expect a China trip to be is here: there's history, mouth-watering cuisine, astonishing landscapes, off-the-beaten track getaways, modern cityscapes and a rich and abundant ethnic backdrop. Unlike the dusty northern Chinese heartland, where the minority presence is often sparse and intangible, China's Southwest is richly peopled by ethnic tribes who bring a unique dimension to China travel. With much of the region refreshingly hedging up against non-Han Chinese civilisations, from the mountains of Tibet through Burma and Laos to Vietnam, the Chinese stamp is rapidly diffused by a minority-rich presence.

Fabled topography ranges from the heavenly landscapes around Yángshuò to the wild mountain scenery of Western Sìchuān and Northern Yúnnán. Celebrated cuisine spans the culinary encyclopedia from the blistering flavours of Húnán through the numbing aromas of Sìchuān, the sweltering hotpots of Chóngqìng to the minority dishes of Guìzhōu and the diverse menus of Yúnnán.

Western journalistic commentary paints a China irrepressibly on the move, striding into an opulent future: a country where staggering GDP figures share the tabloid limelight with stylish models and swanky brand names. You would be forgiven for thinking that Shànghǎi's dazzling renaissance or Běijīng's Olympic buzz somehow summed up China.

China is indeed going places. In 2006, the Three Gorges Dam – the world's largest – was in place three years ahead of schedule. China shot a man into space in 2003, repeated the feat in 2005 and reportedly aims to get a man to the moon by 2024. Currently the world's fourth largest economy, pundits constantly tip China to overtake the US economy within the next few decades. Despite downsizing, the country has the world's largest standing army (which could sponge up the world's largest number of permanent bachelors, a by-product of the one-child policy). China also finds itself at the heart of a potential shift of world power from the West to the East.

While these are all facts of modern China, it can seem like a fantasy to those wandering in off-the-beaten-track minority villages in north Guǎngxī or rural Guìzhōu. Travelling the Southwest is a sheer lesson in scale and a primer in diversity: China is so vast and disparate, it soon becomes clear that the huge progress of the past decades is either concentrated elsewhere or spread very thin.

Like much of the rest of China, the Southwest indeed finds itself pinched between the poverty and powerlessness of the past and the affluence and growing self-confidence of an uncertain future. For some, the fruits of the economic

FAST FACTS: CHINA

Population: 1.3 billion

Life expectancy male/female: 70.4/73.7 years

GDP growth: 10.5% (2006)

GDP per capita: US$7600 (PPP), US$2001 (nominal)

Population below poverty line: 10% (2004 estimate)

Adult literacy: 86%

Internet users: 137 million

Major exports: textiles, clothing, footwear, toys and machinery

Religions: Buddhism, Taoism, Islam, Christianity

Number of Chinese characters: over 56,000

3 1833 05401 8459

boom are tangible and easy to assess, but on other development indicators – democracy, human rights, adequate rural education and healthcare, the rule of law, intellectual property rights and environmental degradation, to name a few – China is either making negligible progress or is indeed stationary (or moving backwards).

The immediate ills of economic restructuring are the stresses and strains of readjustment. China is a work – the biggest on the planet – in progress, with the *lǎobǎixìng* (common folk) frequently voicing discomfort about the direction of economic growth, especially when corruption, land confiscation and pollution remain rampant. Perhaps more than in any other country in the world, wealth is power in China; and the Chinese aspire to wealth to obtain certainty in an often capricious and unpredictable state.

The dismal certainties of the socialist era may have been depressingly familiar, but they were rock-solid. Today's riotous economy is a sink-or-swim set-up with few welfare nets to protect the impoverished or disadvantaged. Affluent pockets such as Liǔzhōu (p189) in Guǎngxī and Xīngyì (p121) in Guìzhōu hedge up against numbing, miserable poverty.

Despite its relative economic isolation and the large disparities between the Southwest and the eastern seaboard, the Southwest remains resiliently conservative. He may be long forgotten in the boardrooms of east China, but Mao's portrait still hangs stubbornly in Dong drum towers in Guǎngxī. Yet China's vast economic potential is making serious inroads. According to some reports Chóngqìng is the world's largest metropolitan area, and money is being shovelled into transport infrastructure throughout the Southwest in a bid to ignite economic potential.

Unlike north and east China, where Godzilla-sized carbon footprints carpet the land, the denizens of lush Southwest China are cleaner and greener. Travellers to Běijīng and Shànghǎi moan perennially about pollution, but – with perhaps the exception of Chéngdū and Chóngqìng – there are fewer surgical masks on the streets of the Southwest, while the rustbelt of the northeast is little more than hearsay.

Despite the rebellious paroxysms of the 20th century, the Chinese are a deeply pragmatic people. The Chinese are respectful and fearful of authority, so you won't see any antigovernment graffiti in China. You won't hear speakers standing on soap boxes to vent their political views (unless they chime with government opinion). Indoctrination, propaganda and censorship are rife, from school textbooks to the broadsheets that are pinned up in public or published on line. Political debate is stifled and most Chinese keep their heads down and work hard for a living. All of this creates a perhaps misleading impression of placidity, but as the Chinese say: 人不可貌相, 海不可斗量; *rén bùkě màoxiàng, hǎi búkě dǒu liáng* – you can't judge a book by its cover.

History

Given its tendency towards colour and vibrancy, it's no surprise that the history of China's Southwest comes at you like an action-packed flick, full of brazen, unpredictable characters and dramatic, untamed scenery. With ruthless warlords, shifting dynasties, foreign intruders and civil turmoil, the Southwest has often served as China's frying pan – the hotbed of many fiery scenes with consequences that sputter out across the country. There's never a dull moment.

Stephan Haw squeezes a very concise and readable account of China's past into 300 pages in *A Traveller's History of China*.

TRADITIONALLY DIVERSE

One of China's earliest settlements was founded in Sìchuān and populated by settlers from the Yellow River basin, the oldest cradle of Chinese civilisation. It was in these very early days that the Southwest was established as a multi-ethnic domain; the whole of the region was inhabited by Thai-related tribes, who were joined by Miao and other migrating tribes around 2000 to 3000 years ago. Much of the west of the region was inhabited by Qiang tribes, ancestors of the Tibetans. By 3000 BC, a distinct culture had evolved in modern day Sìchuān, based on the kingdoms of Shu (which took in Chéngdū, parts of northwest Yúnnán and northwest Guìzhōu) and Ba (centred on the region between Yíbīn and the Three Gorges). By 1200 BC these kingdoms were joined by the agriculturally suave Dian culture around Kūnmíng.

Han Chinese settlers started to trickle into the area in the 5th century BC. As time went by, waves of Han migrants fleeing war, famine and the barbarian invasions of the north slowly shifted the demography of the region and brought it into the Chinese fold. Nevertheless, the region is still home to at least 26 different ethnic groups and, particularly in rural areas, many of their traditions are still very much a part of life. See Minority Cultures (p51) for more information.

IN THE BEGINNING

With each new discovery, archaeologists have continued to push back the year that humans first set up camp in China's Southwest. Some of the earliest multi-celled organisms ever discovered were unearthed in Guìzhōu, with one fossil encasing what is believed to be a 580-million-year-old embryo. The mind boggles. The Chéngjiāng region of Yúnnán has also been fertile ground for soft-bodied fossils, some of which have revealed so much about the evolutionary process that they have been listed as world cultural relics by Unesco. In fact, Yúnnán has established itself as one of Asia's earliest human hangouts, with an eight-million-year-old anthropoid skull dug up from its soil.

TIMELINE

c 3000 BC	604 BC	551 BC
A civilisation is well-established in modern-day Sìchuān, incorporating a number of minority, tribal cultures. It is a period of major advances, including the construction of the Dujiangyan Irrigation System near Chéngdū, still in use today.	Laotzu, the founder of Taoism, is reputedly born. Aged 80, disillusioned, he leaves his job as keeper of the archives at the imperial court, to write his seminal text *The Way and its Power*.	Confucius is born. Within half a century his teachings are deep-seated in Chinese society; however, they also remain at odds with many of the Southwest's minority cultures.

CHINESE DYNASTIES

Dynasty	Period	Site of capital
Xia	**2200–1700 BC**	
Shang	**1700–1100 BC**	Ānyáng
Zhou	**1100–221 BC**	
Western Zhou	1100–771 BC	Hào (near Xī'ān)
Eastern Zhou	770–221 BC	Luòyáng
Qin	**221–207 BC**	Xiányáng
Han	**206 BC–AD 220**	
Western Han	206 BC–AD 9	Xī'ān
Xin	AD 9–23	Xī'ān
Eastern Han	AD 25–220	Luòyáng
Three Kingdoms	**AD 220–80**	
Wei	AD 220–65	Luòyáng
Shu (Shu Han)	AD 221–63	Chéngdū
Wu	AD 229–80	Nánjīng
Jin	**AD 265–420**	
Western Jin	AD 265–317	Luòyáng
Eastern Jin	AD 317–420	Nánjīng
Southern & Northern Dynasties	**AD 420–589**	
Southern Dynasties		
Song	AD 420–79	Nánjīng
Qi	AD 479–502	Nánjīng
Liang	AD 502–57	Nánjīng
Chen	AD 557–89	Nánjīng

SPIRIT OF REBELLION

Home to dissidents, rebels and exiled officials, the final stomping ground of empires on their last legs and the breeding ground of rising empires, the Southwest has nurtured a fierce independent streak since its earliest days. When Chinese dynasties to the north were strong, they expanded and conquered, but whenever they grew weak and withdrew, independent kingdoms sprang up in their wake. Chinese emperors saw the region as a barbarian and pestilent borderland populated by wild and uncivilised tribes who were the first to rebel and the last to be brought back in line. However, it's this rebellious spirit that is the glue that binds the Southwest's history together. Today, while very much a part of China, the Southwest continues to maintain a distinctiveness. This comes from the remaining strength of the region's minority cultures, but is also a result of being so far from the say-so of Běijīng.

221 BC	206 BC–AD 220	c 100 BC
Qin Shi Huang becomes China's first emperor after integrating the Southwest and unifying the country. He runs a brutal, tightly centralised government. The Qin dynasty falls after just 15 years.	Born into a peasant family, Liu Bang conquers China from his base in Sìchuān. The new emperor establishes the Han dynasty which rules for more than four centuries, during which the Sìchuān irrigation system is further developed.	Chinese traders and explorers follow the Silk Road through the Southwest and all the way to Rome. The two empires become major trading partners.

Dynasty	Period	Site of capital
Northern Dynasties		
Northern Wei	AD 386–534	Dàtóng, Luòyáng
Eastern Wei	AD 534–50	Linzhang
Northern Qi	AD 550–77	Linzhang
Western Wei	AD 535–56	Xī'ān
Northern Zhou	AD 557–81	Xī'ān
Sui	**AD 581–618**	Xī'ān
Tang	**AD 618–907**	Xī'ān
Five Dynasties & Ten Kingdoms	**AD 907–60**	
Later Liang	AD 907–23	Kāifēng
Later Tang	AD 923–36	Luòyáng
Later Jin	AD 936–47	Kāifēng
Later Han	AD 947–50	Kāifēng
Later Zhou	AD 951–60	Kāifēng
Liao	**AD 907–1125**	
Song	**AD 960–1279**	
Northern Song	AD 960–1127	Kāifēng
Southern Song	AD 1127–1279	Hángzhōu
Jin	**AD 1115–1234**	Kāifēng, Běijīng
Yuan	**AD 1206–1368**	Běijīng
Ming	**AD 1368–1644**	Nánjīng, Běijīng
Qing	**AD 1644–1911**	Běijīng
Republic of China	**AD 1911–49**	Běijīng, Chóngqìng, Nánjīng
People's Republic of China (PRC)	**AD 1949–**	Běijīng

Nanzhao Kingdom

Throughout history, Yúnnán has been the most independent region of the Southwest and while the Chinese Tang dynasty took control of most of China in 619, Yúnnán remained divided into six independent kingdoms. Nanzhao, the most powerful of these, was established by the Bai people and based at Dàlǐ.

Initially allied with the Tang against the Tibetans, the Tang began to feel that the Bai were getting a little big for their britches and so, in the 8th century, a Tang squad of 80,000 troupes swept south to Dàlǐ to establish control. The Tang were soundly whipped (60,000 of them were massacred) by the Bai.

In the aftermath, the Nanzhao Kingdom established itself as a fully independent entity and took control of a large slice of the Southwest, reaching as far as Hanoi in the southeast, Sìchuān in the north, Zūnyì in the northeast

c 50 BC	AD 221	581–618
Some two and a half centuries after it was discovered by Emperor Shennong, China is the first country to document tea-drinking, primarily for its medicinal benefits.	After the fall of the Han, the Sìchuān warlord Shu Han proclaims himself emperor. One of three claimants to the throne (the Three Kingdoms period), he is eventually defeated by northerners.	Nobleman Yang Jian reunifies China under the Sui dynasty. Under his successor, Sui Yangdi, the dynasty goes into rapid decline. Sui Yangdi is assassinated in 618 by one of his own high officials.

and Nánníng in the east, and during this time they dominated trade routes to India and Burma. They later joined forces with the Tibetans to sack Chéngdū in 829, transported tens of thousands of scholars and artisans back to Dàlǐ, and ruled as the most important kingdom in the Southwest for the next six centuries.

The Emperor and the Assassin (1999) is the epic tale of the first emperor of Qin and his lust for power. Woven with murder, love and political intrigue, this film is beautifully shot and a must-see whether you're a history buff or not.

As time went on, Nanzhao rulers were wowed by the glories of the northern Tang, and Chinese culture began to spread like wildfire into the region. In the 10th century, the Nanzhao kingdom was deposed by ethnic Chinese rulers, however the independent kingdom of Dàlǐ continued right up until the Mongol invasion in 1252, when it was finally incorporated into the Yuan dynasty.

Christ's Kid Brother & Other Rebels

By the mid-19th century, secret societies resisting the ruling Qing dynasty were forced inland by the British. These pirates took to shipping opium up and down the waterways of Guǎngxī and Guìzhōu (p29).

Increasing Han migration continued to force many of the local minority peoples off the best lands. Faced with such extreme hardship and humiliation, exacerbated by crippling taxes, rebellions sparked and spread through the region.

The first major revolt was the Taiping Rebellion, which burst out of Jīntián village (near Guìpíng in Guǎngxī, see p198) in 1851 and swept through Guìzhōu. Comprising forces of 600,000 men and 500,000 women, the Taipings eventually took Nánjīng three years later. The Taipings were led by Hong Xiuquan, a failed examination candidate whose encounters with Western missionaries had led him to believe he was the younger brother of Jesus Christ.

The Taipings forbade gambling, opium, tobacco and alcohol, advocated agricultural reform, and outlawed prostitution, slavery and foot binding. The rebellion took tens of millions of lives before being suppressed in 1864 by a coalition of Qing and Western forces – the Europeans preferring to deal with a corrupt and weak Qing government than a powerful, united China governed by the Taipings.

Before being squashed, the Taipings also hooked up with a large Miao rebellion in Guìzhōu. This rebellious group was led by Zhang Xumei and gained many military victories. By the time it was defeated by the Qing in 1871, it had cost several million deaths.

Another further rebellion to rock Yúnnán was sparked by rivalries between the Muslim and Chinese tin miners. A Muslim army (armed by the British) rose up in 1855 and was led by Sultan Suleiman. It quickly took on an anti-government nature when the Qing authorities sided with the Chinese. The Chinese army (armed by the French) slaughtered tens of thousands of Muslims and crushed the rebellion.

618–907	690–705	880–907
Li Yuan establishes the Tang dynasty. It develops links with Persia, India, Malaysia, Indonesia and Japan; Buddhism flourishes; and the plethora of literature produced earns this era the nickname 'Golden Age'.	Wu Zhao is China's first and only empress. Under her often cruel leadership the empire flourishes. She promotes Confucian scholars, but they force her to abdicate when she advocates Buddhism.	Rebels take the capital of Chang'an in 880, forcing the ruler to flee to Sìchuān. The Tang dynasty survives another 27 years, but is fatally weakened. Smaller, weaker kingdoms fill the political vacuum.

DYNASTIC-BOMBASTIC

In 221 BC, the rule of Qin Shi Huang trickled down into China's Southwest, pulling the area into China's dynastic rule and, for the first time, uniting the Chinese into a single empire. The Qin conquered parts of the Baiyu kingdom in eastern Guǎngxī along with the kingdom of Shu in present-day Sìchuān, where the dynasty's capital was established. While they didn't manage to spread into Yúnnán or Guìzhōu, sovereignty was acknowledged and Qin Shi Huang celebrated by honouring himself with the newly coined title of *huángdì*, or emperor. And thus began a string of dynastic rule that would try again and again (with varying success) to contain the Southwest.

What did dynastic rule mean for China's Southwest? Dynasties often had a difficult time extending their rule into the Southwest, with its rebellious minority groups and rugged terrain. Many didn't even try, while others threw a loose noose around the territory but then turned a blind eye. Very few actually tried to rope the region in.

During the Han dynasty (206 BC–AD 220), the *tǔsī* system was established, whereby a hereditary imperial title was bestowed onto local chieftains or headmen. The Chinese saw this as 'ruling barbarians with barbarians' and as long as local rulers maintained peace and paid their taxes they were largely left to their own devices. This system dominated imperial China's relations with the Southwest for two millennia.

Nevertheless, dynastic rule brought huge changes to China and these often impacted the Southwest in very real ways. The Qin dynasty (221–207 BC) introduced uniform currency, standardised script, weights and measurements, and by digging the Ling Canal in Guǎngxī, created a north–south waterway that was the linchpin in linking the region with the rest of the empire.

The Han dynasty sent exploratory missions through the Southwest to India, establishing the Silk Routes and opening channels of trade that would eventually provide a path for the introduction of Hinayana Buddhism from Burma. The short-lived Sui dynasty (581–618) brought administrative and land reform, a strengthened civil service at the expense of aristocratic privilege, and revisions in law code. The Tang dynasty (618–907) divided the empire into 300 prefectures (州; *zhōu*) and 1500 counties (县; *xiàn*), establishing a pattern of territorial jurisdiction that persists, with some modifications, to this day.

The Song dynasty (960–1279) is remembered for its advances in archaeology, mathematics, astronomy, geography, medicine and the arts. Brought on by the spread of rice cultivation, agricultural productivity boomed and eventually left a surplus of labour that was used to develop secondary industries, such as mining, ceramics and silk manufacture.

The introduction of paper money facilitated the growth of more urban centres and was the turning point in China's development of an urban culture. An educated class of high social standing became a distinguishing

www.chinaknowledge .de/History/history.htm has seemingly bottomless coverage of China's various dynasties and eras, with links to more specific information on everything from the religion to technology and economy of each period.

960–1279	c AD 1000	1211
Zhao Kuangyin begins conquering kingdoms – including Sìchuān – and reunifies China under the Song dynasty. The dynasty coexists with non-Chinese powers who eventually drive it south for its final 50 years, and it falls in 1279.	The major inventions of the premodern world – paper, printing, gunpowder and the compass – are all commonly used in China. Under the Song dynasty, significant advances are also made in natural sciences, medicine, mechanics and mathematics.	Mongol ruler Genghis Khan penetrates the Great Wall and two years later conquers Běijīng to establish the Yuan dynasty. It controls China for less than a century before it is convulsed with rebellion.

feature of Chinese society as Confucianism achieved the dominance it was to retain until the 19th century.

The Yuan dynasty (1271–1368) brought shock waves of refugees to the Southwest as Han Chinese fled from the wrath of Genghis Khan and the Mongols. In addition to this, as many as one million Muslim mercenaries settled in Yúnnán to control and repopulate the devastated countryside. The population boom of the Qing dynasty (1644–1911), brought on by the introduction of New World crops and increasingly efficient famine relief and flood control, also prompted mass migration to the Southwest as land-hungry Han took over aboriginal lands.

Some of these changes, such as migration, had immediate effects. Others, like the introduction of standardised script, took longer to take root in the Southwest, but their effects have been equally pronounced on the cultures of the local people.

A Juggling Game

Dynastic rule was often tyrannical and forceful and, given the strong cultures of the region, it's not surprising that Chinese rule often clashed with independent groups in the Southwest. As their spheres of influence grew or dwindled, the dynasties were continually redrawing the map to include or rub out the Southwest.

The Qin conquered only eastern Guǎngxī and Sìchuān while the Han dynasty swept many of the far-flung vassal states under its skirts, including present-day Guǎngxī and Guìzhōu. Nevertheless, independent kingdoms still held sway in some of the Southwest: the Shu and Ba in Sìchuān, the Dian in Yúnnán and the Nanue around Guǎngxī. During the Three Kingdoms, the Han Shu controlled much of Guìzhōu and Yúnnán, but the region's clan-based settlements were largely left undisturbed. The strong Tang dynasty surged towards the Southwest and built garrison towns like Guìyáng and Ānlóng in the Guìzhōu and Guǎngxī region. Chinese control resumed all the way down to Annan ('the pacified south') in northern Vietnam.

While the Song's strong influence on Chinese culture influenced the Southwest, it had little direct involvement in the region. The Song emperor incorporated Sìchuān into the empire but supposedly drew a line across the Dàdū River on a map of Sìchuān and told his generals to forget about the lands to the south. The Song had few dealings with Yúnnán and, for a while, Zhuang rebels set up a short-lived kingdom in Guǎngxī.

It was during the Yuan dynasty, under the Mongol rule of Kublai Khan, that much of the Southwest was included into the empire. Khan reached Yúnnán (via Lugu Lake) and set up ruling centres at Kūnmíng and Dàlǐ. Both Yúnnán and Guǎngxī were formally brought into the imperial fold and the latter received its modern name for the first time. The China ruled

> Marco Polo traipsed through the Southwest during the Yuan dynasty (1206–1368), travelling from Chéngdū to Kūnmíng and scribbling notes about crocodiles, rice wine and tattooed tribespeople.

1368	1406	1557
Zhu Yuanzhang, an orphan, leads a peasant revolution. He reunifies China and establishes the Ming dynasty, conquering Sìchuān from Mongol rule in 1371 and then pushing south to take Yúnnán.	Ming Emperor Yongle begins construction of the 800 buildings of the Forbidden City. The Imperial Palace takes 14 years to complete by an estimated 200,000 workers.	The Portugese establish a permanent trading post in Macau, after paying a tribute to Běijīng. The next 100 years are considered Macau's golden age, as trade booms between Portugal and China.

by Kublai was the largest empire the world has ever known, stretching from the Ukraine and Persia to the northern limits of Vietnam.

The Ming dynasty saw the formal incorporation of the rest of the Southwest into the Chinese empire as political and military control of the region tightened. In reality though, semi-independent local fiefdoms still commanded their own armies and raised their own taxes throughout much of the Southwest.

Imperial rule was propped up by agricultural garrison-communities run by governors-general whose thankless job was to extend the control of the empire. They did this through various 'pacification campaigns' among the local minorities. One of the bloodiest battles in Guǎngxī's history was fought between imperial troops and Yao tribesmen near Guìpíng in 1465. Yúnnán was equally rebellious and Guìzhōu grew as a heavily garrisoned base for incursions into both provinces. When the Ming finally did fall, the remnants of the declining dynasty clung desperately to power in the Southwest, as the Song had done before them. The last Ming prince made a hopeless last stand in Gāolígòng Shān near the current border with Burma before finally fleeing to Mandalay.

The reign of the Qing was a period of great prosperity, although it was four decades before the dynasty finally stamped out the Ming loyalist forces from the south. A mass migration of Han Chinese into the region took the Qing administration with it.

Oertai, a Manchu nobleman, was made governor-general of Guìzhōu, Yúnnán and Guǎngxī and given a mission to bring the local tribes under imperial control. To accomplish this, he was to abolish the powerful local *tǔsī* (土司; p27) headmen who had been effectively ruling the region for centuries.

Oertai soon had ethnic conflict on his shoulders. An uprising in 1726 led to the beheading of 10,000 Miao tribespeople; a further 400,000 starved to death in an ensuing famine. A similar rebellion is believed to have taken place in 1797 among the Bouyi. Suppressing these rebellions placed an enormous strain on the imperial treasury, ultimately contributing to the end of dynastic rule in China.

'The Ming dynasty saw the formal incorporation of the rest of the Southwest into the Chinese empire.'

WHEN THINGS GOT HAIRY

In the mid-18th century China remained inward-looking and seemingly oblivious to the technological and scientific revolutions taking place in Europe. Before long, the 'hairy barbarians' (Westerners) were landing on their shores and by 1760 they were banging at the gate.

Up in Smoke

The early Qing emperors showed a relatively open attitude towards Europeans in China, but by the 18th century this had changed. Qianlong, ruler

1644	1661–1735	1751
The northern Manchus march into Běijīng and proclaim the Qing dynasty. Shunzhi is installed as its first emperor on 30 October. The Qing dynasty lasts until the end of China's dynastic rule in 1911.	The emperor Kangxi extends Qing rule to the Southwest and leads two major expeditions in the far west. Kangxi's 61-year reign makes him the longest-serving emperor in China's history.	Tibet becomes a Chinese colony. With the fall of the Qing dynasty in 1911, Tibet enters a period of de facto independence until 1950 when China invades (or, from the Chinese perspective, 'liberates').

from 1736 to 1795, imposed strict controls on maritime trade, which from 1757 was limited to the single river port of Guǎngzhōu.

Nevertheless, as the British, Dutch and Spanish pried open the Chinese markets from Guǎngzhōu, trade began to flourish – in China's favour. The British couldn't get enough of China's tea, silk and porcelain, and their shopping far outweighed the Chinese purchases of wool and spices. In 1773 the British decided to balance the books with sales of opium. Opium had long been a popular drug in China, but had been outlawed in the early 18th century.

Despite strong Chinese prohibitions, opium addiction in China skyrocketed and, with it, so did sales. Anti-drug laws were far from effective as many officials were opium addicts and therefore assisted in smuggling the drug into China.

'By the early 19th century the opium trade had grown to the point of shifting the trade balance in favour of the Westerners.'

By the early 19th century the opium trade had grown to the point of shifting the trade balance in favour of the Westerners. Opium had become the main crop among the warlords and minorities of the Southwest; the land and its people were saturated in it. Opium was even used as local currency in some places.

The Chinese Government's attempt to halt the illegal traffic in 1839 brought about the famous Opium Wars. The result was the Treaty of Nanking in 1842, which left Hong Kong in the hands of the British 'in perpetuity'. This was soon followed by the British leasing the New Territories and adjoining Kowloon for 99 years, with the promise that the entire colony would be returned to Chinese control at the end of the lease. This handover took place with much fanfare in 1997.

An Unexpected Dinner Date

As imperial control loosened, the Western powers began moving in. A war with France in 1858 (to avenge the murder of a French missionary in Guǎngxī) and another from 1883 to 1885 allowed the French to maintain control of Indochina and carve out Yúnnán and Guǎngxī as their designated sphere of influence. Wúzhōu to the east was prised open to foreign trade in 1897 and Nánníng followed 10 years later. In 1903 France started to build the railway line from Haiphong and Hanoi to Kūnmíng, a line which would soon become the province's main link to the outside world. By 1911 one million Chinese were riding the train every year.

In the latter half of the 19th century, the British were also creeping closer to China's Southwest. Occupying the Kachin state of northern Burma, they persuaded one of Yúnnán's local *tǔsī* headman to defect to the British cause and thereby snatched a strategic section of land. In 1891, 500 British troops briefly occupied Jǐnghóng and began to toy with the idea of building a railway line from Burma to Yúnnán. When a British commercial agent was killed during an exploratory mission to the Yúnnán–Burma border, the British used

1839	1842	1850
China confiscates and destroys 20,000 chests of opium smuggled into the country by Britain, setting off the first of two Opium Wars. Britain's superior military power overwhelms Qing forces.	Following its defeat in the first Opium War, China gives favourable trading terms to Britain, hands over Hong Kong in 'perpetuity', and allows British missionaries to work in China.	The anti-Qing Taiping Rebellion erupts in Guǎngxī province, but ultimately fails to establish its Christian ideology throughout China. An estimated 20 million civilians and soldiers die in the conflict. Major revolts are defeated elsewhere, including Yúnnán.

his murder as a means to extract more trade concessions from the Qing. In 1900 a British gunboat docked in Chóngqìng for the first time.

By the turn of the century, the European powers were on the verge of carving up China for dinner, a feast that was thwarted only by a US proposal for an open-door policy that would leave China open to trade with any foreign power.

Japanese Invasion

The early 1930s saw a great deal of political upheaval in China, namely between the communists and the Kuomintang (KMT; Nationalist Party). This gave the Japanese the opportunity they'd been waiting for. In September 1931 they invaded and occupied Manchuria, setting up a puppet state with Puyi, the last Manchu emperor. So obsessed were the KMT with the threat of the communists, they did nothing to resist Japan's invasion. The KMT was bitterly criticised for not defending China against the Japanese and eventually the party's leader, Chiang Kaishek, was taken hostage by his own generals in an attempt to force an anti-Japanese alliance with the communists. This did little to halt the advance of the Japanese.

Japan launched an all-out invasion in 1937, taking most of eastern China and advancing as far as Nánníng in central Guǎngxī. Human experiments in biological warfare factories and 'burn all, loot all, kill all' campaigns quickly made it one of the most brutal occupations of the 20th century. By 1939 the Japanese had overrun most of eastern China and had reached Nánníng in central Guǎngxī. China experienced massive internal migrations and was subjected to a process of divide and rule through the establishment of puppet governments.

Ironically, the war proved to be a huge boost to the economy and industrialisation of the Southwest. The KMT was forced into retreat by the Japanese occupation and, from 1938 to 1945, Chóngqìng (p436) became the new seat of the Nationalist government. Then a higgledy-piggledy town piled up on mountains in the upper reaches of the Yangzi River, the city was subjected to heavy Japanese bombardments, but logistical difficulties prevented it being approached by land. Entire factories were shifted upstream and China's best universities relocated to Kūnmíng and Chéngdū, along with an estimated 60 to 80 million Chinese. Guìlín (p154) became a major air-force base.

In 1942 the Japanese overran Burma and cut off the Burma Road. The allies were forced to build another road, this time from Ledo in northeast India. An allied plane service began operating from British India over the Himalayas into the airfields of Kūnmíng and Lìjiāng. The route was extremely hazardous (an average of 13 planes were lost each month) but it ensured supplies until the new road opened in 1944. The Japanese eventually reached Téngchōng in Yúnnán and even got as far as taking Guìlín and Wúzhōu in 1944 before their surrender in 1945.

'The early 1930s saw a great deal of political upheaval in China, namely between the communists and the Kuomintang.'

1894–1931	**1908**	**1912–27**
China and Japan go to war, initially over Korea and then in Manchuria. Japan wins an overwhelming victory and establishes a concession in Manchuria. Modernisers in China begin to work for reform.	Two-year-old Puyi ascends the throne as China's last emperor. In 1911 a revolt led by Sun Yatsen establishes a republic. Puyi is forced to abdicate and is eventually expelled from Běijīng in 1924.	Sun Yatsen hands over the presidency to general Yuan Shikai, who tries to impose centralised rule on the divided nation, and then declares himself emperor. The move fails, and China is divided among regional warlords.

THE EMERGENCE OF A REPUBLIC

China's final dynasty, the Qing, managed to cling to power until 1911. The short-lived Boxer Rebellion, led by a xenophobic group who violently attacked foreigners with the support of secret charms, martial arts and the support of the Qing Court, was defeated in 1900 by a combined British, US, French, Japanese and Russian force. This resulted in the foreign forces levying yet another massive indemnity on the Qing government and the ruling empress finally admitting the reality that China was too weak to survive without reform.

The civil service examinations (based on irrelevant 1000-year-old Confucian doctrines) were abolished, but other reforms proved to be a sham and little changed. Meanwhile, secret societies were in league to bring down the dynasty. To make matters worse for the Qing, the empress died in 1908 and left two-year-old Puyi to take over the throne. The Qing was now rudderless and teetered on the brink of collapse.

As an increasing number of new railways were financed and built by foreigners, public anger grew and gave birth to the Railway Protection Movement that spread and quickly took on an anti-Qing nature. The movement turned increasingly violent, especially in Sìchuān. In 1911 republican revolutionaries saw the large-scale Railway Protection Movement as a vehicle to victory over the Qing and hopped on the back of it. The Republicans soon gained support throughout China and rose to power. Two months later, representatives from 17 provinces throughout China gathered in Nánjīng to establish the Provisional Republican Government of China. China's long dynastic rule had reached its end.

China's Provisional Republican Government was led by Sun Yatsen, a Christian and trained medical practitioner educated in Hawaii and Hong Kong. Sun developed a political programme based on 'Three Principles of the People': nationalism, popular sovereignty and livelihood, and his revolution was supported by Chinese communities abroad, as well as by disaffected members of the Qing army. Following early republican uprisings, Sun had fled China in 1895 and watched his campaign succeed from abroad. In 1911 he returned to his homeland and was named president.

Lacking the power to force a Manchu abdication, Sun had no choice but to call on the assistance of Yuan Shikai, the head of the imperial army. The republicans promised Yuan Shikai presidency if he could negotiate the abdication of the emperor, which he achieved. The favour cost the republicans dearly. Yuan Shikai placed himself at the head of the republican movement and forced Sun Yatsen to stand down.

Yuan lost no time in dissolving the Republican Government and amending the constitution to make himself president for life. When this met with regional opposition, he pronounced himself China's newest emperor in 1915. Yúnnán seceded, taking Guǎngxī, Guìzhōu and much of the Southwest with

Mr China's Son: A Villager's Life is an autobiography written by He Liyi, an English-language teacher. The story chronicles how events of the 20th century played out in a small, Bai minority village in remote Yúnnán. The language is slightly halting but the story is captivating.

1926	1931	1934
Chiang Kai-shek rises to power and leads the Northern Expedition out of Guangdong defeating major warlords one by one and proclaiming the Republic of China with its capital in Nánjīng.	From their concession in Manchuria, Japanese troops conquer China's three northeastern provinces. They proclaim it the new nation of Manchukuo under Puyi as emperor.	Close to defeat in their base in Jiāngxī, the communists stage the year-long Long March, which covers 6000 miles through the Southwest and into Sìchuān. On the way Mao Zedong asserts himself as the communist leader.

it. Forces were sent to bring the breakaway provinces back into the imperial ambit, and in the midst of it all, Yuan died.

Between 1916 and 1927, the government in Běijīng lost power over the far-flung provinces and China was effectively fragmented into semi-autonomous regions governed by warlords.

COMMUNISM

Communism is a word quickly associated with China. For Westerners it often conjures up images of navy blue Mao suits, poverty and colourless cities. However, communism in China has taken many forms and has been far from stagnant. At times flourishing and at times horrific (see boxed text, p196), the influence of the communists has been far-reaching. Like their dynastic predecessors, the communists have struggled in their efforts to 'tame' the Southwest, however their success in bringing the region into the Chinese fold can hardly be denied. Regardless of whether one sees it as positive or negative, the communist impact has doubtlessly been profound.

Soldiers Marching

By the 1920s the KMT had emerged as the dominant political force in eastern China. Headed by Chiang Kaishek (1887–1975), the party had direct control over only about half of the country; the rest, including the entire Southwest, was still ruled by local warlords. The main opposition to the KMT came from the Chinese Communist Party (CCP), made up of Chinese Marxist groups who had joined together in 1921.

At the time, China was heavily laden with social problems: child slave labour, domestic slavery and prostitution, the destitute starving in the streets, and strikes suppressed ruthlessly by foreign and Chinese factory owners. The CCP proposed solutions to these problems, namely the removal of the KMT. Not surprisingly, Chiang became obsessed with stamping out the influence of the CCP. He attempted to expand his own power base by wringing power from the remaining warlords and then, in 1927, he took more direct action and ordered the massacre of over 5000 Shanghai communists and trade union representatives.

In this same year, the CCP became divided in their views of where to base their rebellion against the KMT – in large urban centres or in the countryside. After costly urban defeats, the tide of opinion started to shift towards Mao Zedong (1893–1976), who advocated rural-based revolt and guerrilla warfare. While the campaign met with some success, particularly in Guăngxī, the communist armies remained small and hampered by limited resources. It wasn't until 1930 that the ragged forces had turned into an army of around 40,000, which presented such a serious challenge to the KMT that Chiang waged extermination campaigns against them. He was defeated each time, and the communist army continued to expand its territory.

Li Zhisui, Mao's personal physician, tells us everything from the sexual habits to political views of his patient in *The Private Life of Chairman Mao*. An equally disturbing biography is found in *Mao: The Unknown Story* by Jung Chang (author of *Wild Swans*) and Jon Halliday.

1937

Japan launches full-scale war on China in the north. A second front opens up in Shānghǎi. The Nationalists retreat. Chiang moves his capital to Chóngqìng in Sìchuān. Yúnnán becomes a major route for American aid supplies.

1945–9

A full-scale civil war erupts between Nationalists and communists. At first the Nationalists do well, backed with heavy US aid. But the communists fight back to first take Manchuria and Běijīng, and then Nánjīng.

1949

On 1 October Mao Zedong proclaims the People's Republic of China. Having taken refuge in Sìchuān, Chiang Kai-shek flees to Taiwan. The US places a protective naval blockade around the island to prevent a communist attack.

Chiang's fifth extermination campaign began in October 1933. Many of the communist troops had begun disregarding Mao's authority and instead began meeting Chiang's troops in pitched battles. This strategy proved disastrous. Within a year the communists had suffered heavy losses and were hemmed into a small area in Jiāngxī.

On the brink of defeat, the communists decided to retreat from Jiāngxī and march north through the Southwest to Shaanxi to join up with other CCP armies. Rather than one long march, there were several, as various armies in the south made their way north. En route, the communists confiscated the property of officials, landlords and tax collectors, and redistributed land to the peasants whom they armed by the thousands with weapons captured from the KMT. Soldiers were left behind to organise guerrilla groups that would harass the enemy.

The marches brought together many people who held top positions after 1949, including Mao Zedong, Zhou Enlai, Zhu De, Lin Biao, Deng Xiaoping and Liu Shaoqi. It also established Mao as the paramount leader of the Chinese communist movement. Along the way, the posse took a breather in Zūnyì (p145), Guìzhōu; if you're in the neighbourhood, you can take in some of the sights. Serious Long March history buffs might also check out Lúdìng (p391) in Sìchuān.

> The communists' early strategy was summed up in their four-line slogan: *The enemy advances, we retreat; the enemy camps, we harass; the enemy tires, we attack; the enemy retreats, we pursue.*

The People's Republic

The People's Republic of China (PRC) began as a bankrupt nation in October 1949. Unbridled inflation and a KMT legacy of economic mismanagement left the economy in chaos. The country had just 19,300km of railways and 76,800km of useable roads – all in bad condition. Irrigation works had broken down and livestock and animal populations were dwindling. Agricultural output plummeted and industrial production was half that of the prewar period.

In the Southwest, the KMT leader Ding Zuoshou was still very much at large in southern Yúnnán and it wasn't until two months after the official takeover that the PRC managed to push through to Kūnmíng, at which point Ding fled to Burma and northern Thailand with 1000 of his best troops. Taiwanese supply planes, aided by the CIA, started to fly arms and ammunition into this small base to prepare for a counter-attack on Yúnnán and soon the KMT troops numbered 12,000.

The KMT made a total of seven attempts to retake Yúnnán between 1951 and 1953 but was never successful. Thousands of KMT troops remained in the region until 1961 when 20,000 PRC troops crossed into Burma and finally overthrew the remaining KMT.

With the communist takeover, China seemed to become a different country. Unified by the elation of victory and the immensity of the tasks before them, the communists made the 1950s a dynamic period. They embarked

1957	1958–60	1960
Mao Zedong launches the Hundred Flowers Campaign, encouraging open debate and criticism. But when he and the Communist Party come in for bitter criticism, the liberalisation is replaced by a major 'anti-rightist' purge.	Mao's Great Leap Forward abolishes private property, establishes massive agricultural communes and ramps up steel production through enforced backyard furnaces. The result is disastrous. A famine follows that kills tens of millions.	Mao frowns on the USSR's détente with the USA and Khrushchev's de-Stalinisation. When the Kremlin refuses to give China a prototype atomic bomb and sides with India in a border dispute, Sino–Soviet relations sink.

upon land reform, recognised the role of women and attempted to restore the economy. By 1953 inflation had been halted, industrial production was back to prewar levels, and land had been confiscated from landlords and redistributed to peasants. On the basis of earlier Soviet models, the Chinese embarked on a massive five-year plan that was fairly successful in lifting production. The government also increased its social control by organising people according to work units (单位; *dānwèi*) and dividing the country in 21 provinces, five autonomous regions and two municipalities (Běijīng and Shànghǎi). Around 2200 county governments held jurisdiction over nearly one million party sub-branches. In the Southwest, the province of Xikang was incorporated in Sìchuān (1955) and Guǎngxī became an autonomous region (1958). The Southwest borderlands saw an intriguing and often tense mixture of traditional tribal culture and Soviet-inspired reform.

Relentless Reforms

Despite its initial triumphs, the early decades of the PRC saw the introduction of severe policies which resulted in suffering and growing distrust throughout the country. The Hundred Flowers Campaign showed the population the repercussions of criticising the government (opposite). The Great Leap Forward pushed the country into catastrophic poverty as people followed unquestioning production orders from above (opposite). Undoubtedly, the most ill-contrived reforms came with the Cultural Revolution (1966–76; p36), a purge of the arts, religion and culture that left neighbours and family members attacking one another, cultural relics levelled and a thick layer of fear draped across the populace. The Tiananmen Massacre of 1989, where peaceful pro-democracy protestors were flattened by the PLA's army, erased what moral authority the government still held. Captured by Western media, the CCP had bared its teeth for the world to see.

Like the rest of China, the Southwest was severely impacted by the enforcement of these policies. In addition to this, those Chinese who were condemned and persecuted through the various campaigns were often sent for thought reform and hard labour in the Southwest's remote reaches. These camps served not only to increase Han presence in the region but also reinforced the widespread belief that the Southwest was backward and that living there was a form of punishment. In some regions of China, this is still a commonly held opinion.

Despite the hardships it has brought (or perhaps because of them), the Chinese populace continues to declare strong support for the CCP. Particularly in rural areas, Han Chinese tow the party line with a mighty heave-ho and it's not uncommon to see Mao's portrait in rural households in the Southwest. Minorities, on the other hand, generally show a definite disinterest. Rarely will you find someone willing to question or criticise the government; the results have been shown to be far too severe.

'Political power grows out of the barrel of a gun.' Mao Zedong

1966–76	1971	1973
Mao launches the Cultural Revolution. The Red Guards are directed to stamp out the four 'Olds': of customs, habits, culture and ideas. In Yúnnán, half of the temples are destroyed and 14,000 people are killed.	The US table-tennis team becomes the first American delegation to set foot in China in 49 years. The following year, President Richard Nixon visits, meeting Mao and paving the way for a normalisation of bilateral relations.	Having fallen out of favour during the Cultural Revolution, Sìchuān native and Long March veteran Deng Xiaoping is called back as senior vice-premier. By the end of the decade he emerges as China's de facto leader.

RUNNING (A) RIOT

Mao's extreme views, disastrous Great Leap Forward and opposition to bureaucratisation left him feeling isolated within the Party. To get back into the limelight of leadership, he set about cultivating a personality cult. Evidence of his mammoth success can still easily be found in market stalls across the nation, where Mao-embossed lighters, ashtrays and other random memorabilia continue to be sold. In the early 1960s a collection of Mao's selected thoughts were compiled into the 'little red book'. Studied by People's Liberation Army (PLA) troops and introduced into the general education system, this was to become one of the symbols of the era.

Around this time a play was released criticising Mao and a campaign began against it. The purge of the arts that followed led to the unfathomable Cultural Revolution (文化大革命; Wénhuà Dà Gémìng; 1966–76). Sanctioned by Mao, posters went up at Beijing University attacking its administration and Mao's opposition within the CCP. Before long students were issued red armbands and took to the streets. The Red Guards (红卫兵; Hóngwèibīng) were born. By August 1966 Mao was reviewing mass parades of the Red Guards in Tiananmen Sq, chanting and waving copies of his little red book.

Nothing was sacred in the brutal onslaught of the Red Guards as they rampaged through the country. The 'four olds' – old customs, old habits, old culture and old thinking – were all to be eliminated. Schools were shut down; intellectuals, writers and artists were dismissed, killed, persecuted or sent to labour in the countryside; scientific, artistic, literary and cultural publications ceased; temples were ransacked and monasteries disbanded. Physical reminders of China's 'feudal', 'exploitative' or 'capitalist' past – everything from monuments to musical instruments – were destroyed.

Sometimes for fear of being accused, neighbours and even family members turned on one another in the search for 'capitalist roaders'. Millions of people are estimated to have died through beatings, executions, suicide or denial of medical care. Violence, social disorder and economic upheaval were rife. Dress codes were as strict as under the most rigid religious regime; cropped hair and the blue 'Mao suit' were obligatory. Minority areas were worst affected because they were the most traditional.

By 1967 even Mao had begun to feel that enough was enough, especially in the sensitive border regions of Guǎngxī and Yúnnán, and 'ultra-left tendencies' were condemned. The PLA was championed as the sole agent of 'proletarian dictatorship' and began its own reign of terror. Anyone with a remotely suspect background – from having a college education to a distant cousin living overseas – was sent to the countryside, often in remote areas of Yúnnán or Guìzhōu, for re-education and hard labour.

For Mao, the Cultural Revolution succeeded in re-establishing his power. Some measure of political stability returned during the closing years of the Cultural Revolution. Zhou Enlai, who had supported Mao from the sidelines, exercised the most influence in the day-to-day governing of China. Among other things, he worked towards restoring China's trade and diplomatic contacts with the outside world. In the 1970s China was admitted into the UN, re-establishing formal diplomatic relations with the USA in 1979.

The true legacy of the Cultural Revolution has been an underlying element of fear that continues to run through Chinese society, particularly in those generations that lived through it. Even today, following the party line appears infinitely safer than exposing one's own opinions.

1976	1978	1980
Mao dies, aged 83. The official line surfaces that Mao was 70 percent right and just 30 percent wrong (namely the Cultural Revolution) in his leadership of China. This official verdict still applies today.	Deng opens China up. He first launches market-angled economic reform. The following year he makes a successful visit to the United States. Full diplomatic relations are established.	The one-child policy is introduced to slow China's growing population. It creates an ageing society, and the 'bachelor bomb': 23 million young men who will never find a Chinese wife, due to the practice of female-specific abortions.

Capitalism with Chinese Characters

The final two decades of the 20th century saw a grand reversal of the traditional knee-jerk curtsy to Marxist-Leninist ideology. With the death of Mao Zedong, the celebrated Deng Xiaoping era commenced as he came to power as vice-premier, vice-chairman of the party and chief of staff. Aiming to undo the damage inflicted on China by the Cultural Revolution and decades of post-revolutionary economic mismanagement, Deng unveiled his programme of the 'Four Modernisations' (agriculture, industry, science and defence). In the process, China increased contact with the capitalist economies of the West and opened its doors to foreign visitors.

In rural China the 'Responsibility System' allowed people to sell their agricultural surpluses on the open market and this greatly changed life for the better in the Southwest. In 1993 Deng Xiaoping famously proclaimed that 'to get rich is glorious' as the government began to trim down capital-squandering, state-owned industries. The new 'ideology' was declared: 'socialism with Chinese characteristics'. Deng was hardly an economic guru, but his tinkering unleashed the long-repressed capitalist instincts of the Chinese.

Despite its very real successes, one of the lasting failures of the Deng reform era was its dearth of political evolution. The era directly paved the way to the China of today, with all of its massive impetus and glaring social and political contradictions. Aware of its struggle for its own survival, the Communist Party has increasingly relaxed controls preventing the creation of private wealth. The result is a land of opportunity pumped up by astonishing growth in GDP. While many of the poorer, rural areas of the Southwest are undeniably and uniformly poor, China is also a land marked by a growing divide between the haves and have-nots, a spectacular defeat of the most basic axiom of Marxist and CCP orthodoxy. The supreme irony has been that the very force communism arose to overturn (capitalism) gave the CCP a new lease of life. Even the Southwest is not the land of austerity and starkness that many in the West envisage; urban centres like Chóngqìng and Chéngdū are instead overflowing with shopping centres, fast-food outlets and increasing class divisions. This is communism like you've never imagined it.

Rival gangs of Red Guards fought each other to prove their revolutionary purity. In Guǎngxī, rival groups robbed an ammunition train en route to Vietnam and fought each other with machine guns, bazookas and anti-aircraft guns.

THE 21ST CENTURY

Overall, China has made some astonishing achievements in recent years, putting its first man in space in 2003 (a feat it repeated in 2005), completing the Three Gorges Dam in 2006 – ahead of schedule – and, in the same year, putting finishing touches to a railway to Lhasa in Tibet, a technically challenging feat that some said was impossible. Also in the pipeline are plans for a further 48 airports to meet the massive surge in air travel. How China sees the world, and how the world sees China, has also altered drastically in recent decades as the government's political policies and views maintain their rollercoaster of inconsistencies.

1989	1997	1999
Reform-minded Party Secretary-General Hu Yaobang's memorial turns into a pro-democracy demonstration. Nearly one million people gather in Běijīng's Tiananmen Sq. Martial law is imposed. Hundreds are killed as demonstrators are forcibly dispersed.	On 1 July Hong Kong returns to Chinese sovereignty, followed by the nearby Portuguese colony of Macau two years later. Shipping magnate Tung Chee-hwa is chosen as Hong Kong's first chief executive in a Běijīng-controlled vote.	In April, Falun Gong practitioners protest silently in Běijīng, prompting a crackdown. By July the movement is banned, labelled an ideological and political threat to the Communist Party and State.

The Great Divide

As China grew in stature at the dawn of the 21st century, Deng Xiaoping's successor, Jiang Zemin, claimed popular success on the world stage. During his tenure, Hong Kong and Macau returned to China, Běijīng was successful in its Olympics bid for 2008 and China was steered into the World Trade Organization (WTO). Nevertheless, China's economic picture remained hazy at best, with the lumbering state sector an unresolved burden on the economy.

Groomed to take the seat of power since the early 1990s, Hu Jintao – who became president in 2003 – is China's first modern leader to come into the communist fold post-1949. Hopes that Hu was a reformer were quietly suffocated as the president committed himself to unbending controls over the political opposition and resolved to tighten the management of information. In Hu's bid to purge society of 'liberal elements', the policing of the internet was even more rigorously enforced and many publications were shut down.

Nevertheless, Hu's greatest challenge has been an attempt to rectify the inequalities between the flourishing southeast provinces and the inland provinces, including the land-locked Southwest. Rural protests have increased in recent years, sparked by land confiscations, unemployment, environmental pollution, high taxes and corrupt officials.

According to Chinese government figures, 74,000 riots or demonstrations took place during 2004, up from 58,000 the previous year. To redress the economic imbalance, the government has launched an ambitious Develop the West campaign to lure businesses, investment and graduates to China's poorer western regions.

Going Global

China's growing international profile sits uneasily with its policies of non-intervention. Pragmatically business-minded, Běijīng takes little interest in human-rights abuses in countries it does or does not do business with. For instance, China has befriended nations such as North Korea, Myanmar and Zimbabwe, states widely shunned by the rest of the international community.

In an effort to diversify its sources of oil, China has also invested heavily in Africa and then protected these investments by supporting suspect governments (for instance China opposed UN efforts to impose sanctions on Sudan for the massacres in Darfur). Critics argue that for China to take a leading role in international affairs, it will need to be seen as more than a purely opportunistic player. Sino-US relations continue to be of primary strategic importance, especially as China grows in regional and global importance. Optimists point to the growing interdependence of Chinese and American economic ties, and the more cordial atmosphere of cooperation since the

For a positive take on the effects of a shrinking world, check out *China's Ethnic Minorities & Globalisation* by Colin Mackerras. The book, though fairly academic, offers an in-depth examination of minority peoples' place in the world and their interaction with the Chinese Government.

2001	2002	2003
After more than 15 years of negotiations (the longest in international trade history) China joins the World Trade Organization, opening up its markets to foreign companies and capital.	Jiang Zemin passes the leadership of the Communist Party and the presidency to the 'Fourth Generation', headed by Politburo member Hu Jintao.	China sends its first astronaut, Yang Liwei, into space aboard the *Shenzhou 5* spacecraft. He returns to earth a day later, having completed 14 orbits.

Al-Qaeda attacks of 9/11. Pessimists see Taiwan as a potential flashpoint between the two powers (the US has pledged military support to the island in the event of a Chinese invasion).

In the midst of this sits China's Southwest – where international affairs may seem worlds away. Nevertheless, the effects are strongly felt as China's ever-opening doors allow increasing freedom to foreign travellers; minority cultures, not long ago repressed, are now promoted to encourage cultural tourism. The reclusive spirit of the Southwest has nurtured the growing interest of independent travellers who are, in turn, impacting the region's economy, culture and window on the world.

2006	2006	2008
China completes the Three Gorges Dam, the world's largest hydroelectric power station, providing electric power and flood control to millions. However, 1.5 million people are displaced and environmentalists seriously question long-term ecological effects.	On 1 July the first railway to Lhasa in Tibet begins operation. The line includes the highest track in the world (5072m) and the world's longest tunnel (1338 km).	Běijīng hosts the Summer Olympic Games under a watchful global eye. The opening ceremony is on 8/8/2008, at 8.08pm and eight seconds – in Mandarin, the number eight sounds similar to 'wealth' and 'fortune'.

The Culture

REGIONAL IDENTITY

China's Southwest harbours extremes: the headfirst dive towards modernity that you find in cities such as Chóngqìng, Kūnmíng or Chéngdū, alongside some of the country's most remote, rural communities. The Southwest has traditionally been seen by the rest of China as an outback – full of bandits and backwardness. During Mao Zedong's days in power, it was here that the persecuted were sent as punishment, which seemed to only heighten the rest of the country's disdain for the region. Nevertheless, like most Chinese, the people of the Southwest are fiercely proud of their heritage and homeland. The region's ever-burgeoning tourism industry has recently made it a hot spot for foreign visitors and, increasingly, with Chinese tourists from Shàng-hǎi, Běijīng and Hong Kong. One of the results has been an increase in the region's national reputation as the people of the Southwest place themselves proudly on the world map.

One-fifth of China's population is learning English. It's estimated that within two decades, the total number of Chinese English speakers in China will outnumber native English speakers in the rest of the world.

Most Chinese are passionately nationalist, despite disillusionment with Communist Party policies. They're proud of China's heritage and accom-plishments and are none too shy about saying so. This attitude often sits uneasily with their desire to embrace many things Western, from the English language to pop culture to business ideas. There's worry that Western values may destroy the heart of traditional Chinese culture but there's also a strong drive to transform the insularity that has defined China for hundreds of years. In urban centres, more and more Chinese citizens want to be seen as participants in a global world, progressive and open to new ideas. In rural and minority regions, there's often a strong gap between older generations holding on staunchly to traditional ways and younger people eager for a taste of modernity.

Even with so many changes taking place, traditional values persist, par-ticularly in rural, minority regions (see p51). Many Han Chinese beliefs derive largely from the pervasive influence of Confucian philosophy, which forms the very core of Chinese identity. The Chinese value the importance of the family, the cultivation of morality and self-restraint, with the em-phasis on hard work and achievement. It's assumed that the family as a whole will thrive and prosper if harmony prevails at home. Strong family connections and community ties are what keep the Chinese going, even in times of difficulty.

ETIQUETTE DOS & DON'TS

- Always take your shoes off when entering a Chinese home.
- When meeting a Chinese family, greet the eldest person first as a sign of respect.
- Always present things to people with both hands, showing that what you are offering is the fullest extent of yourself.
- When beckoning to someone, wave them over to you with your palm down, motioning to yourself.
- If someone gives you a gift, put it aside to open later to avoid appearing greedy.
- Never write anything in red ink; it's reserved for letters of protest.
- If you blow your nose into a tissue or hanky, don't let people see you pocketing it. The Chi-nese find this infinitely disgusting and prefer to spit their phlegm out onto the pavement.

LIFESTYLE

The rapid development of the past three decades has raised the living standard for many Chinese, especially the urban population. 'You are what you have' has become the motto for China's new 30-somethings, who see a car and a large apartment as the symbols of success. Also at the forefront of a changing China is the computer-savvy younger generation, who are not only downloading the latest pop songs, games and movies, but engaging in heated debates on blogs and internet chat sites about everything from education to premarital sex.

China's Southwest is largely rural and many people continue to eke out a meagre living on diminishing plots of land. The ability to sell their goods on the open market, however, has generally meant a significant rise in income. An increasing number of rural families are now able to send their children to school, although the cost of tuition and healthcare remain huge and often unsurmountable hurdles for many.

Chinese culture has always revolved around the family, considered the bedrock of a stable and harmonious society and, with some modifications, this remains true today. The traditional family structure of many generations living together is changing, with younger generations moving out to pursue new career and educational opportunities, and urban Chinese increasingly living in tiny apartments. Even so, parents enjoy a very tight bond with their children, and extended family remains important, with grandparents commonly acting as caretakers for grandchildren. Every member of the family has a clear set of responsibilities.

In rural areas, and to a lesser extent in the cities, arranged marriages are still very common. In minority areas, the oldest son often moves out after marrying while the second son remains at home. A women often doesn't live with her husband until she becomes pregnant, although when she does move house, she shifts her responsibilities and allegiances to her new family and, in particular, her mother-in-law. This is partly why daughters are traditionally seen as a financial liability. Divorce, customarily looked down upon in Chinese society, is on the rise, and in urban areas more young people are living together before tying the knot. Nevertheless, marriage is still seen as a union of families rather than individuals.

The one-child policy (see p42) has greatly changed the make-up of the family, and of society overall. Having only one child and greater wealth has meant parents are able provide their children with better education, healthcare, food and clothing. It's also meant that children are often doted upon in a big way, and China's siblingless children are often referred to by outsiders as 'little emperors'. As they grow up, these children bear the responsibility of single-handedly carrying on the family name and traditions, and of caring for their ageing parents and grandparents.

ECONOMY

China's economic advances over recent years have continued to dazzle. In the early 1980s, the government introduced market-oriented reforms and today only a third of China's economy is directly controlled by the state. While this has meant huge state-owned factory shutdowns and mass unemployment, it has vastly reduced waste, increased earnings and improved the standard of living for many. China's economy now sees some of the fastest growth in the world and is the second largest after the US; however, with a vast landmass and a humungous population, the resulting wealth is spread very thin.

Employing over 40% of its workforce, China's agricultural sector is the largest in the world. Its service sector is slowly catching up, accounting for 32.5% of the economy. China's cheap labour costs have turned the country

China has around 123 million internet users.

The communists' 'iron rice bowl' meant that, up until the early 1990s, the government employed everyone – regardless of whether there was enough money (or work) to go around.

YOUR FACE OR MINE?

Loosely defined as status, ego or self-respect, the concept of face is not unfamiliar to most foreigners. Essentially it's about avoiding being made to look stupid or wrong. What you may find unfamiliar is the lengths Chinese people will go to in order to save face. Displays of anger and emotion are great losses of face; however, if a conflict arises, opponents dig in their heels – screaming matches on the streets or in shops are not uncommon. Chinese will assume that you also want to save face and will hand over one of their ready-to-wear excuses should they feel you need it. Try never to accuse someone directly; unless you love to argue, outright confrontation should be reserved as a last resort.

into 'the world's factory', manufacturing most of the world's clothing, electronics and household items. China is also one of the largest importers in the world, buying cars, high-tech products, raw minerals, machineries and equipment, chemicals and petroleum, and is also now a net-importer of food.

Within these statistics, you'll find the reality of life for average Chinese citizens – namely a growing gap between the rich and poor. While this disparity is extremely prevalent in the Southwest, particularly between urban and rural communities, there is also a vast disparity between incomes in the China's poorer west and wealthier east. China's GDP per capita is US$7600 (PPP), US$2001 (nominal); however, the wealth is very much concentrated on the east coast. Covering over 70% of China's landmass, the western reaches of the country sees less then 17% of the total economic output.

While some predict that the Chinese economy will be the world's largest by 2020, this wouldn't necessarily equate to a particularly wealthy nation. As there are around four Chinese for every American, the Chinese would only need a salary of 25% of the average US citizen for China to have the same spending power as the USA. It's often difficult to really know what the true Chinese economic picture is; mass corruption leads to catastrophically inaccurate statistics and also sends as much as 2% of China's GDP into unlawful ends.

POPULATION

The one-child policy and consequential preference for male babies is creating a serious imbalance of the sexes. By 2020, over 40 million men may be unable to find spouses.

China is home to 56 ethnic groups, with Han Chinese making up 92% of the population. While China's minority groups are found throughout the country, the borderland of the Southwest is traditionally home to a greater percentage. (See p51 for more.)

China faces enormous population pressures, despite comprehensive programmes to curb its growth. Over one-third of China's 1.3 billion live in urban centres, putting great strain on land and water resources. It's estimated that China's total population will continue to grow at a speed of 10 million each year, even with population programmes such as the one-child policy. Brought into effect in 1979, the policy's aim is to reduce the population to 700 million by 2050. While the government officially opposes forced abortion and sterilisation, allegations of coercion continue as local officials strive to meet population targets. Rural families are now allowed to have two children if the first child is a girl, but some have upwards of three or four kids. Families who do abide by the one-child policy will often go to great lengths to make sure their child is male; females are often aborted or abandoned to overflowing orphanages. All non-Han minorities are exempt from the one-child policy and consequently in many minority regions of the Southwest you will encounter many more babies and children.

SPORT

The Chinese have a very long, rich sports history, and began stretching and breathing taichi-style over 4000 years ago (see below and p170). From as early as 1066 BC, wealthy Chinese have known the delights of archery, acrobatics, martial arts and wrestling – or at least games that come fairly close to these modern-day incarnations. Polo became the height of fashion around AD 650, along with long-distance running, hunting and a board game similar to contemporary mah jong (麻将; *májiàng*).

During the Song dynasty one of the most well-liked sports involved kicking around a leather ball stuffed with hair. In 2003 the international football association FIFA officially recognised that China was the birthplace of football and, in turn, China turned football crazy. Golf is another sport with a long history – as far back as AD 1200, Chinese were hitting balls into holes in the ground with sticks. The national sport is of course table tennis, which you would assume was discovered by the Chinese, but was in fact an invention of the Victorians.

Modern sports, such as basketball, gymnastics, volleyball and swimming, came to China early in the 20th century when Chinese athletes began participating in international sporting events such as the Olympics and the Asian Games. Today Chinese excel in table tennis, volleyball, gymnastics and women's wrestling, though in the Southwest you're more likely to hear the clicking of mah jong pieces than stadium cheers.

In 2004 the All China Sports Federation recognised video games as a legitimate sport.

China's latest addition to its sports repertoire is cricket, with a five-year plan to introduce it into schools and universities and the hope of qualifying for the 2019 World Cup.

MEDIA

Since the communists took power, China's media has been largely controlled by the government. More recent decades have seen reduced government subsidies to media, bringing an increasing reliance on advertisers. The resulting drive for audiences has brought about more opinionated, open and interesting coverage. Media are increasingly willing to report bold and nearly critical commentary (often focusing on local issues and officials rather than those at a national level) as the government has less financial leverage to wield.

All media in China must be associated with a government body and there remain certain lines that cannot be crossed; questioning the legalities of China's incursion into Tibet or the legitimacy of the Communist Party in general, for example, is not tolerated and can lead to publications being shut down at a moment's notice. Self-censorship is expected in all forms of media and you still come across Western publications being sold with 'sensitive' articles simply torn out. Despite an obsessive desire by the government to control information in state media, this control is being challenged by the rise of text messaging and

---

A SPORTING PHILOSOPHY

Martial arts combine discipline, flexibility, spirituality and defence. Practised in China for centuries, the four most common types are *tàijíquán* (太极拳; usually called taiji or taichi), *gōngfu* (功夫; kung fu) and *qìgōng* (气功). In all forms, respect and responsibility is considered paramount, and fighting is seen as a last resort. *Tàijíquán* is very slow and fluid and its motions mirror everyday actions like gathering water. *Gōngfu* has been made popular through Hong Kong films, is much faster than *tàijíquán* and focuses on self-defence. *Qìgōng* is a form of energy management aimed at maintaining good mental and physical health. *Qìgōng* masters have been known to project their *qì* (energy) in miraculous ways – from healing others to driving nails through boards with their bare fingers.

To catch a glimpse of martial arts in action, head to any green space in the early morning. Practitioners are not likely to be the brazen lads and femme fatales you may be expecting. Instead they're likely to be 90-year-old grannies with their ankles up around their noses.

For details on *gōngfu* and *tàijíquán* schools in Yángshuò, Southwest China, see p169.

GŌNGFŪ

One of China's most potent and popular exports, the art of *gōngfu* has its arcane origins in Hénán province's legendary Shaolin Temple. Popularised by Bruce Lee, Jackie Chan, Jet Li and other exponents of the flying sidekick, *gōngfu* has captivated generations of eager Western aspirants.

The term *gōngfu* is frequently misconstrued in the West. It actually means 'skill', generally in an artistic field. A pianist can be said to have *gōngfu*, as can a calligrapher or a water colourist. In the Western imagination, it is more commonly perceived as the ability to drive one's index finger through the windpipe of an unfortunate assailant, leap onto high rafters with a single bound, or send opponents sprawling with a mere shrug.

China's fighting arts generally divide into hard ('external'; (外家; wàijiā) and soft ('internal'; 内家; nèijiā) camps. It's an oversimplification to see hard styles as training physical strength and soft styles as developing pliancy and internal power by using *qì*, but it's pointing in the right direction. In reality, an immense crossover between hard and soft schools blurs the distinction. The most insubstantial of all the soft schools, taichi or *tàijíquán* (太极拳) – which concentrates its skills on yielding to attacks – is only genuinely soft after years, if not decades, of study; and even then physicality can be hard to fully shake off. Many of the ostensibly harder martial arts – Five Ancestors Boxing (五祖拳; wǔzǔquán) for example – are powered by internal energies that require a heightened state of physical relaxation and serious bouts of *qìgōng*.

Gōngfu – both hard and soft – is closely linked to the practice of *qìgōng* (气功) and the nurturing of *gōng* (skill). A veritable taxonomic system of *gōng* exists. Naturally there is hard *gōng* (硬功; yìng gōng), an essential ingredient if you want snapping iron bars or boulder-smashing with your forehead on your CV, but there's also light *gōng* (轻功; qīnggōng) for featherweight dancing on crushed glass or leaping to astonishing heights. Gecko *gōng* (壁虎功; bìhǔ gōng) is for climbing walls with little effort, tortoise-back *gōng* (龟背功; guībèi gōng) develops a solid back, toad *gōng* (蛤蟆功; hámá gōng) strengthens muscles and flying *gōng* (飞行功; fēixíng gōng) helps with sword routines high up among the bamboo fronds.

For unputdownable reading on martial arts goings-on, grab a copy of the tongue-in-cheek *Way of a Warrior: A Journey into Secret Worlds of Martial Arts*, by John F. Gilbey, find a comfy sofa and prepare to be thoroughly entertained.

internet use. The government's reduced resources to oversee and edit media content has also played a role in somewhat controversial stories (such as the AIDS epidemic in Hénán) making it to press.

Access to TV has exploded in China; around a billion Chinese have access to more than 700 local channels and another 3000 cable channels are available. While the government owns and operates the largest network (CCTV), it garners only 30% of China's audience share.

The internet has also made huge waves in China. Despite the government's attempt to built the 'Great Firewall of China', attempts at monitoring and restricting access have proved largely ineffectual. Chinese internet users can access uncensored news via the China News Digest website, which is produced and maintained by overseas Chinese volunteers. Talk radio has also opened the doors to debate in Chinese cities, as callers air their ideas and debate hot topics without having to reveal their identity; the result has been hugely popular programmes which local government officials are weary to do battle with.

Rainclouds over Wushan (1995) was filmed in a town near Chóngqìng, along the Yangzi. An oddly funny drama with little dialogue, beautiful photography and a rather unsettling tone, it won awards at various film festivals around the globe but lost support from the Chinese government.

RELIGION

In recent decades, the Chinese have been returning to restored temples with armfuls of incense. Perhaps in reaction to the spiritual vacuum created by the Mao years and the materialism of the 1990s, religious followings in all their forms seems to be on the rise. Most minority groups in the Southwest have traditional animist or shamanistic belief systems, which have been subsequently overlaid with Buddhist, Taoist, Confucian and even Christian elements; for more on these, see p54.

In 1982 the Chinese government amended its constitution to allow freedom of religion; however, many would contend that this is really only the case with traditional Chinese beliefs. It also remains true that only atheists are permitted to be members of the Chinese Communist Party (CCP). In general, the government is not overly concerned with religious groups unless they are believed to challenge state doctrine, as did the quasi-Buddhist health system, Falun Gong, whose thousands of practitioners have been menaced into obscurity.

> It's often said that many Chinese are Confucianists during their education, Taoists in retirement and Buddhists as they approach death.

Taoism

It is said that Taoism (道教; *Dàojiào*) is the only true 'home-grown' Chinese religion. The founder of Taoism was a man known as Laotzu (老子; *Lǎozǐ*), who is believed to have been born around 604 BC. At the end of his life Laotzu is said to have climbed onto a water buffalo and ridden west towards what is now Tibet, in search of solitude. En route he was asked by a gatekeeper to leave behind a record of his beliefs. The product was a slim volume of only 5000 characters: the *Tao Te Ching* (道德经; *Dào Dé Jīng; The Book of the Way*).

At the centre of Taoism is the concept of Tao (道; *Dào*). Tao cannot be perceived because it exceeds senses, thoughts and imagination; it can be known only through mystical insight. Tao is the way of the universe, the driving power in nature, the order behind all life and the spirit that cannot be exhausted. Tao is the way people should order their lives to keep in harmony with the natural order of the universe. Today, the most famous Taoist notion is that of the duality of the universe divided into Yin (阴; feminine, dark, passive) and Yang (阳; masculine, bright, busy).

> *I Ching* (易经; *Yìjīng*), or *Book of Changes,* is the oldest Chinese classical text and dates back to antiquity. Stemming from an ancient system of cosmology, it expresses the wisdom and philosophy of early China.

Buddhism

Buddhism (佛教; *Fó Jiào*) was founded in India. The cornerstone of Buddhist philosophy is that happiness can only be achieved by following the 'eight-fold path' to nirvana: a state of complete freedom from greed, anger, ignorance and the various other fetters of existence. When Buddhism entered China from India, its exotic nature was an attraction for many Chinese disillusioned with the formalism of Confucianism. With its elaborate explanations of karma, Buddhism offered answers to the afterlife that neither Taoism nor Confucianism could address. Buddhism also had its share of critics, who saw it as a threat to the Chinese identity. The growth of Buddhism was slowed by persecutions and outright abolishment by various emperors.

Most Buddhists in China follow Mahayana Buddhism – but the Dai of Xīshuāngbǎnnà (see p326) are Theravada Buddhists – like Buddhists in Thailand and Myanmar. Buddhists in the Tibetan areas of western Sìchuān and northwestern Yúnnán practice a unique form of Buddhism called Tantric or Lamaist (喇嘛教; *Lǎma Jiào*). It's heavily influenced by Tibet's pre-Buddhist Bon religion and is much more mystical than other forms of Buddhism, relying heavily on *mudras* (ritual postures), mantras (sacred speech), *yantras* (sacred art) and secret initiation rites. Priests called 'lamas' are believed to be reincarnations of highly evolved beings and are split into two orders: the Red Hat (Kagyupa) or Yellow Hat (Gelugpa) sects. The Dalai Lama is the supreme patriarch of Tibetan Buddhism.

Confucianism

While Buddhism and Taoism give reverence to gods and goddesses who preside over earth and the after life, Confucianism (儒家思想; *Rújiā Sīxiǎng*) deals with the affairs of life but not death. More a philosophy than a religion, Confucianism defines codes of conduct and a patriarchal pattern of obedience for the attainment of harmony and overall good; respect flows upwards from child to adult, woman to man and subject to ruler. Not surprisingly, it was adopted by the state for two millennia.

Confucius was born of a poor family around 551 BC. His ambition was to hold a high government office and to reorder society through the administrative apparatus. At most he seems to have had several insignificant government posts, a few followers and a permanently blocked career. At the age of 50 he perceived his divine mission, and for the next 13 years tramped from state to state offering unsolicited advice to rulers on how to improve their governing. The opportunity to put his own ideas into practice never came, and he returned home to spend his last years teaching and editing classical literature. He died in 479 BC, aged 72. The glorification of Confucius began after his death. Mencius (372–289 BC) helped raise Confucian ideals into the national consciousness with the publication of *The Book of Mencius*. Eventually Confucian philosophy permeated every level of Chinese society.

The website www.confucius.org offers a look at the philosophy that changed the course of China. The grand sage's *Lun Yu* (论语; *Classic Sayings*) is available on the site in 21 languages, along with photos of his calligraphy, speeches and a biography.

Islam

Islam (伊斯兰教; Yīsīlán Jiào) was founded by the Arab prophet Mohammed. Its followers, Muslims, believe there is only one God, Allah, and seek universal brotherhood. Islam was brought to China peacefully by Arab traders and Muslim merchants travelling the Silk Road to China and today it is estimated that Islam is followed by 3% to 5% of China's population. The Southwest has a prominent community of ethnic Chinese Muslims, known as Hui (p227), who settled in the region in the wake of the 13th-century Mongol invasion of Kublai Khan. They are set apart from the Han Chinese by their white skullcaps and avoidance of pork (China's main source of meat). China's Muslims suffered greatly during the Cultural Revolution when many were forced to eat pork and mosques were turned into pigsties. These days you'll encounter mosques and Muslim restaurants throughout the Southwest.

Around 90% of organ transplants in China come from executed prisoners, because Confucian ethics deter most Chinese from donating organs.

Christianity

Christianity arrived in China with the Nestorians in the 7th century; although their influence later died out, they made a considerable impact at the time. The religion later took root when large numbers of Catholic and Protestant missionaries established themselves in the Southwest, following the invasion of China by the Western powers in the 19th century. French Catholics were prevalent in northwest Yúnnán and western Sìchuān and Methodist missions were popular among the Miao of Guìzhōu. You'll find Christian churches in Guìyáng, Móxī (p391), Kāngdìng and elsewhere, including Cizhong Catholic Church in Yúnnán (see p297).

Today Christianity is the fastest growing religion in China, with an estimated following of 3% to 5% of the population (40 to 65 million people). It is estimated that over 200,000 Chinese convert to Christianity each year, a statistic that is thought to reflect an overall religious awakening throughout China. This strong shift away from China's traditional religions may be largely due to Mao's razing of religious practices, leaving people with a clean slate from which many pursued different religions. Christianity's increasing toehold has got the attention of authorities, some of whom see the Western religion as a potential threat. Human rights groups have regularly reported cases of priests and followers suffering harassment and detention. Consequently, many Chinese Christians are practising their faith in small groups in residential houses. This, in turn, is germinating the development of various sects which are at risk of being branded as cults and banned by the government.

Other officials in authority appear to show considerable ambivalence to Christianity, with the religion popping up within the government itself. One telling occasion occurred when ex-president Jiang Zemin was asked what he would do if he could make one last decree before leaving office; he replied 'I would make Christianity the official religion of China.' Many in China see Christianity as the secret of the West's successes.

ARTS

Maoist ideological controls and the Cultural Revolution levelled nasty blows at China's art scene. Since the 1970s a great deal has been done to restore what was destroyed, and vibrant artistic expression is once again prominent in Chinese society. The majority of China's avant-garde artists are based in the eastern cities of Běijīng, Hong Kong, Guǎngzhōu and Shànghǎi; the Southwest sees more reserved, traditional art forms.

Visual Arts

Since its earliest days, China has courted beautiful things. The Chinese began making pottery over 8000 years ago, with handcrafted earthenware primarily used for religious purposes. Jade has been revered since Neolithic times; it was believed to have magical, life-giving properties. Opulent jade suits were placed in tombs, and the elixir of powdered jade was eaten by Taoist alchemists. Bronze and copper have also been long valued and were produced in Yúnnán's Dian kingdom 2500 years ago – everything from drums to mirrors to statuettes depicting mythological beasts; to see some of these, visit Kūnmíng's Provincial Museum (p226).

CALLIGRAPHY

Calligraphy was traditionally regarded in China as the highest form of artistic expression. Even today, a person's character is judged by their handwriting; elegant writing is believed to reveal great refinement. Calligraphy is extremely popular in China and a major area of study. You will encounter calligraphy all over the Southwest – on documents, artworks, in temples, adorning the walls of caves, and on the sides of mountains and monuments.

PAINTING

Traditional Chinese painting is the art of brush and ink applied to *xuān* (宣; paper) or silk. The brush line, which varies in thickness and tone, is the important feature of a Chinese painting, along with accompanying calligraphy. Shading and colour play only a minor symbolic and decorative role. From the Han dynasty until the end of the Tang dynasty, the human figure occupied the dominant position in Chinese painting. Then, from the 11th century onwards, landscape dominated. It was not until the 20th century that there was any real departure from native traditions.

Since the late 1970s, the work of Chinese painters has been arguably more innovative and dissident than that of writers, possibly because the political implications are harder to interpret by the authorities. In the Southwest, Yúnnán in particular has seen an upsurge in contemporary painting and a distinctive style has emerged amongst the Naxi; watch for the stunning work of He Xiang Yun, whose strong colour on handmade paper blends traditional Naxi pictographic elements (see the boxed text, p265) with an expressionist style.

SCULPTURE

Chinese sculpture dates back to the Zhou and Shang dynasties, when small clay and wooden dragons, lions and chimeras were commonly placed in

David Aikman in his *Jesus in Beijing* sees China becoming a predominantly Christian country within the next 30 years, with all the huge implications this would mean for foreign policy and the global balance of power. Chinese Christians are far more pro-American and pro-Israeli than their Buddhist and Taoist and atheist confrères.

tombs to protect the dead and guide them on their way to heaven. Sculptures of humans became more common in succeeding dynasties but it wasn't until China's introduction to Buddhism that sculpture moved beyond tomb figurines to other realms of figurative art. Enormous figures of Buddha, carved directly into the rock, are dotted around China and are a mesmerising sight. To experience the world's largest, head to Lèshān in Sìchuān (p383). Also check out the well-preserved caves in Dàzú County (p453) where a wild assortment of colourful sculptures were created during the Song dynasty.

Literature

China's rich literary tradition is largely out of reach to non-Chinese speakers. Many of the translations of the past decade have produced rather stilted, bland versions of Chinese classics, modern short stories and poetry. In recent years publishing houses have been putting more effort into their translations, though the selection remains limited.

> 'Be dutiful at home, brotherly in public; be discreet and trustworthy, love all people, and draw near to humanity. If you have extra energy as you do that, then study literature.'
>
> CONFUCIUS, *I CHING*

PREMODERN LITERATURE

Prior to the 20th century there were two literary traditions in China: the classical and the vernacular. The classical canon, largely Confucian in nature, consisted of a core of texts written in ancient Chinese that were the backbone of the Chinese education system but nearly indecipherable to the masses. *Analects* (论语; *Lúnyǔ*) is a collection of sayings attributed to Confucius that were remembered by his followers; many consider Arthur Waley's 1938 translation to be the best. Tang China is remembered as China's Golden Age of literature; its two greatest poets had strong connections with the Southwest: Li Bai (or Li Bo) was banished to Guìzhōu early in his career and Du Fu was born in Sìchuān.

The vernacular tradition arose in the Ming dynasty and consisted largely of prose epics written for entertainment. Many of China's vernacular texts are available in translation and can give you an interesting glimpse of life in long-ago China. Try *Water Margin/Outlaws of the Marsh* (水浒传; *Shuǐhǔ*

PAGE TURNERS

While not much of China's contemporary literature has spawned from the Southwest, a number of novels available in translation are set in this region. Others cover themes and events that have strongly influenced the Southwest of today. Grab a mug of green tea and settle down with:

- *Half of Man Is Woman*, by Zhang Xianliang (WW Norton & Co, 1998), a candid exploration of sexuality and marriage in contemporary China, and considered one of the most controversial novels of the 1980s.
- *Please Don't Call Me Human*, by Wang Shuo (Hyperion East, 2000), a mocking look at the failures of China's state security system, which appeals to a broad spectrum of Chinese society despite being banned.
- *The Book and the Sword: Gratitude and Revenge*, by Jin Yong (Oxford University Press, 2004), a suspenseful story revolving around the Red Flower Society (a fictional secret society) and its battle to overthrow the Manchu dynasty; first published in 1955.
- *Blades of Grass: The Stories of Lao She*, (University of Hawaii Press, 1999), a collection of 14 stories containing poignant descriptions of people living through times of political upheaval and uncertainty.
- *Wild Swans*, by Jung Chang (Touchstone Books, 2003), the gripping story of three generations of Chinese women struggling to survive the tumultuous events of 20th-century China, with a good portion of the story set in the Southwest.

Zhuàn) by Shi Nai'an and Luo Guanzhong; *Romance of the Three Kingdoms* (三国演义; *Sānguó Yǎnyi*) by Luo Guanzhong; *Dream of the Red Chamber* (红楼梦; *Hónglóu Mèng*) by Cao Xueqin; or *Journey to the West* (西游记; *Xīyóu Jì*) by Wu Cheng'en.

MODERN & CONTEMPORARY LITERATURE

By the early 20th century, translations of Western novels were available in China, causing Chinese intellectuals to look more critically at their own literary traditions. Calls for a national literature based on vernacular Chinese rather than stultifying classical language grew in intensity. The first major Chinese writer to publish in colloquial Chinese was Lu Xun (1881–1936), who is now regarded as the father of modern Chinese literature. His works were mainly short stories that examined China's inability to drag itself into the 20th century. His most famous tale is *The True Story of Ah Q*.

After China came under the control of the communists, most writing in China tended to echo the CCP line. Following Mao's death, writers dared for the first time to explore the traumatic events of the 20th century that had reshaped the Chinese landscape. China's economic progress has spawned a new generation of authors, who write largely about the loneliness and decadence of urban life. See the boxed text, opposite for more.

The *Three Hundred Tang Poems*, compiled from over 48,000 poems preserved from the Tang dynasty Golden Age, provides Chinese conversation with quotable quotes, much as Shakespeare does in English. See http://etext .lib.virginia.edu/chinese /frame.htm for all 300, along with English translations.

Music

TRADITIONAL MUSIC

The traditional Chinese music scale differs from its Western equivalent. Unlike Western music, tone is considered more important than melody. Music was once believed to have cosmological significance and in early times, if a musician played in the wrong tone, it could indicate the fall of a dynasty. Traditional Chinese musical instruments include the two-stringed fiddle (二胡; *èrhú*), four-stringed banjo (月琴; *yuè qín*), two-stringed viola (胡琴; *húqín*), vertical flute (洞箫; *dòngxiāo*), horizontal flute (笛子; *dízi*), piccolo (梆笛; *bāngdí*), four-stringed lute (琵琶; *pípa*), zither (古筝; *gǔzhēng*) and ceremonial trumpet (唢呐; *suǒnà*).

China's ethnic minorities have preserved their own folk song traditions, which are central in their festivals, weddings and courtship rituals. Epic, historical oral ballads with a reed pipe and round lute accompaniment are especially popular. A trip to Lìjiāng in Yúnnán will give you the chance to appreciate the ancient sounds of the local Naxi orchestra (p270).

For a percussion-heavy earful of tunes from Chinese minorities, look for *Yunnan Instrumental Music* (Hugo) or *Baishibai: Songs of the Minority Nationalities of Yunnan* (Pan).

Chinese Opera

Chinese opera has been in existence since the northern Song dynasty, developing out of China's long balladic tradition and based on popular legends and folklore. Performances were put on by travelling entertainers in teahouses frequented by China's working classes.

Chinese opera draws together diverse art forms, including acrobatics, martial arts, stylised dance and elaborate costumes with four major roles: the female, male, 'painted face' (for gods and warriors) and clown. There are over three hundred types of opera in China. Southwestern varieties, such as Sìchuān (see p368), Ānshùn (p114) and Nuo, arose from contact between Han Chinese garrison communities and local minorities.

POPULAR MUSIC

China's thriving popular-music industry came about in the 1980s and has been greatly influenced by a growing exposure to international music trends. Cui Jian, the singer and guitarist whose politically subversive lyrics provoked authorities, led the way for a slew of gritty bands who hacked away at the

GOING WITH THE FLOW

In the West we think of it as a term meaning 'to dejunk', but feng shui (风水; feng meaning 'wind' and shui meaning 'water') is actually a collection of ancient geomantic principles that sees bodies of water and landforms directing the cosmic currents of the universal *qi* (气). To follow feng shui guidelines is to create a positive path for *qi* which can maximise a person's wealth, happiness, longevity and procreation. Ignoring the principals and blocking the flow can spell disaster. Temples, tombs, houses and even whole cities have been built to harmonise with the surrounding landscape in feng shui fashion. Within a building, the order of rooms and arrangement of furniture can also inhibit or enhance *qi* flow. In recent centuries, the barging through of railways and roads and the construction of high-rises has incensed residents who believe the balance of the geography is being disturbed.

edifice of rock and metal (Tang dynasty) and punk (Underground Baby, Brain Failure). Both Chéngdū and Kūnmíng have thriving music scenes with live performances and overflowing CD shops.

For insight into China's contemporary rock scene and information on the latest bands, go to www .rockinchina.com.

Architecture

China's architectural history stretches back more than 3000 years, making it one of the longest of any civilisation. Traditional four-sided courtyard homes (四合院; *sìhéyuàn*) continue to abound today, particularly in rural towns and villages. Enclosed by grey walls, each room opens into a central courtyard. Originally, the height of the walls, the size of the door and the shape of the door stones all told of the type of merchant, official or family that lived inside. An excellent place to see traditional buildings is in Lìjiāng's Old Town (p267), which has been designated as a Unesco Heritage site for its ancient, well-tended buildings. For something a little more unusual and remote, head to Zhàoxīng (p138), a Dong village in Guìzhōu with beautiful traditional wooden structures such as wind-and-rain bridges, and drum towers, all built without a single bolt or nail.

It was not until the 20th century that Chinese architects began to design Western-style buildings with materials such as steel and glass. The early decades of communism have left behind countless cement-block buildings but these days urban architects seem to be trying to outdo one another with contemporary (and sometimes garish) structures.

Minority Cultures

For anyone in search of unique cultural experiences, China's Southwest is the jackpot. A cultural kaleidoscope of Tibetan, Thai and Burmese peoples injects a vibrant dimension into the region. Get off the beaten track and, with each bend in the road, travellers are likely to encounter new languages and new ways of living. The matriarchal Mosu of Yúnnán, the nomadic Tibetans of Sìchuān, the Yi with their slave-raiding, bandit-style past and the festival-fanatic Miao – journey throughout China's Southwest and the list of who you may bump into goes on and on and on…

Spring of the Butterflies & Other Folktales of China's Minority Peoples contains tales from 10 different minority groups, translated by He Liyi. Its eye-catching illustrations depict traditional dress and culture.

IN CONTEXT

Around 37% of China's Southwest is made up of minorities (compared to 9.4% nationwide) and the region contains almost 50% of China's entire 'minority nationality' population – about 50 million people. China's 107-million-strong minority people are divided into 55 ethnic groups, of which 26 are found in the Southwest, though even these only touch the tip of the iceberg. In remote areas of Yúnnán, random geographical features such as a fast-flowing river or mountain range can result in sharp cultural and ethnic divides. When minority classifications were first drawn up in the early 1950s, Yúnnán alone nominated 260 groups, of which 25 were formally recognised. Some minorities, including the Baima of northern Sìchuān, remain officially unrecognised to this day; others are pigeonholed with another group, such as the Mosu of Yúnnán who are officially classified as Naxi. Group populations range from the 16-million-strong Zhuang of Guǎngxī to the fragile pocket of 5000 Drung people in southwestern Yúnnán.

www.china.org .cn/e-groups/shaoshu gives intriguing cultural information on each of China's recognised minority groups. The site is run by the Chinese government so take it with a bucket of salt.

These minority peoples are far more strategically important to China than mere numbers suggest. Not only do they inhabit sensitive border areas but many also have ethnic kin on the other side of these borders. The Guìzhōu Miao are ethnically the same as the Hmong of Laos and Vietnam; the Yao of Guǎngxī are the Mien of Laos and Thailand; and the Jingpo are known in northern Burma as the Kachin. Also, minority lands contain large reserves of untapped minerals and other natural resources.

BIG BROTHER

China's 56th recognised ethnic group is the Han, who make up a staggering 91.9% of the population. Relations between the minorities and the Han Chinese have always been dicey. The Han Chinese have traditionally regarded non-Han groups as 'barbarians', even though China was itself

---

SENSE A DIFFERENCE?

Nearly every Southwestern destination has something to tantalise your senses:

- **See** – the colourful, rambunctious Miao markets in and around Kǎilǐ (p126)
- **Hear** – the mesmerising clamour of the Naxi Orchestra in Lìjiāng (p270)
- **Smell** – the melting yak-butter candles in Kāngdìng's Tibetan Buddhist temples (p388)
- **Taste** - the spicy lamb kebabs sold by Hui-Muslim restaurateurs in Chóngqìng (p449)
- **Touch** – the blue-and-white batik cloth handmade and sold by the Bai in Dàlǐ (p261)

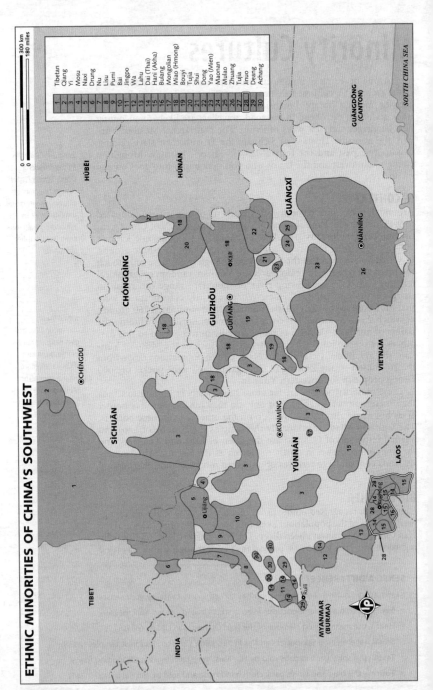

ETHNIC MINORITIES OF CHINA'S SOUTHWEST

1	Tibetan
2	Qiang
3	Yi
4	Mosu
5	Naxi
6	Drung
7	Nu
8	Lisu
9	Pumi
10	Bai
11	Jingpo
12	Wa
13	Lahu
14	Dai (Thai)
15	Hani (Akha)
16	Bulang
17	Mongolian
18	Miao (Hmong)
19	Bouyi
20	Tujia
21	Shui
22	Dong
23	Yao (Mien)
24	Maonan
25	Mulao
26	Zhuang
27	Tujia
28	Jinuo
29	Deang
30	Achang

THREAD OF LIFE *Natuo*

Today I have been to help people planting rice seedlings. This time I helped them; then later when there is water in my paddy, others will come to help me.

We exchange our work. One person is not able to finish cultivating a plot of land; several people doing it together finish it quickly. Doing it in a group heightens your motivation, so we exchange labour.

Old people settled here a long time ago. We live here from generation to generation. Our forefathers Ah Bi and Duojieba have been buried in the village. Now, even their tombs have been trodden flat under a road. We may be the third generation since then.

Of course, it's better to live on the *beizi* (plains). In the *beizi* there are large plots of paddy, while in the mountains the plots are mostly fragmented and small. In the *beizi*, whatever you plant, it yields; while in the mountains, it's harsh for any planting, the land is infertile. Some labour and get food; some labour but in vain. I'm still thinking that we stay here because this is where we belong.

When the old people sewed, I learned from them. Now the price of thread is very high and most people wear Han clothes. Han clothes aren't as warm as Lahu ones. The old generation wears only Lahu clothes. Lahu clothes are better than the Han's. If you wear Lahu clothes and go to plant rice seedlings, it keeps your knees warm.

I don't weave now. One reason is because I have no money to buy the thread – besides, there are many who sell clothes, so you don't have to weave by yourself. Some women still weave cloth.

Most of the young people now don't know how to weave cloth. You just have to labour for others for four to five days, then you can buy a piece of clothing to wear. There are many Han clothes available. But they are a bit too short. The clothes don't cover your waist when you carry firewood on your back. [She sings:]

Take the cotton; use my hands to weave clothes.
We wear them and we feel warm.
Wearing the robe, our necks and shoulders feel warm.
Wearing the clothes we feel warm.
Covering our head with a veil we are beautiful.

The young people like to listen to the people who sing well. Most people can sing. People sing best after they've drunk. Now most people don't know how to sing the songs of the Spring Festival. When people work they sing work songs. When young women and men go out to have fun, they sing love songs. When people send off the spirits, they sing spirit songs. When people die, others sing laments.

It's not only me who knows how to do *jiàohún* (叫魂; calling the spirit); I learned from others. I put rice in a bowl, put an egg on top of it, and take out one [item] of the dead person's clothes. I use a 'call-the-spirit' thread that is brought by the family, and then called the ghost: 'You follow the thread and come back, follow your clothes to come. The sun won't shine on you and the rain won't wet you.'

After this is done, the *jiàohún* thread (spirit thread) would be tied for him, the joss sticks would be burned for the god of the house, the god of the house begged not to hurt him, the sun and the moon asked to protect him.

This [corner of the house] is for burning joss sticks to the god of your house. This ritual is passed on to us from the older generations, so we burn the joss sticks. Even when we have no pain and no disease, we still have to burn the joss sticks in the direction of sunrise.

All the traditions passed on by our older generations – we have to maintain them. As for burning joss sticks, we'll burn when we remember; we won't if we forget.

Natuo lives in Mengba village, Lancang County, Yúnnán and belongs to the Lahu minority group. She is around 80 years old (although she is not sure) and as well as farming rice, she is one of the few people in her village to perform jiàohún.

FORCE OF NATURE

Animists believe that the world is a living being – its rocks, trees, mountains and people all contain spirits which must be in harmony for existence to run smoothly. When this harmony is disrupted, it must be restored, something usually accomplished through the mediation of a shaman. Some shamans are also able to cross over into the spirit world; to divine the future through astrology; and to heal with herbal remedies.

But it's not all left to the shamans. Effort is required by all humans to ensure the goodwill of those spirits found in nature and those of deceased ancestors. Requests for good health, bountiful harvests and successful births are all regularly put before the spirits, with offerings of incense, rice, tobacco, tea and fruit.

Approximately 3% of China's population is animist, the majority of whom belong to minority groups. Others follow folk animism, which is the result of a more dominant religion (such as Buddhism) being introduced into a culture and combined with animism. If you are lucky enough to be invited into the home of a minority family, you will likely see a spirit altar set up in one corner of the room.

ruled by two of these 'minorities' – the Mongols during the Yuan dynasty and the Manchu during the Qing (p27). All nationalities in China are referred to as 'equal brothers', with the Han as the 'eldest brother'; from this stems the belief that (in accordance with Confucian beliefs) it is not only the Han's right, but their duty to watch over and control these younger brothers. History has seen several minority rebellions against Han control, particularly the Muslim and Miao rebellions of the 19th century (see p24).

The Cultural Revolution and the Great Leap Forward were dark times for the minorities. Local languages were outlawed and the 'four olds' (old ideas, old culture, old customs and old habits) were criticised. Religious freedoms were suppressed, and shamans, priests and holy men were arrested. Minorities were forced to cremate their dead, a practice that broke traditional taboos. Local headmen or chiefs were subject to self-criticism and re-education.

These days, while Han chauvinism remains rife, the Chinese authorities paint the minorities as happy, smiling colourful people – and do so with even greater embellishments for the tourism industry. Minorities remain exempt from the one-child policy (they are allowed two) and receive preferential weighting for educational placement – two good reasons why more and more people are registering as belonging to a minority nationality. In total, China's minority population is growing about seven times faster than that of the majority Han Chinese. Local festivals, and cultural life in general, are increasing in strength.

Nevertheless, in reality, minority peoples are often at the lowest rung of the social and economic ladder. Most groups originate from the richer agricultural lands of central China and were pushed first south into the valleys and then up into the mountains of China's Southwest by Han expansion.

Minority areas remain the remotest and least developed parts of China and have generally been passed by in the race to get rich quick. While opium used to be a major cash crop for many minorities (see p29), the communists clamped down hard on this and most are now subsistence farmers.

Integration of the minorities into modern Chinese society is pushed by the government (mainly through demographic dilution) and, in larger, less remote towns, is happening fast. The government often provides pref-

For an academic look at internal colonisation and Han perspectives on minority regions, pick up *Frontier People: Han Settlers in Minority Areas of China*.

Always ask before you get snap-happy. Many minority peoples, such the Yi, believe that cameras steal their soul.

erential economic development to minority regions but rapid economic development generally brings with it immersion in the Han language and social system. Nevertheless, many minority groups are unsurprisingly wary of the majority Han and, particularly in remote villages, remain relatively insular and culturally distinct.

CULTURAL DISTINCTIVENESS

While many minority peoples have mastered Mandarin, the majority of them speak their own languages, which are not taught in schools but are passed from one generation to the next. Most minority groups also use Chinese script as few of these languages have a written form; exceptions include the Yi, Tibetans and Naxi who all have their own ancient scripts. Other groups, like the Miao, have a written code that was established by missionaries during the 18th century.

Many minority cultures are structured on an elaborate set of festivals closely linked to fertility and courtship. The Lusheng Festivals of the Miao (see the boxed text, p104), the Torch Festival of the Yi (see p268) and the Water-Splashing Festival of the Dai (see p326) are just a few of the celebrations that bring animated (and sometimes near-frenzied) atmospheres to quiet, rural communities. While festival-style performances put on especially for tourists can give you a glimpse of this, there's nothing like experiencing the real thing.

Another strong, visual distinction between groups is found in dress. The enormous black hats of the Yi; the elaborate embroidering of the Miao; the plain navy Naxi garments embellished with seven distinctive embroidered circles; the flower headdresses of the Bulang; and the white skullcaps of the Muslims provide a visual feast.

> The Naxi created a written language over 1000 years ago using an extraordinary system of pictographs – the only hieroglyphic language still in use today.

WHEREABOUTS

Western Sìchuān is made up of Tibetans (see p394), mostly Khambas from eastern Tibet or Goloks from the northern Amdo region of Qīnghǎi. Also resident here are small numbers of Tibetan-related Qiang (see boxed text, p396). The south of the province is home to the fascinating Yi people of the Liáng Shān (Cool Mountains), who remained a slave-raiding society strictly divided along caste lines until the end of the 1950s (see p434).

Guìzhōu is dominated by the seven-million-strong Miao (Hmong; see p131) but also populated by the Dong (see p139), known for their dramatic wooden drum towers and bridges, and the Bouyi (see p112), the batik masters of central Guìzhōu. The border with Guǎngxī is home to small groups of Yao and Shui (see p139).

> Guìzhōu's social calendar is packed with more folk festivals than any other province in China.

WHERE TO NEXT?

Find out just how diverse the Southwest's minority cultures really are. Turn to:

- p265, for more on the flexible love affairs and pictographs of the Naxi
- p337, to learn about the turbans, tattoos, teeth-staining and tea-growing practices of the Bulang
- p404, to learn about the ecologically sound (if seemingly gruesome) Tibetan sky burial
- p429, to read about the mystery of the Bo hanging coffins
- p99, for a rundown of the countless festivals of the Miao
- p184, and trek through strings of Dong villages with their distinctive drum towers
- p180, for a spectacular escapade through Zhuang and Yao settlements

Drung girls of north-western Yúnnán have their faces tattooed as a coming-of-age custom. Drung men generally consider tattooed women very beautiful and refuse to marry a woman who is not tattooed.

Northwest Yúnnán has large numbers of Naxi (see p265) and the matrilineal Mosu (see Walking Marriage, p286). The Bai of Dàlǐ have been largely Sinofied over the centuries but were once the most powerful ethnic group in the region (see Nanzha Kingdom, p25). The Bai and the Yi are the two largest minority groups in Yúnnán. The remote border valleys of the Salween River (Nù Jiāng) near Assam in India are Drung, Lisu and Nu areas (see p300).

Xīshuāngbǎnnà has the densest collection of ethnic groups, of which the largest are the Hani (or Akha; see p346) and Dai (see p326). Many smaller groups such as the Lahu (see p340), Wa, Jingpo and Khmer-speaking Bulang (see p337) live in remote settlements and still practise slash-and-burn agriculture. Tiny communities of Pumi, Achang, Jinuo (see p333) and Deang still exist.

Guǎngxī is the most Sinofied province of the Southwest but has communities of Dong, Yao and Mulao in the north.

Environment

From within the cement seas of the Southwest's cities, you may wonder if the urban sprawl has swallowed up all nature had to offer. Fear not. China still has some natural wonders to behold and the Southwest has the lion's share. Spelunkers will be awed by Guìzhōu's Zhijin Cave, one of the world's largest underground labyrinths. Geologists will be perplexed by Guǎngxī's bizarre karst landscape at Guìlín. Hikers after a challenge with views will find it at the holy Éméi Shān, and photographers (and everyone else) will be gobsmacked by the alpine scenery of Jiuzhaigou Nature Reserve. From soaring mountain peaks to lush subtropical forests, from the elusive panda to marauding monkeys, China's Southwest will leave nature-lovers spoiled for choice.

Nevertheless, China is also faced with serious environmental problems. Environmental laws are often unpoliced, and environmentalists are only beginning to gain a voice. Things are improving in some areas but be prepared to encounter heavy pollution, piles of litter and dirty waterways.

THE LAND

China is the third-largest country in the world with an area of 9.5 million sq km. The land surface is like a staircase descending from west to east. The Southwest sits near the top of the stairs, with the mountains of Sìchuān and Yúnnán being an extension of the lofty Qīnghǎi–Tibet Plateau. The highest peak in the Southwest is Gònggā Shān at 7556m; other notable peaks include Kawa Karpo (Méilǐ Xuěshān; 6740m) near Déqīn, and Yùlóng Xuěshān (Jade Dragon Snow Mountain; 5596m) near Lìjiāng.

From these mountains, the land drops down to the Sìchuān Basin and Yúnnán–Guìzhōu Plateau. Melting snow and ice from these highlands tumbles down to form some of the most dramatic gorges in the world, including the famous Tiger Leaping Gorge. In this part of northwest Yúnnán, some of the country's largest rivers pass within 150km of each other, separated by huge mountains: the Salween River (Nù Jiāng), Mekong River (Láncāng Jiāng) and the Upper Yangzi (Jīnshā Jiāng). The Yangzi River (Cháng Jiāng) runs through the Southwest and is, at 6300km, China's longest river. It's also home to the Three Gorges Dam (p458) and the controversial Yangzi Dam Project (p284). Its watershed of almost 2 million sq km – 20% of China's land mass – supports 400 million people.

Below the mountains lies the Sìchuān Basin, known as the Red Basin due to its purple sandstone and shale deposits. This fertile plain averages only 500m in altitude and supports over 100 million people. South of this is the limestone Yúnnán–Guìzhōu Plateau, which takes in eastern Yúnnán, Guìzhōu and western Guǎngxī. At 1000m to 2000m, this eroded carbonate rock produces the weird karst formations of Shílín (the Stone Forest), the caves and waterfalls of Guìzhōu and the famous landscapes of Guìlín and Yángshuò.

Southern Yúnnán and Guǎngxī sit astride the tropic of Cancer. Southern Yúnnán is protected from cold northern winds by the Himalayan mountains and receives moisture-laden air from the Indian Ocean, resulting in a monsoon climate and isolated pockets of tropical rainforest.

WILDLIFE

China's Southwest is endowed with an extremely diverse range of natural vegetation and animal life. Unfortunately, humans have had a considerable impact and much of China's rich natural heritage is rare, endangered or

Earthquakes are not uncommon. A major quake hit Lijiāng in 1996, killing 228 people; another destroyed over 10,000 homes 100km east of Dàlí in January 2000, and western Sìchuān was hit again in 2001. The region's worst quake was in 1970, at the height of the Cultural Revolution, when 15,500 were killed around Tānghǎi.

Many of the region's ethnic groups have traditionally maintained a close and sustainable relationship with their natural environment.

BANKING ON YAKS

Travelling through the northwest of Sìchuān, you'll inevitably encounter the yak. Huge and silent, they'll eye you up from the other side of the bus window as they're herded along by nomadic Tibetans. Unlike you and me, these animals thrive at 1070m to 1220m with a whole lot of fat accumulated just below their heavy wool coat to keep them warm through the frozen winters. Female yaks weigh in at around 360kg while males can reach weights of 1000kg and stand over 1.8m tall.

Tibetans recognised the potential of the yak and began domesticating it over 5000 years ago. There is scarcely an inch of the animal that goes unused: wool for tents, clothes, carpets and rope; skin for shoes, coats and boots; horns for decoration and utensils; fat for candles burned in temples; and the live animal itself for ploughing and threshing. Not to mention the meat and milk – yak meat is surprisingly low in fat, but the milk is around 7%, making the butter and cheese decidedly strong to say the least.

The wild yak, distinguishable by its all-black coat and gargantuan proportions, is now categorised as vulnerable by the World Conservation Monitoring Centre. More commonly seen is the domestic yak, crossbred with dairy cattle in order to produce more milk and better meat. These *dzo*, as they're called in Tibetan, retain their hardiness but are closer in size to a cow than a yak.

While the yak remains the backbone of the Tibetan economy and culture, increased degradation of grasslands and inbreeding have brought about a massive drop in the animals' weight and milk production. To counteract this, a yak sperm bank has opened its doors just north of Lhasa with hopes of raising both the numbers and the quality of the animal, if not the morale of the male yaks.

The website www .wwfchina.org has details of the World Wildlife Foundation's projects for endangered and protected animals in China. You'll also find a kids' page for the budding biologists in the family.

Chinese Taoists and Buddhists believe in ceasing to use protected animals in traditional Chinese medicine (TCM), which they maintain is traditionally based on achieving a balance in nature. What is bad for the environment is bad for the soul.

extinct. Many animals are officially protected, though illegal hunting and trapping continues. A bigger challenge is habitat destruction, caused by encroaching agriculture, urbanisation and industrial pollution. While catching sight of China's rare wildlife in its natural habitat requires a great deal of time, patience and luck, many visitors do include visits to protected parks and research bases for a more guaranteed look at China's elusive residents and blooms. Bird-watching is the exception to the rule; if you're willing to rough it in China's outback, you have a good chance of seeing some rare winged friends.

Animals

The Southwest's wealth of vegetation and variety of landscapes has fostered the development of a great diversity of animals. In mountain regions, you'll have no trouble spotting yaks and macaque monkeys while the lakes of the Yúnnán Plateau are particularly rich in carp: of China's 13 species, 12 are found only here. (Not exactly earth-shatteringly exciting, but an impressive statistic nonetheless.)

ENDANGERED ANIMALS

The Southwest's most exciting wildlife is also its rarest. The stunning snow leopard is found in the most remote reaches of western Sìchuān and is rarely encountered, even by researchers. It preys on mammals as large as mountain goats, but is persecuted for allegedly preying on livestock. Also at risk is the Asiatic black bear and the brown bear; the sika, white-lipped (Thorold's) and diminutive mouse deers; the golden takin; and argali sheep.

While monkeys are a common enough sight in China's Southwest, several are rare and endangered, including the beautiful golden monkey of the southwestern mountains, the snub-nosed monkey of the Yúnnán rainforests and Guǎngxī's rare white-headed leaf monkey. For sheer diversity of wildlife, the tropical area around Yúnnán's Xīshuāngbǎnnà region is one of the richest in China and home to the endangered slender loris, black gibbon, Asiatic Indian elephant, scaly anteater-like pangolin, and the South China tiger, of which only 30 to 80 remain in the world (making it one of the world's 10 most endangered species).

The giant panda is China's most famous mammal and lives in the bamboo-covered slopes of Sìchuān's Himalayan foothills. Of China's 28 panda reserves, 22 are located in Sìchuān. A recent census has revised the world population upwards after an estimated 39 pandas were located in Wanglang Nature Reserve, Sìchuān. Another positive development has been the 'bamboo tunnel', a reforested corridor for the pandas to move between two fragmented patches of forest. Red pandas are also found in Sìchuān and northwest Yúnnán. For more on pandas see the boxed text, p362.

> The giant panda spends up to 16 hours a day eating up to 20kg of bamboo shoots, stems and leaves.

BIRDS

Southwest China has superb bird-watching opportunities, particularly in spring. Cǎohǎi Hú (Caohai Lake), in northwestern Guìzhōu province, supports overwintering black-necked cranes, as well as other cranes, storks and waterfowl. Emerald Pagoda Lake (Bìtǎ Hǎi) and Nàpà Hǎi (Napa Lake) in northwest Yúnnán are also important wintering sites for rare species of migratory birds.

Sìchuān's Jiuzhaigou Nature Reserve is home to rare and endemic Chinese birds, such as the Sìchuān owl. Also in Sìchuān, Wolong Nature Reserve is home to spectacular golden, blood, eared and kalij pheasants, which live on the steep forested hillsides surrounding the main road. As the road climbs towards Beilanshan Pass, watch for eared pheasants and the Chinese monal. The rocky scree slopes at the pass hold partridges, the beautiful grandala and the enormous bearded vulture, which has a 2m wingspan.

> At www.cnbirds.com China Birding can fill you in on overwinter sites, migration routes and the geographical distribution of your feathered friends in China. It also has lots of excellent photos.

Plants

The Southwest's rich flora that has been well utilised over the years. Tea-oil trees, camphor, lacquer, betel nuts, tangerine, pomelo, orange, longan, lychee, kiwis (also known as the Chinese gooseberry), tea, chillies and garlic all grow wild in the region. Three thousand species of medicinal plants are harvested in Sìchuān alone, the most important of which are ginseng, golden hairpin, angelica, fritillary and gastrodia. Xīshuāngbǎnnà in the tropical south has plantations of rubber trees, oil palms, coconuts, cashews, coffee, cocoa, avocados and sapodillas as well as wild tea trees up to 1700 years old.

KILL OR CURE?

Before you swallow that time-honoured remedy, ask for the ingredients. Despite laws banning their capture, protected and endangered animals continue to be led to the chemist counters of China. As traditional Chinese medicine (TCM) makes it big globally, international laws prohibiting the trade of many species have forced practitioners to seek out alternative ingredients. The difficulty lies in getting Chinese consumers to accept such alternatives. Rodent bones just don't come close to the prestige of the tiger bones they're meant to replace.

These days, poachers trading in protected species can find themselves behind bars for up to 15 years, while those found smuggling the internationally revered panda face death. Even consumers can be punished, a law that has been around for some time but only recently enforced. Ingredients to watch for include bear bile, rhinoceros horns, dried seahorse, musk deer, antelope horns, leopard bones, sea lions, macaques, alligators, anteaters, pangolins, green sea turtles, freshwater turtles, rat snakes and giant clams.

The area around Xīshuāngbǎnnà has a diverse and rich flora, with over half of China's protected plants found there. Over 5000 species are known to grow here – up to 100 species in a 250 sq metre area. The tropical forest is, however, under intense strain from slash-and-burn agriculture and is today mostly secondary growth. Only 20% to 30% of the original forest remains.

Most of the world's roses, magnolias, orchids, chrysanthemums and camellias are indigenous to the mountains of western Sìchuān and northwest Yúnnán. At least 600 species of rhododendrons and 650 varieties of azaleas are found in Yúnnán. To see some of the world's rarest azaleas, head to Sìchuān's Wolong Nature Reserve (p375).

The Chinese parashorea, discovered in the 1970s in Xīshuāngbǎnnà and parts of Guǎngxī, is sought after for its timber. It's so fast-growing that the Chinese call it the Wàngtiānshù (Looking at the Sky) tree.

Also endemic to China is the ginkgo tree, a famous living fossil, the unmistakeable imprint of which has been found in rocks 270 million years old. Another prehistoric plant is *Cyathea spinulosa*, a large, woody fern which existed as far back as the Jurassic period. More recently, scientists were somewhat astonished to find specimens of *Metasequoia*, a 200-million-year-old conifer long thought extinct, growing in an isolated valley in Sìchuān. This ancient pine is related to the huge redwoods of North America's west coast. Yúnnán's 'Dragon's Blood Tree' has a life span of up to 8000 years, making it the longest-lived tree on earth. One of the rarest trees indigenous to the area is the magnificent Cathay silver fir, found in isolated groups at Huaping in Guǎngxī. The unique dove tree, or handkerchief tree, grows only in the deciduous forests of the southwest and is becoming increasingly rare.

Apart from rice, the plant probably most often associated with China is bamboo. Some 300 species cover about 3% of the total forest area in China and most of this is located in the subtropical areas south of the Yangzi River. The best place to surround yourself by it is in the Shunan Bamboo Sea of Sìchuān. Bamboo is the favourite nosh of the giant panda and cultivated by the Chinese for building material, food, scaffolding and disposable chopsticks, not to mention furniture and arts and crafts.

NATIONAL PARKS

China has an incredibly diverse range of natural escapes scattered across the country. Since the first nature reserve was established in 1956, around 2000 more parks have joined the ranks, protecting about 14% of China's land area.

The Chinese government site http://china.org.cn has a link to a page covering environmental issues, with regularly updated stories and links. While the content is interesting, it leans heavily on optimism.

Over the past decade, there has been an explosion of nature reserves in the Southwest; Yúnnán alone has over 100 nature reserves, more than any other province. Some reserves protect whole ecosystems while others protect specific rare animals or flora. Others protect geological wonders, such as the limestone terracing at Báishuǐtái (p292) or Shílín (the Stone Forest; p430).

Be prepared to share many of the more popular reserves with expanding commercial development. Tourism is generally welcomed into these reserves with open arms, meaning pricey hotels, more roads, gondolas, hawkers and busloads of tourists. With a little effort, you can often find a less beaten path to escape down but don't expect utter tranquillity.

ENVIRONMENTAL ISSUES

As a developing country with quick-paced industrialisation, it's not surprising that China has some hefty environmental issues to contend with. Unfortunately, China's huge population makes its environmental plights infinitely bigger than those of other nations. With one-quarter of the world's population living on only 7% of the earth's cultivable land, there is incredible pressure on the land's resources. Air pollution, deforestation, melting glaciers, endangered species, and rural and industrial waste are all taking their toll.

TOP NATURE RESERVES

Reserves	Features	Activities	When to Visit	Page
Éméi Shān	luxuriant scenery along a steep, ancient pilgrim route; monkeys; Buddhist sights	hiking, monasteries	May-Oct	p378
Fànjìng Shān	mountainous ecosystems with dove trees; golden monkeys	hiking, monkey breeding centre	May-Oct	p143
Jiǔzhàigōu	stunning alpine scenery & gem-coloured lakes; takins, golden monkeys, pandas	hiking, Tibetan village stays	Jun-Oct	p415
Wòlóng	deep, lush mountain valleys with rare azaleas & bamboo; pandas, golden monkeys, snow leopards, musk deer, golden langurs	panda rehabilitation centre, hiking	Jun-Sep	p375
Sānchàhé	tropical monsoon rainforest home to half of China's protected plant species, 62 species of mammals & 400 species of birds; elephants, gaurs, slow loris, pythons, great pied hornbills, green peafowls	hiking, elephant rehabilitation centre	Jan-Mar	p333

Conservation

Increasingly under the world's limelight with its entry into the World Trade Organization and the 2008 Summer Olympics, China seems to have shifted its policy slightly from one of 'industrial catch-up first, environmental clean-up later' to one that embraces at least a few initiatives for tidying up its environmental act now. Things like natural-gas powered buses tend to be found in urban centres and do little to counteract the countless polluting factories, but are nonetheless a step in the right direction. China is also now a member of Unesco's Man and Biosphere Programme, a signatory to the Convention on the International Trade in Endangered Species and a member of the World Conservation Union. To the government's credit, more than 150 nature reserves have been established in the Southwest alone, protecting about 7% of China's land area. Nevertheless, the tensions between environmental conservation and economic development remain particularly acute, especially as wildlife and natural resources have long been considered mere economic commodities to be exploited.

During the Great Leap Forward, the Four Pests Campaign aimed to eradicate flies, mosquitoes, rats and sparrows. The result was an environmental imbalance with a huge increase in hungry, crop-devouring bugs.

Resources & Pollution

The biggest source of China's air pollution is coal, with major cities lying smothered under great canopies of smog. Coal provides some 70% of China's energy needs and around 900 million tonnes of it go up in smoke every year. Somewhere in China a new coal-fired power station opens every seven to ten days; the result is immense damage to air and water quality, agriculture and human health, and acid rain. As demand quickly outstrips domestic resources of coal, the government has made some effort to seek out alternative sources of energy. Plans to construct natural gas pipelines are underway and taxes have been introduced on high-sulphur coals. It is also proposed that the controversial Three Gorges Dam (p461) will produce up to one-ninth

For a fairly academic but constructive look at China's environmental problems, check out *Green China: Seeking Ecological Alternatives* by Geoffrey Murray and Ian Cook.

GOING GREEN

China has a long tradition of celebrating nature within its frontiers, from landscape paintings to poems dwelling on mountain peaks shrouded in mist. Like many nations of the world, the contradictory China of today eulogises its landscape while simultaneously destroying it.

The green movement in China is relatively new. Waking up to the reality that its citizens had no education or information on ecology, the government has begun bombarding audiences with green directives on TV, from saving water to planting trees to litter disposal. A growing middle class finds itself wooed by adverts for environmentally friendly washing powders and detergents. There has also been an increase in the severity of penalties for violating China's conservation laws, with the death penalty and life sentences not uncommon.

Impressively, the public has also begun to join in the discourse on conservation. Since the advent of China's first environmental nongovernmental organisation (NGO) in the mid-1990s, more than 2000 environmental groups have sprung up. Hundreds of thousands of Chinese now participate in activities ranging from politically 'safe' issues, such as biodiversity protection and environmental education, to cutting-edge environmental activism like dam protests. So far, the government has largely tolerated these activities, perhaps conscious that environmental NGOs can fill gaps in official efforts to protect the environment. However, with little elbow room given for heated debates in the media, it remains to be seen whether or not the government's heavy foot will eventually stamp out this dissent.

In *The River Runs Black* Elizabeth Economy gives a fascinating account of China's environmental crisis. Her perspective is neither melodramatic nor dull, and is very readable.

of China's energy and therefore decrease emissions by 100 million tonnes. The government also has plans to dam the Yangzi in eight places further upriver, including at the popular Tiger Leaping Gorge (see the boxed text, p284). There are also plans to dam the Nu River, see p301.

The country's water isn't faring any better than its air. It is estimated that China annually dumps three billion tonnes of untreated water into the ocean via its rivers, a statement that won't likely shock you if you take a look at some of the water flowing under the bridges. At the end of 2005, around 40% of China's cities had no wastewater-treatment plants and many of those that did have plants didn't use them because local officials resented the cost of running them.

China's rivers and wetlands also face great pressure from siltation due to deforestation and increased run-off, which have brought devastating floods in western Sìchuān and led to a government ban on commercial logging in Sìchuān and Yúnnán. It's hoped that a rise in tourism can earn back some of the billions previously reaped from the lumber trade. Since 2002 two huge diversion projects have been underway as further means of controlling the Southwest's flooding and of moving water from the Yangzi River Basin to drought-prone northern China. A third route, which will necessitate blasting through mountains to link the Yangzi and Yellow Rivers, is proposed for 2010. Opponents call the diversions an overblown Maoist approach; a more moderate solution would be to increase water prices as a means of deterring waste. Prices are currently way below market rates but the government fears that raising them could cause widespread social unrest.

The impact of China's environmental problems doesn't stop at the country's borders – grit from China's desertification has reached as far as Vancouver and San Francisco.

All of this is exacerbated by global warming, which is shrinking the Qīnghǎi–Tibet Plateau's enormous glaciers by 7% each year. This rapid melting will initially increase rivers' water levels, causing widespread flooding, but it's believed it will eventually lead to severe water shortages, droughts and increased sandstorms.

Southwest China Outdoors

China's Southwest is the very icon of the great big outdoors, where huge, voluptuous landscapes insist on an open-air sense of adventure. This is very much an alfresco destination – the Southwest doesn't do stuffy museums or decaying imperial palaces very well. It's not so hot on the Great Wall (it never made it this far south), but the awe-inspiring natural scenery of the Southwest really is something to write home about.

The Southwest isn't, by and large, one of China's big polluters either, so fresh air is a powerful incentive to get out and about. The deserts and arid plains of the north and northwest have no place here – down here it's largely green and intoxicatingly luxurious with a rich diversity of fauna and flora. Unlike other parts of China, it's simple to get off the beaten path and into the big outdoors. And with the sheer variety of landscapes around you – from the dreamlike karst peaks around Yángshuò to the lush vegetation of Xīshuāngbǎnnà and the looming mountains of western Sìchuān – you're spoiled for choice. A sizable and growing crop of outdoor activities can further pepper up any trip to the Southwest and add an adrenaline edge to the fantastic scenery.

GETTING AWAY FROM IT ALL

The rapidly modernising zeal of Běijīng and Shànghǎi – with their hard-edged and futuristic skylines – doesn't make it this far. The Southwest is developing rapidly, but its largely landlocked topography (save for the long Guǎngxī coastline) and the huge distance from China's powerhouse cities corrects expectations that China is a land of shimmering high-rises and breakneck growth.

It is the opportunity to explore the diverse landscapes and vibrant minority cultures of the region that generates its allure, rather than Hong Kong–style modernity. Travellers to Běijīng and Shànghǎi may be initially swept away by their modern guise, but travel through China is ultimately about seeking out the old, the traditional and surviving remnants from earlier dynasties. The Southwest has these in bundles.

Coming to China's Southwest is essentially a nonurban experience. Chóngqìng may be the world's largest metropolitan area, but even this vast city is the gateway to one of China's premier natural phenomena – the awe-inspiring Three Gorges (p458). Most large cities in the Southwest – take Nánníng, Kūnmíng or Guìyáng – are incidental in the bigger picture and serve as launch pads to explorations of the surrounding outdoors.

Han civilisation remains the predominant culture in the Southwest, but if savouring minority culture tops your menu, there isn't much reason to leave the region. The ethnic melange of China's Southwest is unique and far more evident than, say, in northeast China, and it's a principle reason to be here.

Getting out into the open can liberate you from China's hard-nosed entry ticket system for tourist sights. Virtually every official sight in China requires an entrance ticket, often at absurd prices (eg Emerald Pagoda Lake in Yúnnán; p292) that increase way ahead of inflation. Practically every museum in China requires a ticket (which does nothing to promote free education). Although you will be charged at many of the big destinations

The Last Panda, by George Schaller, is the evocative story of a field research team who delve into this elusive animal's habitat in Sìchuān's Wolong Nature Reserve.

in the Southwest, much remains that is gratis, as long as you pack a sense of adventure and are prepared to venture off the tourist trail. There's also all the fun of leaving your guidebook behind and taking off into the unknown; except for the border regions, you won't have to worry too much about where you go, and half the fun of exploring China's Southwest is getting suitably lost.

The Chinese have a high tolerance for synthetic walkways, poured concrete statues and artificiality in general. Westerners do not. This is in sharp contrast with traditional Chinese mores as seen in traditional Chinese painting, where the human presence was minimised. Among young Chinese, there is a growing need to eke out unspoiled areas of natural beauty; but for most Chinese over the age of 40, a kind of communist comfort is drawn from beholding man's indelible impact on the environment.

CLIMATE

As hot and humid as a greenhouse, the Sìchuān Basin has so many foggy days that locals say that the dogs bark in shock whenever they see the sun.

China's Southwest has some of the land's best year-round climate. That said, you want to pick and choose carefully if arriving in the off season. The blistering winter of Běijīng may be a glacial world away from a December trip to Xīshuāngbǎnnà, but at altitude in western Sìchuān or northern Yúnnán, things can get dangerously cold. See p467 for further climate information. Summers in the Southwest are also extremely hot, and although altitude can make things more pleasant, spring and autumn trips are recommended.

BALLOONING

Taking lazily to the skies in hot-air balloons over China's Southwest is feasible. The **Xī'an Flying Balloon Club** (西安飞翔热气球俱乐部; Xīān Fēixiáng Rèqìqiú Jùlèbù; ☎ 0773-882 8444; www.xaballoon.com; 126 Kangzhan Lu; per hr per person Y650) has an office in Yángshuò with hot-air balloons taking to the skies from the Hongqi wharf (红旗码头; Hóngqí Mǎtou) on the Yulong River, around 2km downriver from Yuèliàng Shān (Moon Hill). Flights vary from short vertical lift-offs to hour-long voyages drifting with the wind over the dreamy karst landscape below; for the best views, aim for early morning and evening flights. If you've never experienced a journey in a hot-air balloon, the sublime terrain around Yángshuò can be perfect for a maiden voyage.

BIRD-WATCHING

Keen bird-watchers should carry *The Field Guide to the Birds of China*, by J MacKinnon, which illustrates and describes all 1300 species that have been recorded in China, and gives worthwhile background on their ecology and conservation.

Ornithologists will want to visit the Napa Hai Nature Reserve (p292) between September and March to catch glimpses of black-necked cranes. These cranes can also be seen at Cǎohǎi Hú (p118) at Wēiníng in Guìzhōu province, which sees 100,000 birds passing through in winter (the optimum time to visit is between December and March). Bird-watchers also journey to Wēibǎo Shān (p246) in Yúnnán as it lies on a migratory route. The wetland reserve near Zhiyun Monastery (p272) in Yúnnán is a bird-watching diversion for those in the area. Before visiting reserves, check the latest bird flu situation; see the Health chapter (p496) for more information.

CAVING

The Chinese predilection for caves illuminated by fluorescent rainbow lights grates with Western visitors who prefer their caves *au naturel* and with human impact kept to a minimum. Apart from illuminating stalactites with disco lights, the Chinese delight in naming geological forms with names culled from Chinese myth, religion and superstition; this frequently serves to confuse Westerners as well as robbing the rock form of its spontaneous beauty.

Some caves, such as the Longgong Caves (p113) in Guìzhōu, frequently see a log jam of visitors. For Middle Earth–style effects, try out China's largest cave at Zhijin Cave (p114), also in Guìzhōu.

An organisation with a wealth of information on caving in China is the **Hong Meigui Cave Exploration Society** (www.hongmeigui.net), dedicated to caving in China and which has mounted numerous expeditions to caves around Chóngqìng and throughout Sìchuān, Yúnnán and Guǎngxī. An organisation focussing on the limestone caves around Chóngqìng – rich caving territory – is the **CQOutdoor Caving Team** (☎ 023-6696 1458; www.cqoutdoor.com). Its website is Chinese only at present, but you may be able to get in touch with an English speaker. For guided caving expeditions in the Southwest, also consult **ChinaCaving** (www.chinacaving.com). The company takes teams into karst caves around Lèyè County and Fèngshān County in Guǎngxī province.

CYCLING

Increasing numbers of travellers are cycling into China from Southeast Asia. Cycling through China's Southwest allows you to go when you want, to see what you want and at your own pace. It can also be an extremely cheap, as well as a highly authentic, way to see China.

You will have virtually unlimited freedom of movement and you may also encounter people who rarely if ever come into contact with foreigners. Bear in mind, however, that China's Southwest is a massive chunk of territory (Guǎngxī province, for example, is the size of the UK), and you may wish to alternate your cycling days with trips by train, bus, boat, taxi or even plane, especially if you want to avoid particularly steep regions or areas where the roads are poor.

Yúnnán has 6000m peaks while Guǎngxī has over 1500km of coastline.

Bikechina (www.bikechina.com) is a good source of information for cyclists coming to China, and includes numerous travelogues by cyclists. The Yángshuò-based company offers tours around China's Southwest, ranging from one-day bike tours of Chéngdū to five-day round trips from Chéngdū to Dānbā to eight-day tours around Yúnnán from Kūnmíng to Tiger Leaping Gorge, via Dàlǐ and Lìjiāng. Groups consists of small numbers of cyclists; you can fit in with a range of tours or have a route designed for you. Prices start from around US$90 per person per day.

Biking routes in the Southwest are infinite in number, but be sure to include the journey from Kūnmíng to Dàlǐ, Lìjiāng and on to Shangri-la (Zhōngdiàn), from where you can continue through magnificent scenery on to Lǐtáng in Sìchuān (one week); be prepared for very steep gradients and avoid doing this in winter as the road will be totally snowbound. Numerous roads lead into Tibet (eg via Bātáng from Lǐtáng); despite massive temptation, remember that you are legally not allowed to enter Tibet without a permit. A mammoth bike journey can be undertaken from Kūnmíng in Yúnnán to Chéngdū in Sìchuān. The possibilities are countless, including cycling from Yúnnán into Guìzhōu and then on to Guǎngxī; naturally the rest of China lies beyond. See www.bicycle-adventures.com for recommended cycling routes in the region.

Roads in China's Southwest are generally in good condition, but be prepared for the worst wherever you go. Be aware that lorries (trucks) and cars in China can drive very dangerously. Equipping yourself with a provincial map in Chinese is essential for showing locals to get directions, and for following road signs. Wild dogs can be a menace in more remote areas.

Villages can be widely spaced apart, for example in wilder parts of Sìchuān, and you may need to camp, so taking camping equipment is necessary. Also ensure you have adequate clothing as many routes will be taking you to considerable altitude.

Most areas are now open to foreigners so you won't need a travel permit (the big exception to this is Tibet), although it is worth checking with the local Public Security Bureau before you enter an area you are unsure about.

A basic check list for cycling in China's Southwest includes a good bicycle repair kit, sunscreen and other protection from the sun, waterproofs, camping equipment and maps. For more information on cycling in China, see the Bicycle section in the Transport chapter (p486).

ECOSYSTEM BIODIVERSITY

The opposite of the swirling dust storms of the Taklamakan Desert or the plummeting water table of dry-as-dust Běijīng and Tiānjīn, China's Southwest is a lush and fecund region. Flourishing and well-watered ecosystems abound wherever you glance; Yúnnán alone accounts for at least half of China's animal species (see boxed text, p305). The sheer wealth of regional ecosystem diversity is a dazzling draw card for visitors. Trek to the magnificent ecosystems flourishing around Yúnnán's Mingyong Glacier (p295) or be wowed by the sheer richness of the Nujiang Valley (p297) – home to almost 25% of China's plant and animal species. Explore the primeval forests of Báimǎ Xuěshān (p297) or be simply overwhelmed in spring by the vibrant yellows of Luópíng's fields of canola (p304).

Only about 5% of Yúnnán and Guìzhōu can be considered flat.

Disappear among 30 different types of swaying bamboo in the Shunan Bamboo Sea (p427) for a taste of the utter sublime, or surrender to the jaw-dropping beauty of Jiuzhaigou Nature Reserve (p415), perhaps the most iconic backdrop of China's Southwest. Sìchuān's Huanglong National Park (p414) also harbours some impressive ecosystems, and eager panda-watchers will enjoy trooping off to Wolong Nature Reserve (p375) for fleeting glimpses of the endangered mammal (see also boxed text, p362). The splendid alpine scenery and gorgeous terrain of Yading Nature Reserve (p407) demands exploration by the visitor. Chìshuǐ's (p147) magnificent ferns have their origins way back in the Jurassic. For details on opportunities for bird-watching in China's Southwest, see p64.

HORSE TREKS

China's Southwest has a handful of places where you can ride horses on treks into the hills, principally in Sìchuān and Yúnnán. In Sìchuān, Sōngpān (p411), around Lǎngmùsì (p421), Yading Nature Reserve (p407) and the Tagong Grasslands (p393) are all popular destinations for horse trekking. In Yúnnán, horse treks can also be made up to the Mingyong Glacier (p295) and on Yùlóng Xuěshān (p274) outside Lìjiāng. You may not be able to do too much solo horse trekking or have much freedom of movement, and generally you will be accompanied by a guide.

RIVER JOURNEYS

The Yangzi River (Cháng Jiāng) cuts a dramatic path through Yúnnán and Sìchuān, before pouring out of Chóngqìng to funnel splendidly through the Three Gorges. Despite the completion of the Three Gorges Dam, the journey through the gorges (in between Chóngqìng and Yíchāng) remains one of China's most spectacular trips (p458). The other celebrated river trip is through the splendid karst scenery along the Li River (Lí Jiāng; p166) between Guìlín and Yángshuò. The highlight of the five-hour round trip along the Zuo Jiang Scenic Area (p206) in southwestern Guǎngxī province is the 2000-year-old Zhuang murals at Huāshān. For trekking opportunities in some of Yúnnán's most splendid river-valley scenery, the Nujiang Valley (p297) is second to none.

ROCK CLIMBING

Yángshuò is one of Asia's fastest growing rock-climbing destinations, with massive potential for new routes; see p169 for further details. For loads of tips and hints on climbing, mountaineering and trekking in China, consult www.outdoorschina.com. Yángshuò-based **Karst Climber** (www.karstclimber.com) is another useful climbing operation and source of information for climbs in the Yángshuò region. A guidebook to rock climbing in Yángshuò is available from local shops, detailing recommended bolted routes in the area.

TREKKING

Trekking is essential for a full-on appreciation of the beauty of the South-west (for a local voice on trekking, see p408). Whether it's the Yubeng or Kawa Karpo Treks (see p296), Tiger Leaping Gorge (p281), treks around Fúgòng p299) and other reaches of the Nujiang Valley (p297), hikes up to Dímáluò and Báihànluò (p301), Yading Nature Reserve (p407), or around Lǎngmùsì (p421), tramping through the Southwest can generate the most vivid memories of your trip.

Trekking through borderland territories – where ethnic cultures and languages merge and overlap, and Han China is at its most diluted – allows a unique perspective on the Middle Kingdom. Exploring western and southern Yúnnán province will bring you into contact with a long and meandering international border, where the province comes up against Myanmar, Laos and Vietnam. Travellers to western Sìchuān will find themselves in a largely Tibetan world, in parts very close to the border with Tibet.

Treks can generally be divided into two groups: established treks (where routes are easy to follow, visitor numbers are relatively large and guesthouses and restaurants lie along the trail) and wilderness experiences (where there is no defined route, no accommodation or food, and the thrill of the unexpected waits at every turn). Established treks also vary in difficulty from the simple, but lovely, trek between Píngān and Dàzhài through the Dragon's Backbone Rice Terraces (p181) to more complex and exhilarating, but similarly established, trails such as Tiger Leaping Gorge and Yading Nature Reserve. From a navigation point of view, some of the simplest treks are up sacred peaks such as Éméi Shān (p378) and Qīngchéng Shān (p373).

For wilderness trekking, you will need to set out fully prepared, with detailed maps, tent, stove, sleeping bag, waterproofs and everything you may need to subsist away from civilisation. Climate change is one of the greatest

You will see flowers growing in reckless profusion… For days on end you may tramp over carpets of flowers.

FRANK KINGDON-WARD ON YÚNNÁN; PLANT EXPLORER; C 1911

SAFETY GUIDELINES FOR WALKING

Before embarking on a walking trip, consider the following points to ensure a safe and enjoyable experience:

- Pay any fees and possess any permits required by local authorities.
- Be sure you are healthy and feel comfortable walking for a sustained period.
- Try to obtain reliable information about physical and environmental conditions along your intended route.
- Walk only in regions, and on trails, within your realm of experience.
- Be aware that weather conditions and terrain vary significantly from one region, or even from one trail, to another. Seasonal changes can significantly alter any trail. These differences influence the way walkers dress and the equipment they carry.
- Ask before you set out about the environmental characteristics that can affect your walk and how local, experienced walkers deal with these considerations.

hazards, so time your expedition well and prepare for the worst possible weather. Western Sìchuān offers unrivalled trekking opportunities if you are willing to be self-sufficient and adventurous. The Tagong Grasslands (p393) is great for summer treks, and the area around Dānbā (p395) brings you to fascinating Tibetan and Qiang villages and Qiang watchtowers (see p396). At altitude, Lǐtáng (p402) in Sìchuān is an increasingly attractive trekking destination.

Joining a trekking tour can be expensive and an unattractive option for those who want absolute freedom, but you can take a back seat as all the preparation is done for you, guides are provided and you are looked after. See p475 for recommended tour companies that arrange treks in China's Southwest.

Food & Drink

In China, cuisine is about far more than just filling your belly. It's used as a social lubricant, as an offering to the gods, as a means of showering generosity, and as a conduit for business. A common Chinese saying claims 'for the people, food is their heaven'. This passion for food has shaped Chinese culture, with cooks developing and perfecting their art in even the harshest of living conditions. The result is a triumphant blending of inventiveness, flavour and economy. In all but the remotest corners of the Southwest you'll find a handful of ingredients combined into a cacophony of dishes.

A well-prepared Chinese dish is expected to appeal to all the senses: smell, colour, taste and texture. You can also look for a blending of Yin and Yang, the principles of balance and harmony – bland dishes paired with spicy ones, crisp dishes paired with soft ones. Most vegetables and fruits are Yin foods, generally moist or soft, and are meant to have a cooling effect which nurtures the feminine aspect of our nature. Yang foods – fried, spicy or with red meat – are warming and nourish our masculine side.

China's geographical and climatic differences, together with local cooking styles, have created many different schools of cuisine. Generally, the western school is summed up as spicy although it varies dramatically between provinces and regions. In the north of the Southwest, cuisine has evolved to provide lasting satisfaction in a cold climate (think lard, meat and yak butter) while southern dishes tend to dry out the body through perspiration (think chilli and more chilli), which helps to adjust to the intense humidity.

> www.eatingchina.com is a terrific blog dedicated to the delights of Chinese gastronomy and dishes up recipes and info on tea and holiday foods.

> Chilli peppers came to China from Peru and Mexico during the Ming dynasty and are a concentrated source of vitamins A and C as well as the hallmark of the Southwest's cuisine.

TRAVEL YOUR TASTEBUDS

The most commonly used ingredients in southwestern cuisine are pork, poultry, legumes and soya beans, spiced up with a variety of wild condiments and mountain products such as mushrooms and bamboo shoots. Seasonings are heavy – red chilli, peppercorns, garlic, ginger and onions. Most dishes are stir-fried quickly under extreme heat ('explode-frying') but you'll also find cooking styles like *hóngshāo* (soaked in soy sauce), *yúxiāng* (cooked in a spicy sauce meant to resemble fish) and *tiěbǎn* (served sizzling).

Particularly popular in Sìchuān and Guìzhōu, hotpot is a huge bowl of bubbling, spicy broth that you can warm yourself around while dipping in skewers of veggies, tofu and meat. It's a cheap, tasty way to fill your belly in the winter. For the spicy version ask for *làwèi* (spicy); if you'd like something milder request *báiwèi* (not spicy; and expect a smirk from your server).

In Guǎngxī you'll find Cantonese-style cooking, which tends to be lighter, less spicy and more exotic. Its most popular creations are sweet and sour dishes and dim sum, which has become a Sunday institution worldwide.

While you'll find apples and mandarins throughout much of the region, fruit-lovers should keep on the watch for more exotic varieties, especially in Yúnnán. Lychees, pomelos, longan, rambutan, spodilla, persimmons, dragon fruit and exceptionally sweet pineapple frequently make an appearance in the markets.

You should also have an opportunity to try the region's unique minority dishes. Dai dishes are particularly tasty; try black glutinous rice (really, it's better than it sounds!); sticky rice steamed in bamboo tubes; pineapple and coconut rice; and beef with lemon grass. The Miao use zesty tangerine peel in stir-fries and the Naxi make delicious flatbread that will fill you for a day. In Tibetan communities you may get to try immensely strong yak cheese, *shemre* (rice, yogurt and yak-meat curry) and *tsampa* (roasted barley meal).

STAPLES & SPECIALITIES

In a traditional Chinese meal, grains are always the centrepiece, served with vegetables, soya bean and, if affordable, meat or fish. The principle that a proper meal is based around a staple grain dates back at least to the Shang dynasty (1700–1100 BC) and remains fundamental to Chinese cuisine wherever it is found.

In the Southwest you can expect to eat rice at least once a day but will also have ample opportunity to slurp down rice or flour noodles and munch on local breads like steamed buns and flatbread. For meat you can expect mainly pork and chicken in the cities.

OUR FAVOURITE EATING EXPERIENCES

Damian Harper

Whether the sight of dog meat is finally goading you into vegetarianism or you simply want to feast on inventive Chinese Buddhist cuisine, make a meal of it at Guìlín's Nengren Vegetarian Restaurant (p161). You're on temple grounds so the food is strictly bloodless, but the flavour's full-on.

After three days dieting on backpacker staples, I was overjoyed to bump into the Uighur chef (p173) who made an evening appearance on Yángshuò's Xi Jie to flame up handfuls of chilli-laced *yángròuchuàn* (lamb kebabs), bringing some of the aroma of China's northwest to Guǎngxī.

Tienlon Ho

A great way to while away an afternoon is sipping tea on the 2nd floor of Lǎo Jiē Shí Bā Tī Teahouse (p451). From that roost, you can look out over the old city and still hear the soft strains of the live orchestra that plays downstairs. I especially enjoyed a green tea called *yóng chuān xiù yá* (永川秀芽) that originated during the Ba era and is a great accompaniment to the dried tomatoes and other little bites you order on the side.

A makeshift restaurant on the deck of the lone boat on the bank of the Qu Jiang in Láitān (p456) serves up an extremely fresh catch of the day. The friendly couple that runs Méng Dǎ Yú Qú Jiāng Shuǐ Shàng Cǎo Chuán Yú Zhuāng (蒙打鱼渠江水上草船鱼庄) spends mornings reeling in fish and prawns upriver, which are then kept swimming in a bin on the side of the boat, until they go into the wok and (after a liberal douse of Sìchuǎn peppercorns) onto your plate.

Thomas Huhti

1910 La Gare du Sud (Kūnmíng; p230) is what I had always longed for, a classy Yunnanese food eatery – here in a neocolonial-style building – without indifferent service.

Without a doubt my favourite spot to actually eat out, as in al fresco (becoming rarer as Yúnnán catches up with China's modernisation), is wandering the ubiquitous Jinghong night markets (Jinghong; p330). Plop down, wipe the sweat off, have a cold beer and start smiling as boisterous Chinese on holiday howl for you to party with them.

Eilís Quinn

Neighbourhood locals swear by Xiǎohuī Dòuhuā (Chéngdū; p366), where the modestly sized dishes explode with flavour (and lots and lots of chilli). Picking and choosing among the mysterious list of snacks will be an absolute treat for gastronomic adventurers (I *still* crave its sweet and spicy noodles) but even the everyday dishes like dumplings are fantastic.

Staying with a Miao family in Xìjiāng (p130) you may have one of the most memorable (and lengthy) meals of your life. Miao dishes are colourful with plenty of pickle. It's not too spicy but the cuisine still bursts with vivid tastes. I'd like to tell you what I ate that night in detail, but a Miao custom dictates rice wine be poured down guest's throats continually throughout the meal (no, you don't even need to hold the cup yourself). I woke up the next morning to embarrassingly illegible notes. Don't even ask about the pictures!

In minority regions, duck is often popular, dog is not uncommon, mutton is served in Muslim restaurants and, in very remote, poor areas, you'll even find rat dished up. Vegetables are varied – everything from sweet peppers to mushrooms and aubergine; in the poorest regions you can expect lots (and lots) of cabbage.

Foreigners generally find breakfast the most difficult meal to get their stomach around in China. Locals often have a bowl of rice porridge (*zhōu*; 粥; or *congee*) with pickles and *yóutiáo* (油条; deep-fried dough sticks), along with steamed buns, served plain or with fillings. This is usually washed down with hot soya bean milk.

Other common breakfast dishes include rice-noodle soups, fried peanuts and pork with hot sauce, accompanied with a glass of beer. Just what you had in mind at 7am.

DRINKS
Nonalcoholic Drinks

The Chinese were the first to cultivate tea, and the art of brewing and drinking tea has been popular since the Tang dynasty (AD 618–907). You'll most commonly encounter weak jasmine (*cháshuǐ*) or nonfermented green tea (*lǜ chá*), served on the house in most restaurants and awaiting you in your hotel room.

You'll also find wulong tea (semifermented) and, less commonly, black tea (*hóng chá*). Eight-treasures tea (*bābǎo chá*) is a delicious combination of rock sugar, dates, nuts and tea.

Chinese people will also commonly throw a variety of ingredients – fresh ginger, orange peel, roots and herbs – into empty jars, top it with boiling water and slurp at it all day long. Teahouses serve an outrageous number of teas – many of them are also outrageously expensive so be sure to check the price list before taking a sip.

Coffee has begun making a dent in the Chinese market. In urban centres you'll find cafés serving a semidecent brew. You'll also find packets of instant coffee (including milk and sugar) that act as a good pick-me-up on long, freezing bus rides.

Soft drinks such as Coca-Cola and Sprite are readily found, along with even sweeter local versions. Jianlibao is a Chinese orange-flavoured soft drink made with honey and is definitely the best option.

Mineral water is easy to find, though it's always wise to check the seal. Served in a bottle with a straw, sweet yogurt drinks are available from some shops and street vendors. You'll also find coconut milk, soya bean milk and almond milk.

Alcoholic Drinks

If tea is the most popular drink in the China, beer must be number two. And as with tea, the Chinese have perfected the art of brewing it.

The best-known brand is Tsingtao, which heralds from a brewery in Qīngdǎo that was inherited by the Chinese from the German concession. There are countless other domestic brands to sample: Liquan in Guìlín, Yufeng in Guìyáng, Báilóngtán and KK Beer in Kūnmíng, and Wanli in Nánníng. In minority regions try honey beer, prickly pear beer and Tibetan *chang*, made from barley.

China has produced wine for more than 4000 years, however Westerners are generally disappointed with the results. (Unlike Western producers, Chinese winemakers go to great lengths to achieve oxidation.) Yúnnán has a tradition of making red wine that dates from the Catholic missionaries of the 19th century; watch for the Rouhong and Shangri-la labels.

Indulged in a fiery, chilli-spiced dish and need to cool the fires? Order a can of almond milk. It's delicious and, more importantly, it restores calm to your tastebuds.

Hejie Jiu (Lizard Wine) is produced in Guǎngxi; each bottle contains one dead lizard suspended in clear liquid. Wine with dead bees or pickled snakes is also popular for alleged tonic properties. In general, the more poisonous the creature, the more potent the tonic.

LOCAL REMEDY *Korina Miller*

We'd arrived in the small Tibetan village late and had been lucky enough to find a room in the home of a local family. The brightly painted wooden room was beautiful – but frozen. December in northwest Sìchuān was cold. Very cold. There had to be a local remedy.

We made our way into the kitchen and perched as close as we dared to the wood fire. Amid shy and friendly smiles we were each offered a big bowl of warmth – yak-butter tea.

I am a seasoned tea drinker, having slurped it back since early childhood, and I believe there is little that a good cuppa can't cure. I took a gulp. A big gulp. A big chunky gulp. I kept my smile plastered in place while my taste buds went into a horrified frenzy.

Yak-butter tea is exactly that – tea with salty, incredibly strong yak butter glopped on top. It offers a hearty dose of salt and fat during the winter months and is something of a lifesaver for the Tibetans. But I'd rather I be given my English Breakfast any day. Apparently I'm not so seasoned after all.

I looked at my travelling companion and knew from his bulging eyes and puckered cheeks that he was finding his beverage as challenging as I was. What to do?

Our hostess turned her back and 'pling' went a chunk of yak butter, torpedoed into the fire by my friend. 'Pling. Pling.' The fire sputtered and sizzled but kicked up little fuss. Nevertheless, I couldn't believe my companion's cheek. And I could believe my own even less as I followed suit. 'Pling. Pling. Pling.'

We were finally reaching the bottom of our bowls and smiling with grand relief. Our hostess wandered over and seemed genuinely pleased that we'd nearly polished off our tea. So pleased that she ladled us each out another big serving, slapped the yak butter on top and sat down to join us.

The word 'wine' gets rather loosely translated and many Chinese 'wines' are in fact spirits. Rice wine is intended mainly for cooking rather than drinking. *Baijiu* (white spirits) is extremely popular for toasting at banquets. Made from sorghum, it has a sweet, pungent smell and tastes like paint thinner. If you find yourself invited to a banquet, you will be expected to keep up with the copious toasts of this face-numbing drink, accompanied to loud cries of '*gānbēi*' ('dry the cup'). Be warned: this stuff is strong and hits hard.

The Chinese commonly greet each other with the question '*Nǐ chī fàn le ma?*' ('Have you eaten yet?').

CELEBRATIONS
Holidays

Food is the guest of honour at Chinese holidays and often plays a symbolic role. Noodles are eaten on birthdays and New Year because their long thin shape symbolises longevity. (And consequently it's bad luck to break the noodles before cooking them.)

During the Chinese New Year it's common to serve a whole chicken because it resembles family unity. Fish also plays an important role during New Year celebrations as the word for fish, *yú*, sounds similar to the word for abundance.

Many poor families who can rarely afford meat during the year will save up to serve meat at New Year to symbolise prosperity. Moon cakes (*yuè bǐng*), sweet cakes filled with sesame seeds, lotus seeds, dates and other fillings, are eaten during China's Mid-Autumn Festival, and *zòngzi* (dumplings made of glutinous rice wrapped in bamboo or reed leaves) are eaten during the Dragon Boat Festival.

Banquets

In China, the banquet is the icing on the cake. Important for clinching business deals, welcoming guests and celebrating occasions like weddings, banquets are often a splashy affair. During a banquet, dishes appear in sequence, beginning with cold appetisers and continuing through 10 or more courses.

The host orders far more than anyone can eat; if there are empty bowls this implies a stingy host. Rice is considered a cheap filler and rarely appears at a banquet – don't ask for it; this would imply the food being served is insufficient.

WHERE TO EAT & DRINK

In China, clientele focus on what's in their bowl more than the ambience. Consequently, the way to hunt down a good local eatery is to find one that's busy. Unlikely posters of foreign meals may adorn the wall, the chairs may well be plastic and the lighting glaring, but if it's packed with happy, noisy locals, you can bet the food is good.

To order, you can simply point at dishes that other customers are having or, in places with an open kitchen, you can point to the ingredients you'd like. (Be sure to indicate how many dishes you'd like or you'll get a separate one for each ingredient.) The drawback to this is that you end up eating the same thing again and again; to break the habit, try using the menu in Eat Your Words (p75).

In cities, restaurants around sights and universities will often have English signs and menus, but prices are generally higher and there's often an attempt to gear dishes towards foreign tastes.

The word *fàndiàn* (饭店) usually refers to a large-scale restaurant that may or may not offer lodging. A *cānguǎn* (餐馆) is generally a smaller restaurant that specialises in one particular type of food. The most informal types of restaurants are canteen-style or small hole-in-the-wall eateries with low-end prices and often have some of the best food – watch for *cāntīng* (餐厅), *xiǎochī* (小吃) and *dàpáidàng* (大排档).

Breakfast is served early in China, mainly between 6am and 9am. In larger cities many restaurants serving lunch and dinner open from 11am to 2pm, reopen around 5pm and close at 9pm. In smaller cities, restaurants may close as early as 8pm. Some street stalls stay open 24 hours.

> During its short stay in Chóngqìng (1938–1945), the Chinese Nationalist Government acquired a small army of Sichuanese chefs, many of whom continued on with the government to Taiwan, from where Sichuanese cooking spread across the globe.

Quick Eats

Weekly produce markets, night markets and old town backstreets offer an eyeful and a bellyful too. Hygiene is always a question, so make sure to eat only at the busiest of places to avoid getting sick.

Dumplings (饺子; *jiǎozi*) are a popular snack in China. Similar to ravioli, they're stuffed with meat, spring onion and greens. Locals mix chilli (辣椒; *làjiāo*), vinegar (醋; *cù*) and soy sauce (酱油; *jiàngyóu*) in a little bowl for dipping.

Portable barbeques are used to grill skewers of veggies, tofu and meat; be sure to step in before they're dosed with chilli if you're not keen on spicy foods. At more permanent barbeque stalls, you can prop yourself up at the grill, choose what you like and dip it into tasty sauces.

Other street snacks include fried tofu, tea eggs (soaked in tea and soy sauce), grilled corn-on-the-cob and baked sweet potatoes. Market snacks that most foreigners turn down include chicken feet and pig's ears. Yum, yum.

VEGETARIANS & VEGANS

While vegetarianism can be traced back over 1000 years in China, today it's seen as unusual at best, snobbery at worst. Many Chinese remember all too well the famines of the 1950s and 1960s and these days eating meat (as well

---

EATING DOS & DON'TS

■ Don't wave your chopsticks around or point them at people unless you want to be labelled rude.

■ Don't drum your chopsticks on the sides of your bowl – only beggars do this.

■ Never commit the terrible faux pas of sticking your chopsticks into your rice. Two chopsticks stuck vertically into a rice bowl resemble incense sticks in a bowl of ashes and is considered an omen of death.

■ Don't let the spout of a teapot face towards anyone. Make sure it is directed outward from the table or to where nobody is sitting.

■ Never flip a fish over to get to the flesh underneath. If you do so, the next boat you pass will capsize.

---

as milk and eggs) is a sign of progress and material abundance. Don't be too shocked to find bits of meat snuck into your food.

Strict vegetarians and vegans will find the Southwest a difficult dining date, especially outside urban areas. Vegetables are often plentiful but are generally fried in animal-based oils, and soups and noodle broth are most commonly made with meat stock. If you are willing to turn a blind eye to this, hotpot, barbeques and noodles are often a good way to fill up (nearly) meat-free.

In the most remote, poor areas, the monotony of cabbage and noodles will begin to wear your appetite thin; be sure to bring lots of snacks from the cities. Getting enough salt (something you begin to crave at higher altitudes) is also a challenge as it's generally used only in meat dishes – even crisps are seasoned with chilli rather than salt.

Pure vegan food is best sought at restaurants attached to Buddhist monasteries. The dishes are most often 'mock meat', made from tofu, wheat gluten and vegetables but shaped to look like spare ribs or fried chicken. Just close your eyes and dig in.

> While dropping food is OK, never drop your chopsticks – it's bad luck.

> Swallowing Clouds gets rave reviews. In it, A Zee weaves together knowledge on cooking, culture and language in an insightful, educational, humorous way. You'll find recipes, folk tales and may even come away with the ability to decipher Chinese menus.

HABITS & CUSTOMS

Dining in China is a noisy, crowded affair. Viewed as a way to celebrate togetherness, everything from slurping to spitting out bones is done with enthusiasm and at high volume.

Typically, the Chinese sit at a round table and order dishes from which everyone partakes; it's not unusual for one person at the table to order on everyone's behalf. Don't be surprised if your hosts use their chopsticks to place food in your bowl or plate; this is a sign of friendship.

Remember to fill your neighbours' tea cups when they are empty, as yours will be filled by them. On no account serve yourself tea without serving others first. When your teapot needs a refill, let the waiter know by taking the lid off the pot.

Most Chinese think little of sticking their own chopsticks into a communal dish, though this attitude has changed post-SARS. Most high-end restaurants now provide separate serving spoons or chopsticks to be used with communal dishes.

Never use a personal spoon to serve from a communal plate or bowl. When eating from communal dishes, don't use your chopsticks to root around in a dish for a piece of food. Find a piece by sight and go directly for it without touching anything else.

Probably the most important piece of etiquette comes with the bill: the person who extended the dinner invitation is presumed to pay, though everyone at the table will put up a fight. Don't argue too hard; it's expected that at a certain point in the future the meal will be reciprocated. Tipping is not the norm in China.

EAT YOUR WORDS

See the Language chapter (p501) for pronunciation guidelines.

To save on cooking fuel, meat and vegetables were traditionally chopped into tiny pieces for faster cooking and dishes were served communally to make sure everyone got something to eat.

Useful Words & Phrases

I'm vegetarian.	Wǒ chī sù.	我吃素
I don't eat dog.	Wǒ bù chī gǒuròu	我不吃狗肉
Let's eat!	Chī fàn!	吃饭
Not too spicy.	Bù yào tài là.	不要太辣
Cheers!	Gānbēi!	干杯
chopsticks	kuàizi	筷子
fork	chāzi	叉子
hot	rède	热的
ice cold	bīngde	冰的
knife	dāozi	刀子
menu	càidān	菜单
spoon	tiáogēng/tāngchí	调羹/汤匙
bill (check)	mǎidān/jiézhàng	买单/结帐

Food Glossary
COOKING TERMS

chǎo	炒	fry
hóngshāo	红烧	red-cooked (stewed in soy sauce)
kǎo	烤	roast
yóujiān	油煎	deep-fry
zhēng	蒸	steam
zhǔ	煮	boil

RICE DISHES

mǐfàn	米饭	steamed white rice
ròusī chǎofàn	肉丝炒饭	fried rice with pork
shūcài chǎofàn	蔬菜炒饭	fried rice with vegetables
jīdàn chǎofàn	鸡蛋炒饭	fried rice with egg
jīròuchǎofàn	鸡肉炒饭	fried rice with chicken
xīfàn; zhōu	稀饭; 粥	watery rice porridge (congee)

The delightful children's book *Moonbeams, Dumplings & Dragon Boats*, by Nina Simonds and Leslie Swartz, is filled with recipes from Chinese holidays and will teach you how to make your own mooncakes and dumplings.

NOODLE DISHES

guòqiáo mǐxiàn	过桥米线	across the bridge noodles
mǎyǐ shàngshù	蚂蚁上树	ants climbing tree (noodles and mince-meat)
niúròu miàn	牛肉面	beef noodles in a soup
shuǐjiǎo	水饺	Chinese ravioli
gān bànmiàn	干拌面	dry 'burning' noodles
jiān bǐng	煎饼	egg and flour omelette
chǎomiàn	炒面	fried noodles ('chaomein')
niúròu chǎomiàn	牛肉炒面	fried noodles with beef
huǒguō	火锅	hotpot
jīdàn miàn	鸡蛋面	noodles and egg
qìguō	汽锅	soupy casserole
zhēngjiǎo	蒸饺	steamed shuijiao

BREAD, BUNS & DUMPLINGS

yóutiáo	油条	dough stick
mántou	馒头	steamed bun
bāozi	包子	steamed savoury bun

Some Chinese believe eating pigs' feet regularly will slow down the ageing process.

MEAT & SEAFOOD DISHES

qīngjiāo niúròu piàn	青椒牛肉片	beef with green peppers
gānbiān niúròu sī	干煸牛肉丝	stir-fried beef and chilli
háoyóu niúròu	蚝油牛肉	beef with oyster sauce
shuàn yángròu	涮羊肉	lamb hotpot
chǎo lǐjī sī	炒里脊丝	shredded pork fillet
liūròupiàn	熘肉片	fried pork slices
yāoguǒ jīdīng	腰果鸡丁	chicken and cashew nuts
hóngshāo jīkuài	红烧鸡块	chicken braised in soy sauce
qìguōjī	汽锅鸡	steam-pot chicken
Běijīng kǎoyā	北京烤鸭	Peking duck
gōngbào jīdīng	宫爆鸡丁	spicy chicken with peanuts
biǎndòu ròusī	扁豆肉丝	shredded pork and green beans
guōbā ròupiàn	锅巴肉片	pork and sizzling rice crust
gǔlǎo ròu	古老肉	sweet and sour pork fillets
mù'ěr ròu	木耳肉	wooden-ear mushrooms and pork
qīngjiāo ròupiàn	青椒肉片	pork and green peppers
hóngshāo yú	红烧鱼	fish braised in soy sauce
suāntāng yú	酸汤鱼	sour soup fish
gǒuròu	狗肉	dog meat
yáng ròu	羊肉	goat, mutton
lǎoshǔ ròu	老鼠肉	rat meat

VEGETABLE DISHES

For details on the 23 recognised Sichuanese flavour combinations, the 56 cooking methods and the secrets behind tastes like fragrant fish, sour-sweet and lychee, pick up *Land of Plenty: A Treasury of Authentic Sichuan Cooking*, by Fuchsia Dunlop, written from knowledge gained at a Chéngdū cooking school.

sùchǎo dòuyá	素炒豆芽	fried beansprouts
sùchǎo shūcài	素炒蔬菜	fried vegetables
xiānggū báicài	香菇白菜	bok choy and mushrooms
jiāngzhī qīngdòu	姜汁青豆	string beans with ginger
chǎo fānqié càihuā	炒番茄菜花	fried tomato and cauliflower
mógu chǎo fānqié	蘑菇炒番茄	mushroom and tomato
mù'ěr	木耳	wooden-ear mushroom
fānqié chǎodàn	番茄炒蛋	egg and tomato
yúxiāng qiézi	鱼香茄子	'fish-resembling' aubergine
suānlà tāng	酸辣汤	hot and sour soup
qiézi	茄子	aubergine
hélándòu	荷兰豆	beans
báicài	白菜	bok choy
gānlán	甘蓝	broccoli
càihuā	菜花	cauliflower
sìjìdòu	四季豆	four-season beans
biǎndòu	扁豆	French beans
rǔbǐng	乳饼	goat's cheese
mógu	蘑菇	mushroom
tǔdòu	土豆	potato
nánguā	南瓜	pumpkin
bōcài	菠菜	spinach
yùtou	芋头	sweet potato

BEAN CURD DISHES

shāguō dòufu	沙锅豆腐	tofu casserole
dòufu	豆腐	tofu
málà dòufu	麻辣豆腐	spicy tofu
jiācháng dòufu	家常豆腐	'home-style' tofu
hēimù'ěr mèn dòufu	黑木耳焖豆腐	tofu with wooden-ear mushrooms
dòufu cài tāng	豆腐菜汤	tofu and vegetable soup
cuìpí dòufu	脆皮豆腐	crispy skin tofu
lúshuǐ dòufu	卤水豆腐	smoked tofu
shāguō dòufu	砂锅豆腐	claypot tofu

CONDIMENTS

dàsuàn	大蒜	garlic
jiāng	姜	ginger
làjiāo jiàng	辣椒酱	hot sauce
fēngmì	蜂蜜	honey
yán	盐	salt
jiàng yóu	酱油	soy sauce
táng	糖	sugar

DESSERTS

básī xiāngjiāo	拔丝香蕉	caramelised banana
bābǎofàn	八宝饭	eight-treasures rice
tāngyuán	汤圆	sweet glutinous ball

FRUIT

píngguǒ	苹果	apple
xiāngjiāo	香蕉	banana
lóngyǎn	龙眼	longan
pípa	枇杷	loquat
lìzhī	荔枝	lychees
gānzi	柑子	mandarins
mángguǒ	芒果	mango
lízi	梨子	pear
shìzi	柿子	persimmon
bōluó	菠萝	pineapple
yòuzi	柚子	pomelo
hóngmáodān	红毛丹	rambutan

DRINKS

píjiǔ	啤酒	beer
chá	茶	tea
kāfēi	咖啡	coffee
kāi shuǐ	开水	boiling water
kuàng quán shuǐ	矿泉水	mineral water
hóng pútáo jiǔ	红葡萄酒	red wine
bái pútáo jiǔ	白葡萄酒	white wine
wēishìjì jiǔ	威士忌酒	whisky
fútèjiā jiǔ	伏特加酒	vodka
mǐ jiǔ	米酒	rice wine
báijiǔ	白酒	Chinese spirits
niúnǎi	牛奶	milk
dòujiāng	豆浆	soybean milk
suānnǎi	酸奶	yogurt
guǒzhī	果汁	fruit juice

An old Chinese saying identifies tea as one of the seven basic necessities of life, along with fuel, oil, rice, salt, soy sauce and vinegar. Tea drinking in China was documented as early as 50 BC.

To me wisdom

Lies in being drunk perpetually

And sleeping the rest of the time

LI BAI (701–762)

liǔchéng zhī	柳橙汁	orange juice
yézi zhī	椰子汁	coconut juice
bōluó zhī	菠萝汁	pineapple juice
mángguǒ zhī	芒果汁	mango juice
qìshuǐ	汽水	soft drink (soda)
rède	热的	hot
bīngde	冰的	ice cold
bīng kuài	冰块	ice cube

Gateway Běijīng
北京

In China, all roads and railways lead to Běijīng. There are flights to just about every domestic city of note, as well as air links to most major cities around the world. Unsurprisingly, many people choose to start or end their trip to China in the political and cultural capital, home to some of the country's most essential sights. It's here that you'll find the Forbidden City, the Summer Palace and the Temple of Heaven, while close by is the Great Wall. Even if you're only in the city for a couple of days, that's enough time to get a taste of Běijīng. If you do decide to return, Lonely Planet's *Beijing* city guide will point you in the right direction.

A vast, sprawling city at first sight, Běijīng is actually a fairly easy place to get around. Five ring roads cut through the city, subway lines and overland rail links connect the centre to the far-flung suburbs, and buses and taxis are cheap and plentiful. Běijīng has some of the best restaurants in the country, a huge array of shops to stock up on essentials for your trip and an ever-improving selection of bars and nightlife. Short-term travellers should stay in the area bordered by the third ring road. Sānlǐtún in Cháoyáng District is home to embassies and a wide range of hotels, restaurants, shops and bars. To the west of Sānlǐtún is Dōngchéng District, the heart of old Běijīng with most of the city's remaining *hútòng* – ancient alleyways that crisscross the area. At the southernmost end of Dōngchéng is Wángfǔjǐng, Běijīng's premier shopping district. The areas of Qiánmén and Chóngwén, south of Tiananmen Sq, are convenient for many of Běijīng's most famous sights, but less so for restaurants and nightlife.

The climate in Běijīng is harsh. Summers are hot and humid, while the winter is bitterly cold. Severe air pollution is a problem all year round, but especially at these times, and spring is sandstorm season. The short autumn is the most pleasant time to visit.

INFORMATION
Bookshops
Foreign Languages Bookstore (外文书店; Wàiwén Shūdiàn; ☎ 6512 6911, 6512 6838; 235 Wangfujing Dajie; 王府井大街235号; ⏰ 9am-10pm; ⊛ Wangfujing) An ever-increasing range of English-language novels, nonfiction books and some Lonely Planet guides are available here, as well as maps of Běijīng and beyond.

Wangfujing Bookstore (王府井书店; Wángfǔjǐng Shūdiàn; ☎ 6525 2592; 218 Wangfujing Dajie; 王府井大街218号; ⏰ 9am-9pm; ⊛ Wangfujing) The ground floor of this vast place has a good selection of maps. On the 3rd floor there's a limited range of English-language novels.

Emergency
Ambulance (☎ 120)
Fire (☎ 119)

FAST FACTS

- Area code: ☎ 010
- Population: 15.38 million
- Area: 16,808 sq km

Police (☎ 110)
Public Security Bureau (foreigners' section; ☎ 8402 0101)

Internet Access
You can access the internet at any number of places around town. Most cafés and some bars have wi-fi access.

Beijing Huohu Shiji Internet Café (Běijīng Huǒhú Shìjì Wǎngbā; Chunxiu Lu; ⏰ 8am-midnight)

Maps

Free maps can be found at the various Beijing Tourist Information Centres (opposite)
around town, as well as at most big hotels.
The best English-language map is the *Beijing
Tourist Map* (Y7).

You can buy a *Beijing Tourist Map* at the
Foreign Languages Bookstore and also the
Wangfujing Bookstore (p79).

Media & Internet Resources

There are a number of free English-language
entertainment-listings magazines in Běijīng,
offering the latest on the city's bar, club, music
and restaurant scene. The best of them are
That's Beijing (www.thatsbj.com) and *Time
Out Beijing*.

www.beijingpage.com General information on Běijīng
and some useful links.

www.ebeijing.gov.cn The capital's official website.

www.newsinchinese.com Chinese news in brief, with
word-by-word English translations.

Medical Services

Should you need medical advice or treatment,
Běijīng has some of China's finest medical
facilities.

Beijing Union Hospital (北京协和医院; Xiéhé
Yīyuàn; ☎ 6529 6114, emergency 6529 5284; 53
Dongdan Beidajie; 东单大大街53号) The best
Chinese-run hospital in town. Open 24 hours with a wing
for foreigners in the back building.

International SOS (国际 SOS 救援中心; Guójì SOS Jiùyuán Zhōngxīn; ☎ clinic appointments 6462 9112, dental appointments 6462 0333, 24hr alarm centre 6462 9100; www.internationalsos.com; Bldg C, BITIC Leasing Center, 1 Xingfu Sancun Bei Jie Chaoyang) High-quality but expensive clinic with English-speaking staff and foreign doctors.

Money

Obtaining or changing money in Běijīng is not a problem. The ATMs of the Bank of China and the Industrial and Commercial Bank (ICBC) both accept foreign bank and credit cards. ATMs can be found at the airport, inside most top-end hotels, in many department stores and shopping malls, as well as on most main streets. One useful one to note is the Bank of China branch next to the main entrance of Sundongan Plaza on Wangfujing Dajie.

Foreign currency and travellers cheques can be changed at large branches of the Bank of China, ICBC, CITIC Industrial Bank and China Construction Bank, and at the airport, hotels and several department stores if you show a passport. Advances on credit cards can be obtained at the Bank of China branch at Sundongan Plaza, but there is a 4% commission. Only tourist hotels and upmarket restaurants and shops will accept credit cards.

Citibank (16th fl, Tower 2, Bright China Chang'an Bldg, 7 Jianguomennei Dajie) ATM.

HSBC (ground fl, block A, COFCO Plaza, 8 Jianguomenwai Dajie) Twenty-four hour ATM.

Tourist Information

Visitor assistance in Běijīng lies in the somewhat shaky hands of the **Beijing Tourist Information Centres** (北京旅游咨询服务中心; Běijīng Lǚyóu Zīxún Fúwù Zhōngxīn; ⏰ 9am-5pm). The staff's English skills can be limited, but you'll be able to pick up a free tourist map of Běijīng, lots of leaflets detailing local attractions and at some branches, such as the Cháoyáng one, you can book train tickets. There is also a **Beijing Tourism Hotline** (☎ 6513 0828; ⏰ 24hr), which has English-speaking operators available to answer questions. Useful information centre branches:

Capital Airport (☎ 6459 8148)

Chaoyang (朝阳; ☎ 6417 6627, 6417 6656; chaoyang@bjta.gov.cn; 27 Sanlitun Beilu; 三里屯北路27号)

Dongcheng (东城; ☎ 6512 3043, 6512 2991; dongcheng@bjta.gov.cn; 10 Dengshikou Xijie; 灯市口西街10号)

Xuanwu (宣武; ☎ 6351 0018; xuanwu@bjta.gov.cn; 3 Hufang Lu; 虎坊路3号)

Travel Agencies

Elong (www.elong.net) Popular English-language travel website that offers car, hotel and flight deals.

Kingdom Travel Beijing (Běijīng Wángguó Lǚxíngshè; ☎ 5870 3388; 1815 Shangdu International Centre, 8 Dongdaqiao Lu; ⏰ 9am-6pm Mon-Fri, to 1pm Sat; ⊕ Chaoyangmen) Located near the Landao Shopping Centre, this efficient English-speaking agency can organise air tickets as well as tailor-made packages.

Visas

For visa extensions, head to Běijīng's main **Public Security Bureau** (PSB; 北京市公安局出入境管理处; Gōngānjú; ☎ 8402 0101; 2nd fl, 2 Andingmen Dongdajie; 安定门东大街2号; ⏰ 8.30am-4.30pm Mon-Sat).

DANGERS & ANNOYANCES

Běijīng is an extremely safe place when compared with most similarly sized cities around the world, however, pickpockets do operate on the buses, subways and trains. Be wary of 'students' who try to lure foreigners to overpriced art exhibitions, or to watch traditional tea ceremonies that can cost hundreds of dollars.

SIGHTS

Běijīng's parks are oases in what's a largely concrete city and Běijīngers flock to them from the moment their gates open. **Beihai Park** (北海公园; Běihǎi Gōngyuán; admission Y5, through ticket Y20; ⏰ 6.30am-8pm, buildings to 4pm; ⊕ Tiananmen Xi, then bus 5), northwest of the Forbidden City, is a great place to amble around, grab a beer and a snack, rent a rowing boat, or just people watch. Originally part of Kublai Khan's palace, Beihai is home to a number of interesting temples, including the **White Dagoba**. It's a short hop north from here to **Houhai**, a popular restaurant and bar area centred around another lake. To get to Houhai, head out of the park's northern entrance and cross Di'anmen Xidajie.

With permanent displays of ancient bronzes, Buddhist statues, jade, calligraphy, paintings and ceramics, as well as occasional high-profile exhibitions from abroad, the modern and slickly designed **Capital Museum** (中国首都博物馆; Zhōngguó Shǒudū Bówùguǎn; ☎ 6337 0491; www.capitalmuseum.org.cn; 16 Fuxingmenwai Dajie; 复兴门外大街16号; admission Y20; ⏰ 9am-5pm Tue-Sun; ⊕ Muxidi) stands out from the rest of Běijīng's rather disappointing museums.

When the emperors of the Ming and Qing dynasties were ruling China from the **Forbidden**

City (紫禁城; Zǐjìn Chéng; ☎ 6513 2255; www.dpm.org.cn; adult Nov-Mar Y40, Apr-Oct Y60, Clock Exhibition Hall & Hall of Jewellery each additional Y10; ☼ 8.30am-4pm May-Sep, to 3.30pm Oct-Apr; ◉ Tiananmen Xi or Tiananmen Dong), so-called because the price of uninvited admission was death, it was home to concubines, eunuchs and mandarins as well as royalty. Now, anyone can get into this stunning collection of the best-preserved ancient buildings in China. With 800 buildings and 9000 rooms, it's a vast place (although less than half of it is open to the public) and you could spend days here, but it's possible to explore it in a few hours. There's a good audio tour available for Y40.

It was Mao who said 'he who has not climbed the Great Wall is not a true man'. The Chairman was right. A day trip to the **Great Wall** (长城; Chángchéng) remains an essential part of any visit to Běijīng. Many hotels and hostels run trips to the Wall and some of them come highly recommended, such as those run by Beijing Saga International Youth Hostel (opposite) and Peking Downtown Backpackers Accommodation (opposite). Otherwise, the handiest tours depart from the **Beijing Sightseeing Bus Centre** (北京旅游集散中心; Běijīng Lǚyóu Jísàn Zhōngxīn; ☎ 8353 1111; tickets including admission to the Wall Y90-125), northeast and northwest of Qián-mén alongside Tiananmen Sq. The round-trip takes about nine hours. Watch out for tours that include side-trips to jewellery exhibition halls and traditional Chinese medicine centres, where you'll be pressured into buying gems or 'cures'. Some tours also take in the Ming Tombs; if you don't want to go there, check the itinerary before you book a ticket.

Bādálǐng is the most easily accessible section of the Wall from Běijīng, but it's also the most touristy. **Mùtiányù** is less commercial and has a cable car. **Sīmǎtái** is more dramatic and less visited, but walking this section is not for the faint-hearted; it's very steep and rather precarious in places. **Huánghuā** can be even more hairy, but the views are fantastic.

If you want to visit the Wall under your own steam, then, for Bādálǐng, take bus 919. It leaves from a stop 500m east of Jishuitan subway station and costs Y5 for the two-hour journey. For Mùtiányù, take either bus 916 or 980 from the long-distance bus station next to Dongzhimen subway stop to Huáiróu (Y8), then change to a minibus to Mùtiányù (Y25). To get to Sīmǎtái, take bus 980 (Y10) from the long-distance bus station by Dongzhimen subway and change to a minibus for Sīmǎtái

at Mìyún. For Huánghuā, take bus 916 or 980 (Y8) from the long-distance bus station by Dongzhimen subway to Huáiróu and get off at Míngzhū Guǎngchǎng. Then cross the road and take a minibus to Huánghuāchéng (Y5).

Wandering through Běijīng's **hútòng** is a fascinating way to spend a day. Many of the city's residents still live in these ancient alleyways and to plunge into them is to leave the modern Běijīng of skyscrapers behind. Dating back to the Yuan dynasty (1206–1368), thousands of them run east–west through the heart of the capital and they're home to Běijīng's most vibrant street life.

Most *hútòng* can be found in Dongcheng District. A good place to start is the **Drum Tower** (鼓楼; Gǔlóu; Gulou Dongdajie; ◉ Gulou). Head south down Dianmenwai Dajie and then turn left into any of the alleys and you're in the heart of Běijīng's *hútòng* district. Alternatively, you can tour the *hútòng* from the comfort of a pedicab with the **Beijing Hutong Tour Co Ltd** (☎ 6615 9097, 6400 2787; ☼ tours 8.50am, 1.50pm and 6.50pm May-Oct). Tours depart from a point 200m west of the northern entrance to Beihai Park. Hotels and hostels also organise *hútòng* tours. Typically, they last for three hours and cost around Y180.

Lama Temple (雍和宫; Yōnghé Gōng; 28 Yonghegong Dajie; 雍和宫大街28号; adult Y25, audio guide Y20; ☼ 9am-4pm; ◉ Yonghegong), Běijīng's biggest Buddhist temple, is also its most magnificent. There are five elaborately decorated main halls. The final one, **Wanfu Pavilion**, has a stupendous 18m-high sandalwood statue of the Maitreya Buddha in his Tibetan form.

Home to the capital's main concentration of contemporary art galleries, as well as bars, cafés and restaurants, the **798 Art District** (798 艺术区; Qījiǔbā Yìshùqū; ☎ 6438 4862; 2 & 4 Jiuxianqiao Lu; 酒仙桥路 2 & 4 号; admission free; ☼ galleries 10am-6pm; bus 403 or 909 from Dōngzhímén subway station) makes for a good break from ancient monuments. The art on display is a mixed bag, with the genuinely innovative mingling with the stereotypical. Note that many galleries are closed on Monday.

Summer Palace (颐和园; Yíhé Yuán; ☎ 6288 1144; 19 Xinjian Gongmen, Haidian; 海淀区新建宫门19号; admission Y40-50, audio guides Y30; ☼ 8.30am-5pm; ◉ Wudaokou then bus 375, or direct on bus 303, 330, 332, 333, 346, 362, 718, 801 & 808), the summer retreat for the old imperial court, is a lovely collection of pavilions, temples, lakes, gardens and corridors and is one of Běijīng's finest sites. Located in the far northwest of the city, it's dominated by Kunming Lake. The most notable sights are the **Long Corridor** and on **Longevity Hill**.

The 267-hectare **Temple of Heaven Park** (天坛公园; Tiāntán Gōngyuán; Tiantan Donglu; 天坛东路; low season Y10-30, high season Y15-35, audio tour available at each gate Y40; ☯ park 6am-9pm, sights 8am-6pm; ⊚ Chongwenmen or Qianmen) originally served as the vast stage for the solemn rites performed by the Son of Heaven, as he sought good harvests, divine clearance and atonement for the sins of the people. The temples, altars, walls and halls in the park are a perfect example of Ming dynasty architecture.

The largest public square in the world, the 440,000 sq metres of **Tiananmen Square** (天安门广场; Tiān'ānmén Guǎngchǎng; ⊚ Tiananmen Xi, Tiananmen Dong or Qianmen) lie at the heart of Bĕijīng. Designed as a celebration and projection of Maoist power, the square will forever be associated with 4 June 1989 and the crushing of the democracy movement. The square is at its best early in the morning – there's an elaborate flag-raising ceremony at sunrise – or at night, when it is illuminated.

SLEEPING

Bĕijīng's hotels have improved out of all recognition in recent years. But there's still a shortage of decent budget accommodation, while many of the city's midrange hotels are distinguished only by their uniform blandness. For budget travellers, the centrally located youth hostels are a good bet. If you want to splurge, Bĕijīng has plenty of excellent topend hotels to choose from. Rooms in the more popular places go quickly in peak season, so booking ahead is advisable.

Chóngwén & South Cháoyáng

Leo Youth Hostel (广聚元大饭店; Guǎngjùyuán Dàfàndiàn; ☎ 6303 1595; 52 Dazhalan Xijie; 大栅栏西街52号; 12-bed/4-bed dm Y45/70, d without toilet Y140-160, with toilet Y200-240; ⊚ Qianmen; 💻) Popular bargain hostel in a good location for the sights. OK dorm rooms, simple but passable doubles and a small but lively bar. It's advisable to book ahead here.

Beijing Saga International Youth Hostel (北京实佳国际青年旅社; Bĕijīng Shíjiā Guójì Qīngnián Lǚshè; ☎ 6527 2773; sagayangguang@yahoo.com; 9 Shijia Hutong; 史家胡同9号; dm Y55, d with/without bathroom Y198/180, tr Y210; ⊚ Dengshikou; 💻) Modern, very popular hostel located in a historic *hútòng*. The rooms are well maintained and there's a common rooftop area, a bar, table football and washing machine (Y10 a load). It runs trips to the Great Wall.

Eastern Morning Sun Youth Hostel (北京东方晨光青年旅舍; Bĕijīng Dōngfāng Chénguāng Qīngnián Lǚshè; ☎ 6528 4347; www.hostelsbeijing.com; fl B4, East Bldg, Oriental Plaza, 8-16 Dongdansantiao; 东单三条8-16号; 5-bed dm Y60, d Y120-140, tr Y180, q Y240; ⊚ Wangfujing; 💻) No prizes for the windowless, cramped, claustrophobic rooms here, but the convenient location, late checkout and cheap prices appeal to some. The clean toilets and showers are communal.

Home Inn (如家快捷酒店; Rújiā Kuàijié Jiǔdiàn; ☎ 6317 3366; www.homeinns.com; 61 Liangshidian Jie, Dazhalan; 大栅栏粮食店街61号; d Y178-218; ⊚ Qianmen; 💻) There are 16 branches of this budget-midrange chain scattered around town, but this one's prime location a short walk south of Tiananmen Sq makes it handy for the sights. Double rooms are small but clean. There's a small restaurant.

Tiánshuǐ Lǚguǎn (甜水旅馆; ☎ 6527 9284; 45 Datianshuijing Hutong; 大甜水井胡同45号; d with/without bathroom Y198/180; ⊚ Wangfujing or Tiananmen Dong; 💥) The location in a *hútòng* makes this a pleasant choice; rooms have air-con, TV and shower, but no phone. Room rates drop to Y130 in the slow season. The staff doesn't speak much English.

Cui Ming Zhuang Hotel (翠明庄宾馆; Cuì Míng Zhuāng Bīnguǎn; ☎ 6513 6622; www.cuimingzhuanghotel .com.cn; 1 Nanheyan Dajie; 南河沿大街1号; d/ste Y600/1200; ⊚ Tiananmen Dong) Quiet three-star hotel close to the Forbidden City and the shopping area of Wangfujing.

Peninsula Palace (王府饭店; Wángfǔ Fàndiàn; ☎ 8516 2888; www.peninsula.com; 8 Jinyu Hutong; 金鱼胡同8号; d Y1920; ⊚ Dengshikou; 💻 💥) Top-class restaurants, super-exclusive shops and suitably luxurious rooms make this one of Bĕijīng's best hotels. You can get a *hútòng* tour here with a Tsinghua University professor as a guide, as well as trips to unrestored sections of the Great Wall.

Grand Hyatt Beijing (北京东方君悦大酒店; Bĕijīng Dōngfāng Jūnyuè Dàjiǔdiàn; ☎ 8518 1234; www.beijing.grand.hyatt.com; 1 Dongchang'an Jie; 东长安街1号; d Y2150; ⊚ Wangfujing; 💥 💻 💥) Elegant and stylish, the Hyatt is located in the heart of the Wangfujing shopping area and is just 10 minutes' walk from the Forbidden City and Tiananmen Sq. The rooms are attractive, if not that spacious, there's wi-fi access, and the hotel boasts several top-notch bars and restaurants.

Dōngchéng

Peking Downtown Backpackers Accommodation (东堂客栈; Dōngtáng Kèzhàn; ☎ 8400 2429; www .backpackingchina.com; 85 Nanluoguxiang; 南锣鼓巷85号; 4-/3-bed dm Y65/75, d with/without window Y80/60, all incl breakfast; ⊚ Andingmen; 💻) For backpackers, this place is hard to beat. Located in the lively *hútòng* of Nanluoguxiang, the staff is helpful, the rooms are tidy and there's free breakfast and pickup from the airport (you pay the toll fee). Bike rental costs Y20 a day. Its trips to the Great Wall come recommended.

Bamboo Garden Hotel (竹园宾馆; Zhúyuán Bīnguǎn; ☎ 5852 0088; www.bbgh.com.cn; 24 Xiaoshiqiao Hutong; 小石桥胡同24号; s Y380, d Y680-880, ste Y980; ◉ Gulou) Cosy courtyard hotel close to the Drum and Bell Towers, Houhai Lake and some of Běijīng's most atmospheric *hútòng*. The buildings date back to the late Qing dynasty. Singles are small and ordinary; the double rooms are much more pleasant. The staff can be a little erratic.

Cháoyáng

You Yi Youth Hostel (友谊青年酒店; Yǒuyì Qīngnián Jiǔdiàn; ☎ 6417 2632; fax 6415 6866; 43 Beisanlitun Nan; 北三里屯南43号; dm/d Y70/180; ◉ Dongsishitiao; ⊠ ▢) Located in the heart of Sanlitun's bar ghetto, this decent hostel offers clean and comfortable rooms with air-con (doubles have TV and a phone). There's free breakfast and laundry.

Red House Hotel (瑞秀宾馆; Ruìxiù Bīnguǎn; ☎ 6416 7500; www.redhouse.com.cn; 10 Chunxiu Lu; 春秀路10号; s/tw Y350/400, ste Y600; ◉ Dongzhimen) Close to Sanlitun's bars and restaurants, this place is slightly gloomy but has solid, clean rooms with good bathrooms and offers free breakfast and laundry. You can also rent a bike for Y30 a day.

EATING & DRINKING

Beijing's restaurants are one of the great things about the city. Roast duck may be Beijing's best known dish, but chefs from all around China gravitate to the capital and you can find every genre of Chinese cuisine here. There are an ever-increasing number of foreign eateries providing a taste of home too. Nor will eating out break the bank. It's possible to eat very well very cheaply here and with tens of thousands of restaurants to choose from, you won't have a problem getting a table.

Chóngwén & South Cháoyáng

Megabite (Dàshídài; basement, Oriental Plaza, 1 Dongchang'an Jie; 东长安街1号东方广场; dishes from Y10; ◉ Wangfujing) A busy fast-food emporium that has Cantonese, Yúnnán, Sìchuān, teppanyaki, clay pot, Korean and Indian outlets all under one roof. You can eat well for Y20. You don't pay in cash here; instead, buy a card from the kiosk at the entrance (available in denominations of Y30 upwards) and credits are deducted for each dish you order.

Xiao Wang's Home Restaurant (北京小王府; Xiǎowáng Fǔ; ☎ 6594 3602, 6591 3255; 2 Guanghua Dongli; 光华东里2号楼; meals from Y70; ◈ 11am-

2pm & 5-11pm; ◉ Guomao or Yonganli) This bustling and big restaurant is great for home-style Běijīng cuisine. The chicken wings (Y35) and deep-fried spare ribs with pepper salt (Y48) are excellent, but there's a huge selection of other things to try too. English menu.

Qianmen Quanjude Roast Duck Restaurant (前门全聚德烤鸭店; Qiánmén Quánjùdé Kǎoyādiàn; ☎ 6511 2418; 32 Qianmen Dajie; 前门大街32号; half duck Y84, scallions & sauce Y5; ◈ 11am-1.30pm & 4.30-8.30pm; ◉ Qianmen) Běijīng's oldest and most famous, if not its best, Peking duck restaurant is a vast place that attracts hordes of domestic and foreign tourists. But the duck isn't bad, even if it's a little pricey.

Liqun Roast Duck Restaurant (利群烤鸭店; Lìqún Kǎoyādiàn; ☎ 6702 5681; 11 Beixiangfeng Hutong; 北翔凤胡同11号; roast duck Y98; ◈ 10am-10pm; ◉ Qianmen) Tucked away in a maze of *hútòng* that are disappearing by the day, this might be Běijīng's best duck restaurant. Always busy, it's best to book ahead. The duck is roasted in fruit tree wood–fired ovens and is delicious.

Cháoyáng

Middle 8th (中捌楼餐厅; Zhōngbālóu Cāntīng; ☎ 6413 0629; Sanlitun Zhongjie, Zhongba Lu; 东三里屯中八楼; dishes from Y12; ◈ 11am-2pm & 5.30-11.30pm; ◉ Dongsishitiao then bus 701 heading east) Hip Yúnnán eatery with an authentic, wide-ranging menu. Signature dishes include drunken shrimp (Y22) and braised rice with pineapple in a bamboo shoot (Y12). Rice wine is Y6 a glass. English menu.

Bookworm (书虫; Shūchóng; ☎ 6586 9507; Bldg 4, Sanlitun Nanlu; 三里屯南路; lunch set menu Y78, dinner set menu Y108; ◈ 9am-1am; ◉ Dongsishitiao then bus 701 heading east) Part bar, café, library and restaurant, the Bookworm serves up sandwiches (from Y35) and pasta dishes (from Y45), as well as more substantial fare. You can buy English-language books, including Lonely Planet guides, and magazines here. There's a pleasant roof terrace and wi-fi access.

Pure Lotus Vegetarian (净心莲; Jìngxīnlián; ☎ 6592 3627; inside Zhongguo Wenlianyuan, 10 Nongzhanguan Nanlu; 农展馆南路10号 中国文联院内; meals from Y100; ◈ 9.30am-10pm; ◉ Dongsishitiao then bus 431 heading east; Ⓥ) The monks who run this place consistently come up with the tastiest and most creative vegetarian food in Běijīng, but they charge a lot for it.

Dōngchéng

Passby Bar (过客; Guòkè; ☎ 8403 8004; www.gk01.com; 108 Nanluogu Xiang; 南锣鼓巷108号; beer from Y20, meals from Y40; ◈ 9am-2am; ◉ Andingmen) Something of an institution amongst travellers, this friendly place serves up western and Chinese food. The setting is pleasant, the staff helpful and you can pick up Lonely Planet guides here.

Café Sambal (☎ 6400 4875; 43 Doufuchi Hutong, off Jiu Gulou Dajie; 豆腐池胡同43号, 旧鼓楼大街; dishes from Y35, set lunch Y50; ◷ noon-midnight; ◎ Gulou) Cool Malaysian restaurant located in a cleverly converted courtyard house at the entrance to Doufu Hutong. This place is especially pleasant in summer when you dine under the stars and satellites.

GETTING THERE & AWAY

A number of airlines fly to Chéngdū, Chóngqìng, Kūnmíng and other destinations in China's Southwest. See the Transport chapter for further details (p486).

All trains to China's Southwest depart from **Beijing West Train Station** (北京西站; Běijīng Xī Zhàn; ☎ 6231 6263; East Lianhuachi Rd; 莲花池东路).

There are three trains a day to Chéngdū, leaving at 11.29am, 4.35pm and 10.48pm. Depending on the train, the journey takes between 26 and 32 hours. A hard-seat ticket is Y231, soft-seat Y366. Hard-sleeper tickets cost Y391/405/418 (top/middle/bottom bunk). Soft sleeper tickets are Y615/642 (top/bottom bunk).

Two trains a day run to Chóngqìng, at 4.26pm and 9.28pm. The journey takes between 24 and 30 hours. Hard-seat tickets are Y238, soft-seat Y376. A hard sleeper costs Y401/416/430 (top/middle/bottom bunk); soft sleepers are Y631/658 (top/bottom).

One train runs daily to Kūnmíng, leaving at 6.40pm for the 39-hour trip. A hard-seat ticket costs Y320, soft seat Y509. Hard sleeper tickets are Y539/558/578 and soft sleepers Y852/890.

There is a 24-hour foreigners' ticket office at Beijing West Station on the 2nd floor. Tickets can be bought online at www.china tripadvisor.com and www.china-train-ticket .com, or through hotels and travel agents, but it's cheaper to get them at the station.

There are no buses from Běijīng to Chéngdū, Chóngqìng or Kūnmíng.

GETTING AROUND

The subway (dìtiě) is the best way to get around central Běijīng. The underground dragon moves much faster than the traffic. There are only four lines in existence at the moment, but another five are set to open in the next couple of years. Tickets cost Y3, or Y5 if you are transferring from Line 1 or 2 to Line 13.

Line 1 runs from east to west, cutting through the centre of town. Line 2 is a circle line. Line 13 loops through the north of Běijīng. The Batong Line runs through the eastern suburbs. There are interchange stations between all the lines.

Buses are plentiful and cover much more of the city than the subway, but they make slow progress in the Běijīng traffic. They're best for short hops. Tickets are Y1; you pay the conductor rather than the driver. The routes on bus signs are in Chinese rather than English, so you need to know how many stops you need to go before boarding.

Taxis are everywhere and finding one is only a problem during (infrequent) rainstorms and rush hour. They cost Y10 for the first 3km and then Y2 per kilometre after that. Between 11pm and 6am there is a 20% surcharge added to the fare. All taxis should have and use a meter. Most Běijīng taxi drivers speak little English, but are generally honest.

Bikes are a good way to see central Běijīng, especially the hútòng districts, but heavy traffic on the roads means it can be perilous riding around. Bikes can be hired at Beijing Saga International Youth Hostel (p83), Peking Downtown Backpackers Accommodation (p83) and Red House Hotel (opposite).

To/From the Airport

Běijīng's Capital Airport is 27km northeast from the centre of town, or about 40 minutes to one hour by car. A rail link between the airport and Dongzhimen subway station will be open by the time of the Olympics. Public bus 359 runs from Dongzhimen to the airport (Y3). There are also several express bus lines that run to the airport; all cost Y16. The most useful are Line 3 and Line 2. Both start running at 7.30am, leaving every 15 minutes, and continue until the last flight has arrived in the evening. Line 3 runs from the **Beijing International Hotel** (北京国际饭店; Běijīng Guójì Fàndiàn; 9 Jianguomennei Dajie; 建国门内大街9号) and Beijing Train Station via Chaoyangmen. Line 2 runs to the Aviation Building in Xidan via Dongzhimen.

A taxi from the airport should cost between Y80 and Y100, including the airport expressway toll (Y10). Avoid the taxi touts at the airport who will try and get you into an illegal taxi that will cost Y300 for the trip into town.

Gateway Shànghǎi
上海

No-one visits Shànghǎi with visions in their heads of steep, muddy rice terraces or ethnic minorities circle dancing. Say 'Shànghǎi' to someone, and they're much more likely to imagine something closer to the captivating swirl of sex, fashion, money and neon lights that the city came to stand for in the pre-communist days. And even if reality doesn't always equate with the brand image, Shànghǎi's pulsing metropolis somehow demands a stopover – this is the 21st century, PRC style. So leave the yak in Sìchuān, slip on your best shoes and get ready to do some urban exploring – there's more here to see than you might think.

See Lonely Planet's *Shanghai* guide for additional information.

FAST FACTS

- Area code: ☎ 021
- Population: 15 million
- www.cityweekend.com.cn

INFORMATION
Bookshops
Foreign Languages Bookstore (外文书店; Wàiwén Shūdiàn; ☎ 6322 3200; 390 Fuzhou Rd; 福州路390号; ⏰ 9.30am-6pm, to 7pm Fri & Sat; Ⓜ Middle Henan Rd) The best spot to stock up on reading material.

Emergency
Ambulance (☎ 120)
Fire (☎ 119)
Police (☎ 110)
Public Security Bureau (PSB; 公安局; Gōngānjú; ☎ 6854 1199; 1500 Minsheng Rd; 民生路1500号; ⏰ 9am-5pm Mon-Sat; Ⓜ Shanghai Science & Technology Museum) Near Jinxiu Rd (锦绣路).

Internet Access
Internet cafés are all over town, but there's a frequent turnover of locales. You'll need your passport for ID in most places.

Maps
English maps of Shànghǎi are available at the Foreign Languages Bookstore (see above), major hotel bookshops and occasionally from street hawkers (most of the latter are Chinese-only).

The bilingual *Shanghai Tourist Map*, produced by the Shanghai Municipal Tourism Administration, is free at hotels and Tourist Information Centres (see opposite).

Media & Internet Resources
If you're looking for entertainment ideas, the first thing to do is to grab a free copy of the monthly *That's Shanghai* from a top-end hotel, followed swiftly by issues of *City Weekend*, *Shanghai Talk* or the weekly *SH (8 Days)*. These offer an instant plug into what's on in town, from art exhibitions to club nights to restaurant openings.

The best local websites are listed below.
www.cityweekend.com.cn A good listings site with archived articles.
www.shanghaiist.com Quirky local news blog.
www.smartshanghai.com For fashion, food, fun and frolicking.
www.thatssh.com Always on top of what's happening in Shànghǎi entertainment.

Medical Services
Huashan Hospital (华山医院; Huáshān Yīyuàn; ☎ 6248 9999, ext 2351; 12 Central Wulumuqi Rd; 乌鲁木齐中路12号; Ⓜ Jing'an Temple) Hospital treatment and out-patient consultations are available at the 15th-floor foreigners' clinic; a 24-hour pharmacy is located outside the hospital.

Money
Almost every hotel has money-changing counters. Most tourist hotels, restaurants and banks accept major credit cards. ATMs at various branches of the Bank of China and the Industrial and Commercial Bank of China (ICBC) accept most major cards.

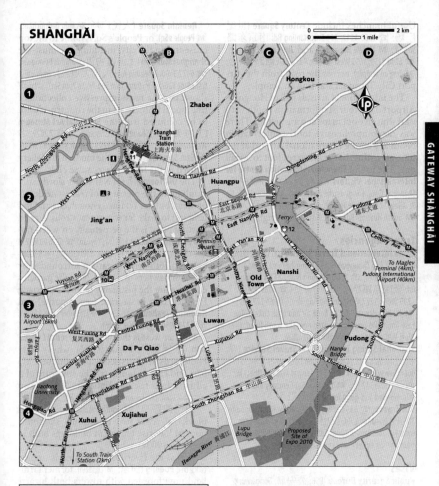

SIGHTS & ACTIVITIES
50 Moganshan Road Art Centre 莫干山路 50号 **1** A2
China Sex Culture Museum
  中华性文化和性健康教育展 **2** C2
Jade Buddha Temple 玉佛寺 **3** A2
Jinmao Tower 金茂大厦 **4** D2
Municipal Historical Museum
  上海城市历史发展陈列馆 ....(see **5**)
Oriental Pearl Tower 东方明珠广播电视塔 **5** C2
Shanghai Museum 上海博物馆 **6** B3
Three on the Bund 外滩三号 **7** C2
Xīntiāndì 新天地 **8** B3
Yuyuan Gardens & Bazaar 豫园 **9** C3

TRANSPORT
Airport City Terminal 机场城市航站楼 **10** A3
Longmen Hotel Ticket Office
  龙门宾馆火车票售票处 **11** B2
Tour Boats 黄浦江游览船 **12** C2

Hong Kong & Shanghai Bank (HSBC; 汇丰银行; Huìfēng Yínháng) has ATMs in the Shanghai Centre (上海商城) on West Nanjing Rd, at Pudong Airport arrivals hall and at 15 East Zhongshan No 1 Rd (中山东一路 15号) on the Bund.

Tourist Information

Tourist Information and Service Centres (旅游咨询服务中心; Lǚyóu Zīxún Fúwù Zhōngxīn) are located near several major tourist sights. The standard of English varies from good to nonexistent and the centres primarily function to book hotel rooms, put you on a tour and sell you souvenirs, but free maps and some information are available.

Useful branches include **Century Square** (世纪广场; ☎ 5353 1117; 561 East Nanjing Rd; 南京东路561号; **M** Middle Henan Rd) and **Jing'an** (静安寺; ☎ 6248 3259; 1699 West Nanjing Rd; 南京西路1699号; **M** Jing'an Temple), across the road from the Airport City Terminal and Jing'an Temple.

The international arrivals hall of Hongqiao Airport has a tourist information booth with staff who give out maps and are helpful. There was no comprehensive tourist information booth at Pudong International Airport at the time of writing, but plans were afoot to install one. The useful **Shanghai Information Centre for International Visitors** (上海国际访问者中心; Shànghǎi Guójì Fǎngwènzhě Zhōngxīn; ☎ 6384 9366; No 2, Alley 123, Xingye Rd; 兴业路123弄2号新天地; **M** South Huangpi Rd) is at Xīntiāndì (right).

Travel Agencies

China International Travel Service (CITS; 中国国际旅行社; Zhōngguó Guójì Lǚxíngshè) East Jinling Rd (☎ 6323 8770; 5th fl, Guangming Bldg, 2 East Jinling Rd; 金陵东路2号); West Beijing Rd (☎ 6289 4510, 6289 8899; 1277 West Beijing Rd; 北京西路1277号; **M** Middle Henan Rd) Can book air and train tickets. The East Jinling Rd branch is located near the south Bund; the West Beijing Rd branch is the head office.

Shanghai Spring International Travel Service (春秋国际旅行社; Chūnqiū Guójì Lǚxíngshè; ☎ 6351 6666; www.china-sss.com; 342 Central Xizang (Tibet) Rd; 西藏中路342号; **M** People's Sq) Centrally located, IATA-bonded and good for air tickets.

STA Travel (☎ 6353 2683; www.statravel.com.cn; Suite 305,158 Hanzhong Rd; 汉中路158号; ☯ 9am-6pm Mon-Fri, 10.30am-3.30pm Sat; **M** Hanzhong Rd) Sells train and air tickets, and can issue ISIC cards.

Visas

Public Security Bureau (PSB; 公安局; Gōngānjú; ☎ 6854 1199; 1500 Minsheng Rd; 民生路1500号; ☯ 9am-5pm Mon-Sat; **M** Shanghai Science & Technology Museum) Handles visas and registrations; 30-day visa extensions cost around Y160. Near Jinxiu Rd (锦绣路).

SIGHTS

Most first-time visitors gravitate towards the **Bund** (外滩; Wàitān; **M** Middle Henan Rd), the picturesque waterfront promenade that embodies old Shànghǎi. Walk the strip, take a cruise on the Huangpu River (see p91) or relax at some fabulous restaurants and bars with views of futuristic Pudong across the river – the most popular address of late is the swish **Three on the Bund** (外滩三号; Wàitān Sānhào; www.threeonthebund.com).

Renmin Square (人民广场; Rénmín Guǎngchǎng; **M** People's Sq), or People's Sq, is home to the top museums in the city, including the must-see **Shanghai Museum** (上海博物馆; Shànghǎi Bówùguǎn; ☎ 6372 3500; 2 Renmin Ave; 人民大道2号; adult/child & student Y20/5; ☯ 9am-5pm Sun-Fri, to 7pm Sat), which showcases the most impressive collection of traditional Chinese art in the country. It's not to be confused with the **Shanghai Art Museum** (上海美术馆; Shànghǎi Měishùguǎn; ☎ 6327 2829; 325 West Nanjing Rd; 南京西路325号; adult/student Y20/10; ☯ 9am-5pm, last entry 4pm), the modern art gallery housed in the former racecourse club.

The **Old Town** (南市; Nánshì) is slowly succumbing to the pressures of real estate development, but has retained enough charm (and temples) to make for some great strolls. A good starting point is the perpetually crowded **Yuyuan Gardens & Bazaar** (豫园; Yùyuán; ☎ 6326 0830; 218 Anren Street; 安仁街218号; adult/child Y30/10; ☯ 8.30am-5.30pm), a 16th-century garden surrounded by souvenir hawkers of all ages. Near the garden's entrance are the justifiably famous Nanxiang Steamed Bun Restaurant (see opposite) and **Huxinting Teahouse** (湖心亭茶馆; Húxīntíng Cháguǎn; ☎ 6373 6950; ☯ 6am-9.30pm).

Further west is the delightful **French Concession** (法国租界; Fǎguó Zūjiè), whose leafy boulevards are bursting with boutiques, hip bars and chic restaurants. The epicentre of it all is style-conscious **Xīntiāndì** (新天地; www .xintiandi.com; cnr Taicang Rd & Madang Rd; 太仓路和马当路的路口; **M** South Huangpi Rd), several blocks of renovated traditional *shíkūmén* houses, low-rise tenement buildings built in the early 1900s.

Across the river from the Bund is unmistakable **Pǔdōng** (浦东; **M** Lujiazui), former farmland now forested with towers both bizarre and breathtaking, including China's tallest buildings, the **Shanghai World Financial Center** (上海环球金融中心; Shànghǎi Huánqiú Jīnróng Zhōngxīn; 100 Century Ave; 世纪大道100号) and the **Jinmao Tower** (金茂大厦; Jīnmào Dàshà; ☎ 5047 5101; 88 Century Ave; 世纪大道88号; adult/child Y70/35, audio tour Y15; ☯ 8.30am-10pm). Choose between the observation deck (88th floor) or drinks in the Cloud 9 Bar (87th floor). Other notable sights include the excellent **Municipal Historical Museum** (上海城市历史发展陈列馆; Shànghǎi Chéngshì Lìshǐ Fāzhǎn Chénlièguǎn; ☎ 5879 1888; basement, Oriental Pearl Tower, 1 Shiji Dadao; 世纪大道1号; admission Y35; ☯ 8am-9.30pm) and the eye-opening **China Sex Culture Museum** (中华性文化和性健康教育展; Zhōnghuá Xìng Wénhuà hé Xìng Jiànkāng Jiàoyùzhǎn;

2789 Riverside Ave; 滨江大道2789号; admission Y20; 8am-10.30pm Mon-Thu, to 10pm Fri-Sun).

Further afield are the **Jade Buddha Temple** (玉佛寺; Yùfó Sì; ☎ 6266 3668; 170 Anyuan Rd; 安远路170号; admission Y20; 8.30am-4.30pm) and the nearby galleries at the **50 Moganshan Rd Art Centre** (Mògānshānlù Wǔshí Hào; 50 Moganshan Rd; 莫干山路50号; admission free), the nexus of the city's art scene.

SLEEPING
Rooms are often marked down considerably; make sure to ask for a discount.

The Bund & Renmin Square
Easy Tour Youth Hostel (上海易途青年酒店; Shànghǎi Yìtú Qīngnián Jiǔdiàn; ☎ 6327 7766; 57 Jiangyin Rd; 江阴路57号; dm/s/d Y50/180/220; People's Sq) The setting and location – just west off Renmin Sq in a building with a bit of history – are up there with the best, but it's a bit drab and some rooms are damp.

Ming Town Hiker Youth Hostel (明堂上海旅行者青年旅馆; Míngtáng Shànghǎi Lǚxíngzhě Qīngnián Lǚguǎn; ☎ 6329 7889; 450 Central Jiangxi Rd; 江西中路450号; dm from Y55, d Y200; Middle Henan Rd;) A short hike from the Bund, rooms include tidy four- and six-bed dorms with pine bunk beds and three good-value luxury doubles.

Captain Hostel (船长青年酒店; Chuánzhǎng Qīngnián Jiǔdiàn; ☎ 6323 5053; www.captainhostel.com.cn; 37 Fuzhou Rd; 福州路37号; dm Y70, d Y450-1200; Middle Henan Rd;) An old turn-of-the-century building off the Bund, the Captain has clean dorms with bunk beds, OK double rooms and a top-floor bar for rum, drunken sailors and long views over the Huangpu River.

Pujiang Hotel/Astor House Hotel (浦江饭店; Pǔjiāng Fàndiàn; ☎ 6324 6388; www.pujianghotel.com; 15 Huangpu Rd; 黄浦路15号; dm Y80, d Y580-1280; Middle Henan Rd) This historic hotel is at the north end of the Bund with loads of stylish midrange rooms. There is also one dorm room, but it's generally full.

Jinjiang Inn (锦江之星旅馆; Jǐnjiāng Zhīxīng Lǚguǎn; ☎ 6326 0505; www.jj-inn.com; 33 South Fujian Rd; 福建南路33号; s/d Y199/239; Middle Henan Rd) This central branch of this hotel chain has bright, airy doubles with shower rooms, some with pleasant views over parkland on the noisier Fujian Rd side.

East Asia Hotel (东亚饭店; Dōngyà Fàndiàn; ☎ 6322 3233; fax 6322 4598; 680 East Nanjing Rd; 南京东路680号; d from Y420; People's Sq) Renovated in 2005, the two-star East Asia Hotel is a popular and long-standing fixture on the cheap Shànghǎi room circuit. Reception is on the 2nd floor through a clothing shop.

Westin Shanghai (威斯汀大饭店; Wēisītīng Dàfàndiàn; ☎ 6335 1888; www.westin.com; 88 Central Henan Rd; 河南中路88号; d from Y2915; Middle Henan Rd;) A stylish component of the Bund Center, this is the best hotel in the district. Home to several top restaurants and the Banyan Tree spa.

French Concession
Mason Hotel (美臣大酒店; Měichén Dàjiǔdiàn; ☎ 6466 2020; www.masonhotel.com; 935 Central Huaihai Rd; 淮海中路935号; s/d Y900/1080; South Shaanxi Rd) From its discreet outward appearance to the small and well-proportioned lobby (with Art Deco–style motifs and casual black leather furniture), this boutique-style hotel is both relaxed and intimate.

Jinchen Hotel (金晨大酒店; Jīnchén Dàjiǔdiàn; ☎ 6471 7000; www.jinchenhotel.com; 795-809 Central Huaihai Rd; 淮海中路795-809号; s & d from Y980; South Shaanxi Rd) Arranged over seven floors, the small, brick Jinchen is excellent, offering clean, tastefully furnished rooms.

Ruijin Guesthouse (瑞金宾馆; Ruìjīn Bīnguǎn; ☎ 6472 5222; www.shedi.net.cn/outedi/ruijin; 118 Ruijin No 2 Rd; 瑞金二路118号; s & d Y1200; South Shaanxi Rd) The Ruijin has elegant grounds and a series of old mansions converted into rooms. Some of the city's most romantic and stylish restaurants and bars charmingly nestle in the gardens.

Pǔdōng
Captain Hostel Zhangyang Rd (船长青年酒店; Chuánzhǎng Qīngnián Jiǔdiàn; ☎ 5836 5966; www.captainhostel.com.cn; 527 East Laoshan Rd; 崂山东路527号; dm Y60, s/d Y198/450; Dongchang Rd;) The Pǔdōng location is less than ideal, though the Captain runs a tight ship.

Grand Hyatt (金茂凯悦大酒店; Jīnmào Kǎiyuè Dàjiǔdiàn; ☎ 5049 1234; www.hyatt.com; 88 Century Ave; 世纪大道88号; d from Y2590; Lujiazui;) No place for those with vertigo, the Grand Hyatt shoots up 33 stylish storeys from the 54th floor of the Jinmao Tower.

EATING
If you're on a budget, look for the innumerable food courts (such as Megabite; 大食代; Dàshídài) in malls everywhere. For a more sophisticated culinary experience, head to the ultra-chic Three on the Bund (see opposite) or the Xīntiāndì complex (opposite), where choices range from traditional Shanghainese to Thai and Italian.

Nanxiang Steamed Bun Restaurant (南翔馒头店; Nánxiáng Mántoudiàn; ☎ 6355 4206; 85 Yuyuan Rd; 豫园路85号; meals Y10-20; 7am-10pm) This eatery serves up the city's most famous dumplings (小笼包).

Vegetarian Life Style (枣子树; Zăozi Shù; ☎ 6384 8000; 77 Songshan Rd; 嵩山路77号; mains Y20-38; Ⓜ South Huangpi Rd) For light and healthy Chinese organic vegetarian food, with precious little oil and creative chefs.

Băoluó Jiŭlóu (保罗酒楼; ☎ 5403 7239; 271 Fumin Rd; 富民路271号; mains Y20-50; Ⓜ Changshu Rd) Join Shanghainese night owls queuing down the street to get into this amazingly busy place. Open till 6am, it's a great place to get a feel for Shànghăi's famous buzz.

Ajisen (味千拉面; Wèiqiān Lāmiàn; ☎ 6360 7194; 327 East Nanjing Rd; 南京东路327号; meals Y30; Ⓜ Middle Henan Rd) Choose from among mouthwatering Japanese noodle dishes via easy-to-use photo menus. Handy branches throughout town.

GETTING THERE & AWAY
Air
Shànghăi has two airports: most international flights operate out of Pudong airport in the southeast, while domestic flights fly out of Hongqiao airport in the west (with occasional exceptions).

Daily domestic flights connect Shànghăi to every major city in China's Southwest (and usually leave several times a day). Prices for these include Chángshā (Y890), Chéngdū (Y1610), Chóngqìng (Y1490), Guìlín (Y1310), Guìyáng (Y1600), Kūnmíng (Y1900), Lìjiāng (Y2430), Nánníng (Y1660), Yíchāng (Y1080) and Zhāngjiājiè (Y1330), but most travel agencies will normally offer discounted fares of up to 40%.

Boat
At the time of writing, boat cruises up the Yangzi River were no longer departing from Shànghăi. Most cruises now only run between Chóngqìng and Yíchāng (Húběi).

Train
Shànghăi is reasonably well connected to the Southwest via rail, though journeys can be epic in duration. The easiest option for buying tickets is at the **Longmen Hotel ticket office** (龙门宾馆火车票售票处; Lóngmén Bīnguǎn huǒchēpiào shòupiàochù; ☎ 6317 9325; Ⓘ 8am-9pm), a short walk west of the **Shanghai train station** (上海站; Shànghǎi zhàn; Ⓜ Shanghai Train Station). You can book sleepers up to nine days in advance here, with a Y5 service charge. You can also buy tickets at the much more chaotic ticket office that is to the southeast of the train station (no service charge). Be aware that some trains may depart from the

South train station (上海南站; Shànghǎi Nánzhàn; Ⓜ Shanghai South Train Station).

Hard sleeper prices for major destinations include: Chángshā (Y272, 18½ hours), Chéngdū (Y259 to Y452, 35 to 45 hours), Chóngqìng (Y475, 42 hours), Guìlín (Y341, 26 hours), Guìyáng (Y405, 32½ hours), Kūnmíng (Y502, 43½ hours) and Nánníng (Y387, 33 hours).

GETTING AROUND
Your best bet for getting around the city is the metro system (tickets Y3 to Y6; for map see http://urbanrail.net/as/shan/shanghai.htm); Lines 1 and 2 cover everywhere of importance, with the exception of the Old Town.

Taxis are also reasonably cheap and easy to flag down, but try to avoid rush hours between 8am and 9am, and 4.30pm and 6pm. The cost is Y11 for the first 3km and Y2.10 for each kilometre thereafter. From 11pm, there's a 10% surcharge.

To/From the Airport
Always check your ticket to be sure which airport you're arriving at or departing from. Buses run from 7am to 11pm.

Hongqiao Airport (虹桥机场; Hóngqiáo Jīchǎng; ☎ 6268 8918) is 18km from the Bund; getting there takes about 30 minutes if you're lucky, or over an hour if you're not. You can take bus 925 from Renmin Sq to the airport. A CAAC bus (Y5) goes from the northeast corner of Central Yan'an Rd and North Shaanxi Rd in the French Concession. Both buses leave the airport from directly in front of the domestic departure hall. Taxis from the centre of town cost from Y50 to Y70, depending on the route taken, traffic conditions and the time of day. Hongqiao Airport is famous for its astonishing taxi queues; sometimes it takes around an hour to get in a taxi.

Pudong International Airport (浦东国际机场; Pǔdōng Guójì Jīchǎng; ☎ 3848 4500) is 30km southeast of the city. **Airport bus 1** (☎ 3848 4500; Y30) runs between Hongqiao and Pudong airports, bus 2 (Y19) runs from Pudong International Airport to the **Airport City Terminal** (机场城市航站楼; Jīchǎng Chéngshì Hángzhànlóu; Ⓜ Jing'an Temple) near Jing'an Temple on West Nanjing Rd, and bus 5 (Y18) goes from the Pudong International Airport to the Shanghai train station via Pǔdōng. A taxi to Pudong International Airport from the city centre (one hour) costs around Y140.

The **Maglev train** (☎ 2890 7777) runs from the Pudong airport to its terminal near the Longyang Rd metro station (one way/return Y50/80). Trains from here run every 20 minutes from 8.30am to 5.30pm and hit warp speed at 430km/h.

Boat

The Huangpu River offers some stirring views of the Bund and the riverfront activity. Most **tour boats** (黄浦江游览船; huángpǔjiāng yóulǎnchuán; ☎ 6374 4461; 219-239 East Second Zhongshan Rd; 中山东二路219-239号; 1hr cruise Y25-Y50, 3½hr cruise Y70-120) depart from the Bund's dock, near East Jinling Rd. Popular 30-minute **cruises** (Y40-70; ☯ 10am-8pm) depart hourly from the Pearl Dock in Lujiazui, Pǔdōng.

For an abbreviated boat tour, catch the **Bund–Pǔdōng ferry** (Y0.50, air-con Y2), which shuttles regularly across the Huangpu River.

Gateway Hong Kong
香港

Hong Kong, a pulsating fusion of two cultures, is like no other city in China, and time has done nothing to diminish its ability to astonish. Even a decade after the return of Hong Kong from British to Chinese sovereignty, this 'meeting of east and west' continues to shake and stir into an invigorating cocktail of colour and aroma, taste and sensation. Hong Kong has something for everyone: shopping malls with bargains galore; romantic vistas across Victoria Harbour or down from the Peak; museums with rich collections devoted to local history and culture; stunning modern architecture; and a seemingly endless choice of restaurants and cuisines. And, despite its size and rapid urbanisation, Hong Kong has a surprising number of accessible beaches and natural retreats for lovers of the great outdoors. It's the perfect place from which to kick off or end a trip to China's Southwest.

For a whole lot more details, see Lonely Planet's *Hong Kong & Macau* guide.

FAST FACTS

- Telephone code: ☎ 852
- Population: 7 million
- www.discoverhongkong.com

INFORMATION
Bookshops
Hong Kong Book Centre (☎ 2522 7064; basement, On Lok Yuen Bldg, 25 Des Voeux Rd, Central; ☺ 9am-6.30pm Mon-Fri, to 5.30pm Sat, 1-5pm Sun Jul & Aug only; MTR Central) Sister store to Swindon Books.

Swindon Books (辰衝; ☎ 2366 8001; 13-15 Lock Rd, Tsim Sha Tsui; ☺ 9am-6.30pm Mon-Thu, to 7.30pm Fri & Sat, 12.30-6.30pm Sun; MTR Tsim Sha Tsui) Swindon is one of the best 'real' bookshops in Hong Kong.

Emergency
Hong Kong is generally very safe but, as with anywhere, things can go wrong.
Ambulance, Fire & Police (☎ 999)
Police Crime Hotline (☎ 2527 7177)
Rape Crisis Line (☎ 2375 5322)

Internet Access
With the plethora of places offering low-cost or free wireless access, including most hotels and all of Hong Kong International Airport, you'll have no trouble accessing the internet with your own laptop. If you didn't bring yours

along, outlets of the Pacific Coffee Company, including its **Central branch** (☎ 2537 1688; www.pacific coffee.com; ground fl, the Work Station, 43 Lyndhurst Tce, Central; ☺ 7am-midnight Mon-Thu, to 1am Fri & Sat, 8am-11pm Sun; bus 13 or 40M), offer free access with a purchase.

Maps
Decent tourist maps are easy to come by in Hong Kong, and even better, they're usually free. The Hong Kong Tourism Board hands out copies of the bimonthly (and somewhat limited) *Hong Kong Map* at its information centres (see opposite).

Universal Publications (www.up.com.hk) produces many maps of Hong Kong, including the 1:80,000 *Hong Kong Touring Map* (HK$22) and the 1:9000 *City Map of Hong Kong & Kowloon* (HK$25), available at most bookshops. **HK City Map** (www.hkcitymap.com) has detailed maps of Hong Kong down to street level, printable from the internet.

Media & Internet Resources
HK Magazine (www.asia-city.com) is a comprehensive free magazine of entertainment listings available Fridays at restaurants, bars, shops and hotels. The free *bc magazine* (www.bcmagazine.net), a biweekly guide to Hong Kong's entertainment scene, is less useful.

Good local websites:
www.12hk.com Hong Kong's 'unofficial guide', with excellent links.

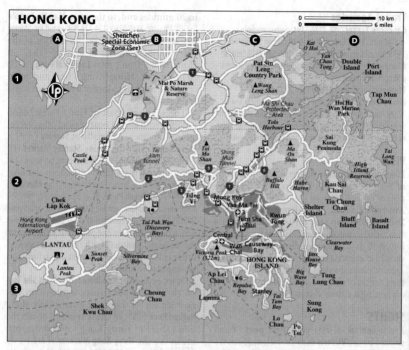

HONG KONG

0 ———————— 10 km
0 ———————— 6 miles

www.hkac.org.hk The Hong Kong Arts Centre's site includes *Artslink*, a monthly listing of performances, exhibitions and art-house film screenings.

www.hkclubbing.com Mandatory surfing before a night out on the town.

www.hkoutdoors.com Hong Kong's answer to the call of the wild.

www.hongkongnews.net Good start for local news.

Medical Services

Medical care is generally of a high standard, but public hospital facilities are stretched and private hospital treatment is expensive. The hospital general inquiry number is ☎ 2300 6555. The hospitals, right, have 24-hour accident and emergency departments or clinics.

Hong Kong Central Hospital (☎ 2522 3141; 1b Lower Albert Rd, Central; MTR Central) Private hospital on Hong Kong Island.

Queen Elizabeth Hospital (☎ 2958 8888; 30 Gascoigne Rd, Yau Ma Tei; MTR Yau Ma Tei) Public hospital in Kowloon.

Money

The unit of currency is the Hong Kong dollar (HK$), which is divided into 100 cents. Travellers can withdraw funds from home accounts using just about any of the numerous ATMs scattered around the territory. The most widely accepted credit cards are Visa, MasterCard, American Express, Diners Club and JCB.

Tourist Information

The **Hong Kong Tourism Board** (HKTB; www.discover hongkong.com) distributes useful pamphlets and publications and has branches at Hong Kong International Airport (see p96; open 7am to 11pm), the Star Ferry Concourse (p96; open 8am to 8pm) in Tsim Sha Tsui, and near Exit F of the Causeway Bay MTR station (open 8am to 8pm). Alternatively, call the **HKTB Visitor Hotline** (☎ 2508 1234) between 8am and 6pm.

Travel Agencies

Concorde Travel (☎ 2526 3391; www.concorde
-travel.com; 1st fl, Galuxe Bldg, 8-10 On Lan St, Central;
◷ 9.30am-5.30pm Mon-Fri, 9am-1pm Sat; MTR Central)
A long-established and highly dependable agency owned
and operated by expats.

Phoenix Services Agency (☎ 2722 7378;
info@phoenixtrvl.com; Room 1404, 14th fl, Austin Tower,
22-26 Austin Ave, Tsim Sha Tsui; ◷ 9am-6pm Mon-Fri, to
1pm Sat; MTR Jordan) One of the best places in Hong Kong
to buy air tickets, get China visas and seek travel advice.

Visas

Hong Kong visas are not required for citizens
of the UK for stays of up to 180 days. Citizens of other European Union (EU) countries,
Australia, Canada, Israel, Japan, New Zealand
and the USA can stay for 90 days without a
visa, while visitors from South Africa are allowed 30 days. Those holding other passports
should check visa regulations on www.immd
.gov.hk/ehtml/hkvisas_4.htm beforehand. See
the Directory chapter (p477) for information
on getting a China visa in Hong Kong.

SIGHTS

From **Central** (中環) your first port of call
should be the **Victoria Peak** (山頂); at 552m it's
the highest point on Hong Kong Island. The
best way to get there is via the thrilling **Peak
Tram** (山頂纜車; ☎ 2522 0922; www.thepeak.com
.hk; one-way/return adult HK$22/33, child & senior HK$8/15;
◷ 7am-midnight), a funicular running every 10
to 15 minutes from the lower terminus behind
St John's Building at 33 Garden Rd, Central,
to the recently renovated **Peak Tower** (凌霄閣)
at the top. The views in clear weather and at
night can be spectacular.

The **Hong Kong Zoological & Botanical Gardens**
(香港動植物公園; ☎ 2530 0154; www.lcsd.gov.hk
/parks/hkzbg; Albany Rd, Central; admission free; ◷ terrace
gardens 6am-10pm; bus 12 or 40M) is a pleasant assembly of fountains, sculptures, greenhouses,
a zoo and aviaries. In nearby **Hong Kong Park**
(香港公園; ☎ 2521 5041; www.lcsd.gov.hk/parks/hkp
/en/index.php; 19 Cotton Tree Drive, Admiralty; admission free;
◷ 6am-11pm; MTR Admiralty) you'll find the splendid **Flagstaff House Museum of Tea Ware** (茶具文
物館; ☎ 2869 0690; admission free; ◷ 10am-5pm Wed-
Mon) in a colonial structure built in 1846.

Other must-see destinations in Central are
the 800m-long **Central Escalator** (中環至半山自
動扶梯; ☎ 2523 7488; admission free; ◷ 6am-midnight;
MTR Central), the longest in the world, which
transports pedestrians up to the Mid-Levels

in 20 minutes and, to the west, **Man Mo Temple**
(文武廟; ☎ 2540 0350; 124-126 Hollywood Rd, Sheung
Wan; admission free; ◷ 8am-6pm; bus 26), one of the
oldest Chinese houses of worship (1847) in
Hong Kong. Don't miss **Lan Kwai Fong** (蘭桂
坊) by night, Hong Kong's best and most
complete bar strip. More of a restaurant scene
is nearby **Soho**.

The southern coast of Hong Kong Island
is dotted with decent beaches and other recreational facilities, especially at **Stanley** (赤柱).
Here you'll also find busy **Stanley Market** (赤
柱市集; Stanley Village Rd; ◷ 9am-6pm; bus 6, 6A, 6X or
260), a covered maze filled with cheap clothing,
toys and bric-a-brac. To the west at **Aberdeen**
(香港仔) is **Ocean Park** (香港海洋公園; ☎ 2552
0291; www.oceanpark.com.hk; Ocean Park Rd; adult/child
HK$185/93; ◷ 10am-6pm; bus 6X, 73 or Ocean Park Citybus
629), a huge amusement park and educational
theme park, complete with roller coasters and
other rides, the world's largest aquarium and
an impressive atoll reef.

Start exploring **Kowloon** from **Tsim Sha Tsui**
(尖沙咀) at the peninsula's southern tip. Renowned for its shopping, particularly along
Nathan Road (彌敦道), this area also boasts the
lion's share of Hong Kong's best museums,
including the **Hong Kong Museum of Art** (香港
藝術博物館; ☎ 2721 0116; http://hk.art.museum; 10
Salisbury Rd, Tsim Sha Tsui; adult/child & senior HK$10/5,
admission Wed free; ◷ 10am-6pm Sun-Wed & Fri, to 8pm
Sat; MTR Tsim Sha Tsui), with Chinese antiquities,
historical paintings and contemporary art,
and the **Hong Kong Space Museum** (香港太空館;
☎ 2721 0226; http://hk.space.museum; 10 Salisbury Rd, Tsim
Sha Tsui; adult/child & senior HK$10/5, admission Wed free;
◷ 1-9pm Mon & Wed-Fri, 10am-9pm Sat & Sun; MTR Tsim Sha
Tsui), with exhibition halls and a planetarium
called Space Theatre (adult HK$24 to HK$32,
child and senior HK$12 to HK$16) showing
between Omnimax films.

The waterfront **Tsim Sha Tsui Promenade** (尖
沙咀海濱長廊), whose **Avenue of the Stars** pays
homage to the Hong Kong film industry, leads
to **Tsim Sha Tsui East** (尖東) and the **Hong Kong
Museum of History** (香港歷史博物館; ☎ 2724
9042; http://hk.history.museum; 100 Chatham Rd South, Tsim
Sha Tsui East; adult/child & senior over 60 HK$10/5, admission
Wed free; ◷ 10am-6pm Mon & Wed-Sat, to 7pm Sun; MTR
Tsim Sha Tsui), which takes visitors on a fascinating wander through Hong Kong's past.

In **Yau Ma Tei** (油麻地), the **Jade Market** (玉
器市場; Kansu & Battery Sts, Yau Ma Tei; ◷ 10am-6pm;
MTR Yau Ma Tei) has scores of stalls that sell all
varieties and grades of jade. Nearby is the

famous **Temple St Night Market** (廟街夜市; Temple St btwn Jordan Rd & Man Ming Lane, Yau Ma Tei; ⏰ 4pm-midnight; MTR Jordan or Yau Ma Tei), the liveliest place in town to bargain for cheap clothes, fake name-brand goods and knockoff CDs and DVDs.

Further north in **Mong Kok** (旺角) is the delightful **Yuen Po Street Bird Garden** (園圃街雀鳥花園; Flower Market Rd, Mong Kok; ⏰ 7am-8pm; Mong Kok KCR East Rail), where birds are 'aired', preened, bought and sold.

If time allows, consider an excursion further afield, perhaps to one of the Outlying Islands or the New Territories. **Lantau** (大嶼山), Hong Kong's largest island, is home to some fine beaches, excellent hiking trails and sights as disparate as the **Tian Tan Buddha** (天壇大佛; Ngong Ping; admission free; ⏰ 10am-5.30pm; Lantau ferry to Mui Wo & bus 2), the largest outdoor Buddha statue in the world, and **Hong Kong Disneyland** (香港迪士尼樂園; ☎ 1-830 830; www.hongkongdisneyland.com; adult/child Mon-Fri HK$295/210, Sat & Sun HK$350/250; ⏰ 10am-9pm Apr-Oct, to 7pm Nov-Mar; MTR Disneyland Resort). A worthwhile destination in the New Territories, a mixed bag of congested 'New Towns' and some surprisingly unspoiled areas and country parks, is **Hong Kong Wetland Park** (香港濕地公園; ☎ 2708 8885; www.wetlandpark.com; Wetland Park Rd, Tin Shui Wai; adult/child HK$30/15; ⏰ 10am-5pm Wed-Mon), a large ecological park near the mainland border with trails, viewing platforms and bird hides as well as cutting-edge exhibition galleries. To get there, take the KCR West Rail to Tin Shui Wai then Light Rail 705 or 706, or catch bus 967 from Admiralty station.

SLEEPING

It's not a hard-and-fast rule but the greatest choice of budget accommodation is in Kowloon.

Hong Kong Hostel (香港旅館; ☎ 2895 1015; www.wangfathostel.com.hk; Flat A2, 3rd fl, Paterson Bldg, 47 Paterson St, Causeway Bay; dm HK$120-150, s/d/tr HK$340/400/500, with shared bathroom HK$250/340/480; MTR Causeway Bay; 🖧 🖵) This excellent series of ever-expanding hostels and guesthouses with 120 rooms is just about the best deal on Hong Kong Island. It's quiet and clean and most of the rooms have private phones, TVs and fridges.

Rent-a-Room (港龍酒店; ☎ 2366 3011; www.rentaroomhk.com; Flat A, 2nd fl, Knight Garden, 7-8 Tak Hing St, Tsim Sha Tsui; dm HK$155-220, s/d/tr/q from HK$360/460/710/920, with shared bathroom from HK$310/370/490/615; MTR Jordan; 🖧 🖵) This fabulous

place has 50 positively immaculate rooms just around the corner from the Jordan MTR station. Each room has shower, safe, TV, telephone and fridge.

The Salisbury (香港基督教青年會; ☎ 2268 7000; www.ymcahk.org.hk; 41 Salisbury Rd, Tsim Sha Tsui; dm HK$230, s HK$760, d HK$860-1060; MTR Tsim Sha Tsui; ✗ 🖧 🖵 🖳) If you can manage to book a room at the YMCA-run Salisbury, you'll be rewarded with professional service and excellent exercise facilities, including a six-lane swimming pool and fitness centre. The 365 rooms and suites are comfortable but simple so keep your eyes on that five-star harbour view.

Alisan Guest House (阿里山賓館; ☎ 2838 0762; http://home.hkstar.com/~alisangh; Flat A, 5th fl, Hoito Ct, 23 Cannon St, Causeway Bay; s HK$280-350, d HK$320-410, tr HK$390-500; MTR Causeway Bay; 🖧 🖵) The 21 well-equipped rooms in this family-run place are spotlessly clean and the multilingual owners are always willing to please.

Booth Lodge (卜維廉賓館; ☎ 2771 9266; http://boothlodge.salvation.org.hk; 11 Wing Sing Lane, Yau Ma Tei; s & d incl breakfast HK$420-1500; MTR Yau Ma Tei; ✗ 🖧) Run by the Salvation Army, this 53-room place is austere and clean but excellent value, especially off-season. Reception is on the 7th floor.

Bishop Lei International House (宏基國際賓館; ☎ 2868 0828; www.bishopleihtl.com.hk; 4 Robinson Rd, Mid-Levels; s HK$600-1040, d & tw HK$720-1210; bus 23, 40; ✗ 🖧 🖵 🖳) This 203-room hotel is hardly luxurious but it's just a short walk to the Zoological & Botanical Gardens and it has its own swimming pool and gym.

Stanford Hillview Hotel (仕德福山景酒店; ☎ 2722 7822; www.stanfordhillview.com; 13-17 Observatory Rd, Tsim Sha Tsui; s & d HK$1000-1600; MTR Tsim Sha Tsui; ✗ 🖧 🖵) This 163-room hotel at the eastern end of Knutsford Tce is a very good choice. It's set back from Nathan Rd in a quiet, leafy little corner of Tsim Sha Tsui, but is close to bars and restaurants.

Hotel LKF (蘭桂坊酒店; ☎ 2850 8899; www.hotel-kf.com.hk; 263 Hollywood Rd, Central; s & d HK$3000-4500; MTR Central; ✗ 🖧 🖵) This stunning 95-room boutique hotel boasts an enviable location just above Lan Kwai Fong (thus the name). Corner rooms (ending in 09) overlook Government House and its gardens and are among the best.

EATING

If you're on a budget, head for the noodle shops of Wan Chai on Hong Kong Island or the Indian 'messes' in Chungking Mansions (36–44 Nathan Rd, Tsim Sha Tsui; metro Tsim Sha Tsui) over in Kowloon. For a more upmarket dining experience and greater choice, check out the Soho neighbourhood. There the world really is your oyster.

Branto Pure Vegetarian Indian Food (☎ 2366
8171; 1st fl, 9 Lock Rd, Tsim Sha Tsui; dishes HK$30-59;
🕐 11am-3pm & 6-11pm; MTR Tsim Sha Tsui; Ⓥ))
This cheap and cheerful Indian club is where to head if
you want to try South Indian vegetarian dishes. Order a
thali, a steel tray of *idlis* (soft rice cakes) and *dosas* (rice
pancakes) with dipping sauces.

Spring Deer (鹿鳴春飯店; ☎ 2366 4012; 1st fl,
Lyton Bldg, 42 Mody Rd, Tsim Sha Tsui; mains HK$60-320;
🕐 11.30am-3pm & 6-11pm; MTR Tsim Sha Tsui) This
is probably Hong Kong's most famous Northern Chinese
restaurant and serves some of the crispiest Peking duck
(HK$280) in town.

Yung Kee (鏞記酒家; ☎ 2522 1624; 32-40 Wellington St; mains HK$78-180; 🕐 11am-11.30pm; MTR
Central) This institution is probably the most famous
Cantonese restaurant in Hong Kong. Yung Kee's roast
goose has been the talk of the town since 1942, and its
dim sum is excellent.

Lin Heung Tea House (蓮香樓; ☎ 2544 4556;
160-164 Wellington St, Central; meals HK$125; 🕐 6am-
11pm; MTR Central) This old-style Cantonese restaurant is
definitely worth a visit for the tableau it offers visitors –
old men reading the newspaper, extended families kibitz-
ing and noshing – and for the authentic dim sum served
from trolleys.

Café Too (☎ 2820 8571; 7th fl, Island Shangri-La Hong
Kong, Pacific Place, Supreme Court Rd, Admiralty; buffet
lunch/dinner Mon-Sat HK$258/358, Sun HK$298/398;
🕐 6.30am-1am; MTR Admiralty) This beautifully
designed food hall has a half-dozen kitchens preparing
dishes from around the world and one of the best buffets
in the territory.

GETTING THERE & AWAY

While neighbouring Guǎngdōng province is
well served by bus, train and ferry from Hong
Kong, the only way to reach China's Southwest directly is by airplane.

Air

At least one flight a day links Hong Kong
International Airport with every major city in
China's Southwest. Sample round-trip fares,
excluding tax and fuel surcharge (for which
you should add about HK$480 return), are
Chéngdū (HK$2400), Kūnmíng (HK$2100),
Chóngqìng (HK$2400) and Guìlín (HK$1480).
There are also cheaper deals, depending on
when and whom you fly, length of stay etc,
but fares will be cheaper still – at least 50%
less than those in Hong Kong – if you travel
to Guǎngzhōu or Shēnzhèn over the border in
Guǎngdōng province. Shēnzhèn's Huangtian
International Airport in particular is easily
reached by bus from Hong Kong and has
flights to just about everywhere in China's
Southwest.

Bus

Several transport companies in Hong Kong
offer bus services to Guǎngzhōu (HK$80 to
HK$100) and Shēnzhèn airport (HK$110),
where you can board flights to the Southwest.
These include **CTS Express Coach** (☎ 2365 0118, 2261
2472; http://ctsbus.hkcts.com) and **Eternal East** (☎ 3412
6677, 2261 0176; www.eebus.com).

Train

Reaching Shēnzhèn over the border in mainland China is a breeze from Hong Kong. Just
board the Kowloon–Canton Railway's East
Rail at Hung Hom station and ride it for 40
minutes to Lo Wu (1st/2nd class HK$66/33);
Shēnzhèn is a couple of hundred metres away.
Its airport is 36km west of the city; a taxi will
cost Y150.

The **Kowloon–Guangzhou express train** (www
.kcrc.com) departs from the Hung Hom station
a dozen times per day; the journey takes 1¾
hours and costs passengers from HK$180.
Tickets can be booked in advance at KCR
stations in Hung Hom, Kowloon Tong and
Sha Tin; from China Travel Service (CTS; 中
国旅行社) agents; or over the phone through
the **Intercity Passenger Services Hotline** (☎ 2947
7888).

GETTING AROUND

The easiest way to get around Hong Kong
is via the **MTR** (Mass Transit Railway; ☎ 2881 8888;
www.mtr.com.hk) metro system. Tickets cost
HK$4 to HK$26 (slightly less if purchased
with a stored-value Octopus card). Trains run
every two to 10 minutes from around 6am to
sometime between 12.30am and 1am daily
on seven lines, including the Airport Express
(see opposite).

The **Star Ferry** (☎ 2366 2576; www.starferry.com
.hk) was once a cheap and easy way to cross
between Central and Tsim Sha Tsui. It's still
the former (HK$1.70/2.20 on the lower/upper
deck), but having moved to a new home at
Pier 7 of the outlying islands ferry terminal in
late 2006 it is no longer very convenient.

Hong Kong taxis are a bargain. Flagfall on
Hong Kong Island and in Kowloon is HK$15
for the first 2km and HK$1.40 for every ad-
ditional 200m. It's slightly less elsewhere in
the territory.

To/From the Airport

Airport Express (☎ 2881 8888; www.mtr.com.hk) trains depart from Hong Kong station (HK$100) in Central every 12 minutes from about 6am to just before 1am daily, calling at Kowloon station (HK$90) in Jordan and at Tsing Yi Island (HK$60) en route; the full trip takes 24 minutes.

Most major areas of Hong Kong Island, Kowloon, the New Territories and Lantau are connected to the airport by bus. Buses A11 (HK$40) and A12 (HK$45) serve major hotel and guesthouse areas on Hong Kong Island, and the A21 (HK$33) does similar areas in Kowloon. Buses run every 10 to 30 minutes from about 6am to between midnight and 1am; the 'N' buses follow the same routes after that.

A taxi from the airport to Tsim Sha Tsui/Central costs around HK$270/340.

Guìzhōu 贵州

Compared with its provincial neighbours, Guìzhōu is like the shy younger sibling everyone knows is there but who no-one pays much attention to. But travellers would still do well to give this mysterious province a chance. The rugged karst landscape, numerous waterfalls and intricate cave networks are all worth exploring, but it's Guìzhōu's lively mix of people that makes the province such a standout destination.

Eighteen different ethnic minorities are spread out over the entire province making up 35% of the entire population. The main groups include the Miao and the Dong in the southeast, the Hui and the Yi in the west and the Bouyi in the southwest. Other major groups include the Shui (Sui), Zhuang and Gejia.

Everything from the clothes and food to the architecture helps give this province a unique flavour. Highlights include the wooden houses of the Miao, the stone houses of the Bouyi and the elaborate wind and rain bridges and towers of the Dong. The diversity of people means Guìzhōu's social calendar is packed and it enjoys more frequent and varied folk festivals than any other province in China. Journeying through remote rural areas and hanging out with locals at these events can end up being the highlight of a trip through China's Southwest.

HIGHLIGHTS

- Hit market day at one of southeast Guìzhōu's **minority villages** (p129) for colours, sights and sounds you'll never forget

- Search out the Jurassic-era dinosaur plants at one of **Chìshuǐ's** (p149) nature reserves

- Get drenched under the ribbon-like water-falls of **Maling Gorge** (p124) and decide for yourself whether or not you like it more than the mighty **Huangguoshu Falls** (p115), Guìzhōu's star attraction

- Visit the wintering fowl at **Caohai Lake** (p118) for a glimpse of the endangered black-necked crane

- Travel to the centre of the earth at spooky **Zhijin Cave** (p114), the largest cave in China

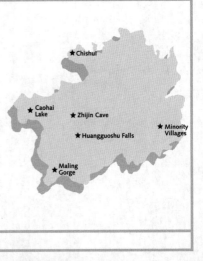

★ Chishui

★ Caohai Lake

★ Zhijin Cave

★ Minority Villages

★ Huangguoshu Falls

★ Maling Gorge

- POPULATION: 39 MILLION

HISTORY

Historically no-one has really wanted much to do with Guìzhōu. Chinese rulers set up an administration in the area as far back as the Han dynasty (206 BC–AD 220), but merely in an attempt to maintain some measure of control over Guìzhōu's non-Chinese tribes. Chinese settlement was confined to the northern and eastern parts of the province and the western areas were not settled until the 16th century, when rapid immigration forced the native minorities out of the most fertile areas.

Another wave of Chinese immigration in the late 19th century brought many settlers from the overpopulated provinces of Húnán and Sìchuān. However, with poor communication systems and transport, development in Guìzhōu was sluggish and the province remained impoverished.

It wasn't until the Sino-Japanese war when the Kuomintang made Chóngqìng their wartime capital that the development of Guìzhōu began: roads to neighbouring provinces were constructed, a rail link was built to Guǎngxī and industries were established in Guìyáng and Zūnyì. Most activity ceased at the end of the Sino-Japanese war and it wasn't until the communists began construction of the railways that industrialisation of the area was revived.

Nevertheless, Chinese statistics continue to paint a grim picture of underdevelopment and poverty for Guìzhōu. Depending on which survey you look at, GDP per capita in Shànghǎi is 10 times higher or more than in Guìzhōu and the province has a reputation as being one of the worst run in China's Southwest.

Still, the government is attempting to change Guìzhōu's fortunes with a big emphasis on tourism. Highways and small regional airports are being built in every possible place to enable fast travel to tourist sights, and minority cultures are aggressively promoted as a local attraction.

Guìzhōu does have one claim to fame: it's the producer of China's beloved Maotai liquor, named for the village of its origin in Rénhuái County. This fiery white spirit is sold in distinctive white bottles with a diagonal red label. Like Yúnnán, Guìzhōu is also a major tobacco-producing area.

CLIMATE

Guìzhōu has a temperate climate with an annual average temperature of 15°C. It's often overcast and rainy and there is little difference between the seasons. Winter lasts from December to February with average temperatures of around 1°C. Autumn lasts from September to November, spring from March to May and summer from June to August, when temperatures average 22°C to 25°C.

FESTIVALS & EVENTS

Exploring minority festivals and markets is one of the main reasons people come to Guìzhōu. Taking place throughout the lunar calendar at various sites, these vibrant celebrations can feature bullfighting, horse racing, pipe playing, comic opera, singing contests and gigantic courting parties. Oh yes, and basketball matches.

The majority of festivals are held on auspicious lunar dates such as the 3rd day of the 3rd lunar month, the 6th of the 6th, the 5th of the 5th and the 9th of the 9th. Most are annual events, though some are held every few years, and others just once a decade.

Kǎilǐ is the springboard for festivals in the Miao and Dong regions of Guìzhōu's southeast. It has the most sophisticated tourist setup and information on festival and market dates is easy to get; the local tourist officials speak a variety of foreign languages and are extremely helpful. However, in other areas, such as the Southwest's Bouyi region, there is little tourist infrastructure and getting information on these events is like pulling teeth. Intrepid travellers may enjoy giving this region a shot anyway, as it provides endless opportunities for off-the-beaten-track discovery.

See the boxed text, p104, for information about some of the more popular events, individual sections in this chapter for information on specific festivals, and the table, p101, for approximate dates in the Gregorian calendar.

LANGUAGE

Mandarin Chinese is spoken by the Han majority. Every minority, whether Miao, Dong or another group, have their own language or dialects. In some minority villages locals speak only limited Mandarin Chinese.

GETTING THERE & AWAY

You can fly to more than 40 destinations within China from Guìyáng's airport, including all major Chinese cities. International destinations include Hong Kong and Bangkok.

A handful of small regional airports have also opened recently; Xīngyì's has flights to

Guìyáng and Shēnzhèn, Huángguǒshù's has flights to and from Guǎngzhōu and Lípíng's has four flights weekly to Guìyáng.

Guìyáng and Chóngqìng are linked by an expressway. Yúnnán is accessible by bus via Wēiníng or on the brand new highway from Xīngyì in the south of the province. From Xīngyì you can also cross into Guǎngxī, which can also be accessed through Cóngjiāng in the southeastern part of the province.

There are daily trains to all major cities in China; sleepers to Chéngdū in Sìchuān or Kūnmíng in Yúnnán are popular options. Trains to Guìlín leave at awkward times and are painfully slow. If you're heading down this way your best bet is to take a train to Liǔzhōu in Guǎngxī and change for a bus to Guìlín there.

CENTRAL GUÌZHŌU

Central Guìzhōu can look a little forlorn, pocked as the coutryside is with endless limestone formations. But despite the appearance of Central Guìzhōu's landscape, this area is the most travelled region of the province and it is also where the province's star sights, such as Huangguoshu Falls, Longgong Caves and Zhijin Cave, as well as its capital city, Guìyáng, are located. The road between Ānshùn and Huángguǒshù is roughly where Bouyi country starts to get interesting, so you could take a break between the must-see destinations to walk the countryside and do a little exploring.

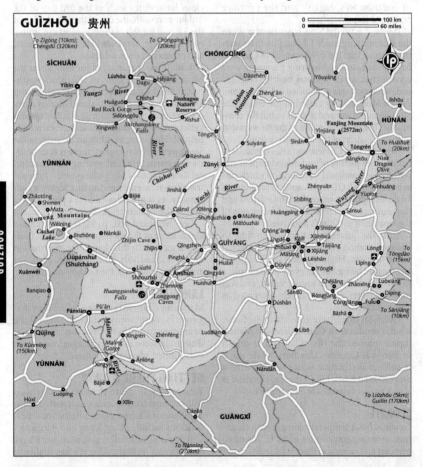

GUÌZHŌU'S FESTIVAL CALENDAR

Use the dates below as a guide to when things really get going in these parts. Always double-check dates with the Kǎilǐ (p126) or the Guìyáng China International Travel Service (p102) before striking off on your own; dates for exactly the same festivals can vary greatly from village to village and the timing of some events is decided by local shamans just a short time before they're to take place.

Dates for some upcoming festivals:

Festival	2008	2009
Hill Leaping Festival	16 Feb	4 Feb
Lusheng Festival	7-22 Feb	26 Jan-10 Feb
Maojie Festival	8 Apr	29 Mar
Sisters' Meal Festival	21-22 Apr	11-12 Apr
Eighth of April	12 May	2 May
Dragon Boat Festival	28 Jun	28 May or 17 Jun
Sixth of June	8 Jul	27 Jul
Giving Worship to the Heavens	16-18 Jul	4-6 Aug
Miao New Year	11 Nov	30 Nov

GUÌYÁNG 贵州

☎ 0851 / pop 1.2 million / elev 1070m

Guìyáng is the provincial capital and a major transport hub for the province, though it's still fairly drab compared with its cousins elsewhere in China's Southwest. It doesn't have the flash of Chéngdū or Chóngqìng, nor the charm of Kūnmíng, but if you plan to spend any amount of time exploring Guìzhōu you'll get to know this place well as you crisscross the province. It's not the worst of fates. There's some interesting sights around town, fantastic street food and lively shopping areas.

Guìyáng means 'precious sun' and may be a reference to the fact that the sun rarely seems to shine through the clouds and drizzle. Otherwise, it has a mild climate year-round, though in recent years it has had some light snowfall and freezing days as late in the year as March.

Orientation

While Guìyáng is a somewhat sprawling kind of place, it remains a manageable size and is easy enough to get around on bus or even by foot. The main commercial district is found along Zhonghua Zhonglu and Zhonghua Nanlu, spreading out along the main roads they intersect. In the south of this area, you'll find the main Bank of China, China Telecom and China Post. If you continue south, you'll reach Zunyi Lu and People's Sq. To the east of here is Jiaxiu Pavilion, a symbol of the city that hovers over Nánmíng Hé.

MAPS

There are no English city maps available but the Chinese-language tourist maps at Xinhua Bookshop are helpful for navigating bus routes.

Information

BOOKSHOPS

Foreign Languages Bookshop (Wàiwén Shūdiàn; Yan'an Donglu) Has a selection of city maps and it's grooming its English collection quite nicely with up-to-date titles: everything from *Sex in the City* to Malcolm Gladwell's *Blink*.

Xinhua Bookshop (Xīnhuá Shūdiàn; Yan'an Xilu) Marginally better in the map department than the Foreign Languages Bookshop.

EMERGENCY

Ensure Chain Pharmacy (Yìshù Yàoyè Liánsuǒ; ☎ 577 3759; cnr Zūnyì Lu & Jiefang Lu; ☼ 8.20am-10pm) Near the train station.

Public Security Bureau (PSB; Gōngānjú; ☎ 590 4509; Daying Lu; ☼ 8.30am-noon & 2.30-5pm Mon-Fri) The place to go to report lost or stolen items and for visa extensions.

INTERNET ACCESS

Internet cafés (Wǎngbā; Longquan Xiang; per hr Y2) Literally dozens of internet cafés line this lane off Hequan Lu.

MONEY

Bank of China (Zhōngguó Yínháng; cnr Dusi Lu & Zhonghua Nanlu) Has an ATM, will exchange money and travellers cheques and offers cash advances on credit cards. Another branch can be found on Zunyi Lu near the train station and another sits on the corner of Wenchang Beilu and Yan'an Donglu.

GUIZHOU

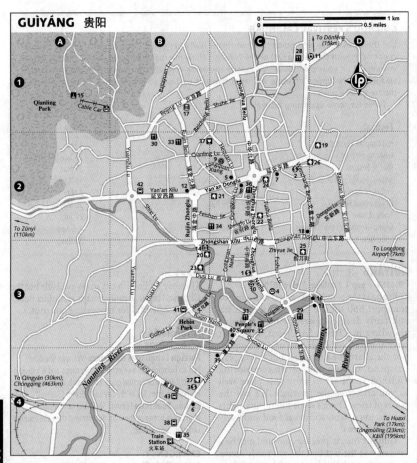

GUÌYÁNG 贵阳

POST & TELEPHONE

China Post (Zhōngguó Yóuzhèng; 46 Zhonghua Nanlu)
Full service, though if you're sending objects overseas the
staff can be a real pain.

Long-Distance Calls (Dusi Lu) Cheap overseas calls can
be made from a small booth here.

TOURIST INFORMATION

China International Travel Service (CITS; Zhōngguó
Guójì Lǚxíngshè; ☎ 690 1660; www.guizhoutour.net; 7th
fl, Longquan Bldg, 1 Hequan Lu; ☺ 9am-5.30pm Mon-Fri)
The friendly English-speaking staff is helpful and can
provide information on festivals.

Guizhōu Overseas Travel Company (GOTC; Guizhōu
Hǎiwài Lǚyóu Zǒnggōngsī; ☎ 586 4898; 28 Yan'an
Donglu; ☺ 9am-6pm) Offers similar services to CITS, but
is more interested in selling tours. Chinese-language tours

to Qīngyán cost Y148. A tour to Huangguoshu Falls and the
Longgong Caves is Y240.

Tourist complaint line (☎ 681 8436) Will a call here
change things? Unlikely. Will it make you feel better? If
you've got one of the English speakers, perhaps.

Dangers & Annoyances

Guìyáng has a reputation among Chinese
as one of China's worst cities for theft. Be
particularly careful in crowded areas such as
the train station, night markets and on local
buses – the favoured haunts of pickpockets.

Sights

PARKS 公园

Qianling Park (黔灵公园; admission Y5; ☺ 6.30am-
9pm) in the northwest of the city is more forest

than park. It's a great escape from the crowds
and city noise and has some lovely paths up to
the **Hongfu Temple** (Hóngfú Sì), a 17th-century
Qing dynasty temple perched near the top of
1300m Qiánlíng Shān. You can save your legs
and take a **cable car** (Y20) up if it's running.
The monastery has a vegetarian restaurant
(open noon to 3pm) in the rear courtyard.
Locals say the park is full of hungry monkeys so keep your eyes peeled. From the train
station area take bus 2.

Elsewhere in the city, **Hebin Park** (河滨公园;
🕑 dawn-dusk) is nowhere near as impressive,
but it's a nice downtown respite, not too far
from People's Sq.

PROVINCIAL MUSEUM 省博物馆

The **Provincial Museum** (Shěng Bówùguǎn; Beijing Lu;
北京路; admission Y10; 🕑 9am-4.30pm) has a going-
out-of-business vibe and criminally lethargic
ticket sellers but it's still worth a stop, especially for travellers pushing off to explore
Guìzhōu's Miao and Dong villages. Exhibits
showcase minority dress and customs from
the Yelang kingdom, believed to have originated in the Warring States Period (475–221
BC). Keep an eye out for displays concerning
the 18th- and 19th-century Miao uprisings
against rapid immigration of Han Chinese
into Guìzhōu.

GUIYANG ART MUSEUM 贵阳美术馆

This **museum** (Guìyáng Měishùguǎn; Ruijin Zhonglu; 瑞金
中路; admission Y15; 🕑 10am-5pm) opened quickly
but seems to have closed just as fast. Its doors

were shut when we dropped by and the lobby
was filled with construction materials, though
it's not clear if they were for renovations or a
change in line of work. Drop by when you're
in town to see what happened. Enter on
Zhongshan Xilu.

Walking Tour

Guìyáng is a pleasant enough place to stroll
around and there are a few pavilions and temples scattered about to give some visual relief
from all the tall grey buildings. Try to take the
more interesting backstreets – not only will
you escape the hair-raising intersections and
roundabouts, you'll also avoid the retired old
guards who maniacally wave red flags at you
every time you attempt to inch off the pavement (they really do seem more aggressive in
Guìyáng than in almost any other city in the
Southwest).

Beginning at **People's Square** (人民广场;
Rénmín Guǎngchǎng), north of the train
station, you'll find one of China's largest,
glistening-white statues of Mao Zedong, as
well as two new Louvre-like glass pyramids,
which mark a massive subterranean Wal-
Mart (a major outing for locals). It's a madhouse here on Friday or Saturday nights when
crowds are so thick it can take a whopping 45
minutes to get from one side of the store to
the other. Outside on the square itself, things
are more pleasant, with lots of families and
people flying kites or visiting in the small gaz-
ebos. Weekday mornings the square is often
flooded with people practising taichi.

GUIZHOU

Just north of here, wander along Yangming Lu, cross a large roundabout, and follow a set of stairs down to the riverside. This walkway is filled with older people playing cards and mah jong. At the end, another set of stairs leads you up to the bridge on which rests **Jiaxiu Pavilion** (甲秀楼; Jiǎxiù Lóu).

On the other side of the river is **Cuìwēi Yuán** (翠微园; admission Y3), a collection of several small pavilions set in a charming garden of bonsai trees, Chinese stones and miniature plum blossoms. The garden was originally a Buddhist abbey built during the Ming dynasty (1425–35), however nowadays it's essentially home to a group of shops selling traditional Miao embroidery; they're interesting to browse through but extremely pricey.

Backtracking across the bridge and heading north up Wenchang Beilu brings you to the Ming dynasty **Wenchang Pavilion** (文昌阁; Wénchāng Gé). It and the old city walls

around it have been beautifully refurbished and the pavilion now houses a very popular local teahouse.

Tours

There are organised tours to Huangguoshu Falls and Longgong Caves that leave daily from People's Sq or the long-distance bus station. Many of the hotels also organise day tours, as do the Guìyáng CITS and GOTC tourist agencies (p102), although they are infrequent off-season. Tours cost from Y240 per person and include transport and admission fees and sometimes lunch.

Festivals & Events

If you're in town during a Bouyi festival, **Huaxi Park** (花溪公园; Huāxī Gōngyuán), 17km south of town, is a good place to head. There's a Bouyi gathering here on the 6th of the sixth lunar month, and on the 15th of the first lunar month (around February) there

MINORITY FESTIVALS

Courtship is the drive behind most of Guìzhōu's minority festivals. There are many elaborate ploys to get boys and girls together, ranging from handing out rice packets with secret messages inside to less subtle games of catch, where crowds of adolescents line up and 'inadvertently' throw the ball at their favourite potential partner until the object of this affection gets the point. Festivals are therefore a time to look your best and flaunt your wealth, which in Guìzhōu means wearing silver jewellery and exquisite embroidery. Girls spend hours preparing for a festival and will often attend accompanied by their mothers, who continually fuss over their daughters and offer advice.

Festivals also serve as a time to meet other clans, pick up news from other villages and generally relax and enjoy life while there is little work to be done in the fields. Glutinous rice cakes, pounded in wooden troughs and dyed with bright colours, are an important festival food. Guests are toasted continually with rice wine, either out of buffalo horns or through straws from a large jug. Important groups are denied entry to some villages until they have downed several shots of rice wine and sung a song.

One of the most common events is the Lusheng Festival, usually held during the first lunar month. Traditional Miao Lusheng celebrations coincide with Chinese New Year, though there's a big official seven-day-long Lusheng Festival that's held yearly on 1 October.

The *lúshēng* (芦笙) is a reed instrument that ranges in length from 1m to 7m. *Lúshēng* competitions are common and various acrobatic styles are performed to the music, such as 'Earthworm Crossing the Mountain'. Activities include playing the *lúshēng* (of course), traditional dancing, beating bronze drums, bullfighting and horse racing. Most dances are little more than slow monotonous shuffles, which people join one by one over the course of an hour or more. Antiphonal singing (echoing duets) is also popular.

Some festivals are held at traditional sites or hills, often called dancing or flower grounds, though many are now held in the less glamorous surroundings of the municipal basketball courts.

Two other common events are the Flower Dance (Tiàohuā), centred around a special flower tree decorated in red silks, and Eating New Rice (Chīxīn Jié) festivals, held to celebrate the harvest by hanging ears of rice and corn in doorways and brewing buckets of rice wine. Dates for these last two festivals change constantly.

are performances of Bouyi opera at Dàzhài (大寨), near Huāxī (花溪).

There are also minor festivals at Tóngmùlǐng (桐木岭), 23km south of Guìyáng, on the 9th of the first lunar month and at Dōngfēng (东风), 15km northeast of Guìyáng, on the 15th of the second lunar month. For details on these and other minor festivals in the region, visit the CITS office in Guìyáng (p102).

Sleeping
BUDGET

Yidu Youth Hostel (Yídū Jiǔdiàn; ☎ 864 9777; fax 863 1799; 9 Zhiyue Jie; 指月街9号; 6-/4-/3-bed dm Y50/60/70, s & d from Y398) Though the six-bed rooms are a real tight squeeze, the rest of the dorms here are great; each one comes with its own shower and toilet and the furniture is all new. Community life is missing though – there's no common room, activities or anything else to tell you this is anything but cheap beds in a nice midrange hotel. Single and double rooms are bright and spacious with pastel green accents and bright orange throw pillows. A complimentary breakfast is included with some room rates.

Jinlóng Dàjiǔdiàn (☎ 528 2321; 61 Yan'an Zhonglu; 延安中路61号; South Bldg s/d Y109/139, East Bldg r Y238-268) Smack in the thick of things, including near the city's tourist offices, this hotel offers a wide choice of rooms in two different wings. Rooms in the eastern ('dōng') building have western toilets, neat showers and sometimes even little loveseats. Things are a little more run down in the south ('nán') building, with squat toilets and lone shower nozzles suspended from the ceilings. All's kept humming by an energetic, unilingual staff.

Yóudiàn Bīnguǎn (Post Office Hotel; ☎ 558 5082; fax 558 5086; cnr 166 Yan'an Donglu; 延安东路166号; d from Y168) This place has a great downtown location and some of the city's best food vendors right outside. Once renovations are done this could be one of the better budget options in town.

Dàxué Lǚguǎn (☎ 670 2348; 180 Baoshan Beilu; 宝山北路180号; d from Y198) This is a bad choice if you want one of the nicest rooms in town. But, with its location on the university campus, it's a good place to consider if you want a 'get-away-from-it-all' feeling at the end of your day, while still being close to the city. It's fun just to wander around and see what campus life is like in Guìyáng. There are so few foreigners here, it's fairly easy to strike up a conversation with curious local students. The staff at the hotel are also lovely and very helpful. Take your time to check out the rooms though – some are pretty grim.

Motel 168 (Mòtài 168; ☎ 816 8168; 2 Shengfu Lu; 省府路2号; r from Y198) Don't let the name put you off: this place is not only cheap (especially with a discount) but it has boutique-hotel aspirations and is an absolute breath of fresh air in stodgy old Guìyáng. The lobby and halls are full of odd angles, lots of mirrors and the occasional disco ball. Not quite as much effort has gone into the surprisingly simple rooms, but there's an interesting flourish in each one, whether it's rounded edges on the furniture, or illuminated white pebbles under the basins. It's all quite enjoyable once you've got past the snobby staff and their dragon-emblazoned black uniforms. This is one of several Motel 168s opened around China by a Shanghai management group.

MIDRANGE

Yùjūnyuàn Bīnguǎn (☎ 597 0701; 71 Zunyi Lu; 遵义路71号; s & d from Y198) This is a welcoming enough place where even security guards give shy smiles and nods once they've gotten used to you. Staff does an admirable job of tending the rooms, despite the obvious wear and tear. Closet-like bathrooms are made entirely of plastic and have tiny little tubs. Conveniently located near the train and some of the major bus stations.

Jīnqiáo Jiǔdiàn (Golden Bridge Hotel; ☎ 582 9958; 2 Ruijin Zhonglu; 瑞金中路2号; d from Y328) Tour groups and frazzled staff trample over ketchup-and-mustard-coloured carpets here, while red-nosed businessmen swarm in and out of 'superior' karaoke facilities 24 hours a day. It's all a bit over the top, but the weathered rooms are tidy and come with tiny balconies.

TOP END

When it comes to top-end accommodation in Guìyáng, nobody's perfect. Two stand out from the crowd, but you'll have to decide which is more important: service or room condition.

Nénghuì Jiǔdiàn (☎ 589 8888; fax 589 8622; 38 Ruijin Nanlu; 瑞金南路38号; d incl breakfast Y520-696; ☒ ☒ ☐) The breakfast buffet here is the best in the city and the rooms are lovely with embroidered pillows and the odd splash of colour. It's also just gotten satellite TV with a good choice of English channels. The room

GUÌZHŌU

and restaurant service here is fine, but the desk staff and even assistant managers can be awkward with foreigners. Some floors are nonsmoking but rooms there are more expensive.

Trade-Point Hotel (Bǎidùn Jiǔdiàn; ☎ 582 7888; www.trade-pointhotel.com; 18 Yan'an Donglu; 延安东路 18号; s/d Y800/900 plus 15% service charge; ✕ ❄ ▯) Nowhere in town is service better than it is here. Trade-Point's business centre is also the only one in downtown Guìyáng where the computers and other facilities consistently work. The rooms are fine and the breakfast buffet extensive, but for the prices it's asking both should be even better. The 13th and 14th floors are nonsmoking.

Eating

Some of the best food in Guìyáng can be found at the night markets. At dusk countless stalls spring up near the train station, all stacked with a huge choice of veggies, tofu and meat. Point at what you like, grab a beer and watch the food be cooked. If you're feeling really adventurous tuck into some steamed pig snout and trotters, a popular local choice. If not, try the local varieties of *shāguō fěn* (砂锅粉), a noodle and seafood, meat or vegetable combination put in a casserole pot and fired over a flame of rocket-launch proportions. The deep-fried skewered potatoes dusted in chilli powder are the best in the province. The position of all the downtown food stalls seems to change from week to week, but there's usually a concentration of snack stalls just after the bridge on the way to People's Sq. A small night market also sets up every evening in a lane just off Ruijin Zhonglu.

Dongjia Family Restaurant (Dòngjiā Shífǔ; ☎ 650 7186; 42 Beijing Lu; 北京路42号; dishes from Y10; ❄ 9.30am-9pm) Waiters here wear either full-silver Miao regalia or indigo tunics and slacks. Every local knows this place, which specialises in minority cooking from all over Guìzhōu. There's no English menu but its book-sized menu is filled with big luscious pictures from the chillies of Miao cuisine to the pickled vegetables of the Dong. The dining room is cosy but undistinguished, except for the giant tree trunk in the middle.

Chishuiqing Jiǔjiā (☎ 552 7525; Xinhua Lu; 新华路; dishes Y12-68; ❄ 9.30am-10pm) This place is casual but beautifully decorated and specialises in dozens and dozens of types of bamboo dishes. So much care has gone into

the menu and décor that the unpleasant wait staff comes as both a shock and a huge disappointment. However, the rest works so well, foodies looking for something a little different may still decide this place is worth taking a risk on.

Yawen Restaurant (Yǎwēn Jiǔlóu; ☎ 528 8811; Gongyuan Beilu; 公园北路; dishes Y18-68; ❄ noon-2pm & 6-10pm) This is popular with locals for its Sìchuān, Guìzhōu and Cantonese dishes. The food can get expensive but it's first rate. The only downsides are a stark white dining room and overly giggly waiters.

Guizhou Long Seafood (Guìzhōu Lóng Hǎiyáng; ☎ 586 3333; 23 Jiandao Jie; 箭道街23号; dishes Y22-58; ❄ 8.30am-late) This place is positively palatial (seriously, there's a huge staircase just inside the entrance like something out of *Gone with the Wind*) and has a huge array of seafood dishes to choose from. There's no English menu, but the bible-sized Chinese one is loaded with pictures to guide your choices.

New Zealand Western Restaurant (Niùxīlán Xīcāntīng; ☎ 651 2086; 157 Ruijin Beilu; 瑞金北路157号; lunch/dinner buffet Y48/58; ❄ 6-9am, noon-2.30pm & 6-9.30pm) What this restaurant has to do with New Zealand is anyone's guess, but the lunch and dinner buffets are enormous, though travellers have given mixed reviews concerning the food quality. The buffets at Aroma Bakery & Café (Beijing Lu; 北京路; open noon to 2pm and 6pm to 9pm) get much better reviews but are far more expensive.

Drinking

UBC Coffee (Shàngdǎo; 185 Ruijin Beilu; 瑞金北路185号; ❄ 9am-2am) There's an extensive coffee and tea menu here, along with the ever popular *zhēnzhū nǎichá* (珍珠奶茶; pearl milk tea). It's a relaxed, friendly place with slightly tacky décor and a grand piano.

At the time of research, about a dozen bars, lounges and clubs had just opened on Hequan Lu north of Qianling Lu. The area hasn't quite taken off yet but it's worth checking out when you're in town to see if things have picked up.

Getting There & Away

AIR

Airline offices in Guìyáng include the **Civil Aviation Administration of China** (CAAC; Zhōngguó Mínháng; ☎ 597 7777; 264 Zūnyì Lu; ❄ 8.30am-9pm), which has helpful English-speaking staff, and **China Southern Airlines** (Zhōngguó Nánfāng Hángkōng Gōngsī;

☎ 582 8429; cnr Zūnyì Lù & Ruijin Nanlu), which also has a booking office.

Destinations include Běijīng (Y1730), Shànghǎi (Y1600), Guǎngzhōu (Y860), Guìlín (Y630), Chéngdū (Y630), Kūnmíng (Y440) and Chóngqìng (Y490). International destinations include Hong Kong and Bangkok.

BUS

Long-distance buses leave from three different stations in Guìyáng, but all have similar destinations at similar times and prices. The main long-distance bus station is on Yan'an Xilu, quite a trek from the train station.

At the time of research, road work between Guìyáng and Zūnyì meant travel times were averaging from five to 8½ hours. If the work is still going on when you arrive, you're far better off taking the train.

The bus stand in the south of town near the train station is a madhouse, and buses only leave when full. Besides destinations in Guìzhōu, it's got all kinds of sleeper buses to places such as Kūnmíng and Guǎngzhōu, but the buses are generally more run down than what you'd find at the stations. The Tiyuguan Long-Distance Bus Station (Tǐyùguǎn Chángtú Chēzhàn) nearby has similar destinations, a fixed schedule and buses in slightly better condition. However, many taxi drivers still don't seem to know much about it – if you tell them you're going to Kǎilǐ, for example, they'll still drop you off at the bus stand even if you tell them you want the Tiyuguan stop.

The Hebin bus depot (Hébīn qìchēzhàn) in the west of town is the place to head for buses to suburban Guìyáng, or towns and villages close to the city.

GUÌYÁNG BUS TIMETABLES

Buses from Guìyáng's Yan'an Xilu bus station:

Destination	Price	Duration	Frequency	Departs
Ānshùn	Y25	1½hr	every 20min	7am-7pm
Chóngqìng	Y124	8hr	6 daily	8am, 9.30am, 11am, 12.30pm, 2pm & 3.30pm
Guǎngzhōu	Y240	17hr	1 daily	6.30pm
Guìlín	Y158	10hr	2 daily	8pm & 9.30pm
Kūnmíng	Y128	12hr	1 daily	9am
Shuǐchéng	Y60-70	4hr	every 30min	7am-7pm
Wēiníng	Y80	7hr	1 daily	9am
Zūnyì	Y25-45	2½hr	every 30-40min	7.30am-7.20pm

Buses from the Tiyuguan long-distance bus station on Jiefang Lu:

Destination	Price	Duration	Frequency	Departs
Chóngqìng	Y80	9hr	1 daily	1.30pm
Kǎilǐ	Y50	2½hr	every 20-30min	7.30am-7.30pm
Léishān	Y40	3hr	1 daily	3pm
Xīngyì	Y70-80	6½hr	hourly	9am-6pm
Zūnyì	Y25-45	2½hr	half-hourly	7am-7pm

Buses from the bus stand:

Destination	Price	Duration	Frequency*	Departs
Ānshùn	Y25	1½hr	every 20min	7am-7pm
Huangguoshu Falls	Y30-40	2½hr	every 40min	7.10am-noon
Kǎilǐ	Y45-50	2½hr	every 40min	7am -6pm

*Average times; buses leave only when full.

GUIZHOU

GUÌYÁNG TRAIN TIMETABLE

Destination	Price	Duration	Frequency	Departs
Běijīng	Y490	29hr	2 daily	7.50am & 8.33am
Chéngdū	Y222	18hr	4 daily	4.01am, 11.51am, 1.30pm & 1.59pm
Chóngqìng	Y135	10-13hr	13 daily	1am-midnight
Guǎngzhōu	Y317	24hr	6 daily	2.27am-12.30pm
Guìlín	Y200	17hr	2 daily	2.13am & 9.31am
Kǎilǐ	Y83	3hr	several daily	24hr departures
Kūnmíng	Y131-155	11-15hr	9 daily	12.30am-midnight
Shànghǎi	Y387	28hr	1 daily	1.56am
Shuǐchéng	Y56-95	4hr	11 daily	24hr departures
Zūnyì	Y62-100	2½-4hr	several daily	24hr departures

TRAIN

Guìyáng's gleaming train station has a modern, computerised ticket office, making it one of the more pleasant places in China to buy a train ticket. However, you'll probably find that it's easier (and quicker) to travel within Guìzhōu by bus.

You can buy tickets four days in advance. Prices listed in the table above are for hard sleepers.

Getting Around

TO/FROM THE AIRPORT

Buses to the airport (Y10; 9am to 11pm) depart from the CAAC office usually two hours before flight departures. They also meet incoming flights during this period and will drop you at any of eight stops downtown. The train station is the terminus. The ride to Guìyáng takes about 20 minutes.

BUS

For city-tour loops take bus 1 and 2 from the train station (they also pass close to the main long-distance bus station). Bus 1 and 2 travel up Zhonghua Beilu and head west along Beijing Lu. Buses cost Y1 and recorded announcements boom out stops in Chinese and (sometimes) English.

TAXI

There is a flat Y10 charge to travel by taxi to anywhere in the city.

AROUND GUÌYÁNG

Qīngyán 青岩

This former military outpost is filled with cobbled streets, old wooden houses and more interesting sights than its small size would

suggest. It makes an excellent daytrip from Guìyáng. A Ming-era settlement, Qīngyán was once a traffic hub between the southwestern provinces. The crisscross of cultures and religions over the centuries has left the town packed with Taoist temples, Buddhist monasteries, Christian churches and menacing watchtowers. There's a Y40 admission fee that includes entrance to the major sites. There's no English-language maps here yet, but an excellent Chinese-language tourist map of Qīngyán has just been put out and is sold at a few stores inside the village.

Enter in the south of town at **Dìngguǎng Mén** (定广门). Near here, you can go up on a portion of the town's old wall where there are some displays of Ming- and Qing-era military costumes.

Just inside the walls is **Bǎisuì Fáng** (百岁坊), an elaborately carved stone gate. Built only recently, the gate was set up in recognition of the abnormally high number of centenarians living in Qīngyán. Continue under the gate and along the main lane. Chinese-English signs point the way to the various sights, including two well-preserved temples, **Cíyún Sì** (慈云寺) and the nearby **Yíngxiáng Sì** (迎祥寺).

Also keep an eye out for the **No 1 Scholar Cave** (赵状元府; Zhào Zhuàngyuán Fǔ), the pavilion set up in honour of Zhao Yijiong, Qīngyán's first scholar of national renown. He topped his imperial examination and went on to become an important official in the Qing administration. His brother was also a notable scholar.

Two wells outside the entrance are said to have been dug by the brothers. Nobody knows who dug which, and the subject is often a lively source of discussion among Chinese tourists. Once you're confident you know which is Yijiong's (most people seem to go with whichever one has more water in it), place your hands in the well for good luck.

Qīngyán's most impressive **Catholic church** (教堂; Jiàotáng) is in the back of town. Sadly, this eerily atmospheric building has been boarded up and the congregation is moving to the nondescript modern white building next door.

There's plenty to eat in Qīngyán and some of the most popular items are pigs' feet and tofu in every conceivable form: from baseball-sized spheres to oblong packages wrapped in leaves. Sweets are also popular including roasted candy (sold everywhere) and sweet potato snacks, either dried or done up as crispy chips.

Be wary of groups of children pushing drawings or paper cranes into your hands. They're often trolling for money and have been known to stomp on visitors' feet or snatch money out of open wallets if they don't think you've been generous enough.

GETTING THERE & AWAY

Only about 30km outside of town, it takes about an hour to get here by bus from Guìyáng. Buses leave regularly from Guìyáng's Hebin Bus Depot (河滨汽车站) for Huāxī (花溪; Y3 to Y5). A minibus will take you the rest of the way to Qīngyán (Y3). If you're dropped off in the new-town area (grey, concrete buildings), just walk towards the walls with the large stone gate.

Nánjiāng Xiágǔ 南江峡谷

This valley located about 90 minutes outside of Guìyáng is beautiful. Waterfalls plunge over its edges and clusters of Bouyi villages nestle among the lush greenery and rice terraces. One long, winding road goes through it all and the scenery seems to go on forever.

This area hasn't been developed for tourism at all and no English is spoken anywhere. However, there are some subtle signs that may slowly change. A couple of viewing pavilions have been built near some of the more attractive and enduring waterfalls and at least one village is opening up a guesthouse.

With its setting right on the river, tiny little **Shuǐtóuzhài** (水头寨) may be the area's most picturesque settlement. It has a handful of beautiful traditional houses, some narrow paths and a pretty little waterwheel. There's one family here that offers room and meals (☎ 745 8059, 1359-503 6521), so you could base yourself in this village and do some walks in the area. At the time of research, construction workers were putting up a modest guesthouse here, which should be open by the time you read this.

About 750m away is **Mǎtóuzhài** (马头寨), a traditional Bouyi village. While it doesn't have as nice a setting as Shuǐtóuzhài, it has traditional homes, a small Buddhist temple and some examples of old tools and farming technology set up along the paths for you to inspect. Foreigners here can make the kids pretty excitable, so brace yourself, especially if you're travelling solo.

Just down the hill from here is **Mùfēng** (木丰), a sprawling modernising town that is the place to go for anything you might want to buy. If you're hungry, go to its **Héxiānxiāng Cānguǎn** (Hexianxiang Restaurant; 河鲜香餐馆; ☎ 754 2210), where the fish hotpot is done with tiny little fish a pinky-length long fresh from the river that crunch like potato chips when you bite into them. Absolutely delicious.

GETTING THERE & AWAY

To get to the places listed above, take a bus from Guìyáng's Hebin bus depot to Mùfēng from where you can walk the kilometre to nearby Mǎtóuzhài and then the 750m or so to Shuǐtóuzhài. However, that's only one small corner of the valley and you may not see some of the waterfalls and more dramatic scenery.

Alternatively, you could hire a car from Guìyáng for half a day to explore the valley and then have the driver drop you off in Shuǐtóuzhài where you could stay the night. From there, you could head down to Mùfēng when you're done and then take the bus back to Guìyáng.

ĀNSHÙN 安顺

☎ 0853 / pop 391,500

Ānshùn is the ideal place to base yourself if you're planning some in-depth exploration of Guìzhōu's major natural sights. Huangguoshu Falls, Longgong Caves and Zhijin Cave are now easy day-trips away thanks to improved roads and bus connections. Ānshùn itself isn't very exciting. The rambling sprawl of buildings here seems to go on forever. However, it can be interesting just to walk around and check out the informal markets that seem to be set up on every other side street, where there's heated bargaining for mundane items such as socks and plastic dishes along with other bric-a-brac.

GUÌZHŌU

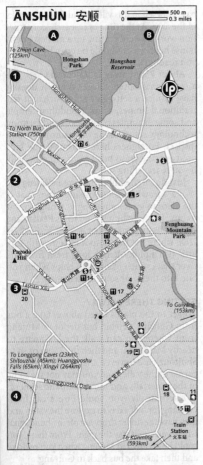

ĀNSHÙN 安顺

0	500 m
0	0.3 miles

Ānshùn's central location has made it western Guìzhōu's commercial hub for centuries – originally for tea and opium, these days for batik and kitchen knives.

A Sunday market found in Ānshùn once drew large numbers of minority villagers from all over the countryside, though in recent years it's of less and less interest. However, most weekends you'll still encounter women villagers in traditional dress on Ānshùn's streets selling vegetables or things such as homemade brooms.

Orientation

The long-distance bus and train stations are 3km and 4km south of downtown respectively. The main commercial and shopping areas are found on Zhonghua Donglu, Gufu Jie and Zhonghua Nanlu.

Information

Bank of China (Zhōngguó Yínháng; cnr Tashan Xilu & Zhonghua Nanlu) Changes cash and travellers cheques and offers cash advances on credit cards. Also an ATM.

China Post (Zhōngguó Yóuzhèng; cnr Tashan Donglu & Zhonghua Nanlu) Tucked next to the China Telecom building.

China Travel Service (CTS; Zhōngguó Lǚxíngshè; ☎ 323 4662, 323 4661; Tashan Donglu; ☯ 9am-5pm Mon-Fri) No English signs outside. Look for a blue sign with yellow Chinese characters.

Internet café (Nanshui Lu; per hr Y2) East off Zhonghua Nanlu.

Long-distance calls You can make cheap long-distance calls from a row of phones in the lobby of the Gōngdiànjú Zhāodàisuǒ (opposite), conveniently located near the long-distance bus station.

Sights & Activities

There's a couple of temples in town worth visiting. **Wén Miào** (Hongxueba Lu; 黉学坝路; admission Y5; ☯ 8am-5pm) is a small but atmospheric Confucian temple in the north of town. The building itself is slightly crumbly and dilapidated and the grounds overgrown, but that just adds to its charm. Keep an eye out for

---

LOCAL VOICES

Some of the countryside around Guìyáng was very isolated, but you can see all the nice roads in the countryside now and visitors probably wonder what they're all doing there. Our government made them to help the villagers. Before, transport was very hard for them; now they like it very much. But other villagers lived very far away in the hills. They had to walk all day down from their village just to get fresh water. Roads couldn't be made in such places. The government had new apartments built close to the new roads instead and moved the villages there. But the buildings weren't well constructed. The roofs leaked. Nothing worked. The villagers didn't like it so they went back up into the hills to their old homes. In the end, the villagers didn't mind walking all day to get water. At least in the villages, their roofs don't leak.

As told by a Guìyáng resident

---

the stunningly intricate carvings winding their way up the various columns. Locals love this place and on weekends the grounds are sprinkled with people drinking tea, reading or sitting on the ground chatting.

Near here is the **Hongshan Reservoir** (虹山水库; Hóngshān Shuǐkù), popular with locals for paddle boating in summer and polar bear swims in winter.

Southeast of Wén Miào, Buddhist **Donglin Temple** (Dōnglíng Sì; Zhonghua Donglu; 中华东路) was built in AD 1405 (during the Ming dynasty) and restored in 1668. It's down a lane off Zhonghua Donglu.

For a peek at the more contemporary side of Ānshùn, **Gufu Jie** is a street of trendy clothing stores and bakeries, and snack stalls that get so packed on weekends it's hard to move. A little further west, the stretch of Zhonghua Nanlu near Zhonghua Donglu is where the city's big commercial stores and shopping centres are located.

The **Wholesale Market of Small Goods in Ānshùn** (Ānshùn Làrǎn Shìchǎng; Zhonghua Nanlu; 中华南路; ☺ dawn-dusk) is the city's main market and probably the most interesting place to prowl.

Festivals & Events

A few minor festivals are held in the Ānshùn area, though they're generally not as spectacular as those held around Kǎilǐ. None of them are worth the trip to Ānshùn alone, but if you happen to be in town already, they are a pleasant diversion and certainly a nice excuse to get out and explore the countryside. Always double-check dates with local tourism officials or the CITS in Guìyáng (p102) before heading off into the wilds to attend any of the following festivities. Dates are known to change from year to year, as well as the location.

Tiàohuā Flower Dance Festival Held in Miao villages during the first lunar month. The main location in Ānshùn is Flower Dance Hill, a few kilometres northwest of town; festivities occur from the 4th to the 6th of the first lunar month. Other gatherings are held at Mǎchǎng and Gāofēng villages (Píngbà County), halfway between Ānshùn and Guìyáng, and in Qīngzhèn town.

Sānyuèsān At Pōgòng (Guānlíng County), 80km southwest of Ānshùn, and at Huǒhuā (Zǐyún County), 100km south of Ānshùn, on the 3rd day of the third lunar month. The festival has different significance depending on what minority group is celebrating it, however, all groups mark it with singing and dancing.

Sìyuèbā 'Ox King' Festival Held at Jiùzhōu and Shuāngbǎo villages, both about 25km east of Ānshùn, on the 8th day of the fourth lunar month.

Liùyuèliù A Bouyi festival at Luohe (Zǐyún County), 67km southeast of Ānshùn, and Lazhai (near Huánglà town), 56km east, on the 6th of the sixth lunar month. Activities include ground opera and singing competitions.

Eating New Rice Festival Held at Huolong and Dagouchang villages, 55km east of Ānshùn, south of the main highway, some time during the seventh or eighth lunar months.

Guìzhōu Batik Festival A state-sponsored festival set up to display (and flog) batik to the tourists. Ānshùn, 28–29 September.

Sleeping

There's a lot of midrange accommodation in Ānshùn geared to Chinese tour groups. Hotels here are generally comfortable but fairly drab and undistinguished.

Gōngdiànjú Zhāodàisuǒ (☎ 332 9124; Zhonghua Nanlu; 中华南路; s & d with bathroom Y78-88, tr Y120) Right across from the Xīxiùshān Bīnguǎn, this place has basic little budget rooms with Chinese toilets and cubby-hole-like showers with no doors. The desk staff is frazzled but kind. Once you've got your key, the journey to your floor begins. Walk through the restaurant

THE BOUYI

The Bouyi, the 'aborigines' of Guìzhōu, are of Thai origin and closely related to the Zhuang of Guǎngxī. Most travellers will come upon them in the Huángguǒshù and Ānshùn areas.

They are generally very poor, in sharp contrast with the postcard images of starched and ironed costumes or ring-of-confidence sparkling teeth. Bouyi dress is dark and sombre, with colourful trimmings. Both men and women wear white- or blue-checked head scarves.

Batik cloth dyeing is one of the many skills of the Bouyi. Batik is made by drawing designs with molten beeswax on a strip of cloth. A variety of instruments is used to produce different shapes with the wax. The fabric is dyed, normally in indigo, and then boiled to remove the beeswax. After it has been rinsed, the pattern of the beeswax remains as the original colour of the fabric. The beeswax is collected and re-used.

The Bouyi are also fine stonemasons. The masonry at Huángguǒshù is intriguing – houses are composed of stone blocks but no plaster is used, and roofs are finished in slate. Bouyi villages often have arched stone bridges and elaborate house entrances. One good place to see stonework is Shítouzhài (石头寨; Stone Stockade village; p117), on the road to the Longgong Caves, near Ānshùn.

Bouyi festivals are usually held on the 'double third' (3rd day of the third lunar month) and 'double sixth'. The Siyueba or Ox King Festival is held on the 8th day of the fourth month, when glutinous rice cakes are offered to ancestors and cattle. The Big Year Festival is held from the 3rd to the 5th of the 12th month. Festivities include lion and dragon dances on top of seven upturned tables, plus courtship games and singing of love songs. Bouyi open-air opera is especially popular during the Big Year and Spring festivals.

dining room to the left of the reception desk. You'll eventually pass a kitchen and then the industrial-sized laundry facilities. The stairs up to the rooms are just after that.

Ānjū Bīnguǎn (☎ 220 1359; train station; 火车站出站口对面; d Y100) Painted a daring powder pink, you'll notice this hotel as soon as you leave the station. Rooms are extremely simple – bathrooms are so small that the sinks are installed over the Chinese toilets and the showerheads are installed over the sinks. Still, this is a fairly popular budget choice and the front desk is fairly friendly.

Fènghuángshān Dàjiǔdiàn (Golden Phoenix Mountain Hotel; ☎ 322 5663; 58 Tashan Donglu; 塔山东路58号; d Y220) Rooms here are memorable for their lively red linen and consistently good-natured staff. Bathrooms can be quite grotty and there are a few wall stains that make you wonder 'what is *that* and how did that get *there*', but despite this, the hotel is certainly one of the more pleasant in town. No English sign outside; enter through the building done up like a Greek bank.

Xixiùshān Bīnguǎn (☎ 221 1888; fax 221 1801; 63 Nanhua Lu; 南华路63号; s/d incl breakfast Y288/328) Standard doubles here are outfitted with everything you could possibly want (big TV, comfortable bed, desk, sitting chairs by the windows), but it's all crammed into such a small space that some of the rooms are ridiculously cramped.

Bathrooms are exactly the opposite – sparsely outfitted and often the same size or bigger than the actual sleeping area. The buffet breakfast is pretty disappointing outside of the high season – noodles are mushy and there's more sauce and condiments than there are things to put them on.

Eating

There are plenty of places to eat in Ānshùn, just little to recommend. Some buildings along Zhonghua Nanlu north of Tashan Lu house restaurants on their 2nd floors, but they seem all but deserted even at peak meal times.

Otherwise, there's a food market (shìchǎng) down an alley off Zhonghua Nanlu, just south of the Bank of China. It's quite fun to wander here and there's usually loud music to go along with the interesting assortment of snacks. There are some great bakeries (miànbāofáng; the one near the corner of Zhonghua Donglu is especially good) and several hole-in-the-wall places on Gufu Jie. A row of forgettable noodle stalls (miàntiáo tān) are located near the train station. There's also a huge supermarket (chāojíshìchǎng) on Zhonghua Nanlu, perfect for picking up snacks for day trips.

Be forewarned: dog is eaten in these parts… lots of dog. You'll see the skinned animals propped up outside restaurants as an enticement to come in for lunch. If you haven't got a taste for canine meat or a desire to try it, learn how to say 'I don't eat dog' (我不吃狗肉; '*Wǒ bù chī gǒuròu*') and practise it well.

Getting There & Away

BUS

There are several bus stations in Ānshùn that are useful to travellers. The north bus station has buses to Zhījīn town (for Zhijin Cave; Y24, 2½ hours, hourly from 7.45am to 5pm) and the west bus station is useful for travelling to Longgong Caves (Y5, 40 minutes, every 20 to 30 minutes from 7am to 5pm).

The long-distance station on the corner of Zhonghua Nanlu and Huangguoshu Dajie has a handful of handy destinations, and the bus stand in front of the train station has buses for numerous provinces in the southeastern part of China.

Buses to Ānshùn leave from every one of Guìyáng's stations (Y25, two hours, every 20 minutes from 7am to 7pm). Any Guìyáng-bound bus out of Xīngyì or Wēiníng will also let you off in Ānshùn if you tell the driver.

TRAIN

From Ānshùn, trains leave daily for Kūnmíng (Y114, 10 hours, 8.50pm), but it's virtually impossible to get sleeper reservations and you might decide to head back to Guìyáng. To

Chóngqìng, there's one train daily (Y120, 12 hours, 9.41pm). To Lìupánshuǐ (for Wēiníng) there are two trains daily at 10.52am and 11.34am (Y22, four hours). Trains leave for Guìyáng all day, though departures are more frequent in the afternoons (Y12, two hours). There are hard seats only so the bus is usually much more comfortable and convenient.

Getting Around

Minibus 1 is the most useful – it zips around town from the train station, up Tashan Donglu and on past the Hóngshān Bīnguǎn. Bus 2 travels between the train station and the north bus station. A seat on a bus costs Y1.

AROUND ĀNSHÙN

Longgong Caves 龙宫洞

The **Longgong Caves** (Lónggōng Dòng; Dragon Palace; admission Y120; ⏰ 8.30am-5.30pm) are a vast network of caves that snake through the hills about 23km away from Ānshùn. Despite the elaborateness of the Longgong park site, it represents only a small portion of the cave network. However, like the Huangguoshu Falls area nearby, this region continues to be aggressively developed for tourism – and signs regularly appear pointing the way to modest new 'scenic sights' within the Longgong area.

The **Dragon Palace Cave**, where an underground river winds its way through a huge

---

BUS TIMETABLES

Buses from Ānshùn's long-distance bus station:

Destination	Price	Duration	Frequency	Departs
Guìyáng	Y25	2hr	every 20min	5.30am-9.40pm
Huángguǒshù	Y10	1hr	every 20min	7.30am-5pm
Kūnmíng (sleeper)	Y100-130	17hr	daily	7am & 1pm
Shuǐchéng	Y35	3½hr	hourly	7am-5.30pm
Xīngyì	Y55	5-6hr	hourly	7am-3.30pm
Zūnyì	Y60	7-8hr	hourly	7am-3pm

Buses to the southeast from the stand outside Ānshùn's train station:

Destination	Price	Duration	Frequency	Departs
Fóshān	Y260	19hr	daily	noon
Fúzhōu	Y360	32hr	daily	noon
Guǎngzhōu	Y240	20hr	daily	noon
Shēnzhèn	Y280	22hr	daily	noon
Xiàmén	Y320	28hr	daily	noon

ĀNSHÙN'S OPERATIC CLAIM TO FAME: DÌXÌ

Everyone's heard of Peking opera, and if you've been travelling round the Southwest for a while, you've probably heard or seen Sìchuān opera as well. What few people know is that Ānshùn, too, has its very own version of the art: ground opera.

Called *dìxì* in Chinese, ground, or 'open-air' opera, as it's sometimes also known, dates back to the Ming dynasty. As part of the performance, actors wrap black see-through cloth over their foreheads and don traditional masks made from bamboo shoots. Up to 50 masks may be used in one opera. The colours of the masks are very symbolic: black denotes righteousness, red symbolises loyalty and bravery, while white indicates evil. Blue and green masks are reserved for monsters or particularly nasty bandits. Banners are also worn on the actors' backs to denote rank, as in the Běijīng Opera.

The operas originally served to drive out evil spirits but have merged with local religious dramas and Han classics such as the Romance of Three Kingdoms and History of the Sui and Tang Dynasties. The plots are livened up by gongs, drums, stilts, flags and displays of martial arts to keep the audience's mind from wandering during the slow bits.

The best time to catch ground opera is during festivals, especially the Spring Festival in January or February. Inquire at Guìyáng's CITS (p102) for more information. (Unless you're a Chinese speaker, Ānshùn's CTS, p110, probably won't be very helpful.) Another form of local opera, *nuó*, is practised by the Tujia people of northeastern Guìzhōu. There's a Nuo Opera Museum in Tóngrén.

---

labyrinth of caves, is Longgong's star attraction. To visit, you have to take a guided (Chinese-only) tour on one of the small boats, which lasts about 40 minutes (though in summer the flood of Chinese tour groups causes a watery gridlock that can draw this out substantially). The guides give a little geological background on the caves, but mostly they just point out the various karst formations with their flashlights and let everyone play 'What does it look like?'. The recorded music and coloured spotlights here can feel a bit over the top at times, but most travellers enjoy drifting through the caves anyway.

Most other sights here will be anticlimactic after the Dragon's Cave and many people continue on to Huangguoshu Falls after finishing their boat tour. But if you want to linger, you can follow footpaths to some of the more modest caves or continue on to **Guanyin Cave** (观音洞; Guānyīn Dòng), the second biggest attraction in the park, about 3km away.

GETTING THERE & AWAY
Local buses depart every hour from Ānshùn's west bus station (Y5 to Y10, 30 to 40 minutes, every 20 to 30 minutes from 7am to 5pm). The last bus returns to Anshun at 5pm.

From March to October, minivans to microvans run all day between Lónggōng and Huángguǒshù (Y15 to Y30, 30 minutes, leaving when full. They run infrequently, if at

all, the rest of the year, but there are always plenty of taxis at the Huangguoshu parking lot that you can take. Not as many hover at Longgong, however, so you may need to wait a while or head back to the main road and flag down a bus.

Zhijin Cave 织金洞
The stunning, *Lord of the Rings*–like stalagmite terrain here is otherwise otherworldly, making this **cave** (Zhījīn Dòng; admission Y120; ☺ 8.30am-5.30pm) one of the most interesting sights in Central Guìzhōu.

Located some 15km outside Zhījīn village, the cave is around 10km long and up to 150m high in some places. Calcium deposits have created an abstract landscape of spectacular shapes and spirals, often reaching from floor to ceiling. Moving from tiny passageways to cathedral-like main halls, it's hard not to be impressed.

Tour guides here are compulsory and start with a minimum of 10 people. Solo travellers visiting outside of peak summer months or on Chinese holidays should be prepared for what can be a very, very long wait. While the tour itself is in Chinese only, you'll be glad to have someone around who knows the way back out of the maze of trails. Tours last about three hours on average. Comfortable shoes with a good grip would be a help here as some of the terrain is very steep and can be slick with water.

GETTING THERE & AWAY

A visit to the cave is an easy day trip from Ānshùn as long as you leave first thing in the morning. Buses depart regularly from Ānshùn for Zhījīn (Y24, 2¼ hours, every 45 minutes from 7.45am to 6pm). Once in Zhījīn, buses or minivans will be clamouring to take you the rest of the way to the cave. The trip will take about 20 minutes and cost between Y8 and Y30 depending on your mode of transport and bargaining skills. Between November and February there are few visitors here so a taxi may be your only option. The last bus leaves Zhījīn for Ānshùn at 6pm, though it's best to show up earlier than that to ensure you get a seat.

Huangguoshu Falls 黄果树大瀑布

Perched in a gorge near Huángguǒshù village, the **Huangguoshu Falls** (Huángguǒshù Dà Pùbù; admission Mar-Oct Y90, Nov-Feb Y70; ⏰ 7.30am-6pm) are the biggest in Asia and the most frequently visited sight in Guìzhōu. The Chinese first explored this area in the 1980s, as a preliminary to harnessing the region's hydroelectric potential. They discovered about 18 falls, four subterranean rivers and 100 caves. Many of these features are being turned into scenic sights so it's likely the region around Huángguǒshù will continue to be developed for tourism for years to come.

Reaching a width of 81m and a height of 74m, the rush of water here in the rainy season (May to October) can be monstrously loud and thrilling to see. The cascade is most spectacular about four days after a heavy downpour. The dry season lasts from November to April and during March and April the flow of water can become a less impressive trickle.

The ticket office and entrance to the falls is off a big new parking lot a couple of kilometres outside of Huángguǒshù village. From here a winding footpath leads down into the ravine. It's a lovely descent among leafy green trees, through some modest pavilions and past lots of hawkers in minority dress who will try to get you to pose for pictures at viewpoints along the way.

The path ends at the **Rhinoceros Pool**, a large pond of water at the foot of the falls. Clouds of spray hover here whatever the season, and when the sunlight hits the mist, the resulting rainbows look as though they are shooting out of the water.

Across the bridge and up the footpath you'll reach **Water Curtain Cave**, where you can walk through a tunnel behind the falls and view the water streaming past. During the rainy season this is almost like walking through a shower and can prove treacherous. Good footwear and waterproofs are recommended at any time of year.

Descending the trail at the other side you'll reach Rhinoceros Pool again. From here you can go back the same way you came or follow the trails on either side of the river to the cable car and take that up to the exit. The lane from here is packed with souvenir stands and leads back to the parking lot.

You can do the whole circuit at a fairly relaxed pace and be done within two to three hours on average. The falls are easiest to reach from Ānshùn but can certainly be done as a day trip from Guìyáng, as long as you leave early in the morning.

The **Star Bridge Scenic Area** (天星桥风景区; Tiānxīng Qiáo Fēngjǐngqū; admission Y30; ⏰ 8.30am-6pm) is about 8km away from Huangguoshu. A visit here involves following a path through a pretty swathe of landscape. It's full of caves, waterfalls, ponds, banyan trees and some tight squeezes between the small karst formations along the trail. There's also a footpath of 365 individual stones laid across the land and bodies of water, each with a day of the year carved into it. When you reach the stone with the same date as your birthday, you're supposed to stand on it and make a wish. You can get here by taxi or minivan from the Huangguoshu Falls parking lot.

If Huangguoshu Falls aren't enough, you could also take a taxi or minivan to some of the other waterfalls in the area. The **Steep Slope Falls** (陡坡瀑布; Dǒupō Pùbù) are 105m wide and 23m high and get their name from the crisscross patterning of sloping waters. They are a couple of kilometres north of Huángguǒshù village. One kilometre downstream of the main falls is the **Luositan Falls** (螺蛳滩瀑布; Luósītān Pùbù), which can be reached on foot from the carpark by following the main road south. The **Dishuitan Falls** (滴水滩瀑布; Dīshuǐtān Pùbù) are a cluster of smaller cascades about 45km west of Huángguǒshù that have gotten good reviews from travellers. They are near the village of Lángdài (郎岱).

In addition to its impressive falls, the area around Huángguǒshù provides an excellent chance to ramble through nearby rural minority areas on foot.

GUÌZHŌU

HUANGGUOSHU FALLS
黄果树瀑布

SLEEPING & EATING

The area around the falls is becoming more and more resort-like each year, with big boxy hotels lining the road to the ticket office and plans for even more accommodation are underway. Though appearing quite grand from the outside, much accommodation here is a disappointment once you get a peek in the rooms – mustiness can be a problem and prices are outrageously inflated even in the low season. Hotels are all open during the off-peak period (November to February), but there are so few overnight visitors at this time that the places are virtually empty and the experience can be a little creepy.

Gōngshāng Bīnguǎn (☎ 359 2315; r from Y288) Not far from the ticket office, rooms here are ultra plain but this is the cheapest place on the road to the falls. Bathrooms have Chinese toilets and water heaters, which, if they've been turned on, ensure a hot shower. The staff here are a plus: young and bubbly, they can be very helpful with local info.

Huángguǒshù Bīnguǎn (☎ 359 2110; d from Y488; 🔀) The closest hotel to the ticket office, this is a big rambling building, with a slickly dressed and well-trained staff, though, unfortunately, not the facilities to match. Some floors have tippy-toe views of the falls and the grounds are lovely, but some rooms are damp and nowhere near worth the price they're asking. Be patient if you decide to bargain here – the discounts don't come easy.

There are lots of restaurants and quick eats around the edge of the parking lot, but the better choices (and cheaper prices) are at one of the hole-in-the-wall eateries on the road veering downhill and westward from here.

There are also plenty of restaurants in Huángguǒshù village near the Catholic church if you feel like a walk.

GETTING THERE & AWAY

Buses to the falls run every 20 minutes from Ānshùn's long-distance bus station (Y10, one hour, from 7.30am to 5pm). The route takes you past the turnoff for Longgong Caves, through the messy town of Zhènníng (镇宁) and around the winding streets of Huángguǒshù village, before letting you off at the parking lot in front of the falls' ticket office.

From Guìyáng, buses to Huángguǒshù leave every 40 minutes from the long-distance bus station (Y30 to Y40, 2½ hours, 7.10am to noon). Guìyáng-bound buses from Xīngyì will also drop you off at the falls.

Leaving the falls, buses for Ānshùn leave when full from the parking lot (Y10, one hour, 7am to 6pm). Guìyáng-bound buses also leave from the parking lot when full between 7am and 6pm (Y35, three hours).

The falls' parking lot is also packed with taxis and microvans for hire. In the peak season, you'll often find minivans shuttling back and forth all day between Huángguǒshù and Longgong Caves.

Huangguoshu Airport only handles flights from Guǎngzhōu (Y890, four weekly) so it won't be of interest to most travelling the Southwest, though flights to and from Kūnmíng and other destinations are likely to be added.

Shítouzhài 石头寨

This **Bouyi village** (admission Y15) isn't far from Huangguoshu Falls and the friendliness of the inhabitants is as much a reason to visit as its lovely setting.

Over 600 years old, this little hamlet is packed with small stone houses, cobbled lanes and friendly locals. Everyone here who isn't farming seems to somehow be involved in batik production, and you may be invited into a villager's home to watch the process. Thankfully, the selling hasn't gotten too aggressive and for the most part you can browse in peace until you see something you like.

This is becoming a popular stop for Chinese tourists and you can see efforts are being made to spruce the place up for travellers; some of the village equipment has bilingual signs explaining its use and the ponds across the street from the village have been landscaped and are dotted with a couple of small waterwheels.

An hour or two would be more than enough to see it all, and a stop here is a pleasant diversion either on your way to or back from Huangguoshu Falls. However, the karst-studded landscape surrounding Shítouzhài is lovely and some travellers may consider hanging around to explore some of the villages spotting the nearby hills or to do some of the lovely walks that would be possible in the area.

SLEEPING & EATING

There's only one guesthouse here open year-round, but others are under construction and should be accepting guests by the time you read this.

Shítouzhài Jǐngqū Zhāodàisuǒ (石头寨景区招待所; ☎ 1376-536 4841; d/tr with shared bathroom Y60/90) Just a few metres inside the village gates and run by a lovely family, this place has simple beds in dark wood rooms. The wooden floors are disturbingly creaky but the shared bathrooms and showers are clean and modern. A single room with a Ming-style 'antique' bed costs Y150.

There's a couple of small restaurants here too, but they are only open in high season months (roughly April to September).

GETTING THERE & AWAY

To get here, take a Huángguǒshù-bound bus from Ānshùn and tell the driver you're going to Shítouzhài (Y5 to Y8, 30 to 40 minutes). You'll be let off at a road forking away from the main highway. Follow the road for about 2km until you reach Shítouzhài. You'll know when you have arrived by the landscaping: there will be a pond with a waterwheel on the right, and, just afterwards, a clutch of stone houses on your left where you'll find the village entrance.

To leave, walk back to the fork in the road. If you're continuing on to Huángguǒshù, most buses heading west will pass the falls; if you're going to Ānshùn, flag down any bus heading eastward.

Other Traditional Villages

If you're interested in visiting still more traditional villages and have plenty of time to endure local transport, you can head out to **Lóujiāzhuāng** (娄家庄), a Miao village 23km northeast of Ānshùn, **Lángdài** (郎岱), 45km west of Huángguǒshù, or **Bawan**, about 50km west of Ānshùn (just south of the Ānshùn–Liùzhī road). Both Lángdài and Bawan are Bouyi villages.

WESTERN GUÌZHŌU

Guìzhōu's west is a mystery to most foreigners, but it has some lovely natural sights that are enticing increasing numbers of travellers to discover the region.

If you're jonesing for a glimpse of the endangered black-necked crane, Wēiníng's Caohai Lake is a hallowed sight for bird-watchers. Further south, some travellers rate a trip to the silvery, thread-thin waterfalls at Xīngyì's Malling Gorge as preferable to the commercialism of Ānshùn's thundering Huangguoshu Falls.

Roads and infrastructure here have improved enormously in recent years, speeding up travel times immensely; there's a small but sleek modern airport in Xīngyì and the road up to Wēiníng is flawlessly smooth.

However, elements of Guìzhōu's 'wild west' reputation remain and there's still a lot here to attract intrepid travellers: English is not spoken at all, foreigners in rural areas will stop traffic and there are real opportunities for off-the-beaten-track exploration of the minority villages.

Many sub-branches of the Miao (Hmong) live here, including the Long-Horned Miao around Liùzhī, named after their enormous protruding hairstyles; the Flowery Miao in the northwest around Wēiníng; and the Black Miao and Bouyi in the southwest around Xīngrén and Xīngyì.

This swath of Guìzhōu is also worth considering as an alternative, little-travelled route to Yúnnán. There are connections to Kūnmíng from Xīngyì and via Xuānwēi from Wēiníng.

WĒINÍNG 威宁

☎ 0857 / pop 57,000

Wēiníng is a rugged little town a couple of kilometres away from Caohai Lake (Cǎohǎi Hú), one of China's premier bird-watching sites.

Though there's not much to see in the town itself, the population is a mix of Han, Miao, Hui and Yi minorities, so there's plenty of atmosphere. A large market is held here every three or four days, which is attended by the Flowery Miao. Evidence of the Hui includes a modern mosque in the north of town and several Muslim restaurants nearby.

There are also remote minority villages in the region, most interesting if you can hunt down a market or festival that may be going on. While not worth the trip to Wēiníng on their own, intrepid travellers may enjoy getting out and exploring some of them and getting to know a bit of the countryside.

Though the centre of town is usually full of life and has a unique energy you just don't feel elsewhere in Guìzhōu, this is still one of the most backward areas in the province. The social problems that go along with that kind of poverty are never far from the surface in Wēiníng.

Caohai Lake 草海湖

Even if it weren't the premier sight for bird-watching in China, Caohai Lake (Grass Sea Lake; Cǎohǎi Hú) would be pretty spectacular. This 20-sq-km freshwater wetland glimmers about 2km away from Wēiníng's central core and when the sun hits the water just so, the effect is gorgeous.

The lake became a national nature reserve in 1992 and is an important wintering site

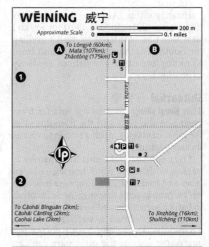

for many migratory birds, the most famous of which is the black-necked crane. The lake is considered a wetland because its average depth is only 2m. Grasses cover 60% of the lake, giving rise to the name Cǎohǎi or Grass Sea.

The lake has a fragile history. It once fed into the Yangzi River (Cháng Jiāng) and has even disappeared several times in the last 3000 years. It was drained during the Great Leap Forward and then again during the Cultural Revolution in order to provide farmland. The experiment was a miserable failure and the land was unusable. The lake was refilled in 1980, but government tinkering with water levels in ensuing years continued to impact both the local environment and villagers' livelihoods.

The government has poured millions of yuán into lake conservation ever since, but some pressing problems remain. Almost a third of Wēiníng's sewage runs into the lake and more than 20,000 people live in the reserve. To encourage local interest in park conservation, some villagers have been hired as park workers, a conservation education programme has been set up and grants have been made available to farmers who wish to set up alternative businesses. One plan for sustainable development involves ecotourism or, more to the point, you.

Boaters and touts will mob you as soon as you arrive at the path down to the lake, offering you a punt around to show you the birds. The official price is Y60 per hour per boat, though you'll have to bargain hard to get them down from starting prices of Y100 or more per person.

Though it's still not possible to walk the entire lake circumference without eventually ending up in patches of swampland, there are extensive trails a good part of the way around. As the cranes often roost quite close to the shore, this is another pleasant way to see the birds and the cacophony of their calls can be fantastic.

Be aware that if you turn down the touts and boaters and decide to walk round the lake instead, they may not leave you alone for the rest of your visit. They have a James Bond–like ability to show up wherever you are in Wēiníng to continue the haggle: your hotel in the morning, the kebab stand in the evening, the bus station as you're trying to leave town.

The lake is particularly beautiful at dusk when the jagged Wumeng Mountain Range frames the silvery sunset. The elevation here is higher though, so bring warm clothes for the cold nights.

The best time to visit the lake is December to March, when the birds are wintering. During this time the northwest enjoys much better weather than the rest of Guìzhōu and there are often clear blue skies in Wēiníng when visibility in nearby Shuǐchéng is down to 200m. However, snow and ice frequently close the road winding up through the hills from Shuǐchéng to Wēiníng, so if you're on a tight schedule it's best to build a couple of extra days into your itinerary just in case the weather doesn't cooperate.

Once you get there, you don't need more than one full day in Wēiníng to explore the lake, but many hard-core bird-watchers or nature-lovers may certainly choose to stay longer.

To get here, you can either walk the 2km from the town centre or take a taxi. Wēiníng's taxis are unmetered so ask how much it will cost first; usually Y3, the fare is sometimes rounded up to Y5 for foreigners. Be careful when you're in the taxis: they're usually dilapidated nightmares and the doors often fly open when the driver takes a corner.

Sleeping

Accommodation in Wēiníng is extremely basic and a lot of times, startlingly unclean. If you're looking for dorm accommodation there's a lot of zhāodàisuǒ (basic lodgings) near the main intersection by the bus station, but conditions can get pretty dirty.

Cǎohǎi Bīnguǎn (草海宾馆; ☎ 622 1511; s/d/tr Y85/50/60) Right on the road, near the path to the lake, the location here is ideal. Rooms are big, have incredibly high ceilings and are furnished with heavy, dark-brown beds, tables and chairs. There's toilets and sinks in each room but showers are communal. The staff here aren't particularly friendly (and often extremely hard to find) but are a pretty good source of local information once you've pinned them down. If you've never been to the hotel before you are likely to walk right by it without even noticing; a taxi from the bus station is your best bet (Y3 to Y5).

Hēijīnghè Bīnguǎn (☎ 622 9306; 18 Jianshe Lu; 建设路18 号; s Y88-128, d Y168) Despite damp, cold rooms and wall stains, this big rambling hotel is the best accommodation in town. Central heating sputters to life with varying degrees of success between 9pm and 10pm. To get here, turn right out of the bus station and cross the intersection. Walk for about half a block and you'll see the hotel on your left.

Eating

There's not a lot of restaurants in town though it's heaving with little four- or five-table hole-in-the-wall eateries. There's a significant Hui population here, so the beef noodles are a consistently tasty dish – try the Muslim restaurants near the mosque.

Cǎohǎi Cāntīng (草海餐厅; dishes from Y5) About 200m east of Cǎohǎi Bīnguǎn, this is a cheap and friendly restaurant, convenient if you are on your way to or from the lake where there are not a lot of places to chow down.

The intersection near Xinhua Bookshop and the long-distance bus station has several hole-in-the-wall stir-fry places as well.

GUÌZHŌU

BIRD-WATCHING ON THE GRASS SEA

Caohai Lake is one of the best places to bird-watch in China; in fact, the World Wide Fund for Nature (WWF) has listed it as one of the top 10 bird-watching destinations in the world.

Up to 100,000 birds winter at the lake between December and March, with 179 different species having been recorded. These include a number of protected species, such as black-necked and hooded cranes, black and white storks, golden and imperial eagles, white-tailed sea eagles, Eurasian cranes and white spoonbills. More common birds easily spotted at the lake include the bar-headed goose, Eurasian widgeon, common pochard, Eurasian coot and black-headed gull.

The lake's star attraction is the black-necked crane. The least known of the 15 types of crane, it is listed by the IUCN (World Conservation Union) as vulnerable, with a global population of around 6000. The birds breed at high altitudes in Tibet, Qīnghǎi and western Sìchuān, and then spend the winter basking in the relative warmth of southern Tibet and the Yúnnán–Guìzhōu plateau. It is thought one important local migration route takes birds from Caohai Lake to Zöigê in northern Sìchuān. Four hundred black-necked cranes currently winter at the lake – the highest number ever recorded and a great improvement on the mid-1970s, when numbers plummeted to only 35.

The cranes have little fear of people and you can often approach to within 10m without disturbing them. Perhaps part of the reason for this is that cranes have long enjoyed an exalted place in Chinese culture as a symbol of happiness and good fortune. You may see statues of cranes in many of China's imperial palaces, such as the Forbidden City in Běijīng.

China's Southwest has several other important crane wintering sites at Dashanbao, Bitahai, Nàpà Hǎi and Huìzé in neighbouring Yúnnán, but Caohai Lake remains by far the easiest and best place to spot them.

The Tuoda Forest, 60km northwest of Caohai Lake, has been set aside as a nature reserve for the protection of the endangered Reeves' pheasant. This bird is unique to China, but owing to widespread deforestation its numbers have declined in recent years and its total population is probably no more than 5000. The male has striking plumage in autumnal golds and browns boldly crisscrossed with black and white; its tail can be up to three times its body length.

Tuoda is a plantation of deciduous and evergreen trees that provides safe feeding and nesting for the pheasants. However, despite its protected status, Tuoda continues to suffer from illegal clearing; recent visitors reported only saplings of oak and pine where once a mature forest supported a good diversity of birds. Reeves' pheasant appears to hang on in Tuoda, but parts of the forest are being converted to agriculture, which almost certainly means local extinction of the bird.

Getting There & Away

Wēiníng's bus station is a broken-down mess and it's hard to believe a place this small can get so chaotic.

From Guìyáng, there's one bus daily to Wēiníng (Y80, seven hours, 9am). If that bus is cancelled (which occurs frequently during winter), you can go to the surprisingly large, modernising city of Shuǐchéng (水城; Y55, 3½ to four hours, every 30 minutes from 7am to 5pm), and from there get a bus the rest of the way to Wēiníng (Y30 to Y40, three to four hours, 9am and noon).

Coming back from Wēiníng, the Guìyáng-bound bus leaves daily at 8.30am. There's no direct bus from Wēiníng to southern Guìzhōu, but if you don't want to backtrack through Guìyáng, take the bus to Shuǐchéng, from where buses leave daily for Xīngyì (Y82, six hours, 8.30am and noon), though by all accounts this may not be the most comfortable ride you've ever been on.

If you want to head to Yúnnán from Wēiníng, a bus goes south to Xuānwēi (Y25, eight hours, 7.30am and 9am). If you catch the 7.30am bus to Xuānwēi, you'll arrive just in time to catch the last bus to Kūnmíng (Y40, eight hours) at 3.30pm, although it's a lot of travelling to do in one day. From Wēiníng, there is also a sleeper bus to Kūnmíng (Y90, 16 hours, 5.30pm).

Alternatively, take the morning bus to Zhāotōng (Y20, three hours, 7.20am and 8am), from where you can hop over to Xīchāng in southern Sìchuān and connect with the Kūnmíng–Chéngdū train line.

AROUND WĒINÍNG

Wēiníng is useful as a base to visit remote Yi and Miao villages in the region, though you'll really have to rough it as facilities are very limited in this area.

If you want to explore, locals recommend **Lóngjiē** (龙街), 60km northwest of Wēiníng. The town of **Jīnzhōng** (金钟), 16km east on the road to Shuǐchéng (水城), is also said to have a great market every three or four days.

On the 5th of the fifth lunar month there is **horse racing** in some Yi villages around Wēiníng and a **Flower Dance Festival** at Mata, featuring crossbow shooting and antiphonal singing. Mata is 107km northwest of Wēiníng and buses to Yúnguì and Lóngjiē pass nearby.

You can reach any of these villages by minibus from the long-distance bus station. Prices depend on the number of travellers they've got and bargaining skills.

These areas are rarely visited by even domestic travellers, let alone foreigners, so it can be extremely difficult to get information and dates on these festivals except from locals once you arrive. (Dates are often also decided locally from year to year.) If you're keen, however, you can contact the Guìyáng CITS (p102), tell the staff what you are interested in and they may be able to ferret out the info for you.

XĪNGYÌ 兴义

☎ 0859 / pop 120,400

Xīngyì doesn't seem like much at first glance. However, the area has become an important gold mining centre (it's the 10th largest gold producer in all of China) and new finds have multiplied the amount of drilling and mineral exploitation in the region. Xīngyì now has one of the more affluent populations in Guìzhōu and that, coupled with the new airport and improved roads, is giving the city a pleasant mini-boom. Unfortunately, despite the development, the city itself is still a bit of a bore, (everything more or less shuts down completely by dark), but the surrounding scenery is definitely worth a visit and the weather here is some of the mildest in Guìzhōu.

Xīngyì is mainly populated by Han Chinese and Hui Muslims, though the surrounding villages are largely made up of Black Miao and Bouyi. Foreign travellers are more or less unheard of here. It's not so easy to suss out local markets and festivals; even the few Xīngyì locals involved in the tourism industry may give you blank looks when you ask (see p123 for more info).

Information

INTERNET ACCESS

Internet access is available from any one of the internet cafés along the upper floor of the ring of buildings surrounding the town's Central Plaza.

MONEY

The **Bank of China** (Zhōngguó Yínháng; Yunnan Donglu; ⊙ 8am-6pm) near Chuanyundong Park will change travellers cheques Monday to Friday in the early morning and in the late afternoon. However, it is not used to foreigners so the transaction may be a long and painful one. Luckily, there's an ATM outside.

POST

You can post your letters from the main China Post office, a five-minute walk northwest of the Pánjiāng Bīnguǎn.

TOURIST INFORMATION

Everything in Xīngyì is geared towards Chinese group tours and there is zilch here to help independent travellers. Even the few local guides have a hard time nailing down festival dates unless they have a long, loooooong lead time. Your best source of travel information for Xīngyì is Guìyáng's CITS (p102); make contact well in advance of your travel dates so the staff has some time to research festivals and the like for you.

Sights & Activities

The most interesting area of town lies in the pedestrian alleys and side streets northeast of **Chuanyundong Park** (Chuānyúndòng Gōngyuán; admission Y1.50; ⊙ dawn-dusk) and leading to the **central plaza** (jiēxīn huāyuán). The central plaza and the small riverside square across from the park are popular meeting places for locals, especially in the evenings.

Chuanyundong Park itself is on the drab side and not really worth your time. The most worthwhile sights in this area are outside Xīngyì city (see p123).

Sleeping

Plenty of budget hotels line the streets around the various bus stations. Service is generally quite friendly but the facilities aren't always the cleanest. Xīngyì's top-end hotel market

GUÌZHŌU

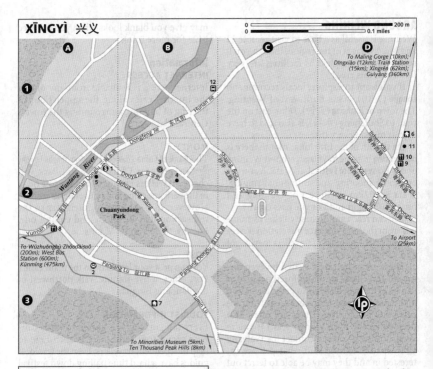

XĪNGYÌ 兴义

is booming thanks to the new airport; these are all centred just outside the city core. The midrange category is the only segment not so well served here.

Wǔzhuāngbù Zhāodàisuǒ (武装部招待所; ☎ 322 4243; 92 Yunnan Jie; 云南街92号; 4-/3-bed dm Y10/15, r Y60, r with shared bathroom Y25-40) The family that runs this hotel is so cheery and kind that they make

staying here worth considering, even if at first glance the facilities might put you off. Rooms will likely be among the most spartan you'll encounter on your trip (they can get damp and drafty in cold weather, too), but it's about the only place along this drag that was enthusiastically accepting foreigners at the time of research. It's also useful if your bus is arriving late or leaving early from the west bus station. There's no name on the sign; look for the bright blue awning with yellow characters.

Pánjiāng Bīnguǎn (☎ 322 3456, ext 8118; 4 Panjiang Xilu; 盘江西路4号; dm/s/d/tr Y50/280/380/380) This hotel is still the most frequent destination in the city for tour groups, meaning its rooms can be booked solid, even in nonpeak periods. Rooms are the generic but comfortable variety you find at such high-volume Chinese hotels, but, at the moment, this is still probably the best midrange option in the city.

Aviation Hotel (Hángkōng Jiǔdiàn; ☎ 312 6666; fax 312 6668; Ruijin Lu; 瑞金路; d incl breakfast Y680; 🖥) Still the best top-end choice in town, this hotel is popular with people visiting for business. It's reliably run, although somewhat inconveniently located on the edge of town.

Eating

Xīngyì residents are the first to admit it: though the town's scenery is terrific, the restaurant scene has a way to go. (As one local resident told us, 'Restaurants? There are many. Are they good? Hmm…not so much.') However, there are some snack foods Xīngyì is well known for that are worth tasting, including *gàngzi miàn* (杠子面), a tasty egg-noodle dish, and *jīròu tāng yuán* (鸡肉汤圆), a soup of small rice dumplings filled with spicy chicken and served in a peppery broth. *Yáng ròu fěn* (羊肉粉; lamb noodles) and *jīdàn gāo* (鸡蛋糕; simple egg cake) are also popular dishes here.

Two of the best places to try some of these dishes are right next door to each other.

Zōu Jīròu Tāngyuán (Ruijin Lu; 瑞金路; dumpling soup Y2-5; noodles small Y3-5, large Y5-7; ☯ 8am-late afternoon) Workers from the nearby shopping centres and businesses flock to this hole-in-the-wall restaurant to fill up on *jīròu tāng yuán* at lunchtime. In addition to serving the hordes, the staff always seems to be busy preparing pickled radishes, huge jars of which sit around the restaurant. Do like the locals do and dump them in the broth to eat with the little rice dumplings.

Laogang Zi Noodle Shop (Lǎogàngzi Miànfáng; ☎ 323 2001; Ruijin Lu; 瑞金路; noodles small Y3-5, large Y5-7; ☯ 8am-4pm or 5pm) Besides the ever popular *gàngzi miàn* there's a list of nine other tasty chicken and beef noodle dishes to try. This simple restaurant has an English sign outside.

There are bakeries (*miànbāo fáng*) all over downtown; one of the best is on the corner of Yunnan Jie and Panjiang Lu.

Getting There & Around

AIR

Xīngyì's new airport is tiny but gleaming. It's a 15- to 20-minute drive from town and the only way to get to or from it is by taxi. The rate will depend on your driver so establish the price before you get in. Many drivers ask for Y15, though don't be surprised if you are hit for as much as Y50.

There are daily services between Guìyáng and Xīngyì (Y1200, 40 minutes), usually two afternoon flights going in both directions. There's also two night flights (again going both ways) between Xīngyì and Shēnzhèn, in Guǎngdōng province, every Thursday and Sunday (Y1050, 35 minutes). New roads between here and Yúnnán have made bus travel so quick and comfortable, the Xīngyì–Kūnmíng flights have been discontinued.

You can buy tickets from **Dàlǐ Guónèi Jīpiào** (☎ 312 0888; 55 Ruijin Lu; ☯ 8am-6pm), right outside the Aviation Hotel.

BUS

There are several bus stations in town, and you may be dropped at any one of them upon your arrival. The **east bus station** (kèyùn dōngzhàn; Hunan Jie) has daily services to Guìyáng (Y92.50, six hours, every 40 to 50 minutes from 8am to 6pm). The same bus will drop you off at Ānshùn (Y65.50, four hours), Huángguǒshù (Y53.50, five hours) or Xìngrén (Y16.50, 45 to 60 minutes). Outside the east bus station are minibuses for Zhēnfēng and Ānlóng.

The west bus station has services to Kūnmíng (Y91.50 to Y109.50, three to five hours, 8am and 8pm). If you're going to the Stone Forest at Shílín in Yúnnán, you can get off the bus a couple of hours before Kūnmíng and save yourself doubling back.

There are also buses to Shuǐchéng (Y82, six hours, 10am, noon and 4pm), where you can spend the night before heading on to Wēiníng for Caohai Lake.

From Guìyáng, there are buses to Xīngyì (Y70 to Y80, 6½ hours, hourly from 9am to 6pm) departing from the Tǐyùguǎn bus station. From Ānshùn there are also hourly buses to Xīngyì (Y55, five to six hours, from 7am to 3.30pm).

TAXI

Xīngyì is a sprawling town and taxis are much quicker and more efficient for getting around than the city buses. The flag fall is Y5.

TRAIN

Xīngyì's nearest train station is 15km northeast of town at Dǐngxiào (顶效). Buses will take you there for Y10 from outside Xīngyì's east bus station.

Five trains leave daily for Kūnmíng departing at 6.10am, 8.13am, 8.40am, 2.15pm and 3.41pm. They take six to seven hours and cost Y100. Trains also stop here en route to Nánníng at 5.01am, 8.20am, 9.16am, 9.33am and 11.42pm (Y120, seven hours).

AROUND XĪNGYÌ

If you want to visit all the following places in one day, a taxi or car hired through your accommodation will likely cost around Y300.

GUÌZHŌU

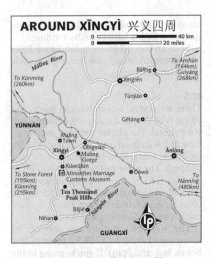

AROUND XĪNGYÌ 兴义四周

Minorities Marriage Customs Museum 民族婚俗博物馆

Set up in a lovely courtyard-style building that was once home to a local Qing officer, the exhibits at this **museum** (Mínzú Hūnsú Bówùguǎn; admission Y15; ✆ 8am-6pm) focus on the clothing and courting rituals of Guìzhōu's minorities.

Some of the displays have English captions but are too bizarrely translated to make much sense; some sound downright naughty (eg 'Girls control their pleasure sowing seeds of love on the village road'.)

Because of this, a little Chinese language skill here would definitely help. However, as many of the rituals are depicted through photographs, anyone with a keen interest in the province's minorities will still enjoy the objects and outfits.

An intriguing ritual to keep an eye out for involves parents drilling holes in their daughter's room so suitors can come and sing to her at night. Once the girl has chosen her man, the holes are sealed up to show the village that the girl is no longer available. Another more disturbing ritual involves a young couple pulling apart a chicken. The direction of the chicken's eyes at the end will tell the families whether the match is a good one (if the eyes go in the same direction) or a bad one (if the eyes are looking in different directions).

The museum is about a 10-minute ride from the centre of Xīngyì and makes a nice diversion on your way to or from Ten Thousand Peak Hills.

You can get to the museum with a taxi or on city bus 1. It's sometimes closed during the day for lunch, so early morning or late afternoon is the best time to catch it open.

Ten Thousand Peak Hills 万峰陵

The karst landscape to the south of Xīngyì is called **Ten Thousand Peak Hills** (Wànfēnglíng; ✆ 334 2299; admission Y61; ✆ 8am-6pm) and the short rolling karst formations of this area seemingly go on forever.

The scenic spot (often called 'the Stone Forest' by locals) is actually just a section where a fancy road has been built around the hills, the various views and karst formations have been given spiffy names, and a ticket booth has been set up. If you arrive by taxi or bus, you'll be ferried around the sight in a golf-cart like touring vehicle while a guide points out the various formations to you, explaining how they change depending on where you are located. (If visiting in cool weather, bring lots of warm clothing: the carts have roofs but no walls so it can get very, very cold.) You can easily make your way around in 30 to 40 minutes.

If you've hired a car for the day and want to see the area in your own vehicle, you can do that, too, although if you have that chance, you'd probably be best to save the admission fee and just ask your driver to spend the day driving you into the hills and stopping at whatever village piques your interest. The Bouyi villages in this area are particularly interesting so you could do some great walks.

You can get to Ten Thousand Peaks either by taxi or on city bus 1.

Maling Gorge 马岭河峡谷

The precarious plunge of **Maling Gorge** (Mǎlínghé Xiágǔ; admission Y60; ✆ 8am-6pm) contains some of the loveliest scenery in Guìzhōu province. Narrow streams of silver water plunge over its sides, and the clouds of spray bouncing on the rocks below look like shattered crystal glass from certain angles. The area is lush with foliage and the walls of the gorge are pocked with exotic calcium formations.

Though becoming more and more popular during the summer, outside of this period the gorge is still a peaceful and quiet place. Many travellers prefer it to Huangguoshu Falls.

From the ticket gate, follow the newly laid stone trail down into the gorge. The trails are well marked and you can spend the better part of a day exploring the waterfalls and caves, crisscrossing the bridges in a loose loop, eventually returning to a steep staircase back up to the parking lot.

A cable car was under construction here at the time of research and should be open by summer 2008.

With the copious amounts of water and mist in the gorge, the trails can become extremely slippery and treacherous, especially during the rainy season. Sturdy shoes and waterproofs are essential. You may also want to bring a torch for the tunnels.

Rafting is becoming a bigger and bigger drawcard here and the activity is offered from roughly March to September, though it completely depends on the water levels and how cold it may be. Don't expect epic whitewater rafting here, as it's a slow descent. The longest route lasts about two hours. All equipment is provided and trips cost roughly Y160 per person. Just follow the signs on the trails to the rafting points.

You can get here either by taxi or on city bus 5. You can also come back on city bus 5, though it is often just as easy to get out on the main road and flag down whatever long-distance bus may be heading into town.

Minority Villages, Festivals & Markets

The region around Xīngyì has plenty of festivals and markets, though at the moment the lack of tourism development in this area means that finding out about them beforehand is challenging, even for locals. The upside is that intrepid travellers will have a ball jumping on and off minibuses to explore.

The **Chabai Singing Festival** takes place on the 21st of the sixth lunar month in a vacant field a few kilometres north of Dīngxiào, just off the main road to Xīngrén. The thwarted ardour of the lovers Cha and Bai is marked by an antiphonal singing contest and an improvised love song competition. The celebration draws not just the locals, but also Bouyi people from nearby Yúnnán and Guǎngxī.

As for markets, you can check out the villages around the little town of **Xīngrén** (兴仁), 45 minutes from Xīngyì (buses leave from Xīngyì's east bus station every 40 to 50 minutes).

Again, though, it's best if you can get a local to find out whether a market is actually going on, because otherwise the villages will be pretty deserted and of not much interest to travellers. **Bālíng** (巴铃), a village 21km east of Xīngrén on the road to Ānshùn, has a reputation for hosting an interesting market every six days that's frequented mainly by Black Miao and Bouyi people.

Other villages with markets every six to eight days include **Túnjiǎo** (屯脚), 18km towards Ānlóng from Xīngrén, and **Gētáng** (戈塘), 41km towards Ānlóng, then 9km west of the main road.

You can get to any of these villages by minivan from Xīngrén.

EASTERN GUÌZHŌU

The rough terrain of eastern Guìzhōu is minority territory and doing a circuit through the area's villages can be one of the most thrilling parts of visiting China's Southwest. No matter what time you come, something, somewhere will be going on, whether it's a colourful market or loud and boisterous festival.

Formerly the stomping ground of intrepid travellers, increasing numbers of people have discovered the region, and much of it can't really be considered off-the-beaten track any more – several of the villages, now wealthy from tourist dollars, are getting pretty slick.

Over 13 different minorities live in the region, technically known as the Qiandongnan Miao and Dong Autonomous Prefecture. Their diversity is fascinating and everything from their languages to their architecture to their food to their dress is different from what you'd see in 'Han' China. The main groups you'll encounter are the Dong, Shui, Miao and Gejia. The landscape, too, is striking, with its lush forests, undulating hills and rice terraces.

If your time is limited, then there are many interesting villages that can be reached as a day trip from Kǎilǐ. If you have more time, it's possible to explore a number of Miao villages in a loop northeast of Kǎilǐ, limiting the amount of backtracking you'll have to do. A journey southeast into Dong territory can also take you in a loop from Róngjiāng, eventually bringing you back to Kǎilǐ or across the border into Guǎngxī province. Zhènyuǎn, Xījiāng and Zhàoxìng are all villages and towns that are definitely worth a visit, and it's worthwhile planning your trip around at least one of the local festivals. In summer, you might also visit Fanjing Shan Nature Reserve, near Guìzhōu's eastern border.

GUÌZHŌU

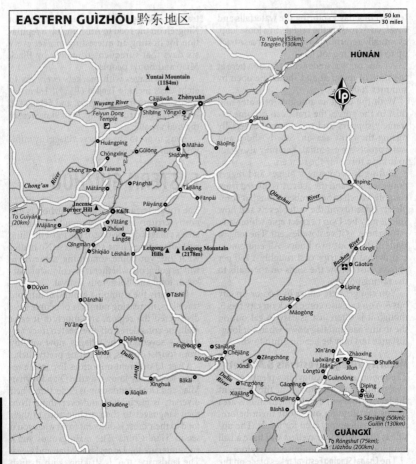

EASTERN GUÌZHŌU 黔东地区

Festivals & Events

Kǎilǐ and surrounding villages host a large number of minority festivals – over 130 annually. February in particular is dominated by more than two weeks of *lúshēng* festivals, held successively in villages in the Zhōi area. The Miao New Year is celebrated around the region, especially in Lángdé and Xījiāng, in the 10th lunar month. Approximate Western dates for the main festivals are given on p101.

KǍILǏ 凯里

☎ 0855 / pop 153,000

Kǎilǐ is the gateway to the fantastic minority territory of eastern Guìzhōu, one of Southwest China's travel highlights. Not much goes on in the city itself but it serves as an excellent base from which to explore the area's Miao and Dong villages. You can either set up in Kǎilǐ and do some day trips, or use it as a launching point for village-hopping your way southeast into Guǎngxī.

Kǎilǐ is about 195km almost directly east of Guìyáng.

Information

Bank of China (Zhōngguó Yínháng; Shaoshan Nanlu) Changes cash, travellers cheques and offers cash advances on credit cards. There is also an ATM here. A second branch on Beijing Donglu will also change cash.

China International Travel Service (CITS; Zhōngguó Guójì Lǚxíngshè; ☎ 822 2506; 53 Yingpan Donglu; ⏰ 9am-5.30pm) If only every CITS in China was like this one! Staff here are universally helpful and have fluent English, French and Japanese speakers. The place for information on minority villages, festivals, markets and organised tours.

China Post (Zhōngguó Yóuzhèng; cnr Shaoshan Beilu & Beijing Donglu) Make international phone calls on 2nd floor.

Internet Café (Wǎngbā; Shaoshan Nanlu; per hr Y2, deposit Y10; 24hr) Near the Kailai Hotel, there's over 100 computers here. If video game–playing locals are camped out at all of them, there's another internet café on Beijing Lu. The Beijing Lu café has a 7-Up sign outside and computers downstairs.

Public Security Bureau (PSB; Gōngānjú; ☎ 853 6113; 26 Yongle Lu; 8.30-11.30am & 2.30-5.30pm Mon-Fri) Deals with all passport and visa inquiries.

Sights & Activities

The only formal sight in Kǎilǐ is its **Minorities Museum** (Guìzhōu Mínzú Bówùguǎn; 宁波路; Ningbo Lu), set up on the 3rd and 4th floors of a large renovated building in the south of town. You'll find maps, examples of minority costumes and other artefacts relating to Guìzhōu's people. Though officially open from 8am to 5pm, the doors are often locked whatever time you turn up. Even so, you can still get a distant look at some of the exhibits from the landing on top of the staircase.

Go back down to the 1st floor of the same building and you can stroll the five dozen or so souvenir stalls set up to hawk minority goods.

Elsewhere, Kǎilǐ has two parks: **Dage Park** (Dàgé Gōngyuán; Big Pagoda Park) is in the north of town, while further southeast, **Jinquanhu Park** (Jīnquánhú Gōngyuán) has a Dong minority drum tower built in 1985.

There's also a **market** on Shaoshan Beilu that, when busy, can be quite interesting.

Festivals & Events

Festivals are one of Guìzhōu's major drawcards and the profusion of them around Kǎilǐ makes this sleepy town the best place to base yourself for exploring them. There is also a huge number of markets held in the villages surrounding Kǎilǐ. Xīnhuá has a huge market every six to seven days. Zhōuxī, Léishān and Táijiāng hold markets every six days. Dates and suggestions are available from the fabulous Kǎilǐ CITS.

Sleeping

Shíyóu Bīnguǎn (☎ 823 4331; 44 Yingpan Donglu; 营盘东路44号; dm/s/d/tr Y26/Y80/120/120) The town's long-time budget favourite, the staff at this hotel are young and friendly. It also has a good location close to both the main bus station and the CITS office. This place is probably a better choice for late-spring to early-autumn stays, as the rooms can get really cold and drafty when the weather cools outside. During major festivals, the dorms and singles fill up very quickly so it's a good idea to reserve ahead.

Guótài Dàjiǔdiàn (☎ 826 9888; fax 826 9818; 6 Beijing Donglu; 北京东路6号; s Y238, d Y258-288) Decorated in blues and greens, the rooms here are quite attractive. This hotel is a popular choice for foreign midrange travellers, despite lethargic, world-weary service.

Kǎilái Jiǔdiàn (☎ 827 7888; fax 827 7666; 21 Shaoshan Nanlu; 韶山南路21号; s/d incl breakfast Y388/328) A favourite with business people and Chinese travellers, this hotel is always pretty crowded and hectic. Rooms are blandly decorated but quite comfortable despite a mould problem beginning in several of the rooms' bathrooms. The buffet breakfast is OK but runs out pretty quickly, so best get down as early as possible for the full selection.

Eating

Snack food is all over Kǎilǐ including crepes, potato patties, barbecues, tofu grills, noodles, hotpot, *shuǐjiǎo* (水饺; Chinese ravioli) and wonton soup. The collection of stalls and eateries on the corner of Yingpan Donglu and Wenhua Beilu are some of the most popular with travellers. Further south, there's a lane heading east off Zhaoshan Nanlu where all kinds of grill and snack stalls set up in the evening; it's worth checking out.

Also check out the alcove off Beijing Donglu, where cafés and restaurants with names such as Bobo and Happy serve up Chinese- and Western-style food with varying degrees of success.

Wàngjiǎo Cāntīng (Beijing Xilu; 北京西路; dishes from Y3; 9am-8pm) Hidden way up on the 3rd floor of a humungous department store, this cafeteria-style eatery is a fun place to eat. Clean and modern, its speciality is all kinds of little snacks, and best of all for those who don't speak Chinese, a lot of the dishes are on display. All you need to do is point to what looks interesting and pretty soon you'll have your own personal feast. There's also a similar place diagonally across from here on the 4th floor of the New Century Plaza shopping

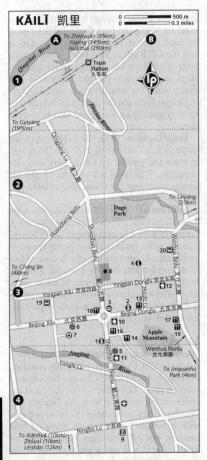

KǍILǏ 凯里

0 .... 500 m
0 .... 0.3 miles

To Zhènyuǎn (85km);
Yùpíng (145km);
Huáihuà (290km)

Qīngshuǐ River

🚉 Train
Station
火车站

Jīnzhòu River

To Guìyáng
(195km)

Qīnglóng Lù 清龙路

To Táijiāng
(25km)

Dage
Park

Huánchéng Beilu

To Chóng'ān
(48km)

Shàoshān Beilu

Wenhua Beilu

Yingpan Xilu 营盘西路

Yingpan Dongli 营盘东路

Beijing Xilu

18

Beijing Donglu 北京东路

Apple
Mountain

Wenhua Nanlu
文化南路

Jìngjìng
River

Yongle Lu

Shàoshān Nanlu 邵山南路

To Jìnquánhu
Park (4km)

To Xiānhuā (10km);
Zhōuxī (10km);
Léishān (12km)

Ningbo Lu 宁波路

centre that locals recommend for the food, though the atmosphere is dismal.

Lǐxiǎng Miànshídiàn (Wenhua Nanlu; 文化南路; dishes from Y5; 🕙 7.30am-7.30pm) Long a popular place with locals, the English menu and friendly family running this place have also made it a popular spot with backpackers. It's a small place with a handful of plastic chairs and tables. The wonton soup and noodles are tasty but the servings are modest, so if you're really hungry, plan to order a lot.

Getting There & Away

BUS

Kǎilǐ is served by two bus stations: the long-distance bus station on Wenhua Beilu has departures to most destinations, but if you

can't find what you're looking for try the local bus station on Yingpan Xilu.

Destinations you can travel to from the local bus station include most of the surrounding villages, such as Lángdé (Y9 to Y10, 45 minutes to one hour), Chóng'ān (Y11, one hour), Májiāng (Y8 to Y10, one hour), Huángpíng (Y13, 30 minutes), Chějiāng, Mátáng and Léishān (Y11, one hour, every 30 minutes from 7am to 7.30pm). Check the bus times when you arrive.

TRAIN

Kǎilǐ's train station is a couple of kilometres north of town but departures are infrequent and the train service slow; you're better off getting the bus. Trains leave round the clock for Guìyáng (Y55), the majority between noon and midnight. These take three to five hours.

For longer distances, it's worth stopping in Guìyáng to secure a reservation. Six trains a day pass through Kǎilǐ on their way to Chóngqìng, and three a day on their way to Kūnmíng (1.51pm, 8.37pm and 8.50pm). You can't get a sleeper reservation in Kǎilǐ so you'll have to pray for intervention from a higher power (the conductor guard). The same advice is valid for east-bound services to Běijīng and Shànghǎi.

BUS TIMETABLES

Buses from the Kǎilǐ long-distance bus station:

Destination	Price	Duration	Frequency	Departs
Cóngjiāng	Y61	6-7hr	6 daily	7am, 8.20am, 9.40am, 11.40am, 1.30pm & 2.30pm
Guìyáng	Y45-51	2½hr	every 20-30min	7.45am-7.15pm
Jǐnpíng (for Lónglǐ)	Y45-70	5hr	every 30-45min	6.10am-4pm
Lángdé	Y8	40min	every 25min	7am-6pm
Lípíng	Y72	7hr	3 daily	7am, 7.40am & 8.40am
Róngjiāng	Y37-47	5hr	every 40min	6.40am-4.40pm
Xijiāng	Y16-18	2½hr	4 daily	9am, noon, 2pm & 4pm
Zhènyuǎn	Y25	3hr	5 daily	7.30am, 9.30am, 11am, 1pm & 2.30pm

Getting Around

Bus fares cost Y0.50 in Kǎilǐ and almost all of the buses departing from the train station follow the same route up Qingjiang Lu, past the long-distance bus station, along Beijing Donglu and down Shaoshan Nanlu to the museum. To the train station take bus 2.

Taxis charge a flat Y5 for anywhere in the city and Y10 to the train station.

AROUND KǍILǏ

The architecture or sights of the villages mentioned following make them worth visiting at any time of year. But there are dozens and dozens of other villages that, though deserted most of the time, are completely transformed during market days (every five to eight days) and are absolutely worth making the effort to get to. (Check with the Kǎilǐ CITS for dates when you arrive.)

However, if you don't have a lot of time for grand overnight trips, there are also dozens of Miao villages within an hour's bus ride of Kǎilǐ that can be visited as day trips. The main attraction is wandering around the countryside, exploring traditional wooden villages and seeing the colourful Miao.

Zhōuxī (舟溪), on the road southwest to Dānzhài (丹寨) and Dūyún (都匀), is a picturesque wooden village with a large Lusheng Festival in the first lunar month shared with nearby **Qīngmàn** (青曼), which provides many musicians for the gathering. Qīngmàn is quiet

the rest of the time, but the dark wood architecture is impressive and there's a hill in the back to climb, passing a small graveyard.

A number of small *lúshēng* festivals are held throughout this region in the first lunar month (usually February). The festivities switch every couple of days between the surrounding villages of Shiqing, Dazhong, Xinguang, Sānjiāng and Yātáng.

The village of **Tónggǔ** (铜鼓), 30km west of Kǎilǐ on the road to Májiāng (麻江), specialises in a form of colourful painting, partly an extension of traditional embroidery designs.

Léishān (雷山) is another village that may be worth checking out and using as a base to explore nearby Leigong Mountain (雷公山; Léigōng Shān; 2178m), which offers some interesting hiking. However, getting there could be a problem; ask at the CITS office in Kǎilǐ.

While the modernisation of some of the villages may disappoint some travellers, many locals say the tourism boom may help preserve some customs. In recent years, as in other poor regions of China, young Miao and Dong have moved in droves to work in boom cities such as Shēnzhèn, Běijīng and Shànghǎi, becoming assimilated into the Han majority. However, some in the Kǎilǐ area villages say that the amount of money tourism is bringing into the region has turned things around in recent years, encouraging young people to maintain their music, dance and customs after seeing how lucrative it can be.

TRADITIONAL GARMENTS

The variety of clothing among the minorities of Guìzhōu provides travellers with a daily visual feast. Clothes are as much a social and ethnic denominator as they are pure decoration. They also show whether or not a woman is married and are a pointer to a woman's wealth and skills at weaving and embroidery.

Many women in remote areas still weave their own hemp and cotton cloth. Some families, especially in Dong areas, still ferment their own indigo paste as well, and you will see this for sale in traditional markets. Many women will not attend festivals in the rain for fear that the dyes in their fabrics will run. Methods of producing indigo are greatly treasured and kept secret, but are increasingly threatened by the introduction of artificial chemical dyes.

Embroidery is central to minority costume and is a tradition passed down from mother to daughter. Designs include many important symbols and references to myths and history. Birds, fish and a variety of dragon motifs are popular. The highest-quality work is often reserved for baby carriers, and many young girls work on these as they approach marrying age. Older women will often spend hundreds of hours embroidering their own funeral clothes.

Costumes move with the times. In larger towns, Miao women often substitute their embroidered smocks with a good woolly sweater and their headdresses look suspiciously like mass-produced pink and yellow Chinese towels.

Xījiāng 西江

Xījiāng is thought to be the largest Miao village and is well known for its embroidery and silver ornaments (the Miao believe that silver can dispel evil spirits). Set in a natural basin, it's bordered by paddy fields, with wooden houses rising up the hillside.

Dawn hikes through the paddies are spectacular and for those looking for more than an afternoon stroll, there's a three-day trek from here to Pàiyáng (排羊), a Miao village north of Xījiāng. This trail winds its way through some remote minority villages and lush scenery. You will probably find accommodation with locals en route, but you shouldn't expect it so come prepared with sleeping bags, food and camping equipment.

Many families offer rooms with dinner for around Y40. This can turn into a festive affair once the neighbours are invited over and the singing performances begin. You can get recommendations from the Kǎilǐ CITS office, but otherwise just go up the main street and ask around. Many of the people running the souvenir stands also offer room and board.

If everyone's full, try the **Yóudiàn Zhāodàisuǒ** (邮电招待所; ☎ 334 8688; dm Y15) near the bus drop-off. Guests say the kindness of the *fúwùyuán* (floor attendants) more than makes up for the grubby facilities.

GETTING THERE & AWAY

From Kǎilǐ's long-distance bus station regular buses go to Xījiāng (Y16 to Y18, 2½ hours,

9am, noon, 2pm and 4pm). Three to four morning buses a day return to Kǎilǐ, or catch a bus to Léishān (Y8, 1½ hours, last bus 5pm) and from there head to Kǎilǐ.

Lángdé 郎德

Nestled among lush green trees, the water-wheels, terrific Miao architecture and cobbled pathways of Lángdé made this village one of the first to become popular with tour groups. It's now a well-oiled machine: the tour buses roll up and the villagers run to their houses to change into festival costumes, and everyone descends on the village square for elaborate singing, dancing and reed flute performances. It may not feel as 'authentic' as some would like, but don't write it off completely. If there aren't any festivals going on when you're in Kǎilǐ, you can at least come here and get a taste of what they're like – seeing all the elaborate silver headdresses alone is pretty impressive. After the performances, the hard sell begins, with locals flogging all kinds of clothes and jewellery. Wandering around the village is also pleasant and there's a terrific 15km trail along the Bala River that will take you through several Miao villages.

GETTING THERE & AWAY

About 20km outside Kǎilǐ, buses pass by here on the way to Léishān (Y7 to Y8). The village is 2km from the main road. To leave the village, get back down to the main road and flag down a bus back to Kǎilǐ.

THE MIAO

The Miao, or Hmong as they prefer to be called, are thought to have migrated 2000 years ago from an area north of the Yellow River. During the course of their migrations, the Miao diversified into subgroups known as Black, Red, White, Blue, Long-Horned and Flowery Miao, after their style of dress. This is, however, largely a Han classification and few Miao use these names among themselves. Many Miao continued their migration beyond China into Laos, Thailand and Vietnam where they are known as the Hmong (or Mong).

The Miao have a reputation as independent-minded and rebellious highlanders. Many Miao joined the armed uprising against the Qing government from 1840 to 1870, which became known as the Miao Rebellion. Numerous Lao Hmong worked covertly for the US government during the American (Vietnam) War and settled in the USA after the fall of Saigon.

A significant number of Miao were converted to Christianity by 19th-century missionaries, who created the first Miao script. Most Miao remain animist, however, with strong elements of ancestor worship. Miao creation stories tell of an ancient flood and also of a mythical bird that hatched the first humans. Tradition also states that the sky is propped up by 12 silver pillars. Miao oral history is full of warrior heroes, many of whom died in uprisings against the Chinese.

Miao women are famous for their embroidery and silver jewellery, with each subgroup employing unique styles. Black Miao, for example, wear 10m-long black turbans, black and purple clothes, and silver 'sideburns', while the Flowery Miao dress predominantly in red, white and yellow. All wear long skirts pleated like an accordion. These skirts, up to 6m long, are starched with rice water and then folded, rolled and stored in a bamboo tube to set the desired number of pleats.

At festival time, Miao women wear stunning silver jewellery, often piling on five or six neck rings, as well as chains, coins, chest locks and multiple headdresses. Girls wear huge horned, silver headdresses and silver crowns resplendent with delicate silver birds, flowers and coins. Silver was originally obtained from melting coins, though the Miao later received an annual silver stipend from the government. Today most of the silver is alloy and, outside festival time, wooden combs and plastic flowers and hairpins are worn as a substitute.

Long hair is particularly sought after, and old or fake hair is sometimes woven into a large headdress. You can even see Miao women buying and selling big bunches of hair in some traditional markets.

Shíqiáo 石桥

This village's name means 'stone bridge' and there are a couple of remarkable ones spanning the nearby river. This is a truly picturesque Miao town, with a main street lined with livestock pens and wooden houses climbing the modest slopes. The village was long famous in the region for its exquisite handmade paper. Though no longer making it for commercial purposes, there is still a small paper-making centre on the edge of town. Villagers there will take you through the traditional paper-making process and may even let you have a go of it yourself. This place is usually only opened if visitors have made prior arrangements or if a tour group has just come through. If you definitely want to see it, get Kǎilǐ's CITS to call ahead for you and check whether it will be open or not when you arrive. It takes about 90 minutes to get here from Kǎilǐ. Buses (Y15) leave every 45 minutes from 7am to 4pm from the local west bus station.

Mátáng 麻塘

This village, 30km from Kǎilǐ, is home to the Gejia, a group that has been identified by the government as belonging to the Miao minority. The Gejia, who have different customs, dress and language, aren't particularly happy about this classification and nor, for that matter, are the Miao. The Gejia are renowned batik artisans and their traditional dress often features batik and embroidery. Their hats (which look a bit like heavily starched napkins) are also made out of batik. The village is incredibly friendly and if you decide to visit, be prepared for the army of women selling handicrafts who will pounce on you as soon as you arrive.

Nearby **Incense Burner Hill** (Xiānglú Shān) hosts a Hill Climbing Festival (on the 19th of the sixth lunar month) to commemorate those who used the hill as a base for the mid-19th-century Miao Rebellion. The one-time temples on the hill either fell into disrepair or were razed during the Cultural Revolution.

GETTING THERE & AWAY

The village is 2km from the main road and buses regularly run past the drop-off point in the direction of Chóng'ān (Y5) and Kǎilǐ (Y7). Just stand on the side of the road and flag down anything that comes your way.

Táijiāng 台江

☎ 0855

The built-up town of Táijiāng is worth a day-trip when its huge **market** gets going every five days, taking over the main street, but also spilling into the interesting backstreets. Contact the Kǎilǐ CITS for exact dates.

Táijiāng is a centre for Miao handicrafts. You can also visit the Wénchāng Gōng (文昌宫), a small temple in the east of town dating from 1892 that now houses a small **Embroidery Museum** (admission Y10). On display are traditional clothing, hats and shoes, all hand-stitched with intricate, beautiful patterns and pictures, though it's likely one of the Miao women will offer to show you their work at their workshop or house.

To get to the museum, turn right at the bus station and head into the centre of town, bearing right at the T-junction. Continue on for a couple of hundred metres to find the museum on your right.

You can also use Táijiāng as a base to visit the nearby villages of Fǎnpái or Shídòng. The Kǎilǐ CITS is excellent for making hotel suggestions, or even better, they may actually be able to fix you up with a homestay in one of the villages. Finally, Táijiāng hosts an interesting lantern festival halfway through the first lunar month.

There are a few hotpot and noodle places along the main street and at the central T-junction. A few restaurants specialise in a kind of communal stir-fry that's worth trying if there's more than one of you.

GETTING THERE & AWAY

The main bus station is in the southwest of town, from where buses run to and from Kǎilǐ every hour or so from 7am until 6pm (Y15, 1½ hours).

To reach Shídòng, head up to the main T-junction and bear left. Minibuses run this route from 7am to 6pm (Y8 to Y10, two hours) and leave when full.

If you're heading to Fǎnpái, you'll find transport along the right-hand branch of Táijiāng's T-junction.

Fǎnpái 反排

This traditional Miao village, hidden high in the hills around Táijiāng, is often shrouded in a fog that makes it seem even more isolated from the rest of the region. The village consists of several hundred **traditional wooden dwellings**, which cloak the steep valley like green moss. In spring, villagers are busy tending the surrounding terraced fields. In the winter chill the kids head off to school carrying mini-braziers full of glowing coals.

The town is noted for its wooden drum dances and has a **festival** on the 2nd day of the second lunar month.

Explore the village and hike in the surrounding hills, following farmers' trails. It's a peaceful, harmonious place where time seems to have stood still – an increasingly rare find in 21st-century China.

To get to Fǎnpái, take a minibus heading from Táijiāng and ask the driver to let you off at Fǎnpái (not Fǎnzhài – that's another village on the same road). The journey costs around Y10 to Y15 and takes 75 minutes.

Shídòng 施洞

Shídòng is a small Miao village on the banks of the Qingshui River, and is famous for its festivals. The two biggest are the **Dragon Boat Festival**, held from the 24th to the 27th of the fifth lunar month, and the **Sisters' Meal Festival** on the 15th of the third lunar month. For approximate Western dates of these festivals, see the boxed text, p101.

At other times this village is quiet except for the **local market**, held every six days, when the backstreets of the old town, east of the main road, and even the banks of the river are filled with stalls and traders.

Women sell inexpensive embroidery and silver all year, and Shídòng is a pretty good place to buy them. There's also a handicraft shop in Lǎotún (老屯), a few kilometres out of town, along the road to Táijiāng.

Minibuses ply the route between Táijiāng and Shídòng all day until dark. The trip takes about 70 minutes and costs around Y15.

Chóng'ān 重安

☎ 0855

Chóng'ān is best known for its bustling **market**, one of the most popular in the region and held every five days. Though this riverside city used to be well known for its nice old town, much of that has disappeared in recent years.

However, there are a few remaining wooden homes and buildings. Among these are **Longevity Hall** (长寿殿; Chángshòu Diàn), recently reincarnated as a pool hall, and the nearby **Cultural Pavilion** (文化堂; Wénhuà Táng), which still holds a 1st-floor library.

Chóng'ān has a **Lusheng Festival** on the 26th of the ninth lunar month and celebrates the **Dragon Boat Festival** on the 26th of the fifth month, although these celebrations aren't as major as Shídòng's.

WALKS

What hasn't changed are the enjoyable short walks around Chóng'ān. Head east from town, towards the bridge to Kǎilǐ; in the high season, you may find some boaters willing to take you to the other side of the river where there are a few remaining **traditional houses**, some of which still have faded red political slogans from the Cultural Revolution emblazoned across their fronts. One by the dockside reads: 'In our hearts Chairman Mao is the reddest of the reddest red suns'. No-one seems to be in any particular hurry to get rid of it.

Longer walks around Chóng'ān will take you to minority villages. From the traditional houses on the south bank of the river, paths lead up the hillside to several Miao villages. If you continue right along the river bank for a couple of minutes and then uphill to the left, you'll eventually come to **Xīnzái** (新宅), an interesting Gejia village.

A second walk begins once you head east over the bridge and out of town, following the main river downstream. You will pass several waterwheels grinding grain in the middle of the river and a workshop of stone carvers by the road. The road sweeps to the left heading north to the Gejia village of **Chóngxīng** (重兴). If you continue straight, you'll pass a carpenters' village. On a hilltop to the left is the village of **Táiwān** (台湾), a blacksmiths' village recognisable by the rhythmic hammering of iron. Chóngxīng is 9km further along this road – your best bet is to hitch with the occasional tractor or truck.

Another hike from Chóng'ān takes you west and upstream. If you continue west along the river bank, you will come to a modern road bridge and a chain suspension bridge, built in 1873 with 16 iron chains. From here you can follow paths along the river bank for about 5km to the **Shengu Pool** (深谷幽溪; Shēngǔ Yōuxī) scenic spot.

SLEEPING

Xiǎojiāngnán Zhāodàisuǒ (小江南招待所; ☎ 235 1208; dm Y30) This hotel gets so-so reviews from travellers concerning its rooms, but fairly good reviews for the travel info it doles out. Staff can help organise anything from boat trips to full-day guided treks to remote Mulao minority villages. The hotel reception displays plenty of photos of the surrounding area to whet your appetite and (sometimes) has English-language maps on hand to give guests.

GETTING THERE & AWAY

Buses between Shībǐng, Huángpíng and Kǎilǐ all pass through Chóng'ān, which means there's a bus almost every half-hour in either direction. Buses to Kǎilǐ run until around 6.30pm.

Huángpíng 黄平

☎ 0855

Huángpíng is home to a huge **market** that transforms the town every five days and attracts both Miao and Gejia people from the surrounding villages.

Also worth a visit is the Taoist temple complex of **Fēiyún Dòng** (飞云洞; admission Y10), built in 1443 and only 12km northeast of town. **Siyueba**, a large festival, is held here on the 8th day of the fourth lunar month. To reach the temple, take any Shībǐng-bound minibus.

GETTING THERE & AWAY

The central bus station has departures to Kǎilǐ from 7.20am until 4.30pm (Y16, 2½ hours) and to Zhènyuǎn from 7am until 4.30pm (Y22). From Kǎilǐ, buses run to Huángpíng from the western bus station from the 6.50am until 5pm. For Shībǐng, catch a Zhènyuǎn-bound bus, which run until about 5.30pm.

EASTERN REGION

This area of southeastern Guìzhōu borders Húnán province, and is where Dong villages start to thin out and Han Chinese settlements take their place.

Lónglǐ 隆里

Set in the midst of some isolated fields, this ancient Han village is over 600 years old and is located close to Guìzhōu's border with Húnán province.

Lónglǐ has a fascinating history. It started out as a military outpost when hundreds of Han soldiers were stationed here during the

GUÌZHŌU

Ming dynasty to protect the kingdom's border from the nearby Miao. Though farming is the primary economic activity these days, most of the village population is directly descended from the original Ming soldiers.

Part of what makes Lónglǐ so charming is that life here is still completely contained within its ancient walls. Though the village's hotel and a modest street of shops are being developed outside the East Gate, everything from the local schools to the police to the mayor's office are found in the village's ancient courtyards and cobbled lanes behind the old fortifications. Located in the middle of endless fields, arriving here really does make you feel like you've landed in the middle of nowhere.

The Y15 entrance fee will be collected from you as you pass the East Gate. The only formal sight within the walls is a museum being set up in the middle of town, though it didn't have much in it at the time of research. However, the village's architecture is exciting enough on its own. Besides atmospheric wooden houses, there are stone pavilions, gates and elaborate decorations painted on many of the traditional buildings.

It takes about an hour to explore it all, though there are lovely walks you could do in the surrounding fields.

Lónglǐ Gǔchéng Jiǔdiàn (隆里古城酒店; ☎ 718 0018; r Y70, r with shared bathroom Y50-60) is the only hotel and restaurant in the village. It's a low-lying modern building completely devoid of character. The employees are fantastic but the rooms are sparse and simple and it gets very cold if you're here during the colder months (the heating doesn't work). The restaurant menu has dishes priced from Y5 to Y13. Located right off the main road, the hotel's Chinese-English sign is the first thing you'll see when you arrive.

GETTING THERE & AWAY
Air
A new airport has been opened about 20km away from Lónglǐ, the government's effort to develop this remote village region for tourism. Though called Liping Airport, it's actually next to a village called Gāotún (高屯) and is closer to Lónglǐ than Líping (黎平). For the moment, service is only between here and Guìyáng. There are four flights a week (Y400, 40 minutes). From here you can take a taxi or bus to Lónglǐ; this trip also takes about 40 minutes.

Bus
There's no direct bus from Kǎilǐ to Lónglǐ. First take a bus from Kǎilǐ's long-distance bus station to the town of Jǐnpíng (锦屏; Y45 to Y70, five hours, every 30 to 45 minutes from 6.10am to 4pm), then get the bus to Lónglǐ from there (Y10, 90 minutes to two hours, every 30 to 40 minutes from 7.40am to 4pm).

Around Lónglǐ
If you decide to base yourself in Lónglǐ, you could also do a day trip to Líping (黎平), about 50km south of here. While this place has modernised much in recent years, making it of less and less interest to travellers, there is still an **ancient street** in town that is fun to spend a couple of hours exploring.

Other than that, the town isn't known for much besides a Long March meeting that took place on 18 December 1934, when Zhou Enlai, Mao and other Communist Party luminaries sat here and discussed their next move – to storm Zūnyì.

Around Líping, there's a wind-and-rain bridge at **Máogòng** (茅贡) and a Dong village at **Gāojín** (高近), both on the road to Róngjiāng.

On the road to Líping near **Gāotún** (高屯), you can explore a number of **limestone caves** (石灰岩山洞; Shíhuīyán Shāndòng) in a scenic area along the Bazhou River (八舟河; Bāzhōu Hé); they're about 10km northeast of Líping. To get there, just get out on the road and flag down a bus. The hotel will tell you what time the buses pass. The trip takes roughly 60 to 90 minutes.

DONG REGION
This is the land of drum towers and wind-and-rain bridges, the epicentre of Dong culture southeast of Kǎilǐ. Village roads here climb into the hills before finally descending into the subtropical Róngjiāng Basin.

Most travellers who make it all the way out here from Kǎilǐ are en route to or from Guǎngxī province. If this isn't in your plans, you can do an interesting loop from Róngjiāng, visiting Líping, Zhàoxīng and Cóngjiāng. The most interesting area is between Cóngjiāng and Zhàoxīng (see p137).

This region has some of the most vivid and exciting **markets** in the whole southeast. The two places listed following are normally practically deserted, but are transformed during market times.

Xiàjiāng (下江) has a fantastic market that attracts hundreds of people from the neighbouring mountain villages. Travelling here on market day is almost as thrilling as the actual market itself. Long before you've reached the village, you'll see Miao and Dong people from riverside villages scrambling into boats and floating all the way down to Xiàjiāng.

The market at **Píngyǒng** (平永), a village located about halfway between Tǎshí (塔石) and Róngjiāng, is great not only because it's an absolute madhouse (so crowded it's sometimes hard to move), but also because it attracts such a diverse mix of people, including many different clans of Miao, Shui and Dong people, all wearing spectacular clothes and jewellery.

It's worth travelling as lightly as possible in these areas, so you can jump off the bus when a particularly interesting village catches your eye. Roads around here are still pretty rough but are slowly being improved. Doing any kind of banking in these parts is not possible so bring your Renminbi with you.

Róngjiāng 榕江
☎ 0855

Róngjiāng is a little, messy concrete city, mainly of interest as a base to visit nearby villages. You are likely to see a number of traditionally dressed villagers here who have come to town to buy or sell goods. The highlight of Róngjiāng is often said to be its Sunday market, though some people say it's not as impressive as it once was. The market takes over a couple of streets just east and parallel to the main road.

The town is clustered around a north–south road; a roundabout and the long-distance bus station are at the northern end, and a local minibus stop is in the south.

SLEEPING & EATING
Róngjiāng has a lot of hotels, but most are pretty battered up.

Míngzhèng Bīnguǎn (民政宾馆; ☎ 662 9108; r Y120-158) This is a worn hotel but is a good back-up address to keep on hand. It usually has rooms available even when the Róngjiāng Bīnguǎn is full. Give the sheets a good look before choosing your room, as sometimes the linen isn't altogether clean.

Róngjiāng Bīnguǎn (榕江宾馆; ☎ 662 4223; r Y220) With a reputation as the best hotel in town, this is the first choice for everyone from business people to Chinese tour groups to foreign travellers. Rooms are still pretty drab, but because of the hotel's popularity, they're usually full anyway. It's best to call ahead and reserve if you're keen to stay here.

There are a number of small restaurants around the bus station and roundabout.

GETTING THERE & AWAY
Róngjiāng's main bus station is in the north of town near the main roundabout. From here, there are three buses daily to Guìyáng (Y98, eight hours).

A range of buses, minibuses and sleepers leave for Kǎilǐ (Y37 to Y47, every 40 minutes from 7am to 4pm). From Kǎilǐ's long-distance bus station, there's a daily service to Róngjiāng (Y37 to Y47, every 40 minutes from 6.40am to 4.40pm). There's frequent service between Róngjiāng and Cóngjiāng from dawn until dusk (Y25 to Y35, two to three hours). Minibuses between Líping, Sāndū and Róngjiāng run all day.

Minibuses leave from the main bus station for many of the surrounding villages, including Xīnghuà and Bākāi. There are numerous connections from there to Sāndū.

Around Róngjiāng
On the road to Sāndū, 25km west of Róngjiāng, **Bākāi** (八开) is a small Dong village with a traditional Sunday market. The one-hour bus ride also passes the villages of **Dùjiāng** (都江), set at a strategically important bend in the river, and **Layou**, a picturesque village on the southern side of the river recognisable by its old humpbacked bridge. You could stop off in these towns and go for a wander if you're interested in exploring some Dong villages.

A more demanding excursion takes you to the villages of **Xìndì** (信地) and **Zēngchōng** (增冲). Xìndì is said to have the largest drum tower in the region, and Zēngchōng the oldest, at 300 years old. There's little, if any, public transport here, so you'll have to hitch or hire a taxi to get there and back. Follow the Cóngjiāng road 23km south to Tíngdòng (停洞), from where a side road leads 23km north towards Tíngdòng and Zēngchōng.

Chējiāng 车江
Built up on one side of a river not far from Róngjiāng, this Dong village's claim to fame is its **drum tower**, supposedly the highest in the region. An entrance fee of Y10 will be collected from you at the village gate.

GUÌZHŌU

THE SHUI

This small ethnic group, originally from the Pearl River region in Guǎngxī, now lives mainly along the Duliu River. They are most easily recognised by their white turbans. While the majority speak and write Chinese, there is an ancient Shui script of about 100 pictographs that is used during shaman practices. Elaborate death taboos and funeral rites ensure a Shui's 12 souls return to their correct place at death.

The Shui Duan New Year Festival is held at the end of the year according to the Shui calendar, around the 10th lunar month. Festivities are held in Shuipan, Dūjiāng (都江) and other villages, and feature fish banquets, drumming and horse racing. The Shui are famous for their bronze drums, many of which were melted down for scrap during the Great Leap Forward.

Jiemao is a singing and courting festival held in the ninth and 10th months of the Shui calendar. It is held in several villages south of Sāndū, including Shuipu and Jiǔqiān (九阡).

Chickens, cows and goats roam freely through the narrow cobbled lanes, as well as some of the most monstrously huge hogs you're ever likely to see.

This village is fun to explore given its rambling set up – no matter how much you walk it, there always seems to be another lane or corner to explore. There's a nice stone path along the riverside, with centuries-old banyan trees leaning over the water. Women are out on the piers washing clothes most afternoons. If you're here in summer, villagers may offer to take you on the river in their boats for a fee.

It's a fascinating village in a lovely setting, but someone needs to get moving on the atrocious garbage problem it appears to be having. There's heaps of the stuff dumped everywhere, including in the middle of some of the loveliest paths and green areas.

The village has a couple of convenience stores but no restaurants. You may be able to arrange a room with a local for around Y40 (whoever is collecting the village entrance fees at the ticket booth may be able to help you out). If not, you'll have to backtrack to Róngjiāng for the night.

GETTING THERE & AWAY

There are several buses daily from Kǎilǐ to Róngjiāng (Y37 to Y47, five hours, every 40 minutes from 6.40am to 4.40pm); from Róngjiāng you can take a minibus or cab to Chējiāng. The ride takes 10 to 15 minutes.

Sāndū 三都
☎ 0855

Sāndū is a medium-sized town about 100km west of Róngjiāng, which could be visited on the way back from Róngjiāng to Kǎilǐ. It's the capital of a Shui autonomous prefecture and

a major market town. Ninety-three per cent of the people in this county are of the Shui minority. Sāndū itself is fairly uninteresting, but is ideal as a base to visit surrounding Shui villages such as **Pǔ'ān** (普安), 26km north, or **Shuǐlóng**, (水龙), 30km south.

Minibuses leave from Sāndū's bus station when full for Dānzhài and Dūyún. Buses run between Róngjiāng, Sāndū and Kǎilǐ all day.

Cóngjiāng 从江
☎ 0855

Cóngjiāng is a fairly nondescript town set on the banks of the Duliu River (Dūliǔ Jiāng). You'll likely have to change buses here if you're heading south to more interesting Dong villages and may have to spend the night if you're aiming for Guǎngxī.

The town is divided by the river. The western side is built up while the eastern side, once a small Dong village, is at an interesting point of convergence between traditional wooden structures and tiled, modern giants.

SLEEPING & EATING

Chūnchéng Lǚguǎn (春城旅馆; ☎ 641 4395; Jiangdong Lu; 江东路; s/d Y60/80) This is about the best of the cheapies. Starkly furnished and slightly battered, bathrooms here have Chinese toilets.

Ténglónggé Bīnguǎn (腾龙阁宾馆; ☎ 641 7777; Jiangdong Qiaotou; 江东桥头; s & d with shared bathroom Y100, s & d with/without heat Y170/150) The town stalwart, this hotel is opposite the bridge on the eastern side of the river. Rooms here are beaten down but serviceable enough.

Jiangdong Lu (江东路) is packed with cheap eats and is the best place to head for food. If you're looking for a meal in Cóngjiāng, it's best not to leave it too late as the town shuts around 7pm or 8pm. A small night market sets up with a few barbecue and hotpot stalls 15 minutes' walk north of the bridge on the western side of town.

GETTING THERE & AWAY

Cóngjiāng has a new bus station about 150m south of the bridge on the eastern side of the river.

Buses running between here and Kǎilǐ have more or less the same schedule no matter which direction you travel (Y61, six to seven hours, six daily at 7am, 8.20am, 9.40am, 11.40am, 1.30pm and 2.30pm). There's frequent service between Róngjiāng and Cóngjiāng from dawn until dusk (Y25 to Y35, two to three hours).

Heading east, there are buses to and from Lípíng between 6.30am and 11.30am. There is no direct link with Zhàoxīng – use the Lípíng route and change at Luòxiāng.

To Guǎngxī, there are five departures for Sānjiāng between 5.40am and 8.20am and then again at 11.30am, 12.30pm and 2.30pm.

Bāshā 岜沙
pop 2140

Bāshā is one of the most unique villages you'll encounter in all of Guìzhōu and is well worth making the effort to get to. Located up the hill from Cóngjiāng, this Miao village is famous for its men who still wear period clothes, carry swords, and wear their long hair rolled up into topknots. Even young boys wear the topknot and carry daggers. Though most say these traditions date from the Ming dynasty, others believe they may date back to the Tang or Song dynasties.

Neither Han culture nor modern technology has made serious inroads here (yet), and nobody, even the villagers themselves, seems sure about why their ancient customs stay so well preserved, though many believe it is simply because of the village's isolation.

The tricky part of a visit here is actually seeing the men, as during the day the majority of them are out hunting or farming. Try to time your visit with a festival for the chance to see the entire village.

It's worth putting aside an entire afternoon to explore Bāshā. It's relatively large with houses perched precariously on the downward sloping hills. As a testament to Bāshā's increasing popularity with tourists, Chinese-English signs now point the way to

various corners of this sprawling settlement and bilingual plaques explain the use of certain buildings. (Take heed though: be sure to knock on a door even if there is a plaque that says 'entrance'. Some residents don't seem to realise yet that their dwellings have been designated 'sights' and they don't take too kindly to visitors making sudden appearances in their living rooms.)

There's an irregularly collected Y15 entrance fee to Bāshā, but if no-one's tracked you down for it by the time you're ready to leave, don't worry about it – it just means the Miao here have decided to give you a *laissez passer*.

There are plenty of hotels and restaurants in Cóngjiāng if you want to spend the night.

GETTING THERE & AWAY

Bāshā is about 10km up the hill from Cóngjiāng. You can walk, take a taxi (around Y15) or take a motorcycle (Y3 to Y5). Arrange a pick-up for coming back or plan to walk back down to Cóngjiāng. Not much transportation hangs around the village. Buses leave Kǎilǐ for Cóngjiāng regularly (Y61, six to seven hours, 7am, 8.20am, 9.40am, 11.40am and 1.30pm).

Cóngjiāng to Zhàoxīng

The beautiful three-hour bus journey east from Cóngjiāng towards Zhàoxīng includes rolling hills and lush terraced fields, groves of tangerine trees and riverboats gliding along the turquoise waters. This route also passes through some of the most interesting villages in southeastern Guìzhōu and it's well worth breaking your trip in at least one.

As the road starts to climb into the hills, about 8km from Cóngjiāng, you'll see the three drum towers of **Gāozēng** (高增), a settlement of three small villages. Another 20km or so brings you to **Guàndòng** (贯洞), the largest village en route. Don't be put off by the ugly concrete blocks on the main street – behind this is an interesting village offering good walks in the surrounding countryside.

Lóngtú (龙图) is another Dong village with several drum towers. A festival, featuring mock battles, is held here over New Year in memory of the ancestral goddess Sasui. North of Lóngtú the road splits left to **Xīn'ān** (新安), a small village with a drum tower on the road to Lípíng, and right to **Luòxiāng** (洛香), on the road to Zhàoxīng and Sānjiāng.

The region holds a *lúshēng* festival and competition in successive villages from the middle of the seventh to the middle of the eighth lunar months.

Transport in this area shouldn't be a problem. Morning buses run from Cóngjiāng to Lípíng and Xīn'ān, and buses run between Cóngjiāng and Luòxiāng from 7.30am to 4.30pm.

Zhàoxīng 肇兴

This gorgeous Dong village is packed with traditional wooden structures, several wind-and-rain bridges and remarkable drum towers. It's a lively place with 700 households, and most villagers continue to wear traditional clothing and speak only their native Dong language.

This is a perfect place to linger for a day or two. The surrounding countryside is lovely and there are a number of walks you could do (ask your accommodation for advice). Even just walking around town in the evening is fascinating. Dong girls and women wash their waist-length hair in the rivers and streams (a sometimes elaborate ritual), while the men always seem to be involved in some kind of new building construction along the main street.

SIGHTS & ACTIVITIES

The main attraction is the village itself, including the five **drum towers**, each built by a different clan, and a number of **wind-and-rain bridges** and **theatre stages**. The village is very active and you'll see people weaving baskets, building homes and embroidering.

There are also a number of pleasant walks around the village and into the countryside. One excellent hour-long walk takes you to the nearby village of **Jìtáng** (纪堂), high in the hills. Follow the dirt road at the edge of town, heading west to Luòxiāng. The road climbs uphill and then branches right, snaking around the terraced valley. Jìtáng has an old drum tower and good views over the valley floor.

From Jìtáng, return by the same route or follow a road that bears right halfway down the hill. Cross into the next valley and then descend slippery paths into the hamlet of **Jílun**, up a side valley from Zhàoxīng. Jílun is a tiny but beautiful Dong village with a single drum tower. Plan half a day for the round trip.

There are also good views of Zhàoxīng from the eastern end of town as the road climbs out of the valley. The hills here offer endless opportunities for exploration.

SLEEPING & EATING

Zhàoxīng is drawing an increasing number of foreign visitors and the main street is developing quickly with several guesthouses, eateries (some with English menus) and bars, though many will not be open in winter.

Wood Guesthouse (侗家木楼旅馆; Dòngjiā Mùlóu Lǚguǎn; r Y30; ☐) With very basic wood rooms and hot showers down in the lobby, this place is family run and the sons are energetic and very helpful.

Zhàoxīng Bīnguǎn (肇兴宾馆; d from Y120; ☒) The most modern digs in the city, staff here dress up in minority costumes and are extremely friendly. Rooms are spic-and-span with tiny gleaming bathrooms.

Be sure to check on the meat of the day, as rat meat (老鼠肉; *lǎoshǔ ròu*) is common in this area. If you plan to do some day walks, it might be a good idea to bring some snacks along.

GETTING THERE & AWAY

From Kǎilǐ you have to travel first to Cóngjiāng (Y61, six to seven hours, 7am, 8.20am, 9.40am, 11.40am and 1.30pm) and change there for a bus to Zhàoxīng (Y15). Direct buses from Cóngjiāng aren't frequent, however, so consider getting on a Lípíng-bound bus and changing halfway (the bus driver will tell you) for a Dìpíng (地坪) bus.

Alternatively, if you're looking to stretch your legs, take a Luòxiāng-bound bus from Cóngjiāng (Y15, two hours) and from Luòxiāng it's a lovely 1½-hour walk along a dirt road to Zhàoxīng, passing through a number of smaller villages en route.

From Zhàoxīng, there is at least one Lípíng–Sānjiāng bus passing through each way. The trip to Sānjiāng, in Guǎngxī, takes about five hours. From there you can catch an onward bus to Guìlín (see p186).

Zhàoxīng to Guǎngxī

There are several buses daily south from Lípíng to Zhàoxīng and on to Dìpíng (also known as Lóngé). The trip takes around four hours. Dìpíng is a Dong village with the best **wind-and-rain bridge** in the region.

From Sānjiāng there are buses that go to Lóngshèng or Guìlín. See p186 for more information.

THE DONG

You will easily spot the Dong by their clothing, headgear and hairdos. Dong men commonly don a black turban, white headband or a black-and-white scarf. In a few traditional villages you may even see men with a shaved head and topknot. On the feet may be straw sandals, and trousers are generally short indigo pants reaching mid-shin. Men working in the fields often tie a wooden tool holder shaped like a boot behind their back.

Dong women typically wear a pleated skirt over skin-tight indigo trousers and embroidered gaiters (or puttees). This is then topped off with an embroidered jacket that is buttoned to the right, as well as a blue-and-black headscarf. The indigo often has a reddish tinge, due to the addition of egg white and blood, and a sheen that comes from beating the cloth with a mallet. The indigo is so dark that many women seem almost drenched in it. Most women wear their hair oiled, wound up in a figure of eight and then held in place with a comb. Many wear silver neck rings.

The Dong people are famed for their wooden architecture and in particular for their drum towers and wind-and-rain bridges, traditionally constructed without nails from the timber of at least 300 fir trees. Most villages have at least one drum tower and this is traditionally used for meetings and festivals.

Larger drum towers have a fireplace underneath the tower, to act as a social centre and meeting point for village elders. The 2m-long drum suspended from the roof rouses the village in case of attack or fire. Drum towers can be up to 15 storeys tall with four, six or eight sides. Multiple towers in a single village indicate that there were originally several settlements, or groupings of clans, which have merged into a larger village unit.

Wind-and-rain bridges, or 'flower bridges', are named after the pavilions that shelter people from the elements, and provide a place to meet, rest and hang out. The best bridges are at Dìpíng in Guìzhōu and Chéngyáng in Guǎngxī. Both drum towers and bridges are decorated with painted Buddhist carvings, often of guardians or symbolic protective animals such as dragons or phoenixes.

The Dong replenish the timber they fell; with each new baby that is born, the parents traditionally plant a tree to be used to build a house when the child reaches adulthood. Because most buildings are made from wood, villages have many fish ponds that double as a water source in case of fire.

Many Dong villages have festivals during the first lunar month. During the Tiaguanren Festival, men from a neighbouring village, dressed as government officials and guards, visit local people who are dressed as bandits, goblins, spiders, beggars and fishermen. Gifts of money are eventually handed out to the actors and to the groups of women who come to sing songs. It's really just an excuse for a huge party.

Another festival, the Caigetang, is held on the 2nd day of the first lunar month and features singing and dancing competitions. Folk songs and oral histories are particularly important to the Dong, as they have no written language.

During the New Year, many Dong women who were married the previous year return with their husband's family to their parents' home, bearing gifts. The New Year in general is a time to remember ancestors, especially the ancient Dong heroine and ancestral goddess Sasui (Grandmother). There are many memorial services to her during this time, especially around Lípíng and Cóngjiāng.

Another activity organised by the Dong, especially in Guǎngxī, is *huapao*. During a game of *huapao* an iron ring wrapped in red floss is blasted out of a metal tube, and in the ensuing rugby-like chaos teams of 12 to 13 players try to wrench it from the opposition and hand it to a judge.

The Dong are especially renowned for their hospitality and fearsome drinking ability. Important guests are often toasted as they enter a village. One spectacular farewell ritual quoted by a local tourism brochure obliges the Dong to 'hang pig heads and tails over the guests, put intestines on everybody and chase after one another with severed pig heads'.

Zhènyuǎn 镇远

☎ 0855 / pop 60,000

This 2000-year-old Han town is picturesquely built up along the banks of the Wuyang River (Wǔyáng Hé) and definitely worth a stop. Though marketed in the provincial tourist literature as Zhenyuan Ancient Town, the city is, despite the lovely setting, generally quite modern and quite ugly. The exception is the old town in the northeastern part of the city. Heavily renovated in the modern-traditional style, this area may not be terribly authentic but it maintains a quiet charm and is near Zhènyuǎn's most interesting sights.

The original town site is on the northern side of the river (traditionally known as Fǔchéng), but the majority of the city sprawl has long since overflowed onto the southern side of the river (an area known as Wēichéng).

Zhènyuǎn grew up as a garrison outpost on the trade route from Yúnnán to Húnán.

You'll need one full day to see all of the town's sights.

INFORMATION

There are several tour operators in the old town, though at the time of research none of the ones open had any English-speaking employees. They all offer the same choice of tours, the most popular being a guided visit to Black Dragon Cave, boat trips down the river (high season only) or a combo package of the two. Prices average from Y50 to Y90 per person but will vary from place to place, depending on whether there's a big group or only you. These are all small operations, so it's best to chat with your fellow travellers when you arrive to get recommendations.

Public Security Bureau (PSB; Gōngānjú; Renshou Xiang)

Zhènyuǎn Miáolíng Lǚxíngshè (☎ 572 0811; 11 Xinglong Jie) This tour operator is open year-round, though day-to-day hours can be irregular in the off-season. It has a good choice of tours, but isn't used to dealing with foreigners.

SIGHTS & ACTIVITIES

The town's main attraction is **Qīnglóng Dòng** (Black Dragon Cave; admission Y30; ☉ 8am-5pm), and it is stun-

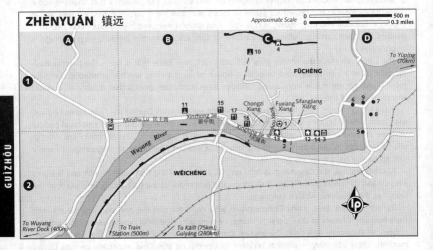

ning. Not a cave at all, the place is actually a complex of Taoist and Buddhist pavilions, temples and grottoes built into the mountain side, which appear to have fused with it over time.

The structures were built during the Ming dynasty (1368–1644) by important scholars and other 'notables'. They were constructed almost on top of each other, and are so densely packed the paths between them are confusing and maze-like. Most of the shrines and statuary were destroyed during the Cultural Revolution, but have been rebuilt, renovated or replaced since.

Don't miss the attractive **Hall of the Great Buddha** and **Zhongyuan Cave**. The **Ziyang Academy** and the **Jade Emperor Pavilion** are high up the slope and have the best views of the old town – great for photo ops.

Just by the exit, the **Longevity Theatre** houses a fantastic collection of models replicating the various dwellings of Guìzhōu's minorities. There are no English captions but the intricate stone and wood structures are worth seeing anyway.

Near here, there's also a place where you can rent **paddle boats** in the summer.

From the complex, cross over the Zhusheng Bridge (Zhùshèng Qiáo) and go through the ornate **pavilion** to the old town.

On your right you'll eventually come to a small **museum** (Xinglong Jie; admission Y10; ☉ 8am-5pm) on the history of the city (look for the entrance guarded by two stone lions).

The best way to explore the old town is to head along either Sifangjiang or Fuxiang Xiang and wander around the tall, layered stone buildings. Many of the houses have quotations from Chairman Mao painted over the entrance archways.

Further west along the northern river bank is the **Tiānhòugōng** (Tianhou Temple). Although the building itself is closed, elderly bird fanciers flock here every Sunday to admire each other's birds and cages.

For an energetic hike, head up the hill north of town to the **Sìgōng Sì**, named after four generals of the Warring States Period (453–221 BC). Bear right near the top, and you'll come to the **old city walls** (gǔchéng qiáng), snaking over the countryside like a shrunken Great Wall of China. There are more defences snaking over hillsides south of town.

The **old walls** on the south side of Wǔyáng Hé are also well preserved and a walkway has been built on them next to the river.

FESTIVALS & EVENTS

The town's mainly Han residents celebrate the Han **Dragon Boat Festival** on the 5th day of the fifth lunar month. To capitalise on tourism, the last several years it's been fixed on 25 May, but double-check this with the Kǎilǐ CITS (p126) before setting off.

SLEEPING

There's plenty of accommodation in the old town, all along Xinglong Jie. Heaps of budget hotels (Y10 to Y15 for dorms, Y60 and less per room) line this road as well, especially where it curves up towards the Zhusheng Bridge. However, at the time of research they all said they didn't have an 'alien permit' so couldn't accept foreign guests, but it may still be worth trying your luck at these places when you arrive. Zhènyuǎn is being aggressively marketed as one of eastern Guìzhōu's top places to visit, so it's hard to believe this antiquated rule right in the heart of its main tourist drag can last much longer.

Gǔchéng Bīnguǎn (☎ 572 7777; fax 572 7888; 4 Xinglong Jie; 兴隆街4号; s/d Y228/268) At the moment, this is the cheapest place in the old town where foreigners can stay. It also has by far the biggest rooms. If you can get a good discount here (you may be able to get up to 50% off), it is worth considering. Just check a few rooms out first; some have a really odd smell in them and others have horrible mould in the bathrooms.

Míngchéng Bīnguǎn (☎ 572 6018; gzzy_zyj@163.com; Xinglong Jie; 兴隆街; d Y318, discounted Y150; ✵) Halls here are so dark you practically need a flashlight to get around. Like most Chinese hotels geared to tour groups, the decoration is uninspired and drab but room conditions are pretty good: the hot water, heaters and air conditioning all work well. Just don't expect much from the staff. They'll cough up local travel information eventually but it doesn't come easy.

Fúchéng Bīnguǎn (☎ 387 7999; www.fchotel.com.cn; Xinglong Jie; 兴隆街; s & d Y328, discounted Y180; ✵) Newly opened, this is the nicest place in town. Spick-and-span rooms are comfortably furnished with clean modern bathrooms. Some of the side rooms have no windows whatsoever, so try to get one facing Xinglong Jie where you can see outside and get lots of natural light.

EATING

Every second business in the old town seems to be a hotpot, noodle or dumpling restaurant.

GUÌZHŌU

If you need snacks for your day trip or long bus rides, there's a **supermarket** (✆ 8am-11pm) just inside the old town gate and a good bakery just outside of it.

GETTING THERE & AWAY
Bus

There's daily service from Zhènyǎn's long-distance bus station to Kǎilǐ (Y25, three hours, 7.30am, 9am, 11am, 1pm, 2.30pm and 3.30pm). If you want to go to Shīdòng, you can take any of these buses and the driver will let you off when he passes through the village. There are no direct buses to Tóngrén; you have to get a bus to Yùpíng (玉坪; Y10, one hour) and then onward transport from there.

Train

Ten trains leave daily for Kǎilǐ (Y60 to Y100, 80 minutes to two hours), departing from between 10am and 11.30pm on their way to Guìyáng. There are no trains to Tóngrén, so you have to go to the railhead at Yùpíng (Y60 to Y100, one hour, 11 trains daily) and take a bus or minibus the rest of the way (Y30, one hour).

The respective schedules are pretty much the same going the other way, from Kǎilǐ to Zhènyǎn or Yùpíng to Zhènyǎn.

Around Zhènyǎn 镇远
WǓYÁNG HÉ 舞阳河

The Wǔyáng Hé (Wuyang River) runs through a scenic area packed with white limestone gorges and weirdly shaped rocks cut by waterfalls and topped with lush green vegetation. There are three mini-gorges along the river – **West Gorge**, **Dragon King Gorge** and **Zhuge Gorge** – plus plenty of spuriously named peaks, the most famous of which is Peacock-Tailed Peak. Boats tour the main river gorges and the side creeks of the Xiangjian and Baishui Rivers.

The docks are 17km west of Zhènyǎn and 1km off the main road to Shībǐng. Ask any of the tour operators (p140) for cruise information.

The Dong minority village of Bàojīng, 41km southeast of Zhènyǎn, celebrates **Sanyuesan** on the 3rd day of the third lunar month with a barbecue fish banquet. The Miao town of Yǒngxī (涌溪), 12km west, celebrates **Double Ninth** on the 9th day of the ninth lunar month.

TÓNGRÉN 铜仁
☎ 5231 / pop 92,100

Think of Tóngrén as northeast Guìzhōu's version of Kǎilǐ: not a destination in and of itself, but rather a small, pleasant city of manageable size that's a pleasant base from which to go further afield. With a pleasant spot on the Jin River (Jīn Jiāng), Tóngrén is the largest town in Guìzhōu's northeast and you will have to pass through here if you're on your way to visit Fanjing Mountain (see opposite).

Information

Bank of China (Zhōngguó Yínháng; Huangcheng Xilu) Changes money and sometimes travellers cheques.

Internet Cafés (per hr Y3) Internet access is available on the 2nd floor of a shopping arcade just off Minzhu Lu, as well as on Jiefang Lu.

Zhōngguó Tiětōng (Jinjiang Lu; ✆ 8am-8pm) You can make cheap international calls from here.

Sights

The small **Nuo Museum** in the southeast of town is devoted to exhibits on *nuó*, a local form of religious opera with animist overtones, similar in many ways to the Bouyi ground opera (see the boxed text, p114). Though nobody was around to unlock the doors at the time of research, this place has, by all accounts, a startling collection of masks worn by *nuó* dancers when they perform.

To get here, walk to Dongshān Sì (East Hill Monastery), take the second right off Jiefang Lu, after Minzhu Lu, and follow the staircase on the left up the hill. Turn left at a group of yellow buildings and continue up the stairs to the top.

Besides the museum, there's not a lot to see in town as most of Tóngrén's old wooden buildings have been demolished.

Minzhu Lu, on the east side of the river, is pedestrianised and filled with bright lights and clothing vendors yelling through megaphones.

Sleeping & Eating

Longfeng Bīnguǎn (☎ 690 1888; Jinjiang Lu; 锦江路; s/d Y188/218; 🖳) The setup here can be odd at times (eg room entrances are sometimes mid-staircase or in an unexpected hall corner), but once you get past that, the furniture and facilities (which include a computer with internet!) are in absolutely pristine condition, although rooms are a bit cramped. Room rates are the same whether your bathroom comes

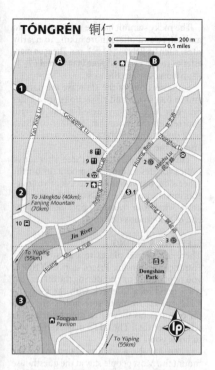

TÓNGRÉN 铜仁

Lu, and for immediate sustenance, tackle the slew of fine but simple restaurants just south of the store.

Getting There & Away
The easiest way to get to Tóngrén is to catch a train to the railhead at Yùpíng (玉坪) and take a bus (Y19 to Y22, one hour) the rest of the way. There's also sometimes minivans or taxis plying the route; they usually charge a minimum of Y30.

There are 11 trains daily in each direction between Yùpíng and Kǎilǐ (Y60 to Y100).

Leaving Tóngrén, buses head to Yúpíng (Y19 to Y22) all day starting at 7am. There are also buses to Kǎilǐ (Y60, six hours, hourly 8.30am to 5.30pm) and Guìyáng (Y110, eight hours, hourly 8am to 4pm).

AROUND TÓNGRÉN
Fanjing Shan Nature Reserve 梵净山自然保护区
This 2572m Buddhist **mountain** (Fànjìng Shān Zìrán Bǎohùqū; admission Y70) is home to the rare golden monkey (jinsihou) and is one of the most important conservation areas in Guìzhōu. Thousands of stairs weave their way through the pristine scenery to a monastery at the top. Not many foreign travellers come here, but it has become a popular trip for Chinese pilgrims and nature lovers.

Set among the Wuling Shan range, this reserve provides a home to over half the province's protected plants and two-thirds of its protected animals. The area was declared a nature reserve in 1978 and incorporated into Unesco's Man and the Biosphere programme in 1986.

with a squat toilet and shower nozzle or a western toilet and closed-in shower, so it's worth checking out your room before paying the deposit. Rooms are often discounted to around Y120.

Jínjiāng Bīnguǎn (522 2341; 8 Jinjiang Lu; 锦江路 8号; s/d/tr Y368/238/228;) This sprawling place is made up of several dispersed buildings, a relic of its glory days as *the* tourist hotel in Tóngrén. It's still grand-enough looking, but some of the essentials are going to pot – several of the showers' drains are completely plugged, flooding the bathroom floors, and the breakfast included in the room rate is a traumatic experience involving sullen wait staff flinging a bowl of cold, limp noodles with a frightening meat topping in front of you. But the *fúwùyuán* (服务员; floor attendants) here are out-of-this-world helpful. If there's a problem they'll fix it; if they can't answer your travel question, they'll find someone who can. Definitely worth the stay despite the hiccups elsewhere at this operation. Discounted rooms usually go for around Y150.

If you're stocking up for Fanjing Mountain, there is a large grocery store on Jinjiang

Though the reserve is home to 300 species of animals, the golden monkey is the most endangered. It is being aggressively protected and a breeding centre at the base of the mountain has been trying to boost the animal's population since 1995. The mountain is home to about 170 of the 15,000 left in the wild. Famous in Chinese mythology as a symbol of longevity, the golden monkey is immediately distinguishable by its blue face. Other animals found on the mountain include protected giant salamanders, musk deer, pangolins (scaly anteater), rhesus monkeys and several varieties of pheasant.

The mountain's most famous flora is the dove tree (Davidia involucrata), 'discovered' by the French missionary Père David. When the tree blossoms in April/May, the flowers look like huge handkerchiefs or doves ready to fly. The vertical 2km forest that blankets the mountain also features subtropical magnolias, Mao bamboo, oaks, myrtles, China fir trees, azaleas and rhododendrons.

Fanjing means 'state of enlightenment and freedom from earthly worries' and has its origins in the 16th century when the mountain was an important Buddhist pilgrimage site. Most of the Ming dynasty temples on the mountainside have since been ruined, though a few were restored in 1992 when access to the mountain was also improved and Chinese tourists gained a renewed interest in the area.

Spring and autumn are the best times to visit the mountain. Spring, in particular, enlivens the summit with azalea blossoms. Summers are generally wet and humid. Though it's technically possible to climb during winter if there hasn't been a heavy snowfall, besides being miserably freezing you'll have to be completely self sufficient. The trail up normally has accommodation and places where you can buy food and drink, but they are all closed from at least December to February.

From the park entrance at Hēiwān (黑湾), you will have to take a minivan or walk the 7km to the Copper Mine, then a further 2.7km to the beginning of the steps at Yu'ao. From here it's a four or more hour climb up 6800 steps past Huixiangping to **Wànbǎo** (Ten Thousand Treasures), where most people stay overnight. From Wànbǎo there are another 300 or so steps to the summit at **Jīndǐng** (Golden Summit) and the weird, layered Mushroom Rocks beyond.

The rocky summit has the remains of an old monastery and offers more hiking to nearby sites, such as **Báiyún** (白云) and **Zhenguo monasteries** to the east and **Nine Dragon Pool** (九龙池; Jiǔlóng Chí) to the west.

Some sections of the staircase are narrow and in bad shape and all sections are a killer on your legs. Give yourself a day to haul yourself up the mountain, another to climb back down, and maybe a third to have a look around the summit.

There are now at least three alternative routes for descending the mountain on the other side, but you'll need to ask at your accommodation or the CITS to make sure you know what your transport options are at the end of the various descents.

SLEEPING & EATING
There are several places to stay at the park entrance in Hēiwān. Prices start at Y100. If you're planning to visit during the off season, it's a good idea to check with the Guìyáng CITS (p102) to make sure hotels are open for business (as they often aren't during the winter months). The CITS may even be able to book you a room.

There are also a number of options on the mountain. Most people stay at the guesthouse at Wànbǎo, though there are hotels lower down the mountain at Copper Mine, Huixiangping and Yu'ao. A sleeping bag would be useful from November until at least March.

You'll find a few basic noodle places and stalls along the trail, but it's a good idea to bring along some of your own food.

GETTING THERE & AWAY
To get to the park entrance, first take a shared taxi from Tóngrén to Jiànkǒu (剑口; Y15, 40 minutes), then a minibus or shared taxi 23km north to the park entrance at Hēiwān (黑湾; Y10, 40 minutes).

Nine Dragon Cave 九龙洞
This 1400m-long karst cave (Jiǔlóng Dòng) is said to be able to hold 10,000 people. It's really off the beaten track but if you're a cave fanatic, it's got to be worth it. To get there, take a bus from Tóngrén's local bus station to Yàngtóu (漾头) and get off a couple of kilometres past the town of Mǎyán (马岩; 15km east of Tóngrén. From here you can cross the Jin River by ferry and walk 15 minutes to the cave entrance. **Guānyīn Shān** lies behind the

cave and is also worth exploring. This sight is still in the process of being developed for tourism so it is worth checking with the Kǎilǐ CITS (p126) for detailed information, or to arrange a guide before you head off.

NORTHERN GUÌZHŌU

The nature reserves around Chìshuǐ are the most pleasant of northern Guìzhōu's destinations. Communist history buffs will also enjoy a pit stop in Zūnyì, with its abundance of revolutionary sites. Taken together, the two cities make up an interesting backdoor route into southern Sìchuān.

ZŪNYÌ 遵义
☎ 0852 / pop 504,000
Mao geeks will love this city, home to a slew of exceedingly well-done sites commemorating a pivotal event in the 20th-century history of the Chinese communist party – the famous Zūnyì Conference. To everyone else, the city is likely to be a great big downer – it's a grim place and not particularly friendly. However, if you're on your way to or from Chìshuǐ, you'll have to overnight here, whether you like it or not.

History
On 16 October 1934, hemmed into Jiāngxī by Kuomintang forces, the communists set out on a Herculean, one-year, 9500km Long March from one end of China to the other. By mid-December they had reached Guìzhōu and marched on Zūnyì. Taking the town by surprise, the communists were able to stock up on supplies and take a breather.

From 15 to 18 January 1935, the top-level communist leaders took stock of their situation at the now-famous Zūnyì Conference. At the meeting, the leaders reviewed their soviet-influenced strategies, which had cost them their Jiāngxī base and caused them large military losses. Mao, who until this time had largely been overshadowed by his contemporaries, was highly critical of the communists' strategy thus far and the resolutions of the conference largely reflected his views. He was elected a full member of the ruling Standing Committee of the Politburo and Chief Assistant to Zhou Enlai in military planning. It would be another 10 years before Mao became the unrivalled leader of the Communist Party, but this event was pivotal in his rise to power.

Information
Bank of China (Zhōngguó Yínháng; Minzhu Lu) Has an ATM and can change cash, travellers cheques and offers cash advances on credit cards.
China Post (☿ 8am-8pm) Go to the end of Zhonghua Nanlu and cross the bridge. The post office is about 200m north on the west side of the street.
Internet café (wǎngbā; Zhongshan Lu; per hr Y2; ☿ 24hr) Look for a blue sign. The café is up a flight of dank stairs on the 2nd floor.
Public Security Bureau (PSB; Gōngānjú; Jinian Sq; ☿ 8.30-11.30am & 2.30-5.30pm) Offers visa extensions.

Sights
COMMUNIST HISTORY SITES
There are numerous sites throughout the Southwest consecrated to the history of 'Red' China, and a lot of them are pretty dull. If the 20th-century history of the Chinese Communist Party isn't your bag, you can skip this place altogether, but for everyone else, the **Zunyi Conference Site** (Zūnyì Huìyì Huìzhǐ; Ziyin Lu; admission Y40; ☿ 8.30am-5pm) is extremely well set up and worth a visit.

Set in a colonial-style house, you'll see the meeting rooms and living quarters of the big-wigs, and rooms filled with CCP memorabilia. Outside, speakers blare revolutionary songs at raucous volumes for your listening pleasure.

Your ticket includes admission to umpteen related sites located nearby. The **Red Army General Political Department** (Hóngjūn Zǒng Zhèngzhì Bù Jiùzhǐ; lane behind Ziyin Lu) has some of the more interesting photos and maps relating to the Long March and Zūnyì Conference. Exhibition halls share the grounds with a **Catholic church** left behind by French missionaries.

Opposite is the **Residence of Bo Gu**, the general leader of the CCP Central Committee at the time of the Zūnyì Conference. Nearby, the **State Bank of the Red Army** (红军银行; Hóngjūn Yínháng) has some terrific money displays and decent English captions.

TEMPLES
Zūnyì has two active Buddhist temples. Built in the 1920s, **Xiangshan Temple** (Xiāngshān Sì) is situated on a small hill in a lively part of town. **Baiyun Temple** (Bǎiyún Sì) is more run-down but still an active place of worship despite its somewhat neglected appearance.

PARKS
Zūnyì is such an overcrowded industrial nightmare, its two parks provide a welcome

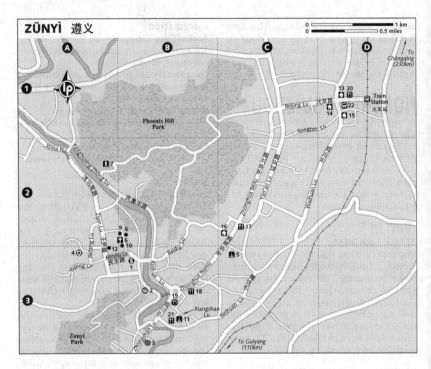

ZŪNYÌ 遵义

respite. **Zunyi Park** (Zūnyì Gōngyuán) is in the west of town and is the smaller of the two, and **Phoenix Hill Park** (Fènghuáng Shān Gōngyuán) is the huge green area in the north. Here you can climb an endless number of stairs up the steep hill for a close look at the epic soviet-socialist style **Monument to the Martyrs of the Red Army**, such a soaring piece of Red Army iconography that it's hard not to be just a little bit impressed.

Sleeping

There's something for every budget in Zūnyì.

Zájì Bīnguǎn (☎ 822 3350; 89 Zhonghua Nanlu; 中华南路89号; d Y158-208) Arriving here is like going to a trendy club – the stairs are black and shiny, there's multicoloured disco lighting across from the elevators, and the staff is young and confident. Once you get to the rooms, they're pretty conservative – make sure you look at several before paying. Two rooms might be identically priced, with one sporting grubby bathrooms and potholed mattresses while another is gleaming and newly outfitted with extras such as comfy loveseats.

Xībù Dàjiǔdiàn (☎ 319 1788; fax 319 1868; Waihuan Lu; 外环路; 汽车客运站旁; s Y158, d Y168-188, tr Y218) Rooms here are only basic affairs, with cramped bathrooms and Chinese toilets. But if you can get a good discount, the location alone makes this place worth considering. Always check the rooms before handing over your deposit. If you don't like what they show you, ask for something on the 9th floor – everything from rooms to halls are in better condition here.

Shíshān Dàjiǔdiàn (☎ 882 2978; fax 882 5861; 108 Beijing Lu; 北京路108 号; s Y196, d with/without bathroom Y336/256, tr Y396) This hotel with the retro-uniformed porters and weathered halls is one of the local standards. A lot of travellers end up here because of its proximity to the bus and train stations. However, its discounts are starting to seem pretty stingy, when you can get a far superior room for the same (discounted) price at the Beautiful Harbour Hotel. Consider the Shíshān Dàjiǔdiàn as a 'back up' instead of a 'go to' option.

Beautiful Harbour Hotel (Jīngténg Lìwān Dàjiǔdiàn; ☎ 864 9898; fax 865 4188; Beijing Lu; 北京路; s/d Y368/468) Almost right across from the long-distance bus station and just a couple of minutes away from the train station, this just-opened hotel is near perfection. Even better, when there are big discounts (sometimes 50%) it's accessible to travellers on most budgets. The rooms are beautiful, with big comfortable beds, and the breakfast buffets wonderful. While the desk staff still aren't too comfortable with foreigners and can be a little frustrating, the assistant managers are fantastic – more generous with discounts and willing to go above and beyond to solve any problems you may have while staying in Zūnyì.

Eating

Street food is your best bet in this town and there are some great hotpot, noodle and grill stalls to be found come dinner time. Some of the best places to look are the lively Xiangshan Lu or the alleys running southeast off Zhonghua Nanlu. For coffee, there's a handful of Western-style cafés at the corner of Zhonghua Beilu and Yan'an Lu. Also be sure to check out the hotpot restaurants south of Xiangshan Temple. The most manic and plentiful choice of hotpot and grill stalls is on Beijing Lu near the bus and train stations.

Getting There & Away

BUS

Useful local buses are 9 and 14, which run from the train station towards Minzhu Lu and the Bank of China. Normally, bus is the quickest and most convenient and comfortable way to reach Ānshùn and Guìyáng. However, major roadworks along this route were causing serious delays at the time of research – the trip to Ānshùn was taking up to 8½ hours, while the trip to Guìyáng took anywhere from five to 10 hours. If the construction is still going on when you arrive, you're better off taking the train. Zūnyì's long-distance bus station has good connections to many destinations in Guìzhōu. For destinations beyond Guizhōu you will have to head to Guìyáng and transfer.

TRAIN

There are regular trains to Guìyáng (Y34, 2½ to five hours, 16 daily), but you're better off catching the bus. Other destinations include Chóngqìng (Y40 to Y47, five to nine hours, 14 daily) and Chéngdū (Y190, 15 hours, 6am, 7.54am, 8.40am and 10.44pm).

CHÌSHUǏ 赤水

☎ 0852 / pop 50,000

Chìshuǐ is fantastic, the locals are shockingly friendly, the surrounding countryside is stunning and it all still has an off-the-beaten-track feel. This isn't much of a place for culture or history tourists, but nature-lovers will have

ZŪNYÌ BUS TIMETABLES

Destination	Price	Duration	Frequency	Departs
Ānshùn	Y60	4–5hr	3 daily	9am, 11am & 3pm
Chìshuǐ	Y90	7–8hr	2 daily	9am & 12.30pm
Chóngqìng	Y30-40	3hr	every 40–50min	7am-7pm
Guìyáng	Y30	2½hr	half-hourly	7am-7pm

a ball exploring Chìshuǐ's unique geography and scenery, which includes bamboo, a prehistoric plant and red earth. The area is especially famous for its spinulosa plants *(suōluó)*, huge woody ferns that grow up to 10m with large umbrella-like leaves. The ferns date from the Jurassic period, 200 million years ago, and have been dubbed 'living fossils' or 'the food of dinosaurs'.

Much of the greenery is gorgeously offset by the red earth in the area, the runoff from which turns rivers and streams red after rainfall, hence Chìshuǐ's name – Red Water.

The only negative here for independent travellers is the hassle involved in getting to some of the scenic spots by public transport. A private car is worth considering, especially if you'd like to see a lot of the countryside and have limited time and Chinese language skills.

Chìshuǐ sits on the east bank of the Chishui River (Chìshuǐ Hé); right across from it is Jiǔzhī (九支), a small crowded town on the Sìchuān side of the border. Historically, the river was important for transporting salt from Zìgòng in Sìchuān to Guìzhōu.

Chìshuǐ has more links with the fertile red basin of Sìchuān than the rocky limestone plateau of Guìzhōu and is an attractive stopover whether you are on the way to or from southern Sìchuān.

Though the locals are extremely warm, there's nothing of particular interest in Chìshuǐ itself, but it's a good base for the surrounding sights.

Sleeping & Eating

Chìshuǐ is a letdown when it comes to accommodation. Many of the rooms are forgettable, expensive and poor value.

Chìshuǐ Yuán Bīnguǎn (赤水源宾馆; ☎ 288 7778; fax 288 7775; Renmin Beilu; 人民北路; s/d Y168/268) This place isn't much, but if you need budget accommodation it's probably the best you can do at the moment. Discounted rooms run from Y100 to Y160, the location is fairly central and the bus station is just down the street. Prepare yourself for lethargic staff, damp rooms, peeling wallpaper and missing shower curtains. On the plus side, it's usually filled with Chinese tour groups, so at least the atmosphere is jovial. To get here, come out of the bus station, turn right, cross Renmin Lu, turn left and walk about 200m.

Zhōngyuè Dàjiǔdiàn (中悦大酒店; ☎ 282 3888, 282 5999; fax 286 0289; 22 Nanzheng Jie; 南正街22号; s/d Y358/398; 🖾) This is the best place in town, though rooms are still generic and forgettable. Plain dark wood furniture is set up on red carpets in rooms either too big or too small to easily accommodate it all. Everything is spotless and nicely kept up, however. The difference between the different classes of rooms is sometimes imperceptible, so there's no need to splurge. Staff here don't speak English at all, but they are mature, professional and helpful despite having almost no experience with foreign guests. Discounted rooms run about Y270.

The area around the Chìshuǐ long-distance bus station has bakeries and a supermarket where you can pick up snacks for long bus rides. There's also a dozen or so food stalls around the corner from the station doing cheap stir-frys and dumplings.

Getting There & Away

Generally, if you are arriving here from somewhere in Guìzhōu, you'll likely be dropped at Chìshuǐ's long-distance bus station (赤水长途客运站; Chìshuǐ chángtú kèyùn zhàn) on Renmin Lu. If you are coming from somewhere in Sìchuān, you will generally be sold a ticket to that province's Jiǔzhī (九支) town. From Jiǔzhī's long-distance bus station (九支长途客运站; Jiǔzhī chángtú kèyùn zhàn) it's a one-minute, Y2 cab ride over the bridge to Chìshuǐ.

Leaving Chìshuǐ for destinations in Guìzhōu, head to Chìshuǐ's long-distance bus station for daily service to Zūnyì (Y85, seven hours, 6.25am and noon), Guìyáng (Y120, ten hours, 6.55am and 8.50am), Chóngqìng (Y60 to Y70, 6.25am, 7.30am, 11am, 12.20pm and 2.35pm), Chéngdū (Y95, 7.50am, 9.55am and 2.45pm), Zhūhǎi (Y13.50, 9.30am and 3.55pm) and Jīnshāgōu (Y11).

At the time of research, delays caused by road construction on main routes from Chìshuǐ were adding between two and four hours to Zūnyì's and Guìyáng's travel times.

Despite being computerised, staff at Chìshuǐ's station still somehow manage to sell tickets for buses that don't exist. If buying tickets in advance, try to verify departure times with a couple of employees first. (Those who check the tickets as you leave the waiting area seem to be more up to date on things than the ticket sellers.)

If you are heading to Sìchuān, your best bet is Jiǔzhǐ's long-distance bus station. From there, there's regular service to the dusty industrial town of Lúzhōu (泸州; Y19, two to three hours, every 20 minutes from 7am to 6pm), from where you can get a bus to Yíbīn (Y27, three hours, every 30 to 40 minutes from 7am to 5pm) and then pick up connections to the rest of Sìchuān.

AROUND CHÌSHUǏ
Sìdònggōu 四洞沟
This **valley** (admission Y30; 8am-6pm) is studded with waterfalls, caves and lush foliage and is the most popular of Chìshuǐ's scenic spots. It's especially famous for the proliferation of spinulosa 'ferns' dotting its paths and is one of the best places to get up close to this prehistoric plant.

Known as 'Four Cave Valley', trails lead up both sides of the valley to the waterfalls, so you can walk up one side of the valley, walk behind the water curtain and return via the opposite trail. You can cover most of the valley in a couple of hours, though intrepid hikers can explore side valleys after the fourth waterfall.

Sìdònggōu is the easiest of Chìshuǐ's scenic spots to get to and is only about 20km away from town. Minivans (Y4, 30 minutes) leave all day from the traffic circle by the long-distance bus station (usually lining up along Renmin Lu just around the right-hand corner from the station). They often have handwritten signs in the windows saying Dàtóng (大同), the village 2km to 3km from the scenic spot. Ask nicely, though, and the drivers will usually take you all the way up the hill to the Sìdònggōu ticket gate. Minibuses head back to Chìshuǐ until dark, though if it's the low season you may have to make your way down the hill to Dàtóng to pick them up. Hours here can be irregular in December and January, so it's a good idea to ask at your accommodation if the site is open or not before heading up.

Shizhangdong Waterfall 十丈洞瀑布
Despite its stature as one of China's largest waterfalls, many travellers (even Chinese ones) have never even heard of this place. At 72m high and 68m wide, **Shizhangdong Waterfall** (Shízhàngdòng Pùbù; 288 1908; admission Y40; 8am-5pm) is surrounded by the unique scenery that's made Chìshuǐ famous and is only a metre or so shorter than Huangguoshu

(see p115). Best of all, it's also much less commercial. The best time to visit is after heavy rain when the falls are at their most thunderous. Water levels are lowest from November to April; it's a good idea to call ahead during this period to confirm the ticket office will be open when you arrive.

Located about 40km from Chìshuǐ, public transport here can be complicated so start your trip early. Minibuses leave from the traffic circle near the long-distance bus station. Ones going directly to Shízhàng village (十丈) seem rare (just a handful a day), but may be more frequent during peak season (Y8 to Y11, one hour). Alternatively, you can take your chances with the drivers promising to get you 'very close'. Be aware that more often than not, you'll find yourself put out near some bridge in the middle of nowhere, having to flag another minibus down to take you the rest of the way. In these cases, you'll finally be let off on the main road at the turn off to Shízhàng. Motorbikes are usually gathered here and will take you to the waterfall ticket booth (about Y20 one way). Until recently, there had been a bus from the long-distance bus station (Y10.50); it may be worth asking if this service has been restarted.

Heading back, get back to the main road and flag down anything heading to Chìshuǐ. Don't leave this too late.

Jinshagou Nature Reserve 金沙沟自然保护区
This reserve (Jīnshāgōu Zìrán Bǎohùqū) was set up to protect a large area of pristine spinulosa forest, but the scenic spot open for tourism is its **bamboo forest** (竹海; zhúhǎi; admission Y25; 8am-5pm). It's a beautiful place, with stone paths crowned with frothy bamboo leaves bobbing in the wind. Best of all, you're very likely to be the only person around. Be careful if you're visiting after rain, as the mossy stone steps going up and down the various hills get *very* slippery.

Minibuses to Jīnshāgōu village (Y11, 1½ hours) leave when full from the traffic circle near Chìshuǐ's long-distance bus station. You may have to transfer once or twice along the way depending on the driver's passenger load (the driver won't go all the way if there are not enough people, but instead farm you off to other drivers along the way). Once you reach the village (where every household seems involved in making bamboo chopsticks in one way or another), the bamboo forest is another

GUÌZHŌU

20- to 30-minute drive away. You will have to negotiate transport with a villager for the winding drive to the top of the hill. You are at their mercy – what you end up paying will depend on your bargaining skills. Chinese tourists seem to manage Y70 for a round trip. In the low season the ticket office is often unstaffed, but don't worry, as you can enter the bamboo forest further up the road. Your driver will know where to drop you off. Enter only where there are stone paths and stick to them – this place is so out of the way that if you get lost you'll be stuck here forever.

Red Rock Gorge 红石野谷

This **gorge** (Hóngshí Yěgǔ; admission Y30; ☯ 8am-5pm) was opened in 2006 and is rapidly becoming one of the most popular sights in the area. It's dotted with small waterfalls and caves and is one of the best places to see the reddened earth that figures so prominently in Chìshuǐ photos and brochures.

Minibuses here leave from the traffic circle near the long-distance bus station (Y7, one hour) when full. Unless it's peak season, it's a good idea to start heading back to Chìshuǐ at around 4pm.

Guǎngxī 广西

Vastly outshone in GDP rankings and cosmopolitan kudos by neighbouring Guǎngdōng – from where most global Chinatowns draw their migrants and Cantonese cuisine – Guǎngxī is hands down the superior travel experience. Money-spinning Guǎngdōng to the east may bask in the lucrative glow of Hong Kong and Shēnzhèn, but in terms of sheer good looks, Guǎngxī's astonishing landscape effortlessly puts its famous neighbour in the shade.

The province conveniently bundles its must-see sights in the northeast, so travellers can breeze from one destination to the next with minimum effort. Famed throughout China and beyond, Guìlín perhaps needs little introduction, but it's nearby Yángshuò that could have you writing a flurry of postcards. Fugitives from China's countless quirks are rapidly won over by the village's folksy charms: a cappuccino or two later and they're ready to admire the out-of-this-world karst scenery, take up kung fu, learn Mandarin, chinwag with the locals, recharge their batteries and prepare to plunge once more into the 'real China'. The Dong villages of Sānjiāng and the rice terraces of Lóngshèng need to be earmarked for earnest exploration, but make sure you also find time to be overwhelmed by the magnificent Detian Waterfall on the Vietnamese border.

Linguists will enjoy being tongue-tied. The *lingua franca* may be Mandarin, but the wooden northern dialect runs into stiff resistance from the sing-song melodies of Cantonese, the patois of choice for many Guǎngxī locals. Off-the-beaten-track forays can result in unforgettable encounters with folk who have never clapped eyes on foreigners, so be on your best behaviour!

HIGHLIGHTS

- Warm to archetypal backpacker culture and China's most dreamlike scenery at **Yángshuò** (p166)

- Get a rush (and bars of Vietnamese coconut candy) alongside the crashing green waters and stupefying scenery of the **Detian Waterfall** (p208)

- Village hop above one of China's most photogenic vistas at Lóngshèng's **Dragon's Backbone Rice Terraces** (p181)

- Trek through a string of Dong villages north of **Sānjiāng** (p184) and swoon before the region's fabulous wind-and-rain bridges

- Dine on Guilin Rice Noodles in **Guìlín** (p154), possibly China's most celebrated tourist city

---

- POPULATION: 44.19 MILLION
- AREA: 236,300 SQ KM

GUĂNGXĪ

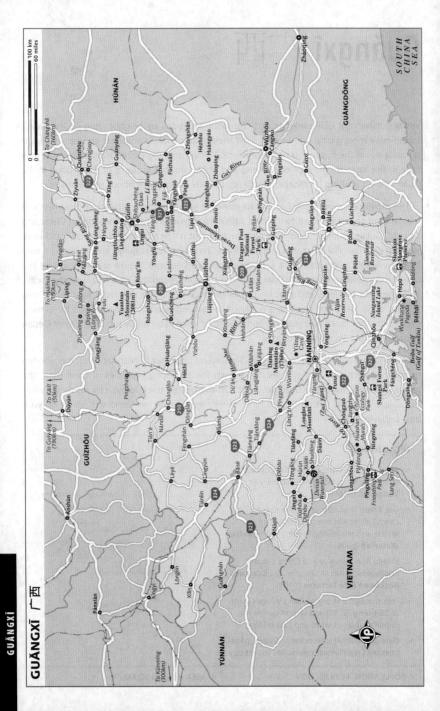

GUĂNGXĪ 广西

HISTORY

Guăngxī first came under Chinese sovereignty when a Qin dynasty army conquered what is now Guăngdōng province and eastern Guăngxī. Like the rest of the Southwest, the region had never been firmly under Chinese control; the eastern and southern parts of Guăngxī were occupied by the Chinese, while a system of indirect rule through chieftains of the aboriginal Zhuang prevailed in the west.

The situation was complicated in the northern regions by the Yao (Mien) and Miao (Hmong) tribespeople, who had been driven there from their homelands in Húnán and Jiāngxī by the advance of Han Chinese settlers. Unlike the Zhuang, who easily assimilated Chinese customs, the Yao and Miao remained in the hill regions, and were often cruelly oppressed by the Han. The tribes and the Han were involved in continuous conflicts. There was a major uprising in the 1830s, and another coincided with the Taiping Rebellion, which began in Guăngxī.

Today the Zhuang people are China's largest minority group, with well over 15 million people concentrated in Guăngxī. In 1955 Guăngxī province was reconstituted as the Guăngxī Zhuang Autonomous Region. The Zhuang are, however, virtually indistinguishable from the Han Chinese, the last outward vestige of their original identity being their linguistic links with the Thai people. Besides the Zhuang, Miao and Yao minorities, Guăngxī is home to smaller numbers of Dong, Maonan, Mulao, Jing (Vietnamese Gin) and Yi peoples. Until very recently, 75% of Guăngxī's population was non-Han.

China's first canal was built in Guăngxī during the Qin dynasty, but the scattered Han were unable use it for economic advantage and the province remained comparatively poor until the 20th century. The first attempts to modernise Guăngxī were made in 1926–27 when the 'Guăngxī Clique' (the main opposition to Chiang Kaishek within the Kuomintang) controlled much of Guăngdōng, Húnán, Guăngxī and Húběi. After the outbreak of war with Japan, the province was the scene of major battles and substantial destruction.

Despite recent improvements in the quality of life in Guăngxī, the province remains one of China's less affluent areas, although the Chinese government's 'develop the west' programme has resulted in large public works expenditure on roads, communications, water conservation and housing.

CLIMATE

Latitudinally, Guăngxī may approximate balmy Florida in the USA, but don't just pack sunscreen and a bathing suit. Average temperatures range from 13°C in January to 28°C in August and pockets of malaria-carrying mosquitoes pose a year-round risk, but there's a clear north–south divide. On the edge of the Yúnnán–Guìzhōu Plateau, Guăngxī province slopes from a higher elevation in the northwest to the lower-lying southeast. Though still subtropical, highlands in the north of the province are more temperate than the steamier south, and winters can be cold and miserable. Much of the annual 150cm to 200cm of rain falls from June to August; less heavy (but more constant) early rains in March bring dismal, cold damp. Note that coastal regions can get hit by typhoons starting in summer. May, September and October are generally the best times to visit.

FESTIVALS

In the region of Sānjiāng, popular festivals include the Bamboo Instrument Competition in Sānjiāng and Dúdòng (first day of the first lunar month), Firecracker and Opera Festivals in Chéngyáng (seventh day of the first lunar month), Méilín (second day of the second lunar month), Dǒujiāng (15th day of the second lunar month), Fùlù/Gǔyí (third day of third lunar month) and Shāyí (fourth day of third lunar month). Bullfighting in Píngliú and Bāxié is staged from the 15th to the 16th of the sixth lunar month. Festivals around Róngshuǐ include the Bamboo Instrument Festival in Róngshuǐ (13th day of the first lunar month), the Ancient Dragon Hill Festival in Xiāngfěn (16th day of the first lunar month) and the New Tree Festival at Yuánbǎo Shān (sixth day of the sixth lunar month).

LANGUAGE

Travellers with knowledge of Mandarin will have few problems navigating Guăngxī's linguistic universe, although the stubborn insistence on local dialects in small villages and rural backwaters can occasionally leave you speechless. Cantonese (Guăngdōnghuà) speakers will be on the same wavelength as the locals in Nánníng, Guìpíng, Wúzhōu, Chóngzuǒ, Píngxiáng, Dàxīn and Bǎisè, although you won't hear it spoken in the northeast around Guìlín, Lóngshèng or around Sānjiāng. The accent and vocabulary of Guǎngxī Cantonese may have Hong Kong Chinese getting all snooty, but mutual comprehension in towns as far-flung as Bǎisè is painless. In Guǎngxī, Cantonese is called *báihuà* (*baakwa* in Cantonese), literally 'white speech', which means 'common speech' as opposed to the *pǔtōnghuà* (Mandarin). You will also see bilingual Chinese–Vietnamese signs in areas nearing Vietnam, and the Zhuang Romanisation system is prominently displayed; it looks like badly spelled pinyin. Rounding out the linguistic patchwork are the numerous minority languages, such as Zhuang, Dong, Xiang, Hmong, Lakkia, Sui, Hakka, Jing (Vietnamese) and Yi, as well as the Chinese Hakka dialect. Stiff resistance to the English language continues unabated, but locals in backpacker ghettos such as Yángshuò compensate with an astonishing grasp of colloquial argot and international slang.

GETTING THERE & AWAY

Airports at Guìlín, Liǔzhōu, Běihǎi and Nánníng provide air links with the rest of China. Arriving in Guìlín by air brings you immediately to Guǎngxī's most intriguing region, putting Yángshuò, Sānjiāng and Lóngshèng within easy reach. International flights from Guìlín go to Hong Kong, Bangkok, Singapore, Kuala Lumpur, Seoul and Fukuoka. You can arrive in Guìlín and Nánníng (and to a lesser extent Liǔzhōu) by air from all over China.

Guǎngxī's principal rail junctions are at Liǔzhōu and Nánníng, through which the province is linked to the rest of China via Húnán, Guìzhōu, Yúnnán and Guǎngdōng. Vietnam is linked to Nánníng by train, which passes through Chóngzuǒ, Níngmíng and Píngxiáng. Bus connections from Guǎngxī run to neighbouring Guǎngdōng, Yúnnán, Guìzhōu, Húnán and beyond.

Despite its southern coastline, boats are only useful for reaching Hǎinán Island from Běihǎi.

GETTING AROUND

Guìlín, Sānjiāng, Róngshuǐ, Bǎisè, Chóngzuǒ, Níngmíng and Píngxiáng are towns that can all be reached by train. Buses fan out across the entire province, following a network of expressways to the principal cities and taking smaller roads for more peripheral destinations. Much of the eastern part of Guǎngxī cannot be reached by rail, so long and painful bus rides are the order of the day. Boats run from Běihǎi to the nearby island of Wéizhōu (p204).

GUÌLÍN 桂林

☎ 0773 / pop 690,000

Eulogised in fantastic terms by Chinese tourist literature and hyped into superstardom by an advertising machine that magnifies its each and every charm (see p202), Guìlín takes its position among the aristocracy of China's top sights with confidence and more than a measure of complacency.

The city of Guìlín is certainly attractive and is a pleasant enough first port of call in Guǎngxī province, although you may only fleetingly glimpse the heavenly beauty cooked up by the ad men and will find that precious few historic relics have survived to the present. For those aching to explore the fabulous karst scenery that undulates in otherworldly fashion across the surrounding countryside, Guìlín's magic is frequently eclipsed by scenic Yángshuò to the south, where there are sure-fire opportunities for lazy exploration in a dreamlike landscape and a friendlier and more finely tuned tourist industry that gaily sets about looking after Western travellers.

A wealthy city enjoying a climate of economic prosperity, Guìlín needs – like all other Chinese tourist cities – to strike the right balance between its evident charms and a booming tourist trade that is ever more in-your-face and relentless in its attentions. Touts and hawkers are highly motivated by the tinkle of tourist capital and some of the towns' sights are both expensive and mediocre, all of which results in a glut of 'best of/worst of' tales of Guìlín.

Nonetheless, Guìlín is pleasantly embroidered with greenery and Osmanthus trees, while the leafy city's extensive air, rail and bus connections make it an excellent base for exploring the northeast of Guǎngxī, where dozens of minority cultures, including large populations of Zhuang, Yao, Miao, Hui and Dong, intermingle and add their stamp to the gorgeous countryside.

The average temperature seems balmy at 20°C, but don't let that fool you. Come winter (December to February) Guìlín can be chilly, miserable and exceedingly damp, with 1900mm of annual precipitation.

History

The prefecture was established in 214 BC during the Qin dynasty but the city was not founded until 111 BC. It developed as a transport centre with the building of the Ling Canal linking the important Pearl and Yangzi river systems. Under the Ming it was the provincial capital, a status it retained until 1914 when Nánníng became the capital. During the 1930s and throughout WWII, Guìlín was a communist stronghold, and its population grew from about 100,000 to more than a million as people sought refuge here. Today it's home to around 690,000 people.

Orientation

The bulk of Guìlín occupies the western bank of the Li River (漓江; Lí Jiāng). The main artery is Zhongshan Lu – divided into southern, middle and northern sections (Zhongshan Nanlu, Zhongshan Zhonglu and Zhongshan Beilu respectively) – running roughly parallel to the Li River on its western side. Guìlín's main train station is situated at the southern end of Zhongshan Lu, with the main bus station to its north.

Closer to the heart of town is Rong Lake (Róng Hú), west of Zhongshan Zhonglu, and Shan Lake (Shān Hú) – the latter of these is romantically graced with charming pagodas – to the east. Northeast of the lakes is Central Sq (Zhōngxīn Guǎngchǎng), the city's focal point and principal shopping and eating district. Many of Guìlín's most popular restaurants and cafés lie scattered along pedestrianised Zhengyang Lu and partially pedestrianised Yiren Lu to the east of Central Sq.

The ancient walled enclosure surrounding Guìlín's Ming dynasty palace (Wáng Chéng) can be found to the north of Jiefang Lu, which crosses Zhongshan Zhonglu at right angles. Heading east, Jiefang Lu traverses Liberation Bridge (解放桥; Jiěfàng Qiáo) to the massive Seven Stars Park. Most of the limestone pinnacles form a circle around the town, though a few of these pop up within the city limits.

Maps

Several reliable maps for Guìlín are hawked citywide, including the *Tour and Communication Map of Guilin* (Y6), which includes some English. Maps of town are also available at Guilin Book City and Daofeng Bookshop.

Information

BOOKSHOPS

Daofeng Bookshop (Dàofēng Shūdiàn; 18 Binjiang Lu; ☾ 9am-10.30pm) Located next to Little Italian, this smart bookstore has a decent range of books, movies and music. Some English titles are in the travel section where a good selection of maps can be found.

Guilin Book City (Guìlín Shūchéng; Zhongshan Zhonglu) Selection of English-language titles on the 3rd floor.

INTERNET ACCESS

Some cafés around town, such as Little Italian (p162) and **Global Mini Café** (Dìqiúcūn Kāfēi Xiǎowū; ☎ 292 7227; 138-2 Zhengyang Lu), offer free internet access. Numerous internet cafés can be found in the alleys near the Jinfeng Hotel, north of Central Sq. Prices kick off from around Y1.5 per hour.

Botanical Garden Internet Bar (Yuánlín Wǎngbā; Zhongshan Nanlu; per hr Y1.5; ☾ 24hr)

Jinhu Internet Café (Jìnhú Wǎngbā; Zhongshan Zhonglu; per hr Y0.8-2; ☾ 24hr)

Wenchang Internet Café (Wénchāng Wǎngbā; Nanhuan Lu; per hr Y2; ☾ 24hr)

INTERNET RESOURCES

A good source of information on the town is www.guilin.com.cn.

MEDICAL SERVICES

Guoyao Pharmacy (Guóyào Dàyàofáng; 19 Nanhuan Lu; ☾ 8am-8pm)

People's Hospital (Rénmín Yīyuàn; Wenming Lu)

MONEY

The Bank of China and the Industrial and Commercial Bank of China generally have ATMs that accept international cards. An ATM that takes international cards can be found at the Lijiang Waterfall Hotel (p160).

Bank of China (Zhōngguó Yínháng; Zhongshan Nanlu; north of train station) Foreign exchange; ATM taking international cards. There also a branch with a foreign exchange on Zhongshan Zhonglu.

Industrial and Commercial Bank of China (Gōngshāng Yínháng; Zhongshan Nanlu) ATM taking international cards.

PHOTOGRAPHY

CD Burning (Wángchéng Bǎihuò; Jiefang Donglu) Several computer kiosks on the 4th floor burn CDs for Y20 per disc.

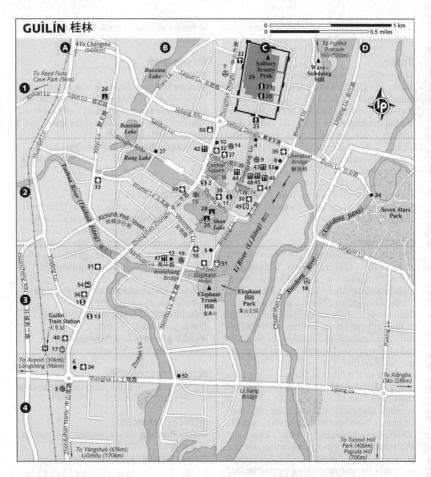

POST & COMMUNICATIONS

China Telecom (Zhōngguó Diànxìn; 53 Zhongshan Zhonglu; ◐ 8.30am-8.30pm) IC cards are available to buy here.

Post Office (Yóujú; 57 Zhongshan Zhonglu; ◐ 8am-7pm) The post office is just north of China Telecom. There's a branch of China Eastern (Dōngfāng Hángkōng; ☎ 311 7788) on the 2nd floor of this post office building. There's also a handy post office branch that can be found just north of the train station on Zhongshan Nanlu.

PUBLIC SECURITY BUREAU

PSB (Gōngānjú; ☎ 582 9930; ◐ 8.30am-noon & 3-6pm Mon-Fri) This is found on the east side of the Li River (Lí Jiāng) and is south off Longyin Lu. This office offers visa extensions.

TOURIST INFORMATION & TRAVEL AGENCIES

There are plenty of Guilin Tourist Information Service Centers (Guìlín Lǚyóu Zīxún Fúwù Zhōngxīn) around town, but they may simply house a young girl chatting on her mobile alongside wilting flyers for city tours, so don't get too excited. One of the better examples can be found next to the South Gate and an efficient counter can also be found at Liangjiang Airport. CITS offices are everywhere, even cropping up downstairs from the Guilin Flowers Youth Hostel (p160).

CITS (Zhōngguó Guójì Lǚxíngshè; ☎ 286 1623; www .guilintrav.com; 41 Binjiang Beilu) Offers tours, including day-long city tours (Y400) and a full-day Li River tour (Y450).

Guilin Tourist Information Hotline (☎ 280 0318)

Dangers & Annoyances

Whether it's a price hike in the cost of a meal or a wildly circuitous taxi ride, many travellers can count on having to deal with overcharging. Stay alert to potential rip-offs and calmly negotiate prices first. Ignore taxi drivers who insist the hotel you plan to stay in is either bad value, run down or full, and come up with alternatives; they are commissioned to take you to pre-arranged hotels. Don't be drawn into even taking a look at the hotel room and insist on choosing somewhere yourself. And keep the word 'calm' in mind no matter what – it's easy to lose your cool and that makes things worse.

Be wary of students wanting to practise English with you. Signs of possible scam artists include a willingness to discuss ways of spending your money. Also, be alert to pickpockets, especially around the train station. We receive a steady stream of letters from fellow travellers warning of scam tour guides and bad experiences in Guìlín.

The explosion of touts in Guìlín has meant that offers of massages, escort services and sex have skyrocketed. Males walking down Zhengyang Lu will have to fend off offers of massage and sex at every turn and it can become tiring.

Sights & Activities

SOLITARY BEAUTY PEAK 独秀峰

At the centre of town, the 152m **pinnacle** (Dúxiù Fēng; ☎ 285 2203; 1 Wangcheng; 王城1号; admission Y50; ⏰ 8am-6pm) affords steep climbs topped with excellent views over Guìlín, the river and surrounding peaks. The entrance fee includes admission to **Wáng Chéng** (靖江王府; Jìngjiāng Wángfǔ; 1 Wangcheng), also known as Jingjiang Prince's City, a 14th-century Ming prince's mansion, dating back to the reign of Hongwu, that was built by the nephew of the emperor, Jing Jiang, and is now home to Guangxi Normal University. During the Qing dynasty, the palace served as the Guangxi Provincial Examination House, and later Sun Zhongshan commandeered the grounds for his northern expedition from here. The entrance to Wáng Chéng is via **Chengyun Gate** on the palace's southern perimeter, which leads to the single-eaved **Chengyun Hall** behind, an examination hall with Solitary Beauty Peak to the north, as well as a small **Confucius Temple** (孔庙; Kǒng Miào). Chengyun Gate itself is accessed via two historic gates, **Zunyi Gate** in the west and **Tiren Gate** to the east. The gate to the south of the palace is **Duanli Gate**, marking the north–south line that runs through the complex.

Buses 1 and 11 go up Zhongshan Beilu past the western side of the peak. Alternatively, take bus 2, which goes past the eastern side along the river. Both buses leave from Guìlín train station.

WAVE-SUBDUING HILL 伏波山

Close to Solitary Beauty Peak and beside the western bank of the Li River, this **peak** (Fúbō Shān; admission Y15; ☉ dusk to dawn) offers fine views of the town. Upon entering through the gate, look out for the large rice pot left behind from the Dingyue Temple – it's big enough to cook rice for 1000 people.

On the southern slope of the hill is **Returned Pearl Cave** (Huánzhū Dòng). The story goes that the cave was illuminated by a single pearl and inhabited by a dragon; one day a fisherman stole the pearl but he was overcome by shame and returned it. A 1000-year-old Buddha image is etched into the wall somewhere in the cave, along with more than 200 other images of the Buddha, most dating from the Song and Tang dynasties. Somewhere, too, is a portrait and autograph by Mi Fu, a famous calligrapher of the Song dynasty. A sad sight is the Sword Testing Stones, which are remnants of stalactites hacked off by soldiers of a warlord showing off their metal and mettle.

Nearby is **Thousand Buddha Cave** (千佛岩; Qiānfó Yán), though the name's an exaggeration – there seem to be a couple of dozen statues at most, dating from the Tang and Song dynasties.

Bus 2 runs past the hill.

FOLDED BROCADE HILL 叠彩山

This **hill** (Diécǎi Shān; admission Y20) affords some of Guìlín's best views, complemented by restored pavilions, some originally dating from the Ming dynasty. Climb the stone pathway that leads you through the cooling relief of Wind Cave (风洞; Fēng Dòng), its walls decked with inscriptions and Buddhist sculptures, some damaged during the Cultural Revolution. Buses 1 and 2 run past the hill.

SEVEN STARS PARK 七星公园

Voted by some travellers as one of Guìlín's star attractions, 137-hectare **Seven Stars Park** (Qīxīng Gōngyuán; park admission Y35, Seven Star Cave admission Y30; ☉ park 6am-9.30pm, caves 8am-5.30pm) sits on the eastern side of the Li River. Cross Liberation Bridge and continue to the end of Jiefang Donglu.

Traversing **Flower Bridge** (花桥; Huā Qiáo) into the park from the main gate, one of the first things you will notice is a political slogan carved deeply and ineradicably into the rock on your left at the end of the bridge; the characters proclaim 'Long Live Mao Zedong Thought' (毛泽东思想万岁). To the north, **Qixia Temple** (Qīxiá Sì) is one of Guìlín's few Buddhist temples, although it is a late-20th-century restoration (it was frequently a victim of war and revolt).

The park was one of the original tourist spots in China's Southwest, and was first opened to sightseers as far back as the Sui dynasty. It takes its name from its seven peaks, which are supposed to resemble the Ursa Major (Big Dipper) constellation. Much of the park is characterised by somewhat disingenuous effects: sculpted rocks, fake waterfalls, concrete paths and swings where you can sit for a photo framed by two peacocks (Y10), but attractive trails wind in and around the hills and you can picnic on the sprawling lawns. Copious English signs steer you around the park to the major sights, or head up to **Round Viewing Pavilion** (Kuàngguān Tíng) to get your bearings and a view of the park.

The park's two highlights are **Seven Star Cave** (七星岩; Qīxīng Yán) – its stalagmites and stalactites coloured by floodlights – and **Dark Dragon Cave** (龙暗洞; Lóngyīn Dòng), with inscribed stelae that date back more than 1500 years. A further attraction is **Camel Peak** (Luòtuo Shān), which indeed resembles a ruminating ship of the desert. View the hill from the front for its two-hump Bactrian camel impersonation or from the rear for its impression of a single-hump dromedary camel. In front of Camel Peak is a weather-beaten podium used by ex-President Bill Clinton when making a speech here; nearby is a sad-looking zoo, eager for both investment and visitors.

For Y50 you can get your wedding photo taken in the park. There is even a small mosque in the grounds.

To reach the park, take bus 10 or 11 from the train station. From the park, free bus 58 runs to Wave-Subduing Hill, Folded Brocade Hill and Reed Flute Cave.

TUNNEL HILL PARK 穿山公园

South of Seven Stars Park and still on the eastern side of the Li River, this **park** (Chuānshān Gōngyuán; admission Y45) is expensive, but rates a mention as many locals insist its cave is superior to those of Seven Stars Park. If you tire of the cave, you can cross the Xiaodong River (小东江; Xiǎodōng Jiāng) – a small branch of the Li – and hike up to a fairly interesting pagoda on **Pagoda Hill** (塔山; Tǎ Shān). Near the summit of the hill is a wind-eroded chasm that supposedly resembles a moonscape from afar.

REED FLUTE CAVE PARK 芦笛公园

Resembling a set from *Journey to the Centre of the Earth* and the garish highlight of the park, **Reed Flute Cave** (Lúdí Gōngyuán; admission Y60; 🕙 8am-6pm) is a huge cave of multicoloured lighting and fantastic stalactites, stalagmites and other geological curiosities. The entrance to the cave was once distinguished by clumps of reeds used by locals to fashion musical instruments, hence the name.

The **Crystal Palace of the Dragon King** grotto can comfortably hold about 1000 people, though many more crammed in here during the war when the cave was used as an air-raid shelter to protect the locals.

Entry is pricey and you may want to try and slip away from the tiresome tour to explore by yourself. Surrounding walks in the park, including those up to Half-Hill Pavilion and across to Lotus Pond, are pleasant.

The park is on the northwestern outskirts of town. Take bus 3 (Y1.50) from the train station to the last stop or hop on free bus 58. Alternatively, it's a pleasant half-hour bicycle ride. Follow the bus route along Lijun Lu, which runs into Xishan Lu and then Taohua Jiang Lu. The latter parallels the small Tao-hua River (桃花江; Táohuā Jiāng) and winds through fields and karst peaks. At Ludi Lu turn left and continue for another 1.2km.

OTHER SIGHTS & ACTIVITIES

At the southern end of Guìlín where the Li River and the Taohua River converge, one of Guìlín's best-promoted sights is **Elephant Hill Park**, where **Elephant Trunk Hill** (Xiàngbí Shān; admission Y25) – unlike other misshapen lumps of rock with tenuous names extracted from Chinese myth – indeed resembles a probos-cidean mammal dipping its snout into the Li River. Visit Water Moon Cave and head up the peak walk to Puxian Pagoda (Pǔxián Tǎ) for views of the park and the picturesque Li River. Cormorant fishing in the Li River is a popular tourist drawcard (Y10). Take bus 2 or freebie buses 57 or 58 to the hill.

The heavily promoted and badly named **Water System in Guilin (Two Rivers and Four Lakes)** (两江四湖; Liǎngjiāng Sìhú; ☎ 288 5898) waterborne tour (adverts carpet the entire city) conveys visitors along a circuit of Guìlín's lakeside and riverside scenery. **Boats** (standard boat adult/child Y149/75, air-con boat adult/child Y155/78, deluxe boat adult/child Y175/88; trip duration 90min) run between the hours of 8am and 10.30pm, departing from Liberation Bridge, nosing up the Li River and under Mulong Bridge to Mulong Lake (木龙湖; Mùlóng Hú), through Baoxian Lake (宝贤湖; Bǎoxián Hú) to Rong Lake and the pagodas of Shan Lake, before drifting down the Taohua River to Wenchang Bridge (文昌桥; Wénchāng Qiáo). Departure and destination points can vary according to the season. Further **boats** (standard boat adult/child Y180/90, air-con boat adult/child Y185/98; trip duration 60min) make briefer circular trips from Mulong Lake to Rong and Shan Lakes. Tickets for both boat trips are available at agents across the city or from the ticket office at the Sun and Moon Twin Pagodas.

A popular tourist trip from Guìlín is the boat to Yángshuò down the Li River. Budget travellers have been put off by the exorbitant ticket prices, presently standing at more than Y400, including lunch and the bus trip back to Guìlín from Yángshuò. If you don't mind joining a Chinese tour group, then you will only have to pay around Y200 for the same service, just without the English-speaking guide.

During the summer, morning tour boats depart from Guìlín from a jetty across the road from the Golden Elephant Hotel at around 8am, although when the water is low you have to take a shuttle bus to Zhújiāng, Mópánshān wharf or Yángdī downriver. For trips booked through hotels, buses usually pick you up at around 7.30am to 8am and take you to the boat. The ticket office for the trip is across the road from the park entrance, on the same side of the street as the Golden Elephant Hotel. The trip lasts all day, and some people find that the time drags towards the end. It's probably not worth it if you're going to be spending any length of time in Yángshuò, where you can organise personalised trips through villagers and more picturesque boat trips to nearby villages.

Famed more for its natural wonders than for its spiritual civilisation, Guìlín has few Buddhist temples of note. A modern-looking and rather gaunt grey stone **Christian Church** (Jīdū Jiàotáng) can be found at 50 Zhongshan Zhonglu. The **Sun and Moon Twin Pagodas** (Rìyuè Shuāng Tǎ; admission Y20; ☺ 8am-10.30pm) elegantly embellish the scenery of Shan Lake. Octagonal seven-storey Moon Pagoda (Yuè Tǎ) is connected to Sun Pagoda (Rì Tǎ) – the world's tallest copper pagoda – by an underwater tunnel. Constructed from a staggering 350 tons of copper (don't climb during lightning storms unless you want to be truly illuminated), the 41m-high Sun Pagoda has nine floors; one of the world's few pagodas equipped with a lift. Artful Chinese *gǔzhēng* (zither) performances are held in the choicely positioned teahouse near the base of Sun Pagoda.

On the northern shore of Rong Lake, the **South Gate** (Nán Mén; 13 Ronghu Beilu) is all that remains of the old city wall. Strikingly illuminated, the gate is one of the features of a pleasant lakeside walk around the shores of Rong and Shan Lakes.

At 8.30pm a nightly artificial **waterfall show** is performed on the north side of the **Lijiang Waterfall Hotel** (Líjiāng Dàpùbù Fàndiàn; ☎ 282 2881; 1 Shanhu Beilu; 杉湖北路1号). If you want to watch early-morning taichi practitioners performing their slow-motion routines to music blaring from speakers, Central Sq is the place.

Tours

There's no shortage of tour operators offering half- or full-day tours of Guìlín's major sights. Ask at any of the towns' plentiful travel agencies, many of which can be found around the train and bus stations and along Binjiang Lu. Prices usually do not include admission fees to individual sights. Alternatively, hire a bicycle or taxi (see p164) for the day to take you around the sights at your own pace.

Festivals & Events

The annual **Dragon Boat Festival** (Duānwǔ Jié), held on the fifth day of the fifth lunar month, sees spectacular dragon boat races along the Li River. Superfit cycling aficionados may like to consider the **Yaoshan Race** (尧山登山赛; Yáoshān Dēngshānsài; ☎ 286 9331; www.guilinyaoshan .com), a gruelling bike race to the top of nearby Yáoshān (尧山) in the east of town.

Sleeping

Hotels are all around the train station area, but few offer comfort or style and the district is devoid of charm. The area on and around

Binjiang Lu and Central Sq is more congenial and puts you closer to the sights and restaurants. In virtually every respect, Yángshuò is a more pleasant place to spend the night.

BUDGET

Backstreet Youth Hostel (Hòujiē Guójì Qīngnián Lǚshè; ☎ 281 9936; guilinhostel@hotmail.com; 3 Renmin Lu; 人民路3号; 6- & 7-bed dm Y40, s & d Y110, tr Y160; ✸ ▣) Way out ahead of other budget competitors, this hostel stands out for its winning location in the heart of things on Renmin Lu, a small street just south of the Sheraton poking west off Binjiang Lu. There's a welcoming lobby area, with rooms arranged with reproduction antique Chinese dark-wood furniture, huge beds in the doubles and pleasant touches such as traditional Chinese knockers on doors. DVDs are available in the foyer for communal viewing on comfy seating. Internet is Y10 for 10 minutes; bike rental is Y20 per day. No phones in rooms. Offers discounts to members.

Guilin Flowers Youth Hostel (Huāmǎn Lóu Guójì Qīngnián Lǚshè; ☎ 383 9625; www.yhaguilin.com; Block 2, 6 Shangzhi Lane, off Zhongshan Nanlu; 中山南路尚智巷6号2楼; dm Y40, s/d/tw without shower Y55/90/90, d & tw with shower Y120; ✸ ▣) Not nearly as pleasant as the Backstreet, this place is at least handy to the train and bus stations, although the district is charmless. The lobby is bright and strewn with comfy sofas draped in throws, and the staff is welcoming. It's a bit hard to find: look out for the Xingye Hotel opposite the train station and follow the alley behind. Bike rental (per half/full day Y15/25, deposit Y250), internet access (three terminals; per hour Y5), pool table, DVDs, wi-fi, bar, small library of unwanted books, laundry room. Offers discounts to members.

Ocean Hotel (Àosēn Jiǔdiàn; ☎ 383 5349; fax 382 5818; 95 Zhongshan Nanlu; 中山南路95号; d Y120) This undersized and unassuming two-star place has surprisingly spacious doubles and twins, discounted temptingly to around Y70 in slacker months. Located north of the train station.

Huali Hotel (Huálì Jiǔdiàn; ☎ 383 6409; fax 382 7103; 257 Zhongshan Nanlu; 中山南路257号; s/d/tr Y220/280/380) One of the better budget hotels in the area, this convenient and popular hotel is well kept, quiet and clean, with doubles often discounted to around Y140. It's located south of the bus station.

Lixin Hotel (Lìxīn Fàndiàn; ☎ 282 2605; 19 Zhongshan Zhonglu; 中山中路19号; s & d Y260, tr Y280) Go for rooms with the best views (called *guānjǐng*

fáng; 观景房) out over Shan Lake to the pagodas. The hotel is located on bustling Zhongshan Zhonglu, with the night market right on your doorstep, although the raucous music from the adjacent shop is a letdown. Rooms are fresh and recently refitted, with fake-wood flooring. Discounts see doubles typically tumble to around Y120.

MIDRANGE

Fengyuan Hotel (Fēngyuán Jiǔdiàn; ☎ 282 7262; 26 Zhongshan Zhonglu; 中山中路26号; d/ste Y280/380; ✷) A standard but affordable and decent midrange hotel with clean rooms and bathrooms, polite service and a good location on the northern cusp of Central Sq at the intersection of Zhongshan Zhonglu and Yiren Lu. Rooms are on the 5th, 6th and 7th floors. Air ticketing available.

Jinfeng Hotel (Jīnfēng Bīnguǎn; ☎ 288 2781; fax 288 2781; north of Yiren Lu & Central Sq; s/d/tr Y388/488/580; ✷) Its central location, tucked away down an alley north of Central Sq, spacious rooms with bathroom, and good discounts (doubles down to around Y150 to Y180), make this place worth considering. The cafés and restaurants of Zhengyang Lu and Yiren Lu are a short walk away.

City Garden Hotel (Chéngshì Huāyuán Jiǔdiàn; ☎ 386 1888; fax 386 1000; 75 Zhongshan Nanlu; 中山南路75号; s/d/ste Y398/498/780; ✷) There's a clean, recently renovated feel at this fresh three-star place spanning eight floors. It has English-speaking staff, a smart lobby area and plush rooms with recently redone bathrooms. Doubles generally drop to around Y200. Just north of the bus station.

TOP END

Hotel Universal (Huánqiú Dàjiǔdiàn; ☎ 282 8228; htlunivs@public.glptt.gx.cn; 1 Jiefang Donglu; 解放东路1号; r with garden-view Y664, r/ste with Li River-view Y830/1245; ✷ ▯) Decorated with reproduction traditional furniture, the stylish lobby interior doesn't extend effectively to the rest of the hotel, where dated rooms and corridors need attention. Take a look at the room first to ensure it has the view you are after as some simply look out onto the road. There's bike rental (per hour/day Y8/50, deposit Y500), though readers have said bikes need attention.

Guilin Bravo Hotel (Guìlín Bīnguǎn; ☎ 289 8888; fax 289 3999; www.glbravohotel.com; 14 Ronghu Nanlu; 榕湖南路14号; d Y1050; ✷ ▯) There's a predominantly Chinese feel to this hotel and it remains one of Guìlín's best, with comfortable rooms and a decent selection of restaurants. Inspect

river-view rooms before paying your deposit as trees growing on the Li River's banks can obscure the view.

Sheraton Guilin (Guìlín Dàyǔ Dàfàndiàn; ☎ 282 5588; www.sheraton.com/guilin; 15 Binjiang Lu; 滨江路15号; d/ste Y1245/2370; ✷ ▯ ▣) It's an old hotel with a dated feel and a thorough refit is needed to add sparkle, but the five-star Sheraton remains one of the better hotels in town with an excellent location. Outdoor swimming pool, gym and sauna. Branch of Air Macau (☎ 286 5400). Wheelchair accessible.

Eating

Celebrated Guìlín dishes include Guilin rice noodles (桂林米粉; *Guìlín mǐfěn*) – found all over China but only true to form here – nun's vegetarian noodles (尼姑素面; *nígū sùmiàn*), Lijiang fish with pine nuts (松子漓江鱼; *sōngzǐ Líjiāng yú*), water chestnut cake (马蹄糕; *mǎtí gāo*), beer duck (啤酒鸭; *píjiǔ yā*), Guilin lotus leaf duck (桂林荷叶鸭; *Guìlín héyè yā*) and Guilin snails (桂林田螺; *Guìlín tiánluó*). Dog meat (狗肉; *gǒuròu*) is highly popular, so check what you are ordering if you want to avoid accidentally devouring Fido and family (see p193). A Qing dynasty speciality, white fermented bean curd is often used to make a sauce for dipping roast pork or chicken. Sanhua wine, actually more like mellow rice firewater, is a favourite local drink, as is local oil tea (油茶; *yóuchá*), which is actually quite salty, with flecks of rice in it. Generally the most exotic food you will come across is eel, catfish, pigeon and dog, although delicacies such as wild boar, lynx, bamboo partridge, giant salamander, crocodile and bamboo rat still crop up on menus.

Wander lively Yiren Lu to the north and east of Central Sq for a great selection of restaurants, cafés and hole-in-the-wall eateries.

Guìlín Rén (☎ 281 0545; www.glr.com.cn; Yiren Lu; 依仁路; from Y5; ✿ 7am-midnight) Cheap set local meals at this ever-popular and handy restaurant designed with a fast-food, no-nonsense approach. Orange-and-white-clad employees even go through motivational songs to boost morale and foster team spirit. There's no English menu, but dishes include three-flavours hotpot (三鲜火锅; *sānxiān Huǒguō*; Y12) and black pepper beef with rice (黑椒牛柳砂钵饭; *hēijiāo niúliǔ shābō fàn*; Y13). Instant coffee served.

Nengren Vegetarian Restaurant (Néngrén Zhāiguǎn; ☎ 286 8845; 6 Lijun Lu; 丽君路6号; meals from Y10;

⊗ 9.30am-2pm & 4.30-8pm; **V**) Fantabulous veggie dishes cooked up within chanting range of the main hall of the Nengren Buddhist Temple on the corner of Xinyi Lu and Lijun Lu. Let the vast menu (Chinese only) take your tastebuds to Nirvana and sample the Nengren vegetable dumplings (能仁斋饺子; *néngrén zhāi jiǎozi*; Y4), the ample curry mock beef noodles (咖喱素牛肉面; *gālí sù niúròu miàn*; Y5) or the straightforward traditional vegetable noodles (传统素面; *chuántǒng sùmiàn*; Y2).

Baiwei Dumpling Restaurant (Bǎiwèi Jiǎoziguǎn; ☎ 210 6743; 9-5 Libin Lu; 漓滨路9-5号; meals Y15-20; ⊗ 6.30am-11pm) Lively, popular and centrally located pocket-sized place busy with diners and a decent menu of wholesome, steaming *jiǎozi* (饺子; dumplings). No English menu.

Yiyuan Restaurant (Yíyuán Fàndiàn; ☎ 282 0470; Nanhuan Lu; 南环路; dishes from Y18; ⊗ 11.30am-2.30pm & 5.30-9.30pm) This outstanding, inexpensive Sichuanese restaurant on Nanhuan Lu has a tasteful all-wood exterior and an English menu. The owner imports all her spices from Sìchuān and you can taste the difference. Try the stir-fried eel with dried chilli and Sichuan spices (Y22).

Aunt (Hǎodàmā; ☎ 286 9999; 中山中路, 八桂大厦; 4th fl, Bagui Mansion, Zhongshan Zhonglu; meals Y20; ⊗ 11am-9pm) Take a pew in this cavernous dining hall and a waitress (some English-speaking) will hand you a card; convey it to the counter of your choice, point and choose from the arranged dishes and your choice goes down on the card – couldn't be simpler. A cornucopia of Chinese and Asian dishes is on view, from *roti prata* (bread; Y12) to scrummy *tāng bāo* (汤包; Y8), lamb kebabs (羊肉串; *yángròu chuàn*; Y3), local Lijiang mussels (Y5 per bowl), stewed carp (烧鲤鱼; *shāo lǐyú*; Y20 each), lashings of *jiǎozi* and fiery bowls of *dan dan* noodles (担担面; *dàndàn miàn*; Y4). Pot of green tea Y1.

Little Italian (Zhèlì; ☎ 311 1068; 18 Binjiang Lu; 滨江路18号; meals Y25; ⊗ 10am-midnight) A simple, modern and relaxing pit stop offering a small mezzanine area, a quiet bar area, pastas, tasty salads, sandwiches and a range of coffees. There's free internet access but you may have to join a queue for the sole terminal. English spoken, plus English menu.

Zhèngyáng Tāngchéng (☎ 285 8553; Zhengyang Lu; 正阳路; meals Y25; ⊗ 11.30am-2.30pm & 5-10pm) Brightly lit and popular soup restaurant with a large selection of local dishes. English menu.

Rosemary Café (Mídiéxiāng; ☎ 281 0063; 1-1 Yiren Lu; 依仁路1-1号; meals Y30) For honest and homely charms, this popular café is a warm beacon to disorientated visitors, with an extensive, heart-warming menu of travellers' favourites and a nightly flock of expat regulars. The Western menu runs dependably to tasty tomato soup, shepherd's pie (Y24), pizza, fish and chips and beyond. Recommended by travellers.

Inaka Japanese Restaurant (Tiánshè Huízhuàn Shòusi; ☎ 139 773 980 85; Yiren Lu; 依仁路) Micro-sized, neat eatery with conveyor-belt sushi creeping past the young and cosmopolitan well-fed of Guìlín; dishes discounted after 9.30pm. It's a short walk along from Rosemary Café in the middle of Yiren Lu at the end of the block of stalls.

Drinking & Entertainment

Ragazza Pub (Yī Rén; ☎ 282 2222; 27 Yiren Lu; 依仁路27号; ⊗ 8pm-2am) Funky and loud with mind-swirling lights and regular live music, this nifty bar on Yiren Lu has been luring Guìlín's young drinkers for more than a decade.

Lijiang Theatre (Líjiāng Jùchǎng; ☎ 285 1280; Binjiang Lu; 滨江路; tickets Y120-180; ⊗ performances 8pm) Show with music, acrobatics and dance, aimed squarely at tourists.

Shopping

For jewellery, clothing, souvenirs and pretty much anything else you can think of, check out Guìlín's cavorting Zhongshan Lu Night Market (桂林市中山路夜市; Guìlínshì Zhōngshān Lù Yèshì). Lit up with bright lights every night from 7pm to 11.30pm along an extensive strip of Zhongshan Zhonglu, all the way from Wumei Lu, north to Jiefang Xilu, there's a strip of stalls selling jade, jewellery, clothing, bags, name chops, perfume and tons of other consumables and trinkets.

Another tourist night market sets up towards the southern end of Zhengyang Lu, but you will have to contend with the persistent *xiǎojiě* (young girls) latching onto males and asking if 'massagey' or, more bluntly, 'sex' is required. For department store shopping, the **Guilin Niko Niko Do Plaza** (cnr Zhongshan Zhonglu & Jiefang Xilu) has a good range of useful stores.

Getting There & Away
AIR

Air tickets can be purchased from the **CAAC Office** (☎ 384 3918 or 384 7252; ⊗ 7.30am-8.30pm) on the corner of Shanghai Lu and Minzhu Lu.

You'll find **Dragonair** (☎ 282 5588, ext 8895) in the Guilin Bravo Hotel.

Guìlín is very well connected to the rest of China (and beyond) by air. Destinations include Běijīng (Y1920), Chéngdū (Y1100), Chóngqìng (Y860), Hǎikǒu (Y840), Guǎngzhōu (Y790), Guìyáng (Y710), Hong Kong (Y1895), Kūnmíng (Y970), Shànghǎi (Y1430) and Xī'ān (Y1220). Seats *may* be available for next-day purchase; you'll need to shop around at different travel agents for discount tickets.

International destinations include regular flights to Seoul (Shǒu'ěr) and Fukuoka, Japan (Fúgāng). Less frequent flights also go to Bangkok, Singapore and Kuala Lumpur; more and more international flights are being added.

Tickets can also be booked through **Guilin Air Service Co Ltd** (17-4 Binjiang Lu), just south of Little Italian.

BUS

Guìlín has numerous connections to a number of destinations in Guǎngxī, Guǎngdōng and as far away as Xiàmén, Fúzhōu and Sānyà from the **main bus station** (Guìlín Kèyùn Zǒngzhàn; ☎ 382 2666) on Zhongshan Nanlu. For short local runs (such as to Yángshuò and Xīng'ān), buses depart from in front of the train station as well as from the bus station. Left luggage is open from 6.30am to 11.30pm and costs from Y3.

TRAIN

Guìlín is not as convenient as Nánníng or Liǔzhōu for train connections (not much starts here) and tickets are harder to come by. Outside national holidays you should have luck, but be prepared to wait an extra day or two for hard sleeper tickets. Guìlín has a main train station and a north train station.

Direct train services from **Guilin train station** (Guìlín Huǒchēzhàn; ☎ 383 3124) include train T6 to Běijīng West (Y401 to Y430, 22 hours, 3.06pm), the K150 to Shànghǎi (Y330 to Y353, 25 hours, 10.11am), the K38 to Guǎngzhōu (Y201 to Y215, 11 hours, 6pm), the K316 to Xī'ān (Y372 to Y399, 25 hours, 5.25pm), the 2055 to Kūnmíng (Y156 to Y169, 22 hours, 8.52am) and the 1557 to Zhànjiāng (hard seat Y76). Other trains run to Liǔzhōu (hard seat Y29), Nánníng (hard seat Y69), Quánzhōu (hard seat Y20) and Xīnxiāng (Y59 to Y67). For Chóngqìng and Chéngdū change trains at Guìyáng.

You can also catch trains K181 and 1337, which depart from Guìlín's **northern station** (Guìlín Běizhàn; ☎ 216 2222), but these are pretty slow, so it might be worth your while going to Nánníng first and buying a ticket there for the direct Nánkūn line to Kūnmíng (15 hours).

Window 7 (☉ 8am to noon and 3pm to 5.30pm) is advertised as welcoming 'foreign guests'.

BUSES FROM GUÌLÍN

Destination	Fare (Y)	Duration (hours)	Departure Time
Bǎisè	155	9	9pm
Běihǎi	170	7	4 per day
Chéngdū	375-395	22	4pm
Chóngqìng	360	16	3pm & 7pm
Guǎngzhōu	160	11	4 per day
Guìpíng	110	6½	9.30am & 4.30pm
Guìyáng	240	11	8pm & 9.30pm
Huáihuà	98	10	2pm
Liǔzhōu	47	2½	every 20min (7am-9.30pm)
Lóngshèng	23	2	every 30min (6.50am-7pm)
Nánníng	88-98	4	every 20min (6.30am-10pm)
Róngshuǐ	38	5	12.30pm
Sānjiāng	27	5	8 per day
Wúzhōu	110	6	6 per day
Xīng'ān	12	1	every 30min (7am-9pm)
Yángshuò	15	1	every 30min (7.10am-8pm)
Zīyuán	25	2	every hr (7.30am-5pm)

Getting Around

TO/FROM THE AIRPORT

Guìlín's Liangjiang International Airport (两江国际机场; Liǎngjiāng Guójì Jīchǎng) is 30km west of the city. CAAC runs buses from the **CAAC Office** (cnr Shanghai Lu & Minzhu Lu) to the airport for Y20, leaving half-hourly from 6.30am to 8.30pm. From the airport, buses run the same hours but may depart later as flights arrive; buses run to the CAAC Office and the Aviation Hotel, via the Tian'e Hotel on Cuizhu Lu. A taxi to the airport costs about Y90 and takes around 40 minutes.

BICYCLE

One of the best ways to get around town is to rent a bike. The youth hostels rent out bikes for around Y20 a day, with a deposit; larger hotels charge more (around Y50 per day). Other bike rental outfits can be found near the bus and train stations and there's another one next to the Overseas Chinese Hotel. The CITS branch downstairs from the Guilin Flowers Youth Hostel rents out bikes (per half/whole day Y15/25). To protect your deposit, always check the bike carefully before renting.

BUS

Most of the city buses that stop in front of Guilin's bus and train stations will get you to the major sights. Buses 51 to 58 are free buses.

Bus 2 Runs from South Stream Park through town passing Elephant Hill Park, Seven Stars Park, Wave-Subduing Hill, Folded Silk Streamers Hill and Guānyīn Pavilion.

Bus 3 Runs from Guilin train station past the bus station to Xishan Park and on to Reed Flute Cave Park.

Bus 9 Runs from Guilin train station along Jiefang Donglu to Seven Stars Park.

Bus 11 Runs from Seven Stars Park across Liberation Bridge, down to the bus and train stations and on to Ping Shan.

Bus 51 From Guilin train station past the main bus station to Central Sq and on to Beiji Sq (北极广场; Běijí Guǎngchǎng) and beyond.

Bus 58 From South Stream Park via Elephant Trunk Hill, Seven Stars Park, Wave-Subduing Hill, Folded Silk Streamers Hill and on to Reed Flute Cave.

A shuttle bus (景点穿梭巴士; jǐngdiǎn chuānsuō bāshì; Y10) runs every 20 minutes between 8.10am and 5.55pm from the CITS office across from the train station, travelling to Elephant Trunk Park, Wave-Subduing Hill, Reed Flute Park, Central Sq, Folk Culture Park, Seven Stars Park and back to the train station.

TAXI

Taxi flagfall is Y7, plus a Y1 petrol charge. If you like the look of a taxi driver, book him or her for the day to whisk you around Guìlín's sights. A car will cost around Y100 for a day-long tour if you don't have the time or the inclination to take to public transport, but remember that few taxi drivers speak any English.

AROUND GUÌLÍN

Jiāngtóuzhōu 江头洲

pop 800

With its gorgeous narrow cobblestone alleyways, bucolic rhythms and pastoral aspect, this peaceful village – located in a region where dialects seem to differ from village to village – has splendid panoramas of ancient houses, ancient lanes and old barns, surrounded by gorgeous countryside and karst peaks. The village – whose inhabitants are all surnamed Zhou (周) – is more than 1000 years old, but it was during the Qing dynasty that the village became famed for its large population of virtuous and righteous officials, who bequeathed Jiāngtóuzhōu its rich architectural heritage. Native sons include the northern Song philosopher and man of ideas, Zhou Dunyi.

Constructed of neatly finished bricks and lining the village's maze of small alleys, Jiāngtóuzhōu's old homesteads are typically characterised by their huge wooden gates, inscribed horizontal boards and spacious courtyards. Look out for faded portraits of Mao Zedong on doorways. On the edges of the village, buildings are simply made of mud bricks.

At the edge of the village as you approach from Jiǔwū and spanning the small Hulong River is the ancient and misshapen arched **Hulong Bridge** (Hùlóng Qiáo), alongside a recently built small brick pagoda. At the head of the village not far from the bridge is the **Ailian Family Temple** (爱莲家祠; Àilián Jiācí; admission Y10), the local ancestral shrine. Within the temple is a huge courtyard containing a couple of dishevelled bìxì (mythical tortoiselike dragons); lovely views extend from the upstairs gallery.

Looking at the temple from outside the gate you are faced with Chinese political slogans from a bygone age: the faded Chinese reads 'The Communist Party forever' and 'Chairman Mao forever'. Throughout the village, other residences are open so you can poke your head around the door for a look-see and appreciate plenty of richly decorated woodwork. Several notable houses can be found along Jinshi Jie (进士街), including the former home of Zhou Ruiqi, a former student leader of the May 4th Movement, at No 38. Inscribed on the doors of the home of Zhou Zerun is another slogan from the Cultural Revolution days.

A popular time to visit the village is during the **Girl's Festival** (姑娘节; Gūniang Jié), held on the 13th day of the 6th lunar month, when the village women dress up in their Sunday best.

If you want to overnight in Jiāngtóuzhōu, the modest **Láishānlǐ Fànzhuāng** (来山里饭庄; ☎ 138 783 119 07; dm Y20) has simple fan rooms without loo. It's on the corner of the road around 500m from the village on the way to Jiǔwū.

To get to Jiāngtóuzhōu, first take bus 100 from Guilin train station or Guilin bus station to Guìlín Běizhàn (桂林北站) on Zhongshan Beilu, north of Beiji Sq (北极广场; Běijí Guǎngchǎng). From Guìlín Běizhàn take a bus through the miserable industrial periphery of Guìlín to the bus station at Língchuān (灵川; Y2, 30 minutes) and transfer to a bus across arable land to Jiǔwū (九屋; Y3, 35 minutes), around 20km from Língchuān. Buses run from between Língchuān and Jiǔwū every 10 minutes between 7am and 5.30pm. From Jiǔwū, it's a 10- to 15-minute walk to Jiāngtóuzhōu.

Dàxū 大圩 (大墟)

Pleasantly situated 18km south of Guìlín on the east bank of the Li River, Dàxū is a riverside Ming and Qing dynasty town that warrants a morning or afternoon's exploration of its characteristic narrow alleyways.

Although the old town originally dates to 200 AD, its commercial history as a river port dates to the Song dynasty, with its greatest period of prosperity arriving with the Ming and Qing dynasties. By the time of the Republic the town had eight major streets.

The area you want to explore is the **Daxu Old Town** (大圩古镇; Dàxū Gǔzhèn), echoing the rattle of mah-jong pieces and the grunting of pigs and replete with absorbing historic

textures, rather than the more modern and characterless part of town. To reach the old town, head south from the bus drop-off point and walk under the railway bridge.

Jiefang Jie (解放街) is a rewarding street of ancient merchant shops and flagstones. The medicine shop at No 40 is worth a look for its medicinal materials and preparations. The **Wanshou Bridge** (万寿桥; Wànshòu Qiáo) is a marvellous old structure with a couple of trees growing out of its side. Originally dating to the Ming dynasty, it was washed away and rebuilt during the reign of Qing emperor Guangxu, events recorded on several plinths along the side of the bridge.

Dongfang Jie (东方街), running from the other side of the bridge, is a similar strip of old shops and houses, running on to the modest brick Yongan Gate. One of the best-preserved residences, the **Former Residence of Liao Jiuli** (廖就利故居; Liào Jiùlì Gùjū; admission Y5) at No 47 is a substantial rice merchant's house with a spacious upstairs chamber where the rice was loaded.

Note the number of bànxīn bànlǎo, hybridised 'half-new, half-old' houses, as locals call them – old houses with recently grafted-on ugly conversions. Elderly Dàxū residents also avow to a magnificent old gate that once stood at Gulou Matou (Drum Tower Dock) that was tragically pulled down during the Cultural Revolution.

Other interesting streets worth browsing include Minzhu Jie (民主街), with its small alleys threading down to the docks. Several small family-run hostels can be found here if you want to spend the night, including a very basic kèzhàn (客栈) at 28 Minzhu Jie with simple beds for Y10.

To reach Dàxū from Guìlín, take a bus (Y5, 30 minutes, every 30 minutes) from the local bus depot around 200m behind the bus station on Zhongshan Nanlu. Alternatively, from the bus station take a Guānyán-bound bus (Y5) that passes by Dàxū. There are also buses (Y10) to Dàxū from the bus station in Língchuān, if you want to combine a trip to Jiāngtóuzhōu and Dàxū. It is also possible to reach Dàxū by bus from Xīngpíng and Yángshuò.

Ling Canal 灵渠

In Xīng'ān County, about 70km north of Guìlín, the Ling Canal (Líng Qú) is described by locals in fabulous terms: 'The north has the Great Wall, the south has the Ling Canal'. Built between 219 and 214 BC during the reign of the first Qin emperor (Qin Shihuang) to transport supplies to his army, the canal is – from a technical point of view – counted among the three great feats of Chinese engineering (along with the Great Wall and the Du Jiang irrigation system in Sìchuān).

The 34km canal links the Xiāng Hé – which flows into the Yangzi River (Cháng Jiāng) and the Li River, which flows into the Zhū Jiāng – thus connecting two of China's major waterways and aiding China's expansion into the Southwest.

You can see the Ling Canal at the market town of **Xīng'ān** (兴安). Two branches of the canal flow through the town, at the northern and southern ends. Come springtime, you'll be elbow to elbow with photographers jockeying for position to snap shots of the peach blossoms lining the canals and spillway.

From Guìlín, buses going to Xīng'ān depart every half hour until 6.30pm (Y8 to Y12, two hours) and hourly express buses going to Quánzhōu (Y10, one hour) also pass through Xīng'ān.

Crown Cave 冠岩

If you need a further subterranean fix, 29km south of Guìlín near Cǎopíng Village (草坪), this **cave** (Guàn Yán; admission Y60) is a 12km-long attraction heavily peddled by Guìlín travel agents. Either walk to the entrance of the cave from the car park or ride the high-speed train cart (Y30) the 3.2km into the cavern. Once inside you can clamber aboard a tourist train, an elevator, or navigate along the 3km of waterways by canoe. If you are lucky enough you may even have time to admire some limestone formations.

South of Crown Cave, Xiāngbā Dǎo (乡吧岛; admission Y20), in the middle of the Li River, is a monolithic theme park of more traditional character focusing on the province's ethnic minority folklore and customs. The island is studded with traditional minority architecture, a central performance area, craft shops, minority-cuisine restaurants, workshops and an entertainment stadium.

Xiāngbā Dǎo is 500m south of Crown Cave and can be accessed by boat from the cave. Some of the Li River tour boats stop off at both the cave and island on their way to Yángshuò.

LI RIVER 漓江

This beautiful river is the shimmering link between Guìlín and Yángshuò and one of the main tourist attractions of the area. A thousand years ago a poet enthused about the scenery around Yángshuò: 'The river forms a green gauze belt, the mountains are like blue jade hairpins'. The 83km stretch between the towns may not quite match this psychedelic vision, but some extraordinary peaks, sprays of bamboo lining the river banks, fishers in small boats and picturesque villages jostle for your attention.

As is the Chinese habit, every feature along the route has been named with a moniker from myth, legend or fancy. **Paint Brush Hill** juts straight up from the ground with a pointed tip like a Chinese writing brush. **Cock-Fighting Hills** stand face to face like two cocks about to engage in battle. **Nine Horse Mural Hill**, past the small town of Yángdì, is a sheer cliff rising abruptly out of the water; there are supposed to be the images of nine horses in the weathered patterns on the cliff face.

A shorter version of this trip can be made between Cǎopíng (草坪) and Xīngpíng (兴坪; see p178), from where buses run regularly to Yángshuò. Take a bus to Cǎopíng (Y8) from the local bus depot around 200m behind the bus station on Zhongshan Nanlu in Guìlín and find a boat owner down by the Li River. Boats take around an hour and a half and cost in the region of Y100 per person. If you take the bus to Cǎopíng, you can stop off at Dàxū (p165) en route.

YÁNGSHUÒ 阳朔

A well-stocked bastion of Western backpacker civilisation, few travellers can voyage around China's Southwest without constant bulletins about Yángshuò. Everyone and his dog has an opinion. Some arrivals groan that Yángshuò is overdone and swamped with tourist mayhem; you will also rapidly gather that the village is not the 'real China' (whatever that means). Indeed some disillusioned sightseers strive to put as much distance between themselves and this small pocket of Guǎngxī as possible.

But for every put-down there's an ebullient paean for its luxurious karst backdrop, its generous bundle of activities, unflagging sense of fun, varied cuisine (read 'backpacker menu'), with-it attitude (a far larger percentage of locals speak good English compared to Shànghǎi or Běijīng), old Banyan trees and Yángshuò's

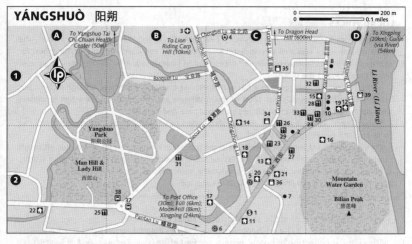

YÁNGSHUÒ 阳朔

INFORMATION
Bank of China 中国银行 1 C2
Café Too & Hostel 自游人旅店 ...... (see 14)
Dr Lily Li .... (see 23)
Kodak Express 柯达 2 C2
People's Hospital 人民医院 3 B1
Public Security Bureau 公安局 4 C1
Red Cherry Internet Café
  红樱桃网吧 5 C2
Xingji Internet Café 星际网吧 6 C2

SIGHTS & ACTIVITIES
Bike Asia .... (see 23)
Budizhen International Kungfu School
  步地真国际功夫馆 7 C2
Cloud 9 Restaurant 聚福楼 ....(see 5)
Former Residence of Xu Beihong
  徐悲鸿故居 8 D1
Jiangxi Guildhall 江西会馆 .... (see 27)
Karst Cafe 9 D1
Lizard Lounge 10 C1
Spider Man Climbing 蜘蛛人攀岩 (see 15)

SLEEPING
Aiyuan Hotel 瑷源宾馆 11 C2
Backstreet Hostel
  桂花巷国际青年旅馆 .... (see 33)
Bamboo House & Hotel 竹林饭店 12 D1
Bamboo House Inn & Café 竹林饭店 13 C2
Café Too & Hostel 自游人旅店 14 C2
Hongfu Palace Hotel .... (see 27)
Hotel Explorer 文化饭店 15 D1
Monkey Jane's Guesthouse
  背包客栈 16 D2
Paradise Yangshuo Resort
  阳朔百乐来度假饭店 17 C2
Seventh Heaven 18 C2
Venice Hotel 威尼斯酒店 19 D1
West Street International Youth Hostel
  西街国际青年旅馆 20 C1
White Lion Hotel 未来恩饭店 21 C2
Yangshuo Li River Hotel
  阳朔漓江饭店 22 A2

EATING
Bar 98 98酒吧 23 C2

Drifter's 旅行者 24 D1
Farmer's Trading Market 农贸市场 .25 A2
Green Lotus Café 年青人咖啡店 ... (see 20)
Kaya Bar 卡雅 26 C1
Le Vôtre 乐德法式餐厅 27 C2
MC Blues 大篷车中西餐厅 28 D1
Meiyou Café 没有饭店 29 C2
Ming Yuan 明园精品咖啡 30 D1
Night Market 夜市 31 B2
Pure Lotus Vegetarian Restaurant
  暗香蔬影素菜馆 32 D1
Red Star Express 红星比萨 33 C1

SHOPPING
Sunshine 100 阳光100西街广场 34 C1
Sunshine 100 阳光100西街广场 35 C1
Vanishing Tribes 36 C2

TRANSPORT
Bus Station 客运总站 37 B2
Private Buses to Guilín, Fúli, Yángdí &
  Xīngping 往桂林, 福利, 杨堤,
  兴坪的班车 38 B2
Wharf 码头 39 D1

excellent ear for the Red Hot Chilli Peppers and other emissaries of Western rock.

If you want your China experience totally unadulterated by Western fads and fashions, Yángshuò will be a nightmare incarnate and the last place to drop your backpack. If, however, you are angling for fun and some of China's most spectacular scenery, Yángshuò could put you in seventh heaven. And with increasing numbers of travellers flocking to Yángshuò on a long-term basis to train in taichi and kung fu in idyllic surrounds, turn their hand to Chinese cooking, grapple with Mandarin in the popular language courses on offer, or scurry out of town on rock climbing jaunts up stunning karst peaks, there's more than enough to fill your travel calendar and you could be here till the cows come home.

Orientation
Yángshuò proper is small and very easy to navigate. The principal street and hub of Yángshuò's tourist cosmos is Xi Jie (西街; West Street) also called 'Foreigner Street', running northeast to the Li River and lined with Western-style cafés, hotels and tourist shops. Just west of the Paradise Yangshuo Resort, Xi Jie loops west, parallel to Pantao

Lu for a short distance of stalls and shops. Heading northeast from Xi Jie is Chengzhong Lu, with a similar collection of hotels, restaurants and shops and itself intersected by busy Diecui Lu. Linked to the southern extremity of Xi Jie, Pantao Lu forms the southwestern boundary of Yángshuò centre and is the main artery to/from Guìlín. The further you go from Xi Jie or from Pantao Lu at its intersection with Xi Jie, the closer you get to Chinese group-tour reality.

Xi Jie is a pedestrian mall, free from bicycles and other traffic.

Dangers & Annoyances

As with Guìlín, rigorously fend off touts who aim to take you on tours or steer you in a half-nelson towards hotels of their choosing. Yángshuò is small with most decent hotels (all English-speaking) clumped together along and off Xi Jie, so finding one that suits you is a piece of cake. Most sights can be visited solo without assistance from pushy guides.

Information

Travel agencies can be found all over Yángshuò and all backpacker-oriented cafés and bars can dispense advice to guests. Also ask at your hotel, but shop around for the best deals.

Bank of China (West end of Xi Jie; 9am-5pm) Foreign exchange and ATM that takes international cards.

Café Too & Hostel (132-3783 1208; 7 Chengzhong Lu; local beer Y7; 8am-midnight) Selection of English paperback fiction.

Dr Lily Li (881 4625; next to Bar 98 on Guihua Xiang) Acupuncture, therapeutic massage, hot cupping, reflexology. Recommended by several readers.

Kodak Express (Xi Jie)

People's Hospital (Renmin Yiyuan; Shenshan Lu)

Post office (yóujú; Pantao Lu; 8am-5pm) Has English-speaking staff and long-distance phone services.

Public Security Bureau (PSB; Gōngānjú; Chengbei Lu) This PSB is well versed in dealing with travellers and has several fluent English speakers. That said, always be calm if taking in a complaint about a local business; losing your cool will get you nowhere. If you need a visa extension you'll have to head further afield; this office doesn't issue them.

Red Cherry Internet Café (Hóngyīngtáo Wǎngbā; 2nd fl, same block as Cloud 9 Restaurant, Chengzhong Lu; per hr Y5; 24hr) Pricey.

Xingji Internet Café (Xīngjì Wǎngbā; Pantao Lu; per hr Y1.5 8am-6pm, per hr Y2 6pm-midnight; 8am-midnight)

Sights

Travellers come to Yángshuò to get out of town and into the countryside that envelops it, but there's loads to do in Yángshuò itself; see opposite for details.

In the southeastern corner of town is Yángshuò's main peak, **Bilian Peak** (Bìlián Fēng; admission Y30). Because it has a flat northern face that is supposed to resemble an ancient bronze mirror, it is also called Bronze Mirror Peak (Tóngjìng Fēng). The peak rises up next to the Li River, in the **Mountain Water Garden** (Shānshuǐ Yuán).

Yangshuo Park (Yángshuò Gōngyuán; admission Y6) is in the western part of town, and here you'll find **Man Hill** (Xíláng Shān; admission Y9), which is supposed to resemble a young man bowing and scraping to a shy young girl represented by **Lady Hill** (Xiǎogū Shān). Other hills nearby are named after animals: **Lion Riding Carp Hill**

(Shīzi Qí Lǐyú Shān), **Dragon Head Hill** (Lóngtóu Shān) and the like.

It's amazing how many travellers come to Yángshuò and don't really see the town, but the area north of Xi Jie and off Chengzhong Lu and Diecui Lu has some great small-town trekking opportunities: back alleys, small markets and throngs of Chinese tourists poking around dozens of shops. The **Former Residence of Xu Beihong** (Xú Bēihóng Gùjū; 17 Xianqian Jie) is one of Yángshuò's few cultural landmarks. Innovative Chinese artist Xu Beihong (1895–1953) is best remembered for his galloping horses that injected dynamism into previously static forms of Chinese brushwork. Admirers of Chinese guildhall architecture can glean something from a visit to the Hongfu Palace Hotel and Le Vôtre Café, both of which occupy sections of the former **Jiangxi Guildhall** (Jiāngxī Huìguǎn), a notable vestige from the Qing dynasty occupying a site along Xi Jie.

A popular evening activity is to take in the **cormorant fishing** on the Li River that usually begins around 7pm to 7.30pm. It is a show for the tourists, but is still entertaining, although the river supports an ever-dwindling supply of fish. Hotels and restaurants usually charge around Y25 per person.

Courses & Activities

Once you have exhausted the splendid countryside, Yángshuò is a premier place to sit back and educate yourself with a course or two.

TAICHI & KUNG FU

With its traditional picture-perfect karst peaks, Yángshuò is a popular place to glean the fundamentals of taichi (*tàijíquán*; see p170). The **Yangshuo Tai Chi Chuan Health Centre** (Baoqan Lu; ☎ 890 0125; www.southchina-taichi.com; ✆ office 7-10am & 4-6.30pm) runs an impressive gamut of taichi routines, from Chen and Yang style forms to push hands and weapons forms, including the sword and sabre. *Qìgōng* is also taught. The principal teacher is Wang Zhiping – whose training was essentially in the vigorous Chen style but who is also adept at Shaolin boxing – who introduces students to taichi via the simplified Yang form. Tuition consists of four hours every day (apart from Sundays) and costs Y40 per hour, Y600 per week or Y1800 per month. Chinese-language lessons are also offered. There's an English speaker available during office hours. The school can also arrange accommodation, but you can of course do that independently. Another popular martial arts school is the **Budizhen International Kungfu School** (☎ 139 773 503 77; budizhenbooking@gmail.com; website under construction; 62 Lotus Lane) where you can get to grips with its distinctive style of Budizhen (步地真) Kung fu (*gōngfu*) taught by Mr Gao. Training – also in taichi and *qìgōng* – is seven days a week, from 9am to 11am and in the evenings from 6pm to 7.30pm.

CLIMBING

Climbing in Yángshuò has mushroomed in popularity over the past decade. There are plenty of climbing outfits in town, and most are ebullient about the rock-climbing potential here, with constant discoveries of new and better peaks. In all around 300 routes can be chosen from, including around 200 bolted routes in the area.

Autumn is the best season for clambering up the karst towers. Across the road from the MC Blues, **Lizard Lounge** (☎ 881 1033; www.china climb.com; 45 Xianqian Jie) is an excellent bar-cum-climbing centre with its own small bouldering wall. Half-day climbs are Y300, including equipment, transport, food, water and guides. **Karst Café** (www.karstclimber.com; 45 Xianqian Jie), just down the road, has one- to 10-day climbing excursions. **Spider Man Climbing** (Zhīzhūrén Pānyán; ☎ 881 2339; www.s-climbing.com; 36 Xianqian Jie) offers half- or whole-day climbing expeditions for Y180 or Y300 respectively. For experienced climbers, multipitch climbs are also offered for Y300, as well as three-day, one week and two-week climbs (Y700/1600/2500). Prices include transport, shoe hire, equipment and guides. You can also pick up equipment here as well as a copy of *Yangshuo Rock Climbing* (Y80). Ask about climbs in the White Mountain area, Baby Frog area and Copper door area. Other rock climbing outfits can be found along Guihua Jie.

CYCLING

In most cases you just need to hire a bike from any of the myriad outlets and head out into the countryside (see p65). If you want to hire a decent and well-maintained mountain bike or join a biking tour, try **Bike Asia** (☎ 882 6521; www.bikeasia.net; 2nd fl, 42 Guihua Lu, above Bar 98), which arranges outings from half-day expeditions to three-day adventures. Two- to four-week cycling expeditions are also arranged through China, Mongolia, Laos, Cambodia, Tibet and Nepal.

KAYAKING

Some travellers identify kayaking trips on the Li River as the highlight of their Yángshuò trip. Putting yourself in a kayak and paddling for three or more hours along a glistening band of water to Yángshuò gives you the freedom to immerse yourself in the lazy Li River panoramas at your own pace. Ask at any of the travel agents or your hotel for details.

COOKING

Cloud 9 Restaurant (Jùfú Lóu; cloud9restaurant03@yahoo .com; Chengzhong Lu) to the south of the Seventh Heaven hotel offers morning or afternoon

---

THE SECRETS OF TAICHI

Characterised by its lithe and graceful movements, *tàijíquán* (太极拳; literally 'Fist of the Supreme Ultimate'), also known as taichi, is an ancient Chinese physical discipline practised by legions of Chinese the land over.

Considerable confusion exists about taichi – is it a martial art, a form of meditation, a *qìgōng* (气功) style or an exercise? In fact, taichi can be each and all of these, depending on what you seek from the art and how deep you dig into its mysteries.

As a straightforward health regimen, taichi strengthens the leg muscles, exercises the joints, gives the heart and cardiovascular system a good workout and promotes flexibility. It also relaxes the body, dissolving stress, loosening the joints and generating a feel of wellbeing.

It may not look demanding, but the 108 movement, 20-minute Yang-style long form is tiring, while the low postures of the Chen style of taichi – closest in essence of all the taichi styles to Shaolin boxing – can be excruciatingly strenuous to perform, and will have your legs shaking with the strain.

Taichi is a superlative system of *qìgōng*, and despite being a moving sequence of *qìgōng* moves, the art is also taught with stationary exercises to circulate *qì*. All of the benefits associated with *qìgōng* come with the practice of taichi.

As a system of meditation, taichi promotes relaxation and makes practitioners feel both centred and focused. Taichi will also introduce you to the meditation techniques of the Taoists as the art is closely allied to the philosophy of Taoism.

Taichi can be trained as a martial art as all the movements are ultimately traceable to the martial arts of the Shaolin Temple, although its effective use as a fighting style requires considerable time and patience, compared with other more direct martial arts. In order to use taichi effectively, the student must learn to relax the body during confrontation, and this involves suppressing instincts to tense up when threatened. Martial arts practice commences with 'push hands', a two-person routine where one student tries to unbalance the other. Push hands develops sensitivity in the hands and teaches the student to relax the body in all situations. If adept at taichi, it is far easier to learn other martial arts, as the student will have learned a way of moving that is common to all of the fighting arts.

Taichi students outdo each other with fables of superhuman exploits by legendary taichi masters, with anecdotes increasingly implausible with each retelling. Stories abound of masters who can crush pieces of ceramic between their fingers, fling their opponents 9m across the room with a shrug or return hardened karate practitioners to square one. Such anecdotes dangle tempting carrots in front of students on their gruelling and elusive path to mastery of their art.

If taking up taichi, a few useful pointers will help you progress in your practice:

- When executing a movement, motion is directed by the waist before moving to the hands (observe a skilled practitioner and see how movement reaches the hands last). The hands never lead the movement.

- When performing a form (as the moving sets are called), keep your head on a level, neither rising nor dipping.

- Practise taichi as if suspended by an invisible thread from a point at the top of your head.

- Don't lean forward or backwards and keep your body vertical.

- Relax your shoulders and let your weight sink downwards.

cooking classes for Y80 a person. Each class starts off with a trip to the Farmers' Trading Market (p174) for fresh ingredients. There are two classes per day, from 9.30am to 11.30am and from 4pm to 8pm.

The **Yangshuo Cooking School** (☎ 137-8843 7286) helps you chuck together a tasty Beer Fish and other local specialities from farmhouse surrounds after going on trips to local markets for ingredients.

LANGUAGE COURSES

With one in two people on earth conversant in either English or Chinese, the time has come to learn Mandarin, so why not do it in Yángshuò? With subsistence costs so low and with all that Yángshuò has to offer, language schools are all the rage. Teaching English is also popular, with schools such as the **Owen Language College** (☎ 881 8555; www.owencollege.com) exchanging free accommodation and meals in exchange for a commitment to teaching students. It's worth considering if you want to stay in Yángshuò for a while.

Sleeping

Travellers tend to arrive in Yángshuò expecting bargain room prices, but remember that it's the market that dictates. Competition generally keeps things somewhat sane, but show up in high season (summer) and you may have to pay the asking price for a bed. In winter, negotiation seems to re-enter the picture in most places. Whatever you do, avoid turning up during the big holiday seasons (first week of May and October and the Spring Festival) – otherwise known as 'Gold Week' (Huángjīn Zhōu) – when rooms prices go through the roof.

The most popular hotels are along Xi Jie, although this can be quite noisy because of late-night drinking binges by travellers in the cafés below, other hotels are more quietly tucked away down small alleys off the main drag. This area definitely has a monopoly on charm, although considerable variety exists among hotels. The Chinese section of town has more white-tiled, midrange options available, but they have little character and neither does the area.

Most of the budget backpacker options on Xi Jie offer very reasonably priced midrange options, and it's generally not essential to book ahead unless it's the holiday period. A number of travellers complain that many of the older hostels suffer from winter damp. To avoid this, check out your room thoroughly before dumping your bags. It seems like every other shop in the streets around Xi Jie has a 'room available' (有房; *yŏufáng*) so pop in and ask, if other places are full. Laundry service is available at most hotels; alternatively, laundries are not difficult to find.

If you want a comfortable sojourn, before you dive into *the* most expensive accommodation option, note that cheap backpacker-friendly hotels have staff with superior and more colloquial English-language skills and sophisticated social skills with foreigners than many of their midrange equivalents that cater more to the Chinese crowd.

BUDGET

Monkey Jane's Guesthouse (Bēibāo Kèzhàn; ☎ 882 1603; monkeyjanesguesthouse@yahoo.com; 28 Lianfeng Zhongxiang; 莲峰中巷28号; dm Y20, s from Y40, tw Y70; ❄) Set back from the Xi Jie action around 80m down Lianfeng Zhongxiang (follow the signs) run-of-the-mill rooms are spread out here over numerous floors, but a worthwhile rooftop bar with good views (with towering peak right behind) is an arm-twister. All rooms come with air-con. Laundry costs Y10 per kg.

Bamboo House Inn & Café (Zhúlín Fàndiàn; ☎ 881 5758 or 882 3222; bamboohouse23@hotmail.com; Guihua Xiang, 23 Guihua Lu; 桂花巷桂花路23号; 5-bed dm with air-con Y20, s/d Y50/60, s/d with air-con Y60/70, s/d with balcony Y80; ❄ 🖳) Down a small lane off Xi Jie, this quiet place has pleasant staff. Dorms are simple and the bathrooms are somewhat primitive but there's laundry (per kg Y12), bike rental (Y10) and free internet. At the time of writing, single and double rooms were undergoing renovation. If a more comfortable stay tops your agenda, try its sister, Bamboo House & Hotel (p172), and enquire about its soon-to-open accommodation in the 20-room block on the other side of Xi Jie.

Backstreet Hostel (Guìhuāxiàng Guójì Qīngnián Lǚguǎn; ☎ 881 4077; 60 Guihua Nanxiang; 桂花南巷60号; 4-6 bed dm Y25, d Y80) An average kind of place needing a dose of tender loving care, with OK rooms, tucked away next to Red Star Express off Xi Jie. Internet (per hour Y3), laundry, kitchen, bike rental (per day Y10), rock climbing (per half day Y180). Doubles are typically Y70, apart from during the feverish holiday season.

West Street International Youth Hostel (Xijiē Guójì Qīngnián Lǚguǎn; ☎ 882 0933; fax 882 0988; 102 Xi Jie;

GUĂNGXĪ

西街1-2号; dm Y25, s & d Y120; ☒ ☐) Rather tatty and unkempt, this functional place could do with a visit from Mrs Mop and a shot of character, but dorm beds are low cost and worth earmarking if other places are jam-packed. Internet access available (per hour Y3).

Bamboo House & Hotel (Zhúlín Fàndiàn; Longmu Xiang, off Xi Jie; 龙母巷, 西街; d Y100-150, family r Y120-180; ☒ ☐) Tucked quietly away down Longmu Alley (Dragon Mother Alley) towards the eastern extremity of Xi Jie, this second branch of the Bamboo Inn (p171) hits all the right notes, with friendly and approachable staff and fine rooms. The granite-clad bathrooms may be an odd selection, but welcome to the comfiest mattresses in Yángshuò's budget domain. Internet access and laundry service available. Its staff speak excellent English and offer good travel advice.

MIDRANGE

Seventh Heaven (☎ 882 6101; fax 882 6101; the7th heavencafe@hotmail.com; 2 Chengzhong Lu; 城中路2号; r Y200-250; ☒ ☐) Tucked away off the main Xi Jie drag, this enjoyable place has pleasant, clean rooms decked out with attractive drapery. There's a bar and restaurant downstairs. All rooms come with balcony, shower, air-con and TV. Free internet use. No phones in rooms.

White Lion Hotel (Wèilái'ēn Fàndiàn; ☎ 882 7778; www.whitelionchina.com; 103 Xi Jie; 西街103号; s/tw/tr Y288/368/488; ☒) Owned by an American who donates money to support kids in education, this agreeable hotel has a courtyard-style interior and although rooms are showing their age, they are pleasant enough with showers, and wooden floors, and baths in the pricier rooms. Discounts see singles fall to Y120 and twins to Y150.

Hotel Explorer (Wénhuà Fàndiàn; ☎ 882 8116; fax 882 7816; jimmyqin@hotmail.com; 40 Xianqian Jie; 县前街40号; s/d/tr with bathroom & air-con Y368/418/548; ☒) Attractively presented in the quaint-old-courtyard look, this popular hotel has fine rooms with large bathrooms and friendly staff. The location off Xi Jie muffles the decibels, and discounts make rooms affordable at all but the busiest times.

Hongfu Palace Hotel (Hóngfú Fàndiàn; ☎ 882 9489; fax 882 9499; 79 Xi Jie; 西街79号; d Y380-480, tr Y660; ☒) Located in part of the historic Jiāngxī Guildhall (p169) on Xi Jie, this pleasant courtyard-style residence maintains its Qing dynasty appearance with original features and spacious doubles. Internet access; ask for discounts.

Aiyuan Hotel (Àiyuán Bīnguǎn; ☎ 881 1966; fax 881 1916; 115 Xi Jie; 西街115号; d Y480; ☒) Friendly staff, a neat disposition and crisp rooms with clean bathrooms make this hotel at the western foot of Xi Jie worth considering, although the adjacent KFC can be noisy. Rooms with hill view are pricier. Discounts bring doubles down to around Y200.

Venice Hotel (Wēinísī Jiǔdiàn; ☎ 881 5898 or 881 5889; 20 Xi Jie; 西街20号; d/tr/ste Y580/680/780; ☒) With elegant and well-maintained rooms, including particularly spacious and stylishly designed family rooms, this hotel at the eastern, quiet cusp of Xi Jie welcomes with a bright and airy courtyard-style lobby area. During slack and slow months, prices of doubles sink affordably to Y120.

Yangshuo Li River Hotel (Yángshuò Líjiāng Fàndiàn; ☎ 881 6966; fax 881 6919; 93 Pantao Lu; 蟠桃路93号; s/d/tr Y680/880/980; ☒) If you want a clean mid-range double with safe, mini-bar, hair dryer and a reasonably smart hotel ambience, this newish place does the trick. But it lacks the ease with foreigners that'll wow you along Xi Jie, and the Pantao Lu area is a bit grim and charmless.

TOP END

Paradise Yangshuo Resort (Yángshuò Bǎilèlái Dùjià Fàndiàn; ☎ 822 2109; www.paradiseyangshuo.com; 116 Xi Jie; 西街116号; d standard/deluxe Y664/913; ☒ ☒) Fine if you want the synthetic Yángshuò experience. Rooms are immaculate and provide a tempting zone of comfort, but the swimming pool, karaoke lounge, massage parlour scream tour group, as do photos of visiting presidents and dignitaries in the lobby. Fish for discounts.

Eating & Drinking

Xi Jie teems with small cafés and bars offering a smorgasbord of Western and Chinese cuisine and perennial travellers' favourites. For anyone who has been on the road around China for a period it's a good excuse to ditch the oily, stir-fried vegetables, *yóutiáo* (fried bread sticks) and weak tea and grab a steaming cup of coffee and a Continental(-ish) breakfast. Cafés tend to open at around 7.30am, serving set breakfasts and serenading hungover guests with soft music, morphing at night into late-night bars, with live music, lashings of alcohol and garrulous crowds.

Most cafés serve reasonable to good fare and travellers will be attracted by their atmosphere.

Some specialities (eg French cuisine) can be found. Keep an eye and a nostril out for Uighur chefs from Xīnjiāng who serve up late-night roast lamb kebabs (羊肉串; *yángròuchuàn*) on Xi Jie. Also look out for street vendors with copper kettles selling black sesame paste (黑芝麻糊; *hēi zhīma hú*), a very sweet and glutinous concoction which will set you back only Y3 per bowl. The vendor puts in the ingredients (osmanthus, lotus seeds, peanuts, black sesame, walnuts and wolfberry) and slops in hot water from the kettle, gives it a stir and there you go. Also look out for sellers of ginger sweets (姜糖; *jiāngtáng*).

As with accommodation, most travellers gravitate to the more laid-back part of town down Xie Jie, where all of Yángshuò's personality is concentrated. Sheer numbers make for fierce competition – and the standard of spoken English is unusually good for China. However, Xi Jie now so seethes with tour groups and touts that quiet alfresco evening dining is pretty much history.

Normally Yángshuò would be too small to warrant a KFC, but Colonel Sanders' empire has given it the thumbs up thanks to the steady stream of tourists; the branch is next to the Bank of China on Xi Jie.

A massive **night market** (Diecui Lu; ♥ from 6pm) gets going across from the bus station. With tents, tables and chairs you can settle in for a sampling of local delicacies such as *tiánluóniàng* (stuffed field snails) whatever the weather. Another smaller night market sets up on Chengzhong Lu. Useful stalls set up during the day across from the bus station on the forecourt in front of Yangshuo Park, selling *píjiǔ yú* (啤酒鱼; beer fish), *málàtàng* (麻辣烫; spicy soup) and clumps of fruit. If you are looking for Chinese restaurants, you can find a cluster at the west end of Xi Jie.

Bars can be safely divided into those that attract Chinese drinkers and those aimed squarely at Westerners, although crossovers exist and some spots cater to foreign diners during the day but lure Chinese punters in the evening. Beers include the unavoidable Guǎngxī-brewed Liquan (漓泉啤酒), plus a foreign gaggle of brews from Heineken to Corona. Western bars run out of steam roughly at the intersection of Chengzhong Lu and Xi Jie, from where Chinese restaurants take the baton.

Bar 98 (Jiǔbā Jiǔbā; ☎ 881 4605; 42 Guihua Lu; 桂花路42号; Liquan beer Y7, large Tsingtao Y12) All-day breakfasts (Y20 to Y24), veggie burgers (Y18), salads and pizzas (Y18 to Y28), no-nonsense ambience and pool table.

Café Too & Hostel (☎ 132-3783 1208; johnnylu668@yahoo.com; 7 Chengzhong Lu; 城中路7号; local beer Y7; ♥ 8am-midnight) This comfortable spot is run by Mr Lu, the resourceful English-speaking owner who has put up a wall or two of English paperback fiction. There's free internet for guests and rooms upstairs (twins with aircon and shower Y70 to Y80) for those keen to dwell beyond earshot of Xi Jie.

MC Blues (Dàpéngchē Zhōngxī Cāntīng; ☎ 882 9222; 40 Xianqian Jie; 县前街40号; local beer Y10, large Tsingtao Y18; ♥ 7am-midnight) Whether it's an early-morning big breakfast or an evening dose of music and chinwagging, this remains one of Yángshuò's most popular venues. The MC Blues Breakfast (Y25) is a serious mouthful: two fried eggs, two slices of toast, bacon, mushrooms, tomatoes, chips, coffee and juice. Pizzas from Y20. The long and lengthy cocktail list runs to grasshopper (Y25); nights draw garrulous crowds.

Meiyou Café (Méiyǒu Fàndiàn; ☎ 881 3676; 86 Xi Jie; 西街86号; local beer Y10) With one of the longest lineages in Yángshuò – which says something at the very least – the Meiyou concocts Western traveller fare and a smattering of Chinese dishes, plus a range of coffees (Blue Mountain coffee, Kaihua etc) and not bad breakfasts. The sign outside saying 'Meiyou Pay FEC' ('No FEC') puts its history in context – FEC (Foreign Exchange Certificates) became extinct in the mid-1990s.

Ming Yuan (Míng Yuán Jīngpǐn Kāfēi; ☎ 134 573 69 680; 50 Xi Jie; 西街50号; minimum charge per person Y15; ♥ 9am-midnight) If the constant bustle of Yángshuò gets too much, creep into this small café. The downstairs tables are a bit cramped, but it's still a quiet slice of civilisation and the cream-of-the-crop for coffee, with a rich range of blends including some more obscure offerings. Short/tall cappuccino Y24/27, short/tall caffe mocha Y27/30, iced coffees and waffles (from Y15). Peaceful mezzanine floor upstairs.

Kaya Bar (Kǎyā; ☎ 398 0180; 47 Guihua Lu; 桂花路47号; beer Y15) Yángshuò had to have a reggae bar, and this is it. Decouple from the village's more hyper drinking holes and decelerate to looped Bob Marley and the occasional reggae party.

Red Star Express (Hóngxīng Bǐsà; 56 Guihua Lu; 桂花路56号; meals Y30) Top pizzas from this eatery newly relocated from its old haunt on Xi Jie.

Splash on the Tabasco, line up a Corona (Y15) or three and sit back to enjoy some wholesome ingredients. For herbivores there's the vegetarian pizza (Y26) while the default option for carnivores is most likely the chilli beef pizza (Y28). The menu continues on into burger, burrito and sandwich territory. If you need to sleep off your pizza, upstairs doubles (with shower and air-con) are Y100.

Green Lotus Café (Niánqīngrén Kāfēidiàn; ☎ 881 2791; 102 Xi Jie; 西街102号; meals from Y18; ☽ 7.30am-midnight) Its walls are covered with the drunken scrawls of travellers, and early morning hangovers get soothed back to normality by soft jazz music. For specialist tastes there's a very brief Israeli menu, otherwise it's standard breakfast fare (Y18 to Y25) with freshly squeezed orange juice and local specialities such as beer fish (Y40).

Drifter's (Lûxíngzhě; ☎ 882 1715; 58 Xi Jie; 西街 58号; ☽ 7.30am-midnight) Does a good morning cuppa and serves Indonesian coffee, otherwise largely indistinguishable from other cafés along Xi Jie.

Le Vôtre (Lèdé Fāshì Cāntīng; ☎ 882 8040; 79 Xi Jie; 西街79号; ☽ 8am-midnight) With its impressive interior (part of the Jiangxi Guildhall) flanked by a dazzling array of Buddhist bodhisattva statues (including a suitably portly Milefo and a large effigy of Guanyin) and hung with portraits of the Marx brothers (Mao Zedong and Zhou Enlai), this is Yángshuò's sole French restaurant.

Pure Lotus Vegetarian Restaurant (Ānxiàng Shūyíng Sùcàiguǎn; 叠翠路; Diecui Lu; meals Y50; ☽ 9.30am-10pm; ⓥ) Aimed at the wealthier tourist bracket ,with semipicturesque views from the terrace at the rear. Pricy Buddhist vegetarian dishes, including Lo Han Zhai (Y35) and braised vegetable balls (Y18).

Farmers Trading Market (Nóngmào Shìchǎng; Pantao Lu) On Pantao Lu, through the archway, this place is open all day and late into the evenings. *Píjiǔyú* (beer fish; per kg Y30) is Yángshuò's most famous dish and in fact this may be the best budget place to buy it. Local Li River fish are cooked up with chillies, spring onion, tomato, ginger and beer. You can find all sorts of stuff here, but you may have to put up with the sight of dogs being skinned, so be prepared.

Entertainment

The top show in town is **Impressions Liu Sanjie** (印象刘三姐; Yìnxiàng Liú Sānjiě; ☎ 881 1982; C/B tickets Y188/320, A tickets Y480-680; ☽ 8-9pm). Directed by movie-maker Zhang Yimou, 600 performers, including local fishermen, take to the Li River and a backdrop of karst hillocks nightly. Twelve surrounding karst peaks are illuminated as part of the show Zhang describes as a 'folk musical'. Travellers give it universal raves. Book through your accommodation and you can usually get tickets for around Y150 to Y180. Most seats are open air and only the most expensive are sheltered – if it's raining you get a plastic raincoat. The show is tweaked every six months or so to keep it fresh.

Shopping

As Yángshuò grapples with the English language, you will note weird shop signs such as 'The case wraps up the person' and other surreal messages. North of Xi Jie a new retail zone called **Sunshine 100** (Guihua Lu; cnr Furong Lu & Diecui Lu), is further commercialising the town.

Yángshuò is a premier tourist bonanza aimed at *wàidìren* (outsiders) flocking here to haemorrhage cash all over the place. Bargain your socks off. Best buys include silk jackets (at much cheaper prices than in Hong Kong), hand-painted T-shirts, scroll paintings, batiks (from Guìzhōu) and name chops. Most travellers suggest shopping in the early evening after all the tour groups have thinned out and prices ease.

Don't forget too that Yángshuò is not simply Xi Jie. Wander around the backstreets, especially north along Binjiang Lu around the Bank of China. There are many places that may not be better than what you'll find on Xi Jie, but they offer the shopper lots more choice. Some of the smarter shops take credit cards.

Vanishing Tribes (☎ 882 6655; www.vanishingtribes .com; 104 Xi Jie; ☽ 9am-midnight) Attractive handicrafts from Dong, Miao, Yao and other ethnic groups, including hand-embroidered shoes and bags, amid piles of glistening, elaborate silver jewellery. It's not cheap (children's shoes start at around Y200), but push for the wholesale price to get bargaining under way.

Getting There & Away

Most travellers arrive in Yángshuò via Guìlín, from where good connections radiate to domestic and even international destinations.

AIR

The closest airport is in Guìlín, and any of the numerous CITS outlets and cafés dispense air tickets relatively cheaply. Check p162 for de-

BUSES FROM YÁNGSHUÒ

Destination	Fare (Y)	Duration	Departure Time
Fúlì	2.5	15min	every 5min
Guăngzhōu	98	10hr	8pm
Guìlín	10	80min	every 10min
Liŭzhōu	32	3½hr	6.30am & 2.40pm
Nánníng	110	6hr	8am & 9am
Shāzi	5	30min	every 20min
Xīngpíng	5.5	1hr	every 15min
Yángdì	8	90min	every 20min

tails on available flights. Cafés and hotels can organise taxi rides from Yángshuò directly to the airport (Y150, one hour).

BUS

Yángshuò's **bus station** (☎ 882 2188) is in the west of Yángshuò at the intersection of Diecui Lu and Pantao Lu, opposite the gate to Yangshuo Park. Regular buses and minibuses run between Yángshuò and Guìlín throughout the day. Buses also head to destinations in Guăngdōng province. Buses to Guìlín go via Pútáo (Y5); buses to Liŭzhōu go via Lìpŭ (Y8).

TRAIN

Yángshuò has no train station, but train tickets for services from Guìlín, Liŭzhōu and Nánníng can be booked at travel agents along Xi Jie or from your hotel. Expect a service charge of anything from Y40 to Y60. Hard sleepers for high-demand routes such as Guìlín to Kūnmíng will cost around Y170 to Y270 (depending on the time of year), but to get tickets like these, you'll have to book at least two to three days in advance – and even further ahead during holidays.

Getting Around

Destinations within town are most easily reached on foot. Single and tandem bike hire is straightforward in Yángshuò and for those with an aversion to exercise, you can even rent electric scooters (Y60; but they have a limited range of around 60km, so check). Most hotels rent out bikes, otherwise you will find rental outlets all over the place, with prices typically ranging from around Y10 to Y15 per day (plus deposit). Think twice if you're asked to fork out a Y400 deposit, waived only if you agree to a 'private' bike tour costing anywhere from Y20 to Y60. Some travellers who've agreed say they've felt hijacked by the guides who were

paid to take them to particular sights whether the travellers wanted to see them or not.

AROUND YÁNGSHUÒ

There are weeks and weeks of possible exploration out there for travellers, including bike, boat, foot or any combination thereof. Summer swimming in the Li River is naturally a temptation, although finding the best and cleanest spot can be tricky and can require foraging around (ask at your hotel).

Moon Hill 月亮山

A limestone pinnacle with a moon-shaped hole, **Moon Hill** (Yuèliang Shān; admission Y9) has some mindblowing views of the surrounding karst countryside. To get to Moon Hill by bicycle, take the highway out of town towards the river and turn right onto the road about 200m before the bridge; Moon Hill is 8.5km from town on your right.

It's a hot and sweaty climb to the top of the 320m peak (with 1251 steps, so reports one focused Frenchman). Once here, you can see **Moon Hill Village** and the 1500-year-old **Big Banyan Tree** (ask the postcard hawkers to point it out).

Black Buddha Caves and Water Caves 黑佛洞和水岩

Not far from Moon Hill are the **Black Buddha Caves** (Hēifó Dòng; half/full tour Y80/120) and **Water Caves** (Shuĭ Yán; half/full tour Y78/108), and you will undoubtedly be intercepted by touts and invited to explore the caverns. Both cave systems are worth a visit and Water Caves have become especially popular.

It is quite easy to get to the caves on a bike, but you can also join one of the many two- and four-hour tours from Yángshuò, which generally include transport, entry and equipment. Keep in mind that official entrance fees

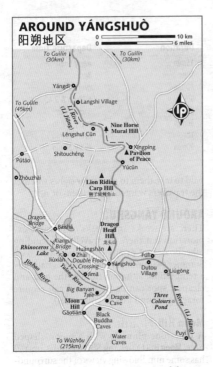

and tours to these caves are just a guideline so bargain all you want.

Other tours can cost from Y25 per head depending on the size of your group and the length of time spent in the caves. At Black Buddha Caves – located just before you reach Moon Hill when coming from Yángshuò – you work your way through caves to subterranean pools and will get completely covered in a vast pool of mud, a squelchy highlight of the expedition. Tours into Water Caves – located several kilometres beyond Moon Hill – enter by boat and take in an underground waterfall and subterranean pools.

Yulong River 遇龙河

The scenery along here equals or even beats that of the Li River. This is the place that usually leaves the biggest impression on most visitors to Yángshuò. Whether it is just meandering along a small farmers' path between the rice paddies or sitting by the river taking in the rural and karst landscape, most travellers fondly remember their time in this river valley.

It is possible to embark on a full-day bike tour of the Yulong River (Yùlóng Hé) and

neighbouring sights, including **Double Flow Crossing** (双流渡; Shuāngliúdù), **Xiangui Bridge** (仙桂桥; Xiānguì Qiáo), nearby **Rhinoceros Lake** (犀牛湖; Xīniú Hú), **Dragon Bridge** and the village of **Jiùxiàn**.

If you seem to be going around in circles, then just ask one of the locals the way back to Yángshuò or follow one of the other independent guides who frequent this area. If you don't fancy heading off independently, then this is a popular trek with Yángshuò's guides who will take you out for the day and even sometimes stop at their home for lunch. This is a good way to see the scenery with an informed local.

If cycling, take care riding along some of those bumpy narrow paths between paddy fields, as it only takes one mistake to end up covered in mud! If you find yourself stranded on the wrong side of the river, look out for bamboo rafts that can ferry you to the other side for around Y5.

DRAGON BRIDGE 遇龙桥

With its higgledy-piggledy steps, this lovely arched **bridge** (Yùlóng Qiáo) was built in 1412 during the Ming dynasty and is among Guǎngxī's largest at 59m long, 5m wide and 9m high. Note how the walls of the bridge lean inwards with age.

It would take a full day to head up to Dragon Bridge and come back on the trails by bike, but definitely worth it. Pack your lunch and some water and enjoy a picnic along the banks of the Yulong River. From Yángshuò, head out towards Moon Hill and, before crossing the bridge over the Yulong River, turn right down the dirt trail.

It is possible to continue along this path (in its variety of forms) and take it all the way to the Dragon Bridge and Báishā (白沙). Don't worry too much if you take a wrong turn as there are innumerable paths running between the Yulong River and the Yángshuò–Báishā road.

Don't be tempted by the Báishā road as it's busy, noisy and dusty. The best part of this trip is not worrying about whether you're wandering down the wrong path, but just enjoying the scenery.

If you want to take the bus to Dragon Bridge, jump on a bus to Jīnbǎo (金宝) from the Yángshuò bus station and ask to get off at the bridge after it stops in Báishā (Y5, 35 minutes).

SHÍTOU CHÉNG, GUĂNGXĪ *Eilís Quinn*

When I first visited Shítou Chéng, it was just after a rainfall. Villagers scampered up and down the hills – it looked so easy despite the slicks of mud. The farmer who agreed to show me around looked at my footwear, shook his head and told me to change into a pair of his rubber boots. Confident in my expensive, state-of-the-art hiking boots, I said no and off we went. Or rather, off he went. Twenty minutes into the ascent I got stuck in the mud and couldn't step out. Muttering 'I told you sos' he came down to pull me out. Ten minutes later, I stepped on a slippery mud patch and slid two metres backwards down the trail. The farmer threw his hands in the air, made exasperated noises and disappeared into the woods. He came out with a long stick, attacked it with his hunting knife, and a few minutes later proudly presented me with a walking stick. I'd like to say it kept me upright for the rest of the walk, but I'd be lying. When we came down from the hill three hours later I was caked in mud. The farmer took me to meet his wife in their orchard and they filled my backpack with apples. 'Tell your friends to come' he said. 'But not after rainfall. It's too much work to stop *lǎowài* [foreigners] from always falling down.'

JIÙXIÀN 旧县

Well worth visiting south of Dragon Bridge is this historic **village** amid the glistening fields not far from Xiangui Bridge; if you haven't brought your bike, it's around Y25 on the back of a motorbike from the bridge or you can fork out around Y150 for a bamboo raft to take you downriver to Jiùxiàn.

The village is well worth exploring for its ancient textures and stony charm. Many of the houses have carved doors, horse-head gables and distinctive rooftop decorations. Old village residents may drag you to their houses for a look, but may also demand money, in which case hand over no more than a few *yuán*. Houses of note include No 88 with a wooden door and large entrance hall. One of the principal structures in this Ming and Qing dynasty village is the **Li Family Ancestral Temple** (黎氏宗祠; Líshì Zōngcí), guarded by village elders. Next to the temple is the **Farmer's Restaurant** (黎氏老根农家饭店; Lí shì Lǎogēn Nóngjiā Fàndiàn; ☎ 0773-877 2715; d with air-con and toilet Y60) if you want to overnight in the area; there is also a terrace restaurant here.

The nearby single-arched 25.8m-long Xiangui Bridge originally dates back to 1123.

Further along the river towards Yángshuò, you may meet guides who offer to take you up to the village remains of **Huángshān Zhài** (黄山寨; Y20) atop a nearby karst peak.

Shítou Chéng 石头城

A fascinating and unusual foray into the countryside to the northwest of Yángshuò accompanies a day trip to this interesting village. Perched among karst peaks to the northeast of Pútáo (葡萄), Shítou Chéng's

gates and walls are largely intact, crowning a limestone peak.

Because of its strategic geography high up in the hills, the village was once a garrison town. Others attest that the walls once housed Qing gangsters who used them as a base from which to extort protection money from villages below. Locals avow that the Japanese decided not to take the village in 1944 as it appeared so imposing.

It's a steep 30- to 50-minute climb up the hill from the village's 'new town' to the 'old town' where the wall begins. Once at the top, it will take another four to five hours to walk around to all four gates.

All the houses in the village are fashioned from the same stone, hence the name of the village (literally 'Stone Town'). The settlement has four main gates at each of the compass points and 18 lesser gates (originally there were 24); little, however, that remains of the soldier's barracks, except a couple of ancient temples, can be hunted down. Seek out a villager to act as a guide to show you around the village as there is usually someone willing to take on the task for a fee of Y30 to Y40. Be warned that visiting Shítou Chéng during or after rain will guarantee a very muddy experience.

To reach Shítou Chéng, take a bus to Pútáo (Y5) from Yángshuò bus station; alternatively, stand on Chengxi Lu and flag down anything heading in the direction of Guìlín and ask to get off at Pútáo. It's also possible to get off at Pútáo on any bus heading to Yángshuò from Guìlín. Once you disembark, you should see a long dirt road heading east. It's another 8km or so to Shítou Chéng, so taking a motorcycle

(Y20) or tractor (Y30) the rest of the way is advisable, which takes around 30 minutes along bumpy, windy, uphill dirt roads. Walking is possible, but the way is unmarked and after a few kilometres people and houses are scarce. If you reach a fork in the road, don't move until someone wanders by who you can ask.

There'll be no stores or restaurants on your way here so bring water and snacks.

You should be able to get a motorcycle ride back to Pútáo from your guide or one of the other villagers after which you can flag down a south-bound bus back to Yángshuò.

Also reachable by motorcycle from Pútáo are the villages of Zhōu Zhài (周寨) and Dōngguā Zhài (东瓜寨).

Li River Excursions

If you're keen on river trips, ask around. There are dozens of touts and guides who will chat to you on the streets of Yángshuò, so ask them for advice on the good, bad and boring stretches of the river.

FÚLÌ 福利

A number of attractive riverside villages are scattered well within range of Yángshuò. A popular trip is to the historic village of **Fúlì**, a picturesque if rather decrepit river town a short distance down the Li River, with stone houses and cobbled lanes. In the old town, Lao Jie (老街; Old Street) is a pleasant strip of houses built from neat brickwork. Cows and calves wander down the alleyways, nosing past tourists. Poke your head into old house interiors, frequently hung with portraits of Chairman Mao. In the south of the village is **Tiānhòu Gōng** (天后宫), a small temple to Mazu. Also known as Tianhou, the goddess Mazu is the patron deity of seafarers and those who make their living on the water. Within the shrine sits a statue of Mazu, and a painted wooden effigy of Guanyin to the rear. Other roads of character in the village are Lǐngbèi Jiē (岭背街), Xīnglóng Jiē (兴隆街) and Zhèndōng Jiē (镇东街). As in the rest of China, even the most ramshackle and impoverished dwellings sport cheerful red couplets that hang vertically on either side of front doors, especially during the Spring Festival. Fúlì is famed for its locally made fans, which you will see on sale. Half the population of Fúlì's considerable population of grandmothers appears to be engaged in

the production of knitted hats and shoes, available for sale everywhere.

Look out for vendors of *yùtou gāo* (芋头糕; tasty, crisp and sweet taro cakes; Y1).

A few expensive daily boats go to Fúlì from Yángshuò; ask in travel agents for better deals and bargains. The most popular way to reach Fúlì is by bike, a trip that takes around an hour. First cycle to Dutou village (渡头村; Dùtou cūn) on the other side of the river and jump onto one of the regular ferries across the water (Y5). It's also possible to reach Fúlì from Xīngpíng by bike. In the summer months you can also reach Fúlì and other villages along the river by inner tube, which can be found from travel agents along Xi Jie in Yángshuò. It takes around three or four hours to get to Fúlì this way. Several places also offer rafting trips and kayak hire, which are both popular options in the warm summer months. Ask at your hotel, at one of the restaurants or at agents in town. A more functional alternative is to take one of the regular buses to Fúlì (Y3, 15 minutes) from Yángshuò bus station. From the drop-off, take a pedicab (Y5) to the old town, or walk.

Market days are good times to visit Fúlì (every third day from the second of each month), but be wary of pickpockets; young males work in groups of three or four, brushing up against travellers and snatching belongings. The eighth day of the fifth lunar month is temple fair day in Fúlì, a fun time to visit.

XĪNGPÍNG & YÁNGDĪ 兴坪和杨堤

Cafés and travel agents also organise boat trips to **Yángdī** and **Xīngpíng**, about three hours upstream from Yángshuò. The mountain scenery around Xīngpíng is even more breathtaking than around Yángshuò, and there are many caves.

As with other traditional villages, wandering around the old section of **Xīngpíng** takes you past historic residences, but you may have to shake off hawkers in relentless pursuit. Xīn Jiē (新街) leads away from the drop off point to Lao Jie (老街), at the end of which is a pleasant café called **This Old Place** (老地方; Lǎo Dìfāng; ☎ 138-7737 8290; 46 Lao Jie) where you can get a bite to eat in relaxing surroundings.

Also within the village is a small **Guandi Temple** (关帝庙; Guāndì Miào), dedicated to the Taoist God of War, dating to the reign of the Qing-dynasty Qianlong emperor. Tucked away down a side street stands an elegant **old stage** (古戏台; Gǔ Xìtái).

From Xīngpíng boats depart for the small, ancient village of **Yú Cūn** (渔村; admission Y25) downriver, although boats (Y30, 20 minutes) leave infrequently if there are not enough people. Alternatively you can fork out Y60 for a bamboo raft to take you there or take the long road behind the hill on foot to the village. Less-visited than Xīngpíng, the village is an attractive settlement of ancient Qing-dynasty houses and narrow alleys.

The authorities have cracked down on private boats between Yángshuò, Xīngpíng and Yángdī, but boats can still be found in Xīngpíng for the round trip to Yángdī (Y50, three hours); if boats are running, touts will hunt you down in town. From Yángdī, you can either walk back to Xīngpíng on the five-hour hike or take a bus back to Yángshuò (Y8, 90 minutes, every 30 minutes); the last bus leaves at 6pm. Alternatively, take a bus (Y8) to Yángdī from Yángshuò bus station and hike or take a boat to Xīngpíng and then bus it back to Yángshuò (last bus 7pm).

To reach Xīngpíng from Yángshuò, either cycle or catch a local bus to Xīngpíng (Y5.5, one hour) from the bus station in Yángshuò.

If you want to spend the night in Xīngpíng, several small *nóngjiā* (农家; family homestead hotels) can be found near the river. During the busy season, they tend to fill up rapidly. The **Riverview Hotel** (Wàngjiāng Fàndiàn; ☎ 870 2276; q per person Y30, tw Y80) is reasonably priced. If you can't find a bed elsewhere, try the **Xingping Inn** (兴平客栈; Xīngpíng Kèzhàn; ☎ 870 3089; s & d from Y50) with small and tidy rooms with squat toilets. It's not near the river but several of the rooms have balconies with limestone peak views.

A 24km **hike** from Yángdī to Xīngpíng, crossing the river at three points, takes you past some of the most superlative views in the region. The entrance fee is Y16 and a moderately fit person can complete it in four to five hours. There are villages and the occasional inn (客栈; *kèzhàn*) along the way where you can pick up essentials, but take water and snacks as little may be open outside of high season.

Set off from the wharf (码头; *mǎtou*) at Yángdī, first crossing the river (Y2) and then walking for around 20 minutes along the river to **Langshi village** (浪石村; Làngshí Cūn), a charming village notable for its ancient buildings. Around half-an-hour from

Langshi village you need to cross the Li River again (Y4), from where it's another 30 minutes or so to another small village, beyond which a road leads past some fabulous river scenery. You'll see **Nine Horse Mural Hill** (九马画山; Jiǔmǎ Huàshān) on the far side of the river as you arrive at the village of **Lěngshuǐ Cūn** (冷水村), where you cross the river once more at the ferry crossing (Y4) and on to Xīngpíng, a long walk through splendid river scenery.

MARKET DAYS
The villages around Yángshuò are best visited on market days, which tend to work on a three-day, monthly cycle. Markets take place every three days starting on the first of the month in Yángdī and Báishā (1, 4, 7 etc) and every three days starting on the second of the month in Fúlì and Pútáo (2, 5, 8 etc), and every three days starting on the third of the month in Yángshuò and Xīngpíng (3, 6, 9 etc). However, sometimes after every third market the next one is in four days, not three. There are no markets on the 10th, 20th, 30th and 31st of the month. If this sounds confusing, you should ask at your hotel or at a café in Yángshuò.

HUÁNGYÁO 黄姚
Found not far from the Guǎngxī–Húnán–Guǎngdōng border and east of the Gui River (桂江; Guì Jiāng), this delightful 900-year old village (admission Y30) lies enveloped in historic charm, its intact architecture, riverside scenes, bridges, ponds, ancient trees, temples, pavilions and spellbinding karst scenery generating an exquisite rural beauty. Guǎngdōng-bound travellers, or those aiming to explore the less-travelled eastern rural fringes of Guǎngxī province, will find the area riveting. Film crews long ago latched onto Huángyáo's good looks, and artists and photographers under the aesthetic spell of the village are a common sight.

The village gets its name from the two families that lived here – one surnamed Huang (黄), the other named Yao (姚). The settlement originally dates way back to the Song dynasty but most buildings go no further back than the Ming, while true prosperity arrived with the Qing dynasty, which bequeathed most of the architecture.

Wandering the maze of stone streets is the best way to explore the village, replete with expertly constructed, painted one-

GUĂNGXĪ

storey brick homesteads, ancestral shrines and fantastically preserved Qing-dynasty buildings. Standout chunks of Ming and Qing architecture include the **Wenming Pavilion** (文明阁; Wénmíng Gé), **Wuyu Temple** (吴宇祠; Wúyǔ Cí), **Dailong Bridge** (带龙桥; Dàilóng Qiáo), **Xingning Temple** (兴宁庙; Xīngníng Miào) and a magnificent **old stage** (古戏台; Gǔ Xìtái). Local opera and songs are performed on the stage on the third day of the third lunar month.

Famed for its *dòufu* (tofu), Huángyáo has a few small restaurants where you can get a bite to eat. If you want to spend the night, numerous hostels in the village can put you up for around Y20 a night. The simple **Huángyáo Yíng Bīnguǎn** (黄姚迎宾馆; ☎ 0774-672 2119) has beds in double rooms for Y20. But if you are looking for something more comfortable, you'll need to overnight in Hèzhōu.

Getting There & Away

Direct buses run every half hour to Huángyáo from Guìlín bus station. The nearest major town to Huángyáo is Hèzhōu (贺州), also called Bābù (八步), which can be reached by bus from Liǔzhōu (Y83) departing at 12.40pm. From Hèzhōu, take a bus (Y6, one hour) to Zhōngshān then jump on a bus (Y8, two hours) to Gǒngqiáo (巩桥), which passes Huángyáo. Alternatively, one bus (Y8) daily from Hèzhōu heads over the hills to Gǒngqiáo 66km away, from where you can jump on a motorised three-wheeler (Y1) to take you the remaining distance to Huángyáo. If coming from the west, it's far more convenient to change buses in Zhōngshān than to continue on to Hèzhōu. A taxi from Hèzhōu to Huángyáo costs around Y100. Zhōngshān can also be reached by bus (Y30, six hours) from Yángshuò, as can Hèzhōu.

LÓNGSHÈNG 龙胜
☎ 0773

The culmination of a two-hour bus trip northwest of Guìlín, the small town of Lóngshèng is the functional and unattractive gateway to one of China's most archetypal and photographed landscapes: the splendidly named Dragon's Backbone Rice Terraces. Sparkling layers of waterlogged terraced fields stubbornly ascend the hillsides in defiance of the region's mountainous terrain, which has compelled generations of farmers to eke out every available scrap of cultivable

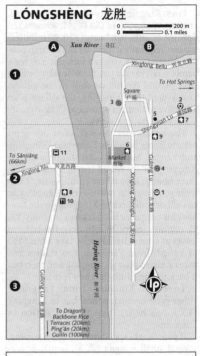

LÓNGSHÈNG 龙胜

To Hot Springs
To Sānjiāng (66km)
To Dragon's Backbone Rice Terraces (20km); Píng'ān (20km); Guìlín (100km)

INFORMATION	
China Post 中国邮政	1 B2
Longsheng Tourism and Information Service Center 龙胜旅游咨询服务中心	(see 9)
Public Security Bureau 公安局	2 B1
Qunxing Internet Café 群兴网吧	3 B1
Xinhua Bookstore 新华书店	(see 4)
Xinhua Internet Café 新华网吧	4 B2

SIGHTS & ACTIVITIES	
Chǔnán Guǎn 楚南馆	5 B1

SLEEPING	
Jīndū Bīnguǎn 金都宾馆	6 B2
Longsheng Hotel 龙胜宾馆	7 B1
Riverside Hotel 凯凯旅舍	8 A2
Tourism Hotel 旅游宾馆	9 B2

EATING	
Meiwei Lamb Restaurant 美味羊肉馆	10 A2

TRANSPORT	
Bus Station 客运站	11 A2

land. The landscape is viewable in a day, but you can spend the night in the village of Píng'ān at the heart of the Dragon's Backbone Rice Terraces and allow yourself more time to visit the sights and make the long trek to the village of Dàzhài.

Well within the geographic and cultural orbit of Guìzhōu and Húnán, the Lóngshèng region is a beguiling patchwork of Dong, Zhuang, Yao and Miao minority villages. Other villages can be visited en route to the less interesting hot springs; jump off the bus (Y5) around 6km from the hot springs and take off into the hills for exploration. One of the very few sights in Lóngshèng itself is the Qing-dynasty **Chǔnán Guǎn** on the corner of Shengyuan Lu and Gulong Lu, a traditional Chinese guildhall built in 1882 by the merchant community.

Information

There's no Bank of China in Lóngshèng and nowhere to change money; change money before you arrive so as not to be caught short.

China Post (Zhōngguó Yóuzhèng; Gulong Lu)

Longsheng Tourism and Information Service Center (Lóngshèng Lǚyóu Zīxún Fúwù Zhōngxīn; next door to the Tourism Hotel on Gulong Lu) Shut at the time of writing.

Public Security Bureau (PSB; Gōngānjú; 5 Shengyuan Lu) Opposite the entrance to the Longsheng Hotel.

Qunxing Internet Café (Qúnxīng Wǎngbā; Xinglong Zhonglu; per hr Y2; ☼ 8am-midnight)

Xinhua Bookstore (Xīnhuá Shūdiàn; Gulong Lu)

Xinhua Internet Café (Xīnhuá Wǎngbā; Gulong Lu; per hr Y2; ☼ 8am-midnight) Behind the Xinhua Bookstore.

Sights

DRAGON'S BACKBONE RICE TERRACES
龙脊梯田

The region around Lóngshèng may be heavily striated with rice fields, but it is only at the Dragon's Backbone Rice Terraces (Lóngjí Tītián) that these feats of farm engineering reach their apogee, layering their way up a string of 500m peaks. A half-hour climb to the top delivers unblemished vistas stepping down the terraced fields below.

Summer rains give the fields their full sparkle, although some travellers have remarked at the beauty of the terraces covered in snow or in October, when the fields are stunningly golden. If visiting in winter and early spring, however, prepare yourself for banks of heavy fog and mist that shroud everything in an impenetrable curtain.

The entrance fee to the terraces (Y50) is collected on the main road along the valley bottom and checked just before the covered bridge.

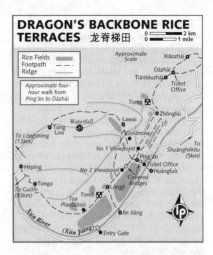

Timetables are liable to fluctuate according to the season, but buses (Y6.5) typically leave from the bus station at Lóngshèng for Píng'ān daily at 7.40am, 9.20am, 11am, 1pm, 3pm and 5pm; in the other direction, buses depart for Lóngshèng from Píng'ān at 7.30am, 9am, 11am, 1pm, 3pm and 5pm, but there may be a later bus leaving at 6.10pm. The trip is only about 20km, however some buses stop midway at the town of Hépíng to try to pull in more passengers, occasionally dragging the trip out to 1½ hours. During the summer, minibuses also regularly leave for the terraces from Lóngshèng between around 7am and 5pm. The bus runs to Huángluò before running wildly uphill to the drop-off point, from where it's a further 15-minute walk uphill to Píng'ān.

PÍNG'ĀN 平安

The lovely Zhuang village of Píng'ān is the centre of operations for any trips around the terraces and hikes into the hills. Uphill from the bus drop-off point, the village is worth exploring prior to launching yourself into the surrounding countryside. There are lovely dry stone walls and reams of tourist souvenirs (including buffalo-horn combs), and Zhuang women standing over cold slabs of dòufu. If your feet need revitalising, there are even places in the village offering foot massages. Several signposts to nearby sights can be found around Píng'ān, but they dwindle the further you get away from the village and the lookouts.

Hunt down the fading Maoist slogan on the rear wall of the building just below the Longji Foggy Resort (龙脊云雾山庄; Lóngjǐ Yúnwù Shānzhuāng) which boastfully declares in faint, red characters: '突出政治用毛泽东思想统帅一切' ('*tūchū zhèngzhì yòng Máo Zédōng Sīxiǎng tǒngshuài yīqiè*'), which literally means 'Stress politics by commanding everything according to Mao Zedong Thought'. The slogan does not appear to have been deliberately artificially preserved through retouching (as is often the case, eg in Chuāndǐxià, outside Běijīng), but seems to have just been left to fade away. To find the house with the ghostly characters, take the right fork past the Li Qing Guesthouse and bear right past the school and the Yànzǐ Shānzhuāng (燕子山庄; Yanzhi Hotel), round the corner to the Longji Foggy Resort and you will find it.

Internet access is available at **View Place Inn** (Lǎnyuè Gé; ☎ 0773-758 3005; per hr Y10) on the way up to the No 2 Viewpoint above the village and at the Ping'an Hotel (per hour Y10).

For accommodation, **Countryside Inn** (乡村旅馆; Xiāngcūn Lǚguǎn; ☎ 0773-758 3020; d with shower Y120) is pretty much the first place you come across on the right hand side of the path. This clean and all-wood place has great, new doubles (no air-con, phone or TV), frequently discounted to around Y80 (and even Y50 to Y60 in winter) and there's a good café serving pizza (Y20 to Y25), French toast (Y12), omelettes (Y6 to Y14), coffee, hot chocolate and other travellers dishes.

Other places include the 16-room **Long Teng Hotel** (龙腾阁; Lóngténg Gé; ☎ 758 3008; d with fan Y15-30, tr with fan Y30), up the steps behind the Countryside Inn, and the nearby **Li Qing Guesthouse** (丽晴旅馆; Lìqíng Lǚguǎn; ☎ 0773-758 3048; fax 0773-758 3021), with outside terrace, rooms with showers and loos and good views, and run by a Zhuang family. Further up towards the No 2 Viewpoint, the **Ping'an Hotel** (平安酒店; Píng'ān Jiǔdiàn; ☎ 0773-758 3198; d Y180-200; 🛜 🖳) has internet access and rooms with air-con, showers and heating, often discounted to Y100.

PÍNG'ĀN TO DÀZHÀI 平安到大寨

Above Píng'ān are the two lookouts, the No 1 Viewpoint, identified by path signs as Nine Dragons and Five Tigers, and the No 2 Viewpoint, also called Seven Stars with Moon. It's a 20- to 30-minute walk up to the No 2 Viewpoint, from where it is a further half an hour to walk to Viewpoint No 1. Accommodation options can be found not far from each spot with beds for around Y70.

From here you can embark on a long and invigorating walk past mountain goats and fabulous scenery all the way to Dàzhài (大寨), from where you can jump aboard a bus back to Lóngshèng. The path to Zhōngliù is pretty straightforward, but from Zhōngliù on there are a few potentially disorientating forks in the road. If you don't want to walk all the way to Zhōngliù and Dàzhài, take the steps down from No 1 Viewpoint and back to Píng'ān. Alternatively, signposts in the other direction lead to the old Zhuang village of Lóngjí and onto Hépíng.

To walk to Dàzhài from No 1 Viewpoint, look out for the signpost that is over a small rise pointing the way to the Yao village of Zhōngliù (中六寨; Zhōngliù Zhài), a small village of wooden houses around 90 minutes away on the path. Follow the stone road through the trees, passing a small wooden pavilion where the stone path peters out before you arrive in a delightful valley. Once here you will need to cross a small wooden bridge before passing another pavilion; at the fork in the road further along, take the lower road that leads downhill to the river; cross the river and continue to the village of Zhōngliù. In Zhōngliù, bear right up the steep steps and out of the village. From this point on, you may have to ask a local or two for directions past the few forks in the road; if you want a local to guide you all the way, there will be no shortage of offers, but you will have to pay (Y20 to Y25). Bank on around two hours (or more for a leisurely walk) for getting from Zhōngliù to Dàzhài.

The next village you will come across is the small Yao village of Tiántouzhài (田头寨) where a few guesthouses can be found, including the **V8 Hostel** (☎ 0773-758 5655), which has simple rooms for Y20 to Y25. Exiting the village, take the path downhill and after half a kilometre or so there's an alternative path leading up to the No 3 Viewpoint, Golden Buddha Summit (金佛顶; Jīnfó Dǐng). Continuing down the path brings you to the Yao village of Dàzhài, where there was considerable building work going on at the time of research. A ticket office in Dàzhài means you can effectively enter at this point and walk all the way to Píng'ān. It is possible to overnight in Dàzhài where there are several inns

(客栈; kèzhàn), such as the **Dazhai Inn** (Dàzhài Kèzhàn; ☎ 0773-758 5601). From Dàzhài, buses run every 30 minutes to Lóngshèng (Y7; 80 minutes) between 7.30am and 5.30pm.

HOT SPRINGS 温泉

Not far northeast from Lóngshèng, the hot springs (wēnquán) are a rather tacky tourist highlight and can be safely missed by the visitor, although buses (Y5) running out there pass through rolling hills sculptured with rice terraces and studded with Yao and Zhuang minority villages. It is possible to desert the bus around 6km to 7km from the hot springs and take off into the hills for some exploring. Beyond the hot springs is the **Longsheng Hot Springs National Forest** (龙胜温泉国家森林公园; Lóngshèng Wēnquán Guójiā Sēnlín Gōngyuán; admission Y20).

Sleeping

It is infinitely preferable to spend the night in the charming village of Píng'ān, rather than overnighting in the town of Lóngshèng, but if you arrive at odd hours, you can try one of the following.

Riverside Hotel (Kǎikǎi Lǚshè; ☎ 751 1335; 5 Guilong Lu; 桂龙路5号; s/d/tr Y15/20/30) Run by a helpful English teacher, rooms are very basic indeed and frigid in winter (although air-con rooms with warm air are possibly in the pipeline). The downstairs restaurant has a simple and basic menu with spare ribs (Y12), sweet and sour pork (Y10) and a smattering of Western items. Ask here about trips to the village of Dìlíng.

Jindù Bīnguǎn (☎ 741 7649 or 751 7649; Xinglong Zhonglu; 兴龙中路; s & d w shower Y30; ✕) Spotless linen, bright and clean rooms, shower and squat toilets. Cross the bridge from the bus station and take the first turn on your left along Xinglong Zhonglu – it's around 70m down on the left hand side. More expensive doubles with bath also available (Y50).

Tourism Hotel (Lǚyóu Bīnguǎn; ☎ 751 7206; 11 Gulong Lu; 古龙街11号; s/d/tr Y120/140/180; ✕) This midrange place has much pricier, large, clean, tiled rooms from the 4th floor up; all have shower but not all have air-con. Rooms are typically substantially discounted, so ask.

Longsheng Hotel (Lóngshèng Bīnguǎn; ☎ 751 2503; Shengyuan Lu; 盛院路; d/tr Y160/300; s/d deluxe Y268/288; ✕) Rooms are perhaps a bit dark, but are pleasant, spacious, well-kept and comfortable enough at this decent two-star hotel; it's easy enough to pick up a double here for Y100 outside of the very busy season.

Eating

In line with its ugly housing, Lóngshèng is unremarkable from a culinary point of view. Street stalls appear around midevening along Xinglong Xilu, offering point-and-choose meals. The Riverside Hotel has a simple menu of Western dishes and Chinese dishes popular with travellers.

Meiwei Lamb Restaurant (Měiwèi Yángròu Guǎn; ☎ 751 8661; Guilong Lu; 桂龙路; hotpot Y28) Not to be confused with the shuàn yángròu, Mongolian hotpots served in Běijīng and the north of China where you scald thin strips of lamb in a boiling broth, the hotpot lamb here is chewier and less flavoursome, but still heart-warming for winter visits. It's a short walk south from the Riverside Hotel.

Getting There & Away

Buses leave Lóngshèng **bus station** (☎ 751 6097) every 20 minutes for Guìlín (Y22, two hours); hourly departures head to Sānjiāng (Y10, two to three hours) between 6.30am and 6pm.

ZĪYUÁN 资源

While most tourists come to Guìlín to float placidly down the Li River, more adrenaline-inducing rides can be made at Zīyuán. Located 107km northeast of Guìlín near Māo'ér Shān (猫儿山; Cat Mountains), Zīyuán is the jump-off point for the wild rafting trip along the Wǔpái Hé. This takes you floating or roaring – depending on water levels – on a trip of around 30km with a drop of about 300m. Another trip of up to 90km along the Zī Jiāng passes lots of villages, cliffs and caves, but requires an overnight stop. Those who don't want to go rafting can visit nearby **Baoding Falls** (宝鼎瀑布; Bǎodǐng Pùbù).

Hotels in Guìlín offer one- and two-day tours to Zīyuán during the warmer months for anything from Y200 for a one-day trip and Y350 for an overnight; weekends are more expensive. Prices are often higher during summer, but it is easier to hook up with a larger tour group. Otherwise head for Zīyuán during summer and make inquires with some of the tour operators in town.

Buses to Zīyuán (Y25, two hours) depart hourly from the Guìlín bus station. You might also consider heading to Lóngshèng from Zīyuán if you've already visited Guìlín.

SĀNJIĀNG DONG MINORITY AUTON-OMOUS COUNTY 三江侗族自治县

☎ 0772

Arriving in the run-of-the-mill township of Sānjiāng (capital of the Sānjiāng Dong Minority Autonomous County) may make you want to jump on the first bus in the return direction, but persist – this is a trip worth taking, as long as you venture out of town. Approximately 20km to the north of town, Chengyang Wind and Rain Bridge and the surrounding Dong villages are peaceful and attractive and make for fascinating exploration, although they are very poor and a reminder of the endemic poverty still afflicting this region of China. Sānjiāng also draws in travellers village-hopping their way into Guìzhōu province. About five hours by bus from Guìlín, Sānjiāng is inhabited mostly by the Dong minority, who comprise more than 50% of the county's population (see p139).

There are few sights in the township of Sānjiāng, although the huge and recently built **Drum Tower** (admission Y10; ⏰ 8.30am-5.30pm) overlooking the river from its elevated perch on the east bank of the Xun River (寻江; Xún Jiāng) can be climbed for views of the town.

Information

The town of Sānjiāng is devoid of a bank where you can change money so make sure you bring enough cash with you. The **Ruyi Internet Cafe** (如意网吧; Rúyì Wǎngbā; Furong Lu; per hr Y2; ⏰ 24hr) is up from the Sanjiang Hotel.

Orientation

Sānjiāng township is divided into east and west by the Xun River. Sānjiāng has two bus stations: Hedong bus station (河东站; Hédōng zhàn) is on the east side of the river on Yagu Lu (雅谷路); the Hexi bus station is over the bridge on the west side of the river, just off Xingyi Lu (兴宜路) as it meets the road from the bridge. Sānjiāng's streets are confusingly devoid of street signs.

Chengyang Wind & Rain Bridge 程阳桥

Overlooking a lush valley dotted with Dong villages and water wheels, this 78m-long, elegant covered **bridge** (Chéngyáng Qiáo; admission Y30) was built in 1912 and is considered by the Dong to be the finest of the 108 such structures in Sānjiāng county. It took villagers 12 years to build. Magnificently hewn from huge, dark fir logs, the bridge's five towers feature multiple storeys with exquisite eaves, and were apparently made without nails. The bridges are characterised by design flexibility, allowing them to be built on any topography. The surrounding terraced fields on either side are irrigated by Dong water wheels, some of which are around 6m tall. The inevitable minority women hawking wares are here as well.

Aimed squarely at tourists, a cultural dance (Mínzú Gēwǔ Biǎoyǎn) takes place in the Ma'an Drum Tower every day at 11am and 3.30pm.

Chéngyáng is a great place to base yourself for a couple of days to explore the surrounding countryside and minority villages. Chengyang Bridge National Hostel (see p186) is a good accommodation option.

From the Sānjiāng bus station, you can catch hourly buses to Línxī, which pass scattered collections of riverside Dong buildings and go right past the bridge, or otherwise take one of the frequent minivan taxis (Y3) that gather outside the bus station. Bus services stop around 6pm in each direction, so if you need to get back to Sānjiāng later than that you'll have to hitch. The first bus of the day to Sānjiāng passes by the bridge around 7.40am.

NEARBY VILLAGES

An excellent walk that leads you through a series of authentic Dong villages can be made after crossing the Chengyang Wind and Rain Bridge. Traversing the bridge immediately brings you to Dong buildings in the villages of **Mǎ'ān Zhài** (马鞍寨) and **Yánzhài** (岩寨). As most of the buildings are made of fir wood, note the ever-present signs in Chinese warning villagers to be constantly vigilant against fire – a constant hazard in these combustible villages; despite this, the old men of the village have few qualms about firing up a vast flaming brazier for heat in the **Ma'an Drum Tower** (马鞍鼓楼; Mǎ'ān Gǔlóu) during winter.

Walking north from Mǎ'ān Zhài soon brings you to the delightful **Helong Bridge** (合龙桥; Hélóng Qiáo), next to the small **Dragon Bridge Dong Hotel** (☎ 133 248 207 06; d Y20-30), which has simple rooms right by the river but no air-con or English spoken. Before crossing the bridge you can carry on into Yánzhài proper, with its ramshackle dwellings offset by a newly constructed drum tower, fashioned from recently felled wood. Further west along the path is the village of **Píngtǎn Zhài** (平坦寨).

Crossing the Helong Bridge, you may be approached by guardians to make a voluntary contribution to the upkeep of the structure. For Y10 and above you get your name carved in a stone plinth. A diverting notice in Chinese on the bridge lists various prohibitions, including a regulation against frying fish within 50m of the bridge. On the other side of the river are fields of crops and the hamlet of **Píng Zhài** (平寨), a lovely village with an old pavilion in its square and flagstone alleyways (so narrow the roofs almost touch). Note the abundance of fire hydrants.

Continue north – along either the riverside path or the main road – for a further 10 minutes or so to **Dōng Zhài** (东寨), passing another recently built drum tower (called the Pingdong Drum Tower). Look out for the the Chengyang Drum Tower just before you reach the bridge over the stream. A substantial old edifice on your right, its interior is hung with a portrait of Mao Zedong (as many drum towers are).

Ahead in **Dàzhài** (大寨) you can cross west over the **Chengyang Puji Bridge** (程阳普济桥; Chéngyáng Pǔjì Qiáo), but you may be once again coerced into contributing restoration funds. There's not much on the other side of the river but a few Dong houses, although a path leads back to Yánzhài if you want to return this way.

Píngpǔ Zhài (平埔寨) is a further 20-minute walk north along the main road, but you can also take the riverside path beside the fields that commence alongside the west bank of the river from Jichang Bridge at the turnoff to the village of **Jíchāng** (吉昌), itself a kilometre or so to the west.

Píngpǔ Zhài is not that pretty and is badly dilapidated, but there are two ancient drum towers here as well as an old theatre stage. The children here are very poor and may follow you in pursuit of loose change.

To get back to Sānjiāng, just flag down any bus (Y5) heading south on the main road.

To Dúdòng 到独峒

For an invigorating and attractive outing that could take you the better part of a day, a walk to the north of Sānjiāng town takes you through a pleasant succession of Dong villages to Dúdòng, which is virtually on the border with Guìzhōu and Húnán. Take a bus from the Hexi bus station in Sānjiāng town to Dúdòng and ask the driver to drop you off at

Zuòlóng (座龙), one hour north of town. The road to Zuòlóng is rough in parts but passes an attractive backdrop of hills contoured with tea bushels.

From the turn-off to Zuòlóng, walk around 500m down the road to the village on the other side of the river, crossable via a string of rocks serving as stepping stones. Among the village's delightful alleys are two **drum towers**, one of which stands near an old theatrical stage (戏台; xìtái) that leans at an awkward angle. At the sight of foreigners and outsiders, children and village elders congregate at the windows of nearby houses. If you want you can continue along the road on the other side of the river to the nearby settlement of Lóng'ān (龙安).

Return to the main road and walk a few kilometres north to **Bāxié** (八协), the next village. As you round the corner into Bāxié, you will arrive at the first of several wind-and-rain bridges. With four towers, the bridge (Gǒngfú Qiáo; 巩福桥) is attractively designed with cross beams decorated with floral motifs. Further along the road, take the stone steps up through the pavilion to your left to the village's seven-eaved drum tower, standing on a small square, topped with a carved bird and facing a traditionally fashioned theatrical stage. Take the steps up to the west of the drum tower for views over the village.

Further along the road is the **Pingliu Cifu Bridge** (平流赐福桥; Píngliú Cìfú Qiáo), which dates to 1861 and the reign of the Qing emperor, Xianfeng. The bridge leads you a short distance ahead to the village of **Píngliú** (平流), where Chinese slogans on walls remind villagers it is a crime not to take their children to school. The local drum tower stands out amid a collection of traditional Dong buildings and houses of more recent construction.

A short walk brings you to **Huálián** (华练), with its namesake bridge (dating originally to 1857) and drum tower rising above the village. At the time of writing, the local wood masons were industriously assembling a new drum tower from fir wood, the material of choice.

Around six kilometres north of Huálián is the settlement of **Bātuán** (岜团). It's quite a walk, but you can jump aboard a passing minibus (Y2). At the village, take the steps down to the magnificent **Batuan Wind and Rain Bridge** (岜团风雨桥; Bātuán Fēngyǔ Qiáo), a black-and-white edifice spanning the river. With fields on either side and superb views downriver, the solidly constructed bridge contains a small shrine to Guandi (here called Guangong), the Taoist God of War. The village also has two drum towers and is currently building a third.

A further 4km from Bātuán, much of it uphill (the walk takes around 50 minutes), **Dúdòng** (独峒) is a busy and rundown town with several restaurants and with pigs roaming its muddy streets. Although much of Dúdòng is modern, a handful of historic buildings can be found in town, including a drum tower, a stage, the Xiapei building (夏培楼; Xiàpéi Lóu) and a bridge. If you want to spend the night, you can check into the **Sky Lake Hotel** (天湖旅馆; Tiānhú Lǚguǎn; ☎ 0772-862 2728) on the main road on the left just before your reach the marketplace after entering the village, which has simple rooms. Ten kilometres north of town the relaxing Dong village of **Gāodìng** (高定) is worth exploring. A motorbike will take you there for around Y10; ask at any of the restaurants in Dúdòng. Buses in the return direction leave hourly from 6am for the journey back to Sānjiāng, past mountains cloaked in firs.

Sleeping

Hotels are plentiful enough in Sānjiāng town, although it is far more pleasant to stay in one of the growing cluster of hotels found by and around the Chengyang Wind and Rain Bridge.

SĀNJIĀNG

Xinglianxin Hotel (兴连新宾馆; Xīngliángxīn Bīnguǎn; ☎ 862 6988; 11 Furong Lu; 芙蓉路11号; s/d/tr/q Y50/78/98/128; ☒) Cheap and clean rooms with air-con, shower (squat loo), TV and heating in this new outfit just up from the Sanjiang Hotel. Look for the sign that simply says 'hotel', next to a Lianhua supermarket branch. Modest discounts available.

Chengyang Qiao Hotel (程阳桥宾馆; Chéngyángqiáo Bīnguǎn; ☎ 861 7431; s Y108-118, d Y138-158; ☒) Next to the Agricultural Bank of China, scuffed rooms are OK here with tiled floor, shower room, air-con and TV, although the road outside can be noisy; rooms can usually be wangled for Y70.

Sanjiang Hotel (三江饭店; Sānjiāng Fàndiàn; ☎ 862 6888; fax 862 6385; 2 Xinhua Lu; 新华路2号; s & d Y218; ☒) On the other side of the river, this smart enough, modern three-star hotel has decent rooms, typically discounted to Y130.

OTHER VILLAGES

Hotels can be found to the west of the Chengyang Wind and Rain Bridge and there's a mushrooming brood in the villages of Yánzhài and Mǎ'ān Zhài just east of the bridge.

Countryside International Hotel (乡村国际旅馆; Xiāngcūn Guójì Lǚguǎn; ☎ 0772-858 2813; fax 858 2813; tw with shower Y30, tr without shower Y30; ☐) After crossing the bridge, turn right and it's straight ahead on your left on the cusp of the small village of Yánzhài. Twin rooms are clean in this newly built place, staff speak English and there's an English menu but no river views. Internet access is Y5 per hour.

Dong Village Hotel (侗家旅馆; Dòngjiā Lǚguǎn; ☎ 0772-858 2421; d with/without shower Y50/40) Excellently located over Chengyang Wind and Rain Bridge and a short walk to the west, with nearby Dong water wheels adding to its riverine charms, this newly built place has neat doubles with first-rate views. No air-con.

Chengyang Bridge National Hostel (程阳桥招待所; Chéngyángqiáo Zhāodàisuǒ; ☎ 0772-858 2468; fax 0772-858 2798; d/tr without shower; Y40/60; ☒) Just to the left of the far side of the bridge and fabulously positioned next to the river, this fine place operates from an original nail-less Dong building (run a metal detector over the woodwork if you want) and is run by amiable manager, Mr Wu Xiaolin. Hydrophiles can swim and bathe in the river during summer months. Laundry service available. Internet access Y5 per hour.

Eating

A strong selection of restaurants lies along Furong Lu (芙蓉路) in the east of Sānjiāng town.

Dòngxiāng Gé (侗乡阁; ☎ 862 5622; 24 Furong Lu; 芙蓉路24号; meals Y50) A welcoming and brightly lit Dong-style restaurant run by an entrepreneur with an eye on the tourist trade. Prices are steeper than you would expect in Sānjiāng, but dishes are appetizing. Square up to a Dong-style beef hotpot (侗家牛排火锅; Dòngjiā niúpái huǒguō; Y38) and Dong-style oil tea fish (侗家油茶鱼; Dòngjiā yóuchá yú; Y38), wave your chopsticks at rabbit hotpot (Y28) or brave a dog-meat hotpot (Y25).

Getting There & Away

BUS

At the time of writing, buses to Sānjiāng town from Lóngshèng were taking around 2½ to three hours on a road that has been two years

BUS TIMETABLE

Destination	Fare (Y)	Duration (hours)	Departure Time
Dúdòng	10	2	9 per day (7.30am-4.20pm)
Guǎngzhōu	152	12	4pm
Guìlín	84	5	7 per day
Línxī	6	1	frequent
Liǔzhōu	35	4	11 per day
Lóngshèng	20	3	21 per day (6.30am-6pm)
Róng'ān	15	1½	18 per day (7.10am-4.50pm)
Róngshuǐ	19	2	1.30pm
Tónglè	8.50	1½	13 per day (7.20am-5.10pm)
Wúzhōu	110	10	3pm

in the re-laying. Hedong bus station on the east side of the river in Sānjiāng town has buses serving Guìlín, Wúzhōu, Lóngshèng and Liǔzhōu. Buses from Lóngshèng arrive at the Hedong bus station; it's a Y2 motor tricycle ride between the two bus stations. Buses to Guǎngzhōu and local destinations such as Línxī and Dúdòng depart from the **Hexi bus station** (河西站; Héxī Zhàn; ☎ 861 2202 or 861 2929) on the west side of the river. With only one bus daily to Róngshuǐ, it is more convenient to first take a bus to Róngān and then take a local minivan to Róngshuǐ.

TRAIN
Sānjiāng's train station is located several kilometres west of town, linked to the town centre by minibuses that run every half-hour throughout the day. Huáihuà, Jíshǒu and Zhāngjiājiè in Húnán (see p212) are accessible by train, putting you within reach of Fènghuáng, Déhāng and Wǔlíngyuán; to the south, the rail line connects with the transport hub of Liǔzhōu.

SĀNJIĀNG TO KĂILĬ
If you have time on your hands, it's worth entering Guìzhōu province through the back door. From Sānjiāng's Hexi bus station parking lot, minibuses leave when full for Dìpíng (Lóng'é; Y14 to Y20), just across the Guìzhōu border. Though the journey takes approximately three hours, prepare for delays that could leave you stranded in Dìpíng for the night. Frequent buses depart Dìpíng for Lípíng (黎平; Y22, five hours).

The journey to Lípíng passes through some beautiful mountains, as well as the fabulous Dong village of Zhàoxīng (p138), the highlight of the trip and definitely worth a visit.

There are also frequent buses from Sānjiāng to Cóngjiāng (从江) in Guìzhōu. The road is good but the route isn't as pretty. However, if you're in a hurry to reach Kăilĭ, there are numerous onward connections that can be made from Cóngjiāng.

Another possibility is to take a train to Tōngdào in Húnán province and from there travel on by bus to Lìpíng.

RÓNGSHUǏ 融水
☎ 0772 / pop 450,000
Another town central to Guǎngxī's minority culture, Róngshuǐ is a possible third node on a Lóngshèng–Sānjiāng–Róngshuǐ loop out of Guìlín for travellers not crossing into Guìzhōu. Thirteen minority groups are represented in this county, with Miao making up 37% of the total. Large numbers of Yao, Zhuang and Dong also live in the county.

Apart from the minority cultural experience, Róngshuǐ's most famous attraction is Yuánbǎo Shān, a couple of hours to the northwest, a rustic mountain with some gorgeous sunrises. While you plan your getaway to surrounding areas, the town itself has a quickly climbed Buddhist mountain.

Orientation
Róngshuǐ is a small town situated on the Rong River (融江; Róng Jiāng). The town's two main streets are the intersecting Shouxing Lu (寿星路) and Chaoyang Lu (朝阳路). None of the roads in town have street signs.

The train line hugs the northern part of town with the station in the northwest about a 20-minute walk west from the centre. The bus station is on Xiangshan Lu (香山路) in the southwest.

Information

A handful of internet cafés for visitors can be found on the corner of Shouxing Lu and Chaoyang Lu.

Sights

LĂOZI SHĀN 老子山

The only sight within the town proper is this hillock (admission Y2) on the southern edge of the central part of town. A short walk uphill from the ticket office brings you past some crudely carved figures of *luóhàn* (Buddhist monks) to the **Tianwang Hall** (天王殿; Tiānwáng Diàn), behind which rises the recently built **Shouxing Temple** (寿星寺; Shòuxīng Sì). You can reach the top of the hill in around 20 minutes for views of the fields and peaks around Róngshuĭ.

To get there, head southeast from the town's only traffic roundabout until the road ends, then local paths will take you by pretty riverside scenes and through village gardens. After 10 minutes you'll cross a stream and see the first of the hawkers at the entrance. Local bus 2 also passes by Lǎozi Shān.

MINORITY VILLAGES 少数民族村落

Many minority villages can be accessed only via waterways from the pier in Róngshuĭ, which is not so easy to do for solo travellers (it can be very expensive) or if you arrive out of season. An alternative you can try is to book one of the minivans outside the bus station to take you around; drivers will charge around Y150 per day (plus fuel). As there's no shortage of Miao culture in the countryside, pick a local bus to anywhere north and you'll be likely to pass at least relatively close to a Miao village; just jump off the bus and look around. Alternatively, you can take an organised tour through one of the travel agents in town; these tours tend to visit villages such as Tiántou Cūn (田头村), the Miao villages of Gōutān (勾滩; Gōutān) and Chánglài (长赖); tours cost from around Y100 for a day tour and they include some tourist-oriented singing and dancing performances and horse fighting shows; boating and rafting trips along the Bei River (贝江; Bèi Jiāng) are also possible.

Sleeping

Bǎotōng Bīnguǎn (宝通宾馆; ☎ 512 9888; 217 Xiangshan Lu; 香山路217号; s Y70, s & d with computer Y120; ☷ 🖳) The clean rooms at this handy

hotel all come with air-con, DVD player, hot water and a shower. Pricier rooms are also equipped with computer terminals and negotiated discounts typically bring rooms down by 30%.

Getting There & Away

BUS

There are buses from the bus station on Xiangshan Lu to Liŭzhōu (Y22, frequent), Nánníng (Y70 to Y85, five per day), Guìlín (Y30, nine per day) and Sānjiāng (Y18, 8.30am). As there's only one daily bus to Sānjiāng it is better to share a ride in a minivan taxi to Róng'ān (Y5, 50 minutes, morning to late afternoon) and then jump on one of the regular buses that connect Róng'ān and Sānjiāng (Y10, 1½ hours). A taxi from Róngshuĭ to Róng'ān costs around Y35.

TRAIN

Róngshuĭ is served by trains between Róng'ān to the north and destinations in Húnán, and Liŭzhōu to the south. Departures to Nánníng (Y28 hard seat), Xiāngfán (Y67 hard seat), Zhāngjiājiè (Y39 hard seat), Jíshŏu (Y31 hard seat) and Huáihuà (Y25 hard seat) all leave in the very early hours of the morning, with the ticket office only open sporadically between 11.30pm and 5.10am.

Getting Around

Most motorcycle-taxi rides in Róngshuĭ cost Y1 to Y2; from the train station to the bus station is Y3, as it's 2km west of the town centre. Otherwise the town is small enough to walk around.

AROUND RÓNGSHUĬ

Yuánbǎo Shān 元宝山

About 75km from Róngshuĭ, the summit of Yuánbǎo Shān rises 2100m over the surrounding plain. Climbable in four to six hours, the peak is surrounded by 3900 hectares of national park, featuring several ambitious trails (lots of steps) and plenty of waterfalls. A highlight is the 'Sea of Clouds', which often shrouds the summit overnight. At dawn, when the clouds clear, Yuànbǎo reddens in what is arguably Guǎngxī's best sunrise scene.

You will probably have to overnight at one of the **wooden huts** (beds Y15-20) on the mountain, since exploring the mountain and getting back in a day is a tall order.

Travel agents in Róngshuǐ can get you on pricey group tours to the mountain (reckon on around Y360 for a three-day tour), otherwise travel there independently, but take adequate food and water.

To get to Yuánbǎo Shān, catch the daily bus departing at noon from Róngshuǐ to the park entrance town of Xiǎosāng (Y10, two hours).

LIǓZHŌU 柳州
☎ 0772 / pop 782,000

The largest city on the Liu River (柳江; Liǔ Jiāng), Liǔzhōu is one of the Southwest's most important train junctions. Attractive karst scenery decorates the outskirts of town and the Liǔzhōu is a modern and wealthy city, but travellers generally find themselves here en route somewhere else.

Information

Several internet cafés can be found in the Yínxīng Shāngyè Chéng on Fei'e Lu west of the south bus station. The Bank of China on Longcheng Lu can change money; the handy Bank of China branch on Fei'e Lu has an ATM. The China Post & Telecom office is next to the Lijing Hotel on Longcheng Lu.

Sights

Liǔzhōu has some pleasant parks, including **Liuzhou Park** (Liǔzhōu Gōngyuán; admission Y3) in the north of the city, **Yufeng Mountain Park** (Yúfēng Shān Gōngyuán) along Fei'e Lu near the main bus station and adjacent to **Ma'an Shan Park** (Mǎ'ān Shān Gōngyuán; admission Y3).

At the time of research, the new **Liuzhou Museum** (Liǔzhōu Bówùguǎn; www.lzbwg.com; cnr Guangchang Lu & Jiefang Beilu) on the northeast corner of Liuzhou Sq had yet to open.

Sleeping

Liǔnán Lǚshè (☎ 361 8813; dm with fan Y10, s with fan Y22-70, tr with fan per bed Y20, d Y70-90) Opposite the train station there's no English sign here, but singles are clean and comfortable enough. Pricier single rooms come with bath and woodstrip flooring; concrete-floored dorms are more spartan.

Nanjiang Hotel (Nánjiāng Fàndiàn; ☎ 361 2988; 304 Fei'e Lu; 飞鹅路304号; s & d Y268-318, tr Y368; 🖃) Also near the train station is this midrange, three-star outfit with good comfy single rooms, women-only rooms (Y298 to Y348) and discounts.

INFORMATION
Bank of China 中国银行	**1** B2
Bank of China 中国银行	**2** B2
China Post & Telephone Office 中国邮政&中国电信	**3** B1
Industrial and Commercial Bank ofChina 工商银行	**4** B1
Internet Cafés 网吧	**5** A2
Kodak Express 柯达	**6** B1

SIGHTS & ACTIVITIES
Liuzhou Park 柳州公园	**7** B1
Liuzhuo Museum 柳州博物馆	**8** B1
Ma'an Shan Park	**9** B2
Yufeng Mountain Park 鱼峰山公园	**10** B2

SLEEPING
Lijing Hotel 丽晶大酒店	**11** B2
Liǔnán Lǚshè 柳南旅舍	**12** A2
Nanjiang Hotel 南疆饭店	**13** A2

EATING
Beijing Jiaozi Restaurant 北京饺子馆	**14** A2

TRANSPORT
CAAC ticket office 民航售票处	**15** A2
Main Bus Station 客运总站	**16** B2
South Bus Station 客运南站	**17** A2

Lijing Hotel (Lìjīng Dàjiǔdiàn; ☎ 280 8888; fax 280 8828; 32 Longcheng Lu; 龙城路32号; d Y388-478; 🖃) Smart, with efficient and polite staff, this four-star hotel is right in the city centre, on the other side of the Liu River. Good English is spoken here and discounts typically bring prices down by 20%.

Eating

Beijing Jiaozi Restaurant (Běijīng Jiǎoziguǎn; ☎ 361 0563; 81 Fei'e Lu; 飞鹅路81号; meals Y15) Bustling and busy dumpling restaurant with bus-loads of *jiǎozi*, handily located just west of the south bus station.

Getting There & Away

AIR

There are flights from Liǔzhōu's Bailian Airport (白莲机场; Báilián Jīchǎng) to Běijīng, Shànghǎi, Guǎngzhōu, Chéngdū, Kūnmíng and other cities. Tickets for flights from here and from Guilín and Nánníng can be bought from the **CAAC ticket office** (Mínháng Shòupiàochù; ☎ 381 0000; 122 Fei'e Lu; ⏰ 8am-8pm). Bus 21 runs to the airport.

BUS

Liǔzhōu has two bus stations; the main bus station (Kèyùn Zǒngzhàn) is located on Wenbi Lu in the south of town. The south bus station (Kèyùn Nánzhàn; ☎ 367 0988) is located east of the train station on Fei'e Lu and serves similar destinations as the main bus station, including two buses to Yángshuò (Y29, 8.50am and 3.30pm) and a bus to Sānjiāng (Y35, 7.25am) and Kǎilǐ (Y122, 3.40pm). The table below refers to trips from the main bus station.

TRAIN

A major rail junction, Liǔzhōu has excellent connections to Chóngqìng (Y75, 6.33am), Beijing West (Y190, 10.49pm), Guilin North (Y26 hard seat), Nánníng (Y51, 8.55am and 4.52pm), Chéngdū (Y99, 9.15pm), Kūnmíng (Y82, 9.55pm), Shànghǎi (Y159, 12.32pm) and Xī'ān (Y122, 2.02pm). Prices are for hard sleepers (midbunk) unless indicated. Connections into Húnán include Zhāngjiājiè (Y53, 10.38pm), Huáihuà (Y40 hard seat) and Jíshǒu (Y47 hard seat).

Getting Around

Liǔzhōu boasts a new fleet of Hyundai taxis; taxis are Y3 at flagfall (plus Y1 petrol tax).

NÁNNÍNG 南宁

☎ 0771 / pop 807,000

Many of China's provincial capitals – think Héféi, Fúzhōu or Nánchāng – are notoriously humdrum and Nánníng is no exception. It ticks all the usual boxes: it's rapidly modernising, increasingly wealthy and in the throes of transformation. The city is green and pleasant enough and waylays visitors questing visas en route to Vietnam, but aside from its excellent museum and a handful of surrounding sights, there's little to deter visitors from pressing on to more scenic parts of the province.

Orientation

Nánníng's grids require only a few blocks to work out. In the north is the train station, from where the main artery – Chaoyang Lu – runs roughly north–south towards the Yong River (Yōng Jiāng), which bisects the city. Halfway down Chaoyang Lu is Chaoyang Garden (Cháoyáng Huāyuán), the geographic centre of town. This is a good place for people-watching and for bus connections to scenic sights outside town. Just north of the river Chaoyang Lu splits into Jiangnan Lu, heading over the Yong Jiang Bridge, and Minzu Dadao, which races east towards the provincial museum and Langdong bus station. Xingning Lu and the west part of Minsheng Lu is pedestrianised.

Information

BOOKSHOPS

Foreign Languages Bookstore (Wàiwén Shūdiàn; Minzhu Lu; ⏰ 9.30am-5.30pm) The usual stale slabs of classic novels peppered with slices of trash fiction and pulp paperbacks.

Xinhua Bookshop (Xīnhuá Shūdiàn; Xinhua Lu)

INTERNET ACCESS

Several internet cafés can be found around the train station area and along pedestrianised Minsheng Lu.

BUSES FROM LIǓZHŌU			
Destination	**Fare (Y)**	**Duration (hours)**	**Departure Time**
Bǎisè	124	8	8.20am & 3.50pm
Běihǎi	110	5	6 per day
Guilín	45	2½	every 30min (7am-9.30pm)
Guìpíng	51	5	6 per day
Nánníng	64	2½	every 10-20min (6am-10pm)
Róngshuǐ	29	2½	every 30min (6.40am-7.40pm)
Yángshuò	30	3½	7.45am

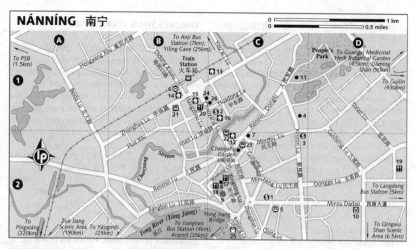

NÁNNÍNG 南宁

Xinxing Internet Café (Xīnxīng Wǎngbā; 2nd fl, Minsheng Lu, per hr Y2; 24hr) Opposite the south door of Àomén Shíjiē (p193).

MONEY
Bank of China (Zhōngguó Yínháng; south of Nanfang Hotel, Chaoyang Lu) ATM that takes Visa, Amex, JCB and Diner's Club cards. The branch on Minzhu Lu gives credit card advances and changes travellers' cheques and cash.

POST & COMMUNICATIONS
China Post (Zhōngguó Yóuzhèng; Minzu Dadao) A handier branch for posting letters is just west of the train station.

PUBLIC SECURITY BUREAU
PSB (Gōngānjú; ☎ 289 1260; Keyuan Dadao; 8am-4pm Mon-Fri) The Foreign Affairs office of the PSB is northwest of the city centre, north of the zoo.

TRAVEL AGENCIES
China International Travel Service (CITS; Zhōngguó Guójì Lǚxíngshè; ☎ 284 5147; 40 Xinmin Lu; 8.30am-

5.30pm Mon-Fri) Only an OK place for independent travellers to get information. Also issues one-month Vietnamese visas (1-/2-/3- day processing Y650/550/450)

Dangers & Annoyances
Child beggars – remotely controlled and guided to their target by grown-up mentors – are common in parts of Chaoyang Lu, even making audacious raids into McDonald's and other fast-food outlets to harass diners.

Sights & Activities
GUANGXI PROVINCIAL MUSEUM 广西自治区博物馆
On Minzu Dadao, the highlight of this fascinating **museum** (Guǎngxī Zìzhìqū Bówùguǎn; admission Y8; 8.30-11.50am & 2.30-5.30pm Mon-Fri, 9am-5pm Sat & Sun) is its magnificent exhibition of ancient Dong bronze drums. Used as sacrificial and ritual vessels and as symbols of power as well as serving as musical instruments, the drums vary in size but are almost all robust and

imposing and finely wrought, with the largest 165cm high. Many of the designs are vivid and realistic, displaying a highly developed knowledge of bronze work. The drums follow a basic type: cylindrical in shape, decorated with frogs, birds, figures and other animals and ornamented with lines radiating concentrically on the lid from a central sun design. Drums are divided into male and female types, with the male drum generating a deeper timbre. Male and female drums can be distinguished by the length of the solar rays and the diameter of the solar design. On view are many different styles of drum, from Lingshan drums with their piggyback-style frog motifs to the Shizhaishan drum type from Yúnnán with its highly decorated patterns. Also on view is a drum mould.

The Guangxi Minority Exhibition has exhibits of the province's plentiful minorities and their traditions, customs and textiles. Learn how the Shui use a water calendar (rather than a solar or lunar calendar) and how a Yao brides cries during her wedding.

In the tree-filled rear garden sit several full-size examples of Dong and Miao houses and a nail-less bridge, complete with pond.

The museum is a quiet, relaxing break from the hectic city streets. There are some English descriptions or you may chance upon one of the English-speaking guides. To get there, walk or take bus 6.

PEOPLE'S PARK 人民公园

Also known as White Dragon Park, this **park** (Rénmín Gōngyuán; 1 Renmin Donglu; admission Y2; ⊗ 9am-6pm) is a pleasant spot for a stroll. Steps facing you as you enter take you up to **Zhenning Fort** (Zhènníng Pàotái; admission Y1) where you can inspect a rusty 122mm **German cannon** on rails, manufactured in the 19th century, taking aim at the southwest. Also within the fort are a couple of smallish smooth-faced *bìxì* (turtlelike dragons) and a Ming dynasty bell. As the blurb insists (with not entirely watertight logic): 'He who has not reached the Zhenning Fort has not reached the Nanning People's Park', and you can't argue with that. There's also the small Shady Botanical Gardens, which features some rare herbs, exotic flowers, a hothouse with local flower varieties, and the requisite 1000-year-old banyan tree. You can also go boating on the lake or take your chances on the roller-skating rink.

QINGXIU SHAN SCENIC AREA
青秀山风景区

This largish scenic area (Qīngxiù Shān Fēngjǐng Qū) to the southwest of Nánníng on the Yōng Jiāng offers lakes, ponds, pavilions, cable cars, viewing platforms and foraging tour groups. A favourite summer retreat since the Sui and Tang dynasties, the park has verdant woods, springs and landscaped gardens with modest but scenic peaks of up to 180m that can be easily scaled.

Local buses 10 and 33 go to the park from the train station, but you still have a fair walk to the entrance. Buses depart when full from the northern side of Chaoyang Garden. It costs Y3 to the front gate or Y11 into the park including admission.

GUANGXI MEDICINAL HERB BOTANICAL GARDEN 广西药用植物园

This fascinating **garden** (Guǎngxī Yàoyòng Zhíwùyuán; admission Y10; ⊗ dawn to dusk) is the largest of its kind in China, with more than 2400 species of medicinal plants (Guǎngxī alone has 5000 species). The botanical gardens will be especially impressive if you are lucky enough to tag along with one of the centre's few English speakers. Stuck in an industrial wasteland northeast of the city, it takes about 30 minutes to get there on bus 101 or 102 from Chaoyang Garden. A taxi from town costs about Y25.

DRAGON BOAT RACES

As in other parts of the Southwest (and Guǎngdōng and Macau), Nánníng stages dragon boat races on the fifth day of the fifth lunar month (sometime in June), when large numbers of sightseers cheer the decorated rowing vessels along the Yōng Jiāng. The rowers pull to a steady cadence of drum beats maintained by a crew member at one end of the boat.

Sleeping
BUDGET

If you don't object to scuzziness, it's worth poking your head into one of the cheap Chinese guesthouses (招待所; zhāodàisuǒ) around the train station area and along Chaoyang Lu. They offer beds for as little as Y10 in a shared room, although not all welcome foreigners.

Yingbin Hotel (Yíngbīn Fàndiàn; ☎ 211 6288; www .ybfd.com; 71 Chaoyang Lu; 朝阳路71号; s Y90-130, d Y100-140, tr/q Y180/200; r with computer Y170-190; 🏠)

Rates dip as low as Y40 for a standard single or Y98 for a computer-equipped version, the latter advertised with free internet, free laundry and free shoe-cleaning. All rooms have air-con, phone, TV and shower except for the cheapie singles and doubles which have fan, TV and shower.

Yutong Hotel (Yùtōng Bīnguǎn; ☎ 242 3285; cnr Jinan Lu & Chaoyang Lu; 济南路和朝阳路交界; s/d Y128/148; ☒) A fresh business hotel of the newly built breed with smart, clean rooms but precious little character. Single rooms come with clean wood floors, digital TV and swish bathrooms with undersink cabinets. Limited English spoken; discounts of around 15% the norm. Look for the modern-looking tower at the intersection of Jinan Lu and Chaoyang Lu.

Railway Hotel (Tiědào Fàndiàn; ☎ 232 3188; fax 242 2572; 84 Zhonghua Lu; 中华路84号; s Y168-188, d Y120-210, tw Y170; ☒) It's service with a scowl at this place, but the location is handy for the train stations, and rooms pass muster, with discounts on the cheapest rooms deflating prices to around Y80. The pricier doubles are large and tidy with bath, but at this price you might as well pay a bit extra and treat yourself at the excellent High Class Hotel opposite.

MIDRANGE

Baohai Hotel (Bǎohǎi Bīnguǎn; ☎ 576 5008; fax 576 5008; 68 Chaoyang Lu; s/d Y300/320; ☒) Once you've recovered from the crummy lift and weird layout with guest rooms lodged away on the 4th and 5th floors of a separate block adjacent to reception, you'll find rooms with acres of space with huge bathrooms; 50% discounts not uncommon.

High Class Hotel (Hǎigélāsī Dàjiǔdiàn; ☎ 579 6888; fax 579 6998; 76 Zhonghua Lu; s & d Y380; ☒) Lovely and spacious double rooms with spotless wood strip floors, smart furniture, supportive mattresses and accommodating staff make this well turned-out hotel the best choice in the train station area. The free breakfast is Chinese-style, and worth it. Discounts regularly bring rooms down to Y160. Highly recommended.

Eating

Nánníng is celebrated for its dog hotpot (狗肉火锅; gǒuròu huǒguō). Wander down Zhongshan Lu for durian, lychee, melons, squid kebabs (Y1), stinky tofu (臭豆腐; chòu dòufu), porridge, endless barbecued meat outlets, dog cadavers spliced in two and swinging from hooks, and roasted sparrows (shāo díquè). Also look out for juàntǒngfěn (steamed noodle pancake wrap with pork and coriander filling served in steaming broth), lǎoyǒumiàn and lǎoyǒufěn (literally 'old friend' wheat or rice noodles). Several restaurants serving dumplings from China's northeast can be found along Huadong Lu near the intersection with Chaoyang Lu.

Tianhong Northeast Jiaozi Restaurant (Tiānhóng Dōngběi Jiǎozi; ☎ 242 8868; 2nd fl, 65 Chaoyang Lu; 朝阳路65号; meals from Y10) There's no English menu at this industrious dumpling restaurant, but don't let that deter you from trying its scrummy jiǎozi. The vegetable jiǎozi (素白菜馅; sùbáicài xiàn) come in at Y2 for six, the chive and egg version (韭菜鸡蛋; jiǔcài jīdàn) only Y2.5 for six; the lamb and onion (羊肉大葱馅; yángròu dàcōng xiàn) are good news at Y4 for a half dozen and, if you still have an appetite, further standard dishes from China's northeast fill out the menu.

Muslim Restaurant (Qīngzhēn Fàndiàn; ☎ 282 1381; 25 Xinhua Lu; 新华路25号; meals Y15-25) Popular and good-value eatery specialising in Chinese Muslim cuisine with a useful English menu.

Àomén Shíjiè (☎ 261 2129; 19 Xinhua Lu; 新华路19号; meals Y25; ⏱ 10am-10pm) Just along from

---

MAN BITES DOG

The history of dog meat (狗肉; gǒuròu; in Cantonese, gauyeuk) consumption in China dates back millennia. Famed among Middle Kingdom residents for its medicinal qualities, canine flesh is especially popular in winter months, as the meat is believed to generate heat and promote bodily warmth. After a spell in Guǎngxī you will get used to the sight of freshly skinned mutts being blow-torched at the wayside, or man's best friend – limbs stiff from rigor mortis – hanging rigidly from hooks in night markets.

Dog meat may make it to the menu across much of China, but not all Chinese participate. The Manchu from China's hearty northeast eschew dog meat because a much-revered pooch once saved the life of Nurhachi, founder of the Manchu state. But travellers to China's Southwest will find dog a standard feature of restaurant kitchens.

the Xinhua bookstore, this gigantic dining hall is lined with hatches where you order your dish, a waitress in tow while you make your choice. There's no English menu, but the wall-mounted photo menu makes ordering a piece of cake. Try the peppery *mápó dòufu* (麻婆豆腐; spicy tofu with crumbs of pork; Y10) or the more straightforward *gōngbào jīdīng fàn* (宫爆鸡丁饭; spicy chicken chunks with rice; Y12) or the tasty *méicài kòuròu bāo* (pork with cabbage; Y15). Dishes are discounted between 2pm and 5pm.

Shaoshanchong Xiang Restaurant (Sháoshānchŏng Xiāngcàiguăn; ☎ 587 1059; 2-16 Sixian Lu; 思贤路2-16号; meals Y30) For sheer OTT novelty and dubious tastefulness, check out this nostalgic Húnán restaurant where signature chili-infused dishes from the home province of Chairman Mao are delivered by gaggles of cheeky, pig-tailed girls in Red Guard uniforms.

Getting There & Away

AIR

Domestic airlines fly all over China from Nánníng, with multiple departures daily to Běijīng (Y2050, three hours five minutes, six per day), Xī'ān (Y1800, three hours 20 minutes, two per day), Shànghăi (Y1660, two hours 20 minutes, four per day), Kūnmíng (Y630, one hour 10 minutes, two per day), Nánjīng (Y1480, three hours, one per day), Chóngqìng (Y940, one hour 20 minutes, one per day), Guăngzhōu (Y730, one hour five minutes, frequent) and Guìyáng (Y630, one hour, two per day). Less frequent departures include Chéngdū (Y1030, 1½ hours, three weekly), Qīngdăo (Y1940, three hours 55 minutes, three weekly) and Hong Kong (Y1900, one hour 10 minutes, three weekly). At the time of writing, the occasional flights to Hanoi (Hénèi) had been suspended.

Civil Aviation Administration of China (CAAC; Zhōngguó Mínháng; ☎ 243 1459; 82-1 Chaoyang Lu; ☷ 24hr) is generally efficient, though travel agencies on the street or in your hotel will have lower prices. From 8pm to 8am doors are barred shut and tickets are sold from the window round the side of the building.

BUS

A **ticket office** (☎ 242 9654 or 242 7619; ☷ 7.30am-9.30pm) for buses from Langdong bus station is located a short walk along Huadong Lu, near the corner of Huadong Lu and Chaoyang Lu, where you can purchase tickets up to 15 days in advance. Just north along Chaoyang Lu and on the same side of the road is a similar **ticket office** (☎ 210 2334; ☷ 6.30am-10pm).

Langdong Bus Station

This **bus station** (埌东客运站; Làngdōng Kèyùnzhàn; ☎ 550 8332, 550 8329) is inconveniently located in the far east of Nánníng. A taxi will cost around Y25 from the train station area; give yourself around 30 minutes to get there; more if it's rush hour.

Vietnam-bound travellers can catch the daily Hanoi-bound bus (Y120, 6½ hours, 8.10am). It will take you to Friendship Pass, after which you cross into Vietnam on foot and then board a Vietnamese bus the rest of the way to Hanoi.

Jiangnan Bus Station

This **bus station** (江南客运站; Jiāngnán Kèyùnzhàn; ☎ 451 9999; 236 Xingguang Dadao) is similarly located out on a limb, way down in the south of town over the Yong River. As well as destinations listed in the table below, numerous destinations in Guăngdōng province are also served. Bus 41 connects Anji Bus Station with Jiangnan Bus Station.

BUSES FROM JIANGNAN BUS STATION			
Destination	**Fare (Y)**	**Duration (hours)**	**Departure Time**
Băisè	65	4	4 per day
Běihăi	58	2½	every 30min (7.30am-9.30pm)
Chóngqìng	260	18	5pm & 6.40pm
Chóngzuŏ	25	1½	Every 40min (8am-6.30pm)
Guìlín	88	4½	frequent
Hong Kong	300	13	9pm
Liŭzhōu	60	3	every 30min (7.30am-9pm)
Yángshuò	100	5½	4.30pm

BUSES FROM LANGDONG BUS STATION

Destination	Fare (Y)	Duration (hours)	Departure Time
Băisè	50	3½	7 per day
Běihăi	58	3	every 20min (7am-9.30pm)
Chéngdū	300	18	2.30pm
Chóngqìng	260	15	2.30pm, 5.30pm & 6.30pm
Chóngzuŏ	20	1½	every 40min
Dàxīn	40	2½	5 per day
Detian Waterfall	90	3½	9am
Friendship Pass	68	2½	8.10am
Guăngzhōu	182	9	frequent
Guìlín	90-100	4½	every 20min (7.30am-11.30pm)
Guìpíng	50	3½	frequent
Guìyáng	160	8	9 per day
Hanoi (Hénèi)	120	6½	8.10am
Hèzhōu	130	8	9 per day
Hong Kong	350	11	9.10am
Kăilĭ	130	12	3.40pm
Liŭzhōu	60	2½	frequent
Píngxiáng	60	2½	frequent
Róngshuĭ	85	7	8.30am & 2pm
Zhōngshān	180	9	frequent
Zīyuán	90	7	9.40am
Zūnyì	200	10	4 per day

Anji Bus Station

Buses leave Anji Bus Station (安吉站; Ānjí Zhàn), north of town, every 15 minutes for Wŭmíng, useful for travellers heading to Yiling Cave (p196). Bus 41 runs between Anji station and Jiangnan station.

TRAIN

Important rail links from the **train station** (☎ 222 2222) include Běijīng (Y499, T6, 28 hours, 9.50am), Chéngdū (Y363, K142, 36 hours, 5.51pm), Guăngzhōu (Y185, K366, 14 hours, 11.55pm), Kūnmíng (Y195, K393, 14 hours, 6.10pm), Shànghăi (Y418, K182, 30½ hours, 9.26am), Xī'ān (Y406, K316, 34½ hours, 10.47am) and Guìlín (Y65, N802, five hours, 8.25am).

The T6 for Běijīng also passes through Liŭzhōu (three hours), Guìlín (five hours), Wŭhàn (17 hours), Zhèngzhōu (22 hours) and Shíjiāzhuāng (26 hours). The K142 to Chéngdū passes through Guìyáng (19 hours) and Chóngqìng (29 hours). The 2012 to Zhāngjiājiè (16 hours) leaves at 7.30pm.

The T905/M2 from Nánníng to Dong Dang (Tóngdēng) in Vietnam departs at 9.15pm, but think twice before hopping on. It takes forever with lengthy delays in Píngxiáng and at customs. The 5517 train for Píngxiáng leaves at 7.58am (four hours 50 minutes).

Getting next-day tickets at the train station doesn't seem to be too problematic. Foreigners can use any window, though technically No 15 is supposed to be 'the one'; window No 16 is the place to go to change tickets.

Getting Around

A CAAC **shuttle bus** (☎ 209 5307; Y15) departs every 30 minutes between 5.30am and 10.30pm from the CAAC office (82-1 Chaoyang Lu) for the 40-minute trip to the airport.

AROUND NÁNNÍNG
Yángměi 扬美

This 17th-century traditional town has been beautifully preserved and has become a popular day trip from Nánníng for Chinese tourists. The town is just 26km west of Nánníng on the Yong River. You could spend a couple of hours just wandering the cobblestone streets admiring the beautiful, historic buildings. There are some descriptions of the

GUĂNGXĪ

REVOLUTION IS NOT A DINNER PARTY

Mao Zedong's famous quip – 'Revolution is not a dinner party' – seemingly fell on a multitude of deaf ears during the chaotic Cultural Revolution. The most gruesome episode in the internecine upheaval, and a strictly taboo subject among Chinese historians, a shocking spate of cannibalism in Guăngxī dragged the Chinese class war down to new depths.

As a result of his research including interviews with witnesses and participants of the atrocities, Chinese dissident novelist Zheng Yi reveals how class enemies were killed and publicly eaten in parts of Guăngxī province during the period of political intoxication that convulsed China between 1966 and 1976. Zheng Yi was initially led to his research by the rumours of cannibalism while he was serving as a Red Guard in Guăngxī during the 1960s.

In his shocking account *Scarlet Memorial: Tales of Cannibalism in Modern China* (Westview Press, 1996), Zheng recounts how a female teacher, Wu Shufang, was killed in May 1968 in Wuxuan County, and her liver cooked and devoured. Her case is but one of many instances of the murder and consumption of teachers, landlords and other members of the bourgeoisie.

The cannibalism was far from clandestine. Rather, it was publicly orchestrated in the form of feasts, with human flesh consumed not to satiate hunger but as the ultimate demonstration of the subjugation of political enemies.

Accusations of state approval remain conjectural and it is possible that these were simply acts of brutality in a corner of China where authority had broken down and nihilism was widespread. The depravity was also arguably an extreme consequence of the dehumanising class hatred and fanaticism instigated by Mao Zedong and his acolytes.

Lu Xun's paranoid protagonist in his seminal *Diary of a Madman* may have imagined himself menacingly surrounded by cannibals, but the modernist author would have been distraught at the prescience of his disturbing tale.

---

history of the town's buildings, but not too much English. Guides will offer their services and you may be lucky to find someone who speaks some English. The best way to get around the town is to hire an ox cart for a half day (Y10). Lunch is available at a couple of restaurants in town or take a packed lunch.

The village used to be a pleasant boat trip away but now buses make the run. Buses leave from a bus stop just north of Chaoyang Garden or from a stop two blocks west of the train station, but only in high season. A taxi to the village will cost Y50 to Y60.

Yiling Cave 伊岭岩

Twenty-five kilometres to the north of Nánníng is **Yiling Cave** (Yílíng Yán; admission Y45; 8am-5pm). The Chinese rarely do caves *au naturel*, so brace yourself for coloured fluorescent lights and in-your-face commercialisation.

When you first arrive at the front gate, wait around for a group to form for a guided tour of the **Zhuang-minority Culture Park**, with its introduction to popular Zhuang culture. Entry is Y45; Chinese-speaking guided tours available.

If you have any time left, then the surrounding countryside is worth exploring.

Minibuses run from Chaoyang Garden most weekends (especially during summer). Alternatively, take bus 41 to the Anji bus station and catch a Wŭmíng (武鸣) bound bus (Y6; every 15 minutes, 6.15am to 10pm) to the cave.

North of Yiling Cave is **Lingshui Springs** (灵水泉; Língshuǐ Quán; admission Y6), essentially a large outdoor mineral swimming pool. To reach the springs, continue on the bus (Y10) past Yiling to Wŭmíng.

Daming Mountain 大明山

A further 1½ hours northeast of Wŭmìng, 90km from Nánníng, **Daming Mountain** (Dàmíng Shān; admission Y20) averages 1200m above sea level, reaching a maximum altitude of 1760m. A popular vacation spot in summer, the temperate climate engenders a population of more than 1700 species of plants. There are several relatively easy walks to nearby scenic lookouts. Most people head up to Dàmíng Shān for the scenery: the deep valley of **Shēnshān Shāngǔ**; the ancient Song pine trees, **Bùlǎosōng** and **Yíngkèsōng**; one of the three waterfalls; **Sacred Girl Peak (Shénnǚ Fēng)**; and of course the highest peak, Dàmíng Shān. Most scenic spots are accessible within a day's hike, however many visitors organise a guide to show them around as paths are poorly marked.

The standard approach is to spend the night in the small forestry village of Dàmíngshān at the foot of the mountain, although if arriving off season it's a good idea to phone ahead. Try the room reservation hotline: ☎ 985 1122.

The **Daming Shan Longteng Guesthouse** (大明 山龙腾宾馆; Dàmíng Shān Lóngténg Bīnguǎn; ☎ 1397 815 3459; r from Y150) is consistently staffed outside of high season, with average rooms but helpful service, and can help you arrange guides and transportation to the mountain.

From Nánníng's Chaoyang Garden, a daily public bus (Y14, 3pm) leaves from Renmin Lu. The bus terminates at Dàmíngshān where you'll find the ticket office, accommodation and a small shop. It is, however, another 27km from here to the top (and Daming Shan Resort) and the bus will only continue up if there are enough paying passengers.

Consider hopping off the bus 5km earlier in **Léijiāng**, where you can find a room and arrange a motorbike (Y50) to take you up to the top early the next day. You can also reach Léijiāng on any Dàhuà-, Mǎshān- or Liǎngjiāng-bound buses from Wǔmìng or Nánníng.

A bus returns to Nánníng from Dàmíng Shān daily at 7.30am. There is sometimes a second bus on weekends.

GUÌPÍNG 桂平

☎ 0775

A friendly and relaxed town, Guìpíng is the modest gateway to the village of Jīntián, birthplace of Taiping leader Hong Xiuquan and cradle of the bloodiest rebellions in history. Things are a bit slow in Guìpíng – the local cinema in 2007 was still screening films about the Sino-Vietnam conflict and the war against US forces in Korea – but locals are affable and climbs up Xīshān get the heart going.

Information

Bank of China (Zhōngguó Yínháng; 448 Guinan Beilu) Foreign exchange and ATM.

China Post (Zhōngguó Yóuzhèng; cnr Renmin Zhonglu & Guigui Beilu) Internet access.

Guiping Tourism Information Service Centre (Guìpíng Shì Lǚyóu Zīxún Fúwù Zhōngxīn; ☎ 338 1833) Just east of the town square; not staffed at time of research.

PSB Exit and Entry Administration Section (Gōngānjú Chūrùjìng Guǎnlǐkē; ☎ 457 2100; 2nd fl, 397 Renmin Zhonglu; ☷ 8am-noon & 2.30-5.30pm Mon-Fri) Can issue visa extensions.

People's Hospital (Rénmín Yīyuàn; Renmin Xilu)

Xinhua Bookstore (Xīnhuá Shūdiàn; Renmin Zhonglu)

Xingji Internet Café (星际网吧; Xīngjì Wǎngbā; Renmin Xilu; per hr Y2; ☷ 24hr) Round the corner from the bus station.

Sights

The enjoyable climb up **Xīshān** (西山; admission Y33) in the west of town can be done in 90 minutes or so; the walk is lovely, so there's little need for the cable car (up/down Y40/15). A succession of pavilions and Buddhist temples awaits ramblers on the way up, including the **Washing Stone Nunnery** (洗石庵; Xǐshí Ān; admission Y2) and the **Longhua Temple** (龙华寺; Lónghuá Sì; admission Y2), which originally dates to the Song dynasty. Note how the bark of the Longlin pine trees resembles the scales of a dragon. The local basketball team run up and down the hill, making you tired just watching them. At the summit is a TV transmitter and a small shrine to Guanyin, the Goddess of Mercy. Hikes from here reach across to neighbouring peaks. Numerous vendors and shops at the base of the peak sell the famous Xishan tea. From the town square to the main gate

is Y2 by three-wheeled motortaxi; otherwise take bus 8.

The attractive nine-storey Ming dynasty **East Pagoda** (东塔; Dōngtǎ) is around 20 minutes on bus 8 (Y2) east of town.

Sleeping

Down the scale of comfort, try any of the hostels near the bus station for beds from around Y10 to Y15.

Nóngyèjú Zhōngxīn Zhāodàisuǒ (☎ 339 1866; Guigui Beilu; 桂贵北路; s with fan without toilet Y30, tr per bed with fan and toilet Y15, d per bed with fan and toilet Y20, tr per bed with air-con and toilet Y35, d per bed with air-con and toilet Y45; 🖭) Right opposite the bus station, this is one of several guesthouses in the vicinity, with cheap and functional rooms facing onto a large couryard.

Gangsheng Hotel (Gǎngshèng Lǚguǎn; ☎ 337 2338; Guigui Beilu; 桂贵北路; s/tw Y108/128; 🖭) Good hotel just north of the bus station with clean, tiled rooms with shower (squat loo); pricier rooms (Y168) come with computer. Discounts shave around 20% off prices.

Guiping Hotel (Guiping Fàndiàn; ☎ 336 9292; 7 Renmin Zhonglu; 人民中路7号; s & d Y220, tr Y250; 🖭) OK if you want reasonable comfort and a plate with Chairman Mao's portrait gazing at you from the shelf. Rooms are spacious and clean, with large shower rooms. Discounts bring rooms down to around Y160 at most times.

Gongde Villa (公德山庄; Gōngdé Shānzhuāng; ☎ 339 3399; Xihan Scenic Area; 西山风景区; s/d/tr Y298/338/368; 🖭) Tucked away at the foot of picturesque Xīshān, this three-star hotel is the most pleasant place to stay, with landscaped gardens, a good restaurant and a ping-pong room.

Eating

Dàpáidàng (大排档; canteen style or small hole-in-the-wall eateries) are liberally scattered along Guigui Lu and Renmin Lu. Cheap claypot restaurants can be found just north of

the bus station exit on Guigui Lu where you can get a cheap claypot rice meal (沙锅饭; shāguō fàn) for about Y5. A string of Sichuan restaurants are just around the corner on the north side of Renmin Xilu, just west of the square, and there's a night market near the China Post office on Renmin Zhonglu.

Getting There & Away

Guìpíng's **bus station** (Kèyùnzhàn; ☎ 338 0032) is on Guigui Lu. To reach Běihǎi, take a bus (Y13) first to the bus station (☎ 0775 422 8007) in Guìgǎng, from where buses (Y75, 9.10am and 2.40pm) to Běihǎi take five hours.

Getting Around

Taxis start at Y3 for the first 2km.

AROUND GUÌPÍNG

Jīntián 金田

Just 23km north of Guìpíng is the town of Jīntián, the birthplace of Hong Xiuquan. Hong was a schoolteacher who declared himself a brother of Jesus Christ and led an army of more than a million followers against the Qing dynasty in the Taiping Rebellion, which was one of the bloodiest civil wars in history. A **museum** (起义纪念馆; Qǐyì Jìniànguǎn; admission Y3; ☼ 8am-5pm) now stands at the site of Hong's home.

The museum has two neglected floors of artefacts and displays tracing the history of the movement. There are no English captions, but a few diagrams and maps will keep you guessing which army went where and when and the exploits of Hong and the God Worshipping Society. The assorted weaponry upstairs may keep you interested.

East of the museum stands a socialist-realist **statue** of Hong – inscribed with the characters 天王洪秀全 (Tiānwáng Hóng Xiùquán; Heavenly King Hong Xiuquan).

Nearby is the site of the **Ancient Barracks** (古营盘; Gǔ Yíngpán) and the **Pledge Rock**

BUSES FROM GUÌPÍNG			
Destination	**Fare (Y)**	**Duration (hours)**	**Departure Time**
Guǎngzhōu	120	7½	3 per day
Guìgǎng	13	70min	frequent
Guìlín	110	5½	4.30pm
Liǔzhōu	60	4	6 per day
Nánníng	50	4	every 3hr (7.30am-8.30pm)
Wúzhōu	40	3	4 per day

OCEAN PERSON

Westerners without Chinese-language skills will be oblivious to the sheer variety of local slang for foreigners. *Lǎowài* (老外) – which literally means 'person from the outside' – or 'foreigner' – remains ubiquitous and you will hear the epithet repeatedly voiced, typically by Chinese men. Despite decades of exposure to Western films, the sudden appearance of Westerners can still spark considerable curiosity. *Wàiguórén* (literally 'person from a foreign country') is a politer alternative and is more popular with children. The most polite formal term is *wàibīn*, which means 'foreign guest'. You will also hear *wàiguólǎo* (外国佬), which also means 'person from a foreign country' but is more colloquial, or nation-specific terms, such as *yīngguólǎo* (英国佬), which means 'a person from England' but is derogatory. You may occasionally hear the Cantonese *saiyan* (西人; *xīrén),* which literally means Westerner, but Běihǎi folk (usually elderly) and Chinese from other areas of Cantonese-speaking Guǎngxī still refer to Westerners as *gwailo* (Mandarin 鬼佬; *guǐlǎo),* a derogatory term that means 'ghost person'. Variants on this are *hakgwai* (Mandarin 黑鬼; *hēiguǐ;* literally 'black ghost') for black people and *gwaipo* (Mandarin 鬼婆; *guǐpó;* literally 'ghost old woman') for western women. Elderly Chinese still refer to the Japanese as *Rìběn guǐzi* (日本鬼子; 'Japanese ghost people'). Perhaps the most courteous term is the seldom-used *yeungyan* (Mandarin 洋人; *yángrén),* which means 'Ocean person', a historical term that identifies Westerners' overseas origins and their first maritime appearance. *Yeung* (mandarin 洋; *yáng;* literally 'ocean') is sometimes used to describe a medley of objects that originated overseas, including matches (洋火; *yánghuǒ;* 'Western fire'), modern houses (洋房; *yángfáng;* 'Western houses'), Western or Arabic numerals (洋码子; *yángmǎzi;* 'Western numerals'), Western style (*yángqì;* 'Western air') and inevitably, Westerners (洋鬼子; *yáng guǐzi;* 'foreign ghosts').

(拜旗石; Bàiqí Shí), where followers made a solemn pledge to join the insurgent ranks. Further along is the **Rhinoceros Pool** (犀牛潭; Xīniú Tán), where the Taiping hid their weapons.

Back 100m or so towards the village, then along a rough dirt road and into the brush is the decaying **old home** of Wei Cheng Hui, another leader of the movement. Here the plotters met and forged their weapons, using the cacophony of flocks of honking geese to mask the sounds of their hammering. The Qing army burned the house, and it wasn't until 1974 that artefacts and fragments of the group's efforts were unearthed. Most relics and memorabilia are kept in Nánjīng, the capital of the Taiping kingdom (1853–64). Today the house lies enshrouded in weeds, behind a locked iron gate.

To get to Jīntián, hop on a bus from Guìpíng bus station (Y4, 40 minutes, every 15 minutes) or from Renmin Lu just west of the square. From the bus drop-off in Jīntián you'll have to backtrack 500m or so over the bridge to where motorcycle taxis are grouped. Go through the red gate there and continue another 4km – a pleasant walk if you've got the time (or Y10 for a round trip in a motorized three-wheeler). The last bus back to Guìpíng departs around 6pm.

Dragon Pool National Forest Park
龙潭国家森林公园

Approximately 20km northwest of town, this **park** (Lóngtán Guójiā Sēnlín Gōngyuán; admission Y50) gives you the opportunity to delve into rustic wilderness and Guǎngxī's only remaining old-growth forest.

From Guìpíng, get the bus to Jīntiáncūn (Y2) and ask the driver to drop you off at the Dragon Pool Park access road (Longtan Lukou). Motorcycle taxis waiting at the intersection will take you to the park for about Y30. A two-day trip via the Forestry Department (☎ 338 0413) in Guìpíng, including guide, food, transport and accommodation, costs about Y200.

BĚIHǍI 北海
☎ 0779 / pop 322,000

An easy-going and friendly port city on the southern coastline of Guǎngxī, Běihǎi (literally 'North Sea') slots into the Chinese tourist consciousness for its Silver Beach, but is also worth visiting for the historic charms of its old quarter and the fun of bouncing over the waves to the island of Wéizhōu off the coast. The town, with its shady, expansive boulevards draped with wide-branched Small Leaf Banyan (小叶榕; xiǎoyè róng) trees and studded with palms, is leafy and green, and locals are amiable and welcoming.

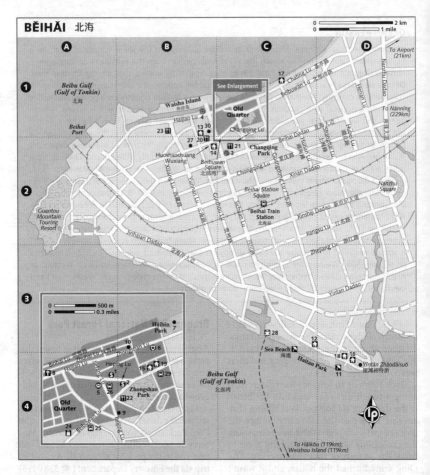

The centre of town is an increasingly affluent and commercially driven domain of department stores and eager young shoppers. Běihǎi may not have the charm of Qīngdǎo in Shāndōng, but the town knocks the spots off dreary Běidàihé in Héběi.

Orientation

Běihǎi sits on a small peninsula on the western end of a larger, east-to-west peninsula jutting off Guǎngxī. The northern coast of the town is home to the bus terminal, department stores and budget lodging options. The main commercial area centres on Beibuwan Sq, with its huge and bizarre Brancusi-esque sculpture ringed by muscled classical figures atop sea creatures.

The southern strip has the new International Ferry Terminal, a couple of upmarket hotels and Silver Beach.

Information

Bank of China (Zhōngguó Yínháng; next to Gofar Hualian Hotel, 1 Beibuwan Xilu) Foreign exchange; ATM. There's another branch with ATM on Heping Lu.

Chonglang Internet Café (Chōnglàng Wǎngbā; Sichuan Lu; per hr Y2; 8am-midnight)

Donghang Internet Café (Dōngháng Wǎngbā; Sichuan Lu; per hr Y1.5; 24hr)

Kodak Express (east of Gofar Hualian Hotel, Beibuwan Xilu; CD burning per disc Y10.

Public Security Bureau (PSB; Gōngānjú; 213 Zhongshan Donglu; 8am-noon & 2.30-5.30pm winter, 3-6pm Mon-Fri summer) Can extend visas.

Tianran Internet Café (Tiānrán Wǎngbā; 4th fl, Xinli Baihuo, Beibuwan Lu; per hr Y1-2.5; ⏱ 24hr)

Xinhua Bookstore (Xīnhuá Shūdiàn; ☎ 303 7988; 3rd fl, Xinli Baihuo, Beibuwan Lu)

Sights & Activities
OLD QUARTER 北海老城
Leading away to the east as Sichuan Lu meets Waisha Island on Beibu Gulf, Zhuhai Lu – formerly a commercial street called Shengping Jie (升平街) – leads you immediately into Běihǎi's quaint and mouldering old quarter (*běihǎi lǎochéng*) of colonnaded streets, fish nets piled on the pavement, old Chinese shop signs composed in full-form Chinese characters and the intermittent rattle of mah jong pieces. Despite the absence of conservation efforts, the entire area has alluring shades reminiscent of Macau and is a rewarding area for a stroll.

A short walk along Zhuhai Lu brings you to the small **Beihai Christ Church** (Běihǎi Jīdūjiào Lǐbàitáng; ☎ 202 4799; 117 Zhuhai Xilu) with its Chinese bibles for sale on the ground floor and small, modern upstairs chapel. Between No 1 and No 3 Zhuhai Xilu was the site of the Sanhuang Temple (三皇庙; Sānhuáng Miào), alas no more.

Zhongshan Lu is also worth wandering along. Dating from 1896, the attractive **former post office** (Dàqīng Yóuzhèng Běihǎi Fēnjú Jiùzhǐ; cnr Zhongshan Donglu & Haiguan Lu; admission Y5) now serves as a simple museum devoted to relics of the Qing dynasty postal system; no English captions.

Just to the southeast of Zhongshan Park as Wenming Lu intersects with Beijing Lu, stands the former **British Consulate Building** (Yīngguó Lǐngshìguǎn Jiùzhǐ), within the grounds of the **No 1 Middle School** (一中; Yīzhōng). Dating

from 1885, the imposing building is a lovely two-storey cream-coloured edifice with verandahs and shutters, flanked by palm trees. A further traditional building can be seen just to the rear, next to the newly built white-tile church. Bus 2 from the train station stops right outside. Nearby Zhongshan Park is a pleasantly green park with several amusement rides for children.

SILVER BEACH 银滩
Southern Thailand it sure ain't, but 1.6km-long **Silver Beach** (Yíntān; admission Y25), about 10km southeast of Běihǎi city centre in Silver Beach Park, has silvery-yellow sand, so-so waters and palm trees, not to mention eclectic architecture. China's mainland beaches are all oddly depressing places, so don't get too energized by the prospect of coming here. If you want, you can jump on a buggy (Y10) on a 6km route past some tacky sights or drive a motorised beach buggy along the sand (10 minutes, one person Y50, two people Y60). You can also get your photo taken while swinging in a suspended chair, with a sign above your head that classifies Silver Beach as 'The Number One Beach on Earth'. Take it or leave it. If you want to go for a swim, swimming areas (open 7am to 7pm) are marked by red buoys, but be warned that Běihǎi's waters can be polluted. Showers and lockers are available just off the boardwalk (Y10 each). On the souvenir front, you can buy a vast conch, a tacky sea-shell wind chime or a rabbit assembled from shells.

Just behind Silver Beach are numerous restaurants and hotels. All are reasonably cheap and simple. The liveliest time to visit is between May and September and during national holidays.

GUĂNGXĪ

THE NUMBER ONE BEACH ON EARTH

Even Guilín – touted as the number one city in Guăngxī – has to contend with the numbing reality of white-tile architecture that makes parts of the city totally indistinguishable from other Chinese towns. Much of the city's history has been obliterated, and apart from the palace at Wáng Chéng, the South Gate and the pavilions on Guilín's karst peaks, it can be tough to get a sense of history.

Tourist hype in China is a branch of mainstream propaganda, where good news is amplified out of proportion and bad domestic news goes unreported (just watch CCTV9). The result is widespread cliché on tourist literature and pervasive deception; rivers are no longer polluted eyesores but 'shimmering ribbons', while industrial towns are miraculously transformed into 'glittering pearls'.

Signs flung up by hawkers on Silver Beach in Běihăi trumpet the modest strip of sand as 'The Number One Beach on Earth' (or more literally, 'The Number One Beach under Heaven'). It is, however, common knowledge that China has some of the dullest beaches on the planet (bar those on Hăinán Island), Silver Beach included. In any honest global ranking, Silver Beach would raise incredulous eyebrows among surfers or sun seekers if it made it into the top 100. But on this southern shore of Guăngxī province, in a land whose citizens still – in the main – rarely venture beyond national frontiers, the beach is served up as the cream of the crop.

The phenomenon can be seen all over China, where you'll be wading into 'The Number One Lake on Earth', jostling with the hordes on 'The Number One Mountain on Earth' and fending off crowds in 'The Number One Temple on Earth'. Just remember, when it comes to hype, China undoubtedly has the 'Number One Overstatement on Earth', so when soaking your toes in the brine off Silver Beach, take it all with a pinch of sea salt.

From Běihăi, walk west from the bus station, bear right at Woping Lu, which branches off behind Běihăi Yíngbīnguăn, and catch bus 3 on the corner of Jiefang Lu (Y2, 15 minutes). A taxi from the centre of town will cost Y20.

HĂIBĪN PARK 海滨公园

If the popular Zhongshan Park is too rocking with senior citizens disco dancing, then head northeast to the more derelict part of town and the northern waterfront where you will find little Haibin Park (Hăibīn Gōngyuán). Inside the park is an expensive **aquarium** (Běihăi Hăidǐ Shìjiè; ☎ 206 9973; admission Y75; ⏰ 8am-5.30pm). Two buildings house seven spacious exhibition halls filled with tanks of strange and colourful fish. Most of the exhibits feature local marine life from the Gulf of Tonkin (Běibùwán).

Sleeping

Centrally located Huoshaochuang Wuxiang (火烧床五巷) is an alley that is literally stuffed with cheap zhāodàisuǒ (招待所; guesthouses) where you can get a bed from around Y20 or an air-con double room for Y35. The alley is found south off Guizhou Lu, west of Beibuwan Sq and just east of the Mingdu Hotel.

BUDGET

Guìhăi Lǚyèbù (☎ 203 0936; 北部湾中路16号; 16 Beibuwan Zhonglu; s with fan without toilet Y28-30, s with air-con and toilet Y40, d with air-con Y50; ☒) Right opposite the main bus station, this handy hotel (no English sign) is simple but well-run, and although staff's English skills are limited it's cheaper than and an improvement on the Taoyuan Hotel round the corner. All rooms come with phone.

Taoyuan Hotel (Táoyuán Dàjiǔdiàn; ☎ 202 0919; 北部湾中路; Beibuwan Zhonglu; s/d from Y70/80, on holidays Y180/200; ☒) A cheap and distinctly average option where weird kitschy Van Gogh and Chen Yifei copies meet dodgy plumbing and a rather scuffed and wanting ambience. Follow the signs down a lane across from the main bus station.

Beihai Hangbiao Hotel (Běihăi Hángbiāo Bīnguăn; ☎ 308 8789; fax 308 8711; 20 Sanzhong Nanli Erxiang, Guizhou Lu; 贵州路三中南里二巷20号; s/d Y200/268; ☒) Clean rooms at this tidy hotel here come with acres of space and cavernous bathroooms. Staff are polite and prices typically drop to around Y100, or Y90 per night for long stays. It's tucked away on the left of an alley off Guizhou Lu, north of the intersection with Beibuwan Lu.

MIDRANGE

Gofar Hualian Hotel (Guófā Huálián Jiǔdiàn; ☎ 308 7888; fax 308 7889; 1 Beibuwan Xilu; 北部湾西路1号;

dY398-468; ⚇ 🖳) Despite the unpleasant brown carpets, rooms are comfortable here and discounts regularly bring the cheaper doubles down to around Y200. The location just down the road from Beibuwan Sq is the real reason to be here, but be warned that the late-night sounds of karaoke indeed 'Go Far'.

TOP END

Shangri-la Hotel (Xiāngélǐlā Dàfàndiàn; ☎ 206 2288; www .shangri-la.com; 33 Chating Lu; 茶亭路33号; d with cityview/seaview Y805/863; ⚇ 🖳) Běihǎi's most luxurious hotel, this lovely 364-room place is located east of the old quarter. It has top-notch service and frequently discounted rates, including perks such as complimentary meals and 6pm checkout. Staff are astonishingly helpful, there's an excellent choice of restaurants and the harbour-view doubles are a treat. Outdoor swimming pool, tennis courts.

SILVER BEACH

If you are visiting Běihǎi to watch the Chinese frolic in the sun, you can stay at Silver Beach. Cheapies such as the **Nánníng Bīnguǎn** (☎ 221 3692; s/d/tr with air-con Y65/80/100; ⚇) in the vicinity of the bus 3 terminus draw in the budget crowd.

Sunshine Holiday Hotel (Yángguāng Dàjiǔdiàn; ☎ 389 5555; fax 389 5556; 2 Yintan Dadao; 银滩大道2号; s/d/tr Y438/468/488; ⚇) Newly built hotel with a fresh and sparkling feel, not far from the bus 3 terminus and within sprinting range of the beach. Outside the peak holiday season rooms typically fall to around Y120.

Eating

Waisha Island (Wàishā Dǎo) is simply awash with large and rather impersonal seafood restaurants and *dàpáidàng*, but prices can be steep in summer; in winter, chefs sit out back smoking and playing mah jong. In the northern section of Yunnan Lu, close to the wharf is Běihǎi's large **seafood market** (Yunnan Lu). This is the place to come if you need to get your hands on dried squid or any other seafood. Buses 2 and 8 from in front of the bus station pass by the market.

Come night time, hordes of cheap *dàpáidàng* operate along Changqing Lu (长青路). Also worth checking out are those along Guizhou Lu. For a hot chocolate, coffee or snack in the wee hours, the McDonald's on Beibuwan Lu is open 24 hours.

Běijīng Jiǎoziwáng (☎ 306 3089; Beibuwan Xilu; 北部湾西路; meals Y25; ⏱7am-2.30pm) For a

much-needed dumpling fix, come here for platefuls of dumplings in all shades, from lamb (羊肉饺子; *yángròu jiǎozi*; Y20), to mushroom (香菇饺子; *xiānggū jiǎozi*; Y16), pork and chives (猪肉韭菜饺子; *zhūròu jiǔcài jiǎozi*; Y12) and beyond.

Dexing Restaurant (Déxīng Jiǔlóu; ☎ 303 3199; 1 Sichuan Lu; 四川路1号; dim sum from Y2; ⏱7am-1.30am) Ensconced on the south side of Beibuwan Sq, this huge restaurant is the place for the full-on Chinese dining experience. It's packed by 9am by punters crowding in to hoover up dim sum (点心; *diǎnxīn*) and other Cantonese favourites.

Coffee Garden (1st fl, Shangri-la Hotel, 33 Chating Lu; 茶亭路33号; meals Y70) If you need a pleasant alternative to the seafood restaurants, this smart restaurant has views over the hotel swimming pool to the Beibu Gulf, polite staff and a menu that includes wild mushroom soup (Y22), American beefburger (Y48) and other popular Western fare.

Getting There & Away

A helpful **ticket office** (☎ 202 8618; ⏱8am-10pm) can be found on the ground floor of the Shangri-la Hotel, selling boat, bus, train and plane tickets. There are also many other travel agencies around town.

AIR

Flights leave throughout the week between Běihǎi and Běijīng (Y1930, daily), Guǎngzhōu (Y760, daily), Hǎikǒu (Y380, four per week), Kūnmíng (Y710, three per week) and Shànghǎi (Y1690, six per week).

BOAT

The **International Ferry Terminal** (Guójì Kèyùn Mǎtóu) serves Hǎikǒu on Hainan Island and nearby Weizhou Island. To Hainan Island, boats (one way; 1st class Y230, 2nd class Y130, 3rd class Y120, budget Y90) leave Běihǎi at 6pm and arrive at Hǎikǒu the following morning at 6am. In the return direction, boats leave Hǎikǒu at 6pm, reaching Běihǎi the following morning at 6am.

BUS

Běihǎi's **Main bus station** (Kèyùn Zǒngzhàn; ☎ 202 2094) is located to the east of Zhongshan Park on Beibuwan Lu. As well as the buses listed below, numerous destinations in Guǎngdōng can be reached from Běihǎi. Regular buses to Nánníng (Y50) also depart from the

BUSES FROM BĚIHǍI			
Destination	Fare (Y)	Duration (hours)	Departure Time
Bǎisè	120	7½	3.45pm & 8pm
Guìgǎng	75	1hr 10min	8.30am & 2.40pm
Guìlín	165	7	4 per day
Liǔzhōu	120	5½	6 per day
Nánníng	55-73	2hr 40min	every 20min from 6am
Píngxiáng	90	7	9.10am & 2.50pm
Wúzhōu	110	7	9am & 6pm

central bus station (Kèyùn Zhōngxīn) to the east of Beibuwan Sq.

The bus to Běihǎi from Guìpíng passes through Yùlín, with its solitary pagoda at the centre of town.

TRAIN
There are two trains a day to Nánníng (Y40, three hours), from where you can connect to destinations beyond.

Getting Around
TO/FROM THE AIRPORT
CAAC buses (Y10, 30 minutes) meet arriving planes and leave two hours before flight departures from the **CAAC building** (Mínháng Dàshà; ☎ 305 1899; Beibuwan Xilu), where plane tickets can also be purchased.

BUS
Bus 1 connects Beibuwan Sq with the main bus station. Bus 2 runs from the train station along Beijing Lu, Beibuwan Lu, along Sichuan Lu and along Haijiao Lu to Dijiao. Bus 3 connects the main bus station with Silver Beach, running via Beibuwan Sq.

TAXI
Taxis are Y5 at flagfall. Getting to Beibuwan Sq from the bus station will cost Y2 by motorbike, Y3 by pedicab or Y6 by taxi. Bus 1 connects Beibuwan Sq with the main bus station.

AROUND BĚIHǍI
Weizhou Island 涠洲岛
Thirty-six nautical miles from Běihǎi, the island of Wéizhōu (www.weizhou.net) is China's largest volcanic island and a tremendous getaway in the Beibu Gulf. Boats from Běihǎi pull in at the wharf at Nanwan Port (南湾港; Nánwān Gǎng), the main settlement in the south of the island from where roads radi-

ate out across the lava-encrusted isle. The island is 6.5km long and 6km wide, so make it a day trip; accommodation is available in Nanwan Port if you miss the last boat back to Běihǎi.

The waters around Wéizhōu contain some of the most diverse coral communities in the area; ask in Nanwan Port about motorboat rides and diving opportunities. Beyond the island's beaches, caves, corals and dormant volcanic scenery, visitors will find a handful of historic sights awaiting exploration. Within Nanwan Port – the former volcanic nucleus of the island – is the **Three Old Women Temple** (三婆庙; Sānpó Miào), but of more interest are the two French-built churches on Wéizhōu, which date to the 19th century. In the northeast of the island is the village of Shèngtáng (盛塘), where the white-washed **Catholic Church** (天主堂; Tiānzhǔ Táng) still attracts worshippers. Roughly on the same latitude but found in a spot towards the other side of the island is the **Holy Mother Church** (圣母堂; Shèngmǔ Táng) in the village of Chéngzǎi (城仔), built in 1880.

The smaller **Xieyang Island** (斜阳岛; Xiéyáng Dǎo) sits in the sea 9 nautical miles to the southeast of Weizhou Island, and can be reached by boat from Nanwan Port.

Tickets for boats to Weizhou Island can be most easily purchased from the **Passenger Ticket Service** (Kèyùn Shòupiào Dàtīng; ☎ 306 6829 or 388 0711) located on Sichuan Lu near the intersection with Beibuwan Lu. Fast boats (one way 1st class Y100, 2nd class Y90, 3rd class Y85) depart at 8.30am, arriving at the island at 10am. Two slow boats (one way Y55 to Y65) depart at 8.30am and arrive at 10.40am and 11.30am. The fast boat returns from Weizhou Island at 3.45pm, arriving in Běihǎi at 5.15pm. The two slow boats leave Weizhou Island at 3.30pm, reaching Běihǎi at 5.40pm and 6.30pm.

Other Sights

Northeast of Běihǎi, a road crosses the peninsula via Hépǔ (合浦), where you can arrange transport to **Shankou Mangrove Reserve** (红树林; Hóngshù Lín), a Unesco-designated Biosphere Reserve.

Halfway along the road between Běihǎi and the reserve, head south towards the coastal town of **Báilóng** (白龙), also called 'Pearl City', where some traditional architecture survives.

You can also take the Nánníng Highway to the north of Běihǎi, and detour 10km east to **Nanguoxing Island Lake** (南国星岛湖; Nánguóxīng Dǎohú). This iridescent-blue body of water is dotted with verdant, sand-edged islands.

At Hépǔ, you can visit **Dongpo Pavilion** (东坡亭; Dōngpō Tíng), 2km to the north, and then head 2km south to **Wenchang Pagoda** (文昌塔; Wénchāng Tǎ). The pavilion was constructed in memory of the famous Song-dynasty scholar and poet, Su Dongpo. Wénchāng Pagoda stands 36m high and was built more than 300 years ago, during the Ming dynasty. Both sites are easily accessible by motorbike taxi (Y5).

CHÓNGZUǑ 崇左

☎ 0771 / pop 330,000 / www.chongzuo.net

At the 122km point along the train line from Nánníng to Píngxiáng is this pleasant, manageable city, well worth a stop for its Ecology Park, distinctive leaning pagoda and Stone Forest.

Orientation

Chóngzuǒ is largely situated south of the Zuo River (左江; Zuǒjiāng) as it loops though town. Jiangnan Lu (江南路; Jiāngnán Lù), the principal road running east–west, is intersected at right angles by busy Xinmin Lu (新民路; Xīnmín Lù). The long-distance bus station is on Yanshan Lu (沿山路; Yánshān Lù), south of the train station on Jiangnan Lu.

Information

Agricultural Bank of China (农业银行; Nóngyè Yínháng; Jiangnan Lu, west of intersection with Xinmin Lu) Can change large units of currency.

Industrial and Commercial Bank of China (工商银行; Gōngshāng Yínháng; west of the train station, Jiangnan Lu) ATM.

Post Office (邮局; Yóujú; Xinmin Lu)

Public Security Bureau (PSB; 公安局; Gōngānjú; 22 Xinmin Lu) Just beyond the bridge to the north along Xinmin Lu.

Xiuxian Internet Café (休闲网吧; Xiūxián Wǎngbā; east side of train station concourse; per hr Y3; ☾ 24hr)

Sights

ZUOJIANG LEANING PAGODA 左江斜塔

This sublime and highly photogenic **pagoda** (zuǒjiāng xiétǎ; admission Y5; ☾ 8.30am-5.30pm), also known as Guilong Pagoda (Guīlóng Tǎ) or Water Pagoda (Shuǐ Tǎ), is approximately 5km northeast of town on Phoenix Lake. Built in 1621 and one of only eight of its kind in the world – leaning, that is – the 18m tower sits atop a rocky outcrop in the lake, a short walk from the entrance.

The tower's 1m lean is evident to observers from the shore. To reach the pagoda, take a skiff (Y2) piloted by an old boat hand across the water; he may even take you for a float around the lake. Once on land, climb up to the pagoda, a white and reddish-brown tiled five-storey tower capped with a Buddhist spire, and ascend the white-washed and brick interior until you can go no higher. Be sure to mind your head on the way down – taller travellers are quite likely to pick up a cranial knock or two if they're not almost bent over double.

Winter can see the water level in the lake so low that the area can be disappointing.

A motorcycle taxi costs about Y10 for the bumpy 25-minute journey to the pagoda, but you may want to arrange for your driver to wait for you.

CHONGZUO ECOLOGY PARK 崇左生态公园

A definite highlight for ecotourists, this excellent **park** (Chóngzuǒ Shēngtài Gōngyuán; ☎ 0771 782 1328; admission Y40) is for the protection of the white-headed leaf-monkey (*Trachypithecus francoisi leucocephalus*), whose numbers equal around 800 in the nature reserve. Accommodation can be found at the park, which can be reached by taking a Shàngsī-bound bus (Y8, one hour) from Chongzuo bus station.

STONE FOREST 石林

About 4.5km from town, Chóngzuǒ's diminutive **Stone Forest** (Shílín; admission Y10) is a rather contrived geological attraction of jagged limestone formations, but the maze of rocks can be surprisingly tranquil, especially if you visit late in the afternoon. It's more than an hour's walk from town. A motorcycle taxi is about Y5.

Sleeping

A few decent hotels can be found near the long-distance bus and train stations.

Jīnyuán Lǚguǎn (金源旅馆; ☎ 783 0894; Jiangnan Lu; 江南路; s Y20-50, tw Y30; 🈺) Very simple rooms, the very cheapest without loo or aircon. It's around 30m on your right on Jiangnan Lu as you exit the train station.

Longhua Hotel (隆华宾馆; Lónghuá Bīnguǎn; ☎ 783 5022; fax 783 5260; Yanshan Lu; 沿山路; s Y40-80, d Y90; 🈺) Handily located just to the west of the long-distance bus station, this place has affordable and clean rooms, the cheapest without air-con.

Yangguang Hotel (阳光大酒店; Yángguāng Dàjiǔdiàn; ☎ 784 0501; fax 784 8498; 36 Jiangnan Lu; 江南路36号; s/d Y218/228, d with computer Y368; 🈺) Reasonable two-star comfort can be found here, with clean and well-furnished rooms and polite staff; the hotel is just east of the train station. Discounts bring singles and doubles down to Y120.

Eating

There's a string of handy, small restaurants on Yanshan Lu across from the Longhua Hotel and the long-distance bus station.

Jiālèjī (家乐基; Jiangnan Lu; meals Y20) Local fastfood style chicken restaurant with tasty, filling burgers, instant coffee and Hollywood movies on looped DVDs; directly opposite the train station.

Getting There & Away

BUS

Buses to Nánníng, Níngmíng and Píngxiáng are more frequent than the train.

The long-distance **bus station** (☎ 782 7995) is located on the north side of Yanshan Lu. As well as the departures listed below, high-speed buses (Y33, two hours) also depart for Nánníng every 40 minutes from 7.50am to 7.30pm.

TRAIN

The train station is located on Jiangnan Lu; the **ticket office** (🕑 8.50-9.50am, 11am-1.30pm & 3-4.15pm) is open irregular hours. Chóngzuǒ is accessible by train from Nánníng and Píngxiáng.

From Nánníng, the 8.00am 5517 leaves Chóngzuǒ at 9.50am, reaching Níngmíng (Y3.50 to Y10) at 10.43am and Píngxiáng (Y7 to Y14) at 11.30am. The slower 8511 sets off from Nánníng at 10.50am, arriving in Chóngzuǒ at 1.34pm, before departing Níngmíng at 2.55pm and arriving in Píngxiáng at 4.10pm.

In the other direction, the 5518 departs Píngxiáng at 2.45pm, arriving in Níngmíng at 3.25pm, Chóngzuǒ at 4.18pm and Nánníng (Y9 to Y18) at 6.05pm.

The 8512 departs Píngxiáng at 10am, Níngmíng at 11.11am and Chóngzuǒ at 12.30pm and reaches Nánníng at 3.25pm.

Getting Around

Taxi fares start at Y3. Motorcycle taxis can get you to most parts of town for Y2.

ZUO JIANG SCENIC AREA
左江风景区

Roughly 190km southwest of Nánníng, Zuǒjiāng Scenic Area (Zuǒjiāng Fēngjǐngqū) provides opportunities to view karst formations, with the added attraction that the region is home to around 80 groups of Zhuang-minority **rock paintings**. The area is also one of the last remaining habitats of the rare whiteheaded leaf monkey.

Níngmíng 宁明

There's no reason to dwell in Níngmíng. The town is the launching point for a Zuǒjiāng adventure but, to be brutally honest, you do not want to spend any longer here than is absolutely necessary.

BUSES FROM CHÓNGZUǑ			
Destination	**Fare (Y)**	**Duration (hours)**	**Departure Time**
Dàxin	17	2	every 15min (6.50am-4.30pm)
Guǎngzhōu	130	8	4pm
Níngmíng	12	2	every 30min (7.30am-5pm)
Nánníng	20-26	2½	every 40min (7.30am-8.40pm)
Píngxiáng	21	1hr 10min	hourly (8.10am-7.10pm)
Shàngsī	22	3½	11.40am
Shuòlóng	15	3	12.40pm & 4.30pm

The River Route

If travelling off season (winter), check that the murals are open as they can close for repair during what is called a restoration period (维修期间; wéixiū qījiān), meaning it is not possible to climb up onto the path to inspect them at close quarters.

The river scenery commences unspectacularly, with flat and low-lying river banks and a few fields thrown out on either side. Locals tend vegetable and flower plots in riverside pools edged with bamboo, while kids splash about in the mud and oxen graze. You will soon pass under the railway bridge and see the hills rising up in the distance. About 45 minutes from Tuólóng, the mountain cliffs suddenly appear directly ahead in a series of monumental and striated slabs of rock.

Just over an hour into the puttering boat journey is the village of **Pānlóng**, where you can visit the **Huashan Ethnic Culture Village** (花山民族山寨度假村; Huāshān Mínzú Shānzhài Dùjiàcūn; ☎ 862 8195; cabins Y120), which is more of a low-key tourist resort with a holiday-camp feel that offers pleasant enough rooms in Dong-style wooden cabins that come with shower, verandah and mosquito-repellent vaporisers (no fan). Tents are also in the pipeline. Hot water for showering is available in the evening. Try to avoid national holidays as the crowds can get noisy. When there is enough of a crowd it is possible to see some traditional Zhuang dancing. A restaurant on site serves traditional local fare for about Y25 per person.

The **Longrui Nature Reserve** (陇瑞自然保护区; Lóngruì Zìrán Bǎohùqū; admission Y20) is directly behind the village. Hiking opportunities here are excellent, although not all parts of the reserve are open. There are some tough sections, but you could definitely spend a whole day poking around in this reserve. Most tourists come with the hope of spying the rare **white-headed leaf monkey** (báitóu yèhóu), also known as the white-headed langur. The resort can easily arrange a guide if you wish (Y30). Ask at the Huashan Ethnic Culture Village about cabins for overnighting within the reserve itself.

The most significant collection of Zhuang paintings is in the **Huashan Murals** (Huāshān Bìhuà; admission Y13) area, another hour's boat ride along the river. A fresco, 170m high and 90m across, groups nearly 2000 reddish figures of hunters, farmers and animals on the brown rock. It is now believed that the Luoyue, the ancestors of the Zhuang, painted these cliffs 2000 years ago during the early Han period (AD 25–220), although it's unclear why. The images are simple, primitive and animistic and rise to a certain height up the cliff face before stopping. It takes five minutes to walk along a path to the end of the cliff. On the 2nd floor of the administration building is a small, dilapidated **museum** (admission Y5) with displays explaining the history of the site, but they're all in Chinese and run down. As mentioned earlier, make sure the murals are open before making the trip, otherwise your boat will simply circle at a considerable distance.

Boat Tours

Boat trips from Tuólóng range from around Y100 to Y200 depending on how many people you're travelling with (and the season). Expect to negotiate extra if you want to stop in Pānlóng. Note that some boat hands only speak Cantonese, but they know you will want to go to Huāshān (花山; fasan, in Cantonese). To save you lugging your bags around, leave them at Níngmíng's bus station before your boat trip.

Sleeping & Eating

If you need to spend the night, accommodation can be found either in Níngmíng or upriver in Pānlóng. Food stalls are strung out at night along Dehua Jie (德华街) towards Xingyuan Jie (兴远街) and cheap and convenient eateries can be found on Dehua Jie near the bus station.

Qìchēzhàn Zhāodàisuǒ (汽车站招待所; ☎ 862 5616; Dehua Jie; 德华街; d/tr with fan per bed Y25/20, d with air-con Y60; ✖) Cheap and conveniently located guesthouse, but you may be woken by early-morning bus departures as it's right next to the bus station.

Yínxīng Bīnguǎn (银兴宾馆; ☎ 0771-863 2688; 38 Dehua Jie; 德华街38号; s Y68-88, d/tr Y98/108; ✖) A short walk west of the bus station on the far side of Dehua Jie, the clean and well-kept tiled-floor rooms come with comfy beds, digital TV, air-con and squat loos. No English sign.

Getting There & Around

If coming from Níngmíng, jump on a motorcycle taxi for the short haul to the bridge at Tuólóng (驮龙) and walk down to the river bank, where rows of boats await. The train from Nánníng and Píngxiáng also stops at Tuólóng train station, from where it's a short walk to the bridge – continue straight along the main road and wander down the path to the right of the bridge. From the bus terminal catch a motorcycle taxi (Y2) and ask the driver to take you to Tuólóng or Huāshān chuán mǎtóu (花山船码头).

From Níngmíng's wharf it is a 1¼ hour boat journey to Pānlóng and another hour downstream to Huāshān. Bank on a round trip of around five hours, including time at the cliff face, but excluding time at Pānlóng and the Lóngruì Nature Reserve.

If you are pressed for time or dislike puttering boats, a road runs along the river from Níngmíng to Pānlóng. A taxi takes about 20 minutes (Y30). Frequent buses run the 43km distance from Níngmíng to Píngxiáng (Y8, every 15 minutes) from 6.40am to 6pm. Buses also depart for Chóngzuǒ (Y12, two hours, 68km, every 20 minutes) from 6.40am to 5pm. To reach Nánníng by bus, go first to Chóngzuǒ and change or take the train from Tuólóng. See p206 for details of trains to Nánníng and Píngxiáng. Air tickets for flights from Nánníng can be bought at the Ningming long-distance **bus station** (☎ 0771-853 7668 or 0771-852 1808). The Ningming bus station is a Y2 motor-taxi ride from the train station.

PÍNGXIÁNG 凭祥
☎ 0771 / pop 100,000

The staging post for onward transport to Vietnam, Píngxiáng is a border trading town rife with bustling markets but little else to see.

Banks are commonplace in Píngxiáng, and changing money is no problem. The **Bank of China** (中国银行; Zhōngguó Yínháng) is on the corner of Yinxing Jie, just south of the bus station. To find the **Tongle Internet Café** (同乐网吧; Tónglè Wăngbā; per hr Y2; ☒ 24hr), come out of the bus station, turn right and take the first turning on your right and it's a short walk up on your right hand side.

If you're heading into China, after crossing the Vietnamese border catch one of the minibuses into Píngxiáng to the bus station, from where there are buses into Guăngxī. The bus station (qìchēzhàn) is a five-minute walk north of Píngxiáng's northern train station, from where there are regular buses to Nánníng (Y70, 2½ hours) between 6.40am and 8.30pm, regular departures to Chóngzuǒ (Y25, 70 minutes) between 7.40am and 6.40pm and regular buses to Níngmíng (Y10, 1½ hours) between 6.50am and 6.30pm.

Minibuses, taxis and motorised pedicabs run to **Friendship Pass** (Yǒuyì Guān) from near the bus and train stations and cost Y10 to Y20, depending on the number of passengers. From Friendship Pass it's another 600m to the Vietnamese border post. Onward transport to Hanoi by train or bus is via the Vietnamese town of Lang Son (Liàngshān), 18km from the Friendship Pass. Remember that Vietnam is one hour behind China; at the time of writing the border post was open till 7pm Vietnam time.

Although there is no real reason to spend the night in Píngxiáng, accommodation is plentiful near the bus station and it's not hard to score a bed in a triple for around Y20; just look for signs saying 'yǒu fáng' (有房). **Yǒuyì Bīnguǎn** (☎ 597 0901; Yinxing Jie; 银兴街; tr per bed Y25, s Y50-60, d Y60-70; ☒) down the alley right opposite the bus station has OK rooms and free internet.

The sit-down **Caidiexuan Bakery** (彩蝶轩蛋糕; Căidiéxuān Dàngāo; ☎ 853 4879; 2 Yinxing Jie; 银兴街2号) next to the Bank of China has filling red-bean-paste buns (红豆包; hóngdòu bāo), egg tarts, some sandwiches and coffee, plus a range of breads and cakes.

DETIAN WATERFALL 德天瀑布

The world's second-largest transnational cataract with a total width of 200m, **Detian Waterfall** (Détiān Pùbù; ☎ 0771-263 6808; www.detian.com; admission Y80; ☒ dawn to dusk) is Asia's largest. It may not be Niagara Falls, but the waterfall is still fantastic and the setting sublime, with its descending levels and powerful cacophony of water. On top of viewing the gorgeous falls spilling down in huge pleats of water into secondary and tertiary cascades, there's the spectacle of the surrounding green hillocks of karst peaks and the added frisson of being on the Vietnamese border.

At the 53rd boundary marker between China and Vietnam, the waterfall drops only 40m, but makes up for it by a more than modest breadth. The Vietnamese got the short end of the cascade stick, with a paltry few ribbons of water falling on their side of the border, while the Chinese have the earth-shaking lion's share of water flow. Despite the tourist pitch which accentuates each season's strong point, the best time to visit is July when you'll be swept away by the waterflow, though water levels are fairly high from May to late September. Show up in November or December and be underwhelmed by the lack of water and constant cloud and fog.

From the entrance, a sightseeing road runs along the river and several trails descend to the banks, where you'll be gently harassed by raft operators offering to take you right into the spray (Y10), but observe the 'no swimming' signs and resist the temptation to breaststroke your way into Vietnam. The Vietnamese segment of the falls, the Ban Gioc Waterfalls (板约瀑布; Bǎnyuē Pùbù), can be seen to the west.

Further up the path are the upper tiers of the waterfall; the air around the **two-step waterfall** (二级瀑布; èrjí pùbù) is said to contain 17,000 negative ions/cu metre – enough perhaps to give you a rush and open your sinuses. Further up is the three-step waterfall where the waters gush into a pool and the green river water cascades beautifully into ribbons.

The trail also follows the river a short distance away from the falls before hooking up with the sightseeing road again. Continue along the road and you will pass a small shrine to Guanyin; further along are steps leading up an old cannon platform, one of 130 built after the Sino-French war. The gun placement is on the top of Yínpán Shān (银盘山), a 90-minute walk uphill.

Further ahead is another cluster of hawkers selling Vietnamese coconut candy, coffee and cigarettes, Vietnamese currency, pirated perfume and aftershave, lumps of marble or tanks made from rifle cartridges. You can also pick up a huge wooden pig for Y500. This is where you will find the **boundary marker** (中越界碑; zhōngyuè jièbēi), also called the Chinese–Vietnamese Number 53rd Boundary Marker (中越53号界碑; zhōngyuè 53 hào jièbēi) between the two countries. The marker is inscribed with the characters '中国广西界' and the French 'Frontiere Sino Annamite'. At the time of writing there was also a sign up in Chinese warning transnationals against introducing bird flu.

For those in a mad rush, buggies can whisk you from the main gate to the boundary marker (single/return Y5/10). If you don't reach the falls till late in the day note that the road has no lights, but you can beg the guard to admit you on the same ticket the next morning if you want to spend the night in the village.

Sleeping & Eating

There's loads of cheap accommodation in the village of Détiān Tún (德天屯) just below the main gate to the falls, but check the rooms first as some can be quite grim. A tourist hotel with views of the falls is inside the main gate. Several dàpáidàng litter the road leading to the main gate – some of which also offer rooms as well as meals. Several of the local hotels also have restaurants.

Détiān Lǚguǎn (德天旅馆; ☎ 0771-377 5098 or 137 685 904 97; 39 Détiān Tún; 德天屯39号) Being renovated at the time of writing, this place is next to a hotel of the same name a short walk down from the main gate.

Détiān Nóngjiā Càiguǎn (德天农家菜馆; ☎ 0771-377 3620; 37 Détiān Tun; 德天屯37号; r Y50) Worth considering only if other places are full or if you need to reserve ahead, as some of its simple rooms have dodgy plumbing. Restaurant downstairs.

Détiān Shānzhuāng (德天山庄; ☎ 377 3570; tw/tr Y500/600, deluxe q Y780; ❄) With the best rooms and views of the falls, this is the most exclusive choice. It's the gates of the scenic area in front of the falls. Expect 20% discounts in winter and quiet periods.

Getting There & Away

Coming from Nánníng or Chóngzuǒ you'll probably need to first get to Dàxīn (大新) and arrange transport from there. The road from Chóngzuǒ to Dàxīn passes through some stunning karst scenery. From Dàxīn, take a pedicab (Y2) to the congregation point at the intersection of Minsheng Jie (民生街) and Lunli Lu (伦理路) for buses to Xiàléi (下雷) which pass through Shuòlóng (硕龙; Y7, one hour), which is where you want to get off. At Shuòlóng jump into a taxivan (Y3) to Détiān (德天). For travellers coming from Jìngxī, any bus to Dàxīn should pass through Shuòlóng, but verify this before getting on. In Shuòlóng, the bus will probably deposit you in front of the 'minibus tree', where rattletrap minibuses or motorcycle taxis run the final lovely 14km, full of eye-catching coloured pools, to Détiān (德天; Y3, 20 minutes). If you're the only passenger going all the way to the falls the driver will probably ask for Y20.

In the return direction, minivans depart Détiān from the car park in Détiān Tún from around midmorning but in the quiet season you may have to wait or book a vehicle for yourself (Y20). If you do want to leave in the evening, you can never really be sure when buses to/from Shuòlóng stop running. There isn't much movement after 5pm.

From Shuòlóng, stand by the road and wait for a bus to pass – there's no way to tell when the next one's coming. Semiregular service is found towards Dàxīn, and therefore Nánníng, but if you want to go towards Jìngxī, the best thing to do is leapfrog villages. First take a Y4 minibus northwest to Xiàléi and then a Y3 minibus to Húrùn (湖润; pronounced Fuyuan here). From there you can get a proper bus for the hour-long ride to Jìngxī. All up, the trip should take around two hours, though taking three hours isn't unheard of.

AROUND DÉTIĀN

Dàxīn 大新

☎ 0771 / pop 350,000

Dàxīn is the usual staging point for Detian Waterfall. A sleepy town, there's not much to see here besides the falls, but you can overnight if you miss the last bus to Shuòlóng. On the western edge of town, left at the big intersection, is the **South Gate** (南门; Nánmén), which locals claim dates from the Zhou dynasty. You can change money at the **Agricultural Bank of China** (农业银行; Nóngyè Yínháng; ☎ 362 3730) on Lunli Lu.

SLEEPING & EATING

Rónghuá Zhāodàisuǒ (荣华招待所; ☎ 362 5271; Minsheng Jie; 民生街; s Y25, d/tr/q per bed Y20/15/6) Very simple place just to the south of the bus station, with no English sign. Pricier rooms have their own loo, all have fan.

Xīndū Dàjiǔdiàn (☎ 362 2011; fax 362 1845; 5 Minsheng Jie; 民生街5号; s/d/tr Y80/70/90) This is a clean and friendly place 100m past the first intersection. It has an abundance of friendly, non-English-speaking staff.

Táoyuán Dàjiǔdiàn (☎ 362 1018; fax 362 1098; 24 Minsheng Lu; 民生路24号; s Y108-128, d Y138; 🅿) Rooms are spacious and clean enough at this more midrange option further down the street.

There are heaps of places to eat – mostly point-and-choose stir-fries and hotpot – out on the street.

GETTING THERE & AWAY

At the time of writing, the bus station at Dàxīn was undergoing renovation and some buses were not running. Express buses to Nánníng (Y40, three hours) should flow pretty much constantly from 5am to 5.30pm. Buses to Xiàléi, which get you to Shuòlóng and Detian Waterfall, depart half hourly (see p209).

JÌNGXĪ & AROUND

☎ 0776 / pop 570,000

With its fine karst scenery, Jìngxī sits somewhat isolated midway between Detian Waterfall and Bǎisè. It looks ugly coming in from the south, but a stroll along the main drag reveals it to be modestly well off, if rather unkempt. Jìngxī has nothing much in the centre of town itself, but nearby are some interesting sights.

Tónglíng, 32km east of Jìngxī, is a scenic valley with impressive scenery boasting cascades, rock formations, waterfalls, natural pools, canyons and boating. To get there catch any bus going to Húrùn, Xiàléi or Dàxīn. Ask the driver to drop you off at the entrance to Tónglíng (Y7) and make sure it is not at the nearby town of Xīnqún. You will need to head back around 4pm as buses are less frequent after that.

Another trip you might consider is to the semipreserved town of **Jiùzhōu**, 16km south of Jìngxī along the road to Dìzhōu. The main attraction is **Jiùzhōu Pavilion** (Jiùzhōu Wénchāng Gé). This is the pagoda you'll see on lots of murals in Jìngxī and across the entire county. To get to Jiùzhōu, hop on the frequent (every 15 minutes) local bus 1 from the intersection next to the Xīngyuán Dàjiǔdiàn (Y2, 15 minutes). The bus drops you off just a short walk from the village.

Calling Rock (Jiàohǎnyán; admission Y6) is another popular local site. It's an impressive limestone cave full of caverns, stalactites, stalagmites and fluorescent lights.

If you need some fresh air after the cave, continue along the main road over the hill to **Goose Spring** (É'quán; admission Y6), a natural spring where you can sit and drink tea while absorbing the surroundings and watching the fish in the spring.

Calling Rock and Goose Spring are both reached on local bus 2, which leaves every 30 minutes (Y1.50, 15 minutes). Just ask the driver to drop you off at the cave and then it's a 600m walk to the entrance.

Getting There & Away

There are two bus stations in Jìngxī: northern and southern. The southern is for local or regional buses and you may be dropped off there. The northern station is more long-distance oriented and has departures to Bǎisè every 20 minutes (Y25, four hours) or hourly express buses (Y35, 3½ hours). There are also frequent buses to Nánníng (Y70, five hours). The entrance is to the right past the reception for the station's hostel.

Most nonexpress buses that depart from the northern station pass by the southern station on their way out of town. It may be just as easy to wait around out the front for your bus. Useful departures from the southern station include: Xiàléi, Dàxīn (for Detian Waterfall) and Húrùn (for Tōnglíng).

BĂISÈ 百色

☎ 0776 / pop 92,000

Worth a swift stopover, the trim and ambitious city of Băisè has a minor buzz to it and a handful of intriguing sights. Its historical significance as a revolutionary base (Deng Xiaoping and the Seventh Route Army established its base of operations in Băisè on 11 December 1929) assures it flocks of domestic tourists doing communist heritage sights, but the city is a pleasant pit stop for travellers taking the train to Kūnmíng or in transit to explorations of the minority towns north of Băisè towards Língyún.

Orientation

Cradled in a nook at the confluence of the Dengbi River (澄碧河; Chéngbì Hé) and the You River (右江; Yòujiāng), the city centre is quite compact, laid out in a quadrant that basically runs northwest to southeast, with Xiangyang Lu running through the centre. The bus station sits at the top of the quadrant. The train station is inconveniently located 6km east of downtown.

Information

Bank of China (中国银行; Zhōngguó Yínháng; Zhongshan Yilu) Foreign exchange and ATM.
Dove (多芬; Duōfēn; ☎ 282 9868; 34 Zhongshan Yilu; CD burning per disc Y15)
Post Office (邮局; Yóujú; Zhongshan Yilu; ◷ 8am-6pm) Near the corner of Jiefang Jie.
Public Security Bureau (PSB; 公安局; Gōngānjú; cnr Zhongshan Lu & Zhongshan Yilu; ◷ 8.30am-noon & 2.30-6pm Mon-Fri)
Youzheng Internet Café (邮政网吧; Yóuzhèng Wǎngbā; per hr Y2; ◷ 24hr) Next to the post office on Zhongshan Yilu.
Xinhua Bookstore (新华书店; Xīnhuá Shūdiàn; Zhongshan Yilu; ◷ 8am-10pm)
Xiuxianzhe Internet Cafe (休闲者网吧; Xiūxiánzhě Wǎngbā; Chengbei Yilu; per hr Y2.5; ◷ 24hr) Just east of the Băisè bus station.

Sights

Wandering the older section of town between Zhongshan Yilu and Aixin Jie is a diversion, as is the historical colonnaded road of Jiefang Jie, from where steps lead down to riverside docks. Before the 1949 revolution this street was the business-activity centre for visiting traders from Guăngdōng.

On Jiefang Jie, the **Baise Uprising Museum** (粤东会馆; Yuèdōng Huìguăn; admission Y15; ◷ 8.30am-5.30pm) traces the movements of Deng Xiaoping and the Seventh Red Army during the 1920s and 1930s, but another reason to visit is to examine the gorgeous architecture of this traditional guildhall that dates from 1720, with its harmonious arrangement of rooms. With their gold figures on a dark red background, the carved cross beams outside the main door are magnificent. Also look up at the ceramic figures arrayed along the roof ridges, still in their original colours. Keep any eye out for the decorative motifs such as bats, plums and carved fish emerging from the walls. The revolutionary displays are rather incidental, unless the period fires you up.

At the corner of Jiefeng Lu Jie and Zhongshan Yilu is the **Lingzhou Guildhall** (灵洲会馆; Língzhōu Huìguăn), now housing an assortment of travel agents. Deng Xiaoping used the Qingfeng Building, down an alley off Xiangyang Lu, as an office when holed up in Băisè.

Over the bridge on the far side of the Dengbi River and up the hill to the east of the **Baise Uprising Memorial** (Băisè Qǐyì Jìniànbēi; 百色起义纪念碑), the **Youjiang Minorities Museum** (右江民族博物馆; Yòujiāng Mínzú Bówùguăn; admission free; ◷ 8.30-11.30am & 2.30-5.30pm) welcomes visitors with a poster of President Hujin Tao visiting Băisè in 2002. The displays of clothes, customs, traditions and musical instruments of regional minorities are hampered by no English captions. Adjacent to the museum is a hall devoted to a diorama of modern Băisè.

Sleeping

Yùnshū Gōngsi Lüshè (运输公司旅社; ☎ 289 4604; 80 Jiefang Jie; 解放街80号; bed in five-bed dm Y6, bed in tr Y7, s Y10-30, d Y16-35) Cheapest of the cheap, this basic hostel tests the lower boundaries of budget and will delight even the stingiest of arrivals. It has scruffy, thin walls and spartan, fan-only rooms, but the location on historic Jiefang Jie can't be beaten.

Jindu Hotel (金都大酒店; Jīndū Dàjiǔdiàn; ☎ 288 1188; fax 288 1193; 29 Chengbei Yilu; 城北一路29号; tw Y228, luxury s/tw Y298/268; ☒) A cut above the rest, the spacious twins at this three-star hotel by the Băisè bus station are decent with commodious wardrobes and well-presented shower rooms where hair driers and carefully folded towels are thoughtful touches.

Eating
The KFC on Zhongshan Yilu can be recommended if only for its super-sonic Panasonic hand driers.

Jinfenghua Coffee Shop (金丰华餐馆; Jīnfēnghuá Cānguǎn; ☎ 282 8080; Xiangyang Lu; 向阳路; meals Y25; ☒ 9am-12.30am) Sit on a windowside swinging seat and flick through the English menu which runs to steaks (from Y28), sandwiches (from Y12), spaghetti (from Y15) and baked rice in bamboo tube (from Y18). The piped muzak is a colossal shame.

Getting There & Away
BUS
The **Băisè bus station** (百色客运站; Băisè Kèyùnzhàn; ☎ 288 1290) is by the intersection of Chengbei Yilu (城北一路) and Xiangyang Lu (向阳路).

TRAIN
Băisè has daily connections that will go to Nánníng (1166, 2006, 5514 and 8566, four hours), Kūnmíng (1165 and 2005, 11 hours) and Guǎngzhōu (1166, 21 hours). The train station is found way out of town, so try to buy your tickets from your hotel, if possible. Bus 1 connects the bus and train stations, via Zhongshan Yilu.

Getting Around
Taxis are Y4 at flagfall. Pedicabs are plentiful, with most trips around the centre of town costing Y2.

AROUND BĂISÈ
Língyún 凌云
A scenic two-hour drive through the mountains following the Chengbi River 80km north of Băisè takes you past some stunning scenery full of attractive minority villages. The town of Língyún is a useful staging post for trips to nearby caves, tea plantations and colourful minority villages. If you have more time, continue on north to the karst landscape of Lèyè (乐业) county. Buses (Y25) leave Băisè hourly for the 90-minute journey.

SIDE TRIP TO HÚNÁN
Travellers doing the northeast of Guǎngxī can delve into southwestern and western Húnán (湖南) province to the north for some more forays into minority villages, crumbling riverside towns and the spectacular landscapes of Wǔlíngyuán.

Minority Villages 侗寨和苗寨
Dong and Miao villages are abundantly scattered around southwest Húnán, some with simple hotels for overnighting travellers. Villages near the border with Guǎngxī include the lovely riverine Dong village of **Dàzhài Cūn** (大寨村), 70km or so from the town of Chéngbù (城步). A short minibus ride (Y2) from the town of Tōngdào (also called Shuāngjiāng; 双江) in southwestern Húnán (just over the border with Guǎngxī), the Dong village of **Huángdù Dòngzú Wénhuàcūn** (皇都侗族文化村) is also worth exploring for its drum tower and wind-and-rain bridge panoramas. A further Dong settlement near Tōngdào is the lovely village of **Yùtouzhài** (芋头寨), 9km outside Băisè.

Fènghuáng 凤凰
A fascinating riverside town of ancient city walls and gate towers, Fènghuáng contains houses on stilts overlooking the river and

BUSES FROM BĂISÈ

Destination	Fare (Y)	Duration (hours)	Departure Time
Běihăi	138	7	7.05am & 4pm
Guìlín	190	9	9.20am
Jìngxī	52	3½	hourly (7am-4.40pm)
Língyún	25	1½	hourly (6.40am-6.30pm)
Liŭzhōu	150	8	7.40am & 5pm
Nánníng	60	4	frequent (6.30am-8pm)

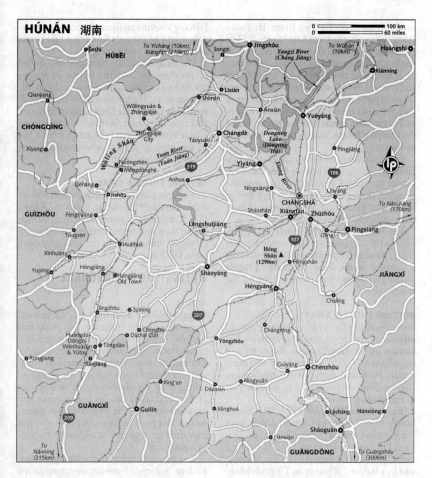

HÚNÁN 湖南

hoary temples dotted about the old town, Fènghuáng can easily fill a couple of days. Home to a lively population of the Miao and Tujia minorities, Fènghuáng's architectural legacy shows distressing signs of neglect, so get to it before it crumbles away. Accommodation is everywhere, from youth hostels to the ubiquitous guesthouses overlooking the Tuo River.

SIGHTS

Strolling willy-nilly around Fènghuáng's old town is the best way to see it. Many of its back alleys maintain an intriguing charm, a treasure trove of old family pharmacists, traditional shops, temples, ancestral halls and crumbling dwellings. Restored fragments of

the city wall lie along the south bank of the Tuo River in the old town and a few dilapidated chunks survive elsewhere.

Several sights can only be visited if you buy the through ticket (Y98), which includes entrance to the **Yang Family Ancestral Hall**, the **Former Home of Shen Congwen**, the **Former Home of Xiong Xiling**, a **boat ride** along the Tuo River, the **East Gate Tower** and other sights. If you don't want to fork out for this, you can still see much of Fènghuáng for free and you can take a boat trip along the river for Y30 from the North Gate Tower. Sights are generally open from 8am to 5.30pm.

Wander along Fènghuáng's restored salmon-coloured **city wall** (城墙; Chéngqiáng) with its defensive aspect along the southern bank of the Tuo River. Half way along its length, the **North Gate Tower** (北门城楼; Běimén Chénglóu) is in a tragic state of neglect, but it remains a magnificent structure. Spanning the river is the magnificent and covered **Hong Bridge** (Hóng Qiáo; admission free). Other significant buildings in the southern part of the old town include the 18th-century walled **Confucian Temple** (Wén Miào; Wenxing Jie) and the **Chaoyang Temple** (Cháoyáng Gōng; 41 Wenxing Jie; admission Y15).

Excellent views of Fènghuáng's riverside buildings on stilts can be seen from the north side of the river. Crossing the river over the stepping stones or the wooden foot bridge brings you to Laoying Shao, a street of bars, cafés and inns overlooking the river.

The **Tian Family Ancestral Temple** (Laoying Shao; admission Y10) is overgrown with weeds. Further along, **Wanshou Temple** (Wànshòu Gōng; admission Y50) is not far from the distinctive **Wanming Pagoda** (Wànmíng Tǎ; admission free), erected right on the river bank.

GETTING THERE & AWAY

Buses from Jíshǒu (Y12, one hour, every 20 minutes) leave from the long-distance bus station on Wuling Donglu. Buses to and from Jíshǒu (吉首; Y12, one hour, frequent) depart from and arrive at the bus station (Kèyùn zhàn) on Juyuan Lu in the new part of Fénghuáng.

Buses from Huáihuà (Y26, 2½ hours, hourly from 7.30am to 5.30pm) depart from the West bus station (Kèyùn Xīzhàn) on Zhijiang Lu. Buses to Huáihuà (Y25, two hours, every 20 minutes) depart from the Minsuyuan bus station (Mínsúyuán Tíngchēchǎng) on Jiangbei Donglu in the north of Fènghuáng. There is one bus a day from Guìlín to Huáihuà (Y92, 12 hours). Trains run from Huáihuà and Jíshǒu to Sānjiāng and Liǔzhōu in Guǎngxī.

Déhāng 德夯

Its seductive riverine setting overlooked by towering, other-worldly karst peaks, the Miao hamlet of Déhāng (admission Y60) northwest of Jíshǒu in western Húnán province offers a tantalising spectrum of treks into picturesque countryside. Rising into columns, splinters and huge foreheads of stone, the local karst geology climbs over verdant valleys layered with terraced fields and flushed by clear streams. Side-stepping

Déhāng's bovine traffic and occasional cowpats might be the only thing that takes your eyes off the gorgeous scenery.

The village itself has been partially dolled up for domestic tourism, but on its fringes the feeling of a pleasant riverside Miao village survives. Highly affordable hotels built from wood also make Déhāng an inexpensive and alluring retreat. Surplus to its charming village views, Déhāng is located within a 164 sq km geological park where magnificent treks thread into the hills.

GETTING THERE & AWAY

The best way to reach Déhāng is to travel via Jíshǒu, south of the village. Buses to Déhāng (Y6, 50 minutes, regular) leave from outside Jíshǒu train station, arriving at and departing (every 20 minutes) from the square/parking lot in Déhāng.

WŬLÍNGYUÁN & ZHĀNGJIĀJIÈ
武陵源和张家界
☎ 0744

Rising sublimely from the misty subtropical forest of northwest Húnán are 243 peaks surrounded by more than 3000 karst upthrusts, a concentration not seen elsewhere in the world. The picture is completed by waterfalls, limestone caves and rivers suitable for organised rafting trips. Nearly two dozen rare species of flora and fauna call the region home and botanists delight in the 3000-odd plant species within this park. Amateur wildlife spotters may even get a gander at a clouded leopard or a pangolin.

Known collectively as the **Wulingyuan Scenic Area** (Wŭlíngyuán Fēngjǐngqū; www.zhangjiajie.com.cn, www.zjjtrip.net), the region encompasses the localities of Zhāngjiājiè, Tiānzǐshān and Suǒxīyu. Zhāngjiājiè is the best known, and many Chinese refer to this area by that name. Recognised by Unesco in 1990 as a World Heritage Site, Wŭlíngyuán is home to three minority peoples: Tujia, Miao and Bai.

A mighty fee of Y245 (students Y165), good for two days with extension, must be paid at the Zhāngjiājiè forest reserve's main entrance just past the village. Admission to other sights within the park can cost extra.

GETTING THERE & AWAY

The most popular access points are Zhangjiajie city (Zhāngjiājiè *shi*) and Zhāngjiājiè village (Zhāngjiājiè *cūn*). The city is near the railway line, while the village is situated nearly 600m above sea level in the Wŭlíng foothills, surrounded by sheer cliffs and vertical rock outcrops.

Zhangjiajie **airport** (☎ 825 3177) is 4km southwest of Zhāngjiājiè city and 40km from the park entrance; a taxi should cost around Y100 to the park. Daily flights include Bĕijīng (Y1340), Shànghăi (Y1330), Guăngzhōu (Y860), Chóngqìng (Y580), Chángshā (Y580) and Xī'ān (Y690).

The train station is 8km southeast of the city. Trains run to numerous destinations, including

Yíchāng, Jíshŏu (Y22 hard seat) and Huáihuà (Y15 to Y37 hard seat, four to 5½ hours).

Minibuses to Zhāngjiājiè village (Y8, 40 minutes) pick up incoming passengers at the car park in front of the train station but can be slow departing; otherwise, take bus 2 to the long-distance **bus station** (☎ 822 2417) on Huilong Lu where buses leave every 15 minutes to Zhāngjiājiè village (Y8). Buses also leave from here for Chángshā (Y120, 11 hours, twice daily), Fènghuáng (Y47, four hours, 8.30am and 2.30pm) and Jíshŏu (Y44, 2½ hours, hourly).

Yúnnán 云南

We've said it before and we'll say it again: if you have time for but one province in China, Yúnnán should be it. Strong words but hyperbole is remarkably understated when describing Yúnnán. No other province can rival Yúnnán's diversity in land and people. Guìzhōu is also an ethnic mosaic, Sìchuān's rivers garner much of the Southwest's glory and Guǎngxī's scenery leaps from every encyclopaedia's entry on China. Yet Yúnnán can top 'em all.

Just gaze at a map. Yúnnán's majestic, and often sacred, peaks thrust from the Tibetan ranges to the north, lush jungle lies a two-day bus ride south and a fertile plain spreads through the rest of the province. It's also home to China's highest number of species of flora and fauna – including 2500 varieties of wild flowers and plants – and known for its mild climate year-round. Indeed, the province's nicknames include 'Kingdom of Plants' and 'Garden of Heavenly Marvellous Flowers'; the capital's nickname is 'Spring City'.

A huge attraction is the province's astonishingly diverse populace. Home to nearly half of all China's ethnic minorities, nearly 50% of the province is non-Han (Han are China's main ethnic group). Village-hop this breathtaking province and greet a new minority group each day, many in time-capsule towns that you'll never forget. Smacks of PR pulp? Well, just be prepared that if you start here, you may never get to another province. It has happened.

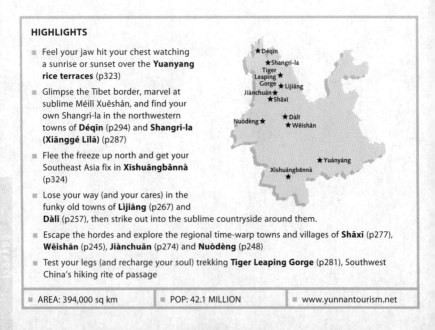

HIGHLIGHTS

- Feel your jaw hit your chest watching a sunrise or sunset over the **Yuanyang rice terraces** (p323)

- Glimpse the Tibet border, marvel at sublime Méilǐ Xuěshān, and find your own Shangri-la in the northwestern towns of **Déqīn** (p294) and **Shangri-la (Xiānggé Lǐlā)** (p287)

- Flee the freeze up north and get your Southeast Asia fix in **Xīshuāngbǎnnà** (p324)

- Lose your way (and your cares) in the funky old towns of **Lìjiāng** (p267) and **Dàlǐ** (p257), then strike out into the sublime countryside around them.

- Escape the hordes and explore the regional time-warp towns and villages of **Shāxī** (p277), **Wēishān** (p245), **Jiànchuān** (p274) and **Nuòdèng** (p248)

- Test your legs (and recharge your soul) trekking **Tiger Leaping Gorge** (p281), Southwest China's hiking rite of passage

| ★Déqīn |
| ★Shangri-la |
| Tiger Leaping ★ Gorge |
| Jiànchuān ★ ★ Lìjiāng |
| ★Shāxī |
| Nuòdèng ★ ★ Dàlǐ |
| ★ Wēishān |
| ★ Yuányáng |
| Xīshuāngbǎnnà ★ |

| ■ AREA: 394,000 sq km | ■ POP: 42.1 MILLION | ■ www.yunnantourism.net |

HISTORY

In the 1960s scientists rocked the anthropological world when they determined that fragments of humanlike teeth discovered by railway engineers in Yuánmóu, northwest of Kūnmíng, belonged to hominids who lived 1.75 million to 2.5 million years ago. This and further discoveries proved what was once considered a wild, isolated region was inhabited before any other in China.

Yúnnán's other great anthropological discovery was of sophisticated Bronze Age cultures around Diān Chí (Lake Dian). First discovered in the 1950s, excavations throughout southeast Yúnnán are filling gaps in a previously unknown period of the province.

It wasn't until the Warring States period (453–221 BC) that the rest of China became interested in the frontiers. Armies invaded twice before Chu general Zhuang Qiao put himself into power as the emperor of the Dian kingdom near Kūnmíng. Though regular contact with the rest of China was still a long way off, it was Zhuang who facilitated eventual expansion and the first large-scale migration.

Qin dynasty emperor Qin Shihuang extended a road from Sìchuān to Qūjìng in northeast Yúnnán and established the first *jun* (prefecture). As the Qin dynasty ceded to the Han dynasty, western Yúnnán was organised within prefectures and the famed Southern Silk Route into Burma and India was established. Meanwhile, Yúnnán was

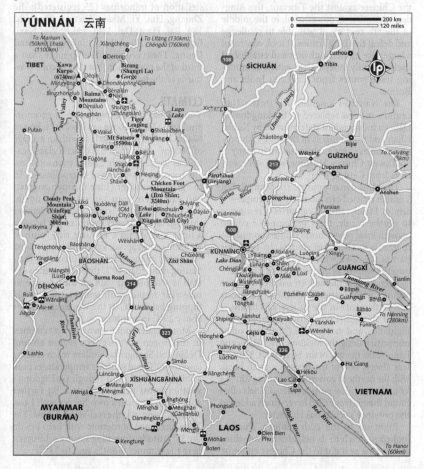

occupied by large numbers of non-Chinese aboriginal people. They lacked good political organisation and their chieftains either obeyed or ignored the emperor.

In the Three Kingdoms period (AD 220–280), a kingdom including parts of Sìchuān was formed when a rebellion by Yúnnán's up-and-coming elite was put down. From this time and throughout the Western Jin period (AD 265–316), Yúnnán crept ever closer to consolidation, and came under the jurisdiction of some sort of Chinese control.

The power base of Yúnnán also shifted slowly – first eastward to Qūjìng, then westward. By the 7th century AD the Bai people had established a powerful kingdom, the Nanzhao, south of Dàlǐ. Initially allied with the Chinese against the Tibetans, this kingdom extended its power until, in the middle of the 8th century, it was able to challenge and defeat the Tang armies. It took control of a large slice of the Southwest and established itself as a fully independent entity, dominating trade routes from China to India and Burma.

The Nanzhao kingdom fell in the 10th century and was replaced by the kingdom of Dàlǐ, an independent state overrun by Kublai Khan and the Mongols in the mid-13th century. Kublai's armies also brought in many of Southwest China's Muslims, who were warriors from Central Asia.

The Ming dynasty purged the Mongols but Yúnnán resisted capitulation to the emperor's armies. Finally, after 15 centuries of resistance to northern rule, the Qing emperor cowed enough local power-brokers into submission to gain a modicum of control. In 1658 this part of the Southwest was finally integrated into the empire as the province of Yúnnán.

Even so it remained an isolated frontier region, with scattered Chinese garrisons and settlements in the valleys and basins, a mixed aboriginal population occupying the highlands, and various Dai (Thai) and other minorities along the Mekong River (Láncāng Jiāng). Like the rest of the Southwest, Yúnnán was always one of the first regions to break with the northern government. During China's countless political purges, fallen officials often found themselves exiled here, which added to the province's rebellious character.

Right up to the 20th century, Yúnnán looked as much to its neighbours Indochina and Burma as it did to the Chinese emperor.

Wracked by ethnic disturbances, including the bloody 1855 Muslim uprising and even bloodier Chinese army put-down, Yúnnán was exploited by local warlords, European powers along the border, and the emperor. It was the death of China, at least in the east, with the arrival of Japanese forces in 1937 that was to ironically augur a better future for Yúnnán. Strategically located away from Japan's forces in the east, the province was used to shuttle material for the Allied war machine. Later, the Red Army would be welcomed by a peasantry that felt it had been ignored long enough.

Today, Yúnnán province looks firmly back in the Chinese fold. It is a province of 42 million people, including a veritable constellation of minorities (25 registered): the Zhuang, Hui, Yi, Miao, Tibetans, Mongols, Yao, Bai, Hani, Dai, Lisu, Lahu, Wa, Naxi, Jingpo, Pumi, Nu, Achang, Bulang, Jinuo and Drung. These groups make up more than a third of the population, but they occupy two-thirds of the land.

CLIMATE

Yúnnán has a stunning range of geomorphology – 76.4m above sea level in Hékǒu to 6740m in the Tibetan plateau with an average of 2000m – and thus the official classification as 'subtropical highland monsoon' really translates as dozens of microclimates. In the grip of summer (June through August) you can freeze your tail off in the north, and in the midst of winter (mid-November through late February) you can get by with a light coat within a 12-hour ride south of Kūnmíng, the capital, which seemingly lacks 'weather', its mean temperature never fluctuating more than 10°C throughout the year. Dàlǐ is also blessed with an ideal temperature year-round, with temperatures rarely dipping below 4°C in the winter months or above 25°C in summer.

More detail about the worrisome extremes: in the frozen northwestern region around Déqīn and Shangri-la, winters reach chilling lows of -12°C and summer temperatures peak at highs of 19°C. And though Guǎngdōng's southernmost peninsula juts a bit further south than Yúnnán's own border with Laos, to most, Yúnnán is the real 'south' China. The Xīshuāngbǎnnà borderline with Laos lies on the 21° latitude – meaning steamy subtropics; here the summer months soar to 33°C.

FESTIVALS IN YÚNNÁN

Festival	Location	Lunar calendar	2008	2009	2010
Water-Splashing Festival	Jǐnghóng, Xīshuāngbǎnnà	(13-15 April fixed in Western calendar)			
Sanyuesan	Western Hills, Kūnmíng	3rd of 3rd	8 April	29 March	16 April
Fertility Festival	Lìjiāng	13th of 3rd	18 April	8 April	26 April
Third Moon Fair	Dàlǐ	15th-21st of 3rd	20-26 April	10-16 April	28 April-4 May
Guanyin Pavilion Festival	Dàlǐ	19th of 3rd	24 April	14 April	2 May
Three Temples Festival	Dàlǐ	23rd-25th of 4th	27-29 May	17-19 May	5-7 June
Guanyin Pavilion Festival	Dàlǐ	19th of 6th	21 July	9 August	30 July
Torch Festival	Shílín, Dàlǐ, Lìjiāng, Chǔxióng	24th of 6th	26 July	14 August	4 August
Guanyin Pavilion Festival	Dàlǐ	19th of 9th	17 October	5 November	26 October

Note: Festival dates are subject to change – check ahead.

LANGUAGE

In addition to Mandarin (which here has been modified into Yunnanese, intelligible to native Mandarin speakers but often not to you!), the other major languages spoken in the Yúnnán province belong to the Tibeto-Burman family (eg the Naxi language), and the Sino-Tibetan family (eg the Lisu language). This, however, is a simplified classification – home to half of China's minority groups, in virtually every county of Yúnnán you pass through you encounter a different language or dialect.

GETTING THERE & AWAY

Air

Kūnmíng is served by all Chinese airlines and has daily flights to most cities. International destinations include but are by no means limited to Hong Kong, Hanoi, Vientiane, Chiang Mai/Bangkok, Rangoon, Osaka and Seoul.

Domestic airports in almost all corners of Yúnnán province are served by daily flights from Kūnmíng (and other major Chinese cities). Keep in mind that some of the following flights are seasonal – meaning you still may be forced to fly first to Kūnmíng and change planes.

The northwest is linked by Shangri-la, Dàlǐ and Lìjiāng. Mángshì and Bǎoshān provide Déhóng prefecture in the southwest with an air link and Jǐnghóng is Xīshuāngbǎnnà's air link.

Dàlǐ airport has flights to Kūnmíng and Guǎngzhōu. From Lìjiāng there are daily flights in high season to Chéngdū, Shànghǎi, Shēnzhèn and Guǎngzhōu (and occasionally Xīshuāngbǎnnà). From Shangri-la, Yunnan Airlines flies to Kūnmíng, Chéngdū, Lhasa, Guǎngzhōu, Shēnzhèn and Guìyáng.

Destinations from Jǐnghóng include Lìjiāng, Shànghǎi, and Guǎngzhōu, as well as direct flights to Bangkok and Chiang Mai in Thailand. Mángshì currently only has flights to Kūnmíng, though at some point flights into Burma should be on offer.

The southeast is now only served by four flights per week to Wénshān on their way to Nánníng, though the flight is absurdly expensive compared to the bus.

Kūnmíng also recently saw the start up of the province's first budget airline – Lucky Air – which hopes to offer cheap flights to/from Dàlǐ and Jǐnghóng, if not other places. We'll see.

Boat

From 2004 to 2006 a number of adventurous foreigners managed to snag rides aboard cargo boats from Jǐnghóng in Xīshuāngbǎnnà to Chiang Saen in Thailand. Chinese authorities liked that not a bit and put a stop to it in October 2006. Coincidentally (?) at the same time a new high-speed passenger boat began running the same route (and stopping off at six ports in between). For more details see the boxed text, p331.

Bus

Roadwise, Yúnnán is what Sìchuān only wishes it were, with a comprehensive and smooth bus network to all major destinations; no other province in Southwest China has laid new roads in the past 10 years as fast as Yúnnán. A few curlicue ribbons still lurk out there if you're planning to head off the well-trodden paths, but these are generally of the serpentine mountain-road variety – you'll get a bit of queasiness perhaps but no tailbone smashing. (The worst are routes between Jǐnghóng and the Dàlǐ, Bǎoshān or Déhóng – for Ruìlì – prefectures.)

Expressways link Kūnmíng with Dàlǐ (and will eventually link with Lìjiāng), south to Bǎoshān and Jǐnghóng, and southeast to Gèjiù, Jiànshuǐ and virtually every other city nearby mentioned in this book. These expressway networks also link Kūnmíng with Sìchuān, Guìzhōu and Guǎngxī, and at the time of writing to the border with Laos (and ultimately Thailand). For Vietnam and Myanmar these cushy highways only get close.

Train

Arriving in (or departing from) Yúnnán by train to Kūnmíng is generally a snap, though, as always, do not expect middle-berth hardsleeper ticket miracles on short notice for the most popular routes.

Railways link Yúnnán to Guìzhōu, Guǎngxī and Sìchuān and further afield throughout the country. Book early for trains to Chéngdū, probably the most popular route, and Guìlín; for the latter, consider the eminently more easily nabbed ticket to Nánníng on the Nankun Railway.

Development of the railways has been slower inside Yúnnán than elsewhere in China; it was only a decade or so ago that the passenger line was extended west to gotta-go-there Dàlǐ (a further extension from Dàlǐ to Lìjiāng was reportedly half-completed at the time of writing).

Yúnnán once had a funky old narrow-gauge rail system for intraprovincial travel in its southeastern counties near Vietnam. This, however, has expired gradually due to ageing infrastructure (nearly a century old!) and chronic landslide issues; the death knell was the cancellation of the wonderfully anachronistic meandering, chugging night train to Hékǒu on the Vietnam border. The provincial government has announced plans to completely overhaul and upgrade the system, along with other Association of Southeast Asian Nations (Asean; the members of which can't seem to agree on whose system to use as a base). This would also, officials claim, eventually include Myanmarr, if they can lay track from Kūnmíng to Ruìlì near the border.

KŪNMÍNG 昆明

☎ 0871 / pop 1.01 million

Yúnnán means 'South of the Clouds', and Kūnmíng, with the apt moniker 'Spring City', couldn't be a better meteorological metaphor for a place far from inclement weather. Indeed, the climate is generally the first thing travellers notice about the place. At an elevation of 1890m, Kūnmíng has a milder climate than most other Chinese cities (and other areas of the province). Winters are short, sunny and dry, though definitely a bit chilly in the shade. Snow isn't entirely unheard of, though spells are quite brief and it'll still be warmer than the north! In summer (June to August) Kūnmíng has more rain but it offers cool respite to anyone coming in from Chéngdū, Chóngqìng or China's tropical neighbours to the south. Indeed, it will be this first breath of fresh air in a long while that will probably begin your infatuation with the city.

Given this fresh climate, it's not surprising that the capital of 'China's Greenhouse' is not unlike one big park, with tree- and flower-lined boulevards every which way. Sure, traffic is worsening by the minute – the Spring City's legendary breezes are having a harder time blowing away the resulting haze – and most of the city's quaint architecture has gone (neon is rare enough however that you can actually see a few stars at night in the heart of downtown), but in the end you'll likely find yourself quite cosy here and spend more time than you'd thought.

Another of Kūnmíng's immediately apparent pluses is the absolute refusal of the populace to be anything but laid-back. There literally is no sense of hurry-up here and the quotient of cell-phone yapping wannabes on boulevards and buses is thankfully on the low end.

Kūnmíng's total population is around 3.5 million, though only about a million inhabit the urban area. At most, minorities account for 6% of Kūnmíng's population, although the farm-

---

WHERE TO FIND OUT MORE

Internet Resources

■ Go Kunming (http://gokunming.com) is run by expats in Yúnnán, specifically Kūnmíng, this site either has what you need or a link to where you can find it.

■ Letters from China (www.voyage.typepad.com/china/yunnan) is a good hub for links to governmental-, transport- and tourism-information sources.

■ Yunnan Explorer (www.yunnanexplorer.com) is an outstanding resource with excellent background articles, maps, and thorough links.

■ Yunnan Tourism (www.yunnantourism.net) is the official site of the Yúnnán provincial government, it provides a good overview – though fairly basic – of all things touristy in the province.

Books

Consider the following brief list of eminent books for Yúnnán- or China-centric reading:

■ Anything by Jonathan Spence, in particular his books *The Search for Modern China* and *God's Chinese Son*.

■ *South of the Clouds: Tales from Yunnan*, edited by Guo Xu and Lucien Miller. This fascinating anthology of Yúnnán tales provides a wonderful thumbnail sketch of the cultural ethos of the province and its people.

■ *Mr China's Son, A Villager's Life*, He Liyi. You cannot possibly be unmoved by this account of a simple man's ordeal during China's 20th-century upheavals. Mr He, a Bai from Dàlǐ, was unlucky enough to have studied English, a crime for which he later found himself sent to the countryside and otherwise persecuted for much of his life. In the end, he wound up sharing his wondrous outlook on life with foreign travellers in his café (now closed) in Dàlǐ.

■ *Soul Mountain*, Gao Xingjian. The Nobel prize winner for literature, Gao weaves a search for his own 'soul mountain' as he wanders about the countryside of Southwest China. Brilliant.

■ Anything by Joseph Rock. Seriously. *The Ancient Nakhi Kingdom of Southwest China* is Joseph Rock's definitive work, along with his Naxi dictionary. For an insight into the man and his work, take a look at *In China's Border Provinces: The Turbulent Career of Joseph Rock, Botanist-Explorer* by JB Sutton, or Rock's many archived articles for *National Geographic*.

■ *The Age of Wild Ghosts: Memory, Violence, and Place in Southwest China*, Erik Mueggler. A compelling account of a Tibetan-Burmese minority community on the fringes – literally and figuratively – of the Han world in the 20th century.

---

ing areas are home to some Yí, Hui and Miao groups. There are also Vietnamese refugees-turned-immigrants who fled the Sino-Vietnamese border clashes that started in 1977.

It's an enormous municipality at some 6100 sq km. The city is surrounded on three sides by the mountain ranges of the Yúnnán-Guìzhōu Plateau; Diān Chí lies to the south.

History

The region of Kūnmíng has been inhabited for around 2000 years, though nearby areas have been populated for millions of years. The tomb excavations around Diān Chí, particularly at Shizhai Mountain near Jìníng on the southern shore, have unearthed thousands of artefacts from the Bronze Age – weapons, drums, paintings, and silver, jade and turquoise jewellery – that suggest a well-developed culture and provide clues to a very sketchy early history of the city.

During the Warring States period the kingdom of Dian was established close to present-day Kūnmíng. The first Chinese prefecture, the Yizhou Jun, was set up in Kūnmíng in 109 BC during the Western Han dynasty. Until the 8th century the town was a remote Chinese outpost, but the kingdom of Nanzhao, centred to the northwest of Kūnmíng at Dàlǐ, captured it and made it their second capital.

In 1274 the Mongols came through, sweeping all before them. Marco Polo gives us a fascinating picture of Kūnmíng's commerce in the late 13th century:

YÚNNÁN

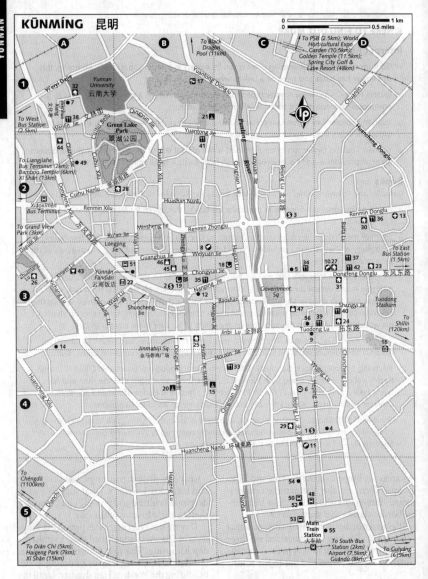

KŪNMÍNG 昆明

0 — 1 km
0 — 0.5 miles

At the end of these five days journeys you arrive at the capital city, which is named Yachi, and is very great and noble. In it are found merchants and artisans, with a mixed population, consisting of idolaters, Nestorian Christians and Saracens or Mohametans...The land is fertile in rice and wheat...For money they employ the white porcelain shell, found in the sea, and which they also wear as ornaments about their necks. Eighty of the shells are equal in value to...two Venetian groats. In this country also there are salt springs...the duty levied on this salt produces large revenues to the Emperor. The natives do not consider it an injury done to them when others have connection with their wives, provided the act is voluntary on the woman's part. Here there is a lake almost a hundred miles in circuit, in which great quantities of fish are caught. The people are accustomed to eat the raw flesh of fowls, sheep, oxen and buffalo…the poorer sorts only dip it in a sauce of garlic…they eat it as well as we do the cooked.

In the 14th century the Ming set up shop in Yúnnánfǔ, as Kūnmíng was then known, building a walled town on the present site. From the 17th century onwards, the history of the city becomes rather grisly. The last Ming resistance to the invading Manchu took place in Yúnnán in the 1650s and was crushed by General Wu Sangui. Wu in turn rebelled against the king and held out until his death in 1678. His successor was overthrown by the Manchu emperor Kangxi and killed himself in Kūnmíng in 1681.

In the 19th century the city suffered several blood baths, as the rebel Muslim leader Du Wenxiu, the sultan of Dàlǐ, attacked and be-

sieged the city several times between 1858 and 1868. It was not until 1873 that the rebellion was finally and bloodily crushed.

The intrusion of the West into Kūnmíng began in the middle of the 19th century and by 1900 Kūnmíng, Hékǒu, Sīmáo and Méngzì had been opened to foreign trade. The French were keen on exploiting the region's copper, tin and timber resources, and in 1910 their Indochina railway, started in 1898 at Hanoi, reached the city.

Kūnmíng's expansion began with WWII, when factories were established here and refugees fleeing the Japanese poured in from eastern China. In a bid to keep China from falling to Japan, Anglo-American forces sent supplies to Nationalist troops entrenched in Sìchuān and Yúnnán. Supplies came overland on a dirt road carved out of the mountains in 1937–38 by 160,000 Chinese with virtually no equipment. This was the famous Burma Road, a 1000km haul from Lashio to Kūnmíng. Today, the western extension of Kūnmíng's Renmin Lu, leading in the direction of Heilinpu, is the tail end of the road. For more on the Burma Road, see the boxed text, p347.

In early 1942 the Japanese captured Lashio, cutting the supply line. Kūnmíng continued to handle most of the incoming aid during 1942–45, when US planes flew the dangerous mission of crossing the 'Hump', the towering 5000m mountain ranges between India and Yúnnán. A black market sprang up and medicines, canned food, petrol and other goods intended for the military and relief agencies were siphoned off.

The face of Kūnmíng has been radically altered since then, with streets widened and office buildings and housing projects constructed. With the coming of the railways, industry has expanded rapidly, and a surprising range of goods and machinery now bears a 'Made in Yúnnán' stamp. The city's exports include steel, foodstuffs, trucks, machine tools, electrical equipment, textiles, chemicals, building materials and plastics.

Orientation

The jurisdiction of Kūnmíng includes four city districts and eight rural counties, which supply the city with fruit and vegetables. The centre of the city is the traffic circle at the intersection of Zhengyi Lu and Dongfeng Lu (this street is also for a few blocks called Nanping Jie).

To the southwest of the intersection, down to Jinbi Lu, the old quarter has given way to Kūnmíng's only area of bustle and neon – best for people-watching. To the north of the intersection is Green Lake Park, a pleasant place for a wander; it contains Yuantong Temple and the Kunming Zoo.

To the east of the city centre intersection is Kūnmíng's major road running north to south, Beijing Lu. At the southern end is the main train station and the long-distance bus station. At about the halfway point, Beijing Lu is intersected by Dongfeng Donglu. This used to be the foreign traveller ghetto where everyone wound up, but today the entire downtown area has somewhere to stay and eat and something to see and do.

MAPS

Scores of maps are available around the bus and train stations and in bookshops; sadly, those with a smattering of English names lack any real detail. The *Yunnan Communications and Tourist Map* (Y10) has got good English labels on the provincial map and on the Kūnmíng city map on the flip side, but this one has become extremely hard to find.

Information

BOOKSHOPS

Mandarin Books & CDs (West Gate, Yunnan University; ☎ 220 6575; ☺ 9am-10pm) Has guidebooks, novels, magazines and a selection of travel writing in English, German, French, Dutch, Italian and some Spanish. Not exactly tons available, but it's better than nothing.

Xinhua Bookstore (Nanping Jie) Provincial and city maps are also found here; most are in Chinese but you'll find something helpful in English.

INTERNET ACCESS

Pretty much every hotel and café frequented by travellers offers email for Y4 to Y10 per hour; try the Camellia Hotel (p228) and the Hump (p228). (Rates at Kūnmíng's zillion internet cafés are Y2 to Y4.) Cloudland International Youth Hostel (p228) has free, albeit occasionally iffy, access (and it's wireless equipped).

MEDICAL SERVICES

Shuanghe Pharmacy (Shuānghè Dàyàofáng; Tuodong Lu; ☺ 24hr) Opposite Yúnnán Airlines.

Yanan Hospital (Yán'ān Yīyuàn; ☎ 317 7499, ext 311; 1st fl, block 6, Renmin Donglu) Has a foreigners' clinic.

MONEY

Bank of China (Zhōngguó Yínháng; 448 Renmin Donglu; ☺ 9am-noon & 2-5pm) Changes travellers cheques and foreign currency and offers cash advances on credit cards. There is an ATM here. There are branches at Dongfeng Xilu and Huancheng Nanlu. A few other banks around town have ATMs which will accept foreign cards; your best bet is to look for branches of the Agricultural Bank of China (中国农业银行), where some travellers have had luck.

POST & TELEPHONE

China Telecom (Zhōngguó Diànxìn; cnr Beijing Lu & Dongfeng Donglu) You can make international calls here.

International Post Office (Guójì Yóujú; 231 Beijing Lu) The main office has a very efficient poste restante and parcel service (per letter Y3, ID required). It is also the city's Express Mail Service (EMS) and Western Union agent.

PUBLIC SECURITY BUREAU

PSB (公安局; Gōngānjú; ☎ 571 7030; Jinxing Huáyuán, Jinxing Lu; ☺ 9-11.30am & 1-5pm) The Foreign Affairs Branch will, with bureaucratic weariness, issue visa extensions in three to five days. The main entrance is off Erhuan Beilu. Buses 3, 25 and 57 will get you within a couple of blocks. Get off the bus at the Jīnxīng Xīmén stop (金星西门站) on Jinjiang Lu, head east two blocks and turn left onto Yuanxi Xiang.

TOURIST INFORMATION

Almost all of the popular backpacker hotels and cafés can assist with travel queries and make ticket reservations (ranging from free to Y20 per ticket). The Camellia Hotel (p228) has four (at last count) agencies, including Mr Chen's Tours (p228) and Ko Wai Lin Travel (p353), offering visa processing, tickets, and some intriguing (if pricey) tours to neighbouring countries.

China International Travel Service (CITS; Zhōngguó Guójì Lǚxíngshè; ☎ 356 6730; 285 Huancheng Nanlu; ☯ 9am-5.30pm) Organises tours. It's not big on dispensing free information, though. French and English spoken.

Tourist Complaint & Consultative Telephone (☎ 316 4961)

Dangers & Annoyances

Kūnmíng is one of the safest cities in China but take special precaution near the train and long-distance bus stations. The area can get seedy at night and there have been reports of travellers having their bags razored.

Sights

TANG DYNASTY PAGODAS 唐代塔

To the south of Jinbi Lu are two Tang pagodas. Neither can be climbed, nor are their temple complexes open, but both are fairly impressive since they age as gracefully as the neighbourhood gentrifies around them. **West Pagoda** (Xīsì Tǎ; Dongsi Jie, 东寺街; admission Y2; ☯ 9am-6pm) is the more interesting. Attached is a compound that is a popular spot for older people to drink tea, chat and thwack mah jong tiles around (if not get a shave and a haircut).

East Pagoda (Dōngsì Tǎ; Shulin Jie, 书林街) – the one slightly off-plumb – was, according to Chinese sources, destroyed by an earthquake; Western sources say it was destroyed by the Muslim revolt.

YUANTONG TEMPLE 圆通寺

One piece of the perfect-for-a-daylong-stroll triumvirate, along with Green Lake Park and the Kunming Zoo (for the views if not the animals' existence), this **temple** (Yuántōng Sì; Yuantong Jie; admission Y4; ☯ 8am-5pm) at the base of Luófēng Hill is the largest Buddhist complex in Kūnmíng and a rare and superb example of Tang dynasty design. Yes, it is pretty cool to wander amid a 1200-year-old temple complex that still draws a fair number of pilgrims. The central courtyard holds a large square pond intersected by walkways and bridges, and at the centre has a Ming dynasty octagonal pavilion which houses a 3m golden Maitreya statue.

To the rear of the temple a much newer hall enshrines a statue of Sakyamuni, a gift from the king of Thailand. Two dragon sculptures

---

OLD KŪNMÍNG

A day or two in the city and you may feel 'old Kunming' is oxymoronic. Nope, not here. Bulldozed traditional architecture ranks among travellers' pettest of peeves (though to be fair who wants to live in a 125-year-old building with rats and no indoor facilities?) and Kūnmíng is like most every other Chinese city in scrambling to save what little extant architecture remains. Besides the much-hyped Flower & Bird Market (see the boxed text, p231), a few pockets of 'real' Kūnmíng do exist.

One place to go to still see little old men puttering about in their funky blue Mao hats or donkey carts parked in front of temples, or even hear everyone speaking the lovely Kūnmíng-accented Yunnanese, is **Guāndù** (官渡). To be precise, one little slice of the district of the same name southeast of downtown – so 'real' that it's technically now a protected national historic park. As one transplant to Kūnmíng aptly put it, 'The only place in Kūnmíng where everyone in the neighbourhood was actually born there.'

Now, living museum this ain't. As of late 2006, crews had pretty much white-tiled the circumferences of the neighbourhood. 'Old' flagstone alleys are being repaved in 'new' brick and 'old' wooden façades are giving way to new (à la the rest of China), and those locked-up pavilions look suspiciously draped in drop cloths for a garish paint job.

But still, it's kind of a kick. When you get off bus 31 (train station all the way to the end), follow the donkey carts. They'll take you to a very laid-back and yes, don't worry, absolutely tourist-free, section of town. A handful of temples (admission to each Y5), pagodas and other historic structures are great fun to track down (new signs in English take away half the fun of puttering about searching for them).

here are a big attraction for pilgrims, and stories and poems about them have been carved into the temple walls.

Behind the hall is a cliff, Putuo Rock, with steps leading up and then inexplicably stopping (for some odd reason that's our favourite part of the temple). Along the way are carved scholastic inscriptions dating back to the Tang dynasty. A brick platform at the base covers two caves inhabited by dragons (it's said the temple was constructed in part to subdue the beasts). There's a wonderful vegetarian restaurant opposite the main temple entrance (see Yuquanzhai Vegetarian Restaurant, p230).

Watch out for pickpockets outside the temple. Whether photos are allowed or not depends on who's minding the place.

KUNMING ZOO 昆明动物园

Close to Yuántōng Sì is the **zoo** (Kūnmíng Dòngwùyuán; admission Y10; 8.30am-5pm), and though the living conditions of the 750 animals are better than at most Chinese zoos (not saying much), obviously most travellers give it a miss. High up on a spiral-shaped hill, you can give the living areas wide berth and strike out into the verdant grounds, which offer commanding views over the city. If you do want a gander at regional fauna, residing here are such Yúnnán rarities as Xīshuāngbǎnnà wild oxen, lesser (red) pandas, leaf monkeys and black-tail pythons; from greater China you'll get the obligatory pandas, tigers, Yangzi alligators, golden monkeys and others. The grounds also use existing city architecture, including a Ming dynasty city wall. The pavilions were constructed to feature all the architectural styles seen throughout Kūnmíng.

The main entrance is at the corner of Yuantong Jie and Qingnian Lu.

YUNNAN PROVINCIAL MUSEUM
云南省博物馆

At the time of writing, this **museum** (Yúnnán Shěng Bówùguǎn; Wuyi Lu; admission Y10; 9am-5pm Tue-Sun) was just having the finishing touches put on its much-needed face-lift; the previous incarnation was as much tomb as museum.

The museum's three major collections will still call this home. The **Bronze Drums Hall** has artefacts from tomb excavations at Jinning (Diān Chí), Wanjiaba (Chǔxióng) and Lijiashan (near Jiāngchuān). The drums date from the Warring States and Western Han periods and are superb. Of 1600 such drums known to exist in the world, China has 1400

and Yúnnán 400, most unearthed at Shizhai Shān near Diān Chí. The ancient drums are brought into a modern context by their use among minorities such as the Yi. For more on Yúnnán's bronze drums see p47 and p191.

The **Ancient Buddhist Art Hall** has examples of the art at Shíbǎoshān, near Dàlǐ, and the murals of Báishā outside Lìjiāng, which are useful if you are thinking of visiting either site.

The **Minority Nationality Hall** mostly consists of photos and fairly tacky shop mannequins (some with blonde hair!) dressed in minority clothes, with examples of embroidery, bags and hats. It gives an idea of Yúnnán's ethnic diversity but you are better off going to Kūnmíng's Nationalities Museum (p237).

KUNMING CITY MUSEUM 昆明市博物馆

The left-hand hall of this **museum** (Kūnmíngshì Bówùguǎn; Tuodong Lu; admission Y5; 10am-5pm Tue-Sun) is packed with swords, spears and surprises like mini bronze ox heads excavated in the Kūnmíng area; you've got pot luck on English captioning (generally none). The right-hand hall houses the highlight of the whole shebang, worth the Y5 itself – an impressive 6.6m pillar engraved with Buddhist scriptures from the kingdom of Dali (AD 937–1253). It's said Prime Minister Yuan Douguang of the Dali kingdom had it constructed for Kūnmíng's military administrator Gao Mingsheng. A dinosaur exhibit inhabits the 2nd floor with the highlight, we kid you not, *Yunnanosaurus robustus;* this area is a bit middling, sadly underrepresenting Yúnnán's paleontological importance.

GREEN LAKE PARK 翠湖公园

Get to this **park** (Cuìhú Gōngyuán; Cuihu Nanlu; 6am-10pm) early in the morning to take a stroll (or

---

FOR THE BIRDS

Some 20 years ago, for whatever reason, red-beaked seagulls started descending on the Diān Chí (Lake Dian) region during their annual southerly migration, and in particular liked Green Lake Park so much that from November to late March they're now a fixture here, not to mention something of a local pet species. Actually, the most fun is when the seagulls arrive in mid- to late November, when you can watch Kunmingites 'flocking' to the waterside in absolute droves to fling bread crusts to the birds.

THE HUI

Wandering about Kūnmíng you can't help but note its Hui (Chinese Muslim) residents. Of the province's approximately 550,000 Hui, Kūnmíng holds the lion's share, with other populations centred in the counties of Xūndiàn and Wēishān (see p245).

In the 13th century Mongol forces swooped into the province to outflank the Song dynasty troops and were followed by Muslim traders, builders and craftsmen. Yúnnán was the only region put under a Muslim leader immediately after Kublai Khan's armies arrived, when Sayyid Ajall was named governor in 1274.

Not long after, mosques all over China were simultaneously raised with the new Yuan dynasty banner. A Muslim was entrusted to build the first Mongol palace in Běijīng and an observatory based on Persian models was also constructed here. Dozens of Arabic texts were translated and consulted by Chinese scientists, influencing Chinese mathematics more than any other source. Yúnnán's Muslims are rightfully proud of their legendary local-boy-done-good Cheng Ho (Zheng He), the famed eunuch admiral who opened up the Chinese sea channels to the Middle East (and who, some believe, may actually have been the first to voyage to the Americas).

Heavy land taxes and disputes between Muslims and Han Chinese over local gold and silver mines triggered a Muslim uprising in 1855, which lasted until 1873. The Muslims chose Dàlǐ (Xiàguān) as their base and laid siege to Kūnmíng, overrunning the city briefly in 1863. Du Wenxiu, the Muslim leader, proclaimed his newly established Kingdom of the Pacified South (Nánpíng Guó) and took the name Sultan Suleyman.

But success was short-lived and in 1873 Dàlǐ was taken by Qing forces and Du Wenxiu was captured and executed. Up to one million people died in Yúnnán alone, the death toll rising to 18 million nationwide. The uprisings were quelled, but they also had the lasting effect of eliciting sympathy from Burma.

perhaps dance with the retired ladies), then chill in one of the lakeside cafés. Sunday is the best time to come. Also try to pay a visit late September to early October for the Lantern Festival, when simply everyone in the city seems to set a paper lantern boat with candle inside adrift on the waters – outstanding photo op!

MOSQUES 清真寺

The oldest mosque in Kūnmíng (or at least on the site where a mosque has sat the longest), the 400-year-old **Nancheng Mosque** (Nánchéng Qīngzhēn Gǔsì; 51 Zhengyi Lu) can be recognised by its telltale greenish onion domes, though the lower floors essentially look like the white-tiled offices that they are! Even worse, in 2005 the once-lively strip of Muslim restaurants and shops selling skullcaps, Arabic calligraphy and pictures of Mecca nearby got its marching orders from the city government and has slowly been dispersing throughout the city. Not much is left. To get to what's left of the Muslim area from the Zhengyi Lu roundabout, walk west past Chūnchéng Jiǔlóu (Spring City Hotel) and then bear left a half-block to a small alley.

Another **mosque** is nearby, wedged between Huguo Lu and Chongyun Jie, and is more

a historical landmark than place of active worship.

CHUÀNG KÙ (THE LOFT)
创库艺术主题社区

West of downtown in a disused factory district are a host of galleries of modern Chinese artists and photographers, along with a handful of restaurants and coffee shops (most rather pricey but worth a look-see for the artwork). The cornerstone of sorts is **TC/G Nordica** (诺地卡; Nuòdìkǎ; ☎ 411 4692; www.tcgnordica.com/en; 101 Xiba Lu; ☯ 5-11.30pm Mon, 1.30-11pm Tue-Sat, noon-4pm Sun), best described as a gallery-exhibition hall-cultural centre. There's even a relaxing restaurant with Scandinavian and Chinese food. (One founder was Swedish, another Chinese – hence the mix). Do check out Nordica's website for a full slate of performances and exhibitions; most weekends something is happening (though if you wish to eat, at times on Friday and Saturday evenings reservations are required).

Activities
The **Spring City Golf & Lake Resort** (春城湖畔度假村; Chūnchéng Húpàn Dùjiàcūn; ☎ 767 1188; www.springcityresort.com), 48km from Kūnmíng on the northeastern shore of Lake Yangzong, is

arguably China's best golf course (can't wait to get furious letters from China's East Coast on that claim). Golf media absolutely gush over some of the signature holes. It features one championship 18-hole course designed by Jack Nicklaus and another designed by Robert Trent Jones Jr, as well as a five-star **resort** (s/d Y1270/1600, villas Y1800-2700) and water-sports centre. A round of 18 holes costs around US$69/89 weekdays/weekends including cart and caddie if you are staying at the hotel, otherwise it's over double this (figure a cool US$250). Club hire is an additional Y200. A one-way taxi from Kūnmíng costs around Y150.

There are plenty of sporting activities, including tennis, golf and boating, on offer at Haigeng Park (p237).

At the end of a hard day's sightseeing let the masseurs in front of Camellia Hotel (right; and many other locations throughout town) ease your aching limbs.

Tours

Several tour outfits cover Kūnmíng and its surrounding sights faster than public minibuses would, but be prepared to pay for them. They generally feature lots of sights most travellers find rather boring (including the ineluctable stopoffs for bathroom breaks in which the toilets just happen to sit at the far end of jade hawkers' corridors). Some tour operators refuse to take foreigners on their tours, claiming the language barrier causes too much trouble. When numbers allow, Kunming Cloudland Youth Hostel (below) has tours.

More central sights like Yuantong Temple are just a short bicycle ride away – it hardly makes sense to join a tour to see them.

Mr Chen's Tours (☎ 318 8114; Room 3116, No 3 Bldg, Camellia Hotel, 154 Dongfeng Lu) can organise trips to almost anywhere you want to go, including flights and overland trips to Lhasa (see p233 for more details).

Sleeping
BUDGET
Kunming Cloudland Youth Hostel (昆明青年大脚氏旅社; Kūnmíng Qīngnián Dàjiǎoshì Lǚshé; ☎ 410 3777; www.cloudland2004.com; cloudland2005@126.com; 23 Zhuantang Lu; 篆塘路23号; 6-/4-bed dm Y20/30; 🖳) The newest of the city's hostels (run by a couple of oh-so-friendly inveterate travellers who know Yúnnán like the backs of

their hands), this place is absolutely charming with a staff that makes a tremendous effort for guests. Dorms are spanking new and comfortable; beds are soft and each comes with an individual locker. Free internet access and loads of extras – fresh cut flowers on the sinks! To get here from the train or long-distance bus station take city bus 64. Get off at the Yunnan Daily News stop (云南日报社站).

Hump (Tuófēng Kèzhàn; ☎ 364 0359; www.thehump hostel.com; Jinmabiji Sq, Jinbi Lu; 金碧路, 金马碧鸡广场; 8-bed dm Y25) Certainly seems like a logical budget option: dorms are enormous and come with individual lockers; there's a basketball court–sized common room and pool and Ping-Pong tables on the terrace; umpteen bars and discos are at your doorstep. What more do you need? Well, quiet for one. (Yeah, a mite thumpy at night.) The authorities also apparently keep a sharp eye on this place for rumoured heretofore bad behaviour, though it's not clear why.

Kunming Youth Hostel (Kūnmíng Guójì Qīngnián Lǚshè; ☎ 517 5395; youthhostel.km@sohu.com; 94 Cuihu Lu; 翠湖路94号; dm Y25, d from Y80) Tucked along a lane beside the Zhengxie Hotel, right by Green Lake Park, the Kunming Youth Hostel is basic but clean and quiet. Dorms have a kind of institutional feel but the staff are friendly. It was slated for a makeover, so it may be a more relaxing environment by the time you read this.

Kūnhú Fàndiàn (☎ 314 3699; 202 Beijing Lu; 北京路202号; dm Y25, s & d Y128) Near the train and bus stations. A fair number of backpackers always end up here though note that the word on the street was that it was soon to close up shop or be renovated to garner another star or two. There are travel services on site and clean though beaten up old dorms. Singles are big but furnished with doll-sized beds – anyone over 1.6m will struggle getting comfortable. The hotel is two stops from the main train station on bus 2, 23 or 47, though it's easy enough to walk there.

Camellia Hotel (Cháhuā Bīnguǎn; ☎ 316 3000; fax 314 7033; www.kmcamelliahotel.com; 96 Dongfeng Donglu; 东风东路96号; dm Y30, d Y188-288; 🖳) This landmark budget option – long the only place backpackers would head for – is of the good news/bad news variety. The downside? Some grubby rooms on offer (though the toilets and showers are decent) and a staff trying (but not always successfully) not to be weary of pesky budget travellers. But with travel services, bicycle hire, foreign exchange, reasonably priced laundry services, and a colossal breakfast buffet, it's all in all not a bad place to find yourself. To get here from the main train station, take bus 2 or 23 to Dongfeng Donglu, then change to bus 5 heading east and get off at the second stop.

MIDRANGE

Yúndà Bīnguǎn (Yunnan University Hotel; ☎ 503 3624; fax 514 8513; d from Y160; 🖳) The university area – laden with foreign-student-centric restaurants, coffee shops, bookshops and the like – makes for a nice home base, and the standard doubles here are a good choice. Staff practically fall all over themselves to help. It's next to the university's west gate.

Míngdū Dàjiǔdiàn (☎ 624 0666; fax 624 0898; 206 Baita Lu; 白塔路206号; s & d Y388, ste 688; 🖳) A rarity in China – a hotel that seems to have given a modicum of thought to its design scheme. Rooms here are done up in a refreshing red-gold colour combo. Bathrooms are spacious and tidy save for the tubs. With decent amenities and service, if you get the usual discount, it's pretty good value.

TOP END

Kunming Hotel (Kūnmíng Fàndiàn; ☎ 316 2063; www.kunminghotel.com.cn; 52 Dongfeng Donglu; 东风东路 52号; s & d Y780, ste Y1419; 🖳) Yet another rarity in China – a hotel that for more than a decade has garnered (quite justifiably) kudos from travellers for its superlative service and upkeep. It's a city-state-sized complex with everything you need and you won't do much better in town. Its most praised restaurant (one of a few) may be the one serving the cuisine of Cháozhōu (the coastal region in eastern Guǎngdōng – lots of veggies in light but delicious sauces).

Sakura Kunming (Kūnmíng Yīnghuā Jiǔdiàn; ☎ 316 5888; 25 Dongfeng Donglu; 东风东路25号; d from Y800; 🖳) This radically revamped monster is opposite the Kunming Hotel; it's a needed step up from its previous incarnation as a fading Holiday Inn. It has some excellent restaurants (Thai and southwestern American–Mexican, along with a popular breakfast-lunch buffet), a Western-style pub, a small health club, pool, and a disco.

Greenland Hotel (Lǜzhōu Dàjiǔdiàn; ☎ 318 9999; www.greenlandhotel.com.cn; 80 Tuodong Lu; 拓东路 80号; s & d incl breakfast from Y945; ste from Y1527; 🖳)

On-the-spot attentive service and nicely appointed rooms are here. However, no room would really cut the mustard after would-be guests have wandered wide-eyed past a staggered fish-filled fountain on the way to the sparkling lobby.

Eating

Kūnmíng is home to all of Yúnnán's fabulous foods, especially in the snack line. Noodle shops will give you a bowl of rice noodles for around Y5 and a bewildering array of sauces with which to flavour the broth – most of them are hot and spicy. Noodles (rice or wheat) are absolutely the chief breakfast option, usually served in a meat broth with a chilli sauce. Everywhere you go in the province you'll find *pàròu ěrsī* (扒肉饵丝), basically interminably braised meat chunks laden atop noodles; toppings vary by shop but the best will have everything under the sun – even ground peanuts and fresh coriander (cilantro).

Regional specialities are *qìguōjī* (汽锅鸡; herb-infused chicken cooked in an earthenware steampot), *xuānwēi huǒtuǐ* (宣威火腿; Yúnnán ham), *guòqiáo mǐxiàn* (过桥米线; across-the-bridge noodles), *rǔbǐng* (乳饼; goat cheese) and various Muslim beef and mutton dishes. *Qìguōjī* is served in dark brown – or even rich purple – casserole pots from Jiànshuǐ County and is imbued with medicinal properties depending on the spices used; *chóngcǎo* (虫草; caterpillar fungus, or pseudo-ginseng) is one. Some travellers wax lyrical about toasted goat cheese – the cheese is actually quite bland and sticks to your teeth.

Gourmands may be interested in a whole banquet based on provincial fungi varietals, or 30 courses of cold mutton, not to mention fried grasshoppers or elephant trunk braised in soy sauce.

Do treat yourself to *mógu* (蘑菇; mushrooms) here. Yúnnán is blessed with infinite varieties, many rare and pricey in other provinces but delightfully common and dirt-cheap here. It's a bounty of 'shrooms come late spring and summer, but many are available year-round. Must try? The otherworldly *cháshùgū* (茶树菇; tea tree mushrooms) grow only in proximity to tea trees and are supposedly – we couldn't agree more – infused with their essence.

Zhènxīng Fàndiàn (Yunnan Typical Local Food Restaurant; cnr Baita Lu & Dongfeng Donglu; 白塔路与东风

ACROSS-THE-BRIDGE NOODLES 过桥米线

Yúnnán's best-known dish is across-the-bridge noodles. You are provided with a bowl of very hot soup (stewed with chicken, duck and spare ribs) on which a thin layer of oil is floating, along with a side dish of raw pork slivers (in classier places this might be chicken or fish), vegetables and egg, and a bowl of rice noodles. Diners place all of the ingredients quickly into the soup bowl, where they are cooked by the steamy broth. As the quote below proves, across-the-bridge noodles is the stuff of which fairy tales are made:

Once upon a time there was a scholar at the South Lake in Méngzì (Southern Yúnnán) who was attracted by the peace and quiet of an island there. He settled into a cottage on the island, in preparation for official examinations. His wife, meanwhile, had to cross a long wooden bridge over the lake to bring the bookworm his meals. The fodder was always cold in winter by the time she got to the study bower. Oversleeping one day, she made a curious discovery. She'd stewed a fat chicken and was puzzled to find the broth still hot, though it gave off no steam – the layer of oil on the surface had preserved the temperature of the broth. Subsequent experiments showed that she could cook the rest of the ingredients for her husband's meal in the hot broth after she crossed the bridge.

Prices generally vary from Y5 to Y15 depending on the side dishes. It's usually worth getting these, because with only one or two condiments the dish lacks zest.

东路交叉路口; dishes from Y5; ⏱ 24hr) Come here for what China used to be like. No, not the food, which is exactly as the name suggests: local food done right in a simple atmosphere. Nah, it's the stonefaced (nay, utterly indifferent at times) service. A blast from the past for any old China hands.

White Pagoda Dai Restaurant (Báitǎ Dǎiwèitíng; 127 Shangyi Jie; 商义街127号; ☎ 317 2932; dishes from Y10; ⏱ 9am-9pm) Dai cuisine moves north here, with a slew of fish dishes and, of course, standards such as pineapple sticky rice and spicy fish wrapped in bamboo shoots, all in a Bǎnnà-themed environment of bamboo and thatching.

Yuquanzhai Vegetarian Restaurant (Yùquánzhāi Cāntíng; Yuantong Jie; 圆通街; dishes from Y10; Ⓥ) Trust us – there is actually no meat in the dishes at this fabulous restaurant, but we know you're still going to write emails insisting there is. The menu – with English – is encyclopaedic, so feel free to ask for help (though there isn't much English spoken). It's across the road from Yuantong Temple.

Brothers Jiang (Jiāngshì Xiōngdì; Dongfeng Donglu; 东风东路; noodles Y10-60) A local fave, this simple place has such good across-the-bridge noodles that there are now several branches throughout the city, most of which are filled to capacity at mealtimes. Pay upfront first at the cash register and make sure you get instructions on the eating process!

Salvador's (萨尔瓦多咖啡馆; Sàěrwǎduō Kāfēiguǎn; Wenhua Xiang; 文化巷; ☎ 822 5457; dishes from Y15; ⏱ early-late) Kūnmíng today is absolutely chock-a-block with Western-style cafés. Most are perfectly fine, but there's a reason this one is always filled. Outstanding coffee and a menu ranging from stick-to-your-ribs breakfast through more solid sustenance – even nod-worthy burritos.

Ma Ma Fu's 2 (Māmǎfù Cāntíng; Baita Lu; 白塔路; dishes from Y15) This branch of the legendary Lìjiāng café is right around the corner east of the Camellia Hotel (and there's a third branch now not far from the Wal-Mart, north of Kunming Cloudland Youth Hostel). Chinese dishes are by far the best, but most people order Western fare like pizza and apple pie.

1910 La Gare du Sud (Huǒchē Nánzhàn; ☎ 316 9486; dishes from Y20) Ensconced cosily in a neocolonial building down an alley south of Jinbi Lu, this place has luscious Yúnnán specialities done up in a classy but relaxed atmosphere. There's an English menu available.

Wei's Pizzeria (Hāhā Cāntíng; ☎ 316 6189; Tuodong Lu; 拓东路; ⏱ 8.30am-9pm; pizzas from Y25, Chinese dishes from Y6) The granddaddy of Kūnmíng's Western-style cafés, down an alley off Tuodong Lu, Wei's has been a sanctuary for many a traveller for good reason: capacious interiors warmed by a wood-fired pizza oven, frosted beer steins, and outstanding food (Western and Chinese).

Hotpot Restaurant (Huǒguō; Renmin Donglu; 人民东路) An absolute madhouse at peak mealtimes, you need to be very aggressive or very brave to muscle your way though the throngs and eventually get fed at this restaurant. Nonetheless, with all the slick restaurant and eateries all over Kūnmíng these days, this is a breath of fresh air.

For self-catering try **Carrefour** (东风西路; Jiālèfú Chāojí Shìchǎng; Dongfeng Xilu). This is a branch of the popular French supermarket chain. They're now in a duel with Wal-Mart (trust us, you'll find them too) so between the two you've got about eight floors of food to gorge yourself on.

Drinking

For laid-back atmosphere, the university area is where you want to be. Wenhua Xiang is a good place to start. Seemingly dozens of superloud bars at Jinmabiji Sq absolutely thump the night away. And for hardcore techno, outrageous prices and all around silliness, the Kundu Night Market along Xinwen Lu has dozens of discos frequented by the young, the rich and the (sometimes) weirdly dressed.

Other places to try:

Café de Camel (Luòtuo Kāfēiguǎn; Tuodong Lu; 拓东路; ☺ 9am-late) A legend started years ago by a Kūnmíng rock-and-roller (dunno if he's still in charge but the atmosphere is still cool), this restaurant-coffee shop doubles as a drinking den on weekends when tables are moved to one side and a DJ plays tunes until dawn.

Speakeasy (Shuōbā; Dongfeng Xilu) A great atmosphere here with a mix of expats and locals. It's not too pricey but not a dive, and doesn't have much of a poseur quotient. It's down the stairs under the blue sign.

Shopping

Well, Kūnmíng isn't on any shopaholic's itinerary but it ain't a total wash. Yúnnán specialities are marble and batik from Dàlǐ, jade from Ruìlì, minority embroidery, musical instruments and spotted-brass utensils.

Other items that make good souvenirs: large bamboo water pipes for smoking angel-haired Yúnnán tobacco and local herbal medicines such as Yúnnán Báiyào (Yunnan White Medicine), which is a blend of over 100 herbs and is highly prized by Chinese throughout the world.

Yunnanese tea is also an excellent buy and comes in several varieties, from bowl-shaped bricks of smoked green tea called *tuóchá*, which have been around since at least Marco Polo's time, to leafy black tea that rivals some of India's best.

One teashop worth checking out is **Tian Fu Famous Teas** (Tiānfú Míngchá; cnr Shangyi Jie & Beijing Lu).

Getting There & Away

AIR

Yunnan Airlines/CAAC (Yúnnán Hángkōng Gōngsī; ☎ 316 4270, 313 8562; Tuodong Lu; ☺ 24hr) issues tickets for any Chinese airline but the office only offers discounts on Yunnan Airlines flights. From 8pm to 8am buy your tickets from the small

---

ONE-STOP SHOPPING

The **Flower & Bird Market** (Huāniǎo Shìchǎng; Tongdao Jie) has long been one of the more enjoyable and relaxing places to stroll in the city. It's also known as *lǎo jiē* (old street) and comprises several downtown blocks surrounded by buildings of immense, gleaming modernity and bustle. Flowers and birds most certainly aren't the main draw here anymore, though on weekends the chirping, yawping and cawing can still be heard a block or more away. This surreal hawkers' ghetto and its mazy neighbourhood walk of stalls is chock-full with flora and fauna (well, again, not so much of these anymore), endless curios, knick-knacks, and doo-dahs (the contents of someone's back hall, it seems, on more than one occasion), some occasionally fine rugs and handmade clothing; and a hell of a lot of weird stuff. (Kurt Cobain or KISS T-shirt? Hmmm.) And you can't help notice that the word 'jewellery' has somehow officially crept into the traditional 'bird and flower' name.

The highlight may lie one block west of the intersection of Guanghua Jie and the pedestrian-only Zhengyi Lu. Here in a creakingly old building is **Fú Lín Táng**, the city's oldest pharmacy. Yep, it's been dishing out the *sānqī* (the legendary Yunnanese cure-all root mixed into tea, which costs about Y20 to Y100 per gram) since 1857.

Ah yes, and 'antiques'. As you'll soon note, 'antiquing' here generally means pawing through layers of crap or fakes. As real antiques it's better to look in the privately run shops on Beijing Lu and Dongfeng Donglu.

ticket window on the left side of the building. Rates given here are posted rates – you rarely have to pay these outside of absolute peak periods. Going through travel agents is a good bet for discounts.

A good one-stop shop for booking flights is the **Sanye International Air Service** (Sānyè Guójì Hángkōng Fúwù Yǒuxiàn Gōngsī; ☎ 353 0773; fax 354 3370; 66-68 Beijing Lu), next door to the long-distance bus station. The office deals with more than 20 international carriers and all the national ones.

Flights are scheduled to depart daily from Kūnmíng for Běijīng (Y1940), Chéngdū (Y830), Chóngqìng (Y840), Guǎngzhōu (Y1290), Guìyáng (Y570), Nánjīng (Y1680), Nánníng (Y710), Shànghǎi (Y2030) and Shēnzhèn (Y1370), Qīngdǎo (Y1730) and Xī'ān (Y1100), among many others.

There is a thrice-weekly flight to Lhasa (Y1970), always via Shangri-la; expect fre-

quency to change often and unexpectedly, so plan ahead.

Within Yúnnán province you can fly to Bǎoshān (Y640), Jǐnghóng (Y780), Lìjiāng (Y660), Mángshì/Déhóng (Y790), Xiàguān/Dàlǐ (Y520), and Shangri-la (Y770).

There are international flights from Kūnmíng flying to most major Asian cities including Hong Kong (Y2108, daily), Vientiane (Y985, Wednesday and Sunday) and Kuala Lumpur (Y2256). A new weekly flight to Osaka had also just been announced at the time of writing.

Foreign airline offices in Kūnmíng include the following:

Dragonair (Gǎnglóng Hángkōng; ☎ 356 1208, 356 1209; 2/F Kǎihuá Guǎngchǎng, 157 Beijing Lu)

Lao Aviation (Lǎowō Hángkōng Gōngsī; Camellia Hotel, 154 Dongfeng Donglu)

Malaysia Airlines (Mǎláixīyà Hángkōng Gōngsī; ☎ 316 5888; Sakura Kunming, 25 Dongfeng Donglu) Office is

KŪNMÍNG BUS TIMETABLE

Destination	Price (Y)	Duration (hours)	Frequency	Departs
Bǎoshān	171-202	7-8	4 daily	8am-9pm
Bǎoshān (sleeper)	142	11	2 daily	7.30pm, 8.30pm
Bīnchuān	77-104	6-8	5 daily	9am, 11am, 3pm, 7pm, 8pm
Chǔxióng	36-41	3-4	half-hourly	7.40am-6pm
Dàlǐ	74-126	5-8	frequent	7.30am-7.30pm
Dàlǐ (sleeper)	95	9	2 daily	9pm, 9.30pm
Gèjiù	64-77	3-4	hourly	8.40am-6.30pm
Jiànchuān	98-125	8	2 daily	8am, 7.30pm (sleeper)
Jiànshuǐ	50	3	half-hourly	7.30am-8pm
Jǐnghóng	185-223	9	4 daily	9.30am, 6pm, 7.45pm, 8.30pm
Jǐnghóng (sleeper)	165	10-11	half-hourly	4-8pm
Lìjiāng	171	9	hourly	7.30am-7.30pm
Lìjiāng (sleeper)	139	10-12	2 daily	8pm, 8.30pm
Liùkù	154	11	daily	6pm
Qiūběi	68	6-7	5 daily	9am, 10.30am, noon, 2.30pm, 8.30pm
Ruìlì	222	13	2 daily	10am, 6pm
Ruìlì (sleeper)	209	15	daily	8pm
Shangri-la	142-161	13-15	1-3 daily	8am, 4.30pm, 6pm
Shangri-la (sleeper)	167	13-15	half-hourly	4-8.30pm
Shípíng	55	3-4	hourly	8am-5pm
Wénshān	86-110	6-7	4 daily	8.40am, 9.20am, 10.30am, 3.40pm
Yuányáng	73-82	6-7	4 daily	10.40am, noon, 7.30pm, 8pm

TRAINS FROM KŪNMÍNG

Destination	Cost (Y)	Train	Duration (hours)	Departs
Běijīng	558	T61	40	10.02pm
Chéngdū	215	K114	18	12.38pm
Dàlǐ	90	N987	9	11.26pm
Emei Town	196	K114	16	12.38pm
Guǎngzhōu	341	K363	25	10.40am
Guìlín	230	2055	20	3.53pm
Nánníng	175	K393	13½	7.03pm
Shànghǎi	502	K79	43	3.07pm
Xī'ān	334	K165	39	6.22pm

All prices listed are for a hard sleeper middle berth on the best (fastest and/or most comfortable) trains.

outside, on your right-hand side approaching the hotel entrance.

Thai Airways International (Tàiguó Guójì Hángkōng; ☎ 351 1515; 68 Beijing Lu) Next to the King World Hotel.

To Tibet

It's now possible to fly to Lhasa from Kūnmíng. However, the situation is the same as in Chéngdū and you must have the requisite permit and travel as part of a group. Mr Chen's Tour (p228) can sort you out with the necessary permits and sign you onto a tour. At the time of writing these packages cost around Y2750.

There are also flights from Shangri-la to Lhasa and it's recently become possible to travel overland from Shangri-la into Tibet (see p291). From Chéngdū Mr Chen can also organise overland travel to Tibet, although some travellers have reported his sales pitch to be better than his trips.

There are also trains to Tibet from Chéngdū for independent travel.

BUS

There seem to be buses leaving from everywhere in Kūnmíng and bus transport can be a little confusing at first. The long-distance bus station on Beijing Lu is the best place to organise bus tickets to almost anywhere in Yúnnán or further afield.

Other stations are found all over the city, but if the main long-distance station doesn't have what you need, start with the east bus station or south bus station, each approximately 2km from the city centre.

Exceptions to this are more local destinations like Diān Chí or even southeastern Yúnnán; see Around Kūnmíng p234 for more details on transport to individual attractions close to the city.

From the sleeper-bus stand closer to the train station you can get sleeper buses to most of the same destinations as the train. Buses tend to be older, so ticket prices are generally cheaper.

Buses to Shílín (Y30 to Y40, two hours, every 30 minutes, 8am to noon) leave from Kūnmíng's **bus station** (Beijing Lu), opposite the long-distance bus station. Make sure you don't get dragged onto one of the tourist buses, unless of course you want to spend the entire morning stopping off at various temples and market stalls en route.

TRAIN

You can buy train tickets up to 10 days in advance, which is good news because at peak times, especially public holidays, tickets sell out days ahead of departure.

Trains no longer serve Hékǒu or anywhere else on the narrow-gauge railway that once served the southeast of the province, though China is working with neighbouring countries to agree on a once-and-for-all rail standard to start rejuvenating the network.

Getting Around

TO/FROM THE AIRPORT

Buses 52 and 67 run between the centre of town and the airport. A taxi averages Y20, depending on where you're going.

GETTING TO VIETNAM

With the closing of the rail line, the most common way to get to Vietnam is by taking a bus from Kūnmíng to the border town of Hékǒu (Y119, 12 hours, 9.45am, 1.30pm, 7.30pm, 8.40pm) and then crossing. Note that some travellers have had their Lonely Planet guides confiscated by officials as they cross the border. We recommend you copy any essential details and cover your guide.

The border checkpoint on the Chinese side (☎ 0873-342 1655) is technically open from 8am to 11pm but don't bank on anything after 6pm.

BICYCLE

Many backpackers hotels and hostels rent bikes for around Y15 per day.

Fat Tyres Bike Shop (☎ 530 1755; 61 Qianju Jie; per day Y20) has a large stock of bicycles including some very good mountain bikes. It also organises Sunday morning bike rides – you need to make reservations ahead of time.

BUS

Bus 63 runs from the east bus station to Camellia Hotel and on to the main train station. Bus 23 runs from the north train station south down Beijing Lu to the main train station. Fares range from Y1 to Y4. The main city buses have no conductors and require exact change.

AROUND KŪNMÍNG

Wonderful sights lie within a 15km radius of Kūnmíng; sadly, however, local transport hasn't quite caught up with people's interest in visiting them. What is available is time-consuming, awkward and very, very crowded. There are few crossovers for combined touring, so it would take something like five return trips to see everything, which would consume three days or more.

Arranging a car and driver through your accommodation or seeing what tours your lodging offers is probably your best bet if you want to see everything fast.

If you don't have much time, the Bamboo Temple (Qióngzhú Sì) and Xī Shān (Western Hills) are probably the most interesting. Both have decent transport connections. Diǎn Chí has terrific circular-tour possibilities of its own. If you have more time, get your hands on

a good map, hire a good bicycle and tour the area on two wheels (but be warned, there are some steep hills lurking out there…).

Bamboo Temple 筇竹寺

This **temple** (Qióngzhú Sì; admission Y10; 🕑 8am-6pm) is definitely one to be visited by sculptors as much as those interested in temple viewing.

Raised during the Tang dynasty, the temple nearly perished in a conflagration in the 15th century. Rebuilt, it wasn't truly restored until the late 19th century, when the abbot employed master Sichuanese sculptor Li Guangxiu and his apprentices to fashion 500 *luóhàn* (*arhat*; noble one). One wonders if he knew what he was getting himself into…

Because Li and his mates pretty much went gonzo in their excruciating, eight-year attempt to perfectly represent human existence in statuary, the result – a fascinating mishmash of superb realism and head-scratching exaggerated surrealism – is stunning. How 'bout the 70-odd surfing Buddhas, riding the waves on a variety of mounts: blue dogs, giant crabs, shrimp, turtles and unicorns? That's *got* to be the highlight. The other realistic depictions resemble the impossible – done with the detail of a split-second photograph: a monk about to chomp into a large peach (the face contorted almost into a scream), a figure caught turning around to emphasise a discussion point, another about to clap two cymbals together, yet another cursing a pet monster. (And this is cool: count the *arhats* one by one to the right until you reach your age – that is the one that best details your inner self. Intriguing, isn't it?)

So lifelike are the sculptures that they were considered in bad taste by Li Guangxiu's contemporaries (some of whom no doubt appeared in caricature), and upon the project's completion he disappeared into thin air.

Unfortunately you have to make do with peering your head round the door as the hall has been closed to visitors to stop local tourists throwing coins at the statues – an act that is thought to bring them good luck (it obviously didn't work). If the temple is quiet when you visit (that's a funny thought) then friendly monks might be persuaded to let you in for a peek inside.

The temple is about 12km northwest of Kūnmíng. Minibuses (Y10, 30 minutes) leave when full from opposite the Yúnnán

Fàndiàn from 7am. Minibuses return regularly to Kūnmíng. A taxi to the temple will cost around Y45.

Diān Chí 滇池

The shoreline of Diān Chí (Lake Dian), to the south of Kūnmíng, is dotted with settlements, farms and fishing enterprises; the western side is hilly, while the eastern side is flat country. The southern end of the lake, particularly the southeast, is industrial.

The lake is elongated – about 40km from north to south – and covers an area of 300 sq km. Plying the waters are *fānchuán* (pirate-sized junks with bamboo-battened canvas sails). It's mainly for scenic touring and hiking, and there are some fabulous aerial views from the ridges at Dragon Gate in Xī Shān; see below).

Grand View Park 大观公园

This **park** (Dàguān Gōngyuán; admission Y10) is at the northernmost tip of Diān Chí, 3km southwest of the city centre. It covers 60 hectares and includes a nursery, a children's playground, rowboats and pavilions. A Buddhist temple was originally constructed here in 1862. The **Grand View Tower** (Dàguān Lóu) provides good views. Its façades are inscribed with a 180-character poem by Qing poet Sun Ranweng, rapturously extolling the beauty of the lake.

Bus 4 runs to the park from Yuantong Temple via the city centre; bus 52 departs from near the Kunming Hotel. At the northeastern end of the park is a dock where you may be able to get a boat (Y5, 40 minutes) to Longmen Village (Lóngmén Cūn) and Haigeng Park (Hǎigěng Gōngyuán). From Longmen Village you can hike up the trail to Dragon Gate and Xī Shān, and catch a minibus back into town from near the summit at the Tomb of Nie Er. From Haigeng Park, take bus 44 to Kūnmíng's main train station.

Xī Shān 西山

Kunmingites like to give you the local creed: 'If you haven't seen Xī Shān, you haven't seen Kūnmíng'. And they have a point. Spread out across a long wedge of parkland on the western side of Diān Chí, Xī Shān (the Western Hills) make a perfectly lovely day trip, full of walking (some very steep sections), exploring and discovering all the temples and other cultural relics. Its hills are also called

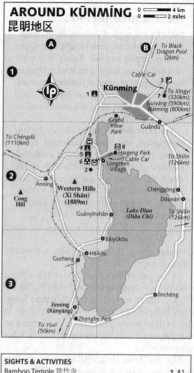

AROUND KŪNMÍNG 昆明地区

0 —— 4 km
0 —— 2 miles

SIGHTS & ACTIVITIES	
Bamboo Temple 筇竹寺	**1** A1
Dragon Gate 龙门	**2** A2
Golden Temple 金殿	**3** B1
Huating Temple 华亭寺	**4** A2
Sānqīng Gé 三清阁	(see 6)
Taihua Temple 太华寺	**5** A2
Tomb of Nie Er 聂耳墓	**6** A2
World Horticultural Expo Garden 世界园艺博览园	**7** B1
Yunnan Nationalities Museum 云南民族博物馆	**8** B2

TRANSPORT	
Gāoyáo Bus Station 高峣客运站	**9** A2

the 'Sleeping Beauty Hills', a reference to the undulating contours, which are thought to resemble a reclining woman with tresses of hair flowing into the sea. (This is certainly more of a draw than the original 'Sleeping Buddha Hills'!)

It's a steep approach from the north side. The hike from Gāoyáo bus station, at the foot of the hills, to Dragon Gate takes 2½ hours, though most people take a connecting bus from Gāoyáo to the top section, or take a minibus direct to the Tomb of Nie Er. It is also possible to cycle to the hills from the city centre in about an hour; to vary the trip,

THE LEGEND OF THE HILLS

The Chinese legend describing the creation of Xī Shān (Western Hills) is one of the most engaging and sad. Before they married, two young lovers who lived in Dragon Gate village at the foot of Luohan Mountain decided to chip stone from the mountain to form a dragon gate, emulating one in northern China.

For years the two toiled but just before completion, the man accidentally broke the tip of a calligraphy brush on a carving. Devastated, he leapt from the cliffs to his death. The young girl was so grief-stricken that her tears filled Diān Chí (Lake Dian). She lay down and turned to stone, forming the rest of Xī Shān.

consider doing the return route across the dikes of upper Diān Chí.

At the foot of the climb, about 15km from Kūnmíng, is **Huating Temple** (Huátíng Sì; admission Y4), a country temple of the Nanzhao kingdom believed to have been constructed in the 11th century. It's one of the largest in the province and its numerous halls have more *arhats*.

The road from Huating Temple winds 2km from here up to the Ming dynasty **Taihua Temple** (Tàihuá Sì; admission Y3). The temple courtyard houses a fine collection of flowering trees, including magnolias and camellias.

Further along the road, near the minibus and cable car terminus, is the **Tomb of Nie Er** (Niè'ér Zhīmù; admission Y1). Nie Er (1912–36) was a talented Yúnnán musician who composed the national anthem of the People's Republic of China (PRC) before drowning in Japan en route to the Soviet Union for further training.

Sānqīng Gé, near the top of the mountain, was a country villa of a Yuan dynasty prince, and was later turned into a temple dedicated to the three main Taoist deities (*sānqīng* refers to the highest level of Taoist 'enlightenment').

From the tomb you can catch a **cable car** (one way/return Y15/30) if you want to skip the fairly steep ascent to the summit. Alternatively a tourist tram takes passengers up to the Dragon Gate for Y2.

Near the top of the mountain is **Dragon Gate** (Lóng Mén; admission Y30). That quote earlier about the Western Hills has a second part: 'And if you haven't seen Lóng Mén, you haven't seen Xī Shān'. Again, there's some validity to this. This is a group of grottoes, sculptures, corridors and pavilions that were hacked from the cliff between 1781 and 1835 by a Taoist monk and coworkers, who must have been hanging up there by their fingertips. At least that's what the locals do when they visit, seeking out the most precarious perches for views of Diān Chí.

The tunnel along the outer cliff edge is so narrow that only one or two people can squeeze by at a time, so avoid public holidays and weekends! Entrance to the Dragon Gate area includes Sānqīng Gé. It's possible to walk up to the Dragon Gate along the cliff path and return via the back routes.

GETTING THERE & AWAY

Minibuses (one way/return Y10/20, one hour, 7.30am to 2pm) leave when full from opposite the Yúnnán Fàndiàn. The only trouble is you could be waiting for ages for the bus to fill up.

It's more reliable to use local buses: take bus 5 from the Kunming Hotel to the terminus at Liǎngjiāhé, and then change to bus 6, which will take you to Gāoyáo bus station at the foot of the hills. Minibuses (Y5) also leave from Liǎngjiāhé and drop passengers off at the Tomb of Nie Er.

To return to Kūnmíng take the bus or scramble down from the Dragon Gate area to the lakeside. Steps lead downhill a couple of hundred metres before Dragon Gate and the Sānqīng Gé area ticket office and end up in Longmen Village (Lóngmén Cūn), also known as Sānyì Cūn. When you reach the road, turn right and walk about 100m to a narrow spit of land leading across the lake. Continuing across the spit, you arrive at a narrow stretch of water and a small bridge. (You could also take the cable car across to Haigeng Park for Y30.) Walk through Haigeng Park's far entrance and catch bus 44 to Kūnmíng's main train station.

If you don't want to pay Y6 to cut through Haigeng Park, you'll have to walk 3km or so from the cable car to the entrance of the Yunnan Nationalities Village or take a taxi (Y10).

Alternatively, bus 33 runs along the western lake shore through Longmen Village, or you can take a boat from Grand View Park.

Yunnan Nationalities Museum 云南民族博物馆

On the northeastern side of the lake, the **Yunnan Nationalities Museum** (Yúnnán Mínzú Bówùguǎn) is worth a visit if you're interested in China's minority nationalities. Its halls display costumes, folk art, jewellery, handicrafts and musical instruments, as well as information – concerning social structure and popular festivals – on each of Yúnnán's 25 minority groups. Closed for renovations at the time of research, it will be reopened by the time you read this.

Golden Temple 金殿

Hidden amid a pine forest on Phoenix Song Mountain is **Golden Temple** (Jīn Diàn; admission Y20; ⏱ 8.30am-5.30pm), a Taoist temple – and actually made of bronze – that was the brainchild of General Wu Sangui. Wu was dispatched by the Manchus in 1659 to quell uprisings in the region but instead turned on the Manchus and set himself up as a rebel warlord, with the Golden Temple as his summer residence. The current structure dates back to 1671; the original Ming temple stood in the same spot but was carted off to Dàlǐ. Out back, there's a 5m-high, 14-ton bell.

Bus 10 or 71 runs here from Kūnmíng's north train station or you can cycle. A cable car (one way/return Y15/25) runs from the temple to the World Horticultural Expo Garden.

World Horticultural Expo Garden 世界园艺博览园

This 218-hectare **garden complex** (Shìjiè Yuányì Bólǎnyuán; ☎ 501 2367; adult/student Y100/50; ⏱ 8am-5pm, last entry at 4pm), about 10km northeast of Kūnmíng near the Golden Temple, was built in April 1999 for the World Horticultural Exposition. The gardens are a mix of pleasant Disney-style topiary work and strangely pointless exhibits left over from the expo; the place is worth a visit if you are interested in gardens and plants, otherwise give it a miss.

Take bus 10 to the terminal. A cable car (Y15) at the back of the gardens can take you to the Golden Temple.

Black Dragon Pool 黑龙潭

This is a rather mediocre **garden** (Hēilóng Tán; admission Y1), 11km north of Kūnmíng, with old cypresses, dull Taoist pavilions and no bubble in the springs. But the view of the surrounding mountains from the garden is inspiring.

Within walking distance is the **Kunming Botanical Institute**, where the flora collection might be of interest to specialists.

Take bus 9 from Kūnmíng's north train station.

Chénggòng County 呈贡县

This county (Chénggòng Xiàn) is an orchard region on the eastern side of Diān Chí. Flowers bloom year-round, with the 'flower tide' in January, February and March. This is the best time to visit, especially the diminutive Dòunán village nearby. Once one of Yúnnán's poorest villages, it now sells more than 400,000 sprays of flowers each day. The village's per capita income went from US$13 to US$415 in four years.

Many Western varieties of camellia, azalea, orchid and magnolia derive from southwestern Chinese varieties. They were introduced to the West by adventuring botanists who carted off samples in the 19th and 20th centuries. Azaleas are native to China; of the 800 varieties in the world, 650 are found in Yúnnán.

During the **Spring Festival** (January/February) a profusion of blooms can be found at temple sites in and around Kūnmíng, notably the temples of Tàihuá, Huátíng, Yuántōng and the Golden Temple, as well as at Black Dragon Pool.

Take bus 5 heading east to the terminus at Júhuācūn, and change there for bus 12 to Chénggòng.

Zhenghe Park 郑和公园

At the southwest corner of Diān Chí, this park (Zhènghé Gōngyuán) commemorates the Ming dynasty navigator Zheng He (known as Admiral Cheng Ho outside China). A mausoleum here holds tablets with descriptions of his life and works. Zheng He, a Muslim, made seven voyages to more than 30 Asian and African countries in the 15th century, in command of a huge imperial fleet. For a bit more detail, see the Hui, p227.

From Xiaoximen bus station take the bus to Jìnníng; the park is on a hill overlooking the town.

Haigeng Park

There are plenty of sporting activities at Haigeng Park – tennis costs Y20/30 per hour in the daytime/evening during the week, and Y24/43 per hour on the weekend. Racket hire costs Y15. There's a driving range with all equipment for hire, and expensive boats available for hire.

SHÍLÍN 石林
☎ 0871

A conglomeration of utterly bizarre but stunning karst geology and a hell of a lot of tourists, this is equally one of the most visited but also most derided attractions in the province. **Shílín** (Stone Forest; ☎ 771 0316; admission Y140) is a massive collection of grey limestone pillars about 120km southeast of Kūnmíng. Split and eroded by wind and rainwater, the tallest of the pillars reaches 30m high. Legend has it that the immortals smashed a mountain into a labyrinth for lovers seeking privacy.

Oft-bemoaned by travellers, Shílín is packed to the gills, every single rock is affixed with a lame name that reads like the purple prose of a high-schooler, and it's pricey. Yet its idyllic, secluded walks are within 2km of the centre and by sunset or moonlight the place becomes otherworldly.

Villages within walking distance from here are populated by the Sani branch of the Yi people and have all been tackily redone for tourists. Less caricaturelike is Lùnán (opposite).

Shílín can easily be done as a day trip from Kūnmíng.

Sleeping & Eating
Shílín doesn't have much in the way of accommodation and what it does offer is overpriced.

Stone Forest International Youth Hostel (Shílín Guójì Qīngnián Lǚguǎn; ☎ 771 0768; dm Y50, s & d small Y120, big Y140) Directly opposite where the buses drop you off, this hostel offers the cleanest, best-value accommodation you will find in Shílín.

Shílín Bìshǔyuán Bīnguǎn (☎ 771 1088; d/tr Y300/360) If you're looking to splash out then the rooms here are quiet and have some good views over Shílín, but you still don't get a lot for your money.

Several restaurants next to the bus stop specialise in duck roasted in extremely hot clay ovens with pine needles. A whole duck costs Y40 to Y50 and takes about 20 minutes to cook – have the restaurant staff put a beer in the freezer and it'll be just right when the duck comes out.

Near the main entrance is a cluster of restaurants and snack bars that are open from dawn to dusk. Check all prices before you order, as overcharging is not uncommon.

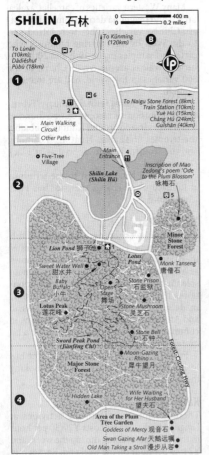

SHÍLÍN 石林

0 ____ 400 m
0 ____ 0.2 miles

To Lùnán (10km); Dàdiéshuǐ Pùbù (18km)

To Kūnmíng (120km)

To Naigu Stone Forest (8km); Train Station (10km); Yuè Hú (15km); Cháng Hú (24km); Guīshān (40km)

Main Walking Circuit
Other Paths

Five-Tree Village

Main Entrance

Shílín Lake (Shílín Hú)

Inscription of Mao Zedong's poem 'Ode to the Plum Blossom' 咏梅石

Minor Stone Forest

Lion Pond 狮子池

Lotus Pond

Sweet Water Well 甜水井

Monk Tanseng 唐僧石

Baby Buffalo 小牛

Open Stage 舞场

Stone Prison 石监狱

Lotus Peak 莲花峰

Stone Mushroom 灵芝石

Stone Bell 石钟

Sword Peak Pond (Jiànfēng Chí)

Moon-Gazing Rhino 犀牛望月

Major Stone Forest

Forest-Circling Hwy

Hidden Lake

Wife Waiting for Her Husband 望夫石

Area of the Plum Tree Garden
Goddess of Mercy 观音石
Swan Gazing Afar 天鹅远嘎
Old Man Taking a Stroll 漫步从容

Entertainment

Sani song-and-dance evenings are organised when there are enough tourists. Shows normally start at around 8pm at a stage next to the Minor Stone Forest but there are sometimes extra performances, so ask at the hotels; performances are free.

There are also Sani performances during the day between 2pm and 3pm. During the **Torch Festival** (July/August), wrestling, bull-fighting, singing and dancing is held at a natural outdoor amphitheatre by Hidden Lake at the back of Shílín.

Getting There & Away

See p233 for details on travelling from Künmíng's bus station to Shílín. In the afternoon there are minibuses waiting at Shílín's car park, leaving when full (Y20).

Minibuses run between Lùnán and Shílín regularly (Y1, 10 minutes). At Shílín, they leave from a stand on the main road. Horse carts cost Y15.

AROUND SHÍLÍN

If you want to get away from the tourist crowds, there are less-visited sights around Shílín.

Larger (300-hectare) rock formations called the **Naigu Stone Forest** (乃古石林; Nǎigǔ Shílín; admission Y40), with karst caves, a large waterfall and an impressive causeway of black volcanic blocks (*nǎigǔ* means 'black' in the local Yi dialect), are 8km northeast of the Major Stone Forest. The easiest way to get to Nǎigǔ is to take a microbus (Y15 one way) or more relaxing horse cart (Y10 return, 45 minutes) from the main road.

Another day-trip option is the impressive **Dàdiéshuǐ Pùbù** (大叠水瀑布; Dadieshui Waterfall; admission Y20), 18km from the Stone Forest. It's a modest 30m wide but it seems larger than its 88m height. Hire a microbus for Y30 from Lùnán, otherwise walk 2km southwest of Lùnán centre, turning left when you see a blue sign, to a small bus stand where microbuses leave for Bǎnqiáo (Y5) and then change for a less frequent microbus – unless it's high season let's say very infrequent – to the falls.

Other places include **Yuè Hú** (月湖; Moon Lake), 15km away and accessible only by hired minibus, and **Cháng Hú** (长湖; Long Lake; admission Y10). To get to Cháng Hú take a bus bound for Guïshān or Lúxī, and get off at Wéizé, from where it's 1.5km to the lake.

Guïshān (圭山), around 40km to the southeast, is an interesting town that has an excellent Sunday market full of Sani traders and is unfrequented by foreign visitors. There is also a remarkable blue church in town that looks like it's been lifted straight from St Petersburg.

LÙNÁN 路南
☎ 0871

Lùnán is a small market town about 10km from the Stone Forest. It's not worth making a special effort to visit, but if you do go, try to catch a market day (Wednesday or Saturday), when Lùnán becomes a colossal jam of donkeys, horse carts and bicycles. The streets are packed with produce, poultry and wares, and Sani women are dressed in their finest.

Sleeping & Eating

Kèxīng Bīnguǎn (客星宾馆; ☎ 779 6725; tr per person Y10, r Y50) On the southwest side of the roundabout is this good budget bet, though it's in need of renovation.

Stone Forest Hotel (石林大酒店; Shílín Dàjiǔdiàn; ☎ 779 8888; fax 779 4887; r incl breakfast Y228-368 + 15%) This high-profile place is right on the central roundabout and has three-star rooms, including transfer from the train station.

There are plenty of restaurants on the street next to the Stone Forest Hotel. The **Línlǎowū Fàndiàn** (林老屋饭店; dishes from Y4) serves good food at bargain prices and there's plenty of fresh produce to point at.

Getting There & Away

Minibuses shuttle between Lùnán and Shílín regularly (Y3, 10 minutes). In Lùnán, flag down anything heading north of the main traffic circle.

Minibuses to Künmíng (Y14, 1½ hours) depart regularly from the west side of Lùnán's main roundabout until around 7pm. For Lúxī (Y12, two hours), catch a through bus at the southeast corner of the roundabout.

JIŬXIĀNG 九乡

The **Jiuxiang Scenic Area** (九乡风景区; Jiǔxiāng Fēngjǐngqū; admission to caves Y30) consists of a series of caves, river gorges and waterfalls. Most visitors take a short boat trip through the Yīncuìxiá (Yincui Gorge) and then follow walkways into Jīnghúnxiá (Jinghu Gorge). After that you enter the main cave hall and proceed through the complex, passing the

Cixiong Waterfall and some impressive limestone terraces. From the exit of the cave a cable car (Y15) takes visitors back to the entrance. There are several other caves in the area. Note that the admission price for this site may be raised, as it's become quite popular.

The area is best visited as a day trip but if you want to spend the night, the **Jiǔxiāng Bīnguǎn** (九乡宾馆; s & d Y80) has decent rooms.

In Yíliáng, 38km away, the **Shuānglú Dàjiǔdiàn** (☎ 0871-753 9444; r Y80-260) on the main highway is a good bet if you can't get back to Kūnmíng. Rooms cost Y260 but may be discounted to as low as Y80.

To get to Jiǔxiāng take a minibus from Kūnmíng's east bus station to Yíliáng (Y8, one hour) and then another from Yíliáng bus station or the road junction to Jiǔxiāng (Y5, one hour). Tour buses occasionally lurk near the Kūnmíng railway station, though the vast majority of them are simply headed for Shílín. If you track one down, the two-hour ride costs Y15.

CHǓXIÓNG 楚雄
☎ 0878 / pop 99,840

Chǔxióng, 185km and two-plus hours west of Kūnmíng, is one of the towns that nearly every Yúnnán visitor grazes transportationally as they whiz toward Dàlǐ, but it's actually not a bad place to hop off for an afternoon of wandering.

Visitors are most intrigued by its heady population of the Yi; indeed, it is the centre of the Yi minority in the county, of which Chǔxióng is the seat. Originally called Elu in the Yi language, the city is also known today as Lùchéng (Deer City). The Yi account for nearly 20% of the city's 400,000 residents; for more information on the Yi see p434. Other minorities with significant populations here include Hui, Bai and Miao.

Chǔxióng's city sights include **Longjiang Park** (龙江公园) in the northern section of the city and **Elu Park** (峨碌公园) in the western part of town. The latter has good views.

Just south of town is the 25m-high **Yan Pagoda** (雁塔), based on the design of the Dayan Pagoda of Xī'ān and dating from the Ming dynasty. It collapsed in an earthquake during the Qing dynasty and was rebuilt.

Buses (Y36 to Y41, three to four hours) depart every 30 minutes from 7.40am to 6pm.

The day trains between Xiàguān and Kūnmíng are the only ones that get you in at a decent time. They depart 8.55am from Kūnmíng and 9.35am from Xiàguān (Y20 hard seat from Kūnmíng) and take 3½ hours.

AROUND CHǓXIÓNG
Zǐxī Shān 紫溪山

This isolated peak in a 12km-long range is 20km west of town. The source of much of Chǔxióng's drinking water, it's a picturesque place famous for the lush red colour of its ubiquitous camellia trees, the cultivation of which dates back more than a millennium (one tree in the park is in fact over 600 years old). The prime minister of the kingdom of Dàlǐ used the mountains as a retreat. When he retired, he built nearly 100 temples, pavilions and nunneries, but earthquakes and wars have left only one – Zǐdìng Sì.

Dàyáo 大姚

About 100km northwest of Chǔxióng is Dàyáo. The feature of this town is one of the oddest-looking pagodas you'll see – the **Bái**

DIGGING IN THE DIRT

Budding palaeontologists and anthropologists will love the Chǔxióng region. Near Lùfēng, in the region's east, bone fragments of palaeo-anthropoids two to eight million years old have been unearthed. Over 120 dinosaurs dating back up to 200 million years have also been found here in what is thought to be one of the world's largest dinosaur burial grounds, and a dinosaur museum has recently been established.

The famed Yuanmou Man was unearthed near Shangnabang village in Yuánmóu, bordering Chǔxióng County, dating Yúnnán's earliest humanlike ancestor to 1.7 million years ago. A large-scale excavation near the Long River unearthed the Dadunzi Neolithic Village. In March 2001 fossilised tusk fragments from a stegadon, or sabre-toothed elephant, were unearthed in nearby Wēishān County.

Most Chinese museums have bronze drums and other relics from nearby Wanjiaba's 2500-year-old eastern Zhou excavation sites. Many of these sites can be visited, though transport is tricky.

Tǎ (白塔; White Pagoda) to the west in Báitǎ Shān. It's hard to ignore its phallic shape, designed to resemble a mallet used to strike an inverted Buddhist bell. The base is an octagonal *samara* (representation of the recurrence of life) while the upper level, reaching 18m, is organised into three structures. The pagoda has a small chink in it, rumoured to be for once-hidden treasure, dislodged during an earthquake.

Dàyáo Zhāodàisuǒ (大姚招待所; ☎ 0878-621 3799; s & d from Y40) is typical of the very cheap local lodging options. Absolutely no frills whatsoever but decent. At least better than any other of the el cheapo options around.

It's easiest to catch a bus here from Chǔxióng, but Kūnmíng's main bus station does have one clunker of a bus per day (Y60, five hours, 7.30am) that heads there.

Shíyáng 石羊

A **Confucian Temple** (孔庙; Kǒng Miào) dating from the Ming dynasty is 33km northwest of Dàyáo, in Shíyáng. It's famed for having supposedly the only intact, original bronze temple statue of Confucius on mainland China. Built in 1709, it is impressive – 2.3m high and 2.5m wide.

Rúguī Fàndiàn (如归饭店; ☎ 0878-637 1089; s & d from Y50) gets most travellers – not that there are that many. Still, it's about as good as it's gonna get here. You can find a few other flophouse guesthouses in Shíyáng with beds from around Y20.

It might be a good idea to go to Xiàguān and/or Dàlǐ via Bīnchuān from Dàyáo if you don't want to slog all the way back to Chǔxióng or Kūnmíng. Bus times are unpredictable.

Yuanmou Earth Forest (Yuánmóu Tǔlín) 元谋土林

Located about 100km north of Chǔxióng, Yuánmóu is the site of famed anthropological excavations and this unique landform. Bizarrely striated sand and clay spires and pillars rise from the flat plains – some formations are so huge they actually resemble cathedrals – and they're given the usual weird names. It's one of Yúnnán's 'Three Forests' along with Kūnmíng's Stone Forest and Xīshuāngbǎnnà's Rain Forest. This freak geology can be found around the region, but is best at Bānguǒ, northwest of Yuánmóu, near the Dongsha River.

There is nowhere to stay at the forest, but Yuánmóu itself has quite a few options with beds from Y15 to Y20.

Buses depart from Yuánmóu for the Earth Forest. In summer you usually do the last leg in a donkey cart. Though Yuánmóu is technically in Chǔxióng County, it's just as close to Kūnmíng and is probably most easily accessed from the capital on any Chéngdū-bound train (hard seat Y35, 4½ hours). Buses don't run all the way to Chéngdū from here. You can also combine it with a trip to Hēijǐng via the train.

HĒIJǏNG 黑井

☎ 0878 / pop 16,155

Most folks' fancies certainly aren't tickled by the thought of visiting an old salt capital. Yet this town approximately 100km northwest of Kūnmíng (it's technically under the administrative umbrella of Chǔxióng County) is, despite the pains in getting there, one of the more perfectly preserved old towns in Yúnnán. Even if the history of salt doesn't interest you, it's got outstanding extant buildings, cool old alleys, and you can even do some sweaty hiking to temples in the hills.

Hēijǐng has been a major producer of the white gold for over a millennium, reaching its zenith during the Ming dynasty, when it accounted for nearly 70% of the imperial salt. The Communist Revolution was pretty much the worst thing that could have happened to the town. After the merchants were driven out and/or executed, salt revenues fell in a big way.

Sights

When you arrive at the gate, you're hit up for the Y30 admission price, which includes entrance to the village, a guide (Chinese only for the nonce), **Dàlóng Cí** (大龙祠; the clan meeting hall) and **Gǔyán Fáng** (古盐坊; an old salt production facility).

This latter site is one of quite a few salt-centric sites in the village and is well worth a visit. You may be surprised how fascinating salt – its history, production, and biochemical necessity – really can be. Seriously. Here you can even pick up a salt souvenir. Earring? Pendant? Don't laugh – cooks from Kūnmíng actually come (or send a gofer) to pick up compressed bowl-shaped blocks of it; apparently, salt is affected geographically like wine – who knew? To get there, just walk east from the village's centre for 15 or so minutes.

Numerous other historical sights relating to sodium chloride are in or near the village, including absolutely pervasive old wells; if you wish, the best one to visit is the **Black Cow Well** (黑牛井; Hēiniú Jǐng) just south of Dàlóng Cí.

Salt aside, just ambling the old flagstone alleys is worth the trip. Wonderfully preserved architecture is everywhere. Temples, ancient gates, old bridges, and on and on. A Ming dynasty **Confucian Temple** (孔庙; Kǒng Miào) is now a primary school. Yeah, the kids love it when a foreigner comes poking around, but there isn't much remaining of the temple itself.

You could also strike off into the hills rising behind the village. Walking northwest from the village centre you'll have to ask for directions to the steps leading up to **Feilai Temple** (飞来寺; Fēilái Sì), not much of a sight but with grand vistas of the river valley. (You can get to the top in 30 minutes or so.) From here you can head east along a ridgeline past a statue and then loop back down into town.

Head in on Sunday; the town has a great market.

Sleeping

One outstanding historic building, now an inn, is the must-stay spot in town, but there are a couple of other preserved courtyard structures that also take guests. Beyond that, more and more standard small family inns and guesthouses are also springing up, most of which have basic singles/doubles with bath from Y40.

Wang Family Courtyard (王家大院; Wángjiā Dàyuàn; ☎ 489 0358; s & d from Y80) A traditional home with courtyard that has been turned into an inn. This one is much more basic than the one listed next, but it's still got decent rooms for the money, especially given the discounts it usually offers.

Wu Family Courtyard (武家大院; Wǔjiā Dàyuàn; ☎ 489 0358; common tr Y120, s/d/ste Y120/180/220) This is the top place in town for good reason. This was the erstwhile home of salt magnate Wu Weiyang, who was executed by the communists in 1949 despite the fact that he had ransomed himself in perpetuity with a cache of silver in 1936. 'Home' may be an understatement – it once had 99 rooms and a propitious 108 entrances. It isn't nearly as

large now but it still holds a huge number of guests and the courtyard and grounds are gorgeous. Discounts are usual outside of summer.

Eating

Salt is the key, no? So you simply must try the *yánmèn jī* (盐焖鸡), chicken that's been soaked and braised epically long in a Hēijǐng salt brine. You might also wish to try *huī dòufu* (灰豆腐), a kind of smoky beancurd, or *niúgānbā* (牛干巴), a local dried and salt-cured beef.

The village doesn't have all that many eateries, but along the one 'main' drag you'll find a handful, including the modest but clean **Jīngxīng Fàndiàn** (井兴饭店; ☎ 489 0506; dishes from Y5), a good place to sample *yánmèn jī*.

Getting There & Away

Your best option from Kūnmíng, sadly, is a slow-ass local train, No 6162 headed for Pānzhīhuā (攀枝花), which leaves the capital at 7.43am and doesn't arrive in Hēijǐng until 1.35pm. At least it only costs Y12. The return train passes through at 12.05pm.

If you want to head west you could switch trains in Guǎngtōng but you're looking at an overnight. From Guǎngtōng you could get on an evening train to Chéngdū but seats are scarce, let alone sleeper berths.

Buses to/from Hēijǐng are a pain in the butt, requiring at least one change – again, Chǔxióng is your best option. A half-dozen buses per day (Y12, two hours) run between Chǔxióng and Hēijǐng.

After getting off the train, indulge in the Y2 horse-cart rides – it's a long slog to the village if you're carrying a bag. From the entrance gate, you can easily walk to the village centre.

XIÀGUĀN 下关
☎ 0872 / pop 136,000

An important FYI: Xiàguān, the capital of Dàlǐ prefecture, is also referred to as Dàlǐ on buses, maps and tickets. So when you hop off your bus, you're probably not in the 'real' Dàlǐ (Dàlǐ Gǔchéng) around 15km north. (Don't worry – if you try to book a hotel room here, you'll probably get asked, uncertainly, if you're sure about that.)

Xiàguān lies at the southern tip of Erhai Lake (Ěrhǎi Hú), about 328km west of Kūnmíng. It was once an important staging post on the Burma Road and is still a key

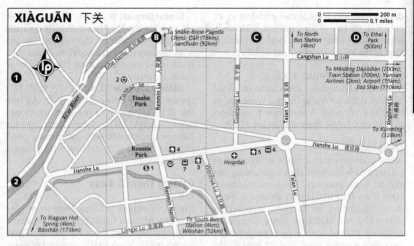

centre for transport in northwest Yúnnán. There is no reason to stay in Xiàguān, you only need to come here in order to catch a bus or train.

To go straight to Dàlǐ, upon arriving in Xiàguān, turn left out of the long-distance bus station, and left again at the first intersection. Just up from the corner is the station for local bus 4, which runs to the real Dàlǐ (Y1.5, 30 minutes) until around 8pm. Bus 8 also runs from the centre of Xiàguān to Dàlǐ's west gate. If you want to be sure, ask for Dàlǐ Gǔchéng (Dali Old City). Both buses make loads of stops along the way, so it's a good way to catch the sights along the west side of Erhai Lake.

Information

The regional **Public Security Bureau** (PSB; Gōngānjú; 21 Tianbao Jie; 8-11am & 2-5pm Mon-Fri) handles all visa extensions for Xiàguān and Dàlǐ. The **Bank of China** (Zhōngguó Yínháng; Jianshe Donglu) changes money and travellers cheques and has an ATM that accepts all major credit cards.

Sights

As far as sights go, there are not many here, yet **Erhai Park** (Ěrhǎi Gōngyuán) does have some worthy vistas of Erhai Lake and surrounding hills. You can reach the park on foot or by motor tricycle for around Y3. Bus 6 goes to the park from the centre of town.

Travel agents around the bus station also sell tickets for day trips up and down Erhai Lake, taking in all the major sights. Prices for the all-day tours start at Y80.

South of the Xi'er River, along Tianbao Jie, is Tiānbǎo Gōngyuán (Tianbao Park), home to the usual brick pathways, old men with birdcages, retiree women exercising, and nary a belching bus in earshot. Most come here for the repaired tombs of the **Pit of 10,000 War Victims.**

The Tang dynasty emperor Tianbao sent wave after wave of troops here in attacks on the Nanzhao kingdom but they were wiped out each time. One general purportedly drowned himself in shame and his spirit haunts a cave on Xieyang Peak west of town (a temple here was built to give it refuge). A park has grown around the peak and it has good views of Xiàguān.

SNAKE-BONE PAGODA (SHÉGŬ TǍ) 蛇骨塔

Good views from here, some 3km north of Xiàguān in Yangping village at the base of Ma'er Peak, but an even better tale. The pagoda was raised in memory of a legendary Bai man who strapped knives to his body and allowed a boa constrictor dragon terrorising Erhai Lake to devour him, which killed the beast. Just south of here, at the base of Xieyang Peak, is **Bǎolíng Sì**, which houses a statue of the local hero and the God of the White Dragon King he killed.

XIAGUAN HOT SPRING 下关温泉

Southwest of Xiàguān, a few kilometres in the suburbs, is this hot spring (Xiàguā Wēnquán) in the Si'er River valley. A small 'resort' with marble bathtubs below waterfalls has been built.

Sleeping

Some travellers stay a night in Xiàguān to catch an early bus from the long-distance bus station, but it's not strictly necessary as buses start from Dàlǐ to Xiàguān around 6.30am. Accommodation in Xiàguān is generally overpriced and midrange, though an excess of hotels at least means you can generally negotiate a pretty good deal, at least in the mid- to top-end places.

Kèyùn Fàndiàn (☎ 212 5286; s & d Y60-120, s/d/tr without bathroom Y30/50/60; ❄) Right next to the main bus station, this place has dirt-cheap rooms with common bathroom and slightly better, though smallish, rooms with private bathroom. Don't expect much but at least the staff are somewhat familiar with foreign guests trying to live on the cheap.

Xiàguān Fàndiàn (Xiaguan Hotel; ☎ 216 1018; 58 Jian-she Lu; 建设路58号; s & d Y100-168; ❄) East of the main bus station, this fading place is still not a bad choice. The opposite of the typical lobby-is-better-than-the-rooms, here the lobby is grim but the rooms aren't bad, particularly if you can score the usual discount down to Y80 or so.

Xiàguān Bīnguǎn (☎ 217 4933; 1 Renmin Lu; 人民路 1号; s & d Y150-288; ❄) Almost directly opposite the main bus station is this option. Though it continually tries to remodel itself into glitz, it still is just better than most other midrange places in town.

Měidēng Dàjiǔdiàn (美登大酒店; ☎ 213 8999; Cangshan Lu, Middle Section; 苍山路中段; s & d Y400-580; ❄) This is one of the best luxury options. A bright lobby atrium leads into the 700-room complex with swimming pool, exercise gym, and restaurant with Chinese and Bai foods.

Getting There & Away

AIR

Xiàguān's airport is 15km from town. The Yunnan Airlines ticket office is inconveniently located near the train station. There are no public buses to the airport; taxis cost Y50 from Xiàguān or Y80 from Dàlǐ. There are three flights daily to Kūnmíng (Y430) and one to Guǎngzhōu (Y1540).

BUS

Xiàguān has five bus stations, which throws some travellers. Luckily, the two main ones are both on the same side of the street, approximately two blocks apart. You might get dropped off at either one. Both have departures throughout the province, so if the long-distance bus station doesn't have a good departure time for you, wander over to the other one.

For Shangri-la (Y50 to Y60, eight to nine hours, every 20 minutes from 6.20am to 8pm) and local destinations you need to

---

XIÀGUĀN BUS TIMETABLE

Buses from Xiàguān's long-distance bus station:

Destination	Price (Y)	Duration (hours)	Frequency	Departs
Bǎoshān	48-58	2½	daily	10.30am
Jiànchuān	20	3½	every 15 min	6.30am-5pm
Jǐnghóng	170	17	3 daily	noon, 2pm, 7.30pm
Kūnmíng	90-126	7	every 40 min	7.50am-7pm
Lìjiāng	41-58	3	5 daily	8.30am, 10am, 2pm, 4pm, 7pm
Mángshì (Lùxī)	98	6-8	1 daily	6pm
Nínglàng	48	8	daily	8pm
Ruìlì	117-131	10-12	2 daily	8.30am, 8.20pm
Téngchōng	85	6	2 daily	10am, 1pm
Yúnlóng	29	3½	every 50 min	7am-4.30pm

catch your bus from the north bus station. Minibuses to Lìjiāng also run regularly from Xiàguān.

To get to Jiànchuān (Y20, 3½ hours) buses run mostly from the north bus station every 15 minutes from 6.30am to 5pm though a few also leave from the main bus station.

Also from the north station but not the main station you can get buses to Bīnchuān for Jīzú Shān. (A third downtown station near the traffic roundabout east of the main bus station also has buses there.)

To get to Wēishān you'll have to slog down to the miniscule south bus station via bus 12 (or a Y8 taxi ride); it's opposite the Kunrui Hotel, near the expressway to Kūnmíng.

Tickets for nearly all destinations can be booked in Dàlǐ.

TRAIN

Four overnight sleeper trains (hard sleeper berths Y67 to Y95) leave Kūnmíng's main train station at 9.25pm, 10.36pm, 11pm and 11.30pm, all arriving in Xiàguān between 5.30am and 8.05am. One day train departs at 8.55am and arrives at 3.54pm; it's cheaper than the night train. Returning to Kūnmíng, trains leave Xiàguān at 8pm, 8.50pm, 9.30pm and 10.20pm. The day train leaves Xiàguān at 9.35am.

Bus 1 goes to the train station from the centre of town.

JĪZÚ SHĀN 鸡足山

Packed with temples and pagodas, **Jīzú Shān** (Chicken-Foot Mountain; admission Y60) is a major attraction for Buddhist pilgrims – both Chinese and Tibetan.

At the time of the Qing dynasty there were approximately 100 temples on the mountain and somewhere in the vicinity of 5000 resident monks. The Cultural Revolution's anarchic assault on the traditional past did away with much that was of interest on the mountain, although renovation work on the temples has been going on since 1979.

Today it's estimated more than 150,000 tourists and pilgrims clamber up the mountain every year to watch the sun rise. Jīndǐng, the Golden Summit, is at a cool 3240m so make sure to bring warm clothing.

SIGHTS & ACTIVITIES

Sights along the way include **Zhusheng Temple** (祝圣寺; Zhùshèng Sì), the most important

temple on the mountain, about an hour's walk up from the bus stop at Shāzhǐ.

Just before the last ascent is the **Magnificent Head Gate** (华首门; Huáshǒu Mén). At the summit is **Lengyan Pagoda** (楞严塔; Lèngyán Tǎ), a 13-tier Tang dynasty pagoda that was restored in 1927.

A popular option for making the ascent is to hire a pony. Travellers who have done the trip claim it's a lot of fun. A **cable car** (admission Y30) to the summit is a good way to cheat, though the ride only starts halfway up.

SLEEPING & EATING

Accommodation is available at the base of the mountain, about halfway up and on the summit. Prices average from Y20 to Y30 per bed. Food gets fairly expensive once you reach the summit so you may want to consider bringing some of your own. There is basic accommodation at **Golden Summit Temple** (金顶寺; Jīndǐng Sì), next to the pagoda – a sleeping bag might be a good idea at this altitude.

GETTING THERE & AWAY

From Xiàguān's north bus station or the bus station a few blocks east of the main bus station take a bus to Bīnchuān (Y11, two hours), from where you'll have to change for a bus or minibus to Shāzhǐ at the foot of the mountain (Y10, one hour).

On the way to Bīnchuān consider a stopover in **Zhōuchéng** (周城), once the administrative centre of the area and another of the important salt capitals. You can check out a 15th-century temple (with a Confucian temple added to it in the 17th century for good measure), ancient bridge and some residual old architecture.

WĒISHĀN 巍山

☎ 0872 / pop 20,670

Some 55km or so south of Xiàguān, Wēishān is the heart of a region populated by the Hui and the Yi. The town was once the nucleus of the powerful Nanzhao kingdom, and from here the Hui rebel Du Wenxiu led an army in revolt against the Qing in the 19th century. Today it's a charming small town with old architecture and strollworthy flagstone streets.

Orientation

The town's central point is the unmistakable **Gǒngcháng Lóu** (拱长楼; Gongchang Tower). North and south of here are pedestrian zones.

To the east five to 10 minutes is the bus station and the road to/from Xiàguān.

Information

No banks can help in town, so stock up in Dàlǐ before you come. **China Post** 中国邮政; Zhōngguó Yóuzhèng; Weicheng Xilu; ☺ 8am-8pm) is just north of the corner of Xixin Jie, about a 10-minute walk west of the bus station. For internet at Y2 per hour, try the café on Weicheng Xilu, located just north of the post office on the opposite side of the street, or the one on Xixin Jie, a couple minutes' walk south.

Sights

Just wandering is all you'll need to do. Besides Gongchang Tower, two other (more modest) historic tower structures are in back alleys a bit north of the bus station. South from Gongchang Tower another 100m, after passing under **Xīnggǒng Lóu** (星拱楼; Xinggong Tower) you'll come to **Menghua Old Home** (蒙化老家; Ménghuà Lǎojiā; admission Y6; ☺ 9am-evening), the town's best preserved slice of architecture. Surrounding a Ming (with Qing additions) compound are rooms filled with the original inhabitants' belongings and other historical artefacts.

Sleeping

Wēishān has loads of options.

Wēishān Bīnguǎn (巍山宾馆; ☎ 0872-612 2655; 52 Dongxin Jie; 东新街52号; d Y40-160; ☒) This government-run place has the cheapest rooms. The lowest-priced ones are actually not that bad. It's a five-minute walk west of the bus station, close to the centre of town.

Yunxi Hotel (云溪会馆; Yúnxī Huìguǎn; ☎ 0872-612 5866; Dongxin Jie; 东新街; d/tr Y120/150; ☒) Not the cheapest in town but, as it had just opened two weeks prior to our visit, it has smashingly fresh rooms (the bathrooms alone are larger than most hotel rooms!) and very friendly staff. Best of all – discounts to around Y60 make it a steal. It's just a hop and skip west of the bus station.

Eating & Drinking

There are quite literally no restaurants in this town other than of the cubbyhole variety. Not a problem, as they're all good. Head north or south of Gongchang Tower to find most of them. Our fave has no name (seriously!) but it's not far south of the tower; it's run by a friendly family. Wherever you are you may see people indulging in a local Yi specialty, baked tea.

Oddly, you'll find a couple of trying-to-be-trendy bars here, including the Hàntáng Jiǔbā (汉唐酒吧), along Ming Jie (明街) north of Gongchang Tower; a beer will be around Y15 at least.

Getting There & Away

Xiàguān's south bus station has buses (Y11, two hours) to Wēishān from 6am to 6pm.

AROUND WĒISHĀN
Wēibǎo Shān 巍宝山

Most tourists to Wēishān – not that there are all that many – are headed for the eminently worthy **Wēibǎo Shān** (Weibao Mountain; admission Y50), about 10km south of town, claimed to be the birthplace of the Nanzhao kingdom. It's a relatively easy hike to all two dozen temples and structures on the mountain (which peaks at around 2500m). During the Ming and Qing dynasties it was the zenith of China's Taoism and you'll find some superb Taoist murals; the most significant are at **Wénchāng Gōng** (文昌宫; Wenchang Palace; No 3 on your entrance ticket) and **Changchun Cave** (长春洞; Chángchūn Dòng; No 1). Along the way you can also espy 50 species of fauna including white pheasant and flying mouse (and the tallest camellia tree in China). Birders in particular go gaga over the mountain and, in fact, the entire county, a node on an international birding flyway.

There is no lodging at the mountain, because it's easy enough to get there from Wēishān.

To get to the mountain from Wēishān you can wait – interminably at times – for shared microvans to leave from a block west of the bus station. If you want to leave straight away, it's easier to just haggle a driver down to around Y40; for Y50 he'll wait there for you.

YÚNLÓNG 云龙
☎ 0872 / pop 8800

Around 150km northwest of Xiàguān and halfway to the Nu Jiang Region, Yúnlóng lies nestled in among the Nu and Yun mountain ranges, populated by more than half a dozen ethnic groups including the Bai, Yi, Miao, Hui, Dai, Lisu and Acang. Most of the press you come across regarding the region mentions an awful lot of mining, but don't let this dissuade a visit. The entire county's scenery – particularly to the north and to the west of the town – can be spectacular; rolling clouds formed from secondary evaporation impelled the name Yúnlóng (literally, 'Cloud Dragon'). In the mountains throughout the county are literally dozens of caves, 'heavenly lakes' and hot springs (along with a lot of interesting ancient bridges). Trouble is, most of these sights are nearly impossible to get to on public transport without flagging something down.

Don't despair, within a handful of kilometres are a couple of outstanding sights: A naturally formed Yin-Yang figure and, further on, a fascinating millennium-old Bai village.

Orientation

Yúnlóng has but a dozen streets and you can cover it in an hour or so. The Bi River (沘江; Bǐ Jiāng) runs along the west side of town north to south (with one tributary splitting off east to west) and everything is referenced to it. The bus station is in the south end of town. Bear left out of the bus station, follow the river, and it'll take you towards slmost everything you need.

MAPS

The lovely map on the bus station wall is the only one you'll find – and its street names don't match those on the actual streets!

Information

Most services are found north of the bus station on Renmin Lu.

Agricultural Bank of China (中国农业银行; Zhōngguó Nóngyè Yínháng; Renmin Lu) They'll smile but be unable to help; stock up on cash before you get here.

China Post (中国邮政; Zhōngguó Yóuzhèng; Renmin Lu) Just west of the PSB.

China Telecom (中国电信; Zhōngguó Diànxìn; Hushan Lu) Exit the bus station and head east 50m; it's on the left.

Jísù Wǎngbā (极速网吧; Jisu Internet Café; Wenbi Lu; per hr Y2) Opposite the Bǐjiāng Bīnguǎn (right).

Public Security Bureau (PSB; 公安局; Gōngānjú; Renmin Lu; ☺ 9.30am-5pm) Unable to help with visa extensions but nice enough anyway.

Sights

If you've got some time to kill, just north of the bus station bearing to the left (before you cross the bridge) sits modestly proud **Panlong Temple** (潘龙寺; Pānlóng Sì), which was shut tight when we showed up.

In the dramatic eyries above the temple sits the town's sentinel **pagoda**, flanked by a **pavilion**. It's a tougher slog to get there than it looks, but the views are grand. In fact,

much of the town is ringed by similar heights and could make for a great day or two of exploring.

Sleeping & Eating

You'll have hardly any problem finding a cheap place to lay your head for the night in Yúnlóng.

Ténglóng Bīnguǎn (腾龙宾馆; ☎ 552 2015; Wenbi Lu; 文笔路; s & d from Y40; 🔲) It certainly doesn't seem like much, with a somewhat riotous canteen-style dining hall next to the reception and faded paint in the hallways. But the rooms themselves are actually perfectly fine and the staff quite helpful.

Bǐjiāng Bīnguǎn (沘江宾馆; ☎ 552 1462; Wenbi Lu; 文笔路; s & d from Y80; 🔲) If you can snag the usual discount down to Y50 (they gave us a suite for this) this is a steal. Everything (usually) works and there's nary a cigarette burn in the carpet.

Yúnlóng Bīnguǎn (云龙宾馆; ☎ 552 4928; Hushan Lu; 虎山路; s & d Y80-280; 🔲) This hotel around 100m east of the bus station is where you'll be led if you stumble off a bus. Spacious compound and attempts at staff professionalism but rooms are the same as everywhere else. You can expect a standard room discounted to around Y60.

For eating, you'll notice an absence of any actual eateries. No problem. Simply walk east from the bus station along Hushan Lu, cross over the bridge and you'll see the town's impressive and laudable 'riverwalk', a flower-shrouded pathway along the dry bed of a Bi River tributary. It isn't a bad stroll, and for most of it you'll find the town's only real eateries – all simple holes-in-the-wall with standard Chinese fare, a few Muslim places, and, careful now, more than one that sells dog (狗肉; gǒuròu; Cantonese, *gauyeuk*). To say 'I don't want to eat dog meat' in Mandarin, it's: *Wǒ bù yào chī gǒu ròu* (我不要吃狗肉).

Getting There & Away

If you're heading for Liùkù in the Nujiang Valley (p297), you'll first have to get on one of two early morning buses for Cáojiàn (漕涧), at the far west end of the Dàlǐ prefecture. From there you'll have to hike uphill one block from where the bus drops you off, turn right (east) and head about 10 more minutes to the highway running through town. From here you can flag down any number of buses

YÚNLÓNG BUS TIMETABLE

Destination	Price (Y)	Duration (hours)	Frequency	Departs
Bǎoshān	35	5	daily	8.20am
Jiànchuān	32	5	daily	8am
Kūnmíng	139	8-9	daily	6pm
Xiàguān	29	3½	16 daily	7am-3pm
Yǒngpíng	16	3	2 daily	9.40am & 14.30pm

(Y13 to Y15, one to two hours) as they pass through. The bumpy and circuitous ride from Yúnlóng (Y22, four hours, 7.30am and 10am) along narrow county roads is a butt-killer, but damn it can be lovely in stretches!

AROUND YÚNLÓNG
Nuòdèng 诺邓
You'll hear much of the 'thousand-year-old village' around these parts, and it refers to this lovely anachronistic hamlet with one of the highest concentrations of Bai in Yúnnán. Nuòdèng, around 7km northwest of Yúnlóng, is unquestionably the highlight to any visit to the area. Ponies and donkeys huff and clop up cool narrow flagstone streets amid buildings which seemingly haven't changed a whole lot since they went up during the Ming and Qing dynasties. A Bai populace indeed – you'll hardly hear Mandarin, let alone English here. Among the myriad architecture you'll find temples, weathered but still proud gates, a Confucian temple now used as a school, ancient burial spots, and the most unretouched Bai courtyards of anywhere in Yúnnán.

And salt. Along with Hēijīng (p241), this village was one of the epicentres of the crucial salt trade. The old Tea Horse Trail (see p277) ponies were lugging not just leafy riches but also white gold as they headed for Tibet, Burma and India. Oh, and the millennial moniker is a bit misleading: the first salt well was set up here as far back as the Han dynasty in the 2nd century AD.

SIGHTS
Entering the village from Yúnlóng, you cross the river and hit the first of the town's many **salt wells**. Grubby today, perhaps, but it was once the lifeblood of dynastic ambition.

Ascending from here you start into your own personal architectural tour. The paths narrow and lead into a wondrous labyrinth of more than 100 ancient dwellings. The village's **salt administration buildings** have got most of the exterior touch ups, not to mention the only English signage you'll see; the interiors, however, are sadly bare. But it's really the nameless dwellings – yeah, they still contain folks living with their chickens with drying peppers everywhere – that make the trip worthwhile. You'll likely be invited in to nose around a few places. Just remember to be polite and not get too animated with the camera.

Of the two shouldn't-be-missed historical spots in the village, first up comes the town's **Confucian Temple**, now home to a primary school. The kids'll eat up a visit from you, even as the teachers try to keep them from getting distracted by the lǎowài (foreigners). Further uphill is the grand old **Yuhuang Pavilion** (玉皇阁; Yùhuáng Gé), built in the 16th century and then rebuilt in the late Qing dynasty after it burned down.

SLEEPING
Gǔcūn Chīzhùdiàn (古村吃住店; ☎ 552 5146; per bed Y10) Smack in the centre of the village, this shop-guesthouse (look for the place with the maps on the wall) doubles as a favourite tea-drinking spot for locals, who linger and slurp their chá (tea) in the shade of a big ol' tree. No frills to be sure but the beds and wash facilities are clean.

Fùjiǎ Liúfāngyuàn (复甲留芳苑; ☎ 552 5032; per bed Y15) At one of the highest points of the village, this original Bai courtyard building is now a cosy little inn-museum run by simply wondrous proprietors who are charming and solicitous. They'll likely pour loads of tea into you and give you a tour of the rooms containing lots of memorabilia and artefacts of the previous owners. More than one traveller has wound up lingering for a week, just wandering about the hills and exploring the old buildings.

(Continued on page 257)

A Hani woman looks out at the spectacular Yuanyang Rice Terraces (p323) in Yúnnán

KEREN SU

Cormorant fishing on the Li River (p166) in Yángshuò, Guǎngxī

DIANA MAYFIELD

KEREN SU

A farmer hangs noodles to dry in a courtyard, Kǎilǐ (p126), Guìzhōu

Live fish for sale in Guìyáng (p101), Guìzhōu

KORINA MILLER

HEIDI LAUGHTON

Market barbecue, Yúnnán (p216)

Zhuang girl drying red peppers on the roof of her house, Lóngjí (p182), Guǎngxī

Old man eating soup and steamed bread (*màntóu*), Yángshuò (p166), Guǎngxī

Waitresses in Lìjiāng (p265), Yúnnán

Dumplings (p73) are a popular snack in China's Southwest

Yak butter, a winter staple of the Tibetan people (p394) in western Sìchuān and northwest Yúnnán

KEREN SU

Long-horned Miao girls in traditional costume to celebrate the Flower Dance Festival (p111), Guìzhōu

Two young Bulang girls enjoying pieces of fruit at a Sunday market in the Xīshuāngbǎnnà region (p324), Yúnnán

BRADLEY MAYHEW

Miao men playing *lúshēng* pipes at a Lusheng Festival in Lángdé (p130), Guìzhōu

JANE SWEENEY

TOM COCKREM

A Bai woman selling batik fabric (p261) in Dàlǐ, Yúnnán

RICHARD I'ANSON

Tibetan man at Horse Racing Festival, Shangri-la (p287), Yúnnán

HEIDI LAUGHTON

A Lisu woman (p297) crossing a river, Yúnnán

Musicians in the Naxi Orchestra (p270) playing traditional instruments, Lìjiāng, Yúnnán

RICHARD I'ANSON

Waterwheel and monument at
entrance to old town, Lìjiāng
(p265), Yúnnán

Backstreets of Lìjiāng (p265), Yúnnán

Riverside, Fènghuáng (p212), Húnán

DIANA MAYFIELD

Three Pagodas, Dàlǐ, Yúnnán (p259)

Chengyang Wind and Rain Bridge (p184), Sānjiāng, Guǎngxī

KRZYSZTOF DYDYNSKI

KEREN

Red Panda, Wolong Nature Reserve (p375), Sìchuān

RICHARD I'ANSON

Visitors on boardwalk alongside Mingyong Glacier (p295), Yúnnán

The mysterious Bo Hanging Coffins (p429) near Yíbīn, Sìchuān

KORINA MIL

(Continued from page 248)

GETTING THERE & AWAY

From Yúnlóng, it's an easy and occasionally picturesque 7km walk to Nuòdèng: follow the river. From the bus station, bear left and walk north along the river. After 100m continue walking past a gas station on your right. After another 100m the road suddenly splits three ways; go the middle route (there will be a white-tiled building in the centre). Near the 2.5km point, you'll pass (but won't likely notice) Tàijítú (below). Note also that at the 3.5km point you'll see a sign with English pointing you to the village. Sadly, the arrow is pointing *the wrong way* (back to Yúnlóng)!

A three-wheeled motorcycle taxi ride there is around Y20.

Tàijítú 太极图

While waltzing along the Bi River towards Nuòdèng, you'll walk right past this amazing coincidence of nature and not even realise it. Or, even if you know it's there, from the ground you can hardly appreciate it.

This is where nature really can seem to be messing with you. The Bi River here is forced into a serpentine roll, and the result, seen from above, is a remarkable naturally formed Yin-Yang symbol. When the weather is right – cooler nights and warmer days, especially November through January according to locals – the mists here are preternaturally lovely. Best photo-op times are mid to late afternoon.

To get to the pavilion at the prime viewing point, you could theoretically hike the seven or so kilometres. The trouble is, it's a long, tedious slog uphill along a gravel road with endless switchbacks. (The rise is only 300m, but it seems like a lot more.) If you're up for it, at the gas station in town head west across the bridge. About 50m after you see a sign saying '天池 22km' go left and up a stone road and start the trek.

Or, more easily, take a three-wheeled motorcycle for Y20.

DÀLǏ 大理

☎ 0872 / pop approx 40,000

Ah, Dàlǐ. Just say the name and watch old China hands grin, thinking of the first of Yúnnán's (nay, China's) backpacker sanctuaries decades ago. Yet today Dàlǐ finds itself getting slagged by quite a few travellers. 'Touristy' has

become a cliché in backpacker discussions and online forums for both Dàlǐ and Lìjiāng and the former is in a losing battle for the hearts and minds of travellers.

Yup, expect a constant friendly invasion of tourists clambering off tour-group buses, way too many souvenir shops, some misguided renovations of streets and structures, and uninterested guesthouse staff – the usual pitfalls of a town gone famous.

Then again, so what? It's still in a stunning location sandwiched between mountains and Erhai Lake and there are still endless fascinating possibilities for exploring and getting to know the region's Bai culture – seriously, if you can't find something to do here, you've got other problems. Just keep wandering the alleys to find your own nook, hike the trails above the town, get on a boat on Erhai Lake or, better, get your hands on a bike and get out of town.

History

Dàlǐ lies on the western edge of Erhai Lake at an altitude of 1900m, with imposing 4000m-tall Cāng Shān (Jade Green Mountains) behind it. For much of the five centuries in which Yúnnán governed its own affairs, Dàlǐ was the centre of operations, and the old city still retains a historical atmosphere that is hard to come by in other parts of China.

The main inhabitants of the region are the Bai, who number about 1.5 million. The Bai people have long-established roots in the Erhai Lake region, and are thought to have settled the area some 3000 years ago. In the early 8th century they grouped together and succeeded in defeating the Tang Imperial Army before establishing the Nanzhao kingdom.

The kingdom exerted considerable influence throughout southwest China and even, to a lesser degree, Southeast Asia, since it controlled upper Burma for much of the 9th century. This later established Dàlǐ as an end node on the famed Burma Road. In the mid-13th century it fell before the invincible Mongol hordes of Kublai Khan.

The influx of Chinese tour groups is changing Dàlǐ's character. The southern part of town has been radically renovated to create a new 'old Dàlǐ', complete with original gates and renovated city walls. Fuxing Lu is now lined with shops catering to Chinese tourists led around by guides dressed up in Bai costumes.

Orientation

Wandering about, you'll see preserved cobbled streets and traditional stone architecture within the town's old walls. Best of all, it's eminently walkable – easy to get your bearings by taking a walk for an hour or so. It takes about half an hour to walk from the South Gate (Nán Mén) across town to the North Gate (Běi Mén). For a good overview of the town and its surroundings you can also walk around the town walls (renovated in 1998).

Huguo Lu is the main strip for cafés – locals call it Yangren Jie (Foreigner's St) – and though every other foreign traveller seems to claim to loathe and avoid it, they're pretty much all there looking for lattes, crispy crust pizzas, cheap garb and bootlegged CDs.

MAPS

Tourist maps of Dàlǐ and the Erhai Lake area are available at street stalls near the corner of Huguo Lu and Fuxing Lu. More useful ones can be picked up at **Mandarin Books & CDs** (Wǔhuá Shūyuàn; Fuxing Lu), along with a great selection of guidebooks and novels in Chinese, English and Dutch.

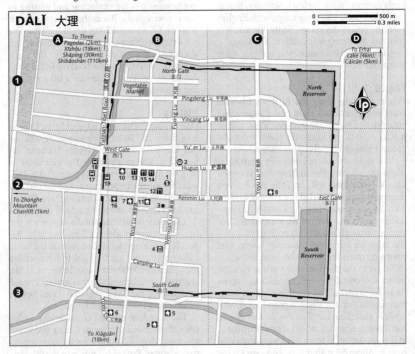

DÀLǏ 大理

Information

All the hotels offer travel advice and can arrange tours and book tickets for onward travel. There are also numerous travel agencies and cafés on Huguo Lu that offer all manner of tours from half-day market trips to full-day trips to Erhai Lake, though it can get expensive unless you can get a group together.

Bank of China (Zhōngguó Yínháng; cnr Huguo Lu & Fuxing Lu) Changes cash and travellers cheques. There is also an ATM here that accepts all major credit cards.

China Post (Zhōngguó Yóuzhèng; cnr Fuxing Lu & Huguo Lu; ☯ 8am-8pm) The best place to make international calls as it has direct dial and doesn't levy a service charge.

China Telecom (Zhōngguó Diànxìn; cnr Fuxing Lu & Huguo Lu; per hr Y2; ☯ 8am-10pm) Internet access. Most hotels also offer free internet access for guests.

Jim's Tibetan Guesthouse (Jímǔ Zàngshì Jiǔdiàn; ☎ 267 1822; 63 Boai Lu; 博爱路63号) Offers a long list of trips, including tours to Muslim markets and Yi minority markets, that are very highly rated by travellers. Jim and his wife Henriette also offer some more unusual trips including trekking in remote areas of Yúnnán and overland travel to Lhasa from Shangri-la (per person from Y5000).

Public Security Bureau (PSB; Gōngānjú; 21 Tianbao Jie, Xiàguān; ☯ 8am-11am & 2-5pm Mon-Fri) No visa extensions here. Period. Years ago the Dàlǐ PSB office started practising its collective stone-faced refusal techniques – most likely because it was simply overwhelmed by backpackers begging second (or third) extensions. Then they shunted off the duties to their colleagues in Xiàguān. (Sigh.) To get there, take bus 4 until just after it crosses the river in Xiàguān. The PSB office is a short walk south from here.

Dangers & Annoyances

The hike up to Zhonghe Temple (Zhōnghé Sì) and along the mountain ridges is super, but there have been several reports of solo walkers being robbed. Sadly, violence has also been a factor in more and more of these robberies. Try to find a partner to walk with.

Be careful on the overnight sleeper bus from Kūnmíng as bags can be pinched or razored. Chain them securely and try cram them under the lower bunk as far back as possible.

Sights

THREE PAGODAS 三塔寺

Around 2km north of Dàlǐ, these **Three Pagodas** (Sān Tǎ Sì; admission incl Chongsheng Temple Y121; ☯ 8am-7pm), are among the oldest standing structures in southwestern China and *the* symbol of Dàlǐ. (Every hotel and restaurant in Yúnnán seems to have a painting or photo of them on the wall.) It's a costly admission price (especially given that you can't actually enter the pagodas), but just watching tourists literally falling off their buses and tearing about to take their snaps nearly makes it worth the price.

The tallest of the three, **Qianxun Pagoda**, has 16 tiers that reach a height of 70m. It was originally erected in the mid-9th century by engineers from Xī'ān. It is flanked by two smaller 10-tiered pagodas, each of which is 42m high.

The temple behind the pagodas, **Chongsheng Temple** (Chóngshèng Sì), also almost makes the admission worth it for the visitor. In traditional Yunnanese style, it has three layers of buildings lined up with a sacred peak in the background. The temple has been restored and converted into a museum chronicling the history, construction and renovation of the pagodas.

DALI MUSEUM 大理市博物馆

The **Dali Museum** (Dàlǐ Shì Bówùguǎn; Wenxian Lu; 文献路; admission Y5; ☯ 8.30am-6pm) is likely the most unvisited tourist spot in the entire region, given the spectacular natural world in which the town is plunked. Nothing else left to do? Give it a shot and you'll see some marble handicrafts (a number of marble stelae grace one wing) and a fairly decent overview of Bai culture.

Festivals & Events

For dates of these festivals, see the boxed text, p219.

Third Moon Fair (Sānyuè Jiē) Merrymaking – along with boatloads of buying, selling and general horse-trading (but mostly merrymaking) – on a human-wave scale takes place during Dàlǐ's outstanding Third Moon Fair, which begins on the 15th day of the third lunar month (usually April) and ends on the 21st day. The origins of the fair lie in its commemoration of a fabled visit by Guanyin, the Buddhist Goddess of Mercy, to the Nanzhao kingdom.

Three Temples Festival (Rào Sānlíng) Just *try* keeping up with the party during this festival. The festival is held between the 23rd and the 25th days of the fourth lunar month (usually falling in May). The first day involves a trip from Dàlǐ's South Gate to Sacred Fountainhead Temple (Shèngyuán Sì) in Xǐzhōu. Here travellers stay up until dawn, dancing and singing, before moving on to Jingui

Temple (Jīnguì Sì) on the shore of Erhai Lake. The final day involves walking – or, occasionally, staggering, or cheating by getting in a horse cart – back to Dàlǐ by way of Majiuyi Temple.

Torch Festival (Huǒbǎ Jié) Held on the 24th day of the sixth lunar month (normally July), this festival is held throughout Yúnnán and is always grand (a ready-made superb photo op if you've got the right lens and film). Flaming torches are paraded at night through homes and fields. Other events include fireworks displays (which go on ad infinitum) and deliriously fun-to-watch dragon-boat racing.

Sleeping

During peak summer months you should brace yourself for a long slog about town in search of a bed, and burnt-out guesthouse staff.

Friends Guesthouse (Dàlǐ Gǔchéng Sānyǒu Kèzhàn; ☎ 266 2888; friendsinn@hotmail.com; 1 Wenxian Lu; 文献路1号; dm Y10, s & d Y50-80) Counting your yuán? Then head to this cheery longtime stand-by. For the price, have an open mind regarding upkeep.

No 3 Guesthouse (Dìsān Zhāodàisuǒ; ☎ 266 4941; Huguo Lu; 护国路; dm Y20; 🖳) A fab staff buzzes about, new wooden furniture fills the rooms with a pleasant pine-like smell, each bunk has a bamboo curtain for privacy, and facilities are immaculate.

MCA Guesthouse (☎ 267 3666; mcahouse@hotmail .com; Wenxian Lu; 文献路; dm Y20, s/d Y100/120; 🖳) Dorms and, well, pretty much everything sport lovely touches like wall art, hardwood floors, and furniture that's actually pleasant to look at; it's almost as if someone cares. Standard rooms have commanding lake views; or you may just wish to loll around the garden and pond. You can also book overland trips to Tibet leaving from Shangri-la here (see p291).

Liùhéyuàn Qīngnián Lǚshè (☎ 267 0701; 415 Renmin Lu; 人民路415号; dm Y20, s & d Y100-200; 🖳) Not much like it in town. Along with loads of extras, each room was designed by local artists and it shows – let's call it funky chic. You'll find a handful of other extras and attitude – of the good sort.

Tibetan Lodge (Dàlǐ Gǔchéng Qīngnián Lǚguǎn; ☎ 266 4177; tibetan_lodge@yahoo.com; 58 Renmin Lu; 人民路58号; s/family ste Y60/160; 🖳) The regular rooms here are a bit cramped (more than necessary space is taken up by those damned unavoidable TVs) but the family suites – ground-floor twins for kids and comfy lofts

for parents – make it worthwhile if you have littl'uns.

Jim's Peace Hotel (Jímǔ Hépíng Jiǔdiàn; www.china -travel.nl; ☎ 267 7824; 13 Yuxiu Lu; 玉秀路中段13号; d Y200; 🖳) Newly opened by a Dàlǐ longtimer, rooms are both sleek and cosy. There's a garden, a roof-top terrace and restaurant and bar below.

If you want the original, **Jim's Tibetan Guesthouse** (Jímǔ Zàngshì Jiǔdiàn; ☎ 267 1822; 63 Boai Lu; 博爱路63号; s & d incl breakfast Y140-200) is still going strong nearby, and you have to check out the great food and company here. Travel services and tours can be booked at both.

Eating

Dàlǐ eateries seem to open almost weekly; and some close just as quickly. Bai food makes use of local flora and fauna – many of which are unrecognisable. However, there are a few things you will most definitely come across. *Ěr kuài* (饵块) are flattened and toasted rice 'cakes' with an assortment of toppings (or plain); these snacks are also found province-wide. 'Milk fan' (乳扇; *rǔshàn*) may not sound appetising, but this 'aired' yogurt/milk mixture (it ends up as a long, thin sheet) is a local specialty and is often fried or melted atop other foods – this is distinct from *rǔbǐng* (乳饼; goat cheese), which is often the sort of cubed cheese you'll get with your tomatoes on salads. Given Erhai Lake's proximity, fish are unsurprisingly a mainstay of most menus. Try *shāguō yú* (沙锅鱼), a claypot fish casserole/stew made from salted Erhai Lake carp – as a Bai touch, magnolia petals might be added.

Bamboo Café (Zízhúwū; ☎ 267 1898; 71 Renmin Lu; 人民路71号; dishes from Y5) Dimly lit and relaxing, this solid place seems to have one of the densest menus you'll find around – the world in a synopsis – but the local faves like Bai fish (Y25) are a great introduction to the local cuisine.

Yunnan Café & Bar (Yúnnán Kāfēiguǎn & Jiǔbā; Huguo Lu; 护国路; dishes from Y5) This town stalwart has always been raved about for its pizza, but you pretty much can't go wrong. The welcoming proprietors really make it special. The breakfasts are well worth the price, especially the Tibetan version (Y18).

Marley's Café (Mǎlì Kāfēiguǎn; ☎ 267 6651; 105 Boai Lu; 博爱路105号; dishes Y5-25) Marley's has always been a cornerstone of the town; now away from the Huguo Lu throngs, it's airier and more relaxing. Well-done food, great service, helpful advice. Check out the Bai banquet on Sunday nights (reserve early).

Tibet Café (Xīzàng Kāfēi; ☎ 266 2391; 42 Huguo Lu; dishes from Y10) A hang-out and thus a good place to eavesdrop or just ask around about what's new, it's also got a solid mix of Tibetan, local and Western food. It's amazingly decorated; you'll feel like royalty sitting in the group dining area. Perhaps the best reason to frequent the place is its pursuits for sustainable development in the Tibetan Kham region.

Jim's Peace Café (Jímǔ Hépíng Cāntīng; ☎ 267 1822; jimsguesthouse@hotmail.com; 63 Boai Lu; 博爱路63号) Folks have always come here as much for laidback Jim as for his great rooms and food. Still, the food is tops. The Tibetan banquet (Y30, minimum four people) in this café is not to be missed, especially when washed down with his 'No 1 special'. See also Jim's Tibetan Guesthouse (opposite).

Drinking

The Western-style restaurants mentioned earlier double as bars. Also worth trying is the **Birdbar** (Niǎobā; ☎ 266 1843; 22 Renmin Lu; 人民路22号), an off-the-main-drag watering hole with a pool table.

Shopping

Huguo Lu has become a smaller version of Bangkok's Khao San Rd. Dàlǐ is famous for its marble and for blue-and-white batik printed on cotton and silk. A lot of the batik is still made in Dàlǐ, and hidden behind many of the shopfronts sit vast vats of blue dye – it's worth asking around at some of the shops to see if you can have a look at how the batik is made. Most of the 'silver' jewellery sold in Dàlǐ is really brass. Occasionally it actually is silver, although this will be reflected in the price.

Most shopkeepers can also make clothes to your specifications – which will come as a relief when you see some of the items of ready-made clothing on offer.

Bargain. Firmly but politely. For those roving salespeople badgering you incessantly, don't feel bad for paying one-fifth of their asking price – that's what locals advise. For marble from street sellers, 40% to 50% is fair. In shops, two-thirds of the price is average. And don't fall for any 'expert' opinions; go back later on your own and deal.

Getting There & Away
AIR

The airport at nearby Xiàguān means Dàlǐ is a mere 45 minutes' flying time from Kūnmíng (see p244). A taxi from Dàlǐ to the airport will cost Y60-Y80 (depending on whether or not the driver thinks you know it's only worth Y60). Alternatively, you can take a bus to Xiàguān and pick up a taxi from there (Y50).

BUS

The golden rule for getting to Dàlǐ by bus is to find out in advance whether your bus is for Dàlǐ or Xiàguān. Many buses advertised to Dàlǐ only go as far as Xiàguān. Coming from Lìjiāng, Xiàguān-bound buses stop at the eastern end of Dàlǐ, let passengers off, then continue to their final destination, from which it's a 20-minute walk to the main guesthouses.

For information on getting to Dàlǐ from Kūnmíng, see p233.

From the bus stop near the West Gate in Dàlǐ there are daily buses to Shangri-la (Y50, eight hours, every 30 minutes from 7.30am to 11am and 7.20pm, 8pm, 8.30pm) and express buses to Kūnmíng (Y106, 9.30am, 10.30am, 4.30pm and 9pm). A slow bus for Kūnmíng also leaves daily at 8am (Y65). Buses to Lìjiāng (Y30 to Y50, every 30 minutes, 7.30am to 7.20pm) also leave from here.

A bus leaves for Shāpíng every Monday morning (Y5, one hour, 9.30am) for the market. At all other times, local buses run regularly to Shāpíng, Xǐzhōu and other local destinations from opposite the bus station in Dàlǐ.

TRAIN

Probably the most popular means of getting to Dàlǐ is the overnight sleeper train from Kūnmíng to Xiàguān (hard sleeper Y93). For more details see p245. Bus 8 runs from Dàlǐ to Xiàguān's train station.

Getting Around

From Dàlǐ, a taxi to Xiàguān airport takes 45 minutes and costs around Y80; to Xiàguān's train station it costs Y30.

Bikes are the best way to get around (Y10 per day). Most of the guesthouses and several other places on Boai Lu rent bikes.

Bus 4 runs between Dàlǐ and central Xiàguān (Y1.50, 30 minutes) every 15 minutes from 6.30am, which means that unless your bus leaves Xiàguān earlier than 7.30am you won't have to stay the night there.

AROUND DÀLǏ

Markets

Usually markets follow the lunar calendar, but shrewd local operators have coopted it into a regular scheme so that tourists have a market to go to nearly every day of the week. See p264 for information on the Monday Shāpíng market. Markets also take place in Shuānglāng (Tuesday), Shābā (Wednesday), Yòusuǒ (Friday; the largest in Yúnnán) and Jiāngwěi (Saturday). Xǐzhōu and Zhōuchéng have daily morning and afternoon markets respectively.

Wāsè also has a popular market every five days with trading from 9am to 4.30pm.

Most cafés and hotels in Dàlǐ offer tours or can arrange transportation to markets for around Y150 for a half day.

Erhai Lake 洱海湖

At the risk of exaggerating excess, this **lake** (Ěrhǎi Hú; Ear-Shaped Lake) has always seemed to have some mystical power to it. Why else would everyone spend so much time cycling around it or ferrying across it? Or just paddling with a local fisher? The seventh-biggest freshwater lake in China at 1973m above sea level and covering 250 sq km, this lake is dotted with trails perfect for bike rides and villages to visit. It's a 50-minute walk from town or a 10-minute downhill jaunt on a bike. Along the way you'll come across a funky old residual residential areas and probably get sidetracked there…

What to do, what to do. A great bike trip is from Dàlǐ to Shāpíng and it can be done in a day. Though the lakeside road may seem the most picturesque, it is too busy and congested to enjoy and you're better off on the secondary road, just to the west of the lakeside expressway. Stop in small villages along the way to buy food and water and you too, like legions before you, will stumble across a forlorn temple or splendid village vista.

Alternately, **Cáicūn** is a pleasant little lakeside village east of Dàlǐ (Y2 on minibus 2) that has a nice local feel to it, as well as the cosy **Darling Harbour Inn** (s & d Y80), with a lovely setting amid camellias; it has a good lounge for relaxing too and the owner speaks some English.

From the village there are regular ferries to **Wāsè** (Y3 to Y5) on the other side of the lake, famed for its market (see above) and for its

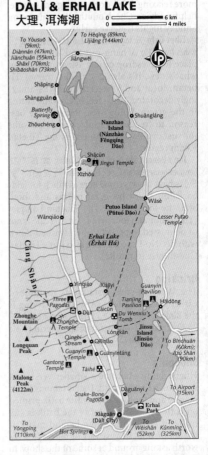

DÀLǏ & ERHAI LAKE
大理、洱海湖

traditional alleys. Plenty of locals take their bikes over. The village also has a few pleasant places to stay.

Ferries crisscross the lake at various points, so there could be some scope for extended touring. Close to Wāsè are **Pǔtuó Dǎo** (Putuo Island; admission to the cave Y12; around Y1 on ferry) and **Lesser Putuo Temple** (Xiǎopǔtuó Sì), set on an extremely photogenic rocky outcrop that is said to have been created by a Bodhisattva (one worthy of nirvana but who remains on earth to help others attain enlightenment) who forgot to finish a bridge between the two islands.

On the eastern shore of Erhai Lake are two temples which couldn't be more different from each other. The somewhat garish white-tiled **Tianjing Pavilion** (Tiānjǐng Gé; admission Y5), also known as the Laotai Temple, wrapped in strings of gargantuan Christmas tree lights, is on a high spot with magnificent views of the lake, especially when the sun shines. Look for the fresco in the ceiling.

On the other side of the bulbous promontory and literally decaying in the weeds amid munching cattle is the better-known **Guanyin Pavilion** (Guānyīn Gé), also known as the Luoquan Temple. According to legend, this was the place where the clandestine lover of a Nanzhao princess was turned into a stone donkey by a master when the princess defied her father's arranged marriage.

Private boat owners at Cáicūn offer return trips to Hǎidōng for about Y100 for the boat.

Just south of the two temples is tiny Jinsu Island (Jīnsūo Dǎo), a canoe-shaped rock 800m by 2000m. It draws tourists mostly for its **Dragon Jade Palace** (admission incl guide Y12), a subterranean network of caves packed with the over-the-top kitsch that is tourist caving in China. Otherwise, just wander around the island through some fairly traditional alleys. After disembarking from your boat (fare Y1), follow the storefronts to the left, and then right on the first alley. You'll come to a small temple and home to a senior citizen centre where old men thwap their plastic checkers around.

North of all the hoopla around Hǎidōng is **Nánzhào Fēngqíng Dǎo** (Nanzhao Island; admission Y22), which has a 7m-high white Buddha and some fairly nice walking trails. It's just a short hop south of **Shuānglǎng** village, a fishing hot spot also known as Double Corridor Village, with interesting old Bai architecture along its alleys. It's probably one of the better versions of a sleepy old Erhai Lake village remaining; those on the western side are pretty much invaded by tourists nonstop. Boats here cost Y50 return.

Other ferries run between Lóngkǎn and Hǎidōng, and between Xiàguān and Jīnsūo Dǎo (Jinsuo Island). Ferries leave early in the morning (for the market) and return around 4pm; timetables are flexible and departures are somewhat unreliable.

Roads now encircle the lake so it is possible to do a loop (or partial loop) of the lake by mountain bike. A few intrepid travellers have leapfrogged these villages, made for Shāpíng's market, then continued all the way around the lake stopping at other markets on the way before boating themselves and their bicycles back to Dàlǐ. Even if you're not into markets you could still do a loop, or partial loop of the lake by mountain bike taking in Xǐzhōu, Zhōuchéng, Shāpíng and Wāsè. You could ride around the lake clockwise from Dàlǐ to Hǎidōng and take the ferry back to Lóngkǎn. A shorter option would be to cycle to Wāsè (57km) and then return to Dàlǐ (via Cáicūn) by ferry.

Plenty of cafés can arrange a horse-and-carriage ride to the lake, then a boat ride to Tianjing Pavilion and Guanyin Pavilion, then Jīnsūo Dǎo or whatever else you dream up. Shop around as prices vary. On the cheaper end, for around Y40 to Y50 per person in a group of around four you can get a round trip to Erhai Lake on a horse-cart, then transport to a couple of spots on the lake. Many possible routes exist, so ask around.

Zhonghe Temple 中和寺

This **temple** (Zhōnghé Sì; admission Y2) is a long, steep hike up the mountainside behind Dàlǐ. To reach the top take the **chairlift** (one way/return Y30/50) up **Zhōnghé Shān** (Zhonge Mountain). Note that the temple may soon also charge Y30, which would keep it on par with the rest of China as it ramps up fees at every attraction in the country. You'll have no trouble whatsoever finding a guy offering pony rides around here; possible tours are infinite but figure on Y70 for a standard ride.

You can also hike up the hill, a sweaty two to three hours for those in moderately good shape (see also Dangers & Annoyances, p259). Walk about 200m north of the chairlift base to the riverbed (often dry). Follow the left bank for about 50m and walk through the cemetery. Follow the path zigzagging under the chairlift. When you reach some stone steps you know you are near the top. Naturally, however, there are oodles and oodles of horse and human paths, dead ends, dry creek beds and the like out there, so you could wind up either hopelessly lost or wonderfully challenged. In fact, this is half the fun of this area – there are tons of tourists around, but it's probably the easiest popular place in the province to lose the crowds.

Branching out from either side of the temple is a trail that winds along the face of the mountains, taking you in and out of steep, lush valleys and past streams and waterfalls.

From Zhōnghé it's an amazing 11km up-and-down hike south to Gantong Temple (below), which serves vegetarian meals for lunch, or to **Qingbi Stream** (Qīngbì Xī), a scenic picnic spot near the village of Qīlǐqiáo 3km from Dàlǐ on the way to Xiàguān. Locals say it's the most picturesque of the 20 or so small creeks. After hiking 4km up a path running close to the river, you'll reach three ponds. There's also a new cable car between the two temples (one way/return Y52/82).

One peak south of Zhōnghé Shān is **Lóngquán Shān**, and halfway up that is Putuo Cliff and Phoenix Cave (Lóngfèngyǎn Dòng), which leads right through the back of the mountain. All in all it's about 9km if you walk from the south gate of Dàlǐ to Lóngquán Shān and then up. There are no really good trails, so figure out how to get there before you go by having a chat with the people who run your guesthouse.

Alternatively, you can spend some more time here on the mountain and stay the night at **Higherland Inn** (Gāodì lǚguǎn; 高地旅馆; ☎ 266 1599; www.higherland.com; dm/s/d Y25/30/50), located just above Zhonghe Temple at 2590m. If you want to get away from the crowds in Dàlǐ then this is the place to do it. The hostel has fabulous views, regular barbecues and bonfire parties and only a handful of rooms (seven), which means it's an incredibly relaxing place to stay. You can reserve rooms at the booking office near the northeast corner of Renmin Lu and Boai Lu in Dàlǐ.

Guanyin Temple 观音堂

This temple (Guānyīn Táng; Y10) is built over a large boulder that locals believe was placed there by Guanyin, the Buddhist Goddess of Mercy, disguised as an old woman in order to block the advance of an invading enemy. On the 19th of the third, sixth and ninth lunar months, people flock here to worship Guānyīn. It is 5km south of Dàlǐ at the base of Foding Peak. If you follow the path uphill for 3km you will come across another temple, **Gantong Temple** (Gàntōng Sì). Built during the Tang dynasty, it once had three dozen subtemples, all of which were destroyed in Qing dynasty uprisings. Supposedly, many poets and government officials retired here as monks, and even an emperor of the Ming dynasty considered being a monk there (he wrote a poem about it instead).

Xīzhōu 喜洲

The sleepy town of Xīzhōu has always been a major stop for wanderers given its well-preserved Bai architecture. Not to mention its location, plunked along the main road north of Dàlǐ. To be honest, this place has gone under the paintbrush quite a bit and is a popular spot for tour buses to unload their hordes to watch 'traditional' Bai dancing in old courtyards. Still, it's a nice place to just wander around. You can catch a local bus from the south gate in Dàlǐ (Y3) or take a taxi (Y30 to Y35) to make the 18km trip. A bicycle trip with an overnight stop in Xīzhōu (there's accommodation in town) is also a good idea.

From here, the interesting town of **Zhōuchéng** (周城) is 7km further north; it too has basic accommodation. This pretty village is also right by the roadside and spreads uphill from a market square, which is dominated by several ancient trees. About 30m uphill along the main street a side alley leads off to the right. A house at the end of the lane on the left sells indigo cloth that it dyes on the spot.

Nearby **Shācūn** (沙村) village is one of the last places on the lake where you might find cormorant fishing. You could easily combine Xīzhōu with a bike trip to Zhōuchéng and Shāpíng market.

Shaping Market 沙坪赶集

Every Monday at Shāpíng, about 30km north of Dàlǐ, there is a colourful Bai **market** (Shāpíng Gǎnjí). The market cranks up around 10am and ends around 2.30pm. You can buy everything from tobacco, melon seeds and noodles to meat, jewellery and wardrobes. In the ethnic clothing line, you can look at shirts, headdresses, embroidered shoes and moneybelts, as well as local batik. Gentlefolks, start your bargaining engines.

Getting to Shaping Market from Dàlǐ is fairly easy. Head out on the road to Lìjiāng and flag down anything heading north. Some of the hotels and cafés in town also run minibuses. By bike it will take about two hours at a good clip.

Butterfly Spring 蝴蝶泉

Butterfly Spring (Húdié Quán) is about 30km north of Dàlǐ. The inevitable legend associated with the spring is that two lovers committed suicide here to escape a cruel king.

After jumping into the bottomless pond, they turned into two of the butterflies that gather here en masse during May.

If you're energetic you could cycle to the spring but most people find it a bit of a tourist trap. Since it is only 4km from Shāpíng, you could also combine it with a visit to the Shāpíng market.

LÌJIĀNG 丽江

new town ☎ 08891, old town ☎ 0888 / old town pop 40,000

Lìjiāng's maze of cobbled streets, rickety-looking wooden buildings and gushing canals suck in nearly 12% of Yúnnán's total tourist population. Yes, those same tour buses disgorging the hordes in Dàlǐ also inevitably call here – and they all manage to get snarled up in epic waves of human jams in the town's tiny alleys.

Seriously – it can at times be like being at a football match in the cheap seats.

But don't let the crowds or any bitchy travellers – and oh Lord are there enough of those – discourage a trip. Like every other tourist-overwhelmed spot on earth, there's still plenty of *there* there. If you look. Get up early enough and it will be just you and a few bun sellers. Then beat a retreat into the delightful labyrinth of the old streets. Soon it will be just you.

In 1996 an earthquake measuring over seven on the Richter scale rocked the Lìjiāng area, killing more than 300 people and injuring 16,000. The Chinese government took note of how the traditional Naxi buildings held up and sank millions of yuán into rebuilding most of Lìjiāng County with traditional Naxi architecture, replacing cement with cobblestone and

---

THE NAXI 纳西

Lìjiāng has been the base of the 286,000 strong Naxi (also spelt Nakhi and Nahi) minority for about the last 1400 years. The Naxi descend from ethnically Tibetan Qiang tribes and lived until recently in matrilineal families. Since local rulers were always male it wasn't truly matriarchal, but women still seem to run the show, certainly in the old part of Lìjiāng.

The Naxi matriarchs maintained their hold over the men with flexible arrangements for love affairs. The *azhu* (friend) system allowed a couple to become lovers without setting up joint residence. Both partners would continue to live in their respective homes; the boyfriend would spend the nights at his girlfriend's house but return to live and work at his mother's house during the day. Any children born to the couple belonged to the woman, who was responsible for bringing them up. The man provided support, but once the relationship was over, so was the support. Children lived with their mothers, and no special effort was made to recognise paternity. Women inherited all property, and disputes were adjudicated by female elders.

There are strong matriarchal influences in the Naxi language. Nouns enlarge their meaning when the word for 'female' is added; conversely, the addition of the word for 'male' will decrease the meaning. For example, 'stone' plus 'female' conveys the idea of a boulder; 'stone' plus 'male' conveys the idea of a pebble.

Naxi women wear blue blouses and trousers covered by a blue or black apron. The T-shaped traditional cape not only stops the basket worn on the back from chafing, but also symbolises the heavens. Day and night are represented by the light and dark halves of the cape; seven embroidered circles symbolise the stars. Two larger circles, one on each shoulder, are used to depict the eyes of a frog, which until the 15th century was an important god to the Naxi. With the decline of animist beliefs, the frog eyes fell out of fashion, but the Naxi still call the cape by its original name, 'frog-eye sheepskin'.

The Naxi created a written language over 1000 years ago using an extraordinary system of pictographs – the only hieroglyphic language still in use. The most famous Naxi text is the Dongba classic *Creation,* and ancient copies of it and other texts can still be found in Lìjiāng, as well as in the archives of some US universities. The Dongba were Naxi shamans who were caretakers of the written language and mediators between the Naxi and the spirit world. The Dongba religion, itself an offshoot of Tibet's pre-Buddhist Bon religion, eventually developed into an amalgam of Tibetan Buddhism, Islam and Taoism. The Tibetan origins of the Naxi are confirmed by references in Naxi literature to Lake Manasarovar and Mt Kailash, both in western Tibet.

Useful phrases in the Naxi language are: '*nuar lala*' (hello) and '*jiu bai sai*' (thank you).

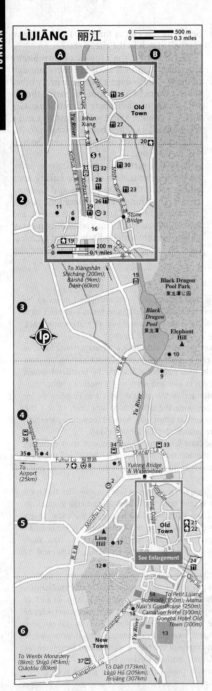

wood. The UN placed all of Lìjiāng County on its World Heritage site list in 1999.

Orientation

Lìjiāng, in northwest Yúnnán, is separated into old and new towns which are starkly different. The approximate line of division is Shīzī Shān (Lion Hill), the green hump in the middle of town that's topped by the Looking at the Past Pavilion. Everything west of the hill is the new town, and everything east is the old town. You *will* get lost in the old town; just follow a stream upstream, all of which lead back toward the centre.

MAPS
Map are everywhere you look, basically. You can get some lovely fold-out maps that are designed to look aged; these are amazingly detailed but, naturally, don't have much English.

Information
Lìjiāng's cafés and backpacker inns are your best source of information on the area. Most have noticeboards and travellers books full of useful tips and advice on surrounding sights, especially the Tiger Leaping Gorge trek.

Bookshops don't have much but you might duck into a chichi hotel and keep an eye out for the *Lijiang Travel Guide*, a tourist rag with relatively up-to-the-minute information on routes, prices and other practical information.

BOOKSHOPS
Mandarin Book & CDs (Lìjiāng Wǔhuá Shūyuàn; Xinhua Jie) Has a fantastic choice of English books and maps on Lìjiāng and the region. Also German, French and other foreign language titles.

CD BURNING
Kodak (Fuhui Lu; per CD Y20)

INTERNET ACCESS
There are lots of places in the old town where you can go online. Prague Café (p269) charges Y5 per hour.

MONEY
Bank of China (Zhōngguó Yínháng; Dong Dajie) This branch is in the old town and has an ATM machine.

POST & TELEPHONE
Many of the backpacker cafés in the old town have IDD lines.
China Post (Zhōngguó Yóuzhèng; Minzhu Lu; ☯ 8am-8pm) Offers Express Mail Service (EMS), so your postcards might actually make it home before you do. Another post office is in the old town just north of Old Market Sq.
China Telecom (Zhōngguó Diànxìn; Minzhu Lu) Next door to China Post; you can make international calls from here.

PUBLIC SECURITY BUREAU
PSB (Gōngānjú; ☎ 518 8437; Fuhui Lu; ☯ 8.30-11.30am & 2.30-5.30pm Mon-Fri) Reputedly very speedy with visa extensions.

TOURIST INFORMATION & TRAVEL AGENCIES
There's a slew of Travel Reception Centres all over the old town but they mostly arrange tours. The best place for info is your accommodation.
China International Travel Service (CITS; Zhōngguó Guójì Lǚxíngshè; ☎ 516 0369; 3rd fl, Lifang Bldg, cnr Fuhui Lu & Shangrila Dadao) Can arrange tours in and around Lìjiāng.
Eco-tours (☎ 131-7078 0719; www.ecotourchina .com) Run by Zhao Fan at the Buena Vista Club (p274). He can organise tours to nearly anywhere you want to go in northern Yúnnán, as well as trekking and camping trips in less well-known areas. Avid bike-riders should check out his free maps of Ljiāng-area cycling trails.

Dangers & Annoyances
It's a pickpocket heyday in the old town, so *always* keep an arm clamped on your valuables. Solo female travellers have also been accosted when walking alone at night in isolated areas of historic Lìjiāng. Take care if travelling alone to isolated sights like Xiàng Shān (Elephant Hill) in Black Dragon Pool Park (Hēilóngtán Gōngyuán); there have been reports of muggings, a few of them violent.

Sights
An interesting local historical tidbit has it that the original Naxi chieftain would not allow the **old town** to be girdled by a city wall because drawing a box around the Chinese character of his family name would change the character from *mù* (wood) to *kún* (surrounded, or hard-pressed).

Hydrophiles will go absolutely gaga over this place. The old town is dissected by a web of arterylike canals that once brought the city's drinking water from Yuquan Spring, in what is now Black Dragon Pool Park. There are several wells and pools still in use around town. Where there are three pools, these were designated into pools for drinking, washing clothes and washing vegetables. A famous example of these is the **Báimǎ Lóngtán** (White Horse Dragon) pool in the south of the old town. You can see one of the original wells opposite the Well Bistro. (Sadly, the days – not too long ago – when you would see locals washing their veggies in the streams after heading home from the market are a bit unthinkable now.)

The town once had several water wheels, though the only one left now is Yulong Bridge

Waterwheel, a reconstructed model at the north edge of the old town. The nearby monument celebrates Lìjiāng's status as a Unesco World Heritage site.

The focus of the old town is **Old Market Sq** (Sìfāng Jiē) Once the haunt of Naxi traders, they've long since made way for tacky souvenir stalls. However, the view up the hill and the surrounding lanes are still extraordinary, just be prepared to share the experience with hundreds if not thousands of other people.

To the west of the square is the **Kegong Archway**, which is the scene of celebrations marking the birthday of the local god Sanduo on the eighth day of the second lunar month (March).

Above the old town is a beautiful **park** that can be reached on the path leading past the radio mast. Sit on the slope in the early morning and watch the mist clearing as the old town comes to life. Here acting as sentinel of sorts for the town, the **Looking at the Past Pavilion** (Wànggǔ Lóu; admission Y15) was raised for tourists at a cost of over one million yuán. It's famed for a unique design using dozens of four-storey pillars – unfortunately these were culled from northern Yúnnán old-growth forests. A path (with English signs) leads from Old Market Sq.

MU FAMILY MANSION 木氏土司府

The former home of a Naxi chieftain, the **Mu Family Mansion** (Mùshì Tǔsī Fǔ; admission Y35; ⏱ 8.30am-5.30pm) was heavily renovated (more like built from scratch) after the 1996 earthquake, using funds from the World Bank. The six main halls and courtyards were rebuilt to resemble a mini Forbidden City, some say deliberately, to reinforce historical Chinese ties to Lìjiāng. The mansion backs onto Shīzǐ Shān. Inadequate captions help non-Chinese speakers not a bit but many travellers find the beautiful grounds reason enough to visit.

BLACK DRAGON POOL PARK 黑龙潭公园

On the northern edge of town is the **Black Dragon Pool Park** (Hēilóngtán Gōngyuán; Xin Dajie; admission Y60, free after 6pm; ⏱ 7am-7pm). Apart from strolling around the pool – its view of Yùlóng Xuěshān (Jade Dragon Snow Mountain) is the most obligatory photo shoot in southwestern China – you can visit the **Dongba Research Institute** (Dōngbā Wénhuà Yánjiūshì) which is part of a renovated complex on the hillside. Here you can see Naxi cultural artefacts and scrolls featuring a unique pictograph script.

At the far side of the pool are buildings used for an art exhibition, a pavilion with its own bridge across the water and the Ming dynasty **Five Phoenix Hall** (Wǔfèng Lóu), a striking Naxi 20m-high edifice dating from 1601 but only moved to its current location in 1979. Its three roofs with eight eaves each are supposedly in the shape of phoenixes.

Trails lead straight up **Xiàng Shān** (Elephant Hill) to a dilapidated gazebo and then across a spiny ridge past a communications centre and back down the other side, making a nice morning hike. See also Dangers & Annoyances, p267.

The **Museum of Naxi Dongba Culture** (Nàxī Dōngbā Wénhuà Bówùguǎn; admission Y5; ⏱ 8.30am-5.30pm) is at the park's northern entrance, and is worth a visit if you have the time. There are displays on Naxi dress and culture, Dōngbā script, Lìjiāng's old town and the dubious claim that the region is the 'real' Shangri-la.

Festivals & Events

The 13th day of the third moon (late March or early April) is the traditional day to hold a **Fertility Festival**.

July brings the **Torch Festival** (Huǒbǎ Jié), also celebrated by the Bai in the Dàlǐ region and the Yi all over the southwest. The origin of this festival can be traced back to the intrigues of the Nánzhào kingdom. A king desired the wife of a subject and so had the man burned to death. Rather than submit to his entreaties, she showed her loyalty by leaping into the fire and immolating herself. The festival isn't quite so sombre.

Sleeping

No shortage of charming Naxi-style lodgings here. It seems that every day a new place opens up (but not that many close). Note that prices can spike in July and August and especially during holidays.

Mama Naxi's Guesthouse (古城香格韵客栈 Gǔchéng Xiānggéyùn Kèzhàn; ☎ 510 0700; 78 Wenhua Lane, Wuyi Jie; 五一街文化巷78号; dm Y15, s & d from Y50; 🖳) This place's enormous popularity derives mainly from Mama's dynamic personality; you'll be glad to have her looking out for you (but go easy on her – she's exhausted). It's packed, a bit chaotic (though well run and clean) but eminently fun. Midnight curfew.

FYI: kitties pretty much have the run of the place.

International Youth Hostel Lijiang (丽江老谢车马店; Lìjiāng Lǎoxiè Chēmǎ Diàn; ☎ 511 6118; 25 Jishan Alley, Xinyi Jie; 新义街 积善巷25号; dm Y20, s Y40-120, d 100-140, tr 150-180) Well-kept rooms of every conceivable variation and touches like flowers or patterned bedspreads set it apart from the generic hostels in town. You can also rent bikes here for Y15 per day. Hot water from 6pm to 2am only.

Dongba Hotel Old Town (东巴客栈; Dōngbā Kèzhàn; ☎ 512 1975; www.dongbahotel.com; 109 Wenzhi Alley; 文治巷109号; dm Y25, s/d/tr from Y60; 🖳) A number of the inns in this 'neighbourhood' of alleys are quite nice and this is the cheapest, which isn't to demean its quality. Good clean dorms and friendly service, well-recommended by numerous travellers.

Good Luck Inn (鸿运客栈; Hóngyùn Kèzhàn; ☎ 512 4748; 21 Huangshan Lane, Xinhua Jie; 新华街、黄山段21号; s & d Y50-80) The town is simply overloaded with 'family-style' inns, and this is a good option: it's hospitable, helpful (despite a dearth of English) and clean.

Carnation Hotel (康乃馨客栈; Kāngnǎixīn Kèzhàn; ☎ 511 1237, 511 7306; ewan_215@yahoo.com.cn; 134 Wenzhi Alley; 文治巷134号; s & d Y50-120, Jul-Aug Y150; 🖳) Smack next to the Dongba Hotel Old Town, this is definitely one of the best in town, with solicitous owners – chatty with some English – and comfy rooms set around a large courtyard. Breakfasts also come recommended.

Moon Inn (新月阁客栈; Xīnyuègé Kèzhàn; ☎ 518 0520; mooninn@163.com; 34 Xingren Xiaduan, Wuyi Jie; 五一街、兴仁下段34号; s & d Y200; i) A casual but mod place, its bright and breezy rooms have wood furniture and fetching colours. The courtyard is lovely and there's a relaxing common room as well. Breakfast Y10, dinner Y20 per person.

Zen Garden Hotel (瑞和园酒店; Ruìhéyuán Jiǔdiàn; ☎ 518 9799; www.zengardenhotel.com; 36 Xingren Lane, Wuyi Jie; 五一街、兴仁段36号; d Y400, 'wedding rooms' Y1400) This sybaritic place, run by a Naxi teacher and decorated with help from her artist brother, is like a sumptuous museum with glittery night views of old Lìjiāng. Amazing attention to detail.

Eating

The following rundown is by no means exhaustive. There are always several 'Naxi' items on the menu, including the famous 'Naxi omelette' and 'Naxi sandwich' (goat's cheese, tomato and fried egg between two pieces of local *bābā*). *Bābā* (粑粑) is the Lìjiāng local speciality: thick flatbreads of wheat, served plain or stuffed with meats, vegetables or sweets. There is simply nothing on earth better for filling your gut before a long day of alley strolling or countryside biking (stick a couple in your pack for bus rides!).

More and more of these places offer free internet for customers; if they do charge, it's around Y5 per hour, though this too is dropping.

Prague Café (Bùlāgé Kāfēiguǎn; 18 Mishi Xiang; 密士巷18号; dishes from Y6; ⏰ from 7.30am) Heading off for the Tiger Leaping Gorge trek? You can't go wrong with the Naxi breakfast (Y22): fried goat cheese, ham and a potato pancake as big as your head will have you all set. Great staff, crowd and atmosphere.

Well Bistro (Jǐngzhuō Cānguǎn; ☎ 518 6431; Mishi Xiang; 密士巷; dishes from Y6; ⏰ 8.30am-late) This well-established landmark of sorts has been serving up solid from-scratch sustenance for going on a decade. Go for the homemade breads and desserts.

Petit Lijiang Bookcafé (☎ 511 1255; 50 Chongren Xiang, Qiyi Jie; 崇仁巷七一街50号; dishes from Y10) Owners Mei and Olivier (a Chinese-Belgian couple whose easygoing nature deftly fits Lìliáng) are great sources of travel info, and the food and atmosphere are so superb you may never leave. Even better, the bookstore has an outstanding collection of English- and French-language titles focusing on Yúnnán and elsewhere in China.

Lamu's House of Tibet (Xīzàngwū Xīcāntíng; ☎ 518 9000; 56 Xinyi Jie; 新义街; dishes from Y10) Lamu has been putting smiles and service before yuán for over a decade and after a few relocations, she has finally nailed her spot in this casual pine-and-bamboo place on the north side of the old town. The upstairs area is great for people-watching, and it's a UN menu; the Tibetan items are all you really need (though the Naxiburger rocks). Do make sure you save room for the desserts though – they are massive.

Blue Page Vegetarian Restaurant (Lányè Sùshí Wū; ☎ 518 5206; Mishi Xiang; 密士巷; dishes from Y10; ⏰ 8.30am-midnight; 🅥) Pretty much everything this place does, it does right. Find nouveau veggie dishes, along with Indian and Chinese, all in a quiet and relaxing atmosphere.

Sakura Café (Yīnghuā Kāfēiguǎn; Xinhua Jie; 新华街; ☎ 312 6766; dishes from Y10; ☯ whenever they wake up till way late) This unbelievably raucous place has gone from subdued and relaxed to utterly *rè nào* (hot and noisy, the way Chinese like it) in half a decade. It is actually one of several other 'Sakura Cafés' also found along this lane; perfectly located to draw in tourists, they absolutely swell with customers at night. You'll hardly hear yourself think at times, but the Korean *bimbab* set meal (Y23) is still outrageously good.

Mama Fu's (Māmǎfù Cāntīng; ☎ 512 2285; Mishi Xiang; 密士巷; dishes from Y10) Streamside dining has been a tradition at Mama Fu's pretty much forever – so popular has her place become she's branched out into Kūnmíng. The Chinese food here is superior to the Western food.

Naku Café (Ākù Kāfēi; ☎ 510 5321; 4 Jishan Xiang, Xinyi Jie; 新义街; dishes from Y20) Not many folks seem to wander into this casual eatery run by some very shy but very friendly staff. Local Naxi dishes outshine the foreign items: the Naxi claypot needs salt but is packed with tofu, potato, turnip, carrots, broccoli and cabbage.

Blue Papaya (Lán Mùguā; ☎ 661 2114; www.thebluepapaya.com; 70 Xinyi Jie; 新义街70号; dishes from Y30) One of the places many folks take the time to write about, this is among Lìjiāng's top casual-chic places. The Italian-centric food – heavy on pasta and fish – is excellent with many, many creative flourishes. The restaurant is also home to a 'cultural exchange academy', offering courses on cooking, massage, taichi and more.

Entertainment

One of the few things you can do in the evening in Lìjiāng is attend performances of the **Naxi Orchestra** (Nàxī Gǔyuè Huì; Naxi Music Academy; ☎ 512 7971; tickets Y100-140; ☯ performances 8pm), located inside a beautiful building in the old town.

All members (26 at last count) are Naxi and play a type of Taoist temple music (known as *dòngjīng*) that has been lost elsewhere in China. The pieces they perform are supposedly faithful renditions of music from the Han, Song and Tang dynasties, and are played on original instruments, some of which were buried during the Cultural Revolution lest they be smashed.

Local historian of note Xuan Ke – he's the guy who originally posited the Shangri-la-is-in-Yúnnán theory – usually speaks for the group at performances (usually – the guy's old, so cut him some slack if he's a no-show; ditto with the drowsy musicians – they're positively ancient and besides, that's half the fun!). In any case, someone will explain each musical piece and describe the instruments. There are taped recordings of the music available; a set of two costs Y30. If you're interested, make sure you buy the tape at the show – tapes on sale at shops around town, and even in Kūnmíng, are often pirated copies.

The government-run **Dongba Palace** (Dong Dajie; tickets Y100-140; ☯ performances 8pm) has a less authentic song-and-dance show.

Getting There & Away

No trains serve Lìjiāng. Yet. Apparently an extension from Dàlǐ was half-finished as of late 2006 – it didn't look it when we there.

AIR

Lìjiāng's airport is 25km southwest of town. Tickets can be booked at the **CAAC** (Zhōngguó Mínháng; ☎ 516 1289; cnr Fuhui Lu & Shangrila Dadao; ☯ 8.30am-9pm). Most hotels in the old town also offer an air-ticket booking service.

From Lijiāng there are oodles of daily flights to Kūnmíng (Y660), three flights daily to Chéngdū (Y1010) and Shànghǎi (Y2560), two flights daily to Shēnzhèn (Y1760) and one daily to Guǎngzhōu (Y1790).

BUS

Lìjiāng has three bus stations: one just north of the old town; the main long-distance bus station in the south; and an express bus station to Kūnmíng and Xiàguān on Shangrila Dadao in the north of town.

From the express bus station there are daily departures to Kūnmíng (Y171 to Y193, 8am, 9am, 10am, 11am and 12.30pm). Two sleeper buses also leave daily for Kūnmíng at 8.30pm; one terminates at Kūnmíng's west station, the other at its south station. Buses also leave here for Xiàguān (Y41 to Y58, 160km, 8am, 11.10am, noon, 2.10pm, 3.50pm and 6.10pm), and daily for Shangri-la (Y45, 8.40am and 2.30pm).

Many buses make the run to Jīnjiāng (Y50), from where you can hop a train to Chéngdū (or Kūnmíng or Hēijǐng), but the bus station where you may be dropped off in Jīnjiāng is 20km from the train station. A bus between the two (there are many) costs Y3.

LÌJIĀNG BUS TIMETABLES

Buses from the north bus station include the following:

Destination	Price (Y)	Duration (hours)	Frequency	Departs
Jinjiāng	Y45-60	8	3 daily	7am, 8am, 11am
Kūnmíng	Y119	8	daily	8pm
Nínglàng	Y23	3-4	6 daily	8am, 9.30am, 10am, 12.30pm, 1.30pm, 2pm
Shangri-la	Y39	5	2 daily	7.50am, 11am
Xiàguān	Y35-37	3½	20 daily	7.30am-6pm

Buses from the long-distance bus station include the following:

Destination	Price (Y)	Duration (hours)	Frequency	Departs
Jiànchuān	16	2-3	every 30-50min	7am-6pm
Kūnmíng	151	12	hourly	8.30-11.30am & 1pm
Kūnmíng (sleeper)	119	8	11 daily	6.30am-9pm
Lúgū Hú	63	7-8	1 daily	9.30am
Nínglàng	23	5	13 daily	8am-4.30pm
Qiáotóu	20	2	daily	1pm
Shangri-la	39	5	15 daily	7.30am-5pm
Wéixī	54	6	2 daily	7.30am, 8.30am
Xiàguān	35-50	3½	27 daily	7.10am-6.30pm

Getting Around

Buses to the airport (Y15) leave from outside the CAAC 90 minutes before flight departures.

Taxis start at Y6 in the new town and are not allowed into the old town (the whole of the old town is pedestrianised).

Bike hire is available at the International Youth Hostel Lijiang (p269; Y15 per day).

AROUND LÌJIĀNG

It is possible to see most of Lìjiāng's environs on your own, but a few agencies do offer half- or full-day tours, starting from Y150 to Y200; it might be worth it if you take one that includes admission fees.

Monasteries

The monasteries around Lìjiāng are Tibetan in origin and belong to the Karmapa (Red Hat) sect. Most of the monasteries were extensively damaged during the Cultural Revolution and there's not much monastic activity nowadays. Nevertheless, the splendid scenery hereabouts make it worth hopping on a bicycle and heading out of town for a look.

PUJI MONASTERY 普济寺

This monastery (Pǔjì Sì) is around 5km northwest of Lìjiāng (on a trail that passes the two ponds to the north of town). The few monks here are usually happy to show the occasional stray traveller around.

FUGUO MONASTERY 富国寺

West of Báishā lies the remains of the temple (Fùguó Sì), once the largest of Lìjiāng's monasteries. Much of it was destroyed during the Cultural Revolution and a couple of remaining buildings were moved to Lìjiāng's Black Dragon Pool Park. Look out for the **Hufa Hall** in the monastery compound; the interior walls have some interesting frescoes.

To get there head west from the main intersection in Báishā until you reach a small village. Turn right at the fork in the road, continue for around 500m then take the next left. Walk up the hill for about 30 minutes and you will come to the monastery ruins.

JADE PEAK MONASTERY 玉峰寺

This small lamasery (Yùfēng Sì) is on a hillside about 5km past Báishā. The last 3km of the track require a steep climb. Lock your bike if you leave it at the bottom.

The monastery sits at the far southwestern foot of Yùlóng Xuěshān (5500m) and was established in 1756. The monastery's main attraction nowadays is the **Camellia Tree of 10,000**

AROUND LÌJIĀNG & SHANGRI-LA 丽江、香格里拉

Blossoms (Wànduǒ Shānchá). Ten thousand might be something of an exaggeration, but locals claim that the tree produces at least 4000 blossoms between February and April. A monk on the grounds risked his life to keep the tree secretly watered during the Cultural Revolution. One camellia in the northwest section is famed as being more than 500 years old.

Not far from Yùfēng Sì is the town of **Yù Hú** (Jade Lake), once the home of Joseph Rock (opposite; when the town was known as Nguluko, not a Chinese name).

On the way to Yùfēng, about 12km from Lìjiāng, is Běiyuè village, the site of another Naxi temple – devoted to Sanduo, a guardian deity – dating from AD 780.

WENBI MONASTERY 文笔寺

Getting to this monastery (Wénbí Sì) requires a steep uphill ride 8km to the southwest of Lìjiāng. There are also some good views and pleasant walks in the near vicinity. The monastery has some distinctive Tibetan features, and dates from 1733. Its two-dozen courtyards once housed 80 lamas. The hill behind the monastery has a sacred cave and spring. In

the cave there's a black rock on which a disciple of Sakyamuni is said to have laid a key, so pilgrims headed to Jīzú Shān (Chicken-Foot Mountain) come to the rock, burn joss, and 'borrow' the key to get to their destination.

ZHIYUN MONASTERY 指云寺

Along the road to Shígǔ, 18km from Lìjiāng by the small Lashi Hai reservoir, is the Zhǐyún Sì (Pointing to the Clouds Monastery), built in 1727. The nearby lake is a **wetland reserve** (admission Y10) popular with birdwatchers, and you may get to see black stork and Chinese mergansers.

Frescoes

Lìjiāng is famed for its temple frescoes. Most travellers probably won't want to spend a week or so traipsing around seeking them out, but it may be worth checking out one or two.

Most of the frescoes were painted during the 15th and 16th centuries by Tibetan, Naxi, Bai and Han artists. Many of them were restored during the later Qing dynasty. They depict various Taoist, Chinese and Tibetan Buddhist themes and can be found on the

JOSEPH ROCK

Travel around Yúnnán long enough and you'll incessantly hear 'Luòkè' (洛克). It's a name – the Sinified version of Rock, Joseph Rock. Absolutely everywhere you go, locals will discuss how 'Luòkè was here in (year)' or 'Luòkè stayed at my grandmother's parents' home'. Etc ad nauseam.

Yúnnán was a hunting ground for famous, foreign plant-hunters such as Kingdon Ward and Joseph Rock. Rock lived in Lìjiāng between 1922 and 1949, becoming the world's leading expert on Naxi culture and local botany. More than his academic pursuits, however, he will be remembered as one of the most enigmatic and eccentric characters to travel in western China.

Rock was born in Austria, the son of a domineering father who insisted he enter a seminary. A withdrawn child, he escaped into imagination and atlases, discovering a passion for China. An astonishing autodidact (he taught himself eight languages, including Sanskrit), he began learning Chinese at 13 years of age. He somehow wound up in Hawaii, and in time became the foremost authority on Hawaiian flora.

Asia always beckoned and he convinced the US Department of Agriculture, and later Harvard University, to sponsor his trips to collect flora for medicinal research. He devoted much of his life to studying Naxi culture, which he feared was being extinguished by the dominant Han culture. He became *National Geographic* magazine's 'man in China' and it was his exploits in northwestern Yúnnán and Sìchuān for the magazine that made him famous.

He sent over 80,000 plant specimens from China – two were named after him – along with 1600 birds and 60 mammals. Amazingly, he was taking and developing the first colour photographic plates in his field in the 1920s! Tragically, containerloads of his collections were lost in 1945 in the Arabian Sea when the boat was torpedoed.

Rock's caravans stretched for 800m, and included dozens of servants (including a cook trained in Austrian cuisine), trains of pack horses, and hundreds of mercenaries for protection against bandits, not to mention the gold dinner service and a collapsible bathtub.

Rock lived in Yù Hú village (called Nguluko when he was there) not far from Báishā. Many of his possessions are now local family heirlooms and his home is now a small **museum** (admission Y5), which got kickstarted in 2004 with a concerted effort by and donations from the Austrian embassy in China. It's open whenever somebody is around.

The *Ancient Nakhi Kingdom of Southwest China* (Harvard University Press, 1947) is Joseph Rock's definitive work. Immediately prior to his death, his Naxi dictionary was also finally prepared for publishing. For an insight into the man and his work, take a look at *In China's Border Provinces: The Turbulent Career of Joseph Rock, Botanist-Explorer* (Hastings House, 1974) by JB Sutton, or Rock's many archived articles for *National Geographic*.

interior walls of temples in the area. However, the Red Guards came through here slashing and gouging during the Cultural Revolution, so there's not that much to see.

In Báishā the best frescoes can be found in **Dabaoji Palace** (Dàbǎojī Gōng; admission Y15; 8.30am-5.30pm), which also has quite nice Naxi artwork and scrolls for sale. Nearby, **Liuli Temple** (Liúlí Diàn) and **Dading Ge** also have some, and in the neighbouring village of Lóngquán, frescoes can be found on the interior walls of **Dajue Palace** (Dàjué Gōng).

BÁISHĀ 白沙

On a plain north of Lìjiāng, near several old temples, Báishā is one of the best day trips out of Lìjiāng, especially if you have a bike. Before Kublai Khan made it part of his Yuan empire

(1271–1368), Báishā was the capital of the Naxi kingdom. It's hardly changed since then – despite being visited by nearly everyone with a guidebook and a bike – and offers a close-up glimpse of Naxi culture for those willing to spend some time nosing around.

We may as well go ahead and name the place 'the Village of Dr Ho' (or He), who has become possibly as famous as any of Lìjiāng County's other attractions. Looking the stereotype of a Taoist physician, he has a sign outside his door: 'The Clinic of Chinese Herbs in Jade Dragon Mountains of Lijiāng'. The author Bruce Chatwin propelled the good doctor into the limelight when he mythologised (nay, borderline romanticised) Dr Ho as the 'Taoist physician in the Jade Dragon Mountains of Lijiāng'. Journalists and photographers (and we) started beating a path to his door, and the rest is quirky history. Kind of a Lìjiāng must-do, and one must say that all the fame hasn't really gone to his head – he's still chatty and friendly and quite serious about listening and prescribing Chinese herbal medicines for what it is that ails you.

Almost directly opposite Dr Ho's clinic is **Café Buena Vista** (Nànà Wéisītā Jùlèbù; ☎ 131-7078 0719; info@ecotour.com), a lovely little café–art gallery run by an artist, Zhao Fan, and his girlfriend. It is also a good place to get travel information (see Eco-tours, p267).

There are a couple of frescoes worth seeing in town and surrounding the area; see p272 for details.

Báishā is an easy 20- to 30-minute bike ride from Lìjiāng. Otherwise take a minibus (Y15) from the corner of Minzu Lu and Fuhui Lu. From Báishā minibuses return to Lìjiāng regularly (Y20).

YÙLÓNG XUĚSHĀN 玉龙雪山

Also known as Mt Satseto, **Yùlóng Xuěshān** (Jade Dragon Snow Mountain; admission adult/student Y80/60; protection fee Y40), 35km or so from Lìjiāng, soars to some 5500m. Its peak was first climbed in 1963 by a research team from Běijīng but is pretty much now overrun daily by the Gore Tex–clad on a mammoth scale.

Dry Sea Meadow (甘海子; Gānhǎizi) is the first stop you come to if travelling by bus from Lìjiāng. A **chairlift** (Y160) ascends to a large meadow at 3050m, which, according to geologists, was actually a lake 2000 years ago. It can often get freezing above even when warm down here at the base of the chairlift: warm coats can be rented for Y30, deposit Y300, oxygen tanks are Y40. (For information on altitude sickness, see p499.)

Cloud Fir Meadow (云杉坪; Yúnshānpíng) is the second stop and a **chairlift** (Y60) takes you up to 4506m where walkways lead to awesome glacier views. Horses can be hired here for Y80.

Views from the two Meadows are pretty impressive, but make sure you get here well before the first chair up at 8.30am. Unless you get a head start on the tour groups, prepare for up to an hour wait to get either up or down the mountain.

Around 60km from Lijiāng, or a 30-minute drive from Dry Sea Meadow, is **Yak Meadow** (牦牛坪; Máoniúpíng) where yet another **chairlift** (Y60) pulls visitors up to an altitude of 3500m

where there are ample hiking opportunities near Xuěhuā Hǎi (Snowflake Lake). Crowds and long waits are almost unheard of here.

And even if you're not a Tiger Woods–wannabe, consider a visit to the **Jade Dragon Snow Mountain Snow Resort** (☎ 573 1888), near the entrance to the mountain, where you can thump a little white ball over 400m at these altitudes! The thin air doesn't help yer slice, however.

At the time of research, camping in the area was not prohibited but it's better to check when you get there as regulations have a tendency to change quicker than the cloud cover.

Bus 7 (Y15 to Y20) leaves for all three spots from the intersection of Minzu Lu and Fuhui Lu in Lìjiāng and passes by Báishā on the way. Returning to Lìjiāng, buses leave fairly regularly but check with your driver to find out what time the last bus will depart.

If you enter the region from the north (Tiger Leaping Gorge) there's no ticket gate.

JIÀNCHUĀN 剑川

☎ 0871 / pop 9685

Travellers taking the alternate route between Lìjiāng and Dàlǐ may hop off the bus in Jiànchuān, head out of the bus station, see the trucks roaring by on busy National Hwy 214, and immediately plan to flag down the first vehicle out of town to the gorgeous mountains and villages surrounding the city.

Don't. Just a few blocks off the ugly main drag, Jiànchuān has some worthy sights of its own. Splendid Qing (and even Ming) architecture lies pretty much untouched – but still in fine shape. Epic tracts of green space offer some great hikes.

The seat of the eponymous county (the one with the highest percentage of Bai in China), Jiànchuān comes to mind for most Chinese as the hometown of Ah Peng, the Bai hero of the movie The Five Golden Flowers. Relics unearthed from Haimenkou, to the south, date to the earliest period of Yúnnán's Bronze Age, something they like to brag about here.

Orientation & Information

National Hwy 214 splits the city north-to-south; you can't miss it for all the dust and traffic. The bus station is along the highway at the south end of town. Three blocks to the north of here is Huancheng Beilu. Most everything you need lies on or between these two roads, including the post office, which is a block north of the highway on Huancheng Beilu, then a block south. East along this same road three blocks is a hospital. Two blocks east of Jìngfēng Gōngyuán (below) is the PSB office. We've yet to find an internet café anywhere in the vicinity; let us know if one pops up.

Sights & Activities

At the north end of Huancheng Beilu is **Jìngfēng Gōngyuán** (景风公园; Jingfeng Park), a meander-worthy park of skyscraperesque (yet droopy) pines, flower-lined paths and some fine historic structures right near the entrance, including a somnolently proud pagoda, a Confucian temple, and a memorial hall to local Bai success stories.

The real highlight in town is the extant Ming and Qing architecture. Nearly two dozen residential courtyards are quite well preserved. An **architectural stroll** is lovely and easy as pie. From Jìfēng Gōngyuán's entrance, veer to the right as you exit and you'll come almost immediately to the little alley Xi Men (West Gate). Head south and just start wending your way up and down blue flagstone alleyways heading every which way. Gorgeous and all the real deal. People are superfriendly; we were invited in to have a look on three separate occasions in three blocks! (Keep in mind that these are people's homes, so don't just barge in and start snapping shots.)

From Jìngfēng Gōngyuán, trails lead straight up into the hills, from where you can supposedly hike (OK, we got lost) the five strenuous kilometres through stands of cypress to the **1000-Lion Mountain of Manxian Forest** (满贤林千狮山; Mǎnxiánlín Qiānshīshān), the name of which lies – it's actually some 3000, the tallest of which stands over 18m tall. It's fairly eerie to be surrounded in the twilight by 3000 lions, stone or not. (Along the way, look for orchids, for which the county is quite well known; three locally grown species have each sold for over Y100,000, though you're not likely to see those on the trails!)

Motorcycle taxi rides cost Y2 to Y3 to most places.

Sleeping & Eating

Ruìhuī Bīnguǎn (瑞辉宾馆; ☎ 452 1970; 214 National Highway; 214国道; d Y60, without bathroom Y40; 🖷) Easy to find. Just head out the bus station door and cross the street, bearing to the right a bit. This place is relatively new, has a friendly staff who'll likely be wide-eyed seeing you waltz in, and offers spotless rooms for next to nothing. Thus, it's often full by midafternoon, so don't dawdle.

Jiànchuān Bīnguǎn (剑川宾馆; ☎ 452 1434; 1 Huancheng Beilu; 环城北路1号; d Y80-100, without bathroom Y50; 🖷) Likely most people will point any foreigner in this direction first. Perfectly fine rooms and a helpful enough staff. It's a block south of Jìngfēng Gōngyuán.

No special eateries stand out. There are perfectly fine restaurants, just not in the old town area. You'll have to head north of Huancheng Beilu to find any.

A few local delicacies are worth asking for. Given its citizenry's prowess at growing flowers, it's unsurprising that Jiànchuān County is purportedly the only place in China to dine on white azalea flowers (白杜鹃花; bái dùjuān huā). At most meals people eat another local speciality: kidney beans (芸豆; yúndòu), prepared in any number of ways. The Bai also make use of the entire bean plant, including the leaves, which are used for the sharp-tasting soup délèmǔzi tāng (得勒母资汤).

Getting There & Away

To get to Shāxī (Y7, one hour) and Shíbáoshān (Y7, 45 minutes), take a small shared van; drivers sit in front of the bus station.

Rumour has it that a new expressway will run between Xiàguān and Shangri-la, passing through Jiànchuān in the near future. No

JIÀNCHUĀN BUS TIMETABLE				
Destination	Price (Y)	Duration (hours)	Frequency	Departs
Kūnmíng	97, 125 (sleeper)	11	roughly hourly	9am-5pm
Lìjiāng	16	2-3	every 30-40 min	6.30am-4pm
Xiàguān	20	3-3½	every 15 min	6.30am-5pm
Yúnlóng	40	6-7	daily	6.40am

work had started as of yet, but if it does, expect delays on these times. (An extension of the train line being built between Dàlǐ and Lìjiāng may also stop here.)

Motorcycle taxi rides cost Y2 to Y3 for most destinations.

AROUND JIÀNCHUĀN

Shíbǎoshān 石宝山

About 75km to the southwest of Lìjiāng (or 110km to the northwest of Dàlǐ) are the **Stone Treasure Mountain Grottoes** (Shíbǎoshān Shíkū; admission Y30; ☑ dawn-dusk). The local tourism bureau loves to tout purported (but anonymous) scholars who compare them favourably with the grottoes of Dūnhuáng, Dàzú, and Dàtóng. We don't know anything about that, but this quite large – expansive but not that high – mountain is lovely, with tracts of old-growth cypress and some fabulous sights. And, yes, this is a Chinese mountain, so there are also the renegade bands of bandit monkeys out there.

There are three temple groups: **Stone Bell** (Shízhōng), the most famous; **Lion Pass** (Shīzi Guān); and **Shadeng village** (Shādēng Cūn).

The Stone Bell monastery group includes some of the best Bai stone carvings in southern China and offer insights into life at the Nánzhào court of the 9th century. One of the best caves features images of Geluofeng, the fourth king of the Nánzhào kingdom. The sculpture of the Eight Kings in China is also among the finest works of Buddhist art in China. And then, ahem, the racy part for which the mountain is rather well known: carvings of female genitalia, which local women visit to boost their fertility. The local tourist PR words, not ours: 'This carving is the only case of engraved vulvas placed on equal terms with the Buddha and God in the world.' Goodness.

On the way to the complex, 6km from the Stone Bell monastery, is the **Bǎoxiàng Sì** (Baoxiang Temple), at the edge of an enormous cliff.

At least 1000 steps lead up to the **Golden Summit Temple** (Jīndǐng Sì) on top of the mountain.

From July 27 to August 1 by the lunar calendar the mountain is home to the genuinely touching **Festival of Songs**, a three-day stretch in which Bai youth come to the mountain and express their love for each other in song. These dates in the western calendar are 27–31 August 2008; 15–19 September 2009; and 5–8 September 2010.

SLEEPING

There is but one hotel on the mountain: **Shíbǎoshān Bīnguǎn** (☎ 478 6093; d Y220; 石宝山 宾馆; ✗) This relatively luxurious place at the mountain's gate is generally empty save for summer weekends, and in off-season you can get at least a 50% discount.

Otherwise, you're looking at extremely basic beds at Baoxiang Temple, halfway up the front of the mountain, or Shizong Temple, halfway up the back of mountain. These are often full.

GETTING THERE & AWAY

To get to Shíbǎoshān, take a bus to Jiànchuān, then hope for a tiny shuttle van from in front of the bus station taking tourists to the mountain. If none are running, you can take one headed toward Shāxī (Y7, 30 minutes; see opposite) and get off at the entrance to the mountain, where you have a 2km hike uphill to the main entrance. (By the way, from where you hop off, look north and you can see both Haba Snow Mountain and Yùlóng Xuěshān. And ignore the dilapidated bus stop here; those buses stopped yonks ago).

If you're coming from Dàlǐ on the old Dàlǐ–Lìjiāng road, you'll have to take a Jiànchuān-bound bus, then get off at the small village of Diànnán, about 8km south of Jiànchuān, where a narrow road branches southwest to the village of Shāxī (opposite), 23km away. You'll just have to wait for a bus for this leg.

Shāxī 沙溪

Arrive in Shāxī and it seems just another dusty village. Walk one mere block east from the one paved road, however, and enter a wormhole. Every step is another decade into a bygone era, the clippety-clops of horse's hooves and bellows of traders highly imaginable. Raised eyebrows at statements such as these are natural, but trust us – this place retains all its centuries of residual charm.

Shāxī was heretofore a crucial node on one of the old tea-horse roads (more like 'caravan routes'), trails of commerce in Yúnnán's precious green gold (especially *pú'ěr chá*; a variety of black tea) that stretched from Yúnnán to Tibet, Nepal, Burma, Laos, Vietnam, and other parts of China. Starting as far back as the Tang dynasty, the routes reached their zenith in the Ming dynasty. Only three caravan oases remain, Shāxī being the best-preserved and the only one with a surviving market (which is on Fridays). Shāxī is endangered by encroaching modernity – a recurring theme for China, despite its historic past – and has been named by international preservationists as one of the world's 100 most precious endangered sites. A good place to get more information is www.shaxi.org.

SIGHTS

All you really need to know about the village is Sideng Jie (寺登街), the ancient town street leading east off the main road (and where all transports drops you off). From here it's a leisurely 10-minute walk to the edge of the village at the **East Gate** (东门; Dōngmén). Along the way you'll come to the central square with its distinctive blue-hued flagstones and pass by a couple of architectural wonders. **Xingjiao Temple** (兴教寺; Xīngjiào Sì) is the only Ming dynasty Bai Buddhist temple and has more than 20 fabulous frescoes, the highlight of which is one of Sakmayuni taming devils. Nearby is the imposing **Three Terraced Pavilion** (三层楼; Sāncénglóu), with graceful upturned eaves and overlapped corners; it's most salient feature, however, is its prominent theatrical **stage** (古戏台; gǔxìtái), a rarity in rural China. The absolute highlight, however, is the **Ouyang Courtyard** (欧阳大院; Ōuyáng Dàyuàn), a superb example of three-in-one Bai folk-architecture in which one wall protected three yards/residences. This, the grandest of all in the village – and there were loads – once included one main house and numerous side houses, a large garden, smaller courtyards, a small stage and even a stable. The stones you stand on date from the Tang dynasty; just think of that. One area today is a modest inn (see Sleeping, following). And this but scratches the surface. Everywhere you turn you'll find a temple or meeting hall, old gate or ancient dwelling still sporting Ming architecture.

But ya gotta get out to taste the real history of the place. The surrounding plains and hills are rife with endless walking opportunities. Exit the East Gate and head south along the Hui River (惠江; Huì Jiāng) five minutes, cross the ancient **Yùjīn Qiáo** (玉津桥; Yujin Bridge) and you're walking the same trail as the horse caravans. (Look hard enough and you'll still be able to see hoofprints etched into the rock, or so it is claimed.)

From Sideng Jie, walk 20 minutes south along the main road coming into town and you'll come to a handful of other historic structures.

SLEEPING

The 'new' part of town along the main road has a couple of inns that are more or less traditional, but you only need them in a pinch. Instead, Sideng Jie has two superb places to place your head for the night.

Tea & Horse Caravan Trail Inn (古道客栈; Gǔdào Kèzhàn; ☎ 0872-472 1051; 83 Sideng Jie; 寺等街83号; dm Y15) Garnering most of the few travellers passing through, this place has basic but spotless rooms and facilities and small but relaxing grounds. If any place in town knows what solo travellers are looking for, it's this one.

Ouyang Guesthouse (三家巷客栈; Sānjiāxiàng Kèzhàn; ☎ 0872-472 2171; Sideng Jie; 寺等街; beds Y15-30) Yes, we know the English sign doesn't match the Chinese one, but who's to quibble? This is one of the most historic structures in the village and the proprietors seem thrilled to be able to extol its virtues.

GETTING THERE & AWAY

Whatever direction you come from you'll pass by Shíbǎo Shān. From Jiànchuān you wait for a shared minivan ride (Y7, one hour) that also stops at Shíbǎo Shān. Theoretically you could hike the last 10km from the mountain to Shāxī, though it isn't all that pretty. Definitely don't try to bicycle it because the rough stone will shred your tyres.

HÈQÌNG 鹤庆

About 46km to the south of Lìjiāng, Hèqìng is just off the main Dàlǐ to Lìjiāng highway. In the centre of the town is the wooden Yúnhé Pavilion, built during the Ming dynasty. You might be able to catch a glimpse of the pavilion as you speed by on the bus from Lìjiāng to Dàlǐ.

BǍOSHĀN & SHÍTOUCHÉNG
宝山, 石头城

☎ 0888 / pop 108 families!

Bǎoshān is a fairly interesting (which is not to say aesthetically pleasant) Naxi village about 125km north of Lìjiāng, but the real reason to endure the hassle of getting here is to continue 24km (one hour) on winding mountain roads to Shítouchéng (the Stone City), a positively charming, time-locked walled village of 108 families, perched on a ledge high above the Yangzi River. At a lower altitude, it's also got a much milder climate than Lìjiāng; it can even get downright hot in summer.

Sights & Activities

From the end of the road there's a 20-minute descent (mostly steps but some stone paths laden with horse apples!) to the village. Once inside the walls, the first left and left again will take you up to a **viewing platform**. The village square at the foot of the entrance gates is the site of occasional Naxi dances in the evenings. The mountain to the north of the town has connections to Kublai Khan, who is said to have crossed the Yangzi here sometime around 1274. Lots of Joseph Rock (p273) lore around here, as well; pretty much every old-timer claims to have had a parent or grandparent assist the explorer on his Yangzi crossings here.

Many of the eaves of the Naxi houses have wooden fish decorating the eves; one reason for this is that the Chinese for fish (*yú*) has the same sound as prosperity (*yú*).

Shítouchéng offers some interesting **treks** for adventurous travellers. Mu Shangwen, the owner of the Mu Family Guesthouse can act as a guide for three- to seven-day treks to Lúgū Lake for Y70 to Y80 per day (solo travellers may get a tiny break). Other guesthouses can arrange guides too. You shouldn't expect any English. You can stay in local houses for the shorter treks. Longer treks may require a tent and requisite gear. There are two main routes; north up the Yangzi River (known here as the Jīnshā Jiāng) to Lābó village and then over the mountains to Yǒngníng, or south to Wúmù and east to Cuìyù, from where you can catch a morning bus to the main Nínglàng–Yǒngníng road.

If you're not planning to head for Lúgú Hú, plenty of day trips are out there as well. Simply striking off on your own in any direction you choose is probably the most common activity. Along the trail to Lúgú Hú some four hours from the Stone City is **Tàizǐ Shān** (太子山), with a couple of caves and a small temple along the way. To get there exit the Stone City main gate (the one you entered when arriving). Cross the small square into the outer village. When you see a sign saying 'Green Food' take a right and then a left.

The path from here winds around a U-shaped bend in the valley and is fairly level. After about a half-hour to an hour, when you've looped back to about the same point as the Stone City, the path rises sharply and you'll encounter some dicey sections, ranging from rock to gravely scree to you've-got-to-be-kidding goat path, with some precariously narrow parts. Must be great fun when raining.

Across the river lie some exceedingly diminutive Pumi villages. Your guesthouse can even ring up a boat to pick you up and show you around for the day, though those slopes are quite steep.

Sleeping

Mu Family Guesthouse (木家客栈; Mùjiā Kèzhàn; ☎ 135-7839 2658; beds Y15) This place in the walled town offers basic but clean rooms with sufficiently comfy beds, and excellent food for about the same price. Pretty much every foreigner who's come to the town – not many, actually – has likely stayed here, so the guesthouse is used to foreigners.

Shíchéng Dìyījiā Kèzhàn (石城第一家客栈; ☎ 519 7511; d Y60, without bathroom Y40) A second guesthouse run by the friendly family of the shared-van driver and his truck-driver brother (see the boxed text, opposite) was just being finished when we visited (they hadn't even made a sign yet). They have a few cosy rooms with private bathroom and hot water and two cheaper rooms with shared bathroom. The balcony outside the rooms has stupendous views of the Yangzi River and the valley below; it's a relaxing place to stargaze and listen to the rushing river. One thing, though: man, they really have some noisy roosters in the morning…

You can bet there will be even more inns by the time you read this. A few more – perfectly fine but without any of the atmosphere of staying inside the village – lie outside the main gate.

Getting There & Away

Only one public bus to Bǎoshān (Y35, five hours) leaves Lìjiāng daily between 8am and 8.30am from the Xiàngshān Shìchǎng market, north of Lìjiāng's Old Town. To get to the market, bus 8 runs east along Fuhui Lu, then north along Xin Dajie to Xiangshan Donglu; the bus stop is opposite the market. From Bǎoshān it's another Y10 and one hour to Shítouchéng.

A small private van does leave from the market at the same time for the same price and goes all the way to the Stone City; it is much quicker, reaching the Stone City in some 5½ hours.

The trouble is that if not enough passengers show up, neither may run; summer weekends are about the only time you're guaranteed to have enough – if not too many.

LAND-SPEED RECORD Thomas Huhti

It was the usual. Get to the bus departure point, which my friend from Kūnmíng had assured me was still the place. *Méi yǒu* (没有; literally 'not have'). Of course. Run around trying to find out where it actually leaves from. An hour later, get to the real place – a grubby market. Bus today? *Méi yǒu*. Already left. What about the little van? *Méi yǒu*. I slurp some noodles while my friend guiltily haggles with a seems-to-be-friendly truck driver, who it turns out is going to the same village. (Also turns out to be the brother of the van driver, who isn't gonna drive up to the village today 'cause…well, just 'cause. 'Cause it's China.) Then he starts up with the old refrain: *mǎ shàng zǒu* (马上走; leaving soon, literally 'horse-on-move/walk'). After a few months in China, one learns to loathe that phrase.

Then the usual of any China journey: another hour of waiting. Troll the streets for an hour. Go to some house to pick up the cargo. No-one there. Wait a half-hour. Guy comes. No key. Fifteen minutes to get key. An hour for two rangy young guys to load literally a tonne of bags into the truck.

Which doesn't start. Monkey around for another half-hour. It coughs and finally chugs. The driver grins the inimitable driver grin.

Finally leave town, but after just 15 minutes, the driver stops and says we should get in back. Now, my paranoia kicks in and I get ready to get in his face, but my friend explains it's either that or we have to pay a Y120 fee for the park that we were going through but not stopping at, the unfairness of which really pisses off my friend. I say I'll pay for both (honestly, I suck at cheating, I'd be sleepless with guilt; plus, Y120 is a lot of money for him). My friend won't budge; he feels it's an insult to extort money from travellers. Now he's really worked up.

So in back we climb atop bags of…white…what? Salt? Chemicals? (The ol' paranoia again…) My friend – true Chinese – tastes it: rock salt for de-icing roads. Well, that's actually pretty cool, considering the pass we're gonna hit. Chug along for 20 minutes, stopping twice for 10 minutes each time so the driver could talk with a local bus driver who had pulled alongside and waved him over – the same bus each time. Who knows why? My friend is still pissed, so I try to assuage him by telling him of one of my other friends, who lives by the Kerouac mantra of 'Avoid the authorities,' but I think I stunk up the translation since I just got that befuddled look I always get.

By now we have another problem – carbon monoxide. Great, I'm in the one truck in China that's airtight. Am I sleepy from the ride, or am I DYING? Me, in a nutshell, there.

Finally hop out a half-hour later. Continue on, with the usual two-hour meal break, fix a flat – only one! – and then get stuck on a mountain road for 90 minutes because another truck had broken down on a hairpin turn. (At least pass out a bunch of smokes I always carry and make new friends – my fave part of China.)

Anyway, finally cross the pass into absolute majesty, two more hours to the village, which is drop-jaw lovely, and wind up staying with the truck driver's wonderful family, sitting on their balcony, drinking tea as they play mah-jong, looking down at the Yangzi River in the moonlight. Who cares if a five-hour trip had just taken nearly 10?

Otherwise, you'll have to do what locals do and hop aboard a supply truck at the same market; it also costs Y35 but can take up to seven hours. Still, they're relatively spacious and fairly comfortable. Here's the huge catch: technically the road to Bǎoshān crosses through the Yùlóng Xuěshān (Jade Dragon Snow Mountain) tourist zone and thus you're gonna get hit up for the Y120 combination fee as you pass the entrance. (Unless, of course, your kindly truck driver offers to stick you in the back of the truck – for a little somethin' for the effort.) You can argue all you want, but park officials will not budge on this.

Vehicles back to Lìjiāng depart Shítouchéng sometime between 8am and 9am (give yourself 30 minutes to haul yourself up the hill) but stop for at least an hour in Bǎoshān to pick up passengers and freight (and eat lunch), finally leaving around 11am or 11.30am. (Line up your ride back when you arrive, just in case.)

An excellent way to leave Shítouchéng is to hike 3½ to four hours to Bǎoshān. If you leave by 7.30am you should arrive in plenty of time to catch the bus from Bǎoshān. The trail follows the Yangzi River past clumps of cacti and after about 1½ hours takes a side valley up to Bǎoshān. After a further 30 minutes the trail crosses a humpbacked bridge to the true right side of the stream. The first half of the trail follows the cliff side and can be dangerous at times so it's a good idea to take a guide; Mu Shangwen (see p278) can act as a guide for around Y30 or introduce you to someone else.

SHÍGǓ & THE FIRST BEND OF THE YANGZI 石鼓和长江第一弯
☎ 0887 / pop 5679

The small town of Shígǔ sits on the first bend of China's greatest river. Shígǔ means 'Stone Drum' and refers to a marble plaque shaped like a drum that commemorates a 16th-century Naxi victory over a Tibetan army. The original stone drum is attributed to Zhuge Liang, the 3rd-century military strategist who crossed the river here during one of his campaigns. Another plaque here celebrates the People's Army crossing of the river here in 1936 during the Long March to the north. Kublai Khan is also said to have crossed the river here on inflated sheepskins.

The view? Well, it is a bend all right and there is a rather nice view. That's about it,

---

> ### THE MOST IMPORTANT HILL IN CHINA
>
> As Simon Winchester notes in his book *The River at the Centre of the World,* China's history hangs in the balance at Cloud Hill, on the first bend of the Yangzi. This pile of rocks in the middle of the oncoming Yangzi River (known here as the Jīnshā Jiāng) funnels China's greatest river north and east into the heartland of China instead of draining south out of China.
>
> Chinese tradition assigns this dramatic U-turn to Yu the Great, China's mythological bureaucrat-deity in charge of water control. Without him, the Yangzi Valley, the cradle of the nation, would never have come into existence and the cultural development of China, and therefore the world, may have been profoundly different.

---

though. Some people love the fact that it isn't a touristified village; others snap a pic and immediately head out. There is a Y4 admission price to the view, though some haven't been asked.

For Shígǔ (Y9, two hours) staff at Lìjiāng's main bus station will likely throw you aboard one of the Jùdiàn (巨甸) bound buses that depart from 7.30am to 4pm. Alternatively, take a 7.30am or 8.30am departure to Wéixī and hop off. It's easily visited in a day. For the return, just wait by the road for any bus passing through. First bend fish are reportedly the tastiest in the region.

LÍMÍNG 黎明
☎ 0887

Halfway to Jùdiàn (巨甸) from Shígǔ a road leads to Límíng and then continues to Líguāng, the heart of a 240-sq-km scenic area of freak geology, with steep flat-topped hills and crags of every conceivable colour vaulting from the river valley floor. There's plenty of hiking potential here, especially to the **Qiānguī Shān** (千龟山; 1000 Turtle Hill), a weird rock phenomenon that is said to resemble 1000 turtles marching off to the sky.

Occasional buses depart for Límíng from the main bus station in Lijiāng. Alternatively take any bus bound for Jùdiàn or Wéixī get off at the turn-off (near Zhōngxīng village) and hitch. Accommodation is available at the bus stop in Límíng.

WÉIXĪ COUNTY 维西县

☎ 0887 / pop (Wéixī town) 4288

Wéixī Lisu Autonomous County lies off the main road to Shangri-la and Déqīn and so gets few visitors but you could visit it as an alternative route to or from Déqīn, or just visit as a return trip from Lìjiāng. It is slated for improvements but this has been said for years; for the moment it's mostly ribbons of roads alternating between decent narrow highway and the occasional place where it has degraded into rough track.

The route can be lovely at times but just be aware that though there are a few sights, practicalities are few and far between. A few bikers have mentioned it as lovely, but demanding. Wéixī itself is a bit of a yawner, except for being one of the few places in China to see the Pumi ethnic minority. The town has loads of cheap guesthouses and hotels, but little traffic and not enough bus tickets, so buy early.

Outside Wéixī, towns are more like microscopic villages – if that – and if there's a guesthouse it may be shut tight. Worse, sudden storms – of rain or especially snow – can leave the road impassable. In 2006 a group of travellers was stranded between Déqīn and Wéixī by a snowstorm that came out of nowhere. They were stuck for four days before anyone even knew they were missing.

The road to Wéixī passes through Jùdiàn, a transport junction where you may have to change buses. Further along is Xīnzhǔ (新主) village in the Héngduàn Shān (横断山). These mountains are a treasure-trove of botany and have been pegged by Chinese scientists as one of the most diverse in the world. A **botanical garden** showcases the dozens of rare species and several thousand-year-old trees in the region.

Some 40km north of Jùdiàn is **Tǎchéng** (塔城), named for the towerlike mountains rising behind the village. Tǎchéng reportedly has many Neolithic ruins, but most tourists come for the cliffside **Bodhidharma Cave & Temple** (达摩祖师洞; Dámó Zǔshī Dòng or Damo Gompa), often translated as the Damo Founder's Cave, 15km east at the elephant-shaped Dámó Shān. Tibetan pilgrims come to circumambulate the temple complex.

Wéixī is pretty much unexplored. The large county sports **Shuoguo Temple** (寿过寺; Shòuguò Sì) and **Pāntiān Gé** (攀天阁), a pavilion 27km north of Wéixī. It also has some lovely Pumi and Lisu villages, including remote Xiánuò village, just over the border in Déqīn County, and **Tónglè** (同乐), near **Yèzhī** (叶枝) town, famous for its minority *achimugua* dance, based on the movements of goats (a nod to the village's heritage).

TIGER LEAPING GORGE 虎跳峡

☎ 0887

Yúnnán's (no, Southwest China's) original trek, Tiger Leaping Gorge (Hǔtiào Xiá) is now the traveller's de facto rite of passage. For very, very good reason. One of the deepest in the world, it measures 16km long and is a giddy 3900m from the waters of Jinsha River (Jīnshā Jiāng; popularly known as the Yangzi River) to the snowcapped mountaintops of Hābā Shān (Haba Mountain) to the west and Yùlóng Xuěshān to the east. And it's preternaturally lovely pretty much everywhere. (The best time to come is May and the start of June, when the hills are afire with plant and flower life.)

Plan on three to four days away from Lìjiāng doing the hike, though it can be done in two. Many travellers have lingered up to a week.

The first rule of business is figuring out what your route is. Finishing south in Qiáotóu allows for quicker transport back to Lìjiāng, but heading north towards Dàjù gives you the option of continuing on to Báishuǐtái. Most people take a Shangri-la–bound bus early in the morning, hop off in Qiáotóu, and hike quickly to stay overnight in Walnut Garden.

You can still see the gorge (if you don't want to trek) by taking a bus to Qiáotóu and then catching one of the ubiquitous microbuses that shuttle people to the main viewpoint 10km away. Cost will depend on your bargaining skills but aim for as close to Y15 as you can. You could even take a taxi (Y50) the 23km from Qiáotóu to Walnut Garden and hitchhike back.

Admission to the gorge is Y50. You can't miss the ticket offices at either end of the gorge.

Dangers & Annoyances

The gorge trek is not to be taken lightly. Even for those in good physical shape, it's a workout. The path constricts and crumbles; it certainly can wreck the knees. When it's raining (especially July and August), landslides and swollen waterfalls can block the paths, in particular on the low road. Half a dozen people – including a

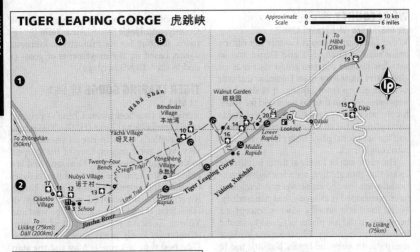

TIGER LEAPING GORGE 虎跳峡

few foreign travellers – have died in the gorge. Over the last decade, a few solo travellers have also been assaulted on the trail.

Check with cafés and lodgings in Lìjiāng for trail and weather updates. Most have fairly detailed gorge maps; just remember they're not to scale and occasionally out of date.

Make sure you bring plenty of water on this hike, 2L to 3L is ideal, as well as plenty of sunscreen and lip balm.

Activities

GORGE TREK

There are two trails: the higher (the older route, known as the 24-bend path); and the lower, the new road, replete with belching tour buses. Only the high trail is worth hiking. Arrows help you avoid getting lost. Then again, as one of our all-time favourite traveller quotes goes, 'Remember the high road leaves less time for drinking beer in Walnut Garden'.

The following route starts at Qiáotóu.

To get to the high road, after crossing through the gate, cross a small stream and go 150m. Take a left fork, go through the schoolyard's football pitch, and join the tractor road. Continue until the track ends and then follow the yellow arrows to the right. It's six hours to Běndiwān or a strenuous eight hours to Walnut Garden. The following list of guesthouses is not exhaustive.

Naxi Family Guesthouse (Nàxī Kèzhàn; dm Y15) Eight kilometres into the trek, this place still gets rave reviews from travellers.

Five Fingers Guesthouse (Wǔzhǐ Kèzhàn; dm Y15) Run by a friendly, enthusiastic family, you can eat with them for Y10.

Halfway Lodge (Zhōngtú Kèzhàn; ☎ 139 8870 0572; Běndiwān; dm Y15) Once a simple home to a guy collecting medicinal herbs and his family, it's now a busy-busy – but cosy and well-run – operation.

Sean's Spring Guesthouse (Shānquán Kèzhàn; ☎ 880 6300; www.tigerleapinggorge.com; dm Y15) This is one of the original guesthouses on the trail and still the spot for lively evenings and socialising. Sean's has electric blankets, mountain-bike hire (Y10 per hour) and can organise camping, guides, and horse trips.

Chateau de Woody (Shānbáiliǎn Lüguǎn; dm Y15) This other original is just fine too.

About 1½ hours from Běndìwān you descend to the road to **Tina's Guest House** (Zhōngxiá Lüdiàn; ☎ 880 6079; dm Y15). Budget more time if you are ascending. A good detour from here leads down 40 minutes to the middle rapids and **Tiger Leaping Stone**, where a tiger is once said to have leapt across the Yangzi, thus giving the gorge its name. The man who restored the path charges Y10.

From Tina's to Walnut Garden it is a 40-minute walk along the road. A new alternative trail to Walnut Garden keeps high where the path descends to Tina's, crosses a stream and a **bamboo forest** before descending into Walnut Garden.

The next day's walk is slightly shorter than the previous day's at four to six hours. There are two ferries and so two route options to get to Dàjù. After 45 minutes you'll see a red marker leading down to the new (winter) ferry (xīn dùkǒu; one way Y10); the descent includes one hairy section over planks with a sheer drop below.

Many trekkers call it a day when they reach the bottom and flag down anything heading back Qiáotóu.

The road to Dàjù and the village itself are pretty uninteresting so you won't be missing anything if you skip it.

If you do decide to head on to Dàjù, it's a hard climb to the car park where you should register with the Lìjiāng PSB (Gōngānjú). The PSB officer offers a car to take you into Dàjù for Y10, avoiding the dull 90-minute walk along the road.

The second, lesser-used option continues along the road from Walnut Garden until it reaches the permanent ferry crossing (Y10). From here paths lead to Dàjù.

If you're doing the walk the other way round and heading for Qiáotóu, walk north through Dàjù, aiming for the white pagoda at the foot of the mountains.

TIGER LEAPING GORGE TO BÁISHUĪTÁI

An adventurous add-on to the gorge trek is to continue north all the way to Hābā village and the limestone terraces of Báishuǐtái. This turns it into a four-day trek from Qiáotóu and

from here you can travel on to Shangri-la. From Walnut Garden to Hābā, via Jiāngbiān, it is seven to eight hours. From here to the Yi village of Sānbà is about the same, following trails. You could just follow the road and hitch with the occasional truck or tractor but it's longer and less scenic. Some hardy mountain bikers have followed the trail but this is really only fun from north to south, elevations being what they are. The best way would be to hire a guide in Walnut Garden for Y50 to Y100 per day, depending on the number of people. For Y100 to Y120 per day you should be able to get a horse and guide. Eventually buses will make the trip, but that is still some time off.

In Hābā most people stay at the **Haba Snow Mountain Inn** (Hābā Xuěshān Kèzhàn; dm Y15), which has toilets and showers. In Sānbà, beds can also be found for around Y15. From Sānbà there is an 8am bus to Shangri-la (Y40, five hours), or you could get off at the turn-off to Emerald Pagoda Lake (Bìtǎ Hǎi) and hike there.

If you plan to try the route alone, assume you'll need all provisions and equipment for extremes of weather. Ask for local advice before setting out.

TIGER LEAPING GORGE VIEWPOINT

If you don't have time to trek the gorge, you can view it from its eastern end near Dàjù. From Dàjù it's a 5km walk to the entry gate or you can take a taxi for Y10. At the car park there's a Y2 entry fee and a walkway leads down to an observation platform.

Sleeping & Eating

Lodging options abound but in peak times – particularly late summer – up to 100 people per day can make the trek, so bed space is short. Be prepared to sleep in a back room somewhere. Supplies of bottled water can be chancy.

QIÁOTÓU

Jane's Tibetan Guesthouse (Xiágǔxíng Kèzhàn; ☎ 880 6570; janetibetgh@hotmail.com; dm/s/d Y15/30/30; 🖳) Jane is one of the gorge's true characters and has all the information on the trek. There are left-luggage facilities and internet access here. It's next to the school at the start of the trek.

Gorged Tiger Café (☎ 880 6300) Run by a local institution (an Australian woman named

THE END OF THE GORGE?

Development is taking its toll on Tiger Leaping Gorge. After three years of Herculean blasting and building, a road was built all the way through the gorge from Qiáotóu to Walnut Garden and a dirt track swings north to Báishuǐtái, joining the road to Shangri-la. Tour buses shuttle up and down the gorge and kitschy stop-off points are always being constructed.

This currently isn't too much of an annoyance for trekkers as the high path climbs way above all of the activity. New plans for resorts, chairlifts, golf courses and the like have been endlessly bandied about.

If only the gorge's annoying new road and its ubiquitous shuttle buses were all. Tiger Leaping Gorge could disappear in a matter of years if plans to build eight dams along 564km of the upper reaches of the Yangzi River go ahead. This is but one of Yúnnán's most controversial dam projects; the other, in the Nujiang Valley (see p297), has put locals equally at odds with the government.

Once completed, the dams along the Yangzi River's upper reaches will flood more than 13,000 hectares of prime farmland, force over 100,000 people (some claim up to a million) to relocate and wash away local culture, history, unique architecture and indigenous plant and animal life.

Officials, naturally, claim that the dams are crucial to sating China's ever-increasing appetite for power. The proposed dams will also divert water to Kūnmíng to help alleviate chronic water shortages (of which anyone who's experienced the capital's 'water blackouts' during winter will be aware). Local officials also hope to garner around US$50 million per annum in tax revenues – double the current figure.

Local opposition has been uniform and ferocious (there have been one or two reports of assaults against officials). They first point out that one of the project's major backers is Li Xiaopeng, the son of Li Peng, the former prime minister who pushed through the controversial Three Gorges Dam project (p461).

But even with every environmental group in China and abroad lobbying against it, it's hard to believe that those in charge will take much notice. At the time of writing the Chinese media reported that preparatory work, including blasting, had already begun and proper construction on the dams was expected to begin by 2008. A good site to keep up to date on the project is www.irn.org.

Margo), this is a welcoming friendly place, though a few travellers have bemoaned the food. Great information source.

The **Youth Hostel** (Qīngnián Lǚguǎn; dm/d Y15/50) on the village's main road is friendly but rooms are subpar at best. There's a **hotel** (d Y280) next the Shangri-la-Qiaotou bus drop-off that seems appealing on the outside (what a shock) but they apparently forgot to include the rooms in its face-lift.

DÀJÙ

Snowflake Hotel (Xuěhuā Fàndiàn; s & d Y20) Rooms are spartan and a bit dark but its friendliness will snag most sweaty TLG trekkers.

Daju Longhu Inn (Dàjù Lónghǔ Kèzhàn; ☎ toll free 888 532 6040; d standard/deluxe without bathroom Y20/50) You may need to stick a smoke into your nostrils in the communal showers and toilets, and the budget rooms are nondescript, but the deluxe ones are quite impressively done up.

Getting There & Away

Transport is ever easier. From Lìjiāng, buses run to Shangri-la every hour or so from 7.30am to 5pm from the long-distance bus station and pass through Qiáotóu (Y20). The last bus to Shangri-la passes through at around 7pm.

At least two buses to Dàjù (Y24, four hours) run in the morning – if they feel like it – from just north of Lìjiāng's old town, by the waterwheel. These return from Dàjù to Lìjiāng at 7.30am and 1.30pm.

Returning to Lìjiāng from Qiáotóu, buses start running through from Shangri-la around 9am. The last one rolls through around 7.40pm (Y20).

Eventually the new highway through the gorge will link Qiáotóu, Walnut Garden and the settlement across the river from Dàjù and then bend north to connect Báishuǐtái, allowing travellers to get to Shangri-la from here.

LÚGŪ HÚ 泸沽湖

☎ 0888

Tranquillity is fast beating a retreat from this forest-lined lake that overlaps the remote Yúnnán–Sìchuān border. The lake, formed by two sinking faults, is fairly high at 2685m and is usually snowbound over the winter months. Villages are scattered around the lake but **Luòshuǐ** (洛水) is the one heavily developed for tourism and is where your bus will drop you off. Essentially, the further you get from Luòshuǐ, the more 'pristine' and 'less touristed' the experience.

Consider heading for Lǐgé (right), a much smaller village on the northwestern shore of the lake. Then again, we've already started getting letters mentioning that it too is becoming 'too touristy'. We politely disagree with that. For now, anyway. (True, maniacal building has started.)

Worry not – there are plenty of fabulous villages. In fact, villages are found throughout the area and it's fairly easy to get yourself lost (in a good way). If you're still looking for remoteness, then just keep village-hopping and you'll find yourself on the Sìchuān side, where little of the action is. Just know that some of the roads around the lake to other villages are pretty rough. Top votes for alternate locations are **Luòwǎ** (洛瓦) and **Wǔzhīluó** (五支罗). Both almost directly opposition Luòshuǐ.

The area is home to several Tibetan, Yi and Mosu (a Naxi subgroup) villages. The Mosu are the last practising matriarchal society in the world (see the boxed text, p286) and many other Naxi customs lost in Lìjiāng are still in evidence here.

The best times to visit the lake are April to May, and September to October, when the weather is dry and mild. Entrance to the lake is Y80.

Sights & Activities

From Luòshuǐ you can visit several islands on the lake by dugout canoe, which the Mosu call 'pig troughs' (zhūcáo). The canoes are rowed by Mosu who also serve as guides and usually take you out to **Lǐwùbǐ Dǎo** (里务比岛), the largest island. From here you can practically wade across to a spit of land in Sìchuān. The second largest island is **Hēiwǎ Dǎo** (黑瓦俄岛). Canoes leave from a beach area to the south of the hotel strip in Luòshuǐ. In Lǐgé any of the hostels can help arrange boat trips. The price will vary wildly, depending on exactly what you want to see, and how many people are in your group. If you're in a group of six to eight people expect to pay around Y10 per person.

Near the bus stop in Luòshuǐ is the worthwhile **Mosu Folk Custom Museum** (摩俗民族博物馆; Mósú Mínzú Bówùguǎn; admission Y20; ☽ hit & miss). The museum is set within the traditional home of a wealthy Mosu family and the obligatory guide will show you around and explain how the matriarchal society functions. There is also an interesting collection of photos taken by Joseph Rock (p273) in the 1920s.

In the outskirts of nearby Yǒngníng is **Zhamei Temple** (扎美寺; Zhāměi Sì), a Tibetan monastery with at least 20 lamas in residence. Admission is free, but a donation is expected. A private minivan costs Y15 per person for the half-hour ride. A bus passes through Luòshuǐ to Yǒngníng (Y5, roughly hourly), or you could opt to walk the 20km or so through pleasant scenery.

Sleeping & Eating

Hotels and guesthouses with doubles from around Y50 line the lakeside in Luòshuǐ. Most have attached restaurants that serve traditional Mosu foods including preserved pig's fat and salted sour fish – the latter being somewhat tastier.

Husi Teahouse (湖思茶屋; Húsī Cháwū; ☎ 588 1170; dm Y15; 🖳) Run by Sichuaner Táng Bīn since 1998, this is one of the original and still the best backpacker hang-outs on the lake. Showers are a bit of a hike from the guesthouse but he's got a fleet of computers with internet, killer coffee, a terrific bar-café and travel info galore. If you're lucky, you'll be in one of four rooms with floor-to-ceiling windows overlooking the lake.

Mósuō Dàjiǔdiàn (摩梭大酒店; ☎ 588 1185; d/cabins 160/400) The nearby Mosu guesthouses will likely have better doubles, but there's a handful of cabins away from the main building worth looking at. They don't have lake views, but each includes a living room, bedroom and bathroom.

LǏGÉ 里格

With its velvet silence and vivid starry nights, arriving in this magical little village after Lìjiāng feels like arriving at the very tranquil end of the earth. Most travellers don't get past Luòshuǐ, so if you do make the effort to come here it will likely be just you, the Mosu and a handful of solo Chinese backpackers.

Set around a bay facing Lǐgé Dǎo (Lige Island), there's a day's worth of exploring to do either in the wilderness or on the lake, but a surprising number of travellers come and just chat, doodle and drink at one of the three waterside cafés.

But do get here as quick as you can. Construction plans are in the works here and one part of the bay looks like it's being readied for the construction of at least a half-dozen two-storey guesthouses.

Sleeping & Eating

Yàsè Dábā Lǚxíngzhě Zhījiā (雅瑟达吧旅行者之家; ☎ 588 1196; dm/d/tr Y20/40/60; 🖳) Recently opened on the edge of the lake, this guesthouse has basic rooms with electric blankets, lovely owners and is just a spit away from the water. The cosy restaurant serves wonderful food: try Lúgū Hú fish (泸沽湖鱼; Lúgū Hú yú) or sausage (香肠; xiāngcháng) along with cold beer and an impressive choice of liqueurs (Baileys anyone?). It can also suggest activities or arrange pretty much any excursion you want here. Bikes cost Y20 per day.

Right around the corner from here, on the south side of this spit of land, is another terrific **guesthouse** (客栈; Kèzhàn; ☎ 588 1015; d from Y30). Waves from the lake lick at the walls of this charming café, it's so close to the water.

It's all headed up by Susan, the fantastically friendly and relaxed owner.

Getting There & Away

Lìjiāng's long-distance bus station has one direct bus a day to the lake (Y63, seven to eight hours, 9.30am) but buy your ticket at least one day in advance as they often sell out. Alternatively, you can go to Nínglàng (宁蒗) from Lìjiāng's north bus station (Y23, three to four hours, six buses daily, 8am to 2pm). From Nínglàng, there's a daily bus to the lake (Y20, three to four hours, 12.30pm). For Lǐgé you will have to change for a minibus in Luòshuǐ (Y8 per person if there's a lot of you though normally they'll try to charge Y10 for the 20- to 25-minute ride).

Leaving Luòshuǐ, the direct bus to Lìjiāng leaves daily at 10am. Again, tickets should be bought at least a day in advance. There's also a daily bus to Nínglàng (Y20, check time when you arrive). From Nínglàng, there's 13 buses daily to Lìjiāng (Y25, 7.30am to 4pm) and one daily to Xiàguān (Y48, 7.50am).

At least one per day also makes the run to Jīnjiāng (Y50), from where you can hop a train to Chéngdū, but the bus station where you may be dropped off is 20km from the train station. A bus between the two (there are many) costs Y3.

The daily bus to Xīchāng (西昌) leaves at 8am (Y60, seven to eight hours). There are also

---

WALKING MARRIAGE

The Mosu are the last practising matriarchal society in the world. This system, whereby kinship and clan names, and social and political positions are passed on through the female line, has fascinated visitors since the area was developed for tourism in the early 1980s. What's proved to be the biggest draw, however, is the Mosu tradition of a 'walking marriage' (走婚; zǒu hūn).

Mosu women never marry nor cohabit; instead women are free to choose as many lovers as they like throughout their lives. Mosu women come of age when they reach 13, after which they no longer have to sleep in the communal living areas but are given their own bedroom. Her lover visits at night and leaves to return to his mother's home in the morning, hence the expression 'walking marriage'.

This idea of such free and easy love has been heavily publicised. Traditionally referred to as Nǚ Guó (Woman's Kingdom), the area of Lúgū Hú was renamed Nǚ'ér Guó (Girl's Kingdom) in order to spice up the romantic and exotic image of the local women.

It's a strategy that's worked. Thousands of tourists have ventured up to this remote area, resulting in the Mosu becoming the richest ethnic minority group in Yúnnán. But it's also had some damaging effects on their culture. 'Walking marriage' has become synonymous with 'one night stand' and many men, in particular Han Chinese, visit the area in the hope of having a walking marriage themselves. This in turn has seen a rise in prostitution in the area, and brothels disguised as karaoke bars now sit on the edge of Luòshuǐ town; the ultimate proof, if it was ever needed, that's there's no such thing as free love.

dozens of minibuses that the prowl the villages around the lake on both the Sìchuān and Yúnnán side if you want to go exploring.

SHANGRI-LA 香格里拉
(ZHŌNGDIÀN 中甸)

☎ 0887 / pop 120,000 / elevation 3200m

Shangri-la (formerly known as Zhōngdiàn, which you'll also see and hear; its Tibetan name is Gyeltang or Gyalthang) is where you begin to breathe in the Tibetan world. (If you can breathe at all, given its altitude.)

One of the most important monasteries in China lies just north of town and the town offers a fantastic dose of Tibet if you can't make it to the real thing. Shangri-la is also the last stop in Yúnnán for more hardy travellers looking at a rough five- or six-day journey to Chéngdū via the Tibetan townships and rugged terrain of western Sìchuān.

How times change. A mere decade ago, Shangri-la was literally a one-yak town, too high and remote to draw in many tourists. Pigs nibbled on garbage-strewn street corners; there was but one place to stay and pretty much nowhere to eat. Then, watching Lìjiāng and Dàlǐ zoom into the tourism stratosphere based on their sublime geographic locations, local and provincial governments started to pay attention to the erstwhile Zhōngdiàn in serious fashion.

Officials declared the town (and by extension the rest of the country) the location of British writer James Hilton's fictional Shangri-la, described in his novel *The Lost Horizon*. Roll your eyes if you wish, but it has worked big time. This is a prime spot for all kinds of tourists – hence the airport and guesthouses springing up seasonally (and skyrocketing entrance fees). Still, it's a wondrous place and well worth a visit.

Plan your visit to this neck of the woods between April and October. There is no point coming here during winter as the city is practically shut down and transportation is often halted completely by snow storms.

Accommodation can be a bit tight around festivals times (see p288), so you may want to arrive a day or two early in order to secure a room.

Information

CD burning is available at Noah Café (p289) for Y10 per CD.

Agricultural Bank of China (Zhōngguó Nóngyè Yínháng; ☎ 822 2567; cnr Changzheng Lu & Xiangyang Lu; ⏰ 8.30am-noon & 2.30-5.30pm Mon-Fri) Can change cash, travellers cheques and usually gives cash advances on credit cards, though some travellers have reported being denied.

China Telecom (Changzheng Lu) There are two telephone offices along this road that offer cheap international phone calls.

Khampa Caravan (Kāngbā Shāngdào Tànxiǎn Lǚxíngshè; ☎ 828 8648; www.khampacaravan.com; Heping Lu) Organises some excellent adventures, from day treks in the surrounding countryside to week-long treks in the remote wilderness. It can also arrange overland travel into Tibet (see p291), as well as flights and permits from Shangri-la to Lhasa. The company also runs a lot of sustainable development programs within Tibetan communities. One of these projects, Trinyi Eco-lodge, is six kilometres southwest out of town and is easy to get to by bike.

Public Security Bureau (PSB; Gōngānjú; ☎ 822 6834; Changzheng Lu; ⏰ 8.30am-12.30pm & 2.30-5pm) Issues on-the-spot visa extensions.

Tibet Café (Xīzàng Kāfēiguǎn; ☎ 823 0282; www .tibetcafeinn.com; Changzheng Lu; internet access per hr Y12) Another great place to go for travel information; it also organises overland travel to Tibet. A particularly worthwhile trip is a visit to its eco-farm, Shangbala, 40km from Shangri-la, where you can spend the evening with a Tibetan family (Y20 per person). All money goes directly to the Tibetan community.

Dangers & Annoyances

Altitude sickness is a real problem here and most travellers need at least a couple of days to acclimatise. Brutal winter weather can bring the town to a complete standstill so try to plan your visit between March and October. Note that with the boom in tourism has come a boom in thievery – pay close attention to your bags and neighbours on buses, especially for those early-in-the-morning dark departures.

Sights

About an hour's walk north of town is the **Ganden Sumtseling Gompa** (Sōngzànlín Sì; admission Y10; ⏰ 7.30am-8pm), a 300-year-old Tibetan monastery complex with around 600 monks, though most of these live and actually work outside the temple. It is by far the most important in southwest China and definitely worth the trip.

Construction on the Gelukpa (Yellow Hat) monastery was initiated in 1679 by the fifth Dalai Lama. Shelled like everything else by the People's Liberation Army (PLA) in 1959 it wasn't reopened until 1981. A half-dozen main buildings include eight colleges, all open – usually – to the public.

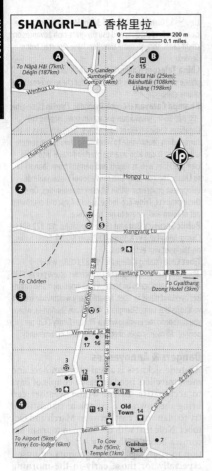

The monks are welcoming, even with more and more tourists coming in. If you're around during special occasions or festivals, you might see Cham, religious dances in which monks wear masks depicting deities, ghosts and animals. Bus 3 runs here from anywhere along Changzheng Lu (Y1). Be advised that the government is planning to raise the admission price to around Y30. It claims that the monastery is getting the bulk of this.

The view of town from the top is gorgeous, and a sunset from here is particularly picturesque among the tinkling bells and the fluttering prayer flags.

Hidden within the old town is the **Scripture Chamber** (Gǔchéng Cángjīngtáng; admission Y5), formerly a memorial hall to the Red Army's Long March. Definitely not much to see here but its one room is worth a look. **Guishan Park** (Guīshān Gōngyuán; admission Y3) is nearby and has a temple at the top with commanding views of the area.

Further south, just outside of and overlooking the old town from an eyrie, is another tiny **temple** presided over by two exceedingly friendly monks. To get here, walk south to the end of Changzheng Lu. Bear left, then take an immediate right. Paths run up across some gardens and along a hill, bypassing a pavilion.

Further north, atop a hill to the west of Changzheng Lu is a **chörten** (Tibetan stupa) with good views of the town.

Besides the sights listed here, Shangri-la is a wonderful place to get off the beaten track with plenty of trekking and horseback riding opportunities, as well as little-visited monasteries and villages. However, the remote sights are difficult to do independently given lack of public transport. You'll need to arrange a guide, or car and driver through your accommodation

Festivals & Events

In mid to late June Shangri-la plays host to a **horseracing festival** that sees several days of dancing, singing, eating and horseracing. Another new festival – usually in September – features minority artists of southwest China.

Sleeping

There are always interesting guesthouses and hostels popping up near the old town and city outskirts. Be aware, however, that despite Shangri-la's often glacial night temperatures, many guesthouses are neither heated nor have 24-hour hot water. Those listed here ostensibly stay open year-round, but verify this with them before you slog your bag down the street in the snow.

Dragoncloud Guesthouse (Lóngxíng Kèzhàn; ☎ 688 7573; www.dragoncloud.cn; 94 Beimen Jie, Jiantang Zhen; 建塘镇北门街94号; dm Y15-25, s & d Y80; 🖳) Large and spacious, this guesthouse has tastefully understated modern rooms and everything is in great shape – including the restrooms and showers. The fireplace in the common area is a godsend. Internet (Y4 per hour) and interesting comings and goings from the nearby old town. Bike rental for Y15 per day.

Shangri-La Traveller Club (Déqīn Zàngdì Guójì Qīngnián Lǚshè; ☎ 822 8671; 98 Heping Lu; 和平路98号; dm/d Y20/50; 🖳) The gregariousness of the staff here makes up (more than enough) for the only downside – the chilling dash from the outdoor shower to your room! You can rent bikes here (Y15 per day) and go online (Y6 per hour).

Kevin's Trekker Inn (Lóngmén Kèzhàn; ☎ 822 8178; www.kevintrekkerinn.com; Tuanjie Lu; 团结路; dm/d Y20/60; 🖳) Run by a diehard traveller, this place has consistently garnered high praise from travellers for its helpful owners and cosy digs. Choose between a traditional Chinese house or a newer Tibetan building. Warmly lit common areas and loads of extras – best might be the flowers the proprietor insists on maintaining on the grounds.

International Youth Hostel (Guójì Qīngnián Lǚshè; ☎ 822 6948; Jiantang Lu; 建塘路; dm/d Y20/80) Spartan and on the chilly side at night, this hostel is in a quiet part of town and run by a lovely family who don't speak English but go out of their way to help.

Gyalthang Dzong Hotel (建塘宾馆; Jiàntáng Bīnguǎn; ☎ 822 3646; www.coloursofangsana.com/gyalthang; s & d in peak season US$90; closed 1 Dec-1 Apr) It's honestly a rare pleasure to write about a high-end place in China that warrants the mention. This is one of them – a fabulous place and one of the best we've seen anywhere in China's Southwest. Some 3km east of town and backed against a 'protector' hill, it's got amazing rooms – call them spiritually chic in design, with subtle rusty oranges and maroons – and exquisite attention to detail throughout.

Eating & Drinking

The Tibet Café (p287) has a popular restaurant, though it's a bit pricey. It also has great bikes for rent.

Noah Café (Nuóyà Kāfēi; Changzheng Lu; 长征路; dishes from Y10) When the weather gets nippy – OK, downright freezing – you can be sure that most people are going to be here for their three squares – if they leave at all. Yup, at last check, this place seemed to be tops – good muesli and pancakes. You can also burn CDs here for Y10.

Cow Pub (Niúpéng Jiǔbā; ☎ 828 5774; Jinlong Jie; 金龙街) The name itself warrants a poke-around in this place whose design scheme is dedicated to cowpokes (Tibetan or otherwise) or at least life in Old Tibet. Subdued but welcoming, you'll find it in the old town.

Artistic Space of the Sacred (Shèngdì Yìshù Kōngjiān; ☎ 823 1309; 16 Cangfang Jie; 仓房街16号) Not your run-of-the-mill joint, this place – is it a bar, an inn? – is run by an artist, and it shows, from the lighting to the colour coordination. Best of all are the inspiring views from the tiered outdoor terraces. A Ming has a gallery full of paintings upstairs and will show you if you ask. He's also set up a four-bed dorm with a Buddhist shrine and a private room with one of the most romantic views in the city.

Have a look around the old town and on Tuanjie Lu for Tibetan and Western restaurants and cafés. Also look out for locally produced Shangri-la wine. French missionaries working in the Mekong area taught the Tibetans wine-producing techniques, a tradition which has fortunately carried on through to today; look for the bottle with a picture of a church on the label.

Getting There & Away

Note that many of the roads leading out of Shangri-la, particularly the road to Emerald Pagoda Lake and Báishuǐtái, take you over 4000m-plus passes. If you fly in direct from Kūnmíng it's important that you give yourself a day or two to acclimatise in Shangri-la.

AIR

There are four flights daily to Kūnmíng (Y830), two a week to Guǎngzhōu (Y1880), and regular flights to Lhasa. Flights for other domestic destinations also leave from this airport but are completely irregular and destinations change from week to week. You can inquire about your destination or buy

SHANGRI-LA – FACT & FICTION

At first it seemed like a typically overstated tourist campaign: 'Shangri-la Found'. Only they weren't kidding. In November 1997 the *China Daily* reported that the Yúnnán Economy & Technology Research Centre had established with 'certainty' that the fabled 'Shangri-la' of James Hilton's 1933 best-seller *Lost Horizon* was, indeed, in Déqīn County.

Hilton's novel (later filmed by Frank Capra and starring Ronald Coleman, Jane Wyatt and John Gielgud) tells the story of four travellers who are hijacked and crash land in a mountain utopia ruled by a 163-year-old holy man. This 'Shangri-la' is in the Valley of the Blue Moon, a beautiful fertile valley capped by a perfect pyramid peak, Mt Karakul. According to Hilton's book, Shangri-la is reached by travelling 'southwest from Peking for many months', and is found 'a few hundred kilometres from a world's end market town…where Chinese coolies from Yúnnán transfer their loads of tea to the Tibetans'.

The Yúnnán Economy & Technology Research Centre based its claim primarily on the fact that Déqīn's Kawa Karpo peak perfectly resembles the 'pyramid-shaped' landmark of Mt Karakul. Also, the county's blood-red valleys with three parallel rivers fit a valley from *Lost Horizon*.

One certainly plausible theory is that Hilton, writing the novel in northwest London, based his descriptions of Shangri-la on articles by Joseph Rock he had read in *National Geographic* magazine detailing Rock's expeditions to remote parts of Lìjiāng, Mùlī and Déqīn. Others believe that Hilton's 'Shangri-la' may just have been a corruption of the word *Shambhala*, a mystical Buddhist paradise.

Tourism authorities wasted little time latching onto the Shangri-la phenomenon and today there are Shangri-la hotels, travel agencies and a Shangri-la airport. Sensing that 'there's money in them there Shangri-la hills', rival bids popped up around Yúnnán. Cízhōng in Wēixī County pointed out that its Catholic churches and Tibetan monasteries live side by side in the valley. One local was even told that she was the blood relative of one of the (fictional) characters! Meanwhile, Dàochéng, just over the border in Sìchuān, had a strong bid based around the pyramid peak of its mountain Channa Dorje and the fact that Rock wrote about the region in several articles. Then there's the town of Xiónggǔ (雄古), a Naxi village 40km from Lìjiāng, which boasts a stone tablet from the Qing dynasty naming the town 'Xianggeli', from where the name Shangri-la is derived.

It's hard for us cynics not to believe that the whole thing has simply been manufactured as a money-making exercise. Provincial authorities had long been preparing for an invasion of tourists into the prefecture to provide an alternative income to the recently banned logging trade. Even Xuan Ke, the original proponent of the Shangri-la theory, laments that the concept has been hijacked for commercial purposes. No amount of reminding that Shangri-la is in a work of fiction will deter local Chinese who are proudly convinced of the authenticity.

And while it may even have been Shangri-la to Hilton and millions of readers, Shangri-la is at its heart surely a metaphor. As a skinny-dipping Jane Wyatt says in the film version of the book, 'I'm sure there's a wish for Shangri-la in everyone's heart…'

tickets at the **CAAC** (Zhōngguó Mínháng; ☎ 822 9901; Wenming Jie).

The airport is 5km from town and is sometimes referred to as Díqìng or Deqen – there is currently no airport at Déqīn. Don't expect to see any taxis here, they are rare around the airport. Shuttle buses (Y10) sometimes wait for incoming flights and will usually drop you right at your hotel. The drivers wear picture ID. If the shuttle bus isn't there you'll have to negotiate with the all the drivers of the black sedans in front of you or call your accommodation to try and arrange something.

BUS

Then, there's everyone's favourite bus-trek: the 'back' door (hardly seems like it with its popularity now) to Chéngdū in Sìchuān, via Xiāngchéng, Lǐtáng and Kāngdìng. It may be the bee's knees as far as travellers' fave roughing-it trips, but be aware that it isn't always a picnic, so be prepared before you go.

You're looking at a minimum of five to six days' travel at some very high altitudes – you'll need warm clothes. Roads are also ass-killing. The first stage of the trip is Shangri-la to Xiāngchéng in Sìchuān. From Xiāngchéng, your next destination is Lǐtáng, though

SHANGRI-LA BUS TIMETABLE

This list is not exhaustive. Loads of other buses ply local- and long-distance routes, most covered in other chapters. You could even take the extraordinary long-haul to Jīnjiāng in Sìchuān from here on an endlessly long sleeper bus.

Destination	Price (Y)	Duration (hours)	Frequency	Departs
Báishuǐtái	23	4	2 daily	9.10am, 2.10pm
Bēnzǐlán	17	3	2 daily	1pm, 2pm
Déqīn	38	6	4 daily	7.20am–noon
Dōngwàng	45	7–8	daily	7.30am
Kūnmíng	167	15	7 daily	4–7.30pm
Lìjiāng	35	4½	13 daily	7.10am–5.40pm
Xiàguān	56	8	hourly	7am–12.30pm
Xiāngchéng	65	8–9	daily	7.30am

if roads are bad you may be forced to stay overnight in Dàochéng. From Lǐtáng, it's on to Kāngdìng from where you can make your way west towards Chéngdū. For more details on these towns see Western Sìchuān & the Road to Tibet (p387).

Few undertake the other options. Take the 8am bus north to Dōngwàng, get off where it turns off the main road and hitch from here. Another option is to take the daily early morning bus to Déróng (Y37), a town with a decent hotel and a couple of nice monasteries just over the border in Sìchuān, and try to catch onward transport to the main Shangri-la–Lǐtáng road from there.

Note that roads out of Shangri-la can be temporarily blocked by snow at any time from November (or even October in some years) to March. If you are travelling at this time bring lots of warm clothes and a flexible itinerary.

For Bēnzǐlán you can also catch the Déqīn bus which passes through Bēnzǐlán on the way. See also individual local destinations for transport details.

TO TIBET

There are now flights from Shangri-la to Lhasa, however the situation is much the same as in Kūnmíng and Chéngdū and travellers must be part of an organised 'group' and have the necessary permits in order to travel. There are three companies in Shangri-la that sell 'packages' to Tibet (around Y2570 per person, including air ticket):

Khampa Caravan (☎ 828 8648; www.khampacaravan .com; Heping Lu)

Tibet Café (☎ 823 0019; www.tibetcafeinn.com; Changzheng Lu)

Tibet Tourism Bureau (Xīzàng Lǚyóujú; ☎ 822 9028; yunnantibettour@yahoo.com.cn; Room 2206, Shangbala Hotel, 36 Changzheng Lu)

These same companies can also organise overland trips from Shangri-la into Tibet via either the northern or southern highway to Lhasa. Likewise, you need official permits in order to do this and these trips don't come cheap (from Y800 to Y1000 per vehicle per day). You're also looking at an eight- to 12-day journey at high altitudes. But holy smoke, what an adventure (and what scenery).

Trips – and costs – vary so it's worth shopping around to see what best suits you. Remember that permits take five days to organise. The Tibet Café has arranged for travellers to start the permit process in Dàlǐ courtesy of the MCA Guesthouse. Traveller's can fax copies of their passports through to Shangri-la from the MCA Guesthouse so by the time they arrive in Shangri-la their permits will be ready to collect. Jim's Tibetan Guesthouse & Peace Café in Dàlǐ (p260) can also organise overland travel to Lhasa.

Getting Around

Buss 1 and 3 zip between the monastery and town (Y1).

AROUND SHANGRI-LA

Approximately 10km southeast of Shangri-la is the **Tiansheng Bridge** (天生桥; Tiānshēng Qiáo; admission Y15), a natural limestone formation, and further southeast, the subterranean **Xiagei hot springs** (下给温泉; Xiàgěi Wēnquán; admission Y15). If you can arrange transport, en route is the

Great Treasure Temple (大宝寺; Dàbǎo Sì), one of the earliest Buddhist temples in Yúnnán.

These sites are wildly popular with Chinese tour groups but many foreign travellers seem uniformly underwhelmed.

Napa Lake (Nàpà Hǎi) 纳帕海

Some 7km northwest of Shangri-la you'll find this seasonal lake (admission Y30) fed by 10 streams and rivers, surrounded by a large grass meadow and mountains on three sides. Nine caves lie in the surrounding mountains; in the hills in the northwest corner of the lake lie the remains of a Ming dynasty temple with fine views.

Between September and March budding ornithologists will like the place: the 2000-sq-m Napa Hai Nature Reserve is home to myriad rare bird species, including a winter community of around 200 black-necked cranes. Autumn is lovely here – azure skies above golden meadows and yaks everywhere.

Outside of these months, the lake dries up and there is little reason to visit. It is worth a bike ride in summer, when you can also hire horses; the rest of the time it's just a marsh. Tents can be rented for around Y25 to Y30 per night in off-peak times (during a festival it may be Y150). The best views are from the high ground to the north and you'll get these from the bus to Déqīn or Bēnzǐlán.

Emerald Pagoda Lake & Shudu Lake 碧塔海和属都海

Some 25km east of Shangri-la, the bus to Sānbà (see Báishuǐtái, following) can drop you along the highway for **Emerald Pagoda Lake** (Bìtǎ Hǎi; admission Y190), which is 8km down a trail (a half-hour by pony). Yes, this is an absolutely laughable admission price, and it was just being introduced at the time of writing. Hopefully there will be enough outcry (and subsequent drop in tourism) for officials to rethink this.

If you do decide to visit, there are lots of hiking options and ponies can be arranged at the lake (Y65 round-trip rides; Y25 to or from southern entrance to/from lake). There is a second, southern entrance, from where it is 2km to the lake. It's possible to rent boats between the two ends of the lake; a motorboat ride runs Y50 per person, or you can haggle down to Y100 or so for five if you're good. Rowboats are cheaper. Tourists come to photograph the island in the middle of the lake

that is ablaze with flowers in June and a riot of autumn colours in October. An intriguing sight in summer is the comatose fish that float unconscious for several minutes in the lake after feasting on azalea petals.

Basic **cabins** (Y15-30) are available at the western end of the lake.

The whopping new entrance fee is also due to the inclusion of Shudu Lake (Shǔdū Hǎi), approximately 10km to the north. More birds, more scintillating blue – you know the deal. The lush carpets of forest are impressive, especially the dragon spruce and silver birch. The name means 'place where milk is found' in Tibetan because its pastures are reputedly the most fertile in northwestern Yúnnán. There certainly is more livestock grazing here than anywhere else. It is possible to hike between the two lakes but it's easy to get lost, so be sure to get precise directions.

Too bad the entrance fee is so high, as it probably puts travellers off a trip to the gorgeous little Tibetan village of **Nírù** (尼迦) to the northeast, close to the border with Sìchuān. (Even if you just wish to meander around those parts, you've gotta fork over the cash for the entrance fee if you're passing through.) One traveller reported hiking from Shudu Lake to Nírù in a day, though you definitely need help knowing where to go. You could also take a daily bus (3pm) to Luòjí (洛吉) and hike/hire a car from there.

Getting to the lake(s) is tricky. You usually have to catch the bus to Sānbà, get off at the turn-off and hitch. Getting back you can wait (sometimes forever) for a bus or hike to one of the entrances or main road and look out for taxis – these guys need a fare back to Shangri-la so you might negotiate a good deal. Emerald Pagoda Lake is one of the more ambitious destinations for a bicycle ride. A taxi will cost around Y200 for the return trip, including Shudu Lake.

Báishuǐtái 白水台

Breathtaking scenery, possible pony rides, and a splendid chain of Tibetan villages leads to **Báishuǐtái** (admission Y30), a limestone deposit plateau 108km southeast of Shangri-la. For good reason has this become probably the most popular slow route between Lìjiāng and Shangri-la.

The terraces, reminiscent of those found in Pamukkale in Turkey or Huánglóng in Sìchuān, are resplendent in sunlight, but can be tough to get to if rainfall has made trails slick. The terraces are around the small Naxi village of Báidì. The highlight of the terraces is a 60m-tall cascade and rock cave. There are sometimes horses for hire up to the terraces for around Y25.

The region is also famed as the birthplace and heartland of Naxi Dongba culture (see p265 for more information) and thus is sacred to the Naxi, so tread ever so lightly.

One adventurous option is to combine a visit to Emerald Pagoda Lake with Báishuǐtái and trek all the way from here to Tiger Leaping Gorge via Sānbà and Hābā villages. You'll need local expertise to find the paths, though a rough road does lead between the villages. It is probably easier to do this route in reverse, since guesthouses in Walnut Grove along the Tiger Leaping Gorge trek can arrange horses and guides. See p283 for further information.

A couple of guesthouses at the nearby towns of Báidì and Sānbà have rooms with beds from Y25; in the off season these can go down to Y10 or so.

From Shangri-la there are two daily buses to Sānbà via Báishuǐtái at 9.10am and 2.10pm (Y23, four hours). Don't count on these always departing. The starting price to charter a microbus from Shangri-la to Báishuǐtái via Emerald Pagoda Lake is Y400 to Y500.

Běnzǐlán & Níxī 奔子栏、尼西

Běnzǐlán gets all the publicity for its wonderful Tibetan gompa, but along the way, roughly halfway to Běnzǐlán and where the highway intersects with the road to Wéixī, consider hopping off in Níxī, famed for its pottery. Some three-quarters of the village's 100-plus families still make the 3km trip to and from local hills, where the clay is said to be sublime, and set to work as they have for centuries.

Běnzǐlán, is the (roughly) halfway point on the way to Déqīn. This laid-back Tibetan village makes an excellent base to explore the wonderful **Dhondrupling Gompa** (东竹林寺; Dōngzhúlín Sì), 22km from Běnzǐlán, heading northwest along the main road. This is one of the most important monasteries in the prefecture. The original temple, built in 1667, was up in Báimáng Xuěshān, but after being destroyed by the PLA in the 1950s, it was rebuilt here, in the lee of the mountain. At its peak, more than 700 monks and 10 'living Buddhas' resided here; now its main

assembly hall and several *kangtsang* (colleges) still house 300 monks and four living Buddhas. There is a **mask dance festival** here in November. There is no entry fee and photos can be taken.

There is lovely scenery in all directions and if you have time it's a great hike to Běnzǐlán. Monks can show you the short cuts. If you enquire politely it might be possible to spend the night at the monastery.

Běnzǐlán has plenty of restaurants and small hotels. All offer decent beds for Y25 to Y30.

Duōwén Lǚguǎn (多闻旅馆; bed Y25) is perhaps the best choice, around the bend in the northern end of town. This Tibetan-style place has a prayer wheel by the entrance and pleasant rooms but fetid toilets; there have been good reports about the family that runs it.

To get to Běnzǐlán take any bus between Shangri-la and Déqīn; buses pass through town between 11am and noon. There are two direct buses a day from Shangri-la (Y17, three hours, 1pm and 2pm). There are daily buses back to Shangri-la. Inquire about times when you arrive.

Bìrǎng Xiágǔ 碧壤峡谷

Worth a visit if you've got loads of time, your butt hasn't been tenderised too much by western Sìchuān buses, and you are well prepared, is impressive **Bìrǎng Xiágǔ** (Birang Gorge; admission Y20), 100km north of Shangri-la. Biodiverse, seems something of an understatement when one takes a gander at the laundry list of flora and fauna contained within. Unesco went gaga when examining the region for placement on its World Heritage sites list in 2003.

It's recently been rechristened Shangri-la Gorge (Xiānggélǐlā Xiágǔ) – along, it seems, with half of the sights in northwest Yúnnán. The gorge itself has dramatic 150m-high sheer walls but the best part is the trail that leads out from the gorge, giving a rare opportunity to do some hiking. Get here quick – shops and restaurants have just been built and the litter is starting to pile up.

Currently you need to stay the night at the gorge or hire your own transport for around Y300. Public buses at 8am from Shangri-la to Wēngshuǐ (翁水; Y30), just north of the gorge, are some of the most hopeless in China, taking up to five hours to cover the 100km and only returning the next morning. You could try and get off the bus to

Xiāngchéng in Sìchuān. You may be able to hitch back in the afternoon in summer.

There is basic accommodation at the **Báimǎ Fàndiàn** (白马饭店; beds Y10) with beds in what is essentially a barn. There is also accommodation at the main gate for Y20, which gets you a proper mattress at least. Bring a sleeping bag in winter and be prepared – we were marooned here for several days after heavy snowfalls in November.

DÉQĪN 德钦

☎ 0887 / pop 60,085 / elevation 3550m

Nestled in the wild west of Yúnnán, among ragged, snowy peaks, Déqīn is the last outpost before Tibet. For borderholics, to the east is Sìchuān, to the west is Tibet and to the southwest is Myanmar. There are sacred mountains seemingly every which way. Intrigued?

This, Yúnnán's northernmost county, is perched at an average altitude of 3550m. One of Yúnnán's – if not China's – most magical mountains, Kawa Karpo (often referred to as Méilǐ Xuěshān) lies to the west of Déqīn. At 6740m, it is Yúnnán's highest peak and straddles the Yúnnán–Tibet border.

During the Tang dynasty, the prefecture was the seat of the Tangbo Tieqiao magistrate, but by the Ming dynasty, Lìjiāng's chieftain held sway. But far-flung Díqìng prefecture was so isolated that it was never really controlled by anyone until the PLA came in force in 1957.

Sparsely populated Déqīn County has only 60,085 people. More than 80% are Tibetan, though a dozen other minorities also live here, including one of the few settlements of non-Hui Muslims in China. A series of recent excavations unearthed stone coffins and tombs with 16 levels dating from the late Han period.

Some travellers are disappointed with the town itself, which is a modern Chinese creation nestling in a side valley of the Mekong River (澜沧江; Láncāng Jiāng), but there's a heavy Tibetan population (head to the market at the top end of town and shoot a few games of pool with the local Tibetans) enlivened by the occasional band of Khampa Tibetans down from the hills on a shopping expedition. And nobody comes here to stay in the town itself – head for the hills!

If you are travelling in winter you are crossing some serious ranges here and at any time from mid-October to late spring, heavy snows can close the roads. Pack sensibly and plan for a snowbound emergency.

Confusingly, Déqīn is the name of the city and county; both are incorporated by the Díqìng Tibetan Autonomous Prefecture. The county seat (and destination of the bus from Shangri-la) is spelled both ways, but you'll also see other variations on signs, maps, whatever. Plus, remember well – as if you could forget – that Déqīn County is also referred to as 'Shangri-la' in an effort to keep tourist dollars flowing up from the other Shangri-la (the erstwhile Zhōngdiàn).

Sleeping & Eating

Pretty much everyone heads for Fēilái Sì (opposite) and environs but the town has a few options.

Deqin Tibet Hotel (德钦楼; Déqīn Lóu; 841 2031; dm/d Y20/70) The most charming accommodation in town. There are bright murals on the walls and ceiling, some gorgeous views from the rooftop terrace rooms and a nice communal sitting area. You'll find this place 200m south of the bus station.

Deqin Dasheng Hotel (德钦大声大酒店; Déqīn Dàshēng Dàjiǔdiàn; d Y468) Up the street on your right after leaving the bus station, this hotel offers huge discounts and is a good choice for those wanting something a bit slicker. Rooms have modern bathrooms and electric blankets – a godsend during the chilly nights. There's an internet café across the street that serves free, bottomless cups of green tea while you surf or email (Y3 per hour).

Wéixī Nóngjiā Fēngwèi (维西农家风味; dishes from Y5) Across from the Deqin Dansheng Hotel, this hole-in-the-wall eatery has the cheapest and some of the best eats in town. It rarely sees tourists, and gets a regular crowd of boisterous locals, particularly for the 7pm news.

Getting There & Away

From Shangri-la to Déqīn, buses leave four times daily between 7.20am and noon (Y38, six hours). The same number of buses return to Shangri-la from Déqīn on a similar schedule.

There isn't any road to the Nujiang Valley (p297). Not yet, anyway. At the time of writing the governments of the Nujiang Valley and Déqīn had apparently goaded the provincial government into shelling out for a new road to link up with Gòngshān, but given the geography, this is proabably a long way off.

YET ANOTHER TIBET BACK DOOR

Déqīn is also a jumping-off point for those looking to slip into Tibet by the back door. There are rumours that the Yúnnán route into Tibet will open up to individual travellers in coming years (of course we've been hearing this annually since 1997 when this town opened), but at the moment travellers can only go to Déqīn, not into Tibet. This route is quite dangerous and the Public Security Bureau (PSB; Gōng'ānjú) keeps a vigilant eye out for foreigners trying to find their way across. Be warned that even if you find a driver to sneak you into Tibet, more than a few travellers have paid half the fare only to have the driver disappear. Just as importantly, if your driver gets caught smuggling you in he will face a large fine and likely confiscation of his driving license.

For details on border crossings into Tibet, see p291.

AROUND DÉQĪN

The Gelukpa (Yellow Hat) sect **Deqin Gompa** is 3km south of Déqīn. The young monks are friendly but there's not a lot to see.

Fēilái Sì 飞来寺

Approximately 10km southwest of Déqīn is the small but interesting Tibetan Fēilái Sì (Feilai Temple; Naka Zhashi, or Trashi, Gompa in Tibetan) devoted to the spirit of Kawa Karpo. There's no charge but leave a donation. No photos are allowed inside the tiny hall.

A further 800m along the main road brings you to a row of **chörten** (stupas) and, weather permitting, breathtaking views of the Méilǐ Xuěshān range, including the 6740m-high **Kawa Karpo** (also known as Méilǐ Xuěshān or Tàizi Shān). A small monument marks the tragic 1991 Sino–Japanese attempt on Kawa Karpo during which 17 people died. The even more beautiful peak to the south is 6054m **Miacimu** (Shénnǚ in Chinese), whose spirit is the female counterpart of Kawa Karpo. Joseph Rock described Miacimu as 'the most glorious peak my eyes were ever privileged to see…like a castle of a dream, an ice palace of a fairy tale'. Locals come here to burn juniper incense to the wrathful spirit of the mountain.

SLEEPING & EATING

This place has gone from deserted to a Chinese backpacker ghetto in a decade. Currently a handful of guesthouses and ultra-laid-back eateries are found here; these come and go like the wind.

Meili Guesthouse (雪山山庄; Xuěshān Shānzhuāng; ☎ 139 8874 0590; www.meililive.com; dm Y20, s & d Y140) This has been around longer than most others

and it's still a well-run place; it's got fabulous views. But then again, everything here does.

Migratory Bird (季候鸟; Jìhòuniǎo; ☎ 689 5030; dishes from Y8) Speaking of views, you are not going to find more breathtaking ones than here at this relaxing bar-café which is pretty much backpacker-central for these parts. If you need to know something, this is where you'll find out. It also does quite a bit of work with disabled Tibetan children.

GETTING THERE & AWAY

To get here from Déqīn a taxi will cost you Y30; alternatively, head out onto the road and flag down anything that moves.

Mingyong Glacier 明永冰川

Tumbling off the side of Kawa Karpo peak is the 12km-long **Mingyong Glacier** (Míngyǒng Bīngchuān; admission Y63, expect price spike if in high season). Over 13 sq km, it is not only the lowest glacier in China (around 2200m high) but also an oddity – it's a monsoon marine glacier, which basically means it has an ecosystem that couldn't possibly be more diverse: you'll see tundra, taiga, broadleaf forest and meadow, all in one hike. A conservation area has been created around the base of the peak. This sucker also hauls, moving an average of 530m per year (that would explain all the ice cracking and thundering). The best views of the glacier are from the road to Míngyǒng as it descends from Fēilái Sì.

For thousands of years the mountain has been a pilgrimage site and you'll still meet a few Tibetan pilgrims, some of whom circumambulate the mountain over seven days in autumn. Surrounding villages are known as 'heaven villages' because of the dense fog that hangs about in spring and summer, even permeating into homes.

Trails to the glacier lead up from Míngyǒng's central square marked by a new *chörten*. After 45 minutes a path splits off down to the (unimpressive) toe of the glacier. Continuing on, after another 45 minutes you get to Tibetan **Tàizǐ Miào** (太子庙), where there is a **guesthouse** (d low season Y100-120, high season Y180). A further 30 minutes along the trail is **Lotus Temple** (莲花庙; Liánhuā Miào), which offers fantastic views of the glacier framed by prayer flags and *chörten*. Horses can also be hired to go up to the glacier (Y150).

If you're coming from Yǔbēng (see boxed text, below), you could also hike to Míngyǒng from Xīdāng in around three hours if you hoof it.

SLEEPING

Beds in all guesthouses are around Y25 to Y30 and toilet facilities are basic. Electricity is iffy so bring a torch or some candles. A handful of new claim-to-be-midrange hotels have gone up in the last half-decade, most of which are uninspiring but still cost Y90 to Y250 for a standard room with bath.

Míngyǒng Shānzhuāng (明永山庄) Up some steps from the main square, where the bus drops you off, is this government-run place with decent dorm rooms. There's a small restaurant here and a pit toilet a short walk out the back.

Biānmǎdìngzhǔ Kèzhàn Further still is this option. This place definitely has the best location in the lovely original settlement and there's a family feel to it.

GETTING THERE & AWAY

From Déqīn, minibuses to Míngyǒng regularly leave from the bridge near the market at the top end of town (Y14, one to two hours). You can also try to rent a car through your accommodation. Returning buses run fairly regularly.

The road from Déqīn descends into the dramatic Mekong Gorge. Six kilometres before

---

THE YUBENG & KAWA KARPO TREKS

A trek to the fabulous **Yubeng Waterfall** (雨崩神瀑; Yǔbēng Shénpù) is an adventurous trip and fast becoming one of the most popular 'other' treks for those dismayed by the numbers of trekkers along the Tiger Leaping Gorge. At the bridge over the Mekong River the road leads 6km to Xīdāng and another 3km or so to a hot spring. Then it's possible to arrange pony hire to take you 25km (four to six hours) to Yǔbēng village, where there are half a dozen basic guesthouses, including **Mystic Waterfall Lodge** (神瀑客栈; Shénpù Kèzhàn; ☎ 841 1082; dm Y20), run by a friendly guide named Aqinpu.

Now, you could – and many do – hike all the way here from Fēilái Sì using local roads and paths. Or use a combination of bus/pony/hiking, the easiest of which would be to bus to Xīdāng, hire a pony (Y100) to the mountain pass two-thirds of the way to Yǔbēng village, then hike the rest.

From Yǔbēng village loads and loads of treks lie out there. (Aqinpu can give you the scoop on all of them.) It's a three- to four-hour trip on foot or horseback to the waterfall. Or, you could head south to a fabulous lake (it's around 4350m high and not easy to find, so take a guide).

Heading back to Xīdāng you could hike east along the Yubeng River, passing through a few groupings of Tibetan huts; you then bend north when you reach the Mekong River and pass through three more 'settlements' before reaching Xīdāng. It's a long, sweaty day and you may need to beg a bed in one of the local huts. Our local friends insist they've done it in around nine or 10 hours, but they're apparently superhuman. Also, it's tough and very easy to get lost in a few spots, so know before you go.

There is a 3pm minibus from Déqīn to Xīdāng (Y14) that returns the next morning at 8am. You could also use the Míngyǒng bus to get back to Déqīn as it passes by Xīdāng at around 3pm or 4pm. A taxi from Fēilál Sì to Xīdāng is around a whopping Y150.

Then there's the legendary Kawa Karpo *kora*, a 12-day pilgrim circumambulation of Méilì Xuěshān. Sadly, half of it is in the Tibetan Autonomous Region, so you'll need a permit to do it; you'll definitely need a guide. Arranging these may be possible in Déqīn but it's not likely; you're better off checking this out in Shangri-la at any of the travel agencies or your accommodation. Better, in Kūnmíng, before heading north, go to the Kunming Cloudland Youth Hostel (p228) and talk to the trekker owners; they can't help with permits but they can find out who can up north.

Míngyǒng the road crosses the Mekong River and branches off to Xīdāng. Nearby is a small temple (Bǎishūlín Miào) and a *chörten*.

Báimǎ Xuěshān 白马雪山

Kawa Karpo gets all the press, but this mountain nature reserve, part of the Hengduan Mountain range, east of Déqīn is impressive. Established in 1985, it's the largest plant and animal reserve in Yúnnán, famous for its dense primeval forests containing many threatened species, including the critically endangered Yúnnán snub-nosed monkey. Botanical gardens and a handful of temples are still on the mountain.

If you are an experienced trekker with a tent, sleeping bag and stove you could get off the Shangri-la–Déqīn bus at the pass and make some fine hikes around the eastern slopes and valleys.

Cizhong Catholic Church
茨中天主教堂

This unexpected church (Cízhōng Tiānzhǔ Jiàotáng), 80km south of Déqīn in the middle of a quiet village (Cízhōng), is based on the design of French cathedrals. (It actually isn't so surprising, given the number of churches to the west in the Nujiang Valley.) Built by French missionaries in 1867, it burned down in 1905 but was reconstructed by the local government over a period of 12 years. Wine is still made from vineyards planted by the missionaries. To get here take any bus bound for Wéixī. There were no guesthouses open (although there used to be one) on a last pass through.

Further south, near the village of **Yèzhī** (叶枝) is where in the 1920s the Lisu developed a syllabic script.

NUJIANG VALLEY
怒江大峡谷

☎ 0886

This epic 320km-long river gorge and its splendid trekking and sublime riverine views make it the most up-and-coming must-see spot in Yúnnán. For the nonce transport is painless but requires lengthy backtracks. You trundle seven hours up the valley marvelling at the scenery, then head back the way you came. Authorities did announce a plan in 2006 to blast a road from the far northern city of Gòngshān to Déqīn, and another from the village of Bǐngzhōngluò into Tibet. Both of these are, given the immense topographical challenges, proabably quite a long way off.

Rewards are immense: explore one of the remotest corners of Yúnnán, sandwiched between the Gāolígòng Shān (Gaoligong Mountain) range and Myanmar to the west, Tibet to the north and the high Bìluó Shān to the east. In addition to the churning Nù Jiāng (Nu River; the Chinese name means Raging River) the region holds nearly a quarter of China's flora and fauna species. The river is crisscrossed by daredevil suspension and cable bridges (in many places people still lug themselves over hand over hand) and the valley is speckled with traditional villages of thatched houses. Here too is yet another of China's controversial dam projects – this one to tame the Nu River, the longest undammed river left in China.

The valley holds an exotic mix of Han, Nu, Lisu, Drung and Tibetan nationalities and even the odd Burmese jade trader. There is a number of Catholic churches, the legacy of hardy French missionaries who arrived here in the 19th century.

The Jiaoye Pass in the west side of the valley was a major route marker for the Hump, the air supply route used during WWII. The remoteness of the region is highlighted by the C-53 plane that crashed in the Piànmǎ region of the valley in 1943 and that remained undiscovered until 1997. Today Piànmǎ is a border crossing (though not for foreigners) and trading post with Myanmar.

LIÙKÙ 六库
☎ 0886 / pop 7800

Liùkù is the humdrum but pleasant capital of the prefecture and an important transport hub, though it's of little intrinsic interest. (At least it's warm here.) You will need to get off the bus and register with a police checkpoint about 2km before town.

Information

China Telecom and China Post are in the town's north, both on Remin Lu.

Agricultural Bank of China (Zhōngguó Nóngyè Yínháng; Chuangcheng Lu) This branch will possibly change money in a pinch but you are safest with US dollars. If the bank is closed try the Nùjiāng Tōngbǎo Dàjiǔdiàn (p298).

YÚNNÁN

Jùlóng Wǎngbā (Chuangcheng Lu; internet access per hr Y2) From Chuangcheng Lu, take a right into the market north of Zhenxing Lu. Go up, take the second left and walk to the end.

Xinhua Bookshop (Xīnhuá Shūdiàn; Renmin Lu) Maps but none in English.

Sights

About 2km along the road to Bǎoshān is the **golden Buddha** that overlooks the town. You'll have to cross the river and follow trails to the top, from where there are fine views of the valley. You can stroll across the foot-bridge west of the bus station and head up the steps into the hills; they're lit up brightly at night.

The best thing might be to just meander along the lovely **riverwalk** on the east side of the Nu River; everyone else in the city does at night (ethnic minorities practise dancing and singing many nights).

The **Mabu Hot Springs**, 12km north of town along the road to Fúgòng, has an attached hotel complex. A Lisu (hair-combing) **festival** is held here on the 15th of the 1st lunar month (March/April).

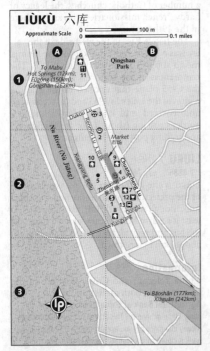

Sleeping

Loads of places exist; few are of much value. If the two budget options listed here don't tickle your fancy, just wander south of the bus station along Chuancheng Lu and take your pick of a few others.

Zhèngfǔ Zhāodàisuǒ (Government Guesthouse; ☎ 362 2589; 153 Renmin Lu; 人民路153号; d Y70-148, s & d without bathroom Y40-50, tr without bathroom Y45-60; 🖳) This guesthouse has tattered everything and indifferent service, but it's the cheapest you'll find.

Yóudiàn Bīnguǎn (Post Hotel; ☎ 362 0500; 193 Chuancheng Lu; 穿城路193号; s & d Y80-150, without bathroom Y60; 🖳) A tad pricier, but in notice-ably better shape (save for the possibility of lingering aroma of smoke).

Shèngbǎolù Dàjiǔdiàn (☎ 363 7888; Xiangyang Lu; 向阳路; s & d incl breakfast Y250-480; 🖳) Superb midrange pricing (if they figure in the usual discount to Y130), a steal for the money, with shy but efficient staff. Rooms are mostly clean as a whistle but they'll let you check more than one if there's even a smidgen of mould.

The top-end choice is probably **Nùjiāng Tōngbǎo Dàjiǔdiàn** (☎ 351 3339; 90 Renmin Lu; 人民路90号; d Y260-420; 🖳), even though the **Nùjiāng Bīnguǎn** (☎ 362 6888; Chuancheng Lu; 穿城路; d Y260-420) in the north of town ostensibly has one more star.

Eating & Drinking

Not much in the way of eateries. For some reason, the town loves its Sìchuān-style **Lǎoyā Tāng** (literally 'Old Duck Soup'), a

LIÙKÙ BUS TIMETABLE

Destination	Price (Y)	Duration (hours)	Frequency	Departs
Bǎoshān	29	3-4	every 30 min	7.30am-3.30pm
Bǐngzhōngluò	65	8	2 daily	6.20am, 8.20am
Fúgòng	23	3½	hourly	6.20am-4.30pm
Gòngshān	55	7	every 45 min	6.30am-1pm
Kūnmíng	157-167	10-11	4 daily	8.30am (express), 6.50pm, 7.30pm, 8.40pm (sleepers)
Xiàguān	52-69	4-6½	every 45 min	6.30am-3pm

stew of duck (natch), carrots, potatoes and other goodies. A good place for it is the aptly named **Sìchuān Lǎoyā Tāng** (319 Chuancheng Lu; 穿城路319号; soup meal for two Y35), north of the bus station.

Just outside the bus station, the trying-to-be-hip **Délāmǔ Xiùkūnbā** (145 Chuancheng Lu; 穿城路145号; beers from Y15) has imported beers and is a decent place to relax.

Getting There & Away

The bus station has luggage storage for Y2 per day, which is useful if you want to travel light up the valley.

If you want to skip Xiàguān and take a side route to Lìjiāng, check out Yúnlóng (see p246), for which you'll likely have to switch buses, probably at Cáojiàn (漕涧) or Yǒngpíng (永平) along the way to Xiàguān.

More buses leave for the Déhóng region. Note that travel times to Bǎoshān (see the boxed text, above), and for Déhóng, should be reduced as ongoing road projects are finished.

FÚGÒNG 福贡

☎ 0886 / pop 4200

Halfway up the valley, the scenery an hour's ride out of town in either direction is probably the best in the valley. The town itself is a scruffy mix of Lisu, Nu and Han Chinese, which bursts into colour every five days with one of Southwest China's best markets.

Activities

North of town the flyspeck village of **Làzàn** (腊咱) is the starting point for one of the valley's best **treks**. From here – a node on one of the old tea-horse roads – you hike up and over the splendid **Sìjì Duōmě** range, then descend to and cross the Mekong River to the equally microscopic hamlet of **Yán Wǎ** (岩瓦). *China Outdoor Exploration* magazine rated it tops in China in

2006. It's not feasible to do it yourself and you'll have a tough time organizing guides locally unless you speak Chinese. It's easier organised in Bǐngzhōngluò (p301). Because of the changing situation with damworks, it's much better to see if your guesthouse in Kūnmíng, Dàlǐ, Lìjiāng, or Ruìlì (or wherever), can do some phonework for you before you get there.

Sleeping & Eating

Zhèngfǔ Zhāodàisuǒ (政府招待所; ☎ 341 1660; Wadi Lu; 娃底路; s/d Y10-50, s & d without bathroom Y10-50, tr without bathroom Y20) Opposite the bus station. Ignore the tamped and threadbare blood-red carpet and you'll do fine. The manager's a cheery old chap amenable to negotiation.

Lèfú Bīnguǎn (乐幅宾馆; Pashan Lu; 帕山路; s & d Y60; ❄) Exit the bus station, turn right, go to the corner, right again and 50m on the opposite side is this better place.

Fúgòng Bīnguǎn (福贡宾馆; ☎ 341 1442; Wadi Lu; 娃底路; s & d Y120; ❄) This one-star is about the best place in town; it's near the Zhèngfǔ Zhāodàisuǒ.

The best restaurants are right by the bus station and the Fúgòng Bīnguǎn. The **Kèyùn Fàndiàn** (客运饭店; Wadi Lu) just east of the bus station is run by a friendly Naxi woman.

Getting There & Away

Buses run hourly to Gòngshān (Y24, 3½ hours) from 10.30am to 4pm, and to Liùkù (Y31, four hours) from 6.30am to 4pm . You can also get buses to Bǎoshān and Xiàguān.

GÒNGSHĀN 贡山

☎ 0886 / pop 16,400

This friendly (if grubby) one-street town is a trading centre for the upper Nujiang Valley. Most people will decamp immediately to Bǐngzhōngluò but it isn't a bad place to spend a (one) night.

YÚNNÁN

> ### ETHNIC GROUPS OF THE NUJIANG VALLEY
>
> The largest ethnic group in the valley are the Lisu (587,000 in Yúnnán). The women are recognised by their black pleated skirt, crimson tunic buttoned to one side, hat of plastic shells and beads and ornamental belt. Lisu men sometimes wear black turbans. The Lisu language belongs to the Yi branch of the Sino-Tibetan group.
>
> There are over a dozen clans, each with their own totems. A **hair-combing festival** is held in the first lunar month and a **harvest festival** in the 10th lunar month. The most spectacular festival is the **Kuoshi Festival** in the second lunar month, when Lisu braves climb barefoot up 30m-high poles, using sword blades as rungs.
>
> The Nu give the valley its name, and number around 26,000. Like the Lisu, the scattered Nu communities grow fields of maize, buckwheat and beans on the hillside and wheat and rice along the valley floors. Also like the Lisu, religion is animist at its heart, with a 19th-century overlay of Catholicism.
>
> The 5500 Drung are related to the Nu but retain a quite different lifestyle. In remoter areas the extended families live in long houses. Traditional dress consists of a toga of woven cloth wrapped over the shoulder. Facial tattooing, once common among older Drung to either gain beauty or luck, or avoid slavers, is slowly dying out. (Check out the fabulous photographs at the Cloudland International Youth Hostel, p228 in Kūnmíng taken by one intrepid photographer who has dedicated half a decade to slogging through the valley to take pictures of the last few dozen women with facial markings.)
>
> The Drung trade medicinal herbs and pelts but are fast being integrated into the modern economy. They have no written language but their spoken tongue is part of the Tibeto-Burman group. Traditionally Drung names consist of the name of the clan, the name of the child's father, a personal name and the infant's position in relation to his siblings. The main **spring festival** involves the sacrifice of a buffalo.

Information

There is a county tourism office kiosk on the west side of the road, north of the bus station. No English spoken here but they're friendly and there's a map of the region (in Chinese) on the wall.

There is one **internet café** (网吧; wǎngbā; per hr Y3). From the bus stop walk back along the highway, cross the bridge and round the corner; it's on your left.

Sights

There is an interesting **Catholic church** (天主教堂) in the southwest of town. At the northern end of the main street is a square selling Nu, Lisu and Tibetan traditional clothes.

When returning to Fúgòng, watch out for the mountain peak with a huge gape in it in the shape of the moon. The crag is two hours south of Gòngshān, 10 minutes north of the village of Lìshādǐ.

Sleeping

There's only one street. This stuff is easy to find.

Bus Station Hotel (交通宾馆; Jiāotōng Bīnguǎn; ☎ 351 1496; s & d Y60, d without bathroom Y30-40) The front desk *is* the bus station so you can roll out of bed and onto a bus. Adequate rooms.

Intergalactic & Small Guesthouse (银河宾馆; Yínhé Bīnguǎn; ☎ 351 1853; s & d Y50) We kid you not, this is the name of the place. Excitable youngsters staff the place and will fall all over themselves to get you to stay; one of them is a veteran of Shangri-la guesthouses and speaks a smattering of English. Cramped but spanking new rooms on an unnamed street.

Xiágǔ Dàjiǔdiàn (峡谷大酒店; ☎ 351 1666; s & d Y200) Forget any other hotel for luxury. This monster opened during our visit. A few bugs were being worked out but rooms are great. Discounts to Y120 are worth it.

There are a few restaurants in town but nothing to get excited about.

Getting There & Away

Minibuses leave every hour or so from 7am to 3.30pm for Fúgòng (Y24, 3½ hours). To Liùkù (Y55, seven hours) buses depart roughly hourly from 6.20am to 11am. There are cramped sleeper buses to Xiàguān (Y96, 14 hours) and Kūnmíng (Y150, forever) every day around 10am. Minibuses leave from north

THE NU RIVER DAM

In 2003 two bombshells – one great piece of news, the other not so great – hit this region. First, Unesco fell all over itself to place the Nu River Valley on its World–Heritage sites list, calling it one of the world's most precious ecosystems of its kind. Then, as is the wont in China, the government announced plans for a series of thirteen dams along the Nu River, the second-longest river in Southeast Asia and one of only two undammed rivers in China. The project would theoretically produce more electricity than even the Three Gorges Dam.

Opposition was immediate and ferocious, led by Unesco, which warned that such a project could warrant the area's delisting; they were joined by over 70 international environmental groups. More amazing was local opposition. Protesting dams in China is a growth industry in itself, but what shocked most was that after more than 50 prominent Chinese (from all walks of life – pop stars to business billionaires) in China spoke out against the dams, and the government was inundated by protests from citizens, they actually backed off in 2004. In 2006 the government, still trying to keep the plan a 'state secret,' announced that it may simply scale back the project to a mere eight dams. Clearly, they were testing the waters of local opinion to see if a compromise could be reached.

Apparently, the government's patience wore thin, because as this book was being prepared for publication, work had started up again in big-time fashion along the valley. And there's no escaping the fact that it will certainly have devastating effects on a region home to half of China's endangered species and 6000 species of flora and fauna. Worse will be the flooding of countless villages and the dislocation of many of the valley's 13 ethnic minority groups from their villages.

---

of the bus station for Bǐngzhōngluò (Y10, one hour) from between 7am and 8am and 5pm or 6pm.

A road is planned from Gòngshān to Déqīn and someday, when it's finally blazed through, it will allow for a smashing loop-trip through northwestern Yúnnán.

AROUND GÒNGSHĀN
Bǐngzhōngluò 丙中洛

It's a smashing treat to head an extra hour (to 90 minutes) through dramatic scenery to this pleasant village, set in a wide and fertile bowl. Hikes around the village absolutely abound, either south along the main road for 2km to the impressive 'first bend' of the Salween River or north along a track more than 15km long that passes through a host of villages and impressive gorges. (Just keep in mind that after Nàqiàluò – 那恰洛 – you're technically entering Tibet, but this is not a border crossing.) But actually just pick a direction and you simply cannot go wrong; just wander down a road or path and enjoy the scenery. You'll find loads of temples and Tibetan Catholic churches and exceedingly friendly people. Another new road from here into Tibet is also in the works. South of the village you have to pay a Y50 entrance fee as it's in a park zone. And do keep one

thing in mind if you're planning on trekking: this isn't Dali, Lijiang, or the Tiger Leaping Gorge. Very, very little English is spoken around here and no one is used to dealing with foreigners.

There are a handful of cheap guesthouses in the village. **Dìyīwān Kèzhàn** (第一湾弯客栈; ☎ 358 1189; s & d without bathroom Y30) is back toward Gòngshān along the main road. Simple rooms but clean.

The friendly, helpful **Chámǎ Kèzhàn** (茶马客栈; Tea Horse Inn; ☎ 358 1277; s & d Y60, tr Y80) has become the go-to spot for good reason. Great rooms and service and it has maps (in Chinese) of the area. There's one double without bathroom for Y40.

Returning to Gòngshān just flag down a minibus (Y10, one hour) as it trolls the streets until around 4pm (or earlier). One bus straight to Liùkù leaves from in front of the Chámǎ Kèzhàn (Y65, eight hours) at around 7.30am or 8am.

Dímáluò & Báihànluò
迪麻洛和白汉洛

About two-thirds of the way between Gòngshān and Bǐngzhōngluò, and a hefty hike across the river from the village of **Pēngdāng** (捧当) into the hills, is the fabulous village of Dímáluò (which is 80% Catholic).

TREKKING THE NUJIANG VALLEY REGION

Looking at maps, hiking over the mountains into the Mekong Valley, particularly from Gòngshān to Yèzhī or Yànmén in Déqīn prefecture seems a snap, but once there it's clear that you need a trustworthy guide and camping equipment. One route from Fúgòng to Yán Wǎ (岩瓦) is covered in the Fúgòng section (see p299). Pilgrimage trekking routes lead from the north of the valley into Tibet to join a pilgrimage circuit of Kawa Karpo (see p296) but again you'd need to arrange this with an expert travel agency.

Excellent places to start for information are the Chámǎ Kèzhàn in Bīngzhōngluò (p301) and especially Alou's Tibetan Lodge in Dímáluò (below) .

Home to **Alou's Tibetan Lodge** (☎ 356 6182; alou dekezhan@yahoo.com; per bed Y10), it's possibly the best spot for a base of exploratory operations. Alou is a local Tibetan guide and conservationist and has been praised for his cultural- and environmental-awareness treks. Meals can be had for Y6 to Y9. Guided treks average around Y60 per day. This is the place to suss out any kind of trekking you want to do in the Nù Jiāng area, but before you head to Dímáluò or Alou's Tibetan Lodge, check whether they are still there. Seriously, that area was slated to be among the first affected by a new dam. Phone/email before you wander into the hills!

A two-hour hike from Dímáluò on the east side of the valley is Báihànluò, which has a 125-year-old Catholic church built in Tibetan style. You can extend this into a trek across the Biluo Mountains to Cízhōng (p297) along the Mekong River. Another lengthier trek leads from Dímáluò north across the mountains toward **Yúnlíng** (云岭), also along the Mekong River. You'll definitely need guides for both.

Drung Valley (Dúlóng Jiāng) 独龙江

Separated from the Nujiang Valley by the high Gāolígòng Shān range and only reached by road in 1999, this is one of the remotest valleys in China. The valley is home to the Drung ethnic group (see the boxed text, p300). The Drung River actually flows out of China into Myanmar, where it eventually joins the Irrawaddy.

At present there are no buses into the valley. You'd have to hire a minivan from Gòngshān for the rough 96km trip to the county capital Dúlóngjiāng. Beyond that, most travel is on foot. There is a County Guesthouse (Xiàn Zhāodàisuǒ) at Dúlóngjiāng.

SOUTHEAST YÚNNÁN

This little-visited corner of Yúnnán has its fair share of interesting sights, a good infrastructure, and at its outer fringes some of the region's most traditional and off-the-beaten-track minority areas. For anyone who wants to avoid the hordes of travellers in Xīshuāngbǎnnà, Dàlǐ and Lìjiāng, this region's highlights – the Mongol community near Tōnghǎi, the traditional architecture of Jiànshuǐ, the golden rapeseed (canola) fields of Luópíng, and the superb terraces of Yuányáng – may well rank as low-key favourites.

LUÓPÍNG 罗平
☎ 0874 / pop 22,510

Coming from Guǎngxī or Guìzhōu in February or March, travellers generally crane their necks out the bus or train windows in these parts, gawking at the resplendent yellows and golds suddenly exploding around them. A halcyon change from the otherwise same-thing-different-kilometre scenery.

That's Luópíng. Or at least *yóucàihuā* (油菜花; canola/rapeseed), the gorgeous and riotously blooming plant for which the area is famed. These flowers also account for much of Southwest China's honey production.

Only that's not all. Outstanding day trips abound, including some of the best waterfalls in western China and worthy river trips where you can do your Huck Finn thing as you pole a raft past Buyi villages and waterwheels, and perhaps top it off with a riverboat cruise into Yúnnán's 'Three Gorges'.

Getting here is easy: it's 240km east of Kūnmíng but it's on a major highway and is a stop on the Nankun Railway heading into Guǎngxī.

Orientation
The town is a bit large but still walkable. On the east end of town is the north–south Yungui Lu, where you'll find the bus station. Just

north of here Wenbi Lu runs west toward the main part of downtown (which you don't need), ending at Jiulong Dadao, which used to be the main drag but is kinda windswept and forlorn now. Three or so kilometres north of here is the train station. Everything you really need is within easy hoofing distance of the bus station.

MAPS

You can get decent maps of Luópíng (Chinese only) at the bus and train stations.

Information

China Construction Bank (中国建设银行; Zhōngguó Jiànshè Yínháng; ☎ 821 5701; Wenbi Lu; 文笔路) West of the traffic circle along Wenbi Lu, friendly if unable to help much. Nor were other banks.

China Post (中国邮政; Zhōngguó Yóuzhèng; Zhōngguó Yóujú; Hongxin Beijie) A block north of the PSB office.

Internet café (网吧; Wǎngbā Guanyin Gejie; per hr Y3) It's not easy to find an internet café in town. The hastily scribbled sign on the window here just says wǎngbā (网吧). It's the closest you'll find to the bus station, along a side street between Baila Jie (白腊街) and Jiulong Dadao (九龙大道).

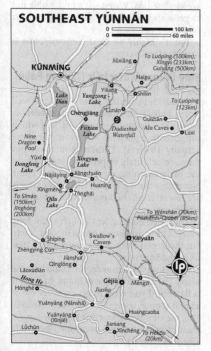

Luoping Tourist Office (罗平旅游局; Luópíng Lǚyóu Jú; ☎ 821 3010; Zhenxing Jie; 振兴街) The staff don't speak English and don't know what to do with you, but they'll give it the old college try!

Public Security Bureau (PSB; 公安局; Gōngānjú; Hongxing Beijie; 红星北街) Not equipped to deal with visa issues but nice enough.

Xinhua Bookshop (新华书店; Xīnhuá Shūdiàn; Zhenxing Jie; 振兴街) This bookshop is not worth much but it does have a few Chinese-only guidebooks.

Sights

Honestly, no one comes here for the city's somewhat drab aesthetics. If you've got time to kill, wander down to **Tàiyèhú Gōngyuán**, where you can paddle a boat or watch the old folk play checkers.

Sleeping & Eating

In February and March you will pay dearly for a room. Note also that massage parlour rows are everywhere and you can expect to hear, 'Hello! Hello' a lot from the working girls on the street and on the phone in your room.

Yúnguì Lǚshè (云贵旅社; ☎ 821 2255; Yungui Lu, Alley 1; 云贵路1巷; s & d from Y20) In a town of scuzzy guesthouses, this is a good choice. Basic but clean and friendly. And you absolutely needn't worry about security, as the proprietor – who chuckles in bemusement at the thought of having foreign guests – has a son on the local police force.

Shānhú Bīnguǎn (山湖宾馆; ☎ 821 2458; Wenbi Lu; 文笔路; s, d & tr Y100-120; 🖥) Not exactly an exuberant staff (hence the fading rooms), but it's still clean and not bad for the price. Discounts to Y80 or so would make it more worthwhile.

Luópíng Dàjiǔdiàn (罗平大酒店; ☎ 822 5788; 336 Yungui Lu; 云贵路336号; s & d incl breakfast Y160-380, without bathroom Y100; 🖥) A newer place that thankfully gets overlooked by tour groups, it's got very well-kept rooms, and a happy staff. Discounts to Y100 are well worth it.

Yāncǎo Bīnguǎn (烟草宾馆; ☎ 821 2967; 98 Wenbi Lu; 文笔路98号; s & d Y228-388; 🖥) Locals will tell you that the nicest hotels are found along Jiulong Dadao in the western part of town. They are mistaken. Recently renovated out of the erstwhile Héngshēng Bīnguǎn (恒升 宾馆), which the signs outside still say, this place has very nice rooms and prompt service. As such, expect it to often be booked solid by tour groups.

Getting cheap eats in town is a snap. The problem is you've got to walk the massage parlour gauntlets to get near any of the eateries along Wenbi Lu west of Yungui Lu. Just west of the traffic circle is a night market that's named well: Barbecue Night Market (Shāokǎo Yèshì). Actually, only a dozen – if that – stalls are set up, but it's great anyway. Our favourite is stall No 4 (or is it 5?) on the left as you go in. It's run by a wonderful woman who sells outstanding noodles. As you move west and/or south from here, places become indoor joints, getting larger, noisier, and far pricier.

Getting There & Away
BUS
The bus station (客运站) has everything you need for local and long-distance trips, including those to areas around Luópíng mentioned on right. Buses to Kūnmíng (Y43, four hours) run roughly half-hourly from 7am to 5.30pm (if not later); this trip will likely be done more quickly in the future as seemingly incessant roadwork is completed.

Heading south, buses leave for Lúxī (Y22, two hours) at 9.05am, 10.30am, 11am, 11.45am and 12.25pm, with one or two more in the afternoon. You can get two buses daily to Qiūběi (Y36, five hours), one at 7.30am and the other at 10.15; the former is a direct bus, the latter runs a more circuitous route via Yànshān (砚山).

You're within spitting distance of Guìzhōu and Guǎngxī here as well, so buses run eastward regularly. The easiest thing to do is hop on one of the zillion buses to Xīngyì (Y22, two hours) in Guìzhōu; they run every 20 minutes or so from 6am to around 6pm.

TRAIN
A half-dozen trains pass through the city each day, but most put you in at ungodly hours (especially when coming from Kūnmíng). From Guǎngxī your best bet is train 181, which passes through most of that province's major stations before dropping you here at 10.30am. The K337 train puts you in at 5am.

From Kūnmíng the best train is K366/3 (Y38 hard seat, 3½ hours), which departs the capital at 10.40am and arrives at 2.08pm.

Getting Around
Taxis cost Y5 to get anywhere. Bus 1 runs from the bus station to downtown.

AROUND LUÓPÍNG
Those Golden Fields of Rapeseed
You could pretty much pick any direction and not go wrong; after all, there's over 200 sq km of the stuff in the county. To kill two birds with one bus trip (as it were) you can hop off a bus to Bǎnqiáo at one of two bus stops along the expressway (remember, this is China) near the Golden Cock Hills (金鸡峰丛; Jīnjī Fēngcóng) and strike off southward along paths winding around the karst peaks. Believe it or not, near the first bus stop coming from Luópíng, a sign in English near the highway sign marking Km 30 actually points you in the right direction! From here you could hop aboard another Bǎnqiáo-bound bus for the Nine Dragon Waterfalls (below).

You could also hop a bus headed toward Niújiē (牛街), a dozen or so kilometres to the north, which has rapeseed fields and several rice terraces.

A caveat: show up in February and March and half of China seems to be here to see the same thing. Hotels are stratospherically priced if not booked out altogether. Buses are sardine tins. Worst – it's impossible not to get a shot of a fellow shutterbug in your camera.

But it's highly worth it. Seriously, this is some fantastic scenery.

Nine Dragon Waterfalls (Jiǔlóng Pùbù) 九龙瀑布
Around 35km northwest of town and well worth a visit is this long series of **cascades** (admission Y50) – hence the name – each of which supposedly represents a dragon (there are actually 10 tiers). Dunno 'bout that, but they are definitely impressive, especially in the early morning mists, unless you come November through April, when water levels are low. It'll still be lovely, but a bit underwhelming.

The waterfalls thunder through a 4km-long valley. The entire drop is only a modest 200m, but the largest cascade is a respectable 110m wide and 56m high.

From the park entrance, you could hike the whole circuit in a couple of hours. Most of it is flat, but if you want to get an overview of all of it at once, some steep steps are involved. Still, the view is well worth it from the top. (A chairlift to the top was overgrown by weeds when we visited.)

GETTING THERE & AWAY

A bit of a hassle, but still doable in a morning or afternoon. From the rear of the Luópíng bus station tour buses (Y15) run in high season to the waterfalls. But you still may have a lengthy wait. Just hop a Bǎnqiáo bus (Y4, 30 minutes) right across the expressway and from there it's a Y5 shared-minivan ride to the entrance. Again, however, in low season, not many people are headed to the waterfalls, so between Bǎnqiáo and the gate (and the return) you may need to break down and just pay Y20 for a private ride, otherwise, it may be a long wait.

Duoyi River (Duōyī Hé) 多依河

Around 35km southeast of Luópíng, the absolutely idyllic Duōyī Hé, fed by five underground springs, wends for a dozen kilometres over some 50 calcified shoals and through a picturesque karst landscape and groves of bamboo. Travellers come in droves to pole a Buyi-style raft (Y10) past villages and everpresent waterwheels. It's equally corny and cool.

To get here, minibuses (Y6, one hour) run from the rear of the Luópíng bus station. You can also get tour bus shuttles in summer that include other sights.

Lubuge Three Gorges (Lǔbùgé Sānxiá) 鲁布革三峡

Six kilometres east of the Duoyi River is a hydroelectric plant atop yet another dam. The backed-up reservoir resulted in three gorges and you can take tour boat rides (Y60). **Diling Gorge** (滴灵峡; Dīlíng Xiá), the best one, is downright lovely; the others – **Lion Gorge** (雄狮峡; Xióngshī Xiá) and **Two-Elephant Gorge** (双象峡; Shuāngxiàng Xiá)– are less so.

Shuttle buses run here from the Duoyi River.

LÚXĪ 泸西

☎ 0873 / pop 28,862

The capital of the eponymous county (of 298,000 people), which produces a wealth of coal and dried red peppers exported throughout China. You'll probably see dozens and dozens of market hawkers here, blankets everywhere, drying peppers in the sun.

Sights

In the northeast section of town stands **Xiushan Hill** (秀山; Xiù Shān), a park known

---

YÚNNÁN'S AMAZING BIODIVERSITY

Hands down, Yúnnán is China's treasuretrove of plants and animals. Yúnnán's timber reserves account for 10% of China's total, over a billion cubic metres of wood. Eighteen-thousand species of higher plants inhabit the province, well over half of China's total. There are 2500 species of ornamental plants, particularly flowers and herbs. In one Yúnnán mountain range over half of China's azalea species can be found. The province's eight key flowers – camellia, azalea, primrose, *Gentiana scabra*, lily, magnolia, orchid and *Meconopsis integrifolia* – are prized throughout the world.

Yúnnán is home to half of China's 1700 fauna species and 80% of the country's endangered species are found only in this province.

---

for its forests and scenery. A 25m-high Mingdynasty hexagonal pavilion sits atop. Behind the park is the impressive **Confucius Temple** (文庙; Wénmiào), which is open weekdays.

The big feature in Lúxī is the **Alu Caves** (阿庐古洞; Ālú Gǔdòng; ☼ 8am-4.30pm; admission Y35, with student card Y25), 3km northwest of town. This set of caves lies ensconced within a large karst formation and takes its name from a resident tribe that inhabited the area during the Song dynasty. The main cavern stretches 3km and is broken into three caves and the crystal-clear Yusun subterranean stream coursing some 800m, 15m underground (look out for transparent fish). This is overall one of the more pleasant experiences in Yúnnán. The last cave looks like a million melted candles.

To get to the caves take minibus 1 from the main Jiuhua Lu; it picks up at the exit of the last cave. Ticket sellers will want you to take a guide who will turn on the cave lights but if you take a torch and lose your group it's great fun exploring (the fenced-in path) by torchlight.

Sleeping & Eating

Zhōngxiù Bīnguǎn (钟秀宾馆; ☎ 662 1078; Jiuhua Lu; 九华路; tr per person Y40, d Y100-206; ▨) One long block from the bus station is this place, where you can generally count on to get doubles discounted by 50%. Best (if you can convince them to give you one) are the Y15 beds in a quad in the No 7 Building just outside the main gate. The No 7 Building is officially known as the Xiàn Zhèngfǔ Zhāodǎisǔo Qīhàolóu. There are a number of other hotels in town.

Ālú Dàjiǔdiàn (阿庐大酒店; ☎ 662 5002; d Y200, d/q without bathroom Y55/75; 🖫) At the entrance to the caves, this modestly posh option is slowly being renovated up, to three-star status, and it has only got a handful of common rooms left. In peak periods – weekends in summer and holidays – expect no discounts (if not higher prices than posted), otherwise you should get a room with bathroom for around Y150.

Yíngxiáng Fàndiàn, opposite the entrance to Building No 7, has good food. There is a group of barbecue places in the market north of the intersection leading to the Zhōngxiù Bīnguǎn.

Getting There & Away
From Lúxī there are lots of buses to Kūnmíng (Y30, 3½ hours) via Lùnán, as well as to other local destinations such as Gèjiù and Qiūběi. Coming from Kūnmíng you can explore the Stone Forest (Shílín; p238), and then either hop on a Lúxī-bound bus, or head into Lùnán, from where buses depart for Lúxī.

AROUND LÚXĪ
If you're heading south for other destinations in southeast Yúnnán, maybe hop off for a look at Mílè (弥勒), about 45km southwest of Lúxī. A few temples dot the town, one of which is home to a huge Buddha, the 20m-high resplendently golden Dàfó (大佛). It's also famous for its Red River cigarette brand, produced from field to carton here. The Báilóng Dòng (White Dragon Cave) is another attraction.

CHÉNGJIĀNG 澄江
☎ 0877 / pop 30,618
On a highland plateau 65km southeast of Kūnmíng, Chéngjiāng is the seat of the county dubbed the 'Land of Milk and Honey' for its agricultural output. The H-shaped county's population is small – only around 125,000 people – and features sizable numbers of Hui, Miao and Yi. The town's picturesque old back alleys make it worth a visit, though it's a bit far from Kūnmíng to do as a day trip. Most Chinese tourists tie in a visit here with Jiāngchuán to the south via Fǔxiān and Xīngyún lakes,

and then perhaps on to Tōnghǎi and Jiànshuǐ. Tourists don't sleep or eat here.

On the east side of Chéngjiāng is a massive Ming dynasty **Confucian Temple** (文庙; Wén-miào). It takes up 20,000 sq metres and the Grand Hall of the Honoured Teacher is over 10m high with seven attached rooms.

Also in Chéngjiāng is **Fengshan Park** at the southern base of Feng Shān, built on the site of a long-disappeared Taoist temple.

For details on getting here from Kūnmíng see p231. Buses (Y15, one hour) from Kunming run every 20 to 30 minutes from the main or east bus stations.

AROUND CHÉNGJIĀNG
The primary point of interest for travellers is **Fǔxiān Hú** (抚仙湖), a north–south oriented lake separating Chéngjiāng from Jiāngchuán. The north shore lies 5km south of Chéngjiāng. Fǔxiān is the deepest lake in Yúnnán (second deepest in China) and though smaller than Diān Chí and Erhai Lake in Dàlǐ, its volume is 12 times that of Diān, and six times that of Erhai. The bluish green hue comes from phosphorous deposits from surrounding soils.

The northern shore is the most developed. **Bōxī Bay** has a beach of sorts and is a popular resort.

Clockwise, starting from the northeast, is **Xiàngbílíng Shān** (象鼻岭山) and once you see it you'll see why its English translation is 'Elephant's Trunk Mountain'. The east side has a number of sulphurous **hot springs** (温泉; wēnquán), some quite large, and even a warm-water river in Jiǔcūn. As you continue south keep your eyes peeled for the **Serene Lake Bridge** (Hǎiyán Qiáo), 17.5km south of Chéngjiāng near Hǎikǒu, a Qing dynasty stone arch bridge also known as Haikou Bridge.

Further south on the western side, a tiny islet called **Solitary Hill** (Gūshān Dǎo) appears. The island was once filled with Ming dynasty temples, a pagoda, pavilions and nunneries, though not much is left (the pagoda was melted down for coins during an uprising). You can normally arrange a boat to take you across to the island.

At the southern tip of the lake, near the village of Hǎimén, a 1km-long river connects Fǔxiān Hú to neighbouring Xīngyún Hú. (What's interesting is that fish from both lakes swim to the confluence of the river and

Fúxiān Hú, but they are said to never pass the point where a boundary rock overlooks the water.) To the west is **Yùsǔn Shān** (Jade Bamboo Shoots Mountain), known for the platter-shaped rock atop the peak that purportedly is always wet.

Getting there is just a matter of flagging down a bus and asking if it's going there.

JIĀNGCHUĀN 江川

☎ 0877 / pop 43,550

Southeast of Yùxī, one hour by bus, lies Jiāngchuān, the seat of a tiny county of the same name. Occupied since the ancient Dian culture, it wasn't controlled by imperial China until well into the Han dynasty. Villages around Jiāngchuān are filled with Chinese archaeologists, as excavation sites here have unearthed prime sites of Dian, Neolithic and Bronze Age cultures, including 25 tombs of the Warring States period in Lǐjiāshān near Wengkiaxiang village.

Located in a small circular basin surrounded by mountains, Yunnanese say the county's topography resembles the shape of a begonia leaf.

At the **Bronze Age Museum** (青铜器时代博物馆; Qīngtóngqì Shídài Bówùguǎn; admission Y10; ☯ 10.30am-4pm), the Lǐjiāshān excavation site is particularly highlighted, featuring the 25 tombs of the Warring States period and Western Han dynasty, from which nearly 1000 pristine Bronze Age relics were removed. The local cult of the bull is plain to see. The earliest coins used in Yúnnán were also unearthed at the site. The museum is a five-minute walk along Xingyun Lu west of the bus station. A big bull statue (a replica of one of the bronzes) sits out front.

The Jiāngchuān bus station is a bit chaotic; you'll have to wait for minibuses to regional destinations to fill. There are frequent departures to Yùxī (Y5, one hour) until around 8pm and to Chéngjiāng (Y15, two hours) every hour or so until early afternoon. Minivans to other destinations may leave from other corners in town, it's a maddening slog around to find them at times.

Coming from or going to Kūnmíng (Y19, two hours) there are a couple of daily services to/from Kūnmíng's east bus station, the last one departing at 4pm. Going to Yùxī (Y5, 45 minutes) first and then to Kūnmíng is easier because Yùxī–Kūnmíng buses run seemingly every 30 seconds.

AROUND JIĀNGCHUĀN

Oval-shaped and somewhat salty, **Xīngyún Hú** (星云湖) is known locally as the Sea of Broad Waves. The lake has a few hot springs along its shoreline, and is famous for its big-headed fish, which is supposedly very tasty in hotpot.

Try taking a motor tricycle from the centre of town to the **Lakeside Park** (滨海公园; Bīnhǎi Gōngyuán), 2km north of town.

TŌNGHǍI 通海

☎ 0877 / pop 44,520

Tōnghǎi, occupied since the kingdom of Dian's inception, reached a zenith during the Nánzhào kingdom, when it was chosen as the military and economic centre of the kingdom that stretched from Tōnghǎi to Hékǒu. When the later Dàlǐ kingdom was founded, the leaders came from Tōnghǎi.

Most Chinese visitors come for its lovely Xiu Shan Park, but for foreigners an added attraction is the fading but still visible traditional architecture of its charming avenues and back alleys. To the north 2km or so is the icy-looking, windswept lake, Qīlù Hú, and a short distance (about 15km) west of town is Yúnnán's only remaining settlement of Mongols. Long famed for their metalworking, dozens of them now sell knives around the bus station.

Sights

Xiu Shan Park (秀山公园; Xiùshān Gōngyuán) is quite lovely – with a mist-shrouded, overgrown, mossy gumdrop of a hill, lush with birds – and not too strenuous for the old ticker. Original construction of temples began as early as the Tang dynasty and by the Ming dynasty it was revered as one of southern China's most sacred Buddhist sites. Later, the **mountain** (admission Y15) became famous because the section behind the summit supposedly 'predicts' the weather.

It's only about 200m high but it has enough paths to occupy you for hours. Five temples, some Taoist Ming dynasty towers and over 20 pavilions provide lots of nooks and crannies. Tablets are marked with over 200 couplets left by ancient writers. The first building on the right is the **Sanyuangong Monastery**, freshly painted after a fire. The **Puguan Sì** and **Yongjin Sì**, higher up, contain a bonsai and camellia garden respectively. From the upper part of the hill a trail leads around the

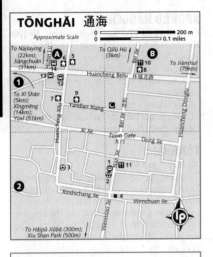

TŌNGHǍI 通海

east side of the hill to the **Báilóng Sì** (White Dragon Monastery), a lovely complex with a small hotel that might make a peaceful place to stay a night.

The views of Qílù Hú and the town are great. Best of all, many of the temples have signs in passable English, giving an insight into the history of the mountain and regional folklore.

Xīshān Park to the west of Tōnghǎi has more trails and a pagoda on its hilltop.

Sleeping

Bless the town for its honesty. This is one of the few places that doesn't slap 'bīnguǎn' on every place to stay and call them hotels.

Jiànhuá Zhāodàisuǒ (☎ 301 7707; Huancheng Xilu; 环城西路; s/d Y40/50) A bit noisy hereabouts but the rooms here are holding up just fine, with bright rooms and good bathrooms.

Jīnhú Lǚguǎn (☎ 301 0190; s & d Y50) Across the street from Jiànhuá Zhāodàisuǒ is this other clean and decent option. Play 'em off each other in your negotiation!

Yùhéng Lǚguǎn (☎ 301 0855; 10 Xi Yandian Xiang; 盐店巷10号; s & d Y50) A fair bit closer to Xiù Shān and definitely in a more interesting neighbourhood – not far from the local mosque – this new place is tucked in an alley with spotless rooms and has a proprietor who seems thrilled to have foreign guests.

Lǐyuè Fàndiàn (☎ 301 1651; 56 Huancheng Xilu; 环城西路56号; s/d with/without bathroom Y100/60, tr Y90;) This longtime stand-by has slightly more upscale rooms and a cheery staff; the standard discounts to Y60 make it really worth the money.

Tong Print Hotel (Tōngyìn Dàjiǔdiàn; ☎ 302 1666; fax 301 6474; North Gate; 北门; s & d Y288;) In a windswept town is a bit of, well, plush comfort. Who'da thunk it? Facilities include a 16th-floor bar with views, a bowling alley, tennis court, sauna, and pool in summer.

Eating & Drinking

Hot and peppery stews cooked in Tōnghǎi-made copper pots are found around town. There are several Muslim restaurants about serving this and other dishes, especially around the main mosque. Itinerant musicians also sometimes sing at restaurants around town.

Nánjiē Cāntīng (7 Nan Jie; 南街7号; dishes from Y2) Tōnghǎi's best-known eatery is along a busy small street leading to Xiù Shān. You pay a couple of yuán for a bowl of noodles served quickly at the back of the restaurant. Or, pick and point and they'll whip it up pronto. It's an excellent meal.

Jiāyuán Dòujiāng (Bei Jie; 南街; dishes from Y2) Wash down any lingering peppers with outstanding soy milk here; it also has excellent across-the-bridge noodles.

Albert's Bar (Xiu Shan Park Gate; 秀山公园大门; drinks from Y8) Albert, the gregarious proprietor at this place, speaks English and is a traveller's best friend, providing internet access and a nice atmosphere after a long day of mountain trudging. Sadly no-one was around when we last visited; hopefully he hasn't left for greener pastures.

YÚNNÁN & KUBLAI KHAN

Travellers to Tōnghǎi are surprised to discover distinct Mongolian dress and non-Han features throughout the town and region. (Not to mention the ornate knives and scabbards sold on every street corner.) In fact there are around 13,000 ethnic Mongolians in Yúnnán; all descended from the army of the great Khan, Kublai.

As part of his campaign in southern China, Kublai and his armies had to enter what today is Yúnnán, one of China's most isolated and long-unconquered regions. In fact, the Mongols thought it a separate country – their name Qandahar for the region is from an Indian language meaning 'Great Country'; it was also called Nánzhào or 'Southern Kingdom' in Chinese (Polo knew it as Caragan). Completely unprepared for the enormity of the land and population opposing them, the Mongol horsemen were also baffled by the strange river-valley topography. Yet Kublai's two armies managed to cross western China mountain by mountain, river by river, opposed by ethnic minority groups at every step. They converged on Dàlǐ and somehow nearly took it without shedding blood.

Khan's armies would not subdue the Song and southern China until 1279, some 70 years after they had made initial advances. In the process they brought Yúnnán into the great Chinese fold. Indeed the inclusion of Yúnnán into the country is considered one of Kublai Khan's greatest achievements as he established the Yuan (Mongol) dynasty. North and south China had been forced to find each other.

Kublai Khan's period was an intriguing one for Chinese culture and society. Kublai was much more open-minded than his Mongol counterparts. He realised Chinese culture had much to offer, and even moved his capital to Běijīng. Once in control in Yúnnán he also left a number of Dai princes in autonomous control. The Chinese were prohibited from most high positions, those being reserved for Mongols. But as a hands-off emperor, Kublai also allowed many aspects of Chinese high culture to flower, the educated elite of Chinese society quietly 'retiring' and concentrating on artistic endeavours.

Getting There & Away

Tōnghǎi's bus station is just south of the Huancheng Beilu and Huangcheng Xilu intersection. But most regional buses leave from a stop west around the corner along Huancheng Beilu at the Hubin Lu intersection. Buses to Jiànshuǐ (Y12, 1½ hours), Gèjiù (Y31, three hours) and Yùxī (Y12, two hours) leave every half-hour or so when full. There are minibuses and plush expresses to Kūnmíng (Y20 to Y33, 2½ hours) every hour or 90 minutes from 8.20am to 6.30pm. To Shípíng (Y18, three hours) buses leave every half-hour or so from 8am to 5pm. Cramped microbuses leave for Jiāngchuān from across the road when full (Y6, one hour).

AROUND TŌNGHǍI
Qìlù Hú 杞麓湖

This indigo-blue lake, 1km north of town, was famed from Tang dynasty times as one of the emperor's eight favourite southeast Yúnnán getaways. The lake once rose much higher along the cliffs of the eastern shoreline and legends tell of how an ancient monk poked a hole in the ground to drain the water for farmers; his story is told at a temple in Xiushan

Park, Tōnghǎi. The easiest option is to travel north of Tōnghǎi to a lakeside park around 3km north of town. You could walk, or a motorcycle taxi would cost around Y5.

Xīngméng 兴蒙

At the base of Feng Shān, in a compact village 14km west of Tōnghǎi just off the main highway, some 4000 Mongolian descendants of members of Kublai Khan's expeditionary force still reside. Over the last 700 years, most have switched from the nomadic rough-riding lifestyle to fishing on Qìlù Hú, but dwindling water levels over the past three decades have forced most onto the land as farmers or builders. Some still forge copperware and a few still hit up likely tourists, trying to sell knives. The traditional stone and sun-dried brick village is still a nice place to wander.

The Mongolian faces and language have been diluted over the years but the dress is still distinct; most people wear green or blue tunics with brightly embroidered sleeves. An annual early-winter festival called **Nadaam** is held here every three years (next one scheduled for 2008), just as it is in summer on the grasslands several thousand kilometres north.

To get here you have to head to the cluster of small buses west of the Tōnghǎi bus station and have someone toss you on one passing through (or relatively near) there. If you're lucky there'll be a small shared van heading there for Y2 per person.

Najiaying Mosque (Nàjiāyíng Qingzhěnsì) 纳家营清真寺

A half-hour by bus up the western shoreline of the lake is the village of Nàjiāyíng, home to one of the oldest mosques in Yúnnán, predating the Ming dynasty. The mosque's three sections include a gate, a courtyard, hall and two flanking rooms that total over 5000 sq metres. The mosque is most impressive if viewed from the heights descending along the road from Jiāngchuān. Any bus to Jiāngchuān from Tōnghǎi will pass through Nàjiāyíng.

JIÀNSHUǏ 建水

☎ 0873 / pop 17,347

Jiànshuǐ really sucks in the tourists with its old-style architecture, friendly folk and a dizzying array of historic sights.

Honestly, those funky old buildings are there. Somewhere. Though yes, you would hardly know it, given the typically polluted and congested outer arteries leading in, then the cheesy face-lift the main downtown streets have been given. Just wander about concentrically and you'll stumble across gems.

Known in ancient times as Butou or Badian, Jiànshuǐ's history dates back to the Western Jin period, when it was under the auspices of the Ningzhou kingdom. It was handed around to other authorities until its most important days as part of the Tōnghǎi Military Command of the Nánzhào kingdom. The Yuan dynasty established what would eventually become the contemporary town.

Jiànshuǐ figured prominently in the 1911 Revolution. On 1 November a group within the army staged a rebellion here inside the Tianjun Temple and established the military government of the Southern Garrison Army. Later, Marshal Zhu De would station his troops here.

Orientation

The eastern perimeter of the city consists of a curved line connecting all the Chaoyang Lus circling the old town; they all link in the east at Chaoyang Gate. The main road downtown is Jinlinan Lu, leading southwest from Chaoyang Gate. Walk due north on Yinghui Lu from Chaoyang Gate 3km to get to the bus station.

MAPS

Shops at the bus station have decent maps, as do several hotels. Most maps are in Chinese but a few now at least have English for streets.

And there's your headache – the street names on the maps don't always match those on the street signs. (Sigh.) Yup, there's been some upgrading of names of late, and even the locals aren't sure what to call the streets! In short, Jinlinan Jie and Jianzhong Lu are one and the same, as are Hanlin Jie/Jianxin Jie and Beizheng Jie/Wenyuan Jie.

Information

There are three no-name **internet cafés** (wǎngbā; per hr Y4) on Yongning Jie, just south of Jinlinan Jie (Jianzhong Lu). No banks yet have ATMs that accept foreign cards, though the many branches of the China Construction Bank (中国建设银行) are supposed to.

The **Jiànshuǐ Travel Agency** (Jiànshuǐ Lǚxíngshè; ☎ 765 2241) can help with information on the surrounding sights but there's little English spoken.

Sights

The following is absolutely not complete. You could spend days and days just poking around all the old buildings and such. Pick up a map and do some exploring.

CONFUCIAN TEMPLE

Jiànshuǐ's tourism linchpin is this famous **temple** (Wénmiào; admission Y20; ☉ 7am-6pm) west of the town centre. Modelled after the temple in Confucius' hometown of Qūfù (Shāndōng province) and finished in 1285, it covers 7.5 hectares and is the third-largest Confucian temple in China. (Actually, some locals employ a flurry of Byzantine mathematics to prove it's the largest. You be the judge.)

The place is so large that you first walk through a gate on Jinlinan Jie (Jianzhong Lu) and all the way around Xue Lake (the Chinese word is actually 'sea') just to get to another gate, then up a walkway before the main structures loom magnificently before you. The structure includes a main hall, two side rooms, two central halls, two pavilions and eight glazed-tile archways. **Dacheng Hall**, the epicentre, is supported by twenty-two 5m-pillars, two engraved with two dragons rising through the mist.

Remarkably, the temple has operated as a school for nearly 750 years and was so successful that over half of all Yúnnán's *jǔrén* (举人; successful candidates in imperial examinations) came from Jiànshuǐ. Many of the names of buildings in Jiànshuǐ use the ideogram *wén*, meaning 'literacy'.

ZHU FAMILY GARDEN

A 10-minute walk east from the Confucian Temple and then left down an alley is an outstanding example of a Qing dynasty traditional ancestral home. The spacious 20,000-sq-metre **complex** (Zhūjiā Huāyuán; ☎ 765 3028; admission Y20; ✷ 7.30am-11pm) comprises ancestral buildings, family homes, ponds and lovely gardens and took 30 years to build. Unsurprisingly, it's now been partially converted into an atmospheric inn.

Travellers will like the small museum in the rear, with dozens of photographs of local architecture, with a heavy focus on bridges. There is also an exhibit on the history of the Zhū family. The Zhū family made its name through its mill and tavern and dabbled in everything from tin in Gèjiù to opium in Hong Kong, eventually falling victim to the political chaos following the 1911 revolution.

ZHÍLÍN SÌ

One of the few remaining examples of intricate woodworking on a large scale, and the largest preserved wooden structure in Yúnnán, this monastery is tucked away in a tiny alley southwest of the Confucian Temple.

Built during the latter stages of the Yuan dynasty, the monastery's distinctive design feature is the brackets between columns and crossbeams. A set of 600-year-old frescoes were recently discovered here, though they have since been moved to local museums.

CHAOYANG GATE

Guarding the centre of town, Chaoyang Gate (Cháoyáng Lóu) – an imposing Ming edifice – was modelled on the Huanghe Tower in Wǔhàn and Yueyang Tower in Húnán and bears more than a passing resemblance to Tiānānmén (Gate of Heavenly Peace) in Běijīng. (You will definitely be told of how it actually predates Tiānānmén.) Recent renovations have resulted in a nice sitting area where

you can grab a tea or beer, a pricier interior teahouse and an upper-floor **exhibit** (admission Y2) of local history. There's no charge to walk up into the gate and admire the building and views close up.

Architecture

Classic architecture surrounds you in Jiànshuǐ, and not just in the old-style back alleys either. Virtually every main street has a historically significant traditional structure. The architecture is especially intriguing because of the obvious mixture of central plans and local styles. Many old buildings, despite official decrees positing them as state treasures, have been co-opted for other purposes and the trick – and truthfully, the great fun – is trying to find them.

A good place to start your explorations is Chaoyang Gate. Head south and then right up a short hill. After 200m on the right is the Grain Bureau (Liángshi Jú). Walk confidently inside, past two old storehouses to the **Chóng-wén Tǎ**, an elegant 14-storey pagoda. From here continue round Guilin Jie and you'll come across four **wells** (井) and a shrine.

Back at Chaoyang Gate, head north and then east to the Workers Club (Gōngrén Jùlèbù). Around the back are several interlocking **lakes**, banked by a throng of elderly card players. A little further east is the former **Fúdòng Sì**, a temple which houses the town's education department.

Sleeping

You'll find a dozen or so basic hotels near the bus station north of town, but who wants to stay there? You could also hoof it west of Chaoyang Gate to snoop out any number of cheap places.

BUDGET

Garden Hotel (Huāyuán Bīnguǎn; ☎ 765 6285; 36 Jinlinan Jie; 金临安街(建中路)36号; s & d Y50-80, without bathroom Y30, tr Y90) It's hit or miss with this place, the epically longtime traveller standby; some find it just fine, others grouse that it's overpriced. Do take a look at a few rooms, as things vary a lot here. Staff are pretty eager to get people back, so you're at an advantage. The street it's on is also known as Jianzhong Lu (建中路).

Wénmiào Bīnguǎn (Temple Hotel; ☎ 765 0996; 89 Ruyi Xiang, Jinlinan Jie; 如意巷、金临安街89号; s & d Y60, without bathroom Y30) One rarely used

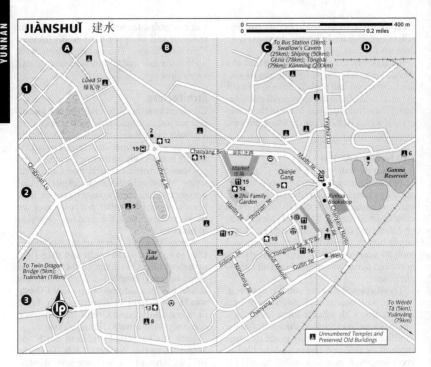

JIÀNSHUǏ 建水

0   400 m
0   0.2 miles

To Bus Station (3km);
Swallow's Cavern
(25km); Shiping (50km);
Gēijiù (78km); Tónghǎi
(79km); Kūnmíng (200km)

Lǜwǎ Sì
绿瓦寺

Qīngyuán Lu

Beizheng Jie

Chaoyang Beilu 朝阳北路

Market
市场

Qianjie
Gang

Mashi Jie

Yinghui Lu

Gulin Jie

Ganma
Reservoir

Hanlin Jie

Shuyuan Jie

Zhu Family
Garden

Xinhua
Bookshop

Chaoyang Nanlu

Jinlian Jie

Nancheng Jie

Yongning Jie 永宁街

Gudor Matou

Gulin Jie

Wells

Xue
Lake

To Twin Dragon
Bridge (5km);
Tuánshān (18km)

Chaoyang Nanlu

To Wénbǐ
Tǎ (5km);
Yuányáng
(79km)

Unnumbered Temples and
Preserved Old Buildings

---

option is this place. Oddly, rooms are good but it's kinda like a homestay otherwise (clamber around a motorbike to get to the rooms). Friendly service and it's near Zhǐlín Sì.

MIDRANGE

There are several good midrange options that offer some character as well as comfort.

Lín'ān Jiǔdiàn (☎ 765 1888; fax 765 4888; Chaoyang Beilu; 朝阳北路; d Y130-170; ☒) A 10-minute walk west of the bus station along Chaoyang Beilu brings you to this place, set off the street and in pleasant gardens. Decent rooms, but not a very intriguing part of the town.

Cháoyáng Dàjiǔdiàn (☎ 766 2401; 6 Chenghuang Miao Jie; 城隍庙街6号; s & d Y158-288; ☒) An erstwhile cheapo guesthouse, it recently was revamped into a comfy three-star hotel with still-fresh-as-daisies rooms with nice detailings. (So get there fast.) The discounts it offers (to Y100 or so) in the off season are a steal. There's a nice restaurant in a traditional-style building, though it seems to hardly ever open.

Huáqìng Jiǔdiàn (☎ 766 6166; 46 Hanlin Jie; 翰林街46号; s & d Y200; ☒) A splendid new hotel,

it basically screams out to welcome foreign guests – hence the ubiquitous signs. It's certainly got the trappings of a cosy guesthouse – bike rental (Y25 per day), a quiet café, cheery staff – everything except cheap rooms. Still, the rooms are smashing, with lovely small patios, and the staff are great. The street it's on is also known as Jianxin Jie (建新街).

Zhūjiā Huāyuán Kèzhàn (☎ 766 7988; s & d Y220-280; ☒) The classiest place in town is this option in the Zhu Family Gardens. Four of the courtyards have been converted into rooms for Y220 and Y280, which, although they are dark, have lovely furniture and traditional old-style beds. It's worth splashing out on the Y280 rooms, as the Y220 ones are really small and pokey.

Eating

Jiànshuǐ is legendary for its *qìguō* (汽锅), a stew made in the county's famed earthenware pots and often infused with medicinal herbs. The cook may make use of the local speciality: grass sprout (草芽; *cǎoyá*), also known as elephant's tooth grass root. It tastes like bamboo. Only found in Jiànshuǐ County, it's often used in broth or fried with liver or pork. Non-meat eaters might find a place that will substitute tofu.

Another local speciality is tonic soup made from bird nests from Swallow's Cavern – don't gulp at the price.

Our friends in Kūnmíng would howl if we were remiss in not touting the glories of Jianshui's barbecue (建水烧烤; *Jiànshuǐ shāokǎo*). And, true, everywhere you look, you'll find lots of cubbyhole restaurants full of braziers roasting meats, veggies, tofu and perhaps goat cheese. A perfect night out is a barbecued meal under the Jiànshuǐ stars with friends.

In the evenings Jinlinan Jie (Jianzhong Lu) becomes a pedestrian area with vendors offering sugar cane, skinned pineapples and kebabs.

Míngchéng Yúlè Zhōngxīn (Yongning Jie; 永宁街; dishes from Y8) serves duck and other local dishes in the shadow of a 1950s communist building.

A restaurant is at the back of the Zhu Family Gardens. In the heat of summer you can dine on a raised platform overlooking the garden. Prices are very reasonable at around Y10 per dish. If you book in advance you don't have to pay the gardens entry fee.

Getting There & Away

Jiànshuǐ has a couple of bus stations. The main one is 3km north of Chaoyang Gate. For very local destinations, you need to head to the second small (regional) bus station ten minutes' walk west at the corner of Chaoyang Beilu and Beizheng Jie.

From the main station there are buses continually leaving for Gèjiù (Y15 to 20, 1½ hours), Yuányáng (Y16, 2½ hours) and Tōnghǎi (Y12, 1½ hours), as well as Méngzì, Shípíng (Y12, one hour) and Kāiyuǎn (Y12, one hour).

Further afield, Kūnmíng is served 7am to 3pm by frequent buses (Y50, three to four hours). Hékǒu-bound travellers have four morning buses (Y47, five hours) between 6am and 11am. The masochistic can take one of the sleepers to Jǐnghóng (Y147, 17 hours), scheduled for 1.30pm and 4.30pm.

AROUND JIÀNSHUǏ
Swallow's Cavern 燕子洞

This freak of nature and ornithology is halfway between Jiànshuǐ and Gèjiù. The karst formations (the largest in Asia) are a lure, but what you'll want to see are the hundreds of thousands of swallows flying around in spring and summer. The **cave** (Yànzi Dòng; admission Y35) is split into two: high and dry, and low and wet. The higher one is so large that a three-storey pavilion and a tree fit inside. Plank walkways link up with other pavilions outside on the rock formations. Look out for the inscribed plaques hanging from the roof at the entrance to the cave. The Lu River runs through the lower cave for about 8km and you can tour the caverns in 'dragon boats'. The cacophony of river and bird is insane.

Getting to the cave is easy…if you can find a bus that takes local roads and not the expressway. Ask at the bus station for any bus bound for Méngzì, Kāiyuǎn or Gèjiù *that passes by the cavern*. Forty-five minutes to an hour later and five to 10 minutes after you pass through Miàndiàn village, at the entrance to another tiny village, you should see signs saying 'Welcome to Swallow's Cave', among other things, all in English. The fare is Y5.

Twin Dragon Bridge 双龙桥

Traditionally styled bridges abound – check out the photos at the Zhu Family Garden (p311) – but you must see this bridge (Shuānglóng Qiáo) across the confluence of the Lu and Tachong Rivers, 5km from the western edge of town. One of the 10 oldest in China, the bridge features 17 arches, so many that it took two periods of the Qing dynasty to complete the project. A three-storey pavilion sits in the middle, with two smaller ones at either end. In the right light at the right times, it's a great photo opportunity.

To get there take minibus 4 from the second bus station (Y1). Note that you have to ask the driver to tell you where to get off the bus and then point you in the right direction. Bus 4 continues to **Huánglóng Sì**, a small temple.

Tuánshān 团山

Some 13km west of the Twin Dragon Bridge is the **Zhang Family Gardens** (张家花园; Zhāngjiā Huāyuán) in Tuánshān. Fascinating little place, this. Some three quarters of the village's families are surnamed Zhang (long story), all descended from forbears who came during the Ming dynasty. Economically astute, they cleaned up in a variety of businesses throughout the Hónghé region, then came home and built exquisite homes famed – justifiably so – for their ornate woodcarvings, calligraphy and paintings. The village is filled with these places – oh yeah, there's one from an interloper family named Mao.

Getting there is a pain. You can wait eternally for a bus from Jiànshuǐ's second bus station; it's easier to plunk down Y28/50 for a one-way/return taxi ride.

Wénbǐ Tǎ 文笔塔

Southwest of town, a few kilometres on the road to Qīnglóng (青龙), this Ming dynasty pagoda is certainly distinctive, shaped like a calligraphy brush. The perimeter of the base matches the height, exactly 31.4m. To get here take a Qīnglóng-bound minibus (Y2) from the northwest side of Chaoyang Gate or take a taxi for Y10. It's a pleasant bicycle ride.

SHÍPÍNG 石屏

☎ 0873 / pop 12,832

Lying approximately 50km west of its better-known sister city Jiànshuǐ, Shípíng has its own cool old town, where you can wander the flagstone streets and alleys. There are a few historical structures of note to scope out, but the real point of interest is Shípíng's famed tofu (bean curd). For more than six centuries, this busy-as-a-bee town has been churning out tonne after tonne of the healthful product.

Many of the 'factories' are simply family-run hole-in-the-wall operations in structures that seem to date from the earliest days of the town. There's nothing quite like it elsewhere.

Orientation

The central part of downtown is a 10-minute walk northwest from the bus station along Huiyuan Lu (汇源路); that is, exit the bus station, cross the street, and turn left. Turn right at the main east–west road, Xishan Lu (西山路). Follow this straight ahead a few blocks till you get to the old town gate. Cross underneath and you'll see a gentrified – kind of – pedestrian area of shops. Turn right immediately and you should be on Xizheng Jie (西正街), which leads directly into the old part of town. The other street of note is Beizheng Jie (北正街)

MAPS

The only map you'll find of Shípíng is at Xinhua Bookshops in other cities in the region. (Shípíng's flyspeck Xinhua Bookshop in the old town is rather barren.) Look for a map titled *Tourist Map of Honghe*; it's got loads of town and city maps in southeast Yúnnán on it, but only the title is in English.

Information

From the corner of Xishan Lu, head east along Huanwen Lu (焕文路) to find a China Post and China Telecom office.

Huazhong Internet Café (华众网吧; Huázhòng Wǎngbā; Xishan Lu, old town; per hour Y2) After passing through the old city gate, instead of turning right into the old town, continue straight ahead some 50m; this place will be on your left.

Sights

In addition to all the tofu goings-on, the town has a few historical architecture tidbits that are worth exploring, both along Beizheng Jie. First up is the **Confucius Temple** (孔庙; Kǒng Miào), which wasn't actually open for viewing at last visit – but the grounds are nice. And it's free. Further south is the extremely old (dating from the Qing dynasty) **No 1 Middle School** (北正街学校; Běizhēng Jiē Xuéxiào), still in use today.

Sleeping

Finding a cheap bed in town shouldn't be too much of a problem, but if you're aiming for mid- to top-end lodgings, Shípíng's stars have

SHÍPÍNG TOFU

Shípíng's tofu purportedly came with Mongol invaders during the Yuan dynasty and the place hasn't let up on producing the stuff since. Wherefore the big fuss? Apparently it's the water, the silky and primevally fresh spring water in these parts (they often tout how the tofu is 'dotted' with it and not grimy tap water or salt water like *other* places).

All the fun in town is just wandering about and scoping out the entire process. In the alley markets you'll see farmers wheeling in and endlessly haggling over the prices of sacks of soybeans. Guys lug pull-carts laden with pre-tofu beans in-between stages of production. The sound of machinery rattles on and on. And there's even some actual tofu being sold.

A few large-scale factories do exist. **Běimén Dòufu Chǎng** (北门豆腐厂; ☎ 485 8730; Ziyan Jie) has been producing the stuff for over six centuries and is probably the most popular stop for belching tour buses and their hordes (they likely won't know what to make of a foreigner). But pretty much everywhere you look you'll find smaller medium-sized factories, and the best, mom-and-pop back-room operations. Just a note: some of the smaller places weren't too keen on visitors, seriously saying they had corporate espionage concerns. Still, most don't mind if you crane your head in a window and watch. Just don't get too frenetic with your camera. You should assume that taking photos of operations is NOT OK, unless they say otherwise.

been somewhat generously assigned. The first block of Xishan Lu east off Huiyuan Lu is the best place to look for cheap digs.

Jíyáng Bīnguǎn (吉洋宾馆; ☎ 485 7198; Xishan Lu; 西山路; s & d Y40-50, without bathroom Y20-30) Coming from the bus station, turn right (east) off Huiyuan Lu onto Xishan Lu, and this is one of the first budget places you'll come to (on the right side of the street). It has quite clean – very well-maintained – rooms, and management that seemed delighted to have foreign friends.

Xǐkèlái Bīnguǎn (喜客来宾馆; ☎ 485 1456; Xishan Lu; 西山路; s/d Y60/70, s & d without bathroom Y40) Neither as spiffy nor quite as friendly as the previous entry (across the street), it's got clean rooms and is popular enough that it's often booked by early evening.

Shípíng Bīnguǎn (石屏宾馆; ☎ 485 5566; 17 Huanwen Lu; 焕文路17号; s & d Y150-280; 🖳) Loads of hotels are scattered through the downtown area, but this is the only even remotely non-dump (or obnoxiously overpriced) one we found, and it's a steal if you can get the standard discount down to Y100. Most rooms have been redone in the not-too-distant past and show actual – gasp – attention to detail. This may be the only bathroom in China that you actually want to spend time in.

Tobacco Hotel (烟草大厦; Yāncǎo Dàshà; ☎ 485 3456; cnr Huiyuan & Xishan Lu; 汇源西山路口; s/d/tr Y160-440; 🖳) Remember this name, because this is what every taxi driver and every clerk in any hotel that can't/won't take you will say. Proudly hailed as the town's superlative

lodging option, it's perfectly fine and there's not a thing wrong with it, other than its rooms aren't any better than those of the Shípíng Bīnguǎn and it's often booked solid with government officials and tour groups.

Eating

For all its tofu boasting, it can be hard to find a place in Shípíng that actually serves the stuff. (After working with tofu all day, perhaps it's understandable people might wish to eat something else.) It's actually hard to find *any* restaurant outside of hotels. The best place to start is in the old town, where you'll find microscopic back-room eateries or street braziers grilling the stuff to smoky perfection. A couple of decent restaurants are also at the east end of Xishan Lu, near the old town gate, including the **Xīndà Jiǔjiā** (新大酒家; ☎ 685 4936; dishes from Y5).

If you do find a place, you're then confronted with the problem of which of the zillion preparations you wish to indulge in. The best thing to do is hit 'em up with your ever-improving Mandarin. Say *Wǒ yào chī Shípíng dòufu* (我要吃石屏豆腐; 'I want to eat Shípíng tofu') and *Qǐng gěi wǒ jièshào* (请给我介绍; 'Please recommend something').

Two ways you can't go wrong are the standards *shāguō dòufu* (砂锅豆腐; claypot beancurd) and *jiān dòufu* (煎豆腐; braised beancurd). One of the best we sampled was Shípíng tofu braised in a sauce of honey and locally produced *báijiǔ* (moonshine). Otherworldly.

SHÍPÍNG BUS TIMETABLE

Destination	Price (Y)	Duration (hours)	Frequency	Departs
Gèjiù	16	2	every 20 min	7am-6pm
Jiànshuǐ	12	1	every 20 min	7am-8pm
Jǐnghóng	130	15	2 daily	3.30pm & 6.30pm
Kūnmíng	55	3-4	15 daily	6am-9.30pm
Tōnghǎi	18	2-3	11 daily	8am-6pm
Yuányáng	52	4	daily	7am

Getting There & Away

To get to Shípíng from Kūnmíng, you can take buses from the main bus station every half-hour to 90 minutes from 7.30am to 5pm. The ride takes three to four hours and costs Y55. Otherwise, buses from cities and towns in southeastern Yúnnán leave for here fairly constantly, though be forewarned that they go to and from Tōnghǎi and up and over mountains at a snail's pace (but the scenery is lovely).

AROUND SHÍPÍNG

If you've got extra time in Shípíng, it might be worth nosing around the vicinity. Plenty of temples and lakeside vistas await. Most head for **Yilong Lake** (异龙湖) just east of town. To the west of town is the **Bǎoxiù** (宝秀) area, with a modest mountain area sporting temples and pagodas.

You can take a local minibus to Bǎoxiù (Y3, 45 minutes), which run regularly when full from the old bus station near the old town gate in Shípíng, but from there to any sights it's a bit tough.

Chat to any taxi driver at the bus station and you can work out an all-day tour with them. It'll run around Y150 (at least) to hit the lake, Bǎoxiù, and Zhèngyíng Cūn (below). One reputable taxi driver/tour guide others have recommended – and we couldn't agree more – is **Liu Jing** (刘晶; ☎ 675 8917, 139 8730 8915). She speaks maybe three words of English but communicates admirably nonetheless and really takes care of you.

Zhèngyíng Cūn 郑营村

Just 10km west of Shípíng, this pleasant village not far south of the road to Bǎoxiù (but a long walk if you're thinking of hopping off a Bǎoxiù-bound bus and hoofing it) is a funky anachronism. Find a variety of ancestral shrines, temples, pavilions and extant

family courtyards here. The architecture is honestly nothing you haven't seen in many other places in China, but the streetscapes are lovely and the populace entirely welcoming (we had one kindly old chap introduce himself, then lead us around for most of a morning letting us into otherwise inaccessible buildings).

Public buses run, but not often if at all, from the old bus station in Shípíng near the old town gate. It's much quicker and easier to hire a taxi, which you can get for Y40 (round trip).

Lǎoxùdiàn 老旭甸

Around 55km south of Shípíng, Lǎoxùdiàn is known as the Fossilised Castle Town. Indeed, the name is not a misnomer – the village features bizarre dwellings, as if the rich clay earth had risen from the ground in a transmogrification of natural architecture. Trouble is, via local transport it isn't easy to get here.

KĀIYUǍN 开远

☎ 0873 / pop 19,248

Once a main transport hub in southeastern Yúnnán, Kāiyuǎn has hit the skids to a certain extent since the demise of passenger rail in this part of the province. Even its narrow-gauge railroad museum's holdings were packed up *in toto* and shipped off to Kūnmíng (a hospital now occupies the train station). Until China and its Southeast Asian neighbours work out the details on the new regional railway network – which doesn't seem to be forthcoming anytime soon – Kāiyuǎn will continue to struggle along as a semibusy industrial city.

There's no real reason to stop here, other than the only local 'sight' **Nán Dòng** (南洞; South Cave) south of town, which was most aptly described by one local: 'Well, yeah, it's a cave, all right.' But if you're headed to the Wénshān region from Jiànshuǐ, Gèjiù, Yuányáng or Shípíng, you'll more than likely have to stop off here and wait for a bus. No biggie, it's got some pretty tree-lined streets and honestly friendly folks.

Sleeping & Eating

No problem at all for lodging. Exit the main bus station and turn left (south). Everything you need is in this direction.

Yuèshèng Bīnguǎn (月盛宾馆; ☎ 316 4676; 162 Xizhong Lu; 西中路162号; s & d Y80-150, s/d/tr without bathroom Y40/40/45; 🖳) This is the first place you'll come to after the bus station; it's about a 10-minute walk from the bus station on your left. Frill-less but perfectly fine and the gregarious staff would love to have you.

Kāiyuǎn Bīnguǎn (开远宾馆; ☎ 316 1336; Nanzheng Jie; 南正街; s & d from Y60; 🖳) If the Yuèshèng Bīnguǎn is full, then continue south to Lingquan Lu (灵泉路) and turn left. Walk ahead a few minutes to Nanzheng Jie. Turn right and 40m ahead on your right is a narrow entrance to this unassuming and slightly somnolent place. Still, it's clean and the staff solicitous.

Diānnán Dàjiǔdiàn (滇南大酒店; ☎ 712 3396; Lingquan Lu; 灵泉路; s & d from Y200; 🖳) A few blocks east of the Kāiyuǎn Bīnguǎn is this, the 'poshest' (quotes necessary) place in town. Rooms aren't exactly flash but at least they're spacious and bright, and service is above par.

A couple of alleys north of Nanzheng Jie along Lingquan Lu (on the southeast side) is a very clean, friendly noodle and dumpling shop that has smiling service and enormous fill-ups (of all varieties of noodles) for around Y4. Every diminutive eatery in this town, truth be told, has the most enormous bowls of noodles we've ever seen.

Getting There & Around

Kāiyuǎn actually has two bus stations: a south station (*nán zhàn*) for southern destinations and a north station (*běi zhàn*), the main one, for others, though there may be some overlap. A taxi ride between the two is all of Y4.

Regionally, the two stations have buses running to/from everywhere every 10 minutes or so. There are zillions of buses to Kūnmíng (Y50 to Y66, three to four hours). To Qiūběi (Y36, 5½ hours) there are buses at 8.10am and 1.05pm though you could also take a Yànshān bus (many departures) and switch there. To Lúxī (Y29, 4½ hours) buses

leave roughly hourly from 8.10am to 6.30pm. To Luópíng (Y42, six hours) buses leave at 7.40am and 9.40am.

GÈJIÙ 个旧
☎ 0873 / pop 35,084

An alpine-esque town set against a backdrop of craggy cliffs. Vistas over a steely blue lake approaching picture-postcard realms. Yes, there's your Gèjiù, the 'Tin City'.

Howzat again? Yes, it is saddled with that grim moniker because of the ore that made it rich as the dickens. Then again, perish those images of mining dust and strip-mining trucks rumbling, for it's an attractive enough city with a European feel (ironic as the tropic of Cancer passes through the northern end of town). The lake is circled by a lovely promenade, there's lots of greenery, boating, and a teahouse or two perched above the water. A park in the southeastern section houses one of the most significant temples in southeast Yúnnán.

Oh, and the tin. Extraction of tin dates from the Han dynasty, though the first commercial enterprise wasn't until 1883, during the Qing dynasty. Tin extraction and smelting still accounts for 95% of Gèjiù's economic base. And the price of tin must be pretty damned high, as you'll see from the costs of things around here.

Orientation

Gèjiù is built on a north–south axis, divided by a lake, Jīn Hú. The bus station is nearly 1.5km from the city centre. The main artery, Jinhu Xilu, branches along the west side of the lake; it becomes Renmin Lu at its first major intersection south of the lake. Jinhu Nanlu leads east from here, along the south shore, 300m to the base of the hills. South of this is the real Gèjiù – three-quarters modern but with a few warrens of old-world architecture. The southern part of the city is buttressed by Baohua Park (Bǎohuá Gōngyuán), the site of Bǎohuá Sì (Baohua Temple).

No maps can be found around the bus station or anywhere else.

Information

Close your eyes, walk 50m and you'll come across an internet café in Gèjiù; all average around Y3 per hour. The largest is the internet café along Jinhu Nanlu on the south side, east of Jinhu Xilu.

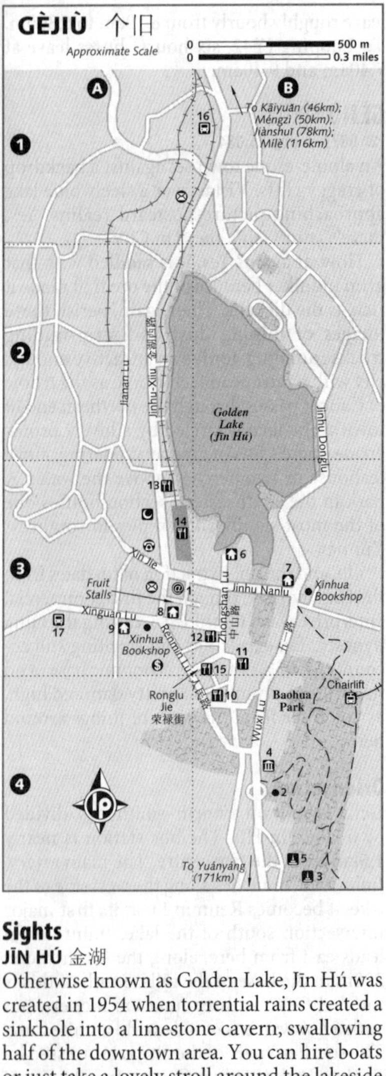

INFORMATION
Internet Café 网吧 ... 1 A3

SIGHTS & ACTIVITIES
Baohua Gate 宝华门 ... 2 B4
Bǎohuá Sì 宝华寺 ... 3 B4
Gejiu Museum 个旧博物馆 ... 4 B4
Monastery 寺庙 ... 5 B4

SLEEPING
Century Plaza 世纪广场酒店 ... 6 B3
Gèjiù Bīnguǎn 个旧宾馆 ... 7 B3
Grand Hotel Honghe 红河大酒店 ... 8 A3
Jiāotōng Bīnguǎn 交通宾馆 ... 9 A3

EATING
Běijīng Fàndiàn 北京饭店 ... 10 B4
Blue Baron 蓝爵士 ... 11 B3
Buffet Restaurant 餐厅 ... 12 B3
French Café 法国楼餐厅 ... 13 A3
Railway Market 火车市场 ... 14 A3
Restaurant of the Tin Metropolis 锡都饭店 ... 15 B3

TRANSPORT
Bus Station 客运站 ... 16 B1
South Bus Station 客运南站 ... 17 A3

Sights

JĪN HÚ 金湖

Otherwise known as Golden Lake, Jīn Hú was created in 1954 when torrential rains created a sinkhole into a limestone cavern, swallowing half of the downtown area. You can hire boats or just take a lovely stroll around the lakeside promenade with every oldster in town.

RAIL LINE 铁路

By the time you read this the city may have made good on its plan to resurrect its defunct narrow-gauge railway line which once went towards Shípíng for tourist excursions (though not all the way to Shípíng). Apparently they're going to have carnival-type attractions at the terminus.

BAOHUA PARK 宝华公园

On the southeastern outskirts of downtown Gèjiù, largish and pretty **Baohua Park** (Bǎohuá Gōngyuán; admission Y2) butts up against Qiling Hill and is built around **Bǎohuá Sì** (Baohua Temple).

The temple was constructed from 1670 to 1675 during the Qing dynasty by a Taoist monk. Later expansions took place in the 20th century. Many of the pavilions and temples have faded but the Lingguan Pavilion, Liang Hall and Baiyuan Tower have all been preserved.

Footpaths wind through the park, taking in some gardens and memorials.

A **chairlift** (one way/return Y15/20; 10am-11pm) up Qiling Hill departs from near the northern entrance to the park. At the top is a restaurant. You could do some good ridge walks around here and walk back to town.

OTHER SIGHTS

If you are headed to Baohua Park, the old town offers interesting backstreets en route to Wuxi Lu. The **Gèjiù Museum** (Gèjiù Bówùguǎn) – which always seems to be closed – has some dull exhibits on local 2000-year-old Eastern Han dynasty excavations. The attached **Caishendian Temple** has some fine statues.

Just up the road, by the entrance to the Baohua Park, is the **Baohua Gate**, also known as the Línyún Gé, built in 1921 by the Republican government.

Sleeping

Budget accommodation is – and has always been – a problem in Gèjiù. Jinhu Nanlu and Xin Jie have a handful of cheap guesthouses, but none accept foreigners. Forget the upper-low end or midrange places you come across along Jinhu Nanlu – they're not worth the money.

Grand Hotel Honghe (红河大酒店; Hónghé Dàjiǔdiàn; ☎ 215 5598; Renmin Lu; 人民路; r Y60-280, without bathroom Y30-50; ﷯) Has always been and still is the best budget option. There is a bewildering array of room choices and prices here – the rate sign looks like an airport departure board.

Jiāotōng Bīnguǎn (交通宾馆; Traffic Hotel; ☎ 216 7028; Xinguan Lu; 新冠路; s/d Y70/80; ﷯) This option, east of the city's regional bus station, seems a bit dark and grim when you enter, but the rooms are actually pretty nice if you want your own bathroom. Best of all, the manager here seems determined to prove the other hotels in town are 'overpriced'. Good sign.

Gèjiù Bīnguǎn (☎ 212 2668; Jinhu Nanlu; 金湖南路; d & tr Y120-288; ﷯) Best used as a last resort for midrange rooms but you can't beat the location.

Century Plaza (Shiji Guǎngchǎng Jiǔdiàn; ☎ 216 8888; www.hh-sj.com; 6-21 Zhongshan Lu; 中山路6-21号; r Y388-1688; ﷯) If you need any proof that the price of tin is high, look no further than the fact that the city has not one but two international-standard luxury hotels within a kilometre of each other. This, the newer one, offers stunning views of the lake in standard rooms and the staff fall all over themselves to help.

Eating

Cheap food is not that easy to find. This town loves its wannabe-chichi, seen-on-the-scene places. However, there are still a few buffet-style restaurants where you pick out three or so dishes and rice for about Y5. The stalls set up around 11.30am and it's all over by 1.30pm. There is a place south of Jinhu Nanlu along Zhongshan Lu.

In the evening, roast beast (and veggies, tofu and goat cheese) can be found at the railway market (nicknamed the 'Barbecue Market') between the south shore of the lake and Jinhu Nanlu, the inside of which is lined with stalls offering braziers to roast your own. Many of these are Muslim.

Blue Baron (Lánjuéshi; ☎ 214 0177; 89 Zhongshan Lu; 中山路; dishes from Y6; ﷯ 11.30am-9pm) This decade-old place serves up pseudo-Western fare and good Chinese, along with coffee, beer and some decent desserts.

French Café (Fǎguólóu Cāntīng; ☎ 213 3688; Jinhu Xilu; 金湖西路; dishes from Y15; ﷯ 9am-noon & 2pm-5.30pm) Not a bit of English here. Or even French. But it does do decent French and Italian food, and the atmosphere is great, housed in an old railroad building (with a nice outside balcony for alfresco dining).

Restaurant of the Tin Metropolis (Xīdū Fàndiàn; Ronglu Jie; 荣禄街; dishes from Y10) and **Běijīng Fàndiàn** (Renmin Lu; 人民路; dishes from Y5), both south of the lake in the rapidly gentrifying old-town district, are the only longtime stand-bys in town for solid Chinese food in a *rènào* (hot and noisy) environment, though sadly the crowds now frequent more chic and trendy places that are pervasive everywhere in this area.

Getting There & Away

To get to Qiūběi you'll have to switch in Kāiyuǎn.

For Jǐnghóng in Xīshuāngbǎnnà buses are being phased out and you'll likely have to go

GÈJIÙ BUS TIMETABLE

Destination	Price (Y)	Duration (hours)	Frequency	Departs
Hékǒu	36	5	hourly	7am-10am (& 3.20pm)
Jiànshuǐ	20	1½	every 10 min approx	6am-6pm
Kāiyuǎn	11	1	every 10 min approx	6am-6pm
Lúxī	34	4	hourly	8am-3.20pm
Tōnghǎi	31	2	3 daily	7.20am, 9.40am, 1.30pm
Wénshān	34	4½	daily	9am
Yuányáng	20	2	3 daily	7am, 7.20am, 7.40am (For Xīnjiē in Yuányáng be sure to specify Yuányáng's Xīnjiē as there's another Xīnjiē locally.)

first to Lùchūn (Y43, six hours) at 6.45am, though they also have epically slow sleepers at 9.10am and 7.30pm.

Buses going to Kūnmíng leave frequently from 6.20am to 10pm with a range of choices (Y30/Y40/48/60 regular/sleeper/Iveco van/luxury coach, five hours).

Another regional bus station is downtown on the southwest end of Xinyuan Lu, serving local sites.

Getting Around

Bus 3 runs from in front of Baohua Park's south entrance all the way along Wuxi Lu to the main bus station north of Jīn Hú. Bus 1 runs north from downtown to the bus station. Bus 2 runs along the east side of Jīn Hú.

AROUND GÈJIÙ

A day trip to **Méngzì** (蒙自) might be worth—for the town's 200-year-old architecture. This town also claims – along with Jiànshuǐ – to being the source of Yúnnán's across-the-bridge noodles. Due to bad roads, the trip takes 1½ hours.

QIŪBĚI 邱北

☎ 0876 / pop 11,418

Qiūběi is, quite honestly, simply a pit stop on the way to Pǔzhěhēi. Grim it isn't by any means. The locals are cheery and helpful and it's fairly relaxed. But given the landscape just outside of town, the ease of transport to get there, and the relative ease of lodging within the park, you'll probably get out as fast as you can.

Orientation & Information

Qiūběi is small enough to walk end to end in 20 minutes; give yourself a couple of hours and you'll have every inch of it reconnoitred. The bus station is on the far north side of town. To get downtown, simply exit the sta-

tion to the right; you're now on Dongzheng Jie (东正街). This becomes Xizheng Jie (西正街) at Caiyun Jie (彩云街). Paralleling Dong/Xizheng Jie is Renmin Lu (人民路); these two run all the way south to Puzhehei Dajie (普者黑大街). That's all you need to know.

We couldn't find one lousy internet café anywhere in this town; trust us, there's nothing else to do here and we spent way too much time looking for a log-in joint.

Sleeping & Eating

At least you'll have little problem finding a place to stay in town. Exit the bus station to the right and bear left at the first intersection. Immediately you'll see the first of the town's cheap guesthouses and hotels – enough for their own phone directory. Few are worth it.

Huìfēng Bīnguǎn (汇丰宾馆; ☎ 412 8266; Dongzheng Jie; 东正街; s & d from Y60; ⊠) Just a block straight ahead out of the bus station, this is among the better of the cheaper options in Qiūběi. Kinda dark interiors but it's clean and as quiet as anything nearby.

Ruìhé Dàjiǔdiàn (瑞和大酒店; ☎ 412 5666; fax 412 6555; Renmin Lu; 人民路; s & d from Y130; ⊠) Qiūběi's original luxury hotel, this is still your best bet for finding anything remotely luxurious. Singles are cramped but in very good shape; twins and doubles are a tad more spacious. Staff are more on the ball than at many similar hotels. To get here, just follow Dong/Xizheng Jie to Caiyun Jie, turn left, then your first left and you're there.

Foodwise, hope you like barbecue (烧烤; shāokǎo) because that's pretty much the only thing you'll find here: braziers flaring on the street, braziers smoking even in eateries. Redolence of searing meat, fish, tofu and veggies.

Our favourite place to eat is **Cǎiyún Fàndiàn** (彩云饭店; Caiyun Jie; dishes from Y2), a lovely tiny

QIŪBĚI BUS TIMETABLE

Destination	Price (Y)	Duration (hours)	Frequency	Departs
Kāiyuǎn	36	5½	2 daily	7.30am, noon
Kūnmíng	63-78	6	every 90 min	8am-9.30pm
Luópíng	32	5-6	7 daily	7.30am, 10am-3pm hourly
Lúxī	38	4	2 daily	8.30am, 10.30am
Wénshān	26	4	hourly	6.20am-5.40pm

place run by a cheerful woman who'll help you sort out what you're hungry for. Plenty of veggies are here for non-meat eaters. You can also get steaming bowls of noodles. It's just north of the corner of Caiyun Jie and Puzhehei Dajie.

Getting There & Away

Note that to get to the Hónghé region you'll need to switch buses in Kāiyuǎn. For Luópíng (Y32, five hours) one direct bus over scenic roads leaves at 7.30am while hourly buses from 10am to 3pm go via Yànshān and take a tad longer.

PǓZHĚHĒI 普者黑
☎ 0876

No time to head for Guìlín or Yángshuò in Guǎngxī? Worry not, for if it's weird and wonderful natural topography (that freaky karst landscape so famed to the east) you're after, this is a grand backup spot. Just 12km outside of Qiūběi, it offers gorgeous scenery – there's nothing like being paddled in a traditional Yi flat-bottomed boat past endless chocolate-drop hillocks, and spelunking innumerable caves.

Now, keep in mind that there's a reason Guìlín and its little sibling Yángshuò are in virtually every coffee-table picturebook the world round…and Pǔzhěhēi ain't. But if you come in the right season – May through early August – it can come pretty close. Endless rivers and streams strewn with gazillions of lotus flowers, upthrusting peaks dense with greenery, and of course tourists chock-a-block on every square inch. (Honestly? Show up November through April and be thoroughly underwhelmed, with brown lotuses choking the waterways, the greenery retreating to reveal rock-scarred crags as if nature's giving you the finger, and stiff winds seemingly always in your face.)

Sights & Activities

Technically, the Pǔzhěhēi region is a vast place, a 165-sq-km spread encompassing, let's see, over 280 karst peaks, five dozen lakes, 250 caves, waterfalls, valleys, ancient rock paintings, and several cremation tomb groups.

You'll only really probably see the main **park section** (admission May-Oct Y100, Nov-Apr Y60), which has but a handful of caves and peaks (embarrassingly adorned for the most part with communications towers) but some nice

waterways. You can probably trudge the whole park area along its few roads in a couple of hours, depending on how quickly/slowly you move. No need to walk, either, as your ticket includes a boat ride on a Yi flat-bottomed canoe and two cave entrances, and after that there are loads of horse carts plodding along whose drivers will endlessly beckon you to haggle for a ride (a couple of yuán is average). If you've done one Chinese caves, one cave is enough here. It's creepily cool and eerily lit as always but they're pretty much the same. The **Buddha Cave** purportedly has the longest reclining Buddha in China.

The rest of the surrounding area could make for some fine bicycle exploring – but you have to lug in your own wheels.

A good time to be here is during the seventh lunar month, when the Yi have their **Face-Painting Festival** blowout. After gorging on roast pig and chicken, everyone runs around to smear ink and soot on each other. The blacker, the better – it guarantees (somehow) a bountiful harvest and safe family. Don't worry – they do it pretty much daily May through the first week of October. Dates for upcoming festivals are: 26–29 July 2008; 14–17 August 2009; 4–7 August 2010.

Sleeping & Eating

Unless you arrive in Qiūběi late in the afternoon or early evening, there's no need to stay there, as the park does have accommodation – dirt-cheap through to apathetically maintained midrange. You can pretty much double any price listed here May through July.

Mínsú Nóngjiā (民俗农家; ☎ 461 8358; Pǔzhěhēi village; per bed Y15) From the final stop of the bus from Qiūběi, walk over the bridge into Pǔzhěhēi village. Look for some characters painted on a cinder-block wall. Here's your cheapest option in the village. Given the price, expect little but it's fine if you can convince them to let you stay (they seemed a bit hesitant).

Pǐnxiānggé Jiǔdiàn (品乡阁酒店; ☎ 461 8064; s & d Y80, without bathroom Y60) This place is one of a handful of modest but comfortable restaurant-hotel options (this one started as a simple shop). From the final stop of the bus from Qiūběi, backtrack towards the park's entrance. A few minutes later on the right side you'll come to this nice little spot with rooms that are very new and clean and a really welcoming owner. There's a spacious but quiet open-air

---

YOU WANT SOME LOTUS WITH YOUR LOTUS?

Remember this word: hé (荷) as in héhuā (荷花; lotus). You're gonna hear it often while here (if you're here May through early August, when Pǔzhěhēi is a blooming garden of lotus flowers). How 'bout some chicken wrapped in lotus leaf? That'd be hébāo (荷包). Remember to have some lotus leaf rice – héyèfàn (荷叶饭). Or for a twist on that how 'bout some sticky-rice stuffed lotus root, the famed nuòmǐ'ǒu (糯米藕)? For breakfast you can't beat a lotus leaf omelette: héyèjiāndàn (荷叶煎蛋).

Right – you're probably sick of lotus by now. No problem, as the other culinary specialty here you needn't even work for. Shuǐshàng shāokǎoděng (水上烧烤等) literally means 'barbecue atop the water (while you wait!)' and indeed, Yi canoes will paddle up and offer you some roast beast (or veggies, even lotus root!).

---

restaurant that's good for hanging out, and the views from the 3rd-floor balconies are superb.

Yínhú Jiǔdiàn (银湖酒店; ☎ 461 0068; s & d from Y180; 🖭) Approximately a kilometre from the main entrance (the bus stops here or you can walk here by staying to the right after you leave the main gate) are a few weary 'midrange' places. This is the best of the lot but they're all pretty much the same. You know: cracked mirrors, dormant lights, rusted tubs. The usual. Still, in off season you can pretty much name your price.

Getting There & Away

Large green buses (Y2, 30 minutes) run to Pǔzhěhēi from Qiūběi whenever full, sometimes half-hourly, sometimes hourly. From the Qiūběi bus station, exit and bear right, then a quick left. One block ahead the buses wait for passengers. You can also pick them up along Dongzheng and Xizheng Jie.

The bus drops you by the ticket office, then it continues on another kilometre or so past the wharf to a tourist zone with a couple of hotels, restaurants and shops. It then backtracks a bit before splitting off and heading to Pǔzhěhēi village proper. To get to other places from Pǔzhěhēi, reverse your trip on the large green buses to Qiūběi, then take a bus from there.

WÉNSHĀN 文山

☎ 0876 / pop 18,753

Wénshān is the capital of the eponymous region in far eastern Yúnnán. One of the poorest regions in the province, it features a heady mixture of Miao and Zhuang people, the latter concentrated near the border with Vietnam. You'll also find quite a few pockets of Yi and Bai people. (The government is hoping that a new airport in Wénshān will be able to jumpstart development.)

Nothing in the city itself really warrants a visit, but you may have to pass through if you're heading for Guǎngxī. This is no bad thing, however, as you could do some grand village explorations in the remotest areas in the east.

Sleeping

Plenty of places to stay around the bus station have singles or doubles for Y40 to Y80.

Jiāotōng Bīnguǎn (交通宾馆; ☎ 219 5518; Huancheng Lu; 环城路; s & d Y80; 🖭) Also near the bus station, this place has perfectly fine standard rooms. Nothing fancy and it's convenient. To get here, head straight north from the central bus station along Puyang Lu.

Getting There & Away

AIR

In late 2006 a new airport opened 23km west of town. Schedules are shaking out but currently flights stop in Wénshān on their way to/from Kūnmíng (Y420) and Nánníng (Y580) on Monday, Tuesday, Friday and Sunday.

BUS

Wénshān actually has three bus stations. Worry not, for they're all along the same road, Kaihua Lu (开化路), which traverses the city from west to east, passing right through downtown. Furthest west is the express bus station. To the east 1km or so is the new central station (新城客运中心; Xīnchéng Kèyùn Zhōngxīn), which has most of what you need. Express buses to Kūnmíng (Y110, six hours) leave at least twice a day from the central station and more often from the express bus station. Regular buses to the capital (Y86, seven to eight hours) leave regularly from

8.40am to 9pm. At least three buses leave daily for Qiūběi (Y26, five hours) but only one per day runs to Luópíng. A dozen buses also run to Hékǒu.

Further southeast (two bridges) is the southern station with departures to smaller, local places.

AROUND WÉNSHĀN
Tuóniáng Jiāng (Tuoniang River)
驼娘江

This tributary of the Pearl River lies in the far eastern tip of Wénshān, and is as far east as you can go in Yúnnán (in fact, you're only around 90km from Bǎisè in Guǎngxī; p211). This river valley is famous for **Bō'ài** (剥隘), a smashingly historic village and once a major node on water trade routes dating back to the Song and Ming dynasties. There are fabulous slate streets, tiny wooden houses and an ancient port where imperial representatives called. Sadly, this place is to be submerged in the near future by dam projects in Guǎngxī.

Forty-two kilometres upstream from the village is a fantastically lovely stretch of the river, popular for boat trips. Oddly craggy cliffs swoop up here to blot out the sun and birds squawk everywhere. And do sample the legendary *Bō'ài kǎoyā* (剥隘烤鸭; Bō'ài roast duck). Whether or not this stretch is affected by the same projects that will devastate Bō'ài is uncertain.

Bàměi 坝美
The fascinating little Zhuang village of **Bàměi** (admission Y35), built around groves of banyan trees, could well argue that Yúnnán's Shangri-la in the northwest is misnamed. Here in one of the most idyllic locations one could imagine sits a village untouched by time (though not always by Chinese tourists). Surrounded by craggy cliffs, it is actually only entered by boat through a kilometre-long cave! In fact, the name in the Zhuang language means 'Cave in the Forest'; history has it that it was founded six centuries ago by a group of Zhuang to escape the lawlessness of one of China's upheavals.

Once in, the picturesque riverine scenery is simply marvellous, with villagers plodding about leading water buffalo and water wheels ubiquitous. And no – zero – electricity. You could also stay with a local family but this is no given.

Bàměi is actually 43km north of Guǎngnán (广南), an uninspiring but friendly town an all-day bus ride from Wénshān. From Guǎngnán you'll have to wait around for enough passengers at the bus station to fill a minivan or hire one yourself. You could also take a bus bound for Bádá (八达), and ask the driver to tell you when to hop off, after which you have a 1km walk to the village. There are very modest but clean enough hotels in Guangnan (s/d from Y50).

And yes, you really do have to enter via a Zhuang-poled boat!

Bābǎo 八宝
Around 160km northeast of Wénshān, Bābǎo is a Zhuang village in one of the more aesthetically pleasing areas of the province. The name means 'Eight Treasures' (as in the soothing tea of the same name) and couldn't be more apt. It is more of a tourist region than a village today but if you can escape the tourist crowds you'll find waterfalls along the Babao River, caves and freak geology (including a fascinating wind-hole literally blown through a rock outcropping), rock paintings and more.

The village is midway between Guǎngnán and Fùníng, best reached from the latter. Try haggling for a ride there. The problem is that it's more oriented toward groups, so it's tough to do solo.

YUANYANG RICE TERRACES
元阳梯田
☎ 0873 / pop 22,631

Picture hill-top villages, the only thing visible above rolling fog and cloudbanks; an artist's palette of colours at sunrise or sunset; spirit-recharging treks through centuries-old rice-covered hills, with a few water buffalo chewing their cud contentedly nearby. Yup, it's kinda hard not to get indulgent when describing these rice terraces (梯田; *tītián*), hewn from the rolling topography by the Hani over centuries. They cover roughly 12,500 hectares and are another of Yúnnán's – nay, China's – most absolutely spectacular sights. Seriously – hiking in the morning mists, you'll swear these pools shimmering with golds and reds are dancing about. An unforgettable experience.

Yuányáng is actually split into two: Nánshā, the new town, and Xīnjiē, the old town, located and hour's bus ride up a nearby hill. Either can be labelled Yuányáng, depending what map you use. Xīnjiē is the one you want, so make sure you are getting off at the right one.

Information

Agricultural Bank of China (中国农业银行; Zhōngguó Nóngyè Yínháng) Gives cash advances on credit cards and changes money but will not cash travellers cheques.

Internet café (山城网吧; Shānchéng Wǎngbā; per hr Y2; ⌚ 24hr) Down the stairs on your left facing the lookout.

Post office (邮局; Yóujú) Go down the stone steps at the south end of Titian Sq (Títián Guǎngchǎng). Turn when you see the road fork behind you.

Sights & Activities

Dozens of villages, each with its own terrace field, spiral out from Xīnjiē. The terraces around each village have their own special characteristics which vary from season to season. A rule of thumb: follow the ever-present photographers.

Duōyishù, about 25km from Xinjie, has the most spectacular sunrises and is the one you should not miss. For sunsets, **Bádá** and **Lǎohǔzuǐ** can be mesmerising.

Maps are available at all accommodation in town. Most are bilingual Chinese-English, though some include Japanese, German and French labels as well.

There's a fleet of minibuses by Xīnjiē's Titian Sq and they leave when full and whiz around the villages but you are much better off arranging a car and driver through your accommodation. It's also easy just to hook up with other travellers and split the cost of chartering a minibus for the day (Y400 to Y450).

Sleeping & Eating

Yuányáng Chénjiā Fángshè (元阳陈家房舍; ☎ 562 2342; dm/s/tr Y10/40/60) This open and breezy guesthouse has spotless rooms with spectacular views of the rice terraces. It's all kept humming by four generations of the same family.

Government Guesthouse (元阳县山城大酒店; Yuányángxiàn Shānchéng Dàjiǔdiàn; s/d Y150/180; ✖) Just off Titian Sq, rooms here are nothing special but the lobby has the best tourist information desk.

Yúntī Dàjiǔdiàn (云梯大酒店; ☎ 562 4858; s/d Y258/328; ✖) These are the swankest digs in town, with clean, modern rooms and a staff used to foreigners.

You'll find plenty of boisterous food stalls in town. **Lǎo Sìchuān Cāntīng Guǎn** (老四川餐厅馆; dishes from Y5; ⌚ 10am-around 11pm) is probably the most popular and it's standing room only some nights. For a more tranquil atmosphere try **Liùjūn Fàndiàn** (六军饭店; dishes from Y4; ⌚ 10am-9:30pm). The food is good and it's the cheapest in town.

Getting There & Away

There are three buses daily from Kūnmíng to Yuángyáng (Y90, 6½ hours, 10.40am, 7.30pm and 8pm). Buses from Yuángyáng (Xīnjiē) back to Kūnmíng leave 10.12am, 5pm and 9pm.

From here destinations include Hékǒu (Y37, four hours), Gèjiù (Y20, two hours), Jiànshuǐ (Y30, four hours) and others.

Or you can take the long way to Xīshuāngbǎnnà. To get there, take the 7.30am bus to Lǚchūn (Y25, four hours), where you'll have wait to get the Jiāngchéng bus at 4pm (Y31, five hours). By the time you arrive, there'll be no more buses but you can stay at the hotel attached to the bus station, which has cheap rooms (dm/d Y10/60). Buses to Jǐnghóng (Y50, 8½ hours) start running at 6am.

This can be a gruelling route over bumpy dirt roads, but it will take you through magnificent scenery. Buses along this route are frequently stopped for routine police checks.

XĪSHUĀNGBǍNNÀ REGION 西双版纳

Xīshuāngbǎnnà (the Chinese approximation of the original Thai name of Sip Sawng Panna, literally '12 Rice-Growing Districts') is located just north of Myanmar and Laos. It's better known as Bǎnnà and has become China's own mini-Thailand, attracting tourists looking for sunshine and water-splashing festivals, hikers readying epic jungle treks, and burned out citizenry (and expats) of China fleeing the congestion (and cold weather) of China's cities.

But despite Bǎnnà's popularity, it rarely seems overwhelmed by tourists – even the capital, Jǐnghóng, is basically an overgrown somnolent town that doesn't seem to get too worked up about things. It is quite easy to lose weeks here...

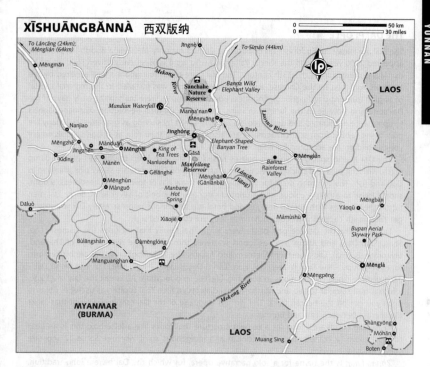

XĪSHUĀNGBĂNNÀ 西双版纳

Environment

Xīshuāngbǎnnà is home to many unique species of plant and animal life. Unfortunately, recent scientific studies have demonstrated the devastating effects of previous government policies on land use; the tropical rainforest areas of Bǎnnà are now as acutely endangered as similar rainforest areas elsewhere on the planet.

The jungle areas that remain contain dwindling numbers of wild tigers, leopards, elephants and golden-haired monkeys. To be fair, the number of elephants has doubled to 250, up 100% from the early 1980s; the government now offers compensation to villagers whose crops have been destroyed by elephants, or who assist in wildlife conservation. In 1998 the government banned the hunting or processing of animals, but poaching is notoriously hard to control.

People

About one-third of the 800,000-strong population found in this region are Dai; another third or so are Han Chinese and the rest is made up of a conglomerate of minorities that include the Hani, Lisu and Yao, as well as lesser-known hill tribes such as the Aini (a subgroup of the Hani), Jinuo, Bulang, Lahu and Wa.

Xishuangbanna Dai Autonomous Prefecture, as it is known officially, is subdivided into the three counties of Jǐnghóng, Měnghǎi and Měnglà.

Climate

The region has two seasons: wet and dry. The wet season is between June and August, when it rains ferociously almost every day. From September to February there is less rainfall, but thick fog descends during the late evening and doesn't lift until 10am or even later.

November to March sees temperatures average about 19°C. The hottest months of the year are from April to September, when you can expect an average of 25°C.

Festivals & Events

During festival times, booking same-day airline tickets to Jǐnghóng can be extremely difficult – even with 17 flights per day. You can try getting a flight into Sīmáo, 162km to the

THE DAI PEOPLE 傣族

The Dai are Hinayana Buddhists (as opposed to China's majority Mahayana Buddhists) who first appeared 2000 years ago in the Yangzi Valley and who were subsequently driven southwards by the Mongol invasion of the 13th century. The Dai state of Xīshuāngbǎnnà was annexed by the Mongols and then by the Chinese, and a Chinese governor was installed in the regional capital of Jinglan (present-day Jǐnghóng). Countless Buddhist temples were built in the early days of the Dai state and now lie in the jungles in ruins. During the Cultural Revolution, Xīshuāngbǎnnà's temples were desecrated and destroyed. Some were saved by serving as granaries, but many are now being rebuilt from scratch. Temples are also recovering their role as village schools where young children are accepted for religious training as monks.

The Dai live in spacious wooden houses raised on stilts, to keep themselves off the damp earth, with the pigs and chickens below. The most common Dai foods are sticky rice (*khao nio* in Dai) and fish. The common dress for Dai women is a straw hat or towel-wrap headdress, a tight, short blouse in a bright colour, and a printed sarong with a belt of silver links. Some Dai men tattoo their bodies with animal designs, and betel-nut chewing is popular. Many Dai youngsters get their teeth capped with gold, otherwise they are considered ugly.

Linguistically, the Dai are part of the very large Thai family that includes the Siamese, Lao, Shan, Thai Dam and Ahom peoples found scattered throughout the river valleys of Thailand, Myanmar (Burma), Laos, northern Vietnam and Assam. The Xīshuāngbǎnnà Dai are broken into four subgroups – the Shui (Water) Dai, Han (Land) Dai, Huayao (Floral Belt) Dai and Kemu Dai – each distinguished by variations in costume, lifestyle and location. All speak the Dai language, which is quite similar to Lao and northern Thai dialects. In fact, Thai is often as useful as Chinese once you get off the beaten track. The written language of the Dai employs a script that looks like a cross between Lao and Burmese.

In temple courtyards, look for a cement structure that looks like a letterbox; this is an altar to local spirits, a combination of Buddhism and indigenous spirit worship. Some 32 separate spirits exist for humans.

Zhang khap is the name for a solo narrative opera, for which the Dai have a long tradition. Singers are trained from childhood to perform long songs accompanied by native flute and sometimes a long drum known as the elephant drum. Performances are given at monk initiations, when new houses are built, weddings, and on the birthdays of important people, and they often last all night. Even if you do understand Dai, the lyrics are complex – if not fully improvised. At the end, the audience shouts 'Shuay! Shuay!' which is close to 'Hip, hip, hooray!'. Even courtship is done via this singing. Some Dai phrases include *doǔzaǒ lǐ* (hello), *yíndíí* (thank you) and *goǐhán* (goodbye).

---

north, or taking the bus. Hotels in Jǐnghóng town are booked solid and prices are usually tripled.

Most people end up in a nearby Dai village and commuting. Festivities take place all over Xīshuāngbǎnnà, so you might be lucky further away from Jǐnghóng.

Tanpa Festival During this festival in February, young boys are sent to the local temple for initiation as novice monks.

Tan Jing Festival Participants honour Buddhist texts housed in local temples in this festival (held between February and March).

Water-Splashing Festival Held in mid-April; washes away the dirt, sorrow and demons of the old year and brings in the happiness of the new. Jǐnghóng usually celebrates it from the 13th to the 15th. Dates in the surrounding villages vary. In Jǐnghóng, the first day of the festival is devoted to a giant market. The second day features dragon-boat racing, swimming races and rocket launching. The third day features the water-splashing freak out. Foreigners get special attention so prepare to get drenched all day. Remember, the wetter you get, the more luck you'll receive.

Tan Ta Festival Held during the last 10-day period of October or November, with temple ceremonies, rocket launches from special towers, and hot-air balloons. The rockets, which often contain lucky amulets, blast off with a curious droning sound, like mini-space shuttles, before exploding high above; those who find the amulets are assured of good luck.

Closed-Door Festival The farming season (from July to October) is the time for this festival, when marriages or festivals are banned. Traditionally this is also the time of year that men aged 20 or older are ordained as monks for a period of time.

Open-Door Festival The season ends with this festival, when everyone lets their hair down again to celebrate the harvest.

JĬNGHÓNG 景洪

☎ 0691 / pop 93,341

Jĭnghóng – the 'City of Dawn' in the local Dai language – is the capital of Xīshuāngbǎnnà prefecture, but don't take that too seriously. It's still an overgrown, drowsy Mekong River jungle town as much as it is a city. Sure, taller buildings are going up and knucklehead neo-phyte tour groups are clambering around here in all directions (great people-watching fun, actually) but it's nonetheless a perfect representation of the laid-back place that Bǎnnà is.

Prepare yourself for searing late-day heat that can put the entire city into a kind of serious slow motion. If you've come from Southeast Asia, no biggie, but if you've acclimatised to higher and nippier elevations in Yúnnán, you'll probably find yourself needing lots of midday siestas.

Information

The travellers' books, staff, and especially other travellers at Mei Mei, Forest and Mekong Cafés (see p329) are by far the best sources of travel tips and trek notes. The best place to make long-distance calls is from the private phone bars along Manting Lu.

Bank of China (Zhōngguó Yínháng; ☎ 213 6228; Xuanwei Dadao); Changes travellers cheques and foreign currency, and has an ATM machine. There's also a branch office on Galan Zhonglu.

China Post & Telecom (Zhōngguó Yóuzhèng & Zhōngguó Diànxùn; cnr Mengle Dadao & Xuanwei Dadao; ◷ 8am-8.30pm)

China International Travel Service (CITS; Zhōngguó Guójì Lǚxíngshè; ☎ 663 8459; Jinghong International Travel Bldg, Mengzhe LuLuandian Jie) Can arrange all manner of one-day tours from Y200 to Y300. However, you're better off going to the Mekong, Mei Mei or Forest Cafés, which will help you with trekking information and put you in touch with English-speaking guides.

Internet cafés (wǎngbā; Manting Lu; per hr Y2) There are about a half-dozen along this street.

Public Security Bureau (PSB; Gōngānjú; ☎ 212 2676; Jingde Lu; ◷ 8-11.30am & 3-5.30pm) Has a fairly speedy visa extension service.

Xishuangbanna Minorities Hospital (Xīshuāngbǎnnà Mínzú Yīyuàn; ☎ 213 0123; Galan Lu) The best bet for having an English speaker available.

ETIQUETTE IN DAI TEMPLES

Around Dai temples the same rules apply as elsewhere: dress appropriately (no tank tops or shorts); take off shoes before entering; don't take photos of monks or the inside of temples without permission; leave a donation if you do take any shots and consider a token donation even if you don't – unlike in Thailand, these Buddhists receive no government assistance. It is polite to 'wai' the monks as a greeting and remember to never rub anyone's head, raise yourself higher than a Buddha figure or point your feet at anyone. (This last point applies to secular buildings too. If you stay the night in a Dai household it is good form to sleep with your feet pointing towards the door.)

Dangers & Annoyances

There have been on-and-off reports from travellers regarding drug-and-rob incidents on the Kūnmíng–Jĭnghóng bus trip. Be careful who your friends are on buses, accept nothing, and leave nothing unattended when you hop off for breaks.

Sights

TROPICAL FLOWER & PLANTS GARDEN
热带花卉园

This terrific **botanical garden** (Rèdài Huāhuìyuán; ☎ 212 0493; 28 Jĭnghóng Xilu; admission Y40; ◷ 7am-6pm), west of the town centre, is one of Jĭnghóng's better attractions. Admission gets you into a series of gardens where you can view over 1000 different types of plant life. Take the path on the left-hand side as you enter the gardens to head towards the lovely tropical rainforest area.

PEACOCK LAKE PARK 孔雀湖公园

This artificial lake in the centre of town isn't much, but the small park (Kǒngquè Hú Gōngyuán) next to it is pleasant. The English Language Corner takes place here every Sunday evening, so this is your chance to exchange views or to engage with the locals practising their English.

MANTING PARK 曼听公园

In the south of Jĭnghóng, **Manting Park** (Mànting Gōngyuán; admission Y15) is not really interesting, even if it is the garden of a former Dai chieftain. The park contains a couple of replica stupas, and you'll probably see Dai dancing

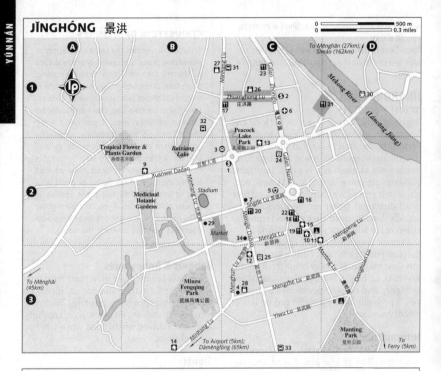

JĪNGHÓNG 景洪

girls (performing a Water-Splashing Festival dance), and a poor elephant in chains.

The temple in the rear of the park, the **Zǒng Fósì** (Wat Bajie in Dai), is the leading regional temple, described by one anthropologist as the 'Ivy League' of temple schools. The temple was built in 1990 and many of its monks have studied in Thailand and speak Thai.

Just before you get to the park entrance is the **Màntīng Fósì**, a temple claimed to date back 1100 years.

Activities
Jǐnghóng's oft-recommended **Blind Massage School** (Mángrén Ànmó; ☎ 212 5834; cnr Mengle Dadao & Jingde Lu; ⏱ 9am-midnight) offers hour-long

TREKKING IN XĪSHUĀNGBĀNNÀ

Treks around Xīshuāngbǎnnà used to be among the best in China: you'd be invited into a local's home to eat, sleep, and drink *báijiǔ* (moonshine). Increasing numbers of visitors have changed this in places. Don't automatically expect a welcome mat and a free lunch just because you're a foreigner, but don't go changing the local economy by throwing money around either.

If you do get invited into someone's home, try to establish whether payment is expected. If it's not, leave an offering (ask at the backpacker cafés what's considered appropriate) or leave modest gifts such as candles, matches, rice etc – even though the family may insist on nothing.

Also take care before heading off, it's a jungle out there, so go prepared, and make sure somebody knows where you are and when you should return. In the rainy season you'll need to be equipped with proper hiking shoes and waterproof gear. At any time you'll need water purification tablets, bottled water or a water bottle able to hold boiling water, as well as snacks and sunscreen.

Seriously consider taking a guide. You won't hear much Mandarin Chinese on the trail, let alone any English. Expect to pay around Y250 per day for a guide.

Forest Café (Sēnlín Kāfēiwū; ☎ 898 5122; www.forest-cafe.org; Ganlan Nanlu, Jǐnghóng) is a great place to start. Sara, the owner, has years of experience leading treks and comes recommended. The other cafés mentioned in this book (Mei Mei Café and Mekong Café) have also been recommended and each emphasises different things.

Try the **Xishuangbanna Travel & Study Club** (Xīshuāngbǎnnà Yóuxué Jùlèbù; Map p328; Mengzhe Lu, Jǐnghóng) for trekking equipment.

massages for Y30. The staff here is extremely kind and travellers give it terrific reports. Head down the lane off Mengle Dadao and climb the stairs on your left up to the 2nd floor.

Sleeping

Banna College Hotel (Bǎnnà Xuéyuàn; ☎ 213 8365; Xuanwei Dadao; 宣慰大道; dm Y15, tw/d per person Y40/50; ⌘) Most travellers are winding up here now, for good reason: clean rooms, efficient service and a smattering of English. Bike rental for Y15 per day, Y150 deposit.

Dai Building Inn (Dǎijiā Huáyuán Xiǎolóu; ☎ 216 2592; 57 Manting Lu; 曼听路57号; dm Y25) Traditional Dai style must mean sweating in the summer, staff a bit uninterested, and thin walls. Still, some people love the place.

Wanli Dai Style Guesthouse (Wǎnlì Dǎiwèi Cāntíng; ☎ 1357 811 2879; Manting Lu; 曼听路; dm Y30) Basic but OK, though the rooms can get stuffy. An approximation of a garden is here and the restaurant is decent.

Dàqingshù Bīnguǎn (☎ 216 1776; Manting Lu, Jinglan Alley 4; 曼听路景兰4巷; s & d Y40-100; ⌘) Set back off of Manting Lu, and thus much quieter, is this new small hotel. Rooms range from smallish to good-sized; the only downer is that the sinks drain onto the floor via a hose. Otherwise it's great. Zilch English but friendly.

Jǐngyǒng Fàndiàn (☎ 212 3727; 12 Xuanwei Dadao; 宣慰大道12号; s & d Y180, s/d without bathroom Y60/80; ⌘) A slight step up between budget and midrange is this place, your best bet for a modicum of comfort and service without busting the bank.

Golden Banna Hotel (Jīn Bǎnnà Jiǔdiàn; ☎ 212 4901; Mengle Dadao; 猛泐大道; s/d Y380/580; ⌘) Though rooms are nondescript, staff are very efficient and offer great deals outside of festival times.

Tai Garden Hotel (Tàiyuán Jiǔdiàn; ☎ 212 3888; fax 212 6060; 8 Minghang Lu; 民航路8号; d Y640 plus 15% tax; ⌘ ⌘) It has quiet grounds replete with its own island, pool, sauna, gym and tennis court. It's full of the sophisticated and the monied, which makes the elegant morning buffet all the more entertaining when it inevitably disintegrates into a rough-and-tumble free-for-all.

Eating

Manting Lu is lined with restaurants serving Dai food, the majority of which dish up Dai dance performances along with their culinary specialities. Dai women thump drums at the entrance and the restaurants are filled nearly every night with tourists generally being festive.

Dai dishes include barbecue fish, eel or beef cooked with lemongrass or served with peanut-and-tomato sauce. Vegetarians can order roast bamboo shoot prepared in the same fashion. Other specialities of this place include fried river moss (better than it sounds and excellent with beer), spicy bamboo-shoot soup and *shāokǎo* (烧烤; skewers of meat wrapped in banana leaves and grilled over wood fires).

Mei Mei Café (曼听路; Měiměi Kāfēitīng; ☎ 212 7324; Manting Lu; dishes from Y5; ☺ 8am-11pm) The institution in town for years and years. Everyone winds up here. How's that for a recommendation?

Forest Café (嘎兰南路; Sēnlín Kāfēiwū; ☎ 898 5122; www.forest-cafe.org; Galan Nanlu; dishes from Y5; ☺ 8.30-10pm) Almost as long as Mei Mei has been around, Sara and her brother have been up the street at the Forest, dishing out healthful foods – try the homemade bread – and the best burgers in Bǎnnà. She also gets raves for her treks.

Méngzì Guòqiáo Mǐxiàn (景德路; Jingde Lu; dishes Y5-20; ☺ 24hr) This breezy, modest restaurant serves up round-the-clock noodles and rice dishes to be washed down with beakers of quenching lemonade (Y4). English menu available.

Lucky Mandalay Restaurant (庄洪路; Lāqià Miǎndiàn Mùsīlín Cāntīng; ☎ 214 1611; Zhuanghong Lu; dishes from Y8) Great Muslim food, tea and ambience in the jade market. Just look for the guys whacking cards on tables outside.

Mekong Café (曼听路; Méigōng Cānguǎn; ☎ 216 2395; 111 Manting Lu; dishes from Y8; ☺ 8am-10pm) The food, smiling service, and travel information are wondrous, but best is the isolated balcony upstairs, your sanctuary from the polluted chaos outside.

Thai Restaurant (曼听路; Tàiguó Cāntīng; ☎ 216 1758; Manting Lu; dishes from Y8) Pounce on it the moment you spy a free seat at this popular Thai restaurant. *Phad thai* devotees literally flock here and the crowds never really thin out. You can also wash the authentic Thai dishes down with some snake whisky if you're feeling brave.

Xīngyuán Lèyuán (嘎兰中路; ☎ 663 2825; Galan Lu; mains from Y10) Dai food without the usual crappy tourist atmosphere; this one overseen (at least originally) by one of the region's best-known traditional Dai singers.

Dining out, as in alfresco, is done nowhere better than it is in Jinghong. Everywhere you go after the heat and torpor of the day wear off, you'll see that tables are thrown onto sidewalks, fish are tossed into aquariums, woks start firing up and the beer is iced, ready for consumption.

Almost anywhere you walk in town, taking a step off a main street will bring you to a great impromptu night market. There is a huge **night food market** by the new bridge over the Mekong where dozens of stalls serve up barbecued everything, from sausages to snails. There are plenty of tables and chairs for those who want to linger at this night market.

BĀNNÀ'S TEA OF CHOICE

Yúnnán is as legendary as any Chinese province for its tea, and *pǔ'ěr chá* (普洱茶), a variety of black tea, may be the king of 'em all. Available all over the province and nationwide, it is legendarily grown in Yúnnán, in particular near Měnghǎi and Sīmáo (though its name comes from a small town near the Laos border). This king of teas was the gold on the old tea-horse road(s) that stretched from Yúnnán into Laos, Burma (Myanmar), Tibet, India and all the way to the Silk Road.

Essentially, the tea's claim to fame is its rich taste acquired from ageing – it, in fact, ferments. The longer it ages, the richer the taste. (This was due in part to the discovery that in order to transport it a long distance, it would need to be steamed and compressed into nuggets or even bowls.) Naturally, some years and seasons are better than others, and each locale in southern Yúnnán claims to produce the finest.

And the higher the quality, the higher the value: a cup in a café can cost on average around Y5, but for the highest quality you can pay nearly Y100,000.

Brewing it is time-consuming but well worth it. You should never drink the first round of steeping and, in fact, the leaves may be reused again and again. No matter what variety, the tea is even favoured by non-tea aficionados for its subtle flavour (and the fact that the leaves are essentially impossible to oversteep):

Then, as always, the health benefits: they're infinite. Of course.

Entertainment

Mengbala Naxi Arts Theatre (Méngbālā Nàxī Yìshùgōng; Galan Zhonglu; 嘎兰南路; tickets Y160; ☻ 8.30pm) This theatre has daily song and dance shows.

YES Disco (Mengle Dadao; 勐肋大道; admission Y10; ☻ 9pm-late) Discos come and discos go, but YES keeps thumping along; you've got a good chance of being heavy-lidded at least one morning here.

Shopping

Market groupies have two terrific places to head for shopping, people-watching and atmosphere. A fabulous fish and produce market is tucked behind some modern buildings across from the long-distance bus station. The **Jade Market** (Yùshìchǎng; Zhuanghong Lu) is nearby, with lots of Burmese and other South Asians hawking their goods alongside locals.

Getting There & Away

AIR

There are several flights a day to Kūnmíng (Y730) but in April (when the Water-Splashing Festival is held) you'll need to book tickets several days in advance to get either in or out.

There are two flights daily in high season to Lìjiāng (Y840). You can also fly to Bangkok (Y1630) and Chiang Mai (Y1630) from here, usually daily.

Tickets can be purchased at the **CAAC Booking Office** (☎ 212 7040; Jingde Lu; ☻ 8am-9pm). Credit cards and travellers cheques are not accepted.

Any café on Manting Lu can buy tickets for you, or go yourself to **Tangshi Travel Agency** (Tángshì Hángkōng Lǚshè; ☎ 212 2766; Mengle Dadao), which has cheap prices.

BUS

The Jīnghóng **long-distance bus station** (Chángtú Kèyùnzhàn; Minhang Lu) is the most useful for long-distance destinations. If you want to explore Xīshuāngbǎnnà, go to the No 2 bus station (Dì'èr Kèyùnzhàn).

There is a new south bus station with many provincial departures; check with your café or hotel to see if your bus starts from there (though most will likely stop at the main bus station) or if they have a better departure time. There is supposed to be a daily bus to Luang Prabang (Laos) from here, but it wasn't running at last visit.

GETTING TO THAILAND

For a couple of years, travellers were having some luck hitching rides on cargo boats heading south into Laos and Thailand, but in November 2006, authorities put the hammer down on that, giving boat operators serious fines (and revoking licenses). New fast ferries leave Jīnghóng Monday, Wednesday and Saturday for the seven-hour ride (Y800) to Chiang Saen in Thailand; plans were to ultimately build up facilities to allow for six stops along the way. Get to the dock on the other side of the Mekong River at 7.30am to start customs proceedings. Also note that this could all change – other ferries have come and gone just as quickly in the past.

If you want to get to the Yuanyang Rice Terraces, first you'll have to take a bus to Jiāngchéng (江城; Y49, 10 hours, 6.30am or 9.20am), overnight and then hop another bus to Lǜchūn (绿春; Y31, five hours), a nice Hani town with a good market, before hopping a bus to Yuányáng (Y25, four hours). You could also take a bus from the main station to Shípíng (15 hours) or Jiànshuǐ (18 hours) and loop back if you're going to those places anyway.

Getting Around

There's no shuttle bus or public transport to the airport, 5km south of the city. A taxi will cost around Y20 but expect to be hit up for up to three times that during festivals.

Jīnghóng is small enough that you can walk to most destinations, but a bike makes life easier and can be rented through most accommodation for Y15 to Y25 a day.

A taxi anywhere in town costs Y5.

AROUND JĪNGHÓNG

Obviously, it's the longer trips that allow you to escape the hordes of tourists and get a feel for what Xīshuāngbǎnnà is about. But even with limited time there are some interesting possibilities. Most destinations in Xīshuāngbǎnnà are only two or three hours away by bus, but generally they are not much in themselves – you need to get out and about. Note that to get to many villages, you'll often first have to take the bus to a primary village and stay overnight there, since only one bus per day – if that – travels to the tinier villages.

JĪNGHÓNG BUS TIMETABLES

Buses from Jīnghóng long-distance bus station:

Destination	Price (Y)	Duration (hours)	Frequency	Departs
Bǎoshān	230	20	daily	noon
Kūnmíng	156-186	9	2 daily	4pm, 7.30pm
Kūnmíng (sleeper)	145-169	9	20 daily	7.30am-7pm
Ruìlì	254	26	daily	9am
Xiàguān	152	18-20	daily	12.30pm

Buses from the No 2 bus station:

Destination	Price (Y)	Duration (hours)	Frequency	Departs
Dàměnglóng	15	3-4	every 20min	6.30am-6.30pm
Gǎnlǎnbà	7.5	¾	every 20min	7.15am-10pm
Jǐngzhēn	11	2	every 20min	7am-6pm
Láncāng	38	5-6	every 30min	6am-4pm
Měnghǎi	11	¾	every 20min	7.30am-1.40pm & 2.20-7pm
Měnghùn	15	1½	every 20min	7am-6pm
Měnglà	33	4-5	every 20min	6.30am-6pm
Mènglián	44	6-7	5 daily	8.30am-noon
Měnglún	14	2	every 20min	7am-6pm
Měnyǎng	7	¾	half-hourly	8am-6pm
Sānchàhé	10-11.50	1½	every 20min	6.15am-6.30pm
Sīmáo	33	5	every 15min every 30min	6.15am-4pm 4-6pm

If you're a serious collector of local market experiences, there are plenty to be found in the region. Like anything else, markets are subjective things, but most people seem to prefer the Thursday market in Xīdìng, then Měnghùn, followed by Měnghǎi.

Biking is grand. First morning? Hop on a bike and strike out in the environs of Jīnghóng. You can't go wrong.

Depending on where you go, you'll get lovely dirt paths interspersed with wide concrete runways, then perhaps a ferry or two across the Mekong River. Travellers in cafés will have the latest info on what roads haven't been bulldozed yet.

Another possible bike ride, for the fit, is from Jīnghóng to Mandian Waterfall (right). Or a much easier bike ride is south along the road to Dàměnglóng; take the left fork near the airport.

About 15km from Jīnghóng is **Manfeilong Reservoir** (曼飞龙水库; Mànfēilóng Shuǐkù), a small lake with a tiny resort. Here you can rent jet skis for Y60 per minute – don't worry, they stop timing every time you fall off.

Some rooms might be available for about Y60. There's not much else to do on the lake, but it's a nice break if you're continuing south.

Mandian Waterfall 曼典瀑布

On the road to Měnghǎi, about 6km to 8km outside Jīnghóng, is a dirt road turn-off to the right near a small market. (If you miss it there should be another fork near Gādōng; take the middle dirt road.) From here it's about 25km to the waterfall (Màndiǎn Pùbù) that is near some Dai villages.

Some of the hills can be really difficult, and during rainy season there's lots of mud. From the end of the dirt road, it's about 45 minutes by foot to the falls.

It's possible to reach other falls but these are dangerous and require dodgy climbs; take a local guide. A round-trip vehicle (big enough for seven) costs around Y120. The only place to stay here is with Dai families. Figure Y30 per person as a top-end price.

Sanchahe Nature Reserve
三岔河自然保护区

This nature reserve (Sānchàhé Zìrán Bǎohùqū), 48km north of Jǐnghóng, is one of five enormous forest reserves in southern Yúnnán. This one has an area of nearly 1.5 million hectares. The part of the park that most tourists visit is **Banna Wild Elephant Valley** (Bǎnnà Yěxiàng Gǔ; admission Y25, with guide Y50), named after the 40 or so wild elephants that live in the valley; it's worth a visit if you want to see something of the local forest. You'll also find displays on tropical birds and butterflies, and peacock shows. Avoid the depressing 'wild' elephant performances for the throngs of shutterbug tourists. A 2km-**cable car** (one way/return Y40/60) runs over the treetops from the main entrance into the heart of the park.

If you want to stay by the park there's a generic **hotel** (d 200) at the main entrance, although it will seem pricy for what you get. Alternatively, you can stay in one of 22 Swiss Family Robinson–type **canopy treehouses** (d Y200) in the heart of the park. Expect a discount, as these are a bit unkempt, though some new highfalutin' ones are planned. A few travellers who have stayed here have reported seeing elephants bathing in the stream beneath them at dawn.

Just about any bus travelling north from Jǐnghóng to Sīmáo will pass this reserve (Y12, one hour). Returning to Jǐnghóng you may have a bit of a wait on your hands at times for traffic to pass by, depending on the time of day.

Měngyǎng 勐养

The much photographed **Elephant-Shaped Banyan Tree** (Xiàngxíng Róngshù) is why most people visit Měngyǎng. It's also a centre for the Hani, Floral-Belt Dai and Lahu, one of the poorest minorities in the region.

Měngyǎng is 34km northeast of Jǐnghóng on the road to Sīmáo.

From Měngyǎng it's another 19km southeast to **Jīnuò** (基诺), which is home base for the Jinuo minority.

Buses from Jǐnghóng's No 2 bus station to Měngyǎng (Y7, one hour) run from 8am to 6pm every 30 minutes.

Měnghǎn 勐罕 (Gǎnlǎnbà 橄榄坝)

If you arrive mid-afternoon, Měnghǎn (or Gǎnlǎnbà as it's sometimes referred to) will be having its daily siesta. But once it cools down, this little place really comes alive and you begin to see why it's such a popular excursion from Jǐnghóng.

It's worth coming by bike (or hiring one in Měnghǎn) as there's plenty of scope for exploration in the neighbourhood.

SIGHTS

The premier 'attraction' in Měnghǎn is the **Dai Minority Park** (傣族园; Dǎizúyuán; ☎ 250 4099; Manting Lu; 曼听路; adult/student Y50/25), which is quite simply part of the town that has been cordoned off and had a ticket booth stuck at the entrance. Tourists can spend the night in villagers' homes and partake in water-splashing 'festivals' twice a day. While the 'park' and Dai architecture are beautiful, spending the night here can feel a bit like you're spending the night in a zoo, albeit a minority one. Despite this, travellers who've come say it's been worth the trip and some have even stayed in touch with their host families.

If you do stay overnight in the park, your ticket is valid for the following day.

Travellers recommend heading to the south of town, crossing the Mekong by ferry (Y2

THE JINUO PEOPLE 基诺族

The Jinuo, sometimes known as the Youle, were officially 'discovered' as a minority in 1979. The women wear a white cowl, a cotton tunic with bright horizontal stripes and a tubular black skirt. Earlobe decoration is an elaborate custom – the larger the hole and the more flowers it can contain the better. Teeth are sometimes painted black with the sap of the lacquer tree, which serves the dual dental purpose of beautifying the mouth and preventing tooth decay and halitosis.

Previously, the Jinuo lived in long houses with as many as 27 families occupying rooms on either side of the central corridor. Each family had its own hearth, but the oldest man owned the largest hearth, which was always the closest to the door. Long houses are rarely used now and the Jinuo sadly seem to be quickly losing their distinctive way of life. The **Temaoke Festival** is held in Jinuo villages on the 6th to 8th of the second lunar month.

YÚNNÁN

GETTING TO LAOS

On-the-spot visas for Laos can be obtained at the border, at Móhàn. Please remember that this could change tomorrow. The price will depend on your nationality (generally US$30 to US$35). The Chinese **checkpoint** (☎ 0691-812 2684; ⏱ 8am-5.30pm) is generally not much of an ordeal. Don't forget that Laos is an hour behind.

Měnglà has one daily bus at 9am running to Luang Nam Tha in Laos (Y32); it takes 90 minutes to the border, where you wait for around an hour to deal with paperwork, before reboarding for the final two-hour leg.

If you miss that, from Měnglà there are also buses to Móhàn every 20 minutes or so from 8am to 6pm.

No matter what anyone says, there should be no 'charge' to cross. Once your passport is stamped (double-check all stamps), you can jump on a tractor or truck to take you 3km into Laos for around Y5. Whatever you do, go early, in case things wrap up early on either side. There are guesthouses on both the Chinese and Lao sides; people generally change money on the Lao side.

with a bike), and then heading left (east). The last ferry returns at 7pm.

SLEEPING & EATING

Beds in a Dai home within the park will cost around Y20 per person. Food is extra. Beds are traditional Dai mats and are usually very comfortable. Most homes will also have showers for you.

Yùnlì Bīnguǎn (运丽宾馆; ☎ 241 0204; Manting Lu; d/tr Y40/60) This is a modern hotel with spotless rooms that all come with their own private balconies.

Dai Family Restaurant (傣家餐厅; Dǎijiā Cāntīng; Manting Lu; mains Y15-18) This place has an English menu on the wall and there are no prices listed, so check before you order as food is a little pricier than elsewhere.

You'll find a handful of Dai restaurants near the Dai Family Restaurant.

GETTING THERE & AWAY

Microbuses to Měnghǎn leave from Jǐnghóng's No 2 bus station (Y8, every 20 minutes, 7am to 6pm). Minibuses also depart from Měnghǎn's bus station for destinations throughout the region. These destinations include Jǐnghóng (Y8), Měnglún (Y10, one hour) and Mengla (Y29, five hours).

It's possible to cycle from Jǐnghóng to Měnghǎn in a brisk two hours or a leisurely three hours, and it's a pleasant ride.

GETTING AROUND

You can rent a mountain bike at the entrance to the Dai Minority Park (Y20 per day) or from one of several bicycle shops along Manting Lu in Jǐnghóng (Y10 per day).

Měnglún 勐仑

Měnglún is the next major port of call east of Měnghǎn. The major attraction is the **Tropical Plant Gardens** (热带植物园; Rèdài Zhíwùyuán; adult/student Y60/40; ⏱ 7am-midnight). The gardens are gorgeous and get high marks from visitors. The 933 hectares of garden are well laid out, and tour groups give it a festive atmosphere, though the concrete paths and guides toting bullhorns quickly dash any hopes of communing with nature. Over 2000 species of tropical plants have been introduced since 1959 and you'll also find every conceivable species existing in Xīshuāngbǎnnà. Look out for *Artiaris toxicana*, which local hunters once used to coat their poisoned arrows. The gardens are over the river, but the entrance is on the northern bank.

To get there, turn left out of the bus station and walk to the first corner. Walk one block and turn left again. You'll come to market hawkers, and a road leading downhill to the right side. Follow this until you reach a footbridge across the Mekong. The ticket booth is just in front of the bridge.

A 10-minute bus ride west of Měnglún towards Měnghǎn, at kilometre-marker 63, is the **Banna Rain Forest Valley** (版纳雨林谷; Bǎnnà Yǔlín Gǔ; adult/student Y20/16), a small but fairly pleasant state-level protected area of forest compete with an aerial walkway (though not as good as the walkway at Bupan outside Měnglà; see opposite). This is primarily a Chinese tourist spot so there's concrete paths and no-smoking signs, but if you get there between 4pm and 5pm you should have the place to yourself. Hopping on a bus back to Měnglún is easy.

There are a couple of lovely Dai villages between Měnglún and the valley. If you have time, continue on the Jīnghóng–Měnglà highway, straight through town for 3km (passing a second entrance to the gardens) to a **forest reserve** (Sēnlín Gōngyuán; 森林公园). There is no word on whether it's open, but it may be ripe for exploring, following all trail etiquette of course.

There are plenty of basic hotels in town, a couple near the park, and one in the park. Every one of them will suffer from dampness and most of them are pretty run-down. It's worth taking a walk around when you arrive to see if anything new has opened up.

The **Bus Station Hotel** (车站招待所; Chēzhàn Zhāodàisuǒ; d Y30) is your best-value option. There's no air-con, but the shared bathrooms and showers are clean and there's a TV in each room.

East of the roundabout, the **Red Bean Hotel** (红豆大酒店; Hóngdòu Dàjiǔdiàn; ☎ 871 6966; s & d Y100; ▧) is relatively new and has great-value rooms. Expect a discount.

The **Friendship Restaurant** (友谊餐厅; Yǒuyì Cāntīng; Main Hwy; dishes from Y8) has lots of dishes made from strange vegetables, ferns and herbs only found locally.

From Jīnghóng's No 2 bus station there are buses to Měnglún (Y14, two hours, every 20 minutes, 7am to 6pm). The buses pass through Měnghǎn. Some travellers have cycled here from Měnghǎn.

From Měnglún, there are buses to Měnglà (Y20 to Y25, 2½ hours, 8.30am to 7.30pm) and Jīnghóng every 30 minutes.

Měnglà 勐腊

The only reason you want to find yourself here is if you're crossing into Laos at Móhān and you can't make it before the border closes. Trust us. Because the bus journey from Jīnghóng, or even Měnglún, will take the better part of a day, you'll probably be stuck here for the night.

There is a **Bank of China** (Zhōngguó Yínháng; ☯ 8-11.30am & 3-6pm Mon-Fri) in the southern half of town that changes cash and travellers cheques but won't give cash advances on credit cards. To change Renminbi back into US dollars, you'll need your original exchange receipts.

If for some godforsaken reason you need to spend more time here, a day trip from Měnglà might include a stop at the **Bupan Aerial Skyway Park** (Wàngtiānshú Zǒuláng; adult/student Y20/17),

a 45-minute bus ride (Y7) to the north. It has a 500m-long rickety walkway 40m above the ground that showcases the rare Chinese parashorea tree (known locally in Chinese as 'Looking at the Sky Tree' because of its height and fast growth). A short trail leads around the forest. Entry includes Y2 life insurance (gulp!). To get here take an hourly minibus to Měngbàn or Yáoqū. The last bus back is around 5.30pm.

About five minutes out of Měnglà town in the direction of the park is a golden **pagoda**

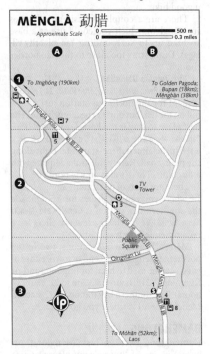

MĚNGLÀ 勐腊

MĚNGLÀ BUS TIMETABLE

Buses from Měnglà's No 2 station:

Destination	Price (Y)	Frequency	Departs
Jǐnghóng	30-34	every 20min	6.20am-6pm
Měnglún	20-24	every 20min	6.20am-6pm
Móhǎn	14	every 20min	8am-6pm
Yáoqū	12	4 daily	8.30am, 10.30am, 2.30pm, 4.30pm

(金塔) on a distant hillside that makes for a good hike.

There are a couple of basic guesthouses in Měngbàn, which you could use as a base to hike up to surrounding **Yao minority villages**. Don't stray too close to the Lao border though.

The **Jīnqiáo Dàjiǔdiàn** (金桥大酒店; ☎ 812 4946; Mengla Beilu; 勐腊北路; d/tr Y50/60; 🖭) is convenient for the north bus station just up the hill on the left, but don't expect much else. The best place to stay is the **Jinxiu Grand Hotel** (Jǐnxiù Dàjiǔdiàn; Mengla Jie; 勐腊街; s & d Y150-280; 🖭 🖭), a self-proclaimed three-star hotel right along the main road. Rarely full and adequate with a discount. There's also an iffy pool.

There are loads of restaurants along Mengla Jie where you can get dishes for Y5. Outside the southern bus station is **Gene's Café** (Mengla Nanlu; 勐腊南路), which a few travellers have recommended for travel advice.

Měnglà has three bus stations: two in the northern (Mengla Beilu) end of town, either of which can be used to head for Jinghong and/or Kūnmíng (Y218, hourly, 8.30am to 11.30am, 14 hours). The southern bus station (No 2 station; Mengla Nanlu) is where you go for Laos.

DÀMĚNGLÓNG 大勐龙

Dàměnglóng (written just 'Měnglóng' on buses) is one of those sleepy places to aim for when you want a respite from the beaten path and a base from which to do some aimless rambling. You won't find much to do in the village itself outside of visiting the Sunday market, but the countryside around the village is peppered with decaying stupas and little villages.

About 70km south of Jǐnghóng and a few kilometres from the Myanmar border, Dàměnglóng is also a good base for hikes and bike rides through the surrounding hills. You can hire bicycles at Dàměnglóng Zhāodàisuǒ for Y15 per day.

The border crossing point with Myanmar (poetically named 2-4-0) has been designated as the entry point for a planned highway linking Thailand, Myanmar and China. Highways have been constructed around here with a vengeance, though the expressway into the three-nation triangle area is only gradually inching this way.

Sights

WHITE BAMBOO SHOOT PAGODA 曼飞龙塔

This **pagoda** (Mànfēilóng Tǎ; admission Y5), built in 1204, is Dàměnglóng's premier attraction. According to legend, the temple was built on the spot of a hallowed footprint left by Sakyamuni Buddha, who is said to have visited Xīshuāngbǎnnà; if you're interested in ancient footprints you can look for it in a niche below one of the nine stupas. Unfortunately, in recent years a 'beautification' job has been done on the temple with a couple of cans of white paint.

If you're in the area late October or early November, check the precise dates of the **Tan Ta Festival**. At this time White Bamboo Shoot Pagoda is host to hundreds of locals whose celebrations include dancing, rocket launchings, paper balloons and so on.

The pagoda is easy to get to: just walk back along the main road towards Jǐnghóng for 2km until you reach a small village with a temple on your left. From here there's a path up the hill; it's about a 20-minute walk. There's an entry fee, but often there's no-one around anyway.

BLACK PAGODA 黑塔

Just above the centre of town is a Dai monastery with a steep path beside it leading up to the **Black Pagoda** (Hēi Tǎ; admission free); you'll notice it when entering Dàměnglóng. The pagoda itself is actually gold, not black. Take a stroll up, but bear in mind that the real reason for the climb is more for the views of Dàměnglóng and surrounding countryside than the temple itself.

Sleeping & Eating

Plenty of cheap options are available for foreigners.

Dàměnglóng Zhāodàisuŏ (大勐龙招待所; dm Y15) This place has basic beds and fragrant bathrooms but the main reason to take note of this hotel is for its bicycle rental (Y15 per day). To get to the hotel, walk uphill from the main highway to where the local government building sits. From there, the hotel is in the grounds to the left, just past some ornamental frogs.

Lai Lai Hotel (来来宾馆; Láilái Bīnguăn; d/tr Y20/30) Simple rooms and a lovely owner meticulous about cleanliness made this hotel the most popular accommodation choice with the Dàměnglóng–to–Búlăngshān trekkers of yore. You'll see the English sign right next to the bus station.

There are a couple of decent restaurants to be found located down from the bus station, near the steps leading up to the Black Pagoda; the Chinese signs proclaim them to be Dai restaurants.

Getting There & Away

Buses for the bumpy ride to Dàměnglóng (Y15, three to four hours, every 20 minutes, 6.30am to 6.30pm) leave from Jǐnghóng's No 2 bus station. Remember that the 'Da' character won't be painted on the bus window. Buses for the return trip run regularly between 6am and 6pm.

THE BULANG PEOPLE 布朗族

The Bulang live mainly in the Bulang Xīdìng and Bada mountains of Xīshuāngbănnà. They keep to the hills farming cotton, sugar cane and *pǔ'ĕr chá* (pu'er tea), one of Yúnnán's most famous exports.

The men wear collarless jackets, loose black trousers and turbans of black or white cloth. They traditionally tattoo their arms, legs, chests and stomachs. The Bulang women wear simple, brightly coloured clothes and vibrant headdresses (atop the black turbans) decorated with flowers. Avid betel-nut chewers, the women believe black teeth are beautiful.

AROUND DÀMĚNGLÓNG

The village of **Xiăojiē** (小街), about 15km north of Dàměnglóng, is surrounded by Bulang, Lahu and Hani villages. Lahu women shave their heads; apparently the younger ones aren't happy about this any more and hide their hair beneath caps.

The Bulang are possibly descended from the Yi of northern Yúnnán. The women wear black turbans with silver decorations; many of the designs are of shells, fish and marine life.

There's plenty of room for exploration in this area, although remember you're not allowed over the border.

MĚNGHĂI 勐海

This modern town is another popular base for exploring the countryside. Grab a bike and head north for the most interesting pagodas and villages.

If you're passing through Měnghăi, it's worth visiting the huge daily produce market that attracts members of the hill tribes. The best way to find it is to follow the early-morning crowds.

If you have to overnight here, just head out in any direction of the bus station to find an inordinate number of hotels; they're all essentially the same – decent.

Buses run from Jǐnghóng's No 2 bus station to Měnghăi (Y11, 45 minutes, every 20 minutes, 7.30am to 1.40pm and 2.20pm to 7pm).

From Měnghăi's bus station there are buses to Búlăngshān (Y18, 9am and 2pm), Xīdìng (Y11, 10.40am and 3.30pm), Měngmăn (Y11, 7.30am, 8.30am, 9.30am and 5pm) and Kūnmíng (Y170 to Y187, 2.30pm, 4.30pm, 5.30pm and 6.30pm), among other destinations. Buses return to Jǐnghóng every 20 minutes until 7pm.

AROUND MĚNGHĂI

In the village of Mànlĕi, about 7km west of Měnghăi, are the **twin pagodas** (双塔), built in 1746. The taller one is 9m, the shorter one 7m. A temple can be visited that sits between them.

Located a few kilometres to the southwest of Manlei (曼垒) is the **Manduan Wat** (曼短) in Mànduăn Village, which dates from approximately 1132. This building is built on 50cm-diameter poles and the heads of each pole are carved into a lotus or painted like a dragon.

Měnghùn 勐混

This quiet little village, located about 26km southwest of Měnghǎi, has a colourful **Sunday market**. The town begins buzzing around 7am and the action lingers on through to noon. The swirl of hill tribespeople, which includes women sporting fancy leggings, headdresses, earrings and bracelets, is enough alone to make the trip worthwhile. Měnghùn also a good place to buy local handicrafts for much cheaper prices than you would find in Kūnmíng (don't haggle too much, these women have yet to learn the idea of over-charging foreigners).

There are several guesthouses here, though none are remarkable. Y40 will get you a double with bathroom and TV but there's no air-conditioning.

Buses departing from Jǐnghóng for Měnghùn (Y15, 90 minutes, every 20 minutes, 7am to 6pm) run from Jǐnghóng's No 2 bus station.

From Měnghùn, minibuses run regularly to Měnghǎi (Y6), Xīdìng (Y11, 1½ hours, 7.10am and 4pm) and throughout the day to Jǐnghóng.

Unless you have a very good bike with gears, cycling to Měnghǎi and Měnghùn is not a real option. The road up to Měnghǎi is so steep that you'll end up pushing the bike most of the way. Cycling from Měnghùn back to Jǐnghóng, on the other hand, is almost entirely downhill.

Around Měnghùn

Near Mànguó Village (曼国), 8km southeast of Měnghùn, is a cluster of **pagodas** (塔) atop Guangjingha Hill. Built in 1746, the grouping is one large, 17m-high pagoda ringed by eight more, beneath which lie the sacred ashes of Bazaiyapa Pasa. You could hire a tractor to get to Manguo for about Y15 return, from where you could walk up the hill. Ask in town for more information.

Xīdìng 西定

This sleepy hillside hamlet comes alive every Thursday for its weekly market, reputedly one of the best in the region. At other times you'll find it almost deserted. To get here by public transport you can either catch one of the two direct buses from Měnghǎi (Y11, 10.40am and 3.30pm) or travel via Měnghùn and change for a bus to Xīdìng. If you want to see the market at its most interesting, you'll really have to get

here the night before. The small guesthouse at the bus station has beds for Y20. Buses from Xīdìng leave twice a day (Y11, 7.20am and 1pm) for Měnghùn. If you miss the bus you can always get a ride on a motorbike (Y30), a spectacular if not hair-raising experience, from the only bike shop in town.

Jǐngzhēn 景真

In the village of Jǐngzhēn, about 14km north-west of Měnghǎi, is the **Octagonal Pavilion** (八角亭; Bājiǎo Tíng; admission Y10), first built in 1701. The original structure was severely damaged during the Cultural Revolution but renovated in 1978 and the ornate decoration is still impressive. The temple also operates as a monastic school. The paintings on the wall of the temple depict scenes from the *Jatatka*, the life history of Buddha.

Frequent minibuses from the minibus centre in Měnghǎi go via Jǐngzhēn (Y11).

MÈNGLIÁN 孟连

☎ 0879 / pop 12,973

OK, fine, so it's not actually in Xīshuāngbǎnnà. Let's not cavil; Mènglián is a quick and worthwhile side trip for anyone attempting the long journey between Jǐnghóng and the Bǎoshān or Déhóng regions. You're also within sniffing distance of Myanmar, but no, you still can't cross in the vicinity.

Mènglián is a big draw for Chinese artists because of its heady dose of minority culture, and the mists rolling through the river valleys of the Bin and Nanlei Rivers and throughout the nature reserve of Gold Mountain (Jīn Shān; also known as Dragon Mountain), rising above the town to the west. (See the mists snaking about the pervasive dragon trees and it isn't hard indeed to imagine dragons, eons ago.)

Of its 16 minority groups, Dai and Lahu are a considerable segment and it's also one of the few places where you experience large numbers of Wa. An old town lined with a few cobblestone walkways rises into the hills.

If you're headed for Jǐnghóng from Déhóng or Bǎoshān and if the roads are washed out somewhere (not unlikely) you may be looking at an overnight stay in Láncāng to the north-east, so what the hey, just bop down.

Information

No information sources, not even an internet café that we could find. The best place to get

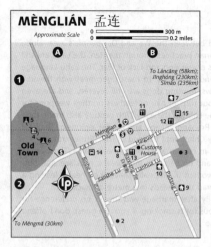

MÈNGLIÁN 孟连

Approximate Scale

0 — 300 m
0 — 0.2 miles

To Láncāng (58km);
Jǐnghóng (230km);
Sīmáo (235km)

Old Town

To Mèngmǎ (30km)

help is at the **Wanderer Café** (Liúlàngzhě Kāfēiguǎn; ☎ 872 5233; Haiguan Lu), where the irrepressibly cheery Han Qing and staff can likely figure out what to do.

Sights

Mènglián has an old town up in the hills and a new, soulless part of town built on a grid pattern, where you'll arrive and sleep. In this lower section of town, in the far southwest, is the **Jīn Tǎ** (Golden Pagoda; admission Y3). You'll find a Buddha statue, other statues, and Dai and Burmese script on the walls.

From here, head back to town and to a small **market** where the roadway is lined with Hani, Dai and Wa farmers.

Now walk west along Menglian Dajie and cross the bridge. Virtually any alley leading up the hill from this point will take you past earthy, traditional mud or wood homes. It's a lovely surprise after the tedium of the new town.

As you head up through the village you'll see the **Zhōngchéng Fósì** (admission Y4), a Dai temple with some pretty gold-leaf designs.

The real attraction in the old town though is the **Menglian Dai People's House Museum** (Mènglián Xuānfǔ Sīshǔ; ☎ 872 3591; admission Y5; ⏰ 9am-5.30pm), the largest and best-preserved of Yúnnán's 18 traditional minority 'clan houses' and used as a residence and meeting hall by the group's elders and high officials. Though Sīmáo now holds sway over the county, Mènglián was once the centre of Dai culture, predating Sīmáo and its rulers, who once lavished gifts on the Dai leader in Mènglián.

This structure was originally built in 1289 during the Yuan dynasty and held 28 generations of Dai rulers. It has since been turned into a museum and the upper floor now features historical artefacts ranging from guns to court clothing and Dai manuscripts. A side room and shrine was once used as quarters for visiting dignitaries.

Further uphill (take a right just before the museum) is the three-storey **Shàngchéng Lóngmiǎn Sì**. This place is the most active temple in town, with two golden pagodas to the side.

Back in the centre of town, the large **central market** is worth a look, especially during the weekly market, held every five days.

Sleeping

For the cheapest digs, exit the bus station onto Haiguan Lu and cross the street; you've got about 20 places to stay in either direction. Take your pick; there are quite a few clean, decent ones.

At midrange places, always but always expect a steep discount (we got around 75% without breaking a sweat) outside holidays and 'busy' season, whenever that is.

Kǒngquè Bīnguǎn (Peacock Hotel; ☎ 872 8895; Haiguan Lu; 海关路; r per person Y30, without bathroom Y10, d Y50-100) Once a solid budget stand-by, this place has faded but at least it's dirt-cheap

THE LAHU

The Lahu people occupy a narrow belt of land between the Wa and Dai people's area, along the Mekong River. Though they've adopted agrarian practices through the Han, the Lahu are still called 'Tiger Hunters' for their one-time prowess at tracking and lack of fear. The Lahu language is of the Sino-Tibetan family; *la* means 'tiger' and *hu* means 'to roast tiger meat with flavour'. Lahu houses all contain shotguns and crossbows; hunting dogs are still revered, and are even buried by families when they die. Hunters still put tufts of hair or feathers on their weapons for every animal they kill. Not limited to animals, the Lahu in the early 18th century also made their presence known to humans, threatening Luang Prabang in Laos, and border regions of Thailand and Burma (Myanmar). They weren't pacified by China until the end of the 19th century.

The Lahu's distinctive dress is similar to that in certain areas of northern China. The women wear a skirt with a high slit, silver ball buttons and no belt. The men wear a necklace coat buttoned on the right and loose pants. Men and women traditionally shave their heads, leaving a tuft of hair called their 'soul'. Women usually wrap their heads in a metre of black cloth.

Customarily, a man lives with his wife's family after marriage and there's no preference for sons. But what the Lahu have always been famous for is smoking. If you're a guest, don't offend by neglecting to offer cigarettes to grandma too.

and staffed with interested workers who are accustomed to dealing with foreign guests.

Kāngfú Bīnguǎn (☎ 872 1243; Menglian Dajie; 孟连大街; s/d Y60/80) Found by exiting the *other* exit from the bus station, this place has clean, smart rooms with squat toilet. Same deal here – nothing flash but perfectly adequate.

Tōngquán Bīnguǎn (☎ 872 6669; Padang Lu; 帕当路; s & d Y180-288, tr Y240; 🖳) Completely renovated only a few years ago, this place is holding up well. Staff were cheery if amazed to see foreigners. Do not even think of paying rack rate here – you can get great deals.

Rúyì Dàjiǔdiàn (☎ 822 3888; 18 Padang Lu; 帕当路18号; s & d Y240; 🖳) Tops in town is this smart complex, with new rooms and super service.

Eating

Wanderer Café (Liúlàngzhě Kāfēiguǎn; ☎ 872 5233; Haiguan Lu; 海关路; food from Y5) What a treat to find this place, which had just opened a week or so before our visit. Owner Nan Qing, a superfriendly Wa woman, will likely find you as she pedals around; if not, do seek this sanctuary out. Sip your fresh-brewed coffee (from Y20) overlooking a lotus pond and listen to awesome music.

Jiāchángwèi Fàndiàn (Haiguan Lu; 海关路; dishes from Y5) This friendly eatery next to the bus station serves good food and will try to accommodate you, though there's no English menu.

Mènglián also has some fine street food. Dai barbecue vendors congregate every afternoon a block west of the bus station but it's all

over by around 6.30pm. You'll see local dried sausages all over town, and the odd Burmese vendor selling *palatar* (Burmese crepe served hot and doused in sweetened condensed milk for Y5). You'll see a couple of small Dai restaurants in the old town, near the Shàngchéng Lóng Miànsì.

Getting There & Away

Buses from the No 2 bus station in Jĭnghóng leave for Mènglián (Y44, six to seven hours) at 8.30am, 10am, 11am, 11.30am and noon. Return buses leave at 8am, 9.30am, 10.30am, 11.30am and 12.30pm.

One bus daily leaves for Xiàguān (Y165, 12 to 14 hours) at 8.30am.

The Mènglián bus station also has tons of buses back up to Láncāng (Y12, one hour, 6.30am to 6pm), from where long-distance transport is easier. Buses for local destinations, including to Fùai and the border area at Měngmǎ (勐马) and Měng'ā (勐阿), leave from a second bus station near the bridge leading to the old town. The border crossing is not open to foreigners.

AROUND MÈNGLIÁN

About 5km from Mènglián, boats can be rented (around Y10) for riverside tours on the Nanlei River. It's also possible to go swimming and to explore caves nearby.

West of Mènglián in the Dai village of Měngmǎ there is another fine pagoda, the **Xiàngyá Tǎ**, and a waterfall about 10km south of the town.

If nothing else, travellers can hop on a Měngǎ-bound bus (Y5, one hour) just to sniff around (but not cross!) the markets around the border area.

Minority Villages

Of the 16 minority groups, you'll mostly encounter Dai, Lahu and Wa. Měngmǎ, near the border, has sizable numbers of Lahu, while Wa are mostly encountered in Fùai to the west or Làlěi to the south. Both Fùai and Làlěi have markets every five days. Buses depart from Mènglián for Fù'ái (Y7, one hour) at 8am, 11am and 4.30pm. When a bus arrives, one leaves. There should be a single afternoon bus to Làlěi at 4pm, which would involve staying the night.

LÁNCĀNG 澜沧
☎ 0879 / pop 7886

Láncāng is a cheerful if not aesthetically pleasing town, a crossroads between Mènglián, Sīmáo and Líncāng, leading to Déhóng and Bǎoshān regions. If you head south to Mènglián you'll often have to switch buses here.

If you arrive on a Sunday, make sure it's early, as the town market is fairly populated and energetic.

Orientation

Láncāng is dissected into a Y-shape by the highway from Jǐnghóng leading to Líncāng, and by the highway south to Myanmar via Mènglián. In the middle sits a large statue – use that for your bearings.

Sleeping & Eating

Shèxìn Bīnguǎn (射鑫宾馆; ☎ 722 5568; Menglang Jie; 勐郎街; s/d Y20/30) Exiting the bus station main entrance, head right, turn right at the first intersection and you'll get to this decent place, where the staff will be amazed to see you. After a bit of bustling about, they'll figure out how to give you a decent, cheap room.

Shùnxīyuàn Bīnguǎn (顺西苑宾馆; ☎ 722 3567; Menglang Jie; 勐郎街; s & d Y60, with bathroom Y100-280; ▨) Cross the street to better digs here, with smart rooms and an attentive staff.

Getting There & Away

To confuse things, Láncāng has three bus stations. From the statue at the crossroads, the main bus station is 100m southeast. Departures to everywhere, in all sorts of buses, leave from here.

To Mènglián there are buses every 40 minutes from 6.30am to 6pm (Y10, one hour). To the Wa settlement of Xīméng (西盟; Y20, four hours) there are buses three or four times a day from all bus stations.

To Jǐnghóng, buses leave hourly or so from 6.30am to 5.30pm (Y34, five to six hours).

Buses depart for Líncāng (Y51, eight to nine hours) and there is a sleeper bus to Bǎoshān (Y148, 20 hours) around 3pm.

Note that the twisting road from Láncāng to Líncāng still can be, as it always has been, a bit brutal, especially during the rainy season. To make it worse, hyperactive border agents search buses a lot.

SĪMÁO 思茅
☎ 0879 / pop 7500

An uninteresting little town, Sīmáo was Xīshuāngbǎnnà's air link with the outside world. Now Jǐnghóng has an airport and only the occasional traveller flies from Kūnmíng to Sīmáo (Y390) to do the final leg to Jǐnghóng by bus if they can't get a flight to Jǐnghóng.

South of Sīmáo is the **Caiyang River Nature Reserve** but apart from that, the scenery between Sīmáo and Jǐnghóng is not exactly a Sumatran jungle, and if you're travelling further afield from Jǐnghóng you'll see plenty of Xīshuāngbǎnnà scenery anyway.

If you do get stuck here, however, east of town is the **Manzhongtian Hot Spring**, set among hundreds of hectares of grassland. Most Chinese tourists come for **Cuiyun Resort** and its oddball karst formations and grottoes, 54km southwest of town.

BĂOSHĀN REGION 保山

Hiking dormant volcanic peaks, dipping in hot springs, peeking about traditional villages. That pretty much sums up this prefecture that was heretofore ignored – at least until the decadent star of Ruìlì (in Déhóng Prefecture) began to wane (and transport became doable).

The eponymous capital is nice enough, but when you say Bǎoshān you really mean Téngchōng, with its residual – less and less but enough to hold interest – old quarters and especially its environs, peppered with minority groups whose villages lie in and around the ancient fire mountains. Located on the other

lonelyplanet.com

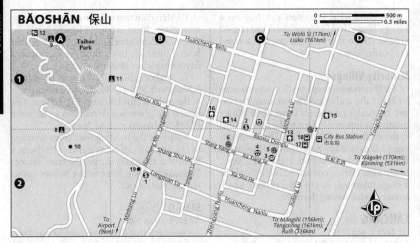

BĂOSHĀN 保山

side of Gāolígòng Shān range, Téngchōng is also prime earthquake territory, having experienced 71 earthquakes measuring over five on the Richter scale since 1500.

As early as the 4th and 5th centuries BC (two centuries before the northern routes through central Asia were established), the Bǎoshān area was an important stop on the southern Silk Road (the Sìchuān–India route). The area did not come under Chinese control until the Han dynasty, when, in AD 69, it was named the Yongchang Administra-

tive District. In 1277 a huge battle was waged in the region between the 12,000 troops of Kublai Khan and 60,000 Burmese soldiers and their 2000 elephants. The Mongols won and went on to take Pagan (in Burma).

BĂOSHĀN 保山

☎ 0875 / pop 22,174

Bǎoshān used to have some funky old architecture and alleys for the visitor to explore. No more. Today it's a bustling up-tempo city with few sights. However, you still may find yourself here, as it is plunked strategically at the centre point of the Déhóng, Nù Jiāng, and Dàlǐ regions.

Marco Polo visited the town in the 13th century when it was known as Yongchang and marvelled at the locals' gold teeth and tattoos. It has innumerable speciality products that range from excellent coffee to leather boots and pepper and silk. Tea connoisseurs might like to try the Reclining Buddha Baoshan Tea, a brand of national repute.

Information

Shops at the long-distance bus station sell maps of Bǎoshān (city and prefecture) that show regional sights in Chinese, with precious few explanations in English.

The **Bank of China** (Zhōngguó Yínháng; Baoxiu Donglu) is west of the bus station (no weekend service), with another branch opposite the Yunnan Airlines office, and the **China Post and China Telecom offices** (Xia Xiang Jie) are not far away. You can get decent internet access at several internet cafés (corner Shang Xiang Jie and Zhengyang Nanlu; corner Xia Xiang Jie and Lancheng Lu; Jiulong Lu, north of bus station) for Y3 per hour.

Sights

Bǎoshān streets are lively and, in a waning few spots, dotted with traditional homes, though the city walls have long since gone. The major sight within easy walking distance of the centre of town is **Tàibǎoshān** and its surrounding **park** (admission Y3).

Just before you head up the steps leading up the hillside you'll see the Ming dynasty **Yuhuang Pavilion** (Yùhuáng Gé) and the attached **Yùfó Sì** (Jade Buddha Temple) on your right. At the top of the steps is the small park and the **Wuhouci Ancestral Temple**, which has a nice garden and teahouse. Wuhou was the title given to Prime Minister Zhuge Liang in the Three Kingdoms period in the kingdom of Shu.

There are paths in the park heading north, west and south. The northern path doubles back to the south and eventually takes you past a very mediocre zoo (best keep walking).

Continuing to the south you will reach **Yiluo Pond** (Yìluó Chí), also known as the Dragon Spring Pond (Lóngquán Chí), with a view of the 13-tiered pagoda known as the **Wénbǐ Tǎ**.

Sleeping

You'll have no problem whatsoever finding budget places to stay in Bǎoshān. Along Baoxiu Donglu are a few Chinese-style hotels, all of which really seem ready to roll out the red carpet for a foreign guest.

Huáli Bīnguǎn (☎ 216 1696; Baoxiu Donglu; 保岫东路; s & d Y100-360, without bathroom from Y30; 🔀) A bit nicer than most cheaper options, this place is set back off the busy main street. Staff are amazed (appalled?) that foreigners would ever wish to stay in a common room, but with some nudging they'll let you. Expect a discount on a room with a bathroom.

Fútài Bīnguǎn (☎ 219 0128; Baoxiu Donglu; 保岫东路; d/tr Y80/90; 🔀) The staff here will likely blow a gasket in excitement to see you wander in. Nice rooms and frenetically cheery staff. Expect to pay Y60.

Huāchéng Bīnguǎn (☎ 220 3999; Jiulong Lu; 九龙路; s/d Y180/220; 🔀) Hands down this is the best value yuán for yuán in town. Once a pioneering, city budget-hotel (shed a tear nostalgically), it's been tastefully revamped into an up(sort of)scale place, with nice appointments and design in the rooms. It was offering huge discounts when we visited, making it a steal.

Lándū Bīnguǎn (☎ 222 2888; www.landuhotel.com.cn in Chinese; Baoxiu Xilu; 保岫西路; r Y240-400; 🔀) If you need any sense of sybaritic comfort in the city, this is it. Great rooms and attentive service. The restaurant is well-regarded locally.

Eating

Alleys off Baoxiu Lu, Shang Xiang Jie and Xia Xiang Jie are good for cheap restaurants. Near the intersection of Baoxiu Xilu and Minhang Lu is Qingzhen Jie (Muslim St), where there are several Muslim (and possibly Burmese, but all the good ones were gone at last check) restaurants.

To the west and around the corner from the Lándū Bīnguǎn is a small street with several coffee shops, one pub, and trying-to-be-chic restaurants.

Getting There & Away

AIR

Travellers are able to fly daily between Bǎoshān and Kūnmíng, though we've never heard of anyone actually doing it. The **Yunnan Airlines/CAAC office** (Yúnnán Hángkōng Gōngsī; ☎ 216 1747) has its office inconveniently located at the intersection of Longquan Lu and Minhang Lu.

Look for a large yellow-tiled building. The **ticket office** (⏰ 8.30am-6.30pm) is on the 1st floor,

BĀOSHĀN BUS TIMETABLE

Destination	Price (Y)	Duration (hours)	Frequency	Departs
Kūnmíng	140-174	7-9	hourly	8am-10pm
Liùkù	29	3-4	every 40 min	6.50am-2.50pm
Ruìlì	47-54	6	hourly	6.30am-2.30pm
Téngchōng	26-40	3-4	every 40 min	8am-6.40pm
Xiàguān	35-44	2½-3	every 45 min	7am-7pm

facing Longquan Lu. The airport is about 9km south of town.

BUS

The sprawling Băoshān long-distance bus station has buses pretty much always to pretty much everywhere in Yúnnán. Buses to Ruìlì pass through Mángshì and Wăndīng. There are also a couple of departures just to Mángshì. For the Nujiang Valley expect the speed to increase as lots of road upgrading is on-going.

There is also a daily sleeper at 6pm to Jǐnghóng (Y180, 20 hours), though it's a rough ride and most travellers opt to take the direct Dàlǐ–Jǐnghóng bus or return to Kūnmíng. If you want to break the trip to Jǐnghóng there are three morning buses (7am, 9am and 10.50am) to Líncāng (Y52) where you can overnight and continue on to Mènglián or Jǐnghóng.

The outside of the bus will always look better on the pricier buses, but the inside won't, and they won't run any faster.

Getting Around

Băoshān can be comfortably explored on foot. A bicycle would ideal to get to some of the sights around Băoshān but there is no evidence of bicycle-hire stands.

Taxis cost Y5 for any ride around the town centre.

AROUND BĂOSHĀN

Just 17km north of town, the **Wòfó Sì** (卧佛寺; Reclining Buddha Temple) is one of the most important historical sights near Băoshān. The temple dates back to the Tang dynasty, and has a history of 1200 years. The reclining Buddha, in a cave to the rear of the temple area, was severely damaged during the Cultural Revolution.

To get to the temple take a microbus (Y2) from stands of drivers lurking near – usually north of – the main bus station to the interesting village of **Bĕimiào** (北庙) and walk or hire a microbus for the rest. A motorcycle with sidecar can take two people there and back from Băoshān for Y40. Taxis ask around Y80.

TÉNGCHŌNG 腾冲

☎ 0875 / pop 13,472

Say Téngchōng and Chinese think 'fire mountain' – as in the Chinese word that means volcano. With 20 volcanoes in the vicinity

and lots of hot springs (p347) there won't be a problem if you're looking for a hot time. (Sorry.)

The town of Téngchōng itself is also worth a quick look-see. For the most part it's a rather drab, grey provincial town, but bizarrely, in the midst of it all, some lanes are still packed with the traditional wooden architecture that used to be commonplace in many towns and cities in Yúnnán. Construction is encroaching on them quickly, however, so you'll need some patience while seeking them out.

Information

Bank of China (Zhōngguó Yínháng; cnr Fengshan Lu & Yingjiang Xilu) Will change cash and travellers cheques. There's also an ATM here.

China Post & Telecom (Zhōngguó Yóuzhèng & Zhōngguó Diànxìn; Fengshan Lu).

Internet café (wǎngbā; Feicui Lu; per hr Y2).

Public Security Bureau (PSB; Gōngānjú; ☎ 513 1146; Yingjiang Xilu; ⏰ 8.30-11.30am & 2.30-5.30pm Mon-Fri) Can help with visa extensions.

Sights & Activities

Much of the city's grand old architecture has been bulldozed but poke around long enough and you will see some fine eye candy, including some funky old temples that had for decades lain dormant but are now being renovated. The best places for a random wander are the backstreets running off Yingjiang Xilu.

There are a couple of small markets with plenty of colour and activity in the mornings. Walking along Fengshan Lu from Feicui Lu, the first side street on the left has a small **produce market**.

Further down on the right is a large, covered **jade market** where you can sometimes see the carving process. Walk east along Yinjiang Xilu and you will come across a larger **produce market** (Chǎnpǐn Shìchǎng; 产品市场) on your right.

A new **museum** was in the works but there's no word on when it was to open.

On the western edge of town is the **Laifeng Shan National Forest Park** (Láifèng Shān Guójiā Sēnlín Gōngyuán; admission Y20; ⏰ 8am-7pm). You can walk through lush pine forests to **Laifeng Temple** (Láifèng Sì) or make the sweaty hike up to the summit where a pagoda offers fine views. There are lots of further hiking possibilities.

In the southwestern suburbs of town, **Xianle Temple** (Xiānlè Sì; admission Y5) is beside the small

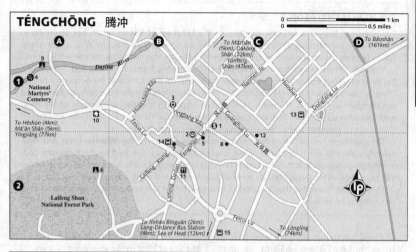

TÉNGCHŌNG 腾冲

Dieshui Waterfall (admission Y20), which makes a good place for a picnic. The area makes a nice destination for a bike ride and you could easily combine it with a trip to Héshùn (p346), a picturesque village 4km outside Téngchōng.

Sleeping & Eating

Téngchōng's accommodation options are fairly spread out. Rooms near the local bus station can get pretty decrepit. Alternatively, try one of the new hotels along Rehai Lu north of the long-distance bus station. It's a less central location, but it's packed with new (clean!) hotels; some have doubles for as little as Y40 per night.

Jīnhǎo Bīnguǎn (cnr Mashi Lu & Rehai Lu; s & d Y60, tr Y70; ⊠) Possibly the biggest and brightest rooms on the entire street. If you're mid-slog through western Yúnnán, the pristine condition of bathrooms here will be cause for unbridled celebration. Head one block north from the long-distance bus station; the hotel is on the right side of the street. Discounted rooms usually go for Y30 to Y40.

Xīnghuá Dàjiǔdiàn (☎ 513 2683; s/d Y220/380; ⊠) It's got cruddy halls with a 'going-out-of-business' vibe, but the rooms themselves are terrific: dark wood, handsome furniture, obscenely big bathrooms. Discounted doubles go for as little as Y120. It's northeast of Laifang Shan National Forest Park.

Food court (cnr Feicui Lu & Laifeng Dadao) Your best option for lunch and dinner. Here you'll find half a dozen restaurants serving up delicious food from morning to night. There's a huge choice of delicious dishes here including *shāokǎo*, grilled fish and chilli crabs.

Getting There & Away

There are two bus stations in Téngchōng: the shiny new long-distance bus station in the south of town and the old local bus station on Dongfang Lu. In general, for destinations north of Téngchōng, head to the long-distance bus station, and for all locations south of town head to the local bus station.

THE HANI (AKHA) PEOPLE 哈尼族

The Hani (also known in adjacent countries as the Akha) are of Tibetan origin, but according to folklore they are descended from frogs' eyes. They are closely related to the Yi as a part of the Tibeto-Burman group; the language is Sino-Tibetan but uses Han characters for the written form.

They are famed mostly for their river-valley rice terraces, especially in the Red River valley, between the Ailao and Wuliang Shan, where they cultivate rice, corn and the occasional poppy. There is a great variety in dress amongst the Hani, particularly between the Xīshuāngbǎnnà and the Hónghé Hani around Yuányáng. Hani women (especially the Aini, a subgroup of the Hani) wear headdresses of beads, feathers, coins and silver rings, some of which are made with French (Vietnamese), Burmese and Indian coins from the turn of the century.

The Hani have two animated New Year celebrations. The seven-day **Misezha** (New Year festival) takes place in the 10th month of the lunar calendar; this is followed by the **Kuzhazha** god-worshipping celebration in the sixth lunar month, lasting three to six days. As part of festivals, the Hani use an ox-hide swing to symbolically ward off bad fortune and augur a favourable year ahead.

The Hani are famed for their hospitality, though whether this endures increasing tourist contact remains to be seen.

The local bus station has daily buses to Ruìlì (Y40, six hours, 7.40am, 8.30am, 10.40am and 11.40am) and Mángshì (Y22, 4½ hours, 7.30am, 10.20am and 1pm), and frequent departures to local destinations.

The long-distance bus station has sleeper buses to Kūnmíng (Y180, 12 hours, eight daily from 3.30pm to 8.10pm). An express bus also leaves for Kūnmíng at 8.30am (Y202, 11 hours). Buses to Bǎoshān (Y28 to Y35, five hours, 7.30am to 5.30pm) leave every 30 minutes. Xiàguān buses leave twice a day (Y87, 10.30am; Y93, 7.40pm).

Buses to local destinations north of Téngchōng (eg Mǎzhàn, Gùdōng, Ruìdián, Diántān or Zìzhi), either leave from, or pass through, Huoshan Lu in the northeast of town.

Getting Around

Téngchōng is small enough to walk around, but a bicycle is helpful for getting to some of the closer sights outside town – the surrounding scenery alone justifies a ride. You can hire a bike from a shop on Guanghua Lu (Y1 per hour).

Bus 2 runs from the town centre to the long-distance bus station.

AROUND TÉNGCHŌNG

There's a lot to see around Téngchōng but getting out to the sights is a bit tricky. Catching buses part of the way and hiking up to the sights is one possibility, while some of the closer attractions can be reached by bicycle.

Your other option is a hired van, which may be affordable if there are several of you; head down to the minibus stand just off the southern end of Huoshan Lu or to the minibus stand for the Sea of Heat in the southwest of town.

Some highlights of the region are the traditional villages that are scattered between Téngchōng and Yúnfēng Shān (Cloudy Peak Mountain). The relatively plentiful public transport along this route means that you can jump on and off minibuses to go exploring as the whim takes you. Several travellers have recommended taking bus 2 to the end of the line south of town; along the route you can see some fine old villages and old architecture.

Héshùn 和顺

Southwest of town is the village of Héshùn, which is well worth a visit. It has been set aside as a retirement village for overseas Chinese, but it's of more interest as a quiet, traditional Chinese village with cobbled streets. There are some great old buildings in the village, providing lots of photo opportunities; a small **museum** (博物馆; bówùguǎn); and a famous old **library** (图书馆; túshūguǎn). There's no admission fee to the village itself but for any 'sights' in the village an all-inclusive fee of Y30 is charged.

Minibuses leave from the corner of Feicui Lu and Laifeng Xiang (Y1.50) in Téngchōng or you can hop on bus 3 that passes nearby. It's an easy bicycle ride out to the village but the ride back is an uphill slog.

Yúnfēng Shān 云峰山

A Taoist mountain located 47km north of Téngchōng, Yúnfēng Shān (Cloudy Peak Mountain; admission Y60), is dotted with 17th-century temples and monastic retreats. Most people take the cable car (one way/return Y30/50), from where it's a 20-minute walk to **Dàxióng Bǎodiàn** (大雄宝殿), a temple at the summit. **Lǔzǔ Diàn** (鲁祖殿), the temple second from the top, serves up great vegetarian food at lunchtime. It's a quick walk down but it can be hard on the knees.

To get to the mountain, go to Huoshan Lu where you can flag down a bus to Ruìdiàn or Diántǎn and get off at the turn-off to Yúnfēng (Y8). Alternatively, take a bus to Gùdōng (Y6) and then a microbus from here to the turn-off (Y2). From the turn-off you have to either hitch, or you can choose to take the lovely walk past the village of Hépíng to the pretty villages just before the mountain. Hiring a vehicle from Téngchōng to take you on a return trip will cost about Y300.

Volcanoes

Téngchōng County is renowned for its volcanoes, and although they have been behaving themselves for many centuries, the seismic and geothermal activity in the area indicates that they won't always continue to do so. The closest one to town is **Mǎ'ān Shān** (马鞍山; Saddle Mountain), around 5km to the northwest. It's just south of the main road to Yíngjiāng.

Around 22km to the north of town, near the village of Mǎzhàn, is the most accessible cluster of **volcanoes** (admission Y20). The main central volcano is known as **Dàkōng Shān** (大空山; Big Empty Hill), which pretty much sums it up, and to the left of it is the black crater of **Hēikōng Shān** (黑空山; Black Empty Hill). You can haul yourself up the steps for views of the surrounding lava fields (long dormant).

Minibuses run frequently to Mǎzhàn (Y5) from along Huoshan Lu, or take a Gùdōng-bound minibus. From Mǎzhàn town it's a 10-minute walk or take a motor tricycle (Y5) to the volcano area.

Sea of Heat 热海

This is a cluster of hot springs, geysers and streams about 12km southwest of Téngchōng. In addition to the usual indoor baths, the **Sea of Heat** (Rèhǎi; adult/student Y30/20, with pool access Y100; ⊙ 7.30am-11pm) features a couple of outdoor hot springs and a nice warm-water swimming pool. If the steep entrance fee puts you off swimming, then you can pay Y30 for a quick dip in the **Měinǚ Chí** (Beautiful Lady Pool) instead. Some of the springs here reach temperatures of 102°C.

The site is a popular local resort and there are several hotels.

THE BURMA ROAD

When Japanese troops occupied northern and eastern China in 1937, the Kuomintang government retreated inland to Chóngqìng. As they looked for supply lines through which to receive Allied reinforcements, they turned back to the ancient overland trade routes with Burma and India, namely the Southwest Silk Road and the old Ambassador's road, once travelled by Marco Polo.

The Kūnmíng–Xiàguān section was built from 1934 to 1935, and in 1937, 200,000 labourers ('coolies' in the parlance of the day) were drafted in to build the section from Xiàguān to Wǎndīng and then on to Mandalay in 1940 via the railhead of Lashio in Burma's Shan state. By February 1939, Allied supplies were being transported by boat to Rangoon, by train to Lashio in northern Burma and then trucked across the jungles and mountain ranges of Burma to Xiàguān and finally Kūnmíng, which rapidly became a major US air base.

In 1942 the Japanese overran Burma and cut the Burma Road and the allies were forced to build another road, from Ledo in northeast India to Bhamo. At one point there were even plans to link Lìjiāng to Assam and US Army engineers went as far as enlisting Joseph Rock's help in mapping the area. The road from Ledo became known as the Stillwell Road, after General Joseph Stillwell, who led the Allied forces in China, Burma and India from his base in Kūnmíng. The road was finally finished in 1944 and disused in 1945.

A short-term stopgap was an air supply line, which ran over the Hump from British India, and over the Himalayan Hump into the airfields of Kūnmíng and Lìjiāng. Over 1000 airmen died crossing the Hump, lost in territory so remote and wild that many bodies have still not been recovered. The US Army is currently investigating two sites in far eastern Tibet as the suspected site of a C-46 plane that crashed in 1946 en route from India.

The importance of the Burma Road diminished after WWII but is enjoying somewhat of a revival, though jade, teak, opium and heroin has replaced the military hardware.

The basic rooms at **Rèhǎi Zhāodàisuǒ** (热海招待所; ☎ 515 0306; d & tr Y80) are a bit damp but come with free access to the hotel's bathing pool (not such a bonus once you've seen it). This place is to the left of the park entrance.

Rehai Grand Hotel (热海大酒店; Rèhǎi Dàjiǔdiàn; ☎ 515 0366; d Y280) has two branches, one within the park and the other just outside the main entrance.

Microbuses leave for Sea of Heat (Y5) when full from the Dongfang Lu turn-off in the south of town.

DÉHÓNG PREFECTURE
德宏州

Déhóng Prefecture (Déhóng Zhōu and Jingpo Autonomous Prefecture), like Xīshuāngbǎnnà, borders Myanmar and is heavily populated by distinctive minority groups. It's in the far west of Yúnnán and is definitely more off-the-beaten track than Xīshuāngbǎnnà.

Most Chinese tourists in Déhóng are here for the trade from Myanmar that comes through the towns of Ruìlì and Wǎndīng – Burmese jade is a popular commodity and countless other items are spirited over the border. The border with Myanmar is punctuated by many crossings, some of them almost imperceptible, so be careful if you go wandering too close.

The most obvious minority groups in Déhóng are the Burmese (normally dressed in their traditional saronglike *longyi*), Dai and Jingpo (known in Myanmar as the Kachin, a minority long engaged in armed struggle against the Myanmar government). For information on etiquette for visiting temples in the region see the boxed text, p327.

Around Déhóng are signs in Chinese, Burmese, Dai and English. This is a border region getting rich on trade – in the markets you can see Indian jewellery, tinned fruits from Thailand, Burmese papier-mâché furniture, young bloods with wads of foreign currency, and Chinese plain-clothes police.

MÁNGSHÌ (LÙXĪ) 芒市 (潞西)
☎ 0692 / pop 15,057

Mángshì is Déhóng's air link with the outside world. It's a large, sprawling town and there's little to see here. Most travellers simply pass through on their way to Ruìlì. If you fly in from Kūnmíng there are minibuses running direct from the airport to Ruìlì and your best bet is to jump into one of these and head south.

If you're planning to fly out of Mángshì then you might have to stay overnight here, in which case there are enough things to keep you occupied for an afternoon or so.

Information

The **Bank of China** (Zhōngguó Yínháng; Dongfeng Lu) changes cash and travellers cheques and gives cash advances on credit cards. There is an ATM machine around the corner from the southern bus station on Weimin Lu.

Sights

Downtown, several temples stand out. **Puti Temple** (Pútí Sì; Zhenguan Lu; admission Y2) dates from 1674 but isn't too impressive nowadays.

Continue on to the next road crossing; the more interesting **Five Clouds Temple** (Wǔyún Sì) is found straight ahead down a mud track. Next to the temple there is a water tank and a tree wrapped in thread to form a spirit trap. It's getting more and more spruced up but is still worth a visit, as much for the mischievous

---

MÁNGSHÌ BUS TIMETABLE

Bus services from Mángshì include the following:

Destination	Price (Y)	Duration (hours)	Frequency	Departs
Bǎoshān	35	4	11 daily	7.20am-3.30pm
Jǐnghóng	239	24	daily	11.30am
Kūnmíng	160-180	10	3 daily	10.30am, 6.40pm, 9pm
Lìjiāng	133	14	daily	5pm
Téngchōng	22	3½	8 daily	7.40am-4.20pm
Xiàguān	80-90	7	2 daily	11am, 8pm
Yíngjiāng	25	3	every 40min	7.30am-4.50pm

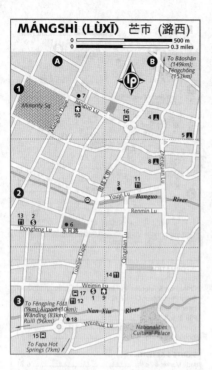

MÁNGSHÌ (LÙXĪ) 芒市 (潞西)

gang of oldsters that set up in front of it, as for the temple itself. Back at the crossroads a left turn will take you a few hundred metres to the **Fóguǎng Sì** (建国路; Foguang Temple) and its cluster of stupas.

Halfway along Youyi Lu, tucked down a side street leading to a primary school, is the 200-year-old **Shùbāo Tǎ** (Embracing Tree Pagoda; admission when anyone is around Y2), so named because over the years it has fused with the surrounding tree. It's only worth a look from a distance, otherwise you'll be hit with an 'admission' ticket.

The town's most interesting **market** is in the north of town, opposite the Jiànguó Fàndiàn, though there is another market just west of the main square.

Not far from the south bus station is the **Nationalities Cultural Palace** (Mínzú Wénhuà Gōng; admission Y3), which is more like a large park full of elderly Chinese practising their taichi. There are a few small exhibits on nationalities and a couple of reconstructed Dai buildings.

About 7km south of town are the **Fapa Hot Springs** (Fǎpà Wēnquán). There are good reports of this site from travellers who have cycled out to them.

If you arrive by plane, en route to town you will pass the attractive **Fēngpíng Fótǎ**, a pagoda 9km southwest of town.

Sleeping & Eating

Chángjiāng Bīnguǎn (☎ 228 6055; 2 Weimin Lu; 为民路2号; s/d 80/100, without bathroom Y50/60; ☒) The impressively well-kept rooms belie the impression one gets from the locale and exteriors. Then again, feel free to snoop around a few – there are some mustier ones to be found.

Xīngjiàn Jiǔdiàn (☎ 228 6788; Jiangguo Lu; 建国路; s & d Y120) Smart hardwood floors and clean bathrooms – that's a good start to this newer, homey hotel, well located down the street from the bus station.

The best places to head for food in Mángshì are the point-and-choose places on Dongfeng Lu located just after the market or along Qingnian Lu. Otherwise try the extremely popular **noodle restaurant** (Tuanjie Dajie) near the southern bus station, where you can get a big plate of fried noodles for Y5.

Fei Ma Movie & TV Bar (Fēi Mǎ Yīngxiàng Gōngzuò Shì; Youyi Lu; 友谊路; ☒ 10am–late) serves coffee and makes valiant stabs at Western cuisine like pizza, serving it all up among the jungle-like décor.

Make sure you try a freshly squeezed lime juice (large/small Y3/2) from one of the numerous stands dotting the town.

Getting There & Away

AIR

The airport is 10km from the city. There are daily flights between Mángshì and Kūnmíng (Y790). There are no buses from Mángshì airport to the town centre so you'll have no choice but to negotiate with the taxi sharks at the airport (Y20 to Y25).

Minibuses to Ruìlì (Y30, two hours) usually wait at the airport for incoming flights. Buses leave the Mángshì **Yunnan Airlines** (Yúnnán Hángkōng Gōngsī; Wenhua Lu; 8.30am–noon & 2.30–6pm) office for the airport around an hour before flight departures.

BUS

There are several bus stations in Mángshì. Both the long-distance bus station in the north of town and the southern bus station offer similar destinations at similar prices and schedules. If you don't find your bus at one, trudge along to the other. A bus stand a block southwest of the southern bus stand has the most frequent departures to Wǎndīng (Y20) and Ruìlì (Y20, 7am to 8pm). Minibuses leave when full so be prepared to wait.

RUÌLÌ 瑞丽

☎ 0692 / pop 13,299

Pity poor Ruìlì. Ruìlì was considered one of the 'it' places in Yúnnán, and young people with money would head here in droves, lured by the implicit promise that 'what-happens-in-Ruìlì-stays-in-Ruìlì'. A rite of passage for anyone living in/passing through Yúnnán was to check out the 'action' in town. Wannabe gangsters mingled with real gangsters, or at least everyone thought they were gangsters. Who the hell knew, so fuelled by dope, drink, and lust was everyone.

Trade with Myanmar fuelled the boom. The border only opened for business in the 1990s but no sooner had it opened than Ruìlì became a hotbed of trade, handling everything from raw goods to gems and arms. In return for the latter, China received huge quantities of heroin, which saw drug-taking and trafficking become part of everyday life. The local government, with help from Běijīng, retaliated and drug dealers were hauled before sentencing panels and then

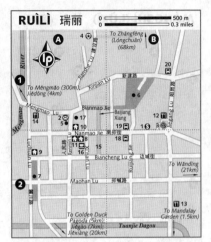

executed. Then trade began expanding, the money flowed to the next hot trade zone, and suddenly all those hot nights didn't seem too hot any more.

These days Ruìlì is, quite honestly, almost sterile. The dance halls and gambling dens are gone and shiny shopping malls and modern hotels stand in their place.

About the raciest thing the average traveller will encounter these days is the odd trader a little overenthusiastically adjusting his sarong. (Well, those pretty lasses haven't all gone, of course.)

But despite the clean-up, Ruìlì has a great mix of Han Chinese, minorities and Burmese traders hawking jade, lively local markets and a laid-back Southeast Asian feel. The minority villages nearby are also reason to come; the stupas are in much better condition than those in Xīshuāngbǎnnà, and it's worth getting a bicycle and heading out to explore.

Another draw for travellers is Myanmar, which lies only a few kilometres away from Ruìlì. Border-crossing restrictions are beginning to relax and although individual tourists are still not allowed to cross, organising permits to take you through the sensitive border area is becoming easier (see p353). New highways laid to facilitate border trade stretch all the way from the border to Mandalay, making what had been a horrible five-day journey much more sane. Foreign travellers may one day be able to re-create the 'Southern Silk Route', of which Ruìlì and Mandalay were a part.

Information

Bank of China (Zhōngguó Yínháng; Nanmao Jie) Provides all the usual services and will let you cash travellers cheques for US dollars in case you're headed to Myanmar.

China Post & Telecom (Zhōngguó Yóuzhèng & Zhōngguó Diànxìn; cnr Mengmao Lu & Renmin Lu) Despite (or perhaps because?) of its border location, sending any kind of package abroad from this branch is a full-on nightmare if not completely impossible. For anything more complicated than buying stamps or making international calls, wait until you move on from Ruìlì.

Dielai Photograph Centre (Diélái Shèyǐng Zhōngxīn; Nanmao Jie) Burns CDs for Y10 per CD. Keep an eye out for the big yellow Kodak sign.

Internet café (wǎngbā; Nanmao Jie, cnr Jiegang Lu; per hr Y2; ⏰ 24hr)

Mandalay Garden (曼德丽花园; Màndélì Huāyuán; ☎ 415 3924; www.mandalaygarden.com; 4 Mangsha Lu; 芒沙路4号) The place to head first if you need information on local travels, tours, bike rentals, and especially those pesky Myanmar overland visas.

Public Security Bureau (PSB; Gōngānjú; Jianshe Lu; ⏰ 8.30-11.30am & 2.30-5.30pm) Just up the road from Ruìlì Bīnguǎn, 500m north of the corner of Nanmao Jie and Renmin Lu.

Ruili Overseas Travel Company (Ruìlì Hǎiwài Lǚyóu Gōngsī; ☎ 414 1880; 27 Nanmao Jie; ⏰ 8-11.30am, 2.30-5.30pm & 7.30-10pm) If it happens to be staffed, you should be able to get information on the local area.

Xinhua Bookshop (Xīnhuá Shūdiàn; Renmin Lu) Sells the *Tourism and Traffic Map of Ruili*, which includes some English.

Dangers & Annoyances

Despite Ruìlì's new look, old problems die hard and prostitution remains an enormous industry in Ruìlì. You don't have to look very hard to see the evidence: brothels disguised as hairdressers fill the town.

All vehicles, including buses, leaving Ruìlì are searched. Authorities are usually more interested in locals, and foreigners are often completely ignored and not even asked for ID. However, some travellers have reported epic grillings bordering on the farcical.

Sights

A visit to Ruìlì is about atmosphere, people-watching, markets and aimless wandering rather than formal sights. It's small enough that you can cover most of it in an hour or so. The huge **market** in the west of town is most colourful by day, especially in the morning, when the stalls are lined with Burmese smokes, tofu wrapped in banana leaves, snack stalls and charcoal sellers. There's also whir of people from nearby minority villages, Burma and far flung places like Pakistan.

At the other end of town, Ruìlì's **jade market** is a hoot and one of the best locations for people-watching. Most of Ruìlì's sights are outside town (see p353), and you'll need a bicycle to get out and see them.

Sleeping

There are some good deals to be found in Ruìlì's hotels, and all the accommodation is within easy walking distance of the main bus station.

Mandalay Garden (曼德丽花园; Màndélì Huāyuán; ☎ 415 3924; www.mandalaygarden.com; 4 Mangsha Lu; 芒沙路4号; dm Y15; 🖥) Might as well call it Moe's Place, that's its de facto name for good reason: Moe, the Burmese owner, is one of those utterly laid-back hosts who brings travellers back to his place just to hang out. It's just the place to chill and soak in the atmosphere of town (and the tons of travel information from other travellers and the staff). There's also a restaurant on site; it's a bit expensive but

---

PAYING THE PRICE

A major problem for the past two decades has been of the poppy-derived variety, Ruìlì being an entry point for Burmese opium headed to Hong Kong. This resulted in a serious IV drug-use problem in the Déhóng region in the 1980s and early 1990s, and a spike in HIV and its pernicious sibling AIDS. According to Unesco reports, China's first AIDS cases (146) were reported in Yúnnán in 1989 (obviously the government was a mite slow in acknowledging the mere existence of HIV), and by 1999 the province reportedly had 44% of all AIDS cases in China.

The province, with Běijīng's help, poured millions of yuán into antidrug efforts along the border with Myanmar. And it had an effect: in the first month it was instituted over 1.8 tonnes of drugs were seized, and new cases of HIV infection have dropped by 30% since 2004.

This is not, of course, to say that the problem has been solved. Those yawn-inducing bus searches are strictly aimed at those attempting to smuggle drugs and if you're dumb enough to possess or – even more insanely stupid – transport, be well aware that the officials do not mess around if they catch you.

---

excellent, serving Burmese, minority, Indian, Japanese and Western food. It can even arrange cooking lessons or hook you up to teach local schoolkids.

Lìmín Bīnguǎn (☎ 414 2249; Nanmao Jie; 南卯街; dm Y20, s & d Y40-80; ✷) There is little to distinguish the singles and doubles, so you might as well go for the cheaper ones. Dorm rooms can get hot and stuffy and the shared bathrooms can be noisy. And certainly expect little from the staff. You can rent bicycles here but some of them are better than others so have a look at a few.

Ruby Hotel (☎ 419 9088; Nanmao Jie; 南卯街; s/d Y80/180) After taking in the bright green exterior and the halls bedecked with pebble-encrusted wall panels, the very plain rooms, while clean, are a minor letdown. No matter, there's more than enough atmosphere at the terrace bar with its thatched huts and floor cushions.

Ruìlì Bīnguǎn (☎ 410 0555; Nanmao Jie; 南卯街; s & d Y200) Across the street from the Ruby Hotel, this place has no fireworks but is comfortingly average. Outside of holidays, rooms rarely go for more than Y100, though deft bargainers have gotten rooms for less.

New Kaitong International Hotel (Xīn Kǎitōng Guójì Dàjiǔdiàn; ☎ 415 777; fax 415 6190; 2 Biancheng Lu; 边城路2号; d Y360, discounted d Y180; ✷ 💻) This is the original luxury hotel in Ruìlì and it offers good discounts which make it a worthwhile option. The outdoor swimming pool is perhaps the best feature and is open to nonresidents for Y10.

Eating & Drinking

For good Burmese food, there are several restaurants in a small alley off Jiegang Lu. The one at the top of the northwestern corner is

particularly good and sees a lot of Burmese patrons. This is also the spot to go for Thai Mekong whisky, served Thai-style with soda water and ice.

There are also lots of Cantonese restaurants here. At night a small but lively market sets up on Baijiang Xiang between Bianmao Jie and Biancheng Lu.

Huafeng Market (Huáfēng Shìchǎng; Jiegang Lu; 姐岗路; dishes from Y4) Ruìlì's version of a traveller's culinary institution is this busy-busy market, where you'll find a huge, thriving outdoor food court with an incredible selection of food, including Thai, Burmese, Chinese and even some Western dishes on offer.

Kūnmíng Guòqiáo Mǐxiàn (昆明过桥米线; Mengmao Lu) You may have had your fill of across-the-bridge noodles (guòqiáo mǐxiàn) while in Kūnmíng, but this place is charming with its dark wood furniture and blue-and-white checked tablecloths. There's a little garden with outdoor seating in back.

Bo Bo's Cold Drinks Shop (Bùbù Lěngyǐndiàn; Baijiang Xiang; drinks from Y3) If Huafeng Market is the institution for eats, then Bo Bo's is the place to go to quaff a beer (or non-alcoholic drink) and chat idly with the longyi-clad Burmese guys. Serves excellent fresh fruit juices and small meals in a bright eating area buzzing with low-key commotion.

Getting There & Away

AIR

Ruìlì has daily flight connections to Kūnmíng via Mángshì, which is a two-hour drive away. See p350 for details. You can buy tickets at

China Eastern Airlines (Dōngfāng Hángkōng Gōngsī; ☎ 411 1111; Renmin Lu; ☒ 8.30am-6pm). Shuttle buses leave daily from the office, three hours before scheduled flights (Y60). You can also use the ticket office to book and reconfirm return flights – do so early as this is an increasingly popular flight.

BUS
There are two bus stations in Ruìlì, the long-distance bus station in the centre of town and the north bus station at the top of Jiegang Lu. Head to the north bus station if you're trying to get to Mángshì (Y20-25, 1½ hours, last bus 6pm, leaves when full); for everything else, you're better off going to the long-distance station.

For local destinations, minibuses and vans leave from the minibus stand near the jade market, or you can just flag one down in the street. Destinations include Wǎndīng (Y5), the border checkpoint at Jiěgào (Y5), and the village of Nóngdǎo (Y8). Buses to Zhāngfēng (Y10, one hour) leave from Xinjian Lu.

TO MYANMAR
To cross from China into Myanmar, travellers must have the correct visa, travel permits and be part of an official 'group'. The group, which might consist entirely of yourself and no-one else, will be escorted from Jiěgào in China to Hsipaw in Myanmar, an eight-hour drive from the border. Once you reach Hsipaw you can wave good bye to your guide and are free to travel on your own further south to Mandalay, Rangoon and so on.

Mandalay Garden (曼德丽花园; Mǎndélì Huāyuán; ☎ 415 3924; www.mandalaygarden.com; 4 Mangsha Lu; 芒沙路4号) Your best source of up-to-the-minute information.

Ko Wai Lin Travel (Map p222; ☎ 0871-313 7555; myanmarwailin@yahoo.com; Room 221, Camellia Hotel, 154 Dongfeng Lu, Kūnmíng) can arrange permit and group travel. Remember it's not possible to organise a visa for Myanmar in Ruìlì and you will have to do this in Kūnmíng at the Myanmar consulate (see p470).

Getting Around
Ruìlì is easily seen on foot, but all the most interesting day trips require a bicycle. Ask at your accommodation for the best place to rent one. A flat rate for a taxi ride inside the city should be Y5, and up for negotiation from there. There are also cheaper motor and cycle rickshaws.

AROUND RUÌLÌ
Most of the sights around Ruìlì can be explored easily by bicycle. It's worth making frequent detours down the narrow paths leading off the main roads to visit minority villages. The people are friendly, and there are lots of photo opportunities. The *Tourism and Traffic Map of Ruili* shows the major roads and villages.

The shortest ride is to turn left at the corner north of the post office and continue out of the town proper into the little village of Měngmǎo. There are half a dozen Shan temples scattered about; the fun is in finding them.

Golden Duck Pagoda 弄安金鸭塔
In the outskirts of town to the southwest, on the main road, this pagoda (Nòng'ān Jīnyā Tǎ) is an attractive stupa set in a temple courtyard. It was established to mark the arrival of a pair of golden ducks that brought good fortune to what was previously an uninhabited marshy area.

Temples
Just past Golden Duck Pagoda is a crossroad and a small wooden temple. The road to the right (west) leads to the villages of Jiěxiàng and Nóngdǎo; on the way are a number of

---

RUÌLÌ BUS TIMETABLE
Buses from Ruìlì long-distance bus station:

Destination	Price (Y)	Duration (hours)	Frequency	Departs
Bǎoshān	45	6	every 30-40min	6am-2.30pm
Jǐnghóng	195	25	daily	8.30am
Kūnmíng	190	16	hourly	8am-8pm
Téngchōng	25	6	every 40-50min	5.40-10.40am
Xiàguān	116	12	hourly	4-8pm

small temples, villages and stupas. None are spectacular but the village life is interesting and there are often markets near the temples.

The first major Dai temple is **Hansha Zhuang Temple** (喊沙庄寺; Hǎnshā Zhuāng Sì), a fine wooden structure with a few resident monks. It's set a little off the road and a green tourism sign marks the turn-off. The surrounding Dai village is interesting.

Another 20 minutes or so further down the road, look out for a white stupa on the hillside to the right. This is **Léizhuǎngxiāng** (雷奘相), Ruìlì's oldest stupa, dating back to the middle of the Tang dynasty. There's a nunnery in the grounds of the stupa as well as fantastic views of the Ruìlì area. Once the stupa comes into view, take the next path to the right that cuts through the fields. You will see blue signs written in Chinese and Dai pointing the way through a couple of Dai villages. When you get to market crossroads at the centre of the main village, take the right path. You'll need to push your bicycle for the last ascent to the stupa. In all, it should take you about 50 minutes to cycle here from Golden Duck Pagoda.

About 2km past the town of Jiěxiàng is **Denghannong Zhuang Temple** (等喊弄庄寺; Děnghǎnnòng Zhuāng Sì), a wooden Dai temple with pleasant surroundings.

It's possible to cycle all the way to Nóngdǎo, around 29km southwest of Ruìlì. There's a solitary hotel in town that has cheap doubles or you can return to Ruìlì on one of the frequent minibuses.

Jiegao Border Checkpoint
姐告边检点

There's not much at this checkpoint (Jiěgào Biānjiǎn Diǎn) but border fanatics will marvel at how everything seems so relaxed on both sides of the – quite literally – bamboo curtain. On a thumb of land jutting into Myanmar, Jiěgào is the main checkpoint for a steady stream of cross-border traffic. As with Ruìlì this place has seen its popular casinos and other dens of iniquity replaced by lemonade stands and cheap electronic shops. To get here, continue straight ahead from Golden Duck Pagoda, cross the Myanmar bridge over Ruìlì Jiāng and you will come to Jiěgào, about 7km from Ruìlì (p353).

Microbuses shuttle between the border and Ruìlì's long-distance bus station when full for Y5 or you can charter one for around Y25 to Y30. Buses continue until late at night.

Wanding Border Checkpoint
畹町边检站

East of Ruìlì lies Wǎndīng (Wǎndīng Biānjiǎn Zhàn), a second checkpoint for crossing into Myanmar. It's not as busy here, nor is it as interesting as Jiěgào, but if you're a serious borderholic then it's worth making the 30-minute drive here just so you can take a photo and say you've been.

Staff at the foreign affairs office of the PSB, just across from the Chinese border checkpoint, seem quite easy-going, and although they will not help you sneak into Myanmar, they are otherwise accommodating. Besides, so underwhelming is the border trade zone here that they look bored enough to have a chuckle at your request.

It's worth climbing up to the north of town to take a look and spend some time at the **Wanding Forest Reserve** (畹町森林公园; Wǎndīng Sēnlín Gōngyuán; admission Y2). There are some pleasant walks. Avoid the zoo, home to three psychotic monkeys, a couple of peacocks and an unidentifiable ball of fur that was either fast asleep or dead.

Local places to stay might be able to provide information on **river trips** that include a barbecue lunch in a minority village. Prices vary depending on the number of participants, but you should be able to do it for around Y50 per person.

Alternatively, it is possible to catch a lift on a boat with locals. Take a minibus in the direction of Mángshì and get off at the bridge that connects with the main Ruìlì–Mángshì road. Travellers have caught boats back to the second bridge closer to Ruìlì and then hitched back to Ruìlì or Wǎndīng. Some very strenuous haggling is required for boat trips.

Minibuses for Wǎndīng (Y10) leave Ruìlì when full, and vice versa.

Golden Pagoda 姐勒金塔

A few kilometres to the east of Ruìlì on the road to Wǎndīng is the Golden Pagoda (Jiělè Jīntǎ), a fine structure that dates back 200 years.

Bàngmáhè 棒麻贺

Another possible cycling route takes you west of Ruìlì, past the old town of Měngmǎo, now a suburb of Ruìlì. After 4km, just past the village of Jiědōng, a turn-off north leads to Bàngmáhè village, a Jingpo settlement with a small waterfall nearby.

Sìchuān 四川

Its capital city pulses with entrepreneurs and bohemians, while mere hours away its grasslands thunder under the hooves of nomadic horsemen and herds of black yaks. This is exactly the sort of mad diversity you'll find all over Sìchuān and part of what makes travel to this province so addictive. There's a mind-whirring number of places to explore and experiences to chase, and no matter how often you come or how long you stay, it always feels as though you've barely managed to scratch the surface. Even the range of cultures is varied, with Tibetan villages tucked among the west's treacherous and frigid mountain terrain eventually melting into comparatively balmy Yi territory in the province's south. This rugged terrain kept Sìchuān isolated for so much of China's history, allowing it to develop its own identity, art forms, unique dialect and world-renowned, tongue-searing cuisine. Writers and painters have celebrated Sìchuān's charms for centuries.

The province's name means 'Four Rivers', a homage to the biggest of the 1300-plus rivers that cut up this massive landmass. The province is also home to the Chūnxī plain of the fertile Sìchuān basin, which supports one of the densest populations on the planet. Investment and exploitation of its vast natural resources are both contributing to Sìchuān's boom, making it one of China's wealthiest provinces and an economic engine of western China. Whatever your passion – nature, culture, adventure, or a mix of all three – you'll be able to indulge it somewhere in Sìchuān.

HIGHLIGHTS

- Lose your breath (both literally and figuratively) among the imposing peaks and Tibetan villages of the **Sìchuān–Tibet Highway** (p393 and p402)

- Take on the vast grasslands of Northern Sìchuān on a horse trek around the remote village of **Lǎngmùsì** (p421)

- Fall under the spell of the rambunctious newborn pandas at Chéngdū's **Giant Panda Breeding Research Base** (p362)

- Get in a ferry and bob past Grand Buddha, the world's largest Buddha statue, in **Lèshān** (p383), before scrambling for an up-close view on dry land

- Ogle the extraordinarily beautiful archaeological exhibits at the most awe-inspiring museum in China's Southwest: **Sānxīngduī** (p373)

- Traipse from temple to temple on **Éméi Shān** (p378) for a sunrise you'll never forget

★ Lǎngmùsì

★ Sìchuān–Tibet Hwy Sānxīngduī ★
★ Chéngdū

Éméi Shān ★ ★ Lèshān

POPULATION: 84 MILLION

SICHUAN

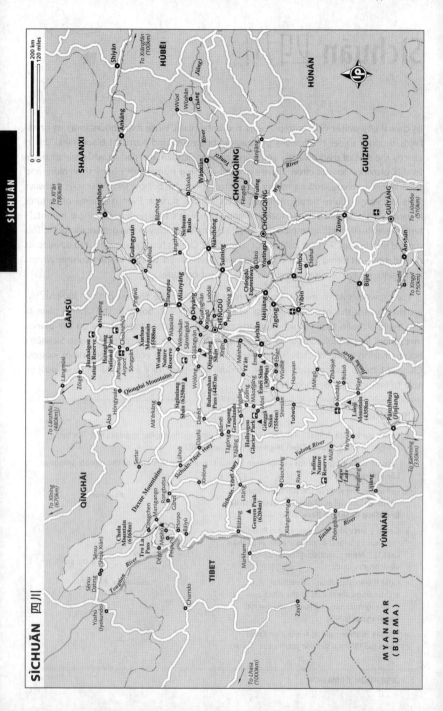

HISTORY

Not until 1986, with the major archaeological discovery of the late-Shang dynasty culture of Shu at Sānxīngduī, northeast of Chéngdū, was the Sìchuān basin's importance to Chinese history fully realised. Never really a backwater as long assumed, it has been the site of various breakaway kingdoms, ever skirmishing with central authority. It was finally wrestled into control and established as the capital of the Qín empire in the 3rd century BC and it was here that the kingdom of Shu (a name by which the province is still known) ruled as an independent state during the Three Kingdoms Period (AD 220–80). The Kuomintang spent its last days in Sìchuān before being vanquished and fleeing to Taiwan. Most recently Chóngqìng split from Sìchuān when it was promoted to the status of municipality in 1997.

During the Warring States period (475–221 BC), a famed engineer, Lǐ Bīng, managed to harness the Du River (Dū Hé) on the Chuānxī plain with his weir system, allowing Sìchuān some 2200 continuous years of irrigation and prosperity. Without exaggeration, this breadbasket region helped to unify (and feed) the nation. Sadly, the Great Leap Forward dealt Sìchuān an especially cruel blow: it's believed that one in 10 people starved.

In 1975, Zhao Ziyang, governor of Sìchuān and the province's first Communist Party secretary, became the driving force behind the agricultural and economic reforms that put Sìchuān back on the map (before he fell from grace and into lifelong house arrest for opposing the use of troops during the 1989 Tiananmen Sq demonstrations). His system (the 'Responsibility System'), whereby plots of land were let out to individual farmers on the proviso that a portion of the crops be sold back to the government, was so successful that it became the national model and was later applied to the industrial sector. As of 2006, this fertile land of 'Heaven's Granary' was still producing over 10% of the nation's grain, soybeans, pork and more.

CLIMATE

Chéngdū and the east have a subtropical, humid monsoon climate with temperatures ranging from 3°C to 8°C in winter (December to February) and 25°C to 29°C in summer (June to August). The Qīnghǎi–Tibet plateau in the west experiences intense sunlight and low temperatures most of the year with temperatures dropping to –9°C in winter and reaching highs of only 17°C in summer.

LANGUAGE

In addition to Mandarin, which is spoken by the Han and the Hui, the other major languages in Sìchuān belong to the Tibeto-Burman family and are spoken by Tibetans and the Yi. Sichuanese is one of the Mandarin dialects; however, the pronunciation is so unique, Sichuanese is near impossible for outsiders (even if they do speak standard Mandarin) to understand.

GETTING THERE & AWAY

For more details about travelling between provinces see Getting Around in the Transport chapter, p486.

Air

Chéngdū's Shangliu Airport is the largest international airport in China's Southwest. Air China and Sichuan Airlines link Chéngdū with all major Chinese cities and fly direct to Lhasa in Tibet. Currently international flights serve Bangkok, Singapore, Hong Kong, Macau, Kuala Lumpur, Kathmandu, Japan, Vienna, Amsterdam and Seoul (and more are always in the pipeline).

Jiuhuang Airport in northern Sìchuān closed in May 2006 for expansion to allow for flights from other major Chinese cities, but should be reopened by the time you read this.

Bus

Sìchuān's provincial government has been throwing hundreds of billions of yuán into highway construction since the mid-1990s as part of China's 'Develop the West' migration plan. High-speed expressways link Chéngdū with Chóngqìng and Lèshān, and the construction of highways to link Chéngdū with Shànghǎi, Běihǎi in Guǎngxī province and Tibet are underway (although to get to Tibet as yet requires superhuman endurance).

Travel to Gānsù is possible via Jiǔzhàigōu and Zöigê. To get to Yúnnán you can travel south via Lèshān, Éméi Shān and Pānzhīhuā on the border, or travel along the southern route of the Sìchuān–Tibet Hwy through both Lǐtáng and Xiāngchéng to Shangri-la (Zhōngdiàn).

Train

Chéngdū is an important railway hub in China's Southwest. Direct trains run to cities such as Běijīng and Shànghǎi. Travel to Kūnmíng in Yúnnán and Xī'ān in Shaanxi tend to be the most popular options, although Chéngdū will eventually have a direct train to Lhasa that will likely be wildly popular. To get to Gānsù you need to change in Hànzhōng, Shaanxi province.

GETTING AROUND

Jiuhuang Airport connects Chéngdū with Sōngpān and Jiǔzhàigōu. The airport was closed for renovation in 2006 but it should be reopened again by the time you read this. New expressways connect Chéngdū with the eastern part of the province, including those from Chéngdū to Lèshān/Chóngqìng. The buses on this side of the province are generally modern and comfortable. Trains in the east have generally been slow and irregular, but in 2006 new high-speed lines to Miányáng, Lèshān and Chóngqìng were being finalised.

Travel in the west of the province can only be done via bus. But make sure you have enough time (and pain medication) – the roads in this part of Sìchuān remain in butt-breakingly awful condition and the buses are, if possible, even worse.

CENTRAL SÌCHUĀN

CHÉNGDŪ 成都

☎ 028 / pop 4 million / elev 500m

Chéngdū is a great city not just because it's a hub for some of Southwest China's great sights, but also because of the interesting mix of people it's attracting these days.

Chéngdū wears its title as the Southwest's economic engine well (though some in Chóngqìng would claim that honour for their city). Investment is not only turning its downtown into a jungle of glimmer with fancy shops and office buildings, but it's also attracting Chinese and expats alike looking to stake out a piece of the pie – many are from the booming east coast looking for the same professional dynamism but with a more relaxed, laid-back lifestyle and less expensive cost of living.

Though Chéngdū is China's fifth most populous city (the greater metropolitan area has just reached 13 million and is growing fast even by China's hyper-standards), it's maintained a certain charm and was rated by several Chinese media as the nation's second most liveable city in 2006.

It's also one of the nicest places for travellers at the moment. Chéngdū is pushing hard for the title of 'Best Tourism City in China' and the mayor is campaigning to get the entire city behind him in welcoming travellers and getting tourist infrastructure and service up to scratch. Billboards and advertisements are everywhere rallying people to the cause and urging them to learn English. Regular visitors to the city will notice a huge increase in people's helpfulness and effort to speak English, from street sweepers to even taxi drivers.

But there are downsides to the boom. The city is choking in exhaust fumes and there are more cars than the streets can comfortably handle. In many ways the growth seems to be faster than what the city can cope with.

Yet there are still pockets of calm. You'll stumble upon markets, countless tiny restaurants specialising in Sìchuān snacks, and parks where old men walk their song birds or hunch over a game of chess (as auburn-haired seen-on-the-scene hipsters yapping on their mobile phones stroll nearby). Add a dash of old-time artisans – cobblers, weavers, itinerant dentists and the like – and you've got your lively yet relaxed Chéngdū.

History

Chéngdū, or 'Perfect Metropolis', has seen the rise and fall of nearly a dozen independent kingdoms or dynasties since its founding in 316 BC; agricultural potential and strategic geography were key to its political power. Yet throughout history it has been equally well known for culture: not by accident did the Tang dynasty poet Du Fu brush his strokes here.

The city is split by the Brocade River (Jǐn Jiāng), a reminder of the city's silk brocade industry, which thrived during the Eastern Han dynasty (AD 25–220). From here the Southern Silk Road guided caravans to the known world. The city's name eventually shifted from Jǐnchéng (Brocade City) to 'Hibiscus City', still used today by locals.

By the time of the Tang dynasty (AD 618–907) the city of Chéngdū had become a cornerstone of Chinese society. Three hundred years later, during the Song dynasty, Chéngdū also began to issue the world's first paper money.

It is also a survivor. Devastated first by the Mongols in retaliation for its fierce resistance, from 1644 to 1647 it was presided over by the rebel Zhang Xianzhong, who set up an independent state in Sìchuān and ruled by terror and mass executions. Three centuries later the city became one of the last strongholds of the Kuomintang.

Orientation

Ring roads circle the outer city: Yihuan Lu (First Ring Rd), Erhuan Lu (Second Ring Rd) and Sanhuan Lu (Third Ring Rd). These are divided into numbered segments *(duàn)*. The main boulevard that sweeps through the centre of everything is Renmin Lu, in its north (北; *běi*), central (中; *zhōng*) and south *(南; nán)* manifestations.

The nucleus of the city is the square that interrupts Renmin Lu, where you'll find the Sìchuān Exhibition Centre, a sports stadium and a colossal Mao statue. Just south is Tianfu Sq, a pedestrianised neon extravaganza and the main shopping district. Note that a new subway system and ongoing plans to relocate government offices and industries are affecting the lay of the downtown land.

MAPS

Tourist maps of Chéngdū, including a handful of English-language ones, abound at train and bus stations, bookshops and newspaper kiosks. City maps in Chinese can be useful for tracing bus routes, though not even the best ones can hope to fully capture the insanity that is Chéngdū's street naming.

Information
BOOKSHOPS
Foreign Language Bookstore (Wàiwén Shūdiàn; Zongfu Lu) Has a good selection of maps and Lonely Planet books.
South West Book Centre (Xīnán Shūchéng; Shangdong Dajie) The best stop for English-language fiction and non-fiction.

INTERNET ACCESS
Well-located options include an internet café on Chunxi Lu, another above the Tourism Passenger Transport Centre, and one on Renmin Beilu, south of the train station. The average charge is Y3 to Y4 per hour. All guesthouses – but not all hotels – have internet access, although few of these are set up to burn CDs or go beyond email.

STREET NAME HEADACHE
Chéngdū is a true Asian city when it comes to its nonchalant disregard of systematic street numbering and naming. When following street numbers in one direction, it's not unusual to meet another set coming the other way, leaving some places with five sets of numbers on their doors. Street names, also, seem to change every 100m or so – with very little apparent logic involved.

Try to bear this approach to street names and numbers in mind when you're looking for somewhere in particular, and rely more on nearby landmarks and relative locations on maps than on street numbers and names.

INTERNET RESOURCES
Chéngdū (www.chengdu.gov.cn) This provincial government website has an OK English version with information on the city and surrounding areas.
Global Doctor Chengdu Clinic (Huánqiú Yīshēng Chéngdū Zhěnsuǒ; ☎ office 8522 6058, 24hr emergency 139-8225 6966; ground fl, Kelan Bldg, Bangkok Garden Apt, Section 4, 21 Renmin Nanlu; ☷ 9-11am & 1.30-3.30pm Mon-Fri) This doctor's clinic has English-speaking staff.
No 3 Hospital (Dìsān Yīyuàn; Dongmen Jie; ☷ 24hr) Helpful staff here with a handful of English speakers who will assist the traveller.

MONEY
Bank of China (Zhōngguó Yínháng; ☎ 8666 0332; Renmin Nanlu; ☷ 8.30am-5.30pm Mon-Fri, to 5pm Sat & Sun) This place changes money and travellers cheques and will offer cash advances on credit cards from Monday through to Friday. Other well-located branches include those on Renmin Zhonglu and just north of the Tourism Passenger Transport Centre. All banks have ATMs and similar hours.

POST & TELEPHONE
China Post (Zhōngguó Yóuzhèng; 71 Shawan Lu; ☷ 8am-6pm) The main international post office is west of the train station. A smaller branch can be found on Dongchenggen Jie near People's Park.

PUBLIC SECURITY BUREAU
PSB (Gōngānjú; ☎ 8640 7067; 136 Wenwu Lu; ☷ 9am-noon & 1-5pm Mon-Fri) The foreign affairs entrance is on Tianzuo Jie; this is the place where you can get visa extensions. The PSB says it's a five-day wait. Period. Consider picking yours up in Lèshān, Kāngdìng, or, best, Sōngpān.

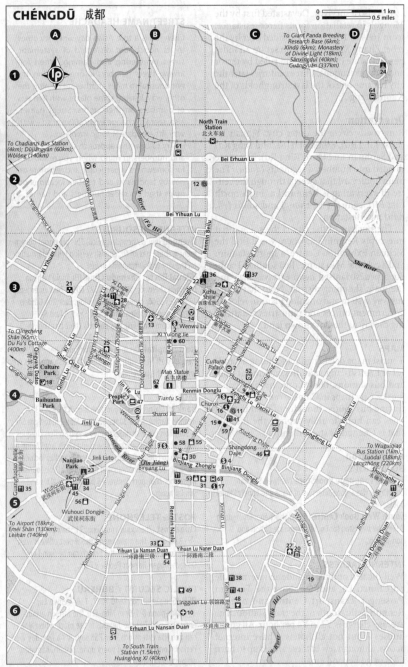

CHÉNGDŪ 成都

SÌCHUĀN

TOURIST INFORMATION

The best source for up-to-the-minute restaurant, bar and entertainment listings is the free magazine *Go West*, found in guesthouses and restaurants, but it goes quickly and isn't always easy to find. It's published every two months.

Tourist booths (Lǚyóu Zīxún Fúwù Zhōngxīn; ☉ 9am-9.30pm summer) These are popping up all over the city in Chéngdū's rush for the 'best tourism city' crown. The best ones are on Chunxi Lu and next door to the Tourism Passenger Transport Centre. The staff often speak English and can be remarkably helpful – once you've pried them away from watching *Desperate Housewives* on the computers.

Tourist hotline (☎ 8292 8555) Free hotline with English-speaking operators.

TRAVEL AGENCIES

Every other building in the city seems to be a travel agency; note also that dissatisfaction with private agencies is a none-too-rare thing, so ask around first. Basically everywhere you can lay your head has a travel agency of some sort.

The more useful travel agencies are at Dragon Town Youth Hostel, Loft and Sim's Cozy Guesthouse; see Sleeping, p364.

Tours offered differ at every place, but many include Hailuogou Glacier Park, Wolong Nature Reserve, Jiuzhaigou Nature Reserve, Éméi Shān and Sōngpān. Also on offer are day trips to the Giant Panda Breeding Research Base and local Sìchuān opera performances.

Prices depend upon the number of travellers but are generally good value.

Agencies can often arrange Yangzi River (Cháng Jiāng) cruise tickets, train and flight tickets and permits to Tibet.

China International Travel Service (CITS; Zhōngguó Guójì Lǚxíngshè; ☎ 8642 8212, 8666 4422; Renmin Nanlu) Arranges pricey tours, including packages to Tibet, and offers train and plane ticket booking for a substantial fee.

Dangers & Annoyances

There have been several reports of foreigners becoming targets for rip-offs and theft in Chéngdū, though violent encounters are rare.

Some travellers have reported having things stolen out of their bicycle basket while they were pedalling.

Sights

GIANT PANDA BREEDING RESEARCH BASE

大熊猫繁殖研究中心

Nearly 50 giant and red pandas live at this centre, one of the most popular sights in the city. Breeding (obviously) is the focus at the **Giant Panda Breeding Research Base** (Dàxióngmāo Fánzhí Yánjiū Zhōngxīn; ☎ 8351 6748; admission Y30; ☉ 8am-6pm) and March to May is the 'falling in love period' (wink wink). In autumn and winter you can

also peer through the glass into the panda 'nursery', which is just adorable – except when the *faux* scientist in the nursery notices tourists' imminent arrival and starts poking the sleeping babies to get them active.

There's also a **museum** at the base with detailed exhibits on panda evolution and habits, as well as a pair of pickled panda genitals in a jar. Exhibits have good English captions. A 15-minute movie plays nearby, explaining panda

---

LIFE ON THE EDGE FOR THE GIANT PANDA David Andrew

The Giant Panda is one of the most instantly recognisable large mammals in the world, and in China you will see its moniker on everything from cigarette packs to souvenir tie pins. But although there are vague references to its existence in Chinese literature going back 3000 years, it was not until 1869 that a remarkable French curate-naturalist, Père Armand David, brought a pelt back to the West and formally described the Giant Panda to the scientific world. Endemic to China, it is now restricted to just five mountain ranges straddling the provinces of Sìchuān, Shaanxi and Gānsù, and is thought to number just 1000 or so individuals in the wild.

One Chinese name for the Giant Panda is *dà xióngmāo* or 'big bear-cat', and it is so unlike other bears that scientists have long debated whether it in fact belongs to the raccoon family, or even whether it should be in a separate family of its own. Recent molecular evidence shows it to be a bear, and like other bears it has a carnivorous ancestry. However, the similarities pretty well end there and almost every aspect of the Giant Panda's ecology and behaviour is adapted to a diet of bamboo. Bamboo is a poor food for a large, warm-blooded animal – it is low in protein and high in indigestible plant fibres, and barely provides enough nutrition to support the panda's metabolism. But it grows as a superabundant food resource in the damp, chilly mountains of Southwest China, and through a suite of adaptations the Giant Panda has overcome the challenge of surviving on what is effectively woody grass.

Most famous of these adaptations is the 'panda's thumb' – not a real thumb, but a modified wrist bone that enables the Giant Panda to strip bamboo leaves from their branches, and to manipulate shoots and stems. Its rounded body shape (by bear standards, at least) and extremities conserve heat in winter, thus enabling the panda to feed year-round without hibernating. Its striking black-and-white colouration and prominent eye patches serve as a warning both to other pandas and to potential predators, since both social and threatening interactions would mean wasting precious energy.

However, the Giant Panda must still ingest an extraordinary amount of bamboo to extract its daily nutrition requirements. And just to make life interesting, every 25 or so years bamboos flower and die en masse, and the pandas must move to other feeding areas to survive. With the increased fragmentation of their natural forest habitat their choices for new feeding sites are limited, and in the mid-1970s more than 130 pandas starved to death when bamboos flowered and died in Mín Shān, Sìchuān.

With world attention focused on the panda's survival, the Chinese government has set up 11 panda reserves in the Southwest and thrown itself behind a captive breeding program. Chinese laws now strictly forbid hunting or tree-felling in Giant Panda habitat. Peasants are offered rewards equivalent to double their annual salary if they save a starving panda, and life sentences or public executions are imposed on convicted poachers. Even though Giant Pandas are notoriously difficult to breed in captivity, Chéngdū's Giant Panda Breeding Research Base (above) has recently had successes with the birth of a number of pandas. But sceptics would rather leave the pandas to their own devices and see more efforts made to preserve natural panda habitat; captive breeding has in only a very few cases been used successfully to save wild populations of large animals. And you can't ignore the profit motive in China's burgeoning economy: Giant Pandas draw a crowd wherever they are displayed and nearly 200 are kept in China's zoos.

mating habits; it includes some disturbing images of a mother panda swatting around her piglet-pink newborn.

Feeding time is around 9.30am and is when the pandas are most active. Once feeding is over, they don't do much besides sleep.

Bus 10 runs out to Qīnglóng, from where you'll have to change for bus 1 to the terminus. From here, hop on a motorised rickshaw to the breeding centre. A lot less hassle are the tours run by most guesthouses for Y50, including the entrance fee. You can also get one of the special tourist buses directly here from the Traffic Hotel. The base is about 10km from the city centre.

WENSHU TEMPLE 文殊院

This Tang dynasty monastery is Chéngdū's largest and best-preserved Buddhist temple. **Wenshu Temple** (Wénshū Yuàn; Renmin Zhonglu; 人民中路; admission Y5; 8am-6pm) has air redolent with incense, a low murmur of chanting, exquisite relief carvings, and, best of all, a sense of serenity and solitude despite the crowds of worshippers who flock to the place. If you only have time for one temple on your visit, this is by far the most interesting.

A vegetarian restaurant and two atmospheric teahouses (see p368) are on the grounds.

A new **pedestrian street** has been set up just south of here with restaurants and souvenir stalls.

TOMB OF WANG JIAN 王建墓

The small, dark and pleasantly spooky **Tomb of Wang Jian** (Wángjiàn Mù; Yongling Lu; 永陵路; admission Y20; 8am-6pm Mar-Oct, to 5pm Nov-Feb) was erected in honour of Wang Jian (AD 847–918), a general who came to power after the AD 907 collapse of the Tang dynasty and later became emperor of the Shu kingdom. He's remembered for ruling in a hands-off manner and for the success of agriculture during his reign.

So far, this is the only mausoleum excavated in China that features above-ground tomb chambers. It's also known for having 24 statues of musicians – a collection now considered to be the best surviving record of a Tang dynasty musical troupe. Excellent English captions explain their musical instruments in detail.

Look around carefully (especially up at the ceiling) for damage caused by tomb raiders believed by archaeologists to have forced their way into the chambers over the centuries.

ZHAOJUE TEMPLE 昭觉寺

This **temple** (Zhāojué Sì; admission Y2; park 6am-6pm, ticket office to 5pm) dates back to the 7th century and has since served as a model for many Japanese and Southeast Asian Buddhist temples.

During the early Qing dynasty, Zhāojué Sì underwent extensive reconstruction under the supervision of Po Shan, a famous Buddhist monk who established the lovely waterways and groves you see here today. The effect is impressive and the grounds are quieter and more spread out than at Chéngdū's other temples.

Little of the temple's original architecture survived the Cultural Revolution, and serious restoration work was only undertaken in the last decade.

There are several pavilions, though all except the imposing prayer hall were being renovated at the time of research.

There's a vegetarian restaurant on the grounds (see p367) and a teahouse next door.

Zhaojue Temple is about 6km northeast of Chéngdū city centre. Loads of buses run to the nearby Zhaojue bus station (Zhāojué chēzhàn) from around town. Cycling there is possible, though you risk asphyxiation from traffic fumes.

TEMPLE PARKS

The **Green Ram Temple** (Qīngyáng Gōng; Qingyang Dadao; 青羊大道; admission Y5; 7am-6.30pm) is the oldest and most extensive Taoist temple in the Chéngdū area. For local visitors, stroking the bronze goat here is a must – it can supposedly vanquish life's troubles and pains. Its odd, ungoat-like companion has no special powers, but is unique in that it combines features of all the Chinese zodiac animals. Another highlight here is an eight-sided pagoda built without bolts or pegs. The 16 pillars inside are covered in elaborate carvings and in total 81 dragons are depicted.

The temple has excellent nightly performances of Sìchuān opera and theatre. You can give the **Culture Park** (文化公园; Wénhuà Gōngyuán; admission free; 7am-10pm) next door a miss. With its mass of teahouses, souvenir stalls and weathered rides for kids, it's noisy, loud and doesn't actually have much green space.

Down the road, you'll find one of the city's most popular scenic spots, set up in honour of the poet Du Fu (AD 712–70), a man who wrote some of the Tang dynasty's most enduring poems. **Du Fu's Cottage** (杜甫草堂; Dùfǔ Cǎotáng; ☎ 8731 9258; 38 Qinghua Lu; 清华路38号; admission Y60; ⏱ 7.30am-7pm Mar-Oct, 8am-6.30pm Nov-Feb) is a park centred around his former residence and is arguably the most beautiful green space in Chéngdū.

Du Fu was born in Hénán but the upheaval caused by the An Lushan Rebellion (756–763), an uprising by a general against Tang rulers, kept the poet on the move. He ended up settling in Chéngdū for four years. During that time, he penned more than 200 poems on the people who lived and worked nearby.

The park is an interesting set up of bamboo paths, streams and pavilions, including a replica of Du Fu's cottage (though there is some dispute over how accurate the placement is). The most recent addition is a modern structure at the north end of the park where you can check out an excavation site of Tang-era objects.

During the high season, shuttle buses sometimes run from the park's north gate to Wuhou temple, free of charge. Audio guides (Y20, plus Y300 deposit) are also available in several languages including English, but they are very popular and run out quickly.

Next to Nanjiao Park (南郊公园; Nánjiāo Gōngyuán; admission Y2; open 6am to 10pm), **Wuhou Temple** (武侯祠; Wǔhóu Cí; admission Y60; ⏱ 6.30am-8pm) is a complex of pavilions and statues commemorating figures from the Three Kingdoms period (AD 220–80). The images and names you'll see most frequently here are Emperor Liu Bei and that of Zhuge Liang, a legendary military strategist known for his wisdom and culture and immortalised in one of the classics of Chinese literature, *The Romance of the Three Kingdoms*.

The temple is surrounded by picturesque gardens and mossy cypresses draped over walkways. It regularly hosts Sìchuān opera performances. **Jinli Luto** to the east is a recently gentrified street (in the 'new-old' style of so many Chinese cities) chock-full of shops, galleries, restaurants, pubs, teahouses and more.

In the southeast of town, near Sìchuān University, is **Wàngjiānglóu Gōngyuán** (望江楼公园; River Viewing Pavilion Park; admission Y20; ⏱ 8am-6pm), a park known for its beautiful bamboo-lined paths and dedicated to the Tang dynasty poet Xue Tao, one of the few women of this period whose work is still celebrated today. The four-storey, wooden Qing pavilion in the heart of the park overlooks Brocade River and was built in her honour. The well nearby is where Xue Tao is said to have drawn water to dye her writing paper. The park also features over 150 varieties of bamboo from China, Japan and Southeast Asia, ranging from bonsai-sized potted plants to towering giants.

PEOPLE'S PARK 人民公园

This **park** (Rénmín Gōngyuán; admission free; ⏱ 6am-8pm) always seems full of life. Locals flock here to practise their singing and dancing and do their exercises. The teahouse draws many visitors (and locals after their taichi practice) for good reason (see p368).

Plopped in the middle of the park's bonsai and perennials is the **Monument to the Martyrs of the Railway Protection Movement** (1911). This obelisk memorialises an uprising of the people against corrupt officers pocketing cash intended for railway construction. People's Park was a private officer's garden, so it was a fitting place to put the structure.

The bunker-like structure across the lake from the teahouse was an underground **funhouse** with a notoriously tacky reputation. It's been closed for some time now and it's not clear when (or if) it will reopen.

SICHUAN UNIVERSITY MUSEUM 四川大学博物馆

The **Sichuan University Museum** (Sìchuān Dàxué Bówùguǎn; East Gate, Sichuan University; 四川大学东大门内) is one of the better museums in the southwest. The collection is particularly strong in the fields of ethnology, folklore and traditional art, and is housed in a swank modern building near the university's east gate. However, it's been closed for some time and no-one seems to know when it will be reopening. Stay tuned.

Sleeping
BUDGET

Chéngdū has a great choice of backpacker-friendly places.

Sim's Cozy Guesthouse (Guānhuá Qingnián Lǚshè; ☎ 8691 4422; www.gogosc.com; 42 Xizhu Shijie; 西珠市街42号; 12-bed dm Y15-20, 4- & 6-bed dm Y25-35, s from Y50, d Y70-200; ✉ 🖥) Run by a backpacker couple (he's Singaporean, she's Japanese), this exceptional hostel is one of the most welcoming you'll find. A stone's throw from the serene Wenshu Temple, the hostel is in a traditional-style building over 100 years old. The rambling halls seem to go on forever and rooms exist in every kind of amenity combination you can imagine (with or without air-con, bathrooms, wi-fi etc). Lovely touches are everywhere, such as lockable boxes in the dorms or TV sets with DVD players in some of the double rooms. There's a lovely pondside bar and the staff are phenomenal. Backpackers will love this place.

Loft (Sīhào Gōngchǎng Qīngnián Lǚguǎn; ☎ 8626 5770; www.lofthostel.com; 4 Tongren Lu, Xiaotong Xiang; 同仁路4号, 小通巷; 4-/6-bed dm Y20/15, s & d with/without bathroom Y120/60; ❄ ❑) This place screams New York chic at every turn and has the coolest setup of any hostel in China's Southwest. Rooms have exposed brick walls, minimalist furnishings and sexy black-tiled bathrooms. There's a massive, high-ceilinged common room with free internet, movies and a pool table. The staff are so relaxed and friendly it's hard to tell at first glance who's an employee and who's a traveller. The chic setup would appeal to both backpackers and midrange travellers. Enter through Café Copenhagen (which, by the way, is great) to reach the front desk.

Holly's Hostel (Jiǔlóngdǐng Qīngnián Kèzhàn; ☎ 8554 8131; hollyhostelcn@yahoo.com; 246 Wuhouci Dajie; 武侯祠大街246号; 4-bed dm with shared bathroom Y20, 6-bed dm with bathroom & air-con Y30, d Y120; ❄) An awesome location near the bustling Tibetan quarter and sweet, helpful staff are the real pluses here. The plain, serviceable rooms don't have the same verve as some of the other hostels, but the complimentary shampoo and amenities in the doubles are a nice touch. A top-floor café serves Western and Chinese food and has a lovely, leafy terrace. Free pickup from the train station; airport pickup is Y70.

Dragon Town Youth Hostel (Lóngtáng Kèzhàn; ☎ 8664 8408; www.dragontown.com.cn; 27 Kuan Xiangzi; 宽巷子27号; dm Y30-40, s Y100-150, d 100-160; ❄ ❑) This building dates from the Qing dynasty and is one of the most atmospheric hostels around. Down a quiet alley, it's got a traditional courtyard and two 'honeymoon suite' rooms featuring antique Chinese furniture. The rest of the rooms are simple, but they're clean and comfortable. The bar here seems perpetually full and is a great place to meet fellow travellers.

Traffic Hotel (Jiāotōng Fàndiàn; ☎ 8545 1017; www .traffichotel.com; 6 Linjiang Zhonglu; 临江中路6号; dm Y30, d/tr Y240/290; ❄) A backpacker standard for

ages, this hotel is old-fashioned but has spotless rooms and every service you could ever imagine, including several travel agencies and an on-site restaurant. The location near the Tourism Passenger Transport Centre can't be beaten and it's got helpful English-speaking staff. It's also near the stop for the new tourism buses.

MIDRANGE

Besides what's listed here, most budget guesthouses have midrange value doubles for bargain prices.

Yùlín Bīnguǎn (☎ 8557 8839; 9 Yihuan Lu, Nansan Duan; 一环路南三段9号; d Y148-280; ❄) There's something for all price ranges here, including one wing with the niftiest midrange digs in town. Though small, the rooms are delightfully set up: the modern bathrooms sparkle with glass sinks and showers and there are flat-screen TVs in every room. The third wing is more expensive with bigger (or do the wall mirrors just make them seem that way?) rooms, which, though pleasant, don't quite seem worth the price. A cheap wing with stinky halls has clean but snoringly bland rooms.

Hóngwǎ Bīnguǎn (☎ 8541 2979; 29 Wangjiang Lu, inside Sichuan University East Gate; 望江路29号, 四川大学东大门内; s/d/tr Y160/260/300; ❄) The starkly plain facilities here are by no means the best in the city, but the location in a peaceful corner of Sichuan University makes it worth considering. The basketball and badminton courts are nearby and you can usually get in on a game, making it easy to meet people and get an up-close look at local university life. Discounted rooms often run Y96 for a single, Y156 for a double.

Xīnchūn Bīnguǎn (☎ 8672 6622; fax 8667 2382; 23 Chunxi Lu, Bei Duan; 春熙路北段23号; s Y280-340, d 340; ❄) Tucked down one of the city's bustling pedestrian shopping streets, you couldn't ask for a more central location than this. The reception staff can get hysterically giddy with foreigners, but if you can put up with that the rooms are awesome – small, sleekly modern and gleaming clean. Outside of high season times, rates are often discounted by 50%.

TOP END

Developers are throwing up first-rate luxury hotels with wild abandon both downtown and in the city's suburbs – if this is what you're after, the selection is phenomenal.

Sofitel Wanda Chengdu (Chéngdū Suǒfēitè Wàndá Dàjiǔdiàn; ☎ 6666 9999, 6680 8899; fax 6666 3333; 15 Binjiang Zhonglu; 滨江中路15号; s & d from Y1500, discounted Y900; ✗ 🔊) From service to facilities, this is the best hotel in town at the moment. Basic rooms are filled with mirrors, exotic vases and naughty 360-degree glass showers looking into the bedrooms. Televisions offer 24-hour channels in almost every major Asian and European language. Best of all, everyone from the hotel electricians to housekeeping to desk staff are friendly and helpful. A stay here would be a memorable experience worth every yuán.

Eating
CHINESE
Chinese people revere Sìchuān's hot and spicy cuisine (see the boxed text, opposite). The most salient pepper flavour is *huājiāo* (花椒; a wild pepper); some love it, while others cringe at its over-the-top numbing effect (rural dentists purportedly use it as an anaesthetic) and say its aftertaste is a bit like a detergent.

You should also learn *xiǎo chī* (小吃; little eats); cheap, quick snacks are the way of life here. Popular for lunch with the on-the-fly lunchtime crowd is *shāokǎo* (烧烤), Sichuanese barbecue. Skewers of meat, veggies and smoked tofu are brushed with oil and chilli and grilled.

Sadly, city officials have begun clearing many streets of itinerant roadside food stalls, so instead of forming night markets many of these stalls have had to either close or move indoors. Yet prowling around you'll still find roadside stalls on back streets, many simply portable grills on bikes.

With more time you can savour *huǒguō* (火锅), though it's becoming a bit of a yuppified sit-down affair. It's similar to fondue: you dip skewered meat and veggies into big woks filled with hot, spiced oil and then into little dishes of peanut oil and garlic. Be forewarned though – hotpot can be *very* hot. Even many Sichuanese can't take it. To prevent the sweats, try asking for *báiwèi* (白味), the hotpot for wimps. Peanut milk, sold in tins, can help arrest the dragonesque results.

Xiǎohui Dòuhuā (☎ 8625 2753; section 12, 86 Xi Dajie; 西大街86号, 附12; dishes Y2-10) Specialising in tofu and noodle snacks in more combinations than you'd ever think possible, eating at this cosy neighbourhood eatery is a sensory thrill. Try the crispy beef beancurd (牛肉豆花; *niúròu dòuhuā*) and steamed beef with rice powder (粉蒸牛肉; *fěnzhēng niúròu*), and don't miss the thick, succulent and spicy sweet noodles (甜水面; *tiánshuǐ miàn*). Note to allergy sufferers: more than half the dishes here are served with some kind of peanut ingredient. The cooks will make them without peanuts, however, if you ask.

Chén Mápó Dòufu (Pockmarked Mother Chen's Bean Curd; Jiefang Lu; 解放路; dishes from Y5) *Mápó dòufu* is served here with a vengeance – soft, fresh bean curd with a fiery sauce of garlic, minced beef, salted soybean, chilli oil and fiery Sìchuān pepper. So popular is this place that a handful of franchise options are now found throughout town.

Yǒngjì Tāngyuán Miànguǎn (☎ 8553 4074; 13 Wuhouci Dongjie; 武侯祠东街13号; noodles Y5, dumplings Y7.50) Steamy and bustling, this little place is right near the Tibetan neighbourhood and is a terrific place to come for monstrous-sized bowls of delicious dumplings.

Lǎozi Hào (☎ 6809 0096; Shuinianhe Lu; 水碾河路; noodles Y5-10) Two brothers run this noodle place and they've turned it into a neighbourhood institution. The modernisation steamroller has forced them to move several times in recent years, but they always find somewhere else in the area to set up – their customers trailing loyally behind them. Try their fiery tomato egg noodles (番茄煎蛋面; *fānqié jiān dànmiàn*) to see what all the fuss is about.

Lóngchāoshǒu Cāntīng (cnr Chunxi Lu & Shandong Dajie; 春熙路与山东大街交叉路口; meals Y5-15) This big, bustling cafeteria-style eatery can be overwhelming, but it's a long-time favourite for sampling Chéngdū snacks. The cheapest option gives you a range of sweet and savoury items, with each price bracket giving you the same deal on a grander and more filling scale. Unfortunately, it hasn't much to offer vegetarians.

Ārè Zàngcān (☎ 8557 0877; 234 Wuhouci Dajie; 武侯祠大街234号; dishes from Y10) Right across the street from Wuhou Temple, this Tibetan restaurant looks fussy on the outside, but the 3rd-floor dining room is actually bright and relaxed with small, simple tables. There's an English menu from which you can choose something simple, such as veggie *momos* (Tibetan dumplings; Y10), or something more elaborate, such as yak stew (Y68). Service is attentive and there's an adjoining outdoor terrace crowded with leafy green plants that's perfect for warm weather alfresco dining.

HOT & SPICY

The Chinese have a saying: 'Shí zài Zhōngguó, wèi zài Sìchuān' (食在中国，味在四川); China is the place for food, but Sìchuān is the place for flavour). Flavour starts with mouth-singeing peppers whose spiciness is believed to help reduce a person's internal dampness caused by the frequent high humidity and rainy weather. Anything from ginger to local spices to a variety of chillis are then added in unending combinations to give each dish its unique character. With such fiery food, the Sichuanese have a reputation for being a little hot-headed and the local women are even referred to as *là mèizi* (spice girls).

The province boasts a repertoire of over 5000 different dishes. The large number may partly be due to the relocation of people and troops from other provinces over the centuries – each group of people brought their own cuisine with them, influencing local dishes along the way.

We'll just start with five of the most popular dishes:

- *huíguō ròu* (回锅肉; boiled and stir-fried pork with salty and hot sauce)
- *gōngbào jīdīng* (宫保鸡丁; spicy chicken with peanuts)
- *shuǐzhǔ yú* (水煮鱼; boiled fish in a fiery sauce)
- *gānbiān sìjìdòu* (干煸四季豆; dry-fried green beans)
- *mápó dòufu* (麻婆豆腐; pock-marked Mother Chen's bean curd)

The last two dishes can be made suitable for vegetarians; just ask for the meat to be left out (不放肉; *bù fàng ròu*).

If you'd rather learn to whip the dishes up yourself, some hostels offer cooking lessons to their guests. Holly's Hostel (p365) needs one day's notice, and for Y100 you'll be taught to cook up your own five-dish Sìchuān feast. Lessons at Sim's Cozy Guesthouse (p364) cost around Y75.

Bāguó Bùyì Fēngwèijiǔlóu (☎ 8509 5888; section 19, 8 Guangfuqiao Beijie; 广福桥北街8号, 附19; main dishes Y38-52; ☑ 10am-9.30pm) Now at a new location, the modern decoration has given this restaurant a slightly clubby vibe. Named after the traditional cotton clothing that was worn by peasants in the eastern part of the province, the Sìchuān food here is hugely popular. There's no English spoken, but the huge plank-like menu is full of glossy multicoloured pictures, so choosing won't be too hard.

VEGETARIAN

A special treat for vegetarians is to head out to Wenshu Temple (p363), where there is an excellent vegetarian restaurant with an English menu (dishes Y6 to Y10).

Zhaojue Temple (p363) also serves up vegetarian dishes for lunch (dishes from Y8, from 11am to 3.30pm). If you're really keen, you might ride out to the Monastery of Divine Light (p373) in Xīndū, 18km north of Chéngdū, in time for lunch (dishes from Y7, 11am to noon).

Most of the Western restaurants also feature vegetarian options on their menus.

WESTERN

The number of Western restaurants springing up in Chéngdū continues to grow. There's over a dozen along Kehua Beilu alone.

Highfly Café (Gāofēi Kāfēi; ☎ 8544 2820; 18 Linjiang Zhonglu; 临江中路18号; dishes from Y12; ☑ 9am-late; 🖳) Along with the Traffic Hotel, this place has been a backpacker mainstay since the '90s. The happy staff get overwhelmed with hipster Chinese at times, but it's a relaxing place with great food; try the delicious calorie-laden fudge brownies. Free internet access.

Peter's Tex-Mex (Pídé Déizhōu Páfáng; ☎ 8522 7965; 117 Kehua Beilu; 科华北路117号; dishes from Y15; ☑ 7.30am-11pm) More than just the best Tex-Mex food in the city, the food served here is among the best you'll have anywhere. Once you've given the *chimichangas* (deep-fried burritos) a pass (it's the only dish they haven't quite pulled off), you can't go wrong no matter what you order. Try the strawberry margaritas (Y40) – slightly tart, they taste like fresh berries. Service is flawless and this place attracts everyone from businessmen to Chinese families and students from nearby Sichuan University.

Grandma's Kitchen & Deli (Zǔmǔ De Chúfáng; ☎ 8524 2835; 73/75 Kehua Beilu; 科华北路73/75 号; mains from Y20) Grandma's has burgers, steaks and salads, but it's the desserts that stand out the most. Shakes and smoothies are also popular and on Sundays this place is packed with families and young children. The deli here also has plenty of fans.

Drinking

TEAHOUSES

There's positively nowhere in China that better represents the culture of tea than Sìchuān does. The 'art' of drinking tea dates back 3000 years, and traditionally the teahouse functioned as the centre of social life: a place where people had haircuts, watched opera performances, played cards, bantered over poetry, had their earwax removed (no kidding) and gossiped about their neighbours. It's a bit like going to the pub today, minus the earwax and opera.

Temple of Mercy (Dàcí Sì; Dacisi Lu; 大慈寺院; tea Y1; ⏰ 10am-6pm) This temple itself doesn't offer much to see, however, its teahouse, with tables piled high with mah jong pieces and teacups, is a perfect place for a lazy afternoon in the sun.

Renmin Teahouse (Rénmín Cháguǎn; People's Park; 人民公园; tea Y5-20; ⏰ 10am-6pm) This is one of Chéngdū's finest. Come and enjoy a most pleasant afternoon over a bottomless cup of stone-flower tea.

Another charming family-type teahouse is in Wenshu Temple (p363), with an amazingly crowded and steamy ambience. This is in addition to the huge tea garden outside – one of the largest and most lively in Chéngdū. If you want to join in, sit on the west side of the path, closest to the main temple, where tea costs Y2. The tea must be greener on the other side of the path where it costs Y10.

PUBS & BARS

Chéngdū has a wild and booming but everchanging nightlife and part of the fun is finding out exactly where it's taking place. Like in Chóngqìng, what's this week's 'must' destination can be next week's ghost haunt. Because clubs and bars change owners, vibes and names so quickly, nightlife in Chéngdū is often more about getting to a particular area and seeing what's going on, rather than heading to a particular club or bar. A copy of *Go West* magazine (see p359) is a good place to start.

Shamrock Irish Bar & Restaurant (Sānyècǎo Àì'ěrlán Xīcān Jiǔbā; ☎ 8523 6158; 4 Duan, 15 Renmin Nanlu; 人民南路15号4段; ⏰ 10am-2am) From atmosphere, to service, to food, to drink, this place is the perfect pub. Expats regularly gather here to watch sports events on the TVs, oohing and aahing over everything from cricket and football to hockey. A pint of Guinness on tap costs Y80.

Roo Bar (Dàdàishǔ Jiǔbā; ☎ 8540 1318; 6 Kehua Jie; 科华街6号; ⏰ 11.30am-2am) Equally boisterous, this place often gets a big student crowd from the nearby university. In addition to your beer here, you can indulge in a burger with beetroot and egg, among other delicacies.

Hemp House (☎ 138-0800 1424; 3rd fl, Oriental Times Mall, Dongmen Daqiao, Dong Dajie; 东大街，东门大桥，东方时代商城3楼; ⏰ 9pm-late) One of the most popular places at the time of research, Hemp House has pool tables and plays everything from house to reggae. The best time to come is Saturday nights when it becomes a dancing free-for-all.

Entertainment

Sìchuān opera is one of the art forms Chéngdū is best known for throughout China. It has a tradition dating back more than 250 years and features slapstick, eyeglass-shattering songs, gymnastics and even fire breathing. Several opera houses are scattered throughout the older sections of town, a couple of which are in temples listed previously (the ones in the temples are pricey and filled with tourists). Many offer daily performances, some are weekends only. No matter where you go, it's a grand, fun-filled experience.

For those new to the genre, weekend shows usually dish up a kind of medley of Sìchuān opera's 'greatest hits', giving you a good overview. Any of the guesthouses will be able to organise tours for a similar price; some even have local connections to possibly get you backstage.

Jinjiang Theatre (Jǐnjiāng Jùyuàn; Huaxingzheng Jie; 华兴正街) This combination teahouse, opera theatre and cinema is one of the more centrally located. High-standard Sìchuān opera performances are given every Saturday and/or Sunday afternoon (Y120 per person), though the teahouse itself often has performances for just Y15!

At the time of research, the best place to head for super-slick discos was the south side of Erhuan Lu, Nansan Duan (二环路南三段).

For the best bars playing hip-hop, reggae and blues, it's best to check out the streets in and around Sichuan University.

Shopping

The main downtown shopping area extends from the eastern end of Renmin Donglu south to Shangdong Dajie, with trendy clothing shops and department stores. Glitzy department store complexes are pretty much ubiquitous now.

South of the river, on a street across from the entrance to Wuhou Temple, is a small Tibetan neighbourhood. While it's not evident in the architecture, it is in the prayer flags, colourful scarves, beads and brass goods for sale. You won't find the variety of things (nor the bargains) that you'll find in the northwest of Sìchuān, but it still makes for an interesting wander.

Qingshiqiao Market (Qīngshíqiáo Shìchǎng; Xinkai Jie; 新开街) This large market is one of the most interesting and busiest places to wander in town. Shops and stalls sell brightly coloured seafood, flowers, cacti, birds, pets and a thousand dried foods.

Tóng Rén Táng (Tong Ren Tang Pharmacy; 1 Zongfu Lu; 总府路1号) Even if your knowledge of Chinese medicine is zilch, this traditional Chinese pharmacy, over 260 years old, is a superb place to just browse and gape at the enormity of knowledge accrued over four millennia.

Outdoor clothing and equipment are a big buy in the city (lots of folks headed into the western hills and Tibet, natch). Mountain Dak Outdoor Sports Club (Gāoshān Hùwài Lǚyóu Tànxiǎn Yòngpǐn) and **Airwolf** (Fēiláng Hùwài; ☎ 8544 2612; 18 Linjiang Lu; 临江路18号; ⏰ 10am-8pm Nov-Feb, to 9pm Mar-Oct) are near Highfly Café. Another half a dozen are to the south along Renmin Nanlu at the corner of Yihuan Lu Nansan Duan. Quality varies: experts don't call a lot of it 'North Fake' for nothing.

Getting There & Away

AIR

Flights internally go everywhere, virtually all the time. Whatever you do, shop around: outside the highest periods posted rates should mean little. Internal destinations include Běijīng (Y1440, 2¼ hours), Chóngqìng (Y380, 45 minutes), Dàlián (Y1810, 3½ hours), Shànghǎi (Y1660, two hours 20 minutes), Guǎngzhōu (Y1300, one hour 50 minutes), Lìjiāng (Y880, one hour), Kūnmíng (Y700, one hour) and Xī'ān (Y630, one hour 20 minutes).

Within Sìchuān there are four flights a day to Jiuhuang Airport (Y700, 40 minutes), the new air link for Jiǔzhàigōu and Sōngpān in northern Sìchuān.

International destinations include Hong Kong (Y2200, 2½ hours), Tokyo (Y3000, 6½ hours), Singapore (Y1900, four hours 20 minutes), Seoul (Y2800, three hours 45 minutes) and Bangkok (Y1700, two hours 55 minutes). Flights should also operate between Amsterdam, Vienna and Macau by the time you read this.

Airline offices in Chéngdū:

Air China (Zhōngguó Mínháng; ☎ 8666 1100; 41, Section 2, Renmin Nanlu; ⏰ 8am-7.30pm)

China Southern Airlines (Zhōngguó Nánfāng Hángkōng; ☎ 8666 3618, 8666 3468; 19 Shangdong Dajie; ⏰ 8.30am-6pm)

Dragon Air (Gǎnglóng Hángkōng Gōngsī; ☎ 8676 8828; Section 1, 15 Renmin Zhonglu) In the Sheraton Chengdu Lido Hotel (Tiānfǔ Lìdū Xǐláidēng Fàndiàn).

Sichuan Airlines (Sìchuān Hángkōng Gōngsī; ☎ 8666 6998, 8666 6768; 1 Fu, 6 Renmin Xilu; ⏰ 8am-9pm)

BUS

Transport connections in Chéngdū are more comprehensive than in other parts of the Southwest. High-speed expressways from Chéngdū to Chóngqìng, Lèshān, Zìgòng and Yíbīn have cut down travel time significantly, and more are always under construction.

The **Tourism Passenger Transport Centre** (Xinnanmen; ☎ 8543 7347, 8544 3617; 57 Binjiang Lu) recently had its name changed from Xinnanmen and though often just called the 'tourist bus station' these days some people still refer to it by its old name. It's in the southern part of town and is the main bus station, with tickets to most places around Sìchuān.

See the boxed text (p370) for bus times. Note that some destinations have departures from more than one station; not all can possibly be listed here so double-check with your guesthouse or hotel.

TRAIN

Train tickets are a hell of a lot easier to land these days, but you still can't count on next-day middle-berth hard sleeper miracles for the most popular routes. Almost all the hostels can book train tickets for a service fee of around Y20.

Daily departures include Kūnmíng (Y248, 18 hours), Éméi (Y22, two hours), Chóngqìng

SÌCHUĀN

(normal/express Y101/125, 11 hours/five hours), Běijīng (Y405, 26 hours) and Xī'ān (Y185, 18 hours). One high-speed train line has recently started between Chéngdū and Miányáng; another to Lèshān was close to being finished at the time of research. Note that the express to Chóngqìng that started in 2006 is nearly as fast as the bus.

Trains leave from Chéngdū for Lhasa every other day at 6.18pm (Y740, 48 hours), but, as always, you must get your permit first. Travel agencies in hostels can help you get it. Most departures of interest to travellers will leave from the North Train Station (Huǒchē Běizhàn).

TO TIBET

You still cannot fly solo to Tibet and so must sign on for a 'tour' in order to get the required Tibetan travel permit. All guesthouses in town offer the service. You may have 20 people in your guesthouse's 'tour group', but you'll never see them again after you deplane.

At the time of research these packages were priced from Y1600 to Y1900 including flights, and were the most cost-effective way of getting into Tibet. CITS runs its own four- to six-day tours (Y2000 to Y4000).

Sìchuān's land borders into Tibet are still closed to foreigners. Some travellers attempt to sneak across but the majority are turned back and fined heavily. Don't believe anyone who says they can drive you to Lhasa; they can't.

Stories of travellers being dumped off in the middle of nowhere once they've crossed the border into Tibet (minus their bags and money) are not uncommon. In 2006 the US State Department was reporting incidents of

CHÉNGDŪ BUS TIMETABLES

Buses from the Tourism Passenger Transport Centre (Xinnanmen):

Destination	Price	Duration	Frequency	Departs
Éméi	Y37	2hr	every 20min	6.40am-7pm
Dūjiāngyàn	Y18	1hr	half-hourly	8.30-11am
Huánglóngxī	Y11	1hr	half-hourly	8am-noon
Jiǔzhàigōu	Y123	10hr	1 daily	8am
Kāngdìng	Y117	7hr	hourly	7am-2pm
Lèshān	Y43	2hr	every 20min	7.10am-7.35pm & 9.30pm

For northern destinations you will need to trek over to the Chadianzi bus station in the northwest of the city.

Destination	Price	Duration	Frequency	Departs
Dūjiāngyàn	Y18	1½hr	every 40min	6.30am-8pm
Jiǔzhàigōu	Y110	12-13hr	3 daily	7.20am, 8am & 4pm
Sōngpān	Y74	8hr	3 daily	6.30am, 7am & 7.30am
Wòlóng	Y20.50-22.50	4hr	1 daily	11.40am
Xiǎojīn	Y46	7hr	4 daily	6.30am, 7am, 7.30am & 8am

For eastern and northeastern destinations your best bet is to try the north bus station, near the north train station. However, to get to Dàzú, you'll most likely need to head to Wuguiqiao bus station outside the Second Ring Rd.

Destination	Price	Duration	Frequency	Departs
Làngzhōng	Y89.50	5hr	every 50min/30min	6.50am-12.30pm/ 4pm-6.30pm
Yíbīn	Y97	4hr	every 40 min	8am-7pm
Zìgòng	Y64	3hr	every 25min	7am-7pm

travellers being physically assaulted by authorities after they were caught.

Getting Around

TO/FROM THE AIRPORT

Shangliu Airport (双流国际机场; Shuāngliú Guójì Jīchǎng) is 18km west of the city. Bus 303 (Y10) is actually an airport bus that leaves from outside the Air China office on Renmin Nanlu. *Another* bus 303 (Y1) – no lie – is a local bus running to/from the north railway station, taking pretty much forever. A taxi will cost around Y70, though if you are leaving early in the morning, before the traffic gets going, it can be as little as Y45.

BICYCLE

Cycling is a great way to get around Chéngdū, although the pollution (and traffic) can be terrible. Guesthouses rent bikes for about Y10 per day. The bikes are in fairly good condition but the usual rules apply: check your bike before you cycle off and make an effort to park it in a designated parking area. Also, see Dangers & Annoyances, p361.

BUS

The most useful bus is 16, which runs from Chéngdū's north train station to the south train station *(nán chēzhàn)* along Renmin Nanlu. Regular buses cost Y1, while the double-deckers cost Y2. Bus 81 runs from the Mao statue in the centre of the city to Green Ram Temple, and bus 12 circles the city along Yihuan Lu, starting and ending at the north train station. Bus 4 runs from the centre of town to Chadianzi bus station and Wuguiqiao bus station.

SUBWAY

In 2006 ground was broken (immediately snarling traffic) on the city's new subway, slated for a 2010 completion. When finished, it will be one of the most extensive in China; expect traffic headaches till the day it's done.

TAXI

Taxis have a flag fall of Y5 (Y6 at night), plus Y1.40 per kilometre. Motorised rickshaws also scuttle around the city and are cheaper, but slower, than cabs. Hailing a cab on Friday and Saturday nights in Chéngdū these days can be even harder than hailing a rush-hour cab in New York City. Brace yourself – it can sometimes take more than an hour.

AROUND CHÉNGDŪ

Luòdài 洛带

☎ 028 / pop 25,000

The winding lanes, soaring guildhalls and atmospheric teahouses of this Hakka village make for a fantastic day trip from Chéngdū. This place has been prettied up for tourists, but by and large it's been done right and is very foreigner-friendly. Many food stands have English menus and listed prices, and there's a fantastic **tourism centre** (Five Phoenix Bldg Visitor's Centre; Wǔfèng Lóu Yóukè Fúwù Zhōngxīn; 五凤楼游客服务中心; ☎ 8489 3693; ☼ 8am-6pm, later in high season) with English-speaking staff. They can help you with accommodation and also give out free bilingual Chinese-English maps marked up with all the sights. The centre's right by the southernmost parking lot.

The main street (老街; Lǎo Jiē) has the lion's share of sights including a slew of guildhalls, built by migrating Hakka groups and named for their respective provinces. The **Guangdong Guildhall** (which now houses a teahouse) and the **Jiangxi Guildhall** are both worth a visit. The moderately interesting **Hakka museum** (admission Y5; ☼ 9am-5pm), filled with photos, maps and some passable English captions, is in the Hubei and Hunan Guildhall.

Don't miss wandering the lanes and cobbled streets.

Located in the suburbs, 38km east of Chéngdū, you can easily visit this town in half a day, but you may wish to make it a full-day trip.

SLEEPING

There isn't much reason to stay overnight, but there's plenty of accommodation available if you need it. What's available is generally serviceable but not big on atmosphere.

The central **Gōngxiāoshè Lǚguǎn** (供销社旅馆; ☎ 8962 6888, 8489 3137; 4 Lao Jie Xia Jie; 老街下街4号; d Y120) has plain rooms with Chinese toilets. There's also a youth hostel across from the Guangdong Guildhall, though despite the white triangle logo, it's not an official member of Hostelling International. It was closed when we passed by, but may be worth checking out when you're in town.

EATING & DRINKING

If you are interested in Hakka food, there's a line of stalls beside the Guangdong Guildhall serving up snacks. Items are labelled in

SÌCHUĀN

THE HAKKA

The Hakka people are known as great wanderers, which is reflected even in their name. 'Hak' is the Cantonese for 'guest' and 'ka' (pronounced 'ga' in Cantonese) means family. In Mandarin, their name is pronounced Kèjiā (客家). Though 1700 years ago they were predominantly found in the Shānxī and Hénán provinces, they were pushed into southern China by various wars and important Hakka communities sprung up in Guǎngdōng, Jiāngxī and Fújiàn provinces.

Though there's no ethnic difference between them and the Han Chinese, the Hakka are distinct through their customs and speech. There are dozens of Hakka dialects that can have as many as seven tones or as little as none. (Standard Chinese has four tones.) Despite their small numbers, the prominence of successful Hakka, both at home and abroad, is a source of great pride. Notables include actor Chow Yun-Fat (1955–), former Chinese leader Deng Xiaoping (1904–1997) and the self-proclaimed son of God and Taiping rebellion star Hóng Xiùquán (1814–1864).

Hakka food is usually pickled. Anthropologists explain its prevalence as a necessity, because when the Hakka settled in new communities most farmland was already being cultivated by the original inhabitants.

The majority of Sìchuān's Hakka population came to the province between the late 17th and early 20th centuries, and number about three million. There are 80 million worldwide.

English as well as Chinese along with the prices, which are all reasonable, averaging around Y5 each.

For beer or cocktails, try the **Chic Courtyard of Dongshan** (东山别院; Dōngshān Biéyuàn; ☎ 8489 3186; 78 Lao Jie Xia Jie; 老街下街78号), though it may only be open during the high season.

GETTING THERE & AWAY

There are frequent buses to Luòdài from Chéngdū's Wuguiqiao bus station and less frequent service from Chéngdū's tourist bus station. The last bus leaves Luòdài for Chéngdū at 6pm. The trip will take at least an hour.

Huánglóng Xī 黄龙溪

☎ 028

With an arresting riverside location, this 1700-year-old village has a network of winding cobbled lanes leading to temples, old wharves and ancient gates. The setting is so unique, the county says upwards of 150 movies have been shot here.

A former military outpost of the ancient Shu kingdom, with its position at the Jinjiang and Luxi Rivers, it later evolved into an important commercial centre, particularly for transporting tea during the Song dynasty.

Many of the buildings here were constructed during the Ming and Qing periods. You can pretty well head off in any direction and find something of interest to explore, from courtyards to ancient banyan trees to interesting old foot bridges.

Boats leave from the **old wharf** (古码头; gǔmǎtou), where you can choose between big traditional-style Chinese boats or little motor boats for hire (Y60 to Y80 per hour). However, they often don't run during the low season. During the high-traffic summer months, you may also find small water taxis that can drop you off at one of the monasteries further along the river. Just make sure you figure out how you're going to get back before sending your water taxi on its way.

Near the old wharf is **Zhènjiāng Sì** (镇江寺), a temple where sailors once came to make offerings when they pulled into port.

There are no maps of the village available yet, however, there is a good wooden sign with an English-Chinese map as you walk into town. If you take a picture of it with your digital camera, you could use this while you're sightseeing, to make sure you don't miss the town's major sights.

SLEEPING & EATING

You'll see some tourist hotels on your way into the heart of the village, but they are generally pretty grim.

Try the rooms above **Lan's Tea** (兰庭; Lán Tíng; ☎ 1330-8199 9757; dm Y25-30, d Y80) instead. Opened by a couple who needed to find a space for their antique furniture, they decided to open a teashop and guesthouse to show it all off. Front facing rooms have lovely little balconies. Showers are communal and the toilets are a hole in the ground in a cubicle just off the courtyard.

Being so near the river, fish and shrimp are popular local dishes. Try the waterside restaurants by the old wharf. Not only do they have the best reputation in town, they also have stunning river views, especially in the evening. Also make sure you try the village speciality: black sesame cake (黑芝麻糕; *hēizhīma gāo*). It's sold on almost every street corner.

GETTING THERE & AWAY

About 40km away from Chéngdū, this is an easy day trip. Buses leave regularly from Chéngdū's tourist bus station (Y11, one hour). The last bus leaves Huánglóng Xī for Chéngdū at 5pm.

Monastery of Divine Light 宝光寺

The **Monastery of Divine Light** (Bǎoguāng Sì; admission Y5; 🕒 8am-5.30pm) was founded in the 9th century, though some parts of this Buddhist complex date from as early as the 1st century. It houses multiple treasures, including a white jade Buddha from Myanmar (Burma), Ming and Qing paintings, calligraphy, a stone tablet engraved with 1000 Buddhist figures and ceremonial musical instruments. The **Arhat Hall**, built in the 19th century, contains 500 2m-high clay figurines of Buddhist saints and disciples (and one of Bodhidharma).

The area in front of the temple has recently been landscaped, creating a large modern square.

The temple is about 18km north of Chéngdū in Xīndū County. Buses run to the monastery from the north bus station and from a stop about 600m east of Chéngdū's north train station from around 6am to 6pm. The trip takes just under an hour. The temple's vegetarian restaurant has a good reputation but is only open 11am to noon.

Sānxīngduī 三星堆

The striking and vast **Sanxingdui Museum** (Sānxīngduī Bówùguǎn; ☎ 0838-550 0349, 0838-565 1550; admission Y80; 🕒 ticket office 8.30am-5pm, museum to 6.30pm) is home to a site some Chinese archaeologists regard as more important than the terracotta warriors of Xī'ān. It houses objects of such exquisite beauty they will be seared in your memory months after you leave.

Throughout the 1900s, farmers were continually unearthing pottery shards and other dirt-encrusted objects at this location, but war and the other well-known distractions of the 20th century kept people from taking much interest in the discoveries. Archaeologists finally launched a full-scale excavation in 1986 and unearthed the proverbial archaeological mother lode – the site of the kingdom of Shu and the cradle of Chinese civilisation in the upper reaches of the Yangzi River.

The objects unearthed range from bells and weapons to bronze trees over 6 feet tall (the latter have to be seen to be believed). The dozens and dozens of masks are the stars of the exhibits, however. They are so sophisticated and complex that they wouldn't look out of place in a modern art gallery or on the cover of an alternative rock or heavy metal album. When you think that many of the objects are up to 4900 years old, it's hard not to get chills.

The English captions here are excellent and this is a sight that will appeal to anyone, whether your interest is history, archaeology, anthropology or art, modern or ancient. The museum grounds are enormous and the exhibits are displayed in two large, modern buildings.

The museum is located 40km north of Chéngdū, west of Guǎnghàn. Get a bus from Zhaojue (or the Tourism Passenger Transport Centre) bus station to Guǎnghàn (Y10, two hours); from there you'll have to hop on bus 1 or 6 (Y2) for the remaining 10km to the site. Get here early: even those who swear they suffer easily from museum fatigue end up staying hours beyond what they'd planned.

Qīngchéng Shān 青城山

The plum- and palm-tree-lined trails of **Qīngchéng Shān** (Azure City Mountain; admission Y60) have made this holy Taoist mountain one of the most popular trips from Chéngdū. Picturesque vistas and dozens of atmospheric temples dot the four-hour return route, along with subtropical foliage.

With a summit of only 1600m, the weather here is better than at Éméi Shān, so the views are far less likely to be obscured by mist and cloud. It's also a far easier climb.

If the front of the mountain is clogged with tourists clamouring for the Yuèchéng Hú (Yuecheng Lake) ferry (Y5) and then the cable car (round-trip Y58), consider heading for **Qīngchéng Hòushān** (Azure City Back Mountain; 青城后山) instead, some 15km northwest of the base of Qīngchéng Shān proper. With over 20km of hiking trails, Qīngchéng Hòushān provides the visitor a more natural environment,

SÌCHUĀN

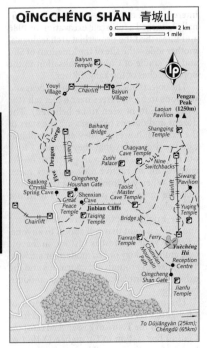

QĪNGCHÉNG SHĀN 青城山

SÌCHUĀN

with **Five Dragon Gorge** (Wǔlóng Gōu) offering dramatic vistas.

Many travellers who come here spend several days. There is a cable car to help with part of the route, but climbing the mountain will still require an overnight stay; you won't want to rush the trip anyway. You can get information on the various walks and routes (though likely in Chinese only) from the ticket office though some employees will be more helpful than others.

SLEEPING & EATING

Besides pricey resort-style (and a few budget) hotels on the road leading up to Qīngchéng Shān's main gate, there are atmospheric temples on the mountain.

Shangqing Temple (上清宫; Shàngqīng Gōng; dm Y50) is a charming wooden building that offers hotel-like facilities. Rooms are basic and clean and have common balconies that look out over the surrounding forests. Its restaurant has a good reputation for quality food.

More restaurants, as well as some snack stands and noodle stops, are scattered along Qīngchéng Shān's trails.

At Qīngchéng Hòushān, there's accommodation in Great Peace Temple (太安阁; Tài'ān Gé) at the mountain's base, or at Youyi Village (友谊村; Yǒuyì Cūn), about halfway up. Dorm beds at both cost around Y20.

GETTING THERE & AWAY

Qīngchéng Shān is some 65km west of Chéngdū. To get there, you have to first travel to Dūjiāngyàn, a town 60km away. At the time of research, construction for the future Chéngdū subway closed the road to Dūjiāngyàn for most of the day. Though there was a one-hour window late in the morning when traffic could head to Dūjiāngyàn, and a one-hour window in midafternoon when traffic could leave Dūjiāngyàn for Chéngdū, these periods were so close together it was impossible to go to Qīngchéng Shān and get back to Chéngdū on the same day. If you are on a tight schedule, ask your accommodation for an update on the construction before heading off.

Buses run to Dūjiāngyàn (Y16, 1½ hours, 7am to 8pm) from Chéngdū's Chadianzi bus station, departing when full, though you should check with your accommodation first on the status of Chéngdū's subway construction and how it's affecting bus service to Dūjiāngyàn. Once you make it to Dūjiāngyàn, it is easy to reach the mountain as numerous minibuses ply the route the rest of the way, stopping first at Qīngchéng Shān (Y4) and then Qīngchéng Hòushān (Y10). The last bus returning to Dūjiāngyàn leaves Qīngchéng Hòushān around 7pm. During the high season there are likely to be buses running directly between Chéngdū's bus stations and Qīngchéng Shān.

Dujiangyan Irrigation Project
都江堰水利工程

The **Dujiangyan Irrigation Project** (Dūjiāngyàn Shuǐlì Gōngchéng; admission Y60; 8am-5pm) is where famed prefect and engineer Li Bing diverted the fast-flowing Min River (Mín Hé) via weirs into irrigation canals in the 3rd century BC. (Chéngdū's riverside parks are actually an extension of the project.) The Min River was subject to flooding at this point, yet when it subsided, droughts could ensue.

Li Bing's idea was to put together an annual maintenance plan to remove silt build-up. Thus the mighty Min was tamed and nary a flood has hit the Chéngdū plain since – a positively Herculean feat, difficult enough to achieve today, let alone then. If it wasn't for Li Bing and his mountain-moving spirit, there would be no Sìchuān as we know it today. Period.

The project is ongoing (and, naturally, modernising); it originally irrigated over a million hectares of land and since 1949 this has expanded to three million hectares. A good overall view of the layout can be gained from **Èrwáng Miào** (Two Kings Temple), which commemorates Li Bing and his son, Er Lang.

This sight gets mixed reviews from travellers: some find the whole thing a waste of time, while others find the historical scope of the project makes it worth the trip. For non-Chinese-speaking people, an English-speaking guide can make all the difference (otherwise you're not looking at much more than coffee-coloured sludge). Occasionally, such guides hang out near the ticket office, or you may consider hooking up with one from Chéngdū, if you can find one that knows their stuff.

GETTING THERE & AWAY

Buses run regularly to Dūjiāngyàn's bus station (in the south of town) from the Chadianzi bus station in Chéngdū (Y18, 1½ hours, 7am to 8pm). Bus 1 runs to the irrigation project from outside the bus station.

The last bus back to Chéngdū leaves around 8pm. There is also a direct bus from Dūjiāngyàn to Wòlóng (Y40.50, 2½ hours) at 8am and 2pm.

At the time of research, construction on the future Chéngdū subway was leaving only a one-hour window late in the morning when traffic could head to Dūjiāngyàn, and a one-hour window in mid afternoon when traffic could return to Chéngdū. Though this may have changed by the time you read this, if you are on a tight schedule, it would be a good idea to check with your accommodation before heading off so you don't get stuck unexpectedly.

Wolong Nature Reserve
卧龙自然保护区

The **Wolong Nature Reserve** (Wòlóng Zìrán Bǎohùqū; admission Y25) is made up of 200,000 hectares of pristine wilderness, set aside by the Chinese government to ensure suitable and protected romping grounds for the Giant Panda.

This UN-designated International Biosphere Reserve is a lovely place for hiking, though trekking here is fairly tough and the trails are faint. Just keep in mind that there's next to no chance you'll see a Giant Panda in the wild here, no matter how long you spend.

For that, head to the park's **Giant Panda Research Centre** (admission Y40; ☻ 8am-6pm), where some 80 pandas have been artificially bred in captivity and live in enclosures. There's a good chance of seeing several baby cubs, no matter what time you visit. You can also visit the nearby **Red-Panda Centre** (Y5), several kilometres further up the mountain, and a **panda museum** (admission Y30; ☻ 8.30am-5pm), with exhibits devoted to the big black-and-white bear-cat as well as some of the reserve's other endangered creatures.

Other animals protected here are the golden monkey, the takin (a big ram-like mammal), deer and snow leopards. The Park Administration Office in Wòlóng village (also called Shawan), at the centre of the reserve, can give information on hiking trails, and researchers at the Conservation Centre (some of whom speak English) are good sources of info on conditions. Be sure to bring your own supplies, including warm clothing.

In spring, the park is closed so that trekkers don't disturb the pandas as they hunt for each other during their mating season. The rainy season is a bad time to be here, as leeches take over the park. Summer is the most popular time to visit. If you can't get to the park, you can check out the utterly cool 'Panda Cam' set up by the reserve on the internet (www.pandaclub.net).

At the Conservation Centre, 6km from Wòlóng village, the **Panda Inn** (☎ 0837-624 3028; fax 0837-624 3014; d Y200) has clean, comfortable doubles with hot showers and heaters. There is also a restaurant in the hotel and barbecue stalls across the road.

GETTING THERE & AWAY

There is usually a bus leaving daily from Chéngdū's Chadianzi bus station to Wòlóng village (Y24, four hours, 11.40am), but at the time of research it wasn't running regularly. If you miss that bus, head over to Dūjiāngyàn from where buses to Wòlóng run twice daily (Y40.50, 2½ hours, 8am and 2pm). If you want to get dropped at the Conservation Centre, rather than Wòlóng village, be sure to tell the bus driver.

Normally, onward buses continue from Wòlóng village over the 4487m Bulangshan Pass to Rìlóng, Xiǎojīn and Dānbà, from where you can catch buses to Kāngdìng. However, bus service along this route was cancelled at the time of research due to ongoing road construction.

LÀNGZHŌNG 阆中

☎ 0817 / pop 112,000

Làngzhōng has Sìchuān's largest grouping of extant traditional architecture and is poised to become a major site as the city develops its old town for tourism.

Located 220km northeast of Chéngdū, Làngzhōng was the capital of Sìchuān for 17 years during the Qing dynasty, and was home to a host of notables throughout history, including astronomer Luo Xiahong, who invented the Chinese calendar.

Don't be put off by the noisy and congested town that greets you when you get off at one of the two bus stations. Just hop in a cab to the old town, where endless photo ops of black-tile roofs, swooping eaves, narrow alleys, flagstone streets and temples atop misty hills across a river await you.

What's so nice about a visit here is that, despite the development, the old town is still inhabited by locals. Vendors weave through the old town's streets hawking fresh bread and vegetables, while school children dash through the alleys, laughing and roughhousing.

Orientation & Information

The town sits on a peninsula surrounded by Jiālíng Hé, and the old town is laid out according to a traditional Tang dynasty plan. Zhangfei Lu is the main artery running roughly north–south through town. At the intersection with Xincun Lu as it heads west, there's a statue memorialising Zhang Fei; the old town is southwest from here.

Banks here don't yet handle travellers cheques or advances on credit cards.

An **internet café** (per hr Y2) is not far from the corner of Dadong Jie and Neidong Jie in the old town.

Sights

There are dozens of sights in Làngzhōng's old town and several more seem to open each year as old houses are renovated and opened to the public, showcasing the town's rich history in advanced learning. Unfortunately, none of

them seem to have English captions so if you don't read Chinese it can be hard to grasp the significance of a lot of what you are seeing. However, as most places are pleasantly set up, it's still fun to flit from one to the other just to soak up the atmosphere. Many people will be happy just wandering the alleys and gaping at the eclectic architecture – a wondrous blend of north China quadrangle and south China garden styles.

Most of the newer sights charge anywhere from Y10 to Y30 entrance fees, however, there are no longer separate entrance fees for the four main sights listed following. Any of these (all open from 8am to 6pm) will sell you a ticket that will get you into all four places for Y50. For more information about sights in the old town, call ☎ 623 8777.

Gòngyuàn (学道街; Xuedao Jie) is the best-preserved imperial examination hall in China. The **Zhang Fei Temple** (张飞庙; Zhāngfēi Miào; Xi Jie; 西街) is the tomb of and shrine to local boy done good Zhang Fei, a respected general during the kingdom of Shu who administered the kingdom from here. Further south is the **Huáguāng Lóu** (华光楼; Huaguang Tower; 大东街; Dadong Jie), with terrific views of the old town's roofs and courtyards, and the nearby **Folk Customs Performance Hall** (民俗博物馆; Mínsú Bówùguǎn; Wumiao Jie; 武庙街), which was being renovated at the time of research.

Across the river to the south and east you can have a grand time exploring. At the foot of Mt Daxiang sits the sedate-looking **Grand Buddha** (大佛寺; Dàfó Sì), one of the largest Buddha statues in Sìchuān. Nearby, among Buddhist statuary, grottoes and caves littering the hillsides, is **No 1 Scholars Cave** (状元洞; Zhuàngyuán Dòng), where two legendary court officials once crammed for their examinations.

Sleeping

Atmospheric accommodation for all budgets is springing up in the old town's historical old houses. All of the following are in Làngzhōng's historical quarter.

Xīnyuè Kèzhàn (欣悦客栈; ☎ 801 6974; 100 Nanjie; 南街100号; s & d with shared bathroom Y40-60) This is a charming mom-and-pop kind of place with small and simple rooms set up around a pretty interior courtyard. Shared bathrooms are basic and clean, but it's the warm and helpful owners that really make this place worth recommending.

Qinjia Courtyard Hotel (秦家大院; Qínjiā Dàyuàn; ☎ 666 4534; 67 Nanjie; 南街67号; r Y100-150) A former government office, this place is both stunning and great value. Rooms are all furnished with some combination of antique-style beds, cabinets and chairs and big modern bathrooms – some even come with charming little sitting rooms. There's no air-con, but rooms have electric blankets. A small restaurant in the middle of the courtyard serves Sìchuān food (dishes Y15 to Y20), and though the atmosphere is intimate, it's geared towards groups rather than individual travellers. No English is spoken here but the owners, though shy, are very welcoming.

Wharf Hotel (水码头客栈; Shuǐ Mǎtou Kèzhàn; ☎ 623 3333; fax 622 5927; 61 Xin Jie; 新街61号; s/d from Y218/288; ☒) If the Qinjia Courtyard Hotel is full, try this place. The rooms don't have as much character, but it's still cosy and atmospheric and is worth it if you can get a discount. Some of the bathrooms are a bit eccentric, however, with Western toilets set smack in the middle of the floor.

Eating & Drinking
As the old town develops for tourism, heaps of restaurants and eateries are springing up here all the time – and the service and welcome in most of them are generally terrific.

One thing you'll notice is the air redolent with essence of vinegar – indeed, everything is pickled here! Famed local fare otherwise includes *zhāngfēi niúròu* (张飞牛肉; local preserved beef) and endless noodle soup variations.

Zhāngfēi Zhuāngyuán (张飞庄园; ☎ 622 9659; 4 Wumiao Lu; 武庙路4号; dishes from Y10) Near the old town gates, this small restaurant is a busy but friendly place. You sit on wooden benches in front of a few long wooden tables. Most people come here for noodles, but the main dishes are equally good. Try the *hóng shāo niúròu* (红烧牛肉; Y12), a delectable mix of beef, potatoes and spicy sauce.

Dàoxiāngcūn Jiǔjiā (稻香村酒家; ☎ 626 6333; Xincun Lu; 新村路; dishes from Y10) The old town has loads of great snacking joints, but this sit-down restaurant with rustic décor, a bit outside the alleys, hearkens back to the old days.

There wasn't a lot going on in the way of nightlife at the time of research, but there is lots of construction in the waterfront area, just south of the Huáguāng Lóu. Some of these little houses getting the once-over look like they are being converted into riverside bars; it would definitely be worth checking out when you are in town to see if they've taken off or not.

Getting There & Away
BUS
The town has two bus stations. The glitzy main one is north of the Zhang Fei statue, but you may be dropped off at the smaller, chaotic one to the south. The main station is more traveller friendly and has the less decrepit buses. It's also the best place to get buses to Chéngdū (Y89.50, five hours, half hourly, 6.30am to 6.30pm). Buses also leave from here for Guǎngyuán (Y41, five to six hours, hourly, 7.30am to 1.30pm, last bus 2pm), from where you have train and bus options towards Xī'ān or west into the rough terrain of northern Sìchuān.

Buses leave Guǎngyuán's station for Làngzhōng on a 'when full' basis from 6am until early evening (Y37 to Y45, four hours). Waits can be long (two hours or more is not unheard of), so it's best to travel between 6am to 9am and noon to 3.30pm when passenger traffic is heaviest. Buy your ticket from window four at the kiosk outside.

GUǍNGYUÁN 广元
☎ 0839 / pop 213,200
The endless low sprawl of this modernising grey city and minor manufacturing centre makes Guǎngyuán a forgettable place. But as it's smack in the middle of the Chéngdū–Xī'ān rail line it's a good jumping off point for some of northeastern Sìchuān's sights. Guǎngyuán is the birthplace of Wu Zetian, China's only female emperor, as well as being on the ancient Shǔdào, or the 'Way to Sìchuān' – which impelled Li Bai (AD 701–762) to brush his famous lines 'The way to Shu is harder than the way to heaven' (to translate it roughly) – sliced right through what is the modern city. These days, Guǎngyuán is famous for having China's largest nuclear weapons-grade plutonium production facility.

Orientation
The city is separated into three chunks, split by Nán Hé (南河) and Jiālíng Jiāng (嘉陵江). The train station and one of the two bus stations sits on the east side of a peninsula formed by the rivers' confluence. Another

bus station is southwest, across a bridge over Nán Hé (any bus from the train station will go there). The main road is Shumen Lu, running through the heart of the city.

Sights

Huangze Temple (皇泽寺; Huángzé Sì; ☎ 360 7017; admission temple Y50, temple & Thousand Buddha Cliff Y65; ⊙ 8am-6.30pm May-Sep, to 6pm Oct-Apr) honours Guǎngyuán-born Wu Zetian (AD 625–705), China's only female emperor. Wu, who ruled during the Tang dynasty from AD 690 until her death, is feted among the temples, pavilions and 1000-odd statues lining Thousand Buddha Cliff on the west bank of the Jiālíng Jiāng.

The exquisite stone carvings, immaculately kept grounds and decent English captions make this a memorable sight, but even so, given that everything can be comfortably seen in under an hour, the ticket price is absolutely insane.

A taxi from the train station to the temple costs Y7.

Sleeping & Eating

Few cheap options (figure Y25 or so for a bed in a common room) exist. Those that do are all in the vicinity of the train station, but it's worth noting that even Chinese visitors on a budget tend to give them a wide berth.

Bāshǔ Bīnguǎn (巴蜀宾馆; ☎ 288 7555; 46 Nanjie; 南街46号; discounted s & d without air-con Y45, with air-con Y65-75) It's about the only cheap hotel in the area and in comparison with what else this town has on offer, this hotel seems nothing short of spectacular. Cosy rooms are spotless, decorated in red and yellow and have simple gleaming bathrooms pumping out reliable hot water. Rack rates run Y140 to Y200, but staff told us the Y45 to Y75 range was pretty much used year-round.

Phoenix Hotel (凤凰大酒店; Fènghuáng Dàjiǔdiàn; ☎ 551 6888; 45 Shumen Beilu Yiduan; 蜀门北路一段 45号; s/d/tr incl breakfast Y200/240/320; ❄) This is a fantastic midrange option, a Y5 cab ride away from the train and bus stations. The decoration is nothing special (standard issue dark wood with white bedding), but everything from the furniture to the carpet to the bathrooms looks like it was done up yesterday. A simple buffet breakfast of rice porridge, egg and vegetables is served from 7am to 9am. Discounts run 25% to 50% off the rack rates.

Lǎo Chéngdū Càiguǎn (老成都菜馆; Jing Xiangzi; 井巷子; dishes Y12-16; ⊙ 10am-10pm) This place is a comfortable pit stop for Sìchuān food. It's right around the corner from the Phoenix Hotel.

Getting There & Away

All trains running between Chéngdū and Xī'ān stop here and are your best option for getting to the latter. Trains to Xī'ān are Y80 and to Chéngdū Y47. Both of Guǎngyuán's bus stations have services to Chéngdū running from 7.40am to 7.20pm (Y98, three to four hours, every 40 minutes or so). From the bus station opposite the train station there is service to Jiǔzhàigōu (Y91, 10 to 12 hours, frequency depends on season), and buses to Xī'ān (Y111, at least six hours) run every 30 to 90 minutes from 7.30am to 5pm. Buses to Làngzhōng leave on a when-full basis between 6am and early evening (Y37 to Y45, four hours). Buses run most frequently from 6am to 9am and noon to 3.30pm.

ZHĀOHUÀ 昭化

If the monotony of grey Guǎngyuán is getting to you, a half-day trip to this pleasant country village makes for a nice change of scene, with its old wooden houses and villagers puttering through the lanes on their way to and from the surrounding fields. The main – and pretty much only – street **Tàishǒu Jiē** (太守街) stretches between famed village gates, fragments of which (they claim) date from the Three Kingdoms era.

Historic buildings are marked with Chinese-only signs, including the old town pharmacy and old town liquor-brewing facility.

To get here, buses (Y9, 40 minutes to one hour) run from Guǎngyuán's southern bus station (not the one at the train station); they leave as they fill up, so you may have a wait. Don't start your trip too late, as return buses taper off in the midafternoon.

ÉMÉI SHĀN 峨眉山

☎ 0833 / elevation 3099m

For many travellers, watching the sun come up at this holy mountain is among their most memorable moments in China and the scenery here has long been considered 'a must' for anyone travelling through Sìchuān.

Along with Pǔtuóshān in Zhèjiāng, Wǔtái Shān in Shānxī and Jiǔhuá Shān in Ānhuī, Éméi Shān is one of China's four famous Buddhist

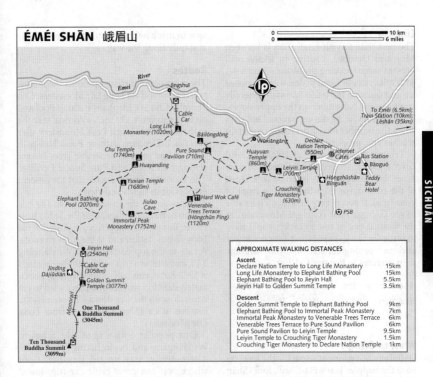

ÉMÉI SHĀN 峨眉山

0 — 10 km
0 — 6 miles

River
Emei Jingshui
Cable Car
Long Life Monastery (1020m) Báilóngdòng
Chu Temple (1740m) Pure Sound Pavilion (710m) Wǔxiāngāng Declare Nation Temple (550m) Internet Cafés Bus Station
Huayanding Huayuan Temple (860m) Bàoguó
Yuxian Temple (1680m) Leiyin Temple (700m) Hóngzhūshān Bīnguǎn Teddy Bear Hotel
Elephant Bathing Pool (2070m) Jiulao Cave Hard Wok Café Crouching Tiger Monastery (630m)
Immortal Peak Monastery (1752m) Venerable Trees Terrace (Hóngchūn Píng) (1120m) PSB

To Éméi (6.5km); Train Station (10km); Lèshān (35km)

Jieyin Hall (2540m)
Jindīng Dàjiūdiàn Cable Car (3058m)
Golden Summit Temple (3077m)
One Thousand Buddha Summit (3045m)
Monorail
Ten Thousand Buddha Summit (3099m)

APPROXIMATE WALKING DISTANCES

Ascent
Declare Nation Temple to Long Life Monastery	15km
Long Life Monastery to Elephant Bathing Pool	15km
Elephant Bathing Pool to Jieyin Hall	5.5km
Jieyin Hall to Golden Summit Temple	3.5km

Descent
Golden Summit Temple to Elephant Bathing Pool	9km
Elephant Bathing Pool to Immortal Peak Monastery	7km
Immortal Peak Monastery to Venerable Trees Terrace	6km
Venerable Trees Terrace to Pure Sound Pavilion	6km
Pure Sound Pavilion to Leiyin Temple	9.5km
Leiyin Temple to Crouching Tiger Monastery	1.5km
Crouching Tiger Monastery to Declare Nation Temple	1km

mountains. Here you'll find lush mountain scenery, plantations of tea trees, scads of temples, and macaques (a type of monkey) famous for harassing hikers for food and relieving them of any object that hasn't been tied down.

On the rare afternoon there is also a phenomenon known as Buddha's Aureole, where rainbow rings, produced by refraction of water particles, attach themselves to a person's shadow in a cloud bank below the summit. Devout Buddhists, thinking this was a call from yonder, used to jump off the Cliff of Self Sacrifice in ecstasy.

Éméi Shān has little of its original temple work left (from 100-odd temples dating from the advent of Buddhism in China). Glittering Jinding Temple (Jīndǐng Sì), with its brass tiling engraved with Tibetan script, was completely gutted by fire. Other temples suffered the same fate, and all were nicked to various degrees by war with the Japanese and Red Guard looting.

However, it's not just the temples that lure people here. The scenery is astounding: fir, pine and cedar trees clothe the slopes, butterflies and azaleas line the paths, while lofty

crags and cloud-kissing precipices beckon in the distance.

A wave of pilgrims and tourists flock here during the peak season, when the number of stalls and hawkers multiply accordingly. However, most of these types of visitors tend to hover around the monasteries, meaning you can still find solitude on the mountain trails.

Along with Lèshān and Jiuzhaigou Nature Reserve, Éméi Shān is on Unesco's list of World Heritage sites.

Tickets

Tickets for Éméi Shān (Y120) include having your mug shot scanned onto the ticket, which is then laminated – a ready-made souvenir. Entry to Declare Nation Temple and Crouching Tiger Monastery at the foot of the mountain do not require this ticket; they have their own admission charges (see p381).

Internet Access

Two large internet cafés are a five-minute walk east of Declare Nation Temple (see p381); the Teddy Bear Hotel (p382) also has internet access.

SÌCHUĀN

Climate

The best time to visit Éméi Shān is between May and October. Visiting in winter will present some trekking problems – iron soles with spikes can be hired to deal with encrusted ice and snow on the trails. Snowfall generally starts around November on the upper slopes. Try to avoid visiting during national holidays when the number of visitors to the mountain reaches epic proportions.

Temperate zones start at 1000m. Cloud cover and mist are prevalent all year round at Éméi Shān and generally interfere with views of the sunrise (or even the hand in front of your face). If you're very lucky, you'll be able to see Gònggā Shān (Gongga Mountain) to the west; if you're not so lucky, you'll have to settle for the less appealing Telecom tower and meteorological station. Some average temperatures in degrees Celsius:

Location	Jan	Apr	Jul	Oct
Éméi town	7	21	26	17
Summit	6	3	12	-1

What to Bring

Definitely not your entire pack – the less you have the happier you will be. Still, Éméi Shān is a tall *and steep* mountain at 3099m, so the weather is uncertain – prepare yourself for sudden changes but don't weigh yourself down. The Teddy Bear Hotel (p382) stores bags for free (other places may levy a small charge).

Monasteries have no heating or insulation, but blankets are provided and some even have (godsend) electric blankets. You can also hire heavy overcoats at the top. Heavy rain can be a problem, as even a light mist can make the slate steps slippery and extremely treacherous. A good pair of rough-soled shoes or boots is a must. Flimsy plastic rainwear is sold on the mountain.

A fixed-length umbrella would be most useful – for the rain, as a walking stick and perhaps as a warning to any brigand monkeys. The Teddy Bear Hotel lends walking sticks out for free. A flashlight is important if you're spending the night or planning to hike at dawn. Food stalls are ubiquitous; nevertheless, extra munchies wouldn't hurt. Finally, don't forget toilet paper.

Travellers have become sick from contaminated water supplies on the mountain, so it's wise to drink only the bottled water available at stands along the way.

Routes

The most popular route up/down the mountain is to ascend via Long Life Monastery, Chu Temple (Chū Sì), Elephant Bathing Pool and on to the summit. On the way down, take the path off towards Magic Peak Monastery after you reach Elephant Bathing Pool. This path will also lead you past Venerable Trees Terrace (Hóngchūn Píng) and Pure Sound Pavilion. The majority of hikers agree that the descent is superior in sights and views.

Buses go up the mountain from the bus station in Bàoguó village, near the Teddy Bear Hotel. Bus routes and prices are posted at the Bàoguó bus station and at the stops en route. A ride to the top costs Y30, to Wǔxiǎngǎng Y10, and a return trip with a number of stops is Y60. Buses run half-hourly from approximately 6am to 5pm, but you don't want to cut it too close on the way down – if you miss the last bus, it's a 15km walk down from Long Life Monastery.

One popular option is to take a bus to Wǔxiǎngǎng and begin hiking from there. Alternatively, stay on till Jìngshuǐ, from where you can get a cable car (up/down/return Y40/30/60, 6am to 6pm) up to Long Life Monastery. From the top of the cable car you can join the route to the summit. Buses run as far up the mountain as Jieyin Hall (接引殿; Jiēyǐn Diàn; two hours), from where it's a steep two-hour hike or five-minute cable car ride (one way/return Y40/70) to the top.

For an epic one-day trek, most hotels can book you on a bus leaving at 3.30am(!), popular with Chinese tourists to 'cheat' and see the sunrise sweatlessly. *But* expect an immense traffic jam at the entrance gate followed by an enormous queue of tourists. Few actually make it in time.

These buses begin to head down from Jieyin Hall around midmorning, stopping at various temples along the way and finally bringing you back to Bàoguó at around 5pm. The round trip costs about Y60 and will probably leave your head spinning.

Duration

Time? Well, you'll be quoted wildly different times by everyone you meet. While you don't require any particular hiking skills, it is a tough climb. It is possible to make it to

MONKEY ETIQUETTE

The monkeys have got it all figured out. If you come across a monkey 'tollgate', the standard procedure is to thrust open palms towards the outlaw to show you have no food. The Chinese find the monkeys an integral part of the Éméi trip and many like to tease them.

The monkey forms an important part of Chinese mythology. There is a saying in Chinese, 'With one monkey in the way, not even 10,000 men can pass', which may be deeper than you think!

Some of these chimps are big, and staying cool when they look like they might make a leap at you is easier said than done. There is much debate as to whether it's better to give them something to eat or to fight them off.

One thing is certain: if you do throw them something, don't be too stingy. They get annoyed very quickly if they think they are being undersold. More than one traveller has told the tragic tale of having their Lonely Planet book ripped to shreds in front of their eyes by an extortive simian.

the summit from Long Life Monastery and back down to Declare Nation Temple in two days, but you must be willing to spend at least 10 hours hiking each day and hope for good weather. The altitude may also play havoc with your breathing and ascending too quickly will only increase this. All up, it's wise to leave yourself three days for the trek.

The approximate distances on the map will give you an idea of what is involved; time yourself on the first kilometre or two and then average out your own probable climbing duration.

Sights
DECLARE NATION TEMPLE 报国寺
Constructed in the 16th century, **Declare Nation Temple** (Bàoguó Sì; admission Y8) features rare plants and a 3.5m-high porcelain Buddha that was made in 1415, which is housed near the Sutra Library.

CROUCHING TIGER MONASTERY 伏虎寺
The renovated **Crouching Tiger Monastery** (Fúhǔ Sì; admission Y10) is hidden deep within the forest. Inside is a 7m-high copper pagoda inscribed with Buddhist images and texts.

PURE SOUND PAVILION 清音阁
Named after the sound effects produced by rapid waters coursing around rock formations, this temple (Qīngyīn Gé) is built on an outcrop in the middle of a fast-flowing stream.

Small pavilions here are great for appreciating the natural music. It's possible to swim here, although the water is only likely to be warm enough during the summer months.

LONG LIFE MONASTERY 万年寺
Reconstructed in the 9th century, **Long Life Monastery** (Wànnián Sì; admission Y10) is the oldest surviving Éméi temple. It's dedicated to the man on the white elephant, the Bodhisattva Puxian, who is the protector of the mountain. This 8.5m-high **statue** is dated from AD 980, cast in copper and bronze and weighs an estimated 62,000kg. If you can manage to rub the elephant's hind leg, good luck will be cast upon you. The statue is housed in Brick Hall, a domed building with small stupas on it and the only building left unharmed in a 1945 fire.

IMMORTAL PEAK MONASTERY 仙峰寺
Somewhat off the beaten track, this monastery (Xiānfēng Sì) is backed by rugged cliffs, surrounded by fantastic scenery and oozing with character. The nearby **Jiulao Cave** (九老洞; Jiǔlǎo Dòng) is inhabited by oversized bats.

ELEPHANT BATHING POOL 洗象池
According to legend, Elephant Bathing Pool (Xǐxiàng Chí) is the spot where Puxian flew his elephant in for a big scrub, but today there's not much of a pool to speak of. Being almost at the crossroads of both major trails, the temple here is something of a hang-out and often crowded with pilgrims.

GOLDEN SUMMIT TEMPLE 金顶寺
This magnificent but clearly recently renovated temple (Jīndǐng Sì) at the Golden Summit (Jīn Dǐng; 3077m) is as far as most hikers make it. Covered with glazed tiles and surrounded by white marble balustrades, the temple now occupies 1695 sq metres. The original temple had a bronze-coated roof,

which is how it got the name Jīn Dǐng (which can also mean 'Gold Top').

It's constantly overrun with tourists, pilgrims and monks, and you'll be continuously bumped and jostled. Sadly, the sun rarely forces its way through the mists up here.

From the Golden Summit it was once common to hike to **Ten Thousand Buddha Summit** (Wànfó Dǐng), but most pilgrims now just take the monorail (a one-hour return ticket costs Y50).

Sleeping & Eating
ON THE MOUNTAIN

The old monasteries offer food, shelter and sights all rolled into one. While some travellers complain about the spartan and somewhat damp conditions, others love what may be as many as a thousand years of character.

A few of the monasteries at key junctions have posted prices, but at others you may well have to bargain with the monks. You can expect to pay between Y20 and Y40 for a bed in a dorm room (the cheapest beds are reserved for pilgrims), with plumbing and electricity provided in those at the higher end of the scale. The following should give you an idea of where to head for the cheapest beds, but expect to pay more in the high season.

Venerable Trees Terrace (洪椿坪; Hóngchūn Píng; dm Y20-30, d Y160) is a good spot, with newer rooms, countless monkeys and fresh landscaping. Other travellers like **Elephant Bathing Pool** (dm from Y20).

Others, including **Declare Nation Temple** (dm from Y20), **Pure Sound Pavilion** (dm Y15-20, d Y150), **Long Life Monastery** (dm Y10-40), **Crouching Tiger Monastery** (dm from Y50), **Golden Summit Temple** (dm Y15-40), Magic Peak Monastery (though some have found the monks here unfriendly hosts) and Leiyin Temple (雷音寺; Léiyīn Sì), have monastery guesthouses. There's also a host of smaller lodgings at Chu Temple (初殿; Chū Diàn), Jieyin Hall, Yuxian Temple (遇仙寺; Yùxiān Sì), Báilóngdòng (白龙洞; White Dragon Cave) and Huayuan Temple (Huáyuán Sì), among others. The smaller places will accept you if the main monasteries are full, often during peak season. Failing those, if night is falling you can kip virtually anywhere, such as in a teahouse or a restaurant. Be prepared to backtrack or advance.

There are also guesthouses and hotels on Éméi Shān, though you can't count on them being open in the off season. They may also give preference to locals over foreigners. On average you can expect to pay between Y150 and Y300 for a room. Most of these guesthouses are clumped behind Golden Summit Temple, to the west. **Jīndǐng Dàjiǔdiàn** (☎ 509 8088, 509 8077; d Y600) is a three-star hotel located at the base of the cable car offering the ultimate luxury: 24-hour hot showers.

Vegetarian meals are included with the price of a bed at many of the monasteries.

Just up from Venerable Trees Terrace, Hard Wok Café is run by a friendly ex-army cook and his wife; find the best coffee on the mountain and fairly decent pancakes (wow!).

Food stalls near the monastery grounds sell biscuits, instant noodles, peanuts and drinks – not to mention a wide variety of fungus. Be wary of teahouses or restaurants serving *shénshuǐ* (神水; divine water), or any tea or food said to possess mystical healing qualities. Miracles are not guaranteed but the price of at least Y10 for the cup of water or tea is.

BÀOGUÓ VILLAGE

Hotels are everywhere on the road leading to the mountain; most are nondescript and overpriced. Have a wander and check out a few options, as prices and room conditions fluctuate.

Teddy Bear Hotel (玩具熊酒店; ☎ 559 0135, 138-9068 1961; www.teddybear.com.cn; dm Y30-35, s & d Y80-150, tr Y180) A long-time backpacker favourite, this is the best place to stay if you are visiting for the first time – and not just because the rooms are spotless. Many of the staff speak English and can tell you anything you want to know about taking on Éméi Shān. Other perks include free laundry, a left-luggage service and a massage when you make it back down the mountain. The café inside is a great place to unwind and swap tall mountain tales.

Hóngzhūshān Bīnguǎn (红珠山宾馆; ☎ 552 5888; d Y580) This hotel has a tranquil setting of lush forests and a view on the edge of a pond, making it worth the splurge for some people.

The street leading up to Declare Nation Temple is lined with restaurants, including *huǒguō* and *shāokǎo* stalls, which begin to appear as evening approaches.

Getting There & Away

Éméi town is the main transport hub for travel to and from the mountain. It lies 6.5km east of Éméi Shān, and 130km southwest of Chéngdū. Buses from Chéngdū's tourist bus station run every 20 minutes to Éméi town (Y33, two hours, 6.40am to 7pm).

BUS
There is no direct public bus between Éméi town and Bàoguó village. If you don't want to catch a taxi (Y20), then take bus 1 from opposite the long-distance bus station (Y0.50). Get off at the first stop, cross the road (past the statue) and then catch bus 5 (Y1) to Bàoguó village.

Heading back to Éméi town, buses leave every 10 minutes from outside Bàoguó's long-distance bus station (Y1, 20 minutes, 7.30am to 7pm). You can also catch a direct bus to Chéngdū (Y36, two hours, hourly from 6.30am to 6pm), Lèshān (Y11, one hour, hourly from 6am to 5pm) and Chóngqìng (Y40, seven hours, 8.30am) from here.

TRAIN
Éméi train station is on the Chéngdū–Kūnmíng line and lies 3.5km from the centre of Éméi town. Bus 4 (Y0.50) runs between the train station and the long-distance bus station. Éméi town has trains to Chéngdū, Kūnmíng and Wūsīhé. A new high-speed train to Chéngdū should be running by the time you read this. The Teddy Bear Hotel can help you out with train times (they change frequently) and booking tickets.

LÈSHĀN 乐山
☎ 0833 / pop 155,930
This small riverside city is home to 'Dàfó', the tallest Buddha in the world and one of Southwest China's most enduringly popular sights.

With new expressways completed, Lèshān is now easily done as a day trip from Chéngdū, though if you want to overnight it there are enough diversions around the city to make it worth your while.

Information
Bank of China (Zhōngguó Yínháng; ☎ 212 5121; Renmin Nanlu) Changes money and travellers cheques and offers cash advances on credit cards. There is also an ATM here.

China Post (Zhōngguó Yóuzhèng; Yutang Jie) Next door is China Telecom where international phone calls can be made.

Internet cafés (wǎngbā; per hr Y2-3) These are scattered throughout downtown (shown on the map).

Mr Yang (☎ 211 2046, 130-3645 6184; richardyangmin@yahoo.com.cn; Yang's Restaurant, 2F,

128 Baita Jie) Has long been the guru of travel information in Lèshān and can organise almost anything (a visit to a local doctor, a local family or nearby villages, calligraphy lessons). One or two travellers have given lukewarm reviews, but the vast majority of feedback has been positive. (That said, the company he is affiliated with in Chóngqìng for Yangzi River cruise tickets has not been so favourably reviewed.) So have a chat with this friendly and interesting character; if you're suspicious, do some homework and see.

People's Hospital (Rénmín Yīyuàn; ☎ 211 9310, after hours emergencies 211 9328; 76 Baita Jie) Has a couple of English-speaking doctors.

Public Security Bureau (PSB; Gōngānjú; ☎ 219 3718; 236 Chunhua Lu; ☒ 9am-noon & 2-6pm Mon-Fri) Two-day visa extensions are typical.

Sights
GRAND BUDDHA 大佛
Carved into a cliff face overlooking the confluence of Dadu River (Dàdù Hé) and Min River (Mín Hé), Grand Buddha (Dàfó) is 71m high, has ears 7m long, insteps 8.5m broad, big toes 8.5m long and fingernails taller than your average human.

A Buddhist monk called Haitong got the ball rolling on the statue's construction in AD 713. He hoped that a giant Buddha would calm the swift currents and protect boatmen from lethal currents in the nearby river hollows.

It worked. During the 90-year construction period, enormous amounts of rock and silt were discarded into the river by sculptors, which ended up filling the river hollows and inadvertently taming the currents. However, for regular folks it's all about the Buddha, and locals still credit his calming influence for taming the waters.

An elaborate water-drainage system is in place inside the sculpture (not visible to travellers, unfortunately) to prevent weathering. It's done a good job on the inside, though on the outside, Dàfó is starting to show his age and soil erosion is an ongoing problem. There was once a building sheltering the statue, but it was destroyed during a Ming dynasty war. Some people think it should be rebuilt; others want to sheath the Buddha in a high-tech plastic bubble.

To really get a sense of the statue's magnitude make sure you visit the platform on top, opposite his head, and then descend the stairway to the feet for the Lilliputian perspective.

THOUSAND BUDDHA CLIFFS 夹江千佛岩

About 30km north of Lèshān and 2.5km west of the train station at Jiājiāng are the **Thousand Buddha Cliffs** (Jiājiāng Qiānfóyán; admission Y35; 8am-5pm). For once, the name is not an exaggeration: over 2400 Buddhas dot the cliffs, dating from as early as the Eastern Han dynasty. The statues show a few signs of wear and tear but, considering their age, are in fairly good condition.

Set in a rather pretty location along a riverbank and on the edge of the countryside, this site takes something of an effort to reach. Catch one of the many buses from Lèshān's central bus station down the bumpy road to Jiājiāng (Y5, one hour). From Jiājiāng bus station, take a pedicab (Y10) or taxi (Y15)

to the site. The last bus returning to Lèshān leaves Jiājiāng at 6pm.

OTHER SIGHTS

The **boardwalk** along Binhe Lu follows the Dadu River from its confluence with the Min River up past Jiāzhōu Bīnguǎn. Popular for strolling in the evenings, if you follow it as far as Jiāzhōu Bīnguǎn, you'll see fan dancers, ballroom dancers and even tango lessons underway in a large square near the intersection with Baita Jie.

Travellers have recommended day trips to villages outside Lèshān, such as **Luóchéng** (罗城), 50km southeast (famed for its old 'boathouse' architecture). Check with Mr Yang.

Tours

Tour boats pass by for panoramic views of the Grand Buddha (hovering in front for about 10 minutes), which reveal two guardians in the cliff side, not visible from land. You currently have a choice of three types of boat from the dockside along Binjiang Lu. Large

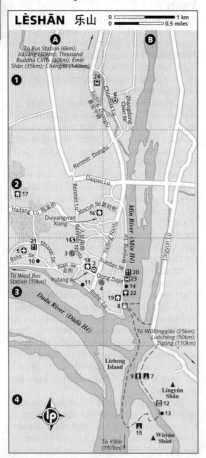

tour boats (Y50; ☻ 7.30am-6.30pm 1 Apr-7 Oct, 8am-5.30pm 8 Oct-31 Mar) and smaller **speedboats** (Y50; ☻ 7.30am-7.30pm) leave regularly throughout the day from the dock near the central bus station.

The third option is to take the bargain ferry (Y3) that leaves from a small dock not far from the Táoyuán Bīnguǎn next to the Sleeping Buddha Tea Pavilion. This cheap option doesn't stop in front of the Buddha but you will still get a good view – you'll just have to be extra quick with your camera. The only drawback is its infrequent departures (every 90 minutes from 7am to 5.30pm April to September, every 90 minutes from 8am to 5pm October to March).

A fun option is the local ferry (Y1) to Lizheng Island, in the middle of the two rivers' confluence. While this doesn't take you to the Buddha itself, it gives you unrivalled views. The ferry leaves regularly throughout the day from Lizheng Gate (look for a stone archway), not far from the Jiāzhōu Bīnguǎn.

The final destination for the boats leaving from the main docks is **Wuyou Temple** (Wūyóu Sì; admission Y10; ☻ 8am-6pm). Like the Grand Buddha, this monastery dates from the Tang dynasty with Ming and Qing renovations. It commands panoramic views and is a museum piece containing calligraphy, painting and artefacts, many with English captions.

Wuyou Temple has a hall of 1000 terracotta *arhat* (Buddhist disciples who have achieved enlightenment) displaying an incredible variety of postures and facial expressions – no two are alike. The *arhat* are housed in the **Luohan Hall**, which dates back to 1909. Inside is also a fantastic statue of **Avalokiteshvara**, the Sanskrit name of the Goddess of Mercy (Guanyin in Chinese).

If you get off the boat at Wuyou Temple, a visit through the temple will take you across Wūyóu Shān and down to a small bridge that crosses over to Língyún Shān (Towering Cloud Hill). Here you can visit **Oriental Buddha Park** (Dōngfāng Fódū Gōngyuán; admission Y40), a newly assembled collection of 3000 Buddha statues and figurines from all around Asia. The park's centrepiece is a 170m-long reclining Buddha, said to be the world's longest. However, this park seems a hasty effort to cash in on Buddha-mania.

Next door is the **Mahaoya Tombs Museum** (Máhàoyámù Bówùguǎn; admission Y5), which has a modest collection of tombs and burial artefacts dating from the Eastern Han dynasty (AD 25–220).

Continuing past the museum and up Língyún Shān brings you to the entrance gate of **Dafo Temple** (Dàfó Sì; admission Y70). This is where you can get right up close to the Grand Buddha, with narrow staircases running head to toe. Avoid visiting on public holidays or weekends, when traffic on the stairs comes to a complete standstill.

To return to Lèshān, you can either catch another boat from the ferry dock near the entrance to the Buddha or take bus 13, which leaves from the same place and will drop you back at Lèshān's dock.

This can take less than 1½ hours from the Lèshān dock, but that's pushing things a lot.

Sleeping

Táoyuán Bīnguǎn (☎ 210 1718; Binjiang Lu; 滨江路; s with shared bathroom Y60, d Y120) Facing the docks, this hotel's location is unbeatable if you want an early morning start to your Grand Buddha visit. Room conditions have deteriorated in recent years, but it's still a backpacker favourite. Tiny shoebox-sized singles are occasionally discounted to Y50, but the shared bathrooms are odorous nightmares. The doubles are OK, but once you've seen the pristine condition of the similarly priced rooms at the Post & Telecommunication Hotel, the prices here will seem outrageous.

Duìyángwān Bīnguǎn (☎ 501 0345; middle section, Duiyangwan Xiang; 兑阳湾巷中段; d Y100-160) Despite having halls resembling corridors in a rickety Chinese hospital, the basic rooms here are OK, though a bit on the damp side. This wouldn't be your first choice, but it's a useful back-up place should other addresses in town be full.

Post & Telecommunication Hotel (Yóudiàn Bīnguǎn; ☎ 211 1788; fax 211 0457; 32 Yutang Jie; 玉堂街32号; r Y138; ☒) The tyranny of basic beige decoration reigns at most Chinese budget hotels, but it was thrown off here during recent renovations and the result is stunning. Rooms have *faux* hardwood floors and neat-as-a-pin modern bathrooms. The white furniture, bedecked with pink or peach upholstery and cushions, won't be everyone's cup of tea, but it certainly makes the rooms bright and cheerful.

Jīnhǎitáng Dàjiǔdiàn (☎ 212 8888, 212 2666; fax 212 2666; 99 Haitang Jie; 海棠街99号; d incl breakfast Y460; ☒) Of the top-end offerings in town, this large, multiwinged hotel is the most successful at delivering clean, comfortable rooms. It's also free of the pervasive dampness present in so many of this town's other hotels. Decoration is humdrum white linen and tired cream-coloured walls, but a discount would definitely make a stay here worth it.

Eating & Drinking

The roads near the docks are the best places to prowl for interesting restaurants and bustling hole-in-the-wall eateries. The western side of Binjiang Lu is particularly good. Another good place to wander is Binhe Lu, where you'll find a handful of teahouses and a number of restaurants.

Yang's Restaurant (Yángjiā Cāntīng; 2F, 128 Baita Jie; 白塔街128号; dishes Y15-25; ☺ 6-9pm) Run by Mr Yang the travel guru (see Information, p383), this restaurant is in the living room of his home. His wife is the chef and serves good local food.

Xībà Dòufu Dàjiǔdiàn (☎ 211 3333; Binjiang Lu; 滨江路; mains Y18-48) For something a little fancy, try this place by the river bank. It's got a large cavernous dining room and specialises in tofu dishes (Y28 to Y48).

For drinks, check out the bar (jiǔbā) just south of where the tour boats leave from. Right on the river, it's got loud music and a lovely outdoor patio. Visit during the warm months – there won't be much going on here otherwise.

Getting There & Away

Expressways link Lèshān to Chéngdū and Chóngqìng; another is being built to Yíbīn.

BUS

Lèshān has two bus stations and both are inconveniently located outside of the downtown core.

You can get onward transport to most places from the long-distance bus station. See the boxed text, below, for bus info. Note that at the time of research, there was no service to Xīchāng in southern Sìchuān from Lèshān. You'll have to head to Chéngdū for onward transport.

If you are coming from Chéngdū, you may be dropped off at the bus station 6km to the north of town. It has daily services to Éméi (Y8, one hour, 7am to 6pm), as well as frequent departures for destinations such as Chéngdū, though these departures are less frequent than those from the long-distance bus station.

There's a third bus station near the downtown docks, but at the time of research it was only being used for tour buses.

TRAIN

No matter that ticket sellers swear blind there is a station here, there simply is no train service to Lèshān. It still means Éméi Shān, or more likely Jiājiāng, both about an hour away by bus. (A new high-speed train is running from Chéngdū to Éméi Shān, but the bus is still faster.)

Getting Around

Buses 1 and 8 run the length of Jiading Lu and connect the pier area with the northern long-distance bus station. Buses run from 6am to 6pm, at roughly 20-minute intervals. Bus 13 runs from Lèshān dock to Wuyou Temple.

Pedicab rides cost from Y2 to Y5. Taxis start at a flat rate of Y3 for the first 3km.

Unfortunately there doesn't seem to be any bicycle hire in Lèshān – or many bicycles at all for that matter. But you probably wouldn't want to take one up and down the stairs at the Grand Buddha anyway.

LÈSHĀN BUS TIMETABLES

Buses from Lèshān's long-distance bus station:

Destination	Price	Duration	Frequency	Departs
Chéngdū	Y39-42	2hr	every 20min	6.30am-7pm
Chóngqìng	Y88	6hr	hourly	8am-5pm
Éméi	Y11	40min	every 15min	7am-6pm
Kāngdìng	Y100	8hr	1 daily	9.30am
Yíbīn	Y59	6hr	5 daily	8.30am-3.10pm
Zìgòng	Y35	5hr	half-hourly	8.40am-5.10pm

WESTERN SÌCHUĀN & THE ROAD TO TIBET

To the north and west of Chéngdū is where green tea becomes butter tea, Confucianism yields to Buddhism and gumdrop hills leap into jagged snow-capped peaks. Much of the area kisses the sky at between 4000m and 5000m high.

To Tibetans and Tibetan-related people (Qiang) this area is part of the province of Kham, which covers the eastern third of the Tibetan plateau. For travellers, it is Tibet sans the 'official' provincial border and all its hassles.

The Sìchuān–Tibet Hwy, begun in 1950 and finished in 1954, is one of the world's highest, roughest, most dangerous and most beautiful roads. It splits into northern and southern routes 70km west of Kāngdìng. As yet, there isn't much in the way of tourist facilities. For more information on Kham visit www.khamaid.org.

Dangers & Annoyances

Towns in these areas experience up to 200 freezing days per year. Summers are blistering by day and the high altitude invites particularly bad sunburn. Lightning storms are frequent from May to October, when cloud cover can shroud the scenic peaks.

If you're planning to attempt to cross into Tibet from Bātáng or Dégé, you may want to reconsider. The Public Security Bureau keeps a close eye on foreigners, and as truck drivers are severely punished for carrying foreigners across the border, they're unlikely to give you a lift. Some travellers have managed to bribe their way in, but at costs that make flying from Chéngdū seem cheap. However, if you're arriving from Tibet into Sìchuān, nobody seems to give a damn.

In 2006 the US State Department was reporting incidents of travellers being physically assaulted by authorities after they were caught attempting to cross into Tibet.

Be forewarned: at the time of writing it was not possible to change money or travellers cheques or to get advances on credit cards in Sìchuān's northwest. The bank in Kāngdìng *sometimes* changes cash and travellers cheques but don't count on it. Better to bring your Renminbi with you.

KĀNGDÌNG (DARDO, DARSEDO) 康定

☎ 0836 / pop 82,000 / elev 2616m

The biggest city in the region, Kāngdìng's core is a mass of busy shopping streets surrounded by eerie, underpopulated clusters of low grey buildings.

Most travellers doing the Tibetan Hwy will need to stay in Kāngdìng at least one night, though there are lots of places to explore in the outlying areas if you want to hang around longer. Kāngdìng is also famous throughout China for a popular love song called the 'Kāngdìng Love Song' that the town's surrounding scenery inspired.

The comma-shaped town is wedged into a deep valley and built up around the confluence of the swift Zheduo and Yala Rivers (known as the Dar and Tse in Tibetan). Gònggā Shān (Gongga Mountain; 7556m) towers nearby.

Kāngdìng has been a trade centre between Chinese and Tibetan cultures for centuries with trading including the exchange of wool, Tibetan herbs and, especially, bricks of tea from Yǎ'ān wrapped in yak hide. It also served as an important staging post on the road to Lhasa, as indeed it still does today.

Kāngdìng was historically the capital city of the local Tibetan kingdom of Chakla (or Chala). It was also later, from 1939 to 1951, the capital of the short-lived province of Xikang, when it was controlled by the opium-dealing warlord Liu Wenhui.

These days, despite being the capital of the Gānzī Tibetan Autonomous Prefecture, Kāngdìng doesn't have much of a Tibetan flavour and is majority Han Chinese.

Information

Agricultural Bank of China (Zhōngguó Nóngyè Yínháng; Xi Dajie; ☼ 9am-5pm Mon-Fri) If its one English-speaking employee is working, this bank will change US dollars, UK pounds and *maybe* travellers cheques. But because it's such a crapshoot, you're better off changing *all* the money you will need before you get to Kāngdìng. No ATMs or credit card advances are available in this city either.

Internet café (wǎngbā; per hr Y2-3; ☼ 8am-midnight) In an alley off Xi Dajie, this internet café has fast connections. You can also get online at Sally's Knapsack Inn (see p389).

Public Security Bureau (PSB; Gōngānjú; ☎ 281 1415; Dongda Xiaojie; ☼ 8.30am-noon & 2.30-5.30pm) Three-to five-day service for visa extensions, but if you sweet-talk *politely*, perhaps the same day.

SÌCHUĀN

Sights

There are several monasteries in and around Kāngdìng. Just behind Black Tent Guesthouse, the quiet **Anjue Temple** (Ānjué Sì; Ngachu Gompa in Tibetan) dates back to 1652 and was built under the direction of the fifth Dalai Lama.

Nanwu Temple (南无寺; Nánwú Sì) belongs to the Gelugpa (Yellow Hat) sect of Tibetan

Buddhism and is the most active monastery in the area with around 80 monks in residence. Set in the south of town on the northern bank of the river, it affords good views of Kāngdìng and the valley. Walk south along the main road, following its bend to the left for 2km. Cross the bridge at the southern end of town and continue on 300m. Next to a walled Han Chinese cemetery is a dirt path that follows a stream uphill to the lamasery.

You can also head up **Pǎomǎ Shān** (跑马山) for excellent views of Kāngdìng, the surrounding mountains and valleys and – if you're lucky – Gònggā Shān. The ascent takes you past oodles of prayer flags, several Buddhist temples and up to a white *chörten* (stupa). You can go up by foot, or on the weathered old cable car (Y30). Take particular care when wandering around Pǎomǎ Shān and try to avoid hiking on your own. A British tourist was murdered here in the spring of 2000 and one or two muggings have been reported.

To reach the hill, bear left at the fork in the road just south of the bus station and walk about 10 minutes until you reach a **monastery** on the left; a stairway leads up the hill from here. A second, more direct route, heads up the hill further south, beginning above the staircase on Dongda Xiaojie.

In the south of town the 400-year-old **Jingang Temple** (金刚寺; Jīngāng Sì) is undergoing renovations. A taxi from the bus station will cost you Y5.

About 5km north of Kāngdìng are the **Erdao Bridge Hot Springs** (二道温泉; Èrdào Wēnquán), where you can have a half-hour bath in slightly egg-smelling, warm, sulphurous water. Take your own towel. You can reach the hot springs by taxi for about Y8.

In town, the **market** (*shìchǎng*) on Dongda Xiaojie is worth a look. On summer evenings, **People's Square** (Rénmín Guǎngchǎng) is filled with dancers boogieing to an eccentric mix of techno and ballroom music.

Festivals & Events

The **Walking Around the Mountain Festival** (Zhuànshān Jié) is the biggest annual celebration in Kāngdìng and one of the best times to visit the city. It takes place on Pǎomǎ Shān on the 8th day of the fourth lunar month to commemorate the birthday of the Historical Buddha, Sakyamuni. During the festival, white-and-blue Tibetan tents cover the hillsides and visitors come from all over western Sìchuān for wrestling, horse racing and the 10-day street fair.

Sleeping

Kāngdìng has a good range of accommodation, including a couple of backpacker-friendly choices.

Black Tent Guesthouse (Gònggāshān Lǚshè; 28 Yanhe Xilu; 沿河西路28号; dm/d Y20/50) By far the most popular place, the atmospheric dorm rooms with wood floors here are cosy. There's one shower and one toilet.

Sally's Knapsack Inn (背包客栈; Bēibāo Kèzhàn; ☎ 283 8377, 130-6007 5296; dm Y20; ☐) Next to Jingang Temple, this laid-back hostel and café has colourful carved wooden beds and the most helpful man in town when it comes to travel info. A taxi from the bus station will cost you Y5.

Qīngyuán Dàjiǔdiàn (☎ 669 9888; Yingbing Dadao; 迎宾大道; d Y380; ✸) Some rooms here are missing lights, electric kettles and room switches. However, once you stumble on an intact room, they're terrific – tremendously comfortable with the works (reliable hot water, heating). Conveniently located right by the bus station, a discounted room may run as low as Y120 to Y150.

Love Song Hotel (Qínggē Dàjiǔdiàn; ☎ 281 3333; fax 281 3111; 156 Dongda Xiaojie; 东大小街156号; d incl breakfast Y580) Service here can be pretty lethargic and dismissive, but the rooms and facilities are the best in town. Discounts are the only real disappointment – even in the low season they aren't substantial. Despite the good condition of the rooms, some travellers may find them overpriced.

Eating

Hotpot is everywhere, as in most Sìchuān tourist towns.

Nine Bowls Vegetable of Country (Jiǔwǎn Nóngjiā Xiāng; ☎ 287 5199; Yanhe Xilu; 沿河西路; dishes from Y5; ⊙ 11am-9pm) You can't miss this cubbyhole place – the sign next door says 'Chóngqìng Strange Taste Fish'! The exceedingly friendly staff is overseen by an equally hospitable manager who speaks decent English. It also has an English menu.

Droma Yudia-Khampa Tibetan Eatery (☎ 282 3463; Xinshi Qianjie; 新市前街; dishes from Y10; ⊙ 9am-9pm) This newer place has a large, warm dining room and comfy seating, and a huge menu of local, Nepali and Western food and even breakfast (though they seem to rise late around here).

Hóngkāng Fàndiàn (☎ 283 5101; 14 Xi Dajie; 西大街14号; dishes Y12-18; ⊙ 9am-10pm) Outstanding Sìchuān food is served in this modest but spotless restaurant – you really can order just about anything off the menu here and not be disappointed. The small dining room is filled with dark wood chairs and tables decked with cheery blue-and-white checked tablecloths. The waiters aren't very friendly, but they're still among the most attentive and professional in town. You'll never have to lift a finger for so much as a tea refill or dropped napkin.

Near the bus station and market are *bāozi* (steamed stuffed buns; 包子) places, great for snacks to take on bus journeys. In the evening, numerous covered stalls set up camp at the northern end of town with arguably the widest selection of skewered meat, veggies and fish in Sìchuān.

Drinking

Tibetan dance halls are the place to go for a night out in Kāngdìng and they make for a very entertaining evening. Traditional Tibetan and Chinese songs, including the famous Kāngdìng Love Song, are performed to ear-splitting techno beats and a very appreciative audience. Try the **Kangba Dancehall** (Kāngbā Dàwǔtái; ☎ 669 3255; Xidakai Lu; 西大开路; drinks from Y20), where you can get up and dance once the performances are finished.

Getting There & Away

An airport is being built on the way to Tǎgōng; it's slated for completion in 2009.

BUS

Improved roads have made Kāngdìng far more accessible. The bus station is in the northeast of town.

If heading south, check whether roadwork near Xīchāng has been completed or not. At the time or research, delays caused by construction on this route were increasing travel times well over the usual seven hours.

See the boxed text, p390, for bus details.

TAXI

Taxis congregate on Xinshi Qianjie, not far from the Chángchéng Bīnguǎn. Trips to Lúdìng cost around Y20.

SÌCHUĀN

KĀNGDÌNG BUS TIMETABLES

Buses from Kāngdìng:

Destination	Price	Duration	Frequency	Departs
Bātáng	Y138	2 days	daily	6.30am
Chéngdū	Y105-117	8hr	half-hourly	6am-5pm
Dānbā	Y43	4hr	daily	7am
Dégé	Y166	24hr	daily	7.30am
Gānzī	Y107	12hr	daily	6.15am
Lèshān	Y72-89	8hr	daily	7am
Lǐtáng	Y80	7hr	daily	6.45am
Tǎgōng	Y33	4hr	daily	6am
Xiāngchéng	Y140	14hr	daily	6am
Xīchāng	Y90	7hr	daily	6am

AROUND KĀNGDÌNG

Mugecuo Lake 木格措湖

There are several mountain lakes and hot springs in the vicinity of Kāngdìng. Lying 21km to the north of town up the Yala Valley, Mugecuo Lake (Mùgécuò Hú) is one of the highest lakes in northwestern Sìchuān at 3700m. Locals boast that it's one of the most beautiful.

Trails around it lead to other smaller lakes such as **Hóng Hǎi** (Red Sea). Also worth checking out is **Qīsè Hǎi** (Seven Colour Lake), which lies a few kilometres before Mùgécuò. It's best not to wander around these parts alone or to stray too far off the path. The area of 'Wild Men's Lake', as Mùgécuò means in Tibetan, is home to wolves and other wild beasts.

There's no public transport to the lake. You'll need to negotiate transport with a taxi or minivan. Prices vary wildly depending on the number of passengers and how long you want to stay. Taxis start at Y200 to Y300. It takes 1½ hours to get to the lake.

Mùgécuò is best done as a day trip from Kāndìng.

Gongga Monastery 贡嘎寺

This monastery (Gònggā – or Konka or Kongkar – Gompa) is situated at the western foot of Gònggā Shān, a mountain increasingly popular with hardcore, experienced mountain climbers.

The monastery was ravaged during the Cultural Revolution but is currently enjoying something of a revival. It is of the Kagyu sect of Tibetan Buddhism and forms part of a pilgrimage route around the holy Minya Konka, the local Tibetan name for Gònggā Shān. The monastery is very remote and can only be reached on foot or with a 4WD.

This trip is difficult but not impossible to do on your own. You first need to get yourself to the trailhead at Liùbā (六巴), a small village. There is no bus service to Liùbā but you may be able to get one heading for Jiǔlóng (九龙). This will take you to the crossroads leading to Liùbā from where you'll have to walk or hitch the remaining 10km. From Liùbā you can hitch or trek the 25 or so kilometres to Yùlóngxī (玉龙溪), where you may be able to arrange accommodation. From here you will have to trek over into the Moxi Valley (磨西山谷; Móxī Shāngǔ), where the monastery is situated.

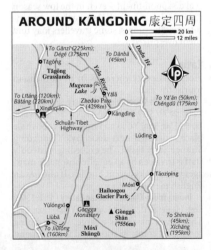

You may be able to stay in the monastery, from where you could do any number of day hikes up and down the Moxi Valley, before retracing your steps back to Kāngdìng. A more difficult option involves following the Moxi Valley downstream (eastwards) for around 60km until you reach the main Lúdìng–Shímián road, where you can flag down a bus.

This is a wild, difficult and untouristed route. Only experienced hikers should attempt it with sufficient food, a tent and warm clothes.

LÚDÌNG 泸定
☎ 0836 / elev 1310m

Lúdìng is a small, bustling town about halfway between Kāngdìng and Móxī. You wouldn't make a point of coming here, but as it's a minor connection point for buses between western Sìchuān and Chéngdū, Lèshān and Móxī, you may end up here all the same.

The only sight is the **Luding Bridge** (泸定桥; Lúdìng Qiáo; admission Y10), a 100m-long chain suspension bridge over the Dadu River (Dàdù Hé), famous throughout China as the site of one of the most famous episodes of the Long March. It's said that 20 communist troops, armed with grenades, supposedly crossed the bridge hand over hand after finding the Kuomintang troops had pulled the planks off the bottom of the structure. There's increasing doubt, however, whether this event actually took place.

The bridge is five minutes' walk from the bus station. Just follow the river into town and you'll find it. There's also a small museum here commemorating the Long Marchers.

Sleeping & Eating
The hotel situation in Lúdìng is good unless you're on a budget; for cheaper digs head for Móxī or Kāngdìng.

Chēzhàn Lǚguǎn (车站旅馆; Bus Station Hostel; ☎ 139-9048 9606; dm Y20, d/tr Y30/60) This hostel is one of the few cheap but decent options.

Lúdìng Qiáo Bīnguǎn (泸定桥宾馆; ☎ 312 8888; d Y480) Across the river from the bus station in the new area of town, this hotel is a good midrange option where you can often get 50% discounts on rooms. It's the building with the large green dome on the roof.

Clustered around the bus station are a number of nondescript restaurants as well as a teahouse, where you can while away your time until the next bus pulls into town.

Getting There & Away
From Lúdìng there are daily buses to Chéngdū (Y92 to Y98, six hours, 6.30am, 10am and 1pm) and Shímián (Y20, three hours, 6am and noon). Minibuses run regularly to Kāndìng (Y20) and Móxī (Y20).

A second route between Éméi Shān and Lúdìng, without doubling back to Chéngdū, runs via Wūsīhé to the south. There is usually one morning bus at 6am from Lúdìng to Wūsīhé (Y20), but if it doesn't appear, jump on the bus to Shímián from where there is frequent onward transport. Once you reach Wūsīhé you'll need to hop on a train to Éméi town. The train departs Wūsīhé in the afternoon, so you shouldn't have to stay overnight here. If you're headed south to Pānzhīhūa or Kūnmíng, you can only buy hard-seat tickets in Wūsīhé and few onward trains stop here.

MÓXĪ 磨西
☎ 0836 / pop 6,000

Móxī, the gateway to Hailuogou Glacier Park (see p392), is nestled in some delicious mountain scenery around 50km southwest of Lúdìng. The village itself isn't much but is pleasant to wander around for an hour or two. Locals are mainly Han Chinese or Tibetan.

Sights
Móxī's older, traditional wooden buildings are at the bottom of the village. Also at this end is a multicoloured **Catholic church** (天主教堂; Tiānzhǔ jiàotáng; admission Y3) where Mao camped out during the Long March. It's open to the public and you will be given an obligatory tour by the old men who look after the place. From here, the village climbs its way up a hill. If you follow the dirt road up, about 200m past the main crossroads on the right is **Guānyīn Gǔ Gompa** (观音古寺), a 400-year-old Bön (Tibetan Buddhist sect) temple that is run by some delightful old women. In the courtyard is a mammoth, gnarled tree around which the temple has been built. Across the road from the temple is a small **pagoda** (塔), from where you can get a view of the surrounding scenery.

Sleeping & Eating
Móxī has plenty of accommodation.

Bīngchuān Fàndiàn (冰川饭店; dm Y25, d Y60) Opposite the entrance to the church, this place has what may be the best glacier views in town. It's also a good choice because staff here are used to dealing with foreigners.

Hǎiluó Fàndiàn (海螺饭店; ☎ 326 6297; d Y80; 🅿) Up the road from the Bīngchuān Fàndiàn, this place has generic budget rooms, but is known for the magnificent views from its rooftop terrace.

There are a number of restaurants, barbecue stalls and hotpot places along the main road and the road leading to the glacier park entrance. Check prices before ordering.

Móxī's shops and fruit stands are well stocked if you need to buy some supplies for a trip to Hǎiluógōu.

Getting There & Away

Most visitors to Móxī arrive on a tour bus. Basically the transport system here entails prowling the village for the inevitable jumble of minibuses and motorbikes, then sorting out prices and drop-offs with the drivers and your fellow commuters.

Most locals scoot around on motorbikes or catch a ride to Lúdìng (Y20) in one of the minibuses that circulate between the two towns. These leave from the crossroads at the top end of town.

There is supposedly a 7am bus to Lúdìng (Y15, two hours), but don't count on it. Ditto Chéngdū (Y95, eight hours, 8.30am). The owner of the Bīngchuān Fàndiàn will be able to help you out with transport. Change at Lúdìng for Chéngdū and Kāngdìng. If you're headed to Shímián, get off the bus at Māozìpíng, on the other side of the bright-orange Rainbow Bridge. From here you can flag down a southbound bus.

To reach Móxī, get off your bus in Lúdìng, from where you can grab a minibus to Móxī (Y20). Travelling from the south via Shímián, get off at Māozìpíng and flag down a minicab to Móxī from there. If you're coming from Yǎ'ān, get the driver to let you off at Gāngǔdì (干谷地), from where you can get a taxi (Y20, one hour).

HAILUOGOU GLACIER PARK 海螺沟冰川公园

Hailuogou Glacier slides – literally – off the eastern slopes of Gònggā Shān to form the lowest glacier in Asia. **No 1 Glacier** (一号冰川; Yīhào Bīngchuān), the main glacier, is 14km long and covers an area of 16 sq km. It's relatively young as glaciers go: around 1600 years old. The top of Hailuogou can offer incredible vistas of Gònggā Shān and the surrounding peaks, all above 6000m, but how much you actually see is entirely up to Mother Nature. Constantly framed with a backdrop of snowy peaks, the surrounding forests are also beautiful, their ecosystems changing as you ascend the mountain.

The entrance to **Hailuogou Glacier Park** (Hǎiluógōu Bīngchuān Gōngyuán; admission Y140) lies in Móxī. The park was once a popular choice for trekking and camping; it used to be possible to ascend the entire mountain by foot or pony, but as the sight has become more commercial this is no longer the case. Nowadays, travellers must take a minibus from the park entrance along a paved road up to **Belvedere** (观景台; Guānjǐngtái), 3km above Camp No 3, via Camps No 1 and 2. From Belvedere the tour groups tend to continue their ascent to the base of No 1 Glacier via cable car (Y160, 8.30am to 4pm).

It is still possible to trek from Belvedere and it's a one- to two-hour walk up to No 1 Glacier. While not a tough climb, the walk is made more difficult as the path has been largely neglected and so at times is hard to follow. On a clear day, however, there are some beautiful views to be had and the trail passes through some lovely forest. En route to the base is the **Waterfall Viewing Platform** (冰川观景台; Bīngchuān Guānjǐngtái) at 3000m. From here you can see the main glacier tongue, plus **No 2 Glacier** (二号冰川; Èrhào Bīngchuān) and **Golden Peak** (金银峰; Jīnyínfēng) at 6368m.

The entrance fee to the park includes a guide, compulsory for all tourists going out on the glacier and handy for keeping you away from deep crevices and melting points. Guides meet you at the base of No 1 Glacier and take you on a 30-minute tour of the glacier, after which you are free to go off and explore.

The park's development means this is no longer the nature getaway it once was. But if your main interest is seeing and even walking across a glacier, then the park is still worth a visit. Come prepared with warm clothes and sunglasses. You'll also need to bring food and water, as you might not find much to buy en route until you reach Camp No 3 and its pricey restaurants. On maps of the park, marked trails may be less than accurate and some may have disappeared.

The rainy season for this area spans July and August, although the locals say they get 200 days of rain a year. (Some travellers who've been here during these summer months are emphatic that it wasn't worth it.) The best time to visit is between late September and November, when skies are generally clear. Autumn colours are particularly beautiful at this time, though it can be cold up at Camp No 3.

Sleeping & Eating

Accommodation options in the park tend to fall into one category: old and overpriced.

Camp No 1 (一号营地; Yīhào Yíngdì; dm Y150) At 1940m, this spot still offers budget dorm beds but conditions are damp and dirty.

Camp No 2 (二号营地; Èrhào Yíngdì; dm Y150) Sitting at 2620m, No 2 has cramped, expensive dorm rooms, although the price does include a dip into the hot springs.

Camp No 3 (三号营地; Sānhào Yíngdì) is the highest camp at 2940m and offers two resort-style hotels. The huge **Jīnshān Fàndiàn** (金山饭店; Golden Mountain Hotel; ☎ 326 6433; r Y160-180) and the new **Jīnshān Dàjiǔdiàn** (金山大酒店; Golden Mountain Grand Hotel; ☎ 326 6383; d Y580) sit side by side and offer the best – and most expensive – accommodation within the park.

The park authorities frown upon camping; in any case there isn't a great deal in the way of flat ground on the way up.

The camps sell some food and drinks, although, out of season, you can only count on this at Camp No 3. Mineral water, soft drinks, beer and instant noodles are usually available at high prices.

Getting There & Away

Turn left at the main crossroads at the top of the hill in Móxī and carry on to the ticket office, about 400m up the road. Móxī itself can be reached by minibus from Lúdìng (see Getting There & Away, opposite, for details).

Minibuses (Y50 return, one hour) start running up the mountain from the park entrance gate at 7.30am and leave as soon as they have more than one passenger. The last bus leaves Belvedere around 7pm and stops at all three camps on the way down.

SÌCHUĀN–TIBET HIGHWAY (NORTHERN ROUTE)

For many, this stretch of the Tibetan Hwy is by far the most thrilling and awe-inspiring. Some 300km longer than the southern route, it crosses Chola Mountain, the highest pass this side of Lhasa. The views are jaw-dropping, the landscape rugged and the cliff-hugging roads are guaranteed to keep your adrenaline pumping for the duration of your journey.

The opportunities for independent exploration are endless. Besides the places listed in this section, almost every major town along this route has an interesting monastery set amongst stunning scenery. Few people make it up this way and you could easily spend a couple of weeks just hopping on and off buses, discovering it all for yourself.

Some of the highway's highlights include the increasingly popular Tagong Grasslands (below), or, for a small detour just off this route, you could head to the splendid little town of Dānbā with its fabulous Qiang watchtowers.

The highway ultimately leads to the border town of Dégé, with its internationally revered printing monastery. It also takes you to the north where it is possible to work your way up to Qīnghǎi province via Sêrxu.

Come prepared with warm clothing. Remember that bus services can be erratic – this is no place to be if you're in a hurry. It's also not possible to change money or travellers cheques, so load up with dosh before you come.

Tagong Grasslands 塔公草原

A trip to the Tagong Grasslands (Tǎgōng Cǎoyuán) will give you a glimpse of remote Tibetan life and some off-the-beaten-track trekking options.

The base for visitors to this area is Tǎgōng town, a small place with a real Tibetan flavour. Some travellers arrange horse treks here, though many just hang out and wander the countryside longer than they'd planned.

The best time to visit is from the beginning of June through to the end of September. There's not much going on during the cold, snowy, off-season months when the area can seem pretty dead. During this period the long slog to get here doesn't seem worth it.

About the only thing to visit in town is the **Tagong Temple** (塔公寺; Tǎgōng Sì; admission Y10). It dates back to the Qing dynasty and blends Han Chinese and Tibetan design elements.

The town is well known for its annual **horse racing festival** (sàimǎhuì), which features thousands of local Tibetan herdsmen along with Tibetan opera and dance performances. It takes place during the eighth lunar month, usually falling in July or August.

SÌCHUĀN

THE TIBETANS

Population: 4.6 million in China and one million in China's Southwest
Location: Western Sìchuān (Gānzī and Ābà Autonomous Prefectures and Mùlǐ Autonomous County); northwestern Sìchuān (Zhōngdiàn and Déqīn Counties); northwest Yúnnán (Déqīn Prefecture)

Western Sìchuān and the extreme northwest of Yúnnán were once part of the Tibetan province of Kham and remain distinctly Tibetan to this day, despite large-scale Han Chinese immigration. Almost the entire region is comprised of Tibetan Autonomous Prefectures, the largest of which centre upon the Ābà, Gānzī, Déqīn and Mùlǐ regions. The grasslands of the extreme northwest of Sìchuān once formed part of the Tibetan region of Amdo, (in)famous for its bandits and caravan-raiders.

Khamba men are seen swaggering along the streets of most settlements west of Kāndìng. Most wear a *chuba* (Tibetan cloak), normally lined with sheepskin and properly worn hanging off the right shoulder. Many wear broad-rimmed cowboy hats (fur-lined hats in winter) and big boots, sporting at least one gold tooth, an amulet around their neck and a knife by their side. Women traditionally wear elaborate coral and amber jewellery and arrange their hair into 108 braids.

Khambas are known as the most religious and warlike of all Tibetans and were depicted by most early travellers as either saints or murderers. In 1959 the region around Lǐtáng saw the fiercest guerrilla resistance to the encroaching Chinese troops and many rebels fled to India and Nepal to organise armed resistance from Mustang (with CIA assistance).

Almost all Tibetans are Buddhists, though northwestern Sìchuān is also a strong centre of Bön, the indigenous pre-Buddhist faith of Tibet. Bön blends the shamanistic spirit worship of rivers, mountains and trees with a veneer of Tibetan Buddhism (which itself has been influenced by the Bön pantheon of gods). Followers of Bön are most easily recognised by the fact that they walk *koras* (pilgrim circuits) and rotate prayer wheels anticlockwise, as opposed to Buddhists who do these things clockwise.

The most famous Tibetan Buddhist monastery in the region is the printing college of Dégé. Many others were destroyed in the 1959 rebellion or during the Cultural Revolution. As you travel through Tibetan territory, you'll see plenty of *chörtens* (Tibetan stupas) and prayer flags adorning the countryside.

Some Tibetan foods you might taste in the region include *tsampa* (roast barley), *momos* (dumplings) and *thugpa* (noodles). Tibetan drinks include yak butter tea and *chang* (Tibetan barley beer).

Lhasa dialect is about as close as you'll come to a lingua franca among the various Kham communities. In western and northern Sìchuān, however, few regular Tibetans, other than monks or the educated, can understand or speak it. Tibetan dialects differ so much from town to town that two Tibetan people living as little as 200km away from each other often have to switch to speaking Chinese in order to communicate.

Basic Tibetan Phrases

Hello.	tashi delek
Thanks.	tujay chay
Goodbye. (if you are leaving)	kaliy shu
Goodbye. (if someone else is leaving)	kaliy pay
What is your name?	kayrang gi mingla karay ray?
My name is…	ngay mingla…ray
I am from (America)	nga (Arig) nay yin
…Australia	…ositaliya
…England	…injiy lungpa
Where is…?	…kaba du?
straight ahead	shar gya
right side	yay chola
left side	yon chola
far	tha ringpo
monastery	gompa
shrine	lhakhang
beautiful	nying-jepo
good	yakpo
boiled water	chu khoma
I don't understand.	ha ko masong

For a comprehensive guide to the Tibetan language, refer to Lonely Planet's *Tibetan Phrasebook*.

There are tons of guesthouses around, but don't expect them all to be open if you show up in the off-season. Wherever you go, prices are fairly uniform: dorms average Y15, rooms with shared bathrooms are around Y60 and rooms with private bathrooms cost around Y100.

Top of the heap is the great **Snowland Guesthouse** (雪城旅社; Xuéchéng Lǚshè; ☎ 286 6098; dm Y25), right next to Tagong Temple. It's got wooden everything and rigid but comfy beds; best are the thick blankets. The shower and facilities are clean.

Sally's Kham Restaurant (康巴餐厅; Kāngbā Cāntīng; ☎ 139-9045 4752; tagongsally@yahoo.com; 🖳) is a goldmine for travellers. It serves Tibetan, Chinese and Western food and has internet access, CD burning, a bakery, and bicycle and sleeping bag rental. Sally speaks English, is about the best source of local travel information and can arrange one- or two-day horse treks for two people or more (Y100 to Y120 per person per day).

One morning bus to Tǎgōng village (on its way to Dàofú) runs daily from Kāngdìng (Y40, four hours, 6am) and drops you outside the temple. During the horse racing festival buses are likely to be more frequent. If you're heading to Gānzī, you can pick up the same bus the next day at about 10am as it passes through town. To Dānbā you'll likely have to take a minivan to Bāměi (Y10, one hour), then another to Dānbā (Y25, two to three hours).

Returning to Kāngdìng, afternoon buses can be flagged down as they pass through Tǎgōng town. You can also catch a minibus on the main street that will take you to Yǎjiāng, from where there are buses to Chéngdū or Lǐtáng.

Dānbā (Lome Dhamkho) 丹巴

☎ 0836 / pop 58,200 / elev 1800m

The area around Dānbā has got to be one of the jewels of western Sìchuān. Set in a gorge, the town is built up along the banks of the Dadu River (Dàdù Hé). Though there's not much to see in the town itself, something about its small compact size and the big roar of the river makes it impossibly charming.

Though technically not on the Sìchuān–Tibet Hwy, Dānbā is nonetheless a good place to take a brief detour – the low elevation means it's unusually warm, a virtual paradise if you have just made your way down from the freezing mountains further west.

Numerous Tibetan and Qiang villages perch in the hills and cliffs in the surrounding countryside along with dozens of ancient stone Qiang watchtowers. With so much to explore, it's ridiculously easy to lose track of time here. Also keep an eye out for families of roly-poly monkeys ambling across villages and (increasingly) the main roads.

There are heaps of places to visit besides what's listed following – though if you don't speak Chinese, it may be difficult to find out about them once you're here. If you're coming from Chéngdū, travellers have been particularly satisfied with the suggestions they've gotten at Sim's Cozy Guesthouse (see p364) for exploring the region.

ORIENTATION & INFORMATION

The narrow town meanders from east to west along the river; the only main road is Sanchahe Lu, paralleling the river. The bus station is in the far west end. Upward (literally) from here you'll find the post office (邮局; yóujú) and **Public Security Bureau** (PSB; 公安局; Gōnganjú; ☎ 353 3710) in the maze of alleys. Continuing on you'll eventually run into a pedestrian street of shops and bakeries. There's an **internet café** (网吧; wǎngbā; per hr Y2) on Guangming Lu (光明路), but it, like the others in town, seem to have the slowest internet connections in all of Sìchuān.

SLEEPING & EATING

There's accommodation for every budget in town.

Xiàngzi Jiǔlóu (巷子酒楼; ☎ 352 3655; 98 Tuanjie Jie; 团结街98号; dm from Y20) Down a dark, body-width-narrow lane, this is a gritty Chinese budget hotel with a slightly rank communal Chinese toilet that's nonetheless pretty cute (the hotel, that is, not the toilet). Flights of narrow steep stairs lead up to the rooms – which are cramped and a little damp but very clean – and a greenhouse-like, glassed-in sitting area with a view of the river. They say they have 24-hour hot water, but water pressure can be so weak it's hard to know one way or the other.

Old Castle Hotel (古堡大酒店; Gǔbǎo Dàjiǔdiàn; ☎ 352 2999; 43 Guangming Lu; 光明路43号; s/d/tr Y680/580/680; ❄) This place has heat, endless hot water, shower pressure that could put out a fire and the most comfortable rooms in town, which may be discounted as low as Y150 if you're lucky.

QIANG WATCHTOWERS & CULTURE

The striking Qiang watchtowers are this area's trademark and many in the Dānbā region are between 800 and 1000 years old. Over 3000 watchtowers were built between the Ming and mid-Qing dynasties alone and 562 from this period are still standing today. The watchtowers come in all sizes depending on their primary use.

Family-built watchtowers averaged between 20m and 30m in height and were mainly used for storing agricultural produce or protecting valuables. Village watchtowers, however, soared as high as 60m. Though occasionally used as places of worship, they mostly served political purposes – protecting Qiang settlements during war, staking out village borders or operating as checkpoints. Fires lit on the towers' rooftops would have warned surrounding villages of impending attack.

Tower entrances are typically up to 10m above the ground, reachable only by ladder that can then be pulled inside preventing access to others.

While the interior of the watchtowers is always rounded, the outside can have anything from four to 13 corners. It's said the only surviving 13-corner watchtower in the Dānbā area is in Pujiadong village.

The Qiang themselves are a small ethnic group that derive their name from a 2000-year-old kingdom ruled by a tribe that is said to have been the progenitor of both the Qiang and Tibetan people. These days, the Qiang and Tibetans live in close proximity in the valleys of northwestern Sìchuān and there are many ethnological and linguistic links between them.

Qiang women wear dresses slit down the sides over blue trousers. Over the top of this, work aprons and black waistcoats are worn. Most women wear black or white turbans and as much silver and amber jewellery as they can afford.

Like their Tibetan cousins, Qiang houses are three-storey constructions. The bottom floor is for livestock, the middle floor for living quarters and the top floor is for storing grain and drying crops. The sharp corners of these fortress-like houses are lined with whitewash and the window frames are painted in bright colours. The sombre stone walls are often lined with bright yellow maize, red chillies and green lucerne drying over the upper balconies.

There are lots of places to eat in Dānbā, but the food is unremarkable with the exception of the dumplings served at **Suíbiàn Xiǎochī** (随便小吃; Tuanjie Jie; 团结街; per bowl Y5), which are terrific. You'll find it roughly at the midpoint between the China Post and PSB.

Wherever you eat, double-check prices, especially around the bus station. Some places charge foreigners over three times the price they charge locals.

GETTING THERE & AWAY

Buses run daily to Kāngdìng (Y42, four hours, 6.30am and 3.30pm), Tǎgōng (Y34, 7.30am), Gānzī (Y92, 7am) and Mǎ'ěrkāng (Y41, 5½ to six hours, 7.30am).

The road between Dānbā and Chéngdū (via Wòlóng) is under construction through to 2008 so the daily bus to Chéngdū (Y92, 6.30am) is sometimes cancelled. Even if it is running during this period, prepare yourself for epic delays running several hours.

Wherever you're travelling to, bus drivers won't go if passenger loads are low. Instead, you'll be passed off to private minivan drivers,

who may then troll maddeningly for more passengers. If you're heading for Kāngdìng you can negotiate with clusters of these drivers at the east end of town; to head towards Tǎgōng, go to the west end.

Around Dānbā

Dozens of Tibetan villages dot the countryside around Dānbā. Some are already very popular with Chinese travellers and quite developed for tourism. Yet all you really have to do is trek out into the surrounding countryside, clamber up some hills and do some solo exploring to get away from it all.

It's possible to stay with locals in most villages. The usual rate is Y50 for one night's accommodation, dinner and breakfast.

If you can arrange it, visit in autumn, when the scenery, a riot of colours, is downright inspirational.

ZHŌNGLÙ ZÀNGZHÀI DIĀOQÚN GÙYÍZHǏ
中路藏寨碉群古遗址

The grey boxlike building near this village's entrance seems sorely out of place amongst the rolling hills and crumbling watchtowers. Once you get past that, however, this village is a pleasant surprise. It's a little more unspoilt and rough around the edges than the popular Jiǎjū Zàngzhài. Short winding trails are bordered by low stone walls, and further on sumptuous scenery promises wonderful walks. A Y15 to Y20 entrance fee is inconsistently collected from visitors.

About 11km from Dānbā, you may be able to negotiate a round-trip taxi ride here for about Y20.

JIǍJŪ ZÀNGZHÀI 甲居藏寨
Proclaimed 'Best Village in China' in 2005 by the Chinese *National Geographic*, this is one of the most visited places in the Dānbā region and is truly worthy of the accolades. Once your vehicle has inched its way up the narrow sliver of cliff-clinging earth posing as a road, the village folds out before you, with clusters of houses tucked into rolling hills.

Home to 150 families, some may find Jiǎjū Zàngzhài a little too slick (tourist money has fixed this place up big time), but the setting is undeniably gorgeous and keen walkers will have a field day exploring the terrain around the village.

There's a small **hotel** (☎ 137-7839 7868, 898 3198) and restaurant in the village, though it's not necessarily open year-round so call first.

Seven kilometres from Dānbā, you can negotiate a round-trip here with taxi drivers for around Y20.

SHUǏQIǍZI CŪN 水卡子村
This village is worth a visit for its exquisite scenery as well as its tiny **selugupa monastery** (Gyalya Yudhom Darjelling Ghen), home to 20 monks and one of the rare temples you'll see in western Sìchuān from this sect of Buddhism. The temple underwent major renovations in 2005, but is between 1000 and 2000 years old, according to the resident monks. You won't need a lot of time to visit the monastery, but could spend some time doing some pleasant walks in the area.

If heading along the road towards Dānbā, you'll pass by a thatch of prayer flags, some boulders and the village stupa, the sight of a heartbreaking accident that recently killed nearly all of the village's young people. Recognising the tourist potential of Shuǐqiǎzi Cūn, a hotel was set up here in 2004 and local young people were invited to do traditional dancing performances. Heavy rains one night caused a catastrophic landslide killing the dancers and destroying the hotel. The village lost 53 people that night and the accident is still much talked about in the Dānbā region.

It takes 45 minutes to reach the village by taxi. Negotiated fees with taxi drivers are usually around Y50 one way, Y80 return.

SUŌPŌ 梭坡
If you're interested in seeing Qiang watchtowers, this is *the* place to come. This village has some of the most remarkable watchtowers in the region; they're in incredible condition and the photo ops are unforgettable.

If you go to the village entrance (across the narrow suspension bridge fluttering with prayer flags), you are likely to be shadowed by the village 'guide'. Despite the laminated ID hanging round his neck, he doesn't do much 'guiding' other than follow you up the steep hills to the towers and relieve you of a Y15 entrance fee on your way down. (Some travellers have said they were hit up for around Y30, but friendly negotiation should usually get him down to Y15.)

Alternatively, you can stop at kilometre marker 147 on the road to the village and head up a dirt road to Suōpō, passing more towers and lovely Tibetan villages on the way. It's about 90 minutes if you don't poke about and are in good shape. Do not shortcut: one residual of the tower fortifications is ridiculously well-designed defensive stone walls full of flesh-ripping brambles.

You can negotiate a round-trip taxi ride here from Dānbā for around Y20.

Gānzī 甘孜
☎ 0836 / pop 61,400 / elev 3394m
A vast sprawl of low wooden houses ringed by the soaring peaks of Chola Mountain, Gānzī is a buzzing little market town populated mostly by Tibetans.

As the capital of the Gānzī (Garzê) Autonomous Prefecture, a growing number of foreigners are sojourning here on their way from Kāngdìng to Sêrxu or on their way west to Dégé. There are endless possibilities for exploration in the surrounding countryside, which is scattered with Tibetan villages and monasteries.

Roads in and out of Gānzī can be notoriously treacherous in winter. Icy roads mean a route littered with overturned trucks and passenger vehicles is not unheard of. If travelling further north or west from here, consider putting off long-haul travel altogether during snowfall. You don't want to be one of those people caught in blizzard conditions between Gānzī and Sêrxu, when your nine-hour trip in a rickety, unheated bus stretches to over 24 hours.

It's a good idea to bring a torch (flashlight) with you too – electricity can be iffy here.

SIGHTS

The **gompa** in downtown Gānzī is a small but thrilling little place for monastery fans. Circled perpetually by praying locals, you'll hear the buzz of chanting and see people doing full body prostrations before you even reach the front door of the prayer hall.

The protector hall at the back is dark and spookily atmospheric. Four glass-enclosed deities are illuminated by dozens of yak-butter candles and the effect is spectacular. Go through the hole in the wall on the left-hand side of the room, and you'll be in a superb corridor filled with Tibetan Buddhist–themed wall paintings that resident monks say are 1000 years old.

To get here, go down the lane running between Dongda Jie and Qinghe Lu.

North of the town's Tibetan quarter you'll find **Garze Gompa** (甘孜寺; Gānzī Sì), a 540-year-old monastery that glimmers with blinding quantities of gold. Encased on the walls of the main hall are hundreds of small golden Sakyamunis – representing all four Buddhist sects. In a smaller hall just west of the main hall is an awe-inspiring statue of Jampa (Maitreya or Future Buddha), dressed in a giant silk robe. The views of town from here are fantastic. There's an inconsistently collected entrance fee of around Y15.

To find the lamasery, take a left out of the bus station and head north for about 10 minutes until you reach the Tibetan neighbourhood. From there, wind your way uphill around the clay and wooden houses. You can also take a taxi (around Y5).

SLEEPING & EATING

At the time of research, we were turned away from every cheap hotel and guesthouse in town and told they didn't accept foreigners. However, some travellers report having had better luck than we did with the guesthouses around the bus station (dorm Y20), so it's worth asking around when you visit.

Ruìfēng Zhùsùdū (瑞丰住宿都; ☎ 752 5465; Binhe Donglu; 滨河东路; s & d Y50) This place has plain, basic rooms with startlingly immense bathrooms, but no hot water. Walk left out of the bus station, hang a right on Chuanzang Lu, continue until you cross the river and turn left onto Binhe Donglu (which reads just 'He Donglu' on the street sign).

Himalaya Hotel (喜玛拉雅宾馆; Xǐmǎlāyǎ Bīnguǎn; 13 Dong Dajie; 东大街13号; ☎ 752 1878; r with/without air-con Y170/150; ❷) The small but spotless, modern rooms at this friendly hotel are the nicest in Gānzī. (Discounted rooms from Y110 to Y120). To reach the hotel, turn left out of the bus station, then right on to Chuanzang Lu. Dong Dajie will be the second major street after you cross the bridge. When you reach Dong Dajie, turn left. The hotel will be on your left-hand side halfway up the street.

Golden Yak Hotel (金牦牛酒店; Jīnmáoniú Jiǔdiàn; ☎ 752 5188, 752 5288; 1 Dajin Tan; 打进滩1号; s & d Y150) Attached to Gānzī's bus station, the Golden Yak has similar rates and discounts to the Himalaya Hotel, but it's not nearly as nice. (It's got electric blankets but no air-con, limited or no hot water and some seriously stinky toilets.) But it's still worth considering for the convenience if you have an early bus the next morning.

Food in Gānzī is pretty mediocre but plentiful nonetheless. There are oodles of hole-in-the-wall restaurants, dumpling stands and noodle places concentrated outside the bus station. The Sìchuān dishes at **Dàbā Zànghàn Yìjiāxīn Fàndiàn** (大巴藏汉一家新饭店; 27 Dajin Tan; 打金滩27号; dishes Y8-10; ☺ 9am-10pm) are generally the tastiest. The lane opposite the station's entrance is also a great place to prowl for food – you'll find a fruit and vegetable market as well as several 'point-and-choose' carts for a cheap on-the-go meal.

GETTING THERE & AWAY

Buses to Gānzī leave Kāngdìng daily (Y106, 10 to 12 hours, 6.15am). A bus to Kāngdìng leaves Gānzī every morning at 6.30am. There are also daily buses to Dégé (Y61, seven hours, 8.30am), Manigango (Y21, two hours, 2.30pm), Dānbā (Y91, 10 hours, 6.30am) and Báiyù (Y70, 6.30am).

Private minivans to Dégé are available for hire – at Y450, they're not a bad deal if there's a group of you.

You can head north from Gānzī to Xīníng in Qīnghǎi province via Sêrxu (Y92, nine hours, 6.30am).

Around Gānzī

For a nice half-day walk, turn right out of the bus station and walk through the Tibetan housing until you reach a bridge festooned with prayer flags running over the Yǎlóng Jiāng. There are endless possibilities for walks on the other side of this bridge. The right path leads through barley fields for 20 minutes to **Dongtong (or Dontok) Gompa** and the impressive **Dingkhor chörten**. The left path leads to **Pongo Gompa** after about an hour or so.

About 7km along the road to Kāngdìng, sheltered in the lee of a hill, is the **Burana Ani Gompa**, a large nunnery by the roadside that might be worth checking out.

Headed 15km west on the road to Dégé, on the north side of the river, is the Gelukpa sect **Beri Gompa**. There are several other monasteries in this pretty area.

Another 15km or so, near the village of Rongbatsa, are the circular walls of **Dargye Gompa** (Dǎjīn Sì) set against white-capped mountains. From here it's a two-hour walk north along the Yǎlóng Jiāng to **Hadhi Nunnery**, home to around 60 nuns.

To reach Beri Gompa and Dargye Gompa, catch the morning bus to Dégé or one of the sporadic local buses heading west.

Manigango 马尼干戈

☎ 0836

Manigango lies halfway between Gānzī and Dégé and is the jumping-off point for Dzogchen Gompa and Yihun Lhatso. Manigango itself is a dusty one-street town that looks unmistakably like the movie set for a Tibetan Western. It's a glorious multicoloured scene with Tibetans on horseback, monks in crimson robes on motorbikes and tractors piled precariously high with pilgrims rattling down the road. It's worth stopping off just for the atmosphere. A horse racing festival is usually held here in the summer. Be warned: Manigango seems to have the biggest population of mangy dogs in China's Southwest and they all come out to play at night.

The town is known in Chinese as Yùlóng or Mǎnígāngē, but it's most commonly referred to by its Tibetan name, Manigango.

SIGHTS

Dzogchen Gompa 竹庆佛学院

This important Nyingmapa monastery (Zhúqìng Fóxuéyuàn), 50km north of Manigango, has a stunning location at the foot of a glacial valley. The recently reconstructed monastery was founded in 1684 and is the home of the Dzogchen school, the most popular form of Tibetan Buddhism in the West. Several important high Nyingmapa lamas, now exiled abroad, originated from nearby valleys.

The site includes the small town, 1.5km off the road, which has a few shops, *chörten* and a chapel with huge prayer wheels. Up the small gorge is the main monastery and 1km further is the *shedra* (monastic college).

Buses to Yùshù and Sêrxu run daily past Dzogchen, but in practice it's easier to hitch. If you do plan to hitch make sure you set out in the morning, as there is little traffic on the roads come the afternoon. If you want to hire a car and driver then it will cost Y250 for the return journey. Getting here you have to cross over Muri La (4633m), so make sure you have some warm clothes, especially if you're hitching in the back of a truck.

Yihun Lhatso 新路海

Thirteen kilometres southwest of Manigango is **Yihun Lhatso** (Xīnlù Hǎi; admission Y20), a stunning holy alpine lake to rival any found in Jiuzhaigou. The lake is bordered by *chörten* and dozens of rock carvings, and the shoreline is sprinkled in places with pure white sand. It's possible to walk an hour or two up the left (east) side of the lakeshore for glacier views. The lake has many great places to camp, though you need to guard against the mosquitoes. To get here you'll have to hitch on Dégé-bound traffic to the turn-off, where there's a bridge and a 1km trail to the lake.

ACTIVITIES

The countryside surrounding Manigango is crying out to be explored and one good way to do it is on horseback. The folks at the Mǎnígāngē Shísùdiàn can help you organise a horse and guide for trekking in the neighbouring areas. Prices usually run at Y200 per day (for horse and guide), but you can probably negotiate. If you plan to go off camping for several days you will be expected to provide meals for your guide as well. Make sure you have all the equipment and food you need before you get to Manigango. There's hardly anything available to buy in town let alone once you've left for the countryside.

SLEEPING & EATING

Manigango was undergoing a construction boom last check, and upgrades were looming (but hopefully not in prices!).

Mǎnígāngē Shísùdiàn (马尼干戈食宿店; dm Y10-20) This is where all the buses stop. It has comfortable basic rooms, but ask for the toilets and they'll point you half a mile up the road – make sure you bring a torch! The staff can help with travel information and bus timetables.

Yùlóng Shénhǎi Bīnguǎn (玉龙神海宾馆; dm Y15-30) Next door to the Mǎnígāngē Shísùdiàn, this hotel is more modern and has its own toilet – bonus! Look for the large red-and-white sign.

The restaurant at the Mǎnígāngē Shísùdiàn serves particularly tasty food and is very cheap. There is a good *niúròumiàn* (beef noodle; 牛肉面) restaurant next door to the petrol station.

The college at Dzogchen Gompa offers beds for Y15 per night, though you need a sleeping bag and your own food. There are a couple of well-stocked shops in the village below.

GETTING THERE & AWAY

A daily bus passes through Manigango at 11am for Dégé (Y35, three to four hours). Coming from Dégé, a bus stops in Manigango at 11am and heads on to Gānzī (Y25, five to seven hours) and Lúhuò (Y50, five hours), where it overnights before heading on to Kāngdìng (Y130) the following morning. A 9am bus leaves daily for Sêrxu.

Dégé 德格

☎ 0836 / pop 58,520 / elev 3270m

Resting in a valley with Chola Mountain to the east and the Tibetan border to the west, Dégé (Dêgê), home of the legendary Gesar, an altruistic king of Ling, is steeped in tradition and still sees little of the outside world. Things are changing, naturally, but it still remains time-locked for the most part. Dégé was renowned for its apothecary monks who developed traditional medicine, but now people come for its famed printing lamasery.

Getting to Dégé is a gruelling haul and buses overturning on the icy, hairpin roads are not uncommon. Altitude sickness is also a very real possibility.

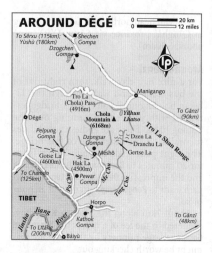

En route you'll see the towering snowy peaks of Chola Mountain stretching up 6168m, and the Xinhua Glacier, which comes down almost to the road at 4100m. Chola Mountain was first scaled in 1988 and you might begin to wonder if your bus driver is attempting to do the same, as the bus grumbles and inches its way uphill to the top of the peaks. At Tro La (Chola) of nearly 5000m, Tibetans on board will throw coloured prayer papers out the window and chant something that you can only hope will carry your bus to safety.

SIGHTS

Bakong Scripture Printing Monastery
德格印经院

At the heart of Dégé and perhaps the heart of the Tibetan world in many respects is this **monastery** (Dégé Yìnjīngyuàn; admission Y25; ⏱ 8.30am–noon & 2-6.30pm), a storehouse for Tibetan culture. Pilgrims circumambulate outside, performing some of the more than 1000 circuits required in the process of cultural development.

The printing house has existed on this site for over 270 years and houses more than 270,000 engraved blocks of Tibetan scriptures (and paintings) from the five Tibetan Buddhist sects, including Bön. Texts include ancient works on astronomy, geography, music, medicine and Buddhist classics. A history of Indian Buddhism, comprising 555 woodblock plates, is the only surviving copy in the world (written in Hindi, Sanskrit and Tibetan).

Built in the Qing dynasty by the 42nd prefect of Dégé, the monastery is revered as one of the three most important Tibetan monasteries (along with Sakya Monastery and Lhasa's Potala Palace) – not surprising since the material stored in Dégé makes up an estimated 70% of Tibet's literary heritage.

Within the monastery hundreds of workers hand-produce over 2500 prints each day. Upstairs, an older crowd of printers produces larger prints of Tibetan gods on paper or coloured cloth that later find their way to hills and temples as prayer flags. If you catch them with a free moment, they'll print you one of your choice for Y10.

Storage chambers are lined floor to ceiling with bookshelves, and a constant thwack emanates from paper-cutting and binding rooms. Protecting the monastery from fire and earthquakes is a guardian goddess, a green Avalokiteshvara (Guanyin).

The entrance fee to the monastery includes a tour guide who is excellent at communicating through pictures if your Chinese isn't up to scratch. The monastery is closed on holidays.

There are three other monasteries in town, including a large one just behind the printing house, which is over 1000 years old.

To reach the printing house, turn left out of the bus station and right over the bridge. Continue up this road to the southeast of town and it will bring you to the monastery's front door.

SLEEPING

True or not, independent travellers may be told that the following place is your only option. That said, a few have had luck getting cheap beds in other hotels – it just depends on the day and the mood of the PSB. Those up here with Tibetan or Chinese guides, however, report few problems getting into the cheapies.

Dégé Bīnguǎn (德格宾馆; ☎ 822 2157; dm Y20, d Y180) Here's where you'll likely be told to go. The dorm rooms are worse than the roads coming in and the doubles are priced laughably high; worse, you may be directed across the street to the expensive wing (Y280).

Wùzī Zhāodàisuǒ (物资招待所; dm Y25) One of the places you may have luck, this guesthouse is located directly opposite the bus station; you'll recognise it from the multicoloured bunting hanging outside.

GETTING THERE & AWAY

Buses to Dégé (Y60, eight to 10 hours) run from Gānzī every two to three days if you're lucky, but most of the time hope for a seat on the daily buses that pass through from other destinations, usually at 8.30am or so.

Private minivans to Gānzī and other places are available for hire (Y450).

Marginally more comfortable buses leave from Kāngdìng for Dégé daily at 7.15am (Y166, 24 hours), stopping overnight in Lúhuò. The return bus stops in Manigango (Y35, three to four hours), Gānzī (Y60, eight to 10 hours) and Lúhuò (Y86, 10 to 12 hours) on the way.

Sêrxu (Shíqú) 石渠

There are two places commonly called Sêrxu (or Sershul): the traditional monastery town to the west (Sêrxu Dzong) and the modern county town of Sêrxu (Shíqú Xiàn), 30km to the east, which has most of the hotels and transport connections.

While you'll probably stop in Shíqú Xiàn en route between Manigango and Yùshù in Qīnghǎi, the huge monastery of Sêrxu Dzong and its intensely Tibetan village, full of wild-haired nomads, is by far the more interesting place and well worth a stopover. There's not a Han Chinese in sight here.

Sêrxu Gompa houses 1200 monks and has two assembly halls, a Maitreya chapel and several other modern chapels, and a *shedra*, with a *kora* path encircling the lot. The road westwards from here towards Qīnghǎi is classic yak and nomad country, passing several long *mani* (prayer) walls and dozens of black yak-hair tents in summer.

In Sêrxu Dzong there's good accommodation at the **monastery guesthouse** (色须寺刚京饭店; sèxū sì gāngjīng fàndiàn; dm Y10-20, tw per bed Y40-50), though the restaurants in town offer better food.

In Shíqú Xiàn there are several decent places, including the **Zháxīkǎ Fàndiàn** (扎溪卡饭店; dm Y40, tw Y120), on the central crossroads, and the monastery-run **Bumgon Choegyeling Monastery Guesthouse** (蒙宜寺九欲归富旅店; Méngyí Sì Jiǔyù Guīfù Lǚdiàn; dm Y20), down the town's main side street.

GETTING THERE & AWAY

Shíqú Xiàn has a 7am bus to Gānzī (Y94, eight hours), via Manigango (Y77), from the bus station in the east of town. To get to Sêrxu

Dzong, take the 8am bus to Yùshù (Y30) from the bus stand in the far west of town.

From Sêrxu Dzong, you'll have to catch a through bus, passing through town at 9am for Yùshù (Y20, four hours), or around 11am for Shíqú Xiàn (Y10, one hour). Coming from Yùshù, it's possible to get off the bus in Sêrxu Dzong, have a look around and then hitch or hire a minivan on to Shíqú Xiàn the same day.

There's no direct bus here from Chéngdū, so you'll have to go first to Gānzī and get the daily bus the rest of the way (Y92, nine hours, 6.30am). Be aware that the road between Gānzī and Sêrxu is extremely treacherous and Sêrxu is frequently snowed in between November and March, cancelling public transit in and out. You are taking your chances if you decide to make this trip in winter, when the nine-hour journey can take up to 36 hours. If the bus gets caught in a blizzard, the driver will stop until daylight, which means you'll be sleeping in an unheated bus all night in sub-zero temperatures. Misery will take on a whole new meaning.

SÌCHUĀN–TIBET HIGHWAY (SOUTHERN ROUTE)

Vast lonely plains give way to razor-peaked mountains on this popular 2140km stretch of the Tibetan Hwy. A trip along this route will take you past imposing Tibetan block homes and nomad settlements, and from the frigid mountain heights of Lǐtáng to the comparatively balmy mildness of Bātáng.

Improving road conditions are also making the Kāngdìng–Lǐtáng–Xiāngchéng–Shangri-la (Zhōngdiàn) back-door route into Yúnnán immensely popular.

As with the rest of northwest Sìchuān, warm clothing is a must. Some travellers experience difficulties with the high altitudes here, so be on the lookout for side effects (see Altitude Sickness, p499) and if you're feeling unwell, head to somewhere lower. There are no money-changing facilities in this region.

Lǐtáng 理塘
☎ 0836 / pop 51,300 / elev 4014m

Lǐtáng has a Tibetan majority and is one of the most atmospheric stops on the southern Sìchuān–Tibet Hwy.

On any given day, dozens and dozens of elderly Tibetans stroll the main streets swinging hand-held prayer wheels and chanting.

Nearby, wild-haired nomads wearing *Mission Impossible* sunglasses and drowning in *chorpas* (traditional long-sleeved Tibetan coats) look on, as they straddle their motorcycles and sell stacks of yak skins.

Though the town is famed as the birthplace of the seventh and 10th Dalai Lamas, there's not much to visit in Lǐtáng itself besides the temple.

The town's core is a forgettable mass of low, ramshackle buildings, but it's ringed by interesting clusters of typical Tibetan houses, and further on the terrain spirals out into rolling hills, epic grasslands and ice-capped peaks.

The town is becoming an increasingly popular base for experienced trekkers looking for off-the-beaten-path routes. For casual hikers, there are also some spectacular walks in the hills. Advice on where to go (ie places that currently aren't being used as grazing pastures, or for sky burials; see p404) must be sought from locals. Be sure to allow yourself time to acclimatise to the altitude before you set out.

Travellers are increasingly being approached at the bus station or outside the Crane Guesthouse by freelance guides offering to organise walks or a visit to a nomad camp. Most travellers have had good experiences, some have been disappointed. Ask around when you arrive to get the latest from other travellers.

Lǐtáng lies at a wheeze-inducing altitude of 4014m. If you find yourself suffering from altitude sickness and can't get out of town, there is a local treatment consisting of medicated pills and rehydration drinks. The women running Crane Guesthouse (opposite) may be able to help you out; however, this shouldn't be considered a remedy and you should still descend to a lower altitude as soon as possible.

November to February is absolutely freezing here. It's also not the ideal time to visit Lǐtáng if you're on a tight schedule – snow storms frequently close the roads during this period, cancelling bus services in and out of town.

INFORMATION

China Post (Zhōngguó Yóuzhèng; Tuanjie Lu Beiduan; ⏰ 9-11.30am & 2-5.30pm)

Internet café (wǎngbā; Tuanjie Lu Beiduan; per hr Y3) Right next to China Post.

Public Security Bureau (PSB; Gōngānjú; emergency ☎ 110; Tuanjie Lu Beiduan)

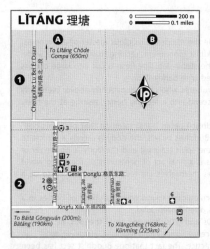

LĪTÁNG 理塘

0 — 200 m
0 — 0.1 miles

To Lītáng Chŏde
Gompa (650m)

Chengxihe Lu Bei Er Duan 城西路北二段

Jiangxi Jie 江西街

Genie Donglu 格聂东路

Shangmao Jie 商贸街

Xingfu Xilu 幸福西路

To Báitǎ Gōngyuán (200m);
Bātáng (190km)

To Xiāngchéng (168km);
Kūnmíng (225km)

SIGHTS & ACTIVITIES

Litang Chode Gompa (理塘长青春科尔寺; Lítáng Chángqīngchūn Ke'ěr Sì; ⏰ irregular) is a Tibetan monastery built in honour of the third Dalai Lama. The town and mountain views from the lamasery are spectacular. The statue of Sakyamuni inside is believed to have been carried from Lhasa by foot. To get here, follow Chengxihe Lu Bei Er Duan north. It's a lovely walk with heaps of traditional stone homes on both sides of the street affording wonderful glimpses of day-to-day Tibetan life. The temple is at the very end of the road.

Báitǎ Gōngyuán (白塔公园; Xingfu Xilu; 幸福西路; ⏰ dawn-dusk) is a *chörten* on the edge of Lítáng. No matter when you come, the area is packed with Tibetans sitting on the grass and praying, or circling the stupa at high speed spinning prayer wheels. Dozens of smaller *chörten* fill the courtyard, which itself is edged with a corridor of prayer wheels. The entrance is on a side street off Xingfu Xilu.

FESTIVALS & EVENTS

The annual **Lítáng Horse Festival** is known as one of the biggest and most colourful of the Tibetan festivals. Every five years an even more spectacular event is staged.

Room prices triple during this period and hotels are booked solid well in advance. The festival usually starts on 1 August and lasts for 10 days, although it's worth checking at the hostels and travel agencies in Kāngdìng or Chéngdū before you head out here.

The festival usually kicks off with an odd mix of hip-hop, Indian and Tibetan dance performances. Arts and crafts displays, trade fairs, and horse stunts so daring it's hard to watch without holding your breath take place the following days.

SLEEPING

Many hotels in Lítáng have no showers or hot water and electricity everywhere can be unreliable. Nobody has central heating. Cheapo hostels (Y10 to Y15 per bed) are found around the bus station.

Safe and Life International Hotel (Píng'ān Shèwài Bīnguǎn; ☎ 532 3861; Xingfu Xilu; 幸福西路; 2-bed dm Y15, s Y30) Right across from the bus station, the location here is ideal if you have an early morning bus or arrive late at night. The owners speak no English but are incredibly kind and eager to help their guests, whether through ferreting out travel info or finding out about activities in the countryside. Rooms are cramped, beat up and can get cold and damp in winter so this may be a better choice for spring or summer stays. A communal shower in the courtyard has hot water from 8am to 11pm and their 1st-floor restaurant has an English-Chinese menu.

Crane Guesthouse (Xiānhè Bīnguǎn; ☎ 532 3850; Xingfu Xilu; 幸福西路; dm Y25, s/d Y156/166) Hands down the backpacker favourite, this place has a welcoming staff. Some speak a little English and they often invite guests to sit around the fire and sip yak butter tea. Two- and three-bed dorms are cosy and the single and double rooms have hot-water showers and heat lamps in the bathrooms. Guests can make long-distance calls from a phone in the main office.

SÌCHUĀN

SICHUĀN

SKY BURIAL

The white cloth is removed from the body while the *tomden* (a religious master of ceremonies) sharpens his large knife. He circles a small Buddhist monument, reciting mantras all the while, and slices into the body lying before him on the stone slab. The flesh is cut into large chunks and the bones and brain are smashed and mixed with barley flour.

The smell of flesh draws a large number of vultures who circle impatiently above. Eventually the *tomden* steps away and the huge birds descend into a feeding frenzy, tearing at the body and carrying it in pieces up to the heavens.

This is sky burial (*tiānzàng*), an ancient Buddhist-Tibetan burial tradition that performs both a spiritual and practical function. According to Buddhist beliefs, the body is merely a vehicle to carry you through this life; once a body dies, the spirit leaves it and the body is no longer of use. Giving one's body as food for the vultures is a final act of generosity to the living world and provides a link in the cycle of life. Vultures themselves are revered and believed to be a manifestation of the flesh-eating god Dakinis.

Practically, this form of burial provides an ecologically sound way to dispose of bodies in a terrain where wood is scarce and the ground is often frozen solid.

The Chinese banned sky burials in the 1960s and '70s. It wasn't until the '80s, as Tibetans regained limited religious rights, that the practice was once again legalised. However, most Han Chinese still regard sky burials as a primitive practice. The fact that one Buddhist sect has been known to keep the tops of the skulls to use as enlarged sacred teacups has often been touted as proof of Tibetan savagery.

In Lhasa, tourists require official permission to attend a sky burial; in the more remote areas of Sìchuān, however, you may well be told where and when the burials are to take place. Nevertheless, local Tibetans have been unsurprisingly offended by travellers who have turned these funerals into tourist outings. Common decency applies – if you aren't invited, don't go, and whatever you do, do not attempt to capture the moment on camera.

High City Hotel (Gāochéng Bīnguǎn; ☎ 532 2706, 532 2338; Genie Donglu; 格聂东路; d/tr Y340/480; 🖳) This is the most upscale accommodation the city has to offer. Rooms here are certainly modern looking but the upkeep in some is surprisingly lax, especially when it comes to the cleanliness of the showers. The hotel cuts off the hot water in winter, but all rooms have heaters. The lobby is a popular place for business people to gather and drink tea. Low-season rates start at Y120.

EATING & ENTERTAINMENT

There are plenty of small, hole-in-the-wall restaurants in Lìtáng, and you can't really go wrong with any of them. Xinfu Xilu, around the Crane Guesthouse, has the best choice of places.

Wánglóng Guàntāngbāo (Genie Donglu; 格聂东路; ☸ 8am-late evening) This is the best place for breakfast. It serves delicious dumplings (饺子; *jiǎozi*; Y3) and bowls of rice porridge (粥; *zhōu*; Y1).

If you want something to do at night, try the bar (*jiǔbā*) behind the High City Hotel. It's a big, saloon-style place that has Tibetan dancing performances on many nights. Opening hours are irregular. Drop by around 9pm to see what (if anything) is going on. Closing time depends entirely on the size of the crowd.

Just north of the bar is a Sìchuān restaurant (*Sìchuān fàndiàn*). It's about the fanciest in town and its food gets good reviews from travellers. It's closed for much of the off-season though.

GETTING THERE & AWAY

Lìtáng's bus station is a chaotic place. You'd be forgiven for believing the staff's sole goal is to make leaving town as difficult as possible. Getting tickets can take a lot of patience (and often a lot of time) so don't leave it until the last minute. The ticket window opens at 2pm.

Buses leave Lìtáng for Kāngdìng (Y81, eight hours, 6.30am), Xiāngchéng (Y62, four hours, 6am) and Dàochéng (Y47, three to four hours, 6am).

There's also a daily bus from Lìtáng to Bātáng (Y60, 6.30am). Normally this trip should take six hours, however, ongoing roadwork between these two cities (which includes blasting tunnels through mountains) means frequent delays and interminable stops in the (usually freezing) middle of nowhere. At the time of research, the trip was averaging 12 to 15 hours. Check with your accommodation (not the infernal 'Construction? What construction?' bus-station staff) for an update on the situation when you arrive.

It looks easy to head north to Gānzī via Xīnlóng from here, but though road work continues, at the time of writing it was still a no-go for public transport.

Bātáng 巴塘
☎ 0836 / elev 2589m

Bātáng is kind of cool, if only because it's the closest town to Tibet (only 32km from the border) open to foreigners. It's a small place, crowded with stores and surrounded by suburbs of lovely ochre Tibetan houses. Bātáng is much lower (so much warmer) than surrounding areas. When it's still the end of winter in Lǐtáng it's already spring in Bātáng.

Roadwork between Lǐtáng and Bātáng (begun in 2004 and continuing indefinitely) is not only wrecking havoc with bus schedules between these two towns, but also with Bātáng's infrastructure; hot water and electricity are frequently cut for hours at a time. A flashlight is essential.

There's no signage in Bātáng. Streets all technically have names but locals don't know what they are. You're better off using landmarks to navigate around this place.

SIGHTS
The Gelugpa sect **Chode Gaden Pendeling Monastery** (巴塘寺; Bātáng Sì) in the southwest of town has 500 resident monks. It's dark, atmospheric and well worth a visit. There are three rooms behind the main hall: a protector chapel, a room with a giant statue of Jampa and a 10,000 Buddha room. Up some stairs via a separate entrance is a room for the Panchen Lama, lined with photos of exiled local lamas who now reside in India. Most images here are new but one upstairs statue of Sakyamuni is claimed to be 2000 years old. An old Chinese hospital is now used as monk accommodation. If the temple's locked, just duck into the kitchen (it always seems to be open) across from the front door and one of the monks will get the key for you.

To get here, follow Wenhua Jie downhill. Keep your nose alert for the smell of butter and follow the odour to the *gompa*'s entrance. This temple is tucked off the street and easy to walk right past.

There are some fine walks around town. Head north to a lovely Tibetan hillside village and then west to a riverside *chörten*. Alternatively, head south from the town centre over a bridge and then east to a hilltop covered in prayer flags and offering views of the town.

SLEEPING & EATING
Jīnshuì Bīnguǎn (金穗宾馆; ☎ 562 2700; 3-bed dm Y30, d high season Y160-180, low-season Y100, d with shared bathroom high/low season Y100/80) Rooms here are in pretty good shape, for the most part very clean and well kept. Furnishing is minimal and beds have simple white covers. Get a back-facing room for views of the surrounding Tibetan village and away from the street karaoke. Turn left coming out of the bus station and continue into town. Take the first right after the huge, hard-to-miss golden eagle statue in the little park area; the hotel's a block down on the left.

W Bīnguǎn (W宾馆; ☎ 562 3132; 1 Jinxianzi Dadao; 金弦子大道1号; d Y68-86) Run by a cool, young Tibetan couple, this is a plain but very clean and bright hotel with decent bathrooms. Just a couple of minutes from the bus station, it's a good bet for early departures or late arrivals. The only downside is its proximity to some thunderously loud karaoke. Walk left coming out of the bus station. The hotel has an English sign and will be on your left.

Xueyu Zhaxi Hotel (雪域扎西宾馆; Xuěyù Zhāxī Bīnguǎn; ☎ 562 3222; Shangmao Jie; 商贸街; r from Y288; ❄) People may try to steer you to this place (the supposed best in town), but, though the air-conditioning is a godsend on cold nights, you'll generally be better off at one of the two budget places we've listed. Though the battered rooms, decorated in an odd mix of beige fleur-de-lys wallpaper and green, yellow and burgundy striped carpets are OK, the bathrooms are often a problem: not all have hot water, shower pressure is almost nonexistent, many of the toilets don't work at all and the stink can be horrendous.

Cuìzhào Miàn (脆诏面; ☺ 8am-8pm) This sparkling clean place is a standout in a town not renowned for good food. Its dumplings in broth (抄手; *chāo shǒu*; Y5) are outstanding, served with a dipping sauce so tasty you could drink it back like juice. Sounds gross, but it's really that good. Turn left coming out of the bus station and follow the main road to the first major intersection. This small eatery will be on your left near the corner before you cross the street.

GETTING THERE & AWAY
There are daily buses to Kāngdìng (Y139, two days via Yǎjiāng, 6am, arrive around 11am) and Chéngdū (Y239, two days via Yǎjiāng, 6am, arrive about 6pm). Yǎjiāng is a cold, tiny town, made up of two cluttered streets. The **Yālóngwān Dàjiǔdiàn** (雅龙湾大酒店; d Y80) at the bus station has electric blankets and is your best lodging option. The restaurant right next door serves Sìchuān dishes and tasty noodles.

The road to Lǐtáng is under heavy-duty construction until god knows when, so expect to be held up for long periods of time (you should bring a good book!). Though frustrating, delays are not as bad as when travelling in the other direction, from Lǐtáng to Bātáng (Y60, 6.30am), which can take up to 15 hours these days.

As Bātáng is closer to the construction areas and buses out of town leave so early, you're usually able to scoot past most of the roadwork before the construction crews wake up and seal everything off. The bus station is a 10-minute walk from the town centre.

Headed west, there are buses at 2pm (Y44, four hours) and afternoon microbuses (Y50) to Markham, 138km away inside Tibet. However, travellers will have problems buying tickets to Markham as the town is officially closed to foreigners.

LĬTÁNG TO SHANGRI-LA (ZHŌNGDIÀN)
This is a back-door route to Yúnnán that takes you through 400km of spectacular scenery from Lǐtáng to Shangri-la (also known as Zhōngdiàn) via Xiāngchéng, where you will have to spend the night.

Xiāngchéng (Chatreng) 乡城
☎ 0836
Xiāngchéng is a tidy little town, its countryside packed with numerous Tibetan villages. Though quickly modernising and expanding, there's not much to see in Xiāngchéng itself. Its **monastery** (桑披罗布岭寺; Sāngpī Luóbùlíng Sì; admission Y15; ❀ 8am-8pm Jul & Aug, to 6.30pm Sep-Jun) on the hill overlooking town, however, is defi-

nitely worth a visit, not only for the views but also for its religious significance.

Destroyed during the Cultural Revolution, the temple reopened in 2002. Putting it back together was a labour of love for locals, both those living in town and villagers from the countryside. A drive to collect donations began in 1996 and carvers and painters started coming in from the countryside to donate their time. Though the main building is completed, construction is ongoing. Villages continue to rotate their 'experts', with a new team replacing the previous one every few days.

The monastery is also important because of a small gold and silver stupa decorated with precious stones in the **Golden Prayer Hall** (Sarthom Kham). The stupa was placed there in honour of one of the Dalai Lama's teachers, who originally hailed from Xiāngchéng and has since passed away. A Chinese tourist put this monastery on the map in 2003 when he alerted the monks that he had seen the reincarnation of the lama in one of the precious stones. The monastery has become increasingly popular ever since, especially with Chinese Buddhists.

These days, this 2nd-floor hall is filled 24 hours a day with people doing full body prostrations in front of the stone. If you want to attempt to see the lama in the stone yourself, ask one of the monks for help. They have a long contraption with a magnifying glass dangling on the end that they'll hold up so visitors can get a good look.

This monastery is at the opposite end of town to the bus station. To find it, follow the dirt track up on the left as you reach the edge of town. A taxi here from the bus station is around Y10.

EATING & SLEEPING
There's something for every budget in Xiāngchéng, all on Xiangcheng Zhengjie, the town's main drag.

Xiangbala Xiangcheng Dreamland Hotel (香巴拉乡城梦乡客栈; Xiāngbālā Xiāngchéng Mèngxiāng Kèzhàn; ☎ 582 5449; 4-5 bed dm/s/d Y20/80/90) This hotel has big, bright spartanly furnished rooms with Chinese toilets and solar-heated 24-hour hot water.

Bamushan Hotel (巴姆山大酒店; Bāmǔshān Dàjiǔdiàn; ☎ 582 5999; Xiangbala Dadao; 香巴拉大道; s/d Y480/460, discounted Y280/160; ❀) Down the street, the Bamushan has standard Chinese business hotel rooms, modern bathrooms, comfortable furnishings, Western toilets and boring, forgettable decoration. Breakfast is sometimes included in the room price.

Xiangbala Dadao, the town's main street, is filled with small, hole-in-the-wall eateries serving filling but generally forgettable Chinese and Tibetan dishes.

GETTING THERE & AWAY

There's one bus daily from Lǐtáng to Xiāngchéng (Y62, four hours, 6am). You can then catch a bus to Shangri-la in Yúnnán province the next day between 7am and 8am (Y90). Going the other way, buses from Xiāngchéng head back to Lǐtáng at around the same time. You can also head to Dàochéng on a bus passing through at around 5pm, though it won't go any further than Xiāngchéng if there's a low passenger load. If this happens, you can usually arrange to share a minivan (Y300) with your fellow turfed-out passengers the rest of the way.

In Shangri-la, there's a daily bus to Xiāngchéng (Y90, 7am). Heading back to Shangri-la, the bus leaves at the same time. The trip's duration will depend on your route. A direct road through the mountains takes six to seven hours. However, it is closed by heavy snow in winter (and sometimes even spring and autumn). During these periods, buses take an alternative route, going via Déróng (得荣; 9½ hours).

Try to buy your onward ticket on arrival in Xiāngchéng, as the ticket office is not always staffed before the first buses leave in the morning.

Dàochéng (Dabpa) 稻城
☎ 0836

Dàochéng is a dull little town, but an important stop for travellers on their way to the Yading Nature Reserve. You'll likely have to spend one night here on your way to the reserve and another on your way back.

However, there are a couple of diversions in town if you have time to kill. **Echu Jie** (俄初街; Échū Jiē) is lined with dozens of multicoloured, traditional houses and has been converted into a pedestrian shopping street. There are also several **internet cafés** (网吧; wǎngbā; per hr Y2-3.50) here.

Xiongdeng Gompa (☲ 8.30am-6pm) is the biggest monastery in the region. There's no bus here but you can take a taxi (around Y40, 30 minutes).

There's also **hot springs** (per person Y10), 4km out of town. Taxis charge about Y20 to get to them.

SLEEPING

If you are visiting between October and March, many of the hotels will be closed or, if open, have their hot water and heat turned off.

Tongfu Hostel (同福客栈; Tóngfú Kèzhàn; ☎ 572 8667, 572 8300; www.inoat.com; 1 Yazhuo Jie; 亚卓街1号; dm Y20, d Y80-100) This backpacker-friendly spot has a young, welcoming owner who speaks a little English and is very helpful with tourist info. The hostel closes in winter, usually from late November to sometime in February.

Jinsui Binguǎn (金穗宾馆; ☎ 572 7179; d Y100-120; ☒) Across the street from the Tongfu, this place is open year-round, has simple rooms and keeps the hot water and electricity running 365 days a year. Hurray!

EATING

There are plenty of places to eat here; just don't leave it too late, as restaurants are often entirely shut down by 8pm.

Khampa Restaurant (康巴藏餐; Kāngbā Zàngcān; dishes Y6-25; ☲ 8.30am-8.30pm) This restaurant has a good selection of Tibetan fare. The thurpa (面块; miànkuài; Y6), a colossal serving of noodles, meat and vegetables, can fuel you for the whole day.

GETTING THERE & AWAY

The bus station opens in the afternoon, usually by 2pm. There are daily buses for Xiāngchéng and Lǐtáng; both trips cost around Y47, leave at 6am and take three hours. A minivan or taxi to either of these places costs Y300.

Yading Nature Reserve 亚丁自然保护区

Stunning alpine scenery, snow-capped peaks and endless opportunities for horse treks draw more and more people to this **nature reserve** (Yàdīng Zìrán Bǎohùqū; admission Y150; ☲ ticket office 8am-6.30pm) each year. The terrain is also dotted with lakes and monasteries and is the reason Dàochéng is increasingly showing up on travellers' itineraries. The ticket office is open year-round, except when snow occasionally closes the road in winter. The best time to visit is autumn when the colours are changing (October is said to be particularly impressive).

SÌCHUĀN

The reserve is based around the three holy peaks of **Jampelyang** (Yāngmàiyŏng Shénshān; 5958m) to the south, **Chana Dorje** (Xiárì Duōjí Shénshān; 5958m) and **Chenresig** (Xiānnàirì Shénshān; 6032m). The mountains are named after the Tibetan Buddhist trinity of Bodhisattvas known as the Rigsum Gonpo. None has ever been climbed. The reserve is a strong contender for the title 'Shangri-la' (see the boxed text, p290).

The region was once part of the old kingdom of Mùlĭ and was visited by the fifth Dalai Lama in the 17th century. Joseph Rock, who counted the corpulent King of Mùlĭ as a close personal friend, visited in the 1930s and first described the famed 'Bandit Monastery', whose 400 monks would regularly head out on plundering expeditions before returning to prayer and contemplation. The monastery, called **Konkaling Gompa** (贡岭寺; Gònglĭng Sì) is en route to the reserve, about 60km from Dàochéng, just before Rìwă.

The most popular way for Chinese tourists to see the reserve is by horse (foreigners who visit here seem to just walk). Horse treks are generally Y180 for the first day, and Y120 to Y150 for each day after that, depending on your bargaining skills. There's very simple accommodation (no heat, no showers) at the **Tsongu Gompa** (冲古寺; Chōnggŭ Sì; r Y40-60). A simple wooden (and as yet unnamed) **guesthouse** (☎ 136-9814 2416; dm Y30) was being built near Tsongu Gompa at the time of research and may be worth checking out. The owner is planning to offer horses for hire to his guests as well.

Three-hours' walk southeast of the monastery is **Luorong Pasture** (洛绒牧场; Luòróng Mùchăng), where there is another tent hotel and restaurant. Three hours past here is a trail to **Niúnăi Hăi** (牛奶海; Milk Lake) at 4720m.

From this point most Chinese tourists return the way they came but it is possible to do a circuit of the mountain if you have camping equipment for one night. From Niúnăi Hăi the *kora* continues for one hour to a 4400m pass, and then branches right to some meadows, a popular place to camp. The next day, two hours' hiking northeast gets you to another higher pass, from where it's a four-hour descent beneath the north face of Chenresig Peak. The trail then passes **Tara Lake** (Drölma Tso) en route back to Tsongu Gompa.

LOCAL VOICES *Aku Anzi, Yi Minority, age 30*

This Lìjiāng resident and full-time trekking fanatic and guide has travelled all over China's Southwest. A restless traveller, he hates picking favourites, but admits there's something about nature in western Sìchuān that just can't be beaten.

How did you get interested in trekking?
I grew up in the mountains near Lúgū Hú [Lugu Lake]; my family were shepherds. I ended up going to university to become a teacher and even had a government job, but I didn't like it so much. Yi people are half-nomad, half-farmer. I need to be a free guy…free like a bird (laughing).

Where's your favourite place to go?
I have many favourites, but Lúgū Hú to Yàdīng is gorgeous. The terrain changes so much. You've got rivers, valleys, forests and, from June to August, you wouldn't believe the beautiful flowers you can see at Yàdīng. It takes two weeks to do on horses. You have to be experienced though. It's a little bit tough.

Any other favourites?
Tagong Grasslands. It's getting very popular but it's absolutely beautiful and very topographically flat so routes there aren't too difficult. Once I trekked with nomads there. I just asked if I could go out with them to their camp and they said 'OK'.

What's so special about western Sìchuān?
There's so much life. In Tibet, the terrain is very harsh. In western Sìchuān it's so varied: there's a lot of green, a lot of holy mountains. I feel like I get a more rich experience.

Where to next?
Hmmm. I think I should go to other provinces and find new routes. I'd also like to go to Dégé. Me and my friends got a jeep and visited about three years ago but didn't stay long enough. There are important temples all over the countryside from every school of Tibetan Buddhism. I'd really like to go back and see more of it.

The reserve is about 110km from Dàochéng and takes about 2½ hours to reach. There is no public transportation here, although someone *occasionally* gets a bus to the park up and running during the high-season summer months, but this service cannot be counted on. Most people just arrange a ride through their accommodation. Alternatively, minivans ply Gongga Lu Yiduan, Dàochéng's main street, all day; fellow travellers will be trolling for a ride here as well, so you could hook up with them and split the cost to the reserve.

NORTHERN SÌCHUĀN

This area of the province is synonymous with stunning nature – a mix of savagely lush forests, the eerily stark beauty of vacant grasslands and icy deep lakes fed by thunderous rivers.

The most popular way for travellers to experience all this is by exploring the Jiuzhaigou or Huanglong nature reserves or, even better, by horse trekking around either Sōngpān or Lǎngmùsì. Whichever way you choose to experience it, you'll never forget a trip here.

Northern Sìchuān is home to the Ābà, Tibetan and Qiāng Autonomous Prefectures. In the extreme northwest, the region around Zöigê and Lǎngmùsì is the territory of the Goloks, nomads who speak their own dialect of Tibetan, distinct from the local Amdo dialect. While these Tibetan destinations are less visited, you can incorporate them into an alternative route into Gānsù.

Most of northern Sìchuān is between 2000m and 4000m in altitude, so make sure you take warm clothing. The grassland plateau in the northwest averages more than 4000m, and even in summer temperatures can dip drastically at night. The rainy season lasts from June to August.

Beyond the Sōngpān–Jiǔzhàigōu route, roads in the region aren't always in the best condition. (And the buses aren't much better.) Roads are particularly hazardous in summer, when heavy rains prompt frequent landslides. You might want to think about planning this trip for the spring or autumn, when the weather is likely to be better.

One thing you are bound to see in the north are the countless logging trucks that shuttle up and down the Minjiang Valley (near Huanglong), stripping the area of its forest. Some sources estimate that up to 40% of the region's

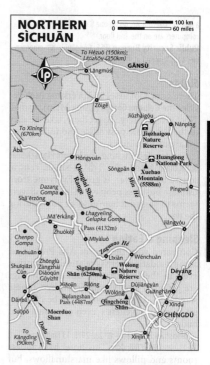

forests have been logged in the last half-decade, causing erosion, landslides and increased levels of silt heading downstream, eventually flowing into the Yangzi River (Cháng Jiāng).

One more time: bear in mind that there is nowhere to change money in this region, so bring sufficient Renminbi.

MǍ'ĚRKĀNG (BARKAM) 马尔康
☎ 0837

Mǎ'ěrkāng is the capital of the Ābà (Tibetan) Autonomous Prefecture. It's a small but surprisingly modern little city built up along the banks of the Suomo River (Suōmó Hé). Predominantly Han Chinese, the main draw of this town is its scenic neighbouring valleys dotted with Tibetan settlements. You could easily spend a couple of days bussing from town into the countryside, stopping where you like to explore some of the surrounding villages.

Information

China Post (Zhōngguó Yóuzhèng; Chongdai Jie) You can also make phone calls from here.

Internet café (wǎngbā; Daerma Jie; per hr Y2-3; ⏱ 24hr) Has terrific high-speed computers. Enter through a lane off Daerma Jie, go up one flight of stairs. The computers are on the 2nd floor.

Public Security Bureau (PSB; Gōngānjú; ☎ emergencies 110; Tuanjie Lu)

Sights

There's not a lot to see in Mǎ'ěrkāng itself besides the **Gelugpa Gompa** (Lǎma Miào), a small Tibetan monastery. To get there, take the alley to the left of the post office and follow it up for about 30 minutes.

For people-watching, the **Leisure Plaza** (Xiūxián Guǎngchǎng; Binhe Lu; 滨河路), a small, central square by the river, is great. Everyone from Chinese business people to Tibetan villagers seems to hang out here at some point during the day.

Sleeping & Eating

Compared with the rest of Ābà Prefecture, accommodation here is relatively expensive, even in the low season. Budget offerings are generally pretty grim (even by Chinese standards), so they won't likely be of interest to most travellers – even ones on a tight budget.

Mínshān Bīnguǎn (☎ 282 2918; 13 Binhe Lu; 滨河路13号; s & d Y160; ☒) This hotel has spotless rooms and pillows like marshmallows, but unreliable hot water. The owners do not bargain – even with Chinese travellers.

Jiarong Hotel (嘉绒酒店; Jiāróng Jiǔdiàn; ☎ 666 6668; 346-430 Dasa Jie; 达萨街346-430号; d Y680; ☒) This is a new place with slick, gleaming rooms and spectacularly posh bathrooms. Discounted prices are between Y260 and Y380.

The cheapo **hotel** (酒店; jiǔdiàn; ☎ 782 4233; Xīzhàn; 西站; dm Y15, d Y60) at the West Bus Station has friendly owners but not-too-clean rooms. In winter, the 10-bed dorm rooms are occupied to near capacity by nomad tribes and can get pretty rowdy. However, if you have an early bus from this station, the place is worth considering. To get here, go up the stairs just outside the bus ticket office.

There are plenty of restaurants in town, though even ones that came recommended were a bit of a let down – even the classic scrambled egg and tomato dish came in the form of a rubbery omelette slapped on a bed of cold tomatoes. Maybe you'll have better luck than we did.

Meigu Jie in the east of town has a huge string of hole-in-the-wall eateries, from claypot stalls to BBQ stands. For fancier

places with more elaborate menus, check out Chongdai Jie in the centre of town.

There's also a good bakery near here on Tuanjie Lu, where you can load up on snacks for day trips and long bus rides.

Getting There & Away

Mǎ'ěrkāng has two bus stations, both outside of the downtown core. The rickety West Bus Station (西站; Xīzhàn) is 2km northwest of downtown; the more modern and busy East Bus Station (东站; Dōng Zhàn) is about 2.5km east of downtown.

You can buy tickets from either no matter where you are going; just make sure to double- and triple-check which station the bus will actually depart from (staff aren't necessarily as helpful as you'd expect in sorting this out).

The East Bus Station is generally the best place to start for the following daily services:

Dānbā (Y41, 5½ hours, 7am), Zöigê (Y63 to Y68, nine hours, 6.30am), Chéngdū (Y89, nine to 10 hours, 6.30am and 9.30am) and Ābà (Y52, five hours, 7am and 11am).

There's sometimes a direct bus to Sōngpān (Y88, 6am). If not, head to Hóngyuán (红原; Y36, three to four hours, 8am), from where you can then catch onward transport.

To reach Mǎ'ěrkāng, there's a daily service from Dānbā (Y41, 5½ to six hours, 7.30am) and Ābà (Y52, five hours, 7am and 11am).

AROUND MǍ'ĚRKĀNG

For intrepid travellers, the forested valley around Mǎ'ěrkāng is sprinkled with Tibetan villages and is well worth exploring. Just get out on the main road and hail down anything buslike heading out of town.

Zhuókèjī (卓克基; Choktse) is a compact Tibetan village around 7km east of town. Just above the cluster of stone houses is a derelict watchtower/fortress that once belonged to a local chieftain and in which Mao Zedong is said to have slept when the Long March passed by.

There are several remote monasteries in the area including **Lhagyeling Gelupka Gompa** (Shuājīng Sì), about 65km east of town.

SŌNGPĀN 松潘
☎ 0837 / pop 71,650

This sleepy town is a popular base for horse treks – an experience right up there with a trip to Jiuzhaigou on the must-do lists of most travellers taking on northern Sìchuān.

Sōngpān's bustling core is contained within the (still intact) old town walls and is thick with tourist shops, Tibetan souvenir stands and some interesting architecture, still holding its own against encroaching development. Keep an eye out for the shockingly ornate covered bridges, a handful of traditional wooden buildings and some truly atmospheric teahouses.

Sōngpān has a long-held reputation for faulty electricity. Though not as bad as it used to be, it's still a good idea to bring a torch. Infrastructure upgrades result in a lack of water from time to time as well.

Spring, summer and autumn are all good times to visit. In winter, expect most midrange and top-end hotels to be closed leaving only unheated budget options. Many backpacker-oriented restaurants and businesses also close during this period. Horse treks are still offered

in winter, but you probably won't want to go for more than a day trip. Travellers who've overnighted during this period describe bone-breaking cold that freezes even the hot water in Thermos flasks.

Information
Agricultural Bank of China (Zhōngguó Nóngyè Yínháng; Shunjiang Lu) There's a pretty good ATM here, but it doesn't work for everybody. This bank won't change travellers cheques, but some people have been able to change American dollars in a pinch – just don't count on it.

China Post (Zhōngguó Yóuzhèng; Shunjiang Lu; ☽ 9-11.30am & 2-5.30pm) On the main street about halfway between the north and south gates.

Internet café (wǎngbā; per hr Y6; ☽ 6am-midnight) On Shunjiang Nanlu just south of the bridge. Emma's Kitchen (p413) has good internet access, too.

Public Security Bureau (PSB; Gōngānjú; ☎ 723 2123; Wenmiao Jie) Renews visas now and has a reputation for efficiency. Some travellers have received same-day service so be nice to the staff! The office is down a side street off Shunjiang Beilu.

Sights
The ancient **gates** from Sōngpān's days as a walled city are still intact, and a couple of outrageously ornate, traditional **covered bridges** span the Min River (Mín Hé). On the far western side of the river is **Guānyin Gé**. Walking up to it will take you through a village-like setting and the small temple offers views over Sōngpān.

Activities
The areas around Sōngpān are dotted with idyllic mountain woods and emerald-green lakes. One of the most popular ways to experience the scenery is by horse trek. Guides can take you out through pristine valleys and peaceful forests, all aboard a not-so-big, very tame horse. Many travellers – from hardy backpackers to families with children – rate this experience as one of the highlights of their travels in Sìchuān.

Treks are organised by **Shun Jiang Horse Treks** (Shùnjiāng Lǚyóu Mǎduì; ☎ 723 1201; Shunjiang Beilu), located about 30m south of the bus station. The guys here have been leading horse treks for years. The vast majority of travellers are utterly happy, but now and again we get reports of lackadaisical if not uninterested (and occasionally gruff) guides. Check with travellers who have recently taken a trip; there will

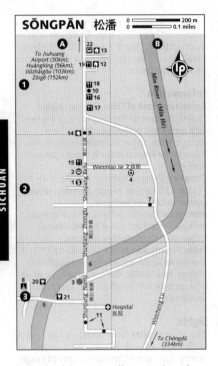

SĪCHUĀN

be loads of them. On offer is anything from one- to 12-day treks and trips can be tailored to suit you.

One of the most popular treks is the four-day trip to **Ice Mountain** (雪玉顶; Xuěyùdǐng), a spectacular ride through as yet unspoilt scenery.

If you're feeling particularly adventurous (and particularly flush) you can make the trip north to Zöigê on horseback, a trek that takes around 12 days. Bear in mind that you will have to cover the cost of the horses on their return journey to Sōngpān, which can make it quite an expensive way to travel.

Rates are very reasonable (Y150 per person the first day, Y100 per person per day after that). You get a horse, three meals a day, tents, bedding, warm jackets and raincoats. The guides take care of everything: you won't touch a tent pole or a cooking pot unless you want to. The only additional charge is entrance to the different sites (Y20 to Y110 each, which can include anything from temples to nature reserves depending on your route), but you will be warned of these before you set out.

As food consists mainly of green veggies, potatoes and bread, you may want to take along some extra snacks for variety.

Shun Jiang Horse Treks now shares the same address and office space with its former rival **Happy Trails Horse Trek Company** (Kuàilè de Xiǎolù Lǚyóu Mǎduì; ☎ 723 1064), which offers similar trips at similar prices.

People may encourage a post-horse-trek visit to the Sōngpān hot springs, but it's better skipped – the springs aren't actually 'hot' at all.

Sleeping

Despite Sōngpān's popularity with travellers, the choice of hotels is surprisingly limited. There are several overpriced tourist hotels inconveniently located far on the outskirts of town (and a couple just outside the southeast part of the old walls), but they are completely closed up in winter, just when you need their central heating and hot water most. Budget accommodation is centred on Shunjiang Beilu around the bus station, where about a dozen places offer dorm beds and cheap private rooms. Figure Y20 to Y30 for a dorm bed, and from Y50 for a simple double room with private bathroom. In the low season, most budget hotels are open but you may have to wait a while for the staff to appear.

Shun Jiang Guesthouse (Shùnjiāng Zìzhù Lǚguǎn; ☎ 723 1201, 723 1064; Shunjiang Beilu; 顺江北路; dm Y20) Run by Shun Jiang Horse Treks, this simple but clean guesthouse is right above its office, which means you can literally roll out of bed and into the saddle.

Sōngzhōu Jiāotōng Bīnguǎn (Songzhou Traffic Hotel; ☎ 723 1818, 723 1258; Shunjiang Beilu; 顺江北路; dm Y25-40, d/tr Y180/150) With so many buses leaving (and arriving) in Sōngpān at ungodly early or late hours, the real selling point of this hotel is its proximity to the bus station (it's so close, in fact, that one of the hotel's indoor halls juts out over the station's waiting room). A double room here can go for as little as Y60 in the low season. Rooms range from perfectly serviceable to slightly dumpy, so have a look at a few options before deciding. Don't count on the hot water either.

Songzhou Ancient Town Hotel (Sōngzhōu Gǔchéng Bīnguǎn; ☎ 132-1984 5998; Shunjiang Beilu; 顺江北路; d Y50) Located above the Yùlán Fànguǎn, rooms in this modest hotel have electric blankets and reliable hot water. Welcoming and helpful staff make this one of the better budget options. The only thing to complain about is the frigid chill that hits the rooms during cold weather – despite the electric blankets, it somehow manages to be even colder inside than it is outdoors. Weird.

Tàiyáng Dàjiǔdiàn (Shunjiang Beilu; 顺江北路) Just outside the north gate, this is the only conveniently located upper-midrange hotel in town. It was closed for heavy-duty gutting and renovation at the time of research, but should be reopened by the time you read this and so may be worth checking out.

Eating

Sōngpān has an excellent assortment of breads for sale, made and sold fresh all day at small stalls on Shunjiang Zhonglu. You'll also see sellers strolling up and down the street here shouldering enormous baskets overflowing with crusty loaves and Tibetan flatbread.

There are also a number of restaurants along Shunjiang Zhonglu, including hotpot and noodle shops. Many have English signs and menus. There's a good bakery along this same street selling bags of cookies and other goodies handy for taking along on day trips.

Lánzhōu Lāmiàn (☎ 723 3916; Shunjiang Beilu; 顺江北路; noodles from Y5; ⏰ 9am-10pm) This unassuming Muslim restaurant has fantastic beef noodles (牛肉面; *niúròu miàn*) perfectly spiced and drowning in fragrant coriander.

Yùlán Fànguǎn (Shunjiang Beilu; 顺江北路; dishes from Y8; ⏰ early-8pm) This is Sōngpān's original hangout for foreign travellers and it remains popular today, despite the mediocre food. There's an extensive English menu offering both Chinese and Western dishes. Don't count on the Western stuff, such as hot chocolate (Y5) or the 'Israeli breakfast' (fried egg, salad and bread; Y10), being available outside of the high season. This place is often open as early as 5am, so it's a good spot to chow down before epic morning bus rides.

Emma's Kitchen (Xiǎo Ōuzhōu Xīcāntīng; ☎ 880 2958; Shunjiang Beilu; 顺江北路; mains from Y10; ⏰ 6.30am-late) This is another popular place for backpackers. Emma is *very* helpful – trust us, she'll find you – and can sort out almost anything from laundry to travel information. During winter, this place is either closed or open irregular hours.

Song in the Mountain (Shunjiang Beilu; 顺江北路; mains from Y10; ⏰ 7am-11.30pm) This small restaurant is run by Sarah, daughter of Fis Took Yang, 'the good guide with the bad eye' at Shun Jiang Horse Treks. Both the Chinese and Western dishes get good reviews from travellers. Sarah is also very helpful if you need general travel information on the area.

Drinking

Teahouses pack the banks of the Min River in the southwest part of town. All have outdoor seating and on a nice day, the clink of cups and hum of gossiping voices give this area a pleasant buzz.

Yíngyuè Cháyuán (⏰ 9am-late) Try this pleasant teahouse, on your right before you cross over the bridge. Its black walls house a pleasant courtyard right next to the river.

Getting There & Away

AIR

Jiuhuang Airport (九黄机场; Jiǔhuáng Jīchǎng) is near Chuānzhǔsì (川主寺), a small town almost halfway between Sōngpān and Jiǔzhàigōu. The airport was closed for renovations at the time of research but should be open by the time you are reading this.

There are no buses to Sōngpān so you'll either have to catch a taxi or go to Jiǔzhàigōu first and catch the early morning bus to Sōngpān the following day. Until recently, the 25-minute taxi ride from Sōngpān to the airport cost Y80, but the price is now set at Y50. However, many taxi drivers still regularly hit travellers up for the old fare, so brace yourself for all sorts of theatrics as they try to cajole the Y80 out of you.

BUS

Sōngpān's bus station is at the northern end of town. There are daily departures to Chéngdū (Y72 to Y76, eight hours, 6am, 6.30am and 7am). You might also be able to grab a seat on a Chéngdū-bound bus from Jiǔzhàigōu or Zöigê that passes through Sōngpān between 8.30am and 10am every day. Buses also leave for Hóngyuán (Y50, five hours, 6.30am) and Zöigê (Y56, six hours, 6.40am and 7.10am). Buses for Jiuzhaigou leave at 7am, 11am and 1pm and will drop you off at either the park entrance (Y27, two hours) or Jiǔzhàigōu town (Y34, two hours 40 minutes to three hours). Buses to Huanglong (Y25, two hours) leave at least once a day from Sōngpān's bus station, though service can be irregular from November through to February. For Lǎngmùsì you will need to change at Zöigê.

From Chéngdū's Chadianzi bus station there are three daily departures to Sōngpān (Y74, eight hours, 6.30am, 7am and 7.30am) and from Jiǔzhàigōu there is a morning departure to Sōngpān at 7.20am.

HUANGLONG NATIONAL PARK
黄龙景区

Bejewelled with sapphire-bright terraced ponds and luxurious emerald-green foliage, **Huanglong National Park** (Yellow Dragon Valley; Huánglóng Jǐngqū; www.huanglong.com; admission Apr–mid-Nov Y200, mid-Nov–Mar Y80; 7am-6pm) is a popular destination for its stunning photo possibilities, fresh air and peaceful walks.

The park's name (Yellow Dragon Valley) is due to the yellow-tinged calcium carbonate and limestone deposits found throughout its 1340 sq km terrain. On land, the layered sheaths of yellowed calcium carbonate are said to look like a dragon's skin. In ponds and lakes, limestone deposits are responsible for the waters' golden shimmer on sunny days.

Legend has it that 4000 years ago a yellow dragon helped the King of the Xia Kingdom,

Xiayu, channel the flood water into the sea, thereby creating the nearby Min River.

Crowned by snowcapped peaks, the park's unique scenery, complex ecosystems and endangered species populations (which include the Giant Panda and the golden snub-nosed monkey) landed Huanglong on Unesco's World Heritage List in 1992.

The best time to visit is in September or October when the autumn colours come out and are reflected in the park's waters to stunning effect. Another great time to visit is during the annual **Temple Fair** (庙会; Miào Huì). Held around the middle of the sixth lunar month (usually July), it attracts large numbers of traders from the Qiang minority. Whatever time you come, keep in mind that the elevation here runs from 3120m to 3570m – meaning thinner air and cooler temperatures than you may expect.

The most spectacular ponds are behind **Huanglong Temple** (黄龙寺; Huánglóng Sì), deep in the valley and 7.5km from the road. (The temple was built to honour the mythical dragon of the King of Xia legend.) A round trip along the footpath here takes about four hours, with the trail returning through dense (and dark) forest. Huanglong is usually less besieged by tour groups than Jiuzhaigou, which some travellers find a huge plus. But while some people rave about the valley's beauty and love the peace and quiet here, others find it disappointing, much preferring the scenery at Jiuzhaigou despite the latter's (at times) overwhelming popularity and rapid commercialisation.

No lodging is allowed in the park any more, and outside all you've got are super overly priced options. The nearby town of Chuānzhǔsì (川主寺) has almost all of the places to stay. Also, you can't count on seeing many food vendors, so it would be sensible to bring along some water and snacks.

Around 56km from Sōngpān, Huanglong is almost always included on the seven-day Jiuzhaigou tours that run out of Chéngdū, as well as on the horse-trekking tours from Sōngpān. From Sōngpān there's usually one morning bus a day to the park (Y25, two hours). However, from November through to February prepare yourself for sporadic or cancelled service. The last bus back to Sōngpān leaves in the early afternoon, usually around 2pm. From Jiǔzhàigōu there's a bus at 7.10am (Y42), but at low-season times (roughly November through to February) service may be irregular or nonexistent. At present, no buses run to the park from Jiuhuang Airport (九黄机场; Jiǔhuáng Jīchǎng). The airport was closed in 2006 for expansion work, but it should be reopened by the time you read this. By then there may also be direct transport added as Huanglong becomes a more popular (and accessible) trip.

JIUZHAIGOU NATURE RESERVE 九寨沟自然保护区

☎ 0837

With thatches of pillowy greenery, delightfully eccentric waterfalls, 'so blue it can't be real' lakes and a terrific network of trails to take you through it all, the Y-shaped valley of this reserve has become one of the most popular sights in Sìchuān. The scenery of **Jiuzhaigou Nature Reserve** (Nine Village Gully; Jiǔzhàigōu Zìrán Bǎohùqū; ☎ 773 9753; www.jiuzhaigouvalley.com; adult/student Apr–mid-Nov Y220/170, mid-Nov–Mar Y80/70; ☉ 7am–6pm) includes forests and meadows roamed by takins, golden monkeys and pandas. All surrounded by snow-capped peaks, the reserve was deemed so impressive it got the attention of the UN, which proclaimed it a World Biosphere Reserve and placed it on Unesco's World Heritage List in 1992, along with nearby Huanglong National Park.

True, the heart-locking ticket price and army of travellers that descends on the reserve daily is off-putting, but take it in your stride, say 'Pish!' and go anyway – it's a national treasure, well worth a splurge of yuán and time, and you'll never forget a visit to this place.

Jiǔzhàigōu means 'Nine Village Gully' and refers to the nine Baima Tibetan villages that can be found in the valley. According to legend, Jiǔzhàigōu was created when a jealous devil caused the goddess Wunosemo to drop her magic mirror, a present from her lover, the warlord God Dage. The mirror dropped to the ground and shattered into 118 shimmering turquoise lakes. Those pools of eye candy are now some of the most photographed scenery in the province.

Trees growing unexpectedly out of the middle of rivers, lakes and waterfalls is another of the park's trademarks. This eccentric flourish to the scenery is caused by fertile pockets of calcium in the waterways, which create impromptu flowerpots.

The park is reached by a modern highway connecting Jiǔzhàigōu town (42km east of the park) with Chéngdū. Over 1.5 million people come here each year and the highway outside the entrance is packed with monstrous resort-style hotels collectively offering over 20,000 beds – with more being added every year.

Over the years, most original residents have been forced to move in order to 'protect' the park. Those who've been allowed to stay put actually work within the park's confines to keep up appearances.

Technically you're not allowed to strike off into the backcountry here, and though the trail network is excellent it can be a bit disheartening in high-season periods when shuttle buses whiz by every 10 minutes depositing dozens and dozens of people at a time to jostle for a picture in front of the same scenic view.

Orientation & Information

Buses from Chéngdū and Sōngpān will drop you at the reception centre and ticket office, just outside the park entrance. If you can produce something remotely resembling a student card you'll be given a discount. The price includes entrance to all areas of the park but does not include the bus pass (high/low season Y90/80), which allows you to hop on and off the shuttle buses running between the park's sights.

The park is 204 sq km and the touring area is set up within its Y-shaped valley. The first leg from the entrance to Nuorilang Falls (where there is a restaurant and cavernous hall selling souvenirs) is 14km. From Nuorilang Falls along the western fork to Swan Lake and the forest is 18km. From Nuorilang Falls to Long Lake along the eastern fork of the valley is 17km.

An ATM at the park entrance accepts major credit cards.

Sights

The first official site inside the park is the Tibetan **Zaru Temple** (Zārú Sì; Zaru Gompa in Tibetan). The bus won't stop here but it is only a short walk up from the ticket office. Turn left at the first fork as you walk up the main road. After a short stroll, the temple will be on your right.

If you continue on the main road, you'll follow **Zechawa River** (Zéchǎwā Hé) to **Sparkling Lake** (火花海; Huǒhuā Hú). This is the first in

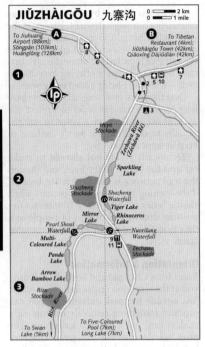

JIǓZHÀIGŌU 九寨沟

0 —— 2 km
0 —— 1 mile

To Jiuhuang
Airport (88km);
Sōngpān (103km);
Huánglóng (128km)

To Tibetan
Restaurant (4km);
Jiǔzhàigōu Town (42km);
Qiáoxíng Dàjiǔdiàn (42km)

Héyè
Stockade

Zechawa River
(Zéchawa Hé)

Sparkling
Lake

Shuzheng
Stockade

Shuzheng
Waterfall

Tiger Lake

Rhinoceros
Lake

Mirror
Lake

Pearl Shoal
Waterfall

Nuorilang
Waterfall

Multi-
Coloured Lake

Zechawa
Stockade

Panda
Lake

Arrow
Bamboo Lake

Rize
Stockade

Rize River

To Swan
Lake (5km)

To Five-Coloured
Pool (7km);
Long Lake (7km)

a series of lakes filled by the **Shuzheng Waterfall** (树正瀑布; Shùzhēng Pùbù) up ahead. As elsewhere in the park, you can stroll along a walkway by the main road or follow a trail on the side of the lake opposite the traffic (the quieter option). On this leg of the valley, the trail is on the eastern side of the river until it reaches the **Nuorilang Waterfall** (诺日朗瀑布; Nuòrìlǎng Pùbù).

Here, the main road branches in two, with the eastern road leading to **Long Lake** (长海; Cháng Hǎi) and **Five-Coloured Pool** (Wǔcǎi Chí), the western road to **Swan Lake** (天鹅海; Tiān'é Hǎi). If you're looking to stretch your legs and clear your lungs, you'd be better off heading along the western route, where you'll find a number of scattered sights and a quiet forest trail leading from **Mirror Lake** (镜海; Jìnghǎi) to **Panda Lake** (熊猫海; Xióngmāo Hǎi). Views from this trail are particularly good, especially of **Pearl Shoal Waterfall** (珍珠滩瀑布; Zhēnzhūtān Pùbù). If you continue past Panda Lake, you will leave the majority of the traffic behind.

The eastern route is almost better done by bus, as the lakes on the way up may be dried out

in winter or when there has been little rainfall and the narrow road sees a great deal of traffic from one end to the other. Nevertheless, the two lakes at the far end are both well worth a visit. Nestled between some dramatic slopes, Long Lake in particular can be jaw-droppingly beautiful, especially on clear days when the sun hits it just so, its reflection piercing the pristine blue water with streaks of gold.

Tours

During summer, various companies in Chéngdū operate tours to Jiuzhaigou and the surrounding area. Most of the trips are advertised for a certain day, but the bus will only go if full. If you are unlucky you may have to spend days waiting, so don't pay first.

A standard tour includes Huanglong and Jiuzhaigou, lasts seven days and starts from Y400 per person. Hotels, food and entry fees are not included in the price. Travel agencies in Chéngdū's Dragon Town Youth Hostel (p365) offer tours, as does the CITS office (p361).

A word of warning: several tour operators in Chéngdū have been blacklisted by travellers for lousy service and/or rudeness. Ask around among travellers to pinpoint a reliable agency.

Sleeping

The strip of road leading to and from the reserve is packed with behemoth-sized upper-midrange and top-end hotels. There's only a tiny handful of budget ones. Expect a huge hike in prices during the high season (July and August) and on all national holidays.

Note that though the park remains open, accommodation, stores and restaurants outside the Jiuzhaigou Reserve start closing up in November and the area becomes a complete ghost town. Things slowly come back to life as March approaches. If you are headed up here during the off season, call ahead to make sure your hotel (and its kitchen) is open.

Otherwise, there's plentiful accommodation in Jiǔzhàigōu town, a small but unbelievably noisy and pushy place of 62,000 people, 42km east of the reserve. There's plenty of cheap but pretty desperate-looking budget accommodation here, but you'll be better off at the slick **Qiáoxíng Dàjiǔdiàn** (侨兴大酒店; ☎ 772 8366; Jiǔzhàigōu Xiànchéng; 九寨沟县城; r with/without bathroom Y350/328; 🖭) on the town's main road to the Jiuzhaigou Reserve. Even when the hotel is heaving with people it gives good discounts – sometimes as low as Y100 for a double with bathroom.

To get to or from here to the park you can try to flag down an eastbound bus (around Y10 to Y15, 40 minutes) or take a taxi (20 minutes). Some cab drivers charge Y30 to Y40 for the trip, others charge Y15 to Y20 per person.

Staying inside Jiuzhaigou Reserve is not allowed, but locals may want to put you up for the night anyway. Think twice before accepting. It's not only illegal, but if you are obviously foreign-looking you and your 'non-exit' from the park are more likely to stand out – especially during the low season. Park rangers have been known to keep remarkable tabs on foreigners and are extremely efficient at rounding up stragglers come closing time, driving them down to the park gates themselves.

Accommodation just outside the reserve includes the following.

Jiùtōng Bīnguǎn (☎ 773 9879; fax 773 9877; dm Y30, d Y100) Next to the bus stop, this spartan space with concrete floors is a long-time standby and still going strong.

YouU Hostel (Yōuyóu Dùjià Liánsuǒ Jiǔdiàn; ☎ 776 3111; www.youuhotel.com; No 4 Bldg, Kangba Linka, Zhangzha Town; 漳扎镇，康巴林卡,风情村4号楼; dm Y40, r Y180) This newly opened hostel is a welcome addition to Jiuzhaigou. Rooms are clean, and it's one of the few places open year-round. Just be warned: though the staff will go out of their way to make you comfortable in winter (including harvesting armfuls of blankets from other rooms), this place is still freezing.

Lántiān Bīnguǎn (☎ 877 8888; d Y120-398, tr Y100-200) Above average detailing and appointments make this place a good bet.

Héyè Yíngbīnguǎn (☎ 773 5555; fax 773 5688; d Y290) Just outside of the park entrance, this hotel has lovely rooms with fancy marble bathrooms.

Sheraton Jiuzhaigou Resort (Xǐláidēng Jiǔzhàigōu Fàndiàn; ☎ 773 9988; fax 773 9666; www.sheraton.com/jiuzhaigou; d Y1200) This is one of the biggest hotels on the block and also one of the poshest. Rooms are elegant and the service is impeccable.

Eating

There isn't a huge choice of restaurants outside the reserve as most tourists tend to eat at their hotels. Several restaurants near the Lántiān Bīnguǎn serve up simple Chinese dishes.

Alternatively there is a good **Tibetan Restaurant** (阿布氆孜; Ābù Lǔzi; ☎ 889 7603, 844 8309; dishes from Y25; 🕙 noon-9pm) that serves very good Chinese and Tibetan food. It's not cheap, but it's a nice place to treat yourself. The restaurant is not very conveniently located and you'll have to get a taxi here (Y10). It's next to Chángqīng Fàndiàn (长青饭店).

Inside the park, you can buy expensive water or snacks in the villages. A restaurant inside the colossal souvenir shop at the reserve's Y-junction at Nuorilang Waterfall offers buffets costing Y25 to Y40 most afternoons. If visiting in the off season, everything is likely to be closed so bring your own water and snacks for the day.

Getting There & Away

AIR

Flights currently operate from Chéngdū (Y700, 40 minutes) to Jiuhuang Airport, with flights to and from Běijīng, Chóngqìng and Xī'ān to be added in the future. The airport was closed for renovations at the time of writing but should be reopened by the time you are reading this.

Buses for Jiǔzhàigōu (Y45, 1½ hours) wait at the airport for arrivals and leave when full. This means that you might have to wait around for a while, as most of your fellow passengers will be hopping off the plane straight onto a tour bus.

Returning to the airport is much easier as a scheduled bus leaves from near the Lántiān Bīnguǎn.

BUS

Chéngdū can be reached in 11 to 13 relatively painless hours. From Chéngdū's Chadianzi bus station there are four daily buses to Jiuzhaigou (Y110, 7.20am, 8am, 8.40am and 2pm); Chéngdū's tourist bus station also has one (Y110, 8am). If you're coming from Gānsù via Zöigê, you'll have to go through Sōngpān. From Sōngpān, buses to Jiuzhaigou leave at 7am, 11am and 1pm. You'll be dropped at the bus station just outside the reserve's entrance (Y27, two hours) or Jiǔzhàigōu town (Y34, 40 minutes from the reserve).

From Jiuzhaigou to Sōngpān (Y28, two to three hours) there is a daily bus that leaves the park at 7.20am; otherwise, flag down buses that start from Nanping and go past the park entrance. The buses won't stop unless you flag them down. The bus station staff will let you know approximately what time the buses will be passing by

You could also head to Jiǔzhàigōu town and catch a bus to Guǎngyuán (Y60, eight hours, 6.30am), gateway to eastern Sìchuān and on the rail line to Xī'ān. However, depending on what route your driver is taking, this can be a lengthy trip along winding roads on some very rickety buses.

Between October and April, snow often cuts off access to Jiuzhaigou for weeks on end. Even at the best of times, transport is not plentiful. Hitching to Jiuzhaigou on tour buses has supposedly happened, but it's a rare occurrence indeed.

Getting Around

You can certainly walk all over the park but given its size there is no way you will be able to see it all in one day. Shuttle buses zip between the park's sights, leaving on a 'when full' basis from just inside the park entrance between 7am and 6pm, just before the park shuts. A high-/low-season day pass costs Y90/80 (a cost that's increasingly being added onto your park entrance ticket). The bus stops at whatever sights you and your fellow passengers want it to. You can either take a quick picture and hop back on the same bus, or linger, wander or hike to the next stop and pick up another shuttle bus later on.

Guides on the buses explain what's coming up next, though in the low season they are usually sleeping and only reluctantly rouse themselves for those not travelling in groups.

The shuttles follow two routes. The main one runs between the entrance and Arrow Bamboo Lake. For transportation between Rhinoceros Lake and Long Lake you'll have to get off the bus and transfer to another shuttle at the Y-junction near Nuorilang Waterfall.

NORTHWEST ROUTE

The epic grasslands in this corner of Sìchuān are smattered with isolated Tibetan towns and villages where life is slow, streets are less crowded and there's a real feeling of being on the edge of the world.

The most popular activities in this region are exploring the monasteries or outdoor activities such as horse trekking, but even just travelling from Ābà to Lǎngmùsì can be a thrill. There's nothing quite like bussing through the grasslands and finding your vehicle swarmed by yak herds as veiled nomads thunder by on horses (or, increasingly these days, on motorcycles).

In the winter months, roads often become impassable and, at an average altitude of 3500m to 4000m, temperatures plummet way past the tolerance levels of most mortals. While still cold, early autumn sees little rain and many clear and sunny skies. In winter, the nomadic Goloks, a Tibetan people, stay closer to main roads and towns and do much of their travel by bus. It makes the trips extremely boisterous and songful but also makes seats hard to get – buy your onward ticket as soon as possible.

The first leg of this route is from Chéngdū to Sōngpān (for more details, see Getting There & Away – Bus, p414). Most travellers take a side trip from Sōngpān to Jiuzhaigou at this point. From Sōngpān you can travel 168km northwest to your next overnight stop in Zöigê, and from there it's worth heading to Lǎngmùsì, just inside the Sìchuān border, for a day or two.

Ābà (Ngawa) 阿坝

Ābà is a lonely-looking place, dwarfed by the vast plains and grasslands that surround it. Qiatang Jie (洽唐街), with a sprawl of one- and two-storey buildings, is this Tibetan town's main artery. On any given day it's flooded with monks, many of them between the ages of six and 15, from the town's monasteries.

Poverty is apparently the reason for the high number of child monks in the area. Locals say sending poor children to the monasteries is the only way for them to get a good education.

There are three dozen or so monasteries hidden in the surrounding countryside, so there's plenty for intrepid travellers to explore in the region besides the town's temples.

There's an **internet café** (per hr Y3; 24hr) on Zhongxin Jie (almost at the corner of Qiatang Jie).

SIGHTS

The fascinating **Kirti Gompa** is a 'must-visit'. It's surrounded by a unique, maze-like network of corridors containing hundreds and hundreds of prayer wheels of all shapes, sizes and designs. Local pilgrims flock here to spin the wheels and pray as they race-walk through the halls. Be very careful not to get in anyone's way. We learned the hard way what happens when you come between a Tibetan grandma and her next prayer wheel…(ouch!).

The **Seru Gompa** near the bus station is also worth a visit for its great two-eyed stupa, the kind usually only seen at monasteries in Nepal. Certain prayer halls here are off-limits to women; if you're a female heading towards a door and a monk starts yelling at you, that's probably why. Visit in the morning if you can, as the buildings are often locked up by the afternoon.

SLEEPING

Accommodation in Ābà is going to be basic no matter how much you spend. No showers and no bathrooms are the rule at most budget accommodation places. Running water (let alone hot water) in these parts can be hit-or-miss too.

Almost all mid- and upper-range hotels cut their water supplies and electricity between October and March. Many close entirely.

Gānxǐ Bīnguǎn (干喜宾馆; dm Y25, d with bathroom Y60) This is about the best of the cheapies and is open year-round. It's pretty gritty but very friendly. Bathroom 'toilets' are holes in the ground. It will be hard to find this place on your own (though centrally located off Qiatang Xijie, the hotel's actual street has no name), so it's best to take a taxi from the bus station (around Y5).

Juomola Guesthouse Hotel (珠峰宾馆; Zhūfēng Bīnguǎn; Qiatang Xijie; 洽唐西街; d with bathroom Y120) Of the hotels open year-round, the drab rooms here are by far the most comfortable. Just don't expect perfection: despite staff claims to

the contrary, running water and hot water are no more reliable here than anywhere else, and though there's air-conditioning in each room, staff couldn't find any of the remote controls at the time of research. The hotel can also get noisy at night with all the customer comings and goings from the great Tibetan café (open 10am to late) on the 2nd floor.

EATING

Ābà's restaurants are concentrated on Qiatang Jie. Surprisingly, many of the Tibetan ones have English menus.

Everest A Tibetan Restaurant (珠藏餐; Zhū Zàngcān; Qiatang Jie; 洽唐街; 10am-10pm) This restaurant, near the corner of Zhongxin Lu, has a big selection of *momos* (Y0.50 a piece) and comfy seating. The menu is exactly the same as at the Tibetan café on the 2nd floor of the Juomola Hotel Guesthouse.

Xuěshān Fàndiàn (雪山饭店; Qiatang Jie; 洽唐街; dishes Y10-15) For Chinese food try this spot between Zhongxin Lu and Pentso Jie. The beef and yellow celery (芹菜牛肉; *qíncài niúròu*; Y15) is particularly good.

GETTING THERE & AWAY

Ābà's bus station is 2.9km from downtown. It has daily services to Mǎ'ěrkāng (Y52, five hours, 7am and 11am) and Zöigê (Y66, six hours, 6am).

Going the other way, there are daily buses for Ābà from Mǎ'ěrkāng (Y52, five hours, 7am) and Zöigê (Y66, six hours, winter/summer 9.30am/9am).

Taxis don't tend to hover at this station, but a city bus is usually on hand to meet arrivals (Y1); it travels straight along the town's main street.

There's an old bus station in the centre of town, but at the time of research it was not in operation.

Taxis are easily hailed around town.

Zöigê 若尔盖
☎ 0839 / pop 59,000

A sparse concrete town in the middle of vast grassland, Zöigê is a sleepy place with a vacant, middle-of-nowhere vibe. Don't despair if you end up here on your way to Lǎngmùsì – it certainly isn't the end of the world. People are friendly, there are heaps of Tibetan teahouses to flop down in and Xiangbala Nanjie (香巴拉南街) is a good street to browse for reasonably priced Tibetan clothing.

While the town's Chinese name is Ruò'ěrgài, it is most commonly referred to by its Tibetan name, Zöigê.

You can visit the **Ta Tsa Gompa** (Daca Si; 达扎寺; Dázhā Sì; ☿ irregular), a Tibetan temple on the northeastern edge of town. You'll have a better chance of finding the buildings open in the morning; much is locked up by noon.

There's also a tiny but spectacular **museum** here with Tibetan artefacts, weapons and the hand print of the fifth Dalai Lama. Because of the items' value, monks don't open the museum for the average traveller – only for VIP guests. But if your visit coincides with a VIP delegation you may be able to tag along.

SLEEPING

Budget offerings in Zöigê are uniformly basic with limited washing facilities and sporadic hot water. Though it can get brutally cold here, it's almost impossible to find accommodation with heating or hot water during winter. Many midrange hotels shut down entirely by mid-December.

Hóngyùn Kèzhàn (鸿运客栈; ☎ 828 2829; Shuguang Jie; 曙光街; dm Y20) Only 100m from the bus station on the same street, this friendly place is ultra basic, but still bright and airy and with very clean rooms. There's communal toilets but no showers on the premises. To get here, walk out of the bus station, cross the street and walk left past Xiangbala Nanjie. The hotel will be on your right just before the next intersection.

Mǎ'ěrtáng Jīnxīn Mùrén Zhījiā Lǚguǎn (玛尔塘金鑫牧人之家旅馆; ☎ 896 8772; 9-10 Mingzhu Jie; 明珠街9-10号; dm Y30, r without bathroom Y60) Its business cards wax poetic (in both Chinese and Tibetan) on love, compassion and world peace, so it's kind of hard not to have a soft spot for this place. Located near a cluster of nice Tibetan teashops, it's got very basic rooms, clean wood floors and a dingy common bathroom with a hot (for most of the time) shower. Turn left out of the bus station, walk 125m or so until Mingzhu Jie and turn left again.

Ruò'ěrgài Fàndiàn (若尔盖饭店; ☎ 229 1041; Shangye Jie; 商业街; r Y200-280; ✷) Tidy rooms here have dirty carpets, cheap furniture and a reliable but limited supply of hot water. To work your room's air-conditioning, you'll have to hunt down the remote control (there's only one for the entire hotel).

The desk staff here are lovely, however, and very helpful. Note that this hotel often shuts down completely in winter. Enter through the lane around the corner on Duoma Beijie (多吗北街).

Ruò'ěrgài Dàjiǔdiàn (若尔盖大酒店; ☎ 229 1998; Shangye Jie; 商业街; r Y428-488) The swankiest option in town, this new hotel has the clean, modern rooms of any other good upper-end Chinese hotel. Though open year-round, it cuts the central heating, hot water and hall lights during winter, making the discount low-season rate of Y140 seem terribly overpriced.

EATING & DRINKING

There are not a lot of memorable eating experiences to be had in Zöigê, but the food is certainly decent enough. This town (and its restaurants) has a tendency to shut down early – don't leave dinner later than 8pm.

There are a couple of good, simple restaurants on Shangye Jie (商业街), both near the Ruòěrgài Fàndiàn.

Lóngxīng Xiǎochī (隆兴小吃; mains Y8-12; ☿ 9am-8pm) This is a terrific place to look out for here. Everything is good, especially the *mápó dòufu* – perfectly spiced and served in huge bowls.

Lóngchéng Shāwú (隆城砂钨; mains Y12-18; ☿ 10am-8pm) A couple of doors down, this restaurant serves killer hotpot dishes – especially the chicken and taro (芋儿鸡; *yù'er jī*; small/large Y12/15) variety.

For yak butter tea (Y10 to Y15 per pot), head to Jingpin Jie (精品街) or Mingzhu Jie (明珠街) where there are several Tibetan teahouses.

GETTING THERE & AWAY

Zöigê's bus station is on Shuguang Jie. It has daily buses to Sōngpān (Y56, six hours, winter/summer 6.30am/6am) and Ābà (Y66, six hours, winter/summer 9.30am/9am).

A spectacular new road to Lǎngmùsì is almost completed (really, it looks like a friggin' airport runway). It's cut down travel between the two places to a 100-minute bus ride (Y25, winter/summer 2.30pm/2pm), though expect hold-ups as they put finishing touches on the road's tunnel.

Despite only taking about 80 minutes by car, many taxi drivers still charge the Y300 to Y400 they demanded when the trip took 3½ hours. Do your best to get a better rate.

Lǎngmùsì (Namu) 朗木寺

☎ 0941

Lǎngmùsì is a fabulous village bookended by alpine scenery to the west and grasslands to the east. Inhabited by Tibetans, Huí Muslims and Han Chinese, it's one of northern Sìchuān's most interesting stops and is becoming as well known for its horse treks as Sōngpān. A massive new expressway between here and Zöigê opened in 2006, cutting travel time between the two places from 3½ hours to 80 minutes.

Lǎngmùsì is best visited in the high season, from spring to autumn. In winter, pretty much all backpacker-oriented accommodation, bars and restaurants are closed, as is the horse trek office.

SIGHTS & ACTIVITIES

Despite Lǎngmùsì's increasing popularity (as evidenced by the dozen or so Western-oriented cafés and bars in town), the surrounding countryside is filled with *gompas*, temples, caves, and hills used for sky burials. Its terrain is just begging to be explored, and the possibilities for walks are endless. Horse treks are also a popular way to see the countryside and can be arranged at **Langmusi Tibetan Horse Trekking** (朗木寺马队; Lǎngmù Sì Mǎduì; ☎ 667 1504). Its opening hours are seasonal; you'll find it on the road perpendicular to the main road, just opposite where the buses drop you off.

You can also check out the **Dacheng Lamo Keri Gompa** at the far end of town from the bus stop. Built in 1413, this monastery is home to about 700 monks who study medicine and astrology in addition to sutras and tantrics. Morning is the best time to find the buildings open.

The 900-year-old **Serchi Gompa** (admission Y16; ☷ irregular) is on a hill opposite the Keri Gompa. Cross the dirt road and follow the smoke up to the monastery.

Keep an eye out for a small **mosque** (清真寺; Qīngzhēn Sì) as you head back to the village. Though locked up when we visited, its exterior is just gorgeous.

SLEEPING

Nomad's Hostel (旅朋青年旅馆; Lǚpéng Qīngnián Lǚguǎn) This backpacker-friendly place is on the main street and is closed in winter.

Yuèlái Bīnguǎn (悦来宾馆; ☎ 667 1509; dm/r Y15/50) Down the sidestreet from the intersection where buses stop, this hotel run by a friendly Huí family has simple but tidy rooms year-round; bathrooms are pretty grubby.

Langmusi Hotel (朗木寺大酒店; Lǎngmùsì Dàjiǔdiàn; ☎ 667 1588; r Y300) At the opposite end of town from the bus stop, this is a lovely new hotel with spotless rooms, friendly staff and two full-time English guides to show guests around. It's open year-round with rates sometimes discounted to Y100 in the low season.

EATING & DRINKING

The main street is packed with restaurants, especially the intersection where the buses stop. Delicious fresh bread is also served everywhere from stands and street carts.

The places mentioned here are backpacker-oriented joints good for food and info, but closed outside of the high season.

Shanghai Times Restaurant & Bar (上海时光; Shànghǎi Shíguāng; ☎ 667 1508; mains Y10-15) This place has an English menu and is right at the crossroads where the buses stop. The kitchen is closed in the low season, but if the lovely owner is around she'll make you a pot of coffee for Y10 and let you hang out anyway.

Leisha's Restaurant (丽莎饭馆; Lìshā Fànguǎn; ☎ 667 1179) Nearby on the main drag, Leisha's has been handing out info to backpackers for years – it's one of the best sources of information in town.

Zàngxiāng Yuán (藏香园; ☎ 667 1349) At the opposite end of town, this is a bar in a traditional building promising whisky, vodka and cold beer. Its massive wooden outdoor terrace is next to a stream – definitely the nicest outdoor seating in town.

GETTING THERE & AWAY

There's daily service to Zöigê (Y12, 1½ hours) and Hézuò (合作; Y28, three hours, 7.30am and 12.30pm) in Gānsù province.

From Zöigê, buses leave for Lǎngmùsì daily (Y25, winter/summer 2.30pm/2pm).

SOUTHERN SÌCHUĀN

Southern Sìchuān has about the quirkiest mix of sites in the whole province, including Gòngxiàn County's hanging coffins, the wackily ornate teahouses and giant dinosaurs of Zìgòng and the outdoor activities and Yi villages of Xīchāng.

Improved transport has made these places more popular with Chinese travellers, but they are still relatively unvisited by foreigners and many hotels in this area, including upscale ones, are terribly shy with their non-Chinese guests.

Altogether, it makes for a fascinating region, worth visiting on its own or taking as a back-door route to Guìzhōu or Chóngqìng.

ZÌGÒNG 自贡
☎ 0813 / pop 693,000

Zìgòng is a pleasant surprise. On the surface, it's much like any other small-sized but modernising Chinese city. But scratch the surface and you'll find Zìgòng's geographical situation has left it with a mix of off-beat sights that range from a nationally renowned dinosaur museum to some of the most ornate and dramatic guild halls you'll see in China's Southwest.

Zìgòng has been important for centuries because of its huge underground salt wells – a mineral refined here for more than 2000 years. As early as the 10th century, boreholes were being drilled thousands of feet into the ground. The salt-laden brine was then brought to the surface, boiled and dried by burning the natural gas that accompanied it.

Salt was a valuable commodity so far from the sea and an important way to both pay and raise taxes. Merchants grew wealthy and decorated the town with halls and temples to protect the source of their wealth.

Today, Zìgòng remains an important centre of salt production.

Information
Bank of China (Zhōngguó Yínháng; Ziyou Lu; ⊙ 8am-6pm) Has an ATM and will change cash, but not travellers cheques.
China Post (Zhōngguó Yóuzhèng; Jiefang Jie) On a pedestrian lane in the centre of town.
Internet café (wǎngbā; Ziyou Lu; per hr Y1.50; ⊙ 24hr)

Sights
ZÌGÒNG DINOSAUR MUSEUM 自贡恐龙博物馆
This **museum** (Zìgòng Kǒnglóng Bówùguǎn; ☎ 580 1235; admission Y40; ⊙ 8.30am-5.30pm) is the pride of Zìgòng. Don't be put off by the battered building and weathered animatronic dinos lurking in the trees and ponds. Inside, the museum has put together a wicked collection of dinosaur skeletons, bones and fossils and those in the main hall are shown off to great effect against dramatic backdrops.

The superstar of them all is the 20m-long **Omeisaurus**, which once weighed in at 40 tonnes. Scientists say its immense weight and huge neck suggest it spent most of its time in marshy bogs or lakes with just its head poking above the surface.

There are also a number of huge, ancient dino bones that are out for visitors to touch, and a football-field-sized interior **excavation site** with a walkway around its circumference. Flurries of small lights illuminate the mishmash of bones – tracing the various spines, legs and flippers of the 170-million-year-old animals is fascinating. There are more bones and fossils upstairs along with exhibits on the history of the excavation and museum itself.

Outside on the museum grounds, a new but much smaller excavation site is under way. At the time of research there wasn't a lot to actually see in it, but it was still interesting to peer over the edge and see how the work was coming along.

Why so many dinosaur bones in Zìgòng? Nobody really knows. They started being uncovered in 1972, at the end of the Cultural Revolution. Excavations started in earnest in the Dashanpu suburbs of Zìgòng, 10km northeast of the town centre. Since then over 100 dinosaurs (kǒnglóng; 'terrible dragons' in Chinese) have been found.

Initially, scientists were puzzled as to why so many fossils were concentrated at one site, but it is now believed that the already dead animals were washed here from the surrounding areas during a massive flood. This created a huge jam of dinosaur carcasses, which were then covered by silt and compressed over the millennia.

To get here from town, catch bus 35 (30 to 40 minutes) heading east on Binjiang Lu and ask to be let off at the museum. A taxi here takes 15 minutes and costs around Y18; it will cost Y28 if the driver takes the expressway and charges you the tolls.

SALT INDUSTRY HISTORY MUSEUM
This **museum** (Zìgòngshì Yányè Lìshǐ Bówùguǎn; ☎ 220 2083; 89 Dongxing Si; 东兴寺89号; admission Y20; ⊙ 8.30am-5.30pm) is devoted to the region's salt industry and does a good job of telling the story through terrific historical photos and modest but effective interactive exhibits. It's all housed in an old guild hall, originally built by salt merchants from Shaanxi in 1736 and later used as a Kuomintang hideout. The building has so many swooping angles and

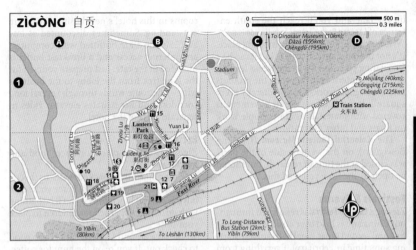

startlingly jaunty carvings, it's more than worth a visit in and of itself. It was most recently renovated in 1872.

Most of the exhibit areas were closed for renovations at the time of research, but a peek behind the construction curtains revealed some sleek new installations and great English captions going up.

Walking Tour

The interesting features that make Zìgòng so much more than just another provincial city are best seen on foot.

Start at the west end of town, where Shigang Jing Lu intersects with Tongxing Lu. **Xiǎoqiáo Jǐng**, one of Zìgòng's ancient salt wells, is on the corner. Though the well itself is filled in, you can still see the wooden poles and pulleys used to haul the brine up to the surface. Black-and-white photos around the base depict fascinating glimpses of old Zìgòng, including the salt wells in action and bustling port scenes.

Walk south to Binjiang Lu for a riverside view and a 300m stretch that's packed with dozens of teahouses.

Wángye Sì, on the river near the Shāwān Fàndiàn, is certainly one of the most impressive temples in town; it's now an excellent teahouse with a view across the river to **Fǎzàng Sì**. Both temples were built to protect the salt trade and to ensure a safe journey for the cargo boats transporting salt downstream.

From here, backtrack past the Shāwān Fàndiàn and take the first right on to Zhonghua Lu, where you will pass a magnificent **teahouse**, so dark and dramatic that it looks out of place amongst the modern nearby buildings.

Continue on along the street until you reach an open paved area, usually packed with all kinds of food stalls, then head uphill along the narrow alley just west of Caideng Jie for a gander through the **Flower & Bird Market**. This area is packed, rain or shine, with elaborate plants and brightly coloured birds. Continue up the lane and you'll reach the south entrance of **Lantern Park** (Cǎidēng Gōngyuán; admission Y1; 7am-11pm), a popular family meeting place. It's not the most attractive park but it can be a fascinating place to visit in the weeks leading up to the Lantern Festival, when the grounds turn into a giant workshop and literally every square kilometre of grass and pavement is covered with materials as craftspeople work on floats and other decorations.

The **Colourful Lantern Museum** (Cǎidēng Bówùguǎn), on the western side of the park, was closed at the time of research, but should be open by the time you read this.

Festivals & Events

Zìgòng's **Lantern Festival** is renowned throughout China and is held over 40 days during the first and second lunar months (normally starting sometime in February). Everything from small lanterns to huge floats are illuminated throughout the city, especially at Lantern Park (Cǎidēng Gōngyuán).

Sleeping

Tiānxiáng Dàjiǔdiàn (☎ 220 9067; 1 Jiefang Lu; 解放路1号; s/d Y60/80) Despite battered, smelly halls, this is a good central budget option with plain, clean rooms – you'll find the best ones on the 5th floor or higher. Cheerful, easygoing staff are another bonus.

Shāwān Fàndiàn (☎ 220 8888; fax 220 1168; 3 Binjiang Lu; 滨江路3号; d Y118-238, ste Y350) This cavernous monster has friendly service and some of the best-value rooms in town. Multicoloured cushions give the rooms a bit of pizzazz, something you don't usually see in this price range. The only caution concerns the bathrooms: some are nursing ferocious rust problems around the drains and pipes. Rooms with a river view are generally around Y20 more expensive than (quieter) digs at the back of the hotel.

Rongguang Business Hotel (Róngguāng Shāngwù Jiǔdiàn; ☎ 211 7777; 25 Ziyou Lu; 自由路25号; s/d Y288/268) One of the newer operations in town, rooms here are low-key and comfortable and many are bright with natural light. Everything is spic-and-span and bathrooms have modern sinks and toilets. Discounts here can be phenomenal, running as low as Y80 to Y120 in the low season.

Xiongfei Holiday Hotel (Xióngfēi Jiàrì Jiǔdiàn; ☎ 211 8888; fax 211 8811; 193 Jiefang Lu; 解放路193号; s & d from Y520;) Reception staff here aren't generally very comfortable with foreigners, but

rooms in this hotel's new business wing are outstanding. Sometimes discounted as low as Y250, most are outfitted with computers and internet access and a breakfast buffet is included in the rate. Just prepare yourself for the long trek from the lobby to the business wing – the route winds through several long corridors and necessitates elevator rides in separate parts of the hotel.

Eating

Zìgòng is a great place for street food and quick eats.

Zhonghua Lu is packed with barbecue (*shāokǎo*) and noodle stalls. Brace yourself if buying around lunch time – you'll be battling with dozens of hyper school children to place your order.

The area around Lantern Park is also good to check out. If you're on the hunt for coffee, there's a Western café (Caideng Jie) opening beside the northern entrance that may be worth checking out. Meanwhile, just south of the park there's a flat paved area where dozens of food stalls set up year-round.

If you want something a bit more formal, head to the southern part of Tongxing Lu, where several indoor, sit-down restaurants specialising in Sìchuān fare line the eastern side of the street.

Drinking & Entertainment

If you are looking for something besides karaoke with your beer, there's not a lot in Zìgòng to recommend. However, teahouses are all over town. Dozens line the edges of the Fuxi River, especially its south bank.

Wángye Sì (Binjiang Lu) A teahouse by day, beer replaces green tea most nights at this former temple. However, the atmosphere is hit or miss. One weekend it may be packed, while the next it doesn't get much more exciting than a few people sitting around playing cards. This place is usually open by 10am at the latest; closing time depends on the crowd.

Getting There & Away

BUS

Zìgòng's long-distance bus station (长途汽车站; Chángtú Qìchēzhàn) is 2km south of the town centre and has daily services to Chéngdū (Y70, three hours, every 40 to 60 minutes from 7am to 7pm), Chóngqìng (Y69, three hours, every 40 to 60 minutes from 6.40am to 6.30pm), Dàzú (Y44, two hours, 8.30am and 2.50pm), Nèijiāng (Y14, 50 minutes, every 30 minutes from 7.20am to 7pm), Yíbīn (Y23, one hour, hourly from 7.30am to 7pm), Lèshān (Y35, three hours, 6.10am and 4.45pm) and Éméi town (Y35, three hours, 6.30am).

TRAIN

With those great bus connections, Zìgòng's train station is fairly quiet. Trains to Yíbīn depart at 3pm (Y9), 4pm (Y4.50) and 5pm (Y4). To Chéngdū there is a morning train at 10.46am (Y35). A night train bound for Chéngdū passes through at 11.46pm, but you can't reserve sleepers in Zìgòng. To Chóngqìng, the train pulls out at 11am (Y25).

Getting Around

A taxi between the town centre and long-distance bus station will cost around Y8. Bus 35 goes out to the Dinosaur Museum.

YÍBĪN 宜宾

☎ 0831 / pop 244,500

Yíbīn may be a bland, bustling city but it's the jumping-off point to some of southern China's most exciting day trips and is a convenient transport hub.

Yíbīn's Min and Jinsha Rivers merge at the eastern end of town to form the Yangzi River, or Cháng Jiāng. The city is known in China for being home to the first port on the Yangzi River.

The city's lost much of its traditional architecture and neighbourhoods to modernisation in recent years. So these days, besides its proximity to some intriguing sights further south, Yíbīn is mostly known for its liquor distilleries, especially Wuliangye (Five Grain Liquor) and Yishouye.

Information

Bank of China (Zhōngguó Yínháng; 45 Nan Jie; ☽ 8.30am–noon & 2–6pm Mon–Fri) Credit card advances and cash exchanges here are no problem. Only one employee in the entire bank is trained to handle travellers cheques. If she's sick, has the day off or is on vacation you're out of luck.

China International Travel Service (CITS; Zhōngguó Lǚxíngshè; ☎ 820 4518; Dongmen; 东门; ☽ 8am–6pm) Located at Yíbīn's old East Gate, staff here aren't too interested in independent travellers, but a couple of the employees may help you out anyway just for a chance to practise their English.

China Post (Zhōngguó Yóuzhèng; Nan Jie) South of the bank.

China Telecom (Zhōngguó Diànxìn, Xi Jie) There are also heaps of other places southwest of the traffic circle where you can make long-distance calls.

Internet café (wǎngbā; 2nd fl, Minzhu Lu; per hr Y2; ☽ 24hr) Best place in town; bright and clean with fast connections and comfy chairs.

Public Security Bureau (PSB; Gōngānjú; ☎ emergency 110; lane off Minzhu Lu)

Sights & Activities

As it lurches towards modernisation, Yíbīn's interesting back streets and traditional wooden architecture have all but disappeared. There's not much of interest in the city itself these days.

The geographical centre of town is the elaborate **Grand Viewing Pavilion** (Dàguān Lóu), with roads leading off in all four directions.

North of here is the **Zhōnggǔ Lóu**, an old bell and clock tower. After its construction in 1932, the city stopped banging drums to indicate the time.

The **East Gate** (Dōng Mén), along the Min River (Mín Hé), is the last remaining example of the traditional city gates. It and the area around it have been heavily renovated and landscaped and are now known as **Shuǐ Dōngmén Guǎngchǎng**. There's also a **teahouse** (cháguǎn) on the grounds here for those who want to linger. Across from here a walkway has been built along the edge of the river, which you can follow, reaching another renovated square and eventually the Jinsha River (Jīnshā Jiāng).

On the other edge of town is **Chuiping Park** (Chuìpíng Gōngyuán), where a less-than-beautiful concrete pagoda gives good views of the city below.

Sleeping

Yíbīn has a big choice of midrange and top-end hotels, but there are not a lot of budget places to recommend – surprising for a city of this size.

Jingmao Hotel (Jīngmào Bīnguǎn; ☎ 701 0888; fax 701 0800; 108 Minzhu Lu; 民主路108号; d Y120) Foreigners send the staff here into near hysterics, so a little Chinese or a phrasebook would be helpful. Once you've got that out of the way, the rooms, though bland and off some terribly dark and neglected halls, are pretty good for this price range.

Jīnyuàn Bīnguǎn (☎ 822 5634; Cishan Lu; 慈善路; s & d Y258) You'll get a warm welcome here as

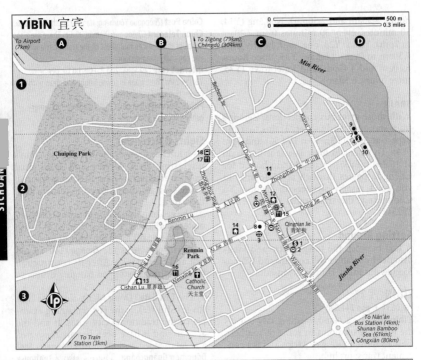

staff are comfortable with foreigners, distinguishing this hotel from a lot of other places in town. The halls can be quite battered, but the rooms, though sometimes on the small side, are clean and tidy. Discounts are as low as Y130 in off-season periods.

Yibin Grand Hotel (Yíbīn Dàjiǔdiàn; ☎ 818 6666; fax 818 6699; 20 Xi Jie; 西街20号; s Y580, d Y418-580; 🖭) Staff can be pretty shy with foreigners, but the bland rooms are quite comfortable and a good buffet breakfast is included in the room rate. The only quibble some may have with this place is the muzak: it's not only blasted into halls, but seems funnelled into some of the rooms as well. Bring earplugs – they might be

the only thing between you and 'Jingle Bells' (the string version, what's more).

Eating & Drinking
The streets of Yíbīn are lined with countless stalls dishing up snacks and fast food from dawn until dusk.

Zhongshui Jing Jie, the road leading up to Beimen bus station, is the best place to hit for noodles – restaurants here have everything from chilli-infused Chinese to coriander-sprinkled Muslim varieties. For dumpling stalls and bakeries head to Wenxiang Jie.

If you are looking for decent coffee, Minzhu Lu just north of Dong Jie seems to have nothing but Western-style cafés, many of which double as bars at night. **Cite Coffee** (Xītídǎo Kāfēi; ☎ 898 1666; 18 Minzhu Lu; 民主路18号; mains from Y16; ◷ 9am-2am) has the nicest atmosphere.

Getting There & Away
AIR
Yíbīn airport, 7km northwest of town, has flights to Kūnmíng (Y510, one hour, two daily, usually evenings), Běijīng (Y1400, two hours 35 minutes, daily), Guǎngzhōu (Y1130, one hour 50 minutes, daily) and Shànghǎi (Y1500, two hours 10 minutes, Monday, Friday and Sunday). At the moment, there are no flights to Chéngdū, Guìyáng, Chóngqìng or Xīchāng.

BUS
Yíbīn has three bus stations – Nán'àn, Beimen and Ximen – though only the former two are likely to be of interest to travellers.

From the Beimen station, there's daily service to Chéngdū (Y97, four hours, every 20 to 50 minutes from 7am to 6pm), Chóngqìng (Y81 to Y95, four hours, every 30 to 50 minutes from 6.45am to 6pm), Lèshān (Y57, four hours, 8.40am) and Zìgòng (Y23, 50 minutes, 7am to 7pm). There are also daily buses for Lúzhōu (泸州; Y27, every 30 to 40 minutes from 7am to 5pm), from where you can continue on to Chìshuǐ in Guìzhōu province. There are no buses heading southwest to either Xīchāng or Kūnmíng.

If going to the Hanging Coffins, the Nán'àn station (南岸汽车站) has buses to Luòbiǎo (Y30, three to four hours, 2pm) and Gǒngxiàn (Y16, two to three hours, every 30 minutes from 6.20am to 7pm). If travelling to the Bamboo Sea, it also has buses to Chángníng (Y11.50, one hour, every 20 minutes from 6.30am to 7pm) and Wànlíng (Y4.50, 20 to 30 minutes, every 20 to 30 minutes from 7am to 5.40pm).

TRAIN
Yíbīn's train station is 3km south of the town centre.

There is an early morning train to Chóngqìng (Y34, nine hours) departing at 6am, as well as an overnight sleeper at 9.22pm (Y74). To Chéngdū there is a slow train leaving at 9.08am (Y28) or a faster one at 10pm (Y47). Two departures a day stop at Zìgòng, the faster one at 9.08am (Y12); however, it's much faster to take a minibus.

AROUND YÍBĪN
Shunan Bamboo Sea 蜀南竹海
This **park** (Shǔnán Zhúhǎi; admission Y63; ◷ ticket office 8am-5.30pm) was made out of one of the largest swaths of bamboo forest in China's Southwest and covers a terrain of 120 sq km.

The scenery, spread out over crumpled hills and modest valleys, is remarkable, with swaying tufts of bamboo bobbing near waterfalls and pools of inky black water. This one-of-a-kind scenery is a major draw for movie and TV directors and many period films and miniseries have been filmed here.

Some 30 types of bamboo are found throughout the park, including Nan, Mao, Golden, Fishpole, Turtleback and Flower Bamboo, all of which have been used to produce everything the local people have needed over the centuries, from needles to furniture to paper to jewellery.

The scenic area was created by cordoning off this bamboo-rich part of the countryside, 61km south of Yíbīn. Though it's called a park, it's almost indistinguishable from other parts of the nearby region except that it has been developed for tourism. For the villagers inside the park, life goes on as usual and you'll see locals everywhere, cutting down bamboo stocks, carrying bamboo bundles on their shoulders and whittling away at it on the side of the roads. Bamboo carvings, dishes or other souvenirs are sold at almost every shop in the area.

The park continues to be developed, and more hotels and shops are added each year. Despite this, the Bamboo Sea still isn't very tourist-friendly for individual travellers, as transportation can be awkward.

Distances between the sights are significant and if you haven't come with a hired car it can be time-consuming to get around. In the high season there are usually private motorcycles and taxis hovering at the entrance so you can negotiate transport. On colder days or slow months, you are likely to be on your own. You can flag down public buses that go from village to village, but this doesn't give you very much flexibility if you want to see some of the more off-the-beaten-track sights.

So, despite having to deal with lots of boisterous tour groups, the high-season summer months are probably the best time to visit – at least the group travellers ensure that hotels and restaurants are open and there's a better

SÌCHUĀN

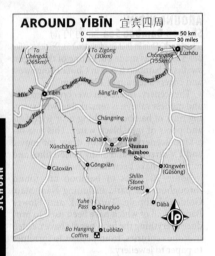

AROUND YÍBĪN 宜宾四周

chance of flagging down rides from one place to another.

The low season is still doable – you'll have the place pretty much to yourself – but it can be a challenge even for the most independent-minded travellers. Many hotels and restaurants are closed, fog devours some of the most picturesque views and constantly hustling for infrequent (and at times very expensive – the drivers know you have no other choice) transportation can be a drain.

Whatever time you visit, the bamboo forest is probably best enjoyed as a one- or two-night trip if you are coming by public transport, though it could certainly be done as a day trip from Yíbīn at a push.

SIGHTS

The ticket gate for the Bamboo Sea is at the western edge of the park. Buses will let you off to buy your ticket before continuing on to Wànlíng village (万岭) where you get off. However, if you see motorcycles or taxis at the entrance, you can negotiate with them instead of continuing on with the bus.

Though some of the sights listed here had posted admission fees of Y5 to Y15 on top of the park entry fee, at the time of research, there was no-one around collecting them from visitors.

In Wànlíng, you can check out the **Bamboo Museum** (竹海博物馆; Zhúhǎi Bówùguǎn; ☎ 820 5146, 498 0561; admission free; ☒ 8.30am-5.30pm). It's a creaky drafty place, but the 1st floor has some wonderful displays of bamboo weap-

ons and the 2nd floor has bamboo clothes, carvings and furniture. Continue south to the waterfalls of **Forgetting Worries Valley** (忘忧谷; Wàngyōu Gǔ) or turn left for the inky pools of **Black Brook Valley** (黑溪; Hēixī) and a rusty old **cable car** (one way/return Y30/40; ☒ 8.30am-5.30pm high season, closed low season), which gives you a worthwhile bird's-eye view of the forest, its pools and waterfalls.

At the top of the cable car is **Looking at the Sea Pavilion** (观海楼; Guānhǎi Lóu), which gives a view down onto the billowing canopy of wispy bamboo heads that give the Bamboo Sea its name. A short walk away is **Jadeite Corridor** (翡翠长廊; Fěicuì Chángláng), a red-dirt road cutting through towering 20m-high bamboo – a scene captured on everything from bus station walls to baseball caps.

If you're looking for some exercise and fresh air, a longer hiking trail ascends between Wànlíng village and **Lóngníng Sì** (龙咛寺), from where you can meet up with the road and carry on to Jadeite Corridor or continue southeast to **Fairy Cave** (仙寓洞; Xiānyù Dòng) or get transport further afield to **Tiānhuáng Sì** (天皇寺).

From Jadeite Corridor you can head back down to Wànlíng by the cable car or along the southern paved road. While this road does offer a few nice views, you aren't going to see a lot more than pavement and bamboo trunks, so you might consider making this 8km trek by flagging down transportation if you don't have any already.

SLEEPING

Hotels in the park are not necessarily open year-round. If you're visiting in the off season, it's a good idea to call ahead, and, if coming in winter, ask if the heat and electricity will be turned on.

New hotels seem to be under construction all over the place, usually around the car parks.

Zhúhǎi Bīnguǎn (Bamboo Sea Hotel; 竹海宾馆; ☎ 498 0000; d from Y170) Overlooking Wànlíng, this weathered hotel is conveniently located and in a beautiful setting.

Shǔnán Bīnguǎn (蜀南宾馆; ☎ 498 0555; d Y228) For something more upscale, try this place on the opposite side of town.

Guānxiānlóu Bīnguǎn (观仙楼宾馆; ☎ 497 0162; r Y280-360) If you want to stay deeper in the park, this hotel is near the Fairy Cave in the park's southeast.

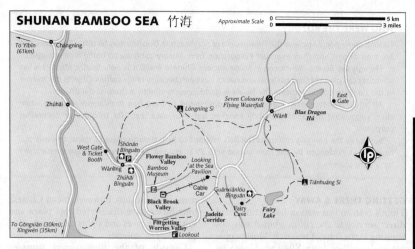

SHUNAN BAMBOO SEA 竹海 Approximate Scale

EATING

Finding something to eat here is no problem – food stalls and simple restaurants are everywhere. There are a number of restaurants around the car park in Wànlǐng, as well as across from the Zhúhǎi Bīnguǎn and near Looking at the Sea Pavilion.

GETTING THERE & AWAY

From Yíbīn's Nán'àn station, take a bus to Chángníng (Y11.50, one hour, every 20 minutes from 6.30am to 7pm), then on to Wànlǐng (Y4.50, 20 to 30 minutes, every 20 to 30 minutes from 7am to 5.40pm), the biggest village inside the Bamboo Sea perimeter.

You may see a posting for a direct bus to the Bamboo Sea from Yíbīn (2.30pm). Not only is this bus service frequently suspended, but it actually only goes to Zhúhǎi (Bamboo) village – several kilometres from the Bamboo Sea's ticket booth and entrance.

Buses back to Chángníng leave Wànlǐng until at least 5pm. Buses from Chángníng back to Yíbīn run until at least 6pm.

Bo Hanging Coffins 悬棺

It's a hell of a slog to get here, but the so-called **hanging coffins** (xuánguān; ☎ 401 1002; admission Y20; ◷ 8am-7pm) are one of the more original sites in Sìchuān and will definitely appeal to travellers looking for something a little offbeat.

Hundreds of wooden coffins were placed in caves and precariously balanced on wooden stakes in the cliffsides of the Deying Valley. Anywhere from 10m to 130m above ground, the coffins are attributed to the ancient Bo people. The oldest coffins date back roughly 1000 years, while the most recent addition was put there only about 400 years ago.

While small numbers of hanging coffins are found in Yúnnán province and other parts of China's Southwest, the largest number and best preserved coffins are here. Once, there were almost 300 of them, though at least one coffin plummets to the ground every 18 months, decreasing their number over the last two decades. Conservationists are working to stabilise the coffins, hoping to preserve the remaining ones.

Nobody really knows why the coffins were put in the cliffs, how they got the coffins up there in the first place or what happened to the Bo people who have since disappeared (see the boxed text, p430). The mystery just adds to the enigma of the place.

While you can see a few of the coffins on a cliff before the entrance gate (ie without buying a ticket), once inside there are a greater number of coffins and stairs that allow you to climb up on the cliff faces for a better look.

You can also check out the small **museum** just inside the grounds near the ticket office. There are some interesting pictures, a skeleton and a couple of coffins you can inspect up close – no English captions though.

There's not much else to do at the site once you've gawked at the coffins, but they do pack enough of a punch to make the trip worth it. You could do some nice walks in the surrounding valley if you wanted to linger.

WHO WERE THE BO?

Though some people believe the Tujia people of northeastern Guìzhōu may be distant relatives, the Bo, their origins and their eventual evaporation from history continue to baffle archaeologists.

Though the Bo are mentioned in some ancient Chinese texts, it is only briefly. Most of what scientists can glean of their customs and habits has been because of the coffins. Objects discovered in the hanging coffins indicate the Bo were good horsemen with a sharp social divide.

All adult skeletons examined were also discovered to have had their teeth removed while alive, suggesting the Bo deliberately knocked out their own teeth for religious or decorative purposes.

Some see the hanging coffins as the Bo's attempt to help their deceased's spirits towards the heavens, as evidenced by one man buried with 29 shirts and 13 trousers, apparent preparation for a long journey.

GETTING THERE & AWAY

Yíbīn's Nán'àn bus station has at times had direct service to the coffins, but it was not running at the time of research. Most people get to the coffins from Yíbīn via Gǒngxiàn (珙县; Y16, two to three hours, every 30 minutes from 6.20am to 7pm). From Gǒngxiàn take another bus south over the Yuhe Pass to Luòbiǎo (洛表; Y13, 2½ hours, every 50 minutes).

The coffins are a further 3km walk south of Luòbiǎo. The bus will drop you at a fork in the road; head down the road on the right.

Buses return hourly to Gǒngxiàn between 6am and 5pm. From there, you can get buses back to Yíbīn until 6.40pm.

The coffins are not easily visited as a day trip. It takes three hours just to get here if you hire a car (Y300 to Y400), and up to five hours by bus – it's doable, but you must leave *early*.

Whether you come by bus or car, the way here, especially between Xúnchǎng (巡场) and Luòbiǎo, will take you through some of the ugliest and most heartbreakingly polluted towns and villages you're likely to see in Sìchuān. Also, road conditions in some places are horrible, especially between Gǒngxiàn and Luòbiǎo.

Stone Forest 石海

Xīngwén's Stone Forest (Shíhǎi Dòngxiāng) is an increasingly popular sight and if you've hired a car, a visit here is a nice add-on to a Bamboo Sea trip. By bus it can be done as a day trip from Yíbīn.

As recently as a few years ago, this could almost have been considered an off-the-beaten-path sight; few people made it out here. Improved roads and tourist develop-ment in the region, however, mean Chinese tour buses have discovered this place and some of the caves and sights can be crowded and noisy in summer.

Outside of the high-season summer months, this place retains some of its rugged, untouched feel. It has some impressive caves and there can be a real primeval feel about the place, though, like the Bamboo Sea, during off-peak periods, it can at times feel almost too deserted.

The big draw here is **Big Funnel Cave** (admission Y50; ⏱ 8am-6pm), an enormous cave with dramatic lighting and limestone formations. Coming out of the cave at the other side there are a few restaurants and souvenir shops, but they will likely be closed outside of the peak season.

There are also plenty of other stone formations outside. The routes are marked with English signs.

GETTING THERE & AWAY

Shílín (石林) village and the Stone Forest can be reached via Xīngwén. To reach Xīngwén (also known as Gǔsòng), take a bus from Yíbīn (Y19.50, three hours, every 90 minutes from 7am to 6pm). You can also reach Xīngwén from Xúnchǎng (Y13, two hours).

From Xīngwén, buses run hourly from the west bus station to Shílín village (Y8, 30 to 40 minutes), 21km away. Be sure to ask for the village itself or you'll be dropped at the entrance to the cave. From Shílín, buses run hourly(ish) back to Xīngwén. Catch them at the crossroads leading into the village.

Xīngwén bus station has regular services to Yíbīn and Xúnchǎng until about 5pm.

If heading from Xīngwén on to Chìshuǐ in northern Guìzhōu, you can get a bus to

Lúzhōu (Y27, three hours) and buy your onward ticket to Chìshuǐ, some 2½ hours east.

XĪCHĀNG 西昌

☎ 0834 / pop 129,200

Squirrelled away in Sìchuān's south, Xīchāng is a terrific little city – clean, laid-back and one of the most welcoming places in the entire province. It's the capital of the Liángshān (Cool Mountains) Yi Autonomous Prefecture so there's great possibility for off-the-beaten-path exploration of the region's Yi villages and surrounding countryside.

Xīchāng is also a great jumping-off point for the back-door route into Yúnnán.

Little of the town's traditional character remains. New construction has left little other than forgettable modern buildings thrown up around vast, soulless boulevards.

For a little more character, you'll have to head up to the northeast of town where there's still some traditional architecture and a mix of Han, Yi and Huí people buying and selling at small markets.

Xīchāng is also home to China's major satellite launching operation – which is why you'll see more space-related statues and souvenirs than usual.

On the edge of town is the large Qiónghǎi Hú, where you can watch the fishermen. There is also a big torch festival here in July.

Mild weather makes the city pleasant to visit year-round, even in the winter months.

Information

Bank of China (Zhōngguó Yínháng; Sanchakou Lu) Changes travellers cheques and cash Monday to Friday from 8.30am to noon and 2pm to 6pm.

China Post (Zhōngguó Yóuzhèng; 45 Chang'an Donglu) Centrally located next to Yóudiàn Bīnguǎn.

Internet café (wǎngbā; Longyanjing Jie; per hr Y2; ☻ 24hr) Head down the lane off Longyanjing Jie. The computers are up the external stairs on the 2nd floor.

Public Security Bureau (PSB; Gōngānjú; ☎ emergency 110; lane off Shita Jie)

Tourist Information Booth (Lǚxíng Zīxún Fúwù Zhōngxīn; ☎ 323 0166; Yuecheng Sq; ☻ 8am-8pm) No English is spoken here but this little booth is still the best source of travel information. It has a touch-screen station with heaps of info about sights, accommodation and transportation, with an 'in English' option.

Xichang International Travel Service (XITS; Xīchāng Lǚxíng Shè; ☎ 610 3155) Down a long, narrow lane off Shengli Nanlu, Yi Duan, this place can arrange tours of the Satellite Launching Centre. However, the office is irregu-larly staffed. If you are lucky, one of the neighbours may offer to phone an employee for you.

Sights

The **old quarter** (古城; gǔchéng) in the northeast is the most atmospheric part of the city. Centred on the south gate of the old walled city, streets here are often overflowing with Yi traders selling vegetables and medicines. Check out the riverside **market** along Shunhe Lu, then stroll along Nan Jie, a narrow street of rickety old wooden buildings clogged with locals.

Shangye Buxing Jie situated nearby is a packed pedestrian-only street of three- and four-storey buildings housing everything from fast-food restaurants to clothing and shoe stores.

Torch Square (Huǒbǎ Guǎngchǎng) in the south of town is also worth a visit. One of the biggest urban projects is going on here, with a huge cultural and arts centre being built along with an outdoor amphitheatre. Still under construction at the time of research, the cultural centre, a sloping grey building with all kinds of odd angles and slashes of red, is shaping up to be a pretty stunning piece of architecture. Locals flock here on weekends to walk and check out the progress.

Qiónghǎi Hú (邛海湖; Qionghai Lake), dotted with villages and parks and surrounded by temples, is the area's most popular site. About 7km from town, bus 22 (Y1) goes directly to the lake. You can spend the whole day just hopping on and off the bus wherever it looks like it might be interesting to explore.

Fishing boats dot the lake year-round and seafood is the local speciality. You'll see people frying up fresh catches at stalls in most of the area's villages. The BBQ fish at **Xiǎo Yúcūn village** (小渔村) has a particularly good reputation.

You can also take boats from one side of the lake to the other – though you may not find anyone around during low-season months. Prices depend on the type of boat and how many people there are, but figure Y15 to Y20 per person for 30 minutes as a starting point. Windsurfing equipment is also available for rent during summer.

The Buddhist and Taoist complex of **Lú Shān** rises from the western shore of the lake. The majority of the eight temples were razed during the Cultural Revolution, however, a walk up the hill takes you past 2000-year-old

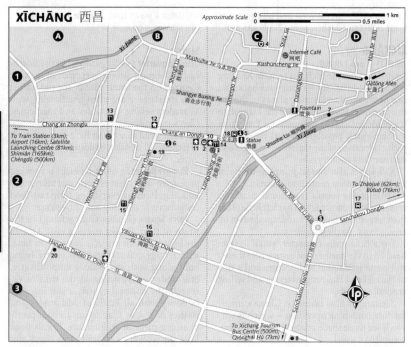

cypress trees that date from the Han dynasty, offering excellent views of the lake and surrounding mountains.

About 15 minutes' walk up Lú Shān lies the **Liangshan Yi Minority Slave Museum** (凉山彝族奴隶社会博物馆; Liángshān Yízú Núlì Shèhuì Bówùguǎn; admission Y30; ☼ 8am-5pm). Captions are in Chinese only, but the collection of weapons, black-and-white photos and detailed local maps are still interesting.

To reach Lú Shān and the museum, take bus 22; the ride takes about 20 minutes. Once you get off, continue walking southeast and take the second small road uphill on the right. This will take you to the bottom of the stairs

leading up the hill. The museum will be on your right.

Sleeping

Xīchāng is drowning in midrange and top-end hotels. There's not a lot of great new budget choices but a couple of old standards are still very good.

Wùmào Bīnguǎn (☎ 322 3186; 13 Chang'an Donglu; 长安东路13号; s & d Y50-80) By far the best budget place in town, the halls here are as cold and clinical as a mental asylum's, but the simple rooms are clean and neat as a pin. Add Y10 if you want one with air-conditioning. The rooms are vastly different in size, decoration and type of toilet (ie squat or Western), but the price difference is often due to something simple such as the newness of the furniture or thickness of the blankets.

Yóudiàn Bīnguǎn (☎ 322 3312; 57 Chang'an Zhonglu; 长安中路57号; s/d Y120/90) Once you get past the somnolent staff and decrepit halls, the rooms here are actually quite nice – clean with big, albeit dark, bathrooms. It also doesn't use the cloying, sickly smelling, pseudo-lemon-scented air freshener that's seemingly *de rigueur* at most other hotels in town.

Yuedu Holiday Hotel (Yuèdū Jiàrì Jiǔdiàn; ☎ 323 4888; 14 Chang'an Lu; 长安路14号; s/d incl breakfast Y300/228) Centrally located, this hotel has a terrific, friendly staff. Though slightly old-fashioned, rooms are in tiptop shape and there's little substantial difference between them and rooms at other hotels in town costing double and triple the price.

Conily Inn (Kāilìlái Jiǔdiàn; ☎ 320 0888; 88 Shengli Nanlu; 胜利南路88号; d incl breakfast Y388-568) This four-star league hotel has the best reputation in town. Though none of the staff speaks English, they're all terrific, from the cleaners to the desk staff. Rooms are clean and comfortable across the board and the difference between the cheap and more expensive doubles is negligible. The only turn-off is the cockroach traps in some rooms.

Eating

A local speciality is *qìguō* (汽锅), an earthenware pot that has its soupy contents heated up by steam through a hole in the middle. Restaurants all over town serve *qìguō*; try the northern end of Shengli Nanlu. Another local treat is steamed oat bread made by Yi people and sold on the roadside in the mornings.

For a more fussy eating experience, try one of the restaurants on Yihuan Nanlu, Er Duan (you'll have no problem spotting them – hosts will be outside dressed up in Yi garb).

Good Wood Café (Kāfēiguǎn Xīcān; ☎ 888 8099; Longyanjing Jie; 龙眼井街; mains Y22-38; ⏱ 9am-2am) This café has an English menu, but the food (whether Chinese or Western) isn't that great (chocolate sundaes come festooned with Pringles potato chips, for example). But the atmosphere is cosy, the chairs plush and it's a good stop for coffee or a beer.

The **JiaJia Supermarket** (Shengli DongLu; ⏱ 8.30am-10pm) is a great place to pick up food for day trips and long bus rides. There's also a good **bakery** (⏱ 9am-7pm) on Wenhui Lu.

Shopping

If your dream is to own a model 'Long March' rocket or a 'The East is Red' satellite, you've definitely come to the right place. There are quite a few shops flogging such space-themed souvenirs alongside bottles of Pepsi-Cola or sacks of sunflower seeds.

Also keep your eyes open for Yi wares – red, yellow and black lacquered bowls and dishes, long pipes and embroidered clothing – though you will find a better selection for better prices at one of the region's surrounding villages or at shops along Qiónghǎi Hú.

Getting There & Away

Xīchāng has become increasingly well connected to the rest of Sìchuān as well as Yúnnán in recent years. However, it is still a good idea to buy your onward ticket as soon as possible if you are on a tight schedule.

It's not uncommon for economy seats on flights to be sold out one to two days in advance.

There are no direct train, bus or flight services heading northeast of here to Yíbīn or Zìgòng.

AIR

Monday to Friday, there are four flights daily from Chéngdū to Xīchāng (Y340 to Y460, one hour, 7.20am and 8.40am; Y480 to Y570, noon and 3.50pm). On Saturday and Sunday only the afternoon flights are offered.

From Xīchāng to Chéngdū, flights leave at 9.05am, 10am, 5.10pm and 6pm, Monday to Friday. Saturday and Sunday flights leave at 1.40pm and 5.35pm. Flights out of Xīchāng are not usually discounted and run between Y480 and Y570.

You can buy tickets at the **plane ticket office** (Hángkōng Shòupiàochù; ☎ 888 8777; Shengli Nanlu Yi Duan; ⏱ 8am-8pm) downtown.

The airport is 16km north of town. A free shuttle bus meets incoming flights and will let you off wherever you want downtown. It takes 15 to 20 minutes to get into town.

A metered taxi from the airport to town costs around Y35, but taxi drivers may hit you up for Y50.

BUS

There are several bus stations in town. Xīchāng's modern and gleaming Tourism Bus Centre (Xīchāng Qìchē Lǚyóu Kèyùn Zhōngxīn) on Sanchakou Nanlu is the main

SICHUAN

YI SLAVE SOCIETY

Each Yi clan belongs to a different caste, which up until the 1950s was the basis of a slave society.

The Black Yi, the aristocrats and landowners, made up 7% of the population and owned 80% of the land. The White Yi made up around 50% of the population and had no freedom of movement. A Black Yi who committed murder could offer a White Yi as compensation to the family of the deceased. The White Yi also had to offer a fixed amount of time each year working in the Black Yi's fields. The lowest of the two classes, the Ajia (33%) and Gaxi (10%), were freely bought and sold as slaves and had no rights.

The Yi were famous for their slave-raiding trips into Han territory. Han traders only dared enter the Liángshān Shān under the protection of a local chief. During the Nationalist era, several powerful Sìchuān warlords were of Yi descent. Slave society existed in the Liángshān region until 1959, when the communists forced the transition to a socialist society.

---

hub and of most use to travellers. There's a daily bus to Chéngdū (Y123, 8.30am), but delays caused by ongoing roadwork means this trip will take a minimum of 12 hours (up from a mere eight). Most people are just taking the train these days. There's also daily service to Lúgū Hú in Yúnnán (Y68, seven to eight hours, 9am – make sure you don't buy a ticket for Sìchuān's Lúgū village by mistake!), Pānzhīhūa (Y40, six hours, 11am), Pǔgé (Y17 to Y26, two hours, every 40 minutes from 7am to 5.40pm) and Kāngdìng (Y88, 6am – nobody seems to know how long this trip takes). There's also a daily sleeper bus for Kūnmíng (Y122, 12 hours, 2pm).

Head to the dark, rickety **East Bus Station** (Kèyùn Dōngzhàn; Sanchakou Donglu) for daily service to Mùlǐ (Y59, eight hours, 7.40am, 8.20am and 9am), Bùtuō (Y21, four to five hours, every 20 minutes from 6.30am to 5pm) and Zhāojué (Y24, two to three hours, every 30 to 40 minutes from 7am to 4.45pm). It can get chaotic here around departure times, with dozens of villagers clamouring for the same tickets.

TRAIN

Xīchāng's train station is a few kilometres west of town (reachable on bus 6), but there's a useful ticket office on Hangtian Dadao Er Duan.

Roadwork between here and Chéngdū means people are abandoning buses for train travel, so hard-sleeper reservations are even more difficult to come by than usual.

There's one train a day to Jiājiāng (for Lèshān; Y100, seven hours) and Chéngdū (Y180, 11 hours), leaving at 3.14am and 11.21pm respectively. There is another train that continues north all the way to Xī'ān

(Y300), departing daily at noon. A notoriously crowded train to Kūnmíng passes through town at 9.50pm (Y120).

AROUND XĪCHĀNG
Satellite Launching Centre
卫星发射中心

China's major **satellite rocket launching centre** (wèixīng fāshè zhōngxīn) is one of Southwest China's more offbeat sites. Located in the Shaba Valley 65km north of Xīchāng, the centre now acts as a commercial venture and has launched several countries' satellites on the back of its Long March rockets.

China's own satellites come under the wonderfully named 'The East is Red' satellite system. The country launched its first satellites during the Cultural Revolution; the first thing it did was broadcast the speeches of Chairman Mao around the world.

Unfortunately, the rockets have had a nasty habit of plummeting back down to earth onto unsuspecting villages. It is believed that there have been several major accidents in the area resulting in a considerable (four-figure) loss of life.

Remarkably enough, Chinese tour groups still regularly visit the launch centre, though foreigners require a special permit to join them. Tourists can visit the control centre, launch pads and the small onsite museum before grabbing a bite to eat in the space canteen. In Xīchāng, the XITS (p431) can arrange tours for around Y118.

XITS will also assist you in applying for your permit, done through the local military rather than the PSB; unfortunately, this can take up to two weeks. Whether you actually get the permit is hit and miss, but it's certainly worth a try. You definitely won't get one if there are any launches imminent or if there have been any recent catastrophes.

The XITS sometimes keeps irregular hours. Contact them well in advance if you are interested in visiting the site so they know to expect you and so you can fax a photo of your passport ahead of time. If you can't get a hold of them, call or go to the Xichang Tourist Booth (p431), where someone might know if any other agency in town has started issuing permits.

Liangshan Yi Autonomous Prefecture 凉山彝族自治州

If you're interested in exploring Yi territory beyond the metropolis of Xīchāng, head out to one of the smaller towns or villages in the area that make up the Liangshan Yi Autonomous Prefecture (Liángshān Yízú Zìzhìzhōu).

Pǔgé (普格), a busy market town populated almost entirely by traditionally dressed Yi, makes a terrific day trip from town. The bus journey to Pǔgé passes through some beautiful scenery and tiny Yi villages where you can hop off for an hour or two until the next bus from Xīchāng passes by.

Buses for Pǔgé (Y17 to Y26, two hours, every 40 minutes from 7am to 5.40pm) leave from Xīchāng's Tourism Bus Centre; the last bus returns from Pǔgé at 5pm.

Other Yi towns in the region include **Bùtuō** (布拖), famous for having perhaps the largest torch festival, and **Zhāojué** (昭觉), which has the highest percentage of Yi in its population. You can reach both towns by bus from Xīchāng (see p433).

If you are headed up to Kāngdìng you will also see many remote Yi villages around **Tuōwū**. It's possible for die-hard explorers to visit more remote Yi towns by heading overland to Lèshān and stopping in Zhāojué.

Luójì Shān 螺髻山

Also in this region is Luójì Shān, a 4358m-high mountain named for its resemblance to a spiral snail shell. With hot springs, waterfalls and glacial lakes, Luójì Shān has become a popular spot for local tourism.

The climb to the top, however, is not as popular, although the steep ascent to the summit is estimated to take only three or four hours. The forested range in which Luójì Shān is situated offers further opportunities for exploration. Places to head for are **Five Colour Lake** (Wǔsè Hú) and **Big Lake** (Dà Hǎizi). April and May are usually the best times for hiking. You need to bring your own camping equipment, all food supplies and a good map of the area. For more information drop into Xīchāng's Tourist Information Booth (p431).

Buses for the mountain leave from Xīchāng's Tourism Bus Station.

Mùlǐ 木里

Mùlǐ is a remote Tibetan Autonomous Prefecture set deep in the 4500m-high Taiyang Mountain Range, or 'Mountains of the Sun', 245km west of Xīchāng. The region has several Tibetan monasteries, including the Mùlǐ Dásì, and backs into the three holy peaks of the Yading Nature Reserve.

You can get a bus to Mùlǐ from Xīchāng's East Bus Station (Y59, eight hours, 7.40am, 8.20am and 9am). You could combine a visit to Mùlǐ with a trip to Lúgū Hú in Yúnnán and then continue on to Lìjiāng.

Chóngqìng 重庆

It's the biggest city you've never heard of. The Capital of Fog. Chóngqìng may not be at the top of your itinerary, but if you're in China's Southwest, odds are you'll end up here. Stay a while. Chóngqìng saves its best for those who take their time.

For 50 years there was little to distinguish Chóngqìng from any of a dozen cities in China – except maybe the pollution. Steel mills spewed soot into the air and sludge into the water. It was said that the rain was black before it hit the ground.

Chóngqìng had been largely ignored since the 1940s, when it served as the wartime capital and was bombed to oblivion. In 1997 Běijīng finally took notice and carved out the Chóngqìng municipality, and poured $200 billion into transforming it.

As a result, Chóngqìng is being paved and polished at breakneck speed. Slick skyscrapers pop up in place of ramshackle, stilt houses, and beauty parlours and motorcycle-repair shops grow out of abandoned bomb shelters. It's the dynamics of old and new, the struggle between the past and the future, that comprise this city's beauty and character.

Chóngqìng's charm is in the easily missed little details. It is Saturday morning on the waterfront and a woman is casting a net into the muddy waters. 'It's true,' she says, 'many days the city is covered in fog. But you know, fog is beautiful. In Chóngqìng, we have a saying: "There is beauty here every three steps."'

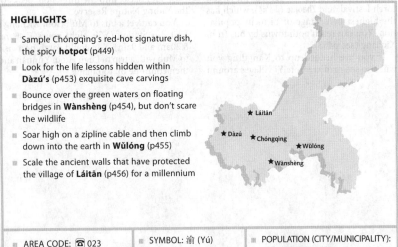

HIGHLIGHTS

- Sample Chóngqìng's red-hot signature dish, the spicy **hotpot** (p449)
- Look for the life lessons hidden within **Dàzú's** (p453) exquisite cave carvings
- Bounce over the green waters on floating bridges in **Wànshèng** (p454), but don't scare the wildlife
- Soar high on a zipline cable and then climb down into the earth in **Wǔlóng** (p455)
- Scale the ancient walls that have protected the village of **Láitǎn** (p456) for a millennium

★ Láitǎn
★ Dàzú ★ Chóngqìng
★ Wǔlóng
★ Wànshèng

| ▪ AREA CODE: ☎ 023 | ▪ SYMBOL: 渝 (Yú) | ▪ POPULATION (CITY/MUNICIPALITY): 4,307,000/31,904,000 |

HISTORY

Modern-day Chóngqìng stands on the site of one of humanity's earliest civilisations. Stone tools and fossils unearthed in the Yangzi River valley show that our upright ancestors roamed here two million years ago, a million years earlier than previously thought.

The first written history comes from the Ba (巴) empire, which inscribed its laws on tortoise shells and built its capital in present-day Chóngqìng. The Ba thrived from the 21st century BC until about 316 BC, when it was conquered by the Qin state. Despite the distance in time, the Ba influence remains strong – the 'hand-waving dance' of the Tujia, the largest minority group in the municipality, is derived from Ba war dances. The character-istic stilt houses of the region were also first built in the Ba era.

Fast forward to 1938, when the Kuomintang hid its wartime capital in Chóngqìng's mountains. Zhou Enlai, Mao Zedong, Chiang Kai-shek and Soong Chingling, communists and Kuomintang alike, came here. In their wake, refugees from all over the country followed, swelling the population to two million. Most of Chóngqìng's current tourist sights are linked to this era.

For a time, this overburdened, war-torn city could not live up to its name. Back in 1189, the local prince, upon becoming Emperor Zhao Dun of the Song dynasty on his birthday, had given Chóngqìng its name in celebration of his 'repeated good fortune'.

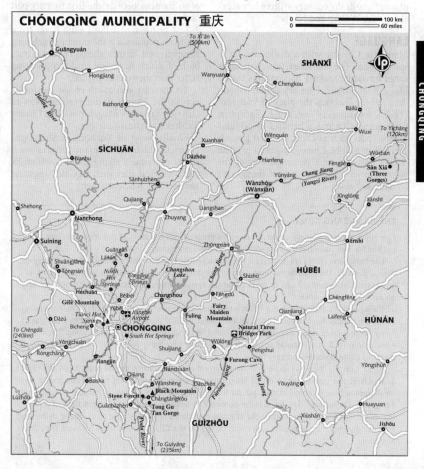

CHÓNGQÌNG MUNICIPALITY 重庆

Finally, recent decades have marked widespread reconstruction and development. New buildings and roads appear daily – a modern library in Shāpíngbà District, a Science and Technology Exhibition Hall in Jiāngběi and a massive Grand Theater perched on the north bank of the Jialing are among the major projects. From the ashes rises China's phoenix, a glass and steel megalopolis.

CLIMATE

Chóngqìng weather has just three settings: sweltering, rainy and foggy. Temperatures hover within a moderate range of 6°C to 20°C most of the year, but from July through September they can top 40°C, earning the city its place as one of the country's 'three furnaces', along with Wǔhàn and Nánjīng.

LANGUAGE

Mandarin Chinese with a distinctive lilt is spoken here. The characteristic accent turns tones upwards, making declarations sound like soft questions. One key colloquialism: 'Méi dé' (没得) takes the place of 'méi yǒu' (没有), meaning 'no' or 'none'. Except in Chóngqìng city and a handful of popular tourist spots such as Dàzú, the best English you'll hear will be Chinese eager to practise 'Hello, how are you?' or vendors vying for your attention. Once they have it, though, it's all hand signals.

ORIENTATION

Chóngqìng is a three-dimensional city, sprawling under and over hilltops and nestled deep into mountainsides. Its streets are so unruly that residents long ago dropped any reference to the sun and made everything relative. Your destination is to be found 'left', 'right', 'straight ahead', 'up', 'down' or 'soon'.

At the city's heart is Yúzhōng District, the densely populated peninsula that juts out between the Jialing River to the north and the Yangzi River (Cháng Jiāng) to the south. The rivers converge at Yúzhōng's eastern tip found at Chaotianmen Dock. Just inland from the dock is the Liberation Monument; the surrounding area of this monument, because of its flatness, became the first touristy part of the city.

Just north across the Jialing River from the main peninsula is the rapidly developing Jiāngběi, and further afield, Yúběi District, both of which have new roads cropping up faster than they can be named.

To the east and south of the peninsula across the Yangzi is the verdant Nán'àn District, the city's oxygen pool and Chiang Kaishek's wartime hide-out.

Finally, west of Yúzhōng is Shāpíngbà District, which has so many universities it seems everyone walking about is under 25, and historical sites such as Gele Mountain and Ciqikou Ancient Town.

THE BANGBANG ARMY

Ever since the first resident could not carry his groceries up the stairs of this mountain city, these porters for hire have been an essential element of Chóngqìng.

The Bàngbàng (棒棒) are named for the characteristic bamboo pole or 'bàng' (棒) they carry on their shoulders. They hustle for work around the docks, bus stations and department stores, offering to climb where no cart or mule could go, carrying loads few could bear and only earning an average Y100 a week.

Their numbers exploded in the 1990s when the government resettlement of the millions living along the Yangzi River began. Today, an estimated 100,000 are members of the city's Bàngbàng Army. Unregulated and poor, they are vulnerable to abuse and misunderstanding. Their lives were glamorised in a popular soap called 'Mountain City Bang Bang Men'. A popular college drinking game involves spotting them.

At 52, Cun Yu Zhun has more grey hair than others in the army, but he says, 'I can still carry as much as the youngsters' – up to 90kg (the eqivalent of four crates of oranges plus a few small appliances). A retired middle-school teacher, he is among a growing number of educated Bàngbàng. On his best day, he says, he earned Y30 delivering a TV to the front desk of a high-rise condominium and hauling bricks at a construction site. But as new roads make deliveries increasingly easy, most days, he waits with others on the Cháotiānmén steps for work that does not come.

Maps

City maps with points of interest and transit lines are updated every few months and come in both English and Chinese. A good one is *Commerce, Traffic and Tour Map of Chongqing*. Pick it up at any newsstand (报刊亭; *bào kān tíng*) for Y5 or stop by Chongqing Book City/Xinhua Bookstore, which offers a comprehensive selection on the 1st floor. Cháotiānmén vendors hawk cheap tourist maps most useful for taping to your dorm wall.

INFORMATION
Bookshops

Chongqing Book City/Xinhua Bookstore (Chóngqìng Shūchéng/Xīnhuá Shūdiàn; 121 Zourong Lu; 🕙 9am-9.30pm) Six stories of printed matter and DVDs that will actually pass customs. A modest foreign-language collection (including English-Chinese novels straight off your high-school reading list) is on the 4th floor. Check out the treasure-trove of Chinese art prints on the 5th.

Internet Access

Internet connections are no longer a rarity. Service at an internet bar (网吧; *wǎng bā*) generally costs a few yuán per hour plus a nominal deposit of Y10 or comes free with a cuppa at many coffee shops.

Frisco Coffee Co (☎ 6775 5992; 1B Paradise Walk, 2nd fl, 23 Yanghe Lu; 🕙 10am-10pm) Good coffee, tasty cheesecake and, free with purchase, wi-fi or access to two terminals in this sunny café in Guānyīn Qiáo.

Readers' Club Internet Café (Dúzhě Jùlèbù; ☎ 6371 6364; 3rd fl, 181 Minsheng Lu; per hr Y2, deposit Y10; 🕙 24hr) Surf for hours completely guilt-free on one of a legion of brand-new PCs, or just enjoy the cushy banquettes and bar service.

SPR Coffee (166 Minzu Rd; 🕙 9.30am-12am) Chinese hipsters in tight jeans come here for the salads, hot dogs and free wi-fi.

Media

Chongqing Currents is a free, fledgling English-language publication that answers expats' burning questions about table manners and where to get a decent beer. Alternatively, *Go West* is a free, Chéngdū-based magazine that also sometimes covers Chóngqìng's bar, restaurant and entertainment scenes. Unfortunately, only a few copies of either bimonthly publication are rationed to major hotels such as the Harbour Plaza, Hilton or JW Marriott. If you don't find them there, you're out of luck.

Medical Services

Chongqing First Aid Centre (Jíjiù Yīliáo Zhōngxīn; ☎ 6369 2253; 1 Jiankang Lu; 🕙 8am-5pm Mon-Fri, 8am-noon Sat & Sun) Provides comprehensive care and 24-hour emergency services (dial clinic) for foreign visitors.

Fuqiao Foot Massage Centre (Jiāfú Fùqiáo; ☎ 38-8399 8666; 3rd fl,12 Yang He Lu; 🕙 24hr) In traditional Chinese medicine, the feet are the gateway to the rest of the body. Try a 60-minute Chinese foot massage for Y50.

Global Doctor Chongqing Clinic (☎ 8903 8837; 7th fl, Suite 701, Hilton Hotel, 139 Zhongshan San Lu; 🕙 9am-5pm Mon-Fri, closed holidays) Provides basic care and 24-hour emergency services (dial clinic) for foreign visitors.

Heping Pharmacy (Hépíng Yàofáng; ☎ 6370 2900; 28 Minquan Lu; 🕙 8am-9.30pm) Has many branches but this is one of the biggest. On-site health advice too.

Money

Bank of China (Zhōngguó Yínháng; 104 Minzu Lu; 🕙 9am-noon & 2-6pm Mon-Fri summer, 1.30-5pm winter) Changes money and advances cash on credit cards. Bring your passport and crisp bills. After a rash of counterfeiting, tellers are extremely wary of foreign currency and, unlike you, they have all day. Thank goodness for the always-courteous 24-hour ATM bank across from Harbour Plaza. Also, many large hotels have exchange desks and ATMs.

Post

Post Office (Yóujú; 104 Minquan Lu; 🕙 8.30am-9pm) Look for the round, green post box out front. The service counter is tucked in back behind the mobile-phone sales counters. Don't expect lines. It's fight or flight if you want to buy stamps, international and domestic calling cards, or Western Union services.

Public Security Bureau

PSB (公安局; Gōngānjú; ☎ 63692043; www.cqga.gov.cn; 555 Huang Long Jie & Wu Huang Lu; 🕙 1.30-5pm) The Entry-and-Exit Bureau issues visa extensions. If you're after anything more unusual, take care of it in Chéngdū. Take bus 461 from Liberation Monument to the last stop and walk west a couple of blocks.

Tourist Information

Chongqing Municipal Tourism Bureau (Chóngqìng Shì Lǚyóu Jú; ☎ 8903 3055; 50 Jiuchikan & Cangbai Lu; 🕙 9am-noon & 1.30-5.30pm) Direct general questions and gripes to this public information office.

Travel Agencies

Your hotel concierge can ferret out better deals on tours and tickets than you can on your own but they will only offer a few choices. Check with a travel agency to find out all that's available.

CHÓNGQÌNG CITY

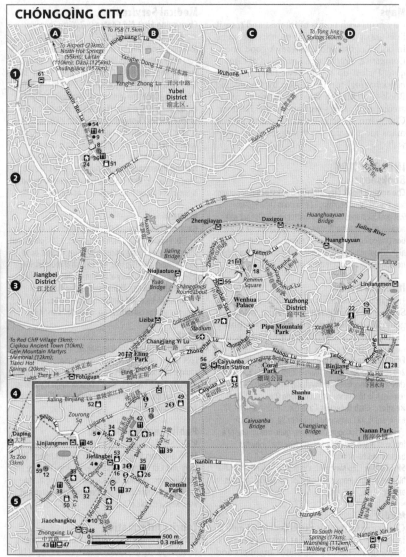

China International Travel Service (CITS; Zhōngguó Guójì Lǚxíngshè; ☎ 6373 0111; www.citscq.com; 25th fl, New York, New York Bldg, 108 Bayi Lu; ☒ 9am-6pm) Handles domestic and international travel for Chinese citizens, so city tours (Y60) and day trips to Dàzú and Wǔlóng (Y220 and up) are cheapest here. Expect booking and tours to be entirely in Chinese.

Chongqing China Travel Service (Chóngqìng Zhōngguó Lǚxíngshè; ☎ 6372 8888; www.ctscq.com;

19F, Tower A, Dushi Plaza, 39 Wusi Lu; ☒ 9am-6pm) Your best bet for booking tours outside the city proper. It says it has English, French, German, Korean, Thai and Japanese speakers on staff.

Harbour Plaza Business/Travel Centre (Hǎiyì Lǚyóu Zhōngxīn; ☎ 6370 0888; 3rd fl, Harbour Plaza, Wuyi Lu; ☒ 8am-11pm) Run by the posh Harbour Plaza hotel (p448), so staff is used to meeting high-maintenance trav-

anywhere ambling tourists frequent, especially bus and train stations and crowded areas such as Cháotiānmén and Liberation Monument.

Scams

Touts will try to make friends with you at the bus or train station. They may suggest a great (cheap!) hotel, by which they are paid to lure you. Avoid the hassle and tell them you've already reserved a room elsewhere, thank you. Sometimes they do have decent recommendations, but most of the time the hotel is already booked up. And if it isn't, it'll be obvious why.

SIGHTS

Chóngqìng's sights are scattered all over town and fall under two major themes: war and revolution; and other events. Many in the first category are west of the peninsula, but the rest are centrally located.

Liberation Monument 解放碑

If you have just a couple of days to spend in the city, **Liberation Monument** (Jiěfàngbēi; Zourong Lu & Minquan Lu; 邹容路和民权路) is the best place to start. First built to commemorate Sun Yatsen's death, the wooden tower's dedication was twice revised to mark the victory over the Japanese in 1947 and the first anniversary of the People's Republic of China in 1950. It's also the site of a spectacle every morning at 6am, when hundreds congregate at its base for taichi practice. Keep an eye out for blue Chinese and English markers pointing the way to major sites and shopping around this area.

Luóhàn Sì 罗汉寺

Just a 10-minute walk from Liberation Monument, this 1000-year-old Buddhist **Arhat temple** (cnr Xinhua Lu & Datong Lu; 新华路和打铜路交叉路口; admission Y5; 8am-5.30pm) stands in stark contrast to the concrete jungle outside its gates.

Luóhàn is the Chinese expression of the Sanskrit *arhat*, which is a Buddhist term for those enlightened disciples who have overcome the bondages of greed, hate and ignorance. The temple's striking feature is a long corridor of Song dynasty rock carvings. Among these carvings are a large bronze Buddha and an Indian-style *jataka* mural of Prince Siddhartha cutting his hair to renounce the world. There are also over 500 terracotta *arhats*, which could not withstand fires, bombs

ellers' needs and many are fluent in English. They can track down English guides for a premium price (city tour Y680).

DANGERS & ANNOYANCES

Chóngqìng is a relatively safe city, but pickpockets, especially children from the western provinces sometimes supervised by nearby adults, are becoming a nuisance. Take care and pollution, and so have been reincarnated a couple times, most recently in 1986.

Once home to 70 monks, there are only around a couple of dozen ascetics in residence these days. We visited during heavy renovations, which when completed will include a vegetarian eatery.

Three Gorges Museum 三峡博物馆

This **natural history and art museum** (Sānxiá Bówùguǎn; ☎ 6367 9066; www.3gmuseum.cn; 236 Renmin Lu; 人民路236号; adult/child Y40/20; ☷ 9am-5pm) covers the cultural history of the civilisations that grew up along the Yangzi's banks. The well-executed exhibits, some of which came from the former Chongqing Museum, warrant at least an afternoon. Check out the splendid Three Gorges Hall for a play-by-play of the first people who settled here all the way through to the construction of the world's largest dam (minus references to the social

upheaval). While English captions are sparse, you can rent an English audio tour for Y10.

On the other side, look across the square at the **People's Hall** (Rénmín Lǐtáng; admission Y5). When built in 1954, it was the tallest building in town and symbolised Chóngqìng's rebirth from backwater war casualty to modern metropolis.

Take light rail or bus 103 from Liberation Monument.

Hú Guǎng Huì Guǎn 湖广会馆

This **guild** (☎ 6393 0287; www.cqhuguang.com; 1 Chang-bin Lu, Bajiaoyuan, 长滨路芭蕉园1号; admission Y30; ☷ 9am-6pm) was the seat of immigrant life 300 years ago in the Qin dynasty. Eager to increase the population in Sìchuān, the government encouraged widespread immigration beginning in AD 316. By the time of the guild, the population was 800,000 and rapidly growing as settlers arrived mostly from the Hú (Húnán and Húběi) and Guǎng (Guǎngdōng and Guǎngxī) provinces, as well as 10 others. People came to the guild for legal processing and to worship and celebrate with other new arrivals.

English guides are available for Y60, though you could easily spend a day wandering on your own through the beautifully restored guild houses and their collections of furniture, art and jewellery.

Also worth checking out are the daily performances on the three opera stages, highlighting some examples of the traditions immigrants brought to Chóngqìng – from the tea art of Xīzàng to the quick-change *biàn liǎn* mask changing of Sìchuān. Free preview performances are put on at 2.30pm. Full performances with tea service are at 8pm (Y98 and up).

The guild is a 15-minute walk from Liberation Monument.

Cháotiānmén Dock 朝天门码头

Cháotiānmén has been one of China's busiest river ports since the Ming dynasty. From the square overlooking the dock, you can watch the jade green Jialing River meet the less photogenic, brown Yangzi. Climb down the steps to the markers along the bank marking the river's rise (eventually 175m) as a result of the Three Gorges Dam down river.

Chongqing Planning Exhibition Gallery 重庆市规划展览馆

This newly renovated **museum** (Chóngqìngshì Guīhuà Zhǎnlǎnguǎn; Chaotianmen Sq; 朝天门广场; admission Y20; ☉ 9.30am-5.30pm Tue-Sun) sets recent local history to flashing lights. As told by models, la-

sers and interactive consoles, the story of the Three Gorges Dam is a rosy one. Downstairs, a separate room is devoted to each of the 43 townships and counties comprising the municipality. Next door, the companion **Museum of Famous Historical Figures** (Lìshǐ Míngrén Guǎn; admission free; ☉ 8am-5pm Tue-Sun) introduces visitors to everyone who was anyone in this town, for example, prodigal son Deng Xiaoping, who grew up just north of Chóngqìng. Both museums' exhibits have many expert English captions.

Ciqikou Ancient Town 磁器口古镇

Perched on a hill overlooking the Jialing River 14km west of the city centre, Ciqikou Ancient Town (Cíqìkǒu Gǔzhèn) dates back almost 1700 years. At its height in the Ming dynasty, it shipped its namesake ceramics, *cíqì*, from the town pier.

Every building has been preserved or restored for tourists, but behind the shops and restaurants, the residents air their laundry and stir rice porridge over charcoal flames. And at 8pm each night, the town crier walks the streets banging a gong to announce all is well. Behind the lacquer is a living, working village – just one adorned with descriptive placards.

A network of alleyways and walking streets comprises the town. Check the map at the two main gates for all the attractions. A few sights not to be missed include **Bǎolún Sì** (宝伦寺; Heng Jie & Ciqikou Zheng Jie; 横街和磁器口正街; admission Y5; ☉ 7am-6pm), one the last remaining of Ciqikou's five temples (another now serves as a primary school). The magnificent main

---

DIÀOJIĂO LÓU 吊脚楼

A striking trait of the Chóngqìng skyline is the traditional stilt houses precariously clinging to the city's steep inclines. *Diàojiǎo* refers to these structures' support pilings, while *lóu* refers to their many levels.

Diàojiǎo lóu are in many ways the predecessor to the modern skyscraper, sprawling vertically rather than horizontally to save space. Their design also serves to keep family units in close quarters despite uneven terrain. They are built on a bamboo or fir frame that is fitted into bore holes drilled into the mountainside. Their thin walls are stuffed with straw and coated with mud to allow for cooling ventilation. This is in contrast to the four-cornered *sìhéyuàn* (四合院) structures typical in northern China, whose design maximises light while shutting in warmth.

The Miao minority continues to live in *diàojiǎo lóu* today, building their houses to jut out over steep riverbanks. The burial ritual of the high-mountain tribes in southern Chóngqìng involves arranging coffins on wooden stilts in the form of these houses fit for the afterlife. In the city, modernisation has turned *diàojiǎo lóu* into a symbol of poverty and as a result they are quickly disappearing. A few examples remain in use today on the cliff overlooking the Yangzi River bridge and around the Eighteen Stairs.

CHÓNGQÌNG

HOT SPRINGS 温泉

Weary souls have for dynasties found rejuvenation soaking in Chóngqìng's hot springs. The Chinese are just re-embracing the luxury travel concept, so amenities at these retreats are often spare, but at least the waters are always soothing.

North Hot Springs (北温泉; Běi Wēnquán; ☎ 6822 0111; admission Y20; ✆ 7am-10pm), nestled at the base of Jinyun Mountain, was once an extremely exclusive, ancient medical retreat and still houses a 5th-century Buddhist temple and gardens. Take bus 502, 503 or 504 to Běibèi (北碚) and then catch bus 520 (Y11).

South Hot Springs (南温泉; Nán Wēnquán; ☎ 6284 6106; admission Y20; ✆ 9am-10pm) is a no-frills assemblage of 40°C sulphur springs. Come here to avoid the crowds. Take bus 302 from Liberation Monument for the 25-minute ride.

Tiāncì Hot Springs (天赐温泉; ☎ 6570 0075; Jiǔlóngpō District; admission Y46; ✆ 24hr) offers the hottest mineral-rich soaks (57°C) in lovely landscaped private pools. About 20 minutes by bus from the North bus station (Y24) or by taxi (Y60).

Tóngjǐng Springs (统景温泉; ☎ 6728 8999; 66 Jin Quan Lu; admission Y60; ✆ 24hr) is the most manicured and modern of the retreats. You can stay for up to a month in an apartment. Single and double rooms go for Y388 and Y468. Take bus 612 from Cháotiānmén between 8am and 11pm for the hour-long trip.

---

building dates back 1000 years to the Northern Song dynasty.

Across from the temple and down the stairway is the small **Trackers' Cultural museum** (纤夫文化; Qiànfū Wénhuà; admission Y2; ✆ 8am-6.30pm), dedicated to the Yangzi's boat trackers. Working in gangs of up to 30, these muscle men employed moves like 'phoenixes nodding their heads', where each dug into the ground with one hand and steadied the rope with the other to haul boats upriver.

The curator, Cheng Wei Bing, was himself a tracker for 30 years and many items including the braided bamboo rope and rainhat are his own gear. There are few English captions here, but there are neat wooden-boat models.

For a quiet walk away from the bustle, head up the path towards **Ma An Mountain** (马鞍山; Mǎ'ān Shān) and get lost among the meandering backstreets.

From Liberation Monument take bus 402, 418, 462 or 702 to Shāpíngbà and then transfer to bus 202 or 843 to Ciqikou. The ride takes about an hour. A taxi takes half the time and costs about Y35.

Red Cliff Village 红岩村

During the Kuomintang–communist alliance against the Japanese in WWII, this **village** (Hóngyán Cūn; admission Y18; ✆ 8.30am-5.15pm) west of the peninsula served as the offices and living quarters of the communist representatives to the Kuomintang.

During the war, almost every one of the Party's major leaders lived here, including Ye Jianying, Zhou Enlai and his wife, Deng Yingchao, and Dong Biwu. After the Japanese surrender in 1945, Mao Zedong also came to Chóngqìng – at the instigation of US ambassador Patrick Hurley – to join in the peace negotiations with the Kuomintang. The talks lasted 42 days and resulted in a formal agreement that Mao later described as 'empty words on paper'.

One of China's better revolutionary-history **museums**, which includes a large collection of wartime photos and furnishings, now stands at this site. Most captions are in Chinese only. Just a short walk from the museum stands the old headquarters of the South Bureau of the Communist Party's Central Committee and the office of the Eighth Route Army, which fought on the frontlines under a strict code of ethics that are still referred to by Chinese parents and school-teachers today.

To get to Red Cliff village, take bus 104 from Linjiang Lu just northwest of Liberation Monument. The ride takes under an hour. A taxi from downtown takes less time and will cost around Y24.

Gele Mountain Martyrs' Memorial 歌乐山烈士陵园

In 1943 the USA and Chiang Kaishek were to sign a secret agreement that set up the Sino-American Cooperation Organisation (SACO), under which the USA helped to train and dispatch secret agents for the Kuomintang. The chief of SACO was Dai Li, the ruthless head of the Kuomintang military secret service, and US Navy Commodore Milton Miles served as deputy chief.

Though the Kuomintang had recognised the Communist Red Army as allies in the struggle against the Japanese invaders, it never recognised the Communist Party as a legal political entity. The Kuomintang held adherents of repressive laws and imprisoned high-ranking and student communists alike in the SACO prisons during the era known as the Bloody Betrayal. On the night before the Kuomintang's withdrawal from the mainland on 29 November, 1949, more than 300 prisoners were marched out and executed. All the **sites** (gēlèshān lièshì língyuán; admission to all sites Y40; 8.30am-7pm) on Gele Mountain relate to these events.

The largest of the 20 prisons on the mountain is **Zhāzǐ Dòng** (渣滓洞; admission Y10). It was here that the highest-ranking prisoners were held under the most punishing conditions. Prisoners were also kept in **Bái Gōngguǎn** (白公馆; admission Y10), a residence turned makeshift internment camp about 20 minutes from Zhāzǐ Dòng (just follow the signs). On display are gory pictures and films about the massacre of communist prisoners. On the way down the hill, check out the **Doghouse** (中美合作狼犬室; Zhōngměi Hézuò Lángquǎn Shì; admission Y5), where the US trained spy dogs. Near the bottom of the hill is the **Martyrs' Memorial** (烈士墓; Lièshì Mù; admission Y10; 8.30am-5pm), on whose peaceful grounds stands a forest of memorial stelae (碑林; bēilín). Included in the Martyrs' Memorial admission is the Hong Yan Spirit Exhibition Hall, a museum filled with more macabre and gory scenes.

Take bus 215 from Linjiang Lu just northwest of Liberation Monument. The ride is about an hour. A taxi is quicker and will cost you Y30. Make sure that the driver knows where you want to get off, as the entrance is not obvious.

Provisional Government of the Republic of Korea 大韩民国临时政府

This small enclave of offices and residences served as the entire **Korean capital** (Dà Hán Mínguó Línshí Zhèngfǔ; 6382 0753; 38 Lián Huā Chí; 莲花池 38号; admission Y20; 9am-5pm) during WWII. In response to brutal colonial rule by the Japa-

nese, the Korean heads of state fled to China in 1909 and formed an alliance. They set up camp in Shànghǎi and eventually moved to Chóngqìng in 1940. The provisional government's plea to President Roosevelt, written in imperfect but plaintive English, hangs in a gallery accompanied by haunting footage of the air raids.

This is within 10 minutes' walking distance of Liberation Monument.

Bomb Shelter 演武厅出入口

You could easily miss the entrance to this **shelter** (Yǎnwǔtīng Chūrùkǒu; admission free; 9am-noon & 2-5.30pm Tue-Sun) save for graphic carvings on its exterior of men, women and children engulfed in flames. Japanese bombers usually flew in by night, following the silver reflection of the moonlight on the Yangzi to pinpoint the city.

A small display of photographs documents the effects of 104 separate air strikes between 1938 and 1943, particularly 5 June 1941 when bombs fell for five hours and killed 2500 people. It is estimated that thousands more suffocated in shelters throughout the city behind caved-in entrances.

The shelter is a very short walk from Liberation Monument.

Stilwell Museum 史迪威将军旧居

Only opened in 2003, this **museum** (Shǐdíwēi Jiāngjūn Jiùjū; admission Y5; 9am-5pm) by Eling Park is something of a novelty in China as it focuses on the American involvement in WWII. It is located in the former VIP guesthouse of the Kuomintang and residence of General Joseph Stilwell, commander of the US forces in the China-Burma-India Theatre and chief-of-staff to Chiang Kaishek in 1942. Stilwell realised early on that a successful resistance required the cooperation of the Kuomintang and communist forces, and it was at his urging that Chiang relented for a time.

Repeated efforts to bring the two sides together in a truly unified front against the Japanese largely failed, Stilwell said later, because of Chiang's obsession with wiping out the communists. Vinegar Joe's caustic personality grated with Chiang and others, so despite major victories including retaking the Burma front and procuring fighter jets for the Chinese air force to fly a key route over the Himalayas, called the Hump, Roosevelt relieved him of command in 1944.

Take the light rail to the Liziba stop or bus 104 from Linjiang Lu just northwest of Liberation Monument. The museum is a five-minute walk up a very steep hill.

Parks

At 345m, **Pipa Mountain Park** (枇杷山公园; Pípa Shān Gōngyuán; 74 Pipa Shan Zheng Jie; 枇杷山正街 74号; admission Y5, temple Y3; 6am-11pm summer, 6.30am-10pm winter) marks the highest point on the peninsula. It's a good place to spend a leisurely afternoon sipping tea, playing chess, and sunning your prized songbirds.

At the neck of the peninsula, **Eling Park** (鹅岭公园; Éling Gōngyuán; Eling Zheng Jie; 鹅岭正街) is not worth a special trip but does offer good views of the skyline if you can't make it east across the Yangzi.

Renmin Park (Rénmín Gōngyuán; Xinhua Lu & Zourong Lu; 新华路和邹容路; 6am-dusk), not to be confused with Renmin Sq, has more wildlife for sale than it has roaming free. Puppies, fish, birds and every other form of pet await adoption, although some are just being babysat for the day.

Head across the Yangzi to get to the least-developed corner of the city and the Nanshan Scenic Area. It contains a number of parks including **Nanshan Park** (Nánshān Gōngyuán), which has spectacular rose and orchid gardens as well as cherry blossoms in bloom from mid-March to early May. On a cool, clear night, the most incredible views of the skyline are from behind the glass of the **Yìkēshù Viewing Platform** (admission Y20; 9am-11pm). Or brave the 20-minute climb up to the **Golden Eagle Garden** (Dàjīnyīng Yuán; admission Y12; 8.30am-11pm), the highest point within the city proper. From the Yangzi River Cable Car, catch bus 320 (Y1.50, running from 8.40am to 5.30pm) on Wuyi Lu just east of Liberation Monument.

WALKING TOUR

This short route takes you through 1800 years of history and the heart of the old city.

Start at the western end of **Tōngyuǎnmén** (**1**; 通远门; cnr Zhongshan Yi Lu & Heping Lu). Only the footstone remains of the original structure, one of nine major and eight minor gates (mén) that have protected the city since the 2nd century BC. It is for these gates that neighbourhoods around the city are still named.

Head up to the top of the gate and walk its length, following the signs to **Drum Tower**

Lane (**2**; 鼓楼巷; Gǔlóu Xiàng). The bronze inscriptions along the way tell the story of Tōngyuǎnmén's construction, the Mongols breach in 1278 AD and a peasant revolt that pushed through in 1644.

Past the aerobicisers and the tea house (you might check out the old tools on display in the courtyard), the **bronze sculpture** (**3**) of a fist on your right commemorates a 1927 military coup in Chóngqìng, in which Yang Shankun's eldest brother was killed at age 27. Follow Drum Tower Lane as it makes a sharp left turn downhill all the way back to Tōngyuǎnmén.

Climb back over the gate and then swing under its arch to head downhill on the right side of Heping Lu (和平路). After about 10 minutes, take the small pedestrian lane just after the exercise park and police stand. When you see the roundabout, cross the street and head to the **viewing balcony** (**4**) to your left.

From this roost, glimpse a view of the old city, with its clay rooftops and lively community built along the winding steps of the Eighteen Stairs (十八梯; Shíbātī). An example of **stilt housing** (**5**) stands on its last legs just to the left (p443).

Head to the right of the platform and down the old stairs, worn smooth by countless climbers carrying goods up from the river to the rest of the city. For more on those climbers, see p438. Behind a metal gate to the left of the stairs is a tunnel several kilometres long. On hot afternoons, the neighbourhood takes advantage of the cool air that pours from the **bomb shelter's** (**6**) mouth over card tables and tea.

As you continue winding your way through the neighbourhood, hang a right on to Xia Hui Shui Gou (下回水沟; Xiàhuíshuǐ Gōu), which makes a sharp turn up the hill back to Zhongxing Lu (中兴路; Zhōngxīng Lù), and then turn right. A few steps on the right is a large **flea market** (**7**; 8.30am-4.30pm), where you'll need a good eye, or at least patience, to spot the finds among the Mao buttons and knock offs. Take a few steps further up the road and rest your feet with onion pancakes at the **Muslim Restaurant of Tian Shan** (**8**; p449) or at the neighbourhood institution **Lǎojiē Shíbātī Teahouse** (**9**; p451).

TOURS

Hotels and travel agencies book pricey day tours around the city for Y680 or to Dàzú for

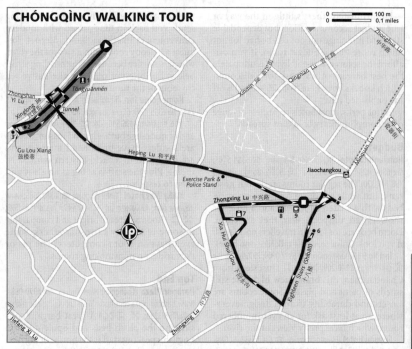

CHÓNGQÌNG WALKING TOUR

WALK FACTS

- **Start** Tōngyuǎnmén
- **Finish** Lǎojiē Shíbātī Teahouse
- **Distance** 2.3km
- **Duration** two hours

Y1550 (see p439). If you enjoy organised fun, an affordable option is a river cruise, which departs nightly from Chaotianmen Dock, March through January. Most cruises sail around the peninsula and pass under both the Jialing and Yangzi bridges, giving you a good look at Chóngqìng by night when the grey is dressed up with a flash of neon.

You can buy tickets for the river cruise at most hotels or the travel agencies around Cháotiānmén including **Chongqing Changjiang Sightseeing** (☎ 6373 5818; fax 6373 0013; 2 Shanxi Lu; with/without dinner Y108/Y80). Cruises board at 6.30pm, serve dinner at 7pm, and cruise from 8pm to 10pm. Just don't expect too much out of the food.

FESTIVALS & EVENTS

Spring Festival (southeast Chòngqìng) Begins on the eve of lunar new year and ends with the lantern festival on the 15th day of the first month of the lunar calendar (mid-January to mid-February). The Tujia put on performances of their hand waving and lantern dances throughout the counties of Shízhù, Péngshuǐ, Qiánjiāng, Yǒuyáng and Xiùshān.

Three Gorges International Tourist Festival (☎ 5823 9314) Happens annually in late May at different sites along the Yangzi. Events include dragon boat races and special sightseeing tours throughout the region.

Autumn Harvest (southeast Chóngqìng, Wànshèng) For the Miao this is a week of bullfights, drumming and song, taking place late October. The celebration is also an opportunity for young people to couple up. Each village builds a giant swing on which couples stand and swing together. If a girl steps on her partner's feet, it's love.

SLEEPING

Chóngqìng may not be a Pearl of the Orient, the Paris of the East, or a modern, Olympic host city. But at least the price of a night's accommodation reflects this – it's up to a third less than what you'd pay in Hong Kong, Shànghǎi or Běijīng.

Unfortunately, there's little in the way of true budget accommodation, but dependable standard midrange options can be had for not much more than a budget room. If you can afford the splurge, top-end living is ultimately the best bargain. Always ask for a discount, which knocks anywhere from 20% to 40% off the published rate.

As for perks, most hotels regardless of range offer complimentary breakfast spreads.

Budget

Huìxiānlóu Hotel (Huìxiānlóu Bīnguǎn; ☎ 6384 5101; fax 6384 4234; 186 Minzu Lu; 民族路186号; dm/s/d Y50/240/320) The regular rooms are, by our nose, rank. But while the dorm rooms (four or six beds with a shared bathroom and a hose for showers) are unspectacular, they are clean. Dorm beds are for foreign travellers only (read: if you look Chinese, don't talk like one here).

Inn No 9 (Jiǔhào Kèzhàn; ☎ 6377 0909; 29 Xinyi Jie; 信义街29号; s/d 140/209; ✗ ✗ 🖳) Just steps from Cháotiānmén, this brand-new high-rise still smells of paint and plaster. Some rooms are closets and durability trumps design everywhere, so at least ask for an even-numbered room, which have pretty views of the river.

Fùyuàn Hotel (Fùyuàn Bīnguǎn; ☎ 6362 7333; 12 Caiyuan Lu; 菜园路12号; s/d Y160/198; ✗) With newly spruced-up rooms, this is the best budget option in town. Right by the Càiyuánbà bus and train stations, it's a great location for late arrivals/early departures but out of the way for everything else. A huge internet café sits just off its lobby (Y2 per hour plus Y10 deposit).

Bāyī Hotel (Bāyī Bīnguǎn; ☎ 6380 5400; fax 6383 4038; 250 Bayi Lu; 八一路250号; s/d/tw Y218/248/248; ✗ 🖳) If you can overlook the spotty red carpeting and grotty bathrooms, rooms here are perfectly fine. The central location, handful of English-speaking staff and internet bar downstairs (Y2 per hour) make up for everything else.

Midrange

Square Hotel (Sàigé'ěr Jiǔdiàn; ☎ 6373 3333; fax 6373 2525; 28 Wusi Lu; 五四路28号; s/d/ste Y250/258/438; ✗ ✗) Planted in the heart of downtown, the location and comfortable rooms make this is a popular place for locals to send their friends. If you're here for an extended stay, deluxe doubles are equipped with kitchenettes. Check in is on the 11th floor.

Hóngyádòng Hotel (Hóng Yá Dòng Jiǔdiàn; ☎ 6399 2888; fax 6399 2999; 56 Cangbai Lu; 沧白路56号; s/d/ste Y398/538/1288; ✗ ✗) This brand-new hotel's traditional Chinese architecture and setting sends you back in time armed with modern conveniences like broadband internet. Request a balcony room with a view of the river, which is noisier because of the bustling street below, but brighter than the alternative – a close-up of the mountain's face.

Homehome Inn (Fènghuáng Jiājū Jiǔdiàn; ☎ 6355 7444; fax 6355 7399; 6 Fenghuangtai, Nanjimen; 南纪门风凰台6号; s/d/tr Y436/516/636; ✗ ✗) At the higher end of midrange but with good reason. Rooms are spotless, have broadband internet, and are decorated in a slick, Eastern minimalist theme. Plus the staff is as big as an army and keen to respond.

Milky Way Hotel (Yínhé Bīnguǎn; ☎ 6380 8585; www .cqyinhe.com; 49 Datong Lu; 大同路49号; s/d Y598/698; ✗ 🖳) Rooms here are bright and comparable to some of the city's five-star affairs. Some even have in-room computers. The major downside: no nonsmoking rooms.

Top End

Harbour Plaza (Chóngqìng Hǎiyì Jiǔdiàn; ☎ 6370 0888; www.harbour-plaza.com/hpcq; Wuyi Lu; 五一路; s/d/ste Y498/768/1298; ✗ 🖳 ✗) A great bargain considering the plush beds and opulent décor. English-speaking staff is the norm. Being next to a huge mall is a plus; everything from shopping to Dance Dance Revolution to ice skating and bowling is at your doorstep.

Chongqing Golden Resources Hotel (Jīnyuán Dà Fàndiàn; ☎ 6795 8888; fax 6795 9999; www.grhotel.cn; 2 Jianxin Bei Lu; 建新北路2号; s/d/ste Y640/723/1536; ✗ 🖳 ✗) The first of a growing legion of ritzy hotels in Jiāngběi District. Rooms overlook Guānyīn Qiáo's parks and the building connects to a kooky underground mall modelled after Caesar's Palace in Las Vegas.

InterContinental Chongqing (Zhōujì Jiǔdiàn; ☎ 8906 6888; www.ichotelsgroup.com; 101 Minzu Lu; 民族路101号; r/ste Y800/1200; ✗ ✗ 🖳 🖳) The city's showy nonpareil not surprisingly has luxurious amenities and impeccable service. The concierge has every single bus route committed to memory for heaven's sake. There's a chichi spa, sapphire-blue indoor pool, and five-room themed suites.

Also recommended:

JW Marriott Chongqing (Wàn Háo Jiǔdiàn; ☎ 8906 6888; 6399 9999; 77 Qingnian Lu; 青年路77号; www .marriott.com; s/d/ste Y530/660/1200; ✗ ✗ 🖳)

Hilton (Xī'ěrdùn Jiǔdiàn; ☎ 8903 9999; www.hilton .com; 139 Zhongshan San Lu; 中山三路139号; r/ste Y1500/2080; ✗ ✗ 🖳)

STREET FOOD PRIMER: THE MOST COMMON TREATS ON THE STREETS

■ *Héchuān táopiàn* (合川桃片): rice-flour wafers flavoured with osmanthus and walnuts; Chinese aristocracy used to mail order this stuff in the 18th century.

■ *Jiāoyán huāshēng* (椒盐花生): the ultimate touring food – peanuts fried with salt and black pepper.

■ *Liáng cíbā* (凉糍粑): round or half moon–shaped rice cakes stuffed with yellow bean and either honey or salt, toasted over a charcoal fire.

■ *Máoxiěwàng* (毛血旺): a butcher's wife's invention that made its debut on the Ciqikou pier. Try this at home! Stew beef stomach, duck blood, pig lung, duck intestine, eel, cured meats, pig heart, bean sprouts, peas, ginger and hot peppers. Serve over noodles.

■ *Máhuā* (麻花): fried wheat-flour twists that come in sweet and savoury breeds.

■ *Mùchuísū* (木捶苏): caramelised sugar made airy by being repeatedly pounded by heavy wooden mallets; the pounding catches air pockets between a thousand folded layers.

■ *Shānchéng xiǎo tāngyuán* (山城小汤圆): the mountain city's favourite treat. Silky soft rice balls floating in a clear soup, with a tasty centre of sesame, red bean, or ground peanut and sometimes served with *láo zāo* (醪糟), fermented rice from the wine-making process.

EATING
Street Food

The drag for cheap eats is **Good Eats Street** (Hǎochī Jiē), the stretch of Bayi Lu between Zourong and Zhonghua Lu. From stalls, carts and underground food courts, loudmouthed vendors dish up spicy noodles, clay-pot stews and beasties on sticks. Lines run deep on weekends. For more on what to eat, see above.

Hotpot

Chóngqìng's most famous dish is *huǒguō* (火锅; see p450). Hotpot is usually cheap, but since it's priced by ingredient the tab adds up quickly. Look for it wherever there are street vendors or small restaurants. Wuyi Lu has a concentrated assortment and is locally known as Huoguo Jie (Hotpot St), or take a walk along Minsheng Lu. Across the Yangzi on Nanan Binjiang Lu, hotpot tends toward the upscale (glass tables and air conditioning).

Qíqí Shànyú Hot Pot (☎ 6379 9369; 2nd fl, 39 Linjiang Lu; 临江路39号; ☽ 10.30am–'whenever') This joint is loud, crowded and serves hotpot so corrosive you tear up just stepping into the dining room. Not surprisingly, it's a local favourite. Paper-thin slices of lamb, freshwater eels (its namesake), and all manner of greens are Y6 to Y11 per heaping plate.

Little Swan Hot Pot (Xiǎo Tiān'é Huǒguō Cāntīng; ☎ 6785 5328; 78 Jianxin Bei Lu; 建新北路78号; per person Y100; ☽ 11am-2pm & 5-9pm) Recommended for those who don't subscribe to the sweating-buckets-perched-on-a-plastic-stool hotpot

experience. There's air-con, tablecloths, and five kinds of broth. Ask to *'zìzhù huǒguó'* (自助火锅), which allows you to choose from 30 different vegetables, meats, vegetables and noodles wheeled to your table. Take bus 112 from Linjiang Lu just northwest of Liberation Monument.

Restaurants

A good place for a sit-down meal is along Nanan Binjiang Lu. The strip is teeming with outdoor patios, hotpot eateries, loud riverboat dining halls and classy restaurants where waiters serve meals in white gloves and surgical masks. It's worth going for the great view of downtown along the boardwalk in Nanan Park alone. Take the Yangzi River Cable Car and then grab a taxi (Y8) or bus 338 west to Haitang Xiaoyue Lu. Walking takes about 20 minutes.

AE&E Restaurant (Àlǐ yǔ àidé Kāfēi Xīcāntīng; meals Y55; Far Eastern Bldg ☎ 8911 8066; 2nd fl, Far Eastern Bldg, Guanyin Qiao; 观音桥远东百货二楼; Metropolitan Plaza ☎ 6371 0088; 1st fl, Tài Píng Yáng department store, Metropolitan Plaza; 大都会广场太平洋百货一楼; ☽ 10am-10pm) The place for ice cream and occasionally misguided Western food.

Muslim Restaurant of Tian Shan (Xīnjiāng Tiānshān Cāntīng; ☎ 6383 3803; 3-7 Zhongxing Lu; 中兴路3-7号; average dish Y10; ☽ 9am-9pm) Serves the dishes of the Silk Road, meaning lots of lamb – braised lamb, stewed lamb and lamb wrapped in buns – eaten with a side of black vinegar and garlic. Try the *lǎng* (Y5), crispy onion pancakes baked to perfection on the side of circular ovens.

CHÓNGQÌNG

VERY HOT, VERY SPICY & A LITTLE TINGLY

The definition of a good dish in this region is one that balances the sensations of *má* and *là*.

Má is the numbing sensation provided by the Sìchuān peppercorn, a tiny black flower with the kick of black pepper and ginger combined with what can only be described as your dentist's anaesthesia. Taken in large doses, it is said, this stuff can kill. But no dish is complete without the searing bite of chilli pepper (of which there are countless varieties), which supply the *là*.

Hotpot (火锅; *huǒguō*; literally 'fire pot') embodies these elements and is therefore Chóngqìng's famed and favourite dish. It's eaten year-round, even on the hottest days, because it is believed the sweat it induces encourages circulation and is a cure for aches and colds.

Best guesses put the birth of hotpot at a meat market on the banks of the Jialing River at the end of the 19th century. Poor boatmen floating by fished the scraps and organs thrown into the river and slow boiled them with plenty of spices to cover up any rancid taste. Enterprising peddlers saw the niche in the market and began selling the soup on the streets. On a long pole, they carried a roving restaurant – a pot of broth, a selection of cheap meats, and utensils and stools.

Today, hotpot is no longer itinerant nor a dish of leftovers. Everything from exotic mushrooms to freshwater crab can go in the pot. To local residents, however, the key remains not what you cook but what you cook it in. Restaurants have their signature broths, and vendors sell congealed lumps of perfectly proportioned Sìchuān peppercorn, chilli peppers and sesame oil to take home.

There are different forms of hotpot throughout China, but no-one eats hotpot quite like the people here. The chilli combinations are much hotter than even those used in neighbouring Chéngdū. If all this sounds too much for your taste buds, ask for the '*yuānyāng*' version, which is divided like a Yin-and-Yang symbol into a spicy side and a mild side (fish or chicken broth). Fish out the peppercorns, and do as the locals do by adding lots of vinegar to your bowl to stop your throat from clenching up from all the hot chillies. Or just tell waiters, '*pà là*' (you're scared of spice). Just don't be surprised if they laugh.

Propitious Winds (Nánfāng Huāyuán Yú Gāo Guǎngchǎng; ☎ 6862 3123; 2nd fl, Hua Yuan Yu Gao Complex; 花园渝高广场二楼; per dish Y16-38; ⏰ 10.30am-11pm) Its outdoor deck draws a lively crowd and its extensive menu of *jiāng hú*, signature local dishes, keeps them coming back. Try the claypots and springwater chicken (泉水鸡).

Lǎo Sìchuān Dàjiǔlóu (☎ 6382 6644; 186 Minzu Lu; 民族路186号; average dish Y38; ⏰ 11.30am-2.30pm & 4-9.30pm) Locals bring visitors here to ease them into the region's spicy cuisine. The reason? 'It's not so spicy', one patron divulged gesturing to his pansy-mouthed Běijīng friend. The food is otherwise pretty authentic, though if you order from the English menu, more likely to be tourist-oriented.

DRINKING

When it comes to Chóngqìng nightlife, a couple of ground rules apply: hotspots all turn over fast and frequently, so you should ask around for the latest obsession; and, in these parts a good time starts with green tea–whiskey cocktails and invariably ends at a KTV (karaoke) bar. So you can consider yourself warned.

Déyì Shìjiè (Minquan Lu & Xinhua Lu; 民权路 和 新华路) Start the night at this massive KTV bar and club complex with a constantly changing line-up of tenants including some of the following venues.

Soho Bar (Sūhé Jiǔbā; ☎ 6379 7776; A1-6 Diyi Shijie; 得意世界 A1-6号; ⏰ 7pm-3.30am) The young and fashionable sway to covers belted out by professional karaoke singers perched on podiums throughout the bar. Pimped-out private KTV rooms are available but must be booked in advance.

True Love (Zhēn'ài; ☎ 6379 7377; www.chongqingjiuba .com; A1, Deyi Shijie; 得意世界 A1; ⏰ 8pm-2am) This eccentric hangout is a lonely-hearts club set to upbeat background music. Theme nights include find-a-date (have your mini-bio ready to read on stage along with your cell-phone number) and Arabian night when belly dancers shimmy around the uncomfortable date you just found.

Pirates Pub (Kǎbùléidēng Hǎidàobā; ☎ 6399 2888; 1st fl, Hóngyádòng, 56 Cangbai Lu; 红崖洞, 沧白路56号; ⏰ 8pm-6am) Serves up the ingenious combination of pirates and disco. Local bands start playing most nights at 9pm but the mutiny doesn't happen until 11pm. Look for three ship's sails.

Dee Dee's Bar (86 Nánpíng Xīnjiē; 南坪新街86号; ☽ 2pm-midnight) Tucked down steps next to the Holiday Inn (Yangzi), this bar remains the hub of the city's expat community thanks in part to its Thursday dart tourneys. Aside from the decent beer and grub, this is the place to gather local knowledge about things like where to get a good milkshake (the word is AE&E Restaurant).

Rúyì Jiǔbā (☎ 6385 8029; 31 Tǐyù Cūn; 体育村31号; ☽ 8pm-7am) While the gay scene in China remains underground, businessmen and labourers alike come here to down pints together and catch lively drag acts. Head down the dark stairs directly across from the lobby of the Hilton on Zhongshan Lu.

Lǎojiē Shíbātī Teahouse (Lǎojiē Shíbātī Chálóu; ☎ 6383 1694; 1 Zhong Xing Lu; 中兴路1号; ☽ 9am-midnight) A teahouse has stood for 600 years here at the top of the Eighteen Stairs. Come for a fresh pot of tea (Y30 to Y50) served with small plates of dried fruit and cakes, and an arresting view of the old city. There's beer available too.

SHOPPING

True local handicrafts like Sìchuān silk embroidery, bicolour stone carvings, and lively flower and brocade Tujia weavings are hard to find in the city proper. Pick up that sort of thing on an excursion.

Hóngyádòng (Linjiang Lu & Cangbai Lu; 临江路和沧白路; ☽ 9am-7pm) Built into the cliffs overlooking the Jialing, this massive complex is a Disney version of the tumbledown houses that once stood in its place. If you have just a day to try local food and pick up souvenirs, it's a fun place to wander around. The handicraft stalls are on the 3rd floor, and food is on the 4th. If you have time in the evening, catch the dynamic dance performance depicting the history of the city in the Bāyú Theatre (tickets Y80 to Y120; 8pm Monday, Wednesday, Friday and Saturday), or head to the ground floor to dance the night away yourself.

Guānyīn Qiáo (Jianxin Bei Lu & Jianxin Dong Lu; 建新北路和建新东路; ☽ most stores 8am-10pm, to 10.30pm Sat & Sun) Ages ago on this spot, Guanyin, goddess of mercy, saved residents from a flood with a lotus bridge. Today, the only magic around here is how your money disappears. Pick up Italian boots in the Las Vegas Underground Sleepless Town and then skip over to

the Hong Kong Center for American designer jeans. For brand names, check out Mào Yè Department Store.

Maison Mode (Měiměi Shídài Bǎihuò; ☎ 6376 7325; 100 Zourong Lu; 邹容路100号; ☽ 8am-10pm) From its perch smack in the middle of Liberation Monument, the poshest department store in town hawks the world's most upscale labels (but for the usual price).

Carrefour (Jiālèfú Cháojíshìchǎng; ☎ 9658 8999; Cangbai Lu & Mianhua Lu; 沧百路和棉花路; ☽ 8.30am-10pm) Gleaming mega-markets are cropping up all over town including a Wal-Mart out in the west 'burbs, but none beat this store's central location and wide assortment of envelopes, cheese and foot baths.

Flower and Bird Market (花鸟市场; Huāniǎo Shìchǎng; across from Marriott; ☽ dawn-dusk) Fragrant herbs and jasmine flowers perfume this open-air market. Vendors hitch in from the countryside with buckets of rare orchids on Sundays. Sadly, birds are no longer sold here. For buyable birds, see p446.

GETTING THERE & AWAY
Air

Chóngqìng's Jiangbei International Airport (重庆江北飞机场; Chóngqìng Jiāngběi Fēijīchǎng) is 25km north of the city centre. You can book domestic flights through **Air China** (Zhōngguó Guójì Hángkōng; ☎ 6787 8538; 30 Jianxin Bei Lu; ☽ 8.30am-6pm) and **China Eastern** (Zhōngguó Dōngfāng Hángkōng; ☎ 7118 1821; www.ce-air.com; 235 Minsheng Lu; ☽ 8.30am-5pm). **Dragonair** (Gǎnglóng Hángkōng; ☎ 6372 9900; Room 2906, Metropolitan Plaza, 68 Zourong Lu; ☽ 9am-5pm) flies to Hong Kong and destinations beyond the mainland. You can also book flights at most hotels and the numerous travel agencies around Liberation Monument (see p439).

There are daily flights to destinations across China, including Chéngdū (Y460; 50 minutes), Kūnmíng (Y820; one hour), Guìyáng (Y490; 45 minutes), Guǎngzhōu (Y1290; 1½ hours), Wǔhàn (Y810; 80 minutes), Shànghǎi (Y1490; two hours), Běijīng (Y1560; two hours 10 minutes), Shēnzhèn (Y1280; two hours) and Hong Kong (Y2639; two hours and 15 minutes). Prices increase during holidays.

Boat

Countless cruises make the run daily from Chóngqìng down the Yangzi River to the Three Gorges and Yíchāng. The cruises have been popular with tourists for dynasties and

CHÓNGQÌNG BUSES

Buses make the following trips from Chóngqìng's bus stations (check related sections for specific stations).

Destination	Price (Y)	Duration	Frequency	Departs
Běibèi	3.50	41min	2 daily	9.59am, 12.59pm
Chéngdū	117	6.5hr	every 30min	6.30am-9.30pm
Dàzú	45	2.5hr	every 30min	6.30am-9.30pm
Éméi	106	2hr	2 daily	9.30am, 11.30am
Héchuān	45	2hr	hourly	9.30am-1.00pm
Jiāngkǒu	65	4.5hr	4 daily	6.30am, 8am, 9.20am, 11.30am
Lèshān	80	2½hr	hourly	7am-6pm
Nánchuān	35	2.5hr	hourly	7.30am-6pm
Tóngnán	50	2hr	2 daily	7.40am, noon

have also inspired masterworks of Chinese literature and art. Major historical sites have disappeared and a few have been transplanted since the Three Gorges Dam opened in 2006. But the mountains remain the stuff of paintings, despite losing 145m and counting to rising waters.

For details on Yangzi River trips see p461. Cruise tickets can be purchased through your hotel or from the agencies around Cháotiānmén, although shop carefully as amenities vary greatly while prices may not.

Bus

The main long-distance bus terminal is **Càiyuánbà bus station** (☎ 6280 5226) located right next to the train station. There are 10 other major bus depots in the city proper, but those of most interest to travellers are **Cháotiānmén** (☎ 6373 6778), **Nánpíng** (☎ 6280 5226) and **North** (☎ 6785 3898) bus stations.

Buses run to Chéngdū (Y112) between 6.30am and 9.30pm, but as this is the busiest route, you can also catch shuttle buses (the plush air-con type) in the mornings in front of Cháotiānmén Dock. Major hotels including the Marriott and Hilton offer vans and buses depending on numbers for Y120.

Train

Càiyuánbà train station (☎ 6386 2607; 1 Caiyuanba Zheng Jie), Chóngqìng's main rail station, is located west of the city centre. You can also check timetables and buy train tickets at the more conveniently located **Cháotiānmén Booking Hall** (☎ 6310 0659; Dock 3; 3号码头; ☒ 7am-10pm) just off Chaoqian Lu.

GETTING AROUND
To/From the Airport

Until the light rail is finished, a taxi is the easiest mode of transportation. Depending on traffic, it will cost Y60 to Y100 (plus tolls). No city buses go directly to the airport, but the Civil Aviation Administration of China (CAAC; Zhōnguó Mínháng) operates a Y15 airport shuttle from 6.30am to 5pm arriving and departing from the Shàngqīngsì (上清寺) roundabout. The ride is free if you fly Sichuan Airlines between Chéngdū and Chóngqìng.

Bus

Local buses in Chóngqìng can be painfully slow and, since the hills mean there are no bicycles, more crowded than those in other Chinese cities. Destinations are posted and also called out by attendants from the side window. As this is undoubtedly confusing, here are key routes to note: 401 runs from Cháotiānmén and Shàngqīngsì via Zhongshan Yi Lu; 402 heads further west from Liberation Monument to Shāpíngbà; 405 runs between Liberation Monument and Guānyīn Qiáo; 102 connects Càiyuánbà bus and train stations with Cháotiānmén; 384 runs from Wuyi Lu just east of Liberation Monument to Nánshān.

Most importantly, watch out! A city-wide ban on car horns to cut down noise pollution has unfortunately turned buses into silent, wheeled predators.

Cable Car

A ride on either of the city's two cable cars – the Yangzi River Cable Car (Y2/4 one-way/

CHÓNGQÌNG TRAINS

Trains travel daily to the following destinations. Express trains are marked with an 'E.'

Destination	Price (Y)	Duration	Frequency	Departs
Běijīng	347/401E	25hrE/33/44hr	3 daily	12.26pmE, 8.18pm, 11.59pm
Chéngdū	113/120E	4.5hrE/9hr	5 daily	8amE, 1pmE, 3.07pmE, 8.55pm, 9.05pm
Guǎngzhōu	208/339E	31hrE/38hr	6 daily	5.35pm, 7.36pm, 9.11pm, 10.36pmE, 12.32am, 1.02am
Guìyáng	73/101E	10hrE/12hr	2 daily	7.45am, 8.03pmE
Kūnmíng	213	21hr	2 daily	12.47pm, 2.42pm
Lhasa	754	47hr	daily	7.20pm
Shànghǎi	458	42hr	daily	8.07pm
Wǔlóng	98/100E	2hr 30minE/ 4hr 35min	2 daily	8.40am, 10.45pmE
Xī'ān	109	13.5hr	daily	9.59am

return, departs 6.30am to 9.45pm) and the Jialing River Cable Car (Y1.5/3, departs 10am to 6pm) – spanning both the Jialing and Yangzi rivers is more fun than functional.

You get a bird's-eye view of the polluting industrial blocks and murky waters from the cable car. The ride north lands you in the middle of major construction projects, so expect a 20-minute walk to civilisation (or catch bus 607). The ride south drops you off about a 20-minute stroll from the Nanan Binjiang Lu eateries.

Car

Companies base rates on time, mileage and car model. Always pricier than public transit, but for a group of two or more the flexibility of having a driver on hand with local knowledge can make this a worthwhile option.

For example, hiring **Chongqing Zulin Company** (重庆租赁公司; Chóngqìng Zūlìn Gōngsī; ☎ 6280 6598; 1 Nanping Dong Lu) for a two-day trip to Wǔlóng runs about Y1500 for a cushy sedan, including tolls but not food, lodging and tip for the driver. Also check with your hotel for car services.

Light Rail

The city has a smooth, new **light rail** (轻轨; qīng guǐ; ⏱ 6.30am-10.32pm) costing Y1 to Y5 depending on how far you go. The only downside is that for now that's not very far. Wave your ticket over the sensor upon entry and stick it in the slot upon exit.

Taxi

The flag falls at Y5 and doesn't move for 3km. The base fare increases to Y6 between 10pm and 6am. Catching a cab is tricky only right before 5pm when drivers change shifts.

Most drivers do not read maps, so if you don't speak Chinese, have your destination written down in Chinese. Cabbies are surprisingly honest, so no need to get suspicious if one makes extra turns. The city is fraught with one-way streets.

AROUND CHÓNGQÌNG

DÀZÚ COUNTY 大足县

The grotto art of Dàzú County, 125km northwest of Chóngqìng, is a designated Unesco World Heritage Site on par with China's most prominent Buddhist cave sites at Dūnhuáng, Luòyáng and Dàtóng.

The exquisite carvings here uniquely reflect the melding in the 9th century of China's three main religions – Buddhism, Taoism and Confucianism – by mixing their beliefs in both sacred and profane scenes. Over 50,000 individual carvings and statues are hidden in 40 sites across the county.

The main groupings are on five mountains, with the most historically important at North Hill and Treasured Summit Hill. The earliest figures in the area were carved in the 7th century during the Tang dynasty with additions continuing through the Song dynasty, 600

CHÓNGQÌNG

years later. Combined tickets for both sites are available for Y120.

Sights & Activities

TREASURED SUMMIT HILL 宝顶山

A Tantric Buddhist monk named Zhao Zhifeng directed that the carvings at **Treasured Summit Hill** (Bǎodǐng Shān; admission Y80; ☉ 8.30am-5.30pm) be cut from a horseshoe-shaped ridge. The results of his 70-year effort, which began in 1179 AD, are some of the most striking examples in the county.

The centrepieces are a 31m-long, 5m-high reclining Sakyamuni Buddha entering nirvana and, next to it, a mesmerising gold Avalokiteshvara (God of Mercy), with 1007 arms reaching out to the suffering multitudes. Many of the other surrounding figures were made in the likenesses of Buddhist preachers and sages – celebrity figures of the time. Others are depictions of the everyman: cowboys enjoy a rest after diligently tending their buffalo; parents care for their children through birth and death; drunkards forget what their wives and children look like and tumble into hell. It's a wonder what those monks were trying to teach us.

Treasured Summit's thoughtful design incorporates the area's natural features directly into the forms. For example, a natural spring that would have gradually washed away a depiction of the nine dragons bathing the baby Buddha was ingeniously channelled through the mouth of a dragon.

Take a minibus (Y5, 45 minutes) about 15km northeast of Dàzú town to Bǎodǐng Shān from 9am to 6pm, departing when full. A motorcycle taxi will take you there for around Y20. As you pass by on the bus, look out for sculptures hidden in the hillsides.

NORTH HILL 北山

Built on the site of a military outpost, **North Hill** (Běi Shān; admission Y60; ☉ 8.30am-5.30pm) contains some of the earliest carvings in the region and was commissioned by the local prefect. The dark niches hold nearly 300 small statues, unfortunately many in poor condition. According to locals, it was unmanaged tourists rather than the usual Cultural Revolution zealots who beheaded them.

Look for the Bodhisattva of Universal Benevolence, whose round features and unassuming posture are said to represent the ideals of Eastern beauty. A steep hike up to the white pagoda (also covered in carv-

ings) earns you a splendid view of the entire county.

North Hill is about a 30-minute hike up from Dàzú town – head straight for the pagoda, which is visible from the bus station.

Sleeping & Eating

There are plenty of hotels in the area but none of them stand out. Sniff for mustiness before checking in.

Dàzú Hotel (Dàzú Bīnguǎn; ☎ 4372 1888; fax 4372 2967; 79 Lónggǎnglóng Zhōnglù; 龙岗龙中路79号; s/d Y200/332) As the regular host of metallurgist conferences, rooms are what you'd expect: perfectly nice, boring and dressed in durable fabrics. The location is central and the staff is used to dealing with tourists. To get here, turn left from the bus station, then at the roundabout take the first road to the right, Binhe Jie (滨河街), which runs along the river. It's a 30-minute walk from the hotel to Běi Shān or a Y10 cab ride.

Finding a bite to eat in Dàzú is no problem. **Buxing Jie** (步行街; the second road branching right at the roundabout) is a charming street lined with restaurants and dumpling carts.

Getting There & Around

BUS

Buses make the 2½ hour trip from Chóngqìng to Dàzú (Y45) every half hour from 6.30am to 9.30pm. Buses back to Chóngqìng follow roughly the same schedule with the last leaving at 6pm.

To get to the sites, take a 10-minute taxi ride (Y12) from Dàzú's long-distance station, also called the **old station** (220 Shuangta Lu; 双塔路 220号), over the bridge to the local bus station to catch a minibus.

TRAIN

Skip the train and save hours and money.

WÀNSHÈNG DISTRICT 万盛区

With native old-growth forests and rare wildlife like the endangered golden monkey, Wànshèng is the closest thing to hinterland in Chóngqìng. Another reason to spend a couple of days here is the fascinating mix of ethnic minorities that have made their home in the foothills along the border with Guìzhōu.

Black Mountain (黑山; Hēi Shān; ☎ 4827 9999; admission Y60, incl Stone Forest Y99; ☉ 8am-6pm) is actually a gorgeous range of mountains crisscrossed by floating bridges and jade-green streams that plummet into waterfalls. To get the most out of your time, enter from the north gate and pay for the electromobile ride (Y20), which saves you a 30-minute walk down an uninspiring paved road. At the end of your three-hour hike, catch the **cable car** (admission Y20; 8am-6pm) up to the south exit of the park.

Not 15 minutes away, the **Stone Forest** (石林; Shí Lín; admission Y60; 7am-4pm) covers 6 sq km of jagged stone outcrops that formed 460 million years ago in very odd shapes. There are interesting fossils to look at too. Residents of the **Miao farming communities** dotted along the base of the mountains put on traditional dance performances here in the summer at 10am and 2.30pm Friday through Sunday.

Head to **Tonggutan Gorge** (铜鼓滩漂流; Tónggǔtān Piāoliú; adult/student Y100/80; 8am-4pm) for an 11km rafting trip down the Podu River, which flows just across the border in Guìzhōu. This is not white-water rafting, but at peak water levels the steepest drop is about two stories. The nearby town, which developed as a result of the salt trade, also has some interesting architectural sites.

Sleeping

Huìxīn Jiǔlóu (汇鑫酒楼; Zi Ru Sq, South Bldg; 子如广场南楼; s/d Y168/198;) The newest hotel in the area also has luxury-level rooms for twice the price as the basic. The friendly staff aims to please and has extensive knowledge of the surrounding area.

Wansheng Hotel (Wànshèng Bīnguǎn; ☎ 4827 0487; 42 Wandong Bei Lu; 万东北路42号; s/d Y188/198;) Rooms haven't been redecorated since calico was in style, but at least they're clean. More importantly, food and everything you may need in town is within walking distance.

Getting There & Around

BUS

From Nánpíng bus station, buses make the 2½-hour trip to Nánchuān (南川; Y35) every hour between 7.30am and 6pm. There are no trains. Don't miss the last bus back to Chóngqìng, which leaves Nánchuān at 5.30pm.

To get to the sites, exit from Nánchuān's main bus station, turn right, and walk 10 minutes to the local bus station to ride a minibus for another hour to Wànshèng. Buses from Wànshèng heading to Black Mountain and Stone Forest (Y5) depart when full

between 7.30am and 5pm. To reach Tonggutan Gorge, you have to take a minibus from Wànshèng to Guānbàzhèn (关坝镇; Y11) departing every 40 minutes between 7am and 6pm and then catch another to Chángtángkǒu (长塘口; Y11), the rafting start point. A taxi directly from Wànshèng is about Y150.

CAR

If all this is too much for you, the Hu family offers great **tours** (☎ 4835 7152, 130 183 32838; 2-day tour Y600) if you can speak some Chinese (they speak absolutely no English and don't have plans to learn so far). They can arrange a home stay or book hotel rooms, buy tickets, share local lore and shuttle you around in their yellow 4WD. Plus, they know invaluable tricks, for example, how to wave down a bus at the expressway toll plaza if you miss the last official bus to Chóngqìng.

WǓLÓNG COUNTY 武隆县

About 194km southeast of Chóngqìng, this county is a vast landscape of sharp peaks, deep gorges and unique geological formations. Geologists named the distinctive and ubiquitous limestone caverns and stone bridges created by subterranean water flows karst (天坑; tiānkēng) formations.

Tiānkēng is the reason this is some of the best terrain in the region for outdoor activities like hiking and climbing, and why the entire county is designated a national geological park.

The three major sites are widely dispersed and take at least two very full days to cover. If your time is limited, start at the Natural Three Bridges, spend the night on Fairy Maiden Mountain, and take on Furong Cave the next day.

About 19km south of town, **Natural Three Bridges** (天生三桥; Tiānshēng Sān Qiáo; admission Y40; 9am-4pm) is an incredible feat of earthly engineering. The scenery is so striking it served as backdrop for a number of major motion pictures, including most recently Zhang Yimou's *Curse of the Golden Flower*. A spring-fed underground river carved out underground passages, which collapsed two million years ago to create the Heavenly Dragon, Green Dragon (the tallest natural bridge in the world at 281m) and Black Dragon bridges. The 30-minute continuous descent into the valley from either of the two entrances is steep. The faint-hearted can catch a bus to an elevator near the Heavenly Dragon bridge.

Fairy Maiden Mountain (仙女山; Xiānnǚ Shān; admission Y50) is named for the column of stone in the shape of a lone lass standing at the top of the mountain. At 2300m, this alpine prairie is a good place to spend a quiet night. There's plenty to do during the day as well, including horseback riding, skiing, and petting the sheep that wander about.

Furong Cave (芙蓉洞; Fúróng Dòng; adult/child Y70/50; ⏰ 9am-4pm) is so massive, it's a wonder that it was only discovered in 1993. The two-hour tour involves a lot of ascending and descending on paved stairs through the main limestone cavern, which is almost 3km in length. The first possible exit is two-thirds of the way through, so be prepared to commit. Naff comparisons of stalagmites to dragons, gods and body parts aside, the tour is spectacular. There are formations not to be seen anywhere else, including a watery pool of pink calcite flowers that look like coral. Afterwards, enjoy the surface by flying 100m above it and the Wu River on a **zipline cable** (速滑; Sùjhuá; Y50; ⏰ 9am-5pm). Or float downriver on a raft (Y70 for three hours) or go for a swim just west of the cave at the **Furong River jetty** (芙蓉江码头; Fúróng Jiāng mǎtou; ☎ 7774 2278; ⏰ 8.30am-8pm April-Oct, 8.30am-6.30pm Nov–March).

Sleeping & Eating

Just east of Renmin Sq in Wǔlóng's city centre is a night market with countless noodle stalls and other street food.

Fairy Maiden Mountain Holiday Hotel (Xiān Nǚ Shān Zhèn, Dà Cǎo Yuán; 仙女山镇, 大草原; ☎ 7773 7657; www.cq-xinhua-hotel.com/zh/xls; s/d Y350/488; ✉ 🖥 🖥) is a sparkling five-star hotel, happy to reward you after a long day of hiking with sublimely soft pillows. Staff can also hook you up with skiing (Y60 per hour, December to February). Book ahead, because if it's full, they may try to cab you over to sister hotel Fairy Maiden Xinhua Manor, which is not quite as swanky but nearly the same price.

Nóngjiālè (农家乐) is a breed of inn that abounds along Wuxian Lu (武仙路), the road up to Fairy Maiden Mountain. A very reasonable fee gets you a huge homemade meal, access to house rice wines and the opportunity to commune with fellow travellers over raucous mah jong late into the night. Bathrooms are always shared and shower

facilities are very basic. Sometimes, the kids' room is converted for your stay. **Róngyí** (蓉怡; per person incl dinner Y27) serves delectable food, sometimes involving a special breed of chicken raised in the mountains.

Getting There & Around

BUS

Buses from Càiyuánbà make the 4½-hour drive to Jiāngkǒu (江口; Y65) four times a day at 6.30am, 8am, 9.20am and 11.30am. Buses also depart from Cháotiānmén twice a day at 8.30am and 6.30pm. When you arrive, you have to walk about 10 minutes to the local bus station to catch a minibus to the sites. All local buses depart when full.

Destination	Price (Y)	Duration	Departs
Fairy Maiden Mountain	15	1hr	9am-4pm
Fúróng Cave	6	30min	9am-4.30pm
Natural Three Bridges	13	1hr	9am-6pm

TAXI

A taxi to the sites will run anywhere from Y60 to Y100. You can also haggle for a motortaxi (about Y20), though this is not recommended as these rides are technically illegal. This is usually not a problem except, say you fell off said bike, and the driver ditched you rather than risk talking to the authorities when the ambulance arrived.

TRAIN

Two trains daily make the trip between Càiyuánbà and Wǔlóng (Y98) at 8.40am (takes about 4½ hours) and the express (2½ hours) at 10.45pm. The last train departs for Càiyuánbà at 9pm. The local bus station is a very short walk downhill from the train station.

LÁITĀN 涞滩

This breathtaking village is actually an ancient military fort that has been encircled by protective walls for over 1100 years. The walls successfully withstood Mongol invaders, but they could not keep out developers who plan to pave over the spring-fed paddies and ancient flagstones to make the area more accessible to tourists. Locals keen on opportunity are not questioning progress, but try catching it before the plastic Buddha vendors show up, at least for comparison's sake.

From the main gate, you can see the town sites first or walk along the wall. Either route will eventually lead you past all the sites.

The central attraction is an imposing 14.6m Song dynasty **Buddha** (二佛寺; Èrfó Sì; admission Y10; 🕑 7am-6pm) carved into the mountainside and flanked by 1014 statues of his disciples. This Buddha is said to be second in size (hence the name, 'èr' for second) to the giant buddha in Lèshān. Almost all of the original poetry and many of the figures' heads were snapped off during the Cultural Revolution, but the Buddha's right hand fell off in the Qing dynasty of natural causes.

Just around the bend is the Tang dynasty **temple** (二佛禅院; Èrfó chányuàn; admission Y5; 🕑 7am-5.30pm). The relief carvings of round-headed figures on the front gate are the oldest in the area and have lasted so long unscathed, locals say, because of their artistry.

A word of caution: this is a superstitious community. Never touch upturned ceramic bowls (or any curiously placed object, for that matter) as these are prayer relics left after a cleansing ritual. If you want to partake in some of your own unexplainable phenomena, the fortune tellers outside the temple are of noted repute. Liú Bànxiān (刘半仙), whose name literally means 'Half Genie', charges Y40 and usually sits on the right-hand side of the road leading out of the temple. He doesn't speak English so give him your birthday and time you were born and record what he says, so that someone can translate your fate later.

When you're ready for some realism, grab a bite in town at a number of friendly restaurants that serve up Láitán's famous rice wine (米酒; mǐjiǔ), or head down the worn steps near the monks' tombs to the river. A local family serves up the day's catch on the fishing boat moored offshore for about Y120 for a meal for four. You can pick your fish from a tank submerged on the side of the boat. The salt-and-pepper river prawns (椒盐虾; jiāoyán xiā) are truly divine.

To reach Láitán, buses leave Càiyuánbà for the hour drive to Héchuān (合川; Y12) hourly between 6am and 9pm. For the 30-minute ride to Lóngshì Zhèn (龙市镇; Y10), transfer to a minibus, which departs when full between 5.30am and 9pm. Then catch another minibus (Y2) for the short ride to Láitán's main gate, departing when full usually between 6am and 9pm but confirm with the driver to be sure.

SHUĀNGJIĀNG 双江

About 160km northwest of Chóngqìng city, this tiny village is packed with architectural sights and is a living homage to their hometown hero, Yang Shangkun. Just keep in mind, unless you're really into buildings, the sites start to blur together and there's not much else in the town, so plan this as a half-day trip.

Buses make the two-hour trip from Càiyuánbà station to Tóngnán (潼南; Y50) twice daily at 7.40am and noon. From Tóngnán, catch minibus 16 (Y2) the last 10km to Shuāngjiāng. Minibuses usually return to Tóngnán until 5pm but check with the driver on your way there to avoid surprises.

On the way in from the Tóngnán bus stop to Shuāngjiāng stands the massive tomb of Yang Shangkun, who died in 1998 after serving as the second president of the PRC. A small-town guy who was nothing if not scrappy, Yang worked his way up the communist ranks only to be imprisoned for 12 years in 1966 after allegedly planting a bug in Mao's office.

His loyalty to the party earned him the presidency in 1988, a position he held during the student uprising in Tiananmen Sq the following year. Most of the sites in Shuāngjiāng were at some point all owned by Yang's family.

From the bus stop, head to the right downhill for the main attractions, which are hidden within the meandering, ancient streets of a section called Jīnlóng Cūn (金龙村). The main drag will take you past several major examples of Qing dynasty houses.

The first is **Tiánbà Dàyuàn** (田坝大院; 48 Zheng Jie; admission Y15; 🕑 8am-6pm), the ancestral home of the Yang family, last inhabited by Shangkun's eldest brother. It is a prototypical sìhéyuàn (四合院), a four-sided house with a courtyard, common in northern China. There's not much by way of exhibits here, but you're free to wander so climb upstairs to the ladies' bedroom and marvel at how anyone with bound lotus feet climbed up and down ladders.

Just down the road is **Yáng'àngōng Jiùjū** (杨闇公旧居; admission Y15; 🕑 8am-6pm), the home of Shangkun's great uncle.

On your way back to the bus, take a rest at **Dingzikou Tea House** (丁字口茶楼; He Jie), one of several tea houses that have been brewing pots since the Qing era.

Cruising the Yangzi

THE THREE GORGES

China's mightiest – and the world's third-longest – river, the 6300km Yangzi (长江; Cháng Jiāng), starts life as trickles of snow melt in the Tánggǔlǎ Shān of southwestern Qīnghǎi before spilling from Tibet, swelling through seven Chinese provinces, sucking in water from hundreds of tributaries and powerfully rolling into the East China Sea north of Shànghǎi.

Few riverine panoramas inspire such awe as the Three Gorges (三峡; Sānxiá). The vast chasms of rock, sculpted over aeons by the flowing mass of water, are the Yangzi River's most fabled piece of geology. Apocryphally the handiwork of the Great Yu, a legendary architect of the river, the gorges – Qútáng, Wū and Xīlíng – commence just east of Fēngjié in Chóngqìng and level out west of Yíchāng in Húběi province, a journey of around 200km.

The imposing chasms span from 300m at their widest to less than 100m at their narrowest pinch. Their attraction is easily hyped, however, and some travellers register disappointment. The construction of the formidable Three Gorges Dam (p461) has furthermore cloaked the gorges in as much uncertainty as their famous mists: will the gorges be humbled, vanishing forever beneath a huge lake, or will they shrug off the rising waters?

The truth lies somewhere in between. Experienced boat hands avow to a stunting of their magnificence, but first-timers – the majority of those on cruises – remain suitably awestruck. The waters have yet to rise to their full stature, but you can gauge the extent of the deluge from the riverside 175m markers, awaiting the water's highest reach. It's also worth noting that the gorges were clipped by 10m or so when the earlier Gezhou Dam in Yíchāng (Húběi province) went up, and seasonal variations in water level can be as much as 50m.

If a consensus emerges from travellers' reports, it is that the temples can be busy with jostling crowds (and overpriced) while the towns and settlements along the Yangzi River are quite modern-looking and uniform. It is the spectacular natural scenery that undoubtedly steals the show, although some find it possible to gorge oneself (excuse the pun) on the canyons. After the shock and awe of their first appearance, the cliffs can become repetitive, especially the overlong Xiling Gorge (Xīlíng Xiá). But if you don't expect to swoon at every bend in the river, the sheer pleasure of journeying downriver is a stimulating and relaxing adventure, not least because of the change of pace and perspective.

The principle route for those cruising the Yangzi River is between Chóngqìng and Yíchāng. The growth of speedier expressways sees fewer passenger boats nosing all the way down from Chóngqìng to Nánjīng or Shànghǎi, and most cruises focus on the Three Gorges themselves. High-season boats (April to May and October to November) can be a scrum; off-season, however, the trip is serene and a great opportunity to observe life on the river from a sedentary perspective – even better if you bring some binoculars with you.

BOATS & TICKETS

When choosing your boat you have three options. The most luxurious passage is on internationally owned tour cruise ships, where maximum comfort and visibility are accompanied by a leisurely agenda. Boats stop at all the major sights for long visits, giving passengers time to tour the

The Three Gorges Dam is designed to withstand an earthquake of seven on the Richter Scale.

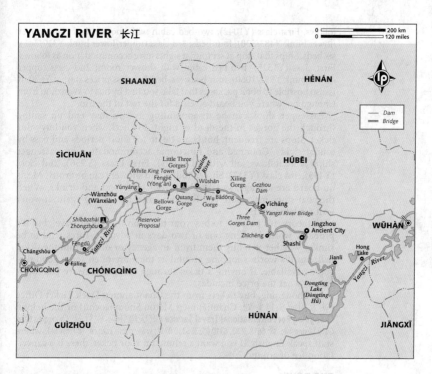

attractions. These boats are ideal for travellers with time, money and negligible Chinese skills. The average number of days for such a cruise is three nights and three to four days.

The fastest route is by hydrofoil, although at the time of writing, direct Chóngqìng–Yíchāng hydrofoils (Y370, 11 hours) had stopped running. Hydrofoils depart from Wànzhōu (Y380, including bus from Chóngqìng to Wànzhōu; Y270 just from Wànzhōu; seven hours) downriver, running to the hydrofoil terminal west of Yíchāng (a further hour by bus from town). Buses linking Chóngqìng and Wànzhōu take three hours.

Hydrofoils are not geared towards tourists so there's no outside seating, but visibility is OK, albeit through Perspex windows. Nonetheless, most passengers use them solely for transportation so while everyone is watching films on TV, you can stand at the door, stupefied by the views. For those who find a day of gorge-viewing adequate, hydrofoils are ideal, although tourist sights are skipped. Food and refreshments are served, but it's a good idea to take along your own snacks and drinks. Hydrofoils make regular but very brief stops at towns (but not sights) along the river to take passengers on board and for disembarkation; check when the boat is leaving if disembarking temporarily.

The third alternative is to board one of the Chinese cruise ships or slow passenger boats that typically depart Chóngqìng in the evening. Chinese cruise ships generally take three days and three nights to reach Yíchāng, while passenger ships take around two and a half days. Some Chinese cruise ships stop at all the sights, others stop at a mere handful, while other vessels stop at none; standards are less professional than the luxury tour ships, but adequate. Tickets for cruise ships not stopping at tourist sights are as

Plans for the Three Gorges Dam date from 1919 when Sun Yatsen (Sun Zhongshan) saw its huge potential for power generation.

follows. First class (Y1042), two-bed cabin with shower; 2nd class (upper /lower bunk Y483/530), four beds; 3rd class (upper/lower bunk Y317/347), six beds. Ships that stop at six tourist sights have accommodation as follows. First class (Y1525), two-bed cabin with shower room; 2nd class (upper /lower bunk Y992/1060), four beds; six-bed 3rd class prices start at Y620. It is also possible to book packages that take you first by bus to Wànzhōu from Chóngqìng, where you board a vessel for the rest of the trip.

Passenger ships can be disappointing as you may end up sailing through the gorges in the dead of night, so check when you buy your ticket. Stops are frequent, but boats tie up for short periods and pass by tourist sights. Cramped and functional accommodation on passenger ships is as follows (all without sights). First Class (Y956), 2nd class (Y495), 3rd class (Y317). Shared toilets and showers can be grotty. Meals on board are average, so take along your own food and drinks. When the boat stops make sure you find out when it's leaving again; it won't wait for latecomers.

In theory, it's possible to buy your ticket on the day of travel, but it's probably worth booking one or two days in advance. Fares tend to be similar whether you buy them from an agency or direct from the ticket hall, but it's worth shopping around as there are often some good discounts available. If buying a ticket through an agent, ensure you know exactly what the price includes.

In Chóngqìng, buy tickets from the Chaotianmen Dock Ticket Office (朝天门码头售票处; Cháotiānmén Mǎtou Shòupiàochù) or the helpful **Chongqing Port International Travel Service** (重庆港国际旅行社; Chóngqìng Gǎng Guójì Lǚxíngshè; ☎ 6618 3683, 6310 0553, 6310 0711; www.cqpits.com.cn; 18 Xinyi Jie), where staff speak English. If you want a refund on your ticket, there is a cancellation fee of around 20%.

THE ROUTE

Most boats travel from Chóngqìng to Yíchāng or Wǔhàn. The Chóngqìng to Yíchāng route is by far the most travelled section of the Yangzi, threading through the Three Gorges and passing the namesake dam. The route can be travelled in either direction, but most passengers journey downstream from Chóngqìng to Yíchāng, a journey that can take anything from 11 hours (hydrofoil) to two nights and two days (passenger ships) or three nights and three days (cruise ships) to even longer tourist cruises. Some vessels soldier on beyond Yíchāng to Wǔhàn and on to Jiǔjiāng, Nánjīng and Shànghǎi, but boat numbers have dwindled in the face of alternative transport and the riverside scenery becomes distinctly ho-hum beyond Yíchāng.

Vessels stop at many of the towns between Chóngqìng and Yíchāng that can also be reached by road, so taking the bus can speed up your journey. If you buy your ticket from an agency, ensure you're not charged up front for the sights along the way as you may not want to visit them all and some of the entrance fees are steep. The only ticket really worth buying in advance is for the popular Little Three Gorges tour, which is often full (see the Wànzhōu to Yíchāng section, p462).

CHÓNGQÌNG TO WÀNZHŌU 重庆 – 万州

The initial stretch is slow-going and unremarkable, although the dismal view of factories gradually gives way to attractive terraced countryside and the occasional small town.

Passing Fúlíng, the next significant town and the first disembarkation point is **Fēngdū** (丰都), 170km from Chóngqìng. Nicknamed the City of

The Yangzi River will deposit over 500 million tons of silt every year into the reservoir behind the dam.

THE DAMNED YANGZI

The Three Gorges Dam is China's biggest engineering project since the construction of the Great Wall. Completed ahead of schedule in May 2006, it will eventually back the Yangzi River up for 550km, flood an area the size of Singapore and wash away the homes of up to two million people. It will rank as the world's largest dam – an epic show of communist might, evidence of man's dominance over capricious nature and the 21st-century symbol of a new superpower.

Located at Sandouping, 38km upstream from the existing Gezhou Dam, the Three Gorges Dam is a cornerstone of government efforts to channel economic growth from the dynamic coastal provinces into the more backward western regions, somehow transforming hinterland into heartland. Measuring 185m high and 2km wide, the dam will have a hydroelectric production capacity equivalent to 18 nuclear power plants.

The dam will improve navigation on the Yangzi River, which already transports 70% of the entire county's shipping, and will be instrumental in flood control, a problem that has claimed more than one million lives in the past 100 years alone.

However, the massive scale of the Three Gorges Dam project has caused disquiet among environmentalists, economists and human-rights activists, arousing some of the most outspoken criticism of government policy since the Tiananmen Sq protests of 1989.

Construction of the dam was incredibly expensive, the initial estimates of US$20 to US$30 billion rising to an eventual US$75 billion. The social implications of the dam are enormous: an estimated 1.5 million people living in inundated areas will have been relocated and, more importantly, given a new livelihood. Environmentalists are perhaps the most vocal in their concerns, as it's thought that as the river slows, so will its ability to oxygenate. The untreated waste that pours into the river from over 40 towns and 400 factories, as well as the toxic materials and pollutants from industrial sites, could well create another world record for the dam: a 480km-long septic tank – the largest toilet in the world.

In addition, the dam will disrupt the environments of such endangered species as the Yangzi River dolphin and Chinese sturgeon. The rising waters will also cover countless cultural artefacts at more than 8000 important archaeological sites. Despite an ambitious plan of relocation and preservation, only one-tenth of all historic sites and relics will be saved.

In 1999, 100 cracks were discovered running the full height of the up-stream face of the dam. Yet despite this, in June 2003 the reservoir was filled to a depth of 127m. Chinese engineers say such problems are common in large dams and that the cracks have been repaired.

Fears about the project were further heightened when information was released about two dams that collapsed in Hénán province in 1975. After 20 years as a state secret, it is now apparent that as many as 230,000 people died when the Banqiao and Shimantan dams collapsed. If a similar accident was to happen on the Yangzi River, the entire population of nearby Yíchāng (480,000 souls) would be dead within an hour.

Planners insist that the Three Gorges Dam has been constructed according to safety regulations that would make such disasters impossible. Still, the collapse of the walls holding back the world's largest storage reservoir in one of the world's most densely populated pieces of real estate is a scenario that must keep even the most gung-ho supporters of the Three Gorges Dam project awake at night.

Ghosts (Guǐchéng; 鬼城), the town faces inundation once all the sluice gates are shut on the Three Gorges Dam. This is the stepping-off point for crowds to belt up – or take the cable car up – **Míng Shān** (名山; admission Y60) and its theme-park crop of ghost-focused temples.

Drifting through the county of Zhōngzhōu, the boat takes around three hours to arrive at **Shíbǎozhài** (Stone Treasure Stockade; admission Y40; ☺ 8am-4pm) on the northern bank of the river. A 12-storey, 56m-high wooden pagoda built on a huge rock bluff, the structure originally dates to the reign of Qing-dynasty emperor Kangxi (1662–1722). Your boat may stop for rapid expeditions up to the tower and for crowded climbs into its interior.

Most morning boats moor for the night at **Wànzhōu** (also called Wànxiàn), a grimy town that rises in steep gradients above the river. Travellers aiming to get from A to B as fast as possible while taking in the gorges can skip the Chóngqìng to Wànzhōu section by hopping on a three-hour bus and then taking either a hydrofoil, passenger ship or cruise ship from the Wànzhōu jetty.

WÀNZHŌU TO YÍCHĀNG 万州 – 宜昌

Boats departing Wànzhōu soon pass the **Zhang Fei Temple** (Zhāngfēi Miào; admission Y20), where short disembarkations may be made. Yúnyáng, a modern town strung out along the north bank of the river, is typical of many utilitarian settlements. Look out for abandoned fields, houses and factories, deserted in advance of the rising waters. Boats drift on past ragged islets, some carpeted with small patchworks of fields, and alongside riverbanks gorgeously striated with terraced slopes, rising like green ribbons up the inclines.

The ancient town of **Fēngjié** (奉节), capital of the state of Kui during the Spring and Autumn and Warring States, overlooks **Qutang Gorge** (瞿塘峡; Qútáng Xiá), first of the three gorges. The town – where most ships and hydrofoils berth – is also the entrance point to **White King Town** (白帝城; Báidìchéng), where the King of Shu, Liu Bei, entrusted his son and kingdom to Zhu Geliang, as chronicled in the *Romance of the Three Kingdoms*.

Qutang Gorge – also known as Kui Gorge (夔峡; Kuí Xiá) – rises dramatically into view, towering into huge vertiginous slabs of rock, its cliffs jutting out in jagged and triangular chunks. The shortest of the three gorges, at 8km in length, Qutang Gorge is over almost as abruptly as it starts, but it is reckoned by many to be the most awe-inspiring. Also the narrowest of the three gorges, it constricts to a mere 100m or so at its narrowest point, where the waters flow at their fastest. The gorge offers a dizzying perspective onto huge strata and vast sheets of rock; the final rise of the water level will undoubtedly rob the gorge of some of its power, but for now the cliffs remain imposing. On the northern bank is **Bellows Gorge** (Fēngxiāng Xiá), where nine coffins were discovered, possibly placed here by an ancient tribe.

After Qutang Gorge the terrain folds into a 20km stretch of low-lying land before boats pull in at the riverside town of **Wūshān** (巫山), situated high above the river. Many boats stop at Wūshān for five to six hours so passengers can transfer to smaller tour boats for trips (Y150 to Y200) along the **Little Three Gorges** (小三峡; Xiǎo Sānxiá) on the Daning River (大宁河; Dàníng Hé). The landscape is gorgeous, and some travellers insist that the narrow gorges are more impressive than their larger namesakes.

Back on the Yangzi River, boats pull away from Wūshān to enter the penultimate **Wu Gorge** (巫峡; Wū Xiá), under a curiously bright red bridge that blots the landscape. Observe how some of the cultivated fields on the slopes overhanging the river reach almost illogical angles, and look out for the markers that signpost the water's highest reach.

Wu Gorge – the Gorge of Witches – is simply stunning, cloaked in green and carpeted in a profusion of shrubs, its cliffs frequently disappearing into ethereal layers of mist. About 40km in length, its cliffs rise to just over 900m, topped by sharp, jagged peaks on the northern bank. A total of 12 peaks cluster on either side, including **Goddess Peak** (Shénnǔ Fēng) and **Peak of the Immortals** (Jíxiān Fēng).

Boats continue floating eastwards out of Wu Gorge and into Húběi province, past the mouth of **Shennong Stream** (神农溪; Shénnóng Xī) and

The Yangzi River has caused hundreds of catastrophic floods, including the disastrous inundation of 1931, in which an estimated 145,000 died.

the town of Bādōng on the southern bank, along a 45km section before reaching the last of the Three Gorges.

At 80km, **Xiling Gorge** (Xīlíng Xiá) is the longest and perhaps least impressive of the gorges. Note the slow-moving cargo vessels on the river, including long freight ships loaded with mounds of coal ploughing downriver to Shànghǎi, their captains alerted to the shallows by beacons that glow from the bank at night. This gorge was traditionally the most hazardous, where hidden shoals and reefs routinely holed vessels, but it has long been tamed, even though river traffic slows when the fog reduces visibility.

The monumental **Three Gorges Dam** (Sānxiá Dàbà; admission Y240) looms up and boats stop so passengers can shuttle across to the dam's observation deck for a bird's-eye view of this mammoth project. Hydrofoils from Chóngqìng and Yíchāng pull in here for passengers to disembark. Boats continue and pass through the locks of the Gezhou Dam (Gézhōu Bà) before completing the journey 30km downstream to Yíchāng.

Directory

CONTENTS

ACCOMMODATION

Hotels in this book are divided into three categories: budget, midrange and top end. The majority of rooms in China are 'twins', two single beds placed in one room. Single rooms (one bed per room; 单间; *dānjiān*) are rare. Double rooms (双人房; *shuāngrénfáng*; also called 标准间; *biāozhǔn jiān*) are often twin, with two beds. Suites (套房; *tàofáng*) are available at most midrange and top-end hotels.

China's Southwest has a wide variety of accommodation options, from rudimentary rooms in cheap family homesteads (农家; *nóngjiā*) to inns (客栈; *kèzhàn*), youth hostels (青年旅社; *qīngnián lǚshè*), cheap Chinese guesthouses (招待所; *zhāodàisuǒ*) and hotels

that range across the spectrum from two- to five-star through budget, midrange and top end. Hotels are called either *bīnguǎn* (宾馆), *jiǔdiàn* (酒店), *dàjiǔdiàn* (大酒店), *fàndiàn* (饭店) or *dàfàndiàn* (大饭店).

Be warned that the star rating at China's hotels can be misleading. Hotels are often awarded four or five stars, when they are patently a star lower in ranking.

When checking into a hotel you must complete a registration form. A copy of this is sent to the local Public Security Bureau (PSB). The form will ask what type of visa you have. For most, the type of visa is 'L', from the Chinese word for travel *(lǚxíng)*. For a full list of visa categories, see p476.

The policy at most hotels is that you check out by noon to avoid being charged extra.

The Chinese method of designating floors is the same as that used in the USA, but different from, say, that in Australia. What would be the ground floor in Australia is the 1st floor in China, the 1st is the 2nd, and so on.

A deposit (押金; *yājīn*) is required at most hotels; this will be either a cash deposit, or your credit card details will be taken. If your deposit is paid in cash, you will be given a receipt, which you should hold on to, for later reimbursement. Credit cards can usually be used for payment at three-star hotels and up, but always check beforehand.

Single males at midrange hotels are routinely pestered on the phone by girls providing massage *(ànmó)*.

Budget

Until recent years, foreigners were barred from very cheap guesthouses as a matter of course, but times have changed and increasing numbers of bargain accommodation options now accept Westerners.

Rooms in family homesteads *(nóngjiā)* – typically family homes in smallish villages and towns with a handful of rooms – cost as little as Y10 a night. English skills will be nonexistent, but you won't get any cheaper. Owners can usually cook up meals and travellers can get closer to the authentic China.

Youth hostels *(qīngnián lǚshè)* typically cluster in the big backpacker destinations,

PRACTICALITIES

■ There are four types of plugs – three-pronged angled pins (as in Australia), three-pronged round pins (as in Hong Kong), two flat pins (US style but without the ground wire) or two narrow round pins (European style). Electricity is 220V, 50 cycles AC.

■ The standard locally published English-language newspaper is the *China Daily* (www.china daily.com.cn). China's largest circulation Chinese-language daily is the *People's Daily (Rénmín Rìbào)*. It has an English language edition on http://english.peopledaily.com.cn. See www .onlinenewspapers.com/china.htm for a more exhaustive list.

■ Imported English-language newspapers such as the *Times, International Herald Tribune, Asian Wall Street Journal, Financial Times* and *South China Morning Post* can be bought from five-star hotel bookshops, as can imported English-language international magazines such as *Time, Newsweek, Far Eastern Economic Review* and the *Economist*.

■ Listen to the BBC World Service (www.bbc.co.uk/worldservice/tuning/) or Voice of America (www.voa.gov). China Radio International (CRI) is China's overseas radio service and broad-casts in about 40 languages. The national TV outfit, Chinese Central TV (CCTV), has an English-language channel – CCTV9. CCTV4 also has some English programmes. Your hotel may have ESPN, Star Sports, CNN or BBC World.

■ China officially subscribes to the international metric system, but you will encounter the ancient Chinese weights-and-measures system that features the *liǎng* (tael, 37.5g) and the *jīn* (catty, 0.6kg), which are both commonly used. There are 10 *liǎng* to the *jīn*.

such as Guìlín (p154), Kūnmíng (p220) and Yángshuò (p166). Expect dorm rooms here to kick off from around Y25 in a four- to six-bed dorm. Hostel facilities will generally include common internet access, washing machine, a DVD machine for common use (with films), notice board, lockers, perhaps a café or bar, and bicycle rental. Beyond dorms, many youth hostels also have single and double rooms. Staff are young, speak good English and can be very helpful for travel advice. Certified youth hostels should carry the 'Hostelling International' logo, but a huge number of independent hostels also exist. For a list of youth hostels in China, see www .chinayha.com and look out for its handy guide listing current hostels (available from youth hostels). Useful online hostel booking websites include www.hostelworld.com and www.hostelbookers.com.

Chinese guesthouses tend to congregate near bus and train stations and can offer beds in shared rooms (typically with shared loo and shower) for as low as Y10 per night. They can be handy but are often grubby and housed in characterless buildings; English skills will be minimal or zero. If looking for a cheap room, always be on the lookout for the characters '有房' (*yǒufáng*; literally 'room available') on boards outside shops and establishments.

Certain temples and monasteries (especially on China's sacred mountains) can provide accommodation. They can be very cheap, but extremely ascetic, with no running water or electricity.

Midrange

Midrange hotels (three to four stars) offer comfort and a measure of style, but are often bland and unimaginative. You should find someone who can speak English, but other language skills are often problematic. When making a choice, opt for Sino-foreign joint-venture hotels over Chinese-owned hotels, wherever possible. Furthermore, opt for newer establishments and chain hotels over older midrange options. Rooms will all come with air-con and may have cable TV or an in-house movie channel and telephone, and should also come with kettle (and coffee sachets), water cooler, safe and minibar, and there should be broadband internet connection. You may receive a free newspaper, but at best only the *China Daily*.

Top End

Whenever possible, aim for luxury international chain hotels that have a proven stand-ard of excellence and quality across the board when opting for top-drawer accommodation.

Staff speaks better English and standards are more closely approximate to international standards, as opposed to top-end Chinese-owned hotels that mainly cater to Chinese guests.

Five-star hotels should be equipped with top-notch sport (including swimming pool and tennis courts), recreational and shopping facilities, and there should be a wide selection of dining options and ATMs that take international cards. Five-star hotel rooms will have a kettle (and coffee sachets), safe, minibar, satellite or cable TV, broadband internet connection, free newspaper (typically the *International Herald Tribune*) and nightly turndown.

Superior comfort should also be available on executive floors, which typically provide free drinks upon arrival and in the afternoon, complimentary breakfast and business facilities. All hotel rooms are subject to a 10% or 15% service charge.

Discounts & Reservations

It is essential to bargain for rooms at reception as discounts are always in force in all but the cheapest accommodation options. Apart from during the busy holiday periods (first week of May and October and Chinese New Year),

rooms should be well below the rack rate and rarely booked out. At reception, discounts of 10% to 50% off the tariff rate are possible, and around 30% is typical. Booking online is an excellent way to secure a good price on a room, and should be the first place you look. Often you actually get a discount by booking through an agency – and these can be substantial, up to 40% to 50% off the walk-in rate (although don't use Chinese online agencies, which simply offer rates you can get from a hotel itself). A useful accommodation website for travellers booking accommodation is **CTrip** (☎ 800 820 6666; www.english.ctrip.com). Airports at major cities may have hotel-booking counters with discounted rates.

BUSINESS HOURS

China officially works a five-day week. Banks, offices and government departments are normally open Monday to Friday (but some banks are open limited hours at weekends as well). Most open around 8.30am, possibly closing for one to two hours in the middle of the day, before reopening until 5pm or 6pm. Saturday and Sunday are both public holidays, but many museums stay open on weekends and close one or two days during the week instead (usually Monday).

HOTEL PRIMER

hotel	fàndiàn/jiǔdiàn/dàjiǔdiàn	饭店/酒店/大酒店
single room	dānjiān	单间
double room	shuāngrénfáng	双人房
triple room	sānrénjiān	三人间
quad	sìrénjiān	四人间
suite	tàofáng	套房
bathroom	wèishēngjiān	卫生间
key	yàoshi	钥匙
lift	diàntī	电梯
visa	qiānzhèng	签证
broadband	kuāndài	宽带
reception	zǒngtái	总台
passport	hùzhào	护照
deposit	yājīn	押金
youth hostel	qīngnián lǚshè	青年旅社
TV	diànshì	电视
telephone	diànhuà	电话
air-con	kōngtiáo	空调
taxi	chūzūchē	出租车
check out	tuìfáng	退房
discount	zhékòu	折扣
toilet paper	wèishēngzhǐ	卫生纸

In Xīshuāngbǎnnà most government buildings operate on the siesta system and working hours are normally around 8am to 11.30am and then 3pm to 6pm or even 8pm.

Travel agencies and foreign-exchange counters in tourist hotels and some local branches of the Bank of China have similar opening hours, but are generally open on Saturday and Sunday as well, at least in the morning. Post offices and telecommunication offices usually stay open to at least 7pm and many are open 24 hours. Internet cafés are either open 8am to midnight, or more popularly, 24 hours.

Many parks, zoos and monuments are also open on weekends and often at night.

Restaurants are generally open from around 10.30am to 11pm or midnight; but some shut at around 2pm and reopen at 5pm or 6pm, others are open through the night. The Chinese are accustomed to eating earlier than Westerners, lunching at around midday and having dinner in the region of 6pm.

Department stores and shops are generally open 10am to 10pm, seven days a week. Note that some businesses in China close for three week–long holidays.

CHILDREN

Children will feel more at home in China's principal points of entry (Hong Kong, Běijīng and Shànghǎi), but could feel out of place in smaller towns and in the wilds of the Southwest.

Baby food, milk powder, nappies and other essentials are widely available in supermarkets. Practically no cheap restaurants have baby chairs and finding baby-changing rooms is next to impossible. Ask a doctor specialised in travel medicine for information on recommended immunisations for your child.

Admission prices to many sights and museums have children's rates, usually for children under 1.1m to 1.3m in height. Always ensure that your child carries a form of ID and a hotel card, in case they get lost.

CLIMATE CHARTS

China's Southwest generally enjoys a pleasant climate, but large regional differences exist; as a general rule temperature is ruled by altitude.

Summer lasts from around May to August. Xīshuāngbǎnnà in southern Yúnnán experiences a mild monsoon during this period, when the most rain falls in Guìzhōu. High spots like Éméi Shān are a great relief from

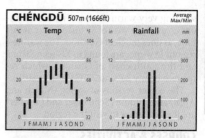

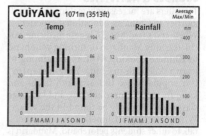

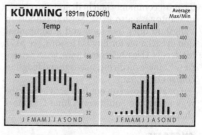

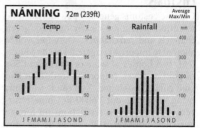

the heat. Sìchuān is foggy and cloudy all the time; Chóngqìng is sweltering.

Winters vary in intensity according to altitude so you'll need to bring a varied wardrobe. In Yúnnán, winters are short and cold north of more clement Kūnmíng, especially as the land ascends into Tibet. Northern Guǎngxī sees temperatures dropping to freezing from November to February. Temperature statistics don't really indicate how cold it can get, so bring very warm clothes. The mountainous areas in the west of Sìchuān freeze at this time, as does much of Guìzhōu. The warmest regions in winter are found in Xīshuāngbǎnnà and the south coast of Guǎngxī, which remains a balmy 24°C to 27°C (75°F to 80°F).

The cooler seasons of spring (March and April) and autumn (September and October) are the best times to visit the region.

COURSES & ACTIVITIES

Travellers are increasingly making the overall journey to China an educational experience. Whether it's traditional Chinese medicine, taichi, learning Mandarin or turning your hand to Chinese cooking, visitors are aiming to learn a skill while in China. Yángshuò (p169) is a popular place to learn both taichi and kung fu, and Chinese cooking and language classes can similarly be found in the village. When selecting a Chinese-language school, talk to other students beforehand. Mandarin is the most commonly taught dialect, but classes in Cantonese also exist. Several schools in Yángshuò offer free food and accommodation in exchange for English lessons; see p171 for details. **Chinastudies.com** (www.chinastudies.com) runs Chinese medicine, massage and fengshui courses in China.

For a rundown on outdoor activities in the region, see the Southwest China Outdoors chapter.

CUSTOMS

Chinese customs generally pay tourists little attention. There are clearly marked 'green channels' and 'red channels'. Duty-free, you're allowed to import 400 cigarettes or the equivalent, two bottles of wine or spirits and 50g of gold or silver. Importing fresh fruit and cold cuts is prohibited. You can legally only bring in or take out Y6000 in Chinese currency. There are no restrictions on foreign currency; however, you should declare any cash exceeding US$5000 (or its equivalent in another currency).

Anything made before 1949 is considered an antique and needs a certificate for export; objects manufactured before 1795 cannot legally be taken out of the country.

Some travellers have had their Lonely Planet guides confiscated at the border for their on-map depiction of Taiwan in a different colour scheme from China. Whatever your opinion on the status of the Republic of China, it may be a good idea to have some scissors handy for on-the-spot editing.

DANGERS & ANNOYANCES

For information on bird flu, consult the Health chapter.

Crime

The China we see in the Western (and Chinese) media – Shànghǎi's glittering high-rises, fleets of black Audis and stock-market winners – is a fabulously warped take on China. For the majority of the population, China remains very poor indeed and yawning disparities between rich and poor generate crime. Guìzhōu province, for example, is very destitute in areas and parts of Yúnnán are impoverished.

Most crime, however, occurs between Chinese people and travellers are generally, but not exclusively, left alone. Visitors are usually victims of petty economic crime, such as theft, rather than serious crime. Incidences of crime increase around the Chinese New Year (p470). Certain cities are worse than others – Guìyáng is notorious.

Hotel rooms are generally safe, but dorms require more care. All hotels have safes and storage areas for valuables – use them.

Violence against foreigners is not common, but does exist. Again, financial motives are in the main and foreigners have been killed for their valuables, or killed when resisting theft. Solo travellers are most at risk, so travel in groups.

If something of yours is stolen, report it immediately to the nearest Foreign Affairs Branch of the PSB. They will ask you to fill in a loss report before investigating the case and sometimes even recovering the stolen goods. For travel insurance purposes (very recommended), it is essential to obtain a loss report.

Photocopy the information page and visa page of your passport in the event of theft.

Scams

Scams are rife in China. Ostensibly friendly types invite you for tea or an expensive meal of snake meat and confess they have no money when the bill arrives, while practising their English on you. Be naturally vigilant when approached by English speakers in the street and don't immediately assume that an approach is a hospitable gesture (but it may be).

Spitting

Campaigns to stamp out the practice have been partially successful in the major urban centres – there is less public spitting in Guǎngzhōu, Shànghǎi and Běijīng these days (some areas impose a Y50 fine), but in the country, the phlegm still flows.

Transport

Your greatest danger will almost certainly be crossing the road, so develop avian vision and a sixth sense. Crossing only when it is safe to do so could perch you at the side of the road in perpetuity, but don't imitate the local tendency to cross without looking. China's roads kill without mercy, with an estimated 600 traffic deaths per day (World Health Organization figures), and are the major cause of death for people aged between 15 and 45. Many cheaper long-distance buses still come without seatbelts. Taxis frequently only have seatbelts in the front passenger seat.

EMBASSIES & CONSULATES
Embassies & Consulates of the People's Republic of China Abroad

For a full list of diplomatic representation abroad go to the Ministry of Foreign affairs website at www.fmprc.gov.cn/eng/.

Australia (www.chinaembassy.org.au) Canberra (☎ 02-6273 4780, 6273 4781; 15 Coronation Drive, Yarralumla, ACT 2600); Melbourne (☎ 03-9822 0604); Perth (☎ 08-9321 8193); Sydney (☎ 02-9699 2216)

Canada (www.chinaembassycanada.org) Ottawa (☎ 613-789 3509; 515 St Patrick St, Ottawa, Ontario K1N 5H3); Calgary (☎ 403-264 3322); Toronto (☎ 416-964 7260); Vancouver (☎ 604-736 3910)

France (☎ 01 47 36 02 58; www.amb-chine.fr; 9 Ave V Cresson, 92130 Issy les Moulineaux, Paris)

Japan Tokyo (☎ 03-3403 3389, 3403 3065; 3-4-33 Moto-Azabu, Minato-ku, Tokyo 106); Fukuoka (☎ 92-713 1121); Osaka (☎ 06-445 9481); Sapporo (☎ 11-563 5563)

Malaysia Kuala Lumpur (☎ 03-242 8495; 229 Jalan Ampang, Kuala Lumpur); Kuching (☎ 82-453 344)

New Zealand Wellington (☎ 04-587 0407; 104A Korokoro Rd, Petone, Wellington); Auckland (☎ 09-525 1589)

Singapore (☎ 65-734 3361; 70 Dalvey Rd)

Thailand (☎ 02-245 7032/49; 57 Th Ratchadaphisek, Bangkok)

UK (www.chinese-embassy.org.uk) London (☎ 020-7636 8845, 24hr premium-rate visa information 0891 880 808; 31 Portland Place, London, W1N 5AG); Edinburgh (☎ 0131-316 4789); Manchester (☎ 0161-224 7480)

USA (www.china-embassy.org) Washington DC (☎ 202-338 6688; room 110, 2201 Wisconsin Ave NW, Washington

DC, 20007); Chicago (☎ 312-803 0098); Houston (☎ 713-524 4311); Los Angeles (☎ 213-380 2508); New York (☎ 212-330 7410); San Francisco (☎ 415-563 9232)

Embassies & Consulates in China
EMBASSIES IN BĚIJĪNG

Embassies in Běijīng are open 9am to noon and 1.30pm to 4pm Monday to Friday, but visa departments often open only in the morning.

Australia (☎ 010-6532 2331; www.austemb.org.cn; 21 Dongzhimenwai Dajie)

Cambodia (☎ 010-6532 2790; fax 6532 3507; 9 Dongzhimenwai Dajie)

Canada (☎ 010-6532 3536; www.beijing.gc.ca; 19 Dongzhimenwai Dajie)

France (☎ 010-8532 8080; www.ambafrance-cn.org; 3 Dongsan Jie)

Germany (☎ 010-8532 9000; www.deutschebotschaft -china.org; 17 Dongzhimenwai Dajie)

India (☎ 010-6532 1908; www.indianembassybeijing .org.cn; 1 Ritan Donglu)

Ireland (☎ 010-6532 2691; fax 6532 2168; 3 Ritan Donglu)

Italy (☎ 010-6532 2131; www.italianembassy.org.cn; 2 Sanlitun Dong Erjie)

Japan (☎ 010-6532 2361; fax 6532 4625; 7 Ritan Lu)

Laos (☎ 010-6532 1224; 11 Dongsi Jie)

Malaysia (☎ 010-6532 2531; fax 6532 5032; 13 Dongzhimenwai Dajie)

Myanmar (Burma) (☎ 010-6532 0359; www.myan marembassy.com; 6 Dongzhimenwai Dajie)

Nepal (☎ 010-6532 1795; fax 6532 3251; 1 Sanlitun Xi Liujie)

Netherlands (☎ 010-6532 0200; fax 6532 4689; 4 Liangmahe Nanlu)

New Zealand (☎ 010-6532 2731; www.nzembassy .com/china; 1 Ritan Dong Erjie)

Singapore (☎ 010-6532 3926; www.mfa.gov.sg /beijing; 1 Xiushui Beijie)

South Korea (☎ 010-6505 2608; www.koreaemb.org.cn; 3rd & 4th fl, China World Trade Center, 1 Jianguomenwai Dajie)

Sweden (☎ 010-6532 9790; www.swedenabroad.com; 3 Dongzhimenwai Dajie)

Thailand (☎ 010-6532 1749; www.thaiembassy .org/beijing; 40 Guanghua Lu)

UK (☎ 010-5192 4000; www.uk.cn; 11 Guanghua Lu)

USA (☎ 010-6532 3831; http://beijing.usembassy-china .org.cn/; 3 Xiushui Beijie)

Vietnam (☎ 010-6532 1155; fax 6532 5720; 32 Guanghua Lu)

CONSULATES IN CHÓNGQÌNG

Canada (☎ 023-6373 8007; 17th fl, Metropolitan Tower, Zourong Lu)

Denmark (☎ 023-6373 6008; 31st fl, Metropolitan Tower, Zourong Lu)

DIRECTORY

Japan (☎ 023-6373 3585; 14th fl, Commercial Wing, Chongqing Hotel, 283 Minsheng Lu)

UK (☎ 023-6369 1500; 28th fl, Metropolitan Tower, Zourong Lu)

CONSULATES IN GUĂNGZHŌU

Australia (☎ 020-8335 5911; fax 8335 0718; Room 1509, 15th fl, Main Tower, Guangdong International Hotel, 339 Huanshi Donglu)

Canada (☎ 020-8666 0569; fax 8667 2401; Room 801, Wing C, China Hotel, Liuhua Lu)

Germany (☎ 020-8330 6533; fax 8331 7033; 19th fl, Main Tower, Guangdong International Hotel, 339 Huanshi Donglu)

Japan (☎ 020-8333 8999, ext 197; fax 8387 8835; 2nd fl, East Tower, Garden Hotel, 368 Huanshi Donglu)

Thailand (☎ 020-8188 6968, ext 310; Room 310, White Swan Hotel, 1 Shamian Nanjie)

UK (☎ 020-8335 1354; fax 8332 7509; 2nd fl, Main Tower, Guangdong International Hotel, 339 Huanshi Donglu)

USA (☎ 020-8121 8000; fax 8121 8428; 1 Shamian Nanjie, Shāmiàn Dǎo)

Vietnam (☎ 020-8330 5911; 2nd fl, B Bldg, Hotel Landmark, Qiaoguang Lu)

CONSULATES IN HONG KONG

Australia (☎ 0852-2827 8881; 23rd fl, Harbour Centre, 25 Harbour Rd, Wan Chai)

Canada (☎ 0852-2810 4321; 11th-14th fl, Tower I, Exchange Sq, 8 Connaught Pl, Central)

Germany (☎ 0852-2105 8788; 21st fl, United Centre, 95 Queensway, Admiralty)

Japan (☎ 0852-2522 1184; 46th & 47th fl, Tower I, Exchange Sq, 8 Connaught Pl, Central)

New Zealand (☎ 0852-2877 4488, 0852-2525 5044; Room 6508, 65th fl, Central Plaza, 18 Harbour Rd, Wan Chai)

UK (☎ 0852-2901 3000; 1 Supreme Court Rd, Admiralty)

USA (☎ 0852-2523 9011; 26 Garden Rd, Central)

Vietnam (☎ 0852-2591 4517; 15th fl, Great Smart Tower, 230 Wan Chai Rd, Wan Chai)

CONSULATES IN KŪNMÍNG

Laos (☎ 0871-317 6624; Room N120, ground fl, Camellia Hotel, 96 Dongfeng Donglu; 🕓 8.30am-noon & 1.30-4.30pm Mon-Fri)

Myanmar (☎ 0871-360 3477; fax 360 2468; www .mcg-kunming.com; B503, Longyuan Haozhai, 166 Weiyuan Jie; 🕓 8.30am-noon & 1-4.30pm Mon-Fri)

Thailand (☎ 0871-314 9296; fax 316 6891; ground fl of the South Wing of the Kunming Hotel, 52 Dongfeng Donglu; 🕓 9-11.30am Mon-Fri)

Vietnam (☎ 0871-352 2669; 2nd fl, Kaihua Plaza, 157 Beijing Lu; 🕓 8am-noon & 2-5.30pm Mon-Fri)

CONSULATES IN NÁNNÍNG

Vietnam (☎ 0771-1551 0562; 1st fl, Touzi Dasha, 109 Minzu Dadao)

CONSULATES IN SHÀNGHĂI

Australia (☎ 021-5292 5500; www.aus-in-shanghai .com.cn; 22nd fl, Citic Sq, 1168 West Nanjing Rd)

Canada (☎ 021-6279 8400; www.shanghai.gc.ca; Suite 604, West Tower, Shanghai Centre, 1376 West Nanjing Rd)

Germany (☎ 021-3401 0106; www.shanghai.diplo.de; 181 Yongfu Rd)

Japan (☎ 021-5257 4766; www.shanghai.cn.emb-japan .go.jp/cn; 8 Wanshan Rd, Hongqiao)

New Zealand (☎ 021-6471 1108; www.nzembassy .com; 15a, Qihua Tower, 1375 Central Huaihai Rd)

UK (☎ 021-6279 7650; www.britishconsulate.sh.cn; 3rd fl, Room 301, Shanghai Centre, 1376 West Nanjing Rd)

USA (www.usembassy-china.org.cn/shanghai) Central Huaihai Rd (☎ 021-6433 6880; 1469 Central Huaihai Rd, entrance on Wulumuqi Rd); Westgate Tower (☎ 021-3217 4650, after-hours emergency number for US citizens 021-6433 3936; 8th fl, Westgate Tower, 1038 West Nanjing Rd)

FESTIVALS & EVENTS

Visiting temples during festival periods will reward you with colourful ceremonies and events. Sights can, however, become rapidly swamped with holidaying Chinese.

The various minorities in China's Southwest each have their own colourful festivals and these are excellent opportunities to appreciate traditional customs, attire and cuisine. Many take place during the winter period when there is little work to be done in the fields and people have more time for festivals. Almost all are dated by the lunar calendar and fall on auspicious dates such as the third day of the third lunar month.

Guìzhōu (especially around Kǎilǐ) and Yúnnán (Dàlǐ and Xīshuāngbǎnnà) have the best of these festivals. For details of local and minority festivals see the start of each province chapter and the Top 10 Festivals section of the Getting Started chapter (p14). With the exception of the Spring Festival, festivals that don't qualify as national holidays (see opposite) include the following:

February

Spring Festival (春节; Chūn Jié) Usually in February – this is otherwise known as Chinese New Year and starts on the first day of the first month in the lunar calendar. Although officially lasting only three days, many people take a week off from work and enjoy big family get-togethers. Be warned: this is China's biggest holiday with transport booked solid. The Chinese New Year will fall on the following dates: 7 February 2008 and 26 January 2009.

Lantern Festival (元宵节; Yuánxiāo Jié) It's not a public holiday, but it is very colourful. Children make (or buy) paper lanterns and walk around the streets in the evening holding them. It falls on the 15th day of the first moon, and will be celebrated on the following dates: 22 February 2008 and 9 February, 2009.

April
Tomb Sweeping Day (清明节; Qīngmíng Jié) A day for worshipping ancestors; people visit and clean the graves of their departed relatives, placing flowers on tombs and burning ghost money. The festival generally falls close to Easter, on 5 April in most years, or 4 April in leap years.

April
Mazu's Birthday (妈祖生日; Māzǔ Shēngrì) Mazu, goddess of the sea, is guardian of seafarers and those who make their living off the seas and waterways. Also called Tianhou (Tin Hau in Cantonese) her birthday is widely celebrated at Taoist temples in coastal regions as far south as Vietnam. Mazu's birthday is on the 23rd day of the third moon; 28 April 2008 and 18 April 2009.

May/June
Dragon Boat Festival (端午节; Duānwǔ Jié) This very popular festival sees crowds watching dragon boat races and eating *zòngzi* (triangular glutinous rice dumplings wrapped in reed leaves). The festival falls on the fifth day of the fifth lunar month; 8 June 2008 and 28 May 2009.

September
Mid-Autumn Festival (中秋节; Zhōngqiū Jié) Also known as the Moon Festival, this is a traditional time to eat tasty *yuè bǐng* (moon cakes) and for families to get together. The festival takes place on the 15th day of the eighth moon, and will be celebrated on the following dates: 14 September 2008 and 3 October 2009.

FOOD

Don't settle for that Chinatown schlock any more, China is where it's at (see p72) and food should top your priorities. It depends on where you travel, but a meal for one at budget eateries should cost under Y20; midrange dining options will cost between Y20 and Y100, while top-end meals can cost anything over Y100.

If you want to eat bread and cakes, look out for bakeries (面包店; *miànbāo diàn*), which are all the rage even in small towns.

GAY & LESBIAN TRAVELLERS

Greater tolerance exists in the big cities than in the more conservative countryside. However, even in urban China it is recommended that gays and lesbians are clandestine about their sexual orientation. On the other hand, recognised gay discos, bars and pubs in big cities appear to function without official harassment, although they tend to keep a fairly low profile.

Check out www.utopia-asia.com/tipschin .htm for loads of tips on travelling in China and a complete listing of gay bars nationwide. You can also contact the **International Gay & Lesbian Travel Association** (☎ 1-954-776 2626; fax 776 3303; www.iglta.com) in the USA.

Useful publications include the *Spartacus International Gay Guide* (Bruno Gmunder Verlag), a bestselling travel guide for gay travellers.

HOLIDAYS

The People's Republic of China has nine national holidays, as follows (Hong Kong and Macau have different holidays):
New Year's Day 1 January
Chinese New Year (Spring Festival) Usually February
International Women's Day 8 March
International Labour Day 1 May
Youth Day 4 May
International Children's Day 1 June
Birthday of the Chinese Communist Party 1 July
Anniversary of the Founding of the People's Liberation Army 1 August
National Day 1 October

Many of the above are nominal holidays that do not result in leave. The 1 May holiday is a week-long holiday, as is National Day on 1 October and the Chinese New Year is also a week-long holiday for many. It's not a great idea to arrive in China or to go travelling during these holidays as things tend to grind to a halt. Room prices all over China rapidly shoot up during the May and October holiday periods. International Women's Day is a half-day holiday for women.

INSURANCE

A travel insurance policy to cover theft, loss, trip cancellation and medical problems is a good idea. Travel agents can sort this out for you although it is often cheaper to find good deals with an insurer online or from a broker. Some policies offer lower and higher medical expense options; the higher ones are chiefly for countries such as the USA, which have extremely high medical costs.

Some policies specifically exclude 'dangerous activities' such as skiing and even trekking. Check that the policy covers ambulances or an emergency flight home. If you have to claim, make sure you keep all documentation. See the Health chapter (p493) for further information on health insurance.

Note that private medical care is limited to large cities and medical care can be rudimentary in smaller towns.

INTERNET ACCESS

Handy internet cafés in towns, cities and destinations are listed under Information throughout this book. Internet cafés tend to cluster near train stations and commercial areas of town. Look for the characters *wǎngbā* (网吧) – or the more rarely used *wǎngluò* (网络) – which mean internet café.

Internet cafés are far easier to find in the Southwest than in Běijīng or Shànghǎi and protocol is also more relaxed down here; you probably won't be asked for ID. From 2007, China was preparing to ban the opening of new internet cafés, so don't expect accessibility to improve.

Online prices are cheap – ranging from as little as Y1 to Y3 per hour, depending on which zone you sit in, but you may have to pay a deposit (usually around Y10). Normally you are given a ticket with a user number and a password (usually a sequence of numbers), which you key into the on-screen box to get online. Internet cafés may operate a nonsmoking policy, but it may not deter your neighbour from puffing away like a madman.

The majority of internet cafés are crowded with teenagers playing games, so things can get noisy and weekends can be totally packed. Opening hours are generally from 8am to midnight or, more commonly, 24 hours.

Youth hostels and other backpacker hotels should have internet access in common areas; if not gratis, rates will be around Y5 per hour.

Objective news and news analysis is feared by the authorities, who strictly control internet content. Even so, most English-language newspapers can be read online, although the BBC News website is invariably inaccessible and you may find other websites unexpectedly becoming blocked; it all depends on the whim of the censors.

Occasionally – as in May 2006 – sites such as Hotmail can go down for long periods, so having a backup email address is a good idea.

LEGAL MATTERS

Anyone under the age of 18 is considered a minor, and the minimum age at which you can drive is also 18. The age of consent for marriage is 22 for men and 20 for women. There is no minimum age that restricts the consumption of alcohol or use of cigarettes. China's laws against the use of illegal drugs are harsh, and foreign nationals have been executed for drug offences (trafficking in more than 50g of heroin can result in the death penalty).

The Chinese criminal justice system does not ensure a fair trial and defendants are not presumed innocent until proven guilty. Note that China conducts more judicial executions than the rest of the world put together, up to 10,000 per year according to some reports. If arrested, most foreign citizens have the right to contact their embassy, see p469.

MAPS

Outside of Hong Kong, English-language maps of towns published in China are uniformly third-rate and rarely have scales; the Southwest is no exception. Ask at concierge desks in five-star hotels for freebie English-language maps, if available. Chinese-language maps are hawked at every turn in tourist towns; look out for transport maps (交通图; *jiāotōng tú*) that list bus routes. New editions are typically annual, but the volume of updated cartographic information is often minimal. Maps can also be bought at newspaper kiosks (报刊亭; *bàokān tíng*) and from bookshops such as Xinhua Bookstore (新华书店; *Xīnhuá Shūdiàn*), branches of which are listed under Information sections throughout the destination chapters in this book.

MONEY
ATMs

In China's Southwest, ATMs that take international cards include branches of the Bank of China and the Industrial & Commercial Bank of China where you can use Visa, MasterCard, Cirrus, Maestro, Plus and American Express (Amex) to withdraw cash. The network largely applies to sizeable towns and cities. Large airports, five-star hotels and some department stores have ATMs.

Counterfeit Bills

Counterfeit notes are a problem in China. Very few Chinese will accept a Y50 or Y100 note without first checking to see if it's a fake. Many shopkeepers will run notes under an ultraviolet light looking for fakes. Visually checking for forged notes is hard unless you are very familiar with bills, but be aware that street vendors may try and dump forged notes on you in large denomination change.

Credit Cards

Credit is not big in China. Foreign plastic is therefore of limited use, but cards used include Visa, MasterCard, Amex and JCB. Don't expect to use them everywhere and always carry enough cash. You should be able to use them at upmarket hotels and restaurants, supermarkets, department stores and shops in tourist towns. Money can also be withdrawn at certain ATMs (see opposite) in large cities on credit cards such as Visa, MasterCard and Amex.

Credit card cash advances have become fairly routine at head branches of the Bank of China. Bear in mind, however, that a 4% commission is generally deducted. The Bank of China does not charge commission on Amex cash withdrawals.

Currency

The Chinese currency is the Renminbi (RMB), or 'People's Money'. Formally the basic unit of RMB is the *yuán* (元), which is divided into 10 *jiǎo* (角), which is again divided into 10 *fēn* (分). Colloquially, the *yuán* is referred to as *kuài* (块) and *jiǎo* as *máo* (毛). The *fēn* has so little value these days that it is rarely used.

The Bank of China issues RMB bills in denominations of one, two, five, 10, 20, 50 and 100 *yuán*. Coins come in denominations of one *yuán*, five *jiǎo*, one *jiǎo* and five *fēn*. Paper versions of the coins remain in circulation. For images of Chinese currency, click on www.chinatoday.com/fin/mon/.

Hong Kong's currency is the Hong Kong dollar and Macau's is the *pataca*.

Exchanging Money

Renminbi is still not freely convertible outside China, but it's easy to exchange money at the airport when you arrive. Foreign currency and travellers cheques can be changed at border crossings, international airports, branches of the Bank of China, tourist hotels, and some large department stores; hours of operation for foreign exchange counters are 8am to 7pm (later at hotels). The official rate is given almost everywhere and the exchange charge is standardised, so there is little need to shop around for the best deal. See the exchange rate table in the Quick Reference inside the front cover and consult a newspaper for the current exchange rate. In some backwaters, it may be hard to change lesser-known currencies – US dollars and UK pounds are still the easiest to change (travellers have also reported seeing Australian dollars go far).

Keep at least a few of your exchange receipts. You will need them if you want to exchange any remaining RMB you have at the end of your trip.

Tipping

In China, almost no-one asks for tips. Many midrange and top-end eateries include their own service charge; cheap restaurants do not expect a tip. Taxi drivers throughout China do expect tips.

Travellers Cheques

These are worth taking with you if you are principally travelling in large cities and tourist areas. Not only will they protect your money against theft or loss, but the exchange rate for travellers cheques (旅行支票; *lǚxíng zhīpiào*) is higher than for cash (around 2% higher). They cannot be used everywhere, however. You should have no problem cashing them at tourist hotels in China, but they are of little use in budget hotels and restaurants. As with credit cards, ensure that you always carry enough ready cash on you. If cashing at banks, aim for the larger banks such as the Bank of China or the Industrial & Commercial Bank of China. Stick to the major companies such as Thomas Cook, Amex and Visa. In big cities they are accepted in almost any currency, but in smaller destinations its best to stick to common currencies such as US dollars or UK pounds.

PASSPORTS

You must have a passport with you at all times; it is the most basic travel document and all hotels will insist on seeing it. The Chinese government requires that your passport be valid for at least six months after the expiry date of your visa. You'll need at least one entire blank page in your passport for the visa.

Have an ID card with your photo in case you lose your passport; even better, make

DIRECTORY

photocopies of your passport. Your embassy may need these before issuing a new one (a process that can take weeks). Also report the loss to the local PSB (公安局; Gōngānjú). Long-stay visitors should register their passport with their embassy.

PHOTOGRAPHY & VIDEO

In large towns and cities, good photographic outlets where you can find colour slide film, a range of batteries and get digital images downloaded to CD or converted to prints are reasonably easy to find. Kodak is the main player in the market, with branches everywhere.

POST

The international postal service is efficient, and airmail letters and postcards will probably take around five to 10 days to reach their destinations. Domestic post is swift.

China Post operates an Express Mail Service (EMS), which is fast, reliable and ensures that the package is sent by registered post. Not all branches of China Post have EMS, so try larger branches.

Apart from local post offices, branch post offices can be found in tourist hotels where you can send letters, packets and parcels, but you may only be able to post printed matter. Other parcels may require a customs form attached at the town's main post office and a contents check. Even at cheap hotels you can usually post letters from the front desk – reliability varies, but in general it's fine.

In major cities private carriers, United Parcel Service, DHL, FedEx and TNT Skypak, have a pick-up service as well as drop-off centres, so call their offices for the latest details.

SHOPPING

Since foreigners are often overcharged in China's Southwest, bargaining is essential. You can bargain (讲价; jiǎngjià) in shops, markets and hotels, but not everywhere. In large shops and department stores where prices are clearly marked, there is usually no latitude for bargaining. In small shops and street stalls, bargaining is expected, but there is one important rule to follow – be polite.

TELEPHONE

International and domestic calls can be easily made from your hotel room (or from public telephones on the street). International phone calls are expensive and it is best to

buy a phone card (opposite). The majority of public telephones take Intergrate Circuit (IC) cards (see below) and only a few take coins. Domestic and international long-distance phone calls can also be made from main telecommunications offices and 'phone bars' (话吧; huàbā).

The country code to use to access China is 86. To call a number in Kūnmíng for example, dial the international access code (00 in the UK, 011 in the USA), dial the country code (86) and then the area code for Kūnmíng (0871), dropping the first zero, and then dial the local number. For telephone calls within the same city, drop the international and area codes (qūhào). If calling internationally from China, drop the first zero of the area or city code after dialling the international access code, and then dial the number you wish to call.

Area codes for all cities, towns and destinations appear in the relevant chapters.

Mobile Phones

Mobile-phone shops (手机店; shǒujīdiàn) such as China Mobile can sell you a SIM card, which will cost from Y60 to Y100 and will include Y50 of credit. When this runs out, you can then top-up the number by buying a credit-charging card (充值卡; chōngzhí kǎ) for Y50 or Y100 worth of credits.

The Chinese avoid the number four – 'sì' – (四; which sounds like but has a different tone from the word for death – 'sǐ'; 死) and love the number eight – 'bā' (八). Consequently, the cheapest numbers tend to contain numerous fours and the priciest have successions of eights.

You can certainly take your mobile phone (手机; shǒujī) to China, but ensure it is unlocked, so you can use another network's SIM card in your phone. Alternatively, global SIM cards are available from airports but you might as well wait till you get to China and visit a branch of China Mobile, which is far cheaper. Contact your network (eg Orange, Vodaphone) to see if your phone can use international roaming in China. If it can, it will probably be expensive; the cheaper option is to obtain a new SIM card in China, but make sure your mobile phone is unlocked first.

Phonecards

For local calls, IC cards (IC 卡; *IC kǎ*) are available from kiosks, hole-in-the-wall shops, internet cafés and from any China Telecom office. They've prepaid cards that can be used in most public telephones, telecom offices and hotels. Some IC cards can only be used locally (depending on where the card was purchased), while other cards can be used throughout China. International calls using IC cards are much more expensive than using Internet Phone (IP) cards.

If you wish to make international calls from your hotel phone, it is much cheaper to use an IP card. International calls on IP cards are Y1.80 per minute to the USA or Canada, Y1.50 per minute to Hong Kong, Macau and Taiwan, and Y3.20 to all other countries; domestic long-distance calls are Y0.30 per minute. You dial a local number, then punch in your account number, followed by a pin number and finally the number you wish to call. English-language service is usually available. IP cards come in various denominations and substantial discounts are offered. IP cards can be found at the same places as IC cards. Some IP cards can only be used locally, while others can be used nationwide, so buy the right card (and check the expiry date).

TIME

The Chinese live by both the Gregorian and the lunar calendar. Time throughout China is set to Běijīng time, eight hours ahead of GMT/UTC. When it's noon in Běijīng it's also noon in Kūnmíng and all other parts of the country. There is no daylight-saving time in China.

When it's noon in Běijīng the time is 2pm in Sydney, 4am in London, 11pm in New York (previous day) and 8pm in Los Angeles (previous day).

TOILETS

Despite proud claims to have invented the first flushing toilet, China has some wicked loos, but in a country of 1.3 billion, that is perhaps unsurprising. When out and about, make a beeline for fast-food outlets, top-end hotels and department stores for more hygienic alternatives or swallow hard and brave the stench. Toilet paper is rarely provided in street-side public toilets so *always* keep a stash with you. Squat toilets are common in budget hotel rooms so if that's not what you want, shop around. In many hotels and buildings, especially old ones, the sewage system can't handle paper. As a general rule, if you see a wastebasket next to the toilet, that's where you should throw the toilet paper; otherwise the loo could choke up and flood.

Hyperventilate before tackling toilets on the older trains, or enter with a strong cigarette.

Remember the following: men 男 *(nán)*; women 女 *(nǚ)*.

TOURIST INFORMATION

Tourist information in many large cities and towns – apart from Kūnmíng – in China's Southwest are rudimentary and of little use. Large cities such as Běijīng and Shànghǎi have more evolved tourist-information infrastructure, but even in Shànghǎi, tourist information facilities are primitive. Backpacker haunts such as Yángshuò (p166) and Dàlǐ (p257) are equipped with helpful English-speaking bar and hotel staff who can offer free advice. Elsewhere, you may have to fall back on your hotel or the China International Travel Service (CITS; 中国 国际旅行社; Zhōngguó Guójì Lǚxíngshè). Most towns and cities have a branch of CITS and addresses and contact details of offices are listed throughout this book, although extracting useful advice can be like pulling teeth from many branches; CITS outfits in traveller havens such as Kǎilǐ (p126) are far more on the ball.

TOURS

Adventure-travel companies that organise treks to China's Southwest include the following:

Active Travel (☎ 64 3-445 2320; www.activetravel .co.nz) New Zealand–based outfit running small-group treks to remote parts of Yúnnán and treks through Tiger Leaping Gorge and beyond.

Bike China (www.bikechina.com) Yúnnán-based company that specialises in bicycle tours of China's Southwest.

Earth River Expeditions (☎ 800-643 2784; www .earthriver.com; 180 Towpath Rd, Accord, NY 12404, USA) Offers rafting and trekking around Tiger Leaping Gorge.

Intrepid Travel (☎ 44 0 1373 826611; www
.intrepidtravel.com; 76 Upper St, Islington, London N1
0NU, UK) Runs a large variety of tours to China's Southwest, including 15-day trips from Běijīng to Kūnmíng via
Chéngdū, 10-day trips from Kūnmíng lassoing in Lìjiāng,
Tiger Leaping Gorge, Dàlǐ and Shangri-la plus five-day
Chinese cooking-oriented trips to Yángshuò.

Journeys International (☎ 800-255 8735, 734-665
4407; www.journeys-intl.com; Suite 3, 107 Aprill Dr,
Ann Arbor, MI 48103-1903, USA) Tours that take in the
highlights of the Southwest.

Mountain Travel-Sobek (www.mtsobek.com) Specialises in rafting and trekking.

Peregrine Adventures (☎ 61 3-8601 4444; websales
@peregrineadventures.com; www.peregrine.net.au; 380
Lonsdale Street, Melbourne, VIC 3000, Australia) Small-
group adventure tours, family, trekking and wildlife tours
to Yúnnán and the Southwest.

White Pearl Associates (www.chinarivers.com) Runs
tours in the Nùjiāng region of Yúnnán that directly benefit
local community organisations and protected areas.

Wild China (www.wildchina.com) Runs a selection of
tours around the Southwest and other parts of China.
Treks include six-day expeditions within Xīshuāngbǎnnà, a
week-long trek to Yading Nature Reserve in west Sìchuān
and a 12-day journey through the minority region of
southeast Guìzhōu.

TRAVELLERS WITH DISABILITIES

As with the rest of the land, China's Southwest
has few facilities for disabled travellers, but
it's not totally impossible. Most hotels have
lifts, so booking ground-floor hotel rooms is
not essential, unless you are staying in very
budget accommodation. Some hotels at the
four- and five-star level have rooms for those
with physical disabilities.

However, roads and pavements make
things very difficult for the wheelchair-bound
or those with a walking disability. Pavements
are often crowded, in a dangerous condition
and have high kerbs. It is recommended that
you take a lightweight chair so you can collapse it easily for navigating around obstacles
or loading into the back of taxis.

You will find loads of useful information
for wheelchair-bound travellers – including
recommended travel agents geared towards
disabled travellers – online at www.disability
travel.com.

VISAS

Apart from citizens from Japan, Singapore
and Brunei, a visa is required for the PRC, but
at the time of writing visas were not required
for most Western nationals to visit Hong
Kong (p94) or Macau. Refer to the Passports
section (p473) for details on passport validity
requirements and what to do in the event of
passport loss while in China.

For most travellers, the type of visa is an L,
from the Chinese word for travel *(lǚxíng)*. This
letter is stamped right on the visa. The L visa
can be either a multiple- or single-entry visa.

Visas are readily available from Chinese
embassies and consulates in most Western
and many other countries. A standard 30-day,
single-entry visa from most Chinese embassies
abroad can be issued in three to five working
days; visa charges vary, but prices have risen
steadily over recent years. Express visas cost
twice the usual fee. You normally pay up front
for the visa, rather than on collection. You can
get an application form in person at the embassy or consulate, or obtain one online from a
consular website (try www.fmprc.gov.cn/eng/–
click on About China, then Travel to China
and then Visa Information). A visa mailed to
you will take up to three weeks. Rather than
going through an embassy or consulate, you
can also make arrangements at certain travel
agencies. Visa applications require at least one
photo (normally a 5cm one). When asked on
the application form, try to list standard tourist
destinations such as Guìlín or Kūnmíng as your
choice is nonbinding.

Thirty-day visas are available at the Macau–
China border at Zhūhǎi. Visas are also available
at the Luóhú border crossing between Hong
Kong and Shēnzhèn, although at the time of
writing this did not apply to US citizens, who
will need to apply in Hong Kong or have a visa
already. A 30-day visa is activated on the date
you enter China, and must be used within three
months of the date of issue. Although a 30-day
length of stay is standard for tourist visas, 60-
and 90-day visas are generally also available.
On request, you can receive a double-entry or
multiple-entry travel visa. If you have trouble
getting more than a 30-day visa, or a multiple-
entry visa, try a local visa-arranging service or a
travel agency in Hong Kong. You need to extend
your visa in China if you want to stay longer.
A Chinese visa covers virtually the whole of
China, although some restricted areas still
exist, which will require an additional permit
(opposite) from the PSB, at a cost.

At the time of writing, Chinese embassies
in the US were no longer accepting mailed
visa applications, so this may mean you will

have to mail your passport to a visa service agency, who will then deal with it.

Many people in the US use the **China Visa Service Center** (☎ 1-800 799 6560; www.mychinavisa.com), which offers impeccable and prompt service. The procedure takes around 10 to 14 days.

The letter specifying what type of visa you have is usually stamped on the visa itself. There are eight categories of visas, as follows:

Type	Description	Chinese name
L	travel	*lǚxíng*
F	business or student	*fǎngwèn*
D	resident	*dìngjū*
G	transit	*guòjìng*
X	long-term student	*liúxué*
Z	working	*rènzhí*
J	journalist	*jìzhě*
C	flight attendant	*chéngwù*

Important note: if you visit Hong Kong or Macau from China, you will need to be on a double-entry or multiple-entry visa to re-enter China or else will have to get a new visa (below).

Getting a China Visa in Hong Kong

Hong Kong is still a good place to pick up a visa for China. China Travel Service (CTS) and any of the other companies listed under Travel Agencies (p94) will be able to obtain one for you or you can apply directly to the **Visa Office of the People's Republic of China** (☎ 0852-3413 2300; 7th fl, Lower Block, China Resources Centre, 26 Harbour Rd, Wan Chai; ☻ 9am-noon & 2-5pm Mon-Fri). Visas processed here in one/two/three days cost HK$400/300/150. Double/six-month multiple/one-year multiple visas are HK$220/400/600 (plus HK$150/250 if you require express/urgent service). Be aware that American and UK passport holders must pay considerably more for their visas. You must supply two photos, which can be taken at photo booths in the Mass Rapid Transit (MTR) and at the visa office for HK$35.

Travel Permits

Travellers to certain areas of a military or sensitive nature require a travel permit (旅行证; *lǚxíng zhèng*), although most of the regions covered in this book are open to foreign travellers.

If you are in any doubt whether an area is restricted, ask at the nearest branch of the PSB. A travel permit for travellers to Tibet is mandatory.

Visa Extensions

Extensions of 30 days are given for any tourist visa. You may be able to wangle more, for reasons such as illness or transport delays, but second extensions are usually only granted for one week, on the understanding that you are on your way out of China. Visa extensions (fees vary depending on nationality) are dealt with by the PSB.

WOMEN TRAVELLERS

Principles of decorum and respect for women are deeply ingrained in Chinese culture. Chinese males are not macho, and there is a strong sense of balance between the sexes. Nonetheless, in its institutions, China is a patriarchal and highly conservative country where virtually all positions of political and state authority are occupied by (old) men.

In general, foreign women are unlikely to suffer serious sexual harassment in China. Try to stick to hotels in the centre, rather than the fringes of town.

Taking a whistle or alarm with you would offer a measure of defence in any unpleasant encounter. If you have to travel alone, consider arming yourself with some self-defence techniques.

Tampons (卫生棉条; *wèishēng miántiáo*) can be found almost everywhere, especially in big supermarkets. It's best to take plentiful supplies of the pill (避孕药; *bìyùnyào*) unless you are travelling to the big cities where brands such as Marvelon are available from local pharmacies.

Transport

CONTENTS

GETTING THERE & AWAY

ENTERING CHINA

There are no particular difficulties for travellers entering China. As a general rule, visas (see p476) cannot be obtained at the border. At the time of writing, visas were not required for most Western nationals to visit Hong Kong or Macau, and some visa-free transits exist. Chinese immigration officers are scrupulous and, by definition, highly bureaucratic, but not difficult or overly officious. Travellers arriving in China will be given a health declaration form and an arrivals form to complete.

Passport

You will not be allowed to enter China if your passport expires within six months. All travellers to mainland China (apart from Hong Kong and Macau residents, who need a permit) will require a visa and a valid passport to enter (see p476). You'll need at least one entire blank page in your passport for the visa. In case of loss or theft, photocopy the information page and visa page of your passport and keep copies in a separate place from your passport. Contact the Public Security Bureau

---

THINGS CHANGE...

The information in this chapter is particularly vulnerable to change. Check directly with the airline or a travel agent to make sure you understand how a fare (and ticket you may buy) works and be aware of the security requirements for international travel. Shop carefully. The details given in this chapter should be regarded as pointers and are not a substitute for your own careful, up-to-date research.

(PSB) and your consulate or embassy in the event of loss or theft.

AIR

For convenience and accessibility, most arrivals are by air, with relatively small numbers of foreign travellers reaching China by sea and overland. The proliferation of direct international flights to China makes air access increasingly convenient, although direct international flights into China's Southwest are largely limited to northeast and Southeast Asia.

Most long-haul international flights to China go via Běijīng, Hong Kong or Shànghǎi; see the Běijīng, Hong Kong and Shànghǎi gateway chapters for details on arriving and spending time in those cities. Flights between Hong Kong and China's Southwest are classed as international.

Airports & Airlines

Hong Kong, Běijīng and Shànghǎi are China's principal international air gateways. **Hong Kong International Airport** (airport code HKG; ☎ 852-2181 0000; www.hkairport.com) is located at Chek Lap Kok on Lantau Island in the west of the territory. Běijīng's **Capital Airport** (airport code PEK; ☎ arrivals & departures 010-6454 1100) has benefited from considerable investment, a new terminal and a further terminal is under construction. International flights to Shànghǎi arrive at **Pudong Airport** (airport code PVG; ☎ 021-6834 1000, flight information 021-6834 6912) in the east; domestic flights use **Hongqiao Airport** (airport code SHA; ☎ 021-6268 8899, 021-6268 3659) in the west of the city. Domestic flights from all gateway cities fly into China's Southwest.

REGIONAL FLIGHTS

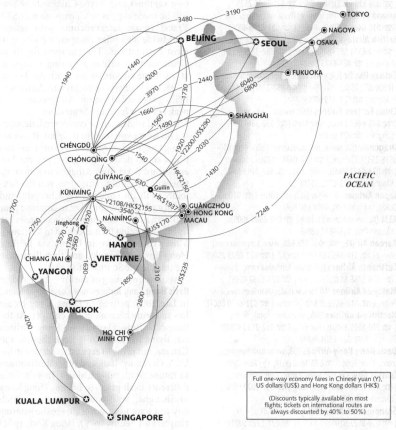

Full one-way economy fares in Chinese yuan (Y), US dollars (US$) and Hong Kong dollars (HK$)

(Discounts typically available on most flights; tickets on international routes are always discounted by 40% to 50%)

TRANSPORT

The cheapest direct ticket deals are generally available from China's international carriers, such as China Eastern.

The number of direct international routes into China's Southwest is growing. Chéngdū's Shangliu Airport has the most international air connections (to/from Hong Kong, Japan, South Korea, Thailand, Singapore, Malaysia and Nepal; flights to Austria, Netherlands and Macau are also in the pipeline). Kūnmíng in Yúnnán similarly has substantial international connections (to/from Hong Kong, Japan, South Korea, Thailand, Vietnam, Myanmar and Laos). Other provincial capitals in China's Southwest with international connections include Guìyáng (to Hong Kong and Thailand). Guìlín's Liangjiang International

Airport has connections to Japan, South Korea, Thailand, Singapore and Malaysia. Nánníng has occasional flights to Hanoi in Vietnam, but at the time of writing these had been suspended.

International and domestic departure tax is included in the price of the ticket.

Airlines flying to and from China include the following:

Air Canada (AC; www.aircanada.ca); Běijīng (☎ 010-6468 2001); Shànghǎi (☎ 021-6279 2999)

Air China (CA; www.airchina.com.cn); Běijīng (☎ 800 810 1111); Shànghǎi (☎ 021-5239 7227)

Air France (AF; www.airfrance.com); Běijīng (☎ 4008 808 808); Shànghǎi (☎ 4008 808 808)

Air New Zealand (NZ; www.airnz.com); Hong Kong (☎ 852-2862 8988)

TRANSPORT

All Nippon Airways (NH; www.ana.co.jp); Běijīng
(☎ 800 820 1122); Shànghǎi (☎ 021-5696 2525)
Asiana Airlines (OZ; www.us.flyasiana.com); Běijīng
(☎ 010-6468 4000); Shànghǎi (☎ 021-6219 4000)
British Airways (BA; www.british-airways.com); Běijīng
(☎ 010-8511 5599); Hong Kong (☎ 852-2822 9000);
Shànghǎi (☎ 021-6375 8866)
Cathay Pacific (CX; www.cathaypacific.com); Běijīng
(10800 852 1888); Hong Kong (☎ 852-2747 1888);
Shànghǎi (☎ 021-375 6000)
China Eastern Airlines (MU; www.ce-air.com); Běijīng
(☎ 010-6464 1166); Hong Kong (☎ 852-2861 0322);
Shànghǎi (☎ 021 95108)
Dragonair (KA; www.dragonair.com); Běijīng (☎ 010-
6518 2533); Chéngdū (☎ 028-8676 8828); Chóngqìng
(☎ 023-6372 9900); Hong Kong (☎ 852-3193 3888);
Shànghǎi (☎ 021-6375 6375)
Japan Airlines (JL; www.jal.com); Běijīng (☎ 010-6513
0888); Shànghǎi (☎ 4008 880 808)
KLM (KL; www.klm.nl) Běijīng (☎ 010-6505 3505);
Shànghǎi (☎ 021-6884 6884)
Korean Air (KE; ☎ 4006 588 888; www.koreanair.com);
Běijīng (☎ 010-8453 8137); Shànghǎi (☎ 021-6275 2000)
Lufthansa Airlines (LH; www.lufthansa.com); Běijīng
(☎ 010-6468 8838); Shànghǎi (☎ 021-5352 4999)
Malaysia Airlines (MH; www.malaysiaairlines.com.my);
Běijīng (☎ 010-6505 2681); Shànghǎi (☎ 021-6279 8607)
Northwest Airlines (NW; www.nwa.com); Běijīng
(☎ 010-6505 3505); Hong Kong (☎ 852-2810 4288);
Shànghǎi (☎ 021-6884 6884)
Oasis Hong Kong Airlines (O8; www.oasishongkong
.com); Hong Kong (☎ 852-3628 0628; ☺ 8am-8pm)
Qantas Airways (QF; www.qantas.com.au); Běijīng
(☎ 010-6567 9006); Hong Kong (☎ 852-2822 9000);
Shànghǎi (☎ 021-6145 0188)
Scandinavian Airlines (SK; www.sas.dk); Běijīng
(☎ 010-8527 6100); Shànghǎi (☎ 021-5228 5001)
Singapore Airlines (SQ; www.singaporeair.com); Běijīng
(☎ 010-6505 2233); Hong Kong (☎ 852-2520 2233);
Shànghǎi (☎ 021-6289 1000)
Thai Airways International (TG; www.thaiairways
.com); Běijīng (☎ 010-6460 8899); Kūnmíng (☎ 0871-
351 1515); Shànghǎi (☎ 021-5298 5555)
United Airlines (UA; www.ual.com); Běijīng (☎ 010-
6463 1111); Hong Kong (☎ 852-2810 4888); Shànghǎi
(☎ 021-3311 4567)
Virgin Atlantic (VS; www.virgin-atlantic.com); Hong
Kong (☎ 852-2532 3030); Shànghǎi (☎ 021-5353 4600)

Tickets

The cheapest tickets to China and Hong Kong
can often be found online or in Chinatown
discount agencies around the world. Other
budget and student travel agents offer cheap
tickets, but the best offers are in agents that

deal with Chinese regularly returning home
(festival times such as the Chinese New Year
will be more expensive). Firms such as STA
Travel (www.statravel.com) with offices
worldwide also offer competitive prices to
most destinations. The cheapest flights to
China are with airlines requiring a stopover
at the home airport such as with Air France
to Běijīng via Paris or Malaysian Airlines to
Běijīng via Kuala Lumpur. Air fares to China
peak between June and September.

Several routes can be considered, depending on where you want to fly from. If you are
flying long haul or round-the-world and can
find a cheap ticket to Bangkok, you can buy
an onward ticket from Bangkok to Kūnmíng,
Chéngdū or Guìlín. This gives you the flexibility to fly into one city (eg Chéngdū) and
out of another (Kūnmíng) or to combine your
trip with one or more regional countries (eg
fly into Kūnmíng then overland to Vietnam).
Most visitors arrive in China via Běijīng,
Hong Kong or Shànghǎi and then fly or take
the train to the Southwest.

With the opening of the long-haul budget
airline **Oasis Hong Kong Airlines** (www.oasishongkong.com)
in late 2006, getting to Hong Kong by air
has suddenly become much cheaper. At the
time of writing, Oasis Hong Kong Airlines
was flying to Hong Kong from the UK and
Canada, but plans to expand its service to the
USA, Germany, Italy and other destinations
in future. With other airlines, there is little
difference in air prices to Běijīng, Hong Kong
or Shànghǎi, so it could depend on which
city you want to stopover in; see the gateway
chapters on Běijīng (p79), Hong Kong (p92)
and Shànghǎi (p86) for further information.
Stopping off in Hong Kong allows you to
sort out your China visa. Domestic tickets
to the Southwest are marginally more expensive from Hong Kong than from Běijīng
or Shànghǎi.

The cheapest available airline ticket is called
an Advance Purchase Excursion (APEX) ticket,
although this type of ticket includes expensive
penalties for cancellation and changing dates
of travel. Tickets listed below are tickets quoted
by airline offices and you will be able to find
cheaper rates through travel agencies.

For browsing and buying tickets on the
internet, try these online booking services:
www.cheapflights.com No-frills website offering
flights to numerous destinations.
www.expedia.com Offers discounted tickets.

CLIMATE CHANGE & TRAVEL

Climate change is a serious threat to the ecosystems that humans rely upon, and air travel is the fastest-growing contributor to the problem. Lonely Planet regards travel, overall, as a global benefit, but believes we all have a responsibility to limit our personal impact on global warming.

Flying & climate change

Pretty much every form of motorised travel generates CO_2 (the main cause of human-induced climate change) but planes are far and away the worst offenders, not just because of the sheer distances they allow us to travel, but because they release greenhouse gases high into the atmosphere. The statistics are frightening: two people taking a return flight between Europe and the US will contribute as much to climate change as an average household's gas and electricity consumption over a whole year.

Carbon offset schemes

Climatecare.org and other websites use 'carbon calculators' that allow travellers to offset the level of greenhouse gases they are responsible for with financial contributions to sustainable travel schemes that reduce global warming – including projects in India, Honduras, Kazakhstan and Uganda.

Lonely Planet, together with Rough Guides and other concerned partners in the travel industry, support the carbon offset scheme run by climatecare.org. Lonely Planet offsets all of its staff and author travel.

For more information check out our website: www.lonelyplanet.com.

---

www.lonelyplanet.com Use the Travel Services to book multistop trips.
www.onetravel.com Offers some good deals.
www.travel.com.au A New Zealand version also exists (www.travel.co.nz).
www.travelbag.co.uk Good for holiday bargains and speciality travel.

To bid for last-minute tickets online, one site to try is **Skyauction** (www.skyauction.com). **Priceline** (www.priceline.com) aims to match the ticket price to your budget.

Discounted air-courier tickets are a cheap possibility, but they carry restrictions. As a courier, you transport documents or freight internationally and see it through customs. You usually have to sacrifice your baggage and take carry-on luggage. Generally trips are on fixed, return-trip tickets and offer an inflexible period in the destination country. For more information, check out organisations such as the **Courier Association** (www.aircourier.org) or the **International Association of Air Travel Couriers** (IAATC; www.courier.org).

Australia

STA Travel (☎ 1300 733 035; www.statravel.com.au) and **Flight Centre** (☎ 133 133; www.flightcentre.com.au) have offices throughout Australia. For online bookings, try www.travel.com.au.

From Australia, Hong Kong is a popular destination and is also the closest entry point into China. Although it's a shorter flight, fares from Australia to Hong Kong are generally not that much cheaper than fares to Běijīng or Shànghǎi. Low-season return fares to Shànghǎi or Běijīng from the east coast of Australia start at around A$1000, with fares to Hong Kong starting from A$910.

Canada

Canadian discount air ticket sellers are known as consolidators and their air fares tend to be about 10% higher than those sold in the USA. Check out travel agents in your local Chinatown for some real deals and browse agency ads in the *Globe & Mail*, *Toronto Star*, *Montreal Gazette* and *Vancouver Sun*. **Travel Cuts** (☎ 800-667-2887; www.travelcuts.com) is Canada's national student travel agency. For online bookings try www.expedia.ca and www.travelocity.ca.

From Canada, **Oasis Hong Kong Airlines** (www.oasishongkong.com) has cheap flights six days a week to Hong Kong from Vancouver from as little as US$275 one-way (plus taxes and charges) in economy. Air Canada has daily flights to Běijīng and Shànghǎi from Vancouver. Air Canada, Air China and China

Eastern Airlines sometimes run very cheap fares. Return low-season fares between Vancouver and Běijīng start at around US$700.

Continental Europe

Generally there is not much variation in air fare prices from the main European cities. The major airlines and travel agents generally have a number of deals on offer, so shop around. **STA Travel** (www.statravel.com) and **Nouvelles Frontières** (www.nouvelles-frontieres.fr) have branches throughout Europe.

Return fares to Běijīng from major Western European cities start at around €900 with Lufthansa, Air France and KLM. Flights to Hong Kong are slightly more expensive, with return fares starting from around €1000 to €1100.

FRANCE

Recommended agencies include the following:
Anyway (☎ 08 92 89 38 92; www.anyway.fr)
Lastminute (☎ 08 92 70 50 00; www.lastminute.fr)
Nouvelles Frontières (☎ 08 25 00 07 47; www .nouvelles-frontieres.fr)
OTU Voyages (www.otu.fr) This agency specialises in student and youth travellers.
Voyageurs du Monde (☎ 01 40 15 11 15; www.vdm .com)

GERMANY

The budget long-haul airline Oasis Hong Kong Airlines are planning to launch direct flights between Cologne–Bonn–Hong Kong and Berlin–Hong Kong in the near future.

Recommended agencies include the following:
Expedia (www.expedia.de)
Just Travel (☎ 089 747 3330; www.justtravel.de)
Lastminute (☎ 01805 284 366; www.lastminute.de)
STA Travel (☎ 01805 456 422; www.statravel.de) For travellers under the age of 26.

ITALY

One recommended agent is **CTS Viaggi** (☎ 06 462 0431; www.cts.it), specialising in student and youth travel.

The very cheap airline **Oasis Hong Kong Airlines** (www.oasishongkong.com) is planning to launch a Milan–Hong Kong direct flight in the near future.

THE NETHERLANDS

One recommended agency is **Airfair** (☎ 020 620 5121; www.airfair.nl).

SPAIN

Recommended agencies include **Barcelo Viajes** (☎ 902 116 226; www.barceloviajes.com) and **Nouvelles Frontières** (☎ 90 217 09 79; www.nouvelles-frontieres.es).

Hong Kong

More than 60 airlines operate between Hong Kong International Airport and about 140 destinations worldwide. Competition keeps fares relatively low, so Hong Kong is a great place to find discounted tickets. For airlines flying to Hong Kong and everything you could ever want to know about Hong Kong International Airport, check out www.hongkongairport .com. Dragonair flies to cities in the Southwest, including Chóngqìng, Chéngdū, Guìlín and Kūnmíng. It is far cheaper to take the train or bus to either Guǎngzhōu or Shēnzhèn and then fly to destinations in the Southwest.

India

STIC Travels (www.stictravel.com) has offices in dozens of Indian cities, including **Delhi** (☎ 11-233 57 468) and **Mumbai** (☎ 22-221 81 431). Another agency is **Transway International** (www.transway international.com).

Japan

Daily flights operate between Tokyo and Běijīng, with one-way fares starting at around US$775. There are also regular flights between Osaka and Běijīng, with one-way fares at around US$600. Daily flights link Shànghǎi to Tokyo and Osaka.

Reliable travel agencies used to dealing with foreigners include the following:
No1 Travel (03-3205 6073; www.no1-travel.com)
STA Travel (www.statravel.co.jp); Osaka (☎ 06-262 7066); Tokyo (☎ 03-5391 2922)

Macau

Air Macau has regular flights to Chéngdū, Guìlín, Kūnmíng and Guìyáng. International flights include Seoul, Bangkok, Manila and Taipei. New long-haul budget airline **Viva Macau** (www.flyvivamacau.com) flies to Jakarta and the Maldives and plans to service destinations including Milan, Moscow, Mumbai, Delhi, Manila and Abu Dhabi. Website www .gomacau.com acts as a consolidator so is a good place to look for cheap fares.

New Zealand

Both **Flight Centre** (☎ 0800 243 544; www.flightcentre .co.nz) and **STA Travel** (☎ 0508 782 872; www.statravel

.co.nz) have branches throughout the country. The site www.travel.co.nz is recommended for online bookings.

International airlines such as Malaysia Airlines, Thai Airways International and Air New Zealand have return fares from Auckland to Shànghǎi for around NZ$1380 during the low season. Return low-season fares to Běijīng start at around NZ$1560.

UK & Ireland

Discount air travel is big business in London. Advertisements for many travel agencies appear in the travel pages of the weekend broadsheet newspapers, in *Time Out*, the *Evening Standard* and in the free online magazine *TNT* (www.tntmagazine.com).

Travel agents in London's Chinatown that deal with flights to China include **Jade Travel** (☎ 0870-898 8928; www.jadetravel.co.uk; 5 Newport Place, London WC2H 7JN), **Sagitta Travel Agency** (☎ 0870-077 8888; www.sagitta-tvl.com; 12-13 Little Newport St, London WC2 7JJ) and **Reliance Tours Ltd** (☎ 0800-018 0503; www.reliance-tours.co.uk; 4th fl, 62 Shaftesbury Ave, Astoria House, London W1D 6LT).

From the UK, the cheapest flights to Hong Kong are with **Oasis Hong Kong Airlines** (☎ 0844 482 2323; www.oasishongkong.com), with one-way daily flights between Gatwick Airport and Hong Kong starting from as low as UK£75 (plus taxes and charges). The cheapest low-season return fares to Běijīng start at around UK£350 with British Airways.

Recommended travel agencies include the following:

Bridge the World (☎ 0870 444 7474; www.b-t-w .co.uk)

Flightbookers (☎ 0870 814 4001; www.ebookers.com)

Flight Centre (☎ 0870 890 8099; flightcentre.co.uk)

North-South Travel (☎ 01245 608 291; www .northsouthtravel.co.uk) North-South Travel donate part of its profit to projects in the developing world.

Quest Travel (☎ 0870 442 3542; www.questtravel .com)

STA Travel (☎ 0870 160 0599; www.statravel.co.uk) For travellers under the age of 26.

Trailfinders (www.trailfinders.co.uk)

Travel Bag (☎ 0870 890 1456; www.travelbag.co.uk)

USA

Discount travel agents in the USA are known as consolidators (although you won't see a sign on the door saying 'Consolidator'). San Francisco is the ticket consolidator capital of America, although some good deals can be found in Los Angeles, New York and other big cities.

From the US west coast, low-season return fares to Hong Kong or Běijīng start at around US$850. Fares to these destinations increase dramatically during summer and Chinese New Year. From New York to Běijīng or Hong Kong, low-season return fares start at around US$890. The supercheap airline **Oasis Hong Kong Airlines** (www.oasishongkong.com) is also planning to launch direct services from Chicago and San Francisco to Hong Kong in the near future.

The following agencies are recommended for online bookings:

www.cheaptickets.com

www.expedia.com

www.itn.net

www.lowestfare.com

www.orbitz.com

www.sta.com (for travellers under the age of 26)

www.travelocity.com

LAND

If you're heading overland from Europe or Asia, it's entirely possible to travel all the way to China and back without having to leave the ground. There are several fascinating routes, including the Vietnam–China border crossing, the Trans-Siberian Railway from Europe, or the exotic Tibet-to-Nepal, Xīnjiāng-to-Pakistan and Xīnjiāng-to-Kazakhstan routes. For more on these routes see Lonely Planet's *China* guide.

It's generally not possible to bring your vehicle into China, although bringing your bicycle should present few problems (although regulations can be capricious). Overland travel between provinces in China's Southwest is largely straightforward, as is transport into the rest of China beyond (see the destination chapters for details).

Border Crossings

China shares borders with Afghanistan, Bhutan, India, Kazakhstan, Kyrgyzstan, Laos, Mongolia, Myanmar (Burma), Nepal, North Korea, Pakistan, Russia, Tajikistan and Vietnam. China also has official border crossings between its special administrative regions, Hong Kong and Macau. The borders with Afghanistan, Bhutan and India are closed. If planning an extensive trip to China overland, make sure you enter China within the given time after your visa is issued (see p476).

TRANSPORT

TRANSPORT

HONG KONG

Hong Kong is an excellent place to enter China overland and there is a variety of options for crossing over the border. From Hong Kong you can reach Guǎngzhōu and virtually any major destination in Guǎngdōng province by bus, from where you can continue by bus or train to destinations in the Southwest. Buses are frequent and run by a multitude of companies and depart from locations around the territory; bus companies include **CTS Express Coach** (☎ 852-2365 0118; http://ctsbus.hkcts.com) and the **Motor Transport Company of Guangdong & Hong Kong** (GDHK; ☎ 852-2317 7900; www.gdhkmtc.com).

To reach Shēnzhèn by train, board the KCR East Rail train at Hung Hom in Kowloon (1st/2nd class HK$66/33, 35 minutes) or at any KCR East Rail station along the way, and ride it to the China border crossing at Lo Wu. From Shēnzhèn you can take a local train or bus to Guǎngzhōu and beyond.

The most comfortable way to reach Guǎngzhōu is via the Kowloon–Guǎngzhōu express train, which covers the 182km route in approximately 1¾ hours. Trains leave Hung Hom station for Guǎngzhōu East 12 times a day between 7.30am and 7.15pm, returning between 8.35am and 9.23pm. One-way tickets cost HK$230/190 in 1st/2nd class for adults and HK$115/95 for children under nine.

Guǎngzhōu has rail connections to everywhere in the Southwest, but it's a major rail bottleneck and it can sometimes be difficult to get an onward ticket leaving the same day or even the next day. This is one city where it's worth trying the **China International Travel Service** (CITS; Zhōngguó Guójì Lǚxíngshè; ☎ 020-8666 6889; 179 Huanshi Xilu; ⏰ 9am-6pm), located near the main train station.

From Hong Kong International Airport buses and boats connect to airports in Macau, Shēnzhèn and Guǎngzhōu, where domestic flights are cheaper. The **TurboJet Sea Express** (☎ 852-2859 3333; www.turbojetseaexpress.com.hk) links Hong Kong International Airport to Shenzhen Airport (HK$230, 40 minutes) seven or eight times daily between 10am and 9.15pm; it also runs to Macau. Buses run by **CTS Express Coach** (☎ 852-2261 2472) and other companies run from Hong Kong International Airport to Guǎngzhōu and other cities in Guǎngdōng.

LAOS

From the Měnglà (p335) district in Yúnnán it is legal to enter Laos via Boten in Luang Nam Tha province if you possess a valid Lao visa. You can now get an on-the-spot visa for Laos at the border, the price of which depends on your nationality (although you cannot get a Chinese visa here). The border doesn't officially close until 5.30pm Běijīng time (and don't forget that Laos is an hour behind), but things often wrap up earlier on the Lao side. As the bus journey from Jǐnghóng to Měnglà takes the better part of the day, you will probably have to stay overnight at Měnglà. For more details, see the boxed text (p334). Lao visas can also be obtained in Běijīng (p469); the Lao consulate in Kūnmíng (p470) issues 15-day tourist visas (valid for two months from date of issue; visa extensions in Laos possible).

MACAU

On the other side of the border from Macau is the Special Economic Zone (SEZ) of Zhūhǎi; the border is open from 7am to midnight. Simply take bus 3, 5 or 9 to the Border Gate (Portas de Cerco) and walk across. A second, less busy crossing is the **Cotai Frontier Post** (⏰ 9am-8pm) on the causeway linking Taipa and Coloane and allows visitors to cross over the Lotus Bridge by shuttle bus (HK$4) to Zhūhǎi. Buses 15, 21 and 26 will drop you off at the crossing.

For buses further afield, the **Kee Kwan Motor Road Co** (☎ 853-933 888) operates from the bus station on Rua das Lorchas, 100m southwest of the end of Avenida de Almeida Ribeiro. Buses for Guǎngzhōu (MOP$70, four hours), from where you can get good connections to the rest of China, depart every half-hour, and for Zhōngshān (MOP$25, 70 minutes) every 20 minutes between about 8am and 6.30pm. There are buses to Guǎngzhōu (MOP$75) and Dōngguǎn (MOP$80) from Macau International Airport.

MYANMAR (BURMA)

Travellers can legally cross the border in only one direction – from the Chinese side into Myanmar at the Jiegao Border Checkpoint connecting Ruìlì (p350) to Muse in Myanmar's Shan State. Land crossings from China are only possible if you join an organised tour group from a Chinese travel agency (eg Ko Wai Lin Travel in Kūnmíng; p225), who can arrange permits. Myanmar visas cannot be arranged in Ruìlì and must be done in Kūnmíng. See p353 for details on journeying to Myanmar. You cannot legally leave Myanmar by this route.

VIETNAM

Travellers can enter Vietnam overland from China and exit Vietnam to China on a standard visa. You cannot obtain visas at the border, but visas for Vietnam can be acquired in Běijīng (p469), Kūnmíng (p470), Guǎngzhōu (p470), or at either CITS (p191) or the Vietnam consulate (p470) in Nánníng; Vietnam also has a consulate in Guǎngzhōu. Chinese visas can be obtained in Hanoi. The Vietnam-China border crossing is open from 7am to 4pm, Vietnam time, or 8am to 5pm, China time. Set your watch when you cross the border – the time in China is one hour later than in Vietnam. There are currently three border checkpoints where foreigners are permitted to cross between Vietnam and China. There is a possibility that others will open in the future. For details of the Beijing–Hanoi train, see below.

Friendship Pass

The busiest border crossing is at the Vietnamese town of Dong Dang, an obscure town (the nearest city is Lang Son 18km to the south) 164km northeast of Hanoi. The closest Chinese town to the border is Píngxiáng (p208) in Guǎngxī province, which is about 10km north of the actual border gate. The only place in Guǎngxī where foreigners can cross is Friendship Pass, known as Huu Nghi Quan in Vietnamese and Yǒuyì Guān in Chinese. Buses and minibuses on the Hanoi–Lang Son route are frequent. For details on reaching Friendship Pass from Píngxiáng, see p208.

Express buses between Píngxiáng and Nánníng are regular and fast (Y60 to Y70, 2½ hours). Píngxiáng is also connected by train to Nánníng, capital of China's Guǎngxī province, 220km away. Train 5518 (Y9 to Y18) to Nánníng departs Píngxiáng at 2.45pm, arriving in Nánníng at 6.05pm. In the other direction, train 5517 departs Nánníng at 8am, arriving in Píngxiáng at 11.30am.

As train tickets to China are expensive in Hanoi, some travellers buy a ticket to Dong Dang, walk across the border and then buy a train ticket on the Chinese side. This isn't the best way because it's several kilometres from Dong Dang to Friendship Pass, and you'll have to hire someone to take you by motorbike. If you're going by train, it's best to buy a ticket from Hanoi to Píngxiáng, and then in Píngxiáng buy a ticket to Nánníng or beyond.

From Nánníng's Langdong bus station, a daily bus (Y68, five hours) runs to Friendship Pass at 8.10am and you can buy a ticket on this bus all the way to Hanoi (Y120, 6½ hours).

Twice-weekly trains run from Běijīng to Hanoi. The T5 leaves Beijing West Train Station at 4.16pm on Monday and Friday, arriving in Hanoi at 8.10am on Wednesday and Sunday. The T6 departs Hanoi at 6.30pm on Tuesday and Friday, arrving in Běijīng at 1.38pm on Thursday and Sunday. The train stops at Shíjiāzhuāng, Zhèngzhōu, Hànkǒu (in Wǔhàn), Wǔchāng (Wǔhàn), Chángshā, Héngyáng, Yǒngzhōu, Guìlín North, Guìlín, Liǔzhōu, Nánníng and Píngxiáng.

Lao Cai–Hékǒu

A 762km metre-gauge railway, inaugurated in 1910, links Hanoi with Kūnmíng; at the time of writing international train services were suspended due to floods and landslide damage; ambitious plans are afoot to upgrade the ageing rail link. The border town on the Vietnamese side is Lao Cai, 294km from Hanoi. On the Chinese side, the border town is Hékǒu, 468km from Kūnmíng. Buses to Hékǒu run from Kūnmíng (Y119, 12 hours, 9.45am, 1.30pm, 7.30pm and 8.40pm; see p234) for more details on crossing the border at Lao Cai–Hékǒu.

Mong Cai–Dōngxīng

Vietnam's third but little known border crossing is at Mong Cai in the northeast corner of the country, just opposite the Chinese city of Dōngxīng.

RIVER

For details on boats between Chiang Saen in Thailand and Jǐnghóng, see the boxed text, p331.

SEA

There are no direct international boats to ports in the Southwest. Weekly ferries link Osaka and Shànghǎi (roughly 44 hours) and twice-monthly services run between Kōbe (Japan) and Shànghǎi (roughly 44 hours). From Tiānjīn, a weekly ferry sails to Kōbe. There are also boats from Qīngdǎo to Shimonoseki every two weeks. Travelling from Korea, international ferries connect the South Korean port of Incheon with Wēihǎi, Qīngdǎo, Tiānjīn (Tánggū), Dàlián and Dāndōng. See

Lonely Planet's *China* guide for more details on all routes.

Hong Kong

Regularly scheduled ferries link the China ferry terminal in Kowloon and/or the Macau ferry pier on Hong Kong Island with a string of towns and cities on the Pearl River delta (but not central Guǎngzhōu or Shēnzhèn).

High-speed ferries run by **TurboJet** (☎ 852-2921 6688; www.turbojet.com.hk) connect the China ferry terminal with Fúyǒng ferry terminal (Shēnzhèn airport) regularly throughout the day. **CMSE Passenger Transport** (☎ 852-2858 0909) has regular services from the China ferry terminal and the Macau ferry pier to Shékǒu, 20km west of Shēnzhèn.

Regular ferries to Zhūhǎi in Guǎngdōng can also be reached from Hong Kong from the China ferry terminal and the Macau ferry pier.

Hong Kong is connected to Macau by two ferry companies that run high-speed vessels virtually 24 hours a day.

Macau

A daily ferry by the **Yuet Tung Shipping Co** (☎ 853-574 478) connects Macau with the port of Shékǒu in Shēnzhèn. Boats run three times a day and take 80 minutes. Tickets can be bought up to three days in advance from the point of departure, which is pier 14, just off Rua das Lorchas and 100m southwest of the end of Avenida de Almeida Ribeiro.

GETTING AROUND

AIR

China's air network is extensive and rapidly growing: its civil aviation fleet is expected to triple in size over the next two decades, with up to 2000 more airliners being added to the existing fleet by 2022. Airports are being built and upgraded all over the land. China is actually running out of airline pilots to fly its growing fleet and foreign pilots have reportedly been hired.

The Civil Aviation Administration of China (CAAC; Zhōngguó Mínháng) is the civil aviation authority for numerous airlines, including for **Air China** (CA; www.airchina.com.cn), **China Eastern Airlines** (MU; www.ce-air.com), **China Southern Airlines** (CZ; www.cs-air.com) and **Sichuan Airlines** (3U; www.scal.com.cn). Sichuan Airlines is based in Chéngdū and China Southern in based in Guǎngzhōu.

CAAC publishes a combined international and domestic timetable in both English and Chinese in April and November each year. This timetable can be bought at some airports and CAAC offices in China. Individual airlines also publish timetables and you can buy these from ticket offices throughout China.

Shuttle buses often run from CAAC offices in towns and cities through China to the local airport.

On domestic and international flights the free baggage allowance for an adult passenger is 20kg in economy class and 30kg in 1st class. You are also allowed 5kg of hand luggage, though this is rarely weighed. The charge for excess baggage is 1% of the full fare for each kilogram. Remember to keep your baggage receipt label on your ticket as you will need to show it when you collect your luggage.

International and domestic departure tax is included in the price of the ticket.

Tickets

You need to show your passport when reserving or purchasing a ticket, and you definitely need it to board the aircraft. Tickets are easy to purchase as at most times there is an oversupply of airline seats (except during major festivals and holidays). Tickets can be purchased from branches of CAAC, travel agents, or from the travel desk of your hotel (the latter will tack on a service charge); it pays to shop around. Discounts are common, except when flying into large cities such as Shànghǎi at the weekend, when the full fare can be the norm; prices quoted in this book are the full fare. Fares are calculated according to one-way travel, with return tickets simply costing twice the single fare.

Children over 12 are charged adult fares; kids between two and 12 pay half-price. Toddlers under the age of two pay 10% of the full fare. You can use credit cards at most CAAC offices and travel agents.

BICYCLE

Most of China's Southwest is ideal for biking, a form of transport that opens up vast areas to exploration and the opportunity to see parts of the region you would miss travelling by bus or train. Minority and rural areas are particularly rewarding, though they are

DOMESTIC FLIGHTS

TRANSPORT

normally pretty hilly, so you will need to be fit. Hiring a bicycle *(zìxíngchē)* in towns such as Guìlín (p154) and Yángshuò (p166) is also an excellent way to get around, but you won't see any bicycles in Chóngqìng (p438), as the gradients are way too fierce.

Refer to the Cycling section in the Southwest China Outdoors chapter (p65) for more details on cycling in this region.

Hazards

Cycling is a popular albeit hazardous means of transport. China's roads – both urban and rural – are lethal, and according to the WHO 600 people a day die in traffic accidents. The exponential increase in vehicle numbers has made cycling increasingly hazardous, so keep you wits about you.

Night riding is particularly dangerous. On country roads look out for tractors, which often have no headlights at all. Chinese bicycles are rarely equipped with lights. Chinese cyclists and pedestrians tend to favour black clothing, which camouflages perfectly with the nightscape.

Dogs, the enemy of cyclists the world over, are less of a problem in China than elsewhere but can be a real menace in Tibetan areas of western Sìchuān and northeastern Yúnnán.

Hire

Established bicycle-hire shops exist in most traveller centres in China's Southwest, the best being at Yángshuò, Dàlǐ, Lìjiāng and Jǐnghóng. In touristy places like Yángshuò

it's even possible to rent electric bikes and scooters.

Most hire shops operate out of hotels popular with foreigners, but independent hire shops also exist. The range of bikes is generally good, but examine your vehicle carefully before handing over a deposit (typically in the region of Y150 to Y500; avoid leaving your passport as deposit).

Day, half-day and hourly hire are the usual options; you can also hire for several days, so touring is possible. Rates for Westerners are typically around Y10 to Y20 per day. Note that some big hotels charge ridiculous rates.

Bike repair shops are everywhere and repairs are cheap.

Off the Road

Most travellers who bring bikes take at least a couple of breaks from the rigours of the road, during which they use some other means of transport. Bicycles can be conveyed by bus, air and train, and even by taxi, although avoid shipping your bike in the build up to and during the Chinese New Year or the major holiday periods.

On the train, your bike won't arrive at the same time as you unless you send it on a couple of days in advance. You will be charged for your bicycle as cargo according to its weight. At the other end it is held in storage for a small daily fee of around Y2 and a small administration fee is payable when you collect it.

Transporting your bike by plane can be expensive, but it's often less complicated than

TRANSPORT

NAVIGATING CITIES

At first glance, Chinese street names can be bewildering, with name changes common every few hundred metres. The good news is that there is some logic to it, and a little basic Chinese will help to make navigating much easier.

Many road names are compound words made up of a series of directions that place the road in context with all others in the city. Compass directions are particularly common in road names. The directions are: *běi* (north; 北); *nán* (south; 南); *dōng* (east; 东); and *xī* (west; 西). So Dong Lu (东路) literally means East Rd, while Xi Jie (西街) means West St.

Other words, which regularly crop up are *zhōng* (central; 中) and *huan* (ring, as in ring road; 环). If you bring them together with some basic numerals, you could have Dongsanhuan Nanlu (东三环南路), which literally means 'east third ring south road' or the southeastern part of the third ring road.

---

by train. Some cyclists have not been charged by CAAC; others have had to pay 1% of their fare per kilogram of excess weight.

BOAT

The best-known river trip is the boat ride through the Three Gorges along the Yangzi River from Chóngqìng (p458). The six-hour Li River (p166) boat trip from Guìlín to Yángshuò is also popular.

BUS

Long-distance buses are an excellent way of getting around China's Southwest. Routes are extensive, tickets easy to get, vehicles are improving, roads are becoming smoother and buses stop in small towns and villages not served by trains or planes. On the downside, prepare for cramped and painful trips on long, time-consuming journeys; appalling and often dangerous driving; and occasional breakdowns that can throw a spanner into your itinerary.

Not all long-distance buses have seatbelts, but all invariably come with looped *wǔdǎ*, kung fu movies or karaoke DVDs with three-dimensional sound. Most buses are now no-smoking, but intransigent male smokers light up regardless on smaller, short-haul routes.

The plushest long-haul coaches have airline-style reclining seats, ample legroom and toilets. Bottles of mineral water are handed out by hostesses on many long-distance routes; but still stock up with snacks.

The shock absorbers on small buses (小巴; *xiǎobā*), minibuses and more ancient long-distance buses are poor, so avoid sitting at the rear of the bus if possible. Long-distance trips can eat into your travel time, so taking a night sleeper (if available) can save time. If you do sit in the back and the road is rough, expect to become

airborne every time the bus hits a bump. Aim for an aisle seat if you have long legs. Chinese tend to avoid sitting next to the *lǎowài* (see the boxed text, p199), so you may have an empty seat next to you on all but the fullest buses.

Minibuses on shorter routes can wait infuriatingly until the bus is full before departing, dawdling at the side of the road and press-ganging hesitant pedestrians onto seats. Consequently what should be a 60-minute trip can take 1½ hours or more. Between towns bus speeds are high, but growing urban traffic can slow things to a crawl as your bus makes its way to and from the local bus station. The smaller the bus the less luggage room. Luggage racks can be wafer-thin and bulky backpacks may have to go on the floor; you'll only find luggage compartments on bigger buses.

Drivers can develop cast-iron bladders from a life of slurping cold tea from jam jars, so toilet stops can be few and far between. As drivers lean on the horn at the slightest sign of movement ahead, things can get cacophonous. Overtaking on blind corners doesn't much faze drivers, so journeys are frequently of the white-knuckle variety.

On long routes, sleeper buses (*wòpùchē*) can be useful for reaching a destination overnight. Bunks can have limited legroom and no luggage storage, however. Try to keep an eye on your valuables.

On some rural routes you'll find *miàndī* (面的) or taxivans that seat around seven. You'll probably run into these on the way to Detian Waterfall in Guǎngxī.

Tickets

Tickets for long-distance buses are easier to obtain than train tickets. Tickets for same-day travel are generally straightforward and usually you can get a seat just before the bus departs, although if there are only one or two departures a day, try to book earlier otherwise you may get a bad seat (towards the rear of the bus) or you may have to wait till the next departure. If possible, book the day before. Optional insurance is provided for an extra Y2 or so. On large buses, seats are generally numbered on the ticket, but if the bus is only half-full you can sit anywhere. When buying tickets, ask what different buses go to your destination; tickets for plusher express buses will be more expensive, but far more comfortable.

Long-distance bus stations are often huge and chaotic. There is often more than one bus station in town, each one generally serving the compass direction of your destination.

Local Chinese maps have a special symbol for a bus station, meant to resemble the steering wheel of the bus.

CAR & MOTORCYCLE

Driving a hire car around China is impossible unless you have a residence permit (p476) and a Chinese driving licence, so don't think you can just jump in a car and blaze off into the wilds. For the latest update, contact **Hertz** (☎ countrywide 800-810 8883; www.hertz.net.cn), but don't expect regulations to relax any time soon. Hiring a motorcycle is similarly impossible unless you have a residence permit. Finding a car with a driver can be arranged through major hotels, CITS or other travel agencies. Parts of the Southwest require hiring a 4WD and driver.

HITCHING

Hitching is never entirely safe in any country in the world, and we don't recommend it. People who do choose to hitch will be safer if they travel in pairs and let someone know where they are planning to go.

Many people have hitchhiked in China, and some have been amazingly successful. It's not officially sanctioned and the same dangers that apply elsewhere in the world also apply in China. Exercise caution, and if you're in any doubt as to the intentions of your prospective driver, say no.

Hitching in China is rarely free, and passengers are expected to offer at least a tip. Some drivers might ask for an unreasonable amount of money, so try to establish a figure early to avoid problems later. There is no Chinese signal for hitching, so just try waving down a truck.

LOCAL TRANSPORT

While China boasts a huge and often ingenious choice of local transport, vehicles can be slow and overburdened, and the transport network is confusing for visitors. Unless the town is small, walking is not usually recommended, since Chinese cities tend to be very spread out. On the plus side, local transport is cheap. Chóngqìng now benefits from a limited light-rail system.

Bus

Apart from bikes, buses are the most common means of getting around in the cities. Services

TRANSPORT

ROAD DISTANCES (KM)

* Distances are approximate

	Chengdū	Chóngqìng	Gèjiù	Guǎngyuán	Guìlín	Guìyáng	Kūnmíng	Nánníng	Wúzhōu
Chóngqìng	340								
Gèjiù	1000	1020							
Guǎngyuán	280	610	1300						
Guìlín	1380	950	1400	1550					
Guìyáng	680	350	670	950	870				
Kūnmíng	770	790	230	1050	1150	450			
Nánníng	1260	930	830	1500	360	850	740		
Wúzhōu	1400	1070	1370	1680	380	980	1270	400	
Xiàguān	850	1050	480	1300	1630	700	260	1000	1530

TRANSPORT

are fairly extensive, buses go to most places and fares are inexpensive (typically Y1). The problem is that they are almost always packed, traffic can be slow and bus routes and signs are in Chinese only.

Taxi

Taxis (出租汽车; *chūzū qìchē*) can be the best way to get around. They are cheap and plentiful and always pursuing customers, so finding one is rarely difficult. Some cities such as Liǔzhōu (p189) sport fleets of new Hyundai taxis.

Taxi rates per kilometre are clearly marked on a sticker on the rear side window of the taxi; flag fall rates vary from city to city and also depend upon the size and quality of vehicle.

Taxi drivers speak little, if any English. If you don't speak Chinese, bring a map or have your destination written down in characters. It helps if you know the way to your destination; sit in the front with a map.

If you encounter a taxi driver you trust or who speaks a smattering of English, ask for his card (名片; *míngpiàn*). You can hire them for a single trip or on a daily basis – the latter is worth considering if there's a group of people who can split the cost.

While most taxis have meters, they are often only switched on in larger towns and cities. If the meter is not used (on an excursion out of town for example), a price should be negotiated before you get into the taxi, and bargaining employed. If you want the meter to be used, ask for *dǎbiǎo* (打表).

It is hard to find rear seat belts in China's older taxis, and front passenger seat belts are so rarely used they are often grimy or locked solid.

Other

An often bewildering array of ramshackle transport options infests China, providing employment for legions of elderly Chinese. The motor tricycle (三轮摩托车; *sānlún mótuōchē*) – for want of a better name – is an enclosed three-wheeled vehicle with a driver at the front, a small motorbike engine below and seats for two passengers behind. They tend to congregate outside the train and bus stations in larger towns and cities.

The pedicab (三轮车; *sānlúnchē*) is a pedal-powered tricycle with a seat to carry passengers.

In some towns (eg Běihǎi) you can get a ride on the back of someone's motorcycle for about

half the price of what a regular four-wheeled taxi would charge. If you turn a blind eye to the hazards, it's a quick and cheap way of getting around. You must wear a helmet – the driver will provide one. Obviously, there is no meter, so fares must be agreed upon in advance.

Prices of all of the above can compare with taxis, however, so check beforehand and bargain. Also note that none of the above offer decent protection in a crash, so taking a taxi is often the more sensible option.

TRAIN

Although crowded, trains are a fantastic way to get around in reasonable speed and comfort. The network covers every province, except Hǎinán Island, with the link to Lhasa in Tibet completed in 2006. At any given time it is estimated that more than 10 million Chinese are travelling on a train in China, except at Chinese New Year when the whole country seems to be on the railway.

Trains are punctual and leave on the dot. A variety of classes means you can navigate as you wish: if you can endure a hard seat, getting from A to B is very cheap. Opting for a soft sleeper means things can get pricey.

The new fleet of trains that run intercity routes is a vast improvement on the old models – they are much cleaner and equipped with air-con. The new 'Z' class express trains are limited to routes between Běijīng and Shànghǎi and Běijīng and Xī'ān: they are very plush, with meals thrown in on some routes, mobile phone charging points and well-designed bunks.

Most trains have dining cars where you can find passable food. Railway staff also regularly walk by with pushcarts offering snacks.

Many train stations require that luggage be X-rayed before entering the waiting area.

Virtually all train stations have left-luggage rooms (寄存处; *jìcún chù*) where you can safely dump your bags for about Y5 to Y10 (per day per item).

An excellent online source of information on China's rail network is www.seat61.com /China.htm, which also has useful links to rail timetables in English, maps of the Chinese rail network and tips on buying tickets.

Classes

Train tickets are calculated simply according the kilometre distance travelled and, on longer routes, the class of travel.

Hard seat (硬座; *yìng zuò*) is actually generally padded, but the hard-seat section can be hard on your sanity – it can be very dirty and noisy, and painful on the long haul. Hard seat on tourist trains, express trains or newer trains is more pleasant, less crowded and air-conditioned.

Since hard seat is the only thing most locals can afford it's packed to the gills. You should get a ticket with an assigned seat number, but if seats have sold out, ask for a standing ticket (无座; *wúzuò*; or 站票; *zhànpiào*), which at least gets you on the train, where you may find a seat or you can upgrade (see below). Because hard-seat tickets are relatively easy to obtain, you may have to travel hard seat even if you're willing to pay for a higher class.

On some short journeys, trains have soft-seat (软座; *ruǎn zuò*) carriages. These trains have comfortable seats arranged two abreast and overcrowding is not permitted. Soft seats cost about the same as hard sleeper and carriages are often double-decker.

Hard-sleeper (硬卧; *yìng wò*) carriages are made up of doorless compartments with half a dozen bunks in three tiers, and sheets, pillows and blankets are provided. It does very nicely as an overnight hotel. There is a small price difference between berths, with the lowest bunk (下铺; *xiàpù*) the most expensive and the top-most bunk (上铺; *shàngpù*) the cheapest. You may wish to take the middle bunk (中铺; *zhōngpù*) as all and sundry invade the lower berth to use it as a seat during the day, while the top one has little headroom and puts you near the speakers. As with all other classes, smoking is prohibited in hard sleeper. Lights and speakers go out at around 10pm. Hard-sleeper tickets are the most difficult of all to buy; you almost always need to buy these a few days in advance.

Soft sleeper (软卧; *ruǎn wò*) is the most comfortable, with four bunks in a closed compartment. Soft sleeper costs around twice as much as hard sleeper (the upper berth is slightly cheaper than the lower berth), so it is usually easier to purchase soft rather than hard sleeper; however, more and more Chinese are travelling this way.

If you get on the train with an unreserved seating ticket, you can find the conductor and upgrade (补票; *bǔpiào*) yourself to a hard sleeper, soft seat or soft sleeper if there are any available.

Reservations & Tickets

The vast majority of tickets are one-way (单程; *dānchéng*) only. Buying hard-seat tickets at short notice is usually no hassle, but you will not always be successful in getting a reserved seat. Tickets can only be purchased with cash.

Tickets for hard sleepers can usually be obtained in major cities, but with more difficulty in quiet backwaters. Don't ever expect to obtain a hard-sleeper ticket on the day of travel so plan ahead and buy your ticket two or three days in advance, especially if you are heading to popular destinations. As a general rule there is an advance-purchase limit of up to 10 days prior to departure.

Buying hard-sleeper tickets in train stations can be trying. Some large stations have windows manned by someone with rudimentary English skills. Purchasing your ticket from the main ticket hall (售票厅; *shòupiàotīng*) – typically accessed by a separate entrance from the departure hall – can be a trial of endurance, especially at the larger train stations. Some stations are surprisingly well run, but others are bedlam. There are windows at large train stations for partial refunds on unused tickets.

If you can't face the queues and uncertainty of getting a sleeper ticket at the train station, turn to your hotel travel desk or travel agent (such as CITS), who can sell you a ticket for a service charge. Telephone booking services exist, but they only operate in Chinese. Many towns and cities also have ticket offices dotted around town where you can obtain train tickets (for a surcharge of around Y5); such outlets are listed in the relevant chapters.

Touts swarm around train stations selling black-market tickets; this can be a way of getting scarce tickets, but foreigners frequently get ripped off. If you purchase a ticket from a tout, carefully check the departure date and the destination. As with air travel, buying tickets around Chinese New Year and the 1 May and 1 October holidays can be hard and prices increase on some routes.

Tickets can also be bought online at www.chinatripadvisor.com or www.china-train-ticket.com, but it's much cheaper to buy your ticket at the station. For trains from Hong Kong to Shànghǎi, Guǎngzhōu or Běijīng, tickets can be ordered online at no mark up from www.kcrc.com.

TRANSPORT

Timetables

Paperback train timetables for the entire country are published every April and October, but they are available in Chinese only (Y5). Even to Chinese readers, working one's way through their Byzantine layout is draining. The resourceful **Duncan Peattie** (www.chinatt.org) publishes an English-language Chinese Railway Timetable, at the time of writing in its 4th edition. Both quick reference and full train timetables are available, as well as supple-ments. The full timetable details 2400 trains, available either in printed form or as two pdf files (for a fee). The quick reference timetable pdf can be downloaded for free. Also consult www.travelchinaguide.com/china-trains/ which allows you to enter your departure point and destination, and gives you the departure times, arrival times and train numbers of trains running that route. Try www.chinahighlights.com/china-trains/index.htm for user-friendly timetables in English.

Health

CONTENTS

Overall China is a reasonably healthy country to travel in, but there are a number of health issues worthy of your attention. Pre-existing medical conditions, such as heart disease, and accidental injury (especially traffic accidents), account for most life-threatening problems. However, becoming ill in some way is not unusual.

Outside of the major cities medical care is often inadequate and food and waterborne diseases are also common. Malaria is still present in the Southwest and high-altitude sickness can be a problem, if you are going to Tibet.

HEALTH ADVISORIES

It's usually a good idea to consult your government's travel-health website before departure, if one is available:

Australia (www.dfat.gov.au/travel/)
Canada (www.travelhealth.gc.ca)
New Zealand (www.mfat.govt.nz/travel)
UK (www.dh.gov.uk) Search for travel in the site index
US (www.cdc.gov/travel/)

In case of accident or illness it's best just to get a taxi and go to hospital directly – try to avoid dealing with the authorities if it is at all possible.

The following advice is a general guide only and does not replace the advice of a doctor trained in travel medicine.

BEFORE YOU GO

Pack medications in their original, clearly labelled, containers. A signed and dated letter from your physician describing your medical conditions and medications (using generic names) is also a good idea. If carrying syringes or needles, be sure to have a physician's letter documenting their medical necessity. If you have a heart condition, bring a copy of your ECG taken just prior to travelling.

If you take any regular medication bring double your needs in case of loss or theft. In China you can buy many medications over the counter without a doctor's prescription, but it can be difficult to find some of the newer drugs, particularly the latest antidepressant drugs, blood pressure medications and contraceptive methods. In general it is not advised to buy medications locally without a doctor's advice.

Make sure you get your teeth checked before you travel, and if you wear glasses take a spare pair and your prescription.

INSURANCE

Even if you are fit and healthy, don't travel without health insurance – accidents do happen. Declare any existing medical conditions you have – the insurance company *will* check if your problem is pre-existing and will not cover you if it is undeclared.

You may require extra cover for adventure activities such as rock climbing. If you're uninsured, emergency evacuation is expensive (receiving bills of more than US$100,000 is not uncommon).

Make sure you also keep all the documentation related to any medical expenses you incur.

HEALTH

HEALTH

RECOMMENDED VACCINATIONS

The World Health Organization (WHO) recommends the following vaccinations for short-term travellers to China:

Adult diphtheria and tetanus Single booster recommended if none in the previous 10 years. Side effects include sore arm and fever. A new ADT vaccine containing pertussis is also available and may be recommended by your doctor.

Hepatitis A Vaccine provides almost 100% protection for up to a year; a booster after 12 months will also provide at least another 20 years protection. Mild side effects such as headache and sore arm do occur in 5% to 10% of people.

Hepatitis B Now considered routine for most travellers. Given as three shots over six months. A rapid schedule is also available, as is a combined vaccination with Hepatitis A. Side effects are mild and uncommon, usually headache and sore arm. In 95% of people lifetime protection results.

Measles, mumps and rubella Two doses of MMR are recommended unless you have had the diseases. Occasionally a rash and flu-like illness can develop a week after receiving the vaccine. Many adults under 40 require a booster.

Typhoid Recommended unless your trip is less than a week. The vaccine offers around 70% protection, lasts for two to three years and comes as a single shot. Tablets are also available; however, the injection is usually recommended as it has fewer side effects. Sore arm and fever may occur. A vaccine combining Hepatitis A and typhoid in a single shot is now available.

Varicella If you haven't had chickenpox, discuss this vaccination with your doctor.

The following immunisations are recommended for long-term travellers (more than one month) or those at special risk:

Influenza A single shot lasts one year and is recommended for those over 65 years of age or with underlying medical conditions such as heart or lung disease.

Japanese B encephalitis A series of three injections with a booster after two years. Recommended if spending more than one month in rural areas in the summer months, or more than three months in the country.

Pneumonia A single injection with a booster after five years is recommended for all travellers over 65 years of age or those travellers with underlying medical conditions that compromise immunity such as heart or lung disease, cancer or HIV.

Rabies Three injections in all. A booster after one year will then provide 10 years' protection. Side effects are rare – occasionally headache and sore arm.

Tuberculosis A complex issue. High-risk adult long-term travellers are usually recommended to have a TB skin test before and after travel, rather than vaccination. Only one vaccine is given in a lifetime. Children under five spending more than three months in China should be vaccinated.

Pregnant women and children should ensure they receive advice from a doctor specialised in travel medicine.

RECOMMENDED VACCINATIONS

Specialised travel-medicine clinics are your best source of information; they stock all available vaccines and will be able to give specific recommendations for you and your trip. The doctors will take into account factors such as past vaccination history, the length of your trip, activities you may be undertaking and underlying medical conditions, such as pregnancy.

Most vaccines don't produce immunity in individuals until at least two weeks after they're given, so visit a doctor six to eight weeks before departure. Ask your doctor for an International Certificate of Vaccination (otherwise known as the yellow booklet), which will list all the vaccinations you've received.

The only vaccine that will be required of you by international regulations is yellow fever. Proof of this vaccination will only be required if you have visited a country that is in the yellow fever zone within the six days prior to entering China. If you are going to be travelling to China directly from South America or Africa, check with a travel clinic as to whether you need yellow fever vaccination.

MEDICAL CHECKLIST

Recommended items for a personal medical kit:

- Antibacterial cream, eg Muciprocin
- Antibiotics for skin infections, eg Amoxicillin/Clavulanate or Cephalexin
- Antibiotics for diarrhoea, including Norfloxacin, Ciprofloxacin, or Azithromycin for bacterial diarrhoea; or Tinidazole for giardia or amoebic dysentery
- Antifungal cream, eg Clotrimazole
- Antihistamine – there are many options, eg Cetrizine for daytime and Promethazine for night-time
- Antiseptic, eg Betadine
- Antispasmodic for stomach cramps, eg Buscopan
- Decongestant, eg Pseudoephedrine
- DEET-based insect repellent
- Diamox if going to high altitudes
- An oral rehydration solution (eg Gastrolyte), diarrhoea 'stopper' (eg Loperamide) and antinausea medication (eg Prochlorperazine)
- Elastoplasts, bandages, gauze, thermometer (but not mercury), sterile needles and syringes, safety pins and tweezers
- Ibuprofen or another anti-inflammatory
- Indigestion tablets, such as Quick Eze or Mylanta
- Iodine tablets (unless you are pregnant or you have a thyroid problem) to purify water
- Laxative, eg Coloxyl
- Paracetamol
- Permethrin to impregnate clothing and mosquito nets
- Steroid cream for allergic/itchy rashes, eg 1% to 2% hydrocortisone
- Sunscreen and hat
- Thrush (vaginal yeast infection) treatment, eg Clotrimazole pessaries or Diflucan tablet
- Ural or equivalent if prone to urinary infections

INTERNET RESOURCES

A wealth of travel health advice is on the internet. For further information, **Lonely Planet** (www.lonelyplanet.com) is a good place to start. The **World Health Organization** (WHO; www.who .int/ith/) publishes a superb book called *International Travel & Health,* which is revised annually and is available online at no cost. Another website of general interest is **MD** **Travel Health** (www.mdtravelhealth.com), which provides complete travel health recommendations for every country and is updated daily. The **Centers for Disease Control & Prevention** (CDC; www.cdc.gov) website also has good general information.

FURTHER READING

Lonely Planet's *Healthy Travel – Asia & India* is a handy pocket size and packed with useful information including pretrip planning, emergency first aid, immunisation, and information on diseases and what to do if you get sick on the road. Other recommended references include *Traveller's Health* by Dr Richard Dawood and *Travelling Well* by Dr Deborah Mills – check out the website (www .travellingwell.com.au).

IN TRANSIT

DEEP VEIN THROMBOSIS (DVT)

Deep vein thrombosis is a condition that occurs when blood clots form in the legs during flights, chiefly because of prolonged immobility. Though most blood clots are reabsorbed uneventfully, some may break off and travel through the blood vessels to the lungs, where they may cause life-threatening complications.

The chief symptom of DVT is swelling or pain of the foot, ankle or calf, usually but not always on just one side. When a blood clot travels to the lungs, it may cause chest pain and difficulty in breathing. Travellers with any of these symptoms should immediately seek medical attention.

To prevent the development of DVT on long flights you should walk about the cabin, perform isometric compressions of the leg muscles (ie contract the leg muscles while sitting), drink plenty of fluids, and avoid alcohol and tobacco. Those at increased risk should wear compression socks.

JET LAG & MOTION SICKNESS

Jet lag is common when crossing more than five time zones; it results in insomnia, fatigue, malaise or nausea. To avoid jet lag try drinking plenty of fluids (nonalcoholic) and eating light meals. Upon arrival, seek exposure to natural sunlight and readjust your schedule (for meals, sleep etc) as soon as possible.

HEALTH

Antihistamines such as dimenhydrinate (Dramamine), promethazine (Phenergan) and meclizine (Antivert, Bonine) are usually the first choice for treating motion sickness. Their main side effect is drowsiness. A herbal alternative is ginger, which works like a charm for some people.

IN CHINA

AVAILABILITY OF HEALTH CARE

There are now a number of good clinics in major cities catering to travellers. Although they are usually more expensive than local facilities, you may feel more comfortable dealing with a Western-trained doctor who speaks your language. These clinics usually have a good understanding of the best local hospital facilities and close contacts with insurance companies should you need evacuation.

Self-treatment may be appropriate if your problem is minor (eg traveller's diarrhoea), you are carrying the relevant medication and you cannot attend a clinic. If you think you may have a serious disease, especially malaria, do not waste time – travel to the nearest quality facility to receive attention.

Buying medication over the counter in China is not recommended, as fake medications and poorly stored or out-of-date drugs are common. To find the nearest reliable medical facility, contact your insurance company or your embassy.

INFECTIOUS DISEASES

Avian Influenza (Bird Flu)

'Bird flu' or Influenza A (H5N1) is a subtype of the type A influenza virus. This virus typically infects birds and not humans; however, in 1997 the first documented case of bird-to-human transmission was recorded in Hong Kong. As of June 2007, there have been 25 confirmed cases of bird flu in China, of whom 15 have died. Currently very close contact with dead or sick birds is the principal source of infection and bird-to-human transmission does not easily occur.

Symptoms include high fever and typical influenza-like symptoms with rapid deterioration leading to respiratory failure and death in many cases. The early administration of antiviral drugs such as Tamiflu is recommended to improve the chances of survival. At this time it is not routinely recommended for travellers to carry Tamiflu with them – rather immediate

medical care should be sought if bird flu is suspected. At the time of writing there have been no recorded cases in travellers or expatriates.

There is currently no vaccine available to prevent bird flu. For up-to-date information check these two websites:

www.who.int/en/
www.avianinfluenza.com.au

Dengue

This mosquito-borne disease occurs in China's Southwest. It can only be prevented by avoiding mosquito bites; there is no vaccine. Dengue-carrying mosquitoes bite day and night, so avoid insects at all times. Symptoms include high fever, severe headache and body ache (previously dengue was known as 'break bone fever'). Some people develop a rash and diarrhoea. There is no specific treatment – just rest and Paracetamol. Do not take aspirin. See a doctor to be diagnosed and monitored.

Hepatitis A

A problem throughout China, this food and waterborne virus infects the liver, causing jaundice (yellow skin and eyes), nausea and lethargy. There is no specific treatment for hepatitis A, you just need to allow time for the liver to heal. All travellers to China should be vaccinated.

Hepatitis B

The only sexually transmitted disease preventable by vaccination, hepatitis B is spread by contact with infected body fluids, including via sexual contact. The long-term consequences can include liver cancer and cirrhosis. All travellers to China should be vaccinated.

HIV

HIV is transmitted via contaminated body fluids. Avoid unsafe sex, blood transfusions and injections (unless you can see a clean needle being used) in China. Always use condoms if you have sex with a new partner and never share needles.

Influenza

Present particularly in the winter months, symptoms of the flu include high fever, muscle aches, runny nose, cough and sore throat. It can be very severe in people over the age of 65 or in those with underlying medical conditions such as heart disease or diabetes – vaccination is recommended for these individuals. There is no specific treatment, just rest and painkillers.

Japanese B Encephalitis

This is a rare disease in travellers; however, vaccination is recommended if spending more than a month in rural areas during the summer months, or more than three months in the country. There is no treatment available and one-third of infected people will die, while another one-third suffer permanent brain damage.

Malaria

For such a serious and potentially deadly disease, there is an enormous amount of misinformation concerning malaria. Before you travel, seek medical advice to see if your trip warrants taking antimalaria medication and if it does, to ensure you receive the right medication and dosage for you.

Malaria has been nearly eradicated in China and is not generally a risk for visitors to the cities and most tourist areas, but it occurs in rural areas in China's Southwest – principally Yúnnán and Guǎngxī bordering onto Myanmar (Burma), Laos and Vietnam and Hǎinán.

There is more limited risk in remote rural areas of Fújiàn, Guǎngdōng, Guǎngxī, Guìzhōu, and Sìchuān. Generally medication is only advised if you are visiting rural Hǎinán, Yúnnán or Guǎngxī.

Malaria is caused by a parasite transmitted by the bite of an infected mosquito. The most important symptom of malaria is fever, but general symptoms such as headache, diarrhoea, cough or chills may also occur. Diagnosis can only be made by taking a blood sample.

Two strategies should be combined to prevent malaria – mosquito avoidance and antimalaria medications. Most people who catch malaria are taking inadequate or no antimalarial medication.

You should always take general insect avoidance measures, to help to prevent all insect-borne diseases, not just malaria. Travellers are advised to prevent mosquito bites by taking these steps:

- Use a DEET-containing insect repellent on exposed skin. Wash this off at night, as long as you are sleeping under a mosquito net. Natural repellents such as Citronella can be effective, but must be applied more frequently than products containing DEET.
- Sleep under a mosquito net impregnated with permethrin.
- Choose accommodation that has screens and fans (if not air-conditioned).
- Impregnate clothing with permethrin in high-risk areas.
- Wear long sleeves and trousers in light colours.
- Use mosquito coils.
- Spray your room with insect repellent before going out for your evening meal.

Rabies

This is an increasingly common problem in China. This fatal disease is spread by the bite or lick of an infected animal – most commonly a dog. You should seek medical advice immediately after any animal bite and commence post–exposure treatment. Having pretravel vaccination means the post–bite treatment is greatly simplified. If an animal bites you, gently wash the wound with soap and water, and apply an iodine-based antiseptic. If you are not prevaccinated you will need to receive rabies immunoglobulin as soon as possible, followed by a series of five vaccines over the next month. Those prevaccinated require only two shots of vaccine after a bite. Contact your insurance company to find the nearest clinic that stocks rabies immunoglobulin and vaccine. It is common to find that immunoglobulin is unavailable outside of major centres – it is crucial that you get to a clinic that stocks immunoglobulin as soon as possible if you have had a bite that has broken the skin.

Schistosomiasis

Also known as bilharzia, this disease is found in the central Yangzi River (Cháng Jiāng) basin. It is carried in water by minute worms which infect certain varieties of freshwater snail found in rivers, streams, lakes and particularly behind dams. The worm enters through the skin and attaches itself to your intestines or bladder. The infection often causes no symptoms until the disease is well established (several months to years after exposure) and damage to internal organs irreversible.

Avoiding swimming or bathing in fresh water where bilharzia is present is the main method of prevention. A blood test is the most reliable way to diagnose the disease, but the test will not show positive until a number of weeks after exposure. Effective treatment is available. There is no way of knowing if water is infected.

HEALTH

STDs

Sexually transmitted diseases most common in China include herpes, warts, syphilis, gonorrhoea and chlamydia. People carrying these diseases often have no signs of infection. Condoms will prevent gonorrhoea and chlamydia but not warts or herpes. If after a sexual encounter you develop any rash, lumps, discharge or pain when passing urine seek immediate medical attention. If you have been sexually active during your travels have an STD check on your return home.

Tuberculosis (TB)

Medical and aid workers, and long-term travellers who have significant contact with the local population, should take precautions against TB. Vaccination is usually only given to children under the age of five, but adults at risk are recommended to have pre- and post-travel TB testing. The main symptoms are fever, cough, weight loss, night sweats and tiredness.

Typhoid

This serious bacterial infection is spread via food and water. Symptoms are a high and slowly progressive fever, headache and it may be accompanied by a dry cough and stomach pain. Be aware that vaccination is not 100% effective so you must still be careful with what you eat and drink. All travellers spending more than a week in China should be vaccinated.

TRAVELLER'S DIARRHOEA

Traveller's diarrhoea is by far the most common problem affecting travellers – between 30% to 50% of people will suffer from it within two weeks of starting their trip. In most cases, traveller's diarrhoea is caused by a bacteria (there are numerous potential culprits), and therefore responds promptly to treatment with antibiotics.

Treatment with antibiotics will depend on your situation – how sick you are, how quickly you need to get better, where you are etc. Traveller's diarrhoea is defined as the passage of more than three watery bowel actions within 24 hours, plus at least one other symptom such as fever, cramps, nausea, vomiting or feeling generally unwell.

Treatment consists of staying well hydrated; rehydration solutions like Gastrolyte are the best for this. Antibiotics such as Norfloxacin, Ciprofloxacin or Azithromycin will kill the bacteria quickly.

Loperamide is just a 'stopper' and doesn't get to the cause of the problem. It can be helpful, for example if you have to go on a long bus ride. Don't take Loperamide if you have a fever, or blood in your stools. Seek medical attention quickly if you do not respond to an appropriate antibiotic.

Amoebic Dysentery

Amoebic dysentery is actually rare in travellers and is overdiagnosed. Symptoms are similar to bacterial diarrhoea, ie fever, bloody diarrhoea and generally feeling unwell. You should always seek reliable medical care if you have blood in your diarrhoea. Treatment involves two drugs: Tinidazole or Metronidazole to kill the parasite in your gut, and then a second drug to kill the cysts. If left untreated complications such as liver or gut abscesses can occur.

Giardiasis

Giardia is a parasite that is relatively common in travellers. Symptoms include nausea, bloating, excess gas, fatigue and intermittent diarrhoea. 'Eggy' burps are often attributed solely to giardia, but work in Nepal has shown that they are not specific to giardia. The parasite will eventually go away if left untreated but this can take months. The treatment of choice is Tinidazole, with Metronidazole being a second option.

Intestinal Worms

These parasites are most common in rural, tropical areas. Some may be ingested with food such as undercooked meat (eg tapeworms) and some enter through your skin (eg hookworms). Infestations may not show up for some time, and although they are generally not serious, if left untreated some can cause severe health problems later. Consider having a stool test when you return home to check for these and to determine the appropriate treatment.

ENVIRONMENTAL HAZARDS
Air Pollution

Air pollution is becoming a significant problem in many Chinese cities due to increasing industrialisation. People with underlying respiratory conditions should seek advice from their doctor prior to travel to ensure they have adequate medications in case their condition worsens. It is very common for healthy people to develop irritating coughs, runny noses etc while in urban Chinese centres as a result of the pollution. It is a good idea to carry symptomatic treatments such as throat lozenges, and cough and cold tablets.

Altitude Sickness

There are bus journeys in Tibet and Qīnghǎi where the road goes over 5000m. Acclimatising to such extreme elevations takes several weeks at least, but most travellers come up from sea level very fast – a bad move!

Acute mountain sickness (AMS) results from making a rapid ascent to altitudes above 2700m. It usually commences within 24 to 48 hours of arriving at altitude and symptoms for AMS include headache, nausea, fatigue and loss of appetite (it very much feels like a hangover).

If you have altitude sickness the cardinal rule is that you must not go higher as you are sure to get sicker and could develop one of the more severe and potentially deadly forms of the disease. These are high altitude pulmonary oedema (HAPE) and high altitude cerebral oedema (HACE). Both of these forms of altitude sickness are medical emergencies and there are no rescue facilities similar to those in the Nepal Himalaya here, so prevention is the best policy.

AMS can be prevented by 'graded ascent' – it is recommended that once you are above 3000m you ascend a maximum of 300m daily and have an extra rest day every 1000m. You can also use a medication called Diamox as a prevention or treatment for AMS after discussion with a doctor experienced in altitude medicine. Diamox should not be taken by people with a sulphur drug allergy.

If you have altitude sickness you should rest where you are for a day or two until your symptoms resolve. You can then carry on, but ensure you follow the graded ascent guidelines. If symptoms are getting worse you must descend immediately before you are faced with a life-threatening situation.

There is no way of predicting who will suffer from AMS but certain factors predispose you to it – rapid ascent; carrying a heavy load and working hard; and having a seemingly minor illness such as a chest infection or diarrhoea. Make sure you drink at least 3L of noncaffeinated drinks daily to stay well hydrated.

The sun is intense at altitude so take care with sun protection and ensure you have adequate clothing to avoid hypothermia – temperatures drop rapidly once the sun goes down and winds can be intense.

DRINKING WATER

- Never drink tap water.
- Bottled water is generally safe – check the seal is intact at purchase.
- Avoid ice.
- Avoid fresh juices – they may have been watered down.
- Boiling water is the most efficient method of purifying it.
- The best chemical purifier is iodine. It should not be used by pregnant women or those with thyroid problems.
- Water filters should also filter out viruses. Ensure your filter has a chemical barrier such as iodine and a small pore size, eg less than four microns.

Food

Eating in restaurants is the biggest risk factor for contracting traveller's diarrhoea. Ways to avoid it include eating only freshly cooked food, and avoiding food that has been sitting around in buffets.

Peel all fruit, cook vegetables and soak salads in iodine water for at least 20 minutes. Eat in busy restaurants with a high turnover of customers.

Heat Exhaustion

Dehydration or salt deficiency can cause heat exhaustion. Take time to acclimatise to high temperatures, drink sufficient liquids and do not do anything too physically demanding.

Salt deficiency is characterised by fatigue, lethargy, headaches, giddiness and muscle cramps; salt tablets may help, but adding extra salt to your food is better.

Hypothermia

Too much cold can be just as dangerous as too much heat. If you are trekking at high altitudes or simply taking a long bus trip over mountains, particularly at night, be aware. At high altitude it can go from being mildly warm to blisteringly cold in a matter of minutes – blizzards have a way of just coming out of nowhere. If you're out walking, cycling or hitching, this can be dangerous.

It is surprisingly easy to progress from very cold to dangerously cold due to a combination of wind, wet clothing, fatigue and hunger,

HEALTH

even if the air temperature is above freezing. It is best to dress in layers; silk, wool and some of the new artificial fibres are all good insulating materials. A hat is important, as a lot of heat is lost through the head. A strong, waterproof outer layer (and a space blanket for emergencies) is essential. Carry basic supplies, including food containing simple sugars to generate heat quickly, and fluid to drink.

Symptoms of hypothermia are exhaustion, numb skin (particularly the toes and fingers), shivering, slurred speech, irrational or violent behaviour, lethargy, stumbling, dizzy spells, muscle cramps and violent bursts of energy. To treat mild hypothermia, get the person out of the wind and/or rain, remove their clothing if wet and replace with dry, warm clothing. Give hot liquids – not alcohol – and some high-kilojoule, easily digestible food. The early recognition and treatment of mild hypothermia is the only way to prevent severe hypothermia, a critical condition requiring medical attention.

Insect Bites & Stings

Bedbugs don't carry disease but their bites are very itchy. They live in the cracks of furniture and walls and then migrate to the bed at night to feed on you. You can treat the itch with an antihistamine. Lice inhabit various parts of the human body but most commonly the head and pubic areas. Transmission is via close contact with an affected person. Lice can be difficult to treat and you may need numerous applications of an antilice shampoo such as permethrin. Pubic lice (crab lice) are usually contracted from sexual contact.

Ticks are contracted after walking in rural areas. Ticks are commonly found behind the ears, on the belly and in armpits. If you have had a tick bite and experience symptoms such as a rash at the site of the bite or elsewhere, fever or muscle aches you should see a doctor. Doxycycline prevents some tick-borne diseases.

WOMEN'S HEALTH

Pregnant women should receive specialised advice before travelling. The ideal time to travel is the second trimester (between 14 and 28 weeks); the risk of pregnancy-related problems is at its lowest and pregnant women generally feel at their best. During the first trimester there is a risk of miscarriage and in the third trimester complications such as premature labour and high blood pressure are possible. It's wise to travel with a companion. Always carry a list of quality medical facilities available at your destination and ensure you continue your standard antenatal care at these facilities. Avoid rural travel in areas with poor transportation and medical facilities. Most of all, ensure travel insurance covers all pregnancy-related possibilities, including premature labour. Malaria is a high-risk disease in pregnancy. WHO recommends that pregnant women do *not* travel to areas with Chloroquine-resistant malaria.

Traveller's diarrhoea can quickly lead to dehydration and result in inadequate blood flow to the placenta. Many of the drugs used to treat various diarrhoea bugs are not recommended in pregnancy. Azithromycin is considered safe.

Supplies of sanitary products may not be readily available in rural areas. Birth control options may be limited so bring adequate supplies of your own form of contraception. Heat, humidity and antibiotics can all contribute to thrush. Treatment is with antifungal creams and pessaries such as Clotrimazole. A practical alternative is a single tablet of fluconazole (Diflucan). Urinary tract infections can be precipitated by dehydration or long bus journeys without toilet stops; bring suitable antibiotics.

TRADITIONAL MEDICINE

Traditional Chinese medicine (TCM) views the human body as an energy system in which the basic substances of *qi* (气; vital energy), *jīng* (精; essence), *xuè* (血; blood, the body's nourishing fluids) and *tiyè* (体液; body fluids; blood and other organic fluids) function. The concept of Yin and Yang is fundamental to the system. Disharmony between Yin and Yang or within the basic substances may be a result of internal causes (emotions), external causes (climatic conditions) or miscellaneous causes (work, exercise, sex etc). Treatment modalities include acupuncture, massage, herbs, diet and *qìgōng* (气功), and aim to bring these elements back into balance. These therapies are particularly useful for treating chronic diseases and are gaining interest and respect in the Western medical system. Conditions that can be particularly suitable for traditional methods include chronic fatigue, arthritis, irritable bowel syndrome and some chronic skin conditions.

Be aware 'natural' doesn't always mean 'safe'; there can be drug interactions between herbal medicines and Western medicines. If using both systems ensure you inform both practitioners what the other has prescribed.

Language

CONTENTS

The official language of the PRC is the dialect spoken in Běijīng. It is usually referred to in the west as 'Mandarin', but the Chinese call it *Putonghua* (common speech). Putonghua is referred to in the Southwest as *hànyǔ* (the Han language), but most of the region's minorities speak their own language and understand Chinese only as a second or even third language.

THE SPOKEN LANGUAGE
Dialects
Discounting ethnic minority languages, China has eight principal dialect groups. The predominant dialect in the Southwest is Sichuanese, though the differences from Putonghua are as much a reflection of regional accent as significant differences in vocabulary. Deng Xiaoping gave most of his speeches in a thick Sichuanese accent. Changes are slight but enough to throw you off course; *hùzhào* (passport) is pronounced 'fuzhao', *méi yǒu* (no; don't have) becomes 'mo de'.

Cantonese is spoken in Hong Kong, Macau, Guangdong and parts of Guangxi.

It differs from Mandarin as much as French differs from Spanish. Speakers of both dialects can read Chinese characters, but a Cantonese speaker will pronounce words very differently. Cantonese also has a more complex tone system than Mandarin, boasting at least seven tones compared with Mandarin's four.

THE WRITTEN LANGUAGE
Chinese is often referred to as a language of pictographs. Many of the basic Chinese characters are in fact highly stylised pictures of what they represent, but most (around 90%) are compounds of a 'meaning' element and a 'sound' element.

So just how many Chinese characters are there? It's possible to verify the existence of some 56,000 characters, but the vast majority of these are archaic. It is commonly felt that a well-educated, contemporary Chinese person might know and use between 6000 and 8000 characters. To read a Chinese newspaper you will need to know 2000 to 3000 characters, but 1200 to 1500 would be enough to get the gist.

Writing systems usually alter people's perception of a language, and this is certainly true of Chinese. Each Chinese character represents a spoken syllable, leading many people to declare that Chinese is a 'monosyllabic language'. Actually, it's more a case of having a monosyllabic writing system. While the building block of the Chinese language is indeed the monosyllabic Chinese character, Chinese words are usually a combination of two or more characters. You could think of Chinese words as being compounds. The Chinese word for 'east' is composed of a single character (*dōng*), but must be combined with the character for 'west' (*xī*) to form the word for 'thing' (*dōngxi*). English has many compound words too, examples being 'whitewash' and 'backslide'.

Theoretically, all Chinese dialects share the same written system. In practice, Cantonese adds about 3000 specialised characters of its own and many of the dialects don't have a written form at all.

CHINESE SAYINGS

Chinese is an extremely rich idiomatic language. Many sayings are four-character phrases that combine a great balance of rhythm and tone with a clever play on the multiple meanings of similar-sounding characters. Perhaps most interesting is how many phrases have direct English equivalents.

缘木求鱼 (yuánmù qiúyú)
Like climbing a tree to catch fish (a waste of time)

问道于盲 (wèndào yú máng)
Like asking a blind man for directions (another waste of time)

新瓶装旧酒 (xīnpíng zhuāng jiùjiǔ)
A new bottle filled with old wine (a superficial change)

坐井观天 (zuòjǐng guāntiān)
Like looking at the sky from the bottom of a well (not seeing the whole picture)

水落石出 (shuǐluò shíchū)
When the tide goes out the rocks are revealed (the truth will come out)

守株待兔 (shǒuzhū dàitù)
Like a hunter waiting for a rabbit to kill itself by running into a tree (trusting to dumb luck)

临阵磨枪 (línzhèn móqiāng)
To not sharpen your weapons until the battle is upon you (to do things at the last minute)

热锅上的蚂蚁 (règuōshàng de mǎyǐ)
Like ants on top of a hot stove (full of worries)

殊途同归 (shūtú tóngguī)
Different roads all reach the same end

同床异梦 (tóngchuáng yìmèng)
To sleep in the same bed but have different dreams (different strokes for different folks)

削足适履 (xiāozú shìlǚ)
Like trimming the foot to fit the shoe

种瓜得瓜 (zhòngguā déguā)
If a man plants melons, so will he reap melons

酒肉朋友 (jiǔròu péngyou)
An eating and drinking friend (fair-weather friend)

晴天霹雳 (qíngtiān pīlì)
Like thunder from a blue sky (a bolt from the blue)

沐猴而冠 (mù hóu ér guàn)
A monkey dressed in a tall hat (a petty official)

燃眉之急 (ránméi zhījí)
A fire that is burning one's eyebrows (extremely urgent)

Simplification

In the interests of promoting universal literacy, the Committee for Reforming the Chinese Language was set up by the Běijīng government in 1954. Around 2200 Chinese characters were simplified. Chinese communities outside mainland China (notably Taiwan and Hong Kong), however, continue to use the traditional, full-form characters.

Over the past few years – probably as a result of large-scale investment by overseas Chinese and tourism – full-form or 'complex' characters have returned to China. These are mainly seen in advertising (where the traditional characters are considered more attractive) and on restaurant, hotel and shop signs.

GRAMMAR

Chinese grammar is much simpler than that of European languages. There are no articles (a/the), no tenses and no plurals. The basic point to bear in mind is that, like English, Chinese word order is subject-verb-object. In other words, a basic English sentence like 'I (subject) love (verb) you (object)' is constructed in exactly the same way in Chinese. The catch with Mandarin is mastering the tones.

MANDARIN

PINYIN

In 1958 the Chinese adopted a system of writing their language using the Roman alphabet. It's known as *pīnyīn* (usually written in English as 'Pinyin'). The original idea was to eventually do away with characters. However, tradition dies hard, and the idea has been abandoned.

Pinyin is often used on shop fronts, street signs and advertising billboards. Don't expect Chinese people to be able to use Pinyin, however. There are indications that the use of the Pinyin system is diminishing.

In the countryside and the smaller towns you may not see a single Pinyin sign anywhere, so unless you speak Chinese you'll need a phrasebook with Chinese characters.

PRONUNCIATION
Vowels

a	as in 'father'
ai	as in 'aisle'
ao	as the 'ow' in 'cow'
e	as in 'her', with no 'r' sound
ei	as in 'weigh'
i	as the 'ee' in 'meet' (or like the 'oo' in 'book' after c, ch, r, s, sh, z or zh)
ian	as the word 'yen'
ie	as the English word 'yeah'
o	as in 'or', with no 'r' sound
ou	as the 'oa' in 'boat'
u	as in 'flute'
ui	as the word 'way'
uo	like a 'w' followed by 'o'
yu/ü	like 'ee' with lips pursed

Consonants

c	as the 'ts' in 'bits'
ch	as in 'chop', but with the tongue curled up and back
h	as in 'hay', but articulated from further back in the throat
q	as the 'ch' in 'cheese'
r	as the 's' in 'pleasure'
sh	as in 'ship', but with the tongue curled up and back
x	as in 'ship'
z	as the 'dz' in 'suds'
zh	as the 'j' in 'judge' but with the tongue curled up and back

The only consonants that occur at the end of a syllable are **n**, **ng** and **r**.

In Pinyin, apostrophes are occasionally used to separate syllables in order to prevent ambiguity, eg the word *píng'ān* can be written with an apostrophe after the 'g' to prevent it being pronounced as *pín'gān*.

Tones

Chinese is a language with a large number of words with the same pronunciation but a different meaning; what distinguishes these 'homophones' is their 'tonal' quality – the raising and lowering of pitch on certain syllables. Mandarin has four tones – high, rising, falling-rising and falling, plus a fifth 'neutral' tone, which you can all but ignore. A good illustration of the importance of getting tones right can be seen with the word *ma*, which has four different meanings according to tone:

high tone	*mā* (mother)
rising tone	*má* (hemp, numb)
falling-rising tone	*mǎ* (horse)
falling tone	*mà* (scold, swear)

Mastering tones is tricky for newcomers to Mandarin, but with a little practice it can be done.

GESTURES

Hand signs are frequently used in China. The 'thumbs-up' sign has a long tradition as an indication of excellence. Another way to indicate excellence is to gently pull your earlobe between your thumb and index finger.

PHRASEBOOKS

Phrasebooks are invaluable, but sometimes seeking help by showing a phrase to someone can result in them wanting to read every page! Reading place names or street signs isn't difficult, since the Chinese name is usually accompanied by the Pinyin form; if not, you'll soon learn lots of characters just by repeated exposure. A small dictionary that includes English, Pinyin and Chinese characters is also useful for picking up a few words.

Lonely Planet's *Mandarin Phrasebook* has script throughout and loads of useful phrases – it's also a very useful learning tool.

ACCOMMODATION
I'm looking for a ...

Wǒ yào zhǎo ...	我要找...
camping ground	
lùyíngdì	露营地
guesthouse	
bīnguǎn	宾馆
hotel	
lǚguǎn	旅馆
tourist hotel	
bīnguǎn/fàndiàn/jiǔdiàn	宾馆/饭店/酒店
hostel	
zhāodàisuǒ/lǚshè	招待所/旅社
youth hostel	
qīngnián lǚshè	青年旅舍

Where is a cheap hotel?
Nǎr yǒu piányi de lǚguǎn?
哪儿有便宜的旅馆?

What is the address?
Dìzhǐ zài nǎr?
地址在哪儿?

LANGUAGE

Could you write the address, please?
Néngbùnéng qǐng nǐ bǎ dìzhǐ xiě xiàlái?
能不能请你把地址写下来？

Do you have a room available?
Nǐmen yǒu fángjiān ma?
你们有房间吗？

I'd like (a) ...
Wǒ xiǎng yào ...   我想要...

  bed
  yī ge chuángwèi   一个床位

  single room
  yìjiān dānrénfáng   一间单人房

  double room
  yìjiān shuāngrénfáng   一间双人房

  bed for two
  shuāngrén chuáng   双人床

  room with two beds
  shuāngrénfáng   双人房

  economy room (no bath)
  pǔtōngfáng   普通房
    (méiyǒu yùshì)   （没有浴室）

  room with a bathroom
  yǒu yùshìde fángjiān   有浴室的房间

  standard room
  biāozhǔn fángjiān   标准房间

  deluxe suite
  háohuá tàofáng   豪华套房

  to share a dorm
  zhù sùshè   住宿舍

How much is it ...?
... duōshǎo qián?   ...多少钱？

  per night
  yī ge wǎnshàng   一个晚上

  per person
  měigerén   每个人

May I see the room?
Wǒ néng kànkan fángjiān ma?
我能看看房间吗？

Where is the bathroom?
Yùshì zài nǎr?
浴室在哪儿？

Where is the toilet?
Cèsuǒ zài nǎr?
厕所在哪儿？

I don't like this room.
Wǒ bù xǐhuan zhèjiān fángjiān.
我不喜欢这间房间

Are there any messages for me?
Yǒu méiyǒu rén gěi wǒ liú huà?
有没有人给我留话？

May I have a hotel namecard?
Yǒu méiyǒu lǚguǎn de míngpiàn?
有没有旅馆的名片？

Could I have these clothes washed, please?
Qǐng bǎ zhèxiē yīfu xǐ gānjìng, hǎo ma?
请把这些衣服洗干净，好吗？

I'm/We're leaving today.
Wǒ/Wǒmen jīntiān líkāi.
我/我们今天离开。

CONVERSATION & ESSENTIALS

Hello.	*Nǐ hǎo.*	你好
	Nín hǎo. (pol)	您好
Goodbye.	*Zàijiàn.*	再见
Please.	*Qǐng.*	请
Thank you.	*Xièxie.*	谢谢
Many thanks.	*Duōxiè.*	多谢
You're welcome.	*Bùkèqi.*	不客气
Excuse me, ...	*Qǐng wèn, ...*	请问，...

(When asking a question it is polite to start with the phrase *qǐng wèn* – literally, 'may I ask?' – this expression is only used at the beginning of a sentence, never at the end.)

I'm sorry.
Duìbùqǐ.   对不起

May I ask your name?
Nín guìxìng?   您贵姓？

My (sur)name is ...
Wǒ xìng ...   我姓...

Where are you from?
Nǐ shì cóng nǎr lái de?   你是从哪儿来的？

I'm from ...
Wǒ shì cóng ... lái de.   我是从...来的

I like ...
Wǒ xǐhuan ...   我喜欢...

I don't like ...
Wǒ bù xǐhuan ...   我不喜欢...

Wait a moment.
Děng yíxià.   等一下

Yes & No

There are no specific words in Mandarin that specifically mean 'yes' and 'no' when used in isolation. When a question is asked, the verb is repeated to indicate the affirmative. A response in the negative is formed by using the word 不 *bù* (meaning 'no') before the verb. When *bù* (falling tone) occurs before another word with a falling tone, it is pronounced with a rising tone.

Are you going to Guilín?
Nǐ qù Guìlín ma?   你去桂林吗？

Yes.
Qù. ('go')   去

No.
Bù qù. ('no go') 不去
No.
Méi yǒu. ('not have') 没有
No.
Bùshì. ('not so') 不是

DIRECTIONS
Where is (the) ...?
... zài nǎr? . . . 在哪儿?
Go straight ahead.
Yìzhí zǒu. 一直走
Turn left.
Zuǒ zhuǎn. 左转
Turn right.
Yòu zhuǎn. 右转
at the next corner
zài xià yīge guǎijiǎo 在下一个拐角
at the traffic lights
zài hónglǜdēng 在红绿灯
map
dìtú 地图
Could you show me (on the map)?
Nǐ néng bùnéng (zài dìtú shàng) zhǐ gěi wǒ kàn?
你能不能(在地图上)指给我看?

SIGNS

入口	*Rùkǒu*	Entrance
出口	*Chūkǒu*	Exit
问讯处	*Wènxúnchù*	Information
开	*Kāi*	Open
关	*Guān*	Closed
禁止	*Jìnzhǐ*	Prohibited
有空房	*Yǒu Kòngfáng*	Rooms Available
客满	*Kèmǎn*	No Vacancies
警察	*Jǐngchá*	Police
警察局	*Jǐngchájú*	Police Station
厕所	*Cèsuǒ*	Toilets
男	*Nán*	Men
女	*Nǚ*	Women

behind	*hòubianr*	后边儿
in front of	*qiánbianr*	前边儿
near	*jìn*	近
far	*yuǎn*	远
opposite	*duìmiànr*	对面儿
beach	*hǎitān*	海滩
bridge	*qiáoliáng*	桥梁
island	*dǎoyǔ*	岛屿
main square	*guǎngchǎng*	广场
market	*shìchǎng*	市场
old city	*lǎochéng*	老城
palace	*gōngdiàn*	宫殿
sea	*hǎiyáng*	海洋

EMERGENCIES
Help!
Jiùmìng a! 救命啊!
emergency
jǐnjí qíngkuàng 紧急情况
There's been an accident!
Chūshìle! 出事了!
I'm lost.
Wǒ mílùle. 我迷路了
Go away!
Zǒu kāi! 走开!
Leave me alone!
Bié fán wǒ! 别烦我!
Could you help me please?
Nǐ néng bùnéng bāng wǒ ge máng? 你能不能帮我个忙?

Call ... !
Qǐng jiào ...! 请叫. . .!
　a doctor
　yīshēng 医生
　the police
　jǐngchá 警察

HEALTH
I'm sick.
Wǒ bìngle. 我病了.
It hurts here.
Zhèr téng. 这儿疼.
I need a doctor.
Wǒ děi kàn yīshēng. 我得看医生.
Is there a doctor here who speaks English?
Zhèr yǒu huì jiǎng yīngyǔ de dàifu ma? 这儿有会讲英语的大夫吗?

I'm ...
Wǒ yǒu ... 我有. . .
　asthmatic
　xiàochuǎnbìng 哮喘病
　diabetic
　tángniàobìng 糖尿病
　epileptic
　diānxiánbìng 癫痫病

I'm allergic to ...
Wǒ duì ... guòmǐn. 我对. . .过敏.
　antibiotics
　kàngjūnsù 抗菌素
　aspirin
　āsīpǐlín 阿司匹林
　bee stings
　mìfēng zhēcì 蜜蜂蜇刺

nuts

guǒrén 果仁

penicillin

qīngméisù 青霉素

antidiarrhoea medicine

zhǐxièyào 止泻药

antiseptic cream

xiāodúgāo 消毒膏

condoms

bìyùn tào 避孕套

contraceptive

bìyùnyào 避孕药

diarrhoea

lā dùzi 拉肚子

headache

tóuténg 头疼

medicine

yào 药

sanitary napkins (Kotex)

fùnǚ wèishēngjīn 妇女卫生巾

sunscreen (UV) lotion

fángshàiyóu 防晒油

tampons

yuèjīng miánsāi 月经棉塞

LANGUAGE DIFFICULTIES

Do you speak English?

Nǐ huì shuō yīngyǔ ma?

你会说英语吗？

Does anyone here speak English?

Zhèr yǒu rén huì shuō yīngyǔ ma?

这儿有人会说英语吗？

How do you say ... in Mandarin?

... zhōngwén zěnme shuō?

... 中文怎么说？

What does ... mean?

... shì shénme yìsi?

... 是什么意思？

I understand.

Wǒ tīngdedǒng.

我听得懂

I don't understand.

Wǒ tīngbùdǒng.

我听不懂

Please write it down.

Qǐng xiěxiàlái.

请写下来

NUMBERS

0	*líng*	零
1	*yī, yāo*	一，幺
2	*èr, liǎng*	二，两
3	*sān*	三
4	*sì*	四
5	*wǔ*	五
6	*liù*	六
7	*qī*	七
8	*bā*	八
9	*jiǔ*	九
10	*shí*	十
11	*shíyī*	十一
12	*shí'èr*	十二
20	*èrshí*	二十
21	*èrshíyī*	二十一
22	*èrshí'èr*	二十二
30	*sānshí*	三十
40	*sìshí*	四十
50	*wǔshí*	五十
60	*liùshí*	六十
70	*qīshí*	七十
80	*bāshí*	八十
90	*jiǔshí*	九十
100	*yībǎi*	一百
1000	*yīqiān*	一千
2000	*liǎngqiān*	两千

PAPERWORK

name

xìngmíng 姓名

nationality

guójí 国籍

date of birth

chūshēng rìqī 出生日期

place of birth

chūshēng dìdiǎn 出生地点

sex (gender)

xìngbié 性别

passport

hùzhào 护照

passport number

hùzhào hàomǎ 护照号码

visa

qiānzhèng 签证

extension

yáncháng 延长

Public Security Bureau (PSB)

gōngānjú 公安局

Foreign Affairs Branch

wàishìkē 外事科

QUESTION WORDS

Who?

Shuí? 谁？

What?

Shénme? 什么？

What is it?

Shì shénme? 是什么？

When?	
Shénme shíhou?	什么时候?
Where?	
Zài nǎr?	在哪儿?
Which?	
Nǎge?	哪个?
Why?	
Wèishénme?	为什么?
How?	
Zěnme?	怎么?

SHOPPING & SERVICES

I'd like to buy ...	
Wǒ xiǎng mǎi ...	我想买...
I'm just looking.	
Wǒ zhǐshì kànkan.	我只是看看
How much is it?	
Duōshǎo qián?	多少钱?
I don't like it.	
Wǒ bù xǐhuan.	我不喜欢
Can I see it?	
Néng kànkan ma?	能看看吗?
I'll take it.	
Wǒ jiù mǎi zhège.	我就买这个
It's cheap.	
Zhè bùguì.	这不贵
That's too expensive.	
Tài guìle.	太贵了
Is there anything cheaper?	
Yǒu piányi yìdiǎn de ma?	有便宜一点的吗?
Can I pay by travellers cheque?	
Kěyǐ fù lǚxíng	可以付旅行
zhīpiào ma?	支票吗?

Do you accept ...?	
... shōu bùshōu?	... 收不收?
credit cards	
xìnyòngkǎ	信用卡
travellers cheques	
lǚxíng zhīpiào	旅行支票

more	
duō	多
less	
shǎo	少
smaller	
gèng xiǎo	更小
bigger	
gèng dà	更大
too much/many	
tài duō	太多

Excuse me, where's the nearest ...?
Qǐng wèn, zuìjìnde ... zài nǎr?
请问,最近的... 在哪儿?

I'm looking for a/the ...	
Wǒ zài zhǎo ...	我在找...
automatic teller machine	
zìdòng guìyuánjī	自动柜员机
bank	
yínháng	银行
Bank of China	
zhōngguó yínháng	中国银行
chemist/pharmacy	
yàodiàn	药店
city centre	
shìzhōngxīn	市中心
... embassy	
... dàshǐguǎn	...大使馆
foreign affairs police	
wàishì jǐngchá	外事警察
foreign exchange office/currency exchange	
wàihuì duìhuànchù	外汇兑换处
hospital	
yīyuàn	医院
hotel	
bīnguǎn/	宾馆/
fàndiàn/	饭店/
lǚguǎn	旅馆
market	
shìchǎng	市场
museum	
bówùguǎn	博物馆
police	
jǐngchá	警察
post office	
yóujú	邮局
public toilet	
gōnggòng cèsuǒ	公共厕所
telephone	
diànhuà	电话
telephone office	
diànxùn dàlóu	电讯大楼
the tourist office	
lǚyóujú	旅游局

change money	
huàn qián	换钱
telephone card	
diànhuà kǎ	电话卡
international call	
guójì chángtú diànhuà	国际长途电话
collect call	
duìfāng fùfèi diànhuà	对方付费电话
direct-dial call	
zhíbō diànhuà	直拨电话
fax	
chuánzhēn	传真
computer	
diànnǎo	电脑

LANGUAGE

email (often simply called 'email')
diànzǐyóujiàn 电子邮件

internet
yīntèwǎng 因特网
hùliánwǎng 互联网 (more formal)

online
shàngwǎng 上网

Where can I get online?
Wǒ zài nǎr kěyǐ shàngwǎng?
我在哪儿可以上网?

Can I check my email account?
Wǒ chá yīxià zìjǐ de email, hǎo ma?
我查一下自己的email, 好吗?

TIME & DATES

What's the time?
Jǐdiǎn zhōng? 几点钟?

... hour ... minute
... diǎn ... fēn ... 点... 分

3.05
sān diǎn líng wǔ fēn 三点零五分

When?
Shénme shíhòu? 什么时候?

now
xiànzài 现在

today
jīntiān 今天

tomorrow
míngtiān 明天

yesterday
zuótiān 昨天

in the morning
zǎoshang 早上

in the afternoon
xiàwǔ 下午

in the evening
wǎnshang 晚上

weekend
zhōumò 周末

Monday
xīngqīyī 星期一

Tuesday
xīngqī'èr 星期二

Wednesday
xīngqīsān 星期三

Thursday
xīngqīsì 星期四

Friday
xīngqīwǔ 星期五

Saturday
xīngqīliù 星期六

Sunday
xīngqītiān 星期天

January
yīyuè 一月

February
èryuè 二月

March
sānyuè 三月

April
sìyuè 四月

May
wǔyuè 五月

June
liùyuè 六月

July
qīyuè 七月

August
bāyuè 八月

September
jiǔyuè 九月

October
shíyuè 十月

November
shíyīyuè 十一月

December
shí'èryuè 十二月

TRANSPORT
Public Transport

airport
fēijīchǎng 飞机场

long-distance bus station
chángtú qìchē zhàn 长途汽车站

subway (underground)
dìtiě 地铁

subway station
dìtiě zhàn 地铁站

train station
huǒchē zhàn 火车站

What time does ... leave/arrive?
... jǐdiǎn kāi/dào? ... 几点开/到?

boat
chuán 船

intercity bus/coach
chángtú qìchē 长途汽车

local/city bus
gōnggòng qìchē 公共汽车

minibus
xiǎo gōnggòng qìchē 小公共汽车

microbus taxi
miànbāochē, miàndī 面包车, 面的

plane
fēijī 飞机

train
huǒchē 火车

I'd like a ...
Wǒ yào yíge ... 我要一个 . . .
one way ticket
dānchéng piào 单程票
return ticket
láihuí piào 来回票
platform ticket
zhàntái piào 站台票
1st class ticket
tóuděngcāng 头等舱
2nd class ticket
èrděngcāng 二等舱
hard-seat
yìngxí/yìngzuò 硬席/硬座
soft-seat
ruǎnxí/ruǎnzuò 软席/软座
hard-sleeper
yìngwò 硬卧
soft-sleeper
ruǎnwò 软卧

When's the ... bus?
... bānchē shénme shíhou lái?
. . . 班车什么时候来?
first
tóu 头
last
mò 末
next
xià 下

I want to go to ...
Wǒ yào qù ...
我要去 . . .
The train has been delayed/cancelled.
Huǒchē wǎndiǎn le/qǔxiāo le.
火车晚点了/取消了
CAAC ticket office
zhōngguó mínháng shòupiào chù
中国民航售票处

boarding pass
dēngjī kǎ 登机卡
left-luggage room
jìcún chù 寄存处
platform number
zhàntái hào 站台号
ticket office
shòupiào chù 售票处
timetable
shíkèbiǎo 时刻表

Private Transport
I'd like to hire a ...
Wǒ yào zū yíliàng ... 我要租一辆 . . .
car
qìchē 汽车
4WD
sìlún qūdòng 4轮驱动
motorbike
mótuōchē 摩托车
bicycle
zìxíngchē 自行车

How much is it per day?
yìtiān duōshǎo qián? 一天多少钱?
How much is it per hour?
yíge xiǎoshí duōshǎo qián? 一个小时多少钱?
How much is the deposit?
yājīn duōshǎo qián? 押金多少钱?
Does this road lead to ...?
Zhè tiáo lù dào ...? 这条路到 . . . ?

road
lù 路
section
duàn 段
street
jiē/dàjiē 街/大街
No 21
21 hào 21号

LANGUAGE

Also available from Lonely Planet:
Mandarin Phrasebook

Glossary

(C) Cantonese; (T) Tibetan

arhat – Buddhist, especially a monk who has achieved enlightenment and passes to nirvana at death; see also *luóhàn*

bābǎo chá – eight-treasures tea
báifàn – rice
báijiǔ – literally 'white alcohol', a type of face-numbing rice wine served at banquets and get-togethers
bāozi – steamed savoury buns with tasty meat filling
běi – north; the other points of the compass are *nán* (south), *dōng* (east) and *xī* (west)
bīnguǎn – tourist hotel
bìxì – mythical, tortoiselike dragon
Bodhisattva – one worthy of nirvana but who remains on earth to help others attain enlightenment
Bön – the pre-Buddhist indigenous faith of Tibet, pockets of which survive in western Sichuān
bówùguǎn – museum

CAAC – Civil Aviation Administration of China
cāntīng – restaurant
cǎoyuán – grasslands
catty – unit of weight, one catty (*jīn*) equals 0.6kg
CCP – Chinese Communist Party, founded in Shànghǎi in 1921
cháguǎn – teahouse
chang (T) – a Tibetan brew made from fermented barley
Chángchéng – the Great Wall
chí – lake, pool
chop – see *name chop*
chörten – Tibetan *stupa*, see *stupa*
chuba (T) – cloak
chūzū qìchē – taxi
CITS – China International Travel Service; deals with China's foreign tourists
CTS – China Travel Service; originally set up to handle tourists from Hong Kong, Macau, Taiwan and overseas Chinese
cūn – village
cūnluò – villages

dàdào – boulevard
dàfàndiàn – large hotel
dàjiē – avenue
dàjiǔdiàn – large hotel
dǎo – island
dàpùbù – large waterfall
dàshà – hotel, building

dàxué – university
dìtiě – subway
dōng – east; the other points of the compass are *běi* (north), *nán* (south) and *xī* (west)
dòng – cave
dòngwùyuán – zoo
dòufu – tofu; beancurd
dzong – Tibetan fort

értóng – children

fàndiàn – a hotel or restaurant
fēng – peak
feng shui – geomancy, literally 'wind and water'; the art of using ancient principles to maximise the flow of *qì*, or universal energy
fēngjǐngqū – scenic area
fó – a Buddha

gǎng – harbour
gé – pavilion, temple
gompa (T) – monastery
gōng – palace
gōngānjú – Public Security Bureau, police
gōngyuán – park
gōu – gorge, valley
gǔ – valley
guān – pass
gùjū – former house, home, residence
gwailo (C) – a foreigner; literally meaning a 'ghost person' and is interpreted as 'foreign devil'

hǎi – sea; also used to mean lake
Hakka – a Chinese ethnic group
Han – China's main ethnic group
hé – river
hú – lake
huājiāo – wild pepper, used in Sìchuān cuisine
Huí – ethnic Chinese Muslims
huǒ chēzhàn – train station
huǒguō – hotpot

IC kǎ – IC card (phone card)
IP kǎ – IP card (phone card)

jiāng – river
jiāo – see *máo*
jiàotáng – church
jiǎozi – stuffed dumpling
jīchǎng – airport

jiē – street
jié – festival
jīn – see *catty*
jì'niànbēi – memorial
jīpiào – air ticket
jiŭdiàn – hotel
jùchăng – theatre
jùn – prefecture

kăoyādiàn – roast duck restaurant
karst – denotes the characteristically eroded landscape of limestone regions, such as the whimsical scenery of Guìlín and Yángshuò
KCR – Kowloon–Canton Railway
Kham – traditional name for eastern Tibet, encompassing western Sìchuān
Khamba – person from Kham
kōngtiáo – air-con, heating
kora (T) – pilgrim circuit
kuài – colloquial term for the currency, *yuán*
kuàizi – chopsticks
Kuomintang – Chiang Kaishek's Nationalist Party, now one of Taiwan's major political parties

lama – a Buddhist priest of the Tantric or Lamaist school; a title bestowed on monks of particularly high spiritual attainment
lăobăixìng – common people, the masses
lăowài – foreigners
liăng – see *tael*
lín – forest
líng – tomb
lóu – tower
lù – road
lŭguăn – hotel
luóhàn – Buddhist, especially a monk who has achieved enlightenment and passes to nirvana at death; see also *arhat*
lúshēng – a reed pipe that features in many festivals in Guìzhōu

mah jong – popular Chinese game for four people, played with engraved tiles
máo – colloquial term for *jiăo*, 10 of which equal one *kuài*
mătou – dock
méiyŏu – 'No', 'There isn't any', 'We don't have'
mén – gate
Miao – ethnic group living in Guìzhōu
miáo – temple
momos – Tibetan dumplings
motor tricycle – an enclosed three-wheeled vehicle with a small motorbike engine, a driver at the front and with seats for two passengers in the back
MTR – Mass Transit Railway, in Hong Kong
mù – tomb

name chop – a carved name seal that acts as a signature
nán – south; the other points of the compass are *bĕi* (north), *dōng* (east) and *xī* (west)

palatar – Burmese crepe
pedicab – pedal-powered tricycle with a seat to carry passengers
Pinyin – the official system for transliterating Chinese script into roman characters
pípa – a plucked string instrument
PLA – People's Liberation Army
Politburo – the 25-member supreme policy-making authority of the *CCP*
PRC – People's Republic of China
prefecture – political subdivision, between a province and a county in size
PSB – Public Security Bureau/Police; the arm of the police force set up to deal with foreigners; see also *gōngānjú*
pùbù – waterfall
Pŭtōnghuà – the standard form of the Chinese language used since the beginning of this century, based on the dialect of Bĕijīng

qì – vital energy (life force) or cosmic currents manipulated in acupuncture and massage
qiáo – bridge
qìchēzhàn – bus station
qìgōng – exercise that channels *qì*
qīngzhēnsì – mosque

rán miàn – 'burning noodles' that are served with onions, chillies, peanuts, chives and a side serving of sauce
rénmín – people, people's
Renminbi – literally 'people's money', the formal name for the currency of China; shortened to RMB

sānlún mótuōchē – motor tricycle
sānlúnchē – pedal-powered tricycle
sēnlín – forest
shāguōfěn – a noodle and seafood, meat or vegetable combination put in a casserole pot and fired over a flame of rocket-launch proportion
shān – mountain
shāokăo – barbecues; skewers of meat wrapped in banana leaves and grilled over wood fires
shĕng – province, provincial
shì – city
shí – rock
shìchăng – market
shíkū – grotto
shòupiàochù – ticket office
shuĭjiăo – a form of steamed *jiăozi*
shuĭkù – reservoir

sì – temple, monastery

sìhéyuàn – traditional courtyard house

stele (stelae) – a stone slab or column decorated with figures or inscriptions

stupa – usually used as reliquaries for the cremated remains of important *lamas*; always walk around stupas clockwise

tǎ – pagoda

tael – unit of weight; one *tael (liǎng)* equals 37.5g; there are 16 *tael* to the *catty*

taichi – the graceful, flowing exercise that has its roots in China's martial arts; also known as *tàijíquán*

tán – pool

thugpa (T) – noodles

tíng – pavilion

tsampa (T) – roasted barley flour (Tibetan)

wǎngbā – internet café

wēnquán – hot springs

xī – west; the other points of the compass are *běi* (north), *nán* (south) and *dōng* (east)

xī – small stream or brook

xiá – gorge

xiàn – county

xiàng – statue

xuěshān – snow mountain

yán – rock or crag

yóujú – post office

yuán – the Chinese unit of currency; also referred to as *Renminbi* or RMB

yuán – garden

zhāodàisuǒ – basic lodgings, a hotel or guesthouse

zhékòu – discount, eg off room price

zhíwùyuán – botanic gardens

zhōng – central

Zhōngguó – China

zìrán bǎohùqū – nature reserve

The Authors

DAMIAN HARPER   Coordinating author, Guǎngxī, Cruising the Yangzi

A growing penchant for *taichi* and a meandering career in book-selling (London, Dublin, Paris) persuaded Damian to opt for a four-year degree in Chinese at London's School of Oriental and African Studies. A year of study in Běijīng and employment in Hong Kong further honed his irrepressible tendencies for wandering, inclinations that have led Damian to contribute to over a dozen guidebooks for Lonely Planet, including *Shanghai, Beijing, Hong Kong, China*, and *Malaysia, Singapore & Brunei*. Married with two children, Damian and his family divide their time between Honor Oak Park in southeast London and China.

MY FAVOURITE TRIP

From Kūnmíng (p220), I'll first tour the towns and villages of the provincial north, and not just the drawcard sights of Dàlǐ (p257) and Lìjiāng (p265), but the lesser-known settlements of Shāxī (p277), Shítóuchéng (p278) and Nuòdèng (p248) before falling for the Yuanyang Rice Terraces (p323) in the southeast of Yúnnán. I'll fly to Guìlín to spend four days exploring the countryside around Yángshuò (p166) before village-hopping to Kǎilǐ (p126) in Guizhōu via Sānjiāng (p184). After flying to Chéngdū from Guìyáng to climb Éméi Shān (p378), I'll visit the ancient village of Huánglóng Xī (p372). Chóngqìng needs to be visited for an authentic hotpot and a chance to see the ancient walled village of Láitān (p456), before contemplating a cruise through the Three Gorges (p458).

Chéngdū
Three Gorges
Huánglóng Xī
Láitān
Éméi Shān
Chóngqìng
Shítóuchéng
Lìjiāng
Nuòdèng
Shāxī
Guìyáng
Kǎilǐ
Dàlǐ
Sānjiāng
Guìlín
Kūnmíng
Yángshuò
Yuanyang
Rice Terraces

LONELY PLANET AUTHORS

Why is our travel information the best in the world? It's simple: our authors are independent, dedicated travellers. They don't research using just the internet or phone, and they don't take freebies in exchange for positive coverage. They travel widely, to all the popular spots and off the beaten track. They personally visit thousands of hotels, restaurants, cafés, bars, galleries, palaces, museums and more – and they take pride in getting all the details right, and telling it how it is. Think you can do it? Find out how at lonelyplanet.com..

TIENLON HO — Chóngqìng

Despite growing up speaking Chinese and packing *màntóu* in her lunchbox, Tienlon Ho first visited China at the ripe age of 21. But Chóngqìng was always in her blood. Her father came there as a child with his mother amid the chaos of bombs. Her mother arrived with her father, an airforce officer called to defend the capital city. In their stories, Chóngqìng was almost mythical. So when she finally saw it herself, Tienlon brought her parents with her. Together they wandered the precipitous staircases and the cavernous bomb shelters of her parents' memories, and she was captivated by the city's history and its people's resilience. Tienlon has travelled extensively throughout China, worked as a lawyer in Hong Kong, and covered food and travel for publications including *GQ* and *Time Out*.

EILÍS QUINN — Guìzhōu & Sìchuān

Eilís Quinn grew up in Vancouver, Canada where visits to that city's massive Chinatown developed a lifelong interest in China and foreign languages. A degree in Chinese studies from Montreal's McGill University finally got her to the Middle Kingdom for real. When she first landed in Southwest China to study at Sichuan Normal University, Chéngdū's airport was a shack and it took two hours on a rickety bus just to get into the centre of town. Back in Canada with degrees in German, Russian and Chinese, she resisted the pull of yet another language degree, opting for journalism instead, and went on to toil in newsrooms across Canada and in New York City. She's now a freelance travel writer based in Montréal and previously authored the Yúnnán, Chóngqìng, Guìzhōu and Guǎngxī chapters for Lonely Planet's *China* guidebook.

KORINA MILLER — History, The Culture, Minority Cultures, Environment, Food & Drink

Korina grew up on Vancouver Island and was lucky enough to have parents who carted her around North America on a number of occasions, leaving her with a well-developed sense of wanderlust. At 18 she left home with her backpack and has been roaming the world ever since. Along the way, she picked up a degree in Communications from Vancouver's SFU and an MA in Migration Studies from Sussex University. She first ventured into China more than a decade ago, researching cooperatives and ecotourism in Shànghǎi and Lìjiāng. Her travels in China have since taken her from the Manchurian border in the north to the Tibetan Plateau in the Southwest. She has written or contributed to more than a dozen LP books, over half of which have been China guides.

CONTRIBUTING AUTHORS

David Eimer first came to China in 1988 on a break from studying law in London. A freelance journalist for a variety of newspapers and magazines in the UK and Australia, he has lived in Běijīng since March 2005. He is the co-author of Lonely Planet's *Beijing City Guide*.

Steve Fallon studied Chinese at Georgetown University in Washington DC and soon found his way to Hong Kong, where he lived for over a dozen years, working for a variety of media and running his own travel bookshop. Steve is now based in London and gets back to Hong Kong annually. He has written or contributed to more than two dozen Lonely Planet titles, including *Hong Kong & Macau* and *China*.

Christopher Pitts studied Chinese in Colorado, Kūnmíng and Táinán, offsetting his years abroad by working in a Chinese bookstore in San Francisco and as an editor in Berkeley. A chance meeting in a Taiwanese elevator wound up letting him off in Paris, where he currently lives with his family, Perrine, Elliot and Céleste. He has written for the Lonely Planet guidebooks *China* and *Shanghai*.

Behind the Scenes

THIS BOOK

This is the 3rd edition of Lonely Planet's *China's Southwest*. The first and second editions (last published in 2002) were both titled *South-West China*. As well as being given a brand new name, this edition has been completely rewritten, as much has changed in this region in the last five years. The original title was researched by Bradley Mayhew and Thomas Huhti (who returned again to write the Yúnnán chapter in this edition). Our second edition was written by Bradley Mayhew, Alex English and Korina Miller (another China-loving author who has joined us again to research this edition). Korina and Thomas were joined by Tien-lon Ho, Eilís Quinn, Christopher Pitts and Steve Fallon. This cast of brilliant and intrepid authors was coordinated by Damian Harper to produce what is undoubtedly the most comprehensive English-language guide to this region of China on the market.

This guidebook was commissioned in Lonely Planet's Melbourne office, and produced by the following:

Commissioning Editors Errol Hunt & Tasmin McNaughtan
Coordinating Editor Amy Thomas
Coordinating Cartographers Diana Duggan & Jody Whiteoak
Coordinating Layout Designer Jacqueline McLeod
Managing Editors Bruce Evans & Suzannah Shwer
Managing Cartographers Julie Sheridan & David Connolly
Managing Layout Designer Sally Darmody
Assisting Editors Sasha Baskett, Michelle Bennett, Louise Clarke, Justin Flynn, Melanie Dankel, Andrea

---

LONELY PLANET: TRAVEL WIDELY, TREAD LIGHTLY, GIVE SUSTAINABLY

The Lonely Planet Story

The story begins with a classic travel adventure: Tony and Maureen Wheeler's 1972 journey across Europe and Asia to Australia. There was no useful information about the overland trail then, so Tony and Maureen published the first Lonely Planet guidebook to meet a growing need.

From a kitchen table, Lonely Planet has grown to become the largest independent travel publisher in the world, with offices in Melbourne (Australia), Oakland (USA) and London (UK). Today Lonely Planet guidebooks cover the globe. There is an ever-growing list of books and information in a variety of media. Some things haven't changed. The main aim is still to make it possible for adventurous individuals to get out there – to explore and better understand the world.

The Lonely Planet Foundation

The Lonely Planet Foundation proudly supports nimble nonprofit institutions working for change in the world. Each year the foundation donates 5% of Lonely Planet company profits to projects selected by staff and authors. Our partners range from Kabissa, which provides small nonprofits across Africa with access to technology, to the Foundation for Developing Cambodian Orphans, which supports girls at risk of falling victim to sex traffickers.

Our nonprofit partners are linked by a grass-roots approach to the areas of health, education or sustainable tourism. Many projects we support – such as one with BaAka (Pygmy) children in the forested areas of Central African Republic – choose to focus on women and children as one of the most effective ways to support the whole community.

Sometimes foundation assistance is as simple as helping to preserve a local ruin like the Minaret of Jam in Afghanistan; this incredible monument now draws intrepid tourists to the area and its restoration has greatly improved options for local people.

Just as travel is often about learning to see with new eyes, so many of the groups we work with aim to change the way people see themselves and the future for their children and communities.

Dobbin, Charlotte Harrison, Kate McLeod, Charlotte Orr, Phillip Tang & Fionnuala Twomey
Assisting Cartographers Csanad Csutoros, Hunor Csutoros, Jacqueline Nguyen, Erin McManus & Malisa Plesa
Assisting Layout Designer Wibowo Rusli
Cover Designer Jane Hart
Project Managers Glenn van der Knijff & Chris Love
Language Content Coordinator Quentin Frayne
Talk2Us Coordinator Margot Kilgour

Thanks to Carolyn Boicos, Dora Chai, Alex Fenby, Mark Germanchis, James Hardy, Rebecca Lalor, Adam McCrow, Celia Wood, Charles Qin & Ji Yuanfang

THANKS
STEVE FALLON

Thanks again to Margaret Leung for her hospitality and support, to James Lee for his skill with a Chinese typewriter and to Neva Shaw for, well, coming back. We missed you. As always, I'd like to dedicate my efforts to my partner, Michael Rothschild, who allows scarcely a day to go by without giving our 'hometown' a passing thought.

DAMIAN HARPER

Thanks firstly to my wife for her support and help, and a big hug to Timothy and Emma for everything. In Guìlín, thumbs up to Zhang Yang for his suggestions and a raised glass to Al, Kurt and Susan at Rosemary Café for their useful pointers. In Yángshuò, cheers to the staff at Bamboo House & Hotel for help and guidance. Jiang Yue, the birthday cake was a real surprise and I'm still speechless with gratitude.

In Dutou village across from Fúlì, Grace and Katie helped me get my bearings, for which I am most thankful. I enjoyed sharing a beer or two with Nicolas Zampiero in Níngmíng; thanks also for your updates. A slap on the back to the sociable old geezer in Xīngpíng (sorry, didn't get your name) who had a tale or two to tell.

Thanks also to the editorial and cartographic staff at Lonely Planet who have helped steer this book in the right direction. Last but not least, I am indebted to all the people of the Southwest who helped make my journey so fascinating and eventful.

TIENLON HO

Thanks to Cheng Wei Bing, Cheng Shifu, Jiang Xin Tian, Huang Ze Ming, Cun Yu Zhun, Zhang Yong Kun, Cun Xiao Yun, Wallace Penny, Qun Joe, the children of Jin Long Cun, and many others who shared their stories. Thanks to Hunt Errol for guiding me through. Thanks to Adams Jon who worked beside me. And finally, thanks to Kao

Wenhuei and Ho Kun. 谢谢妈妈让我发现到处有故事 谢谢爸爸教我述说典故.

THOMAS HUHTI

The following have accumulated boatloads of karma as helpers and/or good-humoured travel mates: Jiang Yingyu, Yang Chunlin and Duan Binbin (Jiànchuān); Abe and Kyra (Kūnmíng); Sinon, Lao Zhang, and the rest at my wondrous Kūnmíng HQ; Billy Zhao, Sim, Maki and urchins (Chéngdū); the inimitable Nan Qing (Mènglián); Liu Jing (Luópíng). And to the people of China in general a huge smile, nod of the head, and deep thank you. Your curiosity, eagerness to help, and especially willingness to smile, make memorable what can be such a slog.

Thanks to all readers who take the time to write in and, especially, help others on the Thorn Tree. Bless Amy, Carlos, Dan, and the rest of my Madison second family for letting me get away with it all yet again (and for their support); and of course my family for their unvanquishable support and bottomless patience.

None of it would be possible mentally without the durability of personal stereos, not to mention the artistry of Chris Whitley, Patty Griffin and Xuan Wei, and the words of Kevin Brockmeier and James Agee. Most of all, thanks to Yuki and Bighead, for being there, even when so far away.

EILÍS QUINN

This research trip was filled with more drama and treachery than a Shakespeare play. Bows, bravos and bouquets are due my fellow passengers on the disaster-prone Lǐtáng–Bātáng bus trip. It was minus 15°C; the roads were closed, the bus blew out in the middle of nowhere; but they never panicked, collected wood and started a fire that kept everybody warm for hours. (For that alone, consider the yak head episode forgiven). I've rarely admired a group of people more. Also a huge thank you to everyone in Sìchuān and Guìzhōu who took time out of their days (often at the last minute) to introduce me to their home towns, take me to meet their families or drive me around at the last minute. Closer to home, a huge *merci*, as always, to Michel for far too many reasons to even begin to list here.

KORINA MILLER

A big shout-out to Errol Hunt for inviting me to join the team, to coordinating author Damian Harper for his support, and to all of my co-authors for doling out information on their regions. To the people of Southwest China, infinite thanks for the countless vivid memories. Thanks to Mike Wilson (my own personal Diane Arbus) and to my parents for unearthing my slides from their storage. Thanks and love to Paul who helped me find the space and time to work, and to Simone whose singing never fails to make me smile.

OUR READERS

Many thanks to the travellers who used the last edition and wrote to us with helpful hints, useful advice and interesting anecdotes:

John Baylis, Andy Carn, Ian Cruickshank, Stephen Eigles, Ben Hill, Judith Karena, Philip Livingstone, Victor Lee, Dirk Leysen, Ines Pauly, Jenny Valk, Jenny and Cor Volk, Nitzan Yudan.

ACKNOWLEDGMENTS

Many thanks to the following for the use of their content:

Globe on title page ©Mountain High Maps 1993 Digital Wisdom, Inc.

Mountain Voices website (www.mountain voices.org), Panos Oral Testimony Programme for the use of the interview with Natuo in Minority Cultures chapter.

Index

INDEX

INDEX

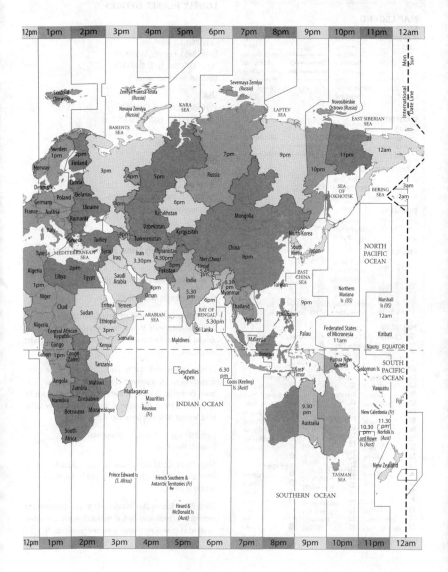

MAP LEGEND

ROUTES

Tollway	Mall/Steps
Freeway	Tunnel
Primary	Pedestrian Overpass
Secondary	Walking Tour
Tertiary	Walking Tour Detour
Lane	Walking Trail
Under Construction	Walking Path
Unsealed Road	Track
One-Way Street	

TRANSPORT

Ferry	Rail
Metro	Rail (Underground)
Monorail	Tram
Bus Route	Cable Car, Funicular

HYDROGRAPHY

River, Creek	Water
Intermittent River	Lake (Dry)
Canal	Lake (Salt)

BOUNDARIES

International	Regional, Suburb
State, Provincial	Ancient Wall
Disputed	Cliff

AREA FEATURES

Airport	Forest
Area of Interest	Land
Beach, Desert	Mall
Building	Market
Campus	Park
Cemetery, Christian	Sports
Cemetery, Other	Urban

POPULATION

◎ CAPITAL (NATIONAL)	◉ CAPITAL (PROVINCIAL)
● Large City	● Medium City
○ Small City	○ Town, Village

SYMBOLS

Sights/Activities	Eating	Information
Beach	Eating	Bank, ATM
Buddhist	**Drinking**	Embassy/Consulate
Castle, Fortress	Drinking	Hospital, Medical
Christian	Café	Information
Confucian	**Entertainment**	Internet Facilities
Golf	Entertainment	Police Station
Islamic	**Shopping**	Post Office, GPO
Jewish	Shopping	Telephone
Monument	**Sleeping**	Toilets
Museum, Gallery	Sleeping	**Geographic**
Point of Interest	**Transport**	Lighthouse
Pool	Airport, Airfield	Lookout
Ruin	Border Crossing	Mountain, Volcano
Taoist	Bus Station	National Park
Trail Head	General Transport	Pass, Canyon
Winery, Vineyard	Parking Area	River Flow
Zoo, Bird Sanctuary	Petrol Station	Waterfall
	Taxi Rank	

LONELY PLANET OFFICES

Australia
Head Office
Locked Bag 1, Footscray, Victoria 3011
☎ 03 8379 8000, fax 03 8379 8111
talk2us@lonelyplanet.com.au

USA
150 Linden St, Oakland, CA 94607
☎ 510 893 8555, toll free 800 275 8555
fax 510 893 8572
info@lonelyplanet.com

UK
72–82 Rosebery Ave,
Clerkenwell, London EC1R 4RW
☎ 020 7841 9000, fax 020 7841 9001
go@lonelyplanet.co.uk

Published by Lonely Planet Publications Pty Ltd
ABN 36 005 607 983

© Lonely Planet Publications Pty Ltd 2007

© photographers as indicated 2007

Cover photograph: farmer working rice field near Yángshuò, Guǎngxī, Daryl Benson/Masterfile. Many of the images in this guide are available for licensing from Lonely Planet Images: www.lonelyplanet images.com.

Printed through The Bookmaker International Ltd
Printed in Hong Kong